AN ANALYTICAL APPROACH TO EVIDENCE

EDITORIAL ADVISORY BOARD
Little, Brown and Company
Law Book Division

RICHARD A. EPSTEIN
James Parker Hall Professor of Law
University of Chicago

E. ALLAN FARNSWORTH
Alfred McCormack Professor of Law
Columbia University

RONALD J. GILSON
Professor of Law
Stanford Law School

GEOFFREY C. HAZARD, JR.
Sterling Professor of Law
Yale University

JAMES E. KRIER
Earl Warren DeLano Professor of Law
University of Michigan

ELIZABETH WARREN
Professor of Law
University of Pennsylvania Law School

BERNARD WOLFMAN
Fessenden Professor of Law
Harvard University

AN ANALYTICAL APPROACH TO EVIDENCE:
Text, Problems, and Cases

RONALD J. ALLEN
Professor of Law
Northwestern University

RICHARD B. KUHNS
Professor of Law
Washington University

Little, Brown and Company
Boston   Toronto   London

Copyright © 1989 by Ronald J. Allen and Richard B. Kuhns

All rights reserved. No part of this book may be reproduced in any form or by any electronic or mechanical means including information storage and retrieval systems without permission in writing from the publisher, except by a reviewer who may quote brief passages in a review.

Library of Congress Catalog Card No. 88-83317

ISBN 0-316-03414-2

MV NY

Published simultaneously in Canada
by Little, Brown & Company (Canada) Limited

Printed in the United States of America

SUMMARY OF CONTENTS

Table of Contents		*vii*
Preface		*xvii*
Acknowledgments		*xxi*
Chapter One	Introduction to the Study of Evidence	1
Chapter Two	Relevancy	101
Chapter Three	The Relationship Between Judge and Jury: Conditional Relevancy, Authentication, and the Best Evidence Rule	161
Chapter Four	The Relevance Rules	213
Chapter Five	The Hearsay Rule	293
Chapter Six	Cross-Examination, Impeachment, and Rehabilitation	493
Chapter Seven	Process of Proof in Civil Cases: Burdens, Presumptions, Judicial Summary and Comment	557
Chapter Eight	Process of Proof in Criminal Cases: Burdens, Presumptions, Judicial Summary and Comment	635
Chapter Nine	Judicial Notice	691
Chapter Ten	Reflections on the Process of Proof	709
Chapter Eleven	Lay Opinions, Scientific Evidence, and Expert Testimony	729
Chapter Twelve	Privileges	759
Table of Cases		809
Table of Authorities		815
Index		823

TABLE OF CONTENTS

Preface   xvii
Acknowledgments   xxi

CHAPTER ONE

INTRODUCTION TO THE STUDY OF EVIDENCE   1

People v. Steele   3
   Preliminary Instructions by the Court   3
   Opening Statement by Mr. Bolling   5
   Opening Statement by Mr. Aspen   10
   Closing Argument of Mr. Elson   81
   Closing Argument of Mr. Aspen   84
   Closing Argument of Mr. Butera   88
   Closing Argument of Mr. Bolling   89
   Judge's Oral Charge   91
   The Verdict   95
PROBLEMS   95

CHAPTER TWO

RELEVANCY   101

A.   RELEVANCY—THE BASIC CONCEPT   101
   Knapp v. State   107

		McQueeney v. Wilmington Trust Co.	109
		NOTES AND QUESTIONS	119
		PROBLEMS	124
B.	A RESTATEMENT OF THE BASIC CONCEPT OF RELEVANCY		126
		PROBLEMS	132
C.	REFLECTIONS ON THE CONCEPT AND SIGNIFICANCE OF RELEVANCY		134
		Nesson, The Evidence or The Event? On Judicial Proof and the Acceptability of Verdicts	134
		Allen, Rationality, Mythology, and the "Acceptability of Verdicts" Thesis	143
		NOTES AND QUESTIONS	158

CHAPTER THREE

THE RELATIONSHIP BETWEEN JUDGE AND JURY: CONDITIONAL RELEVANCY, AUTHENTICATION, AND THE BEST EVIDENCE RULE — 161

A.	THE JUDGE, THE JURY, RELEVANCY, AND AUTHENTICATION		161
		S. Saltzburg and K. Redden, Federal Rules of Evidence Manual	172
		United States v. Carriger	176
		Alexander Dawson, Inc. v. NLRB	179
		PROBLEMS	182
B.	THE BEST EVIDENCE RULE		187
		Seiler v. Lucasfilm, Ltd.	191
		PROBLEMS	195
		Chart: Structure of the Proof Process from the "Relevancy" Perspective	199
C.	REFLECTIONS ON THE RELATIONSHIP BETWEEN JUDGE AND JURY		200
		United States v. Sliker	200

CHAPTER FOUR

THE RELEVANCE RULES — 213

A.	CHARACTER EVIDENCE	215
	1. The Relevance and Possible Uses of Character Evidence	215

Table of Contents

	2. Types of Evidence of Character	218
	3. Limitations on the Types of Evidence That May Be Used To Prove Character	219
	4. The Rationale for Limiting the Use of Specific Acts Evidence To Prove Character	220
	5. Reputation Evidence versus Opinion Evidence	221
	6. A Brief Summary	222
	7. Impeaching Reputation and Opinion Witnesses	223
	PROBLEMS	227
B.	HABIT AND ROUTINE PRACTICE	230
	1. Character versus Habit	230
	2. Business Custom or Routine Practice of an Organization	232
	PROBLEMS	233
C.	EVIDENCE OF SPECIFIC (BAD) ACTS (OF A PARTY)	234
	1. Potentially Admissible Specific Acts Evidence	234
	McCormick's Handbook on the Law of Evidence	234
	2. The "Inclusionary" and "Exclusionary" Approaches to Specific Acts Evidence	240
	3. Specific Acts Evidence, FRE 403, and Preliminary Fact Finding	240
	4. "Round Up the Usual Suspects"—The *Casablanca* Concern	245
	PROBLEMS	246
D.	REFLECTIONS ON SPECIFIC ACTS EVIDENCE	248
	Kuhns, The Propensity to Misunderstand the Character of Specific Acts Evidence	250
	PROBLEMS	263
E.	RAPE SHIELD PROVISIONS	265
	PROBLEMS	270
F.	SIMILAR HAPPENINGS	272
	PROBLEMS	273
G.	INADMISSIBLE TO PROVE "NEGLIGENCE," "LIABILITY," ETC.	274
	1. Subsequent Remedial Measures	276
	PROBLEMS	281
	2. Compromises and Offers of Compromise	281

		PROBLEMS	283
	3.	Payment of Medical and Similar Expenses	284
	4.	Liability Insurance	285
		PROBLEM	286
H.	WITHDRAWN GUILTY PLEAS, PLEAS OF NO CONTEST, AND OFFERS TO PLEAD GUILTY		286
		PROBLEMS	288
I.	"FIGHTING FIRE WITH FIRE"—THE DOCTRINE OF CURATIVE ADMISSIBILITY		289
		PROBLEMS	291

CHAPTER FIVE

THE HEARSAY RULE — 293

A.	RATIONALE AND MEANING		295
	1.	The Hearsay Concept	295
	2.	Hearsay, Lay Opinions, and the Firsthand Knowledge Rule	302
	3.	Multiple Hearsay	303
	4.	Out-of-Court Declarations With No Hearsay Dangers	304
	5.	Out-of-Court Declarations With Sincerity and Narration Problems but No Perception and Memory Problems	308
	6.	Caveat	311
		PROBLEMS	311
	7.	Assertive Nonverbal Activity	313
	8.	Nonassertive Nonverbal Activity	314
	9.	Nonassertive Verbal Activity	320
		PROBLEMS	324
B.	REFLECTIONS ON THE HEARSAY CONCEPT		331
	1.	Disguised Assertions	331
	2.	Classifying Verbal Utterances as Hearsay or Non-Hearsay	332
		PROBLEMS	341
	3.	Classifying State-of-Mind Evidence as Hearsay or Non-Hearsay	344
	4.	Perception, Memory, and State-of-Mind Evidence	346
		PROBLEMS	349

C.	**HEARSAY AND THE CONFRONTATION CLAUSE**	351
	1. The Early Cases	352
	2. The Emerging Right to Confrontation	353
	3. Retrenchment	355
D.	**EXEMPTIONS FROM THE DEFINITION OF HEARSAY**	371
	1. Prior Statements of a Witness Generally	373
	2. Prior Inconsistent and Consistent Statements	373
	3. Preliminary Fact Finding With Respect to Prior Consistent and Inconsistent Statements	374
	4. Prior Statements of Identification	375
	5. The Significance of the Opportunity to Cross-Examine	379
	PROBLEMS	381
	6. Admissions of a Party Opponent Generally	382
	7. A Party's Own Statements	383
	8. Adoptive Admissions	387
	9. Admissions by Agents, Servants, and Employees	389
	10. Co-Conspirators' Admissions	392
	PROBLEMS	398
E.	**THE UNAVAILABILITY EXCEPTIONS: FRE 804**	402
	1. The Meaning of Unavailability	403
	PROBLEM	404
	2. Former Testimony	404
	PROBLEMS	410
	3. Dying Declarations	412
	4. Declarations Against Interest	415
	5. Declarations of Pedigree	419
	PROBLEMS	420
F.	**HEARSAY EXCEPTIONS NOT REQUIRING UNAVAILABILITY: FRE 803**	423
	1. Spontaneous Declarations Generally	423
	2. Present Sense Impressions	424
	3. Excited Utterances	426
	PROBLEMS	429
	4. State-of-Mind Declarations	430
	PROBLEMS	436
	5. Declarations of Physical Condition	439
	PROBLEMS	443
	6. Past Recollection Recorded	444
	PROBLEMS	450

7.	Business Records	451
	PROBLEMS	459
8.	Public Records and Reports	461
	United States v. Oates	462
	Some Thoughts About *Oates*	467
9.	The Absence of Entry Exceptions	472
	PROBLEMS	472
10.	Other Records Exceptions	473
11.	Learned Treatises	474
12.	Judgments	475
13.	The Residual Exceptions	476
	PROBLEMS	478

G. REFLECTIONS ON THE HEARSAY RULE   480
    Note, The Theoretical Foundation of the
    Hearsay Rules   480
    NOTES AND QUESTIONS   489

CHAPTER SIX

CROSS-EXAMINATION, IMPEACHMENT, AND REHABILITATION   493

A. THE VOUCHER RULE   493
    PROBLEMS   496

B. DIRECT AND CROSS-EXAMINATION   498

C. IMPEACHMENT AND REHABILITATION IN GENERAL   502
  1. Impeachment: The Inferential Process   502
  2. Bolstering Credibility   505
  3. Extrinsic Evidence and Impeachment   507
  4. Impeachment and Self-Incrimination   508

D. IMPEACHMENT AND REHABILITATION WITH CHARACTER EVIDENCE   511
  1. Reputation and Opinion Evidence   511
    PROBLEMS   513
  2. Specific Acts Other Than Convictions   515
    PROBLEMS   518
  3. Prior Convictions   519
    Campbell v. Greer   524
    PROBLEMS   529

E.	IMPEACHMENT AND REHABILITATION WITH A WITNESS' PRIOR STATEMENTS	530
	1. Prior Inconsistent Statements	532
	PROBLEMS	536
	2. Prior Consistent Statements	537
	PROBLEMS	540
	3. Impeachment of Experts With Statements in Treatises	541
F.	OTHER IMPEACHMENT TECHNIQUES	542
	1. Bias	543
	PROBLEMS	545
	2. Mental or Sensory Incapacity	547
	PROBLEM	549
	3. Contradiction	549
	State v. Oswalt	553
	QUESTIONS AND PROBLEM	556

CHAPTER SEVEN

PROCESS OF PROOF IN CIVIL CASES: BURDENS, PRESUMPTIONS, JUDICIAL SUMMARY AND COMMENT   557

A.	BURDENS OF PROOF IN CIVIL CASES: THE BURDEN OF PRODUCING EVIDENCE AND RELATED ISSUES	558
	James, Burdens of Proof	565
	NOTES AND QUESTIONS	567
	Chayes, The Role of the Judge in Public Law Litigation	568
B.	THE BURDEN OF PERSUASION	570
	Schechter v. Klanfer	574
	NOTES AND QUESTIONS	576
C.	JUDICIAL SUMMARY OF AND COMMENT ON THE EVIDENCE	578
	NOTES AND QUESTIONS	581
D.	PRESUMPTIONS IN CIVIL ACTIONS	583
	1. The Concept, Such As It Is, of Presumptions	583
	Texas Dept. of Community Affairs v. Burdine	584
	a. Constructing Substantive Rules	591

		b. Allocating Burdens of Persuasion	594
		c. Allocating Burdens of Production	598
		d. Commenting on the Relationship Between Facts	599
		PROBLEMS	605
	2.	Federal Rule 201	609
	3.	The Legislative Role in Structuring the Process of Proof	615
		Usery v. Turner Elkhorn Mining Co. et al.	615
		NOTES AND QUESTIONS	627
E.	REFLECTIONS ON PRESUMPTIONS		629

CHAPTER EIGHT

PROCESS OF PROOF IN CRIMINAL CASES: BURDENS, PRESUMPTIONS, JUDICIAL SUMMARY AND COMMENT   635

A.	THE SCOPE OF THE REQUIREMENT OF PROOF BEYOND REASONABLE DOUBT	636
	Martin v. Ohio	644
	NOTES AND QUESTIONS	652
B.	PRESUMPTION ANALYSIS IN CRIMINAL CASES	652
	Barnes v. United States	653
	County Court of Ulster County v. Allen et al.	658
	Sandstrom v. Montana	669
	Allen, Structuring Jury Decisionmaking in Criminal Cases: A Unified Constitutional Approach to Evidentiary Devices	679
	NOTES AND QUESTIONS	687

CHAPTER NINE

JUDICIAL NOTICE   691

NOTES AND QUESTIONS	697
In re the Marriage of Linda Lou Tresnak and Emil James Tresnak	698
NOTES AND QUESTIONS	703
PROBLEMS	704

CHAPTER TEN

REFLECTIONS ON THE PROCESS OF PROOF   709

NOTES AND QUESTIONS	724

CHAPTER ELEVEN

LAY OPINIONS, SCIENTIFIC EVIDENCE, AND EXPERT TESTIMONY — 729

A. LAY OPINIONS — 729
    PROBLEMS — 733

B. SCIENTIFIC OR SPECIALIZED EVIDENCE — 734
    A True Parable — 739

C. EXPERT WITNESSES — 740
  1. Qualifications — 740
  2. Disclosure of the Bases for an Opinion — 741
  3. Opinions Based on Otherwise Inadmissible Evidence — 742
    PROBLEMS — 749

D. OPINIONS ON AN ULTIMATE ISSUE — 752
    PROBLEMS — 756

CHAPTER TWELVE

PRIVILEGES — 759

A. THE UNIQUE OPERATION OF PRIVILEGE RULES — 760

B. THE HISTORICAL SOURCES AND CURRENT STATUS OF PRIVILEGE RULES — 762

C. CONFIDENTIAL COMMUNICATION PRIVILEGES GENERALLY — 766
  1. Persons and Relationships Covered by a Privilege — 766
  2. Communications—And More? — 767
  3. Confidentiality — 769
  4. Holder of the Privilege — 770
  5. Waiver — 771
  6. The Effect of the Unavailability of the Holder — 773

	7.	Exceptions	773
	8.	Drawing an Adverse Inference From Invoking a Privilege	774
	9.	Unprivileged Confidential Communications	776
		PROBLEMS	776
D.	THE ATTORNEY-CLIENT PRIVILEGE		777
	PROBLEMS		778
	Upjohn Co. v. United States		781
	NOTES AND QUESTIONS		790
	PROBLEMS		798
E.	THE MARITAL PRIVILEGES		799
	Trammel v. United States		799
	PROBLEMS		806
F.	DRAFTING RULES OF PRIVILEGE		806

Table of Cases	809
Table of Authorities	815
Index	823

PREFACE

Two occurrences have significantly affected the law of Evidence in recent years. The first is the adoption of the Federal Rules of Evidence by Congress in 1975. The Federal Rules themselves are the culmination of a long process of creative work by lawyers, judges, scholars, and Congress. Moreover, the Federal Rules have served as a model for the revision of evidence rules in well over half of the states. Thus, the Federal Rules of Evidence are becoming to the law of Evidence what the Federal Rules of Civil Procedure have become to the law of Civil Procedure.

The second occurrence influencing the law of Evidence is the emergence of this area of the law from the shadow of Wigmore and the two generations of codifiers that followed him. Wigmore's ordering and rationalizing efforts were so successful that until recently most scholarship in the field was devoted to filling in the few gaps that he left and to transforming Wigmore's insights into usable, well-drafted rules of evidence. While these efforts were themselves highly successful, they had one unfortunate by-product: Because of the fairly uniform view that all of the fundamental issues had been adequately explored, there was little creative thought about the underlying premises of the law of Evidence. During the last 10 to 15 years, evidence scholars have demonstrated that the fundamental issues have not been resolved. Scholarship over this period has opened new and rich avenues of inquiry, and as a result the field of Evidence has been transformed from being somewhat moribund to being one of the most intellectually exciting fields of study within the purview of the law. To some extent these two occurrences—the adoption of the Federal Rules and the emergence of Evidence from the shadow of Wigmore—have been mutually reenforcing. The Federal Rules of Evidence are the crowning achievement of the codification movement, which, having been attained, freed energies for other pursuits.

This book reflects both phenomena. It concentrates on the Federal Rules, but it does so from the perspective of the ideas underlying those rules.

We have not been content to present merely a mass of doctrines and cases. We have endeavored instead to show the relationship between the theory (or theories) underlying the rules and the rules themselves. This emphasis on the underlying theories reflects our view that the study of any field of law should not consist primarily of ingesting enormous amounts of doctrinal "stew." Rather, the pursuit should be directed toward understanding the conditions that give rise to any form of regulation, whether contained in rules of evidence or in the subtantive rules of some other field.

For the non-litigator this emphasis on underlying theories should give the study of Evidence a richness and depth that would not come from simply learning the rules of evidence. And for the litigator, the emphasis on underlying theories is, in our view, essential for first-rate advocacy. The vast majority of evidentiary issues receive final resolution at the trial court level, and a trial judge is likely to be averse to hearing a long discourse about the theory underlying a particular evidentiary rule. Nonetheless, the lawyer who understands the theory and understands how the rule relates to other rules should be in a better position than the lawyer without this understanding to develop a persuasive argument for how to apply the rule in a particular situation.

There is another factor that has heavily influenced the creation of this book. We believe that the field of Evidence is in large measure a coherent whole rather than an amalgam of virtually unrelated parts. Unlike traditional works on Evidence, we do not treat the various common law categories of Evidence as distinct from one another. Rather, we attempt to show the underlying unity they possess and the ways they relate to each other.

The field of Evidence is primarily concerned with establishing facts for the purpose of resolving disputes. We are concerned that students have a sense of the nature of the process by which facts are established, and consequently we begin in Chapter One with the study of a transcript from a real case. This not only introduces the students to the real process of dispute resolution; it also serves as an effective overview of much of the course to follow.

In Chapter Two we closely analyze the single most important concept in the establishment of facts—relevancy. Chapter Three carries the analysis of relevancy to a deeper plane. Here we work out the relationship between judge and jury, from the perspective of relevancy. More specifically, it is here that we introduce the subjects of conditional relevancy and preliminary fact finding and consider in some detail authentication and the best evidence rule. Chapter Four continues this progress by examining the specific rules of relevancy. In Chapter Five we consider the hearsay rule, which we regard as a specialized rule of relevancy. The inquiry into relevancy-related doctrines continues in Chapter Six, where we consider the subjects of impeachment and rehabilitation.

Examination of the concept of relevancy requires focus on individualized items of evidence, and thus the inquiry in Chapters Two through Six has that focus. In Chapter Seven we move to broader questions related to

Preface

the structure of the trial process. This inquiry begins with the analysis of burden of proof and the related doctrines of presumptions, judicial summary, and judicial comment in civil cases. Chapter Eight continues this line of development by examining the significance of the requirement of proof beyond a reasonable doubt in criminal cases and how that requirement affects the related doctrines introduced in Chapter Seven. Chapter Nine adds the final link to this particular chain through a study of judicial notice. Chapter Ten permits the lessons of these chapters to be reflected upon and presses those lessons a bit further.

In Chapter Eleven we return to the concept of relevancy and consider in detail the specialized relevancy rules governing a subject that has arisen in various contexts throughout the earlier chapters: lay and expert witness opinion testimony. The materials conclude with an examination in Chapter Twelve of rules of privilege.

Despite the substantial amount of text, this book is not a treatise on the law of evidence. We have not attempted to cover "everything." Rather, we have put together materials that we believe will contribute to the effective teaching of Evidence. Our selection of materials has been driven by one criterion alone. We have selected materials that in our judgment are the most effective pedagogical tools. For most of what is covered, we think the best tools are textual discussion followed by problems. Where problems would add nothing to the text, there are no problems; and where cases are helpful, we have included cases.

Throughout the text we quote from the Federal Rules of Evidence and from the Federal Rules' legislative history without giving specific citations. The Federal Rules quoted in the text include amendments through November 1, 1988. The advisory committee appointed by the Supreme Court to draft the rules accompanied each rule with an Advisory Committee Note. The Notes are set forth at 56 F.R.D. 183. The judiciary committees of both the House of Representatives and the Senate held hearings on the Federal Rules. The report of the House Committee is H.R. Rep. No. 650, 93d Cong., 1st sess. (1973), appearing at 1974 U.S. Code Cong. & Admin. News 7075; and the report of the Senate is S. Rep. No. 1277, 93d Cong., 2d sess. (1974), appearing at 1974 U.S. Code Cong. & Admin. News 7051. The Conference Committee report is H.R. Rep. No. 1597, 93d Cong. 2d sess. (1974), and appears at 1974 U.S. Code Cong. & Admin. News 7098.

We are indebted to too many individuals to name who have assisted us in various ways in the creation of this book, but we are especially indebted to our students over the last three years who have labored with us in this effort.

Ronald J. Allen
Chicago, Illinois

Richard B. Kuhns
St. Louis, Missouri

March, 1989

ACKNOWLEDGMENTS

Alfred A. Knopf, Inc. Cather, W., The Professor's House 67-69 (Vintage Books, 1973). Reprinted with permission.

American Bar Association. Rules 1.6, 3.3, and Comment to Rule 1.6. Excerpted from the Model Rules of Professional Conduct, copyright © by the American Bar Association. All rights reserved. Reprinted with permission.

Chayes, The Role of the Judge in Public Law Litigation, 89 Harv. L. Rev. 1281 (1976). Reprinted with permission.

Cleary, E. (ed.), McCormick's Handbook on the Law of Evidence 33, 147-148, 216-217, 554, 558-563, 565, 606, 608, 770, 816-817, 884, 976-977. Reprinted with permission from McCormick's Handbook on the Law of Evidence, Third Edition, copyright © 1984 by West Publishing Company.

Cohen, J., The Probable and the Provable 261 n.6 (1977). Reprinted with permission.

James, Burdens of Proof, 47 Va. L. Rev. 51, 58-61 (1961). Reprinted with permission.

James, Relevancy, Probability and the Law, 29 Calif. L. Rev. 692-693 (1941). Copyright © 1941 by California Law Review, Inc. Reprinted from California Law Review Vol. 29, No. 6, by permission.

Kuhns, R., The Propensity to Misunderstand the Character of Specific Acts Evidence, 66 Iowa L. Rev. 777, 798-799 (1981). Reprinted with permission of the author and the University of Iowa Law Review.

Lempert, R. & Saltzburg, S., A Modern Approach to Evidence 225-226, 384 (1982). Reprinted with permission of West Publishing Company.

Morgan, Presumptions, 12 Wash. L. Rev. 255, 279-281 (1937). Reprinted with permission.

Nesson, The Evidence or the Event?, 98 Harv. L. Rev. 1359-1368 (1985). Reprinted with permission.

Note, The Theoretical Foundation of the Hearsay Rules, 93 Harv. L. Rev. 1787-1791, 1793-1809, 1811-1812 (1980). Copyright © 1980 by the Harvard Law Review Association. Reprinted with permission.

Saltzburg, S., & Redden, K., Federal Rules of Evidence Manual 1005-1010 (4th ed. 1986). Reprinted by permission, copyright © 1986 by The Michie Co.

AN ANALYTICAL APPROACH TO EVIDENCE

CHAPTER ONE

INTRODUCTION TO THE STUDY OF EVIDENCE

The rules of evidence determine the admissibility of evidence, prescribe the qualifications of individuals to be witnesses, and structure the relationships among the various actors at trial. The study of evidence, however, is not just the study of the rules of evidence. Those rules, which give form and content to the process of litigation in our culture, are derivative of our society's views on myriad issues, among them: (1) the appropriate means of resolving disputes; (2) the nature of knowledge, what it means to "know" something, and how knowledge is transmitted to others; (3) the dynamics of small group decision making, and the confidence that we invest in the common person to reach wise and informed judgments that affect the lives of fellow citizens; (4) moral and ethical concerns, such as whether certain individuals (spouses, children, friends) should be required to testify against those close to them, whether convictions in criminal cases, or verdicts in certain civil cases, should be difficult to obtain in order to foster certain values, the extent to which we value repose over correct distribution of wealth (thus determining the difficulty of the hurdle plaintiffs must surmount merely to get a decision on an issue they wish to contest); and (5) the relationship between ideas of justice and efficiency. The vast complex of ideas, principles, customs, and values underlying these concerns are inevitably a part of the study of evidence. Indeed, the rules of evidence are the crystallization of these and related beliefs, concerns, and issues, and to study the rules is to use them as a surrogate for such matters.

The study of evidence will well serve any lawyer, no matter what field that person pursues. Obviously litigators must know—and understand—the rules of evidence in order to use them effectively. It bears remembering that while litigation is virtually always the worst case scenario of any legal transaction, competent lawyers must always be prepared for it no matter what the nature of the relevant legal enterprise happens to be. If a contractual relationship fails or a merger is not consummated and litigation results, what will matter is how well the parties will be able to defend their respective positions. Eventually, that will be determined in significant measure by the effective application of the rules of evidence.

To use the rules effectively, one must understand their meaning and source and purpose. To do so requires that one see the rules in relationship to the issues that give rise to them. Therefore if one intends to be primarily a litigator, it will not do to be content with a merely cursory grasp of the language of the various rules. One must be in a position to work with the rules, to argue for one's position from the perspective of the purposes that underlie the relevant provisions.

For those who do not intend to become litigators, and who are reasonably sure that their legal transactions will never collapse into disputes, it is even more important to see the rules as summaries of underlying issues and to look carefully at those issues. For such individuals, the value of the inquiry lies not in some future utility but instead in its enlightenment of our shared vision of how disputes should be resolved in a civilized society. With that enlightenment may come, indeed we hope will come, disagreement. You may not like all that you see; and if you do not, then you will be in a better position to work for change through the legislative and rule-making processes.

We attempt in these materials to facilitate an inquiry into both the meaning and use of the rules of evidence as well as the issues that underlie them. At times we focus extensively, in fact almost exclusively, on the rules themselves, while at other times we deal quite explicitly with the various issues from which the rules are derived. Upon completion of this inquiry, you should have a thorough understanding of the rules of evidence, as well as considerable appreciation for the concerns that give rise to them.

The rules undoubtedly have their most dramatic impact in the context of litigation where individuals' rights and property are directly at stake. An understanding of the nature of litigation is thus of considerable importance to understanding and evaluating the rules themselves. Consequently, we begin these materials with an edited transcript of a real trial (although names and places have been changed to provide some anonymity to the parties involved). Our intent is to introduce you to the process of litigation by allowing you to study a virtually complete trial. As you read the transcript, try to get a "feel" for what is occurring. Pay attention to the structure of the case, to who is doing what, and why. In addition, consider the various evidentiary issues that are raised, many but not all of which are noted in the footnotes that we have added to the transcript. Another purpose in introducing these materials with the transcript is that it gives an overview of much that is to follow in these materials.

Before you begin reading the transcript, though, remember that much has already occurred. A jury has been selected, and there has undoubtedly been pre-trial maneuvering of various kinds. Such matters may appear to be

Chapter One. Introduction to the Study of Evidence

independent of the trial itself—at least of its truth-determining aspects—but they are not so distinct as they may appear. Judges are informed, and perhaps influenced, by what they learn in the pre-trial stage. Jurors are educated in the voir dire process. And the lawyers learn more about the respective strengths and weaknesses of their own case and that of their opponent. Indeed, this last point cannot be overemphasized. The single most important variable in success at litigation is preparation. If you take away one "rule" of evidence from this course, let it be "prepare, prepare, prepare." As you read the transcript, try to get an insight into how well these lawyers prepared.

THE PEOPLE v. STEELE

THE COURT: Please be seated. You are here for the purpose of trying a case that is a criminal case. Now, this criminal case comes to you by way of an indictment that has been returned by the grand jury of Long County. The indictment charges the defendant with the offense of murder during a kidnapping in the first degree. It is not any evidence. You should give no weight to the fact that an indictment has been returned against the defendant.

At a time before today the defendant has entered a plea of not guilty. You jurors will make a determination of his guilt or innocence. Once I complete these opening remarks counsel for the prosecution and counsel for the defendant, if they wish to do so, will outline for you what they expect the evidence to show. This is called the opening statement by each side. These remarks by the attorneys are intended to familiarize you with what to look for in the way of evidence.[1]

After the opening statements we will begin to hear the evidence in the case. The State of South Dakota will call its witnesses in support of the charge in the indictment.

Now, the evidence that you will consider in this case may be divided into two general categories. The first category will be testimony from a person who is sworn and who sits on this witness stand. The second kind of evidence is called physical evidence. Physical evidence will be some kind of objects or items, documents, something that's tangible, you can hold on to, that are admitted as exhibits into evidence. It will be from this verbal testimony and the exhibits admitted into evidence

---

1. Given that the jury is normally composed of individuals with little or no legal training, what should be explained to them about legal procedures before a trial commences? What should be explained about the law relevant to the particular litigation that is occurring? Very little is typically communicated to the jury by the trial judge before trial commences. Indeed, this transcript contains a more complete set of preliminary instructions than is found in most trials. When you have finished reading it, consider how well it communicates the salient aspects of the experience that the jurors are about to undertake. Note in particular that very little illumination is provided concerning the legal standards relevant to this trial. Why do you suppose that is, and does it make sense?

that you will make your findings of fact and then arrive at your final and true verdict.[2]

You as the jury will be the sole judges of the facts in the case, and you alone have the right to say whether a crime was committed and whether this defendant committed that crime. That will not be my function as the trial judge.[3] As you go about evaluating the evidence and testimony you have several things you can use in determining what these true facts are. First of all, when a witness testifies you may consider whether or not the witness has any interest or any bias in the case. You can take into consideration the manner in which a person answers questions. By that I mean does the person apparently answer the questions in an open manner, or does he seem or appear to be attempting to avoid answering the questions, to evade answering specific questions?

In addition to all of that, you are people of experience, you come into this courtroom possessing common sense. You should use your own common sense, your own experiences, the powers of your observation and hearing, and what you have learned about people to determine the truth and accuracy of the testimony that is presented to you.

My responsibilities will be to see that the trial progresses in an orderly manner. I will rule upon all legal questions that are presented. I have a duty to instruct you as to what the law is, the meaning of the charge against the defendant, the possible verdicts, and what your duties as jurors will be. I am not permitted to hold an opinion or to convey to you any idea that I hold an opinion about the facts of this case or about what the verdict should be. That applies from right now down to the time the trial is ended.[4]

During the course of the trial when I make rulings on objections or questions of law, do not consider my actions and my rulings as any effort to suggest something to you or to hint something to you. My rulings, my actions will be based upon the rules of evidence and procedure in the State of South Dakota.

The attorneys in this case are officers of the court and, being an officer, each attorney has the right and also the duty to make objections

---

2. Are verbal testimony and exhibits the only sources of evidence? What about the jurors' perceptions of the witnesses' demeanors? What of the arguments made by the lawyers? Is there a clear distinction between "evidence" and the "inferences" one draws from the evidence? In this regard notice that the judge will soon instruct the jury to rely on "common sense." Why isn't "common sense" part of the evidence at the trial? Begin to think, in short, about what it means for something to be "evidence."

3. As you read the transcript, see if you think the judge has accurately delineated the roles of judge and jury. Later on in the transcript you will see the judge making rulings on evidence, on occasion excluding offers of evidence. If the jury is the sole judge of the facts, why should a judge exclude evidence?

4. In some jurisdictions, judges have the power to comment on the evidence. This subject is treated in Chapter Seven. As you read the transcript, reflect on what the proper distribution of authority between judge and jury should be. As you will see, that question is one of the mainsprings of the law of evidence.

Chapter One.   Introduction to the Study of Evidence   5

if he believes inadmissible evidence is being offered. But remember that an attorney does not sit in this witness chair, nor is he sworn as a witness. What the attorney says is not evidence. The attorney has the right at the proper time to make an opening statement and to also make a closing argument.

Now, in determining what the facts are and what the verdict should be, I instruct you that you are not to permit any sympathy, any prejudice, or any emotion for or against anyone to influence you.[5]

Until this case is submitted for your deliberations, you cannot discuss the case with anyone, you cannot let anyone talk with you about the case, and that applies even among yourselves; you can't discuss the case or talk about it with anyone or with any other juror. You should keep an open mind and make no decisions about what the facts are or about what the verdict is until, again, you have heard all of the evidence, have heard the closing arguments of the attorneys, and have heard my instructions as to what the law is. It's only after you have all of those things that you are prepared to make findings of fact and then return a verdict.[6]

At this point in time the state has the right to make the first opening statement.

Mr. Bolling?

MR. BOLLING: Thank you, your Honor.[7] May it please the Court, Mr. Aspen, Mr. Butera and you ladies and gentlemen of the jury: I'm Bill Bolling, I'm district attorney here, and the gentleman seated at the table with me is Roy Elson. Mr. Elson is my chief deputy.

This is a rather unique case. Let me say now that the history of our judicial system is that you are the triers of the fact, you are to determine what actually took place. The judge will be the one to tell you what the law is. I may quote some law to you, some other counsel may quote some law to you, but the law that counts and the law that

---

5. Should a juror take into account a personal view of the wisdom or excessiveness of the law that a defendant has been accused of violating? Juries have the power to nullify the law by returning a verdict of not guilty, even if the defendant is factually guilty, and such a verdict cannot be reversed on appeal in order to retry the defendant. Should a jury be instructed on this power? Such questions go to the heart of the justifications for trial by jury; and much evidence law, in turn, results from a desire to regulate the evidence that a jury is permitted to hear. Thus, there is an intimate relationship between the law of evidence and the justifications for jury trials.

6. Why does the judge give this instruction? Does it describe the normal way an individual absorbs information? If not, why is an artificial decision-making process being urged upon the jury?

7. The primary purpose of opening statements is to lay out the case that each party expects to establish through the evidence. This is done in order to give the jury a framework for evaluating the evidence that is produced at trial. Argument over the implications of the evidence is provided in the closing arguments, not here. What other purposes might be served by an opening statement? Could it be used to condition the jury to weaknesses in your, or your opponent's, case? How important is the opening statement in terms of making an impression on the jury? To what extent might jurors be influenced by their impression of the lawyers?

you go by is what the judge gives you in his charge before you go out to make the determination.

Let me say that it would be nice if we had all of the people here who are subjects of this trial. Unfortunately, we can't. So, of necessity, we must piece it together as we find it. I would like to, for just a moment, though, treat this somewhat like we would if we were studying history; that is, with the idea of trying to find out what happened, when it happened, where it happened, how it happened, why it happened, who was involved in it happening.

We would expect the evidence to show that sometime prior to August 31st, 1981, that Mary or Mary Ann McCoy Steele was married to the defendant, Terry Steele, the gentleman seated at the end of the table with counsel at defense table, and that they lived in South Dakota, lived just off of route 147 in what is known as the Pinecrest Community; and on that date, in the early morning hours prior or shortly after daylight, that Mrs. Steele was kidnapped from her home, the home that she had been in that night, rested in. At the time, we expect the evidence to show, that Mrs. Steele was pregnant. In fact, she was nine months pregnant, termed a full baby.[8]

We would expect the evidence to show that the defendant in this cause prior to August the 31st on numerous occasions had sought ways to bring about the death of his wife, Mary Ann Steele, and this included talking with his brothers and even consulting with hired killers, and in fact hiring killers to do the job. And that job included kidnapping her and abducting her from her home, taking her to a foreign place, where her body was dumped; and somewhere in between the time that she was taken from her house until the authorities found her, she was shot, the result of which caused her death.

Now, why did this happen? I can tell you why it happened.

MR. ASPEN: Your Honor, we are going to object to any statements that he's going to make as far as—

MR. BOLLING: We expect the evidence to show that it happened.

THE COURT: Wait just one second, Mr. Bolling; let me rule on the evidence—excuse me—the objection. The objection is sustained. Go ahead.[9]

MR. BOLLING: We expect the evidence to show that the reason that it happened was greed, insurance money, a divorce that he wanted, pos-

---

8. So what? Is this a blatant effort to impassion the jury? If a party is concerned that the adversary may attempt to refer to inadmissible matters, as perhaps the reference to the baby is, a motion in limine can be filed pre-trial to ask the court to direct the adversary not to refer to the inappropriate material. For further discussion of motions in limine, see note 26 infra.

9. What is the basis of this objection? Would this objection apply if the statement "I can tell you why it happened" was made during closing argument? How does, "We expect the evidence to show . . ." change matters? What do you think is the effect on the jury of "sustaining" an objection during the opening phase of a trial?

Chapter One. Introduction to the Study of Evidence 7

sibly love for another woman, which he was already engaged to. There may have been other causes but we expect the evidence to show those.

Now, who all was involved in this? We expect the evidence to show that his brother Mark was involved, his brother Roland was involved, that a person by the name of Amy Lucas was involved, that a person by the name of Manfred Charles Lynch was involved, a person by the name of Travis Sherman was involved, and a person by the name of Earl McGee was involved. Now, those people are not on trial here today because we're only trying one person under our system at this time, so you will only be concerned with Terry Steele as far as the trial itself.

But, to paint the picture, we expect the evidence to show that Terry Steele went to his brother Mark and sought assistance in finding someone to kill his wife, and that ultimately his brother referred him to Manfred Charles, alias Tiny Lynch, who in turn put him in contact with another person by the name of Travis Sherman, who actually met with him and discussed it, even took money but declined to do the job.

We expect the evidence to show that on the morning that the body was found, that this defendant went to the home of this woman that he was engaged to and in her vehicle came back and led an entourage composed of his car, being driven by one of the people who participated in the abduction and killing, and followed by another car, a white Camaro driven by the other person that was involved in it, those persons being Earl McGee and Manfred Charles Lynch. We expect the evidence to show that they drove down the street that he lived on and got out and pointed to the house which was his house, and that the key to his house was on the key ring of his automobile that was turned over to Manfred Charles Lynch or Tiny Lynch.

We expect the evidence to show that a neighbor there in the community of Pinecrest by the name of Elmer Joyce, on his way to work, 7:15 on that morning, saw and observed the vehicle in which not only the defendant, Terry Steele, was in, but his betrothed Amy Lucas, was also riding. In fact, it was her vehicle. And he in his rear view mirror saw behind that vehicle the Steele vehicle, although he didn't observe who was driving it.

We expect the evidence to show that Robert Wallace, another neighbor in that community, saw and observed the Steele car rendezvous with a white Camaro, and because of the early hour and the weather conditions he was unable to identify who the person was but a person got out of the driver's side of the Steele car and went over and conferred with the white Camaro.

We expect the evidence to show that there had been an effort made to get additional insurance and finally to even borrow money, and that that money could not be borrowed without the wife's signature from a local loan company, and that $2500 was borrowed. We expect the evidence to show that part of that $2500 went to pay for the killers to kill Mrs. Steele.

Now, we expect the trial to go rather quickly. We would anticipate and expect the evidence to have Mr. Oliver McCoy, the father of the deceased, to come and tell you about the birth, marriage and burial of his daughter, Mary Steele.[10]

We would expect Mr. Jarvis Nash, a resident of Battle County, to tell you that he was off on the morning of August the 31st, and around 9:15 he was traveling on the road known as Old Foggy Road, and that he saw and observed a white Camaro approaching him, which did more or less a U-turn in the road and sped away from him; and to his left, about 40 feet from the highway, he observed a General Motors car, green in color, and as he stopped to investigate or look at it, he found it was an Oldsmobile; and when he saw a knee inside the car he assumed that there were some children and he didn't go any further but left.

Next we would bring to you and expect the evidence to show Thomas M. Jacobs, who works for the power company there, and that at 11:00—11:05, to be exact—he came by that position and saw the car and stopped and investigated and found the body of Mary Ann Steele and that Investigator Perry of Battle County, actually came to the scene and examined, took pictures, which we expect to introduce to you; and that the pathologist, Dr. Stoddard, who is a pathologist there, conducted a postmortem examination and determined the cause of death to be a bullet wound to the head, shot through the eye of Mary Ann Steele; and, further, that he delivered a full-term baby. We would expect the evidence to show that that baby was buried in the same casket in the arms of the deceased, Mary Steele.[11]

We would expect Captain Holloway to come to the stand and show that he assisted and worked with state police agent, Ed Marshall, and they conferred with one another, and that he would ID or identify some pictures that were taken at the scene.

We would expect the evidence to show Investigator Helms, from the sheriff's office, took into his possession certain ropes and other paraphernalia there at the scene and turned them over to Officer Ed Marshall.[12]

This house was up for sale. We would expect the evidence to show from one Larry Murphy that it had not been shown since August the 31st—excuse me—since August the 25th of 1981 until sometime after the death of Mary Steele.

---

10. Of what possible relevance might such testimony be?

11. The defense objected earlier when the prosecutor transcended the stylistic bounds of opening statements, but there is no objection here. Why? Reconsider note 8 supra.

12. Try to trace these "ropes and other paraphernalia" through the transcript. You will see that they, or at least photographs of them, are argued over at various points in the trial, but their significance is not made clear until closing arguments. Should the prosecution have permitted this ambiguity to persist until that time?

Chapter One. Introduction to the Study of Evidence

We would expect the evidence to show that there were several statements made, and I won't go into those until the appropriate time.

Ladies and gentlemen, this case is based on a state statute that says that if a crime is started in this state, within the county it's started it has what we call venue, which gives the court jurisdiction to try the case, even though it might have been consummated or completed outside of the county. Our laws are such that the legislature sets the laws up to protect the State of South Dakota. The people affected become witnesses. When an act is committed and whenever we read an indictment, it's a crime against the State of South Dakota.

Our law further says when you have a felony, that you have it submitted to the grand jury and the grand jury—

MR. ASPEN: We're going to object to Mr. Bolling quoting the law. The law is expected to come from the Court with regard to this matter.

THE COURT: If it's a matter of the indictment being brought, the objection will be overruled as to that particular part of an opening statement. Any quotation of the law, the objection will be sustained.

MR. BOLLING: The grand jury of this county meets three times a year, 18 members. They return what is known as an indictment. The judge has charged you that the indictment is not evidence in the case, but it does reflect the finding of the grand jury after hearing evidence. If they return a true bill, then they say that the man has to stand trial and there will be a trial to determine whether or not he's guilty.

I want to read to you at this time the indictment the grand jury brought.[13]

> State of South Dakota, Long County, Circuit Court, Spring Term, 1982.
>
> The grand jury of said county charge that before the finding of this indictment, Terry Eugene Steele did intentionally cause the death of Mary Ann Steele by shooting her with a gun, and Terry Steele caused said death during Terry Eugene Steele's abduction of or attempt to abduct Mary Ann Steele with the intent to inflict physical injury upon her, in violation of 13A-5-40 (a)(1) of the Code of South Dakota 1975, as amended, against the peace and dignity of the State of South Dakota.

We expect the evidence to show that a conspiracy existed and that what one does can be attributed to all.

We expect further the evidence to show that this defendant wasn't satisfied that morning that things had gone right, so he went back for the third time to his house but did not go to the house itself, went back to the Pinecrest church, to the back part of the Pinecrest church, where he could have vision of his own house, to make sure that the cars had

---

13. What do you think is the value of reading the indictment to the jury? Why would reading the indictment be more effective than simply reading the Code section that has allegedly been violated?

gone and the men were about to do their deeds, that is, to kill Mary Ann Steele.

I ask you to listen to the evidence as it comes from this stand, at the end listen to the judge's charge, then base your verdict on that.

Thank you so much.[14]

THE COURT: Thank you, Mr. Bolling.

Mr. Aspen?

MR. ASPEN: May it please the Court, Mr. Bolling, Mr. Elson, ladies and gentlemen of the jury: My name is Lane Aspen. Seated at the counsel table with me is Mr. Robert Butera, who is assisting me in the trial of this matter. We were appointed some four or five months ago— to represent Mr. Steele in the charge of murder of Mary Ann Steele during the course of kidnapping. Since that time there have been numerous pleadings filed in this case, numerous motions which have been ruled on by the Court, and as a result those motions have been overruled and we are here today to defend Mr. Steele on a charge of murder of Mary Ann Steele during the course of a kidnapping.

Each of you were charged as jurors because from this witness stand each one of you stated that you could be fair and impartial if you were chosen to sit as a juror in this particular case. That is all that anybody can ask. Based on the evidence that comes from the witness stand, based on the law as the judge charges you the law, then you have to make a decision in this case.

Mr. Steele, as you know from the testimony that you heard here yesterday, or the questions that were asked, was tried for the murder of Mary Ann Steele in Battle County, North Dakota. That case was completed and disposed of February 10th, 1981. We expect the evidence to show that.

MR. BOLLING: We object to the word *tried*. We believe the record shows he pled guilty.

MR. ASPEN: Your Honor, there was a trial.

THE COURT: Just one second.

MR. BUTERA: Your Honor, we move for a mistrial.

MR. ASPEN: We would move for a mistrial at this point.

THE COURT: Just one second. Come over here to the side.

(The Court, Mr. Bolling, Mr. Elson, Mr. Aspen, Mr. Butera, and the reporter went to the side bar and the following proceedings were had outside the hearing of the jury, to wit:)[15]

---

14. Has the State's "picture" been adequately painted? Could it have been done more vividly? Should it have been done more vividly?

15. A "sidebar" is a quick extemporaneous conference or dialogue between the attorneys for each side and the judge who remains seated. It may be initiated by either side or the judge when a point of contention or procedure arises that requires resolution for the smooth functioning of the proceeding. Note that this sidebar is done outside the jury's hearing, as most

Chapter One. Introduction to the Study of Evidence   11

THE COURT: Okay. The objection is sustained. Now, state the grounds of the motion for mistrial.

MR. BUTERA: We feel like the statement Mr. Bolling made has unduly prejudiced the jury. There has been no evidence, nothing put in the record about him pleading guilty to this point; therefore, it's like trying to unring a bell. It's something you can't take away, once they've heard that. So that's the grounds for our objection. I move for a mistrial.

MR. BOLLING: May it please the Court, yesterday when we were having voir dire each and every witness was asked was he aware that the defendant pled guilty.

THE COURT: Every juror.

MR. BOLLING: Juror, yes, sir. Now, that is what the defense counsel asked, it wasn't the state. That is on the record.

THE COURT: The motion for mistrial will be denied. I will instruct the jury to disregard the statement or ground or response, as it may be termed, by the district attorney.

MR. ELSON: We would like to interpose also that the purpose of the opening statement is to explain to the jury what they expect the evidence to show, not just a narrative of anyone—

MR. ASPEN: That's what we expect the evidence to show; we expect the evidence to show that.

MR. BOLLING: Did he have a trial?

MR. ASPEN: He was put to trial in this case.

(The Court returned to the bench and the trial continued as follows, to wit:)

THE COURT: Motion for mistrial will be denied.

Ladies and gentlemen, I will instruct you and you must follow the instructions to disregard the response or objection or comment made by the district attorney just before I asked everyone to come over here to the side of the courtroom. So you are to disregard that. Do not consider that as evidence and do not allow that to sway your deliberations or assessing the evidence in any way.[16]

---

are in order to keep the jury from overhearing what is discussed. That is more efficient than having the jury removed when the parties or the judge anticipate the conference will be short. Federal Rule of Evidence (hereinafter FRE) 104 provides the procedure for handling questions of admissibility of evidence. See in particular FRE 104(c).

16. Counsel for defense was arguing that an instruction to "strike" the prosecutor's remark from the record or to disregard the remark is insufficient to remove its impact from the jury's mind. Such instructions are common in the course of a trial. Do you think jurors are influenced by such remarks, a judge's instruction notwithstanding? If you were entitled to a limiting instruction, would you invariably want one? Note that FRE 105 requires a party who is entitled to a limiting instruction to ask for the instruction. Could a party who failed to request such an instruction claim on appeal that the failure to give the instruction—at least if the right to it were obvious—was plain error? See FRE 103. If a party who is entitled to a limiting instruction does not request it but the judge, on his or her own motion gives the instruction, can the

Please continue, Mr. Aspen.

MR. ASPEN: There was a trial in Battle County; Mr. Steele was put to trial on a charge of the murder of Mary Ann Steele during the course of a kidnapping. That case was disposed of in Battle County on February 10, 1981; we expect the evidence to show this. Mr. Steele was sentenced to life imprisonment. Mr. Steele is presently under the sentence of the State of North Dakota, in their custody, only being loaned to this particular court for this proceeding here.

We expect the evidence to show that Mr. Steele prior to entering a plea or giving his version of the incident which occurred up there, there was an agreement between he and the district attorney's office who was prosecuting this case in Battle County, North Dakota. Based on the agreement, the conclusion was that if he entered a plea of guilty to this charge of murder, which was a lesser included offense of the murder directed by Mr. Steele, which was an aggravating circumstance, that he would be given life imprisonment. We expect the evidence to show that he did in fact agree to take the life imprisonment sentence; he was sentenced, and now he's being brought to trial by this district attorney, this grand jury, controlled by this district attorney, for whatever reason we don't know. Mr. Bolling states to you that the law in South Dakota is such that you can do this, that if a crime begins in South Dakota, then it carries over into North Dakota and you can prosecute. But can you do it based on the Constitution of the United States? We expect the judge to charge you on the evidence—on the law with regard to double jeopardy, and with regard to a plea of autrefois convict, where you've been convicted of the same crime, then you're put to trial again on that crime. The defense contention is we expect the evidence to show this is the same crime, this is the same Mary Ann Steele that was either killed or murdered, that there was a trial in Battle County, this man has been sentenced; now he's being double punished or an attempt to double punish him in Long County simply because, we expect the evidence to show, that this district attorney with his staff was not satisfied with a simple life sentence, they wanted to put him in the electric chair.

We appreciate the concern that you have, but look at the law of

---

party who was entitled to the instruction claim on appeal that the trial judge's action was prejudicial? Should it matter whether the party objected to the trial judge's action at the time? See, e.g., Lakeside v. Oregon, 435 U.S. 333 (1978) (better view is not to instruct over defendant's objection, but doing so is not a constitutional violation).

What methods are available to curtail an attorney's conscious use of "ringing the bell" to introduce otherwise objectionable statements? Remember that jury deliberations take place in private with only the jury present. If the jury did consider the prosecutor's statements in its deliberations after the case is presented, how would the court become aware of it? What are the remedies? See FRE 606. It is very difficult to impeach a jury verdict on the grounds of juror misconduct. An example of the difficulty is presented by the decision in Tanner v. United States, 495 U.S. 929 (1987), where the Court held that intoxication and alleged drug use were not "outside influences" within FRE 606(b), and thus did not provide a basis for reviewing the jury verdict.

the land in which we live. Put yourself in that position. If you had entered a plea of guilty, expecting that that would be the sentence, do you think that man would ever have entered a plea expecting to be put to trial on a death charge in South Dakota? He relied on what they told him in North Dakota. Now they're going to use the same witnesses in this particular court of law to prosecute him for the same crime he's already gotten life for. Is that what you as jurors want in this county? I say not.[17]

Thank you.

MR. BOLLING: I don't know whether we asked for the rule or not.[18] I mentioned it a while ago, but I would ask for the rule, if it hasn't been entered.

THE COURT: The rule has previously been invoked. Any witnesses or anyone or any party, with the exception of the accused and Mr. [Thomas] Holloway [Chief Investigator for the Long County Sheriff's Department], will have to remain outside the courtroom.

Ladies and gentlemen, let me say this one other thing to you in explaining the nature of the proceedings as you will be participating in as a juror. When an attorney says "I object," that means that he is stating under South Dakota rules of evidence and procedure that you are not supposed to hear the answer to the question because it's inadmissible evidence or inadmissible testimony. Now, if I say "sustain the objection," that means that the witness should not answer the question because the answer would be inadmissible evidence, it's something that under the laws of procedure in South Dakota you are not supposed to hear. So if I sustain the objection, you are to disregard any response or statement that the witness starts to make; it's something you are not supposed to hear.

If I say "overrule the objection," then the witness may answer the question and you may consider what the witness says as evidence in the case and you may consider it in your deliberations in determining what the facts are.

The state may call its first witness.

MR. BOLLING: The State will call Dr. Stoddard.

DR. JOHN STODDARD

called as a witness by and in behalf of the State of South Dakota, having been first duly sworn, testified as follows on

17. What is the theory of the defense? When you have finished the transcript and have read the judge's instructions, ask yourself this question once more.

18. The "rule" here refers to a court rule barring the presence of any witness in the courtroom while another witness is testifying. The rationale is that such an injunction precludes a witness from altering or modifying testimony to either explain or dovetail with the testimony of another witness. The objective is to safeguard against the possibility of "contaminating" a witness. See FRE 615.

Direct Examination

Questions by Mr. Bolling:

Q: Doctor, will you state your name for the record, please.
A: Yes, sir. My name is John Stoddard.
Q: What profession or calling do you follow, please?
A: I'm a physician; specifically I have specialty training in pathology.
Q: Doctor, have you had education, background, and experience in this field, qualifying you for this field?
A: In forensic pathology?
Q: Yes.
A: Yes, sir.
Q: Would you tell us what schools you have been to, please, sir?
A: Yes. I attended Ohio University undergraduate school and I went to the University of Michigan Medical School, where I did a residency in pathology, and I have been in private practice of pathology for five years.
Q: Would you tell us in laymen's terms what forensic science is, please, sir?
A: Forensic pathology or forensic medicine involves investigation of medicolegal deaths. These would be deaths that involve either suspicious circumstances or unusual circumstances, violent deaths such as suicides or homicides, or peculiar situations surrounding someone's death.
Q: How long have you been engaged in the practice of medicine, Doctor?
A: Since graduating from medical school will be nine years.
Q: Do you belong to any organizations or medical societies?
A: Yes, sir.
Q: Would you tell us what those are, some of them?
A: I'm a Fellow of the College of American Pathology and a Fellow of the American Society of Clinical Pathology, a Fellow in the American Society of Sitology, a member of the North Dakota Medical Association, a member of the American Medical Association.
Q: Have you also been admitted in the State of South Dakota as well?
A: Right; I'm licensed to practice medicine in both North and South Dakota.
Q: Doctor, during her lifetime did you know Mary Ann Steele?
A: No.
Q: Did you have a body identified to you as being that of Mary Ann Steele?
A: Yes, I did.

MR. BOLLING: We submit to the Court that this witness is qualified as an expert at this time.[19]

---

19. An "expert witness" is a specially qualified person who is empowered under the Rules of Evidence to offer testimony because of special competence in the field of inquiry. FRE 702

Chapter One. Introduction to the Study of Evidence 15

THE COURT: All right. It will be so ruled. The witness will be deemed qualified as an expert in the field of pathology by the Court. Go ahead.

Q: Did you have an occasion to do anything to the remains that were identified to you as that of Mary Ann Steele?
A: Yes, sir, I performed an autopsy.
Q: Could you tell us basically what that consisted of, please, sir?
A: The autopsy consisted of examining the body of the person identified to me as Mary Ann Steele and conducting a full postmortem examination.

MR. ASPEN: Your Honor, at this time we would interpose an objection. There has been no chain of evidence linked up as to the condition of the body prior to the doctor taking charge of the body. At this time we would object to any further testimony in this regard.

THE COURT: Objection will be overruled at this time subject to its being connected up at a later time.[20]

Q: Who identified the body to you, Doctor?
A: There were several law-enforcement officials present at that time, as well as the coroner of the County.
Q: Was Office Perry present?
A: Yes, I believe he was.
Q: I show you what has been marked State's Exhibit 2 and I will ask you to look at that. Are you able, from looking at State's Exhibit 2, to identify that exhibit?
A: I can't specifically identify who the person is without seeing the face. I know that the clothing appears to be the same as what the victim was wearing.

---

defines such a witness "as an expert by knowledge, skill, experience, training, or education, (who) may testify . . . in the form of an opinion or otherwise." See also FRE 703, 705. An expert witness is an exception to the rule that a witness may testify only on the basis of personal knowledge of a matter. See FRE 602. Experts may provide expert opinions in addition to testifying from personal knowledge. However, the strictness of the rule requiring testimony based on firsthand knowledge is relaxed somewhat by allowing lay opinions or "inferences which are (a) rationally based on the perception of the witness and (b) helpful to the clear understanding of his testimony on the determination of a fact in issue." FRE 701. This is a much more important rule than appears at face value. If a lay person were not allowed to give testimony in the form of opinions, how could such a person testify to the speed of a car that was observed, or that a person "winked" at someone else?

Note that the expertise or competence of an expert witness is not assumed; it must be proven to the satisfaction of the court by the party seeking to offer the witness' testimony unless stipulated to by opposing counsel. Consider the role of such witnesses at trial. How could the cause of Mary Ann Steele's death be ascertained with any certainty in the absence of an eyewitness or competent testimony by an "expert"? What would be the impact on our evidentiary system if there were not provisions for "expert witnesses"? Also, is the distinction between "fact" and "opinion" as neatly demarcated as these rules seem to picture it?

The issues raised in this footnote are examined further at the end of this chapter in Problems 2, 3, 10, and 11.

20. What is going on here? Compare this scenario to the discussions later in the transcript concerning photographs.

Q: I show you, then, State's Exhibit 4 and ask you if you can identify that exhibit.
A: Yes. This is the body identified to me as being Mary Ann Steele.
Q: Is that the one that you conducted a postmortem examination on?
A: Yes, it is.
Q: Now, Doctor, what did your examination reveal, please, sir?
A: Would you like me to read the cause of death?
Q: Yes sir, among other things.

MR. ASPEN: Your Honor, we would object as to the cause of death. I think this gentleman is not qualified to testify as to the cause of death.
THE COURT: Objection will be overruled.
MR. ASPEN: Which is a conclusion.[21]
THE COURT: Objection is overruled.

A: The cause of death in this particular case related to a single gunshot wound to the head which entered the brain.
Q: I would like for you to show us on your body, if you would point basically to the point where the entry was and then tell us further about that, please, sir.
A: All right. Well, I'll read the wound track and then I'll demonstrate; perhaps that would be the easiest way.
Q: All right. What you're reading from, were those the notes that were made by you at the time you conducted—
A: This is the written report of the postmortem examination.
Q: All right. Go right ahead, sir.
A: I'm going to read some medical terms but then I'll go ahead and explain exactly what that involved.

    The bullet went through the right eye and, exiting the eye, penetrated the orbit of the eye, specifically the sphenoid bone. It fractured this bone as well as the orbital plate, the frontal bone, proceeded posteriorly and slightly to the left, entered the internal portion of the right frontal cortex of the brain, continued posteriorly and medially and entered the mid-brain and superior portion of the cerebral hemispheres. What this means is that the bullet went in roughly right here at the corner of the eye, proceeded back through the eye, in the orbit, back into the brain, fractured some bones, and I recovered it in the posterior portion of the skull but it was still inside the skull.
Q: So it went in the right eye and around through the brain to the more or less direction of the left rear?
A: That's correct.
Q: In other words, it didn't go in a straight line?

---

21. At one time, expert witnesses were not allowed to offer opinions on "ultimate issues." FRE 704 embraces the more modern view, however, that allows such testimony.

Chapter One. Introduction to the Study of Evidence 17

A: No, it was deflected a little bit by the bone. As it hit the bone it fractured and moved a little bit.
Q: Doctor, let me ask you this. You said the bullet entry was at the right eye?
A: That's correct.
Q: Did it go through the eyeball?
A: That's correct. It nicked just the lower portion of the upper eyelid and upper portion of the lower eyelid, barely nicked both of those surfaces, went right in through the eyeball.
Q: Was there mass bleeding or anything around the wound area itself?
A: There was not a great deal of bleeding, there was a little bit.
Q: A little bit? All right, sir. Now, just one more time before we leave that, Doctor. Would you kind of hold your head down and put your right finger where the bullet went in and your left—

MR. ASPEN: Your Honor, we're going to object to this. He's already demonstrated that one time.
MR. BOLLING: May I get through with the question, please?
THE COURT: Just one minute. Objection is overruled. Go ahead.

Q: Just show us by your two hands the area where it went in and where the bullet was located inside.
A: Right. The bullet went in approximately in this direction right here in the corner of the eye, and I recovered it back here in the back portion, left side, but inside the skull.
Q: Now, Doctor, did you examine or remove any other parts of the body during your postmortem examination?
A: Yes. I recovered a male fetus.
Q: And did that consist, in laymen's terms, of an unborn baby?
A: That's correct.
Q: Doctor, based on your training and experience was that a full-term baby?
A: Yes, sir. The baby weighed approximately eight pounds and two ounces and measured a little over nineteen inches in length. It looked like it was a perfectly normal appearing male infant and under ordinary circumstances I think there would have been a full-term male infant delivered.
Q: Based on your training and experience as pathologist in this particular area, your opinion is the cause of death is what?
A: Of the baby?
Q: No, sir, of the—excuse me—of the body of Mary Ann Steele. I'm sorry.
A: The cause of death was a gunshot wound to the brain.
Q: Now, let's get to the death of the baby, please.

MR. ASPEN: Your Honor, we object as to the death of the baby.
MR. BOLLING: We wouldn't insist on it, Judge.[22]
THE COURT: All right. The objection will be sustained, then, with the withdrawal of the question.

Q: Doctor, did you take any pictures, by any chance?
A: Yes, sir, I did.
Q: Do you have them with you?
A: I took two pictures. I do.
Q: I show you now, Doctor, what has been marked State's Exhibit 4A for purposes of identification and ask you to identify it for us, please, sir.
A: Yes. This is the picture that I took in the autopsy room on the date of the autopsy of the body identified to me as being that of Mary Ann Steele.
Q: Was the autopsy taken at approximately the same time that the picture was taken?
A: The autopsy was taken—the autopsy was performed just after the picture was taken.

MR. BOLLING: At this time we move to introduce—I'm sorry, we'll have to move later on.[23] That's all, sir.

[The defense conducted a short, noncontroversial cross-examination.]

OLIVER MCCOY

[The state's next witness was Oliver McCoy, Mary Ann Steele's father, who identified State's Exhibits No. 2 and 4 as photographs of his daughter. Mr. McCoy then identified State's Exhibit No. 1 as a Cutlas Oldsmobile owned by Terry and Mary Ann Steele and testified about the existence of certain insurance proceeds as noted in the following exchange:]
Questions by MR. BOLLING:

Q: Was there anyone buried in the same casket with your daughter?

MR. ASPEN: Your Honor, we are going to object to this.
THE COURT: Objection will be sustained.[24]

Q: I'll ask you if you are familiar with the insurance that has been collected in this case.

22. Then why was the question asked?
23. Why can't he do it now?
24. Does the jury already know everything the prosecutor wants it to know? What can be done to avoid such tactics?

Chapter One. Introduction to the Study of Evidence 19

MR. ASPEN: Your Honor, we're going to object to the insurance that has been collected in this case; irrelevant and immaterial, has nothing to do with the charge here today.[25]

THE COURT: Come around one moment. (A short discussion was had at the bench between the Court, Mr. Bolling, Mr. Elson, Mr. Aspen, and Mr. Butera, outside the hearing of the jury and the reporter.)

Q: Are you familiar with insurance—

THE COURT: Let me rule on the objection. The objection as to relevancy is overruled; objection on the other grounds is sustained.[26]

---

25. Consider FRE 103. Is Aspen's objection satisfactory to preserve the issue for appeal? The stock objection "irrelevant, incompetent and immaterial" is just that, a stock objection that communicates virtually nothing to the trial judge except the objector's desire to exclude the proffered evidence. Unless that evidence is clearly not admissible for any purpose, the objector must make clear the ground of objection to the trial judge. In addition, evidentiary rulings will virtually never be the basis of appellate reversal if the objector has not been clear, direct, and correct in the objection and if there is any ground upon which the trial judge can be sustained. This is true regardless of what a trial judge rules, in fact. If an objection has been sustained, the losing side must have made clear why the evidence is admissible. In this regard, consider FRE 105. Evidence may be admissible for one purpose or as to one party, but inadmissible for another purpose or as to another party. Also bear in mind that the advocates must be sure that the record adequately reflects the objection, any response to it, and the judge's ruling. It is not unusual, for example, for a sidebar to be held concerning the admissibility of a bit of evidence during which the lawyers make their arguments and the judge rules. If this is held off the record, the lawyers must remember to summarize what occurred for the record when the trial goes back on the record. Failure to "perfect the record" may result in an inability to appeal any asserted error in the trial judge's ruling.

In certain cases, a trial judge or an appellate court will be unable to tell whether the proffered evidence is admissible because the necessary context is lacking. In such cases, the advocate has the duty to make an offer of proof in which the lawyer presents to the judge what evidence is expected to be produced so that the judge can analyze the objected to evidence in that light. See FRE 103(a)(2). Offers of proof may be made in a number of different ways. The lawyer may simply describe for the trial judge what the evidence is going to be. Alternatively, the court may require that the attorney put the relevant witnesses on the stand and ask the appropriate questions of the witnesses. Again, it is the lawyer's obligation to make sure that the record is sufficiently complete so as to preserve any asserted error for appeal. A useful short description of the process of making the record is J. Waltz and J. Kaplan, Making The Record (1982).

The issues dealt with here are probed further in Problems 5 and 7 at the end of this chapter.

26. The "other grounds" are certainly not clear from the objection. What might they have been? The insurance evidence indicates that the insurance company considered the defendant to be guilty of homicide. Use of the evidence for this purpose, however, might be objectionable on hearsay grounds. See FRE 801, 802. The insurance company's action in depriving the defendant of the proceeds of the policy arguably is an out of court statement that the defendant is guilty. The evidence, however, is obviously relevant for another purpose, namely to show that the defendant had a motive for killing his wife. Indeed, the prosecutor referred to the insurance money motive in his opening statement. Why did defense counsel not object to the reference to insurance at that point?

On what grounds other than hearsay might the defendant object to the insurance evidence? See FRE 401-403. Also, see Problem 9 at the end of this chapter.

Perhaps the trial judge's ruling excluding the evidence was improper. If not, perhaps both the prosecution and defense counsel took unnecessary risks with respect to this evidence. If defense counsel were seriously concerned about keeping information about insurance from the jury, they could have filed a motion in limine requesting the judge to order the prosecution

Q: Are you familiar with the insurance that was paid off after the death of your daughter?
A: Yes, sir, I am.
Q: Do you know the amount that was paid?
A: $120,689.53 total.

MR. BOLLING: Your Witness.

Cross-Examination

Questions by MR. BUTERA:

Q: Mr. McCoy, who got the $120,689.53 insurance money?
A: It has been put in certificates for the child of my daughter and the defendant.
Q: Do you have custody of the child?
A: Yes, I do.
Q: Are you the guardian of the child's estate?
A: I am.
Q: As guardian of that child are you in charge of the finances of that child?
A: Through my lawyer, yes.

MR. BUTERA: Nothing further of this witness.[27]

Redirect Examination

Questions by MR. BOLLING:

Q: Did you receive custody of your daughter's child after Mr. Steele was convicted or sometime recently?
A: It was immediately after my daughter's death that we went to a lawyer to see about getting custody of the child. It was done immediately after.
Q: Now, do you know of your own knowledge who would have been the recipient of that money the way the beneficiary was initially made out? Was Mr. Steele the beneficiary of part of that money?
A: That is correct.

MR. BOLLING: We have nothing further.

---

to avoid all questions about insurance. For its part, the prosecution could have avoided mentioning insurance in the opening statement. In extreme cases, reference to clearly inadmissible evidence in an opening statement could lead to a mistrial. In other situations, the failure of a party to produce evidence promised in an opening statement could lead the jury to be skeptical generally about that party's case. In this particular instance, do you think that the defendant should have filed a motion in limine or that the prosecutor should have avoided refering to insurance in the opening statement?

27. Why did defense counsel go into the insurance matter after successfully objecting to the prosecutor's questions about insurance? Could the prosecutor have objected to defense counsel's questions?

JARVIS NASH

[The state's next witness was Mr. Jarvis Nash of La Grange, North Dakota who testified to traveling on Old Foggy Road in Battle County, North Dakota around 9:15 A.M. on August 31, 1981. Mr. Nash testified that while traveling west on Old Foggy Road, he saw a white Camaro turned sideways on the road; he then saw the car straighten up and proceed away from him at a high rate of speed. Mr. Nash then testified to seeing a green car off the left side of the road at the edge of a woods near the spot where the Camaro had been. Nash testified that the green car was then 20 to 40 feet off the road and that he sensed something was wrong and went over to the car to investigate.

[Nash testified that the car was running, the headlights were on, and the windows were fogged up on the inside. He said he saw a "blue jean covered knee" in the back-seat and figured it was a "kid's car" and he was somewhere he ought not be. Nash testified he then got in his truck and left. He also identified the green car as an "Oldsmobile or something of that nature."]

THOMAS M. JACOBS

called as a witness by and in behalf of the State of South Dakota, testified as follows:

Direct Examination

Questions by Mr. BOLLING:

Q: Will you state your full name for the record, please.
A: Thomas M. Jacobs.
Q: Mr. Jacobs, where do you live, please?
A: Hot Springs, Battle County, North Dakota.
Q: Where do you work?
A: Battle County Electric Co-op.
Q: And were you working back on the date of August the 31st, 1981, at approximately 11:05 A.M. that morning?
A: Yes sir, I was.
Q: And where were you working, please, sir?
A: I was traveling on the Old Foggy Road.
Q: Would you tell the Court and jury what you saw or observed there unusual on that morning?
A: Well, I was traveling west on Old Foggy Road. About three-quarters to a mile from U.S. 72 I noticed this green Oldsmobile off the road against a pine tree. I passed the automobile—

MR. ASPEN: Your Honor, we object to the narrative response to the question.[28]

THE COURT: Ask your next question, please.

Q: All right, sir. And what did you do whenever you saw this car, please sir?

A: At first I passed it, then I stopped. Had no intention of stopping but something made me want to stop. I stopped, backed up, and walked down, looked at the automobile.

Q: Tell the Court and jury what you saw or observed when you went over to the car.[29]

A: When I walked down to the automobile I looked in the driver's side—driver's part first, then I looked at the right front fender, which was up against a tree: and as I turned to walk away I looked in the back seat and saw this person laying in the back seat.

Q: And what did you do next, please, sir?

A: I went to the truck, radioed our dispatcher, requested the sheriff to come down.

Q: Did anyone come in response to your call?

A: Yes, sir, Chris Perry, an investigator with Battle County, came.

Q: I show you what's been marked State's Exhibit 1 and I'll ask you if you can identify that exhibit, Mr. Jacobs.

A: Yes sir, I can.

Q: What is it please, sir?

---

28. A direct examination usually takes the form of short, nonsuggestive questions that, when asked and answered in sequence, tell the witness' story efficiently. A narrative response is the witness' account in his own words and chronology without the benefit of the examining counsel's direction. What do you think is the major concern of the defense counsel here? Consider FRE 611, in particular 611(c). A leading question, it is usually said, is one that suggests an answer. That is not a terribly helpful definition, however, for if a question did not suggest an answer, it would be incomprehensible. Obviously, then, it is a matter of the degree to which the question suggests an answer, and the point is that greater latitude to be intrusive is permitted to counsel on cross-examination, when witnesses can be more difficult to deal with because of hostility and self-interest.

As for the specific objection in the transcript, there is nothing that forbids a narrative form of testimony. The trial judge has discretion to ensure that the adversary is not disadvantaged by being unable to anticipate objectionable material. The advantage of a narrative form of questioning, from the point of view of the direct examiner, is that often more information is presented when a witness is given free reign to testify in a narrative. The disadvantage is that it is often less orderly, and more erroneous information may be transmitted.

The issues raised here are probed further at the end of this chapter in Problems 1 and 4.

29. Conducting the direct examination of a cooperative witness can be more challenging than initially meets the eye. The attorney and the witness are likely to have discussed the examination in detail and to have rehearsed—at least several times—both the direct and the probable cross-examination. The difficult task after these rehearsals and after the attorney has become thoroughly familiar with the evidence is for the attorney to appear to have a genuine interest in the questions being asked and to ensure as much as possible that the witness is not merely reciting a rehearsed text but sincerely communicating to the jury. One way to remind a witness to concentrate on communicating with the jury is occasionally to begin a question, as the prosecutor did here, with an admonition to "Tell the jury. . . ."

Chapter One.   Introduction to the Study of Evidence   23

A: That's the Oldsmobile with a South Dakota tag on it. I am sure it's the vehicle I saw off the road there.[30]

Q: Approximately what time was it when you examined—got to the car, in your best judgment?

A: About five minutes after eleven.

Q: And at that time was the motor off or was it running or—

A: The motor was off.

MR. BOLLING: Thank you. You may have the witness.

Cross-Examination

Questions by Mr. BUTERA:

Q: Do you remember which day of the week this was, Mr. Jacobs?
A: Yes sir, it was a Monday morning.
Q: Was it in 1981, or August of 1981, is that when approximately—
A: August 31st, '81.
Q: August 31st, '81.[31] Do you know what the weather was on this particular day?
A: Yes, sir, it was cloudy, threatening to rain. In fact, it was quite a bit of moisture in the air.
Q: Where was the car sitting when you first observed it?
A: It was a ninety-degree angle with the pavement, about 50 foot from the pavement against a pine tree.
Q: Was it rammed into the pine tree or just parked next to it?
A: It was run against the pine tree, right. It did damage to the right front fender.
Q: Right front fender?

---

30. Pay careful attention over the next few pages of the transcript as to how this exhibit is used.

31. The lawyers in this trial are quite skilled interrogators. Pay attention to the style they employ in framing questions and interrogating witnesses. Notwithstanding their skill, on occasion less than the best style is employed. Here we see an example of "echoing" where the lawyer echoes the most recent response of the witness. If done consistently, as often it is by inexperienced attorneys, the practice can become quite annoying and possibly alienate the jury (or at least cause a loss of attentiveness). Echoing can also distract the court reporter, making it more likely that an inexact record will be created. As the preoccupation with "the record" in these footnotes indicates, it is of the utmost importance for the lawyer to be careful in constructing the record. There are a number of mistakes that inexperienced trial lawyers occasionally make that can be avoided by paying careful attention to what is occurring at trial. Think about the following issues:

(a) "overlapping"—if a trial is being conducted with a court reporter, which is still typical today, the reporter cannot accurately record what happens when more than a single person talks at once. In such a circumstance, the careful attorney will be sure to go back and explain "for the record" what transpired; (b) names often cause problems because quite different spellings are often pronounced similarly (e.g. White, Whyte, Wite, Wyatt); (c) figures—when an attorney says "thirty-one-o-four," does this mean 31.4, 31.04, 30,104, or what? Make sure it is clear; (d) gestures—make sure gestures are explained ("let the record show that the witness pointed at the defendant").

A: Yes, sir.
Q: When you came to the vehicle were you able to look inside?
A: Yes, sir, no problem at all.
Q: The windows were clear in there?
A: Right; visibility good.
Q: You said the motor was not running?
A: The motor was not running.
Q: Did you observe whether the motor was warm or cool, or did you observe that?
A: Not until after Chris Perry got there, and it was warm at that time.
Q: This is the first time you've ever observed a car being on the side of the road?
A: In that sort of situation, right.
Q: Now, this road is located in Adams County, North Dakota?
A: No sir, Battle County.
Q: Battle County, North Dakota.
A: Yes, sir.
Q: Did you testify in any of these cases in Battle County, North Dakota?

MR. BOLLING: We object to that question.
THE COURT: Objection will be sustained.[32]
MR. BUTERA: I believe that's all we have, your Honor.
MR. BOLLING: We have nothing further. We ask that this witness be excused.
THE COURT: Any objection?
MR. BUTERA: No, sir.
THE COURT: Thank you for coming, Mr. Jacobs.
MR. BOLLING: Thank you.

[At this point, the court recessed for the noon hour. Before recessing, the judge instructed the jury to avoid discussing the case with anyone, including other jurors. The judge also stressed the importance of retaining an open mind about the facts since the proceedings were not concluded.]

(At 1:20 P.M. the Court, the jury, the defendant, Mr. Bolling, Mr. Elson, Mr. Aspen, Mr. Butera, and all other necessary officers of the court returned to the courtroom and the trial continued as follows, to wit:)

EDWARD CHRISTOPHER PERRY called as a witness by and in behalf of the State of South Dakota having been first duly sworn, testified as follows on

---

32. Why was this objection sustained? Does the judge already know that he is not going to allow a double jeopardy or lack of jurisdiction defense? What does that do to the defense attorneys' theory of the case? Did they have any choice but to proceed as they did?

Chapter One. Introduction to the Study of Evidence

Direct Examination

Questions by MR. BOLLING:

Q: Would you state your full name for the record, please sir.
A: Edward Christopher Perry.
Q: Mr. Perry, where are you employed?
A: Chief investigator with the Battle County Sheriff's Department.
Q: And were you so employed on August 31st and continuous since that date—
A: Yes sir.
Q: —of '81, of the year '81?
A: Yes, sir.
Q: Did you have an occasion to participate in the investigation of the death of Mary Ann McCoy Steele?
A: Yes, sir, I did.
Q: Did that investigation include participating with the Long County authorities as well as elsewhere?
A: Yes, sir.
Q: I'll ask you if you are familiar with a road designated as Old Foggy Road in Battle County, Mr. Perry?
A: Yes, sir, I am.
Q: Did you have an occasion on the date of August the 31st, 1981, to go to that road?
A: I did.
Q: Approximately what time of the day was it when you arrived there, please sir?
A: It was approximately 11:15 A.M.
Q: And who if anyone else was there when you arrived there?
A: When I arrived Mr. Tom Jacobs with the Battle County Electric Co-op was there.
Q: What did you see or observe when you arrived there, please sir?
A: When I arrived the first thing I saw was this green Oldsmobile approximately 50 feet off the roadway up against a tree. Mr. Jacobs was standing approximately 10 feet away.
Q: While you were there did you take any pictures?
A: Yes, sir, I did.
Q: I show you what has been identified as State's Exhibit 1 and I'll ask you if you can identify that, please, sir.
A: Yes, sir.
Q: What is it, please?
A: It's the rear view of the 1978 Oldsmobile Cutlass that belonged to Terry and Mary Ann Steele.
Q: Do you know who took that picture?
A: Yes, sir, I did.

Q: And did you take it there that date?
A: Yes, sir, that very morning.
Q: Does it truly and accurately depict the scene as it existed of that subject matter at that time and place?
A: Yes, sir, it does.

MR. BOLLING: At this time we move to introduce into evidence State's Exhibit 1.
THE COURT: Mr. Aspen, any objection?
MR. ASPEN: We have no objection, your Honor.
THE COURT: It will be admitted into the evidence.[33]

Q: What did you do next, please, sir?
A: As soon as I got out of my vehicle I immediately went to the driver's side of the car and noticed that there was a body laying on the back seat. I immediately opened the door, raised the driver's seat forward, attempted to find a pulse on the lady that was in the back seat, which I failed to get a pulse in the arm. I attempted to find one in the neck area; I was unable to get any pulse there. But I did notice at that time that the body was extremely warm, to the point of being wet under the neck with perspiration.
Q: Continue on, please.
A: As soon as I had determined that there was no heart or heartbeat or pulse or pulse beat, we called the ambulance to the scene.
Q: Now, was the body removed from the car?
A: After several photographs and a crime scene search was made, the body was removed from the car.
Q: I show you what has been marked State's Exhibit 2 and I'll ask you if you can identify that exhibit, please, sir.
A: Yes, sir. This is a photograph made by me from the passenger side of the automobile showing the body laying on the rear seat.

---

33. Pay close attention to the way in which this exhibit was dealt with. There is a universal principle of evidence law that no evidence is admissible until it is shown to be what it purports to be. A witness with firsthand knowledge of the litigated event "purports" to have such knowledge and is qualified to testify upon being shown to have such knowledge. The witness can qualify himself or herself by testifying to the fact that the witness does indeed possess firsthand knowledge of the relevant issues. See FRE 602. Tangible items must also be authenticated. See FRE 901, 902. The witness here is authenticating the photograph. This is also referred to as "laying the foundation" for its admissibility. For a very useful work on the subject of foundations, see E. Imwinkelried, Evidentiary Foundations (1980). Generally speaking, to have an exhibit admitted into evidence, the attorney must first have the exhibit marked for identification by the court reporter. By marking an exhibit for identification and then by referring to the identification mark when the exhibit is used, the attorney can ensure that the record accurately reflects what exhibit is being discussed. The attorney then must lay the necessary foundation to show the exhibit is what it purports to be, offer the exhibit into evidence ("Your Honor, we now offer exhibit 1 into evidence"), and make sure the trial court rules on its admissibility.

The requirement of authentication is a prerequisite to the admissibility of evidence, and thus it is for the judge to decide whether the conditions of admissibility have been satisfied. Consider once more FRE 104. We will return to this rule in Chapter Three.

Chapter One. Introduction to the Study of Evidence 27

Q: Does that truly and accurately depict the scene as it existed that morning on the date we have referred to?
A: Yes, sir, it does.

MR. BOLLING: We move to introduce into evidence State's Exhibit 2.
THE COURT: It will be admitted.

[In a similar fashion, the state laid the foundation for and introduced into evidence State's Exhibit No. 3 and State's Exhibit No. 21 without objection from defense counsel. State's Exhibit No. 3 was a photograph taken from the driver's side of the car showing the face and body of the victim, the contents of her purse, and a shopping bag. State's Exhibit No. 21 was a photograph taken by Perry of the Steele auto's interior showing blood stains on the rear seat, a piece of green plastic wire on the floor board, and a small red toy truck. The state then turned to the sequence of events following the body's removal from the scene:]

Q: Now, after the body was removed did you go with the body to the hospital or wherever they took it?
A: Yes, sir. I followed the ambulance to the Lockhart Medical Center.
Q: Now, prior to the body being removed did you make an examination of the body itself?
A: Yes, sir. As soon as we got the body out of the rear seat and had it laid out on the stretcher, I then attempted to locate any wounds about the head area. At first glance there didn't appear to be any; then I opened the eyelids and found the left eye—I mean, excuse me—the right eye was damaged quite a bit. It appeared to have—that the eyeball was busted.
Q: Do you see any bruises, abrasions, or wounds on the body other than that wound that you have just referred to?
A: No, sir.
Q: After you got to the hospital—you say you went to the hospital—did you follow the body to the area they took it at the hospital?
A: I did, yes, sir.
Q: Do you know Dr. Stoddard?
A: Yes, sir, very well.
Q: Were you present when he performed a postmortem examination?
A: I was, yes sir.
Q: Did you or anyone in your presence identify the body to him as that of Mary Ann Steele?
A: I did, yes, sir.
Q: I'll ask you if at the time the body got to the hospital, if you had an occasion to make other pictures there at the hospital.
A: Yes, sir.

Q: I show you what has been marked as State's Exhibit 4A and I'll ask you if you can identify it, please sir.
A: Yes, sir. This is the body of the person that I identified as Mary Ann Steele in the autopsy room after her clothing had been removed.
Q: Does that truly and accurately depict the body as it existed after the removal of the clothes of Mary Ann Steele?
A: Yes, sir.

MR. BOLLING: At this time we move to introduce into evidence State's Exhibit 4A.

MR. ASPEN: Your Honor, we would object to State's Exhibit 4A, which we've already entered an objection previously, that this photo does not show the body at the time of the—at the crime scene itself, the fact that it would be inflammatory if presented to this jury as evidence. The photo was taken sometime after the body was removed from the vehicle.

MR. BOLLING: May it please the Court, we would show that it was taken immediately after the body was removed from the vehicle and the clothes taken off. May I be allowed to ask a question or two of the witness to substantiate that, your Honor?

THE COURT: Go ahead.

Q: How long after you removed the body was it before it was removed to the hospital?
A: After it was removed from the automobile?
Q: Yes, sir.
A: Approximately five minutes.
Q: All right, sir.
A: Just long enough for me to take two or three more pictures while they were loading her in the ambulance, then we left.
Q: Approximately in time, what length of time was it from the time it left the scene until this picture 4A was taken?
A: It took approximately 10 minutes to drive from the location to the hospital. I would say within 25 to 30 minutes.
Q: Less than half an hour?
A: About that; 25 to 30 minutes.

MR. BOLLING: We again move to introduce State's Exhibit 4A, please.

MR. ASPEN: We renew our objection.

THE COURT: Objection will be overruled on each ground and it will be admitted into evidence as State's Exhibit No. 4A.

Q: I show you now what has been marked State's Exhibit 4 and I'll ask you if you can identify that exhibit.
A: Yes, sir. This is a photograph of the victim taken this same morning shortly after we arrived at the Lockhart Medical Center before the clothing had been removed.

Chapter One. Introduction to the Study of Evidence

Q: You took one before and one after the clothing?[34]
A: Yes sir.
Q: They were about how far apart in time, please, sir?
A: Just the amount of time it took to get her undressed and I would say no more than five or ten minutes.
Q: Does that truly and accurately depict the scene as it existed at the time that you were at the hospital and viewed the remains of Mary Ann Steele on that date, August 31st, 1981?
A: Yes, sir.

MR. BOLLING: We would move to introduce into evidence State's Exhibit 4.
MR. ASPEN: We'll object on the same grounds as State's Exhibit 4A.
THE COURT: On those grounds it will be overruled and it will be admitted into evidence as Exhibit No. 4.

Q: Did you have occasion to look through the automobile itself?
A: Yes, sir.
Q: What if anything did you see or observe there in the car, Officer Perry?
A: Well, while waiting for the arrival of the ambulance, I went over the car and made my photographs, and on the floorboard of the front of the car, next to the accelerator there was a brick lying approximately two inches from the accelerator. In the rear of the floorboard was, as the picture shows, a piece of green plastic wire and a toy truck.
Q: Was this a two- or four-door automobile?
A: Two-door automobile.
   On the floorboard in the rear on the driver's side was a spot of blood. I noticed another spot or two of blood on the passenger's side of the automobile on the edge of the front seat which raises back and forth on a two-door car. It was a couple of spots of blood there, and the blood where her head was lying on the seat.

MR. BOLLING: I have nothing further from Officer Perry.

Cross-Examination

Questions by MR. ASPEN:

Q: Investigator Perry, you stated that there were spots of blood on the floorboard. Was that in the rear?
A: Rear floorboard, yes, sir.
Q: And there was a spot of blood where else did you say?

---

34. What appears to be a relatively innocuous question may be of great significance. Without "before" and "after" photographs, the defense could argue that the state had manipulated the evidence, thus making the photograph inadmissible. This also points out the crucial relationship between pre-trial investigatory techniques and the subsequent admissibility of evidence.

A: On the passenger side on the edge of the seat, the part that raises back and forth on a two-door, on the very edge as you open the door you can see spots of blood on that.

Q: Could you tell in your experience in the investigation of these type matters whether or not the spots of blood appeared to have been placed there by the body being rubbed up against the passenger side of the seat, or whether or not these were sort of a spatter type blood?

A: It was not smeared as it would be, say, putting a body in the car. It looked more just like splattered type blood or just dropped on there.

Q: And also the spot that you found on the driver's side in the back-seat there, on the floorboard, how did that spot of blood appear to be? Was it smeared?

A: It looked probably like one drop of blood. No, it was not smeared. It was almost a round circle.

Q: Did it appear to be a splatter type spot of blood, in your opinion?

A: No. This was very near where the hand was laying off the seat, and there was some blood on the hand and on the purse and the fingers. It's a possibility it dropped off from the fingers.

Q: You stated that the body was warm to the extent that the area under the neck was wet; is that correct?

A: That's correct, yes, sir.

Q: You were there when the postmortem was conducted; is that correct?

A: Yes, sir.

Q: Do you know of your own personal knowledge or did the person who conducted the postmortem establish a time of death?

A: Not while—not during the postmortem, he did not, no.

Q: Do you know of any personal knowledge that you have—

A: He didn't tell me. There was an autopsy report. I don't recall exactly what it said.

Q: Do you have a judgment in your own opinion whether or not the person that you examined, which has been identified as Mary Ann Steele, whether or not death had occurred just prior to your arriving on the scene, or do you have any judgment as to the time of death?

A: I estimated, just from my experience in dealing with deaths, that she probably had been dead no longer than a couple of hours.[35]

Q: The investigation that you made primarily and what you have testified here has to do with the investigation in Battle County, North Dakota—

A: Yes, sir.

Q: —of this death; is that correct?

A: That's correct.

Q: And as far as investigation in South Dakota, did you make any investigation in South Dakota?

---

35. Why is this witness allowed to give such an opinion? This is an example of how the rigors of the evidence rules are relaxed at trial to expedite matters.

Chapter One. Introduction to the Study of Evidence   31

A: Yes, sir, I was part of the investigation in South Dakota.
Q: Mr. Perry, did you perform this investigation for the Sheriff's Department of Battle County, North Dakota, and for the district attorney at that point?
A: Yes, sir.
Q: And did this investigation at that point lead to an indictment of Mr. Terry Steele, in Battle County, North Dakota?
A: It did, yes sir.
Q: Do you know whether or not that case was concluded in Battle County, North Dakota?
A: It was.
Q: It was? Do you know the outcome of that case?
A: Yes, sir, I do.
Q: What was the outcome?
A: Mr. Steele received a life sentence—
Q: On what charge?
A: —on a plea of—
Q: Sir?
A: —murder.
Q: Murder of who?
A: Murder of his wife, Mary Ann Steele.

MR. ASPEN: Your Honor, could we have Mr. Perry on call for recall as a witness in the case?
THE COURT: Do you have any redirect?
MR. BOLLING: No, sir.
THE COURT: Mr. Perry, you will need to remain here in the courthouse subject to being recalled again.

SHERIFF PRENTISS BROOKES

[Sheriff Prentiss Brookes testified to his law enforcement background and credentials totalling over 26 years' experience. Sheriff Brookes testified about his department's investigation of Mary Ann Steele's death beginning with the afternoon of August 31, 1981. He testified that both he and Captain Thomas Holloway of the Sheriff's Department went to the Steele residence to notify the next of kin and found no one at home. Sheriff Brookes then testified that he found Terry Steele's work address from a neighbor and went there to notify Steele of his wife's death. Sheriff Brookes then testified that Captain Holloway and he returned to the Steele residence to secure it for investigative purposes and that his department coordinated with Battle County, North Dakota, law enforcement authorities in investigating Mary Ann Steele's death.

[The defense's cross-examination focused on the limited extent of Sheriff Brookes' personal involvement in the investigation, the fact that he had personally never been to the Old Foggy Road site and the condition of the Steele's house when he and his deputy entered it. The defense also questioned Sheriff Brookes on Terry Steele's reaction when he learned of his wife's death. Sheriff Brookes testified Terry Steele seemed upset.]

Thomas B. Holloway

called as a witness by and in behalf of the State of South Dakota having been first duly sworn, testified as follows on

Direct Examination

Questions by MR. BOLLING:

Q: State your name for the record, please, sir.
A: Thomas Holloway.
Q: Mr. Holloway, where are you employed?
A: Long County Sheriff's Department.
Q: How long have you been employed at the sheriff's office?
A: Approximately three and a half years.
Q: In what capacity are you employed there, please, sir?
A: I'm chief investigator.
Q: Prior to that did you have any law-enforcement experience?
A: Yes, sir.
Q: Where and for how long?
A: I was employed by the district attorney's office in this county for five years as chief investigator.
Q: Now, you heard the sheriff's testimony. Going back to the date of August the 31st, 1981, whenever you learned of Mary Ann Steele's death, after you went back to the house—did you go in on the first trip or the second trip?
A: On the second trip. I did not enter the house—discovered the back door open on the first trip but I did not go inside the residence until the second trip that day.
Q: Now, when you went in tell us what you did, please.
A: The second trip?
Q: Yes, sir.

MR. BUTERA: Your Honor, we object. There has been no foundation.
THE COURT: Objection will be sustained.

Q: Approximately what time was it, Tommy, when you went back?
A: Went back the second time? Approximately two o'clock in the afternoon.
Q: Was anyone else present besides you?
A: Sheriff Brookes and myself.

Chapter One. Introduction to the Study of Evidence 33

Q: Tell us what you did once you went inside, please.
A: I went to the back door. The door was unlocked, so I just turned the handle and went on in. I had to walk around the kitchen table; it was sitting almost directly in front of the rear door of the house. So I walked around to the right of the door, and when I walked around to the right of the door I noticed on the floor a cigarette butt, looked like it had been mashed down on the floor like you would do in a sidewalk, you know, or something like that. I then went on around the kitchen table and went down the hall—
Q: Let me stop you just a minute. Other than that, did the house seem to be in disarray or was it neat or orderly, or how would you term it, other than the cigarette butt?
A: The house was neat and orderly but lived in. There were personal articles laying around but nothing in disarray.
Q: All right.
A: I went down to the left, down the hall to the bedroom that was on the right, and I had to go into the far corner of the bedroom and turn an electric fan off that was there. And then I turned around and retraced my steps, and when I went out the back door I turned the latch and pulled the door shut behind me, locking it, and then we left the house at that time.
Q: Mr. Holloway, I'll show you what's been marked as State's Exhibit 9 and ask if you can identify that, please.
A: This is a black and white photograph of the exterior view of the Steele residence on Pinecrest Drive.
Q: Does that truly and accurately depict the scene as it existed at that time, that dwelling, on August 31st, 1981?
A: Yes, sir.

MR. BOLLING: We would move to introduce State's Exhibit—whatever number that is.
THE COURT: State's Exhibit No. 9, do you have any objection to it?
MR. BUTERA: No, sir.
MR. ASPEN: No objection.
THE COURT: It will be admitted into evidence.

[In a similar fashion, the state had Officer Holloway identify State's Exhibits No. 10 and 11. State's Exhibit 10 was identified as a photograph taken of the Steele driveway and certain tire tracks and marks on the pavement. State's Exhibit No. 11 was identified as a photograph taken of the driveway and sidewalk to the Wallace residence's front door (a neighbor of the Steeles). Both were admitted into evidence without objection. But note the objections to the following exhibit:]

Q: I show you what's been marked State's Exhibit 12. I'll ask you if you can identify that exhibit.

A: Yes, sir. This is a black and white photograph of the bed, bedroom area in the Steele residence, inside the Steele residence.
Q: Does that truly and accurately depict the scene as it existed at the time and place whenever that photograph was taken?
A: Yes, sir.

MR. BOLLING: We move to introduce into evidence State's Exhibit 12.
MR. BUTERA: We would object to this one, your Honor. He failed to lay a predicate.[36]
THE COURT: As to what particular part of the predicate?
MR. ASPEN: The time of the photograph, who took it, et cetera.
MR. BOLLING: I'll be glad to go farther.

Q: Were you present when this was taken, Mr. Holloway?
A: Yes, sir, I was.
Q: Did you take it?
A: No, sir.
Q: But you were present when it was taken?
A: Yes, sir.
Q: And when was it taken, please, sir?
A: It was taken the first.
Q: September 1st?
A: Right, the next day after this.
Q: And who took the photograph?
A: Special Agent Ed Marshall with the State Police Bureau.
Q: Approximately what time of day was it taken?
A: About one o'clock in the afternoon.

MR. BOLLING: We move to introduce into evidence State's Exhibit 12.
THE COURT: Mr. Aspen?
MR. ASPEN: Your Honor, we object unless they can show the house was secured from the time of the first investigation, the first visit, until the photo was taken the following day, based on the remoteness of the photo.
THE COURT: Objection will be sustained at this point.

Q: Mr. Holloway, when you went in and cut off the fan—
A: Yes, sir.
Q: —what date was that?
A: That was the 31st.
Q: And approximately what time was it?
A: About two o'clock in the afternoon.
Q: Was that fan located in the same room that you are referring to here in this State's Exhibit 12?
A: Yes, sir. It was.

36. Pay attention to the treatment of this photograph. What is going on and why?

Q: When you went in to cut off the fan did you have occasion to look at the subject matter portrayed in State's Exhibit 12?
A: Yes, sir.
Q: You say you secured the building as you left?
A: Yes, sir.
Q: The next time that that building was gone into, were you present when it was gone into?
A: I was there shortly after it was gone into, not at the exact time it was entered.
Q: Was the subject matter there then like it was when you cut off the fan, as far as you can tell?
A: Yes, sir.

MR. BOLLING: We would move at this time to introduce State's Exhibit 12.
MR. ASPEN: Your Honor, we still would renew our objection. The officer testified that he did not take the photo but he was present when it was taken, which it was taken September 1st, the day after he stated that the building was secured. In essence, if he can testify as to how the building was secured, then we would probably not object, but we need to know how it was secured.
THE COURT: If that can be established from this witness.
MR. BOLLING: I understand that he locked it.

Q: How was the building secured, Mr. Holloway?
A: The front door was locked, and when I went out the rear door I turned the latch and pulled it shut behind me, tested it, and it locked behind me.

THE COURT: You reoffer the exhibit?
MR. BOLLING: Yes, sir.
MR. BUTERA: May I voir dire the witness as to the question concerning the scene after he left it?
THE COURT: Go ahead.
MR. BUTERA: Were there police or sheriff's department signs put up around the house warning anyone not to enter the house or the property at that time?
THE WITNESS: On the 31st?
MR. BUTERA: Yes, sir.
THE COURT: There was nothing put up there at that time?
THE WITNESS: No sir, it was not.
MR. BUTERA: We would renew our objection at this time, your Honor.
THE COURT: That would be correct, Mr. Aspen, you renew your objection?
MR. ASPEN: Yes, sir, we would renew it, based on the remoteness of the photograph.

THE COURT: Objections will be overruled. It will be admitted into evidence as No. 12 for the State.

[In a similar fashion State's Exhibit 12, a photograph of certain personal items, was admitted into evidence.]

Q: I show you State's Exhibit 7 and I'll ask you if you can identify that exhibit.
A: Yes, sir. That's looking down Pinecrest Drive toward the Steele residence.
Q: I show you what's listed as State's Exhibit 8 and I'll ask you if you can identify that, please.
A: Yes, sir. It's a black and white photograph showing the Steele residence and the driveway and the residence which would be immediately east of the Steele residence on the same side of the road.
Q: And I've asked you previously, you are familiar with that area?
A: Yes, sir.
Q: Does that truly and accurately depict the scene as it exists there at the Steele residence?

MR. BOLLING: We move to introduce into evidence State's Exhibit 8.[37]
MR. ASPEN: We object on the same grounds as State's Exhibit No. 12.
THE COURT: Objection will be sustained until it can be shown that that's the scene as of August 31st, 1981.
MR. BOLLING: May it please the Court, it's my understanding that if the picture is taken at a different time and we can explain the difference, we can still introduce it.

Q: I'll ask you, was this picture taken on August 31st?
A: No, sir, it was not.
Q: When was it taken, if you know?
A: It was approximately a month before the trial in Battle County.
Q: As far as the roads, driveways, the buildings, were they the same on the date that this picture was taken as they were on August 31st, 1981?
A: Yes, sir.
Q: Would the vegetation, then, be the only change, if any?
A: That's correct. There was full vegetation in August, whereas that was last winter, I think it was.

MR. BOLLING: With that, then, we would renew our request to introduce State's Exhibit 8.
THE COURT: Mr. Aspen?
MR. ASPEN: Same objection, your Honor, remoteness of time.

---

37. Does it matter that the lawyer did not wait to get an answer from his witness? If it does not matter here, it might in some other case. This is an example of the attorney not being sufficiently attentive to the record.

Chapter One. Introduction to the Study of Evidence 37

THE COURT: Objection will be overruled. It will be admitted into evidence.[38]

Q: I show you State's Exhibit 5 and ask you if you can identify that exhibit.
A: Yes, sir. It's a black and white photograph of Pinecrest Fundamentalist Church.
Q: And does that truly and accurately depict the scene of Pinecrest Fundamentalist Church as it existed back on August 31st, 1981?
A: Yes sir.
Q: Do you know when that picture was taken?
A: At the same time the other road pictures were taken.
Q: Would the area around the church that's enclosed in there be the same with the exception of the vegetation?
A: Yes, sir.

MR. BUTERA: Your Honor, we would object to this on the grounds as being irrelevant to this matter here.
MR. BOLLING: We'll show relevance by another witness.[39]
THE COURT: All right. The exhibit will be withdrawn at this time, then.

Q: Mr. Holloway, I'll show you what has been marked State's Exhibit 18 and ask you if you can identify that exhibit.
A: Yes, sir.
Q: What is it, please, sir?
A: It's an instant photograph that I made at the parking lot at the Lovett Police Department on 9/4/81 of a vehicle, a pickup truck belonging to Amy Lucas.
Q: Does it truly and accurately depict the scene as it existed at that time and place of that vehicle?
A: Yes, sir, it does.

MR. ASPEN: Your honor, we would object on the relevancy of that photo.
THE COURT: Objection will be sustained at this point.
MR. BOLLING: We'll connect it up later, your Honor.

Q: I'll ask you if you can identify State's Exhibit 19, please.
A: Yes, sir. This is a rear view of the same vehicle. It's a photograph from the rear view of the same vehicle, made at the Lovett Police Department parking lot on 9/4 of '81.

---

38. Has all this time and effort expended upon the exhibits been worth the cost? What might be the alternative?

39. Begin to pay attention to the structure of the state's case: why witnesses are called in a certain order and why they are examined in the order that they are. Here we observe a common problem. A single witness cannot provide a sufficient predicate for the admissibility of evidence. Another witness will be called later whose testimony together with this testimony will suffice to authenticate this evidence. The lawyer, however, has to be sure that each link in the chain is properly forged.

Q: Does that truly and accurately depict the scene as it existed of that vehicle at that time?
A: Yes, sir, it does.

MR. BOLLING: Move to introduce into evidence State's Exhibit 19.
MR. BUTERA: We would object, your Honor, on the same grounds, irrelevant to this point.
THE COURT: Objection will be sustained at this point.
MR. BOLLING: We'll connect it up later.

Q: Mr. Holloway, do you know an officer by the name of Ed Marshall?
A: Yes, sir, I do.
Q: Do you know for whom he works?
A: State Police Bureau.
Q: Did you have an occasion to work with him in the investigation of Mrs. Steele's death?
A: Yes, sir, I did.
Q: Did you have occasion to go outside this county in this investigation?
A: Yes, sir.
Q: Could you tell the judge and the ladies and gentlemen of the jury where this investigation took you, please?
A: To Lovett, North Dakota, several times; Calvery, North Dakota; Woodridge probably half a dozen times; and then numerous times over here.
Q: Did you go to the scene where—the alleged scene where the car was located and the body of Mary Ann Steele located?
A: Yes, I did.
Q: When did you go there, please, sir?
A: It was Monday, a week after the car was found; about the seventh.
Q: When did you commence your investigation of this offense?
A: On the 31st.
Q: And was that investigation spasmodic, continuous, or how?
A: Continuous.
Q: Did you assign any other officers under you in the sheriff's department to perform work on this case?
A: Yes, sir. At different times several of the others worked on it.
Q: Was Investigator Robert Helms one of those officers?
A: Yes, sir.
Q: Could you name some of the other officers that did some work?
A: Deputy Dolton.
Q: Bobby Dolton?
A: Yes, sir. He picked up some items. I can't remember offhand who else was involved in it.
Q: I'll ask you if the South Dakota Crime Lab participated in this investigation.
A: Yes, sir, they did.
Q: And who represented the lab?

Chapter One. Introduction to the Study of Evidence 39

A: Criminalist Ted Randall from the Bartonville lab came down.
Q: Do you have knowledge of any difficulty that Criminalist Randall is having today in his family?
A: Well, yes, sir. To a certain degree, yes, sir.
Q: Would you tell us what the problem is?

MR. ASPEN: Your Honor, we're going to—
MR. BUTERA: Objection. Hearsay.
THE COURT: Objection would be sustained.[40]
MR. BOLLING: We'll withdraw it, then.

---

40. Why would the state ask such a question of this witness? The objection to the question is on hearsay grounds. Briefly, hearsay occurs when a witness is asked to relate what some other person said in order to prove the truth of what that other person said. This witness is being asked to report what Randall, or someone else, said concerning Randall to prove that the matter is true. The hearsay rule forbids this as a means of encouraging individuals with firsthand knowledge to be brought to court to testify. That, in turn, is desirable in order to ensure trustworthiness and to allow the adversary to cross-examine.

There are tactical issues to take into account when deciding whether to object to an opponent's question. First, if a question will not elicit damaging information, there is no reason to weigh the proceedings down with trivial objections. Attorneys should also be wary of imparting the impression to the jury that they have something to hide. Moreover, an objection can often underscore the damaging aspects of an objectionable question, and wisdom may on these occasion dictate silence in the hope that the jury will miss the point. Finally, objectionable questions sometimes will be helpful to one's own case either because the specific answer will be helpful or because the question will "open the door" to one's own testimony that might not otherwise be admissible. See page 20 supra (defense counsel's inquiry about insurance proceeds opened door to prosecutor's questions about the subject).

There are two general types of objections. The first is to the form of the question. For example, the question might be leading, be argumentative, assume facts not in evidence, be compound (that is, asks two or more questions in the guise of one), call for a narrative response, or on cross-examination exceed the scope of the direct. The other type of objection goes to the answer that is likely to be obtained. The answer might be hearsay, violate a dead man's statute, violate the parole evidence or best evidence rules, lack a sufficient foundation, or involve privilege. In each case, the proper procedure is to interpose the objection after the question has been asked, and witnesses must allow the adversary time to interpose the objection. There will be times when such a procedure will be inadequate, such as whenever asking the question itself is as damaging as getting the answer. ("Now, Mr. Smith, isn't it true that you are in fact a wild-eyed anarchist who would betray his own mother to advance your causes, and indeed haven't you already done so?"). The prosecution's reference in this case to the wife being buried with her child in her arms may fit into this category.

At common law, there were in addition to all these rules what were, and are, called rules of competency that would keep a person off the stand entirely. Spouses at common law were incompetent to testify for or against a spouse; interested persons, including parties, could not testify; atheists were incompetent, as were children and the mentally ill. The Federal Rules have eliminated competency as a separate limitation on the admissibility of evidence. Except in diversity cases, FRE 602 is the only competency rule left, limiting testimony to those who have personal knowledge. The word *competency* is now limited to referring to the power of the trial judge to exclude evidence as a result of some other rule of evidence than general relevancy, such as the specific exclusionary rules in Article IV of the Federal Rules. For example, one can say that evidence within the rule against admitting insurance is "incompetent," but all that means is that the judge must decide if the evidence is within the rule or not. Using the word *competent* to refer to the judge's responsibility to administer the rules of evidence is unobjectionable, so long as one bears in mind that little remains of the testimonial incompetencies of the common law.

Q: Mr. Holloway, can you or any of the officers that you worked with ascertain exactly what point and place that the fatal shot was fired into the head of Mary Ann Steele?
A: Not that I know of, no, sir.
Q: I show you what's been marked as State's Exhibit 14. I'll ask you to examine that exhibit and identify it, if you can. What is in the exhibit, please, sir?
A: Looks like some jewelry: earrings, a watch, a necklace; a can of Arid Extra Dry deodorant and an instant—one of those little pocket cameras—not an instant camera but a pocket camera; some personal papers, a vase, a doll, and another vase, personal papers.
Q: Go back to the center area. What did you say that you have identified?
A: A watch, earrings, and a necklace.

MR. BOLLING: You may look at these and pass them around (handing exhibits to a member of the jury).
THE COURT: Any further questions from the witness on direct examination?
MR. BOLLING: Just a minute, Judge.

Q: Mr. Holloway, without going into the elements of a statement, were you present when any statements were made?
A: Yes, sir.
Q: What other officer was present besides you when a statement was made?
A: Sheriff Brookes.
Q: With regards to the statement made to Officer Marshall, were you ever present when any statements were either made or signed in his presence?
A: Yes, sir, I witnessed the signing of a statement.
Q: You witnessed the signing?
A: Yes, sir.
Q: And how many statements did you witness the signing of?
A: One.
Q: One?
A: Yes, sir.
Q: Who was that statement by?
A: Terry Steele.
Q: Terry Steele?
A: Yes, sir.

MR. BOLLING: Thank you. I believe that's all for me.
THE COURT: Cross-examination?
MR. BUTERA: Yes, sir, we have some questions. I would like for the jurors to get through viewing the pictures before I question him.

(A long pause was had in the proceedings while the jurors individually looked at the pictures handed to them by Mr. Bolling, after which the trial continued as follows, to wit:)

Chapter One. Introduction to the Study of Evidence

THE COURT: Mr. Butera?

Cross-Examination

Questions by MR. BUTERA:

Q: You have at all times been an employee of Long County, South Dakota, since at least 1981, September or August of 1981?
A: Yes, sir.
Q: And you have been exclusively an employee of the Long County Sheriff's Department since that time?
A: That's correct.
Q: And those actions that you—this investigation, was it under the auspices strictly of the Long County Sheriff's office?
A: Absolutely, yes, sir.
Q: You weren't aiding or investigating another state's sheriff's department?
A: It was a mutual thing. They were assisting us with our investigation, we were assisting them with theirs.
Q: In other words, you were working with a sheriff's department or the district attorney's office in Battle County, North Dakota?
A: Right.
Q: I'm not saying you were working for them but you were working with them?
A: Working with them, yes, sir.
Q: And you went up there a number of times and their investigators came down here a number of times?
A: That's correct.
Q: And as a consequence of your investigatory efforts in Long County and your cooperation with the investigatory personnel in Battle County, do you know whether or not this led to an indictment against Mr. Terry Steele for the murder of Mary Ann Steele in Battle County, North Dakota.
A: I understand that it did. I've never seen the indictment, but I understand that it did.
Q: Did you hear that on TV or the newspaper, read it in the newspaper?
A: Yes, sir.
Q: You said you were present when Mr. Steele made a statement to the investigators up in Battle County, North Dakota.
A: I wasn't present when the statement was made, I was present when the statement was signed.
Q: Do you recall the date of that signing of the statement by Mr. Steele, Terry Steele.
A: It was September the 4th.
Q: September the 4th, 1981?
A: '81, yes sir.

Q: Do you recall testifying before a grand jury in Long County concerning the Terry Steele case?
A: Yes sir.
Q: Were you subpoenaed as a possible witness in the case against Terry Steele in Battle County, North Dakota?
A: Yes, sir.
Q: And you were subpoenaed to testify in that case if there had been a trial?
A: Yes, sir.
Q: Who were you subpoenaed by?
A: The state.
Q: The state of what?
A: North Dakota.
Q: Was it the district attorney's office up there that initiated it?
A: I'm sure it was; that's the procedure.
Q: Let me ask you one more question about the statement I failed to ask you. The statement that Mr. Steele signed on or about September the 4th of 1981, where was this, where did that signing take place?
A: At the North Dakota state trooper barracks in Woodridge.
Q: Was it in the morning or in the evening?
A: It was in the evening.
Q: How long had you been there prior to the witnessing of Mr. Steele signing the statement?
A: I'm not sure. Probably three or four hours.
Q: Were you actually present when he gave the statement or you just saw him sign it?
A: I came into the room after the statement had been given and saw him sign the statement.
Q: Let me take you back to the day of—I believe it was on a Monday morning, of the 31st of August of 1981, the date of this alleged crime. I believe it was testified that you and Sheriff Brookes went to the house on that particular day. I'm talking about Terry Steele's house.
A: Yes, sir.[41]
Q: What time did you initially go to Mr. Steele's house?
A: I think—it was after lunch; like, say, one o'clock or something like that.

---

41. Compare the form of questioning on cross-examination to that employed on direct examination, and reread FRE 611(c). There are two different approaches to cross-examination. One is the "wide open" rule that allows a cross-examiner to inquire into any matter that is relevant to the trial. The other approach, exemplified by FRE 611(b), is to limit the scope of cross-examination to the scope of the direct. The former rule probably saves some time. The latter preserves the direct-examiner's right to present the evidence as he or she desires. Note that the rules of evidence do not apply to hearings to determine preliminary questions of fact that govern the admissibility of evidence. See FRE 1101 (d)(1). See also FRE 104 (d), which permits an accused to testify as to preliminary matters without waiving the fifth amendment privilege.

Chapter One. Introduction to the Study of Evidence

Q: How many times that day did you go to Mr. Steele's house?
A: Twice.
Q: When you first got the news of the murder of Mary Steele up in Battle County, did you and Sheriff Brookes—what did you do or where did you go?
A: Well, when we first got the message it was on—I had to go to a phone in Stelle and call the office. They requested that I not use the radio for traffic, so I went to a phone in Stelle and I received a message from Battle County that gave me the address and asked me to go find some kinfolks there, that they had this person up there, they didn't know who was kin to her, and so forth.

We then went to the house. I went around to the back door and knocked, and that's when I found the door unlatched. The sheriff went to the front door.
Q: The sheriff was with you at this time?
A: Oh, yes, the sheriff was with me.
Q: Okay. Let me ask you something, Mr. Holloway, let me stop you right there. The first time you went to the house you found the back door was unlocked; is that correct?
A: Yes.
Q: Did you go inside at that time?
A: No, sir, I did not.
Q: Do you recall checking any other doors at that time?
A: Yes, sir. The front door was checked also. It was locked.
Q: Did you discover the fan running then?
A: The sheriff saw the fan when we pulled up in the yard. You know, he said, "There must be somebody here, I see a fan running in the bedroom." So—
Q: Was the window up or down?
A: I think it was up. So we got no response to knocking on the front door, so I said, "Well, maybe they've got the TV going in the back or something." So I went around to the back and beat on the back door. Still no response. Well, I just reached down and turned the knob. When it gave I just saw that the door was unlocked, pulled it back shut, and left.
Q: Did you lock the back door then?
A: No, sir, not at that time.
Q: You just pulled it back?
A: Right.
Q: Mr. Holloway, what time did you initially go to the house again?
A: About one o'clock in the afternoon.
Q: In the afternoon?
A: Right.
Q: And then how long did you stay at the house?
A: Five minutes.

Q: And then you and Sheriff Brookes proceeded to Flagg Buildings then, is that correct?
A: We went to the neighbor's first. I didn't know who lived there but when the boy came to the door I knew him, and I asked him did he know the guy next door and where did he work. And he told us yeah, his name was Terry Steele, and he worked at Flagg Buildings on Fourth Avenue and Pershing Drive in Lovett.
Q: Did you proceed to Flagg Buildings?
A: We drove to Flagg Buildings at that time.
Q: And did you see Mr. Steele when you arrived at Flagg Buildings?
A: Yes, sir.
Q: And did you tell Mr. Steele about the death of his wife at that time?
A: He had just—like I say, five minutes before we got there somebody called him from Woodridge and told him about it, or his cousin came there, or something. I'm not sure, but when I walked up in front of the place it was evident that he already knew about it.
Q: How do you say it was evident that he already knew about it?
A: He appeared to be emotionally upset, yes, sir.
Q: Was he crying and—
A: To a certain degree, yes, sir.
Q: —upset looking, worried looking?
A: Yes, sir.
Q: Now, did you or Sheriff Brookes in your presence, did you have a conversation with Mr. Steele at that time?
A: Yes, sir, I did.
Q: What did you say to Mr. Steele at that time?
A: I showed him my identification, told him who I was, that I was with the Long County Sheriff's Department. And he sat down on the seat of his car there in the yard at Flagg Buildings, and he had the little boy, Ashley, in his arms. And I said, "I take it you've heard about your wife."
Q: And he said, "Yes, I have."
A: I said, "I'm sorry to have to tell you or bring you the news, but before you go to Woodridge I would like to talk to you for just a minute." And I asked him when was the last time he saw his wife, and he told me that she had put him out that morning at nine o'clock at work.
Q: All right. Then did you proceed back to the house shortly thereafter?
A: Well, you know, after that conversation the sheriff stepped up and asked—told him, "Terry, you know your back door was open at your house?" And he said, "No." "And would you want us to go back over there and lock the house, and let you go on to Woodridge?" And he said, "Yeah, I would appreciate it if you would go back over there and lock the house for me."
Q: Then did you and—

Chapter One. Introduction to the Study of Evidence

A: The sheriff and I drove back down on Pinecrest Drive and locked the house.
Q: Approximately what time did you arrive at the house the second time?
A: Between 1:30 and two o'clock probably the latest.
Q: What did you do at that time?
A: Drove up in front of the house, and I walked around through the gate, behind the house, opened the door—
Q: The back door?
A: —back door, walked in, walked around the right side of the kitchen table, down the hall, turned the fan off; turned around and retraced my steps, came out the back door, turned the latch, pulled the door shut behind me, and we left.
Q: And when did you next come back to the house?
A: The next day.
Q: Approximately what time?
A: Around noon.
Q: Now, from two o'clock that afternoon of the 31st until approximately noon of the first, being September the 1st, was the house watched or guarded or marked as a crime scene by the sheriff's department?
A: No, sir.
Q: So there was nobody there to watch the house during that time?
A: No, sir.
Q: No law-enforcement officers, in other words?
A: Correct.
Q: And the day the pictures were made was around noon or the afternoon of the—
A: First.
Q: —of the first?
A: Right; the next day.
Q: Now, after the pictures were made was the house secured then or marked in some way—
A: No, sir.
Q: Then you can't say that the house was not tampered with between the first time you went down there on August the 31st and several days after that; is that correct?
A: All I can say is I saw no difference in the house from when I was there on the 31st until when I was there on the first.
Q: Approximately how long were you in the house on the second occasion that you went down there, when you went in to turn off the fan?
A: The second time on the 31st?
Q: Yes, sir. The first time you didn't go in the house; is that correct?
A: That's correct.
Q: Okay, The second time how long were you inside the house?
A: Probably three minutes or so.
Q: And did you go through the whole house or just a portion of the house?

A: Just on a direct line between the back door and the master bedroom.

MR. BUTERA: I think that's all we have, your Honor.

THE COURT: Thank you, Mr. Holloway. You may step down. We will take about a 10-minute recess.

After recess, the state called Elmer Joyce who was duly sworn as a witness.

Elmer Joyce

[Mr. Joyce testified that he lived on Rockland Drive off I-147 adjacent to Pinecrest Drive. He also said he knew Terry Steele who lived close by.

[Joyce testified that he saw a brown vehicle resembling a van with out-of-state license plates turn off I-147 onto Pinecrest Drive about 7:15 A.M. on the morning of August 31, 1981. Joyce stated that he saw the vehicle while stopped at a stop sign enroute to work in his own auto.

[Mr. Joyce then testified that he saw the Steeles' car come up behind the brown vehicle and park side by side with it in the middle of the road. Mr. Joyce was then shown State's Exhibit No. 7, a picture of Pinecrest Drive going toward I-147, just below the Steele home. Joyce marked on the photograph where he saw the two vehicles. The Court then asked Joyce to stand in front of the jury and point out the spot he had designated on the photograph. The state further asked him to mark the Steele's Driveway on the photograph.

[Joyce next testified that the license tags on the first vehicle had dark colored lettering on a light background, but that he could not designate the state of origin. He then identified the brown vehicle as possibly the one pictured in State's Exhibit No. 18.

[The defense's cross-examination focussed on Joyce's less-than-positive identification of State's Exhibit No. 18 as the vehicle he saw the morning of August 31, 1981. The defense then suggested it might have been the Steele vehicle, an idea that Joyce flatly rejected. Joyce testified he knew the Steele vehicle and it was a medium green Oldsmobile.

[The defense then asked Joyce if he had discussed the case with State's Attorney Bolling and whether he had testified in other legal proceedings. Joyce testified that he spoke with the State's Attorney the morning before and that he had been a witness in the Lynch-McGee case (the other defendants to Mary Ann Steele's murder).

[The court then excused Joyce.]

Robert Wallace

called as a witness by and in behalf of the State of South Dakota having been first duly sworn, testified as follows on

Chapter One.   Introduction to the Study of Evidence   47

Direct Examination

Questions by MR. BOLLING:

Q: State your name for the record, please, sir.
A: Robert Wallace.
Q: Mr. Wallace. Where do you live, please?
A: Fort Tyler Road.
Q: Were you living there back on the date of August the 31st, 1981?
A: No, sir. Then I lived on Pinecrest Drive.
Q: Is that close to the same place that Terry Steele lived?
A: Yes, sir, across the street.
Q: I'll ask you if, calling your attention to the morning of August the 31st, 1981, at the hour of 7:15 or thereabouts, if you saw or observed anything relative to the area of the Pinecrest Church.
A: Yes, sir. I saw the Steele vehicle leave his house and go meet a white Camaro down at the Pinecrest Fundamentalist Church.
Q: What type vehicle did it meet, please, sir?
A: It was around a '68 Camaro, a white color.
Q: Now, did you see or observe anything other than that happen between these two cars?
A: Well, the person in the Steele vehicle got out and went to talk to the person in the Camaro.
Q: I show you what's been marked as State's Exhibit 5 and ask you if you can identify that exhibit.
A: Yes, sir. That's the church where the two cars were.
Q: Does that truly and accurately depict that church and that scene around the church as it existed that day, possibly with the exception of the foliage on the trees?
A: Yes, sir, I would think so.

MR. BOLLING: We move to introduce into evidence State's Exhibit 5.
MR. ASPEN: We renew our objection, your Honor, based on the remoteness of the photo.
THE COURT: Objection will be overruled. It will be admitted into evidence as No. 5 for the state.

Q: I show you what's been introduced as State's Exhibit 6 and I'll ask you if you can identify that exhibit.
A: Yes, sir. This is the scene, the location I was in when I was looking toward the church on Pinecrest Drive.
Q: From that vantage point can you show where you were and where the cars were at the time you saw them?

THE COURT: Stand up and point it out to the jury.
MR. BOLLING: If you will use a pen here and point out as you show it

to the jury. (The witness left the witness stand and stood before the jury box.)

A: Right along here by the road, and the cars were right down here, right past the the first driveway into the church, between the first and the second driveway.
Q: You had come from where, now?
A: From down here up—stopped right here at 147.[42]
Q: And at that time, this road, does that lead down to the Steele house?
A: Yes, sir, my house and the Steele house. I stopped right along here, and the Steele and the other car was right down here in front of the church by these driveways.
Q: What happened after you saw these two cars get together there?
A: Well, the person that was in the Steele vehicle went to talk to the person in the white Camaro.
Q: And then what happened?
A: I went on to town; I don't have any idea; I went on to work.

Cross-Examination

Questions by MR. BUTERA:

Q: What time of the day or night was this that you witnessed these vehicles?
A: Around 7:15 A.M.
Q: Were you on your way to work?
A: Yes, sir.
Q: Were you in your car when you saw this?
A: Yes, sir.
Q: Were you parked at your house or on a side road?
A: I was parked at the stop sign or right past the stop sign right before you enter 147.
Q: How long do you estimate that you stayed there at the stop sign?
A: Thirty seconds to a minute, maybe a minute and a half.
Q: Were you waiting for traffic to pass?
A: Yes, sir.
Q: Were you turning left or right into the main road?
A: Turning back left.
Q: And were you watching the traffic as cars were going by?
A: Well, when I saw the Steele car go to the right it was unusual because it usually heads toward town instead of away from town. I took time out to look and see, you know, if something was wrong, maybe somebody was having some trouble.
Q: How long had the Steeles lived down the street from you, please, sir?
A: Approximately two or three months; I don't know exactly.

---

42. Right where? Has the lawyer paid adequate attention to the record?

Chapter One. Introduction to the Study of Evidence 49

Q: What kind of car did the Steeles have?
A: A green Oldsmobile Cutlass.
Q: Did you recognize the tag number on the car?
A: No, I don't know—I wouldn't know his tag—I don't know my tag number.
Q: That's the only green Oldsmobile you've seen like that?
A: I would think so. In the neighborhood out there. I haven't—
Q: Well, I'm just asking you anywhere, over in Lovett or Bismark or any place else have you ever seen a green Oldsmobile that looked like this one?
A: No, sir.
Q: Did you see who was driving the car?
A: No, I didn't.
Q: Did you see who was driving either car?
A: I know there was a—I think it was a black man driving the Camaro.
Q: The green car, was Mr. Steele driving it or do you know?
A: I don't know.
Q: What makes you think that was Mr. Steele's car?[43]
A: Because it was a car like the Steeles had and it came from their house.
Q: Did you see it pull out of the driveway of the Steeles' house?
A: Yes, I did.
Q: How far is the church from the Steele's house if you went by road?
A: Two or three hundred yards at the most.
Q: Is it a direct route to it?
A: No.
Q: How do you get there?
A: You leave their house and you go up to 147, then you have to turn right to go to the church.
Q: And you observed it coming out of the Steele's house up Pinecrest Drive, or Road, and turning and then going into the church lot?
A: He didn't go into the lot; he just pulled off the road in front of the church.
Q: Do you recall the weather on this particular day?
A: I recall it seemed to be a clear day.
Q: Clear day? Wasn't hazy or foggy or anything?
A: No, sir.
Q: This picture here that you have identified as being the spot where you were, it's a real clear picture. Do you think this was made in the morning or the afternoon?
A: I have no idea.
Q: Well, let me ask you this: This highway here, is this 147?
A: Yes, sir.
Q: Now, is the Pinecrest Church on the east or west side of 147?

43. What do you think of the techniques of cross-examination reflected in this question?

A: West, more or less.
Q: So if I were going down the highway south, then the church would be on this side?
A: Yes, sir.
Q: Did the vehicle pull directly in front of the church or before it got to the church?
A: I don't understand.
Q: When it pulled off the road did it pull right in front of the church or—
A: It was on the other side of the road from the church.
Q: It was on the east side of the road?
A: Uh-huh.
Q: I see.
A: And the Camaro was in the church yard on the west side.
Q: Other than what you've testified here to today and statements that you have made in court, have you made this statement to any other law-enforcement authorities prior to this time?
A: Yes, sir.
Q: Who did you make them to?
A: Tommy Holloway.
Q: Who else?
A: That's it.
Q: Who was present when you made the statement to Mr. Holloway?
A: Tommy and I.
Q: Did you know Mr. Steele prior to the time that he moved on the street with you?
A: No, sir.
Q: What are your normal working hours, please, sir?
A: Eight to five.
Q: When do you leave your house usually?
A: About 7:15 A.M.
Q: Okay. And did you leave your house at the normal time on that particular day?
A: Yes, sir.
Q: How far did you have to drive to get to your place of employment?
A: I think it was around 14 miles.
Q: Was it over in North Dakota?
A: Yes, sir.
Q: What time did you normally arrive at work?
A: About ten minutes till eight.
Q: Were you on time that day or late?
A: On time.

MR. BUTERA: Thank you.
THE COURT: Thank you. You may be excused.
MR. BOLLING: Chief, call the ambulance driver; I forget his name.[44]

44. Who do you think "Chief" is? Does it matter the person is not identified?

Chapter One. Introduction to the Study of Evidence

JAMES BUFORD DOYLE

called as a witness by and in behalf of the State of South Dakota having been first duly sworn, testified as follows on

Direct Examination

Questions by MR. BOLLING:

Q: Will you state your full name for the record, please, sir.
A: James Buford Doyle.
Q: Mr. Doyle, back on August the 31st, 1981 where were you employed?
A: Battle County EMS.
Q: Did you have an occasion on that date to go to the area of the Old Foggy Road and pick up a body?
A: Yes, sir.
Q: Whose body did you pick up, please, sir?[45]
A: Mary Ann Steele.
Q: And where did you take it, please, sir?
A: Lockhart Medical Center.
Q: Do you know Dr. Stoddard?
A: Yes, sir.
Q: Did you turn this body over to Dr. Stoddard?
A: Yes, sir.
Q: Was that body in the same condition when you turned it over to Dr. Stoddard as it was when you picked it up there on Old Foggy Road in Battle County?
A: Yes, sir.

MR. BOLLING: That's all.[46]

Cross-Examination

Questions by MR. ASPEN:

Q: Was the body fully clothed when you picked it up?
A: Yes, sir.
Q: Did any of the clothing seem to be disarranged in any way?
A: No sir.
Q: You did in fact pick up the body on Old Foggy Road in Battle County; is that correct?
A: Yes, sir.

---

45. This is the second time that someone has testified as to whose body was picked up. How does this person know who it was, and why wasn't there an objection on firsthand knowledge grounds?

46. This apparently trivial testimony is more important than it appears. Why?

MR. ASPEN: All right, sir. I have nothing further of this witness.
MR. BOLLING: Call Officer Richard Harmon.

RICHARD HARMON

called as a witness by and in behalf of the State of South Dakota, having been first duly sworn, testified as follows on

Direct Examination

Questions by MR. BOLLING:

Q: Will you state your name, please, sir, for the record.
A: Richard Harmon.
Q: Mr. Harmon, where are you employed?
A: State Police Bureau out of Calvery, North Dakota.
Q: I'll ask you if you had the occasion to work on the case involving the death of Mary Ann Steele.
A: Yes, sir, I did.
Q: When did you first start, please sir?
A: I received a call around noon on August the 31st, 1981.
Q: Where did you proceed to?
A: Woodridge, Battle County Hospital.
Q: When was approximately the first time you saw Terry Steele?
A: I would say it was mid-afternoon; when he arrived at the hospital.
Q: Did you have an occasion to talk with him sometime that day?
A: Yes, sir, later on that night approximately 8:00 P.M.
Q: Where did you talk to him at, please, sir?
A: At Mary Ann Steele's grandparents house, the McCoys, in Woodridge.
Q: And at that time and place in talking with him did you discuss with him facts relative to time periods surrounding the death of Mary Ann Steele?
A: Yes, sir. I told him that I was investigating the death of his wife and could he give me any information that might be helpful, tell me anything that happened on Sunday or Monday leading up to this. And he told me that—you know, he would tell me she was coming to change some pants that she had bought for him that were too large, and I asked him would he write it down for me. While he was writing it down I was talking to Mr. and Mrs. McCoy, and upon completion of the written statement I interviewed him.
Q: All right, sir. Let's go back to just the written part, and I'll ask you to examine State's Exhibit 22 and see if you can identify that, please.
A: Yes, sir. This is the statement that Terry Steele wrote out for me on the night of August 31st, 1981.

Chapter One. Introduction to the Study of Evidence

MR. BOLLING: At this time we would move to introduce into evidence State's Exhibit 22.

MR. ASPEN: We would object.

THE COURT: Objection will be overruled. It's been admitted into evidence.

Q: Mr. Harmon, can you read this statement?
A: Yes, sir.
Q: Would you mind reading it for me?
A: "August 30th, 1981. After a trip to Woodridge . . ." This is Terry Steele writing this. "After a trip to LaGrange, talked about shopping trip next day. Had slacks to exchange, plus Mary wanted to pick up some more things for baby's room and more clothes. I gave her $150.00 in cash to do shopping with.

"August 31st, 1981. Got up at 6:10 A.M., took a shower, sit down, read the newspaper, went out in back yard, fed and watered dogs, picked some tomatoes. Got Mary up about seven o'clock, set down at kitchen table, had a glass of tea, read an article in Redbook magazine.

"We left house at approximately 8:15 to 8:30. Instead of dropping me off at the office Mary let me off at the Chevron station. I bought newspaper at stand, walked across the street to the office. That was about ten minutes till nine. Steve got there about the same time because we were in a hurry to get to the phone because it was ringing.

"Sent Steve to Landmark Ford to have truck inspected. Took two and a half hours.

"Had several customers on property. Sold 10 by 16 gold building.

"Steve went and bought lunch for Ashley and I at Kentucky Fried Chicken. Steve left to work on customer's building.

"Saw Oliver two times during the morning.

"Mary and I talked about"—he added this on at the bottom, meant for it to go up here—"Mary and I talked about taking her mother to breakfast. I called her around ten or 10:30 to see if she had gotten there all right."

Signed by Terry Steele, August 31st, 1981, at 8:15 P.M.

Q: Now, I'll ask you if after he wrote this out you had an opportunity at the same time to talk about other matters relative to his overall condition at the time of her death, like insurance.
A: Yes, sir. I questioned him about the life insurance on Mary Ann Steele; the amount, and who the beneficiaries were; and he told me he only had one policy, with Consolidated Mutual and it was for $120,000.00.
Q: Who was the beneficiary?
A: Terry Steele.
Q: In your discussion did you discuss any of the contents of the car with him?

A: Yes, sir. I had looked at the car earlier on in the afternoon and I asked him about a brick that was laying behind the passenger side—behind the driver's seat in the floorboard. He said that he had put the brick there. Correction. The brick was in the front floorboard, driver's side. I asked him about the brick. He said that he was backing out of his yard several days before, backed over the brick, and instead of throwing it out of the way he picked it up and dropped it in the back floorboard and backed on out. He said he didn't have any idea how it got in the front floorboard.

Q: Did you see or observe anything other than the brick when you examined the car?

A: Yes, sir. I noticed blood on the—blood smears on the dash of the vehicle up around the defroster controls, or radio, in the center of the dash. There were blood smears like somebody had had it on their hands, touched it. Also on the passenger side of the metal strip on the side of the seat, the outside when you open the door and look at it, there was blood on that, just smears. And then in the back floorboard on the mat behind the driver, had a little blood on it, like maybe somebody had it on their foot and stepped in there.

Q: I show you what's been marked as State's Exhibit 21 and ask you if you can identify that exhibit.

A: Yes, sir. This is the inside of the Steele vehicle. You can see the blood in the seat there where Mrs. Steele's head was laying before they moved her. A wire laying behind the driver's side in the back floorboard was in the vehicle.

Q: What kind of wire was that, please, sir?

A: That's electrical wire, heavy electrical wire, a blue or turquoise color.

Q: Do you have any idea about the length of it?

A: Just guessing at it, it's probably five feet long, four or five feet long.

Q: Would you consider it a strong type wire or a weak wire?

A: Very strong.

MR. BOLLING: Your witness.

Cross-Examination

Questions by MR. ASPEN:

Q: Officer Harmon, did you go to the scene and investigate and see the body as it was laying there in the car?

A: No, sir.

Q: You stated that you saw blood stains on the dash?

A: Yes, sir.

Q: Did you see any blood spatters on the right passenger or the—it would be the front seat, the passenger side of the seat, there as you entered the back part of the car?

Chapter One.   Introduction to the Study of Evidence 55

A: Yes, sir, on that metal strip on the passenger side. But I wouldn't call it splatters, it was more like smears.
Q: Did you see anything on the seat itself?
A: On the driver's seat—or the passenger seat?
Q: Yes, sir.
A: I don't remember seeing anything anywhere except on the metal strip.
Q: You stated that on the floorboard of the vehicle it looked like somebody had stepped in blood?
A: Looked like a little blood on the floor mat behind the driver's side like maybe they had it on their foot or something and it smeared down there.
Q: Smeared?
A: Right.
Q: If Mr. Perry testified that it looked like it had just dropped off her hand where she might have been bleeding, would he be incorrect?
A: It didn't look that way to me.
Q: Didn't look that way to you? Could that blood have been smeared by someone else going in and out of the vehicle in the course of the investigation?
A: All I can testify to is the vehicle was locked when I found it—when I went to it, you know. See, they pulled the vehicle from the scene to the service station and locked it inside. I got the key, went down and met the crime lab, had the people at the service station open up the bay where the car was locked up, and I unlocked the car.
Q: So there were several people that had access to it. One would be Chris Perry, is that not correct?
A: He's probably the only one that had the keys to the car.
Q: So he was the first person on the scene; is that correct?
A: As far as I know, yes, sir.
Q: So what he saw would probably be accurate as to the blood and the smears, and so forth; is that correct?
A: Well, what he saw, you know—
Q: It would be more accurate than what you investigated some, what, six hours later, or whatever?

MR. ELSON: Your Honor, I'm going to object to that question. It calls for a conclusion that this witness can't possibly draw; what he could see, whether that would be more accurate, calls for a conclusion about the quality of Perry's eyesight.
THE COURT: If you could be more specific in your questioning, please.

Q: You did not go to the scene with Mr. Perry, did you?
A: No, sir.
Q: What time did you see the car?

A: It was on in the middle of the afternoon after the autopsy was completed and we had left the hospital. I could look back in the case report and give you the exact time, but I would say between three or four o'clock.
Q: And how did you gain entrance to the automobile?
A: I had received a key from the sheriff's department. The sheriff or Chris Perry, one, had the key to the vehicle. It was locked there.
Q: So there were several other people that had access to the car between the time the car was found and the time you actually looked at it around one; is that correct?
A: I don't know. Like I said, my first contact with the vehicle it was locked up. What happened before then I have no idea whatever.
Q: It was not on the scene, was it?
A: No, sir. It was locked up.
Q: At the time that Mr. Steele wrote out this particular statement, which has been marked as State's Exhibit 22, did you require anyone else in your investigation to write out a statement?
A: I hadn't interviewed anybody else in this case at that time other than the doctor that done the autopsy and Investigator Perry.
Q: Had you interviewed any of the other family members?
A: They were all present there during the interview with Terry Steele.
Q: Did you get Mr. Steele to write out this statement in an effort to use this against him in an impeachment if in fact—
A: No, sir. My only concern was, as I told you a while ago, at that time was Mr. Steele. I knew how I would feel if it had been my wife they found, and I was real cautious in talking to Mr. Steele, and I asked him, I said, "Let's go as far as you can with this, if you don't mind writing it down." He held up real well and I got an extensive interview.
Q: Who was present when Mr. Steele gave this statement?
A: Investigator Perry and Mr. and Mrs. McCoy.
Q: Did you ask Mr. and Mrs. McCoy to give a statement as to what they knew about the case?
A: No, sir. They didn't—see, they hadn't had any contact with her that day or the night before.

MR. ASPEN: I don't have anything further of this witness.

RAYMOND W. HELMS

called as a witness by and in behalf of the State of South Dakota having been first duly sworn, testified as follows on

Direct Examination

Questions by MR. BOLLING:

Chapter One. Introduction to the Study of Evidence

Q: State your name and where you are employed, please, sir.
A: My name is Raymond W. Helms; I'm employed with the Long County Sheriff's Department.
Q: Were you so employed on August the 31st, 1981, and continuous since then?
A: Yes, sir, I was.
Q: I'll ask you if you had an occasion to go to a residence identified to you as that of Terry and Mary Ann Steele's and participate in an investigation or some legal work regarding that residence.
A: Yes, sir. On September the 25th, 1981, I went to the residence.
Q: What was the occasion for being there?
A: I served a court order from the probate court so the McCoys could remove personal effects of Mrs. Steele.
Q: Did you take any of the personal effects into your custody at that time?
A: Yes, sir, I did.

MR. BOLLING: At this time your Honor, I would like to ask Ed Marshall to step inside and give something to Mr. Helms, so we might identify it.
I would like the record to show that in the presence of the Court and the jury that he presented a package to Mr. Helms. Now, may I have it so I can mark it?

Q: Mr. Helms, I show you what has been marked State's Exhibit 17 and I'll ask you if you can identify that, please, sir.
A: Yes, sir, I can.
Q: Where did you first see it, please, sir?
A: I first saw the ropes and property laying in front of me in a chair as you go into the master bedroom of the Steele's home from the living room.
Q: Did you take it into your possession?
A: Yes sir, I did.
Q: And what did you do with it, please, sir?
A: I turned it over to Mr. Ed Marshall, SPB investigator.
Q: At the time you turned it over to Mr. Marshall was it in the same condition it was when you took it into your custody?
A: Yes, sir, it is.
Q: Mr. Helms, did you participate further in the investigation of the death of Mary Ann Steele?
A: Yes, sir. At a later date I done a neighborhood canvas.

MR. BOLLING: That's all we have from this witness.

Cross-Examination

Questions by MR. BUTERA:

Q: Investigator Helms, what day did you go to the Steele house to pick these articles up, sir?
A: Friday, September the 25th, 1981.
Q: September the 25th? And were these articles laying out in the open in the house?
A: No, sir. The articles were in the brown paper sack and the brown paper sack was laying in a chair to the right of the entrance door going into the master bedroom.
Q: In other words, they weren't in a closet?
A: No, sir.
Q: They were just laying out there in a paper bag?
A: Yes, sir.
Q: Do you know what these things are?
A: I know this to be rope. I cannot identify this material here. It appears to be a sheepskin type material; I do not know.
Q: Is there anything unusual about these items here?
A: The only thing unusual that I see about the items is that they're split with the ropes run through it, nothing other than that. And they are split up.[47]
Q: Do you know anything about metal buildings or temporary buildings or this type thing?
A: No, sir, I do not.
Q: You don't know whether those were used in the business, in conjunction with the business where some tops of metal buildings would be tied down?
A: I could not say.
Q: Or on the back of a truck, or something, a camper top?
A: I would have no knowledge, no.
Q: When you went to the house on the 25th of September was the house locked or unlocked?
A: The house was locked.
Q: Did you go in the front door or the back door?
A: We made entry through the back door first.
Q: Who is "we"?
A: Me, Mr. McCoy, Mrs. McCoy, two females, and a locksmith.
Q: In other words, the McCoys came down there with you?
A: Yes, sir. The court order was given to me to serve and they followed me down.
Q: Do you remember what the court order told you to take from the house?
A: Personal effects belonging to Mrs. Steele.
Q: And you say you gave these to Ed Marshall from the Battle County sheriff's office?

---

47. Can you make sense of this? Would you be in a better or worse position to do so if you were on the jury? Sitting as an appellate judge? Has the record been sufficiently attended to?

Chapter One. Introduction to the Study of Evidence

A: No sir, I gave them to Ed Marshall who is—Ed Marshall SPB is an investigator.
Q: That's all you gave him?
A: Yes, sir.
Q: But you picked these items up in conjunction with a court order regarding the estate of Mary Steele?
A: That's correct.
Q: Nothing to do with the criminal investigation.
A: No, sir.
Q: But you turned these over to a SPB agent from North Dakota, is that correct?
A: That's correct.
Q: And when you gave these to the SPB agent when did you next see these items?
A: When have I seen them again?
Q: Since you gave them to him.
A: Yesterday when we were reviewing the case.
Q: He's had them up in North Dakota ever since?
A: Yes, sir.
Q: Do you know whether or not he used them in the case against Mr. Steele in Battle County?
A: I have no personal knowledge of it.
Q: Did you testify in that matter in Battle County against Mr. Steele or any of the co-defendants?
A: No, sir, I did not.
Q: Were you there when all the items were removed from the house, when the McCoys were with you?
A: On the 25th I was, yes sir.
Q: Do you recall what was taken out of the house?
A: I have an inventory list. I cannot recall verbatim everything. I have an inventory list of all items that was taken.
Q: Mr. Helms, do you have that list with you today?
A: No, sir, I do not.
Q: Do you know where that list is now?
A: We have a copy of it in the case file but I do not have it with me.
Q: Case file?
A: Yes, sir.
Q: Which case file would that be, please?
A: It would be on the Steele case.
Q: On the inventory that you turned over to the Steeles—excuse me—to the McCoys on this occasion—did you list these rope items on the inventory list that you turned over to them?
A: Not to my knowledge. I cannot remember whether I did or not but I do not think I did.

Q: Did you merely take it upon yourself to get these ropes and turn them over to the SPB agents in North Dakota?
A: Yes, sir, I did.
Q: And you turned nothing else over to them out of the house?
A: No, sir, I did not.

MR. BUTERA: That's all we have, your Honor.
MR. BOLLING: We have nothing further.
THE COURT: Thank you, Mr. Helms. (The witness was excused.) Ladies and gentlemen, It's been a good while since we have had a recess; since 8:30. I'll go ahead and recess the proceedings here in court today.

In this case, under the laws of the State of South Dakota, you will have to remain together this evening until proceedings resume tomorrow.

The instructions that I gave you at lunch time will still apply this evening and for the remainder of the trial.

Again, if there are any kind of accounts of the proceedings here in court in any of the news media, on radio, television or in the newspapers, then you should not read those articles or view them or listen to them; you should ignore them totally. The decisions of fact that you make in this case will be based on what you have heard in this courtroom and the physical items that have been admitted into evidence. They should not be influenced in any way by what other people's accounts are. You are the people who have heard the evidence and you will make the decisions of fact. That is the reason that you are instructed to not listen or observe or in any way be in contact with these accounts that may appear.

At this time I will turn you over to the bailiffs and they will provide the evening accommodations for you. We will bring you back fresh in the morning. Thank you for your participation today. (Recess was had for the day.)

(On the 12th day of January, 1983, the Court, the defendant, Mr. Bolling, Mr. Elson, Mr. Aspen, Mr. Butera, and all other necessary officers of the court returned to the courtroom and the trial continued as follows:)

Edward M. Marshall

called as witness and in behalf of the State of South Dakota, having been first duly sworn, testified as follows on

Direct Examination

Questions by MR. BOLLING:

Chapter One. Introduction to the Study of Evidence 61

Q: Will you state your name, please.
A: My name is Edward M. Marshall.
Q: Where are you employed, Mr. Marshall?
A: North Dakota State Police Bureau.
Q: And were you employed on August the 31st, 1981, with the North Dakota State Police Bureau?
A: Yes, sir, I was.
Q: Now, as part of your assignments were you assigned to work on the investigation of the death of Mary Ann Steele?
A: Yes, I was.
Q: Do you know Terry Steele?
A: Yes, sir.
Q: I call your attention to the date of September the 4th, 1981, and I'll ask you if you saw Terry Steele on that day.
A: Yes, sir, I did.
Q: Where did you see him, please, sir?
A: North Dakota State Patrol barracks in Woodridge, North Dakota.
Q: On that date did he make any type of statement or utterance to you?
A: Yes, sir, he did.
Q: Was it reduced to writing?
A: Yes, sir.
Q: Do you have it with you?
A: Yes, sir, I do.
Q: Could I see it, please?
A: Yes, sir (handing document to Mr. Bolling).

MR. ELSON: It would be marked No. 23.
MR. MARSHALL: The written statement in this portion here. This is a summary as to when I met him, what time. (Court reporter then identified State's Exhibit No. 23.)

Q: Mr. Marshall, I show you what has been marked State's Exhibit 23 and I'll ask you if you can identify it, please, sir.
A: Yes, sir, I can.
Q: What is it, please, sir?
A: It's a waiver certificate signed by myself, by Investigator Chris Perry, and Terry Steele.
Q: When you say "waiver," for the record would you say waiver of what?
A: A waiver certificate pertaining to the Miranda warnings.
Q: His constitutional rights not to testify?
A: Yes, sir.
Q: In addition to what is written there and with regards to the Miranda warning, I'll ask you if any threats or force was used to get Mr. Steele to make a statement.
A: No, sir.

Q: Was there any promise of reward or inducement used to get him to make a statement?
A: No, sir.
Q: Did he voluntarily then sign what purports to be a Miranda waiver that you hold in your hand?
A: Yes, sir.
Q: Where were you when this was signed, please, sir?
A: In an interview room at the patrol barracks in Woodridge.
Q: Who else was present besides Mr. Steele and yourself?
A: Battle County Investigator Chris Perry and I were present in the room with Mr. Steele.
Q: And approximately what time of the day or night was it when you had this conversation with him and he signed the waiver?
A: He signed the waiver at 6:48 P.M.
Q: Now, after having signed the waiver did he make a statement to you?
A: Yes, sir.
Q: Was that statement recorded?
A: By a tape recorder, no, sir. It was recorded in writing.
Q: I mean was it written.
A: Yes, sir.
Q: Who wrote it, please, sir?
A: I did.
Q: Did Mr. Steele read it?
A: Yes, sir.
Q: Did he make any marks on it?
A: Yes, sir. He made—he signed each page of it, initialed each page of it and initialed the corrections or places which I had struck through on the page.
Q: And did he sign it at the conclusion?
A: Yes, sir.
Q: Does it show how long a duration it was from the time that the statement began until it was concluded?
A: Yes, sir. As I said, I advised him of his rights at 6:48 P.M. The—
Q: Excuse me. When you say you advised him of his rights, did you read him the sheet that's attached to the instrument you hold?
A: I first of all read him his rights from a card which I carry in my credentials.
Q: Do you have that card with you?
A: Yes, sir, I do.
Q: Would you get it out and read it now, please sir?
A: Yes, sir. This is what I read to Mr. Steele:

> You have the right to remain silent. Anything that you say can and will be used against you in a court of law. You have a right to talk to a lawyer and have him present while you are being questioned. If you cannot afford to hire a lawyer, one will be appointed to represent you before any ques-

Chapter One. Introduction to the Study of Evidence

tioning, if you wish. You can decide at any time to exercise these rights and not answer any questions or make any statements.

And I asked him did he understand each of these rights as I explained them to him; he said he did.

"And having these rights in mind, do you wish now to talk with me?" And he said yes, he would.

Q: Now, with regards to the waiver of rights as is contained in this instrument marked State's Exhibit 23, consisting of seven pages, which also purports to list his rights, did he read that instrument and that paper?

A: He looked at it. I'm assuming that he did read it. He examined it thoroughly and then signed it. He didn't read it aloud.

Q: Could you relate to the Court, please, how this transpired? After you read him his rights then did you engage in conversation?

A: Yes, sir.

Q: And as you would talk would one write while the other one talked?

A: That portion, yes, sir, came about an hour after I gave him his rights to begin with.

Q: Now, was it at that time that you recorded this instrument?

A: Yes, sir.

Q: Then I'll ask you if this instrument was signed by him as being his statement after it was concluded.

A: Yes, sir.

MR. BOLLING: At this time we would move to introduce into evidence State's Exhibit 23.

MR. ASPEN: Your Honor, we would object to this document based on the fact that it was given at a time when Mr. Steele was under investigation for the charge of murder of Mary Ann Steele in Battle County, North Dakota, a separate and distinct proceeding from this proceeding here today.

THE COURT: All right. On those grounds the objection will be overruled. It will be admitted here in open court in presence of the jury as Exhibit No. 23 for the State.

Q: Will you please read the complete exhibit to the jury, please, sir, including the waiver of rights.

A: "Waiver Certificate. Date: 9/4/81. Time: 6:48 P.M. Place: North Dakota State Patrol Barracks, Lovett, North Dakota.

"I, Terry Eugene Steele, am 29 years of age. My address is Route 10, Box 1557E, Pentelope, South Dakota. I completed the twelfth grade in school.

"I know that Ed Marshall, SPB, and Chris Perry, Battle County investigator, is a special agent with the State Police Bureau. He has told me that: one, I have the right to remain silent; two, anything I say can be used against me in a court of law; three, I have the right to talk to a lawyer and have him present with me while I am being questioned; four, if I cannot afford to hire a lawyer, one will be appointed to represent me before any questioning, if I wish; five, I can decide at any time to exercise these rights and not answer any questions or make any statements.

"I understand my rights. Having these rights in mind, I am willing now to talk about the crime of murder of which I am suspected. I have not been threatened. I have not been promised anything. I have not been forced in any way to answer questions or make a statement."

And below that Terry Eugene Steele's signature appears.

And then below that "Terry Eugene Steele was advised of his rights by me at the time, date, and place shown above. He was not coerced in any manner to say or do anything. He freely and voluntarily waived his rights and agreed to answer questions and make a statement." I witnessed that and Chris Perry, investigator, also witnessed that.

Q: Will you read the statement now?
A: The written formal statement began at 7:50 P.M. on 9/4/81 in the interview room.

"I guess that this thing started about two or three weeks ago. I approached my brother, Mark Steele, of what I had in mind to do. My oldest brother, Ronnie Steele, was in trouble with the authorities already, and Mark got in touch with them and set up a meeting with Ronnie and myself. I told Ronnie that I wanted my wife taken care of because I knew that if I got a divorce I wouldn't be able to keep my son. The meeting took place at Threeforks in Lovett. Money was passed. I gave Ronnie $40.00 to spend the night in a motel. Ronnie left and nothing happened. His job was going to be the 'in between,' if you want to call him that, and he was going to get someone to do it. But, like I said, nothing ever happened.

"When that fell through I got in touch with Mark again and Mark said he knew of somebody else that might do it. He got in touch with these people several times but nothing ever developed. So he finally told me where to go.

"The place that I went to was on 16th Avenue in Lovett in an apartment on the top floor. I drew a map to show it better. I went over there alone about a week before August 31st. Charles was the only one there and I talked to him about it. Charles' nickname is 'Tiny.'

"He then"—excuse me—"He told me that he got in touch with—he told me that he would get in touch with me in the next couple of days. I don't remember the exact date but Tiny and two other blacks came to Flagg Buildings in a 1968 or 1969 Chevy Camaro, solid white. The Camaro had Arizona license plates on it. They stayed in the car and I came out to meet them. The individual that was supposed to actually do it walked off with me and we discussed how it was to be done. I told him that I wanted my wife to look like she had been in an accident. I paid him $100.00 up front and I was supposed to meet them at Tiny's apartment after I got off work. He asked me if I had a pistol to scare her with, to get her in the car. I told him that I would bring it with me when I came to the apartment later that afternoon.

"When I got off work I went by the apartment and discussed how it was to be done and turned over my gun to him. This gun is the only one that I had and it was a .357 Magnum. The instructions that I gave them were that she was to take me to work the following morning, and that he would know what corner to be at to force his way into the car with her. The guy that was supposed to get in the car with her was the one that I gave my gun to but I don't know his name.

"The next morning I stopped by Tiny's apartment to finalize everything. They were supposed to be having transportation problems and I came up with another $300.00 for them to get a car with. I put that money into Tiny's hands directly. That had to be either Tuesday or Wednesday of last week.

"For two days straight Mary came to Woodridge to do some shopping and they never did anything in those two days. I tried to get in touch with them several times but no one was ever there. When I finally got with Tiny again, which was in the latter part of last week, the man that he had found had dropped out of sight. So Tiny said that he and his partner would do it. I don't know the partner's name but he was the one who owned the white Camaro and, by phone conversation, I think that he lives in Flagstaff Hills.

"For a couple of days I didn't hear anything out of Tiny until he called my house Sunday night—(Monday morning)—at two o'clock A.M. He told me that he had his partner there and that he was ready. I told him to call me at the office at nine o'clock A.M.

"I left the house early that morning about six A.M. The brick was already in the back floorboard because I had picked it up from where I had ran over it. I had also placed a blue wire in the back floorboard to be used to tie the steering wheel down.

"I went by Tiny's apartment and explained to him how I wanted it done, and I gave him a phone number of where he could reach me so that I could—so I could turn my car over to him.

"I went over to Amy Lucas's apartment to wait for his call. He called between 7:15 A.M. and 7:30 A.M., I think. I asked Amy to follow me to the Chevron station on Pershing Drive. Tiny and his partner showed up in the white Camaro maybe five or ten minutes before eight o'clock. I got into Amy's truck and they followed me to my house.

"I pulled down Pinecrest Drive and stopped. Tiny's partner was driving my car and he pulled up beside me and I pointed out the house to him. The white Camaro followed my car around the truck and they were side by side in front of my house when I backed the truck onto

Highway 147. I had left the house unlocked but they had my keys and they got in the house with them.

"After I left my house I went to Amy's apartment and stayed there for fifteen minutes or so. Before we went to Amy's, though, we sat in the Chevron station on Pershing Drive and waited for them to go by, but they never came by. So that's when we started to Amy's apartment.

"I had drawn them a map with instructions on where to go but they didn't follow them. After we left Amy's apartment, Amy drove me to the Chevron station where she let me and Ashley out. I got a newspaper at the Chevron station and walked across the street to the Fisca station, where I talked to Mort, the manager.

"After that, I went to Flagg Buildings to go to work. Like I said before, I had given them instructions on what to do but they didn't do it like I wanted them to. They were not supposed to have shot her. They were supposed to have tied down the steering wheel and placed the brick on the accelerator and made it look like an accident where the car went between the two ridges at Rocky Bottom Creek. But they didn't do that. I was as shocked as anyone when I found out about— when I found out that she had been shot.

"The reason that I had this done is that I found out my wife had had an affair with another man and our relationship had just fallen apart. I knew that if I filed for a divorce I probably wouldn't have been able to keep my son. I feel almost certain that the baby she was carrying wasn't mine."

And I asked him a question: "Terry, is there anything that you would like to add or change or delete from this statement?"

Answer: "No. I can read and write and I have read the five pages of this statement and I swear to God that it is the truth."

And I signed my signature, Chris Perry signed his signature, and Terry Steele signed his signature.

Q: All right, sir. Now, how many pages does the statement consist of, please sir?
A: Five pages of that statement.
Q: Are there any drawings or maps affixed as part of that?
A: Yes, sir. After the statement was taken Mr. Steele was in a very cooperative mood and he wanted to assist us in identifying the other people that were involved in this. In the furtherance of that he drew a map or a sketch of where Charles or Tiny, who was later identified as Manfred Charles Lynch, lived. He signed this map too.

[The State then asked Officer Marshall to hold the map up before the jury and identify where Tiny lived. Officer Marshall then returned to the witness stand:]

Chapter One. Introduction to the Study of Evidence 67

Q: Mr. Marshall, did you participate in the arrest of Manfred Charles, alias Tiny Lynch?
A: Yes, I did.
Q: And where was he arrested?
MR. ASPEN: Your Honor, we object to any testimony with regard to the arrest of Tiny Lynch or any other defendant in this cause, as being irrelevant and immaterial to this particular case.[48]
THE COURT: Overruled.
Q: Where was he arrested, please sir?
A: He was arrested in the described apartment.
Q: Now, following taking that statement, did that terminate your relationship at that time and place with Mr. Steele?
A: No, sir, we talked further.
Q: When you were talking further was there anyone else in the room at that time?
A: Yes, sir. Investigator Perry was still in the room. It was a very relaxed type of situation, if you can fathom that, but this is the way it was. He had just confessed to what he knew about the murder and he had gotten a great burden off his shoulders.
MR. ASPEN: Your Honor, we're going to object as to the mental state of the defendant at that particular time.[49]
THE COURT: Objection will be sustained.
THE WITNESS: Your Honor, may I testify—
THE COURT: Just answer his next question, if you will.
Q: What did he say? Instead of what he got off his shoulders, tell us what he said, please, sir.
A: We talked—
MR. ASPEN: Your Honor, we're going to renew our objection to any oral statement that the officer is going to make, based on the fact that the signed statement, which the Court has allowed into evidence, is the best evidence of any statements that were made at that particular point in time.
THE COURT: Objection will be overruled.[50]

---

48. The common law distinguishes relevancy from materiality. Relevance refers to whether an offer of evidence tends to prove that proposition it is offered to prove, and materiality refers to whether the proposition is of significance to the litigation. FRE 401 collapses the two into a single rule.
 Problem 6 at the end of this chapter examines relevancy and materiality.
49. This is an objection to the answer, and not to the question. Observe how the prosecutor avoids the objection.
50. One often finds that there are informal "local rules of evidence" that are followed just as rigorously, if not more so, than the formal rules of evidence. It is conceivable that this particular judge has a tendency to apply a generalized "best evidence" rule, even though he has overruled this particular objection. Nonetheless, bear in mind that there is no such rule of evidence. The best evidence rule concerns the admissibility of writings, and does not extend beyond those confines. See FRE 1001-1007. For an interesting discussion of the extent to which the concern that the "best evidence" be used has influenced other evidentiary rules, see Nance, The Best Evidence Principle, 73 Iowa L. Rev. 227 (1988).

A: We talked in very—some general and some specific areas about the statement of facts that were contained in the statement; and to that he had added verbally that there was a total of $2000.00 that was paid to these people for having Mary Steele murdered. He described $400.00 in his statement that was given before the murder to these subjects, and then there was an additional $1600.00 that he had given to Amy Lucas to make the final payoff after the murder was committed. So a total of $2000.00 was paid by Mr. Steele. There were other areas that we went into but basically that is one specific.

Q: Let me call your attention to the date of the 4th and 28th of '82 and I'll ask you if you were in Battle County on that date.

A: Yes, sir, I was.

Q: Were you with or in the same area in which Terry Steele was on that date?

A: Yes, sir.

Q: And what was the occasion for you to be there and him to be there at that time and place?

A: At that time we were in the process of trying Manfred Charles Lynch and Earl McGee, and Mr. Steele was called to the stand as a witness to testify.

Q: I'll ask you if he made a statement with reference to the abduction of his wife from South Dakota.

A: Yes, sir, he did.

MR. ASPEN: Your Honor, we would object on the grounds that this was in a separate proceeding. The case at that particular point in time, as the record shows, had been concluded wherein Mr. Steele had been charged with the murder of Mary Ann Steele, he had already received a life sentence. At this particular point in time we would object to any statements made in any prior—I mean, any subsequent proceedings whereby there was any promise of reward or any effort made on behalf of the authorities in Battle County to get Mr. Steele to plead guilty in this particular charge, which was already concluded in Battle County. We would renew our objection to any statements made in any proceedings in Battle County, South Dakota, with regard to statements made by Mr. Steele.

THE COURT: Objection is overruled on those bases. As a leading question, rephrase your question.

Q: Were any spontaneous statements made by Mr. Steele?

A: Yes sir. He had refused to testify, based on the fact, as he explained, that there was an implication that other charges might be filed at a later time because of the fact that his wife was abducted from—and taken from South Dakota.

Chapter One. Introduction to the Study of Evidence 69

MR. BUTERA: Your Honor, we're going to object. That's an unresponsive answer to the question Mr. Bolling asked.

THE COURT: Overruled. Go ahead.

A: That she was abducted and taken from Long County, South Dakota, into the State of North Dakota, she crossed the state line.

Q: I show you what has been marked State's Exhibit 17. I'll ask you if you can identify that exhibit, please, sir.

A: Yes, sir, I can.

Q: When did you first see that exhibit, please, sir?

A: I first saw this in the Terry Steele's home on Pinecrest Drive in Long County. It was in this paper sack it was just taken out of, sitting on a chair on the right-hand side of the threshold that leads into the master bedroom. That's the first time that I saw it.

Q: Who was present there besides you on that occasion?

A: Myself, Sheriff Prentiss Brookes, Captain Holloway, Investigator Perry, I believe Agent James Hammon was there, Terry Steele was there, Sandra McCoy, and there may have been a couple of others. I believe that was the 1st of September.

Q: Approximately what time of the day or night was it?

A: It was after lunch, I believe.

Q: Did you have any conversation with Terry Steele, relative to that exhibit?

A: Yes, sir. I saw these ropes and pads and I didn't know what they were, had never seen them before, and I asked Mr. Steele if he knew what they were. He told me that he didn't, that he had never seen them before, had no idea what they were.

Q: And from whom did you get them, please, sir?

A: I got these from Long County Investigator Raymond Helms.

Q: And are those the same ropes and other attachments as you first saw whenever you went there on the first of September.

A: Yes, sir.

MR. BOLLING: We would move to introduce into evidence State's Exhibit 17.[51]

MR. ASPEN: Your Honor, we would object to the introduction of these— I believe it's State's Exhibit 17, based on the fact that the exhibit is irrelevant, it's immaterial, there's been no connection with the death of Mary Ann Steele for which this defendant has been charged.

THE COURT: Objection will be sustained until such time as it can be shown as to the condition of the exhibit now and—[52]

---

51. What is this exhibit? You will find out in the closing arguments. Should more have been done with the exhibit here, though?

52. This is not the first time that the court has helped the prosecutor by suggesting what is missing in the offered proof. In order for an exhibit such as the ropes and pads to be introduced into evidence, proper foundation must be established. Generally, five elements must be present. The exhibit must be (1) relevant, (2) identified visually or through other

Q: Are they in the same condition now as they were at the time you saw them the first time, with the exception of being in this bag?
A: Yes, sir.

MR. BOLLING: We renew our offer.
MR. ASPEN: I would renew the objection, your Honor.
THE COURT: Objection will be overruled. It will be admitted as Exhibit No. 17 for the state.

Q: I show you what's been identified as State's Exhibit 18. I'll ask you if you can identify that, please.
A: Yes, sir, I can. This is a photograph of the truck that belonged to Amy Lucas. This photograph was taken in the parking lot of the Lovett Police Department.

MR. BOLLING: We move to introduce into evidence State's Exhibit 18.
MR. ASPEN: We would object to it unless they can show the time, place, the proper predicate as to who took the photograph—
MR. ELSON: Excuse me, your Honor. That predicate was laid with the prior witness. Officer Holloway testifying and the predicate was laid at that time, when they were identified.
MR. BOLLING: We'll be glad to go ahead and go through it again. It's just a matter of connecting it up, I thought that was the understanding we had.

Q: Were you present when that was taken?
A: Yes, sir, I was.
Q: Does that truly and accurately depict the scene as it existed at the time and place of that subject matter when it was taken?
A: Yes, sir. I recall that Tommy Holloway of the sheriff's department took this photograph.
Q: Do you know when it was taken?
A: Yes, sir. It was taken September 4th, 1981 at 2:40 P.M.

MR. BOLLING: We renew our introduction.
MR. ASPEN: I have no objection.
THE COURT: It will be admitted into evidence, then.

---

senses, (3) recognized by the witness, (4) observed by the witness on the relevant date, and (5) in the same or substantially the same condition as when the witness first saw it. Of these criteria, the last one has not been met, hence the court's ruling not to admit the evidence until the foundation is completed.

In addition to helping on procedural matters, the court can call witnesses and interrogate a witness whether called by the court or not. See FRE 614. And in some jurisdictions, jurors may themselves ask questions or have them asked. Lawyers and judges tend to be wary of encouraging such behavior, but there is some reason to believe that involving the jury somewhat in the evidence production process has beneficial results. Allowing jury questions may help resolve critical ambiguity, as well as help keep the attention of the jurors. For an empirical study of the effect of allowing jurors to ask questions, see Hever and Penrod, Increasing Jurors' Participation in Trials: A Field Experiment with Jury Notetaking and Question Asking, 12 Law & Hum. Behav. 231 (1988).

Chapter One. Introduction to the Study of Evidence 71

Q: I show you, Officer Marshall, State's Exhibit 24 and I'll ask you if you can identify that exhibit, please, sir.
A: Yes, sir. That's a Ziplock bag containing wire which was in the Steele vehicle, and I received that from Mr. Julio Gomez of the state crime lab.
Q: Is it in the same condition now as it was when you got it?
A: Yes, it is.

MR. BOLLING: We move to introduce into evidence State's Exhibit 24.
MR. ASPEN: We would object on the chain of evidence.[53]
THE COURT: Objection will be sustained.
MR. BENTON: That's all we have of this witness.
THE COURT: All right. We will be in recess until 1:15 this afternoon.

(Recess was had for lunch. The court reconvened at 1:11 P.M.)

Cross-Examination

[Mr. Aspen, counsel for the defense, cross-examined Ed Marshall on many of the points raised in Officer Marshall's earlier testimony. Mr. Aspen focused on the circumstances surrounding Steele's confession as set forth in State's Exhibit 23: who else was present at the confession, whether a deal was offered in exchange for Steele's cooperation, and whether the place of Mary Ann Steele's murder was pinpointed by the investigation. Aspen also focused on Terry Steele's written statement and Marshall's participation in both the Battle County and Long County legal proceedings against Terry Steele.

[Officer Marshall acknowledged that he wrote down Terry Steele's statement, but re-affirmed that Steele read and discussed the statement before signing it. Marshall also reiterated that Terry Steele received full Miranda warnings before giving his statement and that Steele at no time requested an attorney. Marshall also denied that any offers of leniency were ever tendered in exchange for Steele's cooperation with the State.

[Marshall testified to no knowledge of where Mary Ann Steele's murder

---

53. "Chain of evidence," or "chain of custody," is a specialized aspect of authentication. When a party wishes to admit an exhibit as evidence, it has to be shown to be what it purports to be and that it has not been tampered with. Accordingly, a foundation must be laid that traces the exhibit through the possession of everyone who had access to it. By showing each step in the process leading from the acquisition of the exhibit to its presentation in court, the judge and jury can appraise the likelihood that the evidence was tampered with. At common law, chain of custody came to be viewed as a separate rule from the normal authentication requirements. The federal rules seem to take the logically correct position that chain of custody is just one variant on those normal authentication rules. See FRE 901, 902. Here the concern is whether the object at issue is the same object previously found in the Steele auto. Generally, there are two ways to demonstrate chain of custody: (1) show the object was in continuous, exclusive, secure possession at all times, and (2) show that the exhibit was uniquely marked and sealed in a container under the control of proper authority. Note that the prosecution does not cure the deficiency in their proffer, nor do they do so later in the case. Does that matter?

actually occurred, but stated the body was found in Battle County, North Dakota. Marshall acknowledged that Steele's written statement described his motives as his wife's affair with another man, his doubts about her unborn baby's parentage, and his desire to have custody of his son in the event of a divorce. But Marshall also stated "the evidence speaks for itself" that Steele's motives were insurance proceeds and marrying Amy Lucas. Finally, Marshall acknowledged that he had testified in legal proceedings against Terry Steele for Mary Ann Steele's murder in both Battle County, North Dakota and Long County, South Dakota.]

Redirect Examination

Questions by MR. BOLLING:

Q: You have been a peace officer for how long?
A: Since 1981—excuse me—1971.
Q: As part of your investigation is it normal that you look for motives from your standpoint as an investigator?
A: Yes, sir.
Q: Would you most likely do that with—

MR. ASPEN: Your Honor, we object. This would call for a mental operation on the part of the witness, what he normally does, and so forth, what he did in this case.

THE COURT: Let him finish his question and then I'll rule on the objection. Go ahead. What's your question?

Q: Is that what you did in this case?
A: Yes, sir.

THE COURT: Just one second. Objection is overruled. The witness can answer the question.

Q: In response to Mr. Aspen's earlier questions, when he referred to what you gave as the motive, what was it you gave as the motive?
A: Gaining insurance money as well as wanting to get rid of his wife so that he could retain custody of his son. He knew he couldn't do that if he divorced her.
Q: Do you know how much insurance money was paid off on this case?
A: In excess of $120,000.00.

MR. BOLLING: Thank you.

Recross-Examination

Questions by MR. ASPEN:

Q: Officer Marshall, do you know who got the insurance money?

A: I don't know whose name it's in. I know that it went to the McCoy family who has custody of Ashley, the son.

MR. ASPEN: I have nothing further.
MR. BOLLING: I do have another question.

Redirect Examination

Questions by MR. BOLLING:

Q: Back on the first time that you went into the Steele residence, was Terry with you?
A: Yes, sir.
Q: Did you see or observe at that point in time any cigarette butts or anything of that nature?
A: In the kitchen area on the linoleum floor there was a crushed cigarette burn; I observed that there.

ALLEN MECUM

The State's next witness was Allen Mecum who was duly sworn.

Direct Examination

[Allen Mecum testified that he worked for Atlantic Discount Company, a consumer finance company in Lovett, North Dakota. He testified that Terry Steele applied for a $2500 loan on August 12, 1981. Mecum identified a copy of the application in court.

[Mecum testified that the application was approved on August 13, 1981, subject to both Steele's and his wife's signature and real estate as collateral. Mecum testified that Terry Steele wanted to know why he needed his wife's signature and twice told him to "forget it," only later to reconsider.

[Mecum then testified the loan was subsequently made when both signatures were furnished. The defense objected to Mecum's testimony on grounds of relevance and materiality; the objections were overruled. The defense then moved for a mistrial which the court denied.]

Cross-Examination

[Mr. Butera, counsel for the defense, focused on Atlantic's normal loan procedure. Mecum acknowledged that a loan secured by jointly held real estate would normally have both names on it. He also acknowledged there was nothing abnormal about this loan and that the check was made out to both parties. The witness was then excused.

[The state then recalled Oliver McCoy as a witness. Thereupon Mr. Aspen asked for side bar outside the hearing of the jury:][54]

THE COURT: State your objection, please.

MR. ASPEN: We would object at this time to the state's recalling Mr. McCoy to the stand as a witness in an effort to elicit some type of testimony which the state is anticipating to be rebuttal type evidence, with regard to some type ropes that were—material that was used or that was found in the home of Terry Steele and Mary Ann Steele, which at this point in time in the trial would be irrelevant and immaterial.

THE COURT: The state has not rested at this point. We are not at the stage of rebuttal testimony. The objection will be overruled.

MR. BUTERA: Your Honor, while we're at the side bar I would like to bring up something about this. The one reason I don't want—that we have an objection to Mr. McCoy testifying is because Mrs. McCoy has been in the courtroom during the part of the trial and then she's been back in the witness chambers with Mr. McCoy. I would like for the Court to inquire whether that's true or not.

THE COURT: As to what?

MR. BUTERA: As to Mrs. McCoy, because she was in the courtroom all morning long and then she has—she was back there part of the morning.

THE COURT: As I understand the nature of the testimony as to what the district attorney wishes to bring forth from the witness, that testimony or the relevant portion of the testimony would have come yesterday afternoon, not this morning. I believe that testimony was from Investigator Helms.

MR. BUTERA: I understand that Mrs. McCoy was in the courtroom at least two or three hours this morning during the testimony of other witnesses, in which the ropes were displayed and were in question.

THE COURT: The objection will be overruled. You may certainly inquire on cross-examination if she had any discussions with anyone.

MR. ASPEN: Your Honor, it's my understanding the state wishes to proffer testimony as to new matter in this case. Is this new matter that the state wishes to offer?

MR. ELSON: Your Honor, I would like to make it clear that during cross-examination of Raymond Helms Mr. Aspen asked if he had any knowledge of whether those ropes could be used or had been used or would be used in the operation of Flagg Buildings. Rather than leave that suggestion with the jury unchallenged, we propose to put Mr. McCoy on the stand and we expect that he would testify that such ropes and pads as those have never to his knowledge been used in the Flagg Buildings, in the operation of Flagg Buildings, and to his knowledge

---

54. See Problem 8 at the end of this chapter, which deals with the procedures for making objections, among other matters.

Chapter One. Introduction to the Study of Evidence 75

they would have no utility in the operation of Flagg Buildings, which is his own business.[55]

THE COURT: Anything further, gentlemen?

MR. BUTERA: The only thing I would like to say is that we haven't put on any conflicting evidence to that. I don't know why—

THE COURT: There's no evidence to say one way or another. The Investigator Helms says, as I recall his testimony, he didn't know.

MR. BUTERA: Your Honor, there isn't any conflicting evidence, there's no evidence—there's nothing that this can conflict with, then.

THE COURT: Objections are overruled.

OLIVER MCCOY

called as a witness by and in behalf of the State of South Dakota having been first duly sworn, testified as follows on

Direct Examination

Questions by MR. BUTERA:

Q: I believe you stated earlier that you owned and operated Flagg Buildings. Is that correct?
A: That's correct.
Q: And that Terry Steele is your son-in-law?
A: Yes, sir.
Q: Mr. McCoy, I show you what's been marked as State's Exhibit 17, I believe—yes, 17. Did you have an occasion in the operation of your business, Flagg Buildings, in moving those buildings or in any way to use things of this nature, State's Exhibit 17?
A: No, sir.

MR. BOLLING: That's all.
THE COURT: Any cross-examination?

Cross-Examination

Questions by MR. ASPEN:

Q: Mr. McCoy, isn't it a fact that Terry actually worked for Economy Portable Buildings of South Dakota, that took over your business?
A: No, sir, he did not. Flagg Buildings has always been owned by me. They knowed—at a time Terry took over the business for me because of a financial situation with me and Economy Portable Buildings. It was never out of my ownership at any time.

---

55. Again, note the care that must be taken by counsel both in structuring one's own case as well as attending to developments that occur during trial.

Q: Okay. Now, let me ask you this with regard to these items which have been marked State's Exhibit 17. You stated that you didn't know what these would be used for. Are you familiar with these type items?
A: I stated that there's never been anything like that used in our operation.
Q: In your buildings?
A: That's right.
Q: Do you handle large type buildings?
A: All types—
Q: What's the smallest type building that you would handle?
A: About six by ten.
Q: In the moving of camper shells for vehicles have you ever seen these type items used to keep from damaging camper shells?
A: No, sir.
Q: Never have. Have you ever seen an item like this in your work?
A: No, sir, positively no.
Q: Do you know where you could acquire something like this?
A: No, I don't.
Q: Is this the first time that you have seen these items?
A: No, sir. I had seen them—I had seen them at the home of my daughter.
Q: When did you first see these items?
A: The first time I remember seeing them was when my wife and I went to the house with the law-enforcement officers to get Mary Ann's things. They were there at that time.
Q: Would that have been on or about September the 25th of '81—or '82?
A: I do not remember the date.

MR. ASPEN: I have nothing further from this witness.

(The witness was excused.)

MR. BOLLING: May it please the court, the state rests.
THE COURT: The state has rested. Defense Counsel has informed me that certain motions are desired to be made by them. Would you present those at this time, please?[56]

[The jury was excused.]

MR. ASPEN: Your Honor, first of all we would inquire of the Court whether or not the Court made a ruling on all motions which we have previously filed in this matter.
THE COURT: The only motions that have not been ruled upon at this

---

56. The prosecution has now completed its case. The court will entertain various motions from defense counsel; after that the defense will present whatever case it chooses to. Before reading the remainder of the transcript, review briefly the prosecution's case and think about what you might do were you defense counsel.

Chapter One. Introduction to the Study of Evidence

point are a motion of former jeopardy or plea of former jeopardy and also a plea of autrefois convict.

MR. BUTERA: A plea of jurisdiction also, your Honor. It should have been ruled on at the end of the state's case.

THE COURT: You bring that up again at this point?

MR. ASPEN: Yes, sir, we also interpose the plea of jurisdiction in that there has been no showing—first of all, we would move to exclude the state's evidence, your Honor, and specifically as grounds for the exclusion of the state's evidence the fact that the state has failed to prove the venue or jurisdiction of the crime itself. The state's evidence clearly from the stand indicates that the officers themselves do not know where the murder occurred, whether it was the State of North Dakota or State of South Dakota. The only thing that Officer Marshall, I believe, testified to was that the body was found in Battle County, North Dakota. Officer Perry testified that the body was warm, having not been dead more than probably two hours, that the body had perspiration marks around the neck indicating that it was a recent death. There has been no statement or no evidence from this witness stand from the State of South Dakota that there was ever a murder which occurred in the State of South Dakota, and we would respectfully request that the plea of jurisdiction be granted, that the state's evidence be excluded with regard to any charge of murder against Mr. Terry Steele.

Next we would move to exclude the evidence based on the fact that the state has failed to make out a case of kidnapping, which is an aggravating circumstance under the charge which is pending against Mr. Terry Steele. There has been no evidence from the witness stand that there was an abduction from the home of Terry Steele. There has been no testimony that anyone saw Mary Ann Steele removed from the home on the morning that she was found in Battle County, North Dakota. For ought that appears, based on the statement introduced by the State of South Dakota, which was written out by Officer Marshall, the person—or the person who actually made the statement, according to Officer Marshall, stated that Mrs. Steele was supposedly—supposed to be en route to her parents in North Dakota. With regard to any type of abduction, we feel the state has failed to make out a case with regard to kidnapping of Mary Ann Steele or forcibly removing her from the home of the Steeles, which was located in Long County, South Dakota, to the spot where the body was found in Battle County, North Dakota.

Your Honor, at this time we would also reassert our motion for plea of double—former jeopardy, in fact, for all the testimony from the witness stand indicates that these officers essentially testified to the same facts in the case which was concluded in Battle County Superior Court, being Case. No. 641, in the Superior Court of Battle County, North Dakota, wherein the defendant, Terry Steele, out of negotiations between he and the district attorney and his attorney at that point entered a plea of guilty to murder of Mary Ann Steele, and on February 10, 1982, was sentenced to life imprisonment; that any testimony with regard to statements obtained or any evidence with regard to the charge of murder of Mary Ann Steele, which was pending in Battle County, North Dakota, that this evidence should not be allowed in this particular court of law in that there has been no proof from the State of South Dakota of any act or any criminal act which has occurred in the State of South Dakota, and, therefore, the charges or the state's evidence should be excluded in this case.

Your Honor, we would move for judgment of acquittal in this cause.

THE COURT: Response by the state?

MR. BOLLING: Yes, sir, may it please the Court. The state relies on Title 15, Section 2-3 where it says, "When the commission of an offense commences in the State of South Dakota and is consummated without the boundaries of the state, the offender is liable to be punished therefore in South Dakota, and venue in such case is in the county in which the offense was commenced, unless otherwise provided by law." We would state to the Court that there has been evidence that the offense was commenced at the Steele residence in Long County.

With regard to the kidnapping we would refer the Court's attention to Title 13A-6-40 in which it says the following definitions apply to kidnapping: "To restrain, to intentionally or knowingly restrict a person's movements unlawfully and without consent, so as to interfere substantially with their liberty by moving him from one place to another, or by confining him either in the place where the restriction commences or in places to which he has been moved. Restraint is without consent if it is accomplished by physical force, intimidation, or deception."

We submit to the Court that this was by deception for the purpose of murder.

THE COURT: These motions and response have been made outside the presence of the jury. The defendant has made a motion to exclude the state's evidence. That motion will be denied. There is a motion to dismiss the case for lack of jurisdiction or a plea to the jurisdiction of this court; that plea and motion will each be denied.

The pleas of former jeopardy and autrefois convict are each denied.

MR. BOLLING: Thank you, your Honor.

MR. ASPEN: May it please the Court, at this time we would call Mr. Terry Steele to the stand for the purpose of perfecting the record with regard to testimony which Mr. Steele would give at this particular trial and hearing on his behalf, out of the presence of the jury; and we would respectfully request that we be allowed to ask Mr. Steele with regard to his constitutional rights as to testimony in this particular matter.[57]

---

57. Consider what is involved here. The defense is "perfecting the record" regarding

Chapter One. Introduction to the Study of Evidence

THE COURT: Is he going to give testimony now, or you just want it into the record advising him of his right to give testimony?

MR. ASPEN: We would go ahead and advise him of his rights with regard to testimony.

THE COURT: There will be no testimony elicited at this point?

MR. ASPEN: No, sir.

THE COURT: All right. Please take the stand.

TERRY EUGENE STEELE

the defendant, having been duly sworn, testified as follows on

Direct Examination

Questions by MR. ASPEN:

Q: State your name for the record, Mr. Steele.
A: Terry Eugene Steele.
Q: Mr. Steele, myself, Lane Aspen, and Mr. Robert Butera, were appointed to represent you in this matter; is that correct?
A: Yes, sir.
Q: And that was back in October of '82?
A: Yes, sir.
Q: All right, sir. Now, have Mr. Butera and myself informed you of your right to take the stand and testify in your own behalf in this matter?
A: Yes, sir.
Q: The fact is you are guaranteed this right under the constitution and nobody can take that right away from you; is that correct?
A: Yes, sir.
Q: You understand that?
A: Yes, sir.
Q: And based on the knowledge that you have the right to take the stand and testify in your own behalf, do you wish to testify in this cause?
A: No, sir.
Q: And you are making that statement or that desire known to the Court of your own volition, without any influence from either myself or Mr. Butera; is that correct?
A: Yes, sir.

Steele's constitutional rights since he has chosen not to testify in his own defense. In this way, the record is clearly established regarding Steele's understanding of the proceedings and his representation by counsel. This provides evidence of Steele's understanding of his rights and minimizes any future challenges based on inadequate and ineffective counsel at trial. Whose benefit is this being done for? Steele's or the lawyers'? Does it make any difference whose benefit is being served?

Q: Do you also understand that you also have the right not to testify, if you so desire, in this particular cause of action?
A: Yes, sir.
Q: Have you had all your constitutional rights read to you at one time or another with regard to your rights to a trial before a jury, and so forth?
A: I'm aware of those.
Q: You are familiar with all those rights?
A: Yes, sir.
Q: And it's your desire not to testify in this particular case; is that correct?
A: No, sir.
MR. ASPEN: Your Honor, I don't have anything further at this point, and we would rest at this point.
THE COURT: Just one second. In regards to this limited matter, does the state have any questions, in regard to his knowledge of his rights that he has to testify or not to testify?
MR. BOLLING: Am I restricted just to his knowledge of whether he has a right to testify or not?
THE COURT: Yes, sir.
MR. BOLLING: No, sir, I have no questions.
THE COURT: Mr. Steele, do you have any questions that you would like to ask me at this point in regard to your rights to testify or not to testify?
THE DEFENDANT: In regards to my right? No, sir, I have no questions.
THE COURT: Thank you. You may step down.
MR. ASPEN: Mr. Steele, let me ask you one further question before you leave the stand. To this point in time are you satisfied with the defense provided by myself and Mr. Butera?
THE DEFENDANT: I couldn't have done better myself.
MR. ASPEN: Does that mean that you are satisfied?
THE DEFENDANT: Yes, sir, I am satisfied.
MR. ASPEN: Your Honor, with the conclusion of that statement by Mr. Steele, we would rest at this point.
THE COURT: Before the jury is brought back in, is there going to be any rebuttal? The defense has rested without any evidence.
MR. ELSON: I don't believe we can rebut the fact that he knows he has a right to testify, your Honor.
THE COURT: All right. Could you come forward a moment, then?

(A short conference was held at the bench between the Court and all counsel.)

THE COURT: The next stage of the proceedings will be closing arguments and then a charge to the jury of the law in this case.

(A recess was had. After the recess, the jury returned to the jury box and the trial continued as follows:)

Chapter One. Introduction to the Study of Evidence 81

THE COURT: The state has announced that it has rested in the presence of the jury. The defense should also, and then I'll instruct them as to the proceedings regarding closing arguments.

MR. ASPEN: Your Honor, at this time the defense would rest.

THE COURT: Ladies and gentlemen, the state has rested and the defense has rested, which brings us to the stage of the proceedings called closing arguments. It is during this period of time that each side has the right to tell you what he believes the evidence has shown or proven or what the evidence has not proven. The attorney will be drawing what he believes are reasonable inferences from the evidence. If by some chance the attorney says something which differs from what you remember as coming from the witness stand, then please remember that the evidence in this case consists of oral testimony from a witness who has been sworn and from the items that have been admitted into evidence as exhibits. It's from these two things that you will make your findings of fact and upon which you will base your verdict. What the attorney says is not evidence; he is merely commenting on the evidence.

If by some chance an attorney says something to you as being a rule of law and it differs from what I say the law is, then take what I say as being the correct statement of law.

Now, the state has the option to begin the closing arguments.

[The closing arguments have been sharply edited to leave in only a few of the more interesting aspects.]

MR. ELSON: Thank you your Honor.

May it please the Court, Mr. Aspen, Mr. Butera, ladies and gentlemen of the jury: my name is Tom Elson; Mr. Bolling introduced me to you at the beginning of the trial.

During the course of the trial my job has been very similar to yours. I have sat and listened to the evidence as it came from the witness stand. But in addition to that I have been taking notes on that evidence, and I feel that it's important at this stage of these proceedings for me to emphasize certain elements that were brought out on the trial of this case. This is for several reasons, because the law is very explicit with regard to criminal matters, that each and every element of a criminal charge must be sustained by legal, competent evidence in order for you to find a verdict of guilty. I would like to point out to you how I believe that the evidence that the State of South Dakota has put on has indeed sustained every aspect of the charge as laid in the indictment and as Mr. Bolling explained to you it would be done at the beginning of this trial.

[At this point, Mr. Elson reviewed and summarized the testimony of each of the state's witnesses and the exhibits admitted into evidence.]

Everything I've talked about up to this point has been about evidence, testimony made from the witness stand. But I would like to talk now about another kind of evidence and that's physical evidence; that's this material that we have arrayed on this desk now. And I would like to talk about why we have physical evidence in a criminal case, because it might be said—and no doubt will be said—by the defense attorneys that the witnesses who testified in this case might have some bias or reason not to tell you the complete truth. It will be up to you to decide whether they are credible, whether they are believable, whether they are worthy of your belief.

But physical evidence is introduced for the purpose of corroborating testimonial evidence,—you have had one opportunity, at least, to look at it and to examine it, but you can take it back to the jury room with you. The photographs are arranged principally in four different groups. The first group is the death scene where Mary Ann McCoy Steele was found in Battle County, North Dakota, showing her position in the car. State's Exhibit 1 is the car itself in the position that it was found, taken from the rear, showing the license plate; and then a series of photographs taken showing Mary Ann McCoy Steele's body in the car before she was removed, State's Exhibits 2 and 3. State's Exhibit 21 is slightly out of order but belongs with this grouping and shows the floor and a wire in the back seat. In each instance these photographs corroborate testimony that you hear from the witness stand.

You heard testimony that Terry Steele told the investigators that he had put a piece of wire and a brick, about which you heard some testimony from Investigator Perry, that he put it in the car for the purpose of having her killers use it to make her death look like an accident. The purpose of that wire in the car, as Terry Steele told the investigator, was to tie down the steering wheel so that the car would go off the road and make her death appear to be an accident. Again, that's corroborative.

Now, at this point you have heard no evidence about the events that actually took place when Mary Ann McCoy Steele's kidnappers and killers approached that house and removed her to where she was ultimately found in Battle County, North Dakota. But you can draw reasonable inferences from what you see, and I will suggest to you now that it is reasonable to infer that her kidnappers took this automobile that belonged to her and her husband and backed it right up to that front door where they could put her in the car with dispatch, so that they didn't have to take a chance on someone passing by and seeing them move from the house all the way to the driveway in her company.

Finally, the last group of photographs shows the interior of the Steele household and, again, it is generally corroborative of testimony that you heard from the witness stand. First of all, it shows a double bed, obviously recently used, slept in. It shows a woman's nightgown,

Chapter One. Introduction to the Study of Evidence 83

a pair of man's pants on the floor. It shows a dresser and a couple of very important items on the dresser, some earrings and a watch, about which SPB Agent Marshall asked the defendant, Terry Steele, on September 1, 1981, "Is that Mary Ann's watch?" "Yes, it is."

"Did she wear it?"

Answer: "She would not have willingly left home without it."

MR. BUTERA: We object, your Honor. That's not in the testimony.

THE COURT: Come over to the side a moment.

(The Court and counsel for both sides went to the side bar and held a conference outside the hearing of the jury. Then the trial resumed.)

THE COURT: The objection is sustained.

Ladies and gentlemen, you are instructed to disregard the last statement as made by the assistant district attorney and not to consider that statement in any of your deliberations or evaluations of the evidence.

MR. BUTERA: We move for a mistrial, based on the misstatement of the facts in the case.[58]

THE COURT: Are there any of you who would not be able to follow the instruction that I just gave you to disregard that statement?[59] Let the record show that all the jurors—or that no juror has responded that they cannot follow the instruction; therefore, the Court deems that all the jury can follow the instruction. Motion for mistrial is denied. Please continue.

MR. ELSON: Let me say this about what you can see in this photograph. A watch is obviously a personal item of jewelry, and I think you can reasonably infer that such an item is most likely to be worn by a person who dresses and leaves the house voluntarily.

The last picture in this series shows the cigarette burn on the floor and again is corroborative of the testimony that you heard from a witness who testified from the witness stand.

---

58. For the third time, the defense moves for mistrial. The defense is arguing that the integrity of the trial is compromised by the prosecution's misstatement of the evidence regarding Mary Ann Steele's watch. Moreover, they are implicitly arguing that an instruction to disregard is insufficient. The Supreme Court in Donnelly v. DeChristoforo, 416 U.S. 637 (1974), held that a closing argument rises to the level of a constitutional violation when it "so infects the trial with unfairness as to make the resulting conviction a denial of due process." Do you think the requisite elements are present here? See United States v. Young, 470 U.S. 1 (1985), finding the prosecutor's comment during closing on his personal belief concerning defendant's guilt to be error, but harmless. For a more egregious case, see Darden v. Wainwright, 477 U.S. 168 (1986). In *Darden*, the prosecutor had called the defendant "an animal . . . [who] shouldn't be let out of his cell unless he has a leash on him" and had stated that he wished the victim had "blown [the defendant's] face off. . . . I wish I could see him sitting here with no face, blown off by a shotgun." Needless to say, such cases call into doubt the seriousness with which *Donnelly* will be taken.

59. How useful is this inquiry? How likely is it a juror at this point would admit to being unable to follow the judge's instructions? For that matter, how many jurors would likely know if they were able to or not?

I want to suggest to you a reasonable inference that can be drawn from the existence of these four links of rope attached to padding. Terry Steele told SPB Agent Marshall that he intended and instructed his wife's killers to make her death look like an accident. If they had to subdue her and bind her in order to get her out of the house, if they used ropes alone they would leave marks on her body, on her arms, on her legs on her neck, however they were attached. It is reasonable to infer that the purpose of these things were to bind her and to pad those bindings so that she would not be marked in the process. We do not know and have no way of knowing, because Mary Ann McCoy Steele is not here to tell us what happened on the morning of August the 31st 1981.

I have reviewed the essential evidence in this case and I think it has produced for you a picture of almost unspeakable horror for the last hours of this 21-year-old girl's life, at a time when she apparently, to all intents and purposes, was a happily married young woman, happily expecting the birth of her second child, to be accosted in her own home by two total strangers who were bent on nothing else but killing her. I submit to you that this evidence is beyond a reasonable doubt that Terry Eugene Steele is guilty as charged in the indictment, and that it is your duty, after deliberating on this evidence, to find him guilty as charged.

The judge will charge you that as you consider this evidence you must consider several alternatives. Terry Steele is charged with murder during the course of a kidnapping in the first degree, and the judge will define for you exactly what kidnapping in the first degree means under the law of South Dakota. And I submit that the evidence proves both of those things. It proves that she was kidnapped and it was kidnap in the first degree, because the only purpose for her being abducted that morning was to kill her. And indeed, they did kill her. The defense will make much in their closing about the fact that we cannot tell you and we cannot show you exactly where and precisely how Mary Ann McCoy Steele met her death; but I submit to you, and the judge will charge you, that under the law of South Dakota if that crime is commenced here in the State of South Dakota—and indeed, we submit it's been proven—if they took her to Tennessee or New York or California or even the moon before they killed her, it makes no difference. It makes no difference where she was killed; that was the culmination of a crime that began right here in Long County, South Dakota. And as a jury of Long County citizens, I ask you to let the word go out from here that Long County does not tolerate this kind of behavior and I ask you to convict the defendant as charged in the indictment to find him guilty.

Thank you very much.

THE COURT: Thank you, Mr. Elson. Mr. Aspen?

MR. ASPEN: May it please the Court, Mr. Elson, Mr. Bolling, ladies

Chapter One. Introduction to the Study of Evidence

and gentlemen of the jury: It comes time for the defense to sum up some of the evidence that we think is pertinent and which has come to you from the witness stand. And just in opening, let me say that the evidence that you have heard from this stand is what you will consider. Anything that I might say that might conflict with what you have heard from the witness stand should not be considered. You should take what the witnesses have said to you with regard to making a determination in this case.

The judge will charge you as to the law as it applies to the facts of this case. Based on the facts and the law, then you have to make a decision whether or not Terry Steele is guilty of murder of Mary Ann Steele during the course of a kidnapping in the first degree.

Now, I submit to you as a defense counsel, as co-defense counsel for Mr. Steele, that the State of South Dakota failed to make out a case with regard to the charge which Mr. Terry Steele stands charged with here today. And let me just read the indictment to you again. "Terry Eugene Steele did intentionally cause the death of Mary Ann Steele by shooting her with a gun, and Terry Eugene Steele caused said death during Terry Eugene Steele's abduction of or attempt to abduct Mary Ann Steele with intent to inflict physical injury upon her, in violation of Section 13A-5-40(a)(1) of the Code of South Dakota, 1975, as amended."

Now, in order to make this case the State of South Dakota must prove that there was a murder committed during the course of a kidnapping. Now, we do not deny that there has been a murder of Mary Ann Steele. As you recall in my opening remarks to you, we indicated to you that Mr. Steele had been prosecuted in Battle County, North Dakota, for the murder of Mary Ann Steele, and he entered a plea of guilty to this charge and was sentenced to life imprisonment. At the present time Mr. Steele is serving this life sentence, even though he's in the courtroom here today. He's on loan from the State of North Dakota for 120 days within which time this trial must commence and the charges be resolved, and he's to be returned to the State of North Dakota to complete his sentence.

Now, let's look at the murder itself. Look at the witnesses that came to you from the stand. Where did these witnesses state that they found the body? They found the body in Battle County, North Dakota, on Old Foggy Road. Where did Mr. Chris Perry state that he found blood spots with regard to the body of Mary Ann Steele? He found some spatters of blood on the right side of the passenger seat as you get into the vehicle, indicating that these were not smear-type spatters but looked like spatters that were caused or thrown there in some particular manner. He also stated that there was a blood spot in the rear portion behind the driver's seat of the car, that the spot could have come from the blood dripping off the hand of Mary Ann Steele. There were also blood spots in the rear seat. At no point in time did he indicate there were any blood spots on the dash of the car. If you recall Officer Ed Marshall's testimony, he stated that there were some smears on the dash and there were also some smears on the door getting into the passenger side of the vehicle. Mr. Chris Perry was apparently the first person on the scene, together with Mr. Jacobs, who investigated the area and the crime scene, and I submit to you that these people would be in the best position to know what happened or to observe exactly the circumstances and the physical evidence at the scene itself.

If you recall the testimony of Mr. Jacobs and also of Mr. Chris Perry, the body appeared to be warm. In other words, I believe his testimony was that it was very warm, to the extent that he could feel wet moisture on the neck of the victim. And if you recall the testimony of Mr. Chris Perry, he said that in his best judgment, based on his experience in law enforcement, Mary Ann Steele had not been deceased or had not died more than two hours prior to the time that he was on the scene. If you recall the testimony, he was there at approximately 11:15 A.M.

I submit to you that, based on the condition of the vehicle at the time that Mr. Jarvis Nash arrived on the scene at approximately 9:15 A.M., that at that point Mary Ann Steele could probably—possibly still be alive. He stated that the windows were fogged up as if somebody had been breathing on the inside. He felt that it was some young people inside and, he didn't want to get involved; he left—but I submit to you, had a close investigation been made at that time, there's a good possibility and a probability that Mary Ann Steele could still have been alive in that vehicle.

What I'm saying to you, ladies and gentlemen of the jury,—based on the testimony, the state's witnesses—that the murder occurred in the State of North Dakota. This gentleman here has pled guilty to the murder of Mary Ann Steele in the State of North Dakota. Now the State of South Dakota proceeds to prosecute him for the same murder of the same individual in the State of South Dakota. Why did the State of South Dakota do this? You've heard the testimony as to when the investigation was done; you've heard the testimony as to the conviction or the guilty plea by Mr. Steele in February of 1982. Mr. Ed Marshall testified that he came before the Long County grand jury in either May or April of 1982, after the conviction in Battle County, and testified before the Long County grand jury. I submit to you that the reason that this case is brought here today is because the district attorney's office, together with his staff and other members of the community, felt Terry Steele didn't get a severe enough penalty; a sentence to life imprisonment was not enough, so therefore we need to run him through this particular court and see if we can't get him the death penalty. I submit that's the only reason that Terry Steele is sitting here today, the

Chapter One. Introduction to the Study of Evidence 87

fact that these individuals felt that this was not severe enough and that he should get death.[60]

I submit to you that the State of South Dakota has failed to make out a charge of kidnapping. They brought ropes or a contraption in here; I asked Mr. McCoy if he knew what they were used for, if they were used on buildings, and he indicated that they were not, that he had never known what they could be used for. Mr. Terry Steele was asked at his home what these were used for, and Terry Steele stated he didn't know, based on Mr. Marshall's testimony. I submit to you that if you tied someone up with these ropes, or these bands, or whatever you want to tie them up with, you're going to leave marks—because you've got to make a loop—unless you've got the complete rope padded; so if the involved party was going to tie somebody up and not leave marks, wouldn't they pad the rope all the way? Would they just leave a portion of it unpadded?

I submit to you that the State of South Dakota has not brought any witness that testified they saw Mary Ann Steele removed from the home, placed in a vehicle, and carried against her will to the State of North Dakota where her body was found. Mr. Elson has referred to some photos of the victim, as well as the scenes. I would ask you to just take these back in the jury room and look at photo State's Exhibit 2 and 3. If you look at State's Exhibit 3, you will see a pocketbook in the left-hand of the victim. Is it reasonable that if somebody has been abducted from their home, would the abductors give a party time to grab their pocketbook and take it with them? As you see the body laying on the seat of this car, it's evident that she's holding a pocketbook in her left hand. Mr. Elson is trying to infer that just because a watch and some earrings were left on a table or a TV set in the home, she left in a hurry.

Mr. Holloway, the investigator that went into the home, stated in essence that the house was not disarrayed. If in fact somebody is taken against their will, don't you think there would be some movement, some chairs turned over, something in disarray about a house that somebody had broken into the house and taken someone against their will? The statement that was introduced into evidence by Mr. Ed Marshall—if you will read through that statement you will see that, in essence, Mary Ann Steele was supposedly stopped en route to Battle County or to the home of her parents, the McCoys. I submit to you that there's not evidence in this case that showed she was taken from the home; that, in fact, she might have been driving her car. We don't know what happened between South Dakota and North Dakota, but we do know that this body was found in Battle County, it was a recent death, that there was no evidence of her body being bruised or abused

---

60. What defense is being relied upon here?

in any way other than the gunshot wound which the doctor testified to. There's a pocketbook in the left had where she's laying on the back seat of the car.

I submit to you that all of the facts, all of the evidence surrounding this case arose of and was completed in the State of North Dakota, and this man has pled guilty to it; he has not denied his guilt in the courts of Battle County, North Dakota. Based on the evidence that's presented here today you should find this defendant not guilty as charged of murder during the course of a kidnapping in the first degree in the State of South Dakota.

I thank you.

THE COURT: Thank you Mr. Aspen. Mr. Butera?

MR. BUTERA: My name is Robert Butera; I have been assisting Mr. Lane Aspen in this matter. We're not in the same practice together, we're both in separate private practices, and we were appointed to this case several months ago. And I want to tell you that Mr. Aspen and I have worked very hard in this case. There has been a lot of evidence, a lot of paperwork, a lot of testimony from another jurisdiction that we had to read. We have researched the law for several months now and I would venture to say that we have probably spent a third of our law practice time for the last several months on this case.

The reason I'm telling you this is because I want to tell you why I started practicing law, and that is because I always wanted to be a lawyer and I always wanted to be in this position here to talk to some jurors, and I appreciate this opportunity to do this and I appreciate living in a country that allows me to do this.

One of the things about our country is the constitution that our country was founded on and the people that drew up that great document some two hundred years ago. If my history is correct, our constitution was drawn up and passed in 1787 in a place called Constitution Hall in Philadelphia in the great state of Pennsylvania. At that time there were 13 states of this great Union. That constitution has been amended several times. I believe it's 29 or 30 times, something like that. The first 10 amendments to that constitution were called the Bill of Rights. They came from a document that was drawn up in England around 1215, called the Magna Carta. Now, what that said was the English people were tired of the way the kings were ruling, so they decided to draw up their own rights, and that's where our Bill of Rights comes from.

One of the 10 Bill of Rights that we have, that we are privileged to be under in in this country, is the fifth amendment, which says in essence that no person shall be subject to the same offense twice; that is, shall not be tried for the same offense twice. They shall not be put in jeopardy of being found guilty of that same offense twice. One time. Now, that's been the law in this country for almost 200 years. That's

Chapter One. Introduction to the Study of Evidence

what our country was founded on. That's why I have worked so hard in this case and why Mr. Aspen has worked so hard in this case. We do not want that right taken away from us. I don't want it taken away from myself, my children, or my grandchildren; I'm certain you don't either, because that's an important right.

[Mr. Butera then reviewed the evidence.]

In closing, I want to say several things to you. I appreciate your presence. I know this has been agonizing for you to sit here and be locked up such a long period of time. But this is important. This is a very important case. It's not only important to Mr. Steele, the defendant, but this case has implications to every citizen of this state and other surrounding states, maybe even for the United States. You may not think so right this minute but I think one day you're going to look back and say you were privileged to serve on this jury.

I want to say one other thing. Mr. Bolling is going to get up here and talk to you and we're not going to have another chance to respond to what Mr. Bolling tells you. But I would like for you to keep in mind the things that I have said and that Mr. Aspen has said to you while Mr. Bolling is talking.

I'll just say one other thing before I leave, that if you have a child and that child does something bad and you spank that child and you punish that child, it's not right to spank that child and punish that child again for the same thing.

Thank you very much.

THE COURT: Thank you Mr. Butera. Mr. Aspen, that completes the defense closing arguments?

MR. ASPEN: That completes our closing arguments.

(A short break was had in the proceedings, after which the trial continued as follows, to wit:)

THE COURT: Mr. Bolling?

MR. BOLLING: We are here today because the grand jury returned an indictment and brought the case before you. The Court will give you the law and see that this is an orderly trial. You will be the finders of the facts. So as far as what the constitution says, what double jeopardy is, or what may have happened in some other state, I'm not concerned with that. We wouldn't be here if he hadn't already ruled on what the law was.

You're going to be determining the facts and that's what I want to talk to you about for just a moment. What is reasonable doubt? "Reasonable doubt" we say is a doubt that you can fasten a reason to. It's not just a whimsy doubt or beyond all absolute certainty.

Now, the state charged in this indictment that on August the 31st, 1981, that that defendant seated at the table with counsel was married to Mary Ann McCoy Steele and that they lived in Long County, and that sometime in the early morning hours, that Mrs. Steele was abducted from her house. We usually don't have people, when they're committing a crime, get on the telephone and call somebody and ask them to come down and be a witness. Many times you'll be unable to get eyewitnesses, even as many as we have had in this case. But let's look at what we've had. We've had neighbors, we've had statements, and we ask you as you come in here to find the facts that happened in this case—to bring with it your common sense. The judge will tell you that you are people of common sense, or you wouldn't be allowed to serve on this jury, and that you can use that common sense in coming to your decision.

So much has been said about the 10 amendments. My thought, as I heard that comment, was that we've got the 10 commandments, too, and one of those says: "Thou shalt not kill." I want to talk to you for just a minute about what I consider a horror story. I want you to, if you will picture a young mother, a young housewife, right in the bloom of life, at the time when everything should be going her way, a time when she should be proud of her accomplishments, proud of her heritage, proud of her child, her husband, her home; and I want you to compare that, as I go through this, to what we find ultimately in Battle County as exhibited in State's Exhibit 4, the dead remains of what purported to be the 21-year-old, 9-months-pregnant woman who had been murdered. That's what we're here about today and that's what it's going to be your job to determine.

Number one: Did Mary Ann McCoy live in Long County in the Pinecrest community? Was she there on the morning of August the 31st, 1981? Was she forcibly abducted through deception or through force? Go back over and think about the evidence that's been submitted to you. There's been comments made on it. Mr. Elson has gone over each person's testimony. We see this beautiful person, out there in the early morning hours, married to a man that you would assume would be protecting her, but instead is fastening himself in an automobile a short distance from his driveway, with another woman, and points out to the murderers where he lives. The keys to the house, that there are locks on there supposedly to secure and protect, are made available to the killers on the car key ring.

No, we see a young woman carrying out God's plan of reproduction, nine-months pregnant, already the mother of one child, there at home where she had a right to be, loving and trusting, having made trips on two occasions, at the insistence of her husband, to Woodridge. And now we see that he's there doing whatever is possible to bring about her death.

Let's for a moment look at supposedly the comments relative to the love of Ashley, the child in this marriage. Was it pride of ownership of a child or was it love that made him want to control him? I submit to you that it was more like $120,689.53 that he wanted to control, rather than a child, and that was the main motive for what we're here on today—greed, if you please.

What was the situation as it existed back then? Here's a man that's hired by the father-in-law in the business; unable to secure, without the assistance of his wife's signature, even $2500.00; and when he does that, by the testimony, he turns $2000.00 of it over to the killers. Could you figure a more gross abuse than to have your wife come up and affix her name so that you could get the money to go down and pay the killers to take her off and put an end to her life? I submit to you that the electric chair was made for a man of that calling and that thinking and that kind of a thought process.

You know, you were selected to represent all the people of Long County whenever you sit as a single juror, and your verdict has to be unanimous. But whenever you return your verdict and you go out on the street and you meet your fellow man, you meet the members of your family, you tell them, "Yes, I sat on a case in Long County. I listened to all the evidence and I weighed it, and I returned a verdict based on the evidence and one that I'm proud of." And when you have done that, then nobody else can say anything about it.

I'm here to tell you that we cannot allow our citizens to be taken, whether they be killed in the house, in an automobile, or in a foreign land. The home has always been a place that we could seek refuge, and there are certain laws that give added protection to those when they're in your house or your place of business.

I submit to you that the state has met its burden in this case. There are some options that the judge will give you, but I submit to you that the appropriate option would be, "We, the jury, find the defendant, Terry Eugene Steele, the defendant in this case, guilty as charged." When you have done that, then you come back and return your verdict here in open court to this judge, then you have done your part. I submit to you that to the best of our ability Mr. Elson and I and the law-enforcement officials involved have done their part.

And I submit to you that the law in this case will be given by the Court, and jeopardy or the constitution are not facts, but things of law. You're concerned with facts and I submit the judge will charge you with that. You determine if she was down there, if she was forcibly taken or deceptively taken; and if, during the course of that deception or force, she was killed—wherever she was killed. And if your answer is yes, then find him guilty as charged in the indictment.

Thank you.

Judge's Oral Charge

[The judge's charge has also been sharply edited to leave in only a few of its more interesting aspects:[61]]

61. The judge did not instruct the jury on the issue of double jeopardy, but he did

THE COURT: Ladies and gentlemen, it's now my privilege and also my duty to instruct you as to what the law is in the case, what your duties will be, and also the possible verdicts and the meaning of the charge against the defendant.

The defendant is charged in the indictment with the offense of murder during a kidnapping in the first degree. This offense is a capital offense under the Code of South Dakota. I will define to you in a few moments exactly what the essential legal elements of this charge and this offense are.

Also included within the offense of murder during a kidnapping in the first degree are the lesser offenses of murder and, separately from that, kidnapping in the first degree. I will define to you in a few moments what those offenses are.

Now, at this stage of the proceedings under the law of South Dakota it is not your concern at this point to be concerned with any punishment that may be imposed upon an offense if you return a verdict of guilty for that offense.

You may not find the defendant guilty of any offense except the one charged in the indictment or the lesser included offense of murder or the lesser included offense of kidnapping in the first degree.

Now, to this charge against him the defendant has entered a plea of not guilty. The law presumes a defendant to be innocent of the offense charged, thus a defendant begins the trial with a clean slate and with no evidence against him. This presumption of innocence will follow a defendant until his guilt is established by the evidence beyond a reasonable doubt. This presumption of innocence alone is sufficient to acquit a defendant unless you are satisfied beyond a reasonable doubt of the defendant's guilt from all the evidence in the case.

The prosecution has the burden of proving every element of the crime charged against the defendant, and in order to find the defendant guilty of the offense you must be satisfied of his guilt beyond a reasonable doubt and to a moral certainty of every element.

A reasonable doubt can be described and defined in this way. It is a fair doubt that is based upon reason and common sense. It arises from the evidence itself. While it is rarely possible to prove anything to an absolute certainty, you should not convict someone upon mere suspicion or guesswork. A reasonable doubt can arise not only from the evidence that is produced but also from a lack of evidence. The burden is upon the prosecution to prove the defendant guilty beyond a reasonable doubt of every essential element of the crime charged. A defendant

---

instruct the jury that South Dakota had jurisdiction of the crime if the jury found that a kidnapping had occurred in South Dakota. The defense objected to the failure to instruct on double jeopardy. What does the court's failure to instruct do to the case for the defense? Should defense counsel have waited to this point to find out what the judge was going to instruct?

Chapter One.   Introduction to the Study of Evidence   93

has the right to rely upon the failure of the prosecution to establish this proof. A defendant may also rely upon evidence brought out on cross-examination of witnesses for the prosecution. The law never imposes upon a defendant in a criminal case the burden of producing any evidence.

Now, note that I did not say that the state is required to bring you evidence to convince you beyond all doubt; it would be almost impossible to prove something to a mathematical or scientific certainty. The law, then, is that the state's burden is beyond a reasonable doubt. That is the burden of proof that's placed upon the state, and they have to do that before they overcome this presumption of innocence.

The term *reasonable doubt* is not so easy to define or to understand, but let me try to explain it to you further in this way. The doubt which would justify an acquittal—that is, a reasonable doubt—it must be an actual doubt, it's not guessing, it's not speculating, it's not surmising or something of that nature. It's not a forced doubt. But a reasonable doubt is that doubt which remains after you have done at least one thing: you have fairly, completely, and honestly considered all of the evidence. In other words, you've sifted the evidence, you have determined what part of it you should believe, you have rejected that part that you don't think is worthy of belief, and putting all of that together, you have this abiding belief of guilty as charged.

On the other hand, if after doing the same things, that is, you sift the evidence, you determine what to believe, you determine what not to believe, and you are afraid, after doing all of that, to convict a person because he might be innocent, you don't want to turn him loose because he might be guilty, then the state has not met its burden of proof and you do have a reasonable doubt. In that event you would have to find the defendant not guilty.

Upon considering all of the evidence or lack of evidence, if you have a reasonable doubt about the defendant's guilt which arises out of any part of the evidence or lack of evidence, you should find the defendant not guilty.

In determining what the true facts are in this case you are limited to the verbal testimony that has been given to you from witnesses that have been sworn and have sat on the witness stand, and also to the physical items that have been admitted into evidence. What the lawyers have said, any statements or arguments made by them during the course of the trial, is not any evidence, so put what they say in a different category from the evidence category.

You should weigh all of the evidence and reconcile it if you can reasonably do so. If there is some conflict in the evidence that is irreconcilable, that you can't reconcile, take the evidence which you think is worthy of belief and give it the weight you think it should have. In doing so, you can take into consideration any interest which a witness might have been shown to have in the outcome of this case.

Part of the evidence in this case that has been presented has been circumstantial evidence. The test of the sufficiency of circumstantial evidence is whether the circumstances as they are proved produce a moral conviction in your minds—that is, a moral belief—to the exclusion of all reasonable doubt of the defendant's guilt. There cannot be a conviction based upon circumstantial evidence unless to a moral certainty it excludes every other reasonable hypothesis except the guilt of the defendant. No matter how strong may be the circumstances, if they can be reconciled with the theory that the defendant is innocent, then the guilt of the defendant is not shown by the full measure of proof that the law requires and the defendant should be acquitted.

Now, all 12 of you must agree before you can reach any verdict in this case. Your verdict must be the verdict of each and every juror. You are the sole judges as to the weight that should be given to the evidence in this case. The judge's duty is to decide the law and the jury's duty is to determine the facts. I have no opinion as to the facts of this case and I don't want you to think from anything that I have said in this charge, any action that I have taken during the trial, or any rulings that I have made that I think one way or the other about the facts of the case. The facts are determined by you.

You should take the testimony of the witnesses and, together with all the proper and reasonable inferences from the testimony and the evidence, apply your common sense and in an honest and impartial way determine what you believe to be the truth. Don't take any suggestions or be influenced in any way because of some chance sighting or other meeting or contact with anyone that you know or that you have seen here in the courthouse or anywhere else.

I will supply to you to take with you to the jury room papers that have the four possible verdicts on them. On each one of them there's a place for the foreman to sign and also a date to be filled in as to when the verdict has been returned. When all 12 of you have reached a unanimous verdict and all 12 jurors are agreed upon the same verdict, then the jury foreman or forewoman, as the case may be, would sign the appropriate verdict form on the line indicated and then date it.

The first thing you should do when you go back to the jury room is to select someone to be a foreman or forewoman. That person's job will be to guide your deliberations and moderate your discussions. Again, when all 12 of you agree upon the same verdict, the foreman would then complete the appropriate verdict form, you would then return into court and announce your verdict.

(At 5:30 P.M. the jury left the courtroom and went to the jury room to begin its deliberations.

Chapter One. Introduction to the Study of Evidence 95

(At 6:15 P.M. the Court, the defendant, Mr. Bolling, Mr. Elson, Mr. Aspen, Mr. Butera, and all necessary officers of the court, but not the jury, returned to the courtroom and the trial continued as follows, to wit:)

THE COURT: I have been informed the jury has returned a verdict. Is the state ready to receive the verdict?

MR. BOLLING: The state is ready, your Honor.

THE COURT: Is the defense ready?

MR. ASPEN: The defense is ready.

THE COURT: Would you bring the jury back in, please. (The jury returned to the courtroom and to the jury box.) Mr. Evans, you are the foreman of the jury?

JUROR PATRICK T. EVANS: Yes sir, the jury has took a verdict—I mean a vote.

THE COURT: Has the jury unanimously decided upon a verdict?

JUROR PATRICK T. EVANS: Yes sir, the jury has unanimously decided upon a verdict.

THE COURT: Would you stand, please, and read the verdict of the jury.

JUROR PATRICK T. EVANS: We, the jury, find the defendant guilty of murder during kidnapping in the first degree as charged in the indictment. This 12th day of January, 1983.

THE COURT: May I see that, please. (The verdict form was passed to the court by the bailiff.) Let me ask if that's the verdict of each and every one of you. (Each and every juror was then queried separately and each juror publicly affirmed the verdict.) The verdict being unanimous and in one of the proper forms, will be received by the Court at this time.

PROBLEMS

1. Bart Trepel sued Fred Pepperberger for libel resulting from an article Pepperberger published in the local newspaper charging that Bart Trepel had "Mafia" connections. Trepel asserted that the story was false and had caused serious damage to his reputation and to his dry cleaning business. To establish these damages, Trepel called Mik Schagel as a witness, and the following testimony was given on direct examination. Is any of it objectionable, and if so, on what grounds?

Q: Your name is Mik Schagel, and you are a former business associate of Bart Trepel, isn't that right?
A: Yes, it is.
Q: And you've known him for about 15 years?
A: Just about; I don't exactly remember when we first met, but I think it's been about 15 years. We met when he was just opening his first dry cleaners outlet. I could tell right away that he was a person I wanted

to do business with; he was dependable, a hard worker, trustworthy. Just an all 'round good guy. And his family is just wonderful. Two lovely kids.

Q: Didn't you in fact meet about 20 years ago when you were both coaching in the Little League?
A: Why, yes, you are right! I had forgotten all about that. Well, it just goes to show you what kind of guy Bart is, spends all of his time on community affairs.
Q: Yes, thank you, and will you tell us, please, about your business relationship with Bart Trepel?
A: Well, it has always been first rate. As I was saying, he's a honest, hard worker. You couldn't find a better person to do business with. It's such a shame that he had to be the subject of that vicious—and let me tell you, completely false—diatribe by that rat Pepperberger.
Q: Has Trepel's reputation and standing in the community been hurt by this article of Pepperberger's?
A: It sure has.
Q: And has he suffered monetary damages, as well?
A: Yes, he has. A lot of people no longer are taking their dry cleaning to him. Just today I overheard two people in the elevator say that they just couldn't risk being associated with someone who might have mob connections, so they were going to take their cleaning elsewhere.

The following exchange occurred on cross-examination:

Q: Isn't it true, Mr. Schagel, that you've harbored a grudge against Mr. Pepperberger ever since he exposed your problems with the IRS a number of years ago?
A: It most certainly is not true. I didn't appreciate his writing those stories, but I didn't threaten him about it, no.
Q: Mr. Schagel, didn't you in fact tell Mr. Pepperberger that if he didn't retract what he had written about you, you were going to put him out of business, legally or illegally?
A: No, it is not true.
Q: And isn't it true Mr. Schagel that you paid some some ruffians to harrass him and his employees?
A: What? Of course not, these are all lies, and if you don't stop it, you'd better watch out.
Q: Watch out for what, Mr. Schagel? Are you going to put me out of business, too?

2. Defendant was driving his car, and crashed into Plaintiff's car at an intersection. Plaintiff alleges that Defendant was driving over the speed limit, was intoxicated, and ran a red light. To establish these facts, Plaintiff wants to call Witness A who was at the scene and will testify that Defendant, when

Chapter One. Introduction to the Study of Evidence 97

he exited his car, was wobbly and looked like he was drunk, and that the smell of alcohol was detectable. Witness B will testify that he was getting his hair cut in a barber shop about a mile away from the accident and observed Defendant's car "whiz by the barber shop going about 70 miles an hour." Witness C will testify that she heard the squeal of tires that could only be made by a car greatly exceeding the speed limit trying to stop quickly, that she looked up and "thought she saw Defendant's car enter the intersection while the light was against him" but she "can't be positive that's so." Witness D, also at the scene, will testify that the first thing Defendant did when he got out of his car after the wreck is walk toward Plaintiff's car, trip over a small piece of wire, get up and say "My God, I need another drink," although Witness D isn't absolutely sure that Defendant said "another."

Can all these witnesses testify accordingly?

3. The heirs of a wealthy old gentleman, Mr. Black, were concerned that he had become unable to take care of himself, and they initiated a competency hearing. At the hearing, a psychiatrist was called who testified after examining Mr. Black that in his opinion the gentleman was suffering from dementia and would be a danger to himself if not committed. Mr. Black's attorney called Billy, a 14-year-old neighborhood child, who testified that he played catch with Mr. Black just about everyday, that Mr. Black never did anything strange, that he was just a kindly old man who never bothered anyone, and that he could take care of himself. Billy knew that, he testified, because Mr. Black often would make lunch for him, and according to Billy, the lunches were "real good and Mr. Black's house was always neat as can be."

Should both witnesses be allowed to testify?

4. P sued D in products liability for injuries sustained when a propane cylinder exploded, allegedly due to the malfunction of a safety relief valve manufactured by D. P called E, an expert engineer who had inspected the cylinder and had in addition conducted some tests on the valve. He testified to those tests on direct examination. On cross-examination, E is asked if he has an opinion as to the cause of the accident, and P objects. What grounds does P have to rely on and what is the proper ruling?

5. At a perjury trial of Defendant, the prosecution called Witness who testified that Defendant had admitted to him that Defendant had lied under oath. On cross-examination, defense counsel asked Witness if he had ever lied under oath, and Witness denied doing so. Defense counsel then asked Witness if he had ever been expelled from any school, and the Prosecution objected on grounds of relevancy. Defense counsel responded: "It sure is relevant. If Your Honor will allow me to continue, I'll demonstrate just how relevant this is." The judge sustained the objection, and Defendant was convicted. Can this ruling justify a reversal?

6. P allegedly was denied promotion because of her race. At trial she offers evidence that the person who was promoted over her was the niece of a supervisor. Admissible or not?

7. The Highbrow Osteopathic Clinic sued Lowbrow Construction Company over the alleged improper construction of a medical clinic. The defendants introduced a document prepared by the plaintiffs that dealt with the construction project but that did not mention any of its alleged problems. The plaintiffs objected on the grounds that the document "should have been offered through a witness" and thus that it had not been authenticated. The judge overruled the objection. On appeal, the plaintiffs argue that their real objection was not to authentication but to the fact that the Lowbrow Construction Company should have been required to establish that problems with the project should have been mentioned in the report. How should this issue be resolved?

8. Susie Slebug, a nurse at the Lazy Bones Rest Home, was indicted for conspiracy to file fraudulent absentee ballots in the names of numerous residents of the Lazy Bones Rest Home. The plan, according to the government, was to sign the absentee ballots using the names of those residents who Susie knew were so ill or incapacitated that they would not vote in the election. At trial, the government produced a parade of virtually senile, emaciated individuals, many of whom could barely understand what was occurring, and a number of whom were quite incoherent and were unable even to hold up their hands to be sworn in. The defense objected to testimony from many of the witnesses on numerous grounds. Some were objected to on the ground that the witness was so far gone mentally that he should be ruled an incompetent witness for lack of personal knowledge and inability to understand the significance of the oath. Others were objected to on the ground that a parade of emaciated elderly citizens was highly prejudicial to the defense. In addition, the defense requested that a hearing on the competency of these individuals be held outside the view of the jury. How should the judge rule?

9. Prior to a trial on conspiracy to convert union funds, Jambo Hoffey filed a motion in limine to exclude certain photographs showing damage to nonunion employers' property on the grounds of authenticity and relevancy. The trial judge reserved ruling, and at trial Hoffey objected to the admission of the photographs on the grounds that they had not been authenticated. The trial judge overruled the objection and admitted the photographs. Hoffey was convicted and now appeals on the ground that the photographs were irrelevant and prejudicial. What result?

10. Helga Holits is suing her employer on grounds of sexual harassment. She has called to the stand Susie Shingles. Counsel for plaintiff has asked Susie to describe the employer's activities. Her response is that he "continually makes advances and is always leering at the women in a lecherous fashion and winking at them." Defense counsel objects on grounds that the answer is not responsive and violates the rule against opinions. What result?

11. Robert Lee is being prosecuted for armed robbery. Lee was arrested one hour after the robbery, at which time he told the police that he had just come from the home of his friend, Bruce Bell, where he had spent the last

five hours playing poker. Before taking Lee to the police station, the arresting officers took him to Bell's house to check out the alibi. After a moment of seeming confusion, Bell did confirm the alibi. Nonetheless, Lee was arrested and charged with the robbery. At a subsequent preliminary hearing Bell testified that at the time of his meeting with Lee and the officers, he noticed that Lee winked at him and that he, Bell, understood this wink to be a signal to provide Lee with an alibi. Lee's counsel has filed a motion in limine objecting on opinion and firsthand knowledge grounds to any trial testimony by Bell as to (a) the supposed reason for Lee's eye movement and (b) Bell's conclusion that the eye movement was a "wink" (i.e., an intent to communicate). How should the court rule?

CHAPTER TWO
RELEVANCY

A. RELEVANCY—THE BASIC CONCEPT

The trial of disputes has as its central goal the accurate resolution of those disputes. This is not to say that other values do not affect the structure of trials or that within the search for truth other values are not accommodated. It is to say, however, that the dominant variable that determines the structure of litigation is the pursuit of factually accurate outcomes. This policy, in turn, rests upon a belief that disinterested fact finders have the capacity accurately to reconstruct prior events if provided with credible evidence. The trial system, in short, pursues the search for truth from the perspective of a correspondence theory of knowledge. We assume that things happen, that what happens is knowable by human beings, and that persons can coherently communicate information about happenings to disinterested third parties who then will draw accurate inferences based upon that information.

This short description of the trial process is brimming with deep and intriguing questions that beg for examination. Is there really a "reality" out there that is independent of the human mind perceiving that reality? Even if there is, does the human condition permit access to that reality, or does the fact that our perceptions of reality are mediated by our senses—that is, by seeing a chair we do not know that there is such an object in front of us; rather, we only "know" that we have received a certain kind of sensory input—doom us to everlasting skepticism in which all we can do is question and never resolve the nature of reality?[1] Suppose, though, that you are

---

1. There was a time when such matters were dismissed by fiat by legal commentators.

convinced that there is a reality and that you can know it. Are you as convinced that your fellow human beings can know it, or do you have doubts about the rationality of the human species? Even if you are a disinterested observer of events, is anyone else? How often have you seen a person's perceptions of an event determined by ideology or wishful thinking? If that is not an uncommon occurrence, what are its implications for the social reconstruction of reality that occurs at trial based upon the testimony of these "irrational" human beings?

Moreover, how much faith do you have in the disinterested third party drawing the appropriate inferences about what happened based upon the evidence of these fallible human beings? Have you found in your experience that the same set of data—such as observations related from one person to another—tends to stimulate similar inferences in those listening to the data? Or are you more impressed with the remarkable divergence of opinion that constantly seems to follow from the presentation of information to a group of individuals? Again, does that increase or decrease your faith in the rationality of human beings?

These questions may at first glance appear to be of the sort that one finds primarily in two settings: philosophy classes and the first year of law school, both of which may seem to specialize in posing interesting but unimportant questions. We suggest, however, that these questions are not only interesting but of great importance. They ask us to consider whether the manner in which we have structured the trial of disputes bears much of a relationship to our beliefs concerning the human condition. To the extent that one has doubts about that matter, one should have serious reservations about continuing the current methods of dispute resolution. On the other hand, to the extent one has greater faith in our capacity rationally to understand and communicate our knowledge about the universe of which we are a part, then one may feel somewhat more sanguine about our present mode of structuring trials.

Although we cannot here pursue these issues in great depth, we suggest that you keep such questions in the back of your mind as you go through the remaining materials in this book. To us, the most important question posed by the study of evidence concerns the rationality of our dispute res-

---

In discussing real evidence, Wigmore in his second edition said:

> It is unnecessary, for present purposes, to ask whether [there is] . . . an inference from the impressions or perceptions of the tribunal to the objective existence of the thing perceived. [Or rather whether analyzing real evidence] differs [from analyzing testimonial evidence] in omitting any step of conscious inference or reasoning [by] proceeding by direct self-perception, or autopsy. . . . The law does not need and does not attempt to consider theories of metaphysics as to the subjectivity of knowledge or the mediateness of perception. It assumes the objectivity of external nature; and, for the purposes of judicial investigation, a thing perceived by the tribunal as existing does exist.

2 J. Wigmore, Evidence in Trials at Common Law §1150 (2d ed. 1923). See also 1 id. at §24, p.223 n.4.

A. Relevancy—The Basic Concept

olution process, and its answer is informed in large measure by one's views of the issues we have just posed. Consequently, we will periodically bring your attention back to such matters as we proceed in this study of the law of evidence. We will also ask you to reconsider your views about the meaning of rationality and to probe whether what you observe in the rules of evidence is designed to advance a coherent understanding of rationality.

Rational outcomes of litigation are advanced in no small measure through the requirement of relevancy. As James Bradley Thayer, upon whose creative shoulders Wigmore erected his Treatise, remarked:

> Observe . . . one or two fundamental conceptions. There is a principle—not so much a rule of evidence as a presupposition involved in the very conception of a rational system of evidence, as contrasted with the old formal and mechanical systems[2]—which forbids receiving anything irrelevant, not logically probative. How are we to know what these forbidden things are? Not by any rule of law. The law furnishes no test of relevancy. For this, it tacitly refers to logic and general experience,—assuming that the principles of reasoning are known to its judges and ministers, just as a vast multitude of other things are assumed as already sufficiently known to them.
>
> There is another precept which should be laid down as preliminary, in stating the law of evidence; namely, that unless excluded by some rule or principle or law, all that is logically probative is admissible. This general admissibility, however, of what is logically probative is not, like the former principle, a necessary presupposition in a rational system of evidence; there are many exceptions to it. Yet, in order to a clear conception of the law, it is important to notice this also as being a fundamental proposition. In an historical sense it has not been the fundamental thing, to which different exclusions were exceptions. What has taken place, in fact, is the shutting out by the judges of one and another thing from time to time; and so, gradually, the recognition of this exclusion under a rule. These rules of exclusion have had their exceptions; and so the law has come into the shape of a set of primary rules of exclusion; and then a set of exceptions to these rules. . . .
>
> In stating thus our two large, fundamental conceptions, we must not fall into the error of supposing that relevancy, logical connection, real or supposed, is the only test of admissibility; for so we should drop out of sight the chief part of the law of evidence. When we have said (1) that, without any exception, nothing which is not, or is not supposed to be, logically relevant is admissible; and (2) that, subject to many exceptions and qualifications, whatever is logically relevant is admissible; it is obvious that, in reality, there are tests of admissibility other than logical relevancy. Some things are rejected as being of too slight a significance, or as having too conjectural and remote a connection; others, as

---

2. Continental legal systems had a specified system of proof. For example, a conviction for a serious crime could only be had upon the presentation of two eyewitnesses or a confession. Circumstantial evidence would not do. But, strong circumstantial evidence constituted a "half-proof" that legitimated the use of torture in order to extract a confession, and so on. For discussions, see J. Langbein, Torture and the Law of Proof: Europe and England in the Ancien Régime (1977); Damaska, The Death of Legal Torture, 87 Yale L.J. 860 (1978); Cohen, Freedom of Proof, in Facts in Law (1983).—Eds.

being dangerous, in their effect on the jury, and likely to be misused or overestimated by that body; others, as being impolitic, or unsafe on public grounds; others, on the bare ground of precedent. It is this sort of thing, as I said before,—the rejection on one or another practical ground, of what is really probative—which is the characteristic thing in the law of evidence; stamping it as the child of the jury system. [J. Thayer, A Preliminary Treatise on Evidence at the Common Law, 264-266 (1898).]

The Federal Rules of Evidence capture Thayer's main point in FRE 402, which provides:

> All relevant evidence is admissible, except as otherwise provided by the Constitution of the United States, by Act of Congress, by these rules, or by other rules prescribed by the Supreme Court pursuant to statutory authority. Evidence which is not relevant is not admissible.

What makes evidence "relevant" is provided by FRE 401:

> "Relevant evidence" means evidence having any tendency to make the existence of any fact that is of consequence to the determination of the action more probable or less probable than it would be without the evidence.

These provisions appear to provide a system of free proof in which the parties may rely upon any evidence that has any logical power whatsoever. In large measure this is so.[3] However, the implications of these two rules must be qualified by those of the third general rule of relevancy, FRE 403:

> Although relevant, evidence may be excluded if its probative value is substantially outweighed by the danger of unfair prejudice, confusion of the issues, or misleading the jury, or by considerations of undue delay, waste of time, or needless presentation of cumulative evidence.

These three provisions structure the approach of the Federal Rules to the question of relevancy. Relevant evidence is any evidence that tends to increase or decrease the chance of "any fact of consequence to the determination of the action" being true (or false, obviously). This definition of relevant evidence combines what the common law perceived as two separate issues: relevancy and materiality. At common law, "relevancy" was limited to the relationship between the evidence that was offered and the proposition it was offered to prove. For example, suppose that the plaintiff in a negligence case involving a car accident offered the testimony of the mother of the plaintiff to prove that the plaintiff had red hair. The mother has personal

---

3. In that regard, consider FRE 102: "These rules shall be construed to secure fairness in administration, elimination of unjustifiable expense and delay, and promotion of growth and development of the law of evidence to the end that the truth may be ascertained and proceedings justly determined."

A. Relevancy—The Basic Concept

knowledge of that fact from personal observation, and thus her testimony is clearly "relevant" to prove the color of the plaintiff's hair. But, what difference does it make what the plaintiff's hair coloration is? None, apparently, and the common law would exclude such evidence on the grounds that the proposition to be proved (the probandum) is not "material" to the cause of action. The evidence, viewed from the perspective of the common law is clearly relevant, because relevancy only went to the relationship between evidence and the proposition it was offered to prove, but it just as clearly is not material because hair coloration is of no significance to the litigation.

Suppose, however, that the case is not one of negligence, but rather involves a trial for an alleged burglary. Suppose further that the victim of the burglary had discovered the burglar in the act, and that as the burglar fled the victim grabbed and ripped some of his hair out by the roots. That hair was black. Would the testimony concerning hair coloration of the defendant by his mother now be admissible? It is just as relevant as it was in the first hypothetical, but in addition it is now material. If the burglar had black hair, which is a reasonable inference given the evidence, the fact that the defendant has red hair would tend to decrease the chance that he committed the crime, a fact that is clearly "material" to the trial. FRE 401 combines these two inquiries into a single rule, but the change is in form only. Under FRE 401, the evidence offered must tend to prove what it is offered to prove, and what it is offered to prove must be of consequence— i.e., material—to the cause of action.

FRE 402 is the necessary second step in the logical ordering of relevancy. It announces that all relevant evidence is admissible, unless there is a specific provision to the contrary, and all irrelevant evidence is not admissible. In an important respect, this rule captures the essence of the Federal Rules, which is to free the evidentiary process from the accumulated constraints of the common law exclusionary rules. In thinking about the nature of relevancy it is important to keep in mind the distinction between admissibility and sufficiency. Evidence is admissible if it has any power to persuade. To be admissible it need not establish the material proposition to the required burden of proof. When thinking about relevancy, you may notice yourself having a tendency to argue against the admissibility of some evidence because it does not "prove" the truth of some material proposition. When you notice this happening, remind yourself that admissibility and sufficiency are two different matters. The first goes to whether the evidence may come in and the second to whether a jury question has been generated.

Against this general background must be read FRE 403, which is a significant qualification of the aspirations of the two previous rules. Here the judicial power to exclude evidence for various reasons is articulated. Although this does modify the unconstrained system of free proof contained in the prior rules, it does so in a way that favors the admissibility of evidence. Relevant evidence is to be excluded only if its persuasive force ("probative value") is *substantially* outweighed by one of the articulated factors. This requires that the probative value of the evidence be compared to the articulated reasons for exclusion and permits exclusion only if those reasons "substantially outweigh" the probative value. Evidence that is unfairly prejudicial or confusing or that will mislead the jury may be excluded. In addition, FRE 403 charges the judge to take into account questions of cost and efficiency, and if the production of evidence causes undue delay, is a waste of time, or is needlessly cumulative, it may be excluded as well. Clearly, this is a rule that favors the admissibility of evidence while concomitantly providing the means of keeping distracting material out of the trial.

While much of FRE 403 is self-evident, a few aspects of it need further consideration. The first is the concept of "unfair prejudice." The phrase is intended to distinguish between the logically probative effect of evidence that is inconsistent with the position of one of the parties, and the effect of evidence that inclines a jury against a party either in violation of some other evidence rule, such as the hearsay rule, or for reasons having nothing to do with the logical power of the evidence. This distinction is quite easy to make in the normal case. For example, assume that the plaintiff entered a lobby of a building, slipped on a wet spot on the floor, fell and broke his leg, and is now suing the owners of the building for negligence in failing to keep the lobby in a safe condition. Could the plaintiff introduce evidence of the condition of the lobby floor at the time of the accident? Clearly so, for that is evidence that tends to increase the probability of a fact of consequence to the determination of the action. This evidence is clearly "prejudicial" to the defendants in the sense that it will increase the probability that the defendants will lose, but it is not "unfairly prejudicial." Rather, the evidence will move the jury toward a rational outcome, and therefore is admissible.

Suppose, by contrast, that the defense wished to introduce evidence that the plaintiff is a child beater, on the ground that child beaters are violent human beings and violent human beings are more likely to injure themselves than nonviolent human beings. Such evidence increases to some extent the probability that the plaintiff's injuries resulted from his own acts rather than the acts of the defendant. Is the evidence admissible? Almost surely not. The evidence may have some tendency to prove that the injuries came from some other source. Nonetheless, the primary value of the evidence would be to incline the jury to return a verdict for the defendant on the ground that the plaintiff is a despicable human being, which is not an appropriate basis for decision. Accordingly, the evidence is "unfairly" prejudicial and should be excluded.

Probative value and unfair prejudice, as exemplified above, are relatively straightforward ideas and not terribly difficult to administer. They become more intractable, however, when evidence has both a proper and an improper aspect. Suppose, for example, that plaintiff sued defendant for injuries resulting from a barroom brawl in which the defendant was allegedly the instigator and the plaintiff was merely trying to protect himself. Should evidence that the defendant is a child beater be admitted? The evidence is

A. Relevancy—The Basic Concept

surely unfairly prejudicial in that it may tend to incline the jury toward a plaintiff's verdict because of the defendant's character. On the other hand, a child beater is likely to possess a vicious character and be a person who is more likely to instigate a barroom brawl than a person who is not a child beater. From this perspective, then, such evidence does tend to make the existence of a fact of consequence to the determination of the action more likely. How should the judge rule on its admissibility? What are the criteria by which probative value and prejudicial impact are calibrated, and how does one determine when the latter "substantially outweighs" the former?

The difficulty is that there does not appear to be a scale upon which the measure of probative value or prejudicial impact may be taken. If that is so, then *a fortiori* no means of calibrating "substantiality" exists. In addition, there is a crucial ambiguity hidden in the use of the word *substantially*, for there are at least two quite different ways to think about the matter. The first is that before evidence is excluded its prejudicial aspects must greatly outweigh its probative aspects; only if the "bad" aspects of the evidence seriously dominate over the "good" should the evidence be kept out. But, why should evidence ever be admitted if its "bad" aspects outweigh the "good"? Admission of such evidence would seem to lead inexorably to "bad" fact finding as the incremental "badness" of the evidence exerts itself. The other way to think about "substantially" is that evidence should be excluded only when the judge is quite confident that the prejudicial aspects of the evidence outweigh its probative value. The rule can be thought of, in other words, as providing a burden of proof to be applied to the admission of evidence that favors wrongful decisions to admit evidence over wrongful decisions to exclude it.

In light of these various ambiguities, how are the courts to proceed? Consider the lessons of the following cases on these issues.

KNAPP v. STATE[4]
168 Ind. 153, 79 N.E. 1076 (1907)

The appellant appeals from a judgment in the above-entitled cause, under which he stands convicted of murder in the first degree. Error is assigned on the overruling of a motion for new trial.

Appellant, as a witness in his own behalf, offered testimony tending to show a killing in self-defense. He afterwards testified, presumably for the purpose of showing that he had reason to fear the deceased, that before the killing he had heard that the deceased, who was the marshal of Hagerstown, had clubbed and seriously injured an old man in arresting him, and that he

---

4. For a fascinating discussion of the *Knapp* case and the appropriate manner of analyzing the questions it raises, see Friedman, Route Analysis of Credibility and Hearsay, 96 Yale L.J. 667, 679 (1987).

died a short time afterwards. On appellant being asked, on cross-examination, who told him this, he answered: "Some people around Hagerstown there. I can't say as to who it was now." The state was permitted, on rebuttal, to prove by a physician, over the objection and exception of the defense, that the old man died of senility and alcoholism, and that there were no bruises or marks on his person. Counsel for appellant contend that it was error to admit this testimony; that the question was as to whether he had, in fact, heard the story, and not as to its truth or falsity. While it is laid down in the books that there must be an open and visible connection between the fact under inquiry and the evidence by which it is sought to be established, yet the connection thus required is in the logical processes only, for to require an actual connection between the two facts would be to exclude all presumptive evidence. Within settled rules, the competency of testimony depends largely upon its tendency to persuade the judgment. As said by Wharton: "Relevancy is that which conduces to the proof of a pertinent hypothesis." 1 Wharton, Ev. §20. In Stevenson v. Stuart, 11 Pa. 307, it was said: "The competency of a collateral fact to be used as the basis of legitimate argument is not to be determined by the conclusiveness of the inferences it may afford in reference to the litigated fact. It is enough if these may tend in a slight degree to elucidate the inquiry, or to assist, though remotely, to a determination probably founded in truth."

We are of opinion that the testimony referred to was competent. While appellant's counsel are correct in their assertion that the question was whether appellant had heard a story to the effect that the deceased had offered serious violence to the old man, yet it does not follow that the testimony complained of did not tend to negative the claim of appellant as to what he had heard. One of the first principles of human nature is the impulse to speak the truth. "This principle," says Dr. Reid, whom Professor Greenleaf quotes at length in his work on Evidence (volume 1 §7n), "has a powerful operation, even in the greatest of liars; for where they lie once they speak truth 100 times." Truth speaking preponderating, it follows that to show that there was no basis in fact for the statement appellant claims to have heard had a tendency to make it less probable that his testimony on this point was true. Indeed, since this court has not, in cases where self-defense is asserted as a justification for homicide, confined the evidence concerning the deceased to character evidence, we do not perceive how, without the possibility of a gross perversion of right, the state could be denied the opportunity to meet in the manner indicated the evidence of the defendant as to what he had heard, where he, cunningly perhaps, denies that he can remember who gave him the information. The fact proved by the state tended to discredit appellant, since it showed that somewhere between the fact and the testimony there was a person who was not a truth speaker, and, appellant being unable to point to his informant, it must at least be said that the testimony complained of had a tendency to render his claim as to what he had heard less probable. . . .

A. Relevancy—The Basic Concept

Judgment affirmed.

The following case presents another example of a court exploring the relevancy of evidence, but it adds an additional dimension to the problem: By what standard should a court of appeals review a relevancy determination of a trial court?

MCQUEENEY v. WILMINGTON TRUST CO.
779 F.2d 916 (3d Cir. 1985)

BECKER, Circuit Judge.

This appeal by the owner and operator of a supertanker from a verdict in favor of plaintiff Francis McQueeney, a seaman aboard the vessel, presents [two] interesting questions in the law of evidence. The first, arising under Fed. R. Evid. 401 and 403, is whether evidence from which it might be inferred that McQueeney has suborned perjury of a proffered witness is admissible as substantive evidence that his claim is unfounded even though the witness never testified. . . . The district court excluded the evidence of subornation of perjury . . . but we conclude that it erred.

Having reached [this] conclusion, we are confronted with the [second] evidentiary question of this case, which arises under Fed. R. Evid. 103(a): What standard of review should a court use in analyzing claims of nonconstitutional harmless error in civil suits? We hold that a court can find that such errors are harmless only if it is highly probable that the errors did not affect the outcome of the case. Applying that standard to the facts here, we find that the errors of the trial court in this case were not harmless. Hence we reverse its judgment and remand for a new trial.

I. BACKGROUND

A. PLAINTIFF'S ACCIDENT, HIS LAWSUIT, AND THE DEPOSITION OF MAURO DE LA CERDA

Appellee McQueeney was a second officer on the T T WILLIAMSBURG, a supertanker owned by appellant Wilmington Trust Company and operated by Anndep Steamship Corporation. McQueeney claims that on March 20, 1981, while the WILLIAMSBURG was docked at Hounds Point, Scotland, he was knocked to the deck while manning a water hose. McQueeney asserts that his fall was caused by both overpressure of the hose and by oil that had been spilled on the deck, making firm footing impossible, and that as a result of his accident, he suffered a herniated cervical disc. . . . The district court conducted a jury trial at the end of which the jury awarded plaintiff a verdict of $305,788.00 against the two defendants.

At trial, McQueeney was his only witness on the issue of liability. On the day the trial was scheduled to begin, however, McQueeney's counsel informed the court that he had just located an eyewitness to the accident, a fellow seaman of McQueeney's named Mauro De la Cerda, who was on board a ship in Freeport, Texas, and was therefore not able to appear as a witness. Counsel requested permission to depose De la Cerda.

The district court granted plaintiff's counsel permission to depose De la Cerda on the conditions that (1) defense counsel be given an opportunity to speak with De la Cerda before deciding whether to travel to Texas, and (2) plaintiff pay costs of defense counsel's trip to Texas if defense counsel chose to make the trip. Defense counsel spoke with De la Cerda by telephone that afternoon and chose to go to Houston. The appropriate arrangements were made, trial was recessed, and the next day De la Cerda was deposed in Houston. His testimony corroborated McQueeney's in all significant respects. Defense counsel, claiming to have been surprised by the deposition testimony because De la Cerda had allegedly told him a different version with respect to several significant facts in their telephone conversation, cross-examined De la Cerda about his statements. However, on both direct and then redirect examination at the deposition, De la Cerda either denied making any statements that contradicted his deposition testimony or testified that his statements of the night before were incorrect and that his current statements were accurate.

When the parties returned to trial, defense counsel moved for leave to withdraw his appearance so that he could testify and impeach De la Cerda's deposition testimony, which he presumed plaintiff would offer at trial. Defense counsel also listed plaintiff's counsel and his associate as witnesses. After a colloquy in the chambers of the district court, plaintiff's counsel and his associate signed affidavits stating that they had not discussed De la Cerda's testimony with him prior to his deposition. The court thereupon denied the counsel's motion for leave to withdraw.

B. Evidence of the Falsity of De la Cerda's Deposition, Plaintiff's Decision Not to Offer It, and the District Court's Ruling

The trial resumed, and McQueeney took the stand. His testimony lasted several days. During cross-examination, and after court had adjourned for the day, defense counsel received crew lists from his client. The lists reflected that De la Cerda had not joined the crew of the WILLIAMSBURG until three months after the alleged accident. The lists proved, therefore, that De la Cerda's "eyewitness" testimony that he had given at his deposition had been fabricated. The next morning, defense counsel brought this information to the attention of the court in a discussion in chambers. After reviewing the crew lists, plaintiff's counsel immediately stated his intention not to use the deposition. Defense counsel rejoined that he intended to use the depo-

A. Relevancy—The Basic Concept

sition to show fraud on the court. Plaintiff's counsel responded that, so long as he was not using the deposition himself, and so long as there was no evidence that McQueeney had perjured himself on the stand, there had been no fraud and the deposition was irrelevant. The district court agreed with plaintiff's counsel and stated that it would not receive the deposition and the crew lists into evidence.

The district court did not articulate the basis for its ruling at trial. However, as appears from the colloquy at the time, the district court felt that so long as the deposition was not introduced by plaintiff, any perjury associated with the deposition was irrelevant to the suit at bar.[3] That this was the court's thinking is evident from its opinion denying defendants' post-trial motion for relief from the judgment or, in the alternative, a new trial. In support of the motion, defendants argued that it was reversible error to bar the deposition and crew lists, but the court ruled that the deposition and crew lists were either irrelevant or only minimally relevant:

---

3. The colloquy was as follows:

MR. BARISH (plaintiff's counsel): . . . I will just not use his deposition. It doesn't affect our case. We'll go in on the plaintiff's case.
THE COURT: All right.
MR. DOWNEY (defendant's counsel): Well, I'm going to have to use the deposition to show a fraud upon the court.
MR. BARISH: By whom?
MR. DOWNEY: By the plaintiff's side of this case.
MR. BARISH: How can you say that?
MR. DOWNEY: Because you've produced a witness—sent me down to Texas last Friday to take a witness who saw an accident, and if my information is correct, the man perjured himself, there's no doubt about it, if he wasn't on that ship to say he saw an accident in March when he didn't join the ship until May. That's serious business, and as defense counsel in this case how can I not bring that to the jury's attention?
MR. BARISH: If I may, your Honor, I think that if what you are saying is accurate that's serious business.
MR. DOWNEY: Yes.
MR. BARISH: But it doesn't affect the plaintiff's case because the plaintiff hasn't perjured himself. And, quite frankly, all it means, as far as I'm concerned, is that I just won't use that deposition. Now there is nothing in that deposition—are you going to introduce into evidence a deposition that supports the plaintiff's case and then say he is not telling the truth?
MR. DOWNEY: Yes, to show a part of fraud.
THE COURT: Well, I'm not going to permit you to do that. I'm going to say to you that if this person perjured himself then we can do one of several things, one of which we can report it to the United States Attorney for perjury, for purposes of perjury, because it was done to influence the outcome of this case. I think that's the appropriate procedure. I don't think we are going to start introducing a document which you think is incorrect and intentionally incorrect in this case.

Now if it's introduced into this case by plaintiff's side then you can bring in the document showing, if you can, that the man wasn't on the ship at the time of the incident and could not have witnessed it, but we're not going to solve all the problems of the world in this case. If it is not brought in then I don't say it's an issue in this case for this jury to consider whether or not the plaintiff is involved. I don't know whether the plaintiff is involved in this matter. That's whose case we're trying. We're trying the plaintiff's case.
MR. DOWNEY: Yes, your Honor.

It is questionable if Mr. De la Cerda's testimony is even relevant, since defendant seeks admission for the mere purpose to impeach and not for the substance of the testimony. Certainly, the confusion of a person's recollection brings little to show whether or not a set of facts occurred in a specific manner. Such testimony would confuse and mislead the jury, because what is at issue here is whether or not certain events did occur, not whether Mr. De la Cerda can remember or has such knowledge. To admit such testimony would not be for any probative value but merely to prejudice the jury against the plaintiff. Surely the probative value of such testimony would be minimal at best and is outweighed by the severe prejudice it would cause at the time of trial.

Thus the court may fairly be said to have excluded the evidence as either irrelevant under Fed. R. Evid. 401, or as relevant but misleading or unfairly prejudicial, in accordance with Fed. R. Evid. 403. . . .

II. DEFENDANT'S PROFFER THAT MCQUEENEY HAD SUBORNED PERJURY

A. THE RULE 401 RULING

The stated purpose of defense counsel's proffer of De la Cerda's deposition, the crew lists for the date of the alleged accident, and defense counsel's own testimony about what De la Cerda had told him the night before the deposition, was to show that the plaintiff had suborned perjured testimony. Defense counsel intended to argue that plaintiff's subornation was evidence of his knowledge of the weakness of his case, and that such knowledge could be taken into account by the jury.

The district court's decision to exclude the evidence as irrelevant is governed by Fed. R. Evid. 401. We review that decision according to the abuse of discretion standard. See United States v. Steele, 685 F.2d 793, 808 (3d Cir.) (once the threshold of logical relevance is satisfied, "the matter is largely within the discretion of the trial court"). We believe that the district court abused its discretion in excluding the proffered evidence. We base our conclusion on common sense, eminent commentators, case law, and the explicit language of Rule 401.

The intuitive appeal of defendants' proffer is immediate. One who believes his own case to be weak is more likely to suborn perjury than one who thinks he has a strong case, and a party knows better than anyone else the truth about his own case. Thus, subornation of perjury by a party is strong evidence that the party's case is weak. Admittedly the conclusion is not inescapable: Parties may be mistaken about the merits or force of their own cases. But evidence need not lead inescapably towards a single conclusion to be relevant; it need only make certain facts more probable than not.

A. Relevancy—The Basic Concept

The evidence of subornation here does cast into doubt the merits of McQueeney's claim, even if it does not extinguish them.[7]

There is ample support among both scholars and courts for this line of argument. Wigmore calls the inference "one of the simplest in human experience":

> It has always been understood—the inference indeed is one of the simplest in human experience—that a party's falsehood or other fraud in the preparation and presentation of his cause, his fabrication or suppression of evidence by bribery or spoliation, is receivable against him as an indication of his consciousness that his case is a weak or unfounded one; and from that consciousness may be inferred the fact itself of the cause's lack of truth and merit. [2 Wigmore §278(2) (Chadbourn Rev. 1979). . . . [See also] McCormick's Handbook on the Law of Evidence §273 at 660 (2d ed. 1972). . . .]

This court has upheld the inference and admitted evidence accordingly. See Newark Stereotypers' Union v. Newark Morning Ledger, 397 F.2d 594, 599 (3d Cir. 1968) ("an attempt by a litigant to persuade a witness not to testify is properly admissible against him as an indication of his own belief that his claim is weak or unfounded or false"). Several other courts of appeals and state appellate courts have done the same. See Great American Insurance Co. v. Horab, 309 F.2d 262, 264 (8th Cir. 1962) (applying rule and citing cases); see also 2 Wigmore §278(2) (Chadbourne Rev. 1979) (collecting cases).

McQueeney points out that *Newark Stereotypers' Union* and *Horab* involved a party's subornation of perjured testimony from a witness who testified at trial, whereas in the case at bar De la Cerda's testimony was never introduced into evidence. This is correct, but it is a distinction of no consequence. Evidence of subornation of perjury is substantive evidence, not mere impeachment material; the inference that one may draw from the subornation does not depend upon anyone else's testimony. The fact that a party suborned perjury is what matters, not the ultimate success or failure of that subornation.

Finally, the explicit language of Fed. R. Evid. 401, which defines as relevant evidence that has "any tendency" to make a difference in the case, provides added reason to permit the materials into evidence. The plain meaning of the Rule demonstrates that the scope of relevant evidence is intended to be broad, and the authorities support such a broad reading. Thus, logic, authority, and the clear language of Rule 401 lead us to the conclusion that the deposition and related testimony were relevant and that the district court abused its discretion in excluding it on relevancy grounds.

---

7. Obviously, the fact that McQueeney may demonstrate at trial that the crew lists were simply mistaken and that De la Cerda was in fact on board the ship, or that De la Cerda was mistaken or disoriented, or that he perjured himself without subornation by McQueeney, does not mean that defendants' proffer must be excluded.

B. The Rule 403 Balance

That the evidence was relevant does not necessarily mean that it should have been admitted. As noted above, the district court, after voicing its doubts that the evidence had any relevance, ruled that even assuming it was relevant, the evidence should not have been admitted because its prejudicial impact would likely outweigh its probative value. This is a standard Fed. R. Evid. 403 balance which we review with substantial deference. Despite this deferential standard, we find that the district court erred, for it underestimated the probative value of the evidence, and misevaluated its prejudicial impact.

The district court assigned virtually no probative value to the evidence of subornation. It should be clear from what we said above, however, that evidence of subornation of perjury may be quite valuable to the defendant in this case. Intuition and the unanimity of the commentators and numerous courts that have considered it suggest not only that subornation of perjury is relevant but that it is powerful evidence indeed. Evidence that McQueeney suborned perjury might well have made the jurors re-evaluate McQueeney's case. Of course, it is not certain that McQueeney did suborn perjury; De la Cerda may have had other reasons for making up his story. But the circumstances of the case and the correlation between McQueeney's story and De la Cerda's deposition suggest that subornation of perjury by McQueeney is a possibility that the jury should have been allowed to consider.

By contrast, although the district court referred to potential confusion and "severe prejudice," and although there was danger of prejudice—the mere suggestion that McQueeney suborned perjury might have led the jury to reflect on his character in an improper manner—it is unlikely that the evidence would result in the "unfair prejudice" proscribed by Rule 403. Moreover, it appears to us that the danger of improper influence was not sufficient to "substantially outweigh[]" the probative value of the evidence, as required by Fed. R. Evid. 403. The court did not articulate any reasons for its finding of prejudice, and this does not appear to us to be the kind of evidence with obvious or overwhelming potential for unfair prejudice. In the absence of a showing of particularized danger of unfair prejudice, the evidence must be admitted. Were we to rule otherwise, evidence could be excluded on an unfounded fear of prejudice and we would effectively preclude all evidence of subornation of perjury.[8]

In sum, the district court misconstrued both elements of the Rule 403 balance hence its balancing exercise was skewed. The court's Rule 403 ruling was thus an abuse of discretion.

---

8. The district court was also concerned that the evidence would confuse the jury because it would lead them to wonder about De la Cerda's integrity rather than about the subjects of the suit—whether McQueeney fell, for what reason, and what his damages were. However, the court could easily have instructed the jury on the limited purposes of the evidence, and thus have avoided any possible jury confusion.

A. Relevancy—The Basic Concept

C. HARMLESS ERROR

Fed. R. Evid. 103(a) states that an evidentiary ruling may not be reversible error "unless a substantial right of a party is affected." It remains for us to consider, therefore, whether the court's decision substantially affected the rights of appellants.

At the outset, we must establish the appropriate standard of review.[10] The analysis is complicated because although there are several cases in this circuit dealing with harmless error in the criminal context,[11] there are none dealing with the standard of review of harmless error in civil cases, and some courts and commentators have argued quite forcefully that the two standards are not the same. We proceed, therefore, by first discussing this circuit's standard of review in harmless error questions in criminal cases. We then consider whether the same standard should apply in civil and criminal cases, and conclude that it should. Finally, we apply the uniform standard to the facts of this case.

1. Criminal Cases

In Government of the Virgin Islands v. Toto, 529 F.2d 278 (3d Cir. 1976), this court stated that an appellate court's harmless error determination requires "perforce (a) resort to probabilities." Id. at 283.[12] Following the lead of former Chief Justice Roger Traynor, the Toto court discussed three possible standards of review for harmless error:

> The reviewing court might affirm if it believes: (a) that it is more probable than not that the error did not affect the judgment, (b) that it is highly probable that the error did not contribute to the judgment, or (c) that it is almost certain that the error did not taint the judgment. [Id.]

The Toto court chose the middle option and thus held that errors in a criminal case are not harmless unless it is "highly probable" that they did not affect a party's substantial rights. Id. at 284. . . .

2. Civil Cases

There are no cases in this circuit analyzing the appropriate standard of review for harmless error in civil cases. Because Toto was a criminal case, there is some question whether its holding applies with full force in the civil context. Although Toto itself did not distinguish between civil and criminal

---

10. Although in this discussion we will often speak of the appellate court's standard of review, our discussion is also relevant to the trial court's harmless error analysis on consideration of post-trial motions.

11. The harmless error standard for constitutional errors differs from the standard for nonconstitutional errors. Our discussion is confined to nonconstitutional errors.

12. For a rather different sort of probabilistic analysis of harmless error, see Kornstein, A Bayesian Model of Harmless Error, 5 J. Legal Stud. 121 (1976).

cases, some courts and commentators argue that it should be more difficult to prove harmless error in the criminal context than in the civil. Others argue that there should be no difference between the standards used in civil and criminal cases. See 1 Wigmore, Evidence §21 (3d ed. 1940) (no distinction between civil and criminal).

Although the courts and esteemed commentators who espouse the position cannot be lightly contradicted, we are unpersuaded by the view that the harmless error standard of review in civil cases should be different from the analogous standard in criminal cases. The case for differentiating the two situations was put most comprehensively by the court in Haddad v. Lockheed:

> (A) crucial first step in determining how we should gauge the probability that an error was harmless is recognizing the distinction between civil and criminal trials. This distinction has two facets, each of which reflects the differing burdens of proof in civil and criminal cases. First the lower burden of proof in civil cases implies a larger margin of error. The danger of harmless error doctrine is that an appellate court may usurp the jury's function, by merely deleting improper evidence from the record and assessing the sufficiency of the evidence to support the verdict below. This danger has less practical importance where, as in most civil cases, the jury verdict merely rests on a more probable than not standard of proof.
>
> The second facet of the distinction between the errors in civil and criminal trials involves the differing degrees of certainty owed to civil and criminal litigants. Whereas a criminal defendant must be found guilty beyond a reasonable doubt, a civil litigant merely has the right to a jury verdict that more probably than not corresponds to the truth.
>
> The civil litigant's lessened entitlement to veracity continues when the litigant becomes an appellant. We conclude that a proper harmless error standard in civil cases should reflect the standard of proof. [720 F.2d at 1459.]

The *Haddad* court thus makes two arguments for imposing a laxer harmless error standard in civil cases than in criminal. The first starts from the undeniable premise that a finding of harmless error by an appellate court infringes on the function of the jury because it puts the appellate court in the position of weighing the evidence before the trial court. The court then proposes that the infringement of the jury's role is less significant in civil than in criminal cases, and that therefore appellate courts reviewing civil cases should be more willing to find errors harmless than they would be if they were reviewing criminal cases. The *Haddad* court's second argument is that the lower burden of proof in civil than in criminal cases implies that society tolerates a greater risk of error in civil than in criminal cases, and that that toleration for error should be reflected in the appellate process as well.

We find neither argument persuasive. The crux of the first argument is that jury verdicts are less worthy of respect in civil cases than in criminal.

A. Relevancy—The Basic Concept

This is so, explains the *Haddad* court, because the civil jury verdict usually rests on a more probable than not standard of proof, whereas the criminal verdict rests on a beyond a reasonable doubt standard. We fail to see the force of the distinction. Verdicts are the result of the same serious deliberation by the jurors no matter what the standard of proof. This is especially so today when, with the proliferation of cases involving civil rights, huge damage awards and forfeitures, the stakes in civil cases are so high, and the infringement of the jury verdict caused by a harmless error finding may be as important in the civil context as in the criminal.

The *Haddad* court's second argument, which also relies on the different standards of proof in civil and criminal cases, is similarly uncompelling. The court once again begins from a sound premise: that the lesser burden of proof in the civil context than in the criminal demonstrates that the impact of falsity is less damaging in civil than in criminal suits for only in the latter is personal liberty at stake. The court goes on to assert that "(t)he civil litigant's lessened entitlement to veracity continues when the litigant becomes an appellant." There is no logical reason, however, that the tolerance for error in the civil context must be compounded by a less stringent standard of harmless error review. Society's tolerance for risk of error in civil cases may have been subsumed in the decision to establish a lower burden of proof in civil cases; further enlargement of the margin of error would therefore distort, rather than reflect, society's wishes. . . .

We are thus unpersuaded by the arguments that the civil and criminal standards of review for harmless error should be different. Moreover, we believe that there are three compelling reasons that the standards should be the same. First, neither Federal Rule of Evidence 103(a) nor 28 U.S.C. §2111 (1982) (the harmless error statute directly applicable to the appellate courts) distinguishes between criminal and civil cases. This implies that Congress intended uniform treatment, and that differentiating civil and criminal standards of review would be contrary to congressional intent.[17]

Second, differentiating the standards might lead to unexpected complications when it is recognized that not all civil cases are alike. Some, like fraud or defamation, require clear and convincing evidence. Because the *Haddad* court apparently believes that the standard of appellate review should

---

17. The Federal Rules of Evidence were originally drafted by a committee and submitted to Congress by the Supreme Court. Congress debated and amended the proposed rules, and eventually passed them in modified form. Pub. L. No. 93-595, 88 Stat. 1926-1937 (1975). The extensive congressional involvement in the rules justifies our reading them as indicative of congressional intent. We also note in this regard that the harmless error provision of the Federal Rules of Civil Procedure, Fed. R. Civ. P. 61, and its criminal analogue, Fed. R. Crim. P. 52(a), provide no hint that the appellate court might use different standards of review in the two situations. The civil rule defines harmful error as that which "appears to the court inconsistent with substantial justice," and the criminal rule defines it as "affect(ing) substantial rights." We do not perceive a clear distinction between the two. Thus, Congress had the opportunity to differentiate the standards, and chose not to do so.

track the burden of proof at trial, it is unclear whether it would require different standards for fraud, defamation, and like cases.[18]

Third, broad institutional concerns militate against increasing the number of errors deemed harmless. Although it is late in the day to pretend that all trials are perfect, perfection should still be our goal. Judge (now Chief Judge) Robinson put the point well:

> The justification for harmless-error rules is singleminded; they avoid wasting the time and effort of judges, counsel and other trial participants. Other considerations enter into the picture, however, when we set out to ascertain what is harmless and what is not. Wisdom of the ages counsels against appellate erosion of the stature and function of the trial jury. Societal beliefs about who should bear the risk of error in particular types of proceedings deserve weight in decisions on harmlessness. Respect for the dignity of the individual, as well as for the law and the courts that administer it, may call for rectification of errors not visibly affecting the accuracy of the judicial process. And the prophylactic effect of a reversal occasionally might outweigh the expenditure of effort on a new trial. [United States v. Burton, 584 F.2d 485, 512-513 (D.C. Cir. 1978) (Robinson, J., dissenting).]

By maintaining a moderately stringent, though not unreasonably high, standard in civil as well as criminal cases, we preserve a strong incentive for the district courts to minimize their errors, and we thereby bolster the integrity of the federal judicial process.

We therefore conclude that the standard of review in civil cases is the same as in criminal, and that, as *Toto* is the law of this circuit with regard to criminal cases, so should it be our guide here.

3. Application of the Toto Standards to the Facts of This Case

Fortunately, the application of the appropriate standard is far easier than the determination of that standard. The district court's refusal to admit the evidence of subornation impaired the defendants' ability to discredit a central element of the plaintiff's case. Moreover, the evidence was critical for the defendants to make their argument on defense of liability; it was potentially the defendants' best evidence and not cumulative. We cannot say that it is highly probable that the trial court's refusal to enter evidence of plaintiff's subornation of perjury did not affect the defendants' substantial rights. Hence, the court's erroneous ruling is grounds for reversal.

---

18. This potential complication demonstrates that the harmless error standard of review is an unwieldy tool with which to attain broad societal objectives. If society wishes to expedite civil trials at the cost of veracity, to make stronger the guarantees of accuracy in criminal prosecutions, or to achieve other goals attainable through fine-tuning of the judicial system, there are more direct ways of doing so than through the byzantine turns of the harmless error standard of review.

A. Relevancy—The Basic Concept

NOTES AND QUESTIONS

1. How did either the trial court or the court of appeals in *Knapp* and *McQueeney* determine whether the evidence offered was relevant to prove a material proposition? Determining the material propositions is easy enough; the law applicable to the cause of action determines the propositions that must be proved by the parties. As the excerpt from Thayer points out, however, there are virtually no rules governing the admissibility of evidence, even though there are numerous exclusionary rules. To decide a question of relevancy requires that the offered evidence be evaluated in the context of the decision maker's knowledge and experience. More particularly, the evidence is evaluated by reference to the generalizations that emerge from the decision maker's knowledge and experience. For example, in *McQueeney* the evidence is relevant because our shared experience is that individuals with weak or invalid claims are more likely than ones with valid claims to attempt to obtain fraudulent evidence. Thus, such an attempt increases the chances that the claim in question was invalid.

The determination of "relevancy," then, is a function of one's knowledge and experience in life. Thus, the advocate wishing to offer or oppose evidence must be prepared to argue for admissibility or exclusion by reference to compelling generalizations. That will also require on occasion that the generalizations be defended, thus pushing back the logical relationships yet one more step. Obviously, we cannot here describe this process in greater detail because each case depends upon the particular evidence in question and the knowledge and experience of the decision maker. Note, however, the wisdom of FRE 401 and 403 when viewed from this perspective. The nature of the relevancy determination could lead to rather idiosyncratic outcomes with individual trial judges reaching remarkably divergent conclusions about the admissibility of evidence because of their own personal views. The Federal Rules admonish the trial judges not to allow this to happen by defining relevancy as "*any tendency* to make the existence of any fact . . . more or less probable. . . ." [Emphasis supplied.] FRE 403, in turn, requires that any such evidence be admitted unless there is a very good reason not to do so. By so strongly favoring admissibility, the rules reduce idiosyncratic exclusions of evidence.[5]

2. There are certain ambiguities in FRE 403. What is the difference between "confusion of the issues" and "misleading the jury," and what is the difference between either of those and "unfair prejudice"? What is the significance of the three uses of the word *or* in the rule? Are there two different grounds of exclusion, one being unfair prejudice "or" confusion of the issues "or" misleading the jury, and the second being undue delay "or"

---

5. There is another limitation on judicial idiosyncrasy that is implicit in the rules. The admissibility of evidence ought to be determined by whether the evidence could influence a reasonable person rather than whether the evidence does, or would, influence the trial judge. This is most obvious in FRE 104(b), which is developed in Chapter Three.

waste of time "or" needless presentation of cumulative evidence? Alternatively, is there simply a list of the relevant six factors justifying exclusion? The significance of this semantic quibble is that, as written, the rule is unclear as to what the phrase *substantially outweighed by* modifies. Is it the first three grounds of exclusion or all of them? In either event, this is an example of sloppy draftsmanship, and it is not the last such that you will come across. The Federal Rules are an impressive achievement, but at many points they read as though they were drafted by committees (which is not surprising since in large measure they were). That creates some stylistic problems as well as ambiguities, such as the one discussed here.

3. The approach of the Federal Rules is typically contrasted with that of Wigmore, who argued that the law distinguished between "logical" and "legal" relevance. 1 J. Wigmore, Evidence in Trials at Common Law §28, at 409-410 (Chadbourn rev.): "[L]egal relevancy denotes . . . something more than a minimum of probative value." It is not altogether clear what this means. Presumably Wigmore was attempting to distinguish between evidence that had some very slight probative value and that which had considerably more persuasive force. Although FRE 401 on its face does not make this distinction, the combined effect of FRE 401 and 403 is consistent with if not identical to the Wigmore approach. If evidence may have a barely perceptible logical effect, it is also likely to be either misleading or lead to delay and waste of time, thus being excludable under FRE 403. At an earlier time there was a concern that the Wigmore approach might lead to confusing the question of admissibility of evidence with the separate question whether the evidence is sufficient to justify a verdict. The question of admissibility goes to logical effect; the question of sufficiency goes to whether a reasonable person could be persuaded by the evidence to the level demanded by the applicable burden of persuasion. A few older cases confused these issues, but it does not appear to be a serious problem today. See Engel v. United Traction Co., 203 N.Y. 321, 96 N.E. 731 (1911).

4. The common law distinguished between two types of relevant evidence: direct and circumstantial. Direct evidence typically is defined as evidence that, if believed, disposes of a material proposition. For example, if an eyewitness testifies that she saw the light was green when the plaintiff's car was in the intersection, that would be direct evidence of the proposition that the light was green. Compare that case to one where a witness testifies that at approximately the time a bank was robbed, he saw the defendant (charged with the bank robbery) running from the vicinity of the bank. This would be viewed as circumstantial evidence of guilt on the grounds that one explanation of the defendant's action is his consciousness of guilt or that he was attempting to escape. See, e.g., State v. Ball, 339 S.W.2d 783 (Mo. 1960). In such a case, though, there are numerous other explanations; and thus even if the fact finder believes the evidence, an inference of guilt does not automatically follow.

Some jurisdictions predicate rules of evidence upon the distinction

A. Relevancy—The Basic Concept

between circumstantial and direct evidence. For example, in criminal cases that are based upon circumstantial evidence an instruction is often given to the effect that the evidence must exclude to a moral certainty every other hypothesis but guilt. Nonetheless, the analytical difference between direct and circumstantial evidence is one of degree only. Typically the inferential chain leading to an inference concerning a material proposition is either stronger or shorter in the case of what normally goes by the label "direct evidence." For example, in the first hypothetical above, the testimony of the witness establishes the material fact if the trier of fact believes the witness observed the event correctly, remembers it, and is presently relating it accurately. These are the standard issues that must be resolved by the fact finder in order to evaluate any evidence, and they are the kinds of issues that people deal with constantly in everyday life.

Compare such "direct" evidence to what normally is called "circumstantial" evidence. Suppose, for example, that a defendant is connected to the scene of a crime based on a number of "circumstances" that indicate, but even if true do not themselves establish, that the defendant was present. For example, assume the crime occurred in Buffalo, New York, and there is evidence that the defendant purchased a ticket for the train to Buffalo. Suppose further that he was observed getting into a cab one-half hour before the train departed, and the cab ride to the station normally takes 15 minutes. In the normal lexicon, these bits of evidence would be "circumstantial" rather than direct evidence that the defendant went to Buffalo because, even if they are both true, it is still possible that the defendant did not go to Buffalo. Thus, not only must the normal issues concerning a witness be resolved, but in addition upon resolution of those issues there are further inferences that must be drawn. There is, in other words, a longer chain of inference in this case than in the normal case of direct evidence.

However, bear in mind that the innocuous sounding phrase *evidence which if believed*, is more complicated than it appears at first glance. How simple is it to know if a witness is telling the truth or if the witness' memory is functioning adequately? Any evidence has associated with it fairly complicated chains of reasoning that make it probative of some material proposition. Some of those chains are longer and some are shorter. Some are stronger in the sense of being more convincing; some are weaker in the sense of being not very persuasive. These are the variables that distinguish circumstantial from direct evidence rather than the simplistic rubric articulated above. Also, do not overlook the fact that circumstantial evidence can often be more probative than direct evidence. A hair found at the scene of the crime that is tied to the defendant by neuron activation analysis is an example of very probative circumstantial evidence, and is probably more reliable than many cases of eyewitness identification that would be labeled "direct" evidence.

5. A doctrine related to those surrounding circumstantial evidence is the rule, still persistent in some jurisdictions, that an "inference upon an

inference" is not allowable. What lies behind this doctrine is the insight that if evidence tends to generate an inference of B and B generates an inference of A (a material proposition), there is a greater risk of error than if there were evidence that tended to prove A without the need to first establish B. The point is that there is a risk of error when B is inferred, and another risk of error when A is inferred from B. To reduce the risk of error, the rule developed in some jurisdictions that forbids "double inferences" of this sort. See, e.g., Waldman v. Shipyard Marina, 102 R.I. 366, 230 A.2d 841 (1967). Generally speaking, the rule makes little sense. At issue is the strength of the connection between the evidence and the final inference of A rather than the number of steps that must be taken to get to that final conclusion. The number of steps may indicate something about the strength of the relationship between the evidence and the material proposition, but little can be said about the matter categorically. Under the Federal Rules, the issue would be whether the evidence had any tendency to establish a material proposition and whether its probative value was so slight as to be misleading or unnecessarily time consuming under FRE 403. That is the proper approach.

6. Evidentiary rulings, especially relevancy rulings, can often mask substantive determinations. Consider the following from James, Relevancy, Probability and the Law, 29 Cal. L. Rev. 689, 692-693 (1941):

> Under modern codes the substantive law confusion is . . . common. . . . Let us analyze a single interesting case, Union Paint & Varnish Co. v. Dean, 48 R.I. 288, 137 A. 469 (1927), an action of assumpsit to recover the purchase price of waterproof roof paint. The defendant relied upon the plaintiff's warranty that the paint would wear for 10 years, breach of which he sought to show by proof that another drum of paint of the same brand, which he had purchased six months earlier, not only had failed to prevent leaks but had ruined the shingles to which it had been applied. The drum of paint in issue, purchased just before leaks developed in the first roof painted, had never been opened. Reversing the trial court, the Supreme Court of Rhode Island held that the defendant's offer of proof (apparently almost the only evidence offered in defense) should have been received, saying:
>
>> If paint of the same brand, sold by the same concern under the same warranty within six months, had proved within that time to be not in conformity with the warranty, in that it was not only not suitable for stopping and preventing leaks but was actually injurious to a roof, a person might well hesitate before using more paint of the same brand when he had no reason to expect the second lot to be any better than the first.
>
> Considered as evidence of the condition of the second drum of paint, proof of the results of use of the first is not very impressive. Waiving any doubts whether the leaks in the first roof were traceable to defects in paint in the first drum, there is no showing whether the defects in the first drum of paint were due to poor ingredients, to a poor formula, or to some error in preparation. If poor ingredients had been used, there is no showing that use of poor ingredients was a policy of, rather than an error of, the plaintiff

A. Relevancy—The Basic Concept   123

company. It is easier to believe that one lot of defective paint went out than it is to believe that plaintiff customarily sold, under a 10-year guaranty, waterproof roof paint which would rot out shingles and cause leaks in six months. And the two drums of paint were probably not out of one lot; certainly there was no showing that they were. Proof of the condition of the paint in the first drum was of negligible value in judging the probable character of the paint in the second, unopened drum. It merely showed that plaintiff company sometimes sold bad paint. If the issue was whether the paint in the second drum was bad, an issue on which the defendant had the burden, the trial judge's ruling seems sound. At worst, the issue is close enough so that an appellate court should not reverse. Yet there is still a ring of reason to the supreme court's statement that "a person might well hesitate before using more paint of the same brand." He would hesitate to risk ruining a second roof even if he only feared that the second drum of paint might be no better than the first. And if he was reasonable in his hesitation, should the plaintiff be allowed to recover even if it could show at trial that the paint in the second drum was perfectly good? The defendant, reasonably hesitant to use the doubtful paint, by now has probably painted all of his roofs with some other paint and has no further use for the drum which he is tendering back to the vendor. If the customer is to be protected, even against proof that the second drum of paint was in fact satisfactory (as the writer should like to do in such a case), a novel rule of substantive law stands revealed behind a somewhat doubtful ruling on evidence.

7. As a general matter, Thayer is correct that relevancy is a function of generalizations that emerge from experience, and that the law does not provide rules of relevance. However, certain patterns emerge in litigation, and what is initially a matter of "common sense" often ends up being articulated in a rule. This process is described in the following passage from State v. LaPage, 57 N.H. 245, 288 (N.H. 1876):

> [A]lthough undoubtedly the relevancy of testimony is originally a matter of logic and common sense, still there are many instances in which the evidence of particular facts as bearing on particular issues has been so often the subject of discussion in courts of law, and so often ruled upon, that the united logic of a great many judges and lawyers may be said to furnish evidence of the sense common to a great many individuals, and, therefore, the best evidence of what may be properly called *common*-sense, and thus to acquire the authority of law. It is for this reason that the subject of the relevancy of testimony has become, to so great an extent, matter of precedent and authority, and that we may with entire propriety speak of its legal relevancy.

In addition to the common law process providing "rules of relevancy," rules of evidence often contain such rules. These tend to be based on the desire to further various policies other than logical relevance, however. Examples of such rules may be found in FRE 404 to 412, which are examined in Chapter Four.

8. Evidence sometimes will be admissible for one purpose or with respect

to one material proposition, but will be inadmissible for another purpose or with respect to a different material proposition. Whenever that occurs, the opponent of the evidence may ask for a limiting instruction that directs the jury to consider the evidence only with respect to its admissible purpose. See FRE 105. This phenomenon is obvious, and thus typically unspoken, with respect to the issue of relevancy. For example, evidence that tends to prove agreement in a contract case but not performance is admissible only on agreement. Since this typically will so clearly be the case, limiting instructions will rarely be asked for.

Some situations involving relevancy do occur with some frequency and call for limiting instructions. Perhaps the most important is where evidence on credibility is admitted that could be used improperly to establish other matters. In a criminal case, for example, if the defendant takes the stand and is impeached based upon his prior record, the jury might infer from his record that he is a criminal type, and thus that it is likely that he committed the offense in question. This would be an improper use of the evidence, and the opponent, in this case the defendant, could ask for an instruction limiting the jury's consideration of the evidence to the proper issue. It is not clear, however, when such an instruction should be asked for. Asking for the instruction tends to emphasize the improper inference, which may be more damaging than simply letting the matter go unnoticed. Furthermore, it is unclear how able or willing jurors are to follow such instructions. Recent empirical work casts some doubt on the extent to which jurors actually ignore evidence that is erroneously offered at trial and that the judge instructs them to ignore, which is somewhat different from but related to the question of whether jurors will properly limit their consideration of evidence admissible for one reason but excludable for another. See Casper, Benedict, and Perry, Juror Decision-Making, Attitudes, and the Hindsight Bias, 13 Law & Hum. Behav.— (1989); Casper, Benedict, and Perry, The Tort Remedy in Search and Seizure Cases: A Case Study in Juror Decision-Making, Law & Soc. Inquiry 279 (1988).

PROBLEMS

1. During a hockey game between two local teams, a fight broke out resulting in physical harm to some of the players. The worst injury was inflicted by one of the player's use of his stick as a weapon. That player was indicted for assault and battery. At his trial, the prosecution produced five witnesses, each of whom testified that the player assaulted the member of the opposing team in an unprovoked way. The prosecution then called a sixth witness who began to testify to precisely the same thing. The defense objected on "403" grounds. What result?

2. Assume the trial judge sustained the defense objection in Problem 1 and that the prosecution rested. The defense then offered evidence to show

A. Relevancy—The Basic Concept

that each of the five witnesses were life-long fans of the team for which the injured player played, and further that there was a long and bitter rivalry between the two teams. The prosecution objected on grounds of surprise, arguing that this evidence was not anticipated and that the prosecution could have produced many more witnesses, undoubtedly some of whom were not life-long fans of the injured player's team, who would testify to the defendant's culpability. What result?

3. D was indicted for the murder of P. The prosecution's case consisted of evidence that D and P had left together to go on a hunting trip; that D returned alone, saying that he and P had had a fight resulting in P's having left their campsite; and that P's body was found with a bullet in his head fired from a deer rifle. The prosecutor wants to introduce evidence that D and P had been in business together; that the business was failing; that there was a life insurance policy for $100,000 on the lives of P and D with their company the beneficiary; that the insurance company had so far refused to pay the face amount; and that D had looked at deer rifles at a local store prior to the hunting trip. Is any or all of this admissible? Does it matter that D will testify to the fact that he and P had gone hunting only with bow and arrow?

4. In Problem 3, the storekeeper where D allegedly looked at deer rifles is called to the stand. When asked if he remembers D coming into his store to look at the guns, the storekeeper replied that he "thought" so, but he "couldn't be sure." D moves to strike the answer from the record and for an instruction that the jury must disregard the answer. What result?

5. P sued D to recover benefits under an insurance policy for an illness from which he was suffering. D relied on the defense of fraud, alleging that P had not been in good health at the time the insurance contract was entered into. To establish the fraud, D attempted to depose P's doctors who had allegedly treated P at approximately the time the insurance was obtained. P refused to waive his physician-patient privilege, however, and thus prevented the insurance company from deposing his former doctors or examining his hospital records. The insurance company offered P's actions as proof of the fraud. Admissible or not? Does it matter whether the insurance company has any other evidence of fraud? — No

6. P is suing D for slander. P wishes to introduce the three individuals who were present when the allegedly slanderous statement was made, all of whom will testify that it was P who slandered D rather than the other way around. P's theory is that the virtually identical testimony of these individuals demonstrates a conspiracy against him, which also tends to prove that the slander occurred. How should the trial judge rule?

7. D, a professor of modern languages and the owner of a "radical" bookstore, was charged with conspiracy and a number of substantive offenses arising out of the bombing of two military recruitment centers. Over objection, the prosecution introduced a book entitled *From the Movement Toward Revolution*, which had on it D's fingerprints, and those of three of D's alleged

co-conspirators. The book's title, but not its substance, was admitted during the government's case in chief. The trial court also admitted the testimony of D's co-conspirators concerning the books that D recommended as well as comments that he had made of a political nature. D testified in his own defense that his store had never sold *From the Movement Toward Revolution*, and he also testified about other "representative books" that could be found in his store that demonstrated that he was a scholarly, humane, and peace-loving man who would not turn to violence. On cross-examination, again over objection, the government secured D's admission that he had read *From the Movement Toward Revolution*. In addition, D was required to read a passage from the book advocating violent insurrection. In closing argument, the government argued that the book was "an architectural manual . . . of urban warfare, and throughout the book there are references to the very thing that these people did."

D was convicted of conspiracy and now appeals on the ground that his objection to the evidence should have been sustained. What result?

B. A RESTATEMENT OF THE BASIC CONCEPT OF RELEVANCY

The essence of the Federal Rules approach to relevancy is that evidence is relevant if it has the capacity to influence a disinterested person on a material proposition. What the infinitive *to influence* means in this context is somewhat vague, though. We know when we have a sense of being "convinced" or "persuaded" or of being placed in "doubt" by an argument or by evidence. But must an analysis of the influence of evidence stop at such an ephemeral point? Some have argued that it must. See, e.g., Hart and McNaughton, Evidence and Inference in the Law 87 Daedalus 40, 44 (Fall 1958): "The adjudicative facts of interest to the law, being historical facts, will rarely be triable by the experimental methods of the natural sciences. . . . For the most part the law must settle disputed questions of adjudicative fact by reliance upon the ambiguous implications of non-fungible 'traces'—traces on human brains and on pieces of paper and traces in the form of unique arrangements of physical objects."

Perhaps Hart and McNaughton are correct that the law must be satisfied with "traces on human brains." Nevertheless, there has been great interest recently in efforts to articulate in a more rigorous fashion what it means for evidence to have persuasive force. These efforts have centered primarily on the implications of a theorem of mathematics known as Bayes' Theorem,[6]

---

6. But see the discussion of inductive probability in L. Cohen, The Probable and the Provable (1977), which offers an alternative to Bayes Theorem.

B. Restatement of the Basic Concept of Relevancy

which provides a rigorous method for combining a person's assessment of the probability of an event with new evidence concerning that event to arrive at a new assessment of the probability of the event.[7] English mathematician Thomas Bayes (1702-1761) demonstrated that the following formula is derivable from the axioms of conventional probability. In the formula,

O(G) = odds of guilt or liability

O(G/E) = odds of guilt or liability given the new evidence (E)

P(E/G) = probability of obtaining the evidence in question if the person is guilty or liable

P(E/not-G) = probability of obtaining the evidence in question if the individual is not guilty or liable

The formula is:

$$O(G/E) = \frac{P(E/G)}{P(E/not\text{-}G)} \times O(G)$$

This formula expresses that the odds of guilt or liability after evidence is received is determined by the relationship between the probability of obtaining the evidence if the person is guilty or liable and the probability of obtaining the evidence if the person is not guilty or liable. In other words, to go from a prior assessment of the odds of liability to an assessment in light of the new evidence requires that the prior assessment be modified in light of the likelihood that the evidence would have been presented at trial if the person is liable as compared to the likelihood that it would have been presented if the person is not liable.

Do not let the discussion of probability theory obscure an important insight here. What makes evidence "relevant" is its capacity to influence the fact finder. That, in turn, is a function of the probability of receiving the evidence if the person is liable as compared to the probability of receiving the evidence if the person is not liable. Take a simple example. Suppose in the hypothetical of the black-haired burglar that the prosecution wished to introduce evidence that the defendant does not like the Chicago Bears. If the defendant is guilty, the probability of receiving this evidence is a function of the proportion of burglars who are Chicago Bears fans, which we shall assume is .95. The probability of receiving the evidence if the defendant is not guilty is a function of the proportion of nonburglars who are Chicago

---

7. For what follows we are indebted to Richard Lempert's work on Bayes' Theorem, which can be found in Lempert, Modeling Relevance, 75 Mich. L. Rev. 1021 (1977). That work was heavily influenced by John Kaplan's article, Decision Theory and the Factfinding Process, 20 Stan. L. Rev. 1065 (1968), which in turn was heavily influenced by Ball, The Moment of Truth: Probability Theory and Standards of Proof, 14 Vand. L. Rev. 807 (1961).

Bears fans, and there is no reason to think that proportion would differ from the proportion of burglars who are fans of the Bears. Thus, the ratio of these probabilities (.95/.95) is 1.0, and 1.0 multiplied by the prior odds of guilt will result in no change in those odds. Therefore, this evidence is irrelevant because it has no impact on the assessment of the odds of guilt.

Contrast this to the testimony about the color of hair of the burglar, and assume that the defendant has red hair as his mother would testify. The probability of receiving the evidence about black hair if the defendant is guilty is very low (virtually .0), precisely because the defendant has red rather than black hair. On the other hand, the chances of receiving the evidence about the burglar having black hair is considerably higher if the defendant is innocent (presumably this probability would be the probability of a person picked at random from the population having black hair, which is fairly high). The ratio of these probabilities is a very small fraction, and thus this evidence tends to reduce significantly the odds of the defendant's guilt. The precise effect would be determined by multiplying this ratio times the prior assessment of the odds of guilt.

We do not suggest that this way of viewing relevance has any value other than a heuristic one. It may help explain how rational people evaluate evidence. Indeed, even as an explanatory effort, it has serious limitations. The formula requires that the decision maker have a preliminary assessment of the odds of guilt or liability *before* the receipt of evidence, and it is unclear what that should be in our system of trials (especially criminal trials). In addition, the probabilities associated with the evidence will virtually always defy quantification. More troublesome still, Bayes' Theorem requires that the decision maker evaluate each bit of evidence as it is introduced, rather than permitting the decision maker to hear all the evidence and deliberate on all of it at the conclusion of the trial process. At trial, by contrast, jurors are explicitly told not to form any generalizations until all the evidence is in. The reason for this is the belief that once opinions are formed they are hard to change. Individuals will rationalize new evidence they hear to make it consistent with their preconceptions. To the extent this is true, the party first producing evidence would have a great advantage at trial, since presumably that evidence will tend to establish that party's case.

The Bayes' Theorem, in short, is an interesting way of thinking about the idea of relevance, even if it is not completely compatible with the trial process. Nonetheless, do not overlook its power. At many points in the trial process the parties have to argue over the implications of the evidence. This requires that the competing generalizations that the evidence permits be compared and contrasted, which, of course, is what Bayes' Theorem is all about. Thus, to argue for the admissibility of evidence requires that an advocate demonstrate to the satisfaction of the trial judge that the competing generalizations permitted by the evidence do not simply cancel each other out (that is, that the likelihood ratio of the Bayes' Theorem is not equal to 1.0), and thus that the generalization of guilt or liability, given the evidence,

B. Restatement of the Basic Concept of Relevancy

is more likely than the generalization of not guilty or not liable (or vice-versa, of course).

Reconsider the hypothetical of the individual running from the scene of the bank robbery. Fleeing is relevant only if it permits a stronger inference (that is, generalization) of guilt than of innocence. If it is just as likely that he was running to catch a bus as to escape being caught, the evidence cannot rationally be relied upon by the fact finder. Bayes' Theorem is merely a formalization of this basic insight.

Bayes' Theorem also provides a useful way to think about the grounds of exclusion under the Federal Rules. Unfair prejudice, confusion, and misleading of the jury exists whenever the jury forms a likelihood ratio that is quite different from what the "true" likelihood ratio is. This can occur whenever the jury misevaluates either component of the ratio for whatever reason.

There is another way to think about the grounds for exclusion that also involves some simple mathematics and that permits taking into account a fact finder's preferences. "Unfair prejudice" describes the situation where the preferences of the fact finder are affected for reasons essentially unrelated to the persuasive power of the evidence to establish the material propositions. Assume that the defendant in the burglary case has been arrested for other offenses in the past and assume further that a prior record has no empirical relationship with the probability that a person has committed a subsequent crime. Suppose evidence of the prior record is admitted at trial. One effect of that evidence may be to reduce the fact finder's concern with accuracy. Given that the defendant has had previous brushes with the law, the fact finder may then think that even if the defendant did not commit the crime charged he undoubtedly committed others, and consequently it would do no great wrong to convict him even if he is innocent of this particular charge. Given the defendant's background, in other words, the "disutility" (i.e., cost) of a wrongful conviction is not what it would be with a person who has never been in trouble with the law.

A fact finder's appraisal of the disutility of one type of error as compared to another can be articulated algebraically.[8] In the formula that follows:

D_g = the disutility of acquitting a guilty person or returning a wrongful verdict for a defendant in a civil case

D_i = the disutility of convicting an innocent man or of returning a wrongful verdict for a plaintiff in a civil case

P = the probability necessary to return a verdict of guilty or liability in a civil case

---

8. We are indebted to Kaplan, Decison Theory and the Factfinding Process, 20 Stan. L. Rev. 1065 (1968) for much of what follows.

A rational decision maker presumably decides issues in such a way as to minimize the disutilities associated with the decision. When the relevant facts are known, that is a simple matter, but in the context of trials the facts are not known with certainty. Therefore, a way must be found to take account of that uncertainty. This can be done through the concept of "expected disutility," which is the disutility associated with a decision multiplied by the probability that the decision is factually accurate. Suppose that there is a disutility of 10 (whatever the units of "disutility" may be) associated with convicting an innocent person and 1 unit of disutility with acquitting a guilty person. How should a decision maker decide when faced with imperfect knowledge? The formula below provides some guidance:[9]

$$P > \frac{1}{1 + \frac{D_g}{D_i}}$$

Plug the figures suggested above into the formula. If $D_g = 1$ and $D_i = 10$, then:

$$P > \frac{1}{1 + \frac{1}{10}} = .91$$

In a criminal case, then, if it is 10 times worse to convict an innocent person than to acquit a guilty person, a jury should vote for conviction only when guilt has been established to a probability of at least .91. Compare this to civil cases. The normal view in civil cases is that the disutility of a wrongful verdict for a defendant is equal to that of a wrongful verdict for a plaintiff. Thus $D_g = D_i$ and the formula reduces to $P > .5$, which is the normal burden of proof in civil cases.

Suppose that in a certain case there is no disutility in convicting an innocent man. A good example is in the novel *To Kill a Mockingbird*, where a heinous crime has outraged the community and someone—it really does not matter much who—must be punished in order to expiate the anger and fear of the community. In such a case, as the value of D_i nears zero, the denominator of the fraction becomes a very large number. Therefore, in order to convict, there need only be a probability P > 1/[a very large number], which equals a very *small* probability. Anyone will do, in short, so long as someone is sacrificed to the community's needs.

Now consider the other side of the coin, where it is the sense of a community that a person has already been punished enough for his or her digressions. For example, consider the case of the president of a small-town bank who has embezzled funds and been caught. The person has lost her

---

9. For elaboration on the source of the formula, see ibid.

B. Restatement of the Basic Concept of Relevancy 131

job and has been disgraced publicly. When brought to trial, the jurors may feel that no more punishment is due. In the formula, D_g (the disutility of acquitting a guilty person) falls to zero. Consequently, the denominator of the fraction approaches 1, and thus the probability needed to convict, P, becomes 1.0. This cannot occur, and the individual is acquitted.

Obviously, these examples and this way of thinking about preferences and prejudice only roughly mirror what occurs in the real world, yet they provide some insights into the decision-making process. The effective advocate will not only provide a compelling factual story, but in addition will to the extent permitted—and much greater latitude will be given in criminal cases—attempt to demonstrate why the costs of a verdict for his or her adversary carries too high a cost. To the extent a party is able to do so, the scales have been tilted in that party's favor.

Whether or not this discussion has been enlightening about the reality of the trial process, it is at least enlightening about one meaning of the word *prejudice* in FRE 403. "Prejudicial" information is that which would tend to make the fact finder balance the disutilities of wrongful decisions in a way inconsistently with that provided by the law. In other words, it would be prejudicial in a civil case to provide information that would tend to influence the jury to the view that it would be five times worse to return a wrongful plaintiff's verdict than a wrongful defendant's verdict. Similarly, because in criminal cases the law requires proof beyond reasonable doubt, it would be prejudicial to admit evidence that would cause the fact finder in a criminal case to decide that it is equally bad to acquit a guilty person as to convict an innocent person.

Note, however, that while this discussion may be enlightening about prejudice, it says very little about when prejudice "substantially outweighs" probative value, which is the standard under FRE 403, and we have little to add to our previous discussion of that issue. To briefly reiterate, there are two relevant variables. The first is the strength of the judge's conviction that evidence will have an inappropriate effect on the jury (which means simply an effect that cannot be logically justified). The second is the magnitude of the illogical effect. A judge will not know for certain that a jury will be inappropriately influenced by evidence; the judge can only appraise the likelihood of the evidence having that effect. Moreover, it seems reasonable to think that some evidence will be more powerful than other evidence in its illogical impact upon the jury. We suggest that "substantiality" is some mix of these two variables. The two extremes are that the trial judge could be convinced beyond reasonable doubt that evidence would have a serious illogical effect. Alternatively, the judge could conclude that there is some small possibility that the evidence would some have some, no matter how slight, illogical effect (which means the *total* effect of the evidence would be to move the jury away from an accurate outcome). "Substantiality" lies somewhere between these two extremes.

Two questions may now be stirring feelings of discontent within you.

First: How can a judge know whether any evidence is relevant and admissible before he or she first hears all the evidence that is to be offered in the case? Whether any piece of evidence will affect an ultimate proposition is a function of all the other evidence that will or may be offered in addition to being a function of the judge's generalizations formed out of his or her knowledge and experience. Suppose, for example, that there was a car accident, and one of the questions was whether the defendant had knowledge that the brakes in the car were bad. Assume further that there is a witness who is willing to testify that he overheard the defendant's mechanic tell the defendant not to drive the car because the brakes were bad. Is that admissible on the question of whether the defendant had notice of the conditions of the brakes? It seems to be, but what if the defendant has evidence that establishes that this witness was in a different state at the time the mechanic purportedly said what he said? Or what if the defendant can show that he is deaf? Or, what if the defendant can show that he immediately took his car to Midas and had the brakes fixed? Without knowing about any of these matters, how can a determination of admissibility be made?

Second: Why is the judge making this determination? Isn't the jury supposed to determine facts? The power to admit or exclude evidence that we have been discussing entails significant control over the fact-finding process. What justifies that control being placed in the hands of the trial judge?

Both of these questions are of great importance, and we examine them in detail in the next chapter. Because they are subtle and complicated, however, it will be useful to fine-tune the lessons of this chapter through the problems that follow and to reflect upon those lessons in the next section. Upon completing those tasks, we will move to the question of the implications of the requirement of relevancy for the relationship between the judge and jury.

PROBLEMS

1. Driver's car ran over Pedestrian, who is now suing Driver for negligence. Among other allegations is one to the effect that Driver was negligent in driving a car that he knew to possess defective brakes. At trial, Pedestrian wants to put Witness on the stand who will testify to overhearing a discussion between Driver and Garage Mechanic that took place prior to the accident. Driver and Mechanic were arguing over a bill for work done to Driver's car. Mechanic had replaced the wiper blades without Driver's permission, and Driver was now refusing to pay for the blades. As Driver was leaving the repair shop, according to Witness, Mechanic yelled at him: "Take your car somewhere else to get the brakes fixed. I never want to see that car again." Will Witness be allowed to testify to this?

2. *D* was indicted for armed robbery. One of his co-defendants turned state's evidence and testified against *D*. That testimony included the fact that

B. Restatement of the Basic Concept of Relevancy 133

D had used a .38-caliber gun during the robbery. At the time of his arrest, D had in his possession a .38-caliber gun. At trial, prosecution wished to adduce evidence of D having this gun in his possession. Admissible or not?

3. A five-count indictment charged D with distributing obscene films. At trial, the government asked the court for permission to show the films to the jury. D objected on grounds of prejudice and offered to stipulate to their obscenity. The government refused the stipulation. The court allowed the the jury to view three of the films, and required the government to accept the stipulation as to the other two. D was convicted and appeals; the government cross-appeals on the issue of the admissibility of the remaining two films. What result?

4. D, who was on trial for bank robbery, was a 38-year-old man of Asian extraction, with a handlebar mustache. He was living with a 23-year-old woman with blond hair, usually worn in pigtails, and he owned a yellow Volkswagen "bug." Witnesses at trial testified that the robber was a 35- to 40-year-old Asian with a handlebar mustache, and after the robbery he was seen entering a yellow Volkswagen driven by a young blond with pigtails. The prosecution also called a statistician to the stand and asked him what the odds would be of the defendant having all the characteristics of the robber but not being the robber. In order to make the calculations, the statistician was told to assume that the probability of the defendant being Asian was 0.2, the probability of having a handlebar mustache was 0.01, the probability of his living with a blond was 0.1, the probability of the blond typically wearing pigtails was 0.2, and the probability of the defendant owning a yellow Volkswagen was .05. The statistician was also instructed to assume that each of these factors was independent of the other. He then testified that the probability of the defendant having each of these characteristics "by chance," and thus not being the robber, is determined by multiplying the separate probabilities of each factor. Therefore, the probability of the defendant not being the robber is $0.2 \times .01 \times 0.1 \times 0.2 \times .05 = .000002$. In closing argument, the prosecutor referred to this figure as proof that the "beyond reasonable doubt" standard had been met. On appeal, D argues that the evidence should not have been admitted. What result?

5. The Flying Friars, a rock group composed of members of a monastery, signed a contract with Fabulous Music, Inc., that called for Fabulous Music to promote the music of The Flying Friars. The Flying Friars came out with a new song entitled Virgin Momma. At about the same time as the song came out, Fabulous Music, Inc., was purchased by new owners who decided they did not wish to maintain the relationship with The Flying Friars. Accordingly, they did not promote Virgin Momma, and they recalled the records that had already been shipped to stores. Prior to the recall, Virgin Momma had reached number 61 on the charts, but after the recall it fell from the charts within two weeks. The Flying Friars sued Fabulous Music, Inc., alleging breach of contract. On the issue of damages, the The Flying Friars offered a statistical study that analyzed the subsequent performance of

every song that had ever reached number 61 on the charts. The study showed that 76 percent of the songs that reached number 61 ultimately reached the top 40; 65 percent reached the top 30; 51 percent reached the top 20; 34 percent reached the top 10; 21 percent reached the top 5; and 10 percent reached number one. Should the analysis be admitted? What arguments can the opponent offer for its exclusion? If it is admitted, what evidence would the opponent want to offer in response?

C. REFLECTIONS ON THE CONCEPT AND SIGNIFICANCE OF RELEVANCY

As Thayer correctly remarked, relevancy—the logical relationship between evidence and the proposition it is offered to establish—appears to be a driving force of the law of evidence. It is the conventional view that accurate outcomes at trial are advanced and the goal of rational decision making achieved in large part through the requirement of relevancy. Here we wish to consider whether the law has made the correct choice in pursuing accuracy and rationality as the primary goals of litigation, and whether in fact those are the choices that have been made. These are the central issues discussed in the following excerpts.

NESSON, THE EVIDENCE OR THE EVENT? ON JUDICIAL PROOF AND THE ACCEPTABILITY OF VERDICTS
98 Harv. L. Rev. 1357, 1359-1368 (1985)

A primary goal of the legal system is to encourage and enable citizens to assimilate legal rules into their behavior. Through trials, society seeks not only to discover the truth about a past event, but also to forge a link between crime and punishment, between wrong and liability. Society attempts, through the judgments of its courts, to project a behavioral message that will influence individuals' conduct. . . .

A trial is ostensibly structured as a truth-seeking process concerned with justice for the parties. Yet it is also a drama that the public attends and from which it assimilates behavioral messages.[14] The court's message to the public at large is: "If you do what the defendant did, you will be doing wrong and you should feel guilty; if you commit such an action, we will judge you

---

14. Cf. Hay, Property, Authority and the Criminal Law, in Albion's Fatal Tree 17 (1975) (describing how the pomp and solemnity of criminal trials in eighteenth-century England induced deference to judicial pronouncements of guilt).

C. Reflections on the Concept and Significance of Relevancy 135

guilty and punish you." The threat of punishment strengthens the moral assertion. Thus, the judicial process inculcates and reinforces standards by which each person should judge himself; the statement about how persons will be judged and punished is a means to that end.

B. A Precondition to Effective General Deterrence: Understanding the Verdict as a Statement About the Event

The deterrent powers of a verdict that a defendant is guilty or liable depends on whether the public views the verdict as a statement about a past event or as a statement about the evidence presented at trial. If a person views the verdict as a determination of what actually happened, he can assimilate the applicable legal rule and absorb its behavioral message. If he regards the verdict as merely a statement about the evidence, he will assimilate only the proof rule, whose deterrent power is far less pronounced. Whether a person regards the verdict as a statement about the event or a statement about the evidence thus becomes a critical issue.

The difference between the two kinds of statements is most clearly explained by a concrete example. Suppose someone flashes a playing card, and we get a quick glimpse of the card. On the basis of this glimpse, we form a belief that the card is not a picture card. The subject matter of our belief is the card, and we make a statement about what happened: "The card that was flashed was not a picture card." We may temper this assertion with uncertainty: "I think that the card flashed was not a picture card." The statement equivocates by describing a state of mind, but the state of mind being described is a belief about the card.[15] If the card in fact turned out to be a king, we would admit that we had been wrong. But suppose we blindly draw a playing card from a well-shuffled deck. Before seeing the card, we would agree that the card is probably not a king. Our statement would express a belief about the evidence that the card is not a king, a belief based on our knowledge about the make-up of the deck, the fairness of the draw, and the laws of probability—not about the unseen card. If the card turned out to be a king, we would not say that we had erred in assessing the probabilities; the discovery is not inconsistent with what we initially believed to be true. We would simply say that on this occasion a relatively improbable event had occurred.[16]

---

15. The statement of belief might be further qualified: "When I identify a card based on a glimpse like this, I am usually right; therefore, I am probably right this time." This probabilistic formulation described the degree of conviction with which the speaker makes his assertion, but the statement is still about the event itself. See generally L. Savage, The Foundations of Statistics (1954) (articulating a theory of statistics based on a subjective view of probability); Tribe, [Trial By Mathematics: Precision and Ritual in the Legal Process] at 1347 (explaining the subjective probabilists' method of converting beliefs into numbers).

16. The subjectivist would reduce this statement to a numerical one, perhaps even to the same probabilistic statement given in note 15. Conversion of the speaker's belief into a statement of probability obscures whether the statement was about the evidence or the event.

The statement about the probability of drawing a king from a shuffled deck is a statement of belief about the evidence. By contrast, the statement based on the glimpse of the card is a statement of belief about the card itself. Similarly, a verdict that a defendant is guilty or liable can be understood either as a statement about the litigated event or as a statement about the evidence presented at trial. In the context of a trial, jurors only hear the statements of witnesses (those who saw the flashed cards) and thus never have firsthand knowledge of the event. Jurors can nonetheless believe that the event happened, making for themselves the inductive leap from the evidence about this event to a statement about what happened.[17] Alternatively, jurors can assess the statements of the witnesses and state, much like the person who drew the card blindly, "On the basis of this evidence, it is more probable than not that the event occurred"; the jurors intend the statement to be one simply about the evidence.

The projection of the verdict as a statement about what happened is the key to conveying the legal rule and its behavioral message. Projecting the verdict as such forges a link between the judicial account of the defendant's transgression and our own behavior. This link is essential to affirming beliefs of the form "If I do X, I will be doing wrong." When similar situations arise in the lives of those who have accepted the verdict as a determination about what happened, these citizens will govern their conduct in accordance with the behavioral rules that they have absorbed.

By contrast, a verdict that people understand as a statement about the evidence communicates a message that may undermine effective general deterrence. The lesson we derive from a verdict that we view as a probabilistic statement about the evidence is: "When current evidence makes violation of the rule appear probable to some specified degree, punishment will follow." This message is accurate, but it does not express the substantive standard that the law is intended to project. The probabilistic message speaks not to what each person knows to be true about his own conduct and his own reality, but to what he thinks society can prove and can thus establish as part of its reality. Probabilistic verdicts thereby incorporate into the substance of their message the practical problems of inductive proof and the epistemological divide between self and other. They transform the substantive message from one of morality ("feel guilty if you do wrong") to one of crude risk calculation ("estimate what you can do without getting caught"). The messages, if assimilated, would have widely divergent consequences. The person who conforms his conduct to the moral code that the rules of law embody is an upright and law-abiding citizen. But the person who routinely

---

All of these statements can be understood as describing the state of mind of the speaker. It is on this basis that a subjectivist would equate them all. Yet they are different statements in that they describe different states of mind—distinguishable by noting what would make the speaker in such a case feel he had been wrong.

17. The juror's statement need not be based on the belief that the event certainly occurred; doubts may remain. The point is that the belief is about what happened, not about the evidence.

C. Reflections on the Concept and Significance of Relevancy

acts on the basis of amoral risk calculations—that is, calculations unaffected by feelings of obligation and guilt—is probably a criminal. He has not been deterred.

These points are easily understood in the context of criminal trials, but they apply equally well to civil factfinding. In a tort action, for example, a jury might find the defendant negligent. Projecting the verdict as a statement about the event is essential to projecting the legal rule that one should not negligently injure others. If a person understands the verdict as a statement about the evidence rather than as a determination about the event, he will assimilate the rule that one should not negligently injure others in a manner that allows them to prove it. Calculation of the problem of proof undermines the behavioral norms embodied in both the civil and the criminal law. It is therefore vital to the civil and criminal systems that the public understand and accept the verdict as a statement about the event itself, rather than as a statement about the evidence.

C. Projecting the Verdict as a Statement About the Event

The public will be inclined to understand the verdict as a statement about what happened if the court is able to project the judgment in that light. A jury may view its verdict either as a statement about the event or as a statement about the evidence. But the court projects the jury's verdict as a statement about the event. In this way, the judicial system is able to inculcate the behavioral message associated with the applicable legal rule.

1. The Role of the Jury.—Ambiguity about the nature and meaning of a jury verdict is inherent in our process of judicial factfinding. Consider the jury finding, "A hit B." The verdict itself provides no indication of the factfinder's inferential process. The factfinder may be stating a belief about what actually occurred. Alternatively, the factfinder may be making a statement about the evidence and expressing his belief about the probability of the truth of the proposition that A hit B.[21] Although the system projects the verdict as a statement about the event, it tolerates some measure of ambiguity as to whether the jury should come to a conclusion about the evidence or the event. Typical jury instructions do not rigorously describe the state of mind a juror must have in order to find a defendant liable or guilty. Civil jury instructions, which ask the jury to determine the likelihood that the defendant violated the law, apparently call upon jurors to make a statement

---

21. The factfinder could not mean that in repeated recreations of the circumstances surrounding the event A would hit B more than half of the time. Neither could the public so construe this statement. The event occurred in a unique context of time and place, shaped by a complex set of physical and psychological factors; there is no simple game-like set-up for which we could imagine repeated trials of the event's occurrence or nonoccurrence. But just as a skilled horseplayer can make a judgment about the odds on a race that will be run only once, so too can a factfinder make a judgment about the probability that a unique event occurred. The factfinder can imagine a setting consisting of all of the known details about the event and assess the betting odds that A hit B.

about the evidence.[22] Criminal jury instructions, on the other hand, require jurors to be convinced beyond a reasonable doubt and thus apparently call upon jurors to convict only on the basis of a belief about what actually happened.[23] But jury instructions are most clearly concerned with the degree of doubt that may attend a verdict, not primarily with an esoteric distinction about whether jurors must actually make an inductive leap to a conclusion about the event.

Both civil and criminal instructions speak to how jurors should feel after the verdict. The criminal instruction says, in effect, "Recognize that you are dealing with a person's life and liberty, and decide he is guilty only if you are confident that you will not be nagged by doubts about the propriety of your decision. Make a decision you can live with." Such emphasis on future repose is what is meant by an "abiding conviction." The civil instruction says, "Give us your best judgment, and then do not worry about it further." Both civil and criminal instructions thus perform their guiding function by conveying appropriate attitudes to jurors and yet remain ambiguous as to whether a verdict is a statement about the evidence or a statement about the event.

The secrecy of jury deliberations also serves to cloud the nature of jury verdicts. Our legal system makes it difficult for parties or the general public to learn about jurors' thought processes. Verdicts are generally inarticulate—guilty or not guilty, liable or not liable—and thus give no indication of a juror's state of mind. Jury deliberations take place in secret, and the rules of evidence severely limit a party's ability to impeach a verdict by attacking jurors' thought processes. As a result, the general public will rarely learn

---

22. A typical jury instruction in a civil action is:

[I]t is proper to find that a party has succeeded in carrying the burden of proof on an issue of fact if, after consideration of all the evidence in the case, the jurors believe that what is sought to be proved on that issue is more likely true than not true.

E. Devitt and C. Blackmar, Federal Jury Practice and Instructions §71.13 (3d ed. 1977). A second such instruction is:

To "establish by a preponderance of the evidence" means to prove that something is more likely so than not so. In other words, a preponderance of the evidence in the case means such evidence as, when considered and compared with that opposed to it, has more convincing force, and produces in your minds belief that what is sought to be proved is more likely true than not true.

Id. §71.14; see also Burch v. Reading Co., 240 F.2d 574, 578-580 (3d Cir.) (holding that a reasonable definition of the preponderance-of-the evidence rule is that facts are more probably true than not), cert. denied, 353 U.S. 965 (1957).

23. A typical jury instruction in a criminal action is:

Proof beyond a reasonable doubt must . . . be proof of such a convincing character that a reasonable person would not hesitate to rely and act upon it in the most important of his own affairs.

. . . If the jury views the evidence in the case as reasonably permitting either of two conclusions—one of innocence, the other of guilt—the jury should of course adopt the conclusion of innocence.

1 E. Devitt and C. Blackmar, supra note 22, §11.14.

C. Reflections on the Concept and Significance of Relevancy

whether the jury regarded its judgment as a statement about the evidence or a statement about the event.

2. The Role of the Judge.—Courts use the ambiguity of the jury verdict to project the verdict as a statement about what happened. Regardless of the thought processes by which jurors arrive at their verdicts, judges in both criminal and civil cases treat jury verdicts as statements about the litigated events. This institutional acceptance of the verdict justifies the imposition of a sanction on the defendant and furthers the inculcation of the applicable legal rule.

The court's post-verdict treatment of the defendant demonstrates its acceptance of the verdict as a statement about the event. A judge does not—at least in theory—mitigate criminal punishment because he doubts the defendant's guilt. The court accepts the jury's verdict as resolving such doubts. Indeed, the imposition of the moral stigma of guilt assumes that the defendant committed the crime, and not merely that the probability is high that he did so. In civil cases as well, the judge orders the jury to impose damages based on its previous finding of liability. The jury does not—again, at least in theory—assess damages that reflect its doubts about what happened. The jury awards damages as if the question of what happened were definitively settled.

Regardless of how a jury reaches its verdict, then, the court will project the judgment as a statement about the litigated event. Public acceptance of this projection, however, depends both on the extent to which members of the public may be predisposed to accept the verdict in a variety of fact-specific situations and on the evidentiary rules and procedures that govern the fact-finding process.

D. PUBLIC ACCEPTANCE OF THE VERDICT

When courts punish a defendant, we want to believe that he is in fact guilty of committing the crime for which he stands convicted. We want to believe that all of the elements of the crime actually occurred. "Why is A in prison for life? Because A stabbed B with an intent to kill B, and he succeeded." We need a belief that the punishment is factually justified, a belief that will permit the courts, with our approval, to impose sanctions without second thoughts. If we do not have such a belief—if we regard the verdict as merely a bet on the probability that A stabbed B—then we cannot feel secure about the imposition of punishment. Our psychological need thus predisposes us to accept the verdict of guilt or liability as a statement about the past event. This acceptance promotes our assimilation of the behavioral message embodied in the underlying substantive rule.

It might appear that a verdict of not guilty or not liable would undercut the behavioral message that is projected when triers of fact find a defendant guilty or liable. A verdict of not guilty or not liable projects a proof rule: "There is insufficient evidence to warrant a conclusion that the defendant committed a wrong." The verdict concerns the evidence rather than the event: It makes no statement about what actually happened. But a verdict of not guilty or not liable will only undermine the legal system's projection of behavioral norms if the public has an independent basis for believing that the defendant did in fact commit the wrongful act. Only in this situation will the public absorb the demoralizing message that it is the proof, rather than the underlying fact, that counts. When there is no basis independent of the trial for believing in the defendant's guilt, a verdict of not guilty poses no danger of subverting the behavioral message that a guilty verdict projects. The general public will continue to accept verdicts that the defendant is guilty or liable as statements about what happened and to assimilate the behavioral norms embodied in the substantive law.

Not everyone, however, accepts verdicts as statements about what happened. A student of judicial process may have a more complex and sophisticated understanding of the meaning of a verdict. Such a person might say, "I do not know whether A killed B, but I do know that there was substantial evidence that A killed B, that A was tried according to procedures I respect, and that A was found guilty by a fairly selected jury. Therefore, I consider his punishment justified." This person makes no judgment about the underlying factual event and forms no actual belief about what happened. But he still accepts the verdict in a way that permits him to put aside what he knows about the details of the evidence. It is true that he accepts the verdict only for the limited purpose of justifying the imposition of the judicial sanction and that his sophistication may largely insulate him from the verdict's behavioral message. Yet he too may feel the ideological impact of the message. Like a theater-goer who knows he is viewing a play and yet still feels its dramatic impact, the sophisticate may be more aware than the average person of the verdict's surrogate quality and yet still be moved by the power of its behavioral norm.

The parties to the litigation are the persons least likely to be predisposed to accept the verdict and to internalize its behavioral message. If they know what actually happened and if the trial result is contrary to their view of the truth, then the verdict will not exemplify for the them the underlying legal rule. Even if the verdict is consistent with what the party knows to be true, it may still fail to inculcate the intended behavioral message. For example, a criminal defendant, even if aware of his guilt, may regard his conviction as a great injustice because of a perceived violation of his procedural rights. For him the message is not, "I am being punished because what I did was wrong," but rather, "I am being punished because courts did not honor my rights." This defendant has not assimilated the behavioral message and is unlikely to do so.

Notwithstanding the various inevitable impediments to the projection of the law's behavioral message through the judicial process, the objective of the trial itself remains clear enough. The trial projects a message that each of us should obey the law. To further this goal, the trial process is

C. Reflections on the Concept and Significance of Relevancy

structured in a variety of ways that encourage the public to accept judicial conclusions as determinations about the litigated events.

II. PROMOTING PUBLIC ACCEPTANCE OF VERDICTS; JUDICIAL MECHANISMS FOR CREATING DEFERENCE

Many of the procedures of our legal system are best understood as ways to promote public acceptance of verdicts. These procedures facilitate both the initial and the continued acceptance of the verdict as a statement about what actually happened. Judges and commentators alike tend to underestimate the role that acceptance of verdicts may play in accounting for certain procedures, preferring instead to rationalize evidentiary and procedural rules as means to advance the search for truth. Many rules are indeed explicable in terms of a truth-seeking rationale. But, on close inspection, some procedures that are rationalized as truth-seeking devices are better understood as means to promote public acceptance of verdicts. . . .

[One example is the] rule governing the defendant's motion for a directed verdict,[36] [which] prevents the legal system from generating unacceptable verdicts. The directed verdict permits the court to withhold from the jury those cases in which a finding of guilt or liability would be patently untenable in light of the case presented by the plaintiff. The trial judge allows a case to go to the jury only if the evidence suffices to support a verdict either way. Giving a case to the jury is tantamount to making a judgment that the jury cannot make an obvious error; such cases fall within a realm of ambiguity that allows the public to defer to any decision the jury reaches.

The extent of public deference to a jury's verdict depends on the kind of evidence presented in the case. The public will usually defer to jury verdicts in cases that depend on the credibility of witnesses. Credibility assessments are subjective and indeterminate; the jurors, by their proximity and attentiveness to the witnesses and evidence, stand in the best position to make these assessments. Most people recognize this circumstance and defer to whatever decision the jurors reach. Thus the structure of the trial process is well suited to induce public acceptance of the verdict in cases that turn on the credibility of witnesses. By contrast, the public has less reason to respect and defer to the jury's judgment in cases involving circumstantial evidence. This evidence is available for anyone to assess, and any interested observer stands in as good a position as the juror to make an evaluation. As a result, acceptance of the verdict in cases involving circumstantial evidence is far less likely to occur.

Indeed, courts often have refused to allow cases based on circumstantial evidence to go to the jury. For example, a defendant charged with house-

---

36. The directed verdict prevents judgment on an issue when the evidence on it is "plainly insufficient to persuade reasonable triers of fact." R. Field, B. Kaplan, and K. Clermont, Materials for a Basic Course in Civil Procedure 108 (5th ed. 1984).

breaking and theft cannot be convicted merely on the basis of proof that his fingerprint was found on an object in the house. The prosecution must also prove that the object was otherwise inaccessible to the defendant. Proof of the fingerprint alone does not dispel reasonable hypotheses consistent with his innocence. Yet a defendant charged with stealing can be convicted on the basis of a witness's identification of him, notwithstanding the existence of a reasonable hypothesis consistent with innocence—namely, that the witness was mistaken. The likelihood of mistaken identity—no matter how convinced the witness may be—may well be greater than the likelihood of the truth of an explanation for the fingerprint that is consistent with the defendant's innocence. And as the circumstantial evidence against a defendant mounts, the circumstantial evidence case increasingly resembles the identification case: A jury could reasonably decide it either way. Yet the identification case will generally reach the jury,[42] whereas the circumstantial evidence case may not.[43] Even though the probability that the defendant is guilty may be higher in the circumstantial evidence case, the basis for deference to the jury verdict is lower, and that factor appears to control the decision whether to permit the case to go to the jury.

We accept the disparate treatment of the inadequate circumstantial evidence case and the identification case because it seems to reflect the difference between speculation and reasonable inference. In the circumstantial evidence case, even if the jury believed all of the evidence, it still could not generate a verdict that the public could understand as other than a bet. The jury would not, we say, have enough information to convict without speculating. By contrast, the identification case permits a conviction because, we say, the jurors can reasonably infer that the identifying witness is telling the truth. But clearly the process of deciding whether to believe a witness could also be understood as a kind of speculation. The difference between unacceptable speculation and reasonable inference is thus not a logical distinction but a functional one: Speculation describes a category of doubts about guilt and liability that the system of judicial proof is incapable of resolving, and reasonable inference describes a category of doubts the system can accommodate. This dichotomy can be understood as a function of the capacities and limitations of the system's mechanisms for creating deference to jurors' decisions and thus for generating acceptable verdicts.

---

42. See Goldstein, The State and the Accused: Balance of Advantage in Criminal Procedure, 69 Yale L.J. 1149, 1156 (1960) ("When . . . X testifies that he saw the accused aim at and shoot Y, and there is no question of defense or justification, the trial judge has no alternative but to submit the case to the jury, unless X or his testimony are inherently incredible.").

43. See, e.g., Borum v. United States, 380 F.2d 595, 597 (D.C. Cir. 1967).

C. Reflections on the Concept and Significance of Relevancy

ALLEN, RATIONALITY, MYTHOLOGY, AND THE "ACCEPTABILITY OF VERDICTS" THESIS
66 B.U.L. Rev. 541, 542-554 (1986)

Much of Professor Nesson's argument is both conventional and uncontroversial. Certainly among the objectives of the legal system are such matters as formulating and enforcing behavioral norms. In addition, the inculcation of those norms occurs in myriad ways, some of which are undoubtedly affected in one manner or another by the process of litigation. What is interesting about Professor Nesson's argument is that he adds to the generally accepted wisdom about these matters the assertion that the process of inculcation is affected by trial verdicts—I assume he means in a significant and direct way for otherwise the argument would be trivial—and in addition that crucial to inculcation is that verdicts be viewed as a statement about what actually happened rather than about what the evidence demonstrates probably happened.

A critical ambiguity is immediately obvious in Professor Nesson's argument. Precisely what is to be projected by or about verdicts is not specified with sufficient clarity. Moreover, when the possibilities are specified and analyzed, the argument is demonstrated to be implausible. . . .

There [are] two possibilities that are candidates for being projected. Professor Nesson may be suggesting that the explicit commands of the substantive law are projected or that the jury's conclusion as to what actually happened is being projected. . . . It does not matter, however, whether Professor Nesson is referring to only one or both of these possibilities, because neither withstands analysis.

Although a significant purpose of the legal system surely is to encourage "citizens to heed the legal rules and to conduct themselves accordingly," there is no evidence to support the proposition that any perceptible amount of communication concerning the substance of those rules or what a jury thinks violates them is a function of the direct effect of litigation on the populace as a whole. The primary message of the results of litigation, both civil and criminal, seems—at least to me—to be that if a person is proven to have violated a legal norm, appropriate verdicts will follow. The content of those norms, however, comes from the constitutional and statutory law of the jurisdiction, and the work-product of the common law system of adjudication, and they along with more general notions of right and wrong are absorbed through complex sociological processes that have their referent in lessons learned in everyday life rather than from the observation of jury verdicts. To be sure, these messages may not be heard very loudly or very clearly, but for a number of reasons neither the intensity nor the clarity is much affected by the results of litigation.

Trials may be "dramas," as he asserts, but they are not sell-outs; they are sparsely attended. A run-of-the-mill trial is just that—run-of-the-mill—

and as a result largely unattended by anyone but the parties and their lawyers. I have sat at length in courtrooms in numerous jurisdictions. My experience has been that in the great majority of the cases, I was the only one in the room other than the actors in Professor Nesson's drama. In addition, I have searched for some evidence—anecdotal or otherwise—that my experience is abnormal. I have found none, and Professor Nesson provides none. This is striking because Nesson is making an empirical rather than an analytical claim, and no basis for it appears to exist.

What he does rely on for support for this crucial aspect of his argument highlights the dubious nature of his central claim. To establish the fact that trial verdicts in modern society have a direct and significant impact on the citizenry, he cites speculation concerning how, in his own words, "the pomp and solemnity of criminal trials in eighteenth-century England induced deference to judicial pronouncements of guilt."[19] A much more accurate picture of the criminal process in twentieth-century United States comes from works such as Professor Mileski's[20] and the Task Force Report on the Courts,[21] which provide no support at all for Professor Nesson's thesis, and I know of no support for the proposition that the public pays any more attention to the process of civil litigation than it does to criminal litigation. Consequently, the acceptability thesis is insupportable regardless whether it refers to the projection of the substantive legal rules or the facts that have been found to violate those rules, since neither is projected by any process with any regularity at all.

Perhaps, though, this is to take his argument too literally. The public does attend some trials—usually ones involving highly controversial issues or events—and the media covers such cases extensively. These are highly unusual cases, however. In contrast to the typical highly publicized case which is meticulously prepared and litigated, a typical criminal court case is disposed of in about a minute and a half, give or take a few seconds. Each of those cases, under Professor Nesson's view, is projecting a behavioral norm, too, but the public is not there to receive it, nor is the public informed of those norms by the media. The great bulk of the projection thus goes unattended. Accordingly, unless Professor Nesson feels that the unusual, controversial, and highly publicized cases carry the weight of his argument, the argument is insupportable.

To be sure, the cumulative effect of verdicts over time may have an

---

19. Nesson at 1360, citing Hay, Property, Authority and the Criminal Law, in Albion's Fatal Tree 17 (1975). Nesson's reliance on Professor Hay's works demonstrates another troublesome aspect of Nesson's work, one to which I return later in this essay. That aspect is its elitist nature. Professor Hay's description, which Nesson cites approvingly, was part of a general condemnation of the manner in which the elite classes in England suppressed and exploited the lower classes. See Linebaugh, (Marxist) Social History and (Conservative) Legal History: A Reply to Professor Langbein, 60 N.Y.U.L. Rev. 212 (1985).

20. Mileski, Courtroom Encounters: An Observation Study of Lower Criminal Court, 5 Law & Soc. Rev. 473 (1971).

21. President's Commission of Law Enforcement and the Administration of Justice, Task Force Report: The Courts (1967).

C. Reflections on the Concept and Significance of Relevancy 145

impact on public perceptions of the requirements of the law, but this does not support the acceptability thesis. Professor Nesson's argument is that there is a relationship between projecting verdicts in cases as statements about the actual events and the success with which the public will assimilate the underlying rule. Although he is unclear about the precise mechanisms he asserts are at work, his argument seems to assume a relatively direct relationship between cases and assimilation. If that is so, an effect that results from long-term, incremental accretion where the passage of time dims any memory of what the precise facts or setting of any particular case may have been cannot be reconciled with his thesis. Thus, it receives no support even from a more plausible assumption about the relationship between verdicts and public perceptions than he seems to embrace.

One can speculate about other ways in which this projection may occur, thus suggesting ways of filling in the empirical gap in Professor Nesson's argument, but none seems to work. The most plausible account yet to be mentioned might be that the parties themselves would act as the projecting agents, and spread the word about the acceptability of jury verdicts as statements about what actually happened. Ironically, Professor Nesson recognizes that the parties are not likely to do so because they are fully aware that a jury's verdict is a statement about the evidence. Moreover, the lawyers and judges are probably aware of this, too, and thus they are not likely to propagate the view Professor Nesson advances, either. As a result, the ones most intimately related to litigation, and virtually the only ones who pay serious attention to it, will surely not concur in the acceptability thesis, leaving it again without its necessary projection mechanism.

There are other factors that Professor Nesson's analysis omits that create even further skepticism about the acceptability thesis. He does not examine, for example, the implications of the fact that most disputes, both civil and criminal, are settled out of court. The ones that go to trial tend to possess a seriously contested matter of law or fact. If that is so, the norms that emerge from such trials are suspect. The facts are not clear or there is a dispute over the law that may only be resolved after extensive appellate review. In light of such ambiguities, it is difficult to see these cases as being successful projectors of society's norms.

Moreover, since Professor Nesson did not address this point, there is no intimation as to why in his view the public would not at best only absorb highly qualified messages from such trials. The only answer to that query indicates the strained nature of the argument. The assertion would have to be made that the public is sufficiently intelligent and aware to garner the overt message of the trial phase of litigation even though it is premised on hotly contested questions of law or fact, but insufficiently intelligent or aware to qualify those messages by a recognition that hotly contested factfinding proceedings often result in erroneous conclusions precisely because it is difficult to say what actually happened. Similarly, "the public" would have to be insufficiently intelligent or aware to qualify the "behavioral norm" that emerges from litigation over a problematic legal rule by reference to the fact that the norm will not emerge until the appellate process is completed. Perhaps Nesson is right in his implicit suggestion that "the public" does possess such highly defined powers of observation and analysis, but I doubt it and know of no evidence to support it.

In short, a crucial component of Nesson's argument stands virtually unsupported. There is no reason to believe that "the public" assimilates messages from trial verdicts in a fashion at all consistent with what the acceptability thesis entails. In addition, there is another component to the thesis that is problematic. The thesis is not just that verdicts project something, but rather they must be construed as projecting a "determination of what actually happened" and not just a "statement about the evidence." In my judgment, this is even more unsupportable than the projection component.

First, Nesson again is somewhat unclear—this time about how these two phenomena differ. At points he implies that a statement about what happened requires that doubts be suppressed about the possibility of error. That is what the word "actually" implies in the passage quoted above. We are told that judges do not mitigate criminal punishment because of doubts about the defendant's guilt and juries do not return verdicts that reflect doubts about what happened.[28] Jurors are told that once they "have decided that an element is probable, they are to consider it established, repress any remaining doubts about it, and proceed to consider the next element." This position is comprehensible, but Nesson rejects it explicitly. He says that "The juror's statement need not be based on a belief that the event certainly occurred; doubts may remain. The point is that the belief is about what happened, not about the evidence." Moreover, "acceptable verdicts" do not require "that the public believes that the factfinder's account is certainly true." Presumably an acceptable verdict can be one that is understood as saying that the defendant (or the plaintiff) "probably" did what he was alleged to have done, so long as the "probably" refers to the event rather than the evidence.

At this point Nesson's argument is quite difficult to follow. It is not acceptable for a verdict to be a statement about the evidence, but it is acceptable to have a statement about what "probably" happened. But, what would a statement about the "evidence" look like? It would be in the form of "Based on all the evidence, what probably happened is X." What, by contrast, would a qualified statement about what happened look like? It would be in the form "After hearing all the evidence, it seems to us that X probably

---

28. Nesson at 1366. [However,] compromise verdicts are a well-known phenomenon in civil trials, and courts often refer to the evidence in determining sentence. See, e.g., Texas v. McCullough, 38 C.L. Rptr. 3137, 3138 (trial judge increased sentence in part because of new evidence that "had a direct effect upon the strength of the State's case at both the guilt and punishment phase of the trial"); Lockhart v. McCree, 106 S. Ct. 1758, at 1769 (defendants may benefit at capital sentencing hearing from "residual doubts" about the evidence).

C. Reflections on the Concept and Significance of Relevancy 147

happened." These statements are not different in any significant way. Indeed, to me they are not different at all. Even if I am wrong in that, however, the difference is obviously minuscule, yet Nesson's argument rests upon the assertion that substantially different effects on "the public" will flow from projecting verdicts as one or the other. He has, in short, invested this non-discernible difference with a mystical effect that there is no reason to believe will, or does, occur.

He asserts there is a difference, however, and [he argues that the difference comes clear in the comparison of the identification of a playing card based on a "quick glimpse" to expressing a belief that a card picked at random is a king]. . . . Even if Nesson is correct that these two examples describe different phenomena, it is hard to imagine that anything of significance rests upon the difference. In both cases factual inferences are being drawn under conditions of uncertainty that entail risks of error. Anyone who is qualified to sit on a jury certainly can perceive that point, as will anyone who may be affected by what those jurors do. More importantly, however, Nesson is wrong that these examples reflect fundamentally different phenomena. His mistake is hidden in the statement that "On the basis of this glimpse, we form a belief that the card is not a picture card." What he fails to ask is how that belief is formed, and it is not formed in any way significantly different from the "belief" that any card picked at random from a deck is a king.

In both cases, the available evidence—what is perceived by the "decisionmaker" at the relevant time—is examined and compared to that person's knowledge and experience. When a person gets a "glimpse" of a card, he or she sees certain attributes of the card. Those attributes are either more consistent with the card being a face card, based upon that person's understanding of what a face card normally looks like, or less consistent, or not determinative. No matter which turns out to be the case however, the conclusion reached will be a function of analyzing what the person perceives in the context of that person's knowledge and experience.

The knowledge and experience used to analyze whether what the person sees indicates that the card is a face card is highly analogous to and in no significant way different from the knowledge and experience brought to bear upon the available evidence in the second of Nesson's hypotheticals. In the second hypothetical, the decisionmaker sees a deck of cards that appears to be a normal playing deck. That observation is filtered through the person's knowledge and experience and an assessment is given, in light of that knowledge and experience, as to the likelihood of drawing a king. Thus, the only difference between the cases is the nature of the evidence available rather than some qualitative difference in the nature of the relevant reasoning process or the kind of conclusion that is drawn.[29]

29. In the second of Nesson's hypotheticals, notions of stochastic probability play a more direct role. Nonetheless, that simply amounts to the fact that the evidence differs in the two cases. In the first, the relevant data are hard to characterize by reference to notions of randomness whereas in the second those notions are more clearly relevant. Nonetheless, a person

These points become clearer if one modifies Nesson's hypotheticals and analyzes them under differing assumptions. Start with the "glimpse" hypo. Nesson is asking us to think of a case where the front side of a card is seen and it appears to bear a face on it. How will a person know that, however? A person will compare the marks on the card to what that person has learned from past experience is a face card, and draw inferences accordingly. If what the person sees is not "clearly" a face, which simply means that the person did not receive unambiguous sensory input, then the person will begin to analogize. Did the observed characteristics look more like a face card or a number card? Were there marks scattered in a way that is not likely to be found on a face card? While this process is occurring, the person is undoubtedly aware that he or she may have either misperceived some of the data—even one who has gotten a "good look" at a card may do that—and in addition is aware of the possibility that the wrong inference may be drawn from what was observed, *if one is forced to draw an inference.*

This is precisely what occurs in the second of Nesson's hypotheticals. The person takes into account what is known about decks of cards and elementary probability theory and, if forced to draw an inference, does so on that basis. That inference may turn out to be in error, and indeed may be in error more often than when one identifies face cards after looking at them. In both cases, however, the process is one of comparing the observable data with one's experience and knowledge and drawing an inference. The only thing that varies is the reliability or nature of the evidence. In fact, the inference drawn in the second of Nesson's hypotheticals could be made much more reliable than the inference drawn in the first. What if the "glimpse" that was obtained in the first hypothetical was a "glimpse" of the back of the card,[34] and what if the deck of cards in the second was one in which all cards lower than a nine had been removed and the question asked was whether the "glimpsed" card in the first case and the drawn card in the second was a face card or not? Undoubtedly, we would have more faith in the answer to the second question.

These modifications of the hypotheticals show that the reliability and nature of the data upon which a decision or judgment or inference rests certainly is a variable. But, that potential variance does not convert one kind of observation into a wholly different kind. Rather, the same kind of mental

---

rationally appraising the two situations will act in highly analogous ways by taking the relevant variables into account in the person's analysis. It just so happens that in one case part of the evidence includes ideas of randomness and in the other it does not, or at least not as much or as explicitly so.

34. The point in the text demonstrates what a fine line Nesson is attempting to draw, as well as why in the end it is unconvincing. He is forced to take the position that there is a fundamental difference between the "events" of getting a glimpse of the front of a card as compared to a glimpse of the back of a card. Turning the card over, in other words, makes a qualitative difference in Nesson's cosmology. In mine it only makes a quantitative one. See also I. Hacking, The Emergence of Probability, 180-185 (1975).

C. Reflections on the Concept and Significance of Relevancy

processes are involved in each. Individuals decide based upon their appraisals of the significance of the available evidence.[35]

In brief, then, both Nesson's conception of the projection of jury verdicts as well as his distinction between statements about evidence and statements about events are highly problematic, and accordingly do not provide much support for the acceptability thesis. Nonetheless, Professor Nesson attempts to draw indirect support for the acceptability thesis by efforts to demonstrate that certain trial procedures are consistent with it. Again, most of these points do not survive on more careful inquiry. Take, for example, his effort to explain the fact that jury deliberations are secret. According to Nesson, "as a result" of jury secrecy, "the general public will rarely learn whether the jury regarded its judgment as a statement about the evidence or a statement about the event." Moreover, he asserts, "Courts use the ambiguity of the jury verdict to project the verdict as a statement about what happened."

This is a bold effort, but it is rather implausible. First, Nesson has only scratched the surface of the incompatibility of normal jury trials with his theory. Jury deliberations are secret, but in addition trials can be messy. There is often directly as well as subtly inconsistent data. Questions of the credibility of witnesses are raised. Memories are impeached. Parties rely on alternative theories and press upon the jury various inferential paths. Without information as to how the jury resolved such matters, how can a verdict project a statement about what actually happened? For rather obvious reasons, the answer cannot be that one looks to the pleadings, for then the acceptability thesis would need to make claims about the dissemination of information concerning the pleadings. In any event, if one looked to the pleadings, one would find both inconsistent pleading as well as alternative pleading.[38] Thus, another problem is uncovered. How can a verdict be viewed as making a statement about what actually happened and projecting a behavioral norm where there are general verdicts in response to inconsistent and alternative pleadings and theories?[39] These questions are not answered.

Nesson follows his analysis of the trial process with certain assertions about how courts project verdicts as statements about what happened by resting judgments on those verdicts. This argument simply begs the question. What it overlooks is that regardless whether he is right or wrong courts will

---

35. Furthermore, even if the conclusion is reached that a person seeing a "glimpse" of a card (presumably the front of the card) is engaged in a fundamentally different epistemological process than one who sees a deck of cards, that conclusion is of little relevance for a system of litigation. At trial, both individuals will be presenting their testimony as to what they observed to fact finders who will not have experienced either event. From the perspective of the fact finder, the observer and his or her testimony is obviously "evidence" of the relevant "event." The strictures of disinterested fact finding would convert, in short, statements about events into statements about evidence.

38. See Fed. R. Crim. P. 9(e)(2).

39. For example, in State v. Williams, 285 N.W.2d 48 (Iowa 1979), the Iowa Supreme Court held that a jury could convict of murder in the first degree upon alternative instructions that either premeditation and deliberation must be found or that a killing was done in the perpetration of a rape and that the jury need not agree on which theory was correct.

rest judgments on those verdicts because that is what the rest of us have instructed them to do as one of their responsibilities in the legal system. The fact that they do what they have been instructed to do provides no support for his thesis whatsoever.

More importantly, the argument overlooks the fact that judges do not take doubt into account because it has already been taken into account in the proof rules. A judge's acceptance of a verdict is not a statement that it is correct or that it is a statement about the litigated event. It is instead a statement that it is rational in light of the evidence and the relevant burden of proof applicable to the cause of action. Indeed, one would expect Nesson to find, and cite, some judges that express concurrence with his views, but he fails to do so. On the other hand, judges talk all the time about "sufficiency of the evidence"[41] and even the Supreme Court of the United States has stated that the purpose of proof rules is to allocate errors.[42] Such judicial activity flatly contradicts the acceptability thesis.

There is one final difficulty with the acceptability thesis. . . . Nesson appears to admit that he is arguing for the projection of a myth. In his own words "Not everyone . . . accepts verdicts as statements about what happened. A student of judicial process may have a more complex and sophisticated understanding of the meaning of a verdict." Thus, the myth of verdicts as statements about what actually happened is being promulgated for the benefit of someone else. That someone else is "the public." Apparently the public is in need of our propagating this myth in order to inculcate the norms we wish to impose upon it. Moreover, the public is apparently sufficiently thoughtless that it will believe that verdicts are statements about the event because we so instruct it, and act on that belief, even though we the instructors know that to be false.

Once again I do not know what the support for this view is, nor do I know who is so gullible as to fall under the sway of this particular mythology. Furthermore, my instincts are precisely the opposite of Nesson's. I certainly suspect that the nonlegally trained individual may not possess great knowledge of the legal process, but that is a problem to be rectified rather than an invitation for manipulation. We should disseminate information about the vagaries of litigation so that people can plan their lives and business with a realistic appraisal of the costs and pitfalls of the process. We should not try to convert in the public's view that messy process into something which it is not by suppressing rather than highlighting the risk of error. We should do this not only out of simple concerns of fairness and honesty but also

---

41. See, e.g., Rogers v. Missouri Pacific R.R., 352 U.S. 500, 503 (1957)("We think that the evidence was sufficient to support the jury finding for petitioner").

42. See In re Winship, 397 U.S. 358 (1970); Addington v. Texas, 441 U.S. 418 (1979). This is significant for the acceptability thesis because if the pronouncements of any court in this country project "behavioral messages" I suspect it is the pronouncements of the Supreme Court, and the Supreme Court's messages cannot be reconciled with Nesson's argument. Thus, if he is right that, on a more general plane, courts project messages, one of the messages that is being projected is that verdicts rest on evidence.

C. Reflections on the Concept and Significance of Relevancy

because "the public" is not so gullible that we will be able to pull the wool over its collective eyes.[48] Efforts to do so are likely to result in the loss of faith in the dispute resolution process as well as in our profession.

Is Nesson too caught up in the symbolic functions of trials? Is Allen too single- or narrow-minded? What are, and ought to be, the purposes furthered by trials? How are they different from, or similar to, other aspects of "public life"? In that regard, consider the following passage from the novel by Willa Cather, *The Professor's House:*

> [T]he door was ajar, and at the moment one of the students was speaking. When he finished, they heard the Professor reply to him.
>
> "No, Miller, I don't myself think much of science as a phase of human development. It has given us a lot of ingenious toys; they take our attention away from the real problems, of course, and since the

---

48. Nesson also argues that the attorney-client privilege furthers the acceptability thesis on the grounds that the privilege allows counsel to "design and present the most plausible defenses, even though they may be false" while at the same time the lawyers "can . . . assert publicly that they do not construct false defenses." Nesson, Acceptability, at 1376-1377. In one sense, this passage captures my discontent with the acceptability thesis. Nesson must be arguing that "the public" will accept that false defenses are not created merely because lawyers can "publicly assert" that false defenses are not created, even though he and I, and anyone who reads any of the extensive literature on the topic or, for that matter, reads or watches the daily news, knows that to be false. All I can say is that Nesson has a remarkable faith in the power of the spoken word on "the public." I tend to have greater faith in the rationality of the public. Nesson certainly receives no support from the Supreme Court on these matters, either. For example, in Nix v. Whiteside, 475 U.S. 157 at—(1986), the Court said that "there is no right whatever—constitutional or otherwise—for a defendant to use false evidence." Similarly, in In re Michael, 326 U.S. 224 at 227 (1945), the Court said: "All perjured relevant testimony is at war with justice, since it may produce a judgment not resting on truth. Therefore, it cannot be denied that it tends to defeat the sole ultimate objective of a trial."

It bears noting that Nesson is in good company, however. Prof. Laurence Tribe in his article, Trial By Mathematics: Precision and Ritual in the Legal Process, 84 Harv. L. Rev. 1329 (1971), argued that quantification of the risk of error in criminal cases should be avoided because such quantification would "undermine the effort, through the symbols of trial procedures, to express society's fundamental commitment to the protection of defendants' rights as a person, as an end in himself." Id. at 1374. Now how, I have always wondered, does Prof. Tribe (and Prof. Nesson following in his footsteps) know that? No support for an empirical assertion is provided. Again, as with Nesson's, it is an argument that upon being unpacked is rife with dubious propositions. It assumes, for example, that those who serve as jurors do not already recognize that there is a risk of error in what they do. In addition, it asserts that if they are so informed, the result will be to undermine symbols of some sort with presumably regrettable consequences. But, what are those consequences? What is the evidence that they will result? For that matter if jurors do recognize the risk of error in what they do, what are those symbols that will fall? Indeed, and most telling of all, why is it that Professor Tribe and Nesson and others contemplating the risk of error—and writing extensively about it—do not bring the symbolic structures crashing to the ground, but communicating that possibility to jurors will? My suspicion is that the answer is that "the public" is not as ill-informed or unintelligent as these arguments assume, and further that social processes are more durable than to be radically effected by the articulation of the obvious fact that mistakes may be made whenever a third party makes decisions based upon that person's analysis of evidence presented to him. See also IA Wigmore on Evidence (Tillers rev. 1983) at 1061-1062 n.22.

problems are insoluble, I suppose we ought to be grateful for the distraction. But the fact is, the human mind, the individual mind, has always been made more interesting by dwelling on the old riddles, even if it makes nothing of them. Science hasn't given us any new amazements, except of the superficial kind we get from witnessing dexterity and sleight-of-hand. It hasn't given us any richer pleasures, as the Renaissance did, nor any new sins—not one! Indeed, it takes our old ones away. It's the laboratory, not the Lamb of God, that taketh away the sins of the world. You'll agree there is not much thrill about a physiological sin. We were better off when even the prosaic matter of taking nourishment could have the magnificence of a sin. I don't think you help people by making their conduct of no importance—you impoverish them. As long as every man and woman who crowded into the cathedrals on Easter Sunday was a principal in a gorgeous drama with God, glittering angels on one side and the shadows of evil coming and going on the other, life was a rich thing. The king and the beggar had the same chance at miracles and great temptations and revelations. And that's what makes men happy, believing in the mystery and importance of their own little individual lives. It makes us happy to surround our creature needs and bodily instincts with as much pomp and circumstance as possible. Art and religion (they are the same thing, in the end, of course) have given man the only happiness he has ever had.

"Moses learned the importance of that in the Egyptian court, and when he wanted to make a population of slaves into an independent people in the shortest possible time, he invented elaborate ceremonials to give them a feeling of dignity and purpose. Every act had some imaginative end. The cutting of the finger nails was a religious observance. The Christian theologians went over the books of the Law, like great artists, getting splendid effects by excision. They reset the stage with more space and mystery, throwing all the light upon a few sins of great dramatic value—only seven, you remember, and of those only three that are perpetually enthralling. With the theologians came the cathedral-builders; the sculptors and glassworkers and painters. They might, without sacrilege, have changed the prayer a little and said, *Thy will be done in art, as it is in heaven.* How can it be done anywhere else *as* it is in heaven? But I think the hour is up. You might tell me next week, Miller, what you think science has done for us, besides making us comfortable." [Pp. 67-69, Vintage Books, 1973.]

Well, what do you think? Compare the Professor's views to those of Mr. Gradgrind in Charles Dickens' *Hard Times*, presented in the following excerpt:

C. Reflections on the Concept and Significance of Relevancy

CHAPTER I: THE ONE THING NEEDFUL

"Now, what I want is Facts. Teach these boys and girls nothing but Facts. Facts alone are wanted in life. Plant nothing else, and root out everything else. You can only form the minds of reasoning animals upon Facts: nothing else will ever be of any service to them. This is the principle on which I bring up my own children, and this is the principle on which I bring up these children. Stick to Facts, sir!"

The scene was a plain, bare, monotonous vault of a school-room, and the speaker's square forefinger emphasized his observations by underscoring every sentence with a line on the schoolmaster's sleeve. The emphasis was helped by the speaker's square wall of a forehead, which had his eyebrow for its base, while his eyes found commodious cellarage in two dark caves, overshadowed by the wall. The emphasis was helped by the speaker's mouth, which was wide, thin, and hard set. The emphasis was helped by the speaker's voice, which was inflexible, dry, and dictatorial. The emphasis was helped by the speaker's hair, which bristled on the skirts of his bald head, a plantation of firs to keep the wind from its shining surface, all covered with knobs, like the crust of a plum pie, as if the head had scarcely warehouse-room for the hard facts stored inside. The speaker's obstinate carriage, square coat, square legs, square shoulders—nay, his very neckcloth, trained to take him by the throat with an unaccommodating grasp, like a stubborn fact, as it was—all helped the emphasis.

"In this life, we want nothing but Facts, sir; nothing but Facts!"

The speaker, and the schoolmaster, and the third grown person present, all backed a little, and swept with their eyes the inclined plane of little vessels then and there arranged in order, ready to have imperial gallons of facts poured into them until they were full to the brim.

CHAPTER II: MURDERING THE INNOCENTS

THOMAS GRADGRIND, sir. A man of realities. A man of facts and calculations. A man who proceeds upon the principle that two and two are four, and nothing over, and who is not to be talked into allowing for anything over. Thomas Gradgrind, sir—peremptorily Thomas—Thomas Gradgrind. With a rule and a pair of scales, and the multiplication table always in his pocket, sir, ready to weigh and measure any parcel of human nature, and tell you exactly what it comes to. It is a mere question of figures, a case of simple arithmetic. You might hope to get some other nonsensical belief into the head of George Gradgrind, or Augustus Gradgrind, or John Gradgrind, or

Joseph Gradgrind (all suppositions, non-existent persons), but into the head of Thomas Gradgrind—no, sir!

In such terms Mr. Gradgrind always mentally introduced himself, whether to his private circle of acquaintance, or to the public in general. In such terms, no doubt, substituting the words "boys and girls," for "sir," Thomas Gradgrind now presented Thomas Gradgrind to the little pitchers before him, who were to be filled so full of facts.

Indeed, as he eagerly sparkled at them from the cellarage before mentioned, he seemed a kind of cannon loaded to the muzzle with facts, and prepared to blow them clean out of the regions of childhood at one discharge. He seemed a galvanizing apparatus, too, charged with a grim mechanical substitute for the tender young imaginations that were to be stormed away.

"Girl number twenty," said Mr. Gradgrind, squarely pointing with his square forefinger, "I don't know that girl. Who is that girl?"

"Sissy Jupe, sir," explained number twenty, blushing, standing up, and curtseying.

"Sissy is not a name," said Mr. Gradgrind. "Don't call yourself Sissy. Call yourself Cecilia."

"It's father as calls me Sissy, sir," returned the young girl in a trembling voice, and with another curtsey.

"Then he has no business to do it," said Mr. Gradgrind. "Tell him he mustn't. Cecilia Jupe. Let me see. What is your father?"

"He belongs to the horse-riding, if you please, sir."

Mr. Gradgrind frowned, and waved off the objectionable calling with his hand.

"We don't want to know anything about that, here. You mustn't tell us about that, here. Your father breaks horses, don't he?"

"If you please, sir, when they can get any to break, they do break horses in the ring, sir."

"You mustn't tell us about the ring, here. Very well, then. Describe your father as a horsebreaker. He doctors sick horses, I dare say?"

"Oh yes, sir."

"Very well, then. He is a veterinary surgeon, a farrier, and horsebreaker. Give me your definition of a horse."

(Sissy Jupe thrown into the greatest alarm by this demand.)

"Girl number twenty unable to define a horse!" said Mr. Gradgrind, for the general behoof of all the little pitchers. "Girl number twenty possessed of no facts, in reference to one of the commonest of animals! Some boy's definition of a horse, Bitzer, yours."

The square finger, moving here and there, lighted suddenly on Bitzer, perhaps because he chanced to sit in the same ray of sunlight which, darting in at one of the bare windows of the intesely whitewashed room, irradiated Sissy. For the boys and girls sat on the face of the inclined plane in two compact bodies, divided up the centre by a narrow

C. Reflections on the Concept and Significance of Relevancy

interval; and Sissy, being at the corner of a row on the sunny side, came in for the beginning of a sunbeam, of which Bitzer, being at the corner of a row on the other side, a few rows in advance, caught the end. But whereas the girl was so dark-eyed and dark-haired that she seemed to receive a deeper and more lustrous colour from the sun when it shone upon her, the boy was so light-eyed and light-haired that the selfsame rays appeared to draw out of him what little colour he ever possessed. His cold eyes would hardly have been eyes but for the short ends of lashes which, by bringing them into immediate contrast with something paler than themselves, expressed their form. His short-cropped hair might have been a mere continuation of the sandy freckles on his forehead and face. His skin was so unwholesomely deficient in the natural tinge, that he looked as though, if he were cut, he would bleed white.

"Bitzer," said Thomas Gradgrind. "Your definition of a horse."

"Quadruped. Graminivorous. Forty teeth, namely, twenty-four grinders, four eye-teeth, and twelve incisive. Sheds coat in the spring; in marshy countries, sheds hoofs, too. Hoofs hard, but requiring to be shod with iron. Age known by marks in mouth." Thus (and much more) Bitzer.

"Now girl number twenty," said Mr. Gradgrind. "You know what a horse is."

She curtseyed again, and would have blushed deeper if she could have blushed deeper than she had blushed all this time. Bitzer, after rapidly blinking at Thomas Gradgrind with both eyes at once, and so catching the light upon his quivering ends of lashes that they looked like the antennae of busy insects, put his knuckles to his freckled forehead and sat down again.

The third gentleman now stepped forth. A mighty man at cutting and drying he was; a government officer; in his way (and in most other people's too), a professed pugilist; always in training, always with a system to force down the general throat like a bolus, always to be heard of at the bar of his little public-office, ready to fight all England. To continue in fistic phraseology, he had a genius for coming up to the scratch, wherever and whatever it was, and proving himself an ugly customer. He would go in and damage any subject whatever with his right, follow up with his left, stop, exchange, counter, bore his opponent to the ropes, and fall upon him neatly. He was certain to knock the wind out of common sense, and render that unlucky adversary deaf to the call of time. And he had it in charge from high authority to bring about the great public-office. Millennium, when Commissioners should reign upon earth.

"Very well," said this gentleman, briskly smiling, and folding his arms. "That's a horse. Now, let me ask you girls and boys: Would you paper a room with representations of horses?"

After a pause, one half of the children cried in chorus, "Yes, sir!" Upon which the other half, seeing in the gentleman's face that Yes was wrong, cried out in chorus, "No, sir!"—as the custom is in these examinations.

"Of course, No. Why wouldn't you?"

A pause. One corpulent slow boy, with a wheezy manner of breathing, ventured the answer. Because he wouldn't paper a room at all but would paint it.

"You must paper it," said Thomas Gradgrind, "whether you like it or not. Don't tell *us* you wouldn't paper it. What do you mean, boy?"

"I'll explain to you, then" said the gentleman, after another and a dismal pause, "why you wouldn't paper a room with representations of horses. Do you ever see horses walking up and down the sides of rooms in reality—in fact? Do you?"

"Yes, sir!" from one half, "No, sir!" from the other.

"Of course, No," said the gentleman, with an indignant look at the wrong half. "Why, then, you are not to see anywhere what you don't see in fact; you are not to have anywhere what you don't have in fact. What is called Taste is only another name for Fact."

Thomas Gradgrind nodded his approbation.

"This is a new principle, a discovery, a great discovery," said the gentleman. "Now, I'll try you again. Suppose you were going to carpet a room. Would you use a carpet having a representation of flowers upon it?"

There being a general conviction by this time that "No, sir!" was always the right answer to this gentleman, the chorus of No was very strong. Only a few feeble stragglers said Yes: among them Sissy Jupe.

"Girl number twenty," said the gentleman, smiling in the calm strength of knowledge.

Sissy blushed and stood up.

"So you would carpet your room—or your husband's room, if you were a grown woman, and had a husband—with representations of flowers, would you?" said the gentleman. "Why would you?"

"If you please, sir, I am very fond of flowers," returned the girl.

"And is that why you would put tables and chairs upon them, and have people walking over them with heavy boots?"

"It wouldn't hurt them, sir. They wouldn't crush and wither, if you please, sir. They would be the pictures of what was very pretty and pleasant, and I would fancy—"

"Aye, aye, aye! But you mustn't fancy," cried the gentleman, quite elated by coming so happily to his point. "That's it! You are never to fancy."

"You are not, Cecilia Jupe," Thomas Gradgrind solemnly repeated, "to do anything of that kind."

C. Reflections on the Concept and Significance of Relevancy

"Fact, fact, fact!" said the gentleman and "Fact, fact, fact!" repeated Thomas Gradgrind.

"You are to be in all things regulated and governed," said the gentleman, "by fact. We hope to have, before long, a board of fact, composed of commissioners of fact, who will force the people to be a people of fact, and of nothing but fact. You must discard the word Fancy altogether. You have nothing to do with it. You are not to have, in any object of use or ornament, what would be a contradiction in fact. You don't walk upon flowers in fact; you cannot be allowed to walk upon flowers in carpets. You don't find that foreign birds and butterflies come and perch upon your crockery; you cannot be permitted to paint foreign birds and butterflies upon your crockery. You never meet with quadrupeds going up and down walls; you must not have quadrupeds represented upon walls. You must see," said the gentleman, "for all these purposes, combinations and modifications (in primary colours) of mathematical figures which are susceptible of proof and demonstration. This is the new discovery. This is fact. This is taste.

The girl curtseyed, and sat down. She was very young, and she looked as if she were frightened by the matter-of-fact prospect the world afforded.

"Now, if Mr. McChoakumchild," said the gentleman, "will proceed to give his first lesson here, Mr. Gradgrind, I shall be happy, at your request, to observe his mode of procedure."

So Mr. McChoakumchild began in his best manner. He and some one hundred and forty other schoolmasters had been lately turned at the same time, in the same factory, on the same principles, like so many pianoforte legs. He had been put through an immense variety of paces, and had answered volumes of head-breaking questions. Orthography, etymology, syntax, and prosody, biography, astronomy, geography, and general cosmography, the sciences of compound proportion, algebra, land-surveying and levelling, vocal music, and drawing from models, were all at the ends of his ten chilled fingers. He had worked his stony way into Her Majesty's most Honourable Privy Council's Schedule B, and had taken the bloom off the higher branches of mathematics and physical science, French, German, Latin and Greek. He knew all about all the watersheds of all the world (whatever they are), and all the histories of all the peoples, and all the names of all the rivers and mountains, and all the productions, manners and customs of all the countries, and all their boundaries and bearings on the two-and-thirty points of the compass. Ah, rather overdone, McChoakumchild. If he had only learnt a little less, how infinitely better he might have taught much more!

He went to work in this preparatory lesson not unlike Morgiana in the Forty Thieves: looking into all the vessels ranged before him, one after another, to see what they contained. Say, good Mc-

Choakumchild: when from thy boiling store, thou shalt fill each jar brimful by-and-by, dost thou think that thou wilt always kill outright the robber Fancy lurking within—or sometimes only maim him and distort him!

NOTES AND QUESTIONS

1. Are trials "public affairs" or are they private affairs in which the public aspect is only incidental? Does it matter, for purpose of constructing trials, which is the more compelling view? To what extent does the fact that private parties submit their personal disputes to public tribunals justify the state's imposing on the parties a dispute resolution process that neither party might otherwise voluntarily chose or justify the furthering of collective goals through the trial medium?

2. What about criminal trials? Are they different from civil trials in relevant ways? Should factual accuracy play a more or less important role in that setting?

3. To what extent should dispute resolution be constructed to advance the peaceful settlement of disputes instead of the accurate resolution of them? See Chafee, Book Review, Wigmore on Evidence, 37 Harv. L. Rev. 513, 519 (1924): "[A] trial is not an abstract search for truth, but an attempt to settle controversy between two persons without physical conflict." Should formulating or expressing community values play a role in the system of litigation? What is or ought to be the role of consistency in decision or is consistency in outcome at odds with any of the other values that might be served by a dispute resolution process?

4. In light of your answers to the previous questions, reconsider the use of juries in negligence cases in which the jury is instructed to apply "the standard of the [relevant] community." Also, what do you think of instructing jurors to apply "contemporary community standards" in obscenity cases? Why should the jury be instructed to apply such standards in those cases but not in others, such as medical malpractice or contract violations cases?

5. Which of the following cases should be permitted to go to a jury for decision:

(a) A person is run over by a cab on a dark, foggy night. The victim testifies that she "thinks," but is not sure, that the cab was operated by the Flash Cab Company. In defense, evidence is offered that during the night in question there were 1000 cabs on the road, of which 50 were owned and operated by Flash Cab Company, and over the previous 18 months, of 2000 complaints filed against cab companies for reckless or illegal operation of cabs, only 100 were filed against drivers working for Flash Cab.

C. Reflections on the Concept and Significance of Relevancy

(b) Same as above, except that the plaintiff has no idea what cab company is the culprit. She does have evidence that of 1000 cabs on the road, 501 are Flash Cabs.

(c) The victim testifies that she is certain that she was run over by a Flash Cab. The defense introduces evidence of an expert that demonstrates that there is a 60 percent chance that her testimony is false. The expert knows this because the expert was able to replicate the conditions of the event and the victim's perceptual abilities in a rigorously controlled experiment.

CHAPTER THREE

THE RELATIONSHIP BETWEEN JUDGE AND JURY: Conditional Relevancy, Authentication, and the Best Evidence Rule

A. *THE JUDGE, THE JURY, RELEVANCY, AND AUTHENTICATION*

As we observed in Chapter Two, only relevant evidence is admissible at trial, and relevancy, in turn, is determined by analyzing the evidence adduced at trial in light of the decision maker's experience, background, and common knowledge. We also saw that the trial judge can exclude evidence that is cumulative or misleading or that does not justify the time required to produce it, which raises at least two serious problems. First, there is a tension between the ideal of the jury as the fact finder and the allocation of authority to the judge to exclude evidence. The trial judge can exercise significant control over the fact finding process by regulating the flow of information to the jury. If a jury is allowed to hear only one side of a case, for example, the odds obviously are going to be substantially increased that the jury will return a verdict for that party.

There is another, more profound, aspect to this tension. We utilize juries in large measure because of a desire that fact finding be informed by the community norms that jurors bring to their tasks, and because of a concern that locating power over fact finding in an elite (the trial bench) risks skewing decisions in favor of the interests of that elite. By permitting the trial judges to regulate the flow of information to the jury, the power to control outcomes is moved at least incrementally in the direction of the judges and away from juries, thus increasing the risk that community norms will suffer and elite interests will benefit.

The second problem that emerges from the concept of relevancy is more prosaic but of great pragmatic importance. The relevancy of any offer of evidence is determined not only by the general knowledge and background of the fact finder, but also by all the other evidence that will be presented at trial. Reconsider an example used earlier. Suppose a case of a car wreck resulting from defective brakes where the plaintiff's theory is that the driver was negligent in driving the car because the driver knew or should have known that the brakes were bad. To prove that the driver was on notice of the condition of the brakes, the plaintiff wishes to offer a mechanic who will testify that he yelled at the driver as the driver was pulling out of the mechanic's gas station, "Be careful. The brakes are bad." That offer of proof certainly seems relevant, but what if the driver can establish that he is completely deaf, and thus could not possibly have heard the mechanic? If that is so, the fact that the mechanic yelled at a deaf driver is not relevant. How, then, can a determination of relevancy of any piece of evidence be made until the judge has heard all the evidence? Indeed, each of the grounds of exclusion in FRE 403 has this aspect.[1]

The issues discussed here are specific examples of a more general dynamic. Rules of evidence, among their many other tasks, regulate and allocate authority to the various actors in the trial drama. It is out of this process of regulation that come at least the initial answers to the two questions that began this inquiry: Why do judges decide questions concerning the relevancy of evidence? How can that be done prior to knowing what all the evidence in a case will be?

The answers to these questions are interesting and subtle, and we will soon turn full attention to them. Before doing so, however, it should be noted that an analogous set of issues exists with respect to questions of law, but the resolution of those issues seems so intuitively obvious as not to require extended consideration. Someone must determine what the law requires, and the judge seems peculiarly well situated to do so. The judge is trained in the law and is under oath to do what the law requires. To give the jury the power to determine what the law requires seems to most observers to be too inefficient and too likely to lead to serious inconsistency in outcome to be worth whatever advantages it might entail.[2]

The primary issue raised by giving the judge the power to determine

---

1. For an interesting example of the common law approach to such problems, see Gila Valley Ry. Co. v. Hall, 232 U.S. 94 (1914). One of the issues was whether the injured party heard a warning given by his supervisor, and was thus put on notice of a dangerous condition. Whether the individual heard the statement seems very much like a question of fact to be decided by the jury. The Court said: "We agree that the testimony was such as to render it a matter of doubtful inference whether Hall heard the conversation; but we think this question of fact was one to be determined by the trial court, and not by the jury. Questions of the admissibility of evidence are for the determination of the court; and this is so whether its admission depend upon matter of law or upon matter of fact." Id. at 103.

2. There have been times in our history when a quite different view was prevalent. Indeed, in some states—Maryland is an example—until recently juries possessed the power to determine what the law is in criminal cases. This allocation of authority was another reflection of distrust of state power. By giving jurors the responsibility to determine the law, the power of state officials is checked in a significant way.

A. The Judge, the Jury, Relevancy, and Authentication 163

the law and to instruct the jury on its requirements is distinguishing questions of law from questions of fact.[3] In the great run of cases, this is not difficult. The law is the collection of rules governing the relationships among individuals in society. On occasion, however, some difficulty is encountered. This occurs either when the legal standards have the effect of obliterating the distinction or when a judgment has been made to transfer the power over a factual matter to the judge by calling the matter a "question of law." Examples of the former situation are negligence and obscenity. In both cases, the legal standards directly incorporate community norms, and consequently one can argue whether a finding of negligence or obscenity is a finding of "fact" or a finding of "law." The real objects of contention in such arguments are who gets to decide the question at issue and what is the appropriate standard of review in the appellate courts (where normally less deference is paid to trial court determinations of law than to determinations of fact at the trial level).

The label "question of law" is also used as a smoke screen by which authority that normally would be vested in juries is transferred to judges. This is typically done if there is a concern that juries will systematically decide cases the "wrong" way, and there is a reciprocal expectation that judges will do the job in a better, more predictable fashion. These cases often seem to reflect special interests exercising their political power in an effort to improve their chances of winning in litigation. Consider, for example, Uniform Commercial Code §2-302, which makes unconscionability a question of law to be decided by the judge. What is it about "unconscionability" that converts such factual matters as "commercial setting, purpose and effect" of a contract clause into questions of law? We suggest that this magical transformation probably was a result more of concern over how juries would decide cases than anything else. Whether our suggestion is correct or not, the point is that on occasion you will see the label "question of law" applied to what are obviously questions of fact, and the reason for so applying the label is to vest power to decide the question in the judiciary.

The proper allocation of authority between judge and jury on questions of fact is also informed by the implications of various policies. The classic treatment of the area is Maguire and Epstein, Preliminary Questions of Fact in Determining the Admissibility of Evidence, 40 Harv. L. Rev. 392 (1927), according to whom authority over fact finding is justifiably allocated to judges in order to (1) reduce the complexity of jury trials, (2) expedite the trial process, (3) increase the predictability of outcomes, (4) preserve issues in a clear and coherent fashion for appeal, (5) insulate juries (and the parties) from unfairly prejudicial evidence, and (6) further the policies of the various exclusionary rules. Each of these reasons makes some sense, although none

---

3. See, e.g., H. Hart and A. Sacks, The Legal Process: Basic Problems in the Making and Application of Law 373-380 (1958).

provides, alone or with any or all of the others, obvious boundaries between the judge and the jury.

Simplifying and expediting trials, if it can be done without damage to the interests of the parties or the goals of the trial system, is certainly a laudable objective (as is its blood relation, "expediting the trial process"), but where is the point at which "simplification" intrudes too far into the appropriate domain of juries? Predictability in outcome is an attractive feature of a system, but only where the input into a system is such that similar outcomes should be expected. In the trial system, by contrast, each case is different, and thus complaints about "inconsistent results" may simply be a surrogate for a general discontent with juries. In any event, again no obvious line is drawn by such a criterion. Preserving issues for appeal is primarily a task for the parties rather than judge (or jury, obviously). Each of these policies, in short, is merely a laudable objective, and none is terribly helpful in providing a limiting principle on the power of juries over facts.

The remaining two points—keeping prejudicial material from affecting fact finding and furthering the policies of the exclusionary rules—may have greater explanatory power. As we have seen, "prejudicial evidence" is evidence that will be misevaluated by the jury. This means that the jurors will either over- or underestimate the persuasive power of the evidence (we include here the effect of evidence on the utility function of jurors), thus increasing the chances of an erroneous verdict as compared to a case where that evidence is excluded. Where we are confident that such a case exists and that excluding evidence is likely to enhance accuracy, there is a persuasive reason to qualify the power of juries over facts by excluding that evidence. The concern for accuracy, in short, trumps the solicitude for jury fact finding.

The other situation in which there is a strong justification for transferring power over facts from jury to judge is when the policies of exclusionary rules would be subverted if juries were to decide the relevant issues. Take, for example, the rule excluding involuntary confessions. It is coherent to let juries decide if confessions are voluntary, and to instruct juries not to rely on a confession if the conclusion is reached that a confession is involuntary. The difficulty is that reasonable doubts may exist as to whether jurors will be able to put the confession out of their minds and not rely on it once a finding of involuntariness is made. Take another example. Again, it is coherent to let juries decide if the conditions of a privilege are met, and to instruct the jury to disregard any material found to be privileged. However, the purpose of privileges is to keep information confidential. By requiring that the information be provided, that purpose is not served, whether or not juries can then disregard the evidence found to be privileged (which many observers doubt). One solution to this problem would be to hold preliminary trials on matters of privilege or on other exclusionary rules with the jury returning preliminary "verdicts" on the privileged character of evidence that one of the parties wished to produce. This strikes most observers as a rather inefficient way to run the trial process, however. Accordingly, power over

A. The Judge, the Jury, Relevancy, and Authentication

the preliminary facts that determine the admissibility of evidence is typically given to the trial judge.

Giving the power to trial judges does not solve all the problems, however. First of all, as we have mentioned, one of the questions is the relevancy of evidence, which cannot be known until all the evidence is in. This problem is obviated by a process of conditional admission, which often goes by the name "conditional relevancy." The judge will admit evidence "conditioned upon" subsequent proof being offered that establishes the relevancy of the first bit of evidence, and so on throughout the trial. Thus, in a contract case, proof of performance (or nonperformance, depending upon who is suing whom) is irrelevant unless there is proof of an agreement, and in many cases, vice versa. It is not a legitimate objection that a party produces evidence of performance before producing evidence of agreement, or again vice versa. Rather, the court will admit such evidence and wait to see whether satisfactory evidence of all the other necessary elements in the cause of action are provided. If there is a gap in the proof of a party, the court will then take the appropriate action if asked to do so by the adversary. Similarly, the court will wait and see if each logical step in the chain of inferences relied upon by the parties is supported by evidence. If, at the end of the production of evidence, certain logical links are unsupported by evidence, the evidence admitted conditionally will be stricken from the record at the motion of the adversary.

Assume that an expert is called in a wrongful death action to give an opinion about cause of death and is asked to assume that the plaintiff was a long-term smoker. The adversary objects on the ground that there is nothing in the record to establish that the plaintiff ever smoked. The proponent responds by asserting that he or she "will connect it up later," which means that the gap in the evidence will be cured at a subsequent point in the trial. Typically the judge will admit the expert's testimony subject to that evidence subsequently being produced. If the evidence is not forthcoming, the expert's opinion will be stricken from the record. What, though, if the adversary is convinced that the evidence will not be produced and is concerned that the jury may be unable to disregard the expert's opinion? In such a case, the adversary will articulate the concerns to the trial judge, who, if convinced that they are serious ones, may require the proponent of the evidence to first produce the evidence upon which the expert's testimony rests. Normally, however, the judge will let each party present the evidence in the manner in which each sees fit.

The doctrine of conditional relevancy has caused much confusion, and the reason for the confusion is that the doctrine itself is confused. The doctrine suggests that there is a special class of cases where the relevancy of one fact depends upon the existence of some other fact. However, this is either false or, alternatively, true of every determination of relevancy (and thus not a separate doctrine). Take the example given above of litigation over a contract, and assume there are only two issues in the case: agreement and performance.[4] The received doctrine of conditional relevancy says that evidence of agreement is "irrelevant" absent evidence of performance, and vice versa. However, this is true in only one instance. If the probability of performance is zero, then and only then does evidence of agreement that makes agreement more probable not raise the probability that the plaintiff should recover. That is so because if the probability of performance really is zero, then we already know that the plaintiff cannot recover, and evidence of agreement is of no consequence. But, if we already know that the probability of performance is zero, there is nothing left to litigate, and so this category of cases tells us nothing about conditional relevancy. If, by contrast, the probability of performance is not zero, then any evidence increasing the probability of agreement increases the chances that plaintiff should win, and thus such evidence is obviously relevant. From this perspective, then, there is no room for an independent doctrine of conditional relevancy to operate.

There is another perspective, though. When evidence is offered, the proponent must indicate why the evidence is relevant. As we discussed in Chapter Two, this entails indicating the generalization that makes the evidence proof of a material fact. The judge's task is to decide whether that generalization may be employed by a jury in its reasoning process, whether it is rational or not. On occasion, the judge will conclude that the generalization may not be relied upon by the jury, and thus that the evidence is inadmissible. This process of the judge considering the permissibility of the underlying generalization, though, occurs with respect to all questions of relevancy, and so once more there is no independent scope for conditional relevancy.

This discussion raises an important point. Assume that a judge decides that an offer of evidence is irrelevant. The proponent of that evidence may then offer further evidence that demonstrates the truth of the generalization necessary for the offer of the first evidence to be relevant. In this respect, the evidentiary process can be "backed up" until the judge is finally convinced that the *unsupported* (by evidence) generalizations that the jury will have to utilize to evaluate the admitted evidence are reasonable. This means, of course, that they are within the common and shared knowledge of reasonable people. Once the judge reaches such a conclusion, all the evidence comes in. If the judge never reaches such a conclusion, all the evidence stays out.

Occasionally, what is normally a preliminary fact that determines the admissibility of evidence, and thus normally for the judge to decide, is also a fact of crucial importance to the case, and thus normally for the jury to decide. Suppose, for example, that a person is charged with rape and defends on the ground that the victim is his wife, whom he cannot rape (which is still the law in many states). When the victim takes the stand, the defendant objects on grounds of the spousal immunity, which prevents spouses from testifying against each other. The preliminary fact to be decided is whether

---

4. For much of what follows we are indebted to the brilliant article, Ball, The Myth of Conditional Relevancy, 14 Ga. L. Rev. 435 (1980).

A. The Judge, the Jury, Relevancy, and Authentication

the two are married, but that is also a fact crucial to the defendant's liability. If the judge decides that a marriage does exist, the jury will be deprived of very important testimony.

Jurisdictions differ in their response to problems such as these. Some would say that the judge must decide the issue, while others would have the jury decide the issue. Nor would it be surprising to see a judge make a preliminary determination for purposes of deciding if the woman can testify, and if she is allowed to testify, instructing the jury to disregard the testimony if it finds that a marriage exits. On the other hand, it also would not be surprising to find a trial judge who has made a preliminary determination of no marriage to simply instruct the jury to acquit if it finds the two to have been married, and not refer to the related evidentiary question.

The relationship between the judge and jury is structured in the Federal Rules by FRE 104, which it is now time to consider:

RULE 104. PRELIMINARY QUESTIONS

(a) **Questions of admissibility generally.** Preliminary questions concerning the qualification of a person to be a witness, the existence of a privilege, or the admissibility of evidence shall be determined by the court, subject to the provisions of subdivision (b). In making its determination it is not bound by the rules of evidence except those with respect to privileges.

(b) **Relevancy conditioned on fact.** When the relevancy of evidence depends upon the fulfillment of a condition of fact, the court shall admit it upon, or subject to, the introduction of evidence sufficient to support a finding of the fulfillment of the condition.

(c) **Hearing of jury.** Hearings on the admissibility of confessions shall in all cases be conducted out of the hearing of the jury. Hearings on other preliminary matters shall be so conducted when the interests of justice require or, when an accused is a witness and so requests.

(d) **Testimony by accused.** The accused does not, by testifying upon a preliminary matter, become subject to cross-examination as to other issues in the case.

(e) **Weight and credibility.** This rule does not limit the right of a party to introduce before the jury evidence relevant to weight or credibility.

The basic point of FRE 104 is that the trial judge is to see that the rules are enforced, including the rule that the jury is primarily responsible for determining the historical facts of the case. There is, however, some ambiguity as to what standards the trial judge is to apply in seeing that the rules are enforced, and there is also ambiguity as to how the potential conflict between the judge's role and the jury's role is to be resolved.[5] Rule 104(b) contains a substantive standard: Evidence depending upon the fulfillment of a condition of fact is admissible if there is evidence "sufficient to support a

---

5. Much of what follows is based on Allen, The Explanatory Value of Analyzing Codifications by Reference to Organizing Principles Other Than Those Employed in the Codification, 79 Nw. U. L. Rev., 1080, 1085-1089 (1984).

finding of the fulfillment of the condition." Rule 104(a), by contrast, does not contain a substantive provision, but the drafters' intent must have been to provide a different one from that of 104(b) or else 104(a) would be superfluous, as indeed the courts are concluding.[6] Thus, the trend seems to be that the preponderance standard is to be employed whenever the question is for the court under FRE 104(a). Note another important difference between 104(a) and (b): The judge is not bound by the rules of evidence, except for privileges, when making a FRE 104(a) determination of the admissibility of evidence. See FRE 1101(d)(1). By contrast, the reference in FRE 104(b) to the "introduction of evidence sufficient to support a finding" indicates that the judge is to make the FRE 104(b) finding on the basis of admitted evidence.

The more difficult issue is to determine which preliminary facts are within FRE 104(a) and which are within 104(b). FRE 104 provides some answers. When a fact is "conditionally relevant" on some other fact (but bear in mind our earlier discussion of this confusing doctrine), evidence of the first fact is admissible if satisfactory evidence of the second fact is offered (with the timing of that offer in the discretion of the judge). In this respect, FRE 104 is quite consistent with its common law predecessors.[7]

There are ambiguities in FRE 104, however. An obvious problem is that it is unclear how it applies to the specific relevancy rules of Article IV. For example, should the judge decide that FRE 411's standards covering liability insurance are met or should such evidence be admitted upon, or subject to, sufficient evidence to support such a finding?[8] The answer comes

---

6. See, e.g., In re Japanese Elec. Prod. Antitrust Litig., 723 F.2d 238 (3d Cir. 1983); James R. Snyder Co. v. Associated Gen. Contractors of America, 677 F.2d 1111 (6th Cir. 1982); United States v. James, 590 F.2d 575 (5th Cir. 1979). The Supreme Court appears to have answered this question in Bourjaily v. United States, 107 S. Ct. 2775 (1987), by holding that FRE 104(a) provides that a court is to decide by a preponderance of the evidence if the conditions of the co-conspirator exception to the hearsay rule, codified in FRE 801(d)(2)(E) are satisfied. The Court spoke in general terms, but it is always possible that subsequent cases will come out differently on different issues.

7. The Advisory Committee Note to FRE 104 in part provides:

If preliminary questions of conditional relevancy were determined solely by the judge, as provided in subdivision (a), the functioning of the jury as a trier of fact would be greatly restricted and in some cases virtually destroyed. These are appropriate questions for juries. Accepted treatment, as provided in the rule, is consistent with that given fact questions generally.

FRE 104(b) does generate a fine theoretical question, though. Its standard—"sufficient to support a finding"—is higher than it need be. One could test relevancy by whether the offered evidence has any power to persuade, even if the power would not be sufficient to support a finding. Indeed, this seems to be the definition of relevancy in FRE 401. Thus, there is a tension between the implications of FRE 401 and FRE 104(b) that reflects the problems inherent in FRE 104(b). The drafters, in other words, did not adequately consider what they were doing, and the rule should be revised.

8. FRE 411 provides:

RULE 411. LIABILITY INSURANCE

Evidence that a person was or was not insured against liability is not admissible upon the issue whether he acted negligently or otherwise wrongfully. This rule does

A. The Judge, the Jury, Relevancy, and Authentication 169

from the recognition, as we develop further in Chapter 4, that most of the "specific relevancy rules" in Article IV are rules of *exclusion* that exist to serve policies that would be defeated by admitting before the jury the evidence relevant to the preliminary question that must be decided, and thus the relevant facts for the operation of any such rules should be decided by the trial judge in order to further the relevant policy choices.[9] Questions of privilege are to be handled similarly, as are the hearsay rule and the rules of impeachment contained in Article VI of the Federal Rules.[10]

The proper approach to witnesses is less clear, notwithstanding the phraseology of the rule. Indeed, there is a tension between FRE 104(a) and FRE 602. FRE 104(a) appears to allocate to the trial judge the authority to determine the qualifications of a person to be a witness.[11] With the exception of expert witnesses, what qualifies a person to be a witness is personal knowledge of the relevant event, thus the implication of FRE 104(a) is that the

---

not require the exclusion of evidence of insurance against liability when offered for another purpose, such as proof of agency, ownership, or control, or bias or prejudice of a witness.

9. Some of the specific relevancy rules are premised upon the lack of probative value of the evidence. This is true for FRE 404, for example, and possibly FRE 406. When that is the case, arguably the appropriate standard is the FRE 104(b) standard.

The Supreme Court in a recent decision embraced in part our view of the relationship between FRE 104 and FRE 404(b). In Huddleston v. United States, 108 S. Ct. 1469 (1988), the Court held that if evidence is admitted for a proper purpose under FRE 404(b), there is no preliminary fact to find. Accordingly, the only responsibility for the judge is to apply the FRE 104(b) standard to ensure relevance (although the court could also exclude the evidence under FRE 403 after a finding of relevance had been made). This confirms the view that relevancy decisions will be subject to the lower standard of FRE 104(b). The Court did not address how a trial court was to decide if evidence is offered for a proper purpose under FRE 404(b), however. Our view is that FRE 104(a) should apply to such decisions, since this entails implementing the nonrelevancy policies of the rule.

One might reasonably wonder whether the functional effect of the difference between 104(a) and (b) justify their existence. In particular, bear in mind that after a court makes a 104(b) ruling, a party can still move to exclude on FRE 403 grounds. If evidence would be admissible under the 104(b) standard but not the 104(a) standard, it is likely to have low probative value. Low probative value, in turn, increases the chances of evidence being excluded under FRE 403.

10. For a discussion, see Kaplan, Of Mabrus and Zorgs—An Essay in Honor of David Louisell, 66 Calif. L. Rev. 987 (1978). The Supreme Court has often allocated to the judiciary the power to decide facts that implicate constitutional values, such as actual malice in first amendment litigation. For a recent example, see Miller v. Fenton, 474 U.S. 104 (1985), holding that the voluntariness of a confession is to be decided independently by the federal courts. For a general discussion, see Monaghan, Constitutional Fact Review, 85 Colum. L. Rev. 229 (1985).

11. At common law, there were, and still are in some jurisdictions, numerous rules of competency that declared that certain types of evidence were not to be used at trial. Examples are spousal testimony, the deadman rule, children under a certain age, and individuals who could not understand the obligations of an oath. The Federal Rules have eliminated all rules of competency but one: the requirement of firsthand knowledge in FRE 602. Nevertheless, the word *incompetency* is still used by courts and commentators to refer to exclusionary rules of evidence, such as those found in Article IV of the Federal Rules. Keep clear the distinction between such a use and the common law meaning of the term, which centered on testimonial incompetency of categories of individuals.

judge must be convinced that a witness possesses firsthand knowledge. FRE 602, however, provides that "[a] witness may not testify to a matter unless evidence is introduced sufficient to support a finding that the witness has personal knowledge of the matter." The standard is that of 104(b) rather than 104(a).[12] The only other subject matters that 104(a)'s "qualification" provision could apply to are the ability of a witness to understand the implications of the oath, the qualification of an expert to testify under FRE 702, and the basis for a lay opinion under FRE 701. To require the trial judge to determine the qualifications of an expert to testify is perfectly sensible. It is not immediately apparent, however, why the standard of 104(b) should be applied to the requirement of personal knowledge for lay witnesses while some other standard is applied to the determination of the justification for a lay opinion under FRE 701, although perhaps this rule can be justified on the ground that jurors are more likely to be misled by expert than lay witnesses, and thus that judges should have greater authority to exclude expert testimony.

The relationship between FRE 104 and FRE 703 is also problematic. FRE 703 states that an expert may testify on the basis of facts or data "reasonably relied upon by experts in the particular field" even if "the facts and data (are) not . . . admissible in evidence," but it fails to specify who should determine reasonableness. Perhaps FRE 702's use of the word *qualified* should again come into play—which is the conclusion the lower federal courts are reaching—or perhaps FRE 104(a)'s phrase *admissibility of evidence* (even though we are talking about otherwise inadmissible evidence) is relevant, or perhaps FRE 703 is somehow analogous to FRE 602, which would imply that FRE 104(b) should govern. Whichever is the better view, the Rules are not much help where they should be and they have left to the courts a number of unnecessary problems to work out.

The testimony of witnesses is not the only type of evidence that may be produced at trial. The parties may also produce real and demonstrative evidence. "Real evidence" refers to tangible items that played some role in the litigated event and from which the jury may draw inferences. Examples are the weapons used in a crime or an appliance that is alleged to have been defective at the time of purchase or within the warranty period. "Demonstrative evidence" refers to tangible items that are helpful to the jury in understanding the litigated event even though the items did not play a role in the event. Examples are charts, maps, and photographs of the relevant scenes. Many courts and commentators no longer distinguish these forms of evidence, and it is not clear that distinguishing them serves a useful purpose. Regardless, no tangible items are admissible at trial without a proper foundation first being laid for their admissibility. Laying the foundation, or "authenticating" the item, requires that the proponent of the evidence demonstrate

---

12. The Advisory Committee Note to FRE 602 states: "It will be observed that the rule is in fact a specialized application of the provisions of Rule 104(b) on conditional relevancy."

A. The Judge, the Jury, Relevancy, and Authentication 171

that the item is what it purports to be and that what it purports to be is relevant to the litigation.

Consider a murder trial where the prosecution wishes to introduce a knife as the murder weapon. Not any knife will do, of course. Whatever the prosecution presents will be relevant to the litigation only if it is the knife that was used in the event (or possibly a facsimile offered for demonstrative purposes). Thus, the prosecution must "authenticate" or "lay the foundation" for the knife's admissibility by showing that it is what it purports to be and that what it purports to be is relevant to the litigation. In this case, the knife "purports to be" the knife used in the murder, and if it is that knife it is certainly relevant to the litigated event. Accordingly, the prosecution has to make a preliminary showing that the knife is the knife used in the murder. Here, of course, the knife would be real rather than demonstrative evidence.

Demonstrative evidence is authenticated in basically the same manner as real evidence, the only difference being that the proponent of demonstrative evidence will normally have to show that the demonstrative evidence will assist the trier of fact in its deliberations. That factor normally will be assumed with real evidence. It would be highly unusual, for example, for a trial court to exclude from evidence a murder weapon on the ground that the jury does not need to observe the weapon for purposes of its deliberations, even if such a conclusion would be accurate. Thus, with demonstrative evidence the advocate must be prepared to convince the trial judge that whatever he or she wants admitted will serve a useful purpose in enlightening the jury's understanding of the relevant events. Some forms of evidence are generally admitted as a matter of course, such as photographs of the scene (assuming they are not misleading in any way, of course). Other types of evidence are more problematic, as the likelihood increases that the evidence may be misleading in one way or the other. Complex charts and graphs often fit into this category, as do complex statistical models.[13]

On its face, FRE 104 is once again unclear as to whether the foundation requirement is a FRE 104(a) or 104(b) issue. Other rules eliminate the ambiguity, however. Consider FRE 901 and 902. FRE 901 makes clear that authentication is a FRE 104(b) issue by explicitly providing the standard "sufficient to support a finding." Thus, FRE 901 is a specific example of the general principle found in 104(b). Note also FRE 902. Here are listed numerous forms of evidence that are self-authenticating, which means that their admissibility need not be accompanied by oral testimony.[14]

The approach of the Federal Rules to the requirement of authentication entails a dramatic change from the common law. At common law, there are numerous special requirements for the admissibility of evidence, most

---

13. A very useful book that presents the various forms of evidence and their respective foundations, and that ought to be consulted by every young trial attorney, is E. Imwinkelried, Evidentiary Foundations (1980).

14. Also note FRE 903, which eliminates an annoying common law constraint upon the admissibility of certain documents.

of which are questions for the judge. The best example is the requirement of chain of custody. At common law, before an item that might be adulterated in any way can be admitted at trial, its proponent must establish the "chain of custody" that leads from the event in question through each person who was in custody of the item to the trial itself. Thus, if the prosecution wishes to introduce an illegal substance that was allegedly seized at the scene of the crime, the trial judge must first be convinced that the substance is the same that was seized and that it has not been modified in any significant way. This can only be done by establishing who first took the substance into custody and to whom it was subsequently transferred, through each transfer of custody, until it finally reaches the court room. If the judge is not convinced that each link in the chain has been established, the evidence is excluded. The Federal Rules change this requirement. Under FRE 901, the question is no longer whether the judge is convinced that the chain of custody has been established; rather, it is whether there is sufficient evidence to support a finding that the matter in question is what its proponent claims it to be, in this case the substance seized at the crime scene.

This change in the common law has not been met with uniform approval. Consider the following:

S. SALTZBURG AND K. REDDEN
Federal Rules of Evidence Manual 1005-1010 (4th ed. 1986)

Rule 901 establishes a general provision that the requirement of authentication or identification as a condition precedent to admissibility is satisfied by evidence sufficient to support a finding that the matter in question is what its proponents claim. If this Rule is read literally, it makes tremendous inroads into common law doctrine, and it greatly simplifies the task of getting evidence before the jury. But as this comment indicates below, it is by no means clear that the changes in the common law that the text of the Rule seems to make are intended by either the Advisory Committee or the Congress.

To understand the problem presented by the general provision of Rule 901(a), consider the case of a psychologist called to testify in support of an insanity defense raised by a criminal defendant. Through the witness, defendant wishes to introduce the results of certain psychological tests. In common law jurisdictions, the first thing that defense counsel will do is establish the qualifications of the expert. The expert will identify the tests and establish their reliability. If he cannot do this to the satisfaction of the Judge, the tests will be excluded. Rule 901(a) may change this. The second sentence of section (a) of the Rule states that the requirement of authentication of the evidence is satisfied if counsel can introduce evidence sufficient to support a finding. Thus, if a reasonable jury can find the tests to be

A. The Judge, the Jury, Relevancy, and Authentication

reasonable psychological tools, which is what the expert claims, it would seem that the evidence should be admitted. The problem is that nothing in the Advisory Committee's Note indicates that this radical change is intended. There are indications that the Rule is designed to simplify the authentication process. But it would be odd if the preexisting process of authenticating tests, experiments, research methods, etc., is completely changed by a Rule that does not squarely address the point and which emerges from a history that fails to indicate that this matter was given sufficient thought. Rule 702 (Testimony By Experts) offers little assistance on this point. Nor does Rule 703.

Another example may help to illustrate the problem with the Rule. Because of the tape recordings made at the White House under former President Nixon, many lawyers, Judges, and scholars have turned their attention to the requirements of authenticating a tape recording. Before the Federal Rules, it was clear that the Judge had to make a finding that the tapes were sufficiently accurate and reliable to be admitted into evidence. Apparently, Rule 901(a) only requires that the Judge ensure that there is enough evidence so that a reasonable jury could find that the tapes are accurate. For a case using this analysis, see United States v. Scully, 546 F.2d 255 (9th Cir. 1976). Was this intended by the drafters? There is no certain way of knowing. Note that, no matter what this Rule requires, federal statutory requirements (e.g., 18 U.S.C. §2518(a) [which regulates the use of information obtained by wiretaps]) may impose extra authentication requirements.

One more example should remove all doubts that there is a problem here. In a typical narcotics case—one, for example, where the defendant is charged with possession of heroin—before the prosecutor is permitted to introduce the narcotics in common law jurisdictions, he is required to demonstrate a chain of custody. Rule 901(b)(1) provides that one of the ways of authenticating evidence is to introduce the testimony of a witness with knowledge. The Advisory Committee's Note states that this subsection contemplates a broad spectrum of evidence including the traditional chain of custody evidence. The problem, however, is that Rule 901(a) can easily be read as doing away with any chain of custody requirement. In pointing this out, we do not intend to suggest that some modification of the traditional requirement would be unwise. We point this out for the purpose of demonstrating that there is a problem in interpretation. Whenever these Rules are applied in a criminal case involving narcotics, the Judge may be called upon to determine whether any chain of custody must be demonstrated. If he interprets Rule 901(a) to permit a loose presentation with gaps that ordinarily would not be allowed, he runs the risk of reversal. The Advisory Committee and the Congress have failed to provide definitive guidance to the Judge in determining what the Rule really means. . . .

A respected Federal Judge has co-authored the following description of Rule 901:

The draftsmen opted to treat authentication and identification as specialized rules of relevance. . . .

This rule does not ignore or repudiate the policy justifications for the authentication requirement. It simply recognizes that where the question is one of probative force or credibility—as it necessarily always is with questions of authenticity and identity—the jury is as competent as the Court.

5 J. Weinstein and M. Berger, Weinstein's Evidence 901(9)[02].

Since the Judge served on the Advisory Committee, he may be correct as to what the Committee intended, although it is by no means clear that Congress was knowledgeable as to this intent when it codified the Rule.

Assuming the accuracy of the description of the intent, we respectfully disagree with the statement of the distinguished author that the Rule envisioned by the Advisory Committee comports with all of the policies underlying all authentication requirements.

We begin with the premise that the confusion found in Rule 901 derives from the confusion that exists even in common law jurisdictions over whether authentication is a problem involving a question of "competency" which must be resolved by preliminary factfinding and decisionmaking by the Trial Judge, or whether it involves a question of conditional relevancy which requires that the Judge only ensure that a *prima facie* case is made before leaving the matter to the jury to resolve. . . . Problems of how to qualify the results of a scientific test, how to justify introduction of an experiment, how to authenticate a tape recording, and how to establish a chain of custody do not lend themselves to one simple solution. In fact, common law jurisdictions, without saying as much, have divided up authentication problems so that some are really problems of relevancy and some involve requirements of preliminary factfinding and judicial screening to insure a minimal level of reliability and safety. Requirements like the chain of custody requirement, for example, are designed to ensure that unnecessary doubts concerning the identity of an object are removed. To eliminate the requirement and to substitute a relevance approach is to change the amount of care required of a party, especially the government in a criminal case. Similarly, to say that a tape recording can be admitted without a preliminary showing that the machine was in good working order, and perhaps also that no one tampered with the tape, is to say that Rule 901 is not as concerned with screening highly powerful evidence in a reasonably careful way as was the common law rule.

We believe that the Advisory Committee's intent is at odds with recent efforts of the Supreme Court to provide minimal guarantees of reliability before certain evidence is offered in a criminal case. See, e.g., Manson v. Braithwaite, 432 U.S. 98 (1977).

Even the text of Rule 901 casts doubt on the proposition that it requires only a bare showing of relevance, and never more, when evidence is authenticated or identified. If this were the case, why would Rule 901(b)(2)

A. The Judge, the Jury, Relevancy, and Authentication

intimate that a nonexpert who becomes familiar with handwriting for purposes of pending litigation should not be permitted to authenticate a challenged writing? We think the rationale for this Rule is that a nonexpert with an interest in litigation might be affected by bias. Since an expert could be retained, there is little reason to assume this risk. If relevance were the sole test, however, any witness with knowledge, no matter how or when it was obtained, ought to be able to identify handwriting.

Consider also Rule 901(b)(6). Assume that a person answers the phone and identifies himself as "John Steven" and that the government later charges someone named John Steven with conspiracy and that proof that he received the call would be helpful to the government's case. The Rule suggests that a jury cannot receive evidence of the conversation on the basis of this foundation. It requires more. In fact, most courts have required something more for some time. But have they done it because they believe that the evidence is not relevant? We think not. Our view is that they recognize how easy it is for one person to say he is someone else and how attractive it might be for people to do just that if it became clear that any statement of identification could be used in litigation against the person identified.

Finally, examine the ancient documents provision in Rule 901(b)(8). If a document is 10 years old, and otherwise meets the standard of the Rule, it is not admitted. Certainly a simple relevance analysis cannot explain this. In our view, the reason that courts demand something more than minimal relevance in some contexts is that the absence of some reliability standard might readily lead to fabrication. . . .

With all due respect, we respectfully submit that there is a better way than this to resolve the problem of how to interpret the Rule. We do not suggest that this is the only way, nor that it is necessarily correct, but we do think it has some merit and is consistent with the thrust of the entire body of the Federal Rules.

Since Rule 104 does not appear to modify the common law, and since Rule 901 does not appear to modify Rule 104, there is no reason to believe that Rule 901 should not be read as codifying a good portion of the common law. The lesson of Rule 901 is that there is more than one way to authenticate evidence. But when it comes to the question of whether the Judge must make a preliminary determination before admitting evidence, as opposed to simply deciding there is enough for the jury to decide whether to rely on the evidence, the best reading of Rule 901 would be to follow the common law, and to modify it in the light of reason and experience. Given that there is no evidence that anyone who played a major part in the drafting of this Rule explicitly stated that the common law would be drastically modified and the supervisory role of the Trial Judge drastically reduced, Judges should await more specific instructions from the Congress or the Supreme Court before abandoning the supervisory role that they played under the common law rules. . . .

Some cases decided under the common law rules have established more stringent foundation requirements for the introduction of tape recordings. In United States v. McMillan, 508 F.2d 101 (8th Cir. 1974), *cert. denied*, 421 U.S. 916 (1975) and United States v. Hassell, 547 F.2d 1048 (8th Cir. 1977), the Court of Appeals established requirements for laying a proper foundation for the introduction of recorded telephone conversations that appear to be more onerous than Rule 901 would seem to require on its face.

Other cases decided both before and after the effective date of the Rules, have suggested that courts will support the view that we urge, which is to follow preexisting common law rules. In United States v. Haldeman, 559 F.2d 31 (D.C. Cir. 1976), *cert. denied*, 431 U.S. 933 (1977), the Court of Appeals held that tape recordings can be admitted with a foundation that eliminates possibilities of misidentification and adulteration "not absolutely, but as a matter of reasonable probability." . . .

The cases appear to be going more in Judge Weinstein's direction than that of Saltzburg and Redden in viewing FRE 901 as a sweeping change of the old common law requirements of authentication. Notwithstanding the wisdom of their views, such a trend is consistent with one of the major thrusts of the Federal Rules, which was to liberalize the admission of evidence. Compare the implications of Rule 901 with FRE 403, for example. What emerges is a general principle that strongly favors the admissibility of evidence. Rule 901 advances that principle by reducing the impediments to admissibility contained within many of the common law's technical requirements for admission. Consider the treatment of the 901 issue in the following cases, paying more attention to the manner in which the courts approach the issue than to the specific conclusions reached.

UNITED STATES v. CARRIGER
592 F.2d 312 (6th Cir. 1979)

LIVELY, Circuit Judge. The defendant was convicted by a jury of evading income taxes for the year 1971. The jury acquitted him of the same charge for 1972. The government sought to prove by the net worth method[1] that Carriger substantially understated his taxable income on the returns which he filed for each of the taxable years for which he was indicted. Prosecution witnesses testified that the defendant owed approximately $13,000 more federal income tax for 1971 than he paid.

---

1. The net worth method was described in detail by the Supreme Court, and its use in tax evasion prosecutions approved in Holland v. United States, 348 U.S. 121 (1954).

A. The Judge, the Jury, Relevancy, and Authentication

I

The net worth method of proof requires the government to establish a taxpayer's "opening net worth" with reasonable certainty. This consists of the taxpayer's assets, at cost, less his liabilities on the last day of the year preceding the one for which taxable income is being reconstructed. The next step involves an analysis of expenditures of the taxpayer during the taxable year and a determination of his net worth at the end of that year. If the net worth at the end of the year plus non–tax-deductible expenditures during the year [minus "opening net worth"] exceeds the amount of taxable income reported, there is an inference that additional taxable income was received. The government must investigate all leads furnished by a taxpayer to explain expenditures or increases in net worth in order to negate the existence of non-taxable sources.

On appeal Carriger contends that the district court erred in excluding evidence by which the defendant sought to attack the accuracy of the prosecution's opening net worth calculation and analysis of 1971 income. In his opening statement counsel for Carriger stated that the defense would show that the defendant's brother paid large amounts of money to the defendant in 1971 and that two promissory notes dated in 1970 were evidence that his brother owed the defendant $24,000.

The defendant's daughter testified that she saw her father count out a large sum of money and hand it to her uncle in 1969 or 1970. An apparently disinterested witness testified that in the spring or summer of 1971 he saw the defendant's brother push a pile of money toward the defendant. Describing the transaction the witness said, ". . . he hollered out ten thousand, and 'Here's the rest' and pushed it to Leland (the defendant), you know." Prior to presenting the above testimony the defendant had sought to introduce as exhibits two promissory notes. Both notes were signed by Vernon Carriger, identified as defendant's brother, and Valada Mason. Both notes were payable to Leland Carriger in annual installments of $1000. One note, for $10,000, was dated March 2, 1970; the other for $14,000, was dated September 10, 1970. The government objected to the introduction of the notes and the objection was sustained.

The promissory notes were first offered during the testimony of an attorney who had represented the defendant's brother and had seen the notes in his office, probably in 1971. Though the witness stated that he was familiar with Vernon Carriger's signature, he was not permitted to testify that the signature on the two notes appeared to be that of Vernon Carriger. The notes were next offered as exhibits during the testimony of another attorney who stated that he represented Vernon Carriger for seven or eight years and had also represented the defendant in tax matters. The witness testified that he was able to recognize the signatures of Vernon Carriger and the other signer of the note, Valada Mason. The witness was not permitted to testify that the signatures on the notes were those of Vernon Carriger and Valada Mason because the district court concluded that there was "no foundation at all" for such testimony. Following this ruling the witness testified that he had seen both signers of the two notes sign their names hundreds of times. He was then permitted to identify the signatures on the notes as those of Vernon Carriger and Valada Mason.

When the two notes were again offered in evidence the objection of government counsel was sustained and they were excluded. The district court held that the tendered exhibits had been adequately identified as purporting to be two promissory notes payable to the defendant and signed by his brother and Valada Mason. However, in concluding that the notes were relevant, but not material, the trial judge stated: "There has been no witness here that has testified as to the purpose, or the execution of these, what the consideration was, why the notes were transferred, how it is material to this lawsuit, how it accounts for any asset or anything else." The court then indicated that the notes could be made material by the testimony of any of the three parties to them or by a lawyer who prepared the notes and could identify the transaction of which they were a part.

The district court correctly determined that the promissory notes were relevant evidence. [See] Rule 401. Since the government's opening net worth contained no indebtedness from Vernon Carriger to the defendant, the notes at least had a tendency to make more probable the fact as claimed by the defendant that the opening net worth was inaccurate for failure to include assets owned by him on December 31, 1970. They also tended to make more probable the claim that some of the defendant's 1971 expenditures came from a non-taxable source—the repayment of a preexisting debt. Since Rule 402, Fed. R. Evid., makes all relevant evidence admissible unless otherwise provided, we must determine whether any exception applies.

In excluding the notes the district court held that they were not material. The Note of Advisory Committee on Proposed Rules appended to Rule 401 criticizes the word *material* as "loosely used and ambiguous." The word *material* does not appear in the Federal Rules and appears to be subsumed into the language of Rule 401, "any fact that is of consequence to the determination of the action." Since the promissory notes related to the central issues in the case they should not have been excluded on grounds of materiality.

In overruling Carriger's motion for a new trial the district court held that "the promissory notes were properly excluded since no foundation was laid for their admission into evidence; . . . ." In its brief the government equates this language with a holding that the notes were excluded for lack of authentication. [See] Rule 901.

The Note of the Advisory Committee appended to Rule 901 states, "Authentication and identification represent a special aspect of relevancy." This comment ties Rule 901 to Rule 104(b), which deals with the admission of evidence where relevancy depends upon fulfillment of a condition of fact. Under this rule the district court was required to make a preliminary deter-

A. The Judge, the Jury, Relevancy, and Authentication 179

mination of whether there was sufficient evidence "to support a finding that the matter in question is what its proponent claims." Rule 901(a). The requirement of the illustration in Rule 901(b)(2) was clearly satisfied by the testimony of the witness who was familiar with the handwriting and signatures of both signers of the notes.

The government argues that exclusion of the notes from evidence was proper because defendant failed to present testimony of a witness with knowledge "that a matter is what it is claimed to be." Rule 901(b)(1). This argument echoes the statement of the district court that testimony concerning the underlying transaction was required to make the notes admissible. Actually the notes were sufficiently identified as promissory notes by their production and no further authentication was required by reason of an applicable provision for self-authentication in Rule 902(9) [which provides for self-authentication of "commercial paper, signatures thereon, and documents relating thereto to the extent provided by general commercial law"].

The Advisory Committee Note and the Report of the House Committee on the Judiciary indicate that "general commercial law" refers to the Uniform Commercial Code. Under Uniform Commercial Code §3-307 mere production of a note is *prima facie* evidence of its validity and of the holder's right to recover on it.

We conclude that the district court erred in requiring further authentication of the promissory notes. Actually, no testimony was required to establish the genuineness of the signatures on the notes. In effect UCC §3-307 creates a presumption that commercial paper offered in evidence is authentic and Rule 902 dispenses with a requirement of extrinsic evidence for admissibility. By requiring proof of the underlying transaction as a condition for admission the district court denied the defendant the benefit of the rule. Of course, admission of the notes would not have established their genuineness or the existence of an indebtedness conclusively. As the Advisory Committee Note states, "in no instance is the opposite party foreclosed from disputing authenticity." In effect the district court required the defendant to prove that the notes were genuine and that a debt existed, whereas only a *prima facie* showing was required to make them admissible. . . .

The judgment of the district court is reversed, and the cause is remanded for a new trial.

ALEXANDER DAWSON, INC. v. NLRB
586 F.2d 1300 (9th Cir. 1978)

PER CURIAM: Alexander Dawson, Inc. (the company), pursuant to section 10(f) of the National Labor Relations Act, petitioned for review of an order of the National Labor Relations Board which found that the company had violated section 8(a)(1) and 8(a)(3) of the Act, 29 U.S.C. §158(a)(1) and (3). The Board cross-petitioned for enforcement. We find that the order is supported by substantial evidence and therefore dismiss the petition for review and grant the Board's petition for enforcement.

FACTS

In 1974 the company began construction of a restaurant and lounge in Las Vegas, Nevada. The company admittedly intended to operate the restaurant on a nonunion basis and so informed its management and supervisors. It realized that maintaining nonunion status could prove difficult because most such establishments in the Las Vegas area were organized and under contract with the Culinary Workers Union. The company consulted attorneys for advice as to how to maintain nonunion status and sent a representative to a conference on that topic. The company informed its supervisors of its desire to remain nonunion and emphasized its policy during the interviewing and hiring processes.

In June, 1975, the Culinary Workers Union Local 226 and the Bartender's Union Local 165 initiated organizational efforts and demanded recognition as representatives of the company's employees. In July, the Local Joint Executive Board of the unions filed an unfair labor practice charge with the Board alleging that the company had violated section 8(a)(1) and 8(a)(3) of the Act, 29 U.S.C. §158(a)(1) and (3) by: (1) interrogating applicants for employment concerning their union sympathies and activities, (2) granting tip subsidies to employees to dissuade them from supporting the union, and (3) discriminating on the basis of union activities by refusing to hire applicants with prior union affiliation or activities.

The Administrative Law Judge (ALJ) found that the company had violated the Act by interrogating employees, granting tip subsidies to discourage union support and by refusing to hire 18 applicants because they were union members or had previously worked in union establishments. He found the evidence insufficient to establish an unlawful refusal to hire as to three other applicants and no improper motive in the discharge of another employee. . . .

The Board adopted the findings and conclusions of the ALJ as to the violations of the Act. . . . Under the order of the ALJ adopted by the Board, the company was required: (1) to cease and desist from interrogating employees, granting tip subsidies and refusing to hire applicants on the basis of their union sympathies, (2) to offer the specified applicants employment in the positions in which they would have been hired absent discrimination and to make them whole through back pay, and (3) to post the usual notices.

I

The company contends that it was error for the Board to find that it had unlawfully refused to hire applicants Dunkle, Hardson, Walters, Chandler,

A. The Judge, the Jury, Relevancy, and Authentication

Mighell, Lewman and Russo, since the finding was based solely on what it argues were improperly admitted, unauthenticated job application forms. These applicants did not testify at the hearing but application forms completed in their names were admitted into evidence. The company contends that the record does not contain any evidence concerning the authorship of the applications and that in the absence of such evidence the writings are not authenticated and are therefore inadmissible.

The ALJ found the documents to be admissible under Rule 901(a) of the Federal Rules of Evidence, which states: "The requirement of authentication or identification as a condition precedent to admissibility is satisfied by evidence sufficient to support a finding that the matter in question is what its proponent claims."[1] The Board specifically agreed with the ALJ's finding of admissibility under Rule 901(a).

The issue for the trial judge under Rule 901 is whether there is *prima facie* evidence, circumstantial or direct, that the document is what it is purported to be. If so, the document is admissible in evidence. It then remains for the trier of facts to make its own determination of the authenticity of the admitted evidence and the weight which it feels the evidence should be given. . . .

The ALJ's finding was based on the similarity of the challenged applications to those filed by applicants who testified and authenticated their own applications. He also noted that the company did not present any evidence to contradict this *prima facie* evidence of authenticity and did not attempt to prove the applications were fraudulently prepared.

The company challenges this basis of authentication, which it terms "authentication by similarity of underlying form," urging there is no such concept. We disagree, based on our understanding of the ALJ's reasoning. The content of a document, when considered with the circumstances surrounding its discovery, is an adequate basis for a ruling admitting it into evidence.

While no witness could specifically testify as to the chain of custody of the seven applications in question (or, indeed, as to the chain of custody of any particular application), the testimony was that a number of applications had (without authority) been taken from the company's premises by two of its employees and given to the union, who then gave them to the General Counsel for the Board. Eleven of the applications in this group were identified by the applicants. It was reasonable for the ALJ to conclude that since all the applications appeared to come from the same source and were on the same form, and since the majority were conceded to be authentic applications for employment, a *prima facie* case of authenticity was established as to the seven remaining documents. We conclude that the ALJ did not abuse his

---

1. The Federal Rules of Evidence are applicable to Board proceedings "so far as practicable." 29 U.S.C. §160(b).

discretion in finding *prima facie* evidence of authenticity and did not err in admitting the applications into evidence.[2]

PROBLEMS

1. Joe Rodgers was injured in 1986 while using an electrical industrial hoist manufactured in 1943 by Smo, Inc. While lifting a heavy concrete form, a "limit switch" failed to stop the upward motion of the hoist, thus causing the cable to snap and the concrete form to fall on Rodgers' foot. Originally the hoist contained a reversing function designed to automatically lower the load being lifted by the hoist in the event the "limit switch" failed. There was no evidence as to the hoist's whereabouts from 1943 until 1976, at which time Rodgers' employer, Concrete Systems, purchased the hoist from New England Manufacturing, a now defunct business. The hoist had been rebuilt to some extent, and the circuitry for the reversing function had been removed. Rodgers sues Smo, Inc., claiming (1) that the literature accompanying the hoist in 1943 inadequately warned users about the reversing function of the limit switch, and (2) that Smo, Inc. breached a continuing duty to warn by failing to provide Concrete Systems with revised literature, a 1980 manual, which explicitly identified the reversing element of the switch.

Rodgers argues that the 1980 manual was the only available evidence of post-sale recognition by Smo, Inc. of the inadequacy of its original literature. Smo, Inc. objects to the admission of the 1980 manual, arguing that the original literature provided adequate warning and that it had no continuing duty to warn Concrete Systems because Smo, Inc. did not know that Concrete Systems possessed the 1943 hoist. Peter D. Grate, the president of Concrete Systems, testifies that he "assumes" he telephoned Smo, Inc. when he bought the hoist, basing his assumption on the fact that he had a "Smo Spare Parts Bulletin" in his files. Nevertheless, Grate concedes that he has no specific recollection of telephoning Smo, Inc. Should the manual be admitted? Suppose Grate remembers contacting Smo, Inc. and informing them that he obtained the hoist. What result?

2. John Carbone is charged with bank fraud and conspiracy to commit bank fraud. At trial, Carbone professes an inability to recall a telephone conversation between him and an alleged co-conspirator. The prosecution, seeking to "refresh his recollection," has him listen to a tape recording of the conversation with a private listening device. After listening to the tape, Carbone denies its authenticity, claiming that the voice on the tape is not

---

2. The ALJ did not misplace the burden of proof on the question of authenticity by noting that the company did not present evidence raising any question concerning the authorship of the applications. Once *prima facie* evidence of authenticity was presented the question of authenticity was before the finder of fact and it remained for the company to rebut the General Counsel's *prima facie* case.

A. The Judge, the Jury, Relevancy, and Authentication

his. The prosecution offers the tape to the judge, asking him to listen to it for voice identification. At sidebar, the judge states "it is clear that it is Mr. Carbone's voice." The prosecution offers the tape into evidence. Defense counsel objects. What result? What if the trial judge was unsure whether the voice on the tape was Mr. Carbone's, at which point the prosecution says "we will introduce expert testimony as to the tape's authenticity." What result?

3. Rizzo Rat was shot while exiting a bar late one night. As he was being transported to the hospital, he said to one of the paramedics, "Doc, I feel pretty bad, but I've felt worse. This is nothing compared to the time in Detroit when I got shot five times. How bad does it look to you, Doc?" The paramedic responded, "Well, you've lost a lot of blood and from the looks of the wound the bullet could be lodged close to your heart." "You don't mean I'm going to die, do you?" screamed Rizzo. "I can't die, Doc, I can't die. Tin Pan Timmy did this to me, Doc, and I can't die until I get even." "I didn't say you were going to die," said the paramedic, "I just said you had lost a lot of blood and I'm worried about where the bullet is lodged." "Doc, Doc, you're right, I don't think I'm going to make it, Doc. Look, Doc, don't let him get away with this if I die, OK Doc? Promise? Don't let him get away with it." At that, Rizzo lapsed into unconsciousness, from which he never recovered.

Tin Pan Timmy was charged with murdering Rizzo Rat. At trial, the prosecution called the paramedic to testify to the conversation he had with Rizzo in the ambulance on the theory that Rizzo made his statements in contemplation of death, and therefore they are within the dying declaration exception to the hearsay rule. The defense objects, arguing that "there is no proof that Rizzo knew he was dying." "That's for the jury to decide," asserted the prosecution. Is it? If it is, how should the judge instruct the jury on the matter?

4. Dick Naxin was on trial for conspiracy to import illegal drugs. At trial, the prosecution wished to produce a tape recording of a conversation between a Jim Booha and Mr. X, the alleged kingpin of the conspiracy; the theory of admission was the co-conspirator's exception to the hearsay rule. Booha and Mr. X discussed at length the manner in which Naxin should smuggle the drugs across the border. During the conversation, Booha and Mr. X also talked of matters that only an intimate of Dick Naxin would know. In addition to the tape, the government had evidence that Naxin had purchased airplane tickets and taken other steps that appeared consistent with the directives implicit in the conversation of Booha and Mr. X. Naxin objected to the admission of the tape on the ground that there had been no proof that he was part of this conspiracy. The government responded by asserting that the tape was proof enough, and in any event some of what was on the tape had been corroborated by independent evidence. How should the trial court rule?

5. Decedent was driving his tractor-trailer rig when it jack-knifed on

the highway, sideswiped a guardrail, and collided with an overpass support. The fuel tank ruptured and caught fire, and flames engulfed the cab area. The severe burns he received caused his death nine days later. A wrongful death action was brought against the manufacturer of the tractor-trailer by Decedent's wife. At trial, defendant offered the testimony of Melvin Myles (a friend of Decedent) and Decedent's wife. The plaintiff objected to Myles being allowed to testify. A hearing was held out of the presence of the jury. Myles testified that he visited Decedent two or three days after the accident and that Decedent told him how the accident occurred. Decedent told Myles that as he was approaching a "real bad curve in the road," his pants had caught on fire from cigarette ashes. As he tried to put the fire out, he lost control of the tractor-trailer and hit the bridge abutment and then the truck caught on fire. The defendant asserted that this statement is not excluded by the hearsay rule, with which the plaintiff agrees. However, the plaintiff argued that Decedent was not competent when the alleged statement was made. According to the plaintiff, Decedent was crazed with pain, and throughout the days following the accident he slipped into and out of consciousness. Even when he was conscious, however, he was in so much pain that he was not mentally competent; therefore, according to the plaintiff, the statement should not come in. The defendant responded by asserting that such matters were for the jury. How should the trial judge handle the matter? What if Decedent survived the fire and had been called as a witness by the defendant to testify about these admissions? Would that make any difference in how the judge should handle the admissibility of the question? Do not worry about the hearsay rule; limit your concern to the relevancy issue.

6. Bill Grimes was injured in an industrial accident and sued his former employer. In order to establish the scope of his damages, he hired a professional video photographer to make a film of him as he went about his everyday affairs. The film, which was taken over an eight-hour period, was 25 minutes long and showed the difficulty with which he performed such everyday functions as driving, operating a fishing reel, and dressing himself. Grimes was also shown hugging his daughter in the film and assisting his quadriplegic brother. Finally, the last five minutes of the film showed Grimes undergoing clinic tests to determine the extent of his injuries. A number of these tests were painful, and Grimes could be seen grimacing as the tests proceeded. When this film was offered at trial, the defense objected. What result?

Suppose the videotape depicted the actions and voices of the plaintiff, his wife, and hospital personnel during a physical therapy session for treatment of burns suffered in the accident and that the tape contained numerous groans, expressions of pain, and wincing facial actions by Grimes, along with scenes showing discolored bandages being removed from his arms. What result?

Suppose that the plaintiff's claim includes the assertion that the accident triggered a severe schizophrenia on his spouse's part resulting from the psy-

A. The Judge, the Jury, Relevancy, and Authentication

chological shock of seeing her husband so badly injured. The wife is declared incompetent and is never present in the courtroom during the trial. After the trial begins, the plaintiff, without notice to the court or to the defendant, videotapes the plaintiff answering questions in his home. The tape also shows the wife to be uncommunicative and partially catatonic, responding to questions with only grunts and groans. Defense counsel objects. What result?

7. Jim Zeal, Stephani Goldstein, and Rhonda Lathrop were sailing a ship, *The Rastafari*. Zeal was the captain and owned the vessel. Goldstein and Lathrop were the crew. They were stopped and boarded by the U.S. Coast Guard on the high seas, some 300 nautical miles southeast of Miama, Florida, and searched. The boarding officers discovered a large quantity of a green leafy substance that turned out to be marijuana. Subsequently, the three were charged with conspiracy to import marijuana into the United States. At trial, the prosecution offered into evidence 11 nautical charts with navigational markings upon them indicating a planned route between Kingston, Jamaica, which the government planned to show was a standard port of call for drug runners, and Miami. The prosecution asserted that the Coast Guard had seized the charts from the boat and that they were relevant to prove the conspiracy of illegal importation. To establish the authenticity of the charts, the prosecution called Ensign Smythe, who testified that he recognized the charts as the ones he seized from the boat and deposited in the safe aboard the Coast Guard cutter. The prosecution also called Agent Orange, who testified that he had brought the charts from the Justice Department offices, where all exhibits are kept pre-trial, to the courthouse. Defense counsel objects to the admissibility of the charts? What result?

In order to link the crew to the conspiracy, the prosecution offered a letter found in the wheelhouse of the *The Rastafari* addressed to all three defendants that read in full: "Dear Grand Banks Lady. I say to you farewell your journey for you carry my greatest treasure. On precious cargo my thoughts are with you. I bid you farewell. Love Julie." The prosecution presented no evidence as to the identity of Julie. Is the letter admissible?

8. Hary Kairys had his U.S. citizenship revoked after the district court found that he had concealed the fact that he had been an armed guard in a Nazi labor camp. To establish that fact, the government relied upon a "personalbogen," which is a German SS identity card. The card bore the defendant's name and his thumbprint, and was found in the Soviet archives in a repository for German SS documents. He appeals on the ground that the government had not authenticated the card, and also asserted that the document was a forgery and contained erasures and inaccuracies. The government also offered into evidence what appeared to be a newspaper dated January 3, 1943, that had an announcement to the effect that Ltd. Kairys had just been transferred to the camp in question. This, too, was objected to on grounds of lack of authentication. What result?

9. Simmons, a longshoreman, sued the owner of a vessel on which he

was allegedly injured. At trial, the owner offered a set of interrogatories purportedly filed by plaintiff in an earlier personal injury action brought by Simmons against the owner of a different vessel. The interrogatories bore the style "James J. Simmons, plaintiff v. Stephen H. Richperson, defendent." The interrogatories did not bear any court stamp and had not been signed or verified by Simmons or his attorney. When asked about them at trial, Simmons denied any knowledge of them. Should they be admitted?

10. Defendant was indicted for illegal manufacture of classified drugs. At trial the government introduced a tape recording between the defendant and one of his suppliers who provided defendant with hard to obtain ingredients from which the defendant manufactured the drugs. The tape was made because the government had discovered the identify of the supplier and had put pressure on him to cooperate, which he agreed to do. At the government's insistance, Supplier called the defendant and recorded the call on tape, while a Drug Enforcement Agency operative listened in. Supplier was killed pre-trial, and the tape was offered through the testimony of the agency operative who testified to how the tape was made, as well as to the fact that it was defendant's voice on the tape. When asked how the tape got from supplier's place of business to the trial, the agent said he did not know. The defense called defendant's father to testify. The father said that to his knowledge the defendant knew nothing about drugs. On cross-examination, his testimony was impeached by calling his attention to a book purportedly authored by the defendant that contained descriptions of drug deals. The father did admit to being familiar with the book, identified the copy presented to him on the stand, and read the title page of the book, where the defendant was identified as the author and as having a copyright in the book. On appeal, defendant asserts the admission of both the tape and the cross-examination on the book were error. What result?

11. Defendant was indicted for cultivation and possession of marijuana. To establish both charges, the prosecution offered photographs that had been seized from defendant's home that showed him posing among tall marijuana plants. The photographs also showed an irrigation device similar to those used on defendant's land, and also depicted certain individuals who had been arrested on or near defendant's land. Defense counsel objected to the admission of the photographs for lack of foundation. What result?

12. The government brought a price fixing charge against D, alleging a conspiracy to fix the price of gasoline. At trial the owner of a gas station testified that D had called him and ordered him to keep his prices high. The owner received a second call 10 minutes later from another of the conspirators who made reference to D's earlier phone call. Should this testimony have been admitted?

13. Sara Barker, a bank teller, is charged with having converted $3000 in travelers's checks. To prove that she signed the checks, the prosecution wants to produce two of her co-workers to testify to the fact that they recognize the handwriting as Barker's. What foundation will the prosecution be required

B. The Best Evidence Rule

to lay before these witnesses will be allowed to testify? Suppose the prosecution wanted to call an expert witness on the matter. What would the foundation be?

14. While waiting for a bus Nanny Johnson met two women who told Nanny that if she "invested" in their company, she would get a five-fold return on her money within six months. Impressed by the possible return on her capital, Nanny agreed to invest, and she and the women went to the main office of her bank to obtain money from Nanny's savings account. Nanny intended to withdraw $25,000, but the bank only had $15,000 in cash. Nanny and the two women proceeded to a branch office, where Nanny withdrew the remaining $10,000, and gave the entire amount to the two women. The two women absconded with the money, but were later caught and charged with obtaining money under false pretenses. At trial, the state produced photographs taken at both banks by automatic surveillance cameras. The state also offered W1 who testified that the pictures taken at the main office accurately depicted the inside of the bank on the day in question, but the state could not produce a witness to testify to the chain of custody of the photographs from the bank to the trial. The state produced W2 who testified that the photos of the branch bank accurately depicted the inside of the branch bank as of the date he started working at the bank, which was 18 months after the alleged crime. He also was able to testify to how the automatic photographic process worked, but not to the chain of custody of the pictures in question. Should the pictures be admitted?

15. George Salova was charged with the distribution of an obscene film. The film portrayed three adult males engaged in various homosexual activities. Prior to trial, Salova engaged the services of Dr. Dahl to conduct a public opinion poll to determine community standards in the county regarding such depictions. The poll asked the respondents their view of community acceptance of sexually explicit materials, but did not ask whether the respondents themselves approved of such matters. In particular, respondents were asked of the community's acceptance of "nudity and actual or pretended sexual activity." These phrases were defined as "total male and/or female nudity, and sexual intercourse including all kinds of sexual variations." Should Dr. Dahl be allowed to testify to the results of the poll? What foundation should first be provided?

B. THE BEST EVIDENCE RULE

Although the Federal Rules have eliminated most of the common law's technical rules concerning the admissibility of various categories of evidence, one of the common law's technicalities was codified in the Federal Rules: Article X creates the federal version of the best evidence rule. At common law, an individual wishing to enter a document into evidence in order to prove the contents of that document had to produce the original or account for its absence. The best evidence rule is another form of a specialized relevancy rule that in many ways is analogous to such matters as chain of custody. When a writing is relied upon, the chances are good that the original will be more trustworthy than a copy. Copies can be adulterated, and the process of copying itself may be not be completely accurate. In order to reduce the possibility of misleading evidence being presented, the common law created a preference for the production of an original document that could be excused only upon quite stringent conditions being met. Those conditions, in essence, were that the proponent never possessed the original or that the original was unavailable for reasons other than the fault of the proponent of the copy.

The best evidence rule has proved to be a pitfall for various reasons. First of all, bear in mind that it is extremely limited. There is no *general* best evidence rule that requires that the "best evidence" of whatever the proponent wishes to prove be offered. Generally speaking, a party may prove its case by any admissible evidence, regardless whether there is other "better" (i.e., more persuasive or reliable) evidence available to the party. The best evidence rule, by contrast, applies only to the offering of a document *in order to prove the contents of the document*. If what is contained in the document may be proved by other means, then the parties may do so. Suppose, for example, that a letter contains an admission by a party that is admissible against that party and would tend to prove liability in a tort suit. If the adversary wishes to rely on the letter to establish the admission, and thus liability, the original of the letter must be produced or accounted for. However, the adversary does not have to rely on the letter and the admission to prove liability. Nor, for that matter, is the letter necessarily required to prove that particular admission. Suppose the writer of the letter said to W, "I am going to write the person I ran over with my car, apologize for doing so, and offer to pay her medical expenses since it was clearly my fault." Assume further that the letter is written. At trial, the admission can be established by the letter, but only if the original is produced or accounted for. However, W can also be called to testify to the oral admission, since W has firsthand knowledge of it. The best evidence rule has no bearing upon W's testimony, and as mentioned above there is no "general" best evidence rule or principle that would prefer the letter as a form of evidence to W's testimony.

Having said just that much about the best evidence rule, you can undoubtedly predict the mess that the common law generated. Does the rule apply only to writings, or alternatively, what is a "writing" for purposes of the rule? When is it necessary to produce a document because of the substantive law? Does the statute of frauds require that written contracts be produced, thus triggering the best evidence rule? What about agreements to sell land? If a writing is going to be used at trial, what is an original? Is a

B. The Best Evidence Rule

copy that is signed, by the use of carbon paper, an original? What about a carbon copy individually signed? What if the parties intended to permit copies to stand as originals? Can the parties by such an act convert a "copy" into an "original"? What are the conditions that excuse producing the original? What if a party inadvertently lost or destroyed the original? If the original is lost, must the *next* best evidence be employed, or will any evidence do? Each of these issues, and many others, produced a plethora of often inconsistent holdings, resulting in a horrible morass. If ever there were an area of the common law that was a testament to the need for statutory change, it was the best evidence rule.

The common law was significantly changed in Article X of the Federal Rules, which you should now carefully consider. FRE 1001 defines various terms. *Writings and recordings* are given a broad definition, and an *original* is defined as the original plus any "counterpart intended to have the same effect by a person executing or issuing it." FRE 1002 provides for the basic best evidence rule, requiring the original of a writing, recording, or photograph, unless an exception is provided. FRE 1003 provides a very important exception that was not known at common law: Duplicates are admissible "to the same extent as an original unless (1) a genuine question is raised as to the authenticity of the original or (2) in the circumstances it would be unfair to admit the duplicate in lieu of the original." FRE 1004 provides the standard catalogue of common law exceptions to the best evidence rule, and the remainder of the rules, with the exception of Rule 1008, deal with various details of which you should be aware but that require no discussion here.

Rule 1008 allocates responsibility for the various preliminary matters associated with Article X. For the most part, the judge is to see that the best evidence rule is administered correctly, and the appropriate standard is that of FRE 104(a). Where, however "an issue is raised (a) whether the asserted writing ever existed, or (b) whether another writing, recording, or photograph produced at the trial is the original, or (c) whether other evidence of contents correctly reflects the contents, the issue is for the trier of fact to determine as in the case of other issues of fact." This allocation is justified by the following comment from the Advisory Committee's Note:

> Most preliminary questions of fact in connection with applying the rule preferring the original as evidence of contents are for the judge, under the general principles announced in Rule 104. Thus, the question whether the loss of the originals has been established, or of the fulfillment of other conditions specified in Rule 1004 is for the judge. However, questions may arise which go beyond the mere administration of the rule preferring the original and into the merits of the controversy. For example, plaintiff offers secondary evidence of the contents of an alleged contract, after first introducing evidence of loss of the original, and defendant counters with evidence that no such contract was ever executed. If the judge decides that the contract was never executed and excludes the secondary evidence, the case is at an end without ever going to the jury on a central issue. . . . The latter portion of the instant rule is designed to

ensure treatment of these situations as raising jury questions. The decision is not one for uncontrolled discretion of the jury but is subject to the control exercised generally by the judge over jury determinations. See Rule 104(b).

The efforts by the drafters explicitly to allocate responsibility is laudable, but not entirely satisfactory. According to Saltzburg and Redden, Federal Rules of Evidence Manual, at 78, the trial court is to determine:

(1) whether an item of evidence is an "original";
(2) whether it qualifies as a duplicate and is thus presumptively admissible;
(3) whether a genuine question is raised as to the authenticity of the original;
(4) whether it would be unfair to admit a duplicate in lieu of an original as provided for in Rule 1003;
(5) whether an original is lost or destroyed;
(6) whether the proponent lost or destroyed evidence in bad faith;
(7) whether an original can be obtained by any available judicial process;
(8) whether proper notice was given a party in control of evidence;
(9) whether evidence goes to a collateral matter or to a controlling issue.

The problem is that some of the judge's tasks overlap with the jury's tasks. Take the simplest example. The jury is to decide if "the asserted writing ever existed" while the judge is to decide if an original is lost or destroyed. But how can the judge decide that an original is lost or destroyed without deciding that an original originally existed? Suppose that P alleges he has an original of a writing, or if it is not an original it is a duplicate. D asserts all originals are lost. Under the rule, the court should decide if all originals are lost, which requires deciding whether this is an original, but the jury is to decide if this is an original. The solution to this problem, presumably, would be for the judge to decide if the writing is a duplicate, and if so admit it if all originals are lost in the judge's view. The jury would then still be permitted to find that what is admitted is or is not the original according to the jury's own lights. If the judge determines that what is offered is not a duplicate, he should admit it nonetheless if there is sufficient evidence to support such a finding (even though the judge disbelieves that evidence) and allow the jury to reach its own conclusion. Indeed, in our view, whenever there is a conflict between the judge's fact finding power over preliminary facts and the jury's role, the solution should be the same: Apply the lower standard of 104(b) and admit the evidence if there is sufficient reason to believe that evidence is what it purports to be (even though the judge does not in fact believe that evidence is what it purports to be). Such an approach

B. The Best Evidence Rule

preserves the jury function, as well as furthers the objective of liberalizing the admission of evidence.

Consider the approach of the court to the best evidence problem in the following case. Reflect also on the complications the rule can generate and see if you can construct an alternative approach to writings that will better secure the goals of the best evidence rule.

SEILER v. LUCASFILM, LTD.
797 F.2d 1504 (9th Cir. 1986)

FARRIS, Circuit Judge:

Lee Seiler, a graphic artist and creator of science fiction creatures, alleged copyright infringement by George Lucas and others who created and produced the science fiction movie *The Empire Strikes Back*. Seiler claimed that creatures known as "Imperial Walkers" which appeared in *The Empire Strikes Back* infringed Seiler's copyright on his own creatures called "Garthian Striders." *The Empire Strikes Back* appeared in 1980; Seiler did not obtain his copyright until 1981....

FACTS

Seiler contends that he created and published in 1976 and 1977 science fiction creatures called Garthian Striders. In 1980, George Lucas released *The Empire Strikes Back*, a motion picture that contains a battle sequence depicting giant machines called Imperial Walkers. In 1981 Seiler obtained a copyright on his Striders, depositing with the Copyright Office "reconstructions" of the originals as they had appeared in 1976 and 1977.

Seiler contends that Lucas' Walkers were copied from Seiler's Striders which were allegedly published in 1976 and 1977. Lucas responds that Seiler did not obtain his copyright until one year after the release of *The Empire Strikes Back* and that Seiler can produce no documents that antedate *The Empire Strikes Back*.

Because Seiler proposed to exhibit his Striders in a blow-up comparison to Lucas' Walkers at opening statement, the district judge held an evidentiary hearing on the admissibility of the "reconstructions" of Seiler's Striders. Applying the "best evidence rule," Fed. R. Evid. 1001-1008, the district court found at the end of a seven-day hearing that Seiler lost or destroyed the originals in bad faith under Rule 1004(1) and that consequently no secondary evidence, such as the post-*Empire Strikes Back* reconstructions, was admissible. In its opinion the court found specifically that Seiler testified falsely, purposefully destroyed or withheld in bad faith the originals, and fabricated and misrepresented the nature of his reconstructions. The district court granted summary judgment to Lucas after the evidentiary hearing.

On appeal, Seiler contends (1) that the best evidence rule does not apply to his works, [and] (2) that if the best evidence rule does apply, Rule 1008 requires a jury determination of the existence and authenticity of his originals. . . .

DISCUSSION

1. APPLICATION OF THE BEST EVIDENCE RULE

The best evidence rule embodied in Rules 1001-1008 represented a codification of longstanding common law doctrine. Dating back to 1700, the rule requires not, as its common name implies, the best evidence in every case but rather the production of an original document instead of a copy. Many commentators refer to the rule not as the best evidence rule but as the original document rule.

Rule 1002 states: "To prove the content of a writing, recording, or photograph, the original writing, recording, or photograph is required, except as otherwise provided in these rules or by Act of Congress." Writings and recordings are defined in Rule 1001 as "letters, words, or numbers, or their equivalent, set down by handwriting, typewriting, printing, photostating, photographing, magnetic impulse, mechanical or electronic recording, or other form of data compilation."

The Advisory Committee Note supplies the following gloss:

> Traditionally the rule requiring the original centered upon accumulations of data and expressions affecting legal relations set forth in words and figures. This meant that the rule was one essentially related to writings. Present day techniques have expanded methods of storing data, yet the essential form which the information ultimately assumes for usable purposes is words and figures. Hence the considerations underlying the rule dictate its expansion to include computers, photographic systems, and other modern developments. . . .

We hold that Seiler's drawings were "writings" within the meaning of Rule 1001(1); they consist not of "letters, words, or numbers" but of "their equivalent." To hold otherwise would frustrate the policies underlying the rule and introduce undesirable inconsistencies into the application of the rule.

In the days before liberal rules of discovery and modern techniques of electronic copying, the rule guarded against incomplete or fraudulent proof. By requiring the possessor of the original to produce it, the rule prevented the introduction of altered copies and the withholding of originals. The purpose of the rule was thus long thought to be one of fraud prevention, but Wigmore pointed out that the rule operated even in cases where fraud was not at issue, such as where secondary evidence is not admitted even though its proponent acts in utmost good faith. Wigmore also noted that if

B. The Best Evidence Rule 193

prevention of fraud were the foundation of the rule, it should apply to objects as well as writings, which it does not. 4 Wigmore, Evidence §1180 (Chadbourn rev. 1972).

The modern justification for the rule has expanded from prevention of fraud to a recognition that writings occupy a central position in the law. When the contents of a writing are at issue, oral testimony as to the terms of the writing is subject to a greater risk of error than oral testimony as to events or other situations. The human memory is not often capable of reciting the precise terms of a writing, and when the terms are in dispute only the writing itself, or a true copy, provides reliable evidence. To summarize then, we observe that the importance of the precise terms of writings in the world of legal relations, the fallibility of the human memory as reliable evidence of the terms, and the hazards of inaccurate or incomplete duplication are the concerns addressed by the best evidence rule.

Viewing the dispute in the context of the concerns underlying the best evidence rule, we conclude that the rule applies. McCormick summarizes the rule as follows: "In proving the terms of a writing, where the terms are material, the original writing must be produced unless it is shown to be unavailable for some reason other than the serious fault of the proponent." McCormick on Evidence §230, at 704. The contents of Seiler's work are at issue. There can be no proof of "substantial similarity" and thus of copyright infringement unless Seiler's works are juxtaposed with Lucas' and their contents compared. Since the contents are material and must be proved, Seiler must either produce the original or show that it is unavailable through no fault of his own. Rule 1004(1). This he could not do.

The facts of this case implicate the very concerns that justify the best evidence rule. Seiler alleges infringement by *The Empire Strikes Back*, but he can produce no documentary evidence of any originals existing before the release of the movie. His secondary evidence does not consist of true copies or exact duplicates but of "reconstructions" made after *The Empire Strikes Back*. In short, Seiler claims that the movie infringed his originals, yet he has no proof of those originals.

The dangers of fraud in this situation are clear. The rule would ensure that proof of the infringement claim consists of the works alleged to be infringed. Otherwise, "reconstructions" which might have no resemblance to the purported original would suffice as proof for infringement of the original. Furthermore, application of the rule here defers to the rule's special concern for the contents of writings. Seiler's claim depends on the content of the originals, and the rule would exclude reconstituted proof of the originals' content. Under the circumstances here, no "reconstruction" can substitute for the original.

Seiler argues that the best evidence rule does not apply to his work, in that it is artwork rather than "writings, recordings, or photographs." He contends that the rule both historically and currently embraces only words or numbers. Neither party has cited us to cases which discuss the applicability of the rule to drawings.

To recognize Seiler's works as writings does not, as Seiler argues, run counter to the rule's preoccupation with the centrality of the written word in the world of legal relations. Just as a contract objectively manifests the subjective intent of the makers, so Seiler's drawings are objective manifestations of the creative mind. The copyright laws give legal protection to the objective manifestations of an artist's ideas, just as the law of contract protects through its multifarious principles the meeting of minds evidenced in the contract. Comparing Seiler's drawings with Lucas' drawings is no different in principle than evaluating a contract and the intent behind it. Seiler's "reconstructions" are "writings" that affect legal relations; their copyrightability attests to that.

A creative literary work, which is artwork, and a photograph whose contents are sought to be proved, as in copyright, defamation, or invasion of privacy, are both covered by the best evidence rule. We would be inconsistent to apply the rule to artwork which is literary or photographic but not to artwork of other forms. Furthermore, blueprints, engineering drawings, architectural designs may all lack words or numbers yet still be capable of copyright and susceptible to fraudulent alteration. In short, Seiler's argument would have us restrict the definitions of Rule 1001(1) to "words" and "numbers" but ignore "or their equivalent." We will not do so in the circumstances of this case.

Our holding is also supported by the policy served by the best evidence rule in protecting against faulty memory. Seiler's reconstructions were made four to seven years after the alleged originals; his memory as to specifications and dimensions may have dimmed significantly. Furthermore, reconstructions made after the release of *The Empire Strikes Back* may be tainted, even if unintentionally, by exposure to the movie. Our holding guards against these problems.

2. RULE 1008

As we hold that the district court correctly concluded that the best evidence rule applies to Seiler's drawings, Seiler was required to produce his original drawings unless excused by the exceptions set forth in Rule 1004. The pertinent subsection is 1004(1), which provides:

> The original is not required, and other evidence of the contents of a writing, recording, or photograph is admissible if
> (1) Originals lost or destroyed. All originals are lost or have been destroyed, unless the proponent lost or destroyed them in bad faith. . . .

In the instant case, prior to opening statement, Seiler indicated he planned to show to the jury reconstructions of his "Garthian Striders" during the opening statement. The trial judge would not allow items to be shown to the jury until they were admitted in evidence. Seiler's counsel reiterated

B. The Best Evidence Rule

that he needed to show the reconstructions to the jury during his opening statement. Hence, the court excused the jury and held a seven-day hearing on their admissibility. At the conclusion of the hearing, the trial judge found that the reconstructions were inadmissible under the best evidence rule as the originals were lost or destroyed in bad faith. This finding is amply supported by the record.

Seiler argues on appeal that regardless of Rule 1004(1), Rule 1008 requires a trial because a key issue would be whether the reconstructions correctly reflect the content of the originals. Rule 1008 provides:

> When the admissibility of other evidence of contents of writings, recordings, or photographs under these rules depends upon the fulfillment of a condition of fact, the question whether the condition has been fulfilled is ordinarily for the court to determine in accordance with the provisions of rule 104. However, when an issue is raised (a) whether the asserted writing ever existed, or (b) whether another writing, recording, or photograph produced at the trial is the original, or (c) whether other evidence of contents correctly reflects the contents, the issue is for the trier of fact to determine as in the case of other issues of fact.[2]

Seiler's position confuses admissibility of the reconstructions with the weight, if any, the trier of fact should give them, after the judge has ruled that they are admissible. Rule 1008 states, in essence, that when the admissibility of evidence other than the original depends upon the fulfillment of a condition of fact, the trial judge generally makes the determination of that condition of fact. The notes of the Advisory Committee are consistent with this interpretation in stating: "Most preliminary questions of fact in connection with applying the rule preferring the original as evidence of contents are for the judge. . . . [T]hus the question of . . . fulfillment of other conditions specified in Rule 1004 . . . is for the judge." In the instant case, the condition of fact which Seiler needed to prove was that the originals were not lost or destroyed in bad faith. Had he been able to prove this, his reconstructions would have been admissible and then their accuracy would have been a question for the jury. In sum, since admissibility of the reconstructions was dependent upon a finding that the originals were not lost or destroyed in bad faith, the trial judge properly held the hearing to determine their admissibility. . . .

Affirmed.

PROBLEMS

1. Blair Wythe was suing his former business partner over some deals that had gone sour. While on the stand testifying to conversations that he

---

2. Lucas conceded the originals existed and Seiler conceded the items he sought to introduce were not the originals. Hence, as subsections (a) and (b) are not in issue, Seiler is arguing that 1008(c) requires that the case be submitted to the jury.

and his former partner had concerning those deals, the defense counsel objected on the grounds that stenographers had been present during the conversations and their notes would be the "best evidence of what was said at the meetings." Must the stenographers' notes be produced?

The first trial ended in a mistrial. Prior to the second trial, Wythe died. His estate pursued the cause of action, however. At the second trial, counsel for the plaintiffs produced Mrs. Wythe and asked her if she remembered what testimony Mr. Wythe had given at the first trial. She responded that she did. She was asked to relate what that testimony had been, and defense counsel objected, again on the grounds that the trial transcript would be the best evidence of the testimony. What result?

2. *D* was tried for burglary. At trial, the government offered photographs of jewelry that had been stolen from the victim's home and found in *D's* possession. The owner of the jewelry identified the jewelry in the photographs as the jewelry that had been stolen from him. A police officer testified that all the jewelry in the photographs had been taken from the defendant. *D* objected to all this evidence on the grounds that the jewelry itself should have been produced or its absence explained, and that the failure to produce the items impaired his right to cross-examine the witnesses against him. How should the court rule?

3. The Department of Agriculture brought suit against Farmer MacDonald to recover the value of loans made to MacDonald under the Farmers Home Administration Act on the grounds that MacDonald had falsified information on the loan applications. To establish the falsification required that the government trace MacDonald's use of the loan proceeds through numerous transactions, which turned out to be quite a complicated matter. The result was a voluminous written record running to over 2000 pages, which after being properly authenticated was admitted into evidence. In order to assist the jury in following the testimony by the government agent who had conducted the investigation, five summary charts were prepared that summarized what was in the 2000-page record. In addition to providing a summary of the various transactions, the charts also labeled certain expenditures and transactions as "questionable." The government moved for the admission of the charts into evidence, but the defense objected on the grounds that the underlying data had already been admitted, thus obviating any need for the summaries, and on the further ground that labeling certain transactions and expenditures as "questionable" was improperly argumentative. In any event, argued the defense, the charts were merely "pedagogical" and should not be allowed to go to the jury room. What result?

4. Bill Hardhat, a former steel employee, filed suit alleging that the defendent denied him a promotion because he was of Mexican-American extraction. To prove damages, Hardhat admitted voluminous financial data to establish his income and expenses for the five years preceding the suit. In addition, he offered a "Summary of Actual Damages" that summarized the financial data and contained a section that projected his future losses.

B. The Best Evidence Rule   197

That section assumed that, without discrimination, Hardhat's income would increase at a rate of 7.0 percent per year, and that there would be an inflation rate of 4.5 percent per year. It also assumed that Hardhat would continue his program of home study, thus qualifying himself for future promotions. Is the summary admissible?

5. Jimmy Pobare tripped on a city sidewalk that was in disrepair and injured himself. He sued the city for negligence in maintaining the sidewalk in an unsafe condition and for failing to warn pedestrians of the dangerous condition of the sidewalk. A state law requires that before a municipality may be sued, a potential litigant must first file with the city a notice of intent to sue and receive from the city's legal department a statement as to why the city is not, or does not believe itself to be, liable. The city moved to dismiss the suit for failure to satisfy this requirement. At a hearing of the motion, the plaintiff took the stand and testified that the necessary notice had been filed, and that the city had responded by denying responsibility for the maintenance of the sidewalk in question. The city objected to the testimony on best evidence grounds, and moved again for dismissal. What result?

6. In 1973, an armed gunman approached a bank teller and demanded all the money in her drawer. She gave him all the cash she had, as well as a small quantity of bait money that is kept in each teller's drawer. "Bait money" is currency the serial numbers of which have been recorded so that it can be identified as coming from the bank, and when bait money is removed from its place in the drawer, a silent alarm is triggered. When that occurred, the bank manager was able to observe and record the license number of the car that turned out to be the getaway car. A check of the registration revealed that the car was owned by Charlie Macaroni. A search warrant was issued for Macaroni's house, which turned up no evidence of the robbery. A couple of hundred dollars in currency was discovered on the premises, but it was not evident that the money came from the bank robbery. The officer executing the search recorded the serial numbers of the bills and then left. He later checked those serial numbers against the numbers of the bait money, and two bills matched. Another search warrant was issued, as well as an arrest warrant. Charlie Macaroni was arrested and his house searched once more. The two bills whose serial numbers matched those of the bank were not discovered, however.

Charlie Macaroni was indicted for bank robbery. At trial, the officer who conducted the search was called to testify in order to connect the defendant to the crime through testimony about the bills found during the first search. The defense objected on the basis of the best evidence rule. What result? Does it matter whether the serial numbers are unique or not? Assume they are not, and that the serial numbers on these bills had been used in three separate years, 1934, 1950, and 1969. What would the significance of that be? Would it matter if a government expert testified that the average life of a bill is 3.5 years, and consequently there was little chance that a bill from 1934 or 1950 still was in circulation? What if he testified that 1934 bills are so rare that their value as collector's items is five times their face value, and that 1950 bills are worth between two and three times their face value, thus further decreasing the odds that any such bills were in circulation?

7. Wallace, the president of a private university, was charged with tax fraud. The government alleges that Wallace abused the non-profit education tax status of the university by using university credit cards to make private purchases. In his defense, Wallace offered computer printouts of all expenditures on the cards in question. The printouts also contained brief explanations of the university-related purpose of each expenditure. Should the printouts be admitted over a best evidence objection? What other problems does this evidence present?

8. Flanagan sues Zeppelin Electric Products, Inc., alleging that an oral agreement was made whereby Flanagan would remove gravel from Zeppelin's lot for consideration of $65 per hour. Flanagan and his crew toiled away until the gravel was completely removed. Zeppelin refused to pay Flanagan's bill, disputing the actual number of hours worked. At trial Flanagan offers into evidence a summary of data transcribed from invoices and tally sheets recorded at the worksite, indicating the number of hours worked by each employee. He claims that most of the invoices and tally sheets were discarded or lost. Defense counsel objects on the ground that the "summaries" violate the best evidence rule, claiming that the so-called tally sheets probably never existed. What result?

9. Bob and Bessie Wright sue the Bolt Oil Co. of Tucson for damages connected with the explosion of their motorhome. While traveling, the Wrights had stopped at defendant's service station to have the propane tanks for their stove filled. They allege that the defendant's employee negligently overfilled the tanks, which caused the explosion. At trial, plaintiffs' counsel offered into evidence a photocopy of a transcription of a statement given by the employee. Apparently, one month after the accident, Earle Hunt, an insurance adjuster, had interviewed the employee and tape recorded the statement in question. Hunt testifies that although he was not certain what happened to the particular tape used to record the statement, many times after transcription the tapes were either reused or discarded. Defense counsel objects on best evidence grounds. Admissible?

The following chart schematically orders the various issues we have been addressing.

B. The Best Evidence Rule

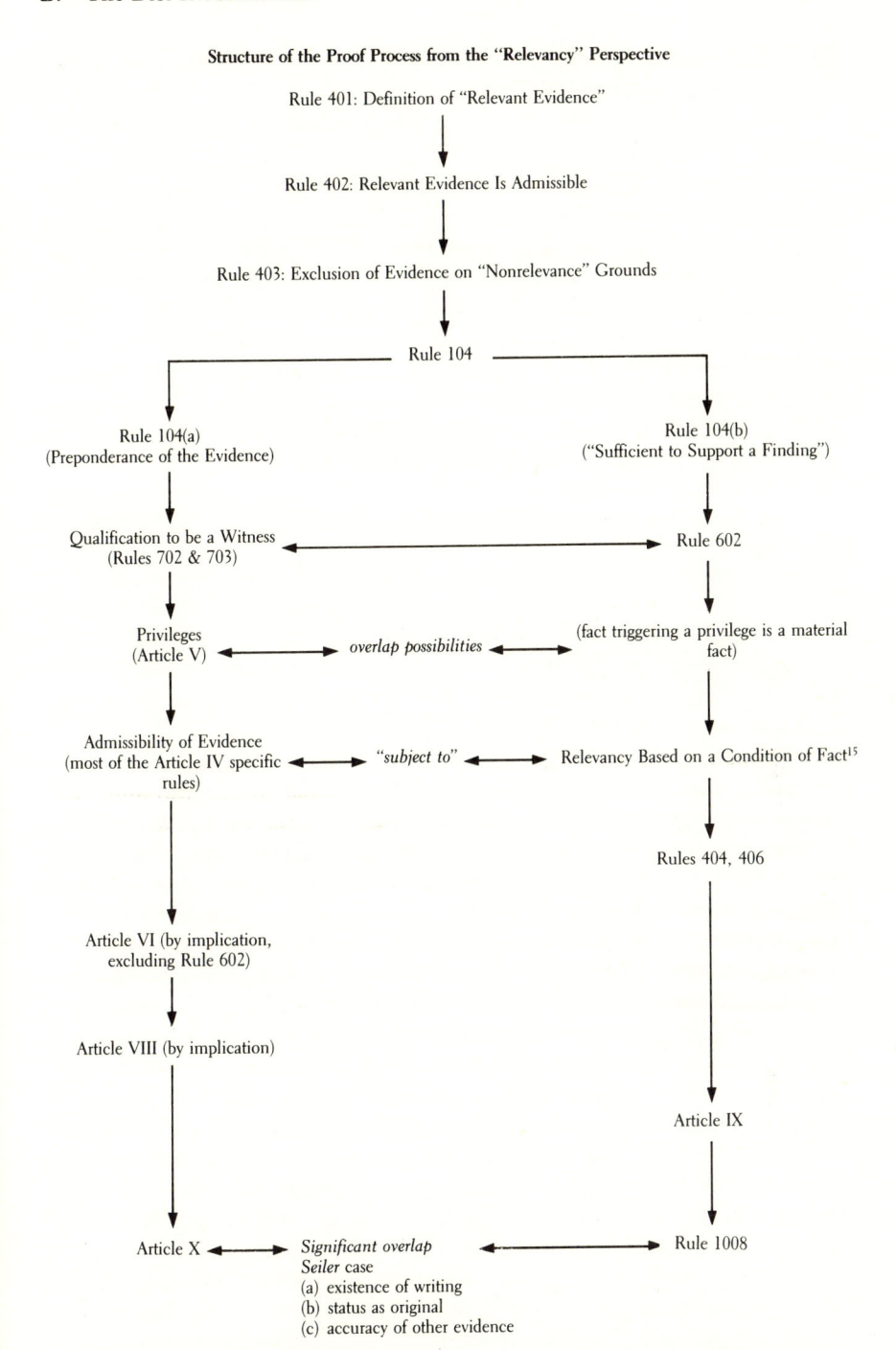

Structure of the Proof Process from the "Relevancy" Perspective

Rule 401: Definition of "Relevant Evidence"
↓
Rule 402: Relevant Evidence Is Admissible
↓
Rule 403: Exclusion of Evidence on "Nonrelevance" Grounds
↓
Rule 104

- Rule 104(a) (Preponderance of the Evidence)
- Rule 104(b) ("Sufficient to Support a Finding")

Rule 104(a) branch:
- Qualification to be a Witness (Rules 702 & 703)
- Privileges (Article V)
- Admissibility of Evidence (most of the Article IV specific rules)
- Article VI (by implication, excluding Rule 602)
- Article VIII (by implication)
- Article X

Rule 104(b) branch:
- Rule 602
- (fact triggering a privilege is a material fact)
- Relevancy Based on a Condition of Fact[15]
- Rules 404, 406
- Article IX
- Rule 1008

Cross-links:
- Qualification to be a Witness ↔ Rule 602
- Privileges ↔ *overlap possibilities* ↔ (fact triggering a privilege is a material fact)
- Admissibility of Evidence ↔ *"subject to"* ↔ Relevancy Based on a Condition of Fact
- Article X ↔ *Significant overlap — Seiler case*
  (a) existence of writing
  (b) status as original
  (c) accuracy of other evidence
  ↔ Rule 1008

15. Presumably this applies to the determination of "relevancy" under FRE 401. Note, however, that the status of FRE 403 is unclear. Is it a 104(a) or a 104(b) question? The cases are not enlightening and merely talk about "judicial discretion" under the rule. For discussion, see note 7 supra.

C. REFLECTIONS ON THE RELATIONSHIP BETWEEN JUDGE AND JURY

The relationship between the judge and the jury is as complicated as the individual life experiences from which the judge and jurors each draw to evaluate the various factual matters that must be resolved during any litigation. In large measure this complex nexus is impossible to capture by the written word, and instead must be observed and experienced. We have tried in this and the preceding chapters to explicate the legal rules and their underlying ideas. What matters, though, is how those ideas are played out in court rooms across the country, and we have given you some examples of that process in the cases and problems. To bring this particular aspect of our inquiry to a close, we ask that you reflect upon the efforts of one of this nation's most distinguished judges to deal rationally with a complex, but not atypical, factual situation and the various evidentiary issues that arise from it.

UNITED STATES v. SLIKER
751 F.2d 477 (2d Cir. 1985)

FRIENDLY, Circuit Judge:

John W. Sliker and Theodore Buchwald appeal from their convictions in the District Court for the Southern District of New York, after a trial before Judge Griesa and a jury, on 19 counts of a 20-count indictment, all related to substantially the same transactions. Excluding the third count, which was dismissed upon the Government's motion, three counts charged the defendants with bank embezzlement in violation of 18 U.S.C. §656, four counts alleged that they committed bank larceny in violation of 18 U.S.C. §2113(b), three counts charged them with transporting stolen property in interstate commerce in violation of 18 U.S.C. §2314, and eight counts alleged that they falsified bank records in violation of 18 U.S.C. §1005. Finally, there was one count alleging a conspiracy to commit these four offenses in violation of 18 U.S.C. §371. Both Sliker and Buchwald received concurrent five-year sentences on the conspiracy and embezzlement charges and on six of the falsification charges; 10 years on each of the larceny and interstate transportation of stolen property charges, also to run concurrently; and five-years' probation for the remaining two falsification counts after they had served these sentences. Carbone received concurrent five-year sentences on each of the first 17 counts, and five-years probation for the final two counts of falsification upon his release from prison. In addition, Carbone was fined $1000 on each of the first 10 counts.

The fraud was perpetrated in January, 1981, through the use of checks issued by the "Bahrain Credit Bank" located in Montserrat, West Indies. In

C. Reflections on the Relationship between Judge and Jury

fact, the bank was a sham, run from the house of Clive Marks, who would claim to represent the bank and would respond affirmatively to inquiries whether the checks were legitimate. By the time it was discovered that the checks were in fact worthless, they would have been cashed.

The Government submitted evidence to establish the following case: In October or November, 1980, defendant Buchwald and Rocco Saluzzi, an unindicted conspirator who was one of the Government's principal witnesses, traveled together from New York to Brussels and endeavored unsuccessfully to use Bahrain Credit Bank checks for the purchase of diamonds. Shortly after their return, Saluzzi met with defendant Carbone, who had apparently helped to finance Saluzzi's Belgian trip, at Carbone's furniture store. Carbone sought permission to give Saluzzi's telephone number to someone whom Carbone wanted Saluzzi to meet. According to Saluzzi, Carbone explained that "(h)e's a pretty interesting guy; he's a good mover of paper and I thought you might want to meet him." Shortly thereafter, Saluzzi received a call from defendant Sliker, who explained that he had obtained Saluzzi's telephone number from Carbone. The two met and Saluzzi told Sliker of his ability to obtain offshore bank checks which could "take" a telephone call or telex; Sliker responded that he had connections for disposing of such checks and encouraged Saluzzi to obtain them as quickly as possible. At a subsequent meeting in Carbone's store, Sliker told Saluzzi that Sliker could "take care of" the checks at the Merchants Bank. According to Saluzzi, Sliker claimed that he could work with Bill Foster, a vice president of the bank, who Sliker stated would be "very cooperative" because Foster was in debt to loansharks for approximately $115,000. Saluzzi then met with Buchwald in order to obtain the checks. Buchwald gave Saluzzi two Bahrain Credit Bank checks, one for $48,760 and the other for $51,240; after Sliker disposed of these as described below, Buchwald gave Saluzzi a third such check for $300,000.

On January 5, 1981, Carbone brought Sliker to the Merchants Bank and introduced him to Foster. Carbone told Foster that Sliker was a good friend and a good businessman and would be a good customer of the Bank. Foster opened an account for Sliker, who deposited $300 in cash.

Sliker returned to the Merchants Bank on January 16, 1981, with a Bahrain Credit Bank check payable to himself in the amount of $48,760, and deposited the check into his account. Foster approved the Bahrain Credit Bank check for immediate credit to enable Sliker to cash a $9,000 personal check; Sliker also opened a savings account by transferring $10,000. Sliker then returned to Carbone's store where Saluzzi was waiting to divide the proceeds. Sliker falsely told Saluzzi he had given $900 to Foster, and another $900 was put aside for Buchwald to give to the source of the checks; the remaining $7,200 was divided equally among Saluzzi, Sliker and Buchwald, who was waiting outside Carbone's store to collect his share. Saluzzi and Buchwald then left together to pay $900 to the source of the checks.

Three days later, on January 19, 1981, Sliker returned to Merchants

Bank and deposited the $51,240 Bahrain Credit Bank check, payable to himself, into his savings account. He then cashed another personal check for $9,000, used a second personal check to purchase a $15,000 Merchants Bank cashier's check payable to an Anthony Filone, and used a third personal check to wire transfer $4,000 to an account at a Maine bank. After these transactions, all but approximately $3,000 of the funds from the first Bahrain Credit Bank check had been removed from Sliker's checking account. Sliker then took the $9,000 he had received in cash and replayed the scenario that had followed the deposit of the first Bahrain Credit Bank check: He met Saluzzi at Carbone's store, falsely told Saluzzi that he had paid Foster $900, put aside another $900 for Buchwald to pay to the source of the checks, and divided the remaining $7,200 in equal shares among himself, Saluzzi and Buchwald; Saluzzi and Buchwald once again left together to pay the source of the checks his share.

On the morning of the next day, January 20, 1981, Foster received a telephone call from an individual purporting to be an officer of the Bahrain Credit Bank, who said he was calling from Montserrat at Sliker's request in regard to three checks the Bahrain Credit Bank had issued to Sliker, the two checks already deposited and another $300,000 check. The caller assured Foster that the checks were properly issued and would be paid on presentation through regular bank channels. That afternoon Sliker went to Merchants Bank with the $300,000 check, payable to himself. He deposited this in his checking account, and Foster approved it for immediate credit. Using a personal check, Sliker purchased five Merchants Bank cashier's checks payable to five different payees, totalling $110,200, and a $100,000 Merchants Bank certificate of deposit; he transferred $60,000 from the checking account into his savings account, and directed that a $10,000 Treasury bill be purchased at the next Federal Reserve auction and paid for with funds from his savings account; finally he cashed another $9,000 personal check. These transactions removed all but approximately $20,000 of the $300,000 from Sliker's checking account. The third $9,000 cash payment was handled in the same fashion as the preceding two. On this occasion Sliker also told Saluzzi that he would give Carbone a few hundred dollars for his part in the scheme.

The scheme was premised on Merchants Bank's sending the checks to Montserrat for processing. The sham bank would then stall or claim never to have received the checks, giving the defendants an opportunity to abscond with the proceeds. With the bad luck which fortunately so often attends criminal enterprises, Foster attempted instead to process the three fraudulent checks through the Federal Reserve Bank. On January 21, 1981, Foster learned that the Federal Reserve Bank, which processes only checks drawn on United States banks, had refused to honor the $48,760 and $300,000 checks deposited by Sliker in his checking account as "not payable in the U.S." Foster also learned that the $51,240 Bahrain Credit Bank check, deposited by Sliker into his savings account, had been refused by the Federal

C. Reflections on the Relationship between Judge and Jury 203

Reserve Bank and, in fact, had already been returned to Merchants Bank. Foster called Sliker who promised to take care of the problem by obtaining new checks or a wire transfer. The next morning, Sliker returned to the Merchants Bank, bringing with him two of the cashier's checks he had obtained on January 20, totalling $42,000. Rather than redepositing these into his checking account, Sliker deposited them into his savings account. He asked Foster to return the $51,240 Bahrain Credit Bank check to him, promising to take it back to the people who had given it to him and obtain a new check on a United States bank or a wire transfer. Foster did so, but agreed to return the other two checks to Sliker when these had been returned to the Merchants Bank only after Sliker had covered the remaining overdraft in the checking account. Foster also asked Sliker to stop writing checks on this account until the matter was resolved. Without Foster's knowledge, however, Sliker returned to the bank that same afternoon and cashed a $7500 check with approval from another officer. Five days later, on January 27, Sliker brought Foster $7500 in cash for deposit into Sliker's checking account; he told Foster that he had obtained the money by collecting on a debt. Despite Foster's request, Sliker continued to write checks on this account.

Of course, these events made depositing any more Bahrain Credit Bank checks at Merchants Bank impossible. However, Sliker did not inform his co-conspirators of the problem, and, to prevent them from learning of it, he was forced to go through the motions one more time. When he returned from the bank empty-handed, Sliker concocted a story that he had seen FBI agents talking to Foster, and that Foster had waved him off; Saluzzi told this to Buchwald. Soon after these events, Saluzzi left New York and lost touch with Sliker, Buchwald and Carbone. Buchwald, in the meantime, was arrested on January 22 by the FBI on unrelated charges. In his possession were a $50,000 Bahrain Credit Bank "Official Bank Draft" and a slip of paper with "Bill," "Merchants Bank NY," and Foster's telephone number on it.[1]

Sliker called Foster on January 30, 1981, promising that a $225,000 wire transfer would arrive from Morgan Guaranty Trust Company. No transfer arrived that day, but Foster credited Sliker's account with that amount anyway. When the transfer still had not been made by February 2, after trying unsuccessfully to contact Sliker, Foster went to Carbone's store and spoke with Carbone about the Bahrain Credit Bank checks. Foster described Carbone as "in shock" and as saying, "I told Jack not to fool around in the bank." Foster also testified that Carbone said he would try to get hold of Sliker and would do his best to straighten out the problem. Foster continued to hide the loss by periodically shifting it among various accounts, but told Carbone and Sliker that something had to be done quickly. In the meantime, Foster took steps to reduce the size of the deficit. Using money Sliker obtained from a friend, as well as the principal from the $100,000 certificate of deposit

---

1. The $50,000 check was one that Buchwald had taken to Belgium for use in his aborted attempt to purchase diamonds.

Sliker had purchased on January 20, Foster reduced the overdraft to approximately $80,000.

Early in July, Carbone requested that Foster come by his store to meet someone, who turned out to be Buchwald. Carbone asked Foster to tell Buchwald what had happened. Foster "gave him the whole story," explaining that Sliker had said that the three bank checks were supposed to represent "a gold transaction." Buchwald replied that "Sliker is full of shit." In November, 1981, Foster resigned from the Merchants Bank. Shortly thereafter he visited Carbone at a restaurant owned by Carbone in Pennsylvania. While Foster was there, Sliker telephoned Carbone and Foster spoke with him. Foster asked Sliker to repay the $80,000 still owed the bank; Sliker requested him to destroy the records or "bury it" at the bank.

Buchwald testified in his own defense. He took the position that although he knew the checks were phoney and were being used to perpetrate a fraud, he did not know that they were to be used to defraud a bank. Carbone also testified and also called three other witnesses. He claimed to have had no knowledge of the fraudulent plan until after it had occurred. Sliker rested his case without testifying or calling any witnesses.

DISCUSSION

Appellants have made numerous challenges to their convictions. We shall . . . deal with issues raised by and relating to each of them individually. . . .

II. Issues Raised by Buchwald . . .

B. *The Bahrain Credit Bank Records*

Buchwald's [complaint] relates to the admission in evidence of papers seized by the Royal Montserrat Police in executing a search warrant on the "Bahrain Credit Bank," which turned out to be the home of Clive Marks, on May 2, 1981. The records included a telephone and address book in which Buchwald's name and telephone number were recorded; a telex relating to Buchwald's Belgian diamond deal; a ledger and index cards that recorded numerous checks issued by the Bahrain Credit Bank, including the three checks deposited by Sliker at Merchants Bank and the check seized from Buchwald incident to his arrest; and a yellow pad diary with several references to Buchwald, Foster, Sliker and the three checks deposited at Merchants Bank. The records were admitted in connection with the testimony of Deputy Superintendent Griffith of the Montserrat Police, who testified that he seized them in the course of his search of Marks' house, and that Marks had been present throughout the search. Griffith testified that Marks had written some of the seized papers, basing his opinion on his

C. Reflections on the Relationship between Judge and Jury

having seen Marks write on two occasions and having observed his signature on travelers' checks that were seized in the search. Buchwald objects that the papers were insufficiently authenticated in that Griffith was not competent to identify Marks' handwriting. . . .

FRE 901(a) provides:

> The requirement of authentication or identification as a condition precedent to admissibility is satisfied by evidence sufficient to support a finding that the matter in question is what its proponent claims.

The Advisory Committee's Notes state that "(a)uthentication and identification represent a special aspect of relevancy. . . . The requirement . . . falls in the category of relevancy dependent upon fulfillment of a condition of fact and is governed by the procedure set forth in Rule 104(b)" under which the judge may conditionally admit the evidence, subject to the jury's ultimate determination as to its genuineness. Hence the rule requires the admission of evidence "if sufficient proof has been introduced so that a reasonable juror could find in favor of authenticity or identification." 5 Weinstein's Evidence, §901(a)(01) at 901-917.

The type and quantum of evidence necessary for authentication is thus related to the purpose for which the evidence is offered. These papers, with their many references to the passing of checks issued by a so-called bank in Montserrat, including the checks used by these defendants to perpetuate the fraud on the Merchants Bank, were offered to prove the part of the scheme that required the existence of a sham offshore bank. The papers were relevant no matter who their author was. All that was needed was sufficient proof for a jury to find that they were connected to the bank that issued the checks used to defraud the Merchants Bank and that the Government alleged was a sham. FRE 901(b)(4) provides that "(a)ppearances, contents, substance, internal patterns, or other distinctive characteristics, taken in conjunction with circumstances" provide a means of authenticating evidence. The contents of these documents, taken in conjunction with Deputy Superintendent Griffith's testimony that they were seized at the purported office of the bank, provided adequate basis to establish their authenticity. . . .

IV. Issues Raised by Carbone

A. *The Sufficiency of the Evidence*

Carbone's first challenge is to the sufficiency of the evidence against him. Starting from the conceded premise that there is no direct proof that he knew of the plan to use checks of the sham Bahrain Credit Bank to defraud the Merchants Bank, he contends that the circumstantial evidence relied on by the Government consisted of four isolated facts—that he introduced Sliker to Saluzzi, that he introduced Sliker to Foster, that his store was used for various meetings between the conspirators, and that Sliker was indebted to him. Carbone argues that, even applying the rules that after a conviction the defendant's burden to show insufficiency is a "very heavy" one, United States v. Carson, 702 F.2d 351, 361, and that the evidence must be viewed in the light most favorable to the Government with all permissible inferences drawn in its favor, the evidence adduced in this case was insufficient for a reasonable jury to find him guilty beyond a reasonable doubt. Carbone places particular emphasis on the absence of proof that he directly benefitted from the scheme, pointing out that the only proof of a direct benefit was Saluzzi's statement that Sliker said that he would pay Carbone a few hundred dollars for his part in the scheme—a rather trifling sum for which to undergo the risk of criminal prosecution.

Although the question is close, we do not accept Carbone's claim. While none of the four pieces of evidence cited by Carbone would alone constitute a reasonable basis for finding him guilty beyond a reasonable doubt, this is not the way in which evidence should be viewed. As we have often said, "pieces of evidence must be viewed not in isolation but in conjunction," United States v. Geaney, 417 F.2d 1116, 1121, for "each of the episodes gain(s) color from each of the others," United States v. Monica, 295 F.2d 400, 401. The evidence takes on a quite different aspect when viewed in this light: Carbone first financed a trip to Belgium by Saluzzi to accompany Buchwald for the purpose of defrauding diamond sellers with phoney Bahrain Credit Bank checks; shortly after the failure of that mission, Carbone arranged the introduction of Saluzzi, who owed Carbone money, to Sliker, who also owed Carbone money and was a "good mover of paper" in Carbone's words; Carbone made his store available for the hatching of a plot to defraud the Merchants Bank, escorted Sliker to the bank to meet his easily gulled friend, Foster, and then on three other occasions made his furniture store available again for the division of loot among the conspirators. A reasonable jury could, of course, conclude that Carbone was the unfortunate victim of deception and coincidence, but we cannot say that an equally reasonable jury could not be convinced beyond a reasonable doubt that Carbone had his finger rather deep in the Merchants Bank pie. Moreover, the Government introduced some further evidence that the jury could have considered in finding Carbone guilty. First, the Government brought out a contradiction to Carbone's exculpatory statement that he had gone to the Merchants Bank on January 5 with Sliker because a bank officer had called while Sliker was with him to tell him that his account was overdrawn.[10] The Government also cast doubt on Carbone's testimony that he was outraged when told of the fraud on February 2, 1981, by playing for the jury a tape recording of a telephone conversation between Sliker and Carbone on January 7, 1982

10. Carbone's reply brief asserts that the account did become overdrawn during the day. However, the bank records cited by Carbone establish not more than that he may have been overdrawn for part of the day on January 2; they also show that any overdraft was ended by the close of business on that day. The uncontroverted testimony was that he went to the bank with Sliker on January 5. In any event, this was an issue for the jury to determine.

C. Reflections on the Relationship between Judge and Jury 207

(of which more hereafter) in which Carbone had a friendly conversation with Sliker and told Sliker that he did not "give a goddam" about Foster's "60, or whatever it was 80"—apparently referring to the portion of the misappropriated money that had not been made good; that "we pushed (it) off to the side, he ain't getting it;" and that "I'm not going to worry about Bill. What you did there, that money is gone." The jury could also have given weight to what it could reasonably have concluded was a lie by Carbone in claiming not to recognize his own voice on the tape, and in at first denying but later admitting that he recognized Sliker's voice, see infra. There was thus enough evidence to justify the jury in concluding that Carbone was guilty beyond a reasonable doubt.[11] . . .

C. The Admission of the Tape of the January 7, 1982 Conversation with Sliker

Carbone makes several arguments relating to the admission into evidence of a tape recording of a telephone conversation between him and Sliker on January 7, 1982, which the Government was allowed to play to the jury during his cross-examination. After Carbone professed an inability to recall the conversation, the prosecutor sought to refresh his recollection by having him listen to a tape of it, stating that if this should fail, he would offer the tape in evidence. After listening to the tape on an earphone, Carbone was asked whether the tape refreshed his recollection; Carbone replied: "Not too much." When asked whether he tape recorded a conversation between him and Sliker, he responded: "I refuse to answer. I'm not sure. I take the Fifth on that one." Questioned whether he recognized his own voice, Carbone answered in the negative, adding "I never heard myself on tape." Questioned whether he recognized Sliker's voice, Carbone answered "(n)ot that much." The prosecutor then offered the tape, asking the judge if he would like to listen to it "for the voice identification." The judge did so, the prosecutor then offered the tape,[12] and Carbone's counsel objected.

At a sidebar conference the judge noted that the tape was very clear and stated that "it is clear that it is Mr. Carbone's voice." Carbone's counsel argued that "(t)he court can't be a witness against my client to authenticate—with regard to voice identification." Observing that "I am just acting as the judge," Judge Griesa overruled this objection. The tape was then played to the jury.[13] In addition to showing cordiality and continued dealings between

---

11. The jury may also have been influenced by Carbone's demeanor, which twice led the judge to reprimand him. Although it is a legitimate factor for the jury to consider, this could not remedy a deficiency in the Government's proof if one existed.
12. The prosecutor wavered as to whether the tape's admissibility for a purpose other than impeachment was as a prior inconsistent statement, which it clearly was not in the sense required by FRE 801(d)(1) or as an admission, which it clearly was, see FRE 801(d)(2). He offered it on both bases.
13. After the tape was played, the prosecutor asked whether the "Bill" referred to on the tape was Bill Foster and Carbone answered affirmatively. An objection by Sliker's counsel that his client's voice had not been authenticated led the prosecutor to question Carbone a second time whether he recognized Sliker's voice on the tape; this time Carbone admitted that he did.

Carbone and Sliker and thus contradicting Carbone's testimony that Sliker's conduct had outraged him and discrediting Carbone's assertion that he had threatened Sliker's life after learning of the fraud, the tape showed that both Sliker and Saluzzi were heavily indebted to Carbone, thereby providing a motive for Carbone to bring them together in an endeavor that might provide them with funds.

Carbone raises two related arguments regarding the authentication of this tape. First, he claims that the judge improperly "testified," in violation of FRE 605, that it was Carbone's voice on the tape. Second, he claims that since no one ever testified before the jury that it was Carbone's voice on the tape, no proper foundation was laid for its admission into evidence. Discussion of these objections requires some preliminary analysis.

In order for a piece of evidence to be of probative value, there must be proof that it is what its proponent says it is. The requirement of authentication is thus a condition precedent to admitting evidence. However, whether a given piece of evidence is authentic is itself a question of fact. Contrary to the first branch of Lord Coke's maxim, *ad quaestionem facti non respondent judices; ad quaestionem juris non respondent juratores* (judges don't answer questions of fact; juries don't answer questions of law), the common law rule was that the judge and not the jury should decide "any preliminary questions of fact, however intricate, the solution of which may be necessary to enable him to determine . . . the admissibility" of evidence. Thayer, Preliminary Treatise on Evidence 258 n.3 (1898) (quoting Gorton v. Hadsell, 9 Cush. 508, 511 (Mass. 1852)). The justification for this principle centered on the supposedly limited abilities of juries and on the circularity of having a jury hear evidence in order to determine whether it should hear the evidence.

Despite the recognized rule we have just described, the maxim that fact finding is for the jury carries considerable force. Leaving too much for the judge to decide would "greatly restrict() and in some cases virtually destroy ()" the functioning of the jury as a trier of fact. FRE 104(b), Notes of Advisory Committee. Thus, exceptions were made to the common law rule stated above. A few courts, for example, allowed the jury to hear dying declarations with instructions to consider the preliminary question whether the declarant spoke with a settled, hopeless expectation of death. Other courts submitted preliminary fact questions on the competence of evidence to the jury where these corresponded with an ultimate disputed factual issue.

FRE 104 retains the principles thus developed at common law. . . . Thus, subsection (a) governs questions concerning the competency of evidence, i.e., evidence which is relevant but may be subject to exclusion by virtue of some principle of the law of evidence, leaving it for the judge to resolve factual issues in connection with these principles. Examples include not only those expressly stated in the rule (privileged information and witness competency), but others such as the hearsay rule, based on the policy of excluding inherently unreliable evidence; the exclusionary rule, designed to ensure the observance by police of fourth or fifth amendment rights; and

C. Reflections on the Relationship between Judge and Jury

many others. Removing factual issues related to determining whether evidence is competent from the jury is based on recognition that the typical juror is intent mainly on reaching a verdict in accord with what he believes to be true in the case he is called upon to decide, and is not concerned with the long-term policies of evidence law.

Subsection (b) provides different treatment for situations in which the relevancy (i.e., probative value) of evidence, rather than its competency, depends upon the existence of a prior fact. Judge Weinstein explains why the Federal Rules leave such issues to the jury:

> This exception to the judge's broad power under Rule 104(a) is based on the theory that these questions of conditional relevance are merely matters of probative force, rather than evidentiary policy, and that the jury is competent to receive the evidence-in-chief and still disregard it if they find the nonexistence of the preliminary fact. [1 Weinstein's Evidence §104(01), at 104-110.]

The requirement that a given piece of evidence be what its proponent claims does not reflect some special evidentiary policy like hearsay rules or privileges. Wigmore described the need for authentication as "an inherent logical necessity." 7 Wigmore §2129, supra, at 703 (emphasis omitted). Authentication is perhaps the purest example of a rule respecting relevance: Evidence admitted as something can have no probative value unless that is what it really is. Thus, the Notes of the Advisory Committee accompanying Rule 901 state that questions concerning authentication are governed by the procedures in Rule 104(b).

Under Rule 104(b), the trial judge may make a preliminary determination as to the prior fact and admit the evidence to the jury's final determination that the prior fact exists. That is what Judge Griesa did here; as he succinctly put it, he was "just acting as the judge." He listened to the tape and determined, based on his own comparison of the voices, that there was sufficient evidence of the prior fact (that the voice on the tape was Carbone's) to admit the evidence for the jury to hear. This is the course which this court has recommended, although it would have been preferable for the judge to have done it in camera. As shown by the Advisory Committee's Note, Rule 605 is addressed to an entirely different situation, namely, situations where the judge presiding at the trial forsakes the bench for the witness stand or engages in equivalent conduct.

The judge's preliminary determination does not, however, finally establish the authenticity of the tape. As with other matters under Rule 104(b), only the jury can finally decide that issue. The judge's admission of the evidence under Rule 104(b) is conditional and "subject to the introduction of evidence sufficient to support a finding of the fulfillment of the condition." FRE 104(b). We thus reach the question whether there was evidence before the jury sufficient to establish that the voice on the tape was Carbone's.

Carbone claims there was not. While the Government does not squarely address the issue in its brief, its basic position must be that hearing the tape after having heard Carbone's voice when he testified provided the jury with sufficient evidence to conclude that the voice on the tape was Carbone's.

FRE 901(a) requires "evidence sufficient to support a finding that the matter in question is what its proponent claims," but does not definitively establish the nature or quantum of proof that is required. Subsection (b) provides illustrations of what will suffice. Subsection (b)(5), dealing specifically with the question of voice identification, states that "[i]dentification of a voice, whether heard firsthand or through mechanical or electronic transmission or recording," can be established "by opinion based upon hearing the voice at any time under circumstances connecting it with the alleged speaker." Carbone argues that the opinion referred to must be that of a witness and not that of the trier of the fact, and the Notes of the Advisory Committee suggest that this is so, as does Judge Weinstein, 5 Weinstein's Evidence, supra, §§901(b)(5)(01), (02). However, subsection (b)(5) is only an illustration and several of the other illustrations do not require opinion testimony and leave it to the jury to make its own comparison. Subsection (b)(3), for example, states that authentication of a writing may be established by "(c)omparison by the trier of fact . . . with specimens which have been authenticated." Similarly, subsection (b)(4) permits a finding of authenticity based on "distinctive characteristics, taken in conjunction with circumstances." See FRE 901(b)(3), (4), Notes of Advisory Committee. We thus see no reason in principle why, in a case like this, where the person whose voice on a tape is to be identified has testified, the jury cannot itself make the comparison. Had the judge put this question to them, that would end this matter. Here, moreover, the Government's case was aided by Carbone's identification of the "Bill" referred to on the tape as Foster and of the other voice as Sliker's, see note 10, supra.

Such difficulty as exists comes from the fact that the question was not specifically put to the jury, which might have assumed that the judge had ruled that the voice was Carbone's, not merely preliminarily, but definitively. However, the jury knew there was an issue since it had heard Carbone disclaim ability to identify the voice as his own, and the judge delivered the appropriate instruction in his general charge to the effect that the jury was the ultimate judge as to all factual issues. We understand the general rule to be that the judge is permitted but not required to deliver a specific instruction to the jury to consider particularly any preliminary question under Rule 104(b). Particularly where, as here, counsel fails to request such an instruction, cf. FRE 105, the decision whether or not to give one lies in the discretion of the trial judge. Undoubtedly it would have been better to have delivered such an instruction here. However, we see no reason why Judge Griesa was required to fear that a juror who, having just heard Carbone testify, thought that the voice on the tape was not Carbone's would have felt constrained to assume that it was. It was thus not an abuse of discretion for

C. Reflections on the Relationship between Judge and Jury

him to have failed to instruct the jury sua sponte that it must specifically decide this issue of authentication. . . .

The judgments of conviction are affirmed.

CHAPTER FOUR
THE RELEVANCE RULES

In addition to having a discretionary rule of exclusion like FRE 403, all jurisdictions have a number of specific exclusionary rules, sometimes referred to as the "relevance rules," which may be invoked to exclude concededly relevant evidence. See FRE 404 through FRE 412. These exclusionary rules are based in part on FRE 403-type considerations (e.g., low probative value, high likelihood of prejudice) and in part on extrinsic policy grounds—that is, on the notion that some desirable social policy will be fostered by the exclusion of relevant evidence and that the benefit of promoting the social policy outweighs the cost of foregoing relevant evidence.[1] For example, the prohibition against evidence of offers to compromise to prove liability, see FRE 408, is based in part on the notion that offers of compromise frequently have very low probative value as evidence of liability. (A person who expects to prevail in a law suit may offer to settle the suit because the cost of settlement is likely to be less than the cost of litigation.) The rule is also based on the notion that private settlement of disputes is socially desirable and that use of offers to prove liability might deter individuals from making settlement offers.

To the extent that a particular relevance rule is based on evidentiary factors (i.e., FRE 403 considerations), the rule represents a judgment that in all or most instances the balance of probative value versus prejudice and other factors is so likely to come out in favor of exclusion that it is not worth the time and the risk of error to engage in the balancing process on a case-by-case basis. To the extent that a relevance rule is based on extrinsic, nonevidentiary policy grounds, there is added reason for exclusion.

1. This same type of social policy rationale is the underlying justification for evidentiary privileges. See generally Chapter Twelve.

As we begin our examination of the relevance rules, you should keep in mind that these rules do not exclude particular types of evidence altogether; rather, they exclude particular types of evidence *for particular purposes*. This is important for two reasons. First, in order to be able to work with the rules, it is not enough to know that there is an exclusionary rule for some particular type of evidence. For example, the offer of compromise exclusionary rule applies only to offers of compromise used to prove liability or fault. Offers of compromise may, subject to FRE 403, be admissible for other purposes. Thus, in order to apply that rule properly, you must ask the question that must always be your first question: *Why* is the evidence relevant; *what* are we trying to prove? Only after you answer that question will you be able to apply a relevance rule.

The second reason for keeping in mind that the relevance rules exclude certain evidence only for certain purposes is to permit you to evaluate the soundness and desirability of the rules. For example, to the extent that one can readily find some alternative permissible theory for the use of evidence that is the subject of a relevance rule, one can with good reason question the desirability of the rule in its present form: If courts usually resolve the FRE 403 balance between the permissible and impermissible use in favor of admissibility with limiting instructions (if requested), and if one doubts the efficacy of limiting instructions, the relevance rule in fact would seem not to be serving its designed purpose. Alternatively, if the FRE 403 balance usually comes out in favor of exclusion, the relevance rule may be stated in a deceptively (and thus perhaps undesirably) narrow manner. On the other hand, it may be that in these impermissible/permissible use situations the evidence is neither almost always excluded nor almost always admitted. If that is the case, perhaps judges are simply applying the FRE 403 balancing test wisely on a case-by-case basis. Or perhaps the inherent difficulty of balancing and the vast discretion of the judge lead to arbitrary and inconsistent results from case to case.

The difficulties in applying FRE 403, of course, are not limited to its application to relevance rule evidence, and by noting these problems here we do not mean to suggest that FRE 403 should be abandoned. Even if FRE 403 is generally desirable, however, it may be that, from a drafting standpoint, we should try to avoid having to resort to FRE 403 if reasonable alternatives are available. If a type of evidence that is the subject of a relevance rule is likely in most cases to be relevant to prove both a proposition for which the evidence is not admissible and one for which it is potentially admissible, it may be desirable to change the relevance rule rather than create a situation that mandates frequent recourse to FRE 403.

Unfortunately we do not now have enough reliable information to be very certain about whether any of the problems suggested in the preceding paragraphs are serious concerns for any particular relevance rule. Perhaps answers to some of the questions will emerge as we gain more experience and sophistication in studying the actual operation of the rules of evidence.

In the meantime, these potential problems should not be ignored. The task of the rule drafter should be to try to come up with the best possible rule in light of the best possible guess (based on logic, empiricism, and intuition) as to how various alternative formulations of the rule are likely to work in practice.

A. CHARACTER EVIDENCE

The Federal Rules governing the use of character evidence, FRE 404 and 405, are quite similar to the common law character evidence rules. Neither the Federal Rules nor their common law counterparts, however, define the terms *character* and *character trait*. In this section we will address some of the problems in determining the scope of what constitutes "character" evidence. Initially, in our discussion we will refer to traits such as honesty, dishonesty, violence, and peacefulness, because we believe that all or most of you and all or most courts would regard these attributes as character traits. For now, this hopefully shared understanding of what constitutes character should be sufficient.

1. The Relevance and Possible Uses of Character Evidence

When evidence of a person's character is relevant in a law suit, it is likely to be relevant in one of two ways. First, a person's character, or a particular character trait, may itself be an essential element of a claim or a defense. For example, if plaintiff sued defendant for libel because defendant had circulated a leaflet claiming that plaintiff was dishonest, a possible defense would be that the statement is true. Since the statement that plaintiff is dishonest is a statement about a character trait of plaintiff, character is an essential element of the defense of truth.

Second, even when character is not an essential element of a claim or a defense, evidence of a person's character may be relevant to help prove what the person did on a particular occasion—that is, to show action in conformity with the character trait. Thus, for example, a defendant charged with embezzlement may offer evidence of his good character for honesty in the hope that the jury will infer that the defendant acted in conformity with that honest character trait on the occasion that is the subject of the prosecution. Here, character is not an essential element of the defense. The defendant may be guilty or innocent regardless of whether the defendant happens to be a generally dishonest or a generally honest person. Evidence of the defendant's character for honesty, however, is relevant in that it is one possible, though not essential, way to help establish the defendant's innocence of the crime charged.

When character is an essential element of a claim or a defense, the party with the initial burden of producing evidence will have to introduce character evidence in order to avoid a directed verdict. When the only relevance of character evidence is to show action in conformity with character on a particular occasion, however, there are good reasons for excluding the evidence altogether.

First, the probative value of character evidence to show action in conformity with character will seldom, if ever, be very great. A person who is generally honest will at least occasionally be less than fully honest; a person whom we may fairly describe as having a violent character will on many occasions react to adverse situations in a peaceful manner. Moreover, if the action in conformity with character about which we are concerned is the subject matter of the litigation (as it typically is), it may be that there were particular stresses on the individual or some other unusual circumstances that increased the likelihood of acting "out of character."

Second, character evidence may be extremely prejudicial, particularly if it is evidence of the character of a party to the law suit. Inherent in the concept of character—or at least in the attributes that most people and most courts think of as character—is a moral quality or sense of rightness or wrongness. Consider, for example, the meaning of the words we use to describe what we refer to as character traits: e.g., "honesty," "dishonesty," "peacefulness," "violence." Evidence that a litigant possesses one of these traits may dispose the jury to decide in favor of that person if it is a positive character trait or against the person if it is a negative one.

Finally, there may be conflicting evidence, and thus doubts, about the nature of the person's character. For example, a person may be extremely conscientious—indeed, obsessive—about avoiding potential accidents around the home (e.g., always checking at least twice before leaving the house to make sure that the iron is unplugged, that the stove is off, and that there are no lit ashes in the ashtrays) and at the same time be quite careless behind the wheel of a car.

Doubts about the nature of a person's character, of course, may exist when character is an essential element of a claim or defense. Moreover, when character is an essential element of a claim or defense, character evidence may have a prejudicial impact that is distinct from its probative value. Consider, for example, a defamation action in which character evidence is offered to prove the truth of the allegedly libelous statement that plaintiff is a dishonest person. The jury may conclude that the evidence is not sufficient to convince them that the plaintiff is a generally dishonest person; yet, at the same time, the jury may dislike the plaintiff enough that they decide in favor of the defendant. When character is an essential element, however, the substantive law makes it necessary to try to determine what the character trait is. When character evidence is being offered only to show

A. Character Evidence

action in conformity with character, it may not be worthwhile to risk the prejudice and to engage in a collateral dispute over what a person's true character is.

Because of these FRE 403-type concerns, the common law and the Federal Rules have a strict prohibition against the use of character evidence to show action in conformity with character, except in very limited situations. For example, FRE 404(a) provides:

> Evidence of a person's character or a trait of character is not admissible for the purpose of proving action in conformity therewith on a particular occasion, except:
>
> (1) *Character of accused.* Evidence of a pertinent trait of character offered by an accused, or by the prosecution to rebut the same;
>
> (2) *Character of victim.* Evidence of a pertinent trait of character of the victim of the crime offered by an accused, or by the prosecution to rebut the same, or evidence of a character trait of peacefulness of the victim offered by the prosecution in a homicide case to rebut evidence that the victim was the first aggressor;
>
> (3) *Character of witness.* Evidence of the character of a witness, as provided in Rules 607, 608, and 609.

The last of the three exceptions in FRE 404(a) is a cross-reference to the impeachment rules, which we will consider in Chapter Six. The first two exceptions, as the terms *accused* and *prosecution* indicate, relate only to criminal prosecutions. Unless the case is a homicide prosecution involving the question who was the first aggressor (FRE 404(a)(2)), these exceptions give the criminal defendant the option to decide whether to open the door to the use of character evidence to show action in conformity with character.[2] In a civil action no party may offer character evidence to show action in conformity with character on a particular occasion (unless the character evidence is offered for impeachment purposes pursuant to FRE 607-609).[3]

Thus far we have considered the use of character evidence to prove an essential element of a claim or a defense and to show action in conformity

---

[2]. In situations in which a criminal defendant has chosen to open the door to character evidence, there is precedent for instructing the jury that character evidence alone may be sufficient to create a reasonable doubt. In increasing numbers, however, courts are taking the position that it is inappropriate to single out character evidence for this type of special instruction. See, e.g., United States v. Burke, 781 F.2d 1234 (7th Cir. 1985).

[3]. FRE 404(a) is substantially a restatement of the common law. The general prohibition against character evidence to show action in conformity with character, the exception embodied in 404(a)(1), and the allowance of some types of character evidence to impeach the credibility of a witness are all consistent with the common law. There is also common law precedent for the exceptions in FRE 404(a)(2). Most of the authority permitting the defendant to open the door to the victim's character, however, exists in the context of a dispute over who was the first aggressor. Some courts do not permit the prosecutor to open the door to character evidence under any circumstances.

A minority common law rule permits defendants in civil actions to open the door to character evidence if the civil action is based on culpable conduct proscribed by the criminal law.

with character. These are the two purposes for which character evidence will usually be relevant. On rare occasions, however, character evidence may be relevant for some other purpose. Reconsider, for example, the defamation action discussed briefly in the text supra. Whereas *character* for honesty (i.e., the kind of person that the plaintiff is) is an essential element of the defendant's defense of truth, *reputation* for honesty (i.e., what people *say* about the plaintiff's honesty) is critical to the plaintiff's claim for damages, which in a defamation action are measured by injury to the plaintiff's reputation. Thus, plaintiff would want to show that his reputation for honesty had suffered as a result of the defamatory statement. The most obvious and direct way to do this would be to have witnesses testify as to what the plaintiff's reputation for honesty was both before and after the alleged defamatory statement. Another possible way to establish reputation for honesty prior to the alleged defamation, however, would be to introduce evidence of the plaintiff's character for honesty—perhaps, e.g., the opinion of a close associate that plaintiff was in fact an honest person. The evidence is relevant, we suggest, because a person whom we know to be honest is more likely to have a reputation for honesty than is a person about whose honesty we know nothing.

There is no reference in the Federal Rules, the Advisory Committee's Notes, or the legislative history to the use of character evidence other than when character is an essential element or when character evidence is offered to show action in conformity with character. The drafters of the Federal Rules seem not to have contemplated the possibility that there will occasionally be other purposes for which character evidence is relevant.

2. Types of Evidence of Character

Once one determines that character evidence is potentially admissible, e.g., because character is an essential element or because one of the FRE 404(a) exceptions applies, the rules of evidence require consideration of the types of evidence that may be offered to establish a person's character. There are three possibilities. First, one might offer specific instances of conduct of the person whose character is in question. One's character, after all, is known to others—to the extent that it is knowable at all—by how one behaves. Second, a witness could offer to testify that in the witness' opinion the person in question has the particular character trait. Finally, a witness could offer to testify that the person has a reputation in the community for having the kind of character trait that is relevant to the litigation. An individual's reputation is what people think or say about the individual, and when reputation evidence is offered to prove character, it is the truth of the reputation that is important. Thus, reputation evidence is hearsay—evidence of what people out of court say about the individual offered to prove the truth of what they say. There is, however, an exception to the hearsay rule for evidence of reputation offered to show an individual's character. See FRE 803(21).

A. Character Evidence

The probative value of opinion or reputation evidence will depend in part on how long, how well, and in what contexts the witness has known (opinion) or has known about (reputation) the person whose character the evidence is offered to prove. The common law (which did not permit opinion evidence at all in most jurisdictions) required that a reputation witness testify to the person's reputation in the community. In theory, this focus on the community as a whole was designed to ensure that evidence be fairly reflective of the views about the person in question. As a practical matter today, however, there will not be many instances in which an individual has a reputation throughout the entire community. Indeed, in our complex, urbanized society, it is not clear what the entire community would be. Courts wisely recognize this fact and permit reputation testimony to be based on what a witness has heard in some relevant community—perhaps the neighborhood where the person lives or the place where the person works.

Even if there is no difficulty in defining the relevant community, there may be a question whether the witness knows or knows about the individual well enough to testify in the form of opinion or reputation. Some common law courts imposed quite rigid foundation requirements on reputation witnesses. The Federal Rules do not deal specifically with this issue. FRE 403, however, provides latitude for trial judges to exclude testimony that is marginally probative because the witness does not have much of a basis for knowing or knowing about the person in question.[4]

3. Limitations on the Types of Evidence That May Be Used To Prove Character

When character is an essential element of a claim or a defense, all three types of evidence—reputation, opinion, and specific acts—are potentially admissible, subject, of course, to FRE 403. See FRE 405(a), (b). If the essential character trait is very general (X is good or bad, as opposed to X is violent or peaceful), everything or almost everything that the person has done is arguably relevant; yet, because of the generality of the character trait in issue, each individual act by itself may be of little probative value. Thus, if the character trait is quite general, specific acts evidence may be the most likely of the three types of character evidence to be excluded on FRE 403 grounds. By contrast, if the character trait is quite specific, there arguably should be a preference for specific acts evidence.

In the limited situations in which it is permissible to use character evidence to show action in conformity with character, the common law

---

4. For a discussion of the common law foundation requirements for reputation and opinion testimony, see Ladd, Techniques and Theory of Character Testimony, 24 Iowa L. Rev. 498 (1939).

permitted only reputation evidence,[5] and the Federal Rules permit only reputation and opinion evidence. See FRE 405(a). Specific acts evidence is not admissible to prove character for the purpose of showing action in conformity with character. See FRE 404(b).

In the rare situations in which character evidence may be relevant for some purpose other than to establish character as an essential element or to show action in conformity with character—e.g., to prove reputation—it is not clear whether the Federal Rules would permit the use of specific acts evidence. On the one hand, FRE 402 provides that all relevant evidence is admissible unless there is a specific exclusionary rule, and the only prohibition against the use of specific acts to prove character is in FRE 404(b), which deals only with specific acts to prove character to show action in conformity with character. On the other hand, FRE 405, after providing in subdivision (a) that reputation and opinion evidence are always potentially admissible to prove character, provides that proof of character may *"also be made"* by evidence of specific acts when character is an essential element of a claim or defense. Arguably there is implicit in this provision the notion that only when character is an essential element can proof also be by specific acts.

4. The Rationale for Limiting the Use of Specific Acts Evidence To Prove Character

The probative value of evidence offered to prove character does not depend on the ultimate purpose for which character evidence is used, and specific acts evidence will frequently be the most relevant form of character evidence. The potentially greater relevance of specific acts evidence, however, may be more than counterbalanced by concerns with prejudice, confusion of the issues, and waste of time. To the extent that specific acts evidence is likely to be more probative of character than reputation or opinion evidence, it is also likely to be more prejudicial in that the jury may have a tendency to decide for or against an individual because that individual is generally good or bad. More importantly, there is always the possibility of a dispute over whether the specific act occurred or whether it occurred in the precise manner suggested by the proponent of the evidence. Thus, if we permitted the proponent to introduce the evidence, we would have to permit the other party to introduce evidence disputing the fact or placing it in a different context. When character is itself an essential element of a claim or defense, it may be reasonable to take the time to litigate fully the occurrence or nonoccurrence of various acts bearing on the character trait. As noted pre-

---

5. The leading case articulating the common law rules with respect to the use of character evidence to prove action in conformity with character is Michelson v. United States, 335 U.S. 469 (1948).

A. Character Evidence

viously, however, the inference from character (regardless of the form of evidence offered) to action on a particular occasion is likely to be weak. As a result, the ultimate value of the character evidence is not likely to be great, even if the specific acts are quite probative of the character trait. Given this probably low ultimate probative value when character evidence is offered to show action in conformity with character, the rules of evidence take the position that it is not worth the time and possible prejudice and confusion of the issues to try to prove or disprove various specific facts that are themselves wholly collateral to the issues at hand.[6]

5. Reputation Evidence versus Opinion Evidence

Normally, when a witness is permitted to testify in the form of opinion, it is permissible to inquire into the underlying bases for the opinion. See, e.g., FRE 705. Indeed, with respect to expert testimony, the common law rule in a number of jurisdictions required the witness to state the bases for an opinion prior to giving the opinion. Because of this standard practice of exploring on either direct or cross-examination the underlying bases for witnesses' opinions, the use of opinion evidence to prove character creates the possibility that opinion testimony about character could lead to testimony about various specific acts that provide the bases for the opinion. If one is willing to permit litigation about the occurrence of specific acts that may be relevant to a character trait, the possibility that opinion testimony may evolve into testimony about specific acts should not be a matter of great concern. If, however, one does not want to engage in this type of specific acts litigation, one might understandably be reluctant to permit opinion testimony to prove character. This is precisely the reason that the majority common law rule prohibited opinion testimony, as well as specific acts testimony, to prove character to show action in conformity with character.

Even though the rule prohibiting opinion evidence to prove character to show action in conformity with character has an understandable objective, it arguably also has an undesirable effect. A witness who is called to testify about a person's character is likely to have rather strong feelings about the person who is the object of the testimony. For example, by far the most common non-impeachment use of character evidence to show action in conformity with character is in situations in which a criminal defendant calls witnesses to testify about the defendant's good character. These witnesses are not likely to be people who have simply heard of the defendant. Rather, they are likely to be people who know the defendant well and think highly

---

6. These same reasons for exclusion of specific acts evidence are applicable to specific acts offered to prove character to show something other than character as essential element or action in conformity with character—e.g., to prove character to show reputation. Thus, even if the Federal Rules do not prohibit the use of specific acts character evidence in this type of situation, there is likely to be a strong FRE 403 argument for exclusion.

of the defendant. They may or may not know much about the defendant's reputation, and they may honestly think they know more than they do about the defendant's reputation: If they have high regard for the defendant, they may find it difficult to imagine that others do not share that view. In short, although the rules of evidence may force these witnesses to couch their testimony in terms of reputation, the real gist of what they are thinking and of what motivates their testimony may well be their *opinion* about the defendant's character.

Recognizing that character witnesses frequently offer opinions in the form of reputation testimony, the drafters of the Federal Rules took the position that these witnesses should be permitted to offer their opinions directly. Thus, FRE 405(a) permits, subject to FRE 403, both reputation and opinion testimony in all instances in which character evidence is admissible. At the same time, however, the drafters recognized the risk that opinion testimony could evolve into specific acts testimony. The Advisory Committee's Note to FRE 405 makes it clear that the use of opinion testimony to prove character to show action in conformity with character should not evolve into litigation about specific acts on which the opinion may be based:

> Opinion testimony on direct in these situations ought in general to correspond to reputation testimony as now given, i.e., be confined to the nature and extent of observation and acquaintance upon which the opinion is based.

6. A Brief Summary

The following chart illustrates the possible purposes for which character evidence may be relevant and the possible methods of proving character:

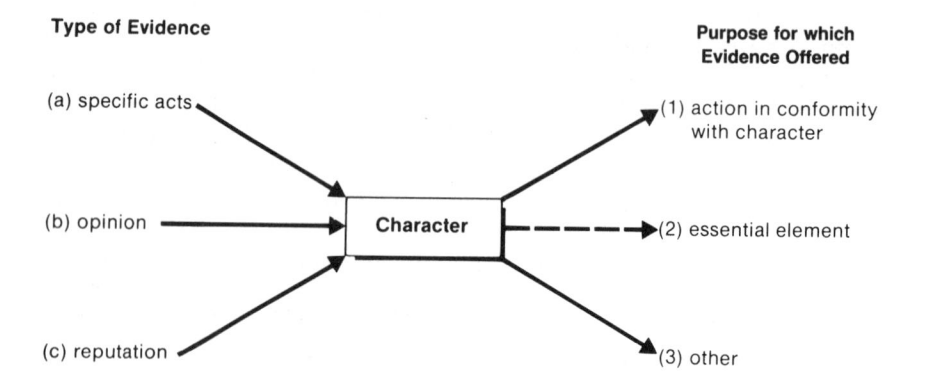

Type of Evidence

(a) specific acts

(b) opinion

(c) reputation

→ Character →

Purpose for which Evidence Offered

(1) action in conformity with character

(2) essential element

(3) other

A. Character Evidence

      (a)(1): Never admissible. FRE 404(b).[7]
      (a)(2): Potentially admissible. FRE 405(b).
      (a)(3): Unclear whether potentially admissible.
(b)(1), (c)(1): Potentially admissible in limited situations provided for in FRE 404(a). FRE 405(a). The common law rule permitted only reputation evidence in these instances.
(b)(2), (c)(2): Potentially admissible. FRE 405(a).
(b)(3), (c)(3): Potentially admissible. FRE 405(a).

7. Impeaching Reputation and Opinion Witnesses

Whenever a party offers character evidence in the form of reputation or opinion testimony, the opposing party is permitted to cross-examine the character witness about relevant specific acts of conduct. See, e.g., FRE 405(a). Assume, for example, that John is charged with criminal assault and that as part of the defense Mary testifies, pursuant to FRE 404(a)(1), that John had a good reputation in the community for peacefulness. The prosecutor, when cross-examining Mary, can ask about various violent acts that John supposedly committed. The purpose of these questions is not to prove John's character for violence. Indeed, since the relevance of John's character is only to show action in conformity with character, FRE 404(b) would prohibit questions about specific acts to prove John's character. Rather, the purpose of the prosecutor's questions is to test Mary's credibility as a character witness: If she denies having heard of the acts of violence, one can infer that

---

    7. Technically, this statement is correct only with respect to the "substantive" as opposed to "impeachment" use of specific acts evidence. As we will consider in detail when we examine the impeachment rules in Chapter Six, it is permissible to use specific acts to prove a witness' bad character for trustworthiness in order to infer that the witness is being untrustworthy on the stand. See FRE 608(b) ("Specific instances of the conduct of a witness . . . may . . . , if probative of truthfulness or untruthfulness, be inquired into on cross-examination of the witness. . . .") See also FRE 609(a) (authorizing the admission of certain convictions "for the purpose of attacking the credibility of a witness . . . if elicited from him or established by public record during cross-examination") Although FRE 609 makes no specific reference to "character" evidence, the use of prior convictions to impeach is generally considered to be a method of impeaching a witness' character for trustworthiness. See, e.g., McCormick's Handbook on the Law of Evidence 93-100 (3d ed., Cleary, 1984). The drafters of the Federal Rules apparently concurred in the view that the use of prior convictions to impeach involved the use of character evidence to show action in conformity with character because FRE 609, along with FRE 608, is listed in FRE 404(a)(3) as providing an exception to the general rule that character evidence may not be used to show action in conformity with a character trait on a particular occasion.
    The drafters of the Federal Rules do not explain—indeed, they were apparently unaware of—the blatant contradiction between FRE 404(a)(3), FRE 608(b), and FRE 609, which together specifically authorize the use of specific acts to prove character to show action in conformity with character, and FRE 404(b), which prohibits, without qualification, the use of specific acts to prove character to show action in conformity with character. Despite this contradiction, courts routinely—and quite correctly, in our view—recognize that the use of specific acts evidence, pursuant to FRE 608 and FRE 609, to impeach a witness' character for trustworthiness is not prohibited by FRE 404(b).

she does not have a very good sense of what John's reputation is; and if she has heard of the acts, one may doubt the truth of her testimony (or question her conception of what reputation for peacefulness means).

There are several restrictions on the content of specific acts questions on cross-examination. First, the specific act must be pertinent to the character trait about which the witness testified on direct examination. For example, in our hypothetical involving Mary's testimony about John's reputation for peacefulness, it would be appropriate to ask about acts of violence but not acts of dishonesty. Questions about acts of dishonesty are not (very) relevant to impeach Mary's testimony, because she limited her direct examination testimony to peacefulness. Even if she knows about or has heard about various acts of dishonesty, her acknowledging that fact would not necessarily diminish the force of her testimony that John has a reputation for peacefulness. After all, John may be or be known as dishonest and, at the same time, be and be known as a peaceful person. Indeed, courts and commentators are likely to say that acts of dishonesty are not relevant to character for peacefulness.

It may be, however, that people who exhibit one bad trait are more likely to exhibit another, particularly if the bad act is an illegal act. A person willing to break one law demonstrates a disrespect for the law in general that may make it more likely that the person would break a different kind of law. Thus, it not clear, for example, that dishonesty is irrelevant to violence. More importantly, even if there is in fact little or no relationship between dishonesty and violence, knowing whether a reputation witness to peacefulness has heard about acts of dishonesty may be relevant to assessing the extent to which the reputation witness knows the defendant's reputation for peacefulness. For example, at least if the dishonest act were one that people were likely to talk about, it seems unlikely that a witness who is thoroughly familiar with a defendant's reputation for peacefulness would not have heard about specific acts of dishonesty.

Despite the arguable relevance of asking Mary about John's dishonesty in order to impeach her testimony about John's peaceful character, there are substantial reasons for not permitting such questions. All questions about specific bad acts offered to impeach character witnesses have a twofold potential for prejudice. First, the jury may not limit the use of the evidence to its legitimate impeachment purpose, but may instead make the impermissible inferences to character and then to action in conformity with character. Second, the jury may be prejudiced against the individual whose character was the subject of the inquiry because that individual appears to be a bad person. Given these dangers, it is arguably appropriate to exclude—on FRE 403, if not FRE 401, grounds—specific acts impeachment questions to character witnesses unless there is a fairly direct (and therefore relatively more probative) link between the particular specific act and the character trait testified to on direct examination.

A second restriction on the use of specific acts evidence to impeach a character witness is that as a matter of relevance—or least FRE 403 bal-

A. Character Evidence

ancing—the questions should be limited to acts that the witness is likely to have known or to have heard about and that occurred during or in fairly close temporal proximity to the time period about which the character witness has testified. For example, if Mary on direct examination testified that she had known John well for five years and was familiar with his reputation during that time, it may not be reasonable to expect that she would have heard about an isolated act of violence that occurred 15 years ago. And even if she had heard about the act, it might not be reasonable to expect a single 15-year-old act of violence to affect her view of John's reputation for peacefulness during the last five years.[8]

A third limitation on the use of specific acts questions relates to the cross-examiner's belief that the specific acts occurred. If the prosecutor had no knowledge about whether John, in our hypothetical, had committed any violent acts, it should be permissible to ask Mary in an unsuggestive manner, "Do you know of any violent acts that John has committed?" However, any but the most general inquiry about specific acts is likely to suggest to the jury that the cross-examiner believes that the act occurred. When such an implication inheres in the question, the cross-examiner must have a reasonable basis for believing that the act occurred.

In discussing this limitation on the cross-examination of character witnesses, the Supreme Court in Michelson v. United States[9] noted that as a matter of logical relevance the requirement should be that the cross-examiner of the reputation witness have a reasonable belief that there were rumors about the act, regardless of whether it in fact occurred. Nonetheless, the Court approved the existing rule requiring the cross-examiner to demonstrate that the act in fact occurred:

> But before this relevant and proper inquiry [here, a question to the defendant's character witness about the defendant's arrest] can be made, counsel must demonstrate privately to the court an irrelevant and possibly unprovable fact—the reality of the arrest. From this permissible inquiry about reports of arrest, the jury is pretty certain to infer that defendant had in fact been arrested and to draw its own conclusions as to character from that fact. The [factual basis for the event requirement] thus limits legally relevant inquiries to those based on legally irrelevant facts in order that the legally irrelevant conclusion which the jury probably will draw from the relevant questions will not be based on unsupported or untrue innuendo. It illustrates Judge Hand's suggestion that the system may work best when explained least. Yet, despite its theoretical paradoxes and deficiencies, we approve the procedure as calculated in practice to hold the inquiry within decent bounds. [335 U.S. at 481 n.18.]

---

8. Assessing whether Mary is likely to have heard of any particular violent act will involve consideration of several factors, e.g., how well and how long Mary has known or known about John, whether John's act is likely to have been the subject of discussion because of the nature of the act, whether John is the kind of person whose activities are likely to be known to people situated similarly to Mary. Questions that are only marginally probative for legitimate impeachment purposes may be excluded because of their inherent prejudice.

9. 335 U.S. 469 (1948).

The common law, which in most jurisdictions permitted a criminal defendant to use only reputation evidence when opening the door to character, was quite exacting about the proper form of specific acts questions on cross-examination. Since the direct examination testimony was limited to what the witness had heard people say about the defendant, asking on cross-examination whether the witness *knew* about some bad act was objectionable. The proper form for the specific acts questions on cross-examination was "Have you heard. . . ?" not "Did you know. . . ?". By contrast, if the jurisdiction happened to permit opinion testimony on direct examination, a witness offering an opinion about the defendant's character presumably would be basing that opinion in whole or in part on personal knowledge. Thus, it would be proper to ask on cross-examination whether the opinion witness knew about specific acts.

If there were ever sound reasons for insisting on the proper form of cross-examination questions about specific acts, those reasons have been seriously eroded by the allowance of opinion as well as reputation testimony on direct examination. The Advisory Committee's Note to FRE 405 asserts that the distinctions in the form of the cross-examination questions "are of slight if any practical significance" and that the second sentence of FRE 405(a) "eliminates them as a factor in formulating questions."[10]

Perhaps the most troublesome aspect of the rule permitting specific acts questions on cross-examination is the apparent unfair advantage that the rule gives to the cross-examiner. Consider, for example, the situation in which a criminal defendant chooses to open the door to character evidence. The defendant is limited to the use of relatively bland reputation or opinion evidence. The prosecutor, however, can ask the character witnesses about all sorts of bad acts that are pertinent to the character trait about which the witnesses have testified. Granted, in theory the purpose of the prosecutor's questions is not to prove the defendant's character but only to impeach the credibility of the character witnesses. And granted, the defendant is entitled to a limiting instruction from the judge. How likely is it, however, that the jury will be able to confine its consideration of the bad acts to the theoretically legitimate impeachment purpose?

If you are skeptical of the jury's ability to perform this mental feat, what could you, as defense counsel, do to blunt the effect of the prosecutor's cross-examination of your character witnesses?

What changes, if any, in the character evidence rules do you think would be appropriate? Consider the following possibilities:

> Leave the rules as they are. After all, the apparent advantage to the cross-examiner (usually the prosecutor, as in our example) arises

---

10. Without the Advisory Committee's Note to tell us, is it really all that clear that the second sentence of FRE 405(a) makes it irrelevant whether the question is "Have you heard. . . ?" or "Did you know. . . ?"?

A. Character Evidence

only after the direct examiner (usually the criminal defendant, as in our example) has chosen to open the door to character evidence.

Permit the direct examiner to use specific acts to prove character to show action in conformity with character.

Prohibit the cross-examiner from asking specific acts questions even for impeachment purposes. See Michelson v. United States, 335 U.S. 469, 488-496 (Rutledge, J., dissenting) (rule permitting specific acts inquiry on cross-examination should be abolished, or at least reformulated to curtail much of such questioning).[11] If such specific acts inquiry were not permitted, the prosecutor would still be free to respond to the defendant's character witnesses by presenting prosecution character witnesses.

Prohibit altogether (except perhaps for impeachment, a matter to which we shall turn later) the use of character evidence to prove action in conformity with character.

In conjunction with the last of these possibilities, consider carefully who is likely to benefit from a rule that permits criminal defendants to open the door to character evidence. Or to put the issue somewhat differently, consider what kinds of people you would like to be able to call as character witnesses if you were a criminal defendant. To the extent that criminal defendants may benefit from the use of character evidence, is the benefit likely to be derived from the content of the character testimony or from the character (and/or reputation) of the character witnesses? If the character of the character witnesses is likely to make the biggest difference, is it desirable to have a rule that, in effect, benefits people primarily because of whom they know?

PROBLEMS

1. Helmer Johanson, an anthropology professor at the local university, has sued Sarah Fuller, a medical student, and Ralph Farnsworth, an old college friend and fellow medical student of Sarah. Helmer had arranged to have Sarah live in his house during the summer while he was excavating in Egypt. One weekend during the summer, Sarah left town to visit her family and gave Ralph permission to use the house. Ralph threw a large rather loud

---

11. The reformulation advocated by Justice Rutledge was the so-called Illinois rule, which limited the specific acts to ones that were similar to the offense for which the defendant was on trial. Justice Rutledge admitted that he preferred abolition of the opportunity for specific acts questions, and he defended the Illinois rule only on the ground that "it has the practical merit of greatly reducing the scope and volume of allowable questions concerning specific acts, rumors, etc., with comparable reduction of innuendo, insinuation and gossip." 335 U.S. at 496.

party that weekend. Helmer claims that Ralph is directly responsible for some damage to the house and that Sarah is liable for the damage because she negligently entrusted the premises to Ralph. Ralph and Sarah, on the other hand, maintain that the damage to the premises existed before Sarah moved in. Helmer calls two former fraternity brothers of Ralph, and they offer to testify about several college fraternity parties during which Ralph caused extensive damage to the fraternity house. Both Ralph and Sarah object to the admission of this testimony. What result?

2. Paul Plant, a candidate for public office, has sued Diane Daniels for defamation for circulating a pamphlet stating that for years Paul has been unfaithful to his wife and that on May 23 Paul stole a pistol from a local sporting good store. Paul testifies that both statements are untrue.

> (a) Paul calls Edgar James, who offers to testify that since the publication of the pamphlet Paul has had a reputation in the community for being a philanderer and for being dishonest.
>
> (b) Diane calls Zelda Young, who offers to testify that she had an affair with Paul last year.
>
> (c) Diane calls Florence Newman, who offers to testify that prior to the alleged defamation Paul had a reputation in the community for being a philanderer and for being dishonest.
>
> (d) Diane calls Winston Hampton, who offers to testify that on two occasions last year when he was with Paul, Paul stole merchandise from a local department store.

Assuming that proper objections are made, which pieces of evidence should be admissible?

3. The defendant has been charged with perjury before a federal grand jury. As part of its case in chief the prosecutor offers the following evidence:

> (a) W-1's testimony that he knows of at least five other occasions on which the defendant had lied.
>
> (b) W-2's testimony that the defendant has a reputation in the community for dishonesty.

As part of the defense, the defendant offers the following evidence:

> (c) W-3's testimony that the defendant has a reputation in the community for honesty.

Assume that there is no objection to the evidence in (c) or that the objection is overruled. On cross-examination of W-3 the prosecutor asks:

> (d) "Did you know that the defendant was convicted of perjury five years ago?"

A. Character Evidence 229

(e) "Have you heard that the defendant was investigated for filing a false income tax return ten years ago?"
(f) "Have you heard that the defendant was convicted of assault last year?" *irrelevant to Credibility*

In rebuttal the prosecution offers the following evidence:

(g) W-4's testimony that in her opinion the defendant is a very dishonest person. *Admissible since the door has been opened*
(h) W-4's testimony that this opinion is based on her having observed the defendant lie and cheat on several previous occasions. *Can't use it b/c its a specific instance*

Which pieces of evidence are objectionable?

4. Dick Davis is charged with the murder of Ralph Green and claims self-defense. After the prosecution has presented its case, Davis offers the following evidence:

(a) W-1 to testify that he and Davis are Elks, that he knows Davis well from weekly meetings, and that Davis has an excellent reputation for honesty among the Elks.
(b) W-2 to testify that Ralph Green has a reputation in the community for violence.
(c) W-3 to testify that two years ago Ralph Green was convicted of aggravated assault, a felony.
(d) W-4 to testify that she told the defendant of three different times that she had seen the victim make unprovoked attacks on other people.

In rebuttal, the prosecution offers the following evidence:

(e) W-5 to testify that Ralph Green has a reputation in the community for peacefulness.
(f) W-6 to testify that Davis has a reputation in the community for violence.

Which evidence is objectionable?

5. Clarence Hill is being prosecuted for the attempted murder of Ted Ellsworth in a jurisdiction that views mere words as potentially adequate provocation. (If Ellsworth had been killed and if the killing were a result of reasonable, adequate provocation, it would be manslaughter, not murder. If the completed act could only be manslaughter, the incompleted act (i.e., the mere wounding) could not be attempted murder.)

Clarence and several eyewitnesses testify as follows: They and Ted Ellsworth were all in a local tavern, and Hill and Ellsworth were at opposite ends of the bar. Ellsworth taunted Hill with racial slurs and derogatory references to Hill's wife. Hill became enraged and shot Ellsworth.

The prosecutor is convinced that these witnesses are lying and wants to introduce the testimony of Ruth Watson that Ellsworth has a reputation in the community for peacefulness, compassion, and absence of racial prejudice. Ellsworth is not available to testify.

Is Ruth Watson's testimony admissible?

B. HABIT AND ROUTINE PRACTICE

1. Character versus Habit

Although FRE 404(a) severely limits the circumstances in which character evidence may be used to show action in conformity with character, the Federal Rules place no restrictions on the use of habit evidence to show action in conformity with habit. Moreover, there is no prohibition against evidence of specific acts to prove habit to show action in conformity with habit. See FRE 406.[12] Consider, for example, Halloran v. Virginia Chemicals Inc.,[13] where one issue was what caused a can of refrigerant to explode. The plaintiff claimed that the explosion was caused by a defect in the product, and the defendant claimed that the explosion resulted from the plaintiff's use of a heating coil, contrary to the instructions on the can. The court held that it was error to exclude evidence of plaintiff's habit of using an immersion heating coil to heat cans of refrigerant.

The primary difficulty posed by rules that restrict the use of character evidence but not habit evidence to show action on a particular occasion is how to distinguish between character and habit.[14] The Advisory Committee's

---

12. FRE 406 is an unusual rule. Whereas most of the Federal Rules are exclusionary provisions, FRE 406 merely announces that evidence is relevant:

> Evidence of the habit of a person or of the routine practice of an organization, whether corroborated or not and regardless of the presence of eyewitnesses, is relevant to prove that the conduct of the person or organization on a particular occasion was in conformity with the habit or routine practice.

As a matter of first impression, the rule seems unnecessary. It does serve an important function, however. Although most jurisdictions today do not limit the use of habit and routine practice evidence, many older cases restricted the use of habit or routine practice evidence to show action in conformity with habit. In some jurisdictions habit evidence could be used for this purpose only if there were no eyewitnesses to the incident in question, and in some jurisdictions the habit evidence was admissible only if corroborated.

13. 41 N.Y.2d 386, 393 N.Y.S.2d 341, 361 N.E.2d 991 (1977).

14. See 1A J. Wigmore, Evidence in Trials at Common Law 1609 n.3 (Tillers rev. 1983):

> Some observers have suggested that a principled distinction cannot be made. See, e.g., 1 Louisell & Mueller, Federal Evidence §156 (1978) ("On a deeper level, it seems that

B. Habit and Routine Practice

Note to FRE 406 quotes with approval the following passage from McCormick's Handbook on the Law of Evidence:[15]

> Character and habit are close[ly] akin. Character is a generalized description of one's disposition, or of one's disposition in respect to a general trait, such as honesty, temperance, or peacefulness. "Habit," in modern usage, both lay and psychological, is more specific. It describes one's regular responses to a repeated specific situation. If we speak of character for care, we think of the person's tendency to act prudently in all the varying situations of life, in business, family life, in handling automobiles and in walking across the street. A habit, on the other hand, is the person's regular practice of meeting a particular kind of situation with a specific type of conduct, such as the habit of going down a particular stairway two stairs at a time, or of giving the handsignal for a left turn, or of alighting from railway cars while they are moving. The doing of the habitual acts may become semi-automatic.

Perhaps as a matter of common usage of the terms *character* and *habit*, most people would agree with the labels that McCormick attaches to his examples. The passage, however, does not tell us what qualitative difference there is between character and habit; nor does it provide us with much of a basis for labeling activity that falls between the fairly extreme examples of generality and specificity. For example, what about evidence that a person (a) is a careful driver, (b) always/usually stops at stop signs, (c) always/usually stops at a particular stop sign? The caselaw suggests that the first and probably the second pieces of evidence would be character evidence and that the last piece

---

the law's concept of character is rooted in the autonomous, free-willing human of the Judeo-Christian tradition, while its concept of habit proceeds from more mechanistic notions akin to the modern behaviorist's idea of the conditioned organism. The occasional confusion of character and habit evidence perhaps represents little more than the overlapping into marginal areas of competing emphases on these two different approaches to human nature." . . .[)]; however, this remark by Louisell and Mueller, while provocative, may be misguided; in the first place, it is by no means incoherent to speak and think of "voluntary habits" since most human habits dealt with under the legal rubric of habit are far removed from the polar form of habitual behavior characterized by involuntary Pavlovian responses to external stimuli and instead involve habits which have been voluntarily assumed and which may also be deliberately abandoned or altered; furthermore, the willingness to admit habit evidence may not reflect the ascendancy of a mechanistic and deterministic theory of human behavior but rather reflect the emergence of a philosophy of man lying at the opposite pole; this is because it is possible that habit evidence has become acceptable because people in the twentieth century are perhaps less prone to confuse the notions of predictability and predetermination; habit evidence may be now admitted precisely because many judges believe that the admissibility of evidence of habit does no violence to cherished beliefs about the capacity of human beings to deliberately regulate and control their conduct; the reviser is inclined to think that the proper historical explanation of habit lies in the direction just sketched since it seems that in nineteenth century intellectual circles there was a far greater fear that systematic descriptions of the course of individual behavior implied the lack of individual autonomy and freedom.

15. The passage appears in slightly modified form in the current edition. McCormick's Handbook on the Law of Evidence 574-575 (3d ed., Cleary, 1984).

of evidence would be habit evidence. That classification, however, is by no means obvious from McCormick's description.

In fact, it is not possible to provide any qualitative distinction between character and habit.[16] There are, however, two factors that both as a matter of common usage and evidentiary principle are helpful in distinguishing between character and habit. The first and, according to the caselaw, the most important distinction is that habit, as opposed to character, tends to be relatively more routine, regularized activity. It is, therefore, more likely to be repeated on any given occasion, and thus more probative of the actor's conduct on a specific occasion.[17] The second distinction is that habit, as opposed to character, tends to be morally neutral and, therefore, nonprejudicial. For example, arriving at work at a certain hour or taking a particular route to work—activities that one would tend to classify as habit—are morally neutral, whereas traits such as honesty, violence, or selfishness, which one would tend to classify as character traits, have a judgmental and, therefore, potentially prejudicial aspect to them.

Focusing on probative value and prejudice provides the proper framework for arguing about and deciding whether evidence should be labeled as habit or character. Relying on these factors, however, will not always provide easy answers to the question whether one is dealing with character or habit. Indeed, the two factors may sometimes cut in different directions. Consider, for example, a case in which the defendant is charged with murdering a prostitute, and the prosecutor wishes to establish that the defendant was with the prostitute on the night of the murder, which happened to be a Thursday. Evidence that the defendant frequently visited the prostitute to prove he visited her on the occasion in question clearly has a judgmental or prejudicial aspect to it. On the other hand, at least if the evidence of visiting the prostitute is quite specific—e.g., visiting her every Thursday at 8 P.M.—the activity is as regular and routine as much of the evidence that gets the label "habit."

2. Business Custom or Routine Practice of an Organization

Business custom or routine practice of an organization is the organizational or institutional counterpart to individual habit. FRE 406 makes it clear that this type of evidence is admissible to show action in conformity with the

---

16. For an excellent discussion of the difficulties in distinguishing between character and habit, see 1A J. Wigmore, Evidence in Trials at Common Law 1624-1630 (Tillers rev. 1983).

17. Closely related to the question whether the type of activity should be regarded as habit evidence is the question whether the evidence offered is sufficient to establish the habit. For example, stopping at a particular stop sign—as opposed to driving carefully or stopping at stop signs generally—would probably be regarded as a habit. Evidence that the driver had stopped at the particular sign on each of the five occasions that the witness had ridden with the driver, however, probably would not be regarded as sufficient to establish that the driver in fact had the habit of stopping at the particular stop sign.

B. Habit and Routine Practice

custom or routine practice on a particular occasion. Like most habit evidence, routine practice evidence is likely to be morally neutral; and because of the regularized, routine nature of the activity, it is likely to be at least as probative of action on a particular occasion as some of the kinds of individual activities that are regarded as habit. There is apt to be a greater need for routine practice evidence, however. Consider, for example, how an insurance company might try to prove that it had mailed a cancellation notice to one of its customers. Almost certainly a copy of the notice will be in the insurance company's files, but it is likely that nobody will have any personal recollection of actually mailing the notice in question. There will be, however, employees of the company who can testify to the routine practice of the company with respect to cancellation notices: that a particular person prepares and signs the notice and places it in a particular box; that another individual routinely takes papers from that box, makes copies and puts them in the appropriate files, puts the original in a stamped addressed envelope, and places the envelope in an outgoing mail basket; and that a third person regularly picks up the outgoing mail and deposits it with the post office.

PROBLEMS

1. Mary Burris has sued John Adkins for injuries received in an automobile accident that occurred at 6 P.M. on Friday, November 23. Mary claims that John was drunk at the time of the accident and that he ran a stop sign. She offers the following evidence:

(a) W-1, one of John's co-workers, to testify that John has intemperate drinking habits;

(b) W-2, another co-worker, to testify that she was absent from work on Friday, November 23, but that on most Fridays after work she and John and several other co-workers go to a tavern near their place of employment and that John usually has three or four beers.

(c) W-3 to testify that he frequently rides in the car with John and that customarily John is a rather careless driver.

(d) W-4 to testify that on the four occasions she has ridden with John, John failed to stop completely for the stop sign at the intersection where the accident occurred.

(e) W-5 to testify that she refuses to ride with John because John is such a bad driver.

Which pieces of evidence are admissible?

2. Alma Peterson has brought a federal civil rights action against James North, a police officer, for fatally shooting her son, Frank. The shooting occurred when North was investigating an automobile accident. North claims that Frank Peterson first shot at him and that the killing was in self-defense.

As part of his defense North offers the testimony of Margaret Kline, a neighbor of Alma Peterson, that she knew of five occasions on which Frank had assaulted other residents in the neighborhood and that in her opinion Frank had been a very violent person. Should this evidence be admitted?

C. EVIDENCE OF SPECIFIC (BAD) ACTS (OF A PARTY)[18]

1. Potentially Admissible Specific Acts Evidence

Even though specific acts are not admissible to prove character to show action in conformity with character, there are a number of purposes for which they may be admissible. See, e.g., FRE 404(b):

> Evidence of other crimes, wrongs, or acts is not admissible to prove the character of a person in order to show action in conformity therewith. It may, however, be admissible for other purposes, such as proof of motive, opportunity, intent, preparation, plan, knowledge, identity, or absence of mistake or accident.

Consider the following description of some of these purposes:

McCORMICK'S HANDBOOK ON THE LAW OF EVIDENCE
558-563 (3d ed., Cleary, 1984)

. . . The permissible purposes include:[10]
(1) To complete the story of the crime on trial by placing it in the

---

18. Nothing in the rules that we are about to discuss or in our analysis of them requires that the acts be *bad* or that they be the acts of *a party*. As a descriptive matter, however, the acts almost always are bad acts, and they usually are the bad acts of a party to the litigation, usually a criminal defendant.

There is a variety of labels for the type of evidence considered here: specific acts evidence, prior bad acts, bad conduct evidence, uncharged misconduct, etc. We will tend to use the term *specific acts*. Regardless of the terminology, the issues are the same.

[10]. The enumerated purposes are not all of the same type. Some are phrased in terms of the immediate inferences sought to be drawn (such as plan or motive) while others are phrased in terms of ultimate facts (such as knowledge, intent or identity which the prosecution seeks to establish. See Stone, Exclusion of Similar Fact Evidence: America, 51 Harv. L. Rev. 988, 1026 (1938) ("Motive, intent, absence of mistake, plan and identity are not really all on the same plane. Intent, absence of mistake, and identity are facts in issue—*facta probanda*. Motive, plan, or scheme are *facta probantia*, and may tend to show an *facta probanda*").

C. Evidence of Specific (Bad) Acts (of a Party)

context of nearby and nearly contemporaneous happenings.[11] The phrases "same transaction"[12] or, less happily, "res gestae"[13] often are used to denote evidence introduced for this purpose.

(2) To prove the existence of a larger plan,[14] scheme[15] or conspiracy,[16]

---

11. United States v. Masters, 622 F.2d 83 (4th Cir. 1980) (upholding admission of taped conversations of the defendant with undercover agents despite reference to other sales and acts on grounds that the evidence was necessary to complete the story of the crime on trial as well as to prove that the defendant was "dealing" . . .); United States v. Ulland, 643 F.2d 537, 540-541 (8th Cir. 1981) (testimony as to financially troubled ventures admissible to show "immediate context" in prosecution for fraud in procuring checks that travelled in interstate commerce); State v. Villavicencio, 95 Ariz. 199, 388 P.2d 245 (1964) (upholding introduction of evidence of sale of narcotics to one person in prosecution for sale to another, where evidence showed that both sales took place at same time and place); State v. Klotter, 274 Minn. 58, 142 N.W.2d 568 (1966) (where guns taken in burglary of sporting goods store and burglary that same night of home of friend of defendant's family located five miles away were found in defendant's possession, the events were "connected closely enough in time, place and manner").

12. United States v. Brooks 670 F.2d 625, 628-629 (5th Cir. 1982) (evidence that marijuana as well as cocaine was found in defendant's car at border patrol checkpoint was properly admitted as proving "an uncharged offense arising out of the same transaction or series of transactions as the charged offense" of possession of cocaine with intent to distribute).

13. United States v. Masters, 622 F.2d 83, 86 (4th Cir. 1980); State v. Price, 123 Ariz. 165, 598 P.2d 985 (1979) ("This principle that the complete story of the crime may be shown even though it reveals other crimes has often been termed 'res gestae.' [W]e choose to refer to [it] as the 'complete story' principle").

14. Compare United States v. Lewis, 693 F.2d 189 (D.C. Cir. 1982) (testimony concerning stolen money orders not charged in indictment admissible to show that defendant was "the mastermind of a common scheme"); United States v. Parnell, 581 F.2d 1374 (10th Cir. 1978), *cert. denied*, 439 U.S. 1076 (previous fraudulent scheme admissible as "direct precursor" of conspiracy to purchase grain with forged cashiers checks); State v. Toshishige Yoshino, 45 Haw. 206, 364 P.2d 638 (1961) (evidence of first robbery admissible in prosecution for second where defendant and others robbed first victim and obtained from him the name and address of their next victim); and State v. Long, 195 Or. 81, 244 P.2d 1033 (1952) (in prosecution for killing owner of truck, proper to prove as part of planned course of action that defendant used truck the next day for a robbery in which he shot an F.B.I. agent while fleeing) with United States v. Dothard, 666 F.2d 498, 504 (11th Cir. 1982) (because a false statement on a U.S. Army Reserve enlistment application, which as the basis of the charge against defendant, and a false statement made to a state driver's license examiner four years earlier were not "so intertwined . . . that they are separate components of a general plan," testimony of state official and prosecutor's comments on defendant's dishonest character constituted reversible error); State v. Manrique, 271 Or. 201, 531 P.2d 239, 242-243 (1975) (previous heroin sales not part of common scheme or plan). . . .

15. On the distinction, if there is one, between "plan" and "scheme," see 2 Louisell & Mueller, Federal Evidence §140 at 140 (1977). The common plan exception includes crimes committed in preparation for the offense charged. United States v. Cepulonis, 530 F.2d 238 (1st Cir. 1976), *cert. denied*, 426 U.S. 922 (testimony that bank robbers shot at a police officer and a passing motorist and evidence of a shotgun not used in the robbery properly admitted to show that defendants' plan was to distract police by firing and that they had assembled weapons for this purpose); United States v. Carroll, 510 F.2d 507, 509 (2d Cir. 1975), *cert. denied*, 426 U.S. 923 (other crimes done to determine if conspirators capable of handling mail truck robbery admissible in prosecution for attempted robbery of the mail truck); United States v. Leftwich, 461 F.2d 586 (3d Cir. 1972), *cert. denied*, 409 U.S. 915 (theft of car admissible in prosecution for robbery accomplished with car). . . .

16. United States v. Bermudez, 526 F.2d 89 (2d Cir. 1975), *cert. denied*, 425 U.S. 970 (upholding admission of "traces of narcotics" and narcotics related equipment seized in home of conspirator six weeks after conspiracy to distribute cocaine ended). . . .

If the "other crimes" evidence is part of the conspiracy charged, then it is direct rather than circumstantial evidence of the offense charged. Consequently, there is no reason to

of which the crime on trial is a part. This will be relevant as showing motive, and hence the doing of the criminal act, the identity of the actor, or his intention.

(3) To prove other crimes by the accused so nearly identical in method as to earmark them as the handiwork of the accused.[17] Much more is demanded than the mere repeated commission of crimes of the same class, such as repeated murders, robberies[19] or rapes.[20] The pattern and characteristics of the crimes must be so unusual and distinctive as to be like a signature.[21]

---

analyze the evidence in terms of the exceptions to the rule excluding "other crimes" evidence. . . .

17. People v. Peete, 28 Cal. 2d 306, 169 P.2d 924, (1946), *cert. denied*, 392 U.S. 790 (prior homicide by defendant accused of shooting the deceased from behind at close range in an attempt to sever the spinal cord admissible to identify defendant as murderer where previous homicide also involved a bullet from behind, severing the spinal cord at the neck); Whiteman v. State, 119 Ohio St. 285, 164 N.E. 51 (1928) (evidence of other robberies by defendants wearing uniforms, impersonating officers and stopping cars, thus "earmarking" them as the perpetrators of the offense charged); Rex v. Smith, 11 Cr. App. R. 229, 84 L.J.K.B. 2153 (1915), described in Marjoribanks, For the Defence: The Life of Edward Marshall Hall 321 (1937) (in this "brides of the bath" case it was shown that the man accused of drowning in the bathtub a woman whom he had bigamously "married" had later "married" several wives who left him their property and whom he then purportedly discovered drowned in the bath).

The phrase of which authors of detective fiction are fond, *modus operandi*, may be employed in this context. . . .

19. United States v. Myers, 550 F.2d 1036, 1046 (5th Cir. 1977), appeal after remand 572 F.2d 506, *cert. denied*, 439 U.S. 847 ("An early afternoon robbery of an outlying bank situated on a highway, by revolver-armed robbers wearing gloves and stocking masks, and carrying a bag for the loot, is not such an unusual crime that it tends to prove that one of the two identified individuals involved must have been the single bandit in a similar prior robbery"). . . .

20. Compare State v. Sauter, 125 Mont. 109, 232 P.2d 731, 732 (1951) (in charge of forcible rape in automobile after picking up victim in barroom, other rapes following similar pickups were "too common . . . to have much evidentiary value in showing a systematic scheme or plan") with McGahee v. Massey, 667 F.2d 1357, 1360 (11th Cir. 1982), *cert. denied*, 103 S. Ct. 255 (where man wearing a white, see-through bikini bathing suit approached a woman sunbathing at beach and raped her, it was within trial court's discretion to permit testimony that twice during the previous month the defendant, wearing a red see-through bathing suit, had exposed himself to other women at the same beach to demonstrate "the manner of operation, identity and type of clothing worn by the defendant"); Williams v. State, 110 So. 2d 654, 663 (Fla. 1959), *cert. denied*, 361 U.S. 847 (that defendant hid in back seat of woman's car at shopping center and fled when woman screamed admissible to prove that six weeks later the defendant raped another woman outside the same shopping center after hiding in the back seat of her car); cf. United States v. Gano, 560 F.2d 990 (10th Cir. 1977) (permissible to show that defendant social worker charged with carnal knowledge of female under age of 16 had sexual relations with the girl's mother and had sold marijuana to mother and given marijuana to daughter).

As the facts of some of these cases may suggest, the courts tend to find distinctive similarities in sex cases more readily than in other situations. See infra note 24. In addition, if the rapist's method of operation is calculated to create the appearance of consent on the part of the victim, the similar acts evidence may be admitted to negate the defense of consent. . . .

21. Compare United States v. Pisari, 636 F.2d 855, 859 (1st Cir. 1981) (use of knife in prior robbery was not sufficient signature or trademark to warrant admission on charge of robbery of postal installation by knife) with United States v. Woods, 613 F.2d 629, 635 (6th Cir. 1980), *cert. denied*, 446 U.S. 920 ("We find the circumstances of this case reveal a 'signature' on the crimes insofar as each was an armed robbery by robbers wearing ski masks, goggles and jumpsuits and using a stolen vehicle for a getaway car"). . . .

C. Evidence of Specific (Bad) Acts (of a Party) 237

(4) To show a passion or propensity for unusual and abnormal sexual relations.[22] Initially, proof of other sex crimes always was confined to offenses involving the same parties, but a number of jurisdictions now admit other sex offenses with other persons,[24] at least as to offenses involving sexual aberrations.[25]

(5) To show, by similar acts or incidents, that the act in question was not performed inadvertently, accidentally,[26] involuntarily,[27] or without guilty

---

22. Woods v. State, 250 Ind. 132, 235 N.E.2d 479 (1968) (other acts of rape and incest with same victim admissible to show "depraved sexual instinct"); State v. Schut, 71 Wn.2d 400, 429 P.2d 126 (1967) (prior acts of incest with victim admissible to show lustful inclination toward victim). . . .

24. Lamar v. State, 245 Ind. 104, 195 N.E.2d 98 (1964); State v. Schlak, 253 Iowa 113, 116, 111 N.W.2d 289, 291 (1961) (evidence that defendant accused of sexually molesting a 15-year-old girl had attacked others upheld as showing his motive—"to gratify his lustful desire by grabbing or fondling young girls"). . . .

Some courts do not admit evidence of sex crimes with other victims as revealing an incriminating propensity, but achieve a similar result by stretching to find other exceptions to the rule against extrinsic character evidence applicable. Findley v. State, 94 Nev. 212, 577 P.2d 867 (1978) (evidence that defendant, charged with placing his hand on the "private parts" of a young girl, had behaved similarly with two women nine years earlier allowed to show intent or lack of mistake where defendant testified and denied the act). . . .

25. State v. McFarlin, 110 Ariz. 225, 517 P.2d 87 (1973) (overruling cases establishing an unqualified propensity rule). Defining aberrant sexual activity presents a considerable problem. At least one state has retreated further, entirely withdrawing its more lenient treatment of evidence of other sex crimes. Commonwealth v. Shively, 492 Pa. 411, 424 A.2d 1257, 1259-1260 (1981), overruling Commonwealth v. Kline, 361 Pa. 434, 65 A.2d 348 (1949).

26. United States v. DeLoach, 654 F.2d 763, 768-769 (D.C. Cir. 1980), *cert. denied*, 450 U.S. 1004 (in prosecution for submission of false information to procure a labor certificate for an alien where defendant disavowed knowledge of codefendant's false submissions, testimony of other aliens that defendant had swindled them by falsely promising to secure labor certificates was admissible to undercut "his defense of mistake"); United States v. Ross, 321 F.2d 61 (2d Cir. 1963), *cert. denied*, 375 U.S. 894 (where defendant charged with securities fraud claimed he was an unwitting tool of his employer, it was proper to show on cross-examination that he had drifted among firms engaged in selling worthless securities by similar methods); United States v. Johnson, 634 F.2d 735 (4th Cir. 1980), *cert. denied*, 451 U.S. 907 (evidence that physician accused of tax evasion submitted fraudulent medicaid billing properly admitted to rebut her claim that she was too devoted to patients to worry about finances); . . . United States v. Witschner, 624 F.2d 840, 843 (8th Cir. 1980), *cert. denied*, 449 U.S. 994 (in prosecution for mail fraud based on submitting fraudulent medical insurance claims, evidence relating to patients not mentioned in the indictment admissible to show "that the submission of the false medical reports was not an accident"); United States v. Harris, 661 F.2d 138, 142 (10th Cir. 1981) (where father accused of murdering eight-year-old son claimed that fatal injuries occurred because he tripped while carrying the child on his shoulders, evidence of many bone fractures sustained by the infant months before were admissible, since "particularly in child abuse cases" the "admissibility of other crimes, wrongs or acts to establish intent and absence of mistake or accident is well established"); People v. Williams, 6 Cal. 2d 500, 58 P.2d 917 (1936) (where defendant accused of larceny by posing as a customer standing near owner of bag and taking purse from bag while owner was shopping, testimony of detectives that defendant took another purse from another woman's bag in the same manner admissible to refute defendant's claim that he picked the purse off the floor, thinking it lost). . . .

27. United States v. Holman 680 F.2d 1340, 1349 (11th Cir. 1982), *reh'g denied*, 691 F.2d 512 (other smuggling incidents to rebut defense of coercion); . . . United States v. Hearst, 563 F.2d 1331 (9th Cir. 1977), *reh'g denied*, 573 F.2d 579, *cert. denied*, 435 U.S. 1000 (evidence of other crimes to negate anticipated defense of duress by publisher's daughter held for ransom by terrorist group and charged in bank robbery committed by the group).

knowledge.[28] The similarities between the act charged and the extrinsic acts need not be as extensive and striking as is required under purpose (3), and the various acts need not be manifestations of a unifying plan, as required for purpose (2). *not an element of the substantive crime but it's relevant*

(6) To establish motive.[30] The evidence of motive may be probative of the identity of the criminal[31] or of malice or specific intent.[32] An application of this principle permits proof of criminal acts of the accused that constitute admissions by conduct designed to obstruct justice[33] or avoid punishment

---

28. United States v. Rubio-Gonzalez, 674 F.2d 1067, 1075 (5th Cir. 1982) (record of illegal entries and deportations of defendant that revealed that defendant had migrated along the same path from the same part of Mexico as did the illegal aliens whom he was charged with concealing was admissible to show that he knew that these persons had entered the United States illegally); United States v. Wixom, 529 F.2d 217 (8th Cir. 1976) (evidence that defendant accused of distributing heroin had distributed an ounce of heroin on another occasion properly admitted to show that he knew he was distributing heroin). . . .

30. United States v. Haldeman, 559 F.2d 31, 88 (D.C. Cir. 1976), *cert. denied*, 431 U.S. 933 (evidence of conspiracy of government officials to break into psychiatrist's office to obtain records of an opponent of government's war policy admissible to show motive for Watergate cover-up conspiracy); United States v. Wasler, 670 F.2d 539, 542 (5th Cir. 1982) (evidence of fraudulent loans admissible to show motive for allegedly fraudulent extension of loan by manager of federal credit union, since "[h]ad Wasler not managed to reduce his monthly payments, a default on the unauthorized loans might well have raised questions whose answers would have proved unpleasant"); United States v. Cyphers, 553 F.2d 1064 (7th Cir. 1977), *cert. denied*, 434 U.S. 843 (testimony that shortly after a bank robbery a defendant asked a government informer to purchase $1000 worth of heroin for him admissible to show motive for robbery; . . . People v. Cardenas, 31 Cal. 3d 897, 184 Cal. Rptr. 165, 169, 647 P.2d 569, 573 (1982) (evidence of narcotics addiction erroneously admitted to show financial motive for attempted robbery of food store, noting that "Prior cases have upheld the admission of [such evidence] where obtaining narcotics was the direct result of the crime committed" but not "where the object of the charged offense was to obtain money or an item other than narcotics"); State v. Green, 232 Kan. 116, 652 P.2d 697, 701 (1982) ("where a marital homicide is involved, evidence of a discordant marital relationship, and of defendant's previous ill treatment of his wife, including his prior threats to kill her, is competent as bearing on the defendant's motive and intent"). . . .

31. State v. Green, 232 Kan. 116, 652 P.2d 697, 701 (1982) (where the "defendant claimed in essence that someone had broken into his wife's house to rob her and inflicted the fatal wounds prior to his arrival . . . evidence of the defendant's prior assaults on his wife was of great probative value on the issue of identity").

32. United States v. Benton, 637 F.2d 1052, 1056 (5th Cir. 1981), *reh'g denied*, 645 F.2d 72 ("While motive is not an element of any offense charged . . . appellant's knowledge that Zambito might implicate him in the Florida homicides constituted a motive for appellant wanting to kill Zambito. . . . This evidence of motivation was relevant as tending to show the participation of appellant in the crime and to show malice or intent which are elements of the crimes charged"). . . .

33. People v. Spaulding, 309 Ill. 292, 141 N.E. 196 (1923) (killing sole eyewitness to crime); State v. Shaw, —Mont.—, 648 P.2d 287 (1982) (testimony that defendant threatened prosecution's key witness admissible to prove consciousness of guilt; State v. Trujillo, 95 N.M. 535, 624 P.2d 44 (1981) (flight and escape); Gibbs v. State, 201 Tenn. 491, 300 S.W.2d 890 (1957) (in prosecution for murder, evidence that defendant also killed daughter when she discovered body admissible (along with evidence that defendant had killed husband first, then the wife when she discovered this) to show motive and as "inseparable components of a completed crime"). . . .

C. Evidence of Specific (Bad) Acts (of a Party) 239

for a crime,[34] or of the crimes that motivated the interference with the enforcement of the law.[35]

(7) To establish opportunity, in the sense of access to or presence at the scene of the crime[37] or in the sense of possessing distinctive or unusual skills or abilities employed in the commission of the crime charged.[38]

(8) To show, without considering motive, that defendant acted with malice, deliberation, or the requisite specific intent.[39]

(9) To prove identity.[40] Although this is indisputably one of the ultimate purposes for which evidence of other criminal conduct will be received, the need to prove identity should not be, in itself, a ticket to admission. Almost always, identity is the inference that flows from one or more of the theories just listed. The second (larger plan), third (distinctive device), and sixth (motive) seem to be most often relied upon to show identity.

---

34. People v. Gambino, 12 Ill. 2d 29, 145 N.E.2d 42 (1957), cert. denied, 356 U.S. 904 (escape and attempted escape while awaiting trial); State v. Brown, 231 Or. 297, 372 P.2d 779 (1962) (stealing cars to escape). . . .

35. State v. Simborski, 120 Conn. 624, 182 A. 221 (1936) (evidence that defendant, who was accused of murdering police officer who was seeking to arrest him, had committed two burglaries a short while before was admissible to show motive and as res gestae); People v. Odum, 27 Ill. 2d 237, 188 N.E.2d 720 (1963) (evidence in a murder prosecution that an earlier indictment for a different crime had named the deceased as a witness against defendant).

37. United States v. DeJohn, 638 F.2d 1048, 1053 (7th Cir. 1981) (testimony of YMCA security guard and city police officer revealing that on other occasions defendant had obtained checks from a mailbox at YMCA was "highly probative of defendant's opportunity to gain access to the mailboxes and obtain the checks that he cashed" with forged endorsements).

38. United States v. Barrett, 539 F.2d 244 (1st Cir. 1976) (evidence admissible to show familiarity with sophisticated means of neutralizing burglar alarms).

39. Compare . . . United States v. Mitchell, 666 F.2d 1385, 1388 (11th Cir.) [sic], cert. denied, 457 U.S. 1124 (testimony that defendant, who was charged with defrauding federal agency by selling part of mortgaged corn crop, was told upon delivering more corn to coop that payments would have to be issued jointly with the agency and that he responded by saying that he would take his corn elsewhere was admissible to prove intent to defraud) with United States v. Foskey, 636 F.2d 517, 524 (D.C. Cir. 1980) ("The mere fact that a person was [arrested] in the company of another who possesses drugs simply is not sufficient to justify a conclusion that he himself knowingly possessed drugs [when arrested together with the same person] two-and-one-half years later," since "the linchpin element of intent in the prior incident" is missing) and United States v. Guerrero, 650 F.2d 728, 734 (5th Cir. 1981) (error to admit testimony of a patient who had obtained a prescription from defendant physician accused of illegally dispensing controlled substances to an undercover agent to the effect that defendant had a reputation for being free with pills and that she obtained and used the pills for non-medical purposes after giving a false medical history, since "absent some evidence that defendant acted with unlawful intent in prescribing to [the witness patient], it cannot be said that [her] testimony is in any way relevant to the question of his intent in prescribing to [the undercover agent]"). Also compare State v. Featherman, 133 Ariz. 340, 651 P.2d 868, 873 (App. 1982) (to prove that defendant murdered his estranged wife, where decomposed body was found in garbage dump, testimony that defendant had hit her over the head with a baseball bat two months prior to her death was admissible as "directly relevant to his intent the night she was killed") with State v. Robtoy, 98 Wn. 2d 30, 653 P.2d 284, 292 (1982) (evidence of unrelated murder ten months earlier erroneously admitted to prove premeditation since it only shows a propensity for premeditated murder). . . .

40. State v. King, 111 Kan. 140, 206 P. 883 (1922) (evidence that bodies of missing persons were on defendant's premises and that their effects were in his possession admissible to prove that he had killed an employee who had disappeared, whose effects were in defendant's possession, and whose burned body was found 10 years later on defendant's premises).

2. The "Inclusionary" and "Exclusionary" Approaches to Specific Acts Evidence

Some jurisdictions follow the "inclusionary" rule for specific acts evidence. See, e.g., FRE 404(b): Although specific acts are inadmissible to prove character to show action in conformity with character, they "may . . . be admissible for other purposes, *such as* proof of motive, opportunity, intent," etc. (emphasis added). Other jurisdictions follow the "exclusionary" rule: Specific acts evidence is excludable unless offered for one of a specified number of purposes. The list of permissible purposes typically includes some or all of the purposes listed as examples in FRE 404(b).

One difficulty with the exclusionary rule is that occasionally litigants will offer highly probative specific acts evidence that does not fit neatly into one of the preexisting catagories. In such a situation, a court is faced with the undesirable alternatives of excluding important evidence or bending the catagories almost out of recognition.[19] Another difficulty with the exclusionary rule in practice is that once an acceptable category is found, many courts, at least in older decisions, treat the evidence as automatically admissible despite substantial FRE 403-type problems. For example, specific instances of bad conduct engaged in by a criminal defendant—and this is the most typical type of specific act evidence—is inherently prejudicial: Jurors, in addition to using the evidence for whatever legitimate purpose it may have, may consider the defendant to be a generally bad person, who perhaps did not pay adequately for prior indiscretions or who, if not convicted, may be prone to engage in similar conduct again. As a result jurors may be less willing than they otherwise would be to consider seriously a possible reasonable doubt about the defendant's guilt of the crime charged. Furthermore, there may be some question about the nature or extent of the defendant's involvement in the prior bad acts. Thus, permitting the prosecution to introduce evidence of the act raises the possibility of time-consuming and confusing litigation about the occurrence or non-occurrence of a collateral event.

Proponents of the inclusionary approach to specific acts evidence have argued that their formulation of the rule is more likely to lead courts to consider seriously the FRE 403-type problems. As a matter of first impression, we fail to see why this should be so. Nonetheless, the reality is that decisions interpreting and applying FRE 404(b) and similar state rules do give serious consideration to FRE 403-type problems.

3. Specific Acts Evidence, FRE 403, and Preliminary Fact Finding

Since FRE 403 is a rule that favors admissibility (probative value must be "substantially outweighed" by countervailing factors), and since there is a

---

19. Not surprisingly, the appellate caselaw suggests that judges usually choose the latter alternative.

C. Evidence of Specific (Bad) Acts (of a Party)

long tradition of admitting extremely prejudicial specific acts evidence for noncharacter purposes, it may be that FRE 403 is not often going to be a barrier to admissibility. There is, however, at least one type of situation in which FRE 403 has been successfully invoked. When the evidence is offered to establish a proposition that is not seriously contested in the case, a growing number of courts have relied on FRE 403 to exclude the evidence. Consider, for example, the following situation:

> The defendant is being charged with knowing possession of marijuana. The prosecutor offers evidence that the defendant knowingly possessed marijuana two years ago on the ground that this prior possession is evidence of the defendant's knowledge, which is one of the elements of the offense.

If the defendant never suggested lack of knowledge but instead claimed that the marijuana belonged to somebody else, there would be little need for the evidence to prove knowledge. It seems likely that the jury would infer knowledge from the fact of possession and from the failure to deny knowledge.[20] Moreover, if the evidence were admitted, there is the risk that the jury would consider it in two improper ways: First, the jury might infer that because the defendant possessed marijuana once before, the defendant is the kind of person who has a propensity to possess marijuana and, therefore, probably possessed it on this occasion. This particular chain of inferences, however, is probably prohibited by the first sentence of FRE 404(b).[21] Second, even if the jurors entertain a reasonable doubt about whether the defendant possessed marijuana on the occasion that resulted in the present prosecution, the jurors may be willing to forgo that doubt in order to convict and remove from the streets someone who is involved with drugs. The lack of need for the evidence[22] coupled with the possibility of misuse of the evidence by the jurors would justify a decision to exclude the prior possession evidence on FRE 403 grounds.[23]

20. The jury will be told that the defendant has the right not to testify and that the prosecutor has the burden of establishing each element beyond a reasonable doubt. To what extent do you believe that these instructions tend to undermine our assertion that there is little need for the prior possession evidence in order to establish knowledge beyond a reasonable doubt?

21. We say "probably" because we sometimes find the distinction between what is prohibited by the first sentence and what is permitted by the second sentence to be quite elusive. See pages 248-263 infra.

22. As we suggested previously, see pages 132, 162 supra, the probative value of evidence for the purpose of FRE 403 balancing should be assessed in terms of the need for the evidence in light of other evidence. Thus, even if one believes there is a very strong inferential link between prior knowing possession and present knowledge, the evidence, in context, may be regarded as having low probative value.

23. If the trial judge disagrees with our assessment of the FRE 403 balance, could the defendant keep the prior possession evidence out by stipulating that the requisite knowledge exists?

The effect of such a stipulation would be to remove the knowledge element from the jury, which is in effect a partial waiver of the right to a jury trial. Can the defendant make such a waiver binding on the prosecutor? The answer with respect to the broader question

On the other hand, if the defendant in our hypothetical claimed not to know that the substance was marijuana, evidence of the defendant's knowing prior possession would be quite important. We suspect that in this situation most courts would permit the prosecutor to introduce the evidence.

If it is the defendant's claimed lack of knowledge that shifts the FRE 403 balance in favor of admissibility, the proper order of proof would require the prosecutor to wait until there had been some suggestion of lack of knowledge. While this suggestion conceivably could come from the cross-examination of prosecution witnesses, it is most likely to come from the examination of the defendant during the presentation of the defense. Thus, the proper time for the prosecutor's evidence would probably be the rebuttal. If the prosecutor knows in advance that the defendant will claim lack of knowledge, however, there is no harm as a practical matter in letting the prior act evidence come in as part of the prosecutor's case-in-chief.

Another important aspect of balancing probative value of specific acts evidence against the FRE 403 countervailing factors is closely connected to a preliminary fact-finding issue on which courts are divided. Concerns with the potential prejudicial impact of specific acts evidence and with the time and possible confusion that may result from litigating collateral issues have led some state and federal circuit courts to impose a high standard of proof on the offering party: As a condition of admissibility, the proponent of the evidence must establish, by clear and convincing evidence, (a) that the person allegedly responsible for the act in fact committed the act and (b) (if culpability in the commission of the act is important to its relevance, as it usually is) that the person did so culpably. In other words, culpable involvement is an FRE 104(a)-type preliminary fact that must be established by clear and convincing evidence, an unusually high standard of proof.

Other courts, following the lead of the fifth circuit in United States v. Beechum[24] have taken the position that the nature and extent of the person's involvement in the specific act is a matter of conditional relevance to be decided pursuant to FRE 104(b). The preliminary fact requirement is satisfied as long as the jury could find that the person was culpably involved in the act. In Huddleston v. United States,[25] the Supreme Court resolved the conflict in the federal circuits by adopting the *Beechum* position.

As a matter of logical relevance, we believe that in most instances the *Huddleston/Beechum* approach to the preliminary fact issue is the correct

---

whether there will be a bench trial or jury trial is "No." The prosecutor can insist on a jury trial even if the defendant prefers a bench trial. See Singer v. United States, 380 U.S. 24 (1965) (proper to deny defendant's demand for bench trial; right to jury trial may be waived with agreement of prosecutor and court, but right to jury trial does not include right to demand the opposite, a bench trial). But cf. Faretta v. California, 422 U.S. 806 (1975) (sixth amendment right to counsel includes right to waive counsel and proceed pro se). Assuming that *Singer* is still good law (and it was cited with approval in *Faretta*), what, if any, bearing should it have on the stipulation question?

24. 582 F.2d 898 (5th Cir. 1978).
25. 108 S. Ct. 496 (1988).

C. Evidence of Specific (Bad) Acts (of a Party)

one.[26] Consider, for example, the typical situation in which specific acts evidence is offered against a criminal defendant to show knowledge or intent. The relevance of the evidence depends upon the defendant's culpable involvement in the act. Any doubt about whether the defendant committed the act with the requisite knowledge or intent should be an issue for the jury to resolve. If the jury believes that the defendant committed the act with culpable intent, the jury will consider the evidence for whatever it is worth.[27] If the jury believes that the defendant was not culpably involved in the act, the only logical thing for the jury to do is to disregard completely the evidence as proof of the defendant's knowledge or intent.

Application of the FRE 104(b) standard to the question of culpable involvement in acts other than those that are the subject of the current litigation may appear at first blush to provide inadequate protection to the party against whom the evidence is offered. Satisfying FRE 104(b), however, is only one condition of admissibility. The judge must still weigh the probative value of the evidence against the countervailing FRE 403 factors, and the very same factors that arguably justify the strict clear and convincing evidence standard are germane to the judge's FRE 403 determination: The prejudicial impact of the evidence will be the same regardless of what preliminary fact standard is applied; if there is a dispute about the person's culpable involvement in the acts, there is the risk of time-consuming and perhaps distracting litigation about a collateral matter; and to the extent there are doubts about the person's culpable involvement in the specific acts, the evidence has decreased probative value. Careful consideration of these issues in terms of FRE 403 on a case-by-case basis could have the desirable result of excluding specific acts evidence only in those situations in which there has been a reasoned determination that the admission of the evidence will be more harmful than helpful. By contrast, application of the clear and convincing evidence test could result in the exclusion of relevant specific acts evidence with minimal FRE 403 problems that happen not to meet the clear and convincing standard.

Despite the logical soundness of the *Huddleston/Beechum* approach to specific acts evidence, it does not necessarily follow that that approach is preferable to the clear and convincing evidence requirement. One may be skeptical about the ability of trial judges to balance wisely on a case-by-case basis factors that are impossible to quantify with much precision, or one may believe that the balancing is so elusive that it cannot be done wisely. If so, there may be merit to the clear and convincing evidence rule because it

---

26. Actually, we cannot think of a situation in which it would not be the proper approach. We are reluctant to make absolute statements about whether FRE 104(a) or FRE 104(b) applies to a particular type of preliminary fact, however. Instead, we believe it is appropriate in each case to inquire whether the preliminary fact is critical to the relevance of the evidence.

27. The jurors, of course, may also consider the evidence in an improperly prejudicial way. For example, they may be more willing to disregard a reasonable doubt if they believe the defendant is a bad person. This is a matter for resolution under FRE 403's probative value vs. prejudice balancing formula.

diminishes the need for balancing. Although the admissibility of specific acts evidence under either approach should ultimately depend upon balancing probative value against the countervailing FRE 403 factors, the clear and convincing evidence approach eliminates the need for FRE 403 balancing in those situations in which the preliminary fact test is not satisfied. To put the matter somewhat differently, the cost of applying the clear and convincing evidence test is the occasional exclusion of relevant evidence with minimal FRE 403 problems; the cost of using the FRE 104(b) preliminary fact standard and then relying on FRE 403 is the increased opportunity for improper and/or inconsistent application of FRE 403 on a case-by-case basis. If the latter cost is greater, it would be desirable to have the clear and convincing evidence test as a limitation on the judge's discretionary FRE 403 balancing.

One might counter that the clear and convincing evidence test is itself imprecise and that the trial judge may have as much difficulty applying it as applying FRE 403. We agree that the task of applying the clear and convincing evidence standard may sometimes be difficult. We believe, however, that that task is likely to be easier—and as a result, hopefully less subject to divergent, seemingly arbitrary results—than the task of applying FRE 403: Both the clear and convincing evidence test and FRE 403 require a quantification of probative value—the former for the purpose of determining whether the clear and convincing standard has been met and the latter for the purpose of comparison of probative value with countervailing factors. The clear and convincing evidence test, however, does not initially require a consideration or quantification of the FRE 403 countervailing factors, and it does not require making a judgment about how to compare units of probative value with units of prejudice, confusion, and time consumption.

Another factor to consider in evaluating the two competing approaches to preliminary fact finding for specific acts evidence is the extent to which the formulation of the test provides a subtle mindset favoring or opposing admissibility. By erecting a high standard of proof as a condition of admissibility, the clear and convincing evidence test can, and perhaps should, be understood as a warning about the dangers of specific acts evidence; by contrast the *Huddleston/Beechum* low standard of proof coupled with reliance on FRE 403, a rule favoring admissibility, can, and perhaps should, be understood as an invitation to admit specific acts evidence in the absence of a good reason for exclusion. To the extent that these messages have an impact on judicial decision making, one would expect more specific acts evidence to be admissible under *Huddleston/Beechum* than under the clear and convincing evidence test. Moreover, since the application of FRE 403 or the application of any standard of proof is inherently imprecise, it may be that the subtle message of the rule has more impact than its substantive content. If so, a choice between *Huddleston/Beechum* and the clear and convincing evidence test should be based on one's sense about whether judges need to be encouraged to admit or discouraged from admitting specific acts evidence.

On the other hand, perhaps a judge's general attitude about the ad-

C. Evidence of Specific (Bad) Acts (of a Party)

mission of specific acts evidence is determined more by factors external to the rules of evidence than by the wording of any particular rule. If so, then perhaps the most important objective of any rule is to provide the framework for reasoned argument and deliberation about the issues that should affect admissibility—an objective that in our view would be better served by the *Huddleston/Beechum* rule than by the clear and convincing evidence test.

Regardless of the standard of proof for preliminary fact finding, there may be a question about how to apply the standard in cases involving multiple specific acts. Consider, for example, the following situation:

> A defendant has allegedly been culpably involved in several specific acts that are offered for some legitimate noncharacter purpose. The acts are all similar, but viewing each act in isolation, there is not clear and convincing evidence—or even evidence sufficient to support a finding—of the defendant's culpable involvement with respect to any single act. Nonetheless, the defendant is the only identifiable person present at the time the incidents occurred, and it seems unlikely that all of the incidents would have occurred in the absence of the somebody's culpable involvement. In this situation, there would appear to be reason to believe—perhaps even a high probability—that the defendant was culpably involved in one or more of the incidents, even though we do not know which one(s). From the fact that the defendant committed one or more of the acts, we can then make an inference about the defendant's intent, knowledge, motive, etc. with respect to the crime charged.

Depending on the nature of the specific acts and the evidence of the defendant's involvement in them, one might be able to urge successfully that the evidence should be inadmissible on FRE 403 grounds. We submit, however, that the evidence should not be excluded merely because there is not clear and convincing evidence—or evidence sufficient to support a finding—of the defendant's culpable involvement in any particular incident. In this type of situation the appropriate focus of attention for preliminary fact finding should be the acts in the aggregate rather than the individual acts.

4. "Round Up the Usual Suspects"—the *Casablanca* Concern[28]

Among the general population, evidence of prior crimes may be relevant in a propensity sense to show guilt. Criminal defendants who go to trial, how-

---

28. The reference is to the movie *Casablanca* starring Humphrey Bogart, Ingrid Bergman, and Claude Rains; more particularly the reference is to Claude Rains' order at the end of the film to "round up the usual suspects." We wish the idea to associate the points made here with *Casablanca* were our own. Unfortunately, it is not. See R. Lempert and S. Saltzburg, A Modern Approach to Evidence 211 n.56 (1st ed. 1977).

ever, do not constitute a random sample of the general population. The investigatory process tends to focus on "known" criminals—the usual suspects. As a result, the percentage of people who are known to have committed prior bad acts is much larger for the universe of criminal defendants than for the general population. This may simply reflect reasonable use of propensity inferences by the investigators. But the fact remains that the selection process is biased toward charging people who have committed prior bad acts. Unless the jury realizes that any criminal defendant is much more likely to have committed prior bad acts than a randomly selected person from the general population, it may overestimate the probative value of specific acts evidence.

Even if jurors recognize the selection bias, there is a further problem. Only a small percentage of people charged with criminal conduct actually go to trial. Most cases are disposed of by guilty pleas, and it may be that defendants who have committed known prior bad acts and who do not plead guilty are disproportionately innocent. The fact that prior bad acts may be admissible against a defendant for non-character purposes may encourage guilty (and even some innocent) bad act defendants to plead guilty. On the other hand, the guilty defendant who has not committed prior bad acts can go to trial without risking the possibility that the jury will be (improperly) influenced by such evidence. In short, in the absence of an incentive for bad act defendants to go to trial (e.g., a severe mandatory penalty for recidivists), prior bad acts evidence may not be probative of guilt for the universe of defendants who go to trial. Indeed, such evidence may be probative of innocence!

PROBLEMS

1. Bart Morris is charged with murder for the fatal shooting of his wife Donna. Bart claims that the shooting was accidental. Several prosecution witnesses testified that in the weeks before the shooting Bart and Donna had not gotten along well and had been involved in numerous loud arguments. The witnesses attributed the tension between Bart and Donna to Bart's frustration over his inability to obtain a job as a police officer and to his financial dependence on Donna. The prosecutor then offered the testimony of Bart's former wife, Lisa, that eight years earlier in another city, when she was married to Bart, he became violent and seriously wounded her with a pistol after he had failed a police academy qualifying examination. Bart objects to the admissibility of this evidence on the grounds that (a) it is improper character evidence, (b) its probative value is substantially outweighed by its prejudicial impact, and (c) he was tried and acquitted of attempted murder for the shooting of his former wife. How should the court rule?

2. Jack Winters is charged with the rape of Frances Dugan. According to the prosecution's evidence, the rapist scaled an ivy-covered wall and

C. Evidence of Specific (Bad) Acts (of a Party) 247

entered Frances' second-story apartment through an open window at approximately 2 A.M. He was wearing black leather pants, a ski mask, and a Grateful Dead T-shirt. He bound the victim's hands with clothesline, stuffed a silk scarf in her mouth, and raped her. The assailant was over six feet tall—probably about 6' 4"—but the victim never saw his face. The prosecution now offers the following evidence:

(a) The testimony of Amy Diller that six weeks *after* the Dugan rape she was raped in her second story apartment at approximately 4 A.M. The assailant, who gained access through an open window, was wearing black or green leather pants, a T-shirt, and a ski mask. He tied her hands with one silk scarf and stuffed another in her mouth. He then raped her. As he was about to leave, she managed to free her hands and pull off the ski mask. She got a good look at her assailant and is convinced that he is the defendant.

(b) The testimony of Darlene Short that two weeks before the Dugan rape she heard a noise outside the window of her second-story apartment. When she went to investigate, she saw a man starting to enter the window. She screamed, and he jumped to the ground and fled. She couldn't see his face because he was wearing some kind of mask, but she is sure he was over six feet tall.

Should the foregoing evidence be admissible?

3. Willis Lang is being prosecuted for conspiracy to defraud the Acme Insurance company by making a false claim for an allegedly stolen car. Jim Scully has testified for the prosecution that he and Lang agreed to have Scully steal Lang's Lincoln Continental and for the two of them to share the proceeds from the sale of the Continental and from the insurance money that Lang would get from Acme. According to Scully, he began to feel guilty about the scheme and reported it to the police. Scully now offers to testify, over Lang's objection, that two months ago Lang asked him to arrange to have a warehouse that Lang owned destroyed by fire. Should the evidence be admitted?

4. Lester Wise was convicted of mail fraud, but he failed to appear for sentencing. He is now being prosecuted for his failure to appear, and he claims insanity as a defense. The prosecutor offers evidence that during the period of his absence Lester was actively involved in a scheme to defraud two trucking companies. Is the evidence admissible?

5. Lyle Rose has filed a federal civil rights action against several county corrections officers. On April 15, when Rose was incarcerated awaiting trial, he was badly beaten by several inmates. He claims that the reason for the beating was that several days earlier the defendants spread the word among the inmates that Rose was a snitch. The defendants offer evidence that prior to the time of the alleged snitch rumor Rose was involved in other fights with inmates. Is the evidence admissible?

6. Barry English is charged with bank robbery. The prosecution offers to show that Barry's joint checking account with his father was overdrawn by $10,000 and that Barry had forged his father's name on several bad checks. Is the evidence admissible?

7. Linda Turner is charged with selling two ounces of cocaine to Tom Peters. The prosecution offers the following evidence:

(a) Tom's testimony that Linda sold him the two ounces of cocaine on November 17.

(b) Tom's testimony that Linda began selling cocaine to him six years ago when he was in the ninth grade.

(c) The testimony of Tom's friend, Irv, that when he was in junior high school, he and several of his friends had purchased cocaine from Linda.

Linda has objected to all of this evidence. How should the court rule?

8. Della Tripp is charged with possession and sale of narcotics. As part of her defense she offers to testify that she has never been arrested or convicted for anything more serious that a minor traffic violation. Should the prosecutor's objection to this testimony be sustained?

D. REFLECTIONS ON SPECIFIC ACTS EVIDENCE

The use of specific acts evidence has been and continues to be the subject of frequent litigation and substantial scholarly commentary. Much of this writing raises more questions than it answers. Consider, for example, the following passage from McCormick's Handbook on the Law of Evidence (3d ed., Cleary, 1984), which is the introduction to the previously excerpted[29] description of permissible uses for specific acts evidence:

> Unless and until the accused gives evidence of his good character, the prosecution may not introduce evidence of (or otherwise seek to establish) his bad character. . . .
>
> This broad prohibition includes the specific and frequently invoked rule that the prosecution may not introduce evidence of other criminal acts of the accused *unless the evidence is introduced for some purpose other than to suggest that because the defendant is a person of criminal character, it is more probable that he committed the crime for which he is on trial.* As [FRE 404(b)] . . . indicates, there are numerous other uses to which evidence of criminal acts may be put, and those enumerated are neither mutually exclusive nor collectively exhaustive. Subject to such caveats, examination is in order of the

---

29. See pages 234-239 supra.

D. Reflections on Specific Acts Evidence

principal purposes for which the prosecution *may introduce evidence of a defendant's bad character.* [Id. at 557-558 (emphasis added).]

Does the first italicized clause use the term *character* in a different sense than the second clause? Are the two clauses inconsistent? In McCormick's view, does the second sentence of FRE 404(b) authorize the use of specific acts for various *noncharacter* purposes, or does it authorize the use of specific acts to prove character to show something other than action in conformity with character?

Since the Federal Rules do not define character, perhaps the preceding questions raise issues more of semantics than substance. Nonetheless, it would be helpful to rational discourse if there were general agreement about the appropriate terminology to use in discussing specific acts evidence, particularly since it is frequently unclear what FRE 404(b) permits and what it prohibits. Compare, for example, the cases cited with approval in nn. 26, 27, 28, and 39 of the previously excerpted passage from McCormick's Handbook on the Law of Evidence[30] with the following passage, which occurs a few pages earlier:

> [E]vidence that an individual is the kind of person who tends to behave in certain ways almost always has some value as circumstantial evidence as to how he acted (and perhaps with what state of mind) in the matter in question. By and large, persons reputed to be violent commit more assaults than persons known to be peaceable. Yet, evidence of character in any form—reputation, opinion from observation, or specific acts—generally will not be received to prove that a person engaged in certain conduct *or did so with a particular intent on a specific occasion.* [Id. at 554 (emphasis added).]

Can you reconcile the cases described in the footnotes with this passage of text?

Consider also the following two passages from McCormick, in which he characterizes the prohibition against the use of character evidence to show action in conformity with character as a prohibition against the use of "propensity" evidence. First, in discussing specific acts evidence McCormick notes: "Evidence of other crimes brought forth as circumstantial proof of guilt for the offense charged is sometimes called 'extrinsic offense evidence.' . . . The rule against such evidence is also called the 'propensity rule' to emphasize the reasoning that the rule seeks to prevent."[31] Second, in elaborating on the "propensity rule," McCormick asserts:

> [E]ven if one or more of the valid purposes for admitting other crimes evidence is appropriately invoked, there is still the need to balance its probative value against the usual counterweights. *When the sole purpose of the other crimes*

---

30. See pages 237, 239 supra.
31. McCormick's Handbook on the Law of Evidence 557 n.7 (3d ed., Cleary, 1984).

evidence is to show some propensity to commit the crime at trial, there is no room for ad hoc balancing. The evidence is then unequivocally inadmissible— this is the meaning of the rule against other crimes evidence. But the fact that there is an accepted logical basis for the evidence other than the forbidden one of showing a proclivity for criminality may not preclude the jury from relying on a defendant's apparent propensity toward criminal behavior. Accordingly, most recent authority recognizes that the problem is not merely one of pigeonholing, but of classifying and then balancing. [Id. at 565 (emphasis added).]

Compare these passages with the cases in the footnotes to McCormick's description of the permissible uses of specific acts evidence. Is the propensity concept helpful in distinguishing between what FRE 404(b) prohibits and permits? Consider the following:

KUHNS, THE PROPENSITY TO MISUNDERSTAND THE CHARACTER OF SPECIFIC ACTS EVIDENCE
66 Iowa L. Rev. 777, 779-796, 798-799 (1981)

Although the various formulations of the specific acts prohibition do not attempt to define the term "character," it appears to have two commonly understood attributes. First, "character" probably includes only those qualities of personality that have some moral overtone, which connotes something good or bad about a person. The term frequently has this meaning as a matter of common usage, and ascribing such a meaning to it for the purposes of the specific acts prohibition is consistent with the concern over the potentially prejudicial impact of specific acts evidence. Pursuant to this understanding of character, morally neutral acts could never fall within the specific acts prohibition because they would not be relevant to prove character.

The second attribute of character is suggested by the fact that the prohibition against specific acts evidence to prove character is limited to showing action in conformity with character. This limitation implies a belief that character has an impact on how one behaves. Or, to put it somewhat differently, proof of a person's character trait is proof that a person has a propensity to behave in a particular manner. Indeed, the terms "character" and "propensity" are often used interchangeably, and the prohibition against specific acts evidence is frequently described as a prohibition against the use of specific acts for propensity purposes. . . .

[N]either the concept of propensity nor the concept of character is helpful to an understanding of how courts have ruled or should rule on the admissibility of specific acts evidence. . . .

D. Reflections on Specific Acts Evidence

I. PROPENSITY EVIDENCE

To substantiate the proposition that the concept of "propensity inference" does not provide a viable basis for distinguishing between admissible and inadmissible specific acts evidence, the analysis in this part will examine the nature of the inferential process of proof involved in the use of specific acts evidence. To facilitate this examination, the inferential process is divided into five categories: (1) traditionally prohibited propensity inferences; (2) permissible individualized propensity inferences from a defendant's bad conduct; (3) permissible generalized propensity inferences from a defendant's bad conduct; (4) permissible generalized propensity inferences from a defendant's neutral conduct; and (5) permissible generalized inferences from the conduct of third persons. The analysis will show that the inferential process is identical in the first two categories and that the remaining categories present only minor variations of the same basic inferential process.[21]

A. TRADITIONALLY PROHIBITED PROPENSITY INFERENCES

An initial difficulty in comparing the inferential process involved in the supposedly prohibited use of specific acts for propensity purposes with the inferential processes involved in the legitimate uses of specific acts evidence is that there are relatively few examples of impermissible "propensity evidence." The question whether specific acts evidence is admissible arises most frequently in the context of a prosecutor's offer to prove that a criminal defendant has committed various bad acts. A published opinion addressing the question of admissibility is likely to exist only if the defendant is convicted and appeals on the ground that the evidence was improperly admitted. An appellate court, however, may simply state that the admission of the evidence, if improper, was harmless error. Moreover, even an opinion holding that the specific acts should not have been admitted can avoid the question whether the evidence required an impermissible propensity inference. The court may simply explain that regardless of whether the evidence should have been excluded on that ground, the trial judge abused his discretion in admitting marginally probative, extremely prejudicial evidence.

Nonetheless, there would probably be a general consensus that the following example illustrates an impermissible propensity inference: The defendant is charged with murdering his wife by stabbing. He admits being present at the time of the fatal incident, but claims that a third person stabbed his wife. To show that the defendant was the assailant, the prosecutor offers

---

21. Because each category is so similar to the others, there may be disagreement over whether a particular illustrative example has been properly classified. Such a disagreement, however, would support rather than detract from the central point of the analysis: The nature of the inferential process involved in the use of specific acts evidence is so similar in all cases that it cannot be used as a device to distinguish between admissible and inadmissible specific acts evidence.

to prove that on several previous occasions the defendant had become involved in fistfights with neighbors.

The relevance of the fistfight evidence is clearly dependent upon a propensity inference: The fact that the defendant has been violent on previous occasions shows that he—at least in comparison to people who have not been violent—has a propensity for violence, and from this propensity the fact finder is asked to infer that the defendant was violent on the occasion in question. Moreover, all of the factors that justify excluding some specific acts evidence are present. If the defendant disputes his involvement in the fistfights, there may be time-consuming and distracting litigation of collateral issues. The fact finder may be more willing to return a guilty verdict after hearing the evidence simply because the defendant appears to be a bad person. Finally, the probative value of several fistfights with neighbors to prove a deadly assault with a knife against one's spouse is not great.

For the purpose of comparing the fistfight hypothetical with other uses of specific acts evidence, it is important to note three aspects of the inferential process of proof involved in linking the prior assaults to assault on the occasion in question. First, the fact finder is asked to make an "individualized" propensity inference in the sense that the defendant's propensity for violence is not a propensity shared by the populace at large. Rather, it is the defendant's prior violent behavior which shows that he, unlike most other people, tends to be violent.

Second, the relevance of this individualized propensity inference, like the relevance of any other inference from evidentiary facts to proof of ultimate facts at issue in litigation, depends on an assumption about the relationship among various phenomena or events in the real world. Consider, for example, a murder prosecution in which the homicide occurred at 10:00 P.M. in Fresno, California, and the defendant shows that at 8:00 P.M. Pacific Standard Time on the same day he was in Bangor, Maine. The defendant's evidence is relevant to prove that he did not commit the crime because of the assumption, based on common experience, that a person cannot travel from Bangor to Fresno in only two hours. Similarly, if a witness testifies that he saw the defendant stab her husband, that evidentiary fact is relevant to prove the ultimate fact that the defendant indeed did stab her husband because of the assumption that it is more likely that on any given occasion a person is speaking truthfully rather than falsely. This assumption about truthtelling is based on our common experience in dealing with people and the conclusion from that experience that people are more often than not truthful. In like manner, the individualized propensity inference in the fistfight hypothetical is based on the assumption, derived from common experience, that a person who has been violent on some occasions is more likely than a person who has not been violent to behave violently on any given occasion.

Finally, in some instances the underlying assumption about the relationship among various phenomena or events in the real world is itself

D. Reflections on Specific Acts Evidence

dependent upon a propensity inference. For example, the assumption that an individual is more likely than not to tell the truth is based on common experience which demonstrates that people generally have a propensity for truthtelling. Similarly, in the fistfight hypothetical, the defendant's prior violence is relevant to show violence on a particular occasion only if the fact finder assumes that people generally—or at least people similarly situated with the defendant in an identifiable manner—who have been violent on some occasions have a propensity to be violent on other occasions. Indeed, whenever the relevance of a piece of evidence is dependent upon an assumption about how people behave, the assumption necessarily encompasses a propensity inference: The behavior of third persons generally or of a particular individual on other occasions is relevant to show the individual's behavior on the occasion in question only if the fact finder assumes that the behavior is of a type that people have a propensity to repeat.

B. PERMISSIBLE INDIVIDUALIZED PROPENSITY INFERENCES FROM A DEFENDANT'S BAD CONDUCT

Courts traditionally have permitted the use of specific acts evidence to show intent or absence of accident. Thus, in order to show malice, the prosecutor may be able to introduce evidence that a murder defendant had previously beaten the victim. Or in a theft prosecution in which the defendant claims to have picked up an apparently lost wallet, the prosecutor may be able to show that in similar circumstances the defendant had in fact stolen wallets from other individuals.

In both examples the prior acts evidence may have a prejudicial impact on the fact finder, and a dispute about the defendant's involvement in the prior acts could result in time-consuming, distracting litigation of collateral issues. Nonetheless, the probative value of prior assaults on the same victim to show malice or prior similar thefts to rebut the defendant's claim that he found a lost wallet is probably somewhat greater than the probative value of prior fistfights in the previously discussed hypothetical. It would arguably be appropriate, therefore, to conclude that the greater probative value justifies admitting the evidence.

One cannot, however, distinguish the fistfight hypothetical from the malice and theft cases on the ground that only the former involves a propensity inference, for the inferential process of proof is identical in all three situations. From the defendant's prior fistfights, assaults on the victim, or thefts the fact finder is asked to make an individualized propensity inference: Because the defendant committed the bad acts in the past, he has a propensity to commit the kind of act in question (or to do so with the requisite criminal intent).

Moreover, in each case, the individualized propensity inference is based on an assumption about human behavior that encompasses a more general propensity inference. Just as people who have committed violent acts on some occasions are more likely than people who have not been violent to act violently on other occasions, people who have manifested a culpable mental state on some occasions are more likely than people who have not manifested such a mental state to behave culpably on other occasions.[32]

C. Permissible Generalized Propensity Inferences from a Defendant's Bad Conduct

The preceding fistfight and intent hypotheticals have been characterized as involving an "individualized" propensity inference because the propensity ascribed to the defendant is not a propensity ascribed to the populace at large or to any independently identifiable group. Rather, at least from the immediate perspective of the fact finder, the propensity is ascribed to the defendant *because* of his specific acts.

In contrast to these examples of individualized propensity inferences, some traditionally permissible uses of specific acts evidence involve what might be characterized as a "generalized" propensity inference. In these latter cases, it seems appropriate to regard the fact finder as beginning with the assumption that individuals in some identifiable group have a propensity to behave in a particular manner. Proof of the defendant's specific act merely identifies the defendant as being included in or specifically excluded from the relevant group.

Consider, for example, the commonly recognized use of specific acts evidence to prove the identity of the defendant as the perpetrator of a crime. Evidence that a defendant had previously assaulted another victim by forcing the victim to disrobe, binding the victim's hands and feet with vines of ivy, tying the ivy in an unusual knot, and with a silver penknife proceeding to inflict stab wounds that formed the letter "V" on the victim's chest would probably be admissible to identify the defendant as the perpetrator of an assault carried out in a similar manner.

There are two ways to characterize the relevance of this other crime evidence. First, one might regard the similar assault as showing that the defendant has an individualized propensity for committing assaults in a unique manner. The inferential process of proof involved in viewing the evidence

---

32. On some occasions specific acts evidence that requires the fact finder to make an individualized propensity inference may pose no threat of prejudice. Consider, for example, a case in which the defendant is charged with a liquor store robbery which occurred at 6:00 P.M. To show that the defendant was probably in the vicinity of the store at the time of the robbery, the prosecutor offers to prove that the defendant regularly rode home from work on a bus that passes by the liquor store shortly before 6:00 P.M. From the fact that the defendant had ridden the same bus in the past, the fact finder is asked to infer that the defendant has a propensity, not shared by people generally, for riding on the same bus. This individualized propensity inference, is based on the more general propensity inference that people who ride the same bus on some occasions are likely to do so on other occasions. Because the act of riding a bus is morally neutral, there is no potential for prejudice. . . . Indeed, the morally neutral quality of the activity coupled with its apparently routine, regularized nature would probably lead courts to place the evidence in the habit rather than the character category. . . .

D. Reflections on Specific Acts Evidence 255

in this manner is identical to the inferential process of proof in the previously described uses of specific acts evidenced.[37] Alternatively, one might argue that, regardless of the defendant's propensities, the other crime is relevant to identify the defendant simply because no other person would be likely to commit the crime charged in the same unusual manner. In other words, the similarity in methods of perpetration is better explained by the theory, derived from common experience, that one individual (who we happen to know is the defendant) probably committed both crimes, rather than the theory that two individuals may have fortuitously perpetrated the crimes in the same manner. This view of the evidence, however, necessarily requires a generalized propensity inference. The only factor that makes commission of the other crime relevant to identify the perpetrator of the charged crime is the assumption that some individual had a propensity to commit both crimes, and this assumption is dependent upon the inference that people generally have a propensity *not* to perpetrate a crime in the same unusual manner in which another person has perpetrated a crime. Thus, proof that the defendant committed the prior crime places him outside the universe of people who share this generalized propensity. At the same time, such proof identifies the defendant as the individual having a propensity to commit the crime in an unusual manner.[38]

A similar inferential process of proof is involved in cases in which the prosecutor offers to prove that a criminal defendant has intimidated a witness or attempted to obstruct justice in some other manner. In one sense the obstruction evidence may be marginally relevant in a manner that would require the fact finder to make an individualized propensity inference. Proof that the defendant committed an illegal act by obstructing justice shows a propensity to act illegally, from which one can infer that the defendant acted illegally by committing the crime charged. Traditionally, however, obstruction evidence is not admitted for that purpose. Rather, it is admitted because the obstruction is viewed as an admission by the defendant that he is guilty of the crime charged. Yet, the obstruction evidence is relevant as an admission only if one assumes that guilty criminal defendants in general have a propensity to obstruct justice in order to avoid the consequences of a possible guilty verdict. Proof of the defendant's obstruction identifies the defendant

---

37. Because the defendant has committed one unusual assault, the fact finder is asked to infer that the defendant has a propensity, not shared by people generally, to commit such assaults. This individualized propensity inference is based on the more general propensity inference that people who are violent on some occasions are more likely than people who have not been violent to behave violently on the occasion in question.

38. Cf. Carter, The Admissibility of Evidence of Similar Facts, 70 L.Q. Rev. 214, 229 (1954):

> [T]he similar fact evidence shows only that the accused had the common characteristic at [the time the prior crime was committed]. The commission of the crime [charged] shows only that the [perpetrator of the crime charged] had that characteristic at a particular but different time. . . . The accused is "identified" [as the perpetrator of the crime charged] . . . because the accused had the characteristic on previous occasions and he therefore is likely to have still had it on the instant occasion.

as belonging to the class of people—in this case, guilty defendants—who share a generalized propensity.[41]

For several reasons, the fact that the preceding identity and obstruction hypotheticals may appropriately be characterized as involving only a generalized propensity is not a sufficient basis for distinguishing them from impermissible uses of specific acts evidence. First, the distinction between individualized and generalized propensity inferences obviously cannot account for the existing state of the law. As the analysis in the preceding section demonstrated, courts sometimes admit specific acts evidence that requires the fact finder to make an individualized propensity inference.

Second, the factors that justify exclusion of some specific acts are not necessarily minimized simply because the propensity inference is a generalized one. The problems of prejudice, time-consumption, and distraction of the fact finder from the central issues of the case exist because bad acts evidence is offered against the defendant, not because of the nature of the propensity inference.[43]

Moreover, the probative value of the bad acts evidence is not dependent upon the nature of the propensity inference. Of course, in the absence of empirical data, one can make only an intuitive guess based on common experience about the probative value of any propensity inference. It seems plausible, however, to view the individualized propensity inference in the previously discussed intent hypotheticals as at least as strong, if not stronger, than the generalized propensity inference underlying the use of specific acts of obstructing justice to show guilt. Innocent defendants may have nearly as great a propensity as guilty defendants to obstruct justice simply because they fear possible conviction. On the other hand, when a prior crime is offered to prove the defendant's identity as the perpetrator of the crime charged, the unusual manner in which both crimes were committed may make the evidence highly probative.[45]

---

41. An almost identical propensity inference is often the key to the relevance of specific acts evidence offered to show motive. . . . Consider, for example, a case in which the defendant is charged with the murder of a police officer who was approaching the defendant on the street. To show that the defendant had a motive for the killing and, therefore, committed the act or did so intentionally, the prosecutor offers evidence that 15 minutes before the killing the defendant had broken into a house. See State v. Simborski, 120 Conn. 624, 630, 182 A. 221, 224 (1936). To the extent that the evidence is relevant to show motive and not merely that the defendant is the type of individual who engages in antisocial behavior, the relevance of the evidence is dependent upon the assumption that people generally have a propensity to avoid situations that they perceive as the first step toward arrest and possible conviction. Or, on a more general level, the propensity to avoid arrest may be characterized as a propensity to maximize freedom of action. Proof of the robbery does not ascribe an individualized propensity to the defendant but rather it identifies him with a group of people who have a propensity to avoid contact with the police.

43. Some generalized propensity inferences can be characterized in terms that are sufficiently broad to make them appear on their face neutral. See note 41 supra. If the propensity inference cannot be articulated in neutral terms, however, it is only because the specific act which gives rise to the propensity inference is itself not neutral.

45. The probative value of similar crimes evidence to identify the defendant as the perpetrator of the crime charged probably depends not only on the uniqueness of the manner

D. Reflections on Specific Acts Evidence

Finally, although the distinction between individualized and generalized propensity inferences may be helpful in describing the manner in which the fact finder is likely to view specific acts evidence, the distinction itself is in one important sense illusory. In terms of the nature of the inferential process of proof, there is simply no qualitative difference between an individualized and a generalized propensity inference. Rather, the distinction is solely a function of how one initially describes the relevant inference. For example, in the previously discussed fistfight hypothetical, the characterization of the inference from prior assaults to violence on the occasion in question as an individualized propensity inference was based on the premise that the fact finder is likely to view the evidence as showing that the defendant, unlike most other people, has a propensity for violent behavior. As the analysis pointed out, however, this view of the evidence is necessarily dependent upon the assumption, derived from common experience, that people who have been violent on some occasions have a propensity to be violent on other occasions. If one initially focuses on this general assumption, then proof of defendant's prior violence merely identifies the defendant as being within the relevant group of people sharing a generalized propensity. In short, the necessary inferences in the process of proof are identical regardless of whether one initially focuses on a generalized or an individualized propensity inference.

D. PERMISSIBLE GENERALIZED PROPENSITY INFERENCES FROM A DEFENDANT'S NEUTRAL CONDUCT

In some instances, traditionally admissible specific acts evidence that requires the fact finder to make a generalized propensity inference poses, at least in theory, no threat of prejudice. Consider, for example, a situation in which a prison escapee claims that his flight was a spontaneous response to duress, and the prosecutor then offers to prove that the prisoner had arranged to have a car waiting outside the prison wall at the time of the escape. The specific acts involved in arranging for the car constitute plans made in preparation for the escape, and to rebut the duress claim the fact finder is asked to infer that individuals who plan a certain course of action tend to follow through with those plans.

This propensity inference is similar to the generalized propensity inferences discussed in the preceding section: The propensity for acting in conformity with one's intentions is an attribute that the fact finder, on the basis of common experience, would tend to ascribe to people generally, and the defendant's actions merely suggest what the particular intention is. In contrast to the specific acts in all of the previously discussed hypotheticals,

---

in which the crimes are perpetrated but also in part on the degree of publicity given to the means of perpetrating the crime or crimes that occurred earlier in time. The fact that an unusual method of perpetrating a crime is a matter of public knowledge may increase the likelihood that two or more individuals would perpetrate crimes in the same unusual manner.

however, making arrangements for a car to be at a particular location at a specified time is "neutral." It is not a crime to engage in such conduct, nor is the conduct morally blameworthy. Thus, proof of the specific acts would not have a prejudicial impact on the factfinder. Moreover, since the specific acts that show the defendant's propensity are themselves neutral, the characterization of the propensity manifested by those acts—in this case a generalized propensity to follow through with one's intentions—is also necessarily neutral and, therefore, nonprejudicial.[50]

A similar situation may arise when the prosecutor offers specific acts evidence to show a defendant's knowledge. If a defendant accused of heroin possession claims that he did not know that the substance was heroin, the prosecutor would be permitted to rebut this claimed lack of knowledge by showing that the defendant on previous occasions had knowingly possessed heroin. From knowledge on a previous occasion, the fact finder is asked to infer knowledge on the present occasion, and this is a type of generalized propensity inference: A person who has obtained knowledge of some fact has a propensity to retain that knowledge.[53] As was true in the escape hypothetical, the propensity inference here is a neutral one, and at least if the act of prior possession occurred in the defendant's capacity as a former narcotics officer or in some other legal context, evidence of the prior possession would not itself be prejudicial.

Despite the absence of a potential for prejudice in the preceding examples, the concerns underlying the exclusion of some specific acts evidence are not diminished simply because the relevant specific acts and, therefore, the relevant propensity inferences are neutral. If there is a dispute about the act or nature of the defendant's involvement in the act, the problem of distracting the fact finder with possibly time-consuming litigation of a collateral matter remains. More importantly, the specific acts that give rise to the neutral propensity inference may not themselves be neutral. The specific instances of prior possession by the heroin defendant are likely to have been

---

50. The particular intent—intent to escape—inferred from the planning activity is not "neutral" in the sense of being non-culpable, but it is neutral in the sense of being non-prejudicial [within the meaning of FRE 403's "unfair prejudice"]. Proof of this intent is essential to establish the defendant's guilt.

53. One might argue either (1) that possession is not an *act* or (2) that obtaining knowledge is not a *physical* act, and that, therefore, the specific acts evidence rules should be inapplicable to this situation. The first argument should be rejected because it is the mental process of obtaining knowledge that is relevant to the case, and the second argument is only another way of stating that the activity in question is neutral: One does not normally associate moral culpability with the mere acquisition of knowledge. As the following textual analysis will point out, the theoretically neutral nature of the prior activity is not a sufficient basis for distinguishing between admissible and inadmissible evidence of prior activity.

In fact, courts and commentators traditionally treat prior possession—at least if it is illegal—as being governed by the specific acts evidence rules. See [R. Lempert and S. Saltzburg, A Modern Approach to Evidence (1977) 220; United States v. Wixom, 529 F.2d 217, 219-220 & n.2 (8th Cir. 1976), discussed in S. Saltzburg and K. Redden, Federal Rules of Evidence Manual 141-142 (2d ed. 1977)]. See also Fed. R. Evid. 404(b) (defining specific acts evidence rule in terms of "other *crimes*, wrongs, or acts") (emphasis added).

D. Reflections on Specific Acts Evidence

instances of illegal possession, and the prison escapee's activity in arranging for a car may have included a plan to have a stolen car at the prison wall. Although the illegal nature of these prior acts is not itself relevant to the required propensity inference, informing the fact finder of the illegality of the acts creates the same potential for prejudice that inheres in the other uses of specific bad acts.

There may, of course, be instances in which the illegality of the specific act is sufficiently incidental that the illegality need not be mentioned to the fact finder. Perhaps, for example, the escapee's plan to have a car outside the prison wall could be adequately explained without any reference to the car theft. In other cases, however, it may be impossible to present adequate proof of the acts without at least an implicit suggestion of their illegality. Consider, for example, the possibility of introducing evidence of prior heroin possession without specific details showing that the possession was illegal. The fact finder may in any event assume that the possession was illegal, in which case avoiding more detailed information about the incident would not minimize the potential prejudice. Alternatively, the fact finder may expect that any proof of prior possession will encompass details of the possession. In such a situation, the unexplained failure to present the details may lead the fact finder to disbelieve a truthful assertion of prior possession.

There undoubtedly will be instances in which the probative value of a neutral propensity inference coupled with the practical necessity of explaining the illegal nature of the prior act that gives rise to the inference will outweigh the countervailing concerns of prejudice, consumption of time, and distraction from the central issues of a case. The point to be made here is simply that the existence of a theoretically neutral specific act and propensity inference does not necessarily minimize any of the concerns that exist in contexts in which bad acts are relevant in a propensity sense.

E. PERMISSIBLE GENERALIZED INFERENCES FROM THE CONDUCT OF THIRD PERSONS

In a relatively small number of cases in which specific acts evidence is offered, the relevance of the evidence arguably is not dependent on a propensity inference. Consider, for example, a murder prosecution in which the state's theory is that the victim was killed with a .38-caliber pistol, and the prosecutor offers to prove that two days prior to the murder the defendant stole such a pistol. Or consider a prosecution for theft from a liquor store in which the prosecutor offers evidence that two hours before the theft the defendant held up a filling station in the same neighborhood.

The evidence in each case is admittedly relevant in a propensity sense. The fact finder might infer that people who steal guns have a propensity to murder or that people who hold up filling stations have a propensity to steal from liquor stores. The relevance of the evidence, however, is not dependent upon these propensity inferences. Mere possession of the weapon shows the ability of the murder defendant to commit the homicide. Similarly, presence in the neighborhood shows the ability of the theft defendant to commit the crime.

If evidence in either of these examples is offered solely to show that the defendant had the ability to commit the crime, there are two bases for characterizing evidence as falling outside the propensity prohibition. First, the prohibition is applicable only to specific acts evidence, and possession or presence arguably is not an "act" within the meaning of the prohibition. Second, evidence that shows only the physical capability of committing an act does not show a tendency to commit the act and, therefore, is arguably not "propensity" evidence.

Nonetheless, the relevance of the evidence ultimately depends upon an inference that is at least very similar to the previously described propensity inferences. For example, just as the fact finder may be asked to infer, on the basis of common experience, that people who behave violently on some occasions are more likely than other people to behave violently on a specific occasion, the fact finder is asked to infer, on the basis of common experience, that people who possess the instrumentalities for committing a crime or who are near the scene of a crime are more likely than other people to commit the crime.

Even if one does not attach the propensity label to evidence offered to show the ability of a defendant to commit a crime, there is no practical justification for distinguishing such evidence from the previously discussed proof of theoretically neutral acts that require a neutral generalized propensity inference. In both instances, the evidence shares the following characteristics: First, there are potential problems of time consumption and distraction of the fact finder in litigating possibly disputed collateral issues; second, the illegal or "bad" nature of the specific acts is not critical to the relevance of the evidence; third, it may nonetheless be practically impossible to explain adequately the relevance of the evidence without reference to the illegal nature of the acts; fourth, if the illegality is explained to the fact finder, the evidence is potentially prejudicial; and fifth, in some instances the probative value of the evidence may outweigh the countervailing concerns of prejudice, consumption of time, and distraction of the fact finder.[60] . . .

---

60. These same factors are present in one type of situation in which specific acts evidence is offered for what is clearly in theory a non-propensity purpose. Occasionally, courts will admit evidence of other crimes committed in close physical and temporal proximity to the crime charged to help complete the story of the crime charged. See State v. Villavicencio, 95 Ariz. 199, 201, 388 P.2d 245, 246 (1964). Apparently the theory underlying this use of specific acts evidence is that in the absence of the evidence, the fact finder would have an incomplete and possibly misleading picture of the nature of the defendant's involvement in the crime charged. See United States v. Carrillo, 561 F.2d 1125, 1127 (5th Cir. 1977). See generally Saltzburg, A Special Aspect of Relevance: Countering Negative Inferences Associated with the Absence of Evidence, 66 Calif. L. Rev. 1011 (1978).

D. Reflections on Specific Acts Evidence

II. THE MEANING OF CHARACTER

The initial discussion of the prohibition against the use of specific acts to prove character to show action in conformity with character suggested two attributes inherent in the concept of character: a connotation of some moral quality and an implication about the manner in which an individual is likely to behave. As the preceding analysis has shown, however, there is not and probably should not be an absolute prohibition against the use of specific bad acts for propensity purposes. Thus, in giving content to the prohibition against the use of some specific acts evidence, one cannot simply equate character evidence with propensity evidence. All character evidence offered to show action in conformity with character is propensity evidence, but not all propensity evidence is character evidence. The question, therefore, necessarily arises whether one can give some additional independent content to the term character or character trait.

There would appear to be only two substantially overlapping factors that may be helpful in distinguishing character evidence from other bad acts propensity evidence. First, case law and scholarly commentaries dealing with specific acts evidence suggest that the character label is used when the evidence has an indirect bearing on an issue and, therefore, a relatively low probative value. For example, evidence of a defendant's previous assaults on third persons offered to prove that the defendant was the first aggressor would probably be regarded as impermissible character evidence. Evidence of previous assaults by the defendant on the murder victim, however, might not be regarded as character evidence. Second, simply as a matter of common usage, describing a particular propensity as a character trait may seem more appropriate in some instances than in others. Thus, an individual's propensity for violence demonstrated by assaults on various third persons might readily be described as a character trait for violence. In contrast, violence directed only against a particular individual arguably does not manifest a propensity that is commonly thought of as a "character trait."

This general sense of what constitutes character is an inadequate basis for distinguishing between permissible and impermissible uses of specific acts evidence for propensity purposes. First, it is simply too imprecise for meaningful application on a case-by-case basis. For example, even if one concludes that in a murder prosecution evidence of the defendant's assaults on random third persons would be regarded as inadmissible character evidence but that previous assaults on only the victim would be viewed as non-character and, therefore, potentially admissible evidence, how should the following evidence be classified: previous assaults against only those third persons who, like the murder victim, are (a) all redheads, (b) all members of the same family, (c) all between the ages of four and six, (d) all between the ages of 20 and 25? Perhaps it would be appropriate to view the fact that the various victims happened to be between the ages of 20 and 25 to be fortuitous and, therefore, to place the character label on this evidence. It is less clear, however, which, if any, of the other proofs of specifically directed violence should be regarded as manifesting a character trait.

Second, and more importantly, the general sense of what constitutes a character trait is not sufficiently related to the factors which justify excluding some specific acts evidence. The prohibition against use of specific acts to prove character to show action in conformity with character encompasses one of these factors: Specific act character evidence tends to have a relatively low probative value. There is no necessary relationship, however, between some independently derived notion of what constitutes a character trait and problems of prejudice, time consumption, and distraction of the fact finder from the central issues of the case. The time consumption and distraction concerns arise whenever the prior acts are numerous or there is a dispute about the nature of the act or a party's participation in it. These potential problems are in no way dependent upon whether the acts tend to show something that might be labeled a character trait.

Similarly, the potential for prejudice from specific acts evidence is not related to the question whether the evidence is offered to prove character or to show some other fact. Potential prejudice exists whenever there is a danger that the fact finder will be influenced not simply by the probative value of the evidence but also by its conclusion that a party is a bad person and, therefore, particularly deserving of punishment. Any bad act, of course, has the potential for influencing the fact finder's decision in such a manner, and thus in one sense any specific bad act is evidence of a general character for badness. Yet, it is clear from the established precedent for permitting bad acts to be used in a propensity sense to prove such issues as motive, intent, or identity that this general way in which bad acts tend to show character is not sufficient to place the acts within the character evidence prohibition.

The primary determinants in applying the character prohibition appear to be the probative value of the specific acts evidence and whether the relevant propensity can, as a matter of common usage, readily be labeled as a character trait. Prejudice, however, is not a function of either of these factors. The degree of prejudice associated with any specific act evidence is a function of how the fact finder is likely to respond to the badness of the act. Consider, for example, two prosecutions for heroin possession. In one case the defendant claims he did not know the substance was heroin. In the other the defendant claims that the heroin was in the sole possession of his companion. To rebut the first defendant's claimed absence of knowledge, the prosecutor offers to prove that the defendant had previously sold heroin to school children. To establish the second defendant's possession the prosecutor offers to prove that on two previous occasions the defendant had possessed heroin. The latter evidence is more likely than the former to fall within the character evidence prohibition,[67] but in the eyes of the fact finder the sale of heroin to school children is likely to be more prejudicial. . . .

67. Compare United States v. Bloom, 538 F.2d 704, 711 (5th Cir. 1976) (Tuttle &

D. Reflections on Specific Acts Evidence

III. THE FEDERAL RULES APPROACH TO SPECIFIC ACTS EVIDENCE

... Rule 404(b) contemplates the use of a balancing test to evaluate the admissibility of specific acts evidence falling outside the character prohibition, and as a result, the rule recognizes that on some occasions specific acts evidence which is not character evidence will be inadmissible. Therefore, the term *character* cannot be simply a label attached to all inadmissible specific acts evidence. As noted previously, however, if "character" is given some independent content, the only thing that is likely to distinguish specific act character evidence from other specific act propensity evidence is the relatively low probative value of the former. In short, the only functional purpose served by the prohibition against specific acts to prove character to show action in conformity with character is to exclude evidence of low probative value.

No other federal rule of evidence serves a similar purpose. Rather, the entire thrust of the Federal Rules is to favor the admissibility of even marginally probative evidence unless there is some important reason to exclude it. The basic definition of relevance in rule 401 requires only a minimal relationship between an item of evidence and the proposition it is offered to prove, and rule 402 provides that "all relevant evidence is admissible, except as otherwise provided." . . . Rule 403 provides that relevant evidence "may be excluded if its probative value is *substantially outweighed*" by countervailing considerations such as prejudice or consumption of time, and each of the specific exclusionary provisions in the Federal Rules, except the provision in rule 404(b), is based primarily on factors other than low probative value. For example, the hearsay rule is based on the premise that the fact finder may not fully appreciate the extent to which out-of-court declarations may be fabricated or inaccurate; the prohibition against introducing evidence of offers of compromise to show liability is based primarily on the ground that exclusion of this evidence facilitates out-of-court settlements; the restrictions on the use of prior convictions to impeach a witness are based [in] large measure on the potentially prejudicial impact of such evidence.

PROBLEMS

1. Courts and commentators almost uniformly deal with specific acts evidence as if there were some clear-cut distinction between the impermissible use of propensity or character evidence and the permissible other uses

---

Clark, JJ., concurring specially), *cert. denied*, 429 U.S. 1074 (1977) (prior narcotics sales evidence offered to show " 'a willingness of the defendant to deal in drugs generally' " is improper character evidence) (quoting trial judge) with People v. Cervantes, 177 Cal. App. 2d 187, 190, 2 Cal. Rptr. 107, 109 (1960) (evidence of other similar narcotics offenses admissible to show "defendant's knowledge of the narcotic nature of the substance").

of specific acts evidence. Consider for example, the following discussion of the use of specific acts to prove intent:

> Evidence of prior similar crimes comes in to show that the act was not done innocently but was done with the requisite criminal intent. Recall the example of the man who claims he poisoned another by mistake and consider how the jury will evaluate this story when it learns that the victim was the third person to be poisoned due to the defendant's "mistake." Obviously, such evidence may be highly probative on the issue of intent. It also may be necessary because there may be little other evidence available to counter the defendant's claim of honest error. . . . The major safeguard which can be expected of courts in this area is that they be sure that an issue of intent has been fairly raised in the case before admitting such evidence. An instruction on the limited use which may be made of such evidence is, of course, appropriate, though it may be of limited value. [R. Lempert and S. Saltzburg, A Modern Approach to Evidence 225-226 (2d ed. 1982).]

Draft an appropriate limiting instruction for the defendant.

2. Martha Woods is charged with the murder of her eight-month-old pre-adoptive foster son, Paul. Paul was placed with Ms. Woods when he was five months old. Up to that time he had been a normal, healthy baby. On five occasions during the first month that he was with Ms. Woods, Paul suffered instances of gasping for breath and turning blue from lack of oxygen. On the first four occasions, he responded to mouth-to-mouth resuscitation. On the last occasion he went into a coma and died a week later.

On each occasion Paul was in Ms. Woods' custody and only she had access to him. On each occasion Paul was taken to the hospital, and on the first four occasions he was released after several days observation in apparently good health. A pathologist testified as an expert witness for the prosecution that Paul's death was not accident or suicide. The witness said he was 75 percent certain that Paul's death was homicide caused by smothering, and he attributed the 25 percent doubt to the possibility of some disease currently unknown to medical science.

The government offers to prove Ms. Woods has had custody of or access to nine children who suffered a minimum of 20 episodes of cyanosis (a blue coloring due to lack of oxygen). Three of the children were her own; two were adopted; two were relatives; and two were children of friends. Seven of the nine children died.

Should the evidence be admitted?

3. Smith is being prosecuted for unlawfully possessing a silver dollar that he knew was stolen from the mails. The government has introduced evidence that Smith was a mailman; that the postal authorities suspected him of stealing from the mails; that they planted a letter containing a silver dollar in a mailbox on Smith's route; that when Smith returned to the station with mail from the box, they discovered that the letter had been opened and resealed; that Smith was then arrested; and that the silver dollar was found

E. Rape Shield Provisions

in his pocket. In his defense Smith testified that the silver dollar dropped out of the envelope; that he had planned to turn it over to his supervisor at the station; but that he had forgotten to do so. As part of its rebuttal the prosecution wishes to introduce into evidence two credit cards that were found in Smith's wallet at the time of the search. The cards do not have Smith's name on them. The government is prepared to prove that the cards were issued to third persons who happen to be on Smith's mail route, and that these third persons never received the cards. Smith has objected to the admissibility of the credit card evidence. What result?

4. Shirley Adams is being prosecuted for sale of heroin to an undercover agent. She claims entrapment as a defense and testifies that the undercover agent, a former lover, pressured her for months to supply him with heroin and that she agreed to do so only after he threatened to commit suicide if she persisted in her refusal. To rebut the entrapment defense, the government offers to prove that on at least four occasions in the last two years Shirley sold heroin to third persons. Should the government be permitted, over Shirley's objection, to introduce this evidence?

5. You have been appointed to an Advisory Committee that has been asked to consider revision of the Federal Rules of Evidence. Your particular assignment is FRE 404(b). Please supply the committee with at least two possible alternatives to the current provision and be prepared to discuss the relative merits of the existing rule and your alternatives.

6. Defendant has been charged with "intentionally having sexual contact with a minor with the intent to become sexually aroused or gratified." During its case in chief the prosecution introduced evidence that Defendant lured a three-year-old girl into his home, fondled her, and gave her a piece of candy. Defendant testified in his own behalf and denied the incident. On rebuttal, the prosecution offers the testimony of a 12-year-old girl that a week before the alleged incident with the three-year-old girl, the defendant offered the witness $20 if she would come into his home and expose herself. Should the evidence be admitted?

E. RAPE SHIELD PROVISIONS[32]

Until fairly recently, many courts were quite liberal in permitting defendants who were charged with rape and other sexual assault offenses and who claimed that the alleged victim consented to the sexual contact to introduce

---

32. The literature on rape, rape prosecutions, and rape shield provisions has grown exponentially over the last few years. For a sampling of some of the works see S. Brownmiller, Against Our Will: Men, Women and Rape (1975); Estrich, Rape, 95 Yale L.J. 1087 (1986); Letwin, "Unchaste Character," Ideology, and the California Rape Evidence Laws, 54 S. Cal. L. Rev. 35 (1980); Berger, Man's Trial, Woman's Tribulation, 77 Colum. L. Rev. 1 (1977).

evidence of the victim's sexual history. The most common form of prior sexual history evidence was reputation testimony, but a number of jurisdictions also permitted specific acts evidence.

We will turn momentarily to an examination and critique of the theories that courts relied on to admit evidence of rape victims' prior sexual conduct. First, however, it is appropriate to address what always should be the initial consideration in dealing with any piece of evidence: the basic notion of relevance.

We have never taught an evidence class without encountering some students—and occasionally a majority of students—who adamantly maintain that evidence of the victim's prior sexual history is irrelevant to the issue of consent. We readily concede that some types of prior sexual conduct evidence may not increase the likelihood that the victim consented on a particular occasion. For example, if we knew that the victim's only prior consensual intercourse was in the context of a marriage relationship, the more reasonable inference may be that she would *not* have consented to intercourse with a defendant who is not her husband. (Similarly, in a homicide prosecution if we knew that the victim had been violent only after drinking and that the victim had not been drinking at the time he was killed, the victim's prior violence may be probative of the fact that the victim was not the first aggressor.) Furthermore, it seems reasonable to hypothesize that a sexually experienced woman is less likely than a sexually inexperienced woman to send "mixed signals" about whether she is consenting. Thus, when a defendant's claim of consent is based on evidence that is arguably ambiguous about consent (e.g., "She said, 'No,' but from the way she treated me I knew she really didn't mean it."), the alleged victim's prior consensual sexual conduct with third persons may be more probative of lack of consent than consent. We are skeptical, however, of the proposition that the victim's prior sexual history has no bearing on the consent question.

The concept of relevance with which we have been dealing explicitly and implicitly throughout the course rests on the premise that individuals have a propensity to behave in particular ways and that we can arrive at reasonable conclusions about historical facts by taking these propensities into account. For example, at the most basic level, when a witness says that event X occurred, we regard the witness' statement as relevant to establish that X occurred because we assume that individuals generally have a propensity to tell the truth. Similarly, a premise underlying the character evidence rules is that individuals have propensities to behave in particular ways and that if we know something about the individuals' conduct on some occasions, we can make reasonable—although sometimes admittedly quite weak—inferences about their conduct on other occasions.

Given this pervasive reliance on the premise that we can infer something about an individual's conduct on some occasions if we know how the individual behaved on other occasions, it seems appropriate, at the very least, to place the burden of proof on those who claim that sexual history has no

E. Rape Shield Provisions

bearing on sexual conduct on a particular occasion. (Because of the probable low probative value of much past sexual conduct evidence and the substantial countervailing concerns, it may well be appropriate to place the burden—perhaps a very heavy burden—with respect to the question of admissibility on the proponent of the evidence. This, however, is a question that is distinct from the relevance question.)

The rape defendant's right to introduce reputation evidence about the victim's prior sexual conduct was regarded until recently as an application of the general principle, codified in FRE 404(a)(2), that a defendant can introduce evidence, in the form of reputation testimony, of the victim's character to prove action in conformity with that character trait by the victim.[33] In other words, just as a homicide defendant claiming self-defense could introduce evidence of the victim's reputation for violence to suggest that the victim was the first aggressor, it was regarded as appropriate for the rape defendant claiming consent to introduce evidence of the victim's reputation for promiscuity or lack of chastity to suggest that she consented to the intercourse.

The theoretical justification for introducing evidence of specific instances of the victim's consensual sexual intercourse was more varied. Some courts claimed that the evidence was admissible to show the victim's "intent"; some courts admitted the evidence to "impeach" the credibility of the rape victim without bothering to explain what relationship existed between consensual sexual intercourse and general truth telling; still other courts frankly admitted that the specific acts evidence was being used in a propensity sense or that it was being used to show character. These latter courts took the position that there was an exception to the propensity/character rule for evidence of prior sexual conduct—an exception, incidently, that was not limited to sexual history of alleged rape victims. Courts would also frequently permit prosecutors to introduce evidence of a criminal defendant's prior sexual misconduct in sexual assault prosecutions.

Whatever may be the merits of permitting a criminal defendant to introduce evidence of a victim's character for violence or permitting the prosecution to admit evidence of a sexual assault defendant's prior misconduct, there are substantial reasons to be concerned about the liberal admissibility of an alleged rape victim's sexual history. The ability to introduce evidence of the victim's sexual history gives the defendant the opportunity to try to make the victim and the victim's character the focal point of the litigation. The prospect of a degrading and humiliating examination by defense counsel may discourage many victims from cooperating with prosecutors;[34] in cases that are tried, there may be disputes about whether the

---

33. The Federal Rules also permit the use of opinion testimony. See FRE 405(a); pages 218-222 supra.
34. The humiliation and degradation of rape victims cannot be attributed solely—or perhaps even primarily—to liberal rules of admissibility for prior sexual conduct. Disbelief of, disrespect for, and insensitivity toward rape victims has existed throughout the criminal justice system. See S. Brownmiller, Against Our Will: Men, Women and Rape 408-420 (1976); Comment, Rape Laws: Sexism in Society and Law, 61 Calif. L. Rev. 919 (1973).

victim in fact engaged in the conduct that is attributed to her. In addition, there are the risks that the jury may overestimate the probative value of the prior sexual history evidence on the question of consent and that the jury may be willing to acquit a clearly guilty defendant because the victim "got what she deserved."[35] Finally, there is the problem that prior sexual history will frequently be of no more than marginal relevance to the question whether the victim consented on the occasion in question. Indeed, as we noted earlier, one of the principal reasons that the rules of evidence severely restrict the use of character to show action in conformity with character is that the strength of the inference from character to action on a particular occasion is almost invariably weak. We can think of no reason to believe that the inference from prior consensual intercourse—at least if the activity is with third persons—to consent with the defendant is a particularly strong propensity inference.

In theory, FRE 403 and its common law counterparts are adequate devices for taking into account these concerns that warrant caution in the use of evidence of a rape victim's prior sexual conduct. Concern with the sensibilities and humiliation of the rape victim is not, strictly speaking, an evidentiary concern and not something that one could readily fit within the FRE 403 factors. A proper application of FRE 403, however, would result in the exclusion of much of the prior sexual history evidence. Thus, the need for special concern about the rape victim would be diminished.

In practice, many individuals perceived—correctly, we believe—that courts were often too willing to admit marginally probative, highly prejudicial evidence of the victim's prior sexual activity in rape and other sexual assault prosecutions. The response to this perception has been the adoption of "rape shield" rules or statutes that specifically address and limit the situations in which evidence of a victim's prior sexual conduct may be admitted. Every jurisdiction now has some form of rape shield provision.

The federal rape shield provision, FRE 412, was not part of the Federal Rules when they were promulgated in 1975. It was added by statute in 1978.[36] Since rape is predominantly a state criminal offense, FRE 412 is not particularly significant as a *federal* rule. It has, however, become significant as a model for the states to consider in developing rules of evidence. FRE 412 provides:

> (a) Notwithstanding any other provision of law, in a criminal case in which a person is accused of rape or of assault with intent to commit rape, reputation or opinion evidence of the past sexual behavior of an alleged victim of such rape or assault is not admissible.
>
> (b) Notwithstanding any other provision of law, in a criminal case in which a person is accused of rape or of assault with intent to commit rape, evidence of a victim's past sexual behavior other than reputation evidence

---

35. See H. Kalven and H. Zeisel, The American Jury 249-254 (1966).
36. Privacy Protection for Rape Victims Act of 1978, Pub. L. No. 95-540, 92 Stat. 2046.

E. Rape Shield Provisions

or opinion evidence is also not admissible, unless such evidence other than reputation or opinion evidence is—

(1) admitted in accordance with subdivisions (c)(1) and (c)(2) and is constitutionally required to be admitted;[37] or

(2) admitted in accordance with subdivision (c) and is evidence of—

(A) past sexual behavior with persons other than the accused, offered by the accused upon the issue of whether the accused was or was not, with respect to the alleged victim, the source of semen or injury; or

(B) past sexual behavior with the accused and is offered by the accused upon the issue of whether the alleged victim consented to the sexual behavior with respect to which rape or assault is alleged.

(c)(1) If the person accused of committing rape or assault with intent to commit rape intends to offer under subdivision (b) evidence of specific instances of the alleged victim's past sexual behavior, the accused shall make a written motion to offer such evidence not later than fifteen days before the date on which the trial in which such evidence is to be offered is scheduled to begin, except that the court may allow the motion to be made at a later date, including during trial, if the court determines either that the evidence is newly discovered and could not have been obtained earlier through the exercise of due diligence or that the issue to which such evidence relates has newly arisen in the case. Any motion made under this paragraph shall be served on all other parties and on the alleged victim.

(2) The motion described in paragraph (1) shall be accompanied by a written offer of proof. If the court determines that the offer of proof contains evidence described in subdivision (b), the court shall order a hearing in chambers to determine if such evidence is admissible. At such hearing the parties may call witnesses, including the alleged victim, and offer relevant evidence. Notwithstanding subdivision (b) of rule 104, if the relevancy of the evidence which the accused seeks to offer in the trial depends upon the fulfillment of a condition of fact, the court, at the hearing in chambers or at a subsequent hearing in chambers scheduled for such purpose, shall accept evidence on the issue of whether such condition of fact is fulfilled and shall determine such issue.[38]

(3) If the court determines on the basis of the hearing described in paragraph (2) that the evidence which the accused seeks to offer is relevant and that the probative value of such evidence outweighs the danger of unfair prejudice,[39] such evidence shall be admissible in the trial to the extent an order made by the court specifies evidence which may be

---

37. The "constitutionally required" phrase is a reference to the due process right of a criminal defendant to present a defense. An evidentiary rule that unreasonably restricts a criminal defendant's ability to present probative exculpatory evidence may be unconstitutional as applied to that defendant. See Chambers v. Mississippi, 410 U.S. 284 (1973). See also Davis v. Alaska, 415 U.S. 308 (1974).—Eds.

38. If the preliminary fact is indeed one of conditional relevance, why should FRE 104(b) not apply?—Eds.

39. Note that this is a reverse FRE 403 balancing test. The probative value must outweigh the prejudice, not vice versa. The effect is to put the burden with respect to the balancing on the proponent of the evidence. For another reverse FRE 403 balancing test, see FRE 609. —Eds.

offered and areas with respect to which the alleged victim may be examined or cross-examined.

(d) For purposes of this rule, the term "past sexual behavior" means sexual behavior other than the sexual behavior with respect to which rape or assault with intent to commit rape is alleged.

FRE 412 raises a number of issues. For example, FRE 412(a) makes no reference to constitutionally required evidence, apparently because the drafters could not conceive of a situation in which that possibility might arise. As a result, the motion and offer of proof requirement in FRE 412(b), on its face, does not apply to reputation or opinion evidence of prior sexual conduct. It is clear, however, that a statute or evidentiary rule cannot override the constitution. Thus, constitutionally required reputation or opinion evidence would be admissible. If a defense counsel plans to offer reputation or opinion evidence on the theory that it is constitutionally required, should counsel make the motion and offer of proof described in FRE 412(b)?

How broadly or narrowly should one interpret "past sexual behavior?" Does it encompass nude dancing? Dressing in a "sexy" manner? Verbal solicitation of sex?

Normally a person making an offer of proof knows what the offered evidence will establish. Of what should the offer of proof consist if defense counsel wants to cross-examine the alleged victim and is not sure what her answers will be?

The major potential problems with rape shield provisions—including FRE 412—is that they may be drawn so narrowly that they exclude evidence that should not be excluded and that they tend to elevate questions of admissibility to constitutional issues.[40] On the other hand, if the provisions are not drawn fairly narrowly, they do not adequately address the evil they were designed to remedy: the perceived abuses of discretion by courts that permitted the liberal use of prior sexual conduct evidence. The difficult task for the rule drafter is to find some reasonable middle ground between a rule that is too restrictive and a rule that grants too much discretion to the judge. Consider whether the drafters of FRE 412 arrived at an appropriate balance.

PROBLEMS

1. Bill Smith has been charged with the forcible rape of Jane Edwards. If Jane in fact consented to the intercourse, Bill is not guilty. Moreover, if he reasonably believed (or in some jurisdictions unreasonably but honestly believed) that Jane was consenting, he is not guilty.

Bill offers the following evidence:

---

40. The drafters of the original Federal Rules made conscious efforts to avoid constitutional issues. See, e.g., FRE 803(22) and the Advisory Committee Note.

E. Rape Shield Provisions

(a) His own testimony that on several previous occasions he had had consensual sexual intercourse with Jane.

(b) The testimony of W-1 and W-2 that Jane had said she wanted to go to bed with Bill and they had told Bill about Jane's statement.

(c) The testimony of W-3 and W-4 that they had had consensual sexual intercourse with Jane and that they had told Bill about their activities with Jane.

(d) The testimony of Bill and the other witnesses that Jane has a reputation in the community for promiscuity.

For what purposes are the above pieces of evidence relevant? Which pieces of evidence would be admissible under the Federal Rules *prior to* the adoption of FRE 412? Which pieces would be admissible *after* the adoption of FRE 412? Is FRE 412 desirable?

2. John Jones is being prosecuted for the rape of Elvira Golden. The evidence establishes that Jones gave Golden a ride home from a bar on the night of the alleged rape and that Golden and Jones had not met prior to that night.

Golden testified that she had merely accepted a ride home with Jones, that he forced her to let him into her apartment, that he pulled out a knife and threatened to kill her if she did not have intercourse with him, that she offered verbal resistance and tried once to run away, and that she did not offer physical resistance to the intercourse because he was too strong and had the knife.

Jones, on the other hand, testified that Golden solicited him and took him to her apartment where they had consensual sexual intercourse, that an argument developed over the price for her services, and that he left without paying.

Jones offers several witnesses to testify that Golden has a reputation in the community for being a prostitute. Is the evidence admissible?

3. Agatha Lewis has brought an action for damages against Brian Bellows, who, she alleges, transmitted AIDS to her. Agatha establishes with blood test evidence that she did not have the AIDS virus 18 months ago, that she now has the virus, and that Brian has the virus. Agatha testifies that she is not an intravenous drug user, that she has not had a blood transfusion, and that the only person with whom she has had intimate sexual contact subsequent to the negative AIDS test is Brian. She further testifies that she met Brian at a party; that they went to his apartment after the party and had sexual intercourse; that she had sexual intercourse with him two or three additional times in the next two weeks; and that she had no further contact with him. In his defense, Brian admits that he met Agatha at a party. He claims that he gave her a ride to her apartment after the party and that he did not on that night or on any other occasion have sexual intercourse with Agatha. In rebuttal Agatha offers the testimony of three women that during

the past year they met Brian at parties or single's bars and had brief sexual affairs with him. Should this evidence be admitted?

4. The defendant is charged with raping his 13-year-old niece. On cross-examination of the niece the defendant wishes to inquire about two previous charges of sexual assault that she made against the defendant and two charges of sexual assault that she made against her step-father, all of which she recanted. Should the court allow the inquiry?

F. SIMILAR HAPPENINGS

Courts, commentators, and casebook authors typically treat evidence of similar happenings or non-happenings—e.g., evidence of other people slipping and falling on the same allegedly slippery floor where plaintiff fell, or evidence that other people did not fall—as a distinct category of evidence.[41] The attempts to introduce similar happenings evidence frequently occur in similar types of situations,[42] and the evidentiary concerns regarding admissibility are frequently similar. Thus, it is reasonable that lawyers, judges, and commentators would focus on similar happenings evidence in existing cases for its value as precedent; and as a result of this focus, it is understandable that within the law of evidence there would be a tendency to treat similar happenings as a distinct type of evidence. Analytically, however, there is no need for a distinct similar happenings rule, and there is none in the Federal Rules.

The problems raised by the attempt to introduce similar happenings evidence can be dealt with adequately by asking the same kinds of questions one must ask with respect to other evidence:

> First, why is the evidence arguably relevant? (The most likely answers will be to show that an event in dispute did or did not occur, to show the meaning of a contract provision, to show that one of the parties knew or should have known about some allegedly unsafe condition, or in the case of sales of allegedly similar property, to show value.)
>
> Second, if the evidence is relevant, is there some specific exclu-

---

41. See, e.g., Robitaille v. Netoco Community Theatres of North Attleboro, 305 Mass. 265, 25 N.E.2d 749 (1940); McCormick's Handbook on the Law of Evidence 578-592 (3d ed., Cleary, 1984); C. McCormick, J. Sutton, and O. Wellborn, Cases and Materials on Evidence 123-166 (6th ed. 1987).

42. For example, McCormick's Handbook on the Law of Evidence divides the discussion of similar happenings evidence into the following categories: Other claims, suits, or defenses of a party; other misrepresentations and frauds; other contracts and business transactions; other sales of similar property as evidence of value; and other accidents and injuries. Handbook 578-592 (3d ed., Cleary, 1984).

F. Similar Happenings

sionary rule that makes it inadmissible? E.g., is the evidence inadmissible hearsay? If the similar happenings constitute conduct by a person whose conduct is presently in issue, is the evidence (i) inadmissible character evidence (first sentence of FRE 404(b)), (ii) potentially admissible habit evidence (FRE 406), or (iii) potentially admissible specific acts evidence (second sentence of FRE 404(b))?

Third, if the evidence is relevant and not inadmissible pursuant to some specific exclusionary rule, is the evidence inadmissible because its probative value is substantially outweighed by FRE 403 factors?

In one respect the foregoing approach is preferable to an attempt to classify and treat evidence in terms of similar happenings. Discussions of similar happenings evidence frequently include both (a) evidence that involves no propensity issues and thus no need to look to FRE 404-406 (e.g., evidence that third persons fell on a walkway to prove that the walkway was unsafe) and (b) evidence whose relevance depends on a propensity inference (e.g., evidence of filing fraudulent similar claims to prove that the present claim is fraudulent). The inclusion of propensity evidence in the same general category with the non-propensity evidence may lead some courts and lawyers to overlook the need to analyze similar happening propensity evidence in terms of FRE 404-406.

PROBLEMS

1. The Friendly Furnace Company sold Frank Olson a new Acme Furnace and installed it for him. Six months later the furnace blew up and caused extensive damage to Frank's house. The Acme Furnace Company has gone out of business, and Frank is suing the Friendly Furnace Company for damages on the theory that Friendly improperly installed the furnace. At trial, Frank offers to show that four other furnaces installed by Friendly also blew up. Three of the explosions occurred before Frank's furnace blew up and one subsequent to the explosion of Frank's furnace.

For what purpose(s) is the evidence arguably relevant? Should the evidence be admitted? What, if anything, might Frank be able to show to strengthen his argument for admitting evidence of the other explosions?

2. Grace Jacobson has sued Don May for personal injuries that she claims to have received falling down an allegedly dangerous staircase in May's apartment building. May offers to show that in the last five years Grace Jackson has filed four similar personal injury actions against other apartment owners. Assume alternatively that (a) there is and (b) there is not evidence that the other claims are fraudulent. In either case, is the evidence admissible?

3. Pamela King has sued the Whoopie Amusement Park for personal injuries she sustained riding on Whoopie's roller coaster. According to Pamela's testimony a tree limb hit her in the face when she was riding on the

roller coaster. The force of the blow broke her glasses and pieces of the lens were lodged in her eye. As part of its defense Whoopie offers the testimony of the amusement park manager (a) that during the entire summer up to the time of plaintiff's injury nobody had complained about low hanging branches along the path of the roller coaster and (b) that on the day plaintiff was injured over 1000 other persons rode the roller coaster without incident. For what purposes is the defendant's evidence relevant? Should it be admitted?

G. INADMISSIBLE TO PROVE "NEGLIGENCE," "LIABILITY," ETC.

Several relevance rules provide that certain evidence is not admissible to prove negligence or culpability or liability, but that the evidence may be admissible to prove other matters such as ownership, control, or bias of a witness. See FRE 407 (subsequent remedial measures), FRE 408 (compromises and offers of compromise), FRE 409 (payments or offers to pay medical and other similar expenses), and FRE 411 (liability insurance).

Each of these rules is based in part on the notion that the evidence will usually have very slight probative value on the question of negligence or fault and that there are countervailing FRE 403 considerations that warrant exclusion. These countervailing considerations include a concern that admission of the evidence to prove negligence or fault may tend to mislead the jury or confuse the issues: Jurors may reasonably expect that the evidence they hear has a bearing on what they are supposed to decide. Thus, if they hear evidence that in fact has very low probative value, they may be misled into thinking that the evidence is more probative than it really is. Moreover, if the jurors happen to have only a vague understanding of their task, they may confuse the issues and consider the evidence in an improper manner. For example, evidence of design change following an accident may be more probative of the feasibility of making the change than of whether the defendant was culpable at the time of the accident. In such a case, there is a risk that jurors may infer, incorrectly, from the admission of the evidence that the issue is feasibility rather than fault. Similarly, if evidence of liability insurance is admitted, jurors may infer, again incorrectly, that it is proper for them to place the loss on the insured rather than on the party who was at fault. In addition, at least with respect to the liability insurance rule, there is a concern with unfair prejudice: Jurors may understand exactly what they are supposed to do but nonetheless be inclined to find an insured person liable regardless of fault in order to compensate an injured party.

The rules excluding evidence to prove liability or fault also traditionally have been justified on the ground that we do not want to discourage individuals from engaging in socially desirable conduct. In other words, there

G. Inadmissible to Prove "Negligence," "Liability," Etc. 275

is a concern that admitting evidence of subsequent remedial measures, offers of compromise, payment of medical expenses, or maintaining liability insurance to prove fault would discourage individuals from engaging in such conduct.[43]

Consider whether these traditional justifications provide a sufficient basis for excluding relevant evidence. At least with careful instructions about the proper uses of the evidence, is it likely that jurors will overestimate the probative value of the evidence or become confused about the issues? With respect to the desire not to deter socially desirable behavior, to what extent do you think individuals take into account—or even know—the rules of evidence when they make decisions about subsequent repairs, offers of compromise, or payment of medical expenses? (The answer may depend to a substantial extent on whether the individual has sought the advice of counsel before engaging in the activity.) And with respect to the liability insurance rule, is it not likely that the jury frequently will assume that a defendant in a civil action is insured? If so, FRE 411 may be more harmful to uninsured defendants than it is helpful to insured defendants.

An additional but less frequently articulated rationale for these exclusionary rules is that, regardless of deterrence, prejudice, or confusion, we do not want to "punish" or disadvantage individuals for doing good things. This rationale is most frequently associated with the exclusionary rule for payment of medical expenses, sometimes referred to as the "good Samaritan" rule. We suggest, however, that the rationale is equally applicable to—and perhaps more compelling than the deterrence rationale for—the limitations on the use of remedial measure, compromise, and liability insurance evidence.

Each of the rules that prohibits evidence to prove negligence or liability articulates the prohibition differently: FRE 407 excludes evidence "to prove negligence or culpable conduct"; FRE 408 excludes evidence "to prove liability for or invalidity of the claim or its amount"; FRE 409 excludes evidence "to prove liability for the injury"; and FRE 411 excludes evidence "upon the issue whether [a] person acted negligently or otherwise wrongfully." Similarly, the illustrations of possible permissible uses of the evidence vary from rule to rule. Compare, for example, FRE 407 (evidence of subsequent remedial measures may be admissible "for another purpose, such as proving ownership, control, or feasibility of precautionary measures, if controverted, or impeachment") with FRE 411 (evidence of liability insurance may be admissible "for another purpose, such as proof of agency, ownership, or control, or bias or prejudice of a witness").

There is no indication in the legislative history that these differences in language were intended to convey different notions about what is prohibited or potentially admissible. In part the differences in the lists of permissible

---

43. The traditional justification for the confidential communication privileges is similar. See Chapter Twelve.

uses is probably a function of the fact that the most common alternative uses will vary from rule to rule. Beyond this, the explanation for the different terminology in the various rules is probably that different committees drafted each rule and that no committee made a serious effort to see that language was consistently used from rule to rule. In any event, the differences in language demonstrate at the very least a lack of attention to detail. For example, why does FRE 407 refer to "negligence or culpable conduct" when FRE 411 speaks in terms of whether a person "acted negligently or otherwise wrongfully"? How broadly or narrowly should one read the exclusion to prove "liability" in FRE 409 and FRE 411? When one party claims that another party is liable for some injury, is not all relevant evidence offered against the allegedly liable party offered, in some sense, to prove "liability"? What does "if controverted" modify in FRE 407, and why does this language appear there and not in FRE 411? Why does FRE 407 read "such as proving" while FRE 411 reads "such as proof of"? And why is there no list of alternatives in FRE 409? Lack of care in drafting even on inconsequential matters inevitably raises the question about care in drafting generally and about how much reliance one should place on the particular language in any rule.

As you consider the following text and problems dealing with the rules that prohibit evidence to prove negligence or fault, keep in mind a question that we raised at the outset of this chapter: To what extent, as a practical matter, does the potential use of evidence for purposes other than to prove negligence or fault undermine the justifications for the rule?

1. Subsequent Remedial Measures

When a person takes steps to alter a condition or object that caused an injury, there are likely to be several possible explanations for the alteration. For example, there may have been a post-injury advancement in the state of the art in the field that permitted the alteration, or the person who made the alteration may have done so out of desire to minimize similar injuries in the future. In this latter case, one possible inference to draw is that the person who made the alteration realized that the object or condition prior to the alteration posed an unreasonable risk of injury. In order not to discourage people from taking such remedial action,[44] however, FRE 407 excludes evidence of the alteration for this purpose:

> When, after an event, measures are taken which, if taken previously, would have made the event less likely to occur, evidence of subsequent measures is not admissible to prove negligence or culpable conduct in connection with the event. This rule does not require the exclusion of evidence of sub-

---

44. See FRE 407, Advisory Committee Note.

G. Inadmissible to Prove "Negligence," "Liability," Etc. 277

sequent measures when offered for another purpose, such as proving ownership, control, or feasibility of precautionary measures, if controverted, or impeachment.

An issue that has divided both federal and state courts is whether evidence of subsequent remedial measures should be admissible in strict liability or products liability actions in order to prove that a product was defective. Courts excluding subsequent remedial action evidence in these cases maintain that the "encouraging repairs" rationale is equally applicable to strict or products liability actions. Courts reaching the opposite result assert that a product defect is something different from negligence or culpable conduct. In addition, they argue that the policy of encouraging repairs would not be frustrated by admitting the evidence. This argument is based on the following reasoning: Even though admission of evidence of subsequent remedial action may increase the likelihood of liability in those cases in which the evidence is admitted, failure to correct an alleged defect will increase the number of injuries. The potential liability from the increased number of lawsuits will inevitably be greater than the somewhat increased likelihood of liability in a relatively smaller number of lawsuits. Therefore, a rational person who was a potential products liability defendant would take the subsequent remedial action regardless of what the rules of evidence provide.

Before analyzing these competing views, we wish to make clear—largely by way of avoidance—precisely what we mean and do not mean when we speak of a strict or products liability action. There may be—or at least there could be—situations in which liability turns solely on a showing of injury and causation without regard to any fault or culpability on the part of the defendant. On the other hand, in some types of actions to which the term *products liability* is attached, it is not sufficient to establish that the defendant's product was the cause of the plaintiff's injury. In these cases, an important question is whether the product was defective, and in at least some of these cases a finding of defect implies some sort of fault or culpability because the notion of defect is relative. In other words, in these cases a defective product is one that is more dangerous or less fit for its intended use than one might reasonably expect it to be; if the product is more dangerous or less fit than one might reasonably expect it to be, that condition exists because the maker of the product made design or manufacturing or other decisions about the product that were less reasonable than they could have been; and failing to measure up to the standard of reasonableness is acting culpably.

As we trust the ensuing text will make clear, our analysis does not depend upon the extent to which any particular cause of action that is labeled strict or products liability happens to conform to or be a variant of one or the other of the foregoing characterizations. Thus, we have no need to state with any precision what a "strict liability" or a "products liability" action is.

As a matter of logical relevance, we believe that courts admitting remedial measure evidence in strict or products liability cases are wrong to do so on the ground that the concept of defect is unrelated to notions of negligence or culpability. Assuming that there is no question of feasibility (in which case the remedial measure evidence would be admissible even in a negligence action), the evidence must be offered to show something beyond the mere fact that the allegedly defective item could have been made in a different manner, for merely to acknowledge that the item could have been made differently would be to introduce evidence to establish a proposition that is not an issue in the case. For what other purpose related to defect might the evidence be relevant? We submit that probably the only and certainly the most likely inference to draw from the remedial measure evidence is the very inference that FRE 407 prohibits in negligence cases: The remedial measure is an admission of some degree of fault or culpability in the original making of the allegedly defective item. We will leave for others the questions when and whether some degree of culpability is or should be relevant to the question of liability in what courts characterize as strict or products liability actions. Our only point here is that, in the absence of a question of feasibility, subsequent remedial evidence offered to show defect is either (probably) not relevant at all or relevant to show some degree of culpability. If the former is true, the evidence should be excluded pursuant to FRE 402, and there should be no need to consider further the ramifications of FRE 407.

Both courts that admit and courts that exclude subsequent remedial measure evidence in strict or products liability cases assume that the evidence is relevant to the question of defect. We will proceed with this same assumption, which, as we have suggested, has as a necessary concomitant the proposition that culpability is relevant to the question of defect. As a result, the language of FRE 407 would appear to mandate exclusion of subsequent remedial evidence. One should be cautious, however, about what content to give the phrase "culpable conduct" in FRE 407. Despite the fact that proof of defect logically involves proof of some degree of culpability, courts commonly characterize products liability actions as involving something quite different from the ordinary notions of fault or culpability associated with negligence actions. Perhaps the drafters of FRE 407 had this common usage in mind; perhaps they intended that "culpable conduct" refer not to the culpability that inheres in the concept of defect but rather to the other traditional types of culpability such as recklessness, gross recklessness, knowing conduct, and purposeful conduct. Unfortunately, there is nothing in the legislative history of FRE 407 to indicate what the Advisory Committee or Congress thought about the use of subsequent remedial evidence in strict or products liability cases. Furthermore, as we have already pointed out, there appears to have been very little attention paid in the drafting process to the terminology used to describe what FRE 407—or FRE 408, 409, or 411— excludes. Nonetheless, it is coherent both to concede that proof of defect involves proof of culpable conduct and, at the same time, to question whether the Advisory Committee and Congress intended for the "culpable conduct" language in FRE 407 to apply to strict and products liability actions.

G. Inadmissible to Prove "Negligence," "Liability," Etc.

Given the ambiguity of the language in FRE 407, it may be helpful to consider the extent to which the policies underlying FRE 407 would be advanced by excluding subsequent remedial measure evidence to prove defects. It may well be, as courts admitting remedial measure evidence have maintained, that a careful cost/benefit analysis would lead the potential products liability defendant to take subsequent remedial action most of the time regardless of the rules of evidence. We suspect, however, that the same may be true of the potential negligence defendant. In any event, there is one factor that makes the "encouraging repairs" rationale for FRE 407 even more applicable to products liability claims than to negligence claims. To the extent that there is a difference between "typical" products defendants and "typical" negligence defendants, the former are likely to be large corporate or institutional defendants, whereas the latter are likely to be individuals or small businesses. The large corporate defendant is more likely than the individual or small business defendant to have the motivation and resources to engage in a serious cost/benefit analysis, and that analysis may at least occasionally suggest that costs can be minimized by not taking remedial action. Consider, for example, the following report of the Ford Motor Company's response to accidents involving Ford Pintos:

> A Cleveland couple whose 1973 Pinto exploded in flames after a rear-end collision yesterday sued Ford Motor Co. and the other driver for $5.1 million. . . .
> [The couple's lawyer] said documents submitted with the suit show that Ford decided to risk losses in lawsuits from such accidents, rather than stage a massive recall of cars.
> One document, called the Grush-Saunby memo, was obtained from Ford in previous court actions elsewhere. In it Ford engineers did a cost analysis comparing the losses the company could expect in court with the cost of recall. Anticipating 180 burn deaths a year, the engineers projected court-adjudicated losses at $49.5 million, the document shows. The cost of recall was pegged at $137 million. [Cleveland Plain Dealer, March 31, 1979, at 8-A, col. 1.]

Unless one can be reasonably certain either (1) that the impact of the rules of evidence will always be an insignificant factor in the product defendant's cost/benefit calculation or (2) that punitive damages will be assessed in a manner that will always make the cost of not taking the subsequent remedial measure more expensive than taking the measure, the failure to exclude subsequent remedial measures evidence is more likely to deter products defendants than negligent defendants.

On the other hand, if one focuses on the notion that it is undesirable to "punish" an individual for doing something "good" as the rationale for FRE 407, and if one continues to regard the typical products defendant as a large corporation and the typical negligence defendant as an individual or small business, it is arguably appropriate to admit subsequent remedial measure evidence in the products case and exclude it in the negligence case. If an individual defendant's alleged negligence arises from activities around the defendant's home or perhaps in conjunction with the family business, it seems understandable to regard the subsequent remedial action as a "good" deed and to refrain from "punishing" or "hurting" the individual by using the deed as evidence of liability. By contrast, it is arguably appropriate to characterize the subsequent remedial measure of the large, impersonal corporate products defendant as a calculated, amoral economic judgment rather than as a morally "good" deed. To the extent that this characterization is apt, it is arguably not (as) unseemly to use evidence of the remedial measure against the large corporate defendant.

Of course, not all products defendants will be large corporations, and not all negligence defendants will be individuals or small companies. Moreover, the same incident will frequently give rise to both a negligence claim and a strict or products liability claim. If evidence were admissible to establish that the product was defective but not to establish that the defendant was negligent, would the jury be able to appreciate the distinction? Alternatively, would it be desirable to try the two causes of action separately or to impanel two juries and have only one hear the subsequent remedial measure evidence? If the answer to both of the preceding questions is "No," does this fact suggest that ensuring *uniform treatment* of subsequent remedial measure evidence in both negligence and in strict or product liability actions should be an important objective? If so, what should the rule be?

In fact, evidence of subsequent remedial measures even in negligence actions is frequently admissible for some purpose other than to prove negligence:

> The ingenuity of counsel in suggesting other purposes has made substantial inroads upon the general rule of exclusion. Thus evidence of subsequent repairs or changes has been admitted as evidence of the defendant's ownership or control of the premises or his duty to repair where these are disputed; as evidence of the possibility or feasibility of preventive measures, when properly in issue; as evidence, where the jury has taken a view, or where the defendant has introduced a photograph of the scene, to explain that the situation at the time of accident was different; as evidence of what was done later to show that the earlier condition as of the time of the accident was as plaintiff claims, if the defendant disputes this; as evidence that the faulty condition later remedied, was the cause of the injury by showing that after the change the injurious effect disappeared; and as evidence contradicting facts testified to by the adversary's witness. [McCormick's Handbook on the Law of Evidence 816-817 (3d ed., Cleary, 1984).]

Given the multitude of potential uses for subsequent remedial measures evidence, perhaps the best explanation for the decisions admitting such evidence in strict and product liability actions to prove defect is that they represent one more inroad on an antiquated and not very significant exclusionary provision.

G. Inadmissible to Prove "Negligence," "Liability," Etc.

PROBLEMS

1. Tammy Parks is suing the Ace Rifle Company for injuries she received from a bullet wound when a model 003 Ace rifle being cleaned by her stepfather accidentally discharged. Tammy claims that Ace is strictly liable for a defective safety on the rifle. The safety had to be off when the bolt was being moved to unload the rifle. At trial, the Ace vice president for marketing testified that the model 003 Ace rifle was the safest rifle on the market. Tammy seeks to introduce evidence that subsequent to her injury Ace changed the design on the model 003 so that the bolt could be used to unload the rifle while the safety was on. Should the evidence be admitted?

2. Lisa Evans is suing the Jones Mfg. Co. for the wrongful death of her husband, Edward. Edward suffered a severed torso when a co-worker turned on an industrial bailing machine, manufactured by the defendant, when Edward was inside the hopper attempting to clear a jam. Lisa wishes to introduce evidence that after Edward's death

   (a) Jones Mfg. Co. fired the individual responsible for designing safety features on the bailer; and
   (b) Edward's employer, Loman Industries, modified the bailer by installing an access door to the hopper and by making the bailer inoperable when the access doors were open.

Should Jones' objection to these pieces of evidence be sustained?

3. Eugene Wright is suing the Loop Ladder Co. for personal injuries that he received when a ladder on which he had been standing fell to the ground with him on it. Eugene claims that a plastic tip on the ladder was too weak and that it broke, causing the ladder to fall. The defendant claims that the plastic tip broke from the impact of the fall or at some later time. An expert witness testifies for the defendant that the tip was adequate for its purpose. Plaintiff offers evidence that shortly after his accident, the Loop Ladder Company substituted a strengthened plastic cap on all of its ladders. Should this evidence be admitted? Would it make any difference in your analysis if the expert were a Loop employee who had authorized the change in the plastic tip?

2. Compromises and Offers of Compromise

FRE 408 provides:

> Evidence of (1) furnishing or offering or promising to furnish, or (2) accepting or offering or promising to accept, a valuable consideration in compromising or attempting to compromise a claim which was disputed as to either validity or amount, is not admissible to prove liability for or invalidity of the

claim or its amount. Evidence of conduct or statements made in compromise negotiations is likewise not admissible. This rule does not require the exclusion of any evidence otherwise discoverable merely because it is presented in the course of compromise negotiations. This rule also does not require exclusion when the evidence is offered for another purpose, such as proving bias or prejudice of a witness, negativing a contention of undue delay, or proving an effort to obstruct a criminal investigation or prosecution.

The third sentence of the rule makes it clear that a party cannot insulate from discovery documents and information that would otherwise be discoverable merely by making reference to or relying on such evidence in the compromise negotiations—a result that courts probably would reach even without this sentence in the rule. The fourth sentence is the standard acknowledgment that offers of compromise may be admissible for purposes other than to prove liability or the amount of a claim.

The second sentence of FRE 408 is a significant departure from the common law rule, which excluded only statements of offer and acceptance and not statements of fault made in the course of compromise negotiations. The Advisory Committee offers the following justification for the change:

> The practical value of the common law rule has been greatly diminished by its inapplicability to admissions of fact, even though made in the course of compromise negotiations, unless hypothetical, stated to be "without prejudice," or so connected with the offer as to be inseparable from it. . . . An inevitable effect is to inhibit freedom of communication with respect to compromise, even among lawyers. Another effect is the generation of controversy over whether a given statement falls within or without the protected area. These considerations account for the expansion of the rule herewith to include evidence of conduct or statements made in compromise negotiations, as well as the offer or completed compromise itself.

One might add that the effect of the common law rule was largely to penalize individuals who, unaware of the rules of evidence, would attempt to negotiate settlements themselves rather than deal through lawyers, who presumably would know to couch any fault-like statements in hypothetical terms.

Consider whether FRE 408's expansion of the common law rule is desirable. The primary motives for compromising a claim will frequently be a desire to avoid the costs of litigation or the risk of losing (or foregoing) a good deal more than the person loses (or forgoes) in compromising the claim. Thus, the probative value of the evidence as an admission of fault or liability will often be quite low. As a result, the cost—in terms of foregoing relevant evidence—of applying the common law rule was not likely to be great. By contrast, FRE 408's extension of the exclusionary provision to clear-cut statements of fault shields highly probative evidence from the fact finder.

G. Inadmissible to Prove "Negligence," "Liability," Etc.

PROBLEMS

1. Jean Wilson has sued Henry Davis for injuries she received in an automobile accident. According to Jean's complaint she was headed west on a two-lane road when Davis, who was heading east, crossed the road into her lane of traffic and hit her. Davis claims that he had been taking necessary evasive action to get out of the way of a another car that had suddenly pulled in front of him from a side street at a very slow rate of speed. The driver of the third car, John Knight, has testified for the plaintiff that Davis was responsible for the accident. Davis offers to show that he had filed suit against Knight for damage to his automobile and that Knight had paid Davis $200 to settle the suit, in which Davis had asked for $400. Should this evidence be admitted over plaintiff's objection? *Biases witness*

2. Jimmy King, a 10-year-old, was seriously injured when he hit a chuck hole with the moped he was riding and a piece of glass from the windshield shattered and pierced his right eye. Jimmy's parents have brought suit against Glassmate, Inc., the manufacturer of the windshield, and against the windshield wholesaler. Glassmate cross-claimed against the wholesaler and brought third-party actions against the retailer and the manufacturer of the lucite used in the windshield. After the jury selection and before the trial began, the plaintiff settled with the wholesaler, the retailer, and the lucite manufacturer, and those parties were dismissed from the suit. At the outset of the trial, the judge made the following comment to the jury:

> The plaintiff has made an election in this case, which is not that unusual, that it wishes to proceed against the one defendant only, and there is a procedure available to do that. The way it works is that the plaintiff can accept nominal payment, it was ten dollars in this case, and then they are excused from further participation in the case.
>
> Now the effect of that is that, depending on what the evidence is, their contribution to the cause of this occurrence may still be submitted to the jury or it may not. That's a decision I will have to make at some point. You may have to make a decision in that respect. We will see how that goes later in the case. But I didn't want you speculating on why they were not here and be concerned as to whether the Court had made a ruling on the merits of the case, which I have not, or speculate on whether the plaintiff had received substantial monies, which they have not. I wanted you to know the full facts of the matter.

Was the judge's comment appropriate? *No — Leigh says it was idiotic*

3. Joyce Lange is suing the estate of Jarvis Smith for injuries that she received as a passenger in Smith's automobile when it was involved in a head-on collision with a vehicle driven by Richard Robbins. Both Smith and Robbins died as a result of the crash. Joyce had initially sued Robbins' estate as well, but that claim was settled without trial. In the suit against Smith, there was testimony that both Smith and Robbins had been drinking

prior to the accident, and there was conflicting evidence about which defendant was driving on the wrong side of the road. One of the plaintiff's witnesses was Ellen Robbins, the widow of Richard Robbins. She testified that her husband had been driving on the right side of the road, and that the Smith vehicle crossed the center line and ran into them. On cross-examination of Ellen Robbins, the defendant brings out the fact that in an earlier deposition Ms. Robbins said she was not sure which vehicle crossed the center line. The defendant now seeks to establish that at that time of that deposition Mr. Robbins estate was being sued by the plaintiff and that that suit was settled. Should the evidence be admitted?

3. Payment of Medical and Similar Expenses

Just as evidence of a subsequent repair or evidence of offering to pay a certain sum to settle a claim may be regarded as an implied admission of fault or liability, paying another person's medical expenses may be an implied admission of fault. For reasons that "parallel those underlying Rules 407 and 408,"[45] however, FRE 409 provides:

> Evidence of furnishing or offering or promising to pay medical, hospital, or similar expenses occasioned by an injury is not admissible to prove liability for the injury.

In one significant respect FRE 409 differs from FRE 408: Statements made in conjunction with the payments—including statements of fault—are *not* excluded. According to the Advisory Committee:

> This difference in treatment arises from fundamental differences in nature. Communication is essential if compromises are to be effected, and consequently broad protection of statements is needed. This is not so in cases of payments [governed by FRE 409], where factual statements may be expected to be incidental in nature.

What do you think of the Advisory Committee's distinction?

Although FRE 409, unlike FRE 407, 408 and 411, does not include an illustrative list of possible permissible uses for evidence of medical and similar payments, the common law counterpart to FRE 409 permitted evidence for other purposes. For example, in a dispute over where the plaintiff's injury occurred, a court admitted evidence of the defendant's payment of medical expenses to prove that the injury occurred on defendant's premises. See Great Atlantic & Pacific Tea Co. v. Custin, 214 Ind. 54, 13 N.E.2d

---

45. FRE 409, Advisory Committee Note.

G. Inadmissible to Prove "Negligence," "Liability," Etc.

542 (1938). There is no indication in the legislative history that the drafters of FRE 409 intended to depart from the common law in this respect.

FRE 409 is rarely invoked, perhaps because there are not enough good Samaritans among us. If there were, an issue that would undoubtedly arise in applying FRE 409 is what constitutes "similar expenses." For example, should evidence of paying to have an automobile repaired or paying subsistence income while an individual is recuperating from injury be excluded?

4. Liability Insurance

Of all of the specific relevance rules, FRE 411, which prohibits the introduction of evidence "that a person was or was not insured against liability . . . on the issue whether the person acted negligently or otherwise wrongfully," is perhaps the least important. Liability insurance is so pervasive that it is doubtful that individuals obtain or forego obtaining liability insurance because of the possible admissibility of evidence regarding insurance; and it is doubtful that individuals act more or less carefully because they have or do not have liability insurance. Admittedly, there may be a serious concern that jurors would be unfairly prejudiced by evidence about the existence or nonexistence of liability insurance in that they may be disposed to impose damages because of insurance or to forego or minimize damages out of sympathy for the uninsured. Particularly in light of the negligible probative value of liability insurance on the question of fault, however, FRE 403 arguably provides ample protection against the unwarranted use of such evidence. Moreover, as we suggested earlier, excluding evidence of absence of insurance may lead the jury to draw the erroneous conclusion that a party is insured; and if a party happens to be insured, it is quite likely that the evidence will be admissible to prove something other than negligence or wrongful conduct. For example, if there is a dispute over whether the defendant is responsible for or has control over the condition or instrumentality that caused the plaintiff's injury, the fact that the defendant had liability insurance may be admissible to prove responsibility or control; if, as is frequently the case, an insurance investigator testifies about the results of an investigation, evidence that the investigator represents a company that insures one of the parties will probably be admissible both as part of the general background information about the witness and as an indication of the possible bias of the witness. In addition, during the jury selection process, it is appropriate in many jurisdictions to ask the prospective jurors if they or any friends or relatives work for insurance companies. The theoretically legitimate reason for such questions is to identify jurors who may have a particular bias because of their own or their relatives association with an insurance company. A likely impact of the questions, however, is to suggest to jurors that one or both parties was insured, and the jury may then be influenced in it's decision on the basis of the assumptions it has made about insurance.

PROBLEM

1. Greg Gross has sued the state for personal injuries and severe damage to his Mercedes Benz sports car that occurred when the car hit a deep pothole and then careened out of control into an embankment. The plaintiff's theory is that the state was negligent in not providing any warning about the condition of the road. In order to alleviate possible bias of jurors who might be inclined to decide in favor of the state in order to avert the need for a tax increase, the plaintiff offers to show that the state carries liability insurance for the kind of injuries that he suffered. Should the evidence be admitted?

H. *WITHDRAWN GUILTY PLEAS, PLEAS OF NO CONTEST, AND OFFERS TO PLEAD GUILTY*

FRE 410 provides:

> Except as otherwise provided in this rule, evidence of the following is not, in any civil or criminal proceeding, admissible against the defendant who made the plea or was a participant in the plea discussions:
> (1) a plea of guilty which was later withdrawn;
> (2) a plea of nolo contendere;
> (3) any statement made in the course of any proceedings under Rule 11 of the Federal Rules of Criminal Procedure or comparable state procedure regarding either of the foregoing pleas; or
> (4) any statement made in the course of plea discussions with an attorney for the prosecuting authority which do not result in a plea of guilty or which result in a plea of guilty later withdrawn.
> However, such a statement is admissible (i) in any proceedings wherein another statement made in the course of the same plea or plea discussions has been introduced and the statement ought in fairness be considered contemporaneously with it, or (ii) in a criminal proceeding for perjury or false statement if the statement was made by the defendant under oath, on the record and in the presence of counsel.

Once a defendant has pled guilty, the defendant may withdraw the plea only with the permission of the court. The standards for permitting withdrawal of a plea typically are not articulated with any degree of specificity, but there must be "cause" or some good reason to permit the withdrawal. A court is likely to permit withdrawal of a plea if there is reason to believe

H. Plea Negotiations

that the plea is inaccurate because the defendant is innocent and/or if it appears that the defendant's rights were violated in the process of procuring the plea. To the extent that the concern is with the violation of the defendant's rights, exclusion may be necessary in order to make the remedy for the violation meaningful. If the prosecutor could respond to a withdrawn plea by using that plea against the defendant in a subsequent proceeding, the value of withdrawal as a remedy would often be substantially undermined. To the extent that the concern is with the reliability of a plea, the fact that a judge has already determined that the plea is unreliable casts doubt on the plea's probative value. Moreover, full relitigation of the reliability issue could be time consuming and could, as a practical matter, force the defendant to take the witness stand. If one can reasonably anticipate that the admission of marginally probative evidence will induce a defendant who would prefer not to testify to waive the fifth amendment right to remain silent, it is arguably appropriate to exclude the evidence in the first instance.

Only some jurisdictions permit pleas of no contest, and where they are permitted, the court usually must approve the pleas. Pleas of no contest are by their nature compromises. They constitute an acquiescence to a criminal conviction without an admission of guilt or a determination of guilt after an adjudicatory trial. Their compromise nature makes uncertain their probative value to prove that the person committed the acts charged. Moreover, to use a no contest plea for this purpose would tend to undermine the initial value of the plea.

Federal Rule of Criminal Procedure 11, which is referred to in FRE 410(3), governs plea bargaining and the judicial acceptance or rejection of guilty pleas. Fed. R. Crim. P. 11(e)(6) contains the same exclusionary provisions codified in FRE 410.

FRE 410(4) is the counterpart in the criminal negotiating process to FRE 408's prohibition against using evidence of attempts to settle or compromise civil claims. As a matter of general principle, and perhaps even as a matter of practical reality, one may question the soundness of such a rule. An offer to plead guilty, at least if the plea is to a relatively serious charge, may have more probative value than the offer to settle—even for a substantial amount of money—a civil claim. Moreover, the offers to plead guilty that are excluded by FRE 410 usually occur in the context of plea negotiations, and there are several reasons why settling or compromising criminal charges may be regarded as undesirable and, therefore, something to be deterred. First, the possibility of pleading guilty to a charge that is substantially less severe than the crime initially charged may have the undesirable effect of pressuring an innocent individual to plead guilty in order to avoid the risk of possible conviction on the more serious charge. Second, the possibility of a plea to a lesser charge may have the arguably undesirable effect of undermining a legislatively dictated mandatory sentence for the crime initially charged or of limiting the range of the judge's sentencing discretion. Finally, a consequence of encouraging or even condoning plea bargaining is the possibility of unfairness or at least the appearance of unfairness from what are or seem to be inconsistent and arbitrary plea bargaining decisions from case to case by prosecutors. This, in turn, may lead to cynicism about or disrespect for the criminal law and perhaps undermine the force of criminal prohibitions and sanctions as general deterrents.[46]

Despite these concerns, the Supreme Court has acknowledged that plea bargaining is an acceptable method for disposing of criminal cases,[47] and the reality is that plea bargaining is pervasive in the criminal justice system. Depending on the jurisdiction, anywhere from 70 percent to 95 percent of all criminal charges are disposed of by guilty plea, and many of these pleas are the result of plea negotiations. Moreover, the criminal justice system does not have the resources to process the current and ever increasing volume of cases without heavy reliance on guilty pleas. Thus, as a practical matter, plea bargaining is a fact of life, and in light of this reality, it may be at least as important to encourage guilty pleas as it is to encourage settlement of civil cases.

Just as excluding statements made in conjunction with offers to settle civil suits may facilitate the negotiating process, excluding statements made in conjunction with inadmissible pleas may facilitate arrangements for those pleas. Furthermore, Federal Rule of Criminal Procedure 11(d) requires the court, as a condition of initially accepting a plea of guilty or no contest to "address[] the defendant in open court [and] determin[e] that the plea is voluntary." Thus, if a plea is to be excluded, it seems reasonable to exclude statements made in conjunction with the plea.

Consider the last sentence of FRE 410, which contains two exceptions to the general rule of exclusion for statements made in conjunction with plea discussions. Do you think the exceptions are wise? Would you add others?

PROBLEMS

1. Eddie Felman was convicted following a jury trial of extortion and conspiracy to extort money. During the course of earlier plea discussions with the prosecutor, Eddie gave the prosecutor several leads to other people supposedly involved in the conspiracy, and these leads turned out to be false. At Felman's sentencing, the prosecutor, in urging that the judge impose a stiff sentence, stated that Felman had been uncooperative. The prosecutor then offered to establish that during the plea negotiations Felman had supplied false information to the authorities. Felman objects on the ground that FRE 410 bars the use of statements made during plea discussions. What result?

---

46. Cf. pages 134-142 (Nesson acceptability thesis).
47. See Santobello v. New York, 404 U.S. 257 (1971).

I. Curative Admissibility

2. Sam Whitty was arrested for sale of cocaine. After receiving and waiving his *Miranda* rights, Whitty indicated that he was anxious to cooperate with the police if they would see to it that he was not treated harshly. The officers responded that they would do what they could for Whitty, and he proceeded to tell them that he had purchased the cocaine from Tom Carver. At Whitty's trial the prosecution calls a police officer, who offers to testify about Whitty's statement. Whitty objects on the ground that it was a statement made during plea negotiations. What result?

3. Gerald Zook has been charged with reckless driving and failure to yield the right of way, both misdemeanors, for his involvement in an automobile accident in which the driver of the other car was severely injured. Gerald is anxious to avoid creating any evidence that may be harmful to him in a civil suit that he expects the driver of the other car to file. At the same time, however, he is not seriously interested in contesting the two traffic offenses. The jurisdiction does not permit pleas of no contest. What are your recommendations with respect to the traffic offense charges?

I. "FIGHTING FIRE WITH FIRE"—THE DOCTRINE OF CURATIVE ADMISSIBILITY

The doctrine of curative admissibility—sometimes referred to as "fighting fire with fire"—permits a party to introduce normally inadmissible evidence in response to the opposing party's introduction of or attempt to introduce inadmissible evidence. Consider, for example, a case in which the plaintiff has sued a local restaurant for food poisoning that allegedly resulted from unsanitary conditions in the kitchen. During the direct examination of the restaurant owner, defense counsel asks the owner to tell the jury about special awards for cleanliness that the restaurant has received over the last five years. The plaintiff could object on the ground that this question calls for inadmissible character or propensity evidence. Having an objection sustained and even having the jury admonished to disregard the question, however, may be of little benefit to the defendant. At least some jurors are likely to assume that awards were received and to draw the improper propensity inference. Indeed, plaintiff's counsel may reasonably believe that the best way to minimize this possibility is not to object at all. In this type of situation, regardless of whether the plaintiff objected to the question, it arguably would be appropriate to permit the plaintiff, in rebuttal, to introduce evidence of citations the restaurant has received from the health department for unsanitary conditions. Although this evidence normally would also be objectionable on character/propensity grounds, allowing it to come in will provide some antidote to the defense counsel's improper evidence. Maintaining a "balance of errors" or permitting the plaintiff "to fight (the defendant's) fire with fire" may contribute to accurate fact finding. Moreover, this remedy is considerably more efficient than the alternatives of declaring a mistrial or reversing a judgment on appeal.

In other situations, the propriety of permitting a party to "fight fire with fire" is less clear. Consider, for example, a defendant who forgoes an adequate opportunity to object to excludable hearsay evidence. Should this failure to object be sufficient to permit the defendant to introduce, over the plaintiff's objection, excludable hearsay evidence? What would be the impact on trials and on litigation strategy if the curative admissibility doctrine were applied this broadly?

Most, but not all, jurisdictions recognize some version of the curative admissibility doctrine, and although there is no Federal Rule of Evidence dealing with the subject, federal courts both before and after the adoption of the Federal Rules have invoked the doctrine. McCormick's Handbook on the Law of Evidence 147-148 (3d ed., Cleary, 1984) provides the following summary:

> Because of the many variable factors affecting the solution in particular cases the decisions do not lend themselves easily to generalizations, but the following conclusions, having some support in the decisions, are submitted as reasonable:
>
> (1) If the incompetent evidence sought to be answered is immaterial and not prejudice-arousing, the judge, to save time and to avoid distraction of attention from the issues, should refuse to hear answering evidence; but if he does hear it, under the prevailing view, the party opening the door has no standing to complain.
>
> (2) If the evidence, though inadmissible, is relevant to the issues and hence probably damaging to the adversary's case, or though irrelevant is prejudice-arousing to a material degree, and if the adversary has seasonably objected or moved to strike, then the adversary should be entitled to give answering evidence as of right. By objecting he has done his best to save the court from mistake, but his remedy by assigning error to the ruling is not an adequate one. He needs a fair opportunity to win his case at the trial by refuting the damaging evidence. . . .
>
> (3) If again the first incompetent evidence is relevant, or though irrelevant is prejudice-arousing, but the adversary has failed to object or to move to strike out, where such an objection might apparently have avoided the harm, then the allowance of answering evidence should rest in the judge's discretion. He should weigh the probable influence of the first evidence, the time and distraction incident to answering it, and the possibility and effectiveness of an instruction to the jury to disregard it. However, here various courts have indicated that introduction of the answering evidence is a matter of right.
>
> (4) In any event, if the incompetent evidence, or even the inquiry eliciting it, is so prejudice-arousing that an objection or motion to strike cannot have erased the harm, then it seems that the adversary should be entitled to answer it as of right.

I. Curative Admissibility

PROBLEMS

1. Ralph Eastman is being tried for possession of cocaine. After the prosecution has presented its case, Eastman takes the witness stand and on direct examination testifies as follows:

Q: Mr. Eastman, do you live alone?
A: No, I share an apartment with Ed Higgins.
Q: Do you both have access to the entire apartment?
A: Yes.
Q: Does the cocaine that is the subject of this prosecution belong to you?
A: No.
Q: Did you ever have this cocaine in your possession?
A: No.
Q: Were you aware that the cocaine was in your apartment?
A: No.
Q: Have you ever in your life possessed cocaine?
A: No, never. I have never messed with any drugs.

After the defense presents the rest of its evidence, the prosecutor, in rebuttal, offers the testimony of Jack Evans that on one occasion last year at a party he snorted cocaine with Ralph Eastman and that when they were college roommates five years ago they smoked marijuana regularly. Defense counsel objects to the admission of the evidence. What result?

2. Janice Goodman has sued the Acme insurance company to collect the proceeds on a fire insurance policy that covered her recently destroyed boutique. The insurance company defends on the ground that the fire was the result of arson procured by Janice. Police Officer Adams, a defense witness, testified that he had arrested Janice for arson. In rebuttal, Janice offers to prove, over the insurance company's objection, that the complaint which led to the arrest was dismissed. Admissible?

3. Wigmore expressed approval of the position taken by some courts that the doctrine of curative admissibility is available only if the party seeking to invoke the doctrine did *not* object to the initial inadmissible evidence. Professor Tillers, the reviser of the first volume of Wigmore's treatise on evidence, approves of those decisions that permit "fighting fire with fire" in situations in which there has been an objection to the evidence. In addition, Tillers suggests that if one had to choose between an objection rule or a no objection rule, it would be preferable to require making an objection a condition of invoking the curative admissibility doctrine. 1 J. Wigmore, Evidence in Trials at Common Law §15, pp.731-733 & n.2 (Tillers rev. 1983). With which view do you agree?

CHAPTER FIVE
THE HEARSAY RULE

The rule prohibiting hearsay—assertions made by declarants out of court and offered in court to prove the truth of the matters asserted—is a relatively recent development in the law of evidence, and it is directly related to the development of the adversary system and the modern jury trial.

The earliest English "juries" consisted of citizens who were summoned to decide disputes on the basis of their own personal knowledge of the litigants and the facts. At least by the early sixteenth century it was well established that the jurors, if they did not have personal knowledge of all the relevant facts, could go out into the community and make inquiry of persons who did know the facts. Only rarely would witnesses give testimony in court. In short, reliance on hearsay was the norm rather than the exception.

Throughout the sixteenth century it became increasingly more common for juries to base decisions in whole or in part on evidence presented by witnesses who testified in court. Concomitantly, litigants in increasing numbers raised objections to the use of hearsay evidence. For example, in the celebrated 1603 treason conspiracy trial of Sir Walter Raleigh, an important part of the prosecution's case was the affidavit of Lord Cobham, an alleged co-conspirator, who was not called as a witness. When Raleigh objected that Lord Cobham, who was available, should be produced to testify in court, the prosecutor's only response was to call as a witness Dyer, a pilot. Dyer testified to facts of which he admittedly had no personal knowledge but that had been told to him out of court by a Portuguese gentleman. On the basis of this hearsay evidence Raleigh was convicted.[1]

Despite objections of the type made in Raleigh's trial, hearsay evidence

---

1. There was no legal basis for Raleigh's demand that Lord Cobham be produced as a witness. See 5 J. Wigmore, Evidence in Trials at Common Law 22 (1974 Chadbourn ed.)

continued to be freely admitted well into the seventeenth century. Decisions excluding hearsay evidence begin to appear with frequency only in the last quarter of that century, and even these decisions acknowledge that the prohibition against hearsay is not absolute. The use of hearsay to corroborate in-court testimony continued to be common.

Modern versions of the hearsay rule likewise are not absolute. There are a number of exceptions to the rule in every jurisdiction. The Federal Rules, for example, contain the basic prohibition against hearsay evidence in FRE 802 and then proceed in FRE 803 and FRE 804 to list nearly 30 exceptions to that prohibition. In addition, FRE 801(d) lists several exemptions from the definition of hearsay, which are functionally no different from hearsay exceptions.[2] In due course we will examine the most important of these exceptions and exemptions. Initially, it is important to understand what constitutes hearsay and what justifications exist for excluding hearsay.

As we begin that inquiry, there are two things you should keep in mind. First, as you will see shortly, any brief definition of hearsay is deceptively simple and misleading. Determining whether a particular piece of evidence is hearsay requires one not merely to apply a written formula to a given piece of evidence but to understand the reasons for the hearsay prohibition—reasons that are captured only imperfectly in any brief definition. Second, keep in mind that the classification of evidence as hearsay or not hearsay is not necessarily determinative of admissibility. Non-hearsay evidence may be inadmissible for some other reason (e.g., privilege), and hearsay evidence may fall within one of the exceptions to the hearsay rule. Thus, you should reserve your judgment about the desirability of the hearsay rule until you have had an opportunity to examine the exceptions to the rule, and for the present, you should not let your subjective desire to admit or exclude a particular piece of evidence influence your evaluation whether the evidence is hearsay.

Once one identifies what constitutes hearsay, there are a number of options from a rule-drafting standpoint for articulating circumstances under which hearsay evidence may be admissible. At one extreme, there could be a limited number of specific exceptions. At the other extreme, there could be a cautionary rule, perhaps similar to FRE 403, which does nothing more than admonish a judge to be wary of hearsay and to exercise discretion to admit "good" hearsay. The Federal Rules take a middle ground between these extremes: In addition to a number of specific exceptions, there is a residual exception for hearsay statements "not specifically covered by the [specific] exceptions but having equivalent circumstantial guarantees of trustworthiness." See FRE 803(24) and 804(b)(5).

2. See also FRE 703, which permits an expert to offer an opinion based on information not otherwise admissible into evidence, and FRE 705, which authorizes disclosure of information upon which an expert relies. If the disclosed information is otherwise inadmissible hearsay, FRE 703 and 705 may have the effect of creating an additional hearsay exception. We explore this matter further in Chapter Eleven. See pages 742-749 infra.

A. RATIONALE AND MEANING

1. The Hearsay Concept

To understand the concept of hearsay, it is important first to look closely at the inferential process involved in assessing the credibility and accuracy of assertions generally. Consider a situation in which an acquaintance, Sally, tells you or writes to you that she saw a gray Honda run through a red light and hit a pedestrian. If you know that Sally is trustworthy and a careful observer with a good memory, you probably would have little doubt about what happened. Indeed, unless you had some particular reason for disbelieving Sally, you would probably regard her statement as some (although not conclusive) proof that the gray Honda had run the red light. The reason this is so is because on the basis of our common experience we have found that more often than not people are truthful. (Consider the chaos in which we would live if people were untruthful half or more of the time!)

Of course, in any given case this assumption about truthtelling may not be correct. The assumption that Sally's (or anyone else's) assertion is a truthful, accurate recounting of some event requires us to make two inferences, either or both of which may be wrong. First, from the fact that Sally said the Honda went through the red light, we must infer—if we are to give any credit to the statement—that Sally honestly believes that the Honda ran through the red light. If Sally is trying to deceive us (a *sincerity* problem), her words will not reflect her actual belief. Similarly, if she has inadvertently used the wrong words (a *narration* problem) or if her words are subject to more than one interpretation (an *ambiguity* problem), her words may not reflect her actual belief. To put the matter somewhat differently, if there is a sincerity problem or a narration or ambiguity problem, the belief that we as listeners attribute (or that jurors would attribute) to Sally will not necessarily be what she is actually thinking.

As a practical matter, narration and ambiguity problems are probably fairly rare in oral or written statements. A narration problem is likely to exist only if the declarant is attempting to communicate in a language that is somewhat unfamiliar to the declarant or if the declarant inadvertently omits a critical word (e.g., the word *not* in a written statement). An ambiguity problem is likely to exist only if the declarant is using slang that is somewhat unfamiliar to the hearer/reader or if it is unclear from the context what the declarant is intending to assert. For example, if a person says, "Jon had a great catch," is the reference to fishing or baseball? Frequently, but not always, the answer will be clear from the context within which the statement is made. In short, narration problems arise when the declarant inadvertently chooses the wrong words; ambiguity problems arise when the hearer/reader misinterprets what the declarant is thinking and, in terms of the declarant's language, accurately communicating. In either case, the result is the same:

Although the declarant may be sincere, the inference from the declarant's words that the hearer/reader draws about the declarant's belief is incorrect.

The second possibly wrong inference about Sally's statement involves the relationship between what Sally believes she witnessed and what actually happened. We must infer that her belief is an accurate reflection of the fact that the Honda ran through the red light. This will not be the case if Sally did not observe the incident accurately (a *perception* problem), or if at the time she made the statement, she had forgotten that the gray car had been a Saab (a *memory* problem).

The relationship between an event and a person's words about that event may be illustrated with a "testimonial triangle":[3]

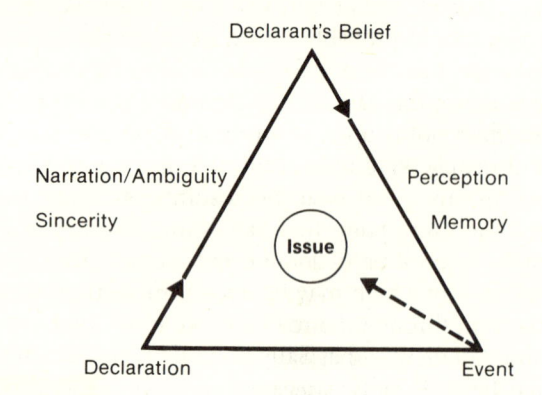

```
                    Declarant's Belief

   Narration/Ambiguity                Perception

   Sincerity                          Memory
                         Issue

          Declaration              Event
```

The left leg of the triangle represents the inference from the declarant's words to the declarant's belief, an inference that requires reliance on the declarant's sincerity and narrative ability. The right leg represents the inference from the declarant's belief to what caused that belief, an inference that requires reliance on the declarant's perception and memory.

"Perception," as used here, includes impressions received from any of the sensory organs. For example, the incorrect identification of an odor or the erroneous hearing of another's words would be a perception problem. In our Honda hypothetical, if the person listening to Sally incorrectly hears her words, that is a perception problem of the hearer. Sally's inadvertent use of the wrong words would be Sally's narration problem. If Sally were color blind and perceived the light to be red when it was in fact green, that would be Sally's perception error.

In order for Sally's declaration "I saw the gray Honda run through the red light" to be relevant to prove that the Honda did run through the red

---

3. The testimonial triangle concept was first popularized for the academic legal community by Professor Lawrence Tribe in his article Triangulating Hearsay, 87 Harv. L. Rev. 957 (1974). For a much earlier version of the triangle, see C. K. Ogden and I. A. Richards, The Meaning of Meaning 10-12 (1927). For a recent version of the triangle that is substantially similar to the one used here, see R. Lempert and S. Saltzburg, A Modern Approach to Evidence 350-353, 357-359 (2d ed. 1982).

A. Rationale and Meaning 297

light, we must make the inferences illustrated by both legs of the testimonial triangle.

The dotted line running from the lower right hand corner of the triangle to "Issue" represents some further inference that may be necessary in order for evidence to be relevant to the resolution of some ultimate fact in a law suit. In our Honda hypothetical, there is no need to draw any further inferences about what happened; running the red light is the ultimate relevant historical fact. The only remaining task is to decide, in view of whatever other evidence there may be, whether the Honda did run the red light (i.e., whether to believe Sally) and if it did, whether running the red light violated the requisite standard of care.

In other situations, additional factual inferences may be necessary. Consider, for example, a homicide prosecution in which one of the elements of the crime is the act of shooting the victim. George offers to testify that within a split second of hearing the sound of a gun shot and seeing the victim fall to the ground, he observed the defendant, Henry, holding a smoking gun. George's testimony, in terms of our testimonial triangle, is relevant to prove that immediately following the sound of a gun shot and the fall of the victim, Henry, who was within George's field of vision, was holding a smoking gun. And for the evidence to be relevant in this manner, we necessarily must rely on George's narrative ability, sincerity, perception, and memory. From the facts that Henry was holding a smoking gun immediately after the sound of a gun shot and the fall of the victim, however, it does not necessarily follow that Henry shot the victim. Even if we assume that other evidence will show that a fatal bullet wound was the reason for the victim falling, it may be that someone other than Henry shot the victim. That person may have put the murder weapon in Henry's hand, or perhaps Henry was independently shooting at something else (a possibility that might or might not be shown to be highly unlikely by ballistics tests on the gun and the fatal bullet). Nonetheless, despite these possibilities, it is reasonable to infer from the fact that Henry was holding a smoking pistol immediately after the victim fell to the ground with a fatal gun shot wound that Henry shot the victim. It is this inference that is illustrated by the dotted line on the triangle. It is an inference that is necessary in order to make the evidence ultimately relevant to a provable proposition in the case; but it is not an inference that requires any further reliance on George's narrative ability, sincerity, perception, or memory.

The base of the triangle is simply a base. There is no direct relationship between words spoken and the event that they describe.

Returning to the Honda hypothetical, if we knew with absolute certainty that Sally was lying or using the wrong words or that she misperceived or had forgotten what happened, Sally's statement would not be relevant to prove that the gray Honda ran the red light. We do not and cannot know these things for sure, however; and, as noted earlier, we do know on the basis of our common experience that more often than not people are truthful and accurate in their statements. Thus, Sally's statement is relevant to prove that the gray Honda went through the red light, even though it may turn out that we ultimately decide that the Honda did not run the light.[4]

Now consider two variations of how Sally's information about the Honda might be communicated to the jury. First, assume that Sally herself is called as a witness and in response to a question on direct examination offers to testify, "On June 1, I observed the gray Honda run a red light and hit a pedestrian." Next, assume that three weeks after the accident Sally made the above statement to her friend George, that George was called as a witness, and that he offered to testify in response to a question on direct examination, "On June 21, Sally told me that three weeks ago she had seen a gray Honda run a red light and hit a pedestrian." The first piece of evidence would be welcome in any courtroom in America, but the second piece of evidence is just as clearly hearsay. In the words of FRE 801(a)-(c), it is an "oral assertion" made by the "declarant" (Sally) "other than while testifying at the trial," and it is being "offered in evidence to prove the truth of the matter asserted." Moreover, there is no traditionally recognized exception to the hearsay rule for this evidence.

In terms of the testimonial triangle, the non-hearsay alternative (i.e., Sally's in-court testimony) requires a trip around only one triangle:

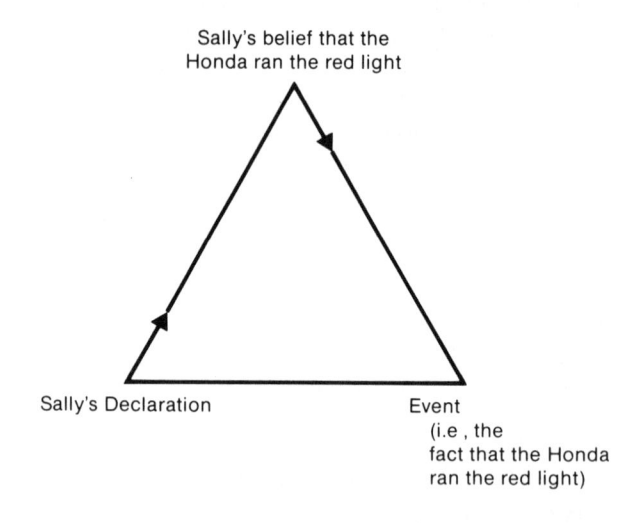

```
              Sally's belief that the
              Honda ran the red light
                       /\
                      /  \
                     /    \
                    /      \
                   /        \
                  /          \
                 /            \
                /_____\
    Sally's Declaration        Event
                               (i.e., the
                               fact that the Honda
                               ran the red light)
```

George's testimony about what Sally said requires us to take trips around two triangles:

---

4. One may be able to identify limited situations in which individuals are more likely than not to be dishonest or inaccurate. Even if this is not possible, there may be situations in which an individual makes an assertion that seems patently inconsistent with current scientific or common experiential knowledge. For example, a person might report having seen the Statue of Liberty step down from her pedestal and go for a swim in the East River, or one of the servants at the marriage at Cana might report that Jesus turned water into wine (see John 2:1-11). If such an individual were willing to testify in court to these events, would it be appropriate for the judge to exclude the evidence on relevance grounds?

A. Rationale and Meaning

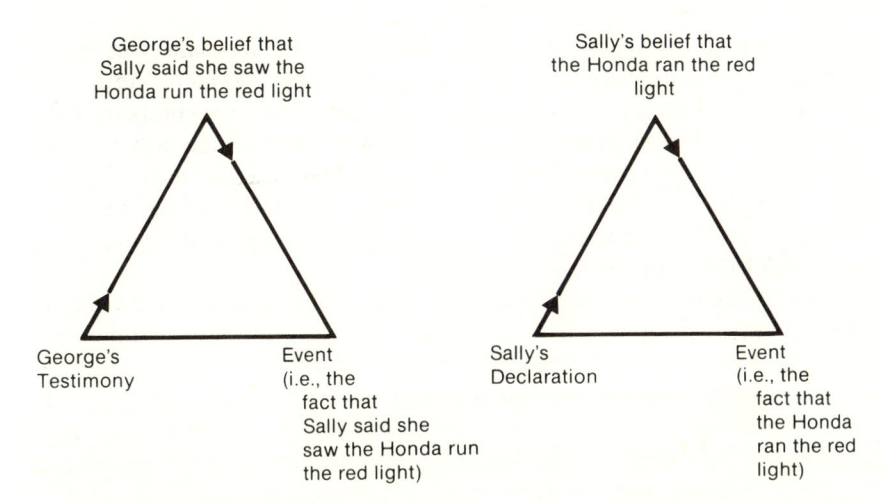

[Diagram: Two triangles illustrating hearsay analysis.

Left triangle — apex: "George's belief that Sally said she saw the Honda run the red light"; bottom-left: "George's Testimony"; bottom-right: "Event (i.e., the fact that Sally said she saw the Honda run the red light)".

Right triangle — apex: "Sally's belief that the Honda ran the red light"; bottom-left: "Sally's Declaration"; bottom-right: "Event (i.e., the fact that the Honda ran the red light)".]

As we have seen, the mere fact that Sally makes a statement about a gray Honda running through a red light is relevant—at least in the minimal FRE 401 sense—to prove that a gray Honda in fact did run through a red light. Why should this relevant information be so welcome in one context and completely excludable in the other?

The most common answer to this question focuses on three factors that tend to minimize the possibility of sincerity, narration/ambiguity, perception, or memory problems being unnoticed by the jury when the assertion is made by the declarant "while testifying at the trial."[5] First, whereas the out of court declaration may or may not be made under oath, the witness in the courtroom is always under oath, thereby theoretically minimizing the possibility of a sincerity problem. Moreover, the solemnity and formality of the proceedings may cause the witness to be particularly careful about properly narrating the event. Second, the jury is able to observe the demeanor of the in-court witness. Observing how the witness responds and reacts to questions, particularly on cross-examination, may give the jurors a somewhat better sense of the witness' sincerity, narrative ability, perception, and memory than they would get from having the content of the statement related to them by some third person. Third, and most important, the in-court witness is subject to

---

5. On their face the rules of evidence apply equally to jury trials and to bench trials. In fact, however, the rules—including the hearsay rule—tend to be applied much less rigidly in bench trials. This is so in part because of the theory that judges will sort out, in their own minds, the admissible from the inadmissible evidence before arriving at a decision and in part because of the belief that judges, as a result of their training and experience, are more likely than jurors to be sensitive to the weaknesses in some types of evidence. For example, we trust judges more than juries with hearsay. Do you think that these are sufficient reasons for relaxing the rules of evidence in bench trials? Even if your answer is no, there is an additional, very practical reason for less rigid evidence rules at bench trials. Sometimes a judge will have to know what the evidence is in order to make a proper ruling on the objection. Once the judge has heard the evidence and heard arguments about its admissibility, it may make little difference whether the judge in a bench trial formally excludes the evidence at the time it is offered.

cross-examination, which may clarify ambiguity, reveal mistakes in narration, weaknesses in perception or memory, or attempts to fabricate.

Some witnesses, of course, may beat the system and lie with persuasion and impunity. But to recognize that possibility is to recognize only that our adjudicatory system is not perfect. It may very well be true, as Dean Wigmore asserted and as most trial lawyers believe, that in the context of our adversary system, cross-examination is "beyond any doubt the greatest legal engine ever invented for the discovery of truth."[6]

On the other hand, cross-examination is not the only vehicle for getting at these potential problems. It may be possible, for example, to show with extrinsic evidence that a hearsay declarant has made inconsistent statements, or is biased against one of the parties, or has a bad character for trustworthiness. See FRE 806 ("When a hearsay statement . . . has been admitted in evidence, the credibility of the declarant may be attacked . . . by any evidence which would be admissible for those purposes if declarant had testified as witness.") Furthermore, the touted benefits of effective cross-examination may not always contribute to accurate fact finding. Cross-examination leads to the explicit exposure of falsehood much less frequently in real life than in "Perry Mason." Thus, the greatest benefit of cross-examination may be the intuitive sense it can give the jury about a witness' general credibility. If so, it is worth considering whether this intuitive sense is likely to be accurate. Some individuals, because of their personalities or their fear of being the center of attention in a public trial, may appear to be less than forthright witnesses, when in fact they are only shy or nervous.

In any event, the primary justification for excluding hearsay evidence is that cross-examination is not available to help evaluate the strength of the inferences from the out-of-court declarant's words to the declarant's belief to the "truth" of what happened in the real world. When we get to the exceptions to the hearsay rule, we will see that most of the exceptions are based in large measure on the theory that the circumstances under which the declaration was made tend to minimize one or more of the potential problems inherent in the inferences from declaration to belief and from belief to truth.

Other rationales have been offered for the hearsay rule, but they are generally considered to be of marginal significance. For example, it has been suggested that without the hearsay prohibition, jurors might be confused as to whether a witness is speaking from firsthand knowledge or relating the statement of another. It would seem, however, that any ambiguity about this point could be readily clarified on either direct or cross-examination of the witness. Another argument for excluding hearsay is that the witness on the stand might have misunderstood what the hearsay declarant said or might have fabricated the existence of the hearsay declarant. Cross-examination is available, however, to test the sincerity and hearing ability of the witness.

---

6. 5 J. Wigmore, Evidence in Trials at Common Law 32 (Chadbourn ed. 1974) 32.

A. Rationale and Meaning

Unless there is some reason to believe that witnesses are more likely to lie about the existence of hearsay declarants than about other things or more likely to misunderstand what hearsay declarants say than to misunderstand or misperceive other things, this rationale for the hearsay rule is not particularly strong.[7]

Of course, if the hearsay declarant is available, it may be desirable to have the declarant testify at the trial, both to avoid the possibility that another witness might misreport or fabricate the existence of the hearsay declaration and to obtain the benefits of oath, demeanor, and cross-examination. Moreover, it may be desirable to require the person who wants to rely on the hearsay declarant's information to call that person to the witness stand. An opposing party might understandably be reluctant to call the hearsay declarant after the hearsay had already been admitted, because the declarant might simply reaffirm and re-enforce the substance of the hearsay. But what if the hearsay declarant is not available to testify? Now we are talking not about whether a particular piece of evidence will be presented to the jury in hearsay form or by the person with firsthand knowledge of the events; rather, we are talking about whether the jury will hear the evidence at all. (As we will see shortly, some of the hearsay exceptions are applicable if, but only if, the hearsay declarant is unavailable. See FRE 804.) Even in the absence of unavailability, how critical is the opportunity to cross-examine? After all, there are other ways to explore possible weaknesses in the inferences from declaration to belief to truth.

It is still much too soon for you to be formulating any definitive judgments about the issues suggested in the preceding paragraph. You should, however, keep those issues in mind as you continue through the remaining hearsay materials. For now be sure that you understand the following:

1. Hearsay is a person's statement (a) that is made at a time other than while the person is testifying at the hearing in which the statement is offered and (b) that is offered to prove the truth of the matter asserted in the statement.
2. Even if the hearsay declarant is also the witness, testimony about the out-of-court declaration to prove the truth of the declaration falls within the basic definition of hearsay. See FRE 801(c). The following evidence, for example, would be hearsay:

> To prove that the blue car did not stop at a stop sign, Mary offers to testify: "I remember telling my friend, Sue, that the blue car ran a stop sign."

> Since the hearsay declarant is in fact subject to cross-examination, some commentators have argued that evidence of this type should

---

7. For a suggestion that witnesses may tend to misunderstand or misperceive what declarants say more frequently than they misunderstand or misperceive other things, see Note 3 at page 489 infra.

not be regarded as hearsay.[8] On the other hand, it has been suggested that cross-examination is most valuable when it is contemporaneous with the assertions whose validity it is testing. It has also been suggested that exempting a witness' prior declarations from the hearsay rule would provide an undesirable incentive for witnesses to rely on prior prepared statements in their testimony.[9]

3. A hearsay statement may be oral, as was the Portuguese gentleman's in Raleigh's case and Sally's in our hypothetical, or it may be written, as was Lord Cobham's in Raleigh's case.

4. The primary justification for excluding hearsay is that there is not an opportunity to cross-examine the hearsay declarant to determine if there are sincerity, narration/ambiguity, perception, or memory problems. (We shall refer to these problems as the "hearsay dangers.")

5. Although, as we shall see shortly, the hearsay rule, like other legal rules, has some rather fuzzy edges, the manner in which the rule is applied is quite rigid. In most jurisdictions, if the evidence is determined to be hearsay, it is not admissible unless it happens to fall within one of the specific exceptions to the hearsay rule. In some jurisdictions, there are some quite flexible exceptions, see, e.g., FRE 803(24), and there is a smattering of decisions that have approved the admissibility of apparently reliable hearsay not falling within any specific exception to the rule.[10] For the most part, however, the focus is exclusively on the questions whether the evidence is hearsay and if so, whether the conditions of some hearsay exception have been satisfied.

2. Hearsay, Lay Opinions, and the Firsthand Knowledge Rule

We have previously encountered the lay opinion rule (see FRE 701) and the firsthand knowledge rule (see FRE 602). Here we address briefly the relationship between those rules and the hearsay rule.

Consider a situation in which Ellen is prepared to testify, "The defendant ignored a stop sign and hit the plaintiff's car in an intersection." Assuming that Ellen's information is not fantasy or the result of ESP, there are three possible bases for her belief: First, she may have observed the entire incident; second, she could have overheard somebody else say what happened; or third, on the basis of her observation of the position of the cars after the

---

8. See, e.g., Morgan, Hearsay Dangers and the Application of the Hearsay Concept, 62 Harv. L. Rev. 177, 192-193 (1957).

9. The Federal Rules create what is in effect an exception to the hearsay rule for some prior statements of a witness by specifically exempting those statements from the definition of hearsay. See FRE 801(d)(1), which we will examine in detail shortly.

10. See, e.g., Dallas County v. Commercial Union Assurance Co., 286 F.2d 388 (5th Cir. 1961).

A. Rationale and Meaning

accident, she could have concluded that the defendant's car must have run the stop sign. If the second variation were true, Ellen would in effect be relating a hearsay statement; and in the last variation, if she were required to relate only what she saw, the jury would be as able as she is to draw the relevant conclusions. Thus, in this last variation, Ellen's testimony would be subject to the same criticism as an impermissible lay opinion.

If one had reason to believe that either the second or third variation was true, what should the proper objection be? The answer depends on the form in which the question is asked to Ellen (or the form in which she responds, if the objection is not made until she has answered). If Ellen is asked about (or if she responds with) what somebody else said, the objection would be hearsay. If Ellen is asked about (or if she appears to be relating) what she observed, then the objection would be lack of firsthand knowledge. An impermissible lay opinion objection is generally reserved for those situations in which it would be impermissible for any lay witness to give the testimony in question. (To put the matter somewhat differently, a lack of firsthand knowledge objection is, in effect, an individualized lay opinion objection.)

It may be that Ellen is using language that sounds as if she has firsthand knowledge but that opposing counsel believes she is in fact relating the substance of a third person's statement. In this situation, because of the form of the testimony, the initial objection would still be lack of firsthand knowledge. The objecting attorney should then immediately ask the judge to permit inquiry, outside the presence of the jury, into the basis for Ellen's testimony. If this inquiry reveals that Ellen is in fact relating hearsay, the objecting attorney can then change the objection to hearsay. (An initial hearsay objection, although technically improper, might not be fatal. What is important, as a practical matter, is for the attorney to make some objection that will get the judge's attention and permit inquiry, outside the presence of the jury, into the basis for the witness' knowledge. Once the basis of knowledge is established, it should be relatively easy for the parties to address the question why the evidence should or should not be admissible.)

3. Multiple Hearsay

On some occasions evidence will contain multiple hearsay. Consider, for example, the plaintiff's attempt to prove that the gray Honda went through a red light by offering a properly authenticated letter that was written by George and that contains the statement "Sally told me that the gray Honda ran the red light." Here we care about the sincerity, narration, perception, and memory of both Sally and George, and neither of them is on the witness stand subject to cross-examination.

If the plaintiff called George to testify from present memory about what Sally said, we would have single hearsay. If the plaintiff called George to the stand to authenticate the letter, however, we would again have multiple hearsay. We continue to be concerned with the truth of what Sally said. In addition, although George is now subject to cross-examination, we are concerned about the truth of George's statement in the letter, and this statement in the letter was made "other than while testifying at the trial or hearing."

In multiple hearsay situations, the evidence will be inadmissible unless there is a hearsay exception for each part of the hearsay. See, e.g., FRE 805 ("Hearsay included within hearsay is not excluded under the hearsay rule if each part of the combined statements conforms with an exception to the hearsay rule provided in these rules.")

4. Out-of-Court Declarations With No Hearsay Dangers

Not all out-of-court declarations are hearsay. A critical aspect of the definition of hearsay is that the declaration be offered to prove the *truth* of the matter asserted. Many out-of-court declarations are relevant without regard to their truth. Consider, for example, the following in-court testimony of Sally about an out-of-court declaration: "One morning several months ago when I was getting gasoline at the service station, I heard the mechanic say to the driver of a gray Honda, 'Your brakes are in bad shape. It would be dangerous for you to drive that Honda.'" If the attorney representing the driver of the Honda objected to Sally's testimony on the ground of hearsay, the opposing counsel might well respond as follows: "Your honor, we are not offering this evidence to prove that the brakes were in fact bad. Rather, we are offering the evidence to prove only that the words were spoken—to prove that the defendant had notice of a possibly dangerous condition before he got into his car and drove through the red light. One of the things that we must prove in order to prevail is that the defendant either did have or should have had notice of the dangerous condition of his car. This is direct evidence of the proposition that he did have such notice."

This response to the objection is perfectly appropriate. The evidence is relevant in a non-hearsay way to a provable proposition in the case: notice. When used solely for this purpose, none of the hearsay dangers exists. We do not care what was in the mind of the mechanic, much less whether something in the mechanic's mind corresponded to some event in the real world. As a result, we have no reason to be concerned about the mechanic's memory, perception, sincerity, or narration, and, thus, no need to be concerned about whether the mechanic is subject to cross-examination. Of course, we do care whether the mechanic spoke any words (is Sally lying?), whether Sally heard the words correctly, and whether, at the time of her testimony, Sally remembers accurately what was said. Furthermore, we care about whether the mechanic's words were spoken loudly enough for the driver of the Honda to hear, and we care about whether the words were spoken in apparent seriousness or in a joking manner. We can deal with all

A. Rationale and Meaning

of these concerns, however, through the direct and cross-examination of Sally. Indeed, there is no particular reason to believe that the mechanic would be in any better position to shed light on these matters than Sally. He may be just as apt to lie about whether he made the statement, and his recollection of the content of the warning and whether it was said loudly and seriously enough to be given credence is not likely to be any better than Sally's.

Perhaps the driver had some particular reason for disregarding the mechanic's warning. For example, the driver may have known from previous dealings with the mechanic that the mechanic frequently gave very serious sounding warnings as a joke or that this mechanic was particularly unreliable. If such is the case, the driver can take the stand or call the mechanic or other witnesses to the stand in order to try to demonstrate why it was reasonable for the driver to disregard the notice. The reasonableness of the driver's disregarding the notice, however, does not depend on the mechanic's narration, perception, or memory at the time the words of notice were spoken. Moreover, while the reasonableness of the driver's disregarding the notice may depend upon the mechanic's *apparent* sincerity, it does not depend upon the mechanic's *actual* sincerity. As we noted, anybody who heard the warning is as capable as the mechanic of recalling and testifying about the apparent sincerity with which the warning was spoken.

The inferential process involved in the use of the mechanic's out-of-court declaration to show notice can be illustrated in the following manner with the testimonial triangle:

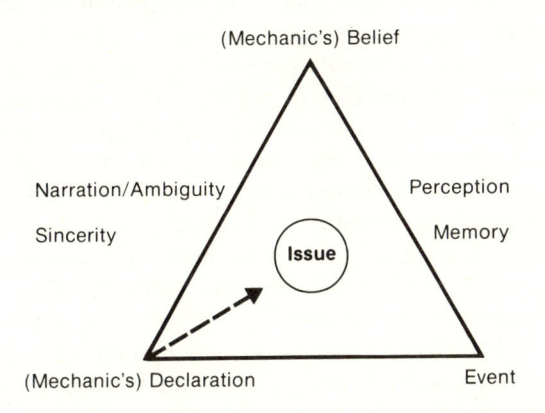

```
                    (Mechanic's) Belief
                           /\
                          /  \
                         /    \
        Narration/Ambiguity   Perception
                       /        \
           Sincerity  /          \  Memory
                     /   Issue    \
                    /   →          \
                   /_____\
         (Mechanic's) Declaration    Event
```

The dotted line from the lower left-hand corner to the Issue represents the inference involved in the use of the mechanic's declaration: From the fact that the mechanic spoke the words, we infer that the driver of the Honda heard or should have heard the words; the relevance of the evidence does *not* depend upon making either of the inferences illustrated by the two legs of the triangle.

(Our concern about Sally's sincerity, narration, perception, and memory—like our concern with any other in-court witness who testifies to some prior event or declaration—could be illustrated by another triangle. See the diagram at page 299 supra. Because an in-court witness is subject to cross-examination, however, the need to make the inferences illustrated by the triangle for the in-court witness is never a basis for exclusion of the witness' testimony. Thus, we have not bothered to include the triangle that illustrates the inferential process with respect to Sally.)

Sally's testimony, of course, is also relevant to prove that the brakes on the Honda were in fact bad, and for this purpose the evidence is clearly hearsay: If the question is the condition of the brakes, we care about the sincerity, narration, perception, and memory of the mechanic, who is not on the witness stand subject to cross-examination. Depending on the circumstances of the making of the statement, there may be an available hearsay exception. See FRE 803(1), (2). See also FRE 801(d)(2)(B). For now, we wish to assume that no hearsay exception applies to the mechanic's declaration.

The fact that the evidence is relevant but excludable as hearsay for the purpose of proving that the brakes were bad does not necessarily mean that the evidence is inadmissible. Rather, we have a situation that arises frequently in the law of evidence: A particular piece of evidence has relevance with respect to two distinct provable propositions, but it is admissible with respect to only one. In this type of situation, as we have seen before and will see again, the question of admissibility is ultimately one of discretionary balancing for the trial judge. See, e.g., FRE 403. Is the benefit of the evidence for the admissible purpose (here, notice) outweighed by the danger that the jury, even after being given limiting instructions, will use the evidence in a significant way for its inadmissible purpose (here, to prove bad brakes)?

Another fairly common type of out-of-court declaration that does not implicate any of the hearsay dangers is a declaration that is itself a legally operative fact. For example, if Paul says to Sarah out of court, "I offer to sell you my horse for five hundred dollars," Sarah—or Paul or anyone else who heard the words—could testify to what Paul said in an action to establish that there was a contract for the sale of the horse. The words are themselves the offer, and anyone who heard them can testify that they were spoken, just as any eyewitness to an automobile accident could testify that the gray Honda ran a red light. No memory or perception problem is pertinent with respect to Paul, because he is not relating some fact that he has observed. Moreover, under the objective theory of contracts there can be no sincerity or narration/ambiguity problem, for we do not have to make any inference from Paul's out-of-court declaration to his belief or intent. The mere fact that he said the words in a manner that the offeree might reasonably be expected to take seriously is sufficient to establish a valid offer. The fact that Paul may have been joking or may have misspoken is irrelevant to the question whether there was an offer. And whether the words were spoken in an apparently serious manner is something about which anyone who

A. Rationale and Meaning

heard the words can testify and be fully cross-examined. (Subjective intent or understanding may be relevant to the issue of mutual mistake. Mistake, however, becomes an issue only after there has been evidence of an offer and an acceptance.)

As the preceding discussion suggests, the critical first step in trying to determine whether an out-of-court declaration is hearsay is to ascertain precisely why the evidence is relevant. More specifically, it is essential to focus on the inferences the fact finder must make in linking the out-of-court declaration to some provable proposition in the case. If the evidence is relevant without regard to the declarant's belief, it is not hearsay. On the other hand, if the relevance of the evidence depends on inferring something about the belief of the declarant and then the relationship between that belief and some event in the outside world, we probably have a case of hearsay. We will see shortly, however, that there are some situations in which the evidence is not hearsay, despite the necessity for making both inferences illustrated by the testimonial triangle.

Some texts and study aids provide a laundry list of out-of-court declarations that are not hearsay, e.g., declarations to show notice and declarations that are legally operative facts. We strongly urge you to avoid relying on such lists for two reasons. First, and most important, one cannot tell whether an out-of-court declaration is hearsay merely by focusing on the substantive purpose for which the declaration is offered. Consider, for example, a slight variation on the preceding notice hypothetical:

> On the question of notice, George offers to testify, "Several days ago Sally told me that she heard the mechanic at her service station warn the driver of a gray Honda that his brakes were bad."

As in the earlier version of the hypothetical, we are not concerned with the mechanic's sincerity, narration, perception, and memory; and we are concerned with Sally's sincerity, narration, perception, and memory. She may have been lying; she may not have heard the warning correctly; or she may not have remembered accurately the content of the warning when she related it to George. In our current variation of the hypothetical, however, Sally is not available for cross-examination; and the fact that George is subject to cross-examination does nothing to alleviate the hearsay dangers with respect to Sally. In terms of the traditional definition of hearsay, we are relying on the truth of Sally's out-of-court assertion that words of warning were spoken. Thus, this evidence, although offered to show notice, is hearsay.

The second reason for being skeptical of laundry lists of out-of-court declarations that are not hearsay relates to one's ability to understand thoroughly and to evaluate the desirability of the hearsay rule. As we have said, the key to understanding hearsay is to focus on the inferential process involved in the use of out-of-court declarations. In doing so, it is helpful, we believe, to avoid insofar as possible organizing schemes that lump together declarations that implicate different types of inferences. The laundry lists, however, almost invariably include some, but only some, of the declarations that fit an inferential pattern that we have yet to consider and to which we now turn.

5. Out-of-Court Declarations With Sincerity and Narration Problems but No Perception and Memory Problems

Thus far, we have seen only two types of out-of-court declarations: (1) those whose relevance depends upon making both the inference from declaration to the declarant's belief and the inference from that belief to some event that caused the belief, and (2) those whose relevance depends upon neither of these inferences. There is, however, a third type of out-of-court declaration— one whose relevance depends upon making the inference from declaration to belief, but not the declaration from belief to what caused the belief. In other words, in considering the relevance of these declarations, we face potential sincerity and narration/ambiguity problems, but no perception or memory problems. Consider, for example the following pieces of evidence:

> To prove that Sam was insane, John offers to testify, "I heard Sam assert that he was King George III."
>
> To prove that Mary was not feeling well last Tuesday morning, Ruth offers to testify, "Last Tuesday morning Mary told me that she had a headache."
>
> To prove that Kathy disliked baseball, Jim offers to testify that he heard Kathy exclaim, "I hate baseball. I'm never going to another baseball game in my whole life."

In each of the preceding examples the relevance of the evidence requires us to draw an inference from the out-of-court declaration to the state of mind or belief of the out-of-court declarant. The first piece of evidence is relevant only if we infer that Sam sincerely believes he is King George; the second piece of evidence is relevant only if we infer that Mary is sincere in her statement that she feels a pain in her head; and the last piece of evidence is relevant only if we infer that Kathy sincerely believes she will not go (or at least will not particularly enjoy going) to another baseball game. In none of the examples, though, do we have any perception or memory problems; there is no particular event that needs to have been perceived and remembered by the declarant in order for the evidence to be relevant.

We turn again to the testimonial triangle to illustrate these out-of-court declarations. The relevance of the evidence is dependent upon making the inference illustrated by the left leg of the triangle (i.e., there are potential sincerity and narration/ambiguity problems), but the evidence is relevant to

A. Rationale and Meaning

```
                    Declarant's Belief
                           ▲
                           ┊
                          ╱▼╲
                         ╱   ╲
        Narration/Ambiguity ╱     ╲  Perception
            Sincerity    ╱  ┌───┐  ╲   Memory
                        ╱   │Issue│   ╲
                       ╱    └───┘    ╲
                      ╱_____╲
                 Declaration            Event
```

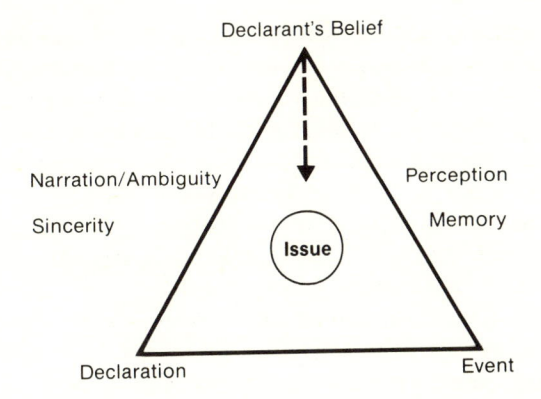

prove a factual issue in the case without regard to the inference illustrated by the right leg of the triangle (i.e., there are no perception or memory problems).

We deal elsewhere with the question whether declarations of the type just illustrated should be classified as hearsay and what implications the answer to that question has for the hearsay rule in general.[11] For now, two things are important about these types of declarations:

1. By considering carefully why a particular out-of-court declaration is relevant, you should be able to identify those situations in which the relevance of the evidence depends upon making an inference about the declarant's belief without the necessity for making a further inference about the correspondence between that belief and some event that may have occurred outside the mind of the declarant.

2. The hearsay rule will never be a reason for excluding declarations that require the fact finder to make an inference about the declarant's state of mind without making a further inference about some event that caused that state of mind. This is so because there is a hearsay exception, which we will consider in more detail later, for declarations of a person's then-existing (i.e., at the time of the declaration) state of mind, emotion, or physical sensation. See, e.g., FRE 803(3). Thus, if a court determines that the declaration is hearsay, the proponent of the evidence can rely on the exception. The exception in effect neutralizes the hearsay objection. If the evidence is to be excluded, it must be for some other reason.

In some jurisdictions, the hearsay exception for declarations of a person's then-existing state of mind has a special requirement that the declaration be

---

11. See pages 344-349 infra.

made under circumstances indicating that the declaration is trustworthy.[12] In jurisdictions having such a requirement, it may be advantageous for the proponent of these state-of-mind declarations to characterize the evidence as not hearsay, whereas it may be advantageous for the opponent of the evidence to characterize the declarations as hearsay. Because the classification of these state-of-mind declarations as hearsay or not hearsay bears no necessary relationship to the likely hearsay dangers,[13] we believe that a trustworthiness requirement, if it exists, should apply regardless of whether the declaration is labeled as hearsay.

As a matter of academic curiosity at this point, you may find it interesting that courts and commentators tend to attach the hearsay label to those declarations that directly assert a mental state. For example, in a husband's alienation of affection action, the wife's out-of-court declaration "I no longer love my husband" or "I feel alienated from my husband" would probably be regarded as hearsay, but because of the state-of-mind exception it would not be excludable hearsay. On the other hand, if the fact finder must circumstantially infer the declarant's state of mind from a statement that purports to assert something other than the declarant's state of mind, courts and commentators tend to regard the declaration as not hearsay. For example, in the alienation of affection action, the wife's out of court statement "My husband is a slob" would probably be regarded as not hearsay. In explaining this classification, the court or commentator might reason that we are not trying to prove the truth of the proposition that the husband is a slob; rather, we are making a circumstantial inference about the wife's alienation.

For reasons that we develop later,[14] we see no value, even at a descriptive level, in the classification of state-of-mind declarations as direct or circumstantial. For now, we wish only to point out two things that the classification does *not* imply. First, the term *circumstantial* should not be understood as implying a diminution in hearsay dangers or as being an adequate substitute for rigorous analysis of potential hearsay dangers. For example, in our alienation of affection hypothetical, the declaration "My husband is a slob" is relevant to show alienation because it is either (1) a direct assertion of the wife's belief that the husband is a slob, from which belief we infer alienation or (2) a somewhat unusual way of attempting to articulate directly a sense of alienation (i.e., the wife may not believe her husband is a slob but may be so characterizing him in order to manifest her dislike of or alienation from him). In both cases there are hearsay dangers associated with the left leg of the testimonial triangle, as there are in the declaration "I feel alienated from my husband."

Second, in situations involving only potential sincerity and narration/ambiguity problems, as well as in situations involving all of the hearsay

---

12. See, e.g., Cal. Evid. Code §1252. See generally McCormick's Handbook on the Law of Evidence 837 (3rd ed., Cleary, 1984).
13. See pages 344-346 infra.
14. Ibid.

A. Rationale and Meaning

dangers, it should make no difference to the analysis whether the out-of-court declarant actually says "I believe," "I feel," "I know." If these or similar words are not actually expressed, they are nonetheless implicit in any attempt to communicate a thought. Whether the words are actually articulated by the declarant has no bearing on the nature and extent of the hearsay dangers and should have no bearing on the classification of the declaration as hearsay or not hearsay.

Incidentally, it is the so-called circumstantial declaration of one's state of mind that frequently gets included in the laundry list of types of out-of-court statements that are not hearsay. (If you are a compulsive list maker, you may find it helpful, despite our earlier admonition, to make such a list. If so, please keep in mind that, notwithstanding lists and labels, the relevance of the declarations "My husband is a slob" (not hearsay) and "I feel alienated from my husband" (hearsay) to prove alienation both depend upon an inference that involves potential sincerity and narration problems, whereas the relevance of the declaration "Your brakes are bad" (not hearsay) to prove notice does not require such an inference.)

6. Caveat

If you go to other sources to increase your understanding of hearsay, be particularly wary of statements that classify evidence as hearsay or not hearsay because of the need to rely or not to rely on the out-of-court declarant's "credibility." Although "credibility" implies a concern with the hearsay dangers, it is not a carefully used term of art. Indeed, use of the word *credibility* often disguises sloppy analysis of the inferential process involved in the use of out-of-court declarations.[15]

PROBLEMS[16]

As you proceed to examine the following hypotheticals, consider, first, why the evidence is relevant: Does the relevance depend on inferences both from the declaration to the belief of the declarant and from the belief to some event that has occurred? Or does the relevance depend on making only the first of these inferences? Or is the evidence relevant without regard to either inference? (There can never be a situation in which the relevance of the evidence depends on making the inference from belief to some event in

---

15. See Park, McCormick on Evidence and the Concept of Hearsay: A Critical Analysis Followed by Suggestions to Law Teachers, 65 Minn. L. Rev. 423 (1981).
Similar problems arise with the use of the term *truth* in defining hearsay. See pages 344-346 infra.
16. Some of the evidence that is hearsay in the following problems may fall within an exception to the hearsay rule and thus not be excludable by the hearsay rule. For now you should ignore this possibility and focus solely on the question whether the evidence is hearsay.

the real world without first making the inference from declaration to belief.) Next, if either or both of the inferences we have been discussing is involved, consider how significant the hearsay dangers really are and whether there is good reason to be concerned about the admissibility of such evidence.

1. Marge Sawyer has sued Dr. Ellen James for malpractice. Sawyer claims that James negligently neglected to remove a sponge during an operation and that the sponge has caused various internal injuries and infections. One of Sawyer's witnesses is a medical student, who offers to testify, "I observed the operation that Dr. James performed on Ms. Sawyer. As the operation was nearing completion, I heard one of the nurses say, 'A sponge is missing.'" Dr. James' attorney objects on the ground that the evidence is hearsay. What result?

2. Sarah Hillman is suing Carole White for slander. Ms. Hillman calls Alice Franks, who offers to testify, "Carole told me that Sarah Hillman had engaged the services of a male prostitute." Is the evidence hearsay?

3. In the same action as in Problem 2, Carole White calls Allan Brown, who offers to testify, "Sarah Hillman has a reputation in the community for being a loose woman and for visiting prostitutes." Is the evidence hearsay?

4. John and Mary Smith had a son, Brent, who was born on August 20, 1946. John and Mary were killed in an plane crash, and their son, if he survived them, was entitled to inherit their entire estates. In a probate proceeding in December, 1988, an individual offers to testify as follows to establish his right to inherit the assets of John and Mary Smith: "My name is Brent Smith. I was born on August 20, 1946. I am 44 years old. I am the son of John and Mary Smith." Is any of this testimony objectionable as hearsay?

5. Vance Graham is being prosecuted for the attempted murder of his wife Sharon. During the prosecutor's direct examination of Police Officer Dan O'Malley, the following transpires:

Q: Have you ever seen or had any dealings with the defendant, Vance Graham, before today?
A: Yes.
Q: Would you please explain to the jury your prior contact with the defendant?
A: On the evening of August 15, I observed the defendant standing in his front yard with a sawed-off shot gun, and I arrested him.
Q: Was there any particular reason that you happened to be in the vicinity of the defendant's residence?
A: Yes, I had just received a radio call from our dispatcher. She reported that neighbors had called complaining of a loud fight and the sound of gun shots at the Graham house.

A. Rationale and Meaning

DEFENSE COUNSEL: Objection, your honor. That's hearsay. We ask that the jury be instructed to ignore that last answer and that it be stricken from the record.

How should the court rule?

6. To prove that the transfer of a ring from Alan to Betty was a gift and not a temporary loan, Betty offers to testify that as Alan handed her the ring he said, "I am giving you this ring as a gift." Is the evidence hearsay?

7. Wilbur Johnson, an inmate at the state penitentiary, has been charged with murder of another inmate. The prosecution's theory is that Johnson aided and abetted the actual killers by supplying them with a knife from the commissary. Johnson's defense is duress, and he offers to testify that the alleged murderers threatened to kill him if he did not supply the knife. The prosecution objects on hearsay grounds to Johnson's testimony about what the alleged killers said. What result?

8. Robert Marsh has been charged with passing a bad check. The check was payable to Marsh and drawn on the account of one Jerome Henshaw. The prosecution's theory is that Henshaw is a fictitious person invented by Marsh. Marsh claims that Henshaw was a 6' 8" construction worker, for whom he had done some odd jobs, and that the check was payment for those jobs. To establish that there is no Jerome Henshaw the prosecution offers the following evidence:

(a) The testimony of several long-time residents of the community that they had never seen a 6' 8" construction worker in the community;

(b) The testimony of several long-time residents of the community that they had never met anyone or heard of anyone named Jerome Henshaw;

(c) The testimony of the local sheriff that he had made a thorough investigation in the community and on the basis of his investigation he was convinced that there was no such person as Jerome Henshaw.

Is any of this evidence objectionable as hearsay?

7. Assertive Nonverbal Activity

Thus far all of our examples of hearsay have involved oral or written assertions, but in some instances hearsay is completely nonverbal. Consider, for example, the following testimony offered by a police officer in an assault prosecution: "When I arrived at the scene of the fight, I asked who threw the first punch, and one of the women who was present pointed at Jim Harris, the defendant, who was wearing a red shirt." Through her nonverbal conduct, the woman, in intent and in effect, appears to be asserting that Harris threw the first punch. All of the hearsay dangers are present: The woman may have been lying (a sincerity problem); the arm movement may have been an involuntary tic that was not intended to express the intent that it appears to express (an ambiguity problem); the woman may not have seen clearly who threw the first punch (a perception problem); and she may have forgotten who threw the first punch by the time the officer asked (a memory problem). Indeed, in terms of the inferential process involved in using this evidence to prove that Harris threw the first punch, there is no relevant difference between the intentional pointing and a verbal response that identifies Harris (e.g., "It was Jim Harris," or "It was the man in the red shirt."). Furthermore, it is clear that all courts would regard this nonverbal conduct as hearsay. The Federal Rules accomplish this result in FRE 801(a) by defining a "statement" as "(1) an oral or written assertion or (2) *nonverbal conduct of a person, if it is intended by the person as an assertion.*" [Emphasis added.]

8. Nonassertive Nonverbal Activity

Sometimes when the relevance of nonverbal conduct implicates the hearsay dangers, the conduct is not intended by the actor as an assertion. Consider the following hypothetical:

> Ben Jacobsen, a 50-year-old former railroad fireman is charged with homicide for fatally shooting a derelict who had been sleeping in a box car in an infrequently used area of the switching yard. The crime occurred at approximately 11 A.M. on Tuesday, July 23. Jacobsen claims that he is not guilty, and he wants to offer evidence suggesting that two teenage boys committed the crime. He calls to the stand Harry Winters, a railroad employee, who offers to testify as follows: "Shortly after 11 A.M. on Tuesday, July 23, I observed two teenage boys near the box car. They were running away from it."

Since the crime took place in an infrequently used area of the switching yard, the mere fact that someone other than the defendant was present at that location is relevant—at least in a minimal FRE 401 sense—to prove that the defendant did not commit the crime: The presence of another person shows that there was somebody else who could have committed the crime. If the evidence is offered for this purpose, there are no hearsay dangers. We simply have the direct testimony of a witness that he observed two teenagers in a particular location. For this purpose, however, there would be no need to admit the "running away" portion of the employee's testimony; the first sentence quoted above would be sufficient. If you were representing the defendant, would you be content to admit into evidence only the first sentence of the switchman's testimony, or would you want the jury to hear the "running away" part of the switchman's testimony as well?

A. Rationale and Meaning

We think the answer is quite obviously that the attorney would want the entire statement introduced, and this is because flight from the scene of a crime is evidence that suggests the guilt of those who are fleeing. But consider carefully how this evidence of flight is relevant to show guilt: First, from the conduct of fleeing, we infer that the boys believe they are guilty. Second, from their belief in their guilt we infer that they are guilty.

The first inference raises potential sincerity and ambiguity problems: The boys may be innocent but intentionally trying to draw suspicion on themselves so that the actual guilty party, Jacobsen, will not be blamed (sincerity); or they may be innocent and running away because they are afraid or do not want to get involved with the police (ambiguity). The second inference raises potential perception and memory problems: The boys may have been playing with a gun and may have thought they shot the derelict, when in fact somebody else—perhaps Jacobsen—did (perception); or if they had been drinking and were perhaps knocked unconscious momentarily in a fight between themselves or with the derelict, they may have forgotten precisely what happened (memory).

If any of the foregoing possibilities is true, the evidence, despite its appearance, is not in fact exculpatory for the defendant. Similarly, one teenager's out-of-court verbal assertion "I shot the derelict" would not be exculpatory in fact, despite its appearance, if the teenager were lying or had misused the English language or if the teenager had misperceived or inaccurately remembered what happened. In short, the very same inferences—and, as a result, the very same potential hearsay dangers—that inhere in using for their truth out-of-court oral or written assertions or nonverbal conduct intended as an assertion also inhere in using the flight evidence to show guilt.

There is another problem that exists with the flight evidence, but it is not a hearsay problem: Perhaps the teenagers were not "fleeing" from the scene of the crime but were jogging by when the witness happened to notice them. A prosecutor concerned with this possibility in our hypothetical should object on the ground that the witness was offering an impermissible lay opinion. See FRE 701. If the objection were sustained, the defense lawyer would then have to ask questions that hopefully would get the witness to break down the flight "opinion" or conclusion into its component parts. For example, the witness might be asked to describe precisely the location of the teenagers in relation to the crime scene, the direction in which they were going, and how fast they were going. On the other hand, if the judge believed that the witness' description of the teenagers' activity as "flight" captured something important about what they were doing that could not easily be broken down into more detailed component parts, the judge should overrule the objection.[17] If the judge were to overrule the objection, the prosecutor

---

17. See generally pages 729-733 supra (discussion of lay opinions).

still could explore on cross-examination exactly what the witness meant by "flight."

Because the inferential process involved in using the flight evidence to show guilt is similar to the inferential process involved in the use of ordinary hearsay, there is precedent—particularly in older decisions—for treating the flight evidence as hearsay. Indeed, the view that nonassertive conduct is hearsay is sometimes described as the common law position. The judicial precedent for excluding nonassertive conduct on hearsay grounds, however, is in fact quite sporadic. The absence of a stronger exclusionary precedent is due in part to the fact that nonassertive conduct classified as hearsay will not be excluded by the hearsay rule if one of the hearsay exceptions applies. One quite common type of nonassertive conduct is flight, and for reasons that we will be discussing shortly, when the prosecutor offers evidence of the *defendant's* flight, that evidence, if classified as hearsay, would fall within the admissions exception. Another reason for the sporadic precedent undoubtedly is that the hearsay nature of nonassertive conduct is often not immediately obvious. Thus, attorneys fail to see the possibility of a hearsay objection.

The modern trend, as exemplified by the Federal Rules, is to exempt the flight evidence from the hearsay prohibition. The Federal Rules accomplish this result by defining nonverbal conduct as a "statement" within the meaning of the hearsay rule only if the conduct is "intended . . . as an assertion." FRE 801(a). Although we suggested earlier the possibility that the teenagers may have been fleeing with the specific intent of trying to draw suspicion to themselves, this possibility seems quite remote. It is much more likely that they were not trying to assert or to communicate anything by their flight. Thus, in a jurisdiction that had adopted the Federal Rules, a court, at least in the absence of some particular reason to believe that these teenagers were intentionally trying to draw suspicion to themselves, would classify the flight evidence as not hearsay.

In determining whether any particular conduct is nonassertive or is intended as an assertion, the judge must rely on intuition and common sense in the same way that the judge must rely on intuition and common sense in determining whether a particular piece of evidence is probative of the proposition for which it is offered. There will be some close cases, and there may occasionally be situations in which there is reason to believe that conduct that is normally nonassertive is in fact assertive. This might be the case, for example, in our flight hypothetical if the prosecutor presented evidence to the judge that the fleeing teenagers were Jacobsen's sons, that they loved their father dearly, that they had never engaged in criminal conduct, that their father had prior assault convictions, that they realized they were being watched, and that they feared their father would be sent to prison if he were caught.

In resolving close cases and determining whether apparently nonassertive conduct may have been assertive, the judge must make a preliminary fact

A. Rationale and Meaning

determination. See, e.g., FRE 104(a). If the judge is not sure in a particular case whether conduct is assertive or nonassertive, what should the decision be? See FRE 801, Advisory Committee Note ("The rule is so worded as to place the burden upon the party claiming that the intention existed; ambiguous and doubtful cases will be resolved against him and in favor of admissibility.") To what language in FRE 801 is the Advisory Committee referring? What precisely is or should be the nature of the burden? Would the Advisory Committee Note have been more helpful if it described the burden of proof in more traditional terms—e.g., "preponderance," "clear and convincing evidence," or "proof beyond a reasonable doubt"?

An important reason for the exclusion of nonassertive conduct from the definition of hearsay is suggested in our discussion of the flight hypothetical: the probable absence of any sincerity danger. Indeed, if we knew for sure that an actor was not trying to assert or to communicate the belief that the offeror of the evidence wants to attribute to the actor, it would necessarily follow that there was no sincerity problem. One can be insincere only when one attempts to communicate a particular belief.

Contrary to the view of the Federal Rules Advisory Committee, there is nothing inherent in nonassertive conduct that tends to reduce or eliminate the other hearsay dangers.[18] As we shall see when we turn to the exceptions to the hearsay rule, however, the probable absence of one or more of the hearsay dangers is a principal justification for many of the exceptions. For example, the primary justification for FRE 803(2), the excited utterance exception, is that a declaration made under the stress of an exciting event is likely to be made spontaneously and without opportunity to fabricate.[19]

A second reason for treating nonassertive conduct as not hearsay (and for many of the exceptions to the hearsay rule[20]) is "necessity"—the notion that foregoing relevant evidence, because of some hearsay dangers, is too great a price to pay because it would be very burdensome or perhaps even impossible to obtain other, "better" evidence on the same point. With respect to nonassertive conduct, the concern is that nonassertive conduct is so pervasive and so often relied on as a matter of course in our everyday lives that we would be giving up too much relevant evidence by classifying such conduct as hearsay. For example, if we look out the window and see people wearing heavy overcoats, we assume it is cold outside; if a north-bound vehicle proceeds through an intersection with a traffic light, we assume the light is green for that vehicle; if we see people on the street begin to put up

---

18. Surprisingly and unaccountably, the Advisory Committee Note to FRE 801 asserts: "Admittedly [nonassertive conduct] is untested with respect to the perception, memory, and narration (or their equivalents) of the actor, but the Advisory Committee is of the view that these dangers are minimal in the absence of an intent to assert. . . ."

19. It is also true that the relative contemporaneity of the declaration to the event tends to reduce any memory problem. On the other hand, the exciting event may very well augment perception problems.

20. See, e.g., pages 412-413 infra (discussion of dying declaration exception); pages 451-452 infra (discussion of business records exception).

their umbrellas, we assume it has begun to rain. In these situations, the individual actors (probably) are not trying to assert that it is cold, that the light is green, or that it is raining. Our assumption that these facts are true, however, is based on an implicit inference about the actors' beliefs and on a further inference that their beliefs are an accurate reflection of some event or occurrence in the real world.[21]

Another reason for treating nonassertive conduct as not hearsay stems from the fact that attorneys sometimes are not immediately sensitive to the hearsay characteristics of such evidence. If a rule treating nonassertive conduct as hearsay would be only sporadically applied, the rule arguably ought not exist at all.

Whether these reasons are sufficient to exclude nonassertive conduct from the hearsay prohibition has long been the subject of academic debate.[22] One concern relates to the process of classifying conduct as assertive or nonassertive. The necessity under the Federal Rules approach of determining whether conduct is nonassertive inevitably entails the risk that an improper decision will be made, either because the actor has cleverly disguised an assertion (e.g., flight intended to draw suspicion on oneself) or because the court misunderstands the concept of nonassertiveness.[23] Even if judges reach

---

21. Cf. A. Christie, Curtain 74-75 (1975):

[Hercule Poirot, explaining to Hastings why the mere presence of X, a suspected murderer, led him to believe that a murder would be committed at Styles:] "If a lot of war correspondents arrive suddenly in a certain spot of Europe, it means what? It means war! If doctors come from all over the world to a certain city—it shows what? That there is to be a medical conference. Where you see a vulture hovering, there will be a carcass. If you see beaters walking up a moor, there will be a shoot. If you see a man stop suddenly, tear off his coat and plunge into the sea, it means that there, there will be a rescue from drowning.

"If you see ladies of middle age and respectable appearance peering through a hedge, you may deduce that there is there an impropriety of some kind! And finally, if you smell a succulent smell and observe several people all walking along a corridor in the same direction, you may safely assume that a meal is about to be served!"

I considered these analogies for a minute or two, then I said, taking the first one: "All the same, one war correspondent does not make a war!"

"Certainly not. And one swallow does not make a summer. But one murderer, Hastings, does make a murder."

That, of course, was undeniable. But it still occurred to me, as it did not seem to have occurred to Poirot, that even a murderer has his off times. X might be at Styles simply for a holiday with no lethal intent. Poirot was so worked up, however, that I dared not propound this suggestion. I merely said that the whole thing seemed to me hopeless. . . .

22. See, e.g., Falknor, The "Hear-Say" Rule as a "See-Do" Rule: Evidence of Conduct, 33 Rocky Mt. L. Rev. 741 (1964); Falknor, Silence as Hearsay, 89 U. Pa. L. Rev. 192 (1940); Finman, Implied Assertions as Hearsay: Some Criticisms of the Uniform Rules of Evidence, 14 Stan. L. Rev. 682 (1962); Maguire, The Hearsay System: Around and Through the Thicket, 14 Vand. L. Rev. 741 (1961); Morgan, Hearsay and Non Hearsay 48 Harv. L. Rev. 1138 (1935); Seligman, An Exception to the Hearsay Rule, 26 Harv. L. Rev. 146 (1912).

23. If at this point you are having some difficulty with the concept of nonassertiveness, your own difficulty is testimony to the fact that the concept is not necessarily an easy one to grasp. In any event, we will see shortly that the question whether conduct should be classified as nonassertive is sometimes quite tricky.

A. Rationale and Meaning

the correct result most of the time, the Federal Rules approach requires the expenditure of time and effort to argue and decide the question whether conduct is nonassertive. Treating all conduct—both assertive and nonassertive—as hearsay at least has the virtue of making such a determination unnecessary. (On the other hand, if attorneys and judges tend not to recognize the hearsay features of nonassertive conduct, the Federal Rules approach may result in more uniform treatment of nonassertive conduct.)

A second, and perhaps more substantial, concern with the Federal Rules approach to nonassertive conduct relates to the hearsay dangers inherent in nonassertive conduct. As noted previously, there is nothing about nonassertive conduct that tends to minimize perception or memory problems. The nonassertiveness—if a correct decision is made on that issue—eliminates only the sincerity problem. The very thing that eliminates the sincerity problem, however, inevitably augments the ambiguity problem: We do not have a sincerity problem because we are confident that the individual is not trying to assert the belief we want the fact finder to attribute to that individual; but because the individual is not trying to communicate that belief, there is often a substantial risk that the proponent of the evidence (and the jury) may attribute an incorrect belief to the actor. For example, in our flight hypothetical, the possibility that the teenagers were fleeing because they did not want to get involved with the police seems quite plausible. Similarly, in our example of the north-bound car going through the intersection, it is unlikely that the driver is intending to assert that the light is green, but it is nonetheless possible that we are incorrect in ascribing to the driver a belief that the light is green. It may be that the light is red, that the driver knows the light is red, and that because of some emergency the driver feels compelled to ignore the red light. In short, with what appears to be nonassertive nonverbal conduct, we can be reasonably confident that there is not a sincerity problem, but we have no guarantee that other hearsay dangers are minimized. Moreover, whereas narration and ambiguity are not often serious problems with oral and written declarations, there may be substantial ambiguity problems with nonassertive conduct.

The necessary concomitant of a substantial ambiguity problem is low probative value. In other words, to the extent that the actor's conduct can reasonably be explained without attributing to the actor the belief that the offeror of the evidence wants the jury to attribute to actor, the evidence has decreased probative value for the purpose for which it is offered. At some point the probative value may be so low that a court applying the Federal Rules could rely on FRE 403 to exclude the evidence. There are not likely to be many situations in which the probative value of nonassertive activity is so slight that an FRE 403 argument for exclusion would prevail, however. Thus, it is appropriate to consider whether, in view of the differences in the hearsay dangers between assertive and nonassertive activity, cross-examination is any less important in the nonassertive activity situation.

An out-of-court actor who was clever enough to engage in what appeared to be nonassertive conduct in order to deceive someone may be clever enough to lie with impunity on the witness stand. It would certainly be helpful, though, to know whether the belief that we want to attribute to the presumably honest nonassertive actor is the correct one, and this information would be easily ascertainable if the actor were available in court. Moreover, it is generally thought that cross-examination is most effective in exposing perception and memory problems,[24] neither of which is minimized in any way by the fact conduct is nonassertive.

On the other hand, we have hearsay exceptions for declarations that may contain serious perception[25] or memory[26] problems, and cross-examination may not be essential for dealing adequately with the ambiguity problem. By suggesting in closing argument the specific ways in which the nonassertive conduct is ambiguous, an attorney can give the jury some concrete sense of how probative the evidence is. That sense, of course, is not as good as knowing for sure what motivated the conduct, but at least the attorney's argument can provide plausible, understandable possibilities with which the jury can grapple. In other words, with respect to the ambiguity problem, the jurors will probably have some intuitive sense of the likelihood that the alternative scenarios suggested by the attorney are true. By contrast, it may be very difficult, in the absence of cross-examination, to give the jury any concrete sense of the magnitude of other hearsay dangers. An attorney could suggest that a declarant may be insincere or may have misperceived or forgotten what happened. In the absence of any extrinsic evidence impeaching the credibility of the declarant, however, the jury would have no way to evaluate how likely it is that such a problem exists in any particular instance.

Even if the foregoing considerations militate against excluding all nonassertive conduct, it does not necessarily follow that the Federal Rules position is desirable. It would be possible, for example, to define hearsay as including both assertive and nonassertive conduct, to create a hearsay exception for nonassertive conduct, and to condition the applicability of that exception on the unavailability of the actor. Do you think such an alternative would be preferable to the Federal Rules?

9. Nonassertive Verbal Activity

Frequently, evidence that is characterized as nonassertive has a verbal component. Indeed, Wright v. Doe d. Tatham,[27] the nonassertive conduct case

---

24. See, e.g., Morgan, Hearsay Dangers and the Application of the Hearsay Concept, 62 Harv. L. Rev. 177, 188 (1948) ("While cross-examination can and occasionally does reveal insincerity and peculiarities in the use of language, experience in the courtroom demonstrates that its most important service is in exposing faults in perception and memory.")
25. See, e.g., FRE 803(2) (excited utterance exception), discussed at pages 426-429 infra.
26. See, e.g., FRE 804(b)(2) (dying declaration exception), discussed at pages 412-415 infra.
27. 5 Clark & Finnelly 670, 47 Rev. Rep. 136 (H.L. 1838).

A. Rationale and Meaning

most frequently cited and discussed by evidence scholars,[28] involves verbal conduct. *Wright* was a will contest between the heir at law and the beneficiary under the will of the decedent, John Marsden. In order to show that Marsden was competent at the time he executed his will, Wright, the beneficiary, offered into evidence several business letters and a personal letter that had been written to Marsden by individuals who were no longer alive. The nature of the inferences that Wright hoped the fact finder would draw from this evidence (and that one must draw in order for the evidence to be relevant to the question of Marsden's testamentary capacity) should by now be familiar: From their conduct of writing and sending the letters to Marsden, one may infer that the letter writers honestly believed that Marsden was competent; and one may infer further that the writers' beliefs were accurate reflections of Marsden's mental state. All of the hearsay dangers are potentially present. Perhaps the letter writers knew that Marsden was incompetent and, believing that Marsden was about to make them beneficiaries in his will, wrote the letters for the specific purpose of creating evidence of Marsden's competence (sincerity); perhaps the writers knew Marsden was incompetent but simply hoped to bolster his spirits by writing (ambiguity); perhaps they did not accurately perceive how strangely Marsden was behaving the last time they saw him (perception); or perhaps at the time they wrote the letters, they had forgotten about Marsden's strange behavior (memory).[29]

As was true in our earlier flight hypothetical and in the other examples of nonassertive nonverbal conduct, it seems highly unlikely that the out-of-court actors—here the letter writers—were attempting to assert or communicate the belief that the offeror of the evidence wants the fact finder to attribute to the actors—here a belief that Marsden was competent. As a result, there is probably no sincerity danger. There is nothing inherent in this evidence that tends to reduce the other hearsay dangers, however; and there would appear to be a substantial ambiguity problem: The bolstering spirits explanation for the letters seems quite plausible. In short, we have an example of nonassertive conduct with a verbal component.

We use the term *nonassertive* to describe the verbal conduct in *Wright* both because it is a convenient shorthand and because the term is frequently used to describe the evidence in *Wright* and similar cases. Before proceeding

---

28. See, e.g., Maguire, The Hearsay System: Around and Through the Thicket, 14 Vand. L. Rev. 741 (1961).

29. There is another relevance problem, which has nothing to do with the hearsay dangers: The letters appear to reflect the proposition that the letter writers, *at the time they wrote the letters*, believed Marsden was competent, and the legal issue is the competency of Marsden at the time he executed the will. If the letters were written long before or after the execution of the will (or more precisely, if the behavior of Marsden that the letter writers presumably perceived in order to have a basis for believing Marsden to be competent occurred long before or after the execution of the will), their probative value as evidence of Marsden's competence—completely apart from the hearsay dangers—may be quite low. (In fact there was a substantial time gap. One letter was written 39 years before the execution of the will; another was written 37 years before the execution of the will; and a third was written 26 years before the execution of the will!)

further, however, it is important to note that the term is technically inaccurate and potentially misleading. Almost every verbalization is a manifestation of an intent to assert something; thus, the likely presence or absence of a sincerity problem does not usually depend upon whether the declarant is intending to make an assertion. Rather, the likely presence or absence of a sincerity problem is a function of whether the purpose for which the evidence is offered is identical or similar to or quite different from what the declarant was trying to assert.

Nonassertive verbal conduct may pose one hearsay risk not posed by nonassertive nonverbal conduct. Even though we are not using the verbal conduct evidence to prove the truth of any particular verbal assertion (e.g., we are not trying to prove the truth of any particular assertion in the letters in *Wright*), the mere fact that words are being used creates the risk that the words may be misused, which is a narration problem. This possibility of a narration problem, however, should not be a sufficient basis to distinguish, for the purposes of admissibility, between verbal and nonverbal nonassertive conduct. The most common type of narration problem—misuse or omission of a single word or phrase—is not likely to be critical to the proper characterization of the speaker's or writer's general activity. For example, in *Wright* if the author of either a business letter or a friendly letter inadvertently omitted the word *not* in a sentence, that omission would probably not be important to our ability to characterize the letter as a personal letter or a business letter and to evaluate the probative value of the letter on the question of Marsden's competence.

To summarize, the hearsay dangers that inhere in nonassertive verbal conduct are almost identical to the hearsay dangers that inhere in nonassertive nonverbal conduct. If nonassertive nonverbal conduct is not hearsay, nonassertive verbal conduct should also be not hearsay.

Not surprisingly, courts, rule makers, and commentators agree that the admissibility of nonassertive conduct does not and should not depend upon whether the conduct is in whole or in part verbal. For example, the justices in *Wright*, after analogizing the letter writing evidence to evidence of nonassertive nonverbal conduct, concluded that all nonassertive activity—both nonverbal and verbal—should be regarded as hearsay;[30] and it is clear from the Advisory Committee's Note to FRE 801 that under the Federal Rules, both the letter writing evidence in *Wright* and the flight evidence in our earlier hypothetical would be classified as *not* hearsay:

> Subdivision (a).... The effect of the definition of "statement" is to exclude from the operation of the hearsay rule all evidence of conduct, verbal or nonverbal, not intended as an assertion. The key to the definition is that nothing is an assertion unless intended to be one.
>
> It can scarcely be doubted that an assertion made in words is intended

---

30. *Wright* is reproduced in the Supplement.

A. Rationale and Meaning

by the declarant to be an assertion. Hence verbal assertions readily fall into the category of "statement." Whether nonverbal conduct should be regarded as a statement for the purposes of defining hearsay requires further consideration. [Assertive conduct is and should be treated as hearsay; however, nonverbal conduct not intended as an assertion is excluded from the definition of statement because] situations giving rise to the nonverbal conduct are such as virtually to eliminate questions of sincerity. Similar considerations govern nonassertive verbal conduct and verbal conduct which is assertive but offered as a basis for inferring something other than the matter asserted, also excluded from the definition of hearsay by the language of subdivision (c).

What is not entirely clear is how, under the Federal Rules (and similar codifications), one arrives at the non-hearsay classification of nonassertive conduct with a verbal component. Consider carefully FRE 801(a), (c):

> (a) Statement. A "statement" is (1) an oral or written assertion or (2) nonverbal conduct of a person, if it is intended by the person as an assertion. . . .
> (c) Hearsay. "Hearsay" is a statement, other than one made by the declarant while testifying at the trial or hearing, offered in evidence to prove the truth of the matter asserted.

FRE 801(a)(2) exempts nonassertive *nonverbal* conduct from the definition of hearsay by limiting the definition of "statement" to "nonverbal conduct of a person, if it is intended by the person as an assertion." This same language cannot exempt the evidence in *Wright* because the evidence is not "nonverbal." Moreover, the "if intended . . ." language in FRE 801(a) appears to modify only subsection (2), and not subsection (1), which includes within the definition of statement "an oral or written assertion." Indeed, the term *assertion* implies an intent to communicate, and thus it seems nonsensical to speak of an assertion that is not intended as an assertion.

One could avoid the anomaly of having to deal with assertions that are not intended as assertions by reading "assertion" to mean "expression," "utterance," "verbiage," or some other term that does not imply (at least as strongly) an intent to communicate.[31] Or perhaps one could maintain that the letters in *Wright* do not constitute "statements" within the meaning of FRE 801(a) because only some expressions are assertions. It seems a bit odd, however, that the rule drafters, particularly in a definitional section, would

---

31. At the time the Federal Rules were drafted, there was precedent for such language. See Cal. Evid. Code §225 (" 'Statement' means (a) oral or written verbal expression or (b) nonverbal conduct of a person intended by him as a substitute for oral or written expression."); Uniform Rule of Evidence 62(1) (" 'Statement' means not only an oral or written expression but also non-verbal conduct of a person intended by him as a substitute for words in expressing the matter stated."). But see Uniform Rule of Evidence 62, Comment ("The definition of 'statement' makes it clear that it is intended to include as hearsay the conduct of a declarant, whether verbal or non-verbal, where it amounts to a communication *or* an expression.) (emphasis added).

expect one either to substitute a term for the one chosen by the drafters or to create and define a new term in order to give content to the rule.

Instead of trying to rely on FRE 801(a) to exempt nonassertive verbal conduct from the definition of hearsay, one could look to FRE 801(c): Arguably the letter writing evidence in *Wright* (and other nonassertive verbal conduct) is not hearsay because the evidence is not being offered to prove the "truth" of any particular assertion.[32]

Unfortunately, the Advisory Committee's Note to FRE 801 is not very helpful about which of these means should be used to classify as non-hearsay evidence like that in *Wright*. Reconsider the previously quoted excerpt from the Advisory Committee's Note. The first paragraph states, without explanation, that nonassertive verbal conduct is excluded from the definition of hearsay by FRE 801(a), the definition of statement. Consider, however, the last sentence of the excerpt, which speaks of "verbal conduct" that is "also excluded" from the definition of hearsay by virtue of FRE 801(c). Does the "also excluded . . ." clause apply only to "verbal conduct which is assertive" or to both "nonassertive verbal conduct" and "verbal conduct which is assertive"? If it applies to both, the sentence is inconsistent with the sentence in the first paragraph. If the "also excluded . . ." clause applies only to "verbal conduct which is assertive," what is the difference between "nonassertive verbal conduct" and "verbal conduct which is assertive but offered as a basis for inferring something other than the matter asserted"? (One answer may be that the "verbal conduct which is assertive . . ." language refers to the kinds of out-of-court statements that implicate no hearsay dangers (e.g., the notice hypothetical at page 304 supra). The correctness of this answer, however, is dubious. The sentence in which the "verbal conduct which is assertive . . ." clause appears is in a paragraph dealing generally with conduct that does implicate hearsay dangers, and the very sentence in question is specifically drawing an analogy to nonassertive nonverbal conduct, which implicates hearsay dangers.)

The ambiguity in the Advisory Committee's Note may be due at least in part to the Advisory Committee's failure to focus clearly on the difference between (1) a declarant's intent and (2) the purpose for which a declaration is being offered into evidence.[33] In any event, as noted previously, it seems clear from the Advisory Committee's Note that the drafters' intent was somehow to exclude from the definition of hearsay verbal activity that we have characterized (and that is commonly characterized) as "nonassertive."

---

32. See Finman, Implied Assertions as Hearsay: Some Criticisms of the Uniform Rules of Evidence, 14 Stan. L. Rev. 682, 684 n.8 (1962) (in discussing applicability of similar Uniform Rule of Evidence to hypothetical based on *Wright*, author concludes that letter writing evidence would be "statement" but would not be hearsay because not offered to prove truth of contents of letters).

33. See text at note 30 supra.

A. Rationale and Meaning

PROBLEMS

1. Ralph Benson and Jerry Jackson owned a small yacht, which they kept docked during the summer months at their cabin on Leech Lake near Walker, Minnesota. On the morning of June 15, Ralph, his wife, and two children set off across the lake in the yacht. A storm suddenly arose on the lake, and nobody has seen the Benson family or the yacht since that morning. In a suit by Jackson against the company that insured the yacht against damage or loss due to bad weather, the insurance company relies on a clause in the policy that permits recovery only if the yacht was navigable at the time of the loss. To prove that the yacht was navigable, Jerry Jackson offers to testify, "On the morning of June 15 I observed Ralph Benson carefully inspect the yacht, place his wife and children on board, and set off across the lake." Counsel for the insurance company objects to this testimony on the ground that it is hearsay. How should the court rule?

2. Kevin Perkins is being prosecuted for arson for setting fire to a local retirement home. An eye witness has testified that the person who set the fire was wearing a mask, gloves, and a heavy coat, all of which he discarded in a nearby alley as he fled. The prosecution then calls Ellen Woodbine, who offers to testify as follows: She raises and trains dogs and specializes in the training of bloodhounds. Within several hours of the fire at the retirement home, the sheriff asked her to come with one of her dogs to the alley where the mask and other items had been discovered. She arrived with "Old Blue," her most accomplished dog. After Old Blue got the scent from the mask, coat, and gloves, he led her and the sheriff around and through town, finally ending up at the edge of town in front of Kevin Perkins' log cabin. When Perkins came to the door, Old Blue ran up to him and barked loudly, which indicated that he was the person whose scent was on the items in the alley. Old Blue has been used in similar tracking roles over the past 10 years and has never been known to make a mistake.

Should this evidence be excluded on the ground that it is hearsay? On any other ground?

3. In a probate proceeding, Alexis Caldwell is attempting to establish that she is a daughter of the decedent. She offers

   (a) her own testimony about how the decedent always treated her as a family member, and
   (b) authenticated letters written by the decedent to Alexis during summers when she was away at summer camp and during her years at college. The letters are all friendly, chatty notes with various items of community and family news. Two letters begin, "My dearest daughter. . . ." The others all begin, "Dear Alexis. . . ."

Should these items of evidence be admissible over a hearsay objection?

4. Ed Stephens is being prosecuted for murder. The prosecution, after marking a shirt for identification and establishing that the victim's blood type was the same as the blood type of stains on the shirt, offered the following testimony of Officer Emily James: "The day after the killing, I was following leads on various possible suspects. I went to the Stephens' home, and found only Mrs. Stephens there. I asked her if she would give me the shirt her husband was wearing the previous evening, and she handed me the shirt that has been marked as an exhibit." Defense counsel has objected to this testimony on the ground that it is hearsay. What result?

5. Pedestrian v. Driver involves a claim for personal injuries. Pedestrian asserts that in addition to her medical bills and the pain and suffering she underwent during the period of recovery, she experienced great pain from the moment of the accident until an anesthetic was administered at the local hospital. Driver, on the other hand, claims that Pedestrian was unconscious from the moment of impact until several hours later when she awoke in the recovery room at the hospital. To prove consciousness and pain and suffering immediately after the accident, W offers to testify as follows for Pedestrian: "Within 30 seconds of the accident I was at Pedestrian's side. She was lying on the ground, and I shouted to a passerby, 'Get help; she's unconscious.' At that moment Pedestrian said, 'I'm not unconscious, and I'm in great pain.'"

Is the evidence hearsay?

6. A petition has been filed praying for the commitment of your evidence professor on the ground that the professor is mentally incompetent. In order to prove that your professor is (in)sane, you and several other students offer to testify that the professor gave a brilliant lecture on the intricacies of the hearsay rule. Should a hearsay objection to this testimony be sustained?

7. Gary Frazer is being prosecuted for the murder of Sheila Foley. The prosecution established that Sheila and two of her girlfriends, Debbie Duckett and Patricia Goodin, had been drinking at a local bar. Sheila claimed to be tired and went out to the car, which was owned by Patricia Goodin. A short time later, Sheila returned to the bar. She then went back to the car, and she was not seen again by her girlfriends. She did not return home that night. Her body was discovered a week later. During the presentation of its case, the prosecution called the two girlfriends. The following occurred during the examination of the Debbie Duckett:

Q: While you and Patty were playing pool, did you have any communication with Sheila at all, do you recall?
A: Yes.
Q: And what did that concern?

DEFENSE COUNSEL: Object to that as calling for a hearsay answer.
THE COURT: Overruled. Go ahead.

A. Rationale and Meaning

A: She said she was going to go out to the car for a while. . . .
Q: And after she entered [the tavern], what, if anything happened?
A: She—We were standing by the corner of the bar and she came up and said that Gary Frazer wanted her to give him a ride home.

DEFENSE COUNSEL: Excuse me. I want to interpose an objection, and ask the objection be allowed to precede the answer, as I couldn't anticipate the witness would testify as to conversations with Sheila Foley. At this time I would object to the question and the answer as it calls for hearsay.
THE COURT: Overruled. . . .

Patricia Goodin testified, inter alia, as follows:

Q: Was there any conversation at all about Sheila going outside that you recall?
DEFENSE COUNSEL: Objection, Your Honor. It calls for hearsay evidence.
THE COURT: Overruled. Go ahead.
A: After we sat there for awhile, she said that she wanted to go out in the car and lay down, she was tired, and we asked her if she wanted to go home, and she said she didn't want to go home yet. . . .
Q: And did Sheila Foley relate anything to you at all?
A: She . . .
DEFENSE COUNSEL: Object, Your Honor. It calls for hearsay.
THE COURT: Overruled. Go ahead.
A: She said that Gary Frazer was out in my car and he wanted her to give him a ride home.
Q: Did she specifically say "Gary Frazer"?
A: Yes.
Q: No question in your mind about that?
A: No.
Q: And what did you say to her?
A: I told her, no, that he was a creep and I didn't want him in my car.

Were the trial judge's rulings correct?

8. Bob Jones is being prosecuted for the attempted murder of his wife, Marsha, who is still in a coma as a result of the beating she received. The assault took place at about 10 P.M. on July 17 in the back yard of the Jones' home in suburban Eastdale. Mr. Jones claims that an intruder entered the yard and began beating Marsha when she refused his demand for her diamond ring and pendant. Jones further claims that he frightened off the intruder before the police arrived. The Jones' home is located in a cul-de-sac on a seldom traveled street.

One of the prosecution's first witnesses is Police Officer Jeremy Cork, who offers to testify as follows: "I was driving through Eastdale on my usual patrol when, shortly before 10 P.M. on July 17, I received a call on my police radio. The dispatcher said, 'Get to the Jones' residence right away. One of the neighbors just called to report a fight in the backyard. Bob Jones is beating his wife again.' "

Defense counsel has objected to the foregoing evidence on the ground that it is hearsay. How should the court rule?

9. Tim Grady and Eric Young are being tried jointly for bank robbery. Following the robbery, a teller identified Young from a photograph, and he was taken into custody. Grady was arrested several days later. During the presentation of its case, the prosecution offers the following testimony of Officer Peter Simmons:

Q: What did you do after you were assigned to the case?
A: I interrogated Eric Young.
Q: Did he make a statement?
A: Yes. He admitted his involvement in the robbery, and he told me who his accomplice was.
Q: Who did he tell you his accomplice was?

COUNSEL FOR GRADY: Object, Your Honor. Hearsay.
THE COURT: Sustained. Proceed.

Q: What did you do as a result of the interrogation?

COUNSEL FOR GRADY: Same objection.
THE COURT: Overruled. Proceed.

A: I arrested Tim Grady.

Were the court's rulings proper?

10. Sondra Evers is suing Ace Department Store for personal injuries sustained when she fell down the steps leading to the bargain basement. Sondra claims that the steps were unusually and dangerously slippery.

(a) Sondra calls Bertha Barlow, who offers to testify as follows: "On the day Ms. Evers had her accident, I was working behind the cosmetics counter, which is located near the bottom of the steps. About a half hour before the accident I overheard one shopper exclaim to her companion, 'I almost fell down those stairs!' "

(b) Ace Department Store calls Karen Larson, who offers to testify: "I am the general manager of the Ace Department Store and I was at the store from 8 A.M. until 5:30 P.M. on the day Ms. Evers fell. Neither on that day nor on any other day did I receive any complaints about the condition of the stairs leading to the bargain basement."

A. Rationale and Meaning

Should either piece of evidence be excluded on the ground that it is hearsay?

11. In his law suit against Emily Haskins, Stan Boswell alleges that he loaned Emily Haskins $500, which he claims she has not repaid. In her answer Emily alleged that she repaid the debt in full. Stan claims that he did not receive any payment from Emily, or, in the alternative, that any payment he did receive was a separate gift and not a repayment of the loan.

(a) As part of her defense, Emily offers to testify: "On February 23 [which was admittedly after the loan had been made], I came to Stan Boswell's office and gave him five $100 bills. As I was handing him the money, I said, 'Stan, here is the five hundred dollars I owe you.'"

(b) As part of his rebuttal, Stan calls his accountant, Mary Lee, who offers to testify: "I was with Stan Boswell on February 23 when Emily Haskins came into his office. I heard Emily say as she handed Stan $500 dollars, 'Stan, here is a little gift for you.'"

Is either piece of evidence hearsay?

12. Paula White is suing Willy Harris for personal injuries resulting from a pedestrian-vehicle accident at an intersection with a malfunctioning traffic light. The vehicle involved in the accident sped away without stopping. Paula claims that Willy was the driver of the vehicle and that he negligently drove through the intersection and hit her.

To prove that Willy owned the vehicle that hit her, Paula offers the following evidence:

(a) A certified copy of the Department of Motor Vehicle records indicating that Willy is the registered owner of a white 1984 Oldsmobile sedan bearing the license number WYZ-287; and

(b) A photograph of a white Oldsmobile sedan bearing the license number WYZ-287 along with the following testimony of Velma Pickering: "I am an amateur photographer, and I happened to be at the intersection when Paula White was hit by a hit-and-run driver. Things happened so fast that I don't remember anything about the car that hit Ms. White. I did have my camera with me, though, and I took a picture of the car that hit Paula as it was leaving the scene. I went home immediately and developed the film in my darkroom. This is the photograph that I took."

To prove that the driver of the vehicle had not been negligent, Willy offers the following evidence:

(c) Al Gamble to testify as follows: "I was at the intersection when the accident occurred. The traffic light was not operating, and a policeman was directing traffic. A few seconds before the vehicle that hit Ms. White entered the intersection, I observed the policeman turn toward Ms. White and raise his arm and outstretched palm in her direction."

Should a hearsay objection to any of this evidence be sustained?

13. Lyle Tingly is being prosecuted for the murder of his wife, June. The prosecution established that Mrs. Tingly was stabbed to death while resting or sleeping in her bed, that she died instantaneously from the stab wounds, and that the time of death was approximately 9:30 P.M. on Tuesday, November 23. To establish that Mr. Tingly was home at the time of the stabbing, the prosecution offers the following evidence:

(a) The testimony of Robert Goodheart, Mrs. Tingly's lover: "Whenever Mr. Tingly was not at home in the evening, June would turn on a lamp that sat on a table in front of the second story window immediately over the front porch. Turning the lamp on was a signal that it was safe for me to come to see her."

(b) The testimony of Emma Glover, a neighbor: "I remember keeping an eye on the Tingly house the night of November 23, because I heard some loud shouting early in the evening. I distinctly recall that the lamp in front of the window above the front porch was not on."

Is any of this evidence objectionable hearsay?

14. Prosecution of Betty Wilson for maintaining a house where betting occurs. A police officer offers to testify that as he was executing a warrant for the search of the house in question, he answered the telephone and heard the voice at the other end of the line say, "This is D.T.; put $25 on Rosebud in the fifth." Ms. Wilson's attorney objects that the evidence is hearsay. How should the court rule?

15. Harold Benson is charged with the robbery of a liquor store. The proprietor of the liquor store did not get a good look at the robber, and Harold claims he was in another part of the city shortly before 2 P.M., when the robbery occurred. The prosecution has several witnesses who observed Harold in the vicinity of the liquor store, and the prosecution wishes to prove that these observations were made around 2 P.M. Consider whether any of the following eyewitness testimony is objectionable on hearsay grounds:

(a) "I bumped into the defendant outside the liquor store. Instead of looking where I was going, I was looking at my watch, which read 2 P.M."

(b) "I saw the defendant come out of the liquor store just as the chimes on the bank clock across the street struck twice."

(c) "It was two o'clock when I saw the defendant leaving the liquor store. I know it was two o'clock because I was just getting on the bus that I take to work every day, and the bus regularly comes at 2 P.M."

(d) "I had just finished watching my favorite soap opera, *One Life to Live*, when I stepped outside and observed the defendant leaving the liquor store. It must have been about 2 P.M. because the soap opera runs from one to two."

(e) "I was talking on the telephone with the defendant's wife when I looked out the window and exclaimed, 'Why, there's Harold across the street by the liquor store,' and she said, 'I wonder why he's there. It's two o'clock and he's supposed to be across town.'"

(f) "I had just called the local telephone number for the time and was told that it was 2 P.M. Then I stepped outside and saw the defendant near the liquor store."

(g) "I had been weeding in the garden for several hours. I looked at the sun dial, which said 2 P.M., and then stepped out into the street. That's when I saw the defendant in front of the liquor store."

B. REFLECTIONS ON THE HEARSAY CONCEPT

1. Disguised Assertions

In some instances, evidence that is classified as nonassertive activity is in fact evidence of assertive behavior. Consider, for example, Albert's testimony that Greta was arrested for robbery to prove that Greta committed the robbery. The officers who arrested Greta may have been making the arrest because they observed Greta commit the robbery. If so, we believe, it is appropriate to regard their conduct as their own intended assertion that Greta committed the robbery. Alternatively, the officers may have been executing a warrant or acting in response to a victim's allegation, and not consciously trying to assert anything about her criminal activity. If this is the case, the officers are making the arrest only because somebody—probably the individual who signed the complaint or the officer who signed the affidavit accompanying a warrant application—made a specific assertion that Greta robbed the bank. In either case, the apparently nonassertive activity of the immediate actors (i.e., the arresting officers) is occurring only because of and is, in effect, a symbolic manifestation of a direct assertion of the proposition that the evidence is being offered to prove. The evidence, therefore, should be regarded as hearsay.

Consider also Mary's testimony that John's driver's license was revoked, which is offered to prove that John is an unsafe driver. It may well be that the person who engaged in the paperwork that officially revoked John's license was not trying to assert anything about how John drives. Nonetheless, the revocation is occurring only because somebody—presumably the judge who found John guilty of a traffic offense—asserted that John engaged in some illegal driving activity. Even if revocation were a discretionary rather than a mandatory penalty, the fact remains that the revocation occurred only because of the finding (i.e., the assertion) of guilt. Moreover, it is irrelevant to the hearsay analysis that the ultimate proposition (unsafe driving) is somewhat different from the specific assertion manifested by the revocation (a traffic violation). The truth of the specific assertion is critical to the relevance of the evidence for the ultimate proposition. (In terms of the testimonial triangle, the inference from specific infraction to bad driving would be illustrated by an arrow going from the bottom right corner of the triangle to the "Issue" in the center of the triangle.) If a license can be revoked for some offenses that are not indicative of bad driving, this fact merely weakens the probative value of the specific assertion to prove the ultimate proposition. Thus, the revocation evidence, like the arrest evidence, should be regarded as hearsay.

Our characterization of the arrest and revocation evidence as assertive is either a minority position or a refinement that most discussions of nonassertive activity do not bother to make. McCormick classifies the revocation evidence as nonassertive.[34] He also classifies the following evidence as nonassertive:

> The payment by underwriters of the amount of an insurance policy to prove that a ship was lost.
> The placing of an institutionalized person in a non-venereal ward to prove that the inmate is not infected.[35]

2. Classifying Verbal Utterances as Hearsay or Non-Hearsay

Perhaps the most difficult problem in classifying evidence as hearsay or non-hearsay is determining what to do with an out-of-court verbalization that potentially implicates all hearsay dangers (i.e., that requires a trip over both legs of the testimonial triangle) and that is being offered to establish a proposition that is not precisely the same as the proposition(s) specifically articulated in the verbalization. At one extreme, there will be some relatively easy cases where the evidence is being offered to prove something quite

---

34. McCormick, The Borderland of Hearsay, 39 Yale L.J. 489, 491 (1930).
35. Id. at 490, 496 n.17. See also Finman, Implied Assertions as Hearsay: Some Criticisms of the Uniform Rules of Evidence, 14 Stan. L. Rev. 682, 683 n.4 (1962) (citing institutionalization evidence as nonassertive). Morgan, on the other hand, characterizes the institutionalization evidence and the revocation evidence as assertive. In the same discussion, however, he also includes as another example of supposedly assertive activity "conduct of boys following a woman on the street and making fun of her" to prove her appearance was abnormal. Morgan, Hearsay Dangers and the Application of the Hearsay Concept, 62 Harv. L. Rev. 177, 190 (1948).

B. Reflections on the Hearsay Concept

different from anything that the declarant may have been intending to assert.[36] *Wright v. Doe d. Tatham* is such a case, and at least evidence scholars have little difficulty equating *Wright* with situations involving nonassertive nonverbal conduct: If nonassertive nonverbal conduct is not hearsay, evidence of the type in *Wright* should also be not hearsay.

At the other extreme there will be some pieces of evidence that quite clearly should be classified as hearsay even though they are being offered to prove something different from what the words of the out-of-court declaration actually articulate. Consider, for example, the following case: To prove that Bob robbed a bank, a witness offers to testify that George, in the context of a discussion about Bob, said, "Well, at least I never robbed a bank." Here, of course, we are not trying to prove the truth of the proposition that George did not rob a bank; nonetheless, the evidence should be regarded as hearsay because it seems clear from the context of the conversation that George is intending to assert the precise proposition that the evidence is being offered to prove, namely that Bob robbed a bank. George has chosen a somewhat unusual way of expressing that proposition, but this unusual manner of expression in no way diminishes any of the hearsay dangers. In short, if one is confident that the declarant is intending to assert the truth of the proposition that the evidence is being offered to establish, the declaration should be classified as hearsay, regardless of the words that the declarant happens to use.[37]

A general principle that would achieve the non-hearsay classification in *Wright* and the hearsay classification of our bank robbery declaration might be stated as follows:

---

36. As we noted earlier in the discussion of nonassertive conduct, one can never be absolutely certain that the declarant or actor is not intending to assert the very proposition that the evidence is being offered to prove. Nonetheless, in some instances one can feel quite confident, on the basis of common experience, that the declaration or conduct was not intended as an assertion of the proposition it is offered to prove.

37. One might argue that it is undesirable to burden the hearsay rule with the necessity of trying to ascertain the declarant's true intent. Indeed, proponents of the position that nonassertive conduct should be treated as hearsay have made this argument. See, e.g., Finman, Implied Assertions as Hearsay: Some Criticisms of the Uniform Rules of Evidence, 14 Stan. L. Rev. 682, 686-688 (1962).

In the nonassertive conduct context, the effect of accepting the argument would be to preclude the use of relevant evidence because of concerns with (1) the burden of having to make an intent finding and (2) the possible admission of evidence with sincerity (as well as other) hearsay problems as the result of an erroneous intent finding.

If one were to take the position that it is undesirable to try to determine a declarant's actual intent in the context of a case like our bank robbery hypothetical, the question remains what impact that decision should have on the hearsay classification. Ignoring intent and looking solely at the words spoken to see if the evidence was offered to prove the truth of those words would tend to result in the admission of evidence with substantial sincerity (as well as other) hearsay problems. Thus, unless one wishes to abandon the hearsay rule altogether (which is certainly a defensible position) or unless one is content to have the protection of the hearsay rule operate in a haphazard manner, the answer should be clear: The evidence is excluded simply because the fact finder is required to make the inferences from declaration to belief to truth, regardless of the declarant's actual intent.

> When an out-of-court declaration is used to prove something different from the truth of the declarant's verbalization, the evidence is hearsay if, but only if, the truth of the specific proposition that the declarant is intending to assert is critical to the relevance of the evidence.

This principle is consistent in theory with the objective of the Federal Rules in distinguishing between assertive and nonassertive activity: If the truth of what the declarant intends to assert is critical to the relevance of the evidence, we obviously have a sincerity problem even if the evidence is being offered to prove something different from what the words articulate; and if the evidence is relevant without regard to the truth of what the declarant was trying to assert, we do not have a sincerity problem. Moreover, it may be that the drafters of the Federal Rules intended this to be the test for classifying hearsay.[38] We suggest, however, that it is frequently impossible to be reasonably certain about what a declarant is intending to assert. As a result, application of the foregoing principle as a test for determining what declarations are hearsay may result in the admission of evidence with substantial sincerity risks.[39]

Consider, for example, a slight variation on the *Wright* case: To prove that X was competent at the time she executed her will, A offers a business letter written to X by Y, the primary beneficiary, at approximately the same time that the will was executed. The letter asks X to join Y in a relatively trivial business deal, makes certain factual assertions about the state of the economy, and includes several references to the extremely able manner in which X had recently negotiated several large contracts. As in *Wright*, the relevance of the letter to prove X's competence does not depend upon the truth of any particular assertion in the letter. Thus, pursuant to the previously suggested test the evidence would be not hearsay, unless one concludes that Y, by writing this particular letter, was intending to assert that X is competent. Given the facts that Y was the beneficiary, that the proposed business deal was relatively trivial, and that Y specifically mentioned X's able performance, one might reasonably draw that conclusion—but, we submit, without a high degree of certainty.

(If the facts in the preceding hypothetical do not, in your view, reasonably suggest that there may have been an intent to assert that X was competent, add the facts that Y knew he was the beneficiary, that Y knew there were doubts about X's mental competence, and that the predominant tone of the letter was praise for X's recent achievements. On the other hand, if in your view the facts given make it easy to conclude that Y was intending

---

38. It is impossible to tell from the language of the rule or from the Advisory Committee Note precisely what the drafters had in mind. See pages 323-324 supra.

39. This proposition and the following analysis are based on the premise that the hearsay rule (including the exclusion of nonassertive activity from the definition of hearsay) is itself fundamentally sound. One may question that premise, as indeed we do later. See pages 336-337 infra.

B. Reflections on the Hearsay Concept

to assert that X is competent, make the proposed business deal an important one and minimize the extent of the praise for X's past activities.)

Consider also various hortatory declarations such as "Watch your step!" offered to prove that the sidewalk was icy or "Accept only cash" offered to prove that the payor was in financial difficulty. When a hortatory declaration is offered to prove some historical fact, the declaration is being offered to prove something other than the proposition that the words articulate; and since a hortatory declaration cannot be true (or false) in the way that an historical fact can be true, it seems appropriate to say that the relevance of the evidence is not dependent upon the "truth" of the assertion. Thus, all hortatory declarations offered to prove historical facts are not hearsay, unless the declarant happens to be using a hortatory form to express an intended assertion of some historical fact. For example, the person who declares "Accept only cash" may be trying to assert the historical fact that the payor is in financial difficulty. One cannot be very certain, however, whether that is the case.

The assertion that hortatory declarations are not hearsay, of course, is nothing more than a definitional fiat. One could just as easily say that all hortatory declarations offered to prove historical facts are hearsay. We have not chosen this latter alternative because it seems clear to us that most evidence scholars regard at least some—and perhaps most—hortatory declarations offered to prove historical facts as not hearsay under the Federal Rules approach to nonassertive activity.

The primary problem underlying the hypothetical variation of *Wright* and various hortatory declarations is factual uncertainty about what the declarant is intending to assert and, therefore, uncertainty about the extent to which there is a sincerity risk.[40] Factual uncertainty may exist because there is a good deal of conflicting evidence or because there is an absence of evidence. In the context of verbalizations that may or may not be intended as assertions of the propositions they are offered to prove, the uncertainty is likely to stem from the absence of evidence. For example, one is likely to be limited to whatever inferences can be drawn simply from the context within which the declaration was made.

The traditional legal device for dealing with uncertainty about factual issues is the burden of proof standard. By assigning the burden to one party instead of the other (e.g., the party claiming that there is not an intent to assert what the evidence is offered to prove) and by deciding how heavy the burden should be (e.g., a preponderance of the evidence or beyond a reasonable doubt), one can allocate the risk of erroneous decisions in a manner designed to minimize costs.

One obvious cost is inaccurate fact finding. That is not always the only cost that one considers in establishing burdens of proof, however. In criminal

---

40. There may also be some disagreement, if not acknowledged uncertainty, among judges and scholars about the normative criteria for giving content to the concepts assertive activity and nonassertive activity. See note 42 and accompany text infra.

cases, for example, the traditional view is that we regard the cost of an erroneous conviction as greater than the cost of an erroneous acquittal, and, therefore, that we place a heavy burden on the prosecutor.

In the context of developing a burden of proof rule for whether verbalizations are intended assertions of what they are offered to prove, inaccurate fact finding on the intent question would appear to be the only relevant cost. The goal should be to minimize the risk of erroneous determinations by the judge about what the declarant was intending to assert. (Whether minimizing the risk of error on this question ultimately helps in minimizing the risk of incorrect factual determinations by the jury is another matter. To raise that issue, however, is to question the hearsay rule, a subject that is beyond the scope of this immediate inquiry.)

Although burdens of proof are most commonly discussed in relation to ultimate facts that determine the outcome of a lawsuit, burdens of proof inevitably are a part of preliminary fact finding by the judge. In some contexts, the role of burdens of proof in preliminary fact finding is specifically recognized and sometimes litigated.[41] Frequently, however, little or no attention is paid to burdens of proof for preliminary fact finding. For example, neither the Federal Rules nor, for the most part, the Advisory Committee's Notes deal with the burden of proof for various preliminary facts. One notable, but not very helpful exception, is the Advisory Committee's Note to FRE 801:

> When evidence of conduct is offered on the theory that it is not a statement, and hence not hearsay, a preliminary determination will be required to determine whether an assertion is intended. The rule is so worded as to place the burden upon the party claiming that the intention existed; ambiguous and doubtful cases will be resolved against him and in favor of admissibility. The determination involves no greater difficulty than many other preliminary questions of fact.

What wording in the rule places the burden on the party claiming that an intention existed? Assuming that there is such a burden, does "conduct" include "nonassertive verbal conduct"? It apparently does not include "verbal conduct which is assertive but offered as a basis for inferring something other than the matter asserted," which, the Advisory Committee's Note asserts, is "excluded from the definition of hearsay by the language of subdivision (c)." It is not clear, however, what the difference is between "nonassertive verbal conduct" and "verbal conduct which is assertive but offered as a basis for inferring something other than the matter asserted."

Even if the Advisory Committee's Note articulates a desirable burden

---

41. See, e.g., Bourjaily v. United States, 107 S. Ct. 2775 (1987), discussed at pages 394-397 infra (preliminary facts required to satisfy coconspirator admission provision must be established by preponderance of the evidence); Lego v. Twomey, 404 U.S. 553 (1972) (prosecution required to prove voluntariness of confession by preponderance of the evidence).

B. Reflections on the Hearsay Concept

of proof rule with respect to what appears to be nonassertive nonverbal conduct, it does not necessarily follow that the same rule should apply to verbalizations offered to prove something different from what the words on their face articulate. It may well be that such verbalizations will frequently be more difficult than non-verbal conduct to classify as assertive or nonassertive. If so, and we believe that this is likely to be the case, one might want a different burden-of-proof rule to govern resolution of the question whether the verbalizations should be classified as hearsay.

The failure of the Advisory Committee's Note to address clearly the burden of proof question with respect to nonassertive verbal conduct may not be a serious deficiency. In order to make an intelligent decision about the appropriate burden of proof standard, one needs to know—or at least have a general sense of—two things: first, the extent to which there are likely to be sincerity risks in the use of declarations that articulate something different from the proposition they are offered to prove; second, how much error (i.e., sincerity risk) we are willing to tolerate. In fact, we do not know, nor are we likely to know, much about incidence of actual sincerity risk; and even if we had this information, it is far from clear that there would be general agreement about how much risk to tolerate.

For example, if one is serious about the hearsay rule, it is by no means clear that a 49 percent possibility of there being a sincerity problem should be sufficient to permit admissibility. Yet, in theory, this would be the result if one of the parties had to establish by only a preponderance of the evidence that the verbalization was or was not intended as an assertion of the proposition that it is offered to prove.

It is also not clear that a higher burden of proof would be desirable. For example, if the proponent had to prove by clear and convincing evidence (e.g., 75 percent probability) that the verbalization was not intended as an assertion of the proposition it is offered to prove, the possibility that a sincerity problem would inhere in admitted evidence would be only 25 percent. In most situations in which the declarant's intent is open to question, however, it may be impossible for the proponent of the evidence to meet such a high standard. If in fact the excluded evidence was disproportionately free from sincerity problems, the high standard of proof would detract from rather than contribute to accurate fact finding.

We realize, of course, that any rational process of determining intent or the likelihood of a sincerity problem inevitably involves a decision about the probability that a particular intent exists. If there is not a reasonable likelihood of consensus on what the standard should be, however, there may be no harm in leaving the standard unarticulated. On the other hand, if the developing caselaw seems inconsistent and contradictory, a specifically articulated standard of proof rule may become a desirable way of promoting uniformity. Our own view is that, at least for the present, it is unnecessary to try to develop a specific burden of proof rule to govern the question whether conduct is assertive or nonassertive.

Regardless of what the standard of proof is and whether it is specifically articulated, it is important to keep in mind the following propositions when dealing with a declaration offered to prove a proposition that is somewhat different from the actual verbalization:

1. *Almost every verbalization constitutes an intent, in some sense, to assert something.*

The terms *intent* and *assert* both imply the making of a conscious choice. Thus, it would be reasonable to regard an unconscious verbalization—e.g., sleep-talk, or perhaps even talking to oneself while walking down the street—as a kind of verbalization that does not constitute an intent to assert something.

Some verbalizations may constitute conscious attempts to communicate something but there may not be an immediate object of the communication. Consider, for example, a person praying aloud in an apparently empty church, or making an entry in a private diary. Each person is making a conscious attempt to articulate particular thoughts and, it would seem, to communicate those thoughts to the cosmos or to one's god or to posterity. Does the fact that the declarant is not intending to communicate—at least at the moment—to another human being suggest that the declaration should not be regarded as an "assertion" for the purposes of FRE 801(a)?

Other verbalizations that are conscious attempts to communicate may have as their immediate purpose the communication of something other than an historical fact or a particular belief or feeling. Consider the out-of-court declaration expressing the greeting, "Hello, John," offered to prove that John was present. The expression may be quite spontaneous, and it may be likely that the declarant is simply intending to express a greeting and not trying to assert the proposition "John is present." Nonetheless, the declarant, at some level of consciousness, it would seem, is trying to communicate not merely a general greeting to another human being but a personalized greeting to the specific person, John; and in the identification of the person as John, all of the hearsay dangers potentially exist. Is a greeting, even when made to a specifically identified person, likely to be sufficiently spontaneous (and therefore not likely to be insincere) that we should it equate it with the nonassertive activity in a case like *Wright*?

2. *To the extent that every verbalization constitutes an intent to assert something, there is no meaningful qualitative distinction between "nonassertive verbal conduct" and a "verbal assertion offered to prove something other than the truth of the matter asserted."*

Although we have adopted the customary usage by characterizing some verbal activity as "nonassertive," we have also noted that such a characterization is imprecise and potentially misleading. Verbal activity may well be "nonassertive" in the sense that it does not constitute an intent to assert the particular proposition it is offered to prove, but at the same time, the ver-

B. Reflections on the Hearsay Concept

balization may be an intended assertion of some other proposition. For example, the letter writing activity in *Wright* is frequently characterized as nonassertive, but it is only nonassertive in the sense that the letter writers were not intending to assert anything about Marsden's competence. They presumably were intending to assert specific propositions set forth in the letters.

Some discussions of the hearsay concept use the term *implied assertion*. Sometimes that term seems to be a synonym for "nonassertive conduct," and sometimes it is used a bit more narrowly to describe some or all *verbal* activity that is offered to prove something different from what the words themselves articulate. The term *implied assertion*, like the term *nonassertive conduct*, is potentially misleading in that the verbalization is likely to constitute an express assertion of some proposition. Moreover, just as we find no meaningful qualitative distinction between "nonassertive conduct" and assertions "offered as a basis for inferring something other than the matter asserted," we see no reason to try to create a bright line distinction between "nonassertive conduct" and "implied assertions."

3. When the verbalization is identical to or is closely related to the proposition that the evidence is offered to prove, there is a relatively high probability of a sincerity risk and not much of an ambiguity danger.

4. The sincerity problem may be greater when the apparently intended assertion is closely related to, rather than identical to, the proposition that the evidence is offered to prove.

Consider, for example, what Mary would say if she wanted to make people believe that a particular company was insolvent. Particularly if she wanted to convey the *false* impression that the company was insolvent, she might not assert that proposition directly. Instead, she might make assertions about specific unpaid debts, or she might urge an agent to demand cash and not accept a check from the company.

One might argue that the example here is no different from the "Well, at least I never robbed a bank" hypothetical, and that in both cases the declarant is intending to assert the very proposition that the evidence is being offered to prove. Perhaps that is correct. At least some evidence scholars, however, maintain that the "demand cash" example may be classified as not hearsay.[42]

5. Disagreement about whether conduct is assertive or nonassertive may

---

42. See Finman, Implied Assertions as Hearsay: Some Criticisms of the Uniform Rules of Evidence, 14 Stan. L. Rev. 682, 687 n.16 (1962) (citing Maguire, The Hearsay System: Around and Through the Thicket, 14 Vand. L. Rev. 741, 766 n.82 (1961) for the proposition that the case requires scrutiny to determine on which side of the line it falls; McCormick, The Borderland of Hearsay, 39 Yale L.J. 489, 490-491[, 495 n.17] (1930) as maintaining the evidence should be not hearsay; and Morgan, Hearsay Dangers and the Application of the Hearsay Concept, 62 Harv. L. Rev. 117, 190-191 (1948) as maintaining that the evidence should be hearsay.)

stem at least in part from disagreement about the definitions of those terms rather than from factual uncertainty about the actor/declarant's intent.

Frequently, scholars have been less than precise in articulating exactly what the differences are between activity that is labeled "assertive" and activity that is labeled "nonassertive."[43] For example, some of the disagreement about the "demand cash" evidence may stem not so much from different assumptions about what the declarant in fact believes or is thinking but rather from different views about how the declarant's belief or thought should be characterized. In other words, in order to determine whether the evidence is being offered to prove what the declarant intended to assert, we must know what we mean by "intent." In view of the rationale for the hearsay rule and for the exclusion of nonassertive activity from the definition of hearsay, we believe that the key to resolving this issue is to focus on the question whether the declaration is one that appears to raise sincerity risks.

6. When the verbalization is offered to prove something quite different from the articulated proposition, there is a relatively high probability of an ambiguity risk and not much of a sincerity danger.

7. Perception and memory dangers inhere in the inference that the belief attributed to the declarant corresponds with some event in the real world. The extent of these dangers is not affected by the similarity or difference between the declarant's actual words and the belief that we attribute to the declarant because of those words.

In light of the foregoing propositions, it seems to us that a rational hearsay rule that categorizes nonassertive nonverbal conduct as not hearsay should tend to classify evidence of the type described in Proposition 3 as hearsay and to classify evidence of the type described in Proposition 6 as not hearsay.[44] Whether the Federal Rules (and other similar statements of the hearsay rule) are likely to accomplish this objective is uncertain. On the one hand, FRE 801 is probably flexible enough—or perhaps ambiguous enough would be more apt—to accomplish the desired goal. In a case like *Wright*, one can characterize the letter writing as nonassertive conduct and therefore not an assertion, or one can say that the letters are not being offered to prove the truth of any particular assertion contained in them. In a case in which the declarant's words are closely related to the proposition that the evidence is being offered to prove, one can argue that the declarant, in effect, is asserting that proposition.

43. See, e.g., the citations in the preceding footnote, especially the Morgan excerpt.
44. We realize the phrases *closely related* (Proposition 3) and *quite different* (Proposition 6) are far from precise. We also realize that a decision maker, whether deliberately or not, inevitably applies some burden of proof standard in determining whether certain propositions have been sufficiently established. We have already suggested, however, why we believe there is no need for specific articulation of a burden of proof standard for determining nonassertiveness; for the same reasons, we do not believe that attempts to articulate the substantive standard more precisely are likely to be of much benefit.

B. Reflections on the Hearsay Concept

On the other hand, the language of FRE 801 may detract from rational classification of the types of evidence considered here. First, and most obviously, although the reasons for excluding hearsay relate to the risks inherent in the inferences from declaration to belief to event, the rule itself is not worded in terms of those inferences. Instead, the language of the rule focuses on the "truth" of the matter asserted, and thus seems to invite classifying as not hearsay some declarations that may pose substantial sincerity risks. This problem is compounded by the fact that the rule can (and perhaps should) be read as excluding a case like *Wright* from the hearsay classification by reasoning that the letters are not offered for their "truth,"[45] rather than by reasoning that the letters, for the purpose offered, do not constitute a "statement." Since *Wright* is analogous to a case of nonassertive nonverbal conduct, it would seem appropriate to be able to rely on the same part of the rule to reach the desired result in the two cases. Treating likes differently—even if the ultimate result is the same—can only contribute to confusion and misunderstanding about the hearsay rule.

Even if FRE 801 detracts from—or at least does not contribute to—a clear understanding and classification of some types of nonassertive activity, it does not necessarily follow that the rule should be revised. One objective of any codification scheme should be to provide rules that are as clear and as simple as possible, and this objective is particularly important with respect to codifications of evidentiary principles, which frequently must be applied quickly in the charged atmosphere of an ongoing trial. It may be that FRE 801 functions quite well for the vast majority of hearsay issues that arise. Moreover, a rule that dealt more consistently with nonassertive activity might, because of the complexity of its wording, be more difficult to understand and apply properly in run-of-the-mill cases.

As an experiment, we suggest that you try your hand at drafting a hearsay rule that both (a) meets our criticisms of FRE 801 and (b) is not significantly longer or more complex than FRE 801. (If you feel that you have succeeded in this task, we urge you to send us copies of your proposals.)

PROBLEMS

1. Julius Darcey is suing Divine Inspiration College, a local unaccredited institution, for breach of contract. Darcey claims that he had an oral one-year agreement to teach remedial English and that he was fired in December, after the first semester. The College claims that part of the

---

45. See Finman, Implied Assertions as Hearsay: Some Criticisms of the Uniform Rule of Evidence, 14 Stan. L. Rev. 682, 684 n.8 (1962) (applying Uniform Rule of Evidence 62 to hypothetical based on *Wright* and concluding that evidence not hearsay because letters not offered to prove truth of matter asserted). But see pages 323-324 supra (suggesting that *Wright* may be an example of "nonassertive verbal conduct" excluded from the definition of hearsay because it is not a "statement" within the meaning of FRE 801(a)).

contract was a promise on Darcey's part to refrain from the use of narcotic drugs during the term of the agreement. To prove that Darcey had been using drugs, the College offers the following testimony of, Ashley Horsely, one of Darcey's former students: "Last December 31, I visited Professor Darcey at the State Drug Rehabilitation Center, where he is a patient." Darcey's counsel has objected to Ms. Horsely's testimony on the ground that it is inadmissible hearsay. How should the court rule?

2. Bob Williams is being prosecuted for bank robbery. The prosecutor calls Amy Jackson, who offers to testify: "The day before Bob Williams was arrested my husband, George, and I spent the entire evening talking about Bob, who was George's co-worker. During that conversation my husband said, 'Well, at least I never robbed a bank.'" Is the evidence hearsay?

3. Assume that the bank robbery in the preceding problem occurred in Chicago on January 2. Several weeks after the robbery when the police were interviewing Joan Williams, Bob's wife, Joan stated that she and her husband were in St. Louis on January 2. As part of its case against Williams, the prosecution offers overwhelming evidence that Bob Williams was in Chicago on January 2 along with a police officer's testimony about Joan's statement that Bob had been in St. Louis. Should the defendant's hearsay objection to what Joan said be sustained?

4. Mary Dugan is being prosecuted for the murder of her boyfriend. To prove that she committed the homicide, the prosecution calls Francis Waterman, who offers to testify as follows: "Several weeks ago as I was walking through what I thought was a deserted forest I noticed a woman sitting on a tree stump in a clearing. It was the defendant, Mary Dugan. I'm sure she didn't see me. I didn't mean to be eavesdropping, but I couldn't help overhearing her. She was sobbing quietly as she said, apparently to herself, 'I only wanted to frighten him; I didn't mean to kill him.'" Is this evidence hearsay?

5. Glen Thompson is being prosecuted for the rape of Joyce Evers. The prosecution offers evidence that two days after the rape Marvin Evers, Joyce's husband, ran into Glen Thompson on the street and that Evers immediately assaulted and severely beat Thompson. Is the evidence admissible?

6. Andy Powers is being prosecuted for the theft of his grandmother's cow, which he sold to a man named Green. Powers' defense is that he was acting with his grandmother's authority when he sold the cow. To rebut this claim, the prosecutor offers the following testimony of Green: "I obtained the cow on Monday and agreed to pay Mr. Powers the following Friday. On Tuesday, Mr. Powers' grandmother came to me and demanded that I return the cow to her."

Should defense counsel's hearsay objection be sustained?

7. John Scalzi is charged with conspiracy to sell narcotics. Scalzi was visiting the home of friends, Kathy and Robert McDaniel, when the police arrived to execute a search warrant. During the course of the search they observed what appeared to be narcotics in plain view on the coffee table and

B. Reflections on the Hearsay Concept

arrested Scalzi as well as the McDaniels. At Scalzi's trial, Officer Jaksch, who was one of the officers executing the warrant, offered to testify as follows:

Q: Did anything unusual happen during the search?
A: Yes, the telephone rang, and I answered it. There was a female voice at the other end of the line.
Q: What did she say?
A: She asked if John was there, and I said that he had just left.
Q: Did she say anything else?
A: Yes, she asked if John had taken care of business. I asked her what she meant, and she asked if John had gotten it bagged up. I said yes.
Q: Are you familiar with the street jargon "got it bagged"?
A: Yes, I am.
Q: What does that mean to you?
A: On the street, "bagged" is a term for packaging of narcotics for sale, basically for transportation.

Is any of the foregoing testimony objectionable hearsay?

8. Pete Storms, an inquisitive three year old, was intrigued by Pepper, a large, unruly Black Labrador that lived next door. One morning Pete stuck his hand through the wire mesh in Pepper's dog run in order to pet the dog. A voice cried out "Beware of the dog!" but the warning came too late, and Pete lost his right hand. Pete's parents have brought a tort action against Bruce LaPac, Pepper's owner. Bart Bartlett and Cara Carlson, both of whom witnessed the biting incident, have different recollections about who shouted the warning.

(a) To prove that Pepper was a dangerous, vicious dog, Bart Bartlett offers to testify that he heard a neighbor shout, "Beware of the dog!"

(b) To prove that Bruce LaPac had notice that Pepper was a dangerous dog, Bartlett offers to testify as in (a).

(c) To prove that Bruce LaPac had notice that Pepper was a dangerous dog, Cara Carlson offers to testify that she heard LaPac shout "Beware of the dog!"

(d) To prove that Pete Storms had notice that Pepper was a dangerous dog, Cara offers to testify as in (c).

Assuming you represent LaPac, what objections could you make to the preceding evidence?

9. Roger Sullivan has been charged with murder for stabbing to death William Newport. Newport was killed in the den of his home late in the afternoon on November 3. Kathy Newport, the decedent's teenage daughter, offers to testify as follows: "I arrived home from school at about 4:15 P.M on November 3 and went into the kitchen to do my homework. I heard two sometimes rather loud male voices coming from the study, and I recognized

one voice as my father's. After a short time, I saw my mother pull her car into the driveway. I could not see the front door from where I was seated, but as the door opened, I heard my mother say, 'Hello, Roger. It's nice to see you. Can you stay and have dinner with us?' I heard a male voice respond, but I couldn't make out who it was or what was said. A few seconds later, my mother came into the kitchen and said, 'I just passed Roger Sullivan at the front door. He seemed quite agitated.' My mother and I chatted for a while, and then we went into the den where we found my father. He was dead."

Is any of Kathy's testimony objectionable hearsay?

3. Classifying State-of-Mind Evidence As Hearsay or Non-Hearsay

As noted previously, evidence offered to show a declarant's state of mind (i.e., evidence whose relevance requires making the inference illustrated by the left leg, but not the right leg, of the testimonial triangle) tends to be classified as hearsay only if the declaration is a direct assertion of the state of mind to be proved. Consider, for example, a will contest case in which the testator has left his entire estate to Harold, one of his three sons. Harold's brothers have challenged the will on the ground that Harold exercised undue influence over the testator. To rebut the claim of undue influence, Harold offers witnesses to testify that prior to the time of the alleged undue influence the testator said, "I prefer Harold over my other sons" and "Harold is the finest of my three sons." According to McCormick, the declaration "I prefer Harold" should be classified as hearsay, and the declaration "Harold is the finest of my sons" should be classified as not hearsay. With respect to the latter declaration, McCormicks's explanation is that we are not trying to prove that Harold is in fact the finest son; rather, we are simply inferring a preference for Harold.[46]

Since there is a hearsay exception for declarations of a declarant's then-existing state of mind, the labeling of declarations offered to show the declarant's then-existing state of mind as hearsay or not hearsay, as McCormick recognized, is purely academic in terms of admissibility. Nonetheless, the traditional labeling, illustrated by McCormick's hypothetical about Harold, is both troublesome and instructive. It is troublesome because the hearsay dangers that inhere in the non-hearsay declaration ("Harold is my finest son") are at least as great or greater than the hearsay dangers that inhere in the hearsay declaration ("I prefer Harold"). The labeling is instructive because it demonstrates how the divergence between a rule's rationale (i.e., concern

---

46. See McCormick's Handbook on the Law of Evidence 591 (2d ed., Cleary, 1972). The hypothetical does not appear in the third edition of McCormick's hornbook. There is nothing in the third edition, however, to suggest that the editors have repudiated anything said about the hypothetical in the second edition. See McCormick's Handbook on the Law of Evidence 843 (3rd ed., Cleary, 1984).

B. Reflections on the Hearsay Concept

with certain specific aspects of the inferential process of proof) and the rule's words (i.e., an undefined reference to the "truth" of the matter asserted) can lead to silly conclusions.

McCormick's labeling the declaration "I prefer Harold" as hearsay and the declaration "Harold is the finest of my sons" as not hearsay is admittedly understandable if one merely applies the language of the hearsay rule in an unthinking, mechanical manner: We are trying to prove (the "truth" of the proposition) that the testator prefers Harold, and we are not trying to prove (the "truth" of the proposition) that Harold is the finest son. From a concern with the underlying rationale for the hearsay rule, however, the classification makes no sense.

First, McCormick ignores the fact that "truth" in the "normal" hearsay situation involving perception and memory problems (as well as sincerity and narration/ambiguity problems) is something quite different from the "truth" of the declarant's state of mind. In normal hearsay situations, "truth" refers to the occurrence of some historical fact; in the state of mind situations, "truth" refers only to the state of mind of the declarant. Thus, in terms of potential hearsay dangers, the relationship between the "finest son" and "prefer Harold" statements is much closer than the relationship between the "prefer Harold" statement and normal hearsay statements.

Second, McCormick is incorrect in stating that only the "prefer Harold" statement is "dependent for its value upon the veracity of the declarant."[47] The "finest son" statement is relevant to show preference for Harold in two ways, both of which require the same reliance on the testator's veracity as the "prefer Harold" statement does. First, one can infer that the testator honestly believes that Harold is the finest son and then make the further inference that, therefore, the testator must prefer Harold. Alternatively, one can infer that because the testator says nice things about Harold, regardless of whether the testator believes them to be true, the testator must prefer Harold. From this perspective, we do not care whether the testator sincerely believes that by some objective standard Harold is the finest son. If we assume, however, that the testator does not sincerely believe Harold is the finest son, consider how the evidence can be relevant to show a preference for Harold. The only reasonable answer, we submit, is that the testator is lying about Harold's objective qualities as a means of intending quite specifically and sincerely to assert a preference for Harold.

Third, the actual hearsay dangers are greater in the declaration that McCormick regards as not hearsay. First, there is such a close—although not completely coincidental—relationship between the "finest son" and "preference" statements (i.e., the possible implication of preference is so obvious in the "finest son" statement) that the risk of an intentionally deceitful communication of preference—i.e, the risk of a sincerity problem—is pretty much the same with both statements. Indeed, the risk may be greater with

---

47. McCormick's Handbook on the Law of Evidence 591 (2d ed., Cleary, 1972).

the "finest son" statement.[48] Second, the "finest son" statement raises a significant ambiguity problem that does not exist with the "prefer Harold" statement: Perhaps the testator believes that Harold is the finest son by some objective standard but nonetheless does not prefer Harold. Willy Loman, if pressed, would probably have to say that Hap was his finer—or at least more successful—son, but Willy clearly preferred Biff;[49] Big Daddy would probably have to admit that Gooper was his more successful son, but Big Daddy preferred Brick.[50]

If one assumes that we do not necessarily have to rely on the testator's sincere belief that Harold is the finest son, the ambiguity occurs in the inference from declaration to the belief that we attribute to the testator.

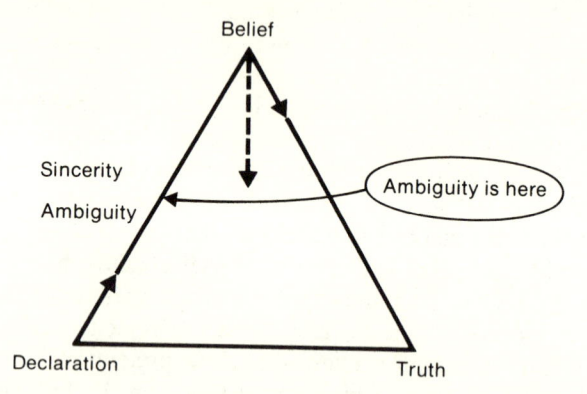

```
                    Belief
                     /\
                    /  \
                   / ↓  \
         Sincerity/      \
                 /        \  ← Ambiguity is here
         Ambiguity\        \
                 /          \
                /_____\
           Declaration      Truth
```

On the other hand, if we assume that the relevance of the evidence depends on the sincere belief that Harold is the finest son, the "ambiguity" technically could be regarded as not presenting a hearsay problem; rather the ambiguity inheres in the inference from belief (i.e., finest son) to provable proposition (i.e., preference).

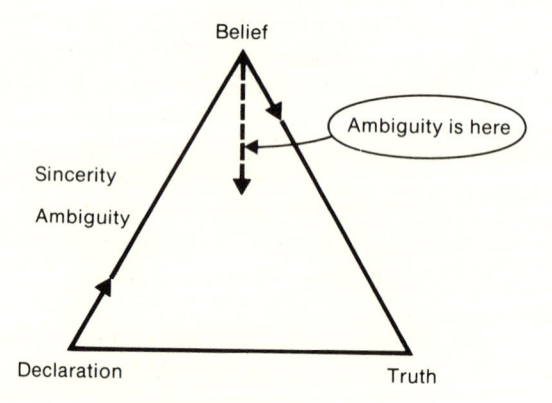

```
                    Belief
                     /\
                    /  \
                   /    \  ← Ambiguity is here
         Sincerity/  ↓   \
                 /        \
         Ambiguity         \
                 /          \
                /_____\
           Declaration      Truth
```

48. See page 339 supra.
49. See A. Miller, Death of a Salesman.
50. See T. Williams, Cat on a Hot Tin Roof.

B. Reflections on the Hearsay Concept

In either case, as noted previously, there is a sincerity problem that is identical to the sincerity problem in the declaration "I prefer Harold."

4. Perception, Memory, and State-of-Mind Evidence

Standard discussions of the concept of hearsay draw a sharp distinction, as we have thus far, between (1) out-of-court declarations offered to show a declarant's then-existing state of mind, and (2) out-of-court declarations offered to show the "truth" of some historical fact. The former, which are not excluded by the hearsay rule (either because they are not hearsay or because they fall within the state-of-mind exception), are characterized as involving potential sincerity and narration/ambiguity problems but not perception and memory problems. In fact, however, perception and memory problems inhere in all declarations of a person's then-existing state of mind.

Consider, for example, Joan's out-of-court declaration, "I have a severe headache." There is obviously a potential sincerity problem. Joan may be lying about her headache, which she is using as an excuse for avoiding a boring cocktail party. There is also obviously (although perhaps less probably) a narration problem. Joan may have felt "heartache" instead of headache and used the wrong word to express her feeling. If Joan used the wrong word, it may simply have been a slip of the tongue. It may, however, have been the result of faulty memory or perception. Joan's—or any declarant's—choice of a word to express a feeling is necessarily based on having *perceived* (by reading or listening) the word used in various contexts and having *remembered* what the word means. Indeed, it may not even be appropriate to distinguish between a "slip of the tongue" and a perception or memory problem. One could perhaps characterize a slip of the tongue as a momentary perception/memory lapse.

Consider also the declarations "I prefer Harold" and "Harold is the finest of my sons" in McCormick's will contest hypothetical. How can we be sure that the declarant meant to say "Harold" rather than "Henry"? The declarant may have inadvertently used the wrong name, or because of a confused *memory*, the declarant may have thought that the preferred son, Henry, was named Harold.

The possible confusion about Harold could be of two types. First, assuming that the declarant's preference is based on which son had been the more loving, the declarant, at the time of his declaration, may have believed that Harold had been the more loving son, but this belief may have been based on inaccurate memory of how his sons behaved toward him. Second, the declarant may have accurately remembered which son (e.g., the first born) had been more loving, but the declarant may have been confused about (i.e., may not have remembered accurately) the name of that son. The first type of mistake would not be relevant to the issue at hand. If there were a preference for Harold at the time of the declaration, that fact would be relevant to rebut the claim of undue influence, regardless of what the basis for that preference was. (The mistake, however, might be relevant for another purpose, e.g., to show general testamentary incapacity.) The second type of mistake is relevant to our present inquiry: If the declarant did not mean to express a preference for Harold, then the evidence does not in fact help to prove what it is offered to prove: the true intent of the declarant.

Uncorrected slips of the tongue are fairly uncommon, and perhaps it is not very likely that a person will forget the meanings of words or that a person will incorrectly remember the names of family members. In similar contexts, however, bad memory about a person's name or some other fact may be somewhat more likely. Consider, for example, the following situation:

> Alan has just been hired as the new foreman of a construction crew. Because George, a well-liked, long-time employee, was passed over for the foreman job, there was some animosity toward Alan. After only two days on the job, Alan was killed in a scuffle with Bill, one of the crew members. There were no eyewitnesses to the fight. Bill has been charged with murder and claims self-defense.
>
> To rebut the claim of self-defense, Alan's widow, Marcia, offers to testify as follows: "The first night that he came home from the job Alan talked about what a rough crew it was and how there seemed to be a lot of animosity. He said he was especially worried about [the person whose name he thought was] Bill and that he, Alan, was going to be sure to keep his distance from Bill."
>
> The prosecutor argues that this evidence is relevant to show Alan's state of mind (fear of Bill) for the purpose of inferring that Alan was not likely to be the first aggressor.

Even if the bracketed portion of Marcia's testimony is deleted, it seems to us reasonable to suggest that Alan might not have accurately remembered the names of the crew members after working with them for only one day. Or perhaps when Alan was introduced to Phil, another crew member, Alan did not hear the name correctly and thought that "Phil" was "Bill."[51] The

---

51. Of course, it is also possible that the person who introduced Phil to Alan incorrectly identified Phil as Bill. If we knew that Alan's sole basis for believing a person to be Bill was the fact that somebody said to Alan, "This person is Bill," then Alan's statement arguably should be excluded because we are relying on the truth of what the out-of-court introducer said. Indeed, whenever a person identifies an individual by using a name, the identifier is inevitably relying on the sincerity, narrative ability, perception, and memory of other people. That is how we "know" that a person has a particular name. Usually, however, the law does not regard in-court testimony that identifies either the witness or someone else by name as hearsay. As a practical matter this is so because it would often be difficult or impossible to get coherent stories from witnesses if they could not refer to people by name. As a theoretical matter, this is so because one's knowledge about a particular person's name may be based on information that would be regarded as not hearsay, at least under the Federal Rules approach to hearsay. For example, an out-of-court exclamation "Oh, Bill!" might not be regarded as an intended assertion of the proposition "This is Bill;" the failure on the part of a person being

B. Reflections on the Hearsay Concept

bracketed language merely emphasizes these possibilities. In short, regardless of whether Alan explicitly acknowledges it, there are potential memory and perception problems in his expression of fear about Bill.

Consider whether the memory and perception problems that inhere in what traditionally is labeled a narration problem are usually likely to be less serious—or less amenable to discovery by cross-examination—than the more obvious or direct perception and memory problems illustrated by the right leg of the testimonial triangle. If so, then the traditional distinction between inadmissible hearsay and admissible declarations of one's then-existing state of mind may be appropriate. It may be, however, that the extent to which there are risks of faulty memory or perception is not closely related to the question whether the memory and perception problems exist in the inference from declaration to belief (i.e., in the narration problem) or in the inference from belief to fact believed. If that is the case, what justification is there for placing outside the hearsay prohibition declarations of one's then-existing state of mind? Or, to ask the question from a different perspective, if declarations of a person's then-existing state of mind are not excluded by the hearsay rule, what justification is there for a rigid rule of exclusion (subject, of course, to specified exceptions) for out-of-court declarations offered to prove the truth of some historical fact?

Regardless of your answers to the preceding questions, it should be clear that whenever the relevance of an out-of-court declaration depends upon making an inference about the declarant's state of mind all four hearsay dangers are potentially present. Moreover, the extent to which there is a reasonable likelihood that any one hearsay danger exists in a particular case does not necessarily depend upon whether the declaration is offered to prove the truth of some historical fact. Thus, despite the traditional learning, there is no hard qualitative line, in terms of the rationale for the hearsay rule, that can be drawn between declarations of one's then-existing state of mind and declarations of historical facts.

PROBLEMS

1. Susan Peach has sued Tim Downy for personal injuries and property damage sustained when Downy's car crossed the center line and ran into Peach's car. The immediate cause of the accident was the blow out of the left front tire on Downy's car. Peach claims that Downy was negligent in that he knew or should have known about the unsafe condition of the tire.

---

introduced as Bill to protest his name probably would be regarded as nonassertive activity suggesting the correctness of the identifier's introduction. Moreover, since most of the time one knows an individual's name from repeated exposure to the name in various contexts, the basis for knowing a name is likely to be highly reliable. Thus, it is unlikely that Alan, if he were alive, would be prohibited from testifying that a particular crew member was Bill. If it could be shown that Alan's sole basis for knowing the name was a single introduction, however, a reasonable argument for excluding the evidence could be made.

Consider which, if any, of the following pieces of evidence should be classified as hearsay if offered to prove Downy's knowledge:

(a) Sam Walsh, a mechanic at a local service station offers to testify, "On the morning of the accident I saw Tim Downy when he was purchasing gasoline at our station, and I told him that the left front tire on his car might blow at any time."

(b) Jane Corey, the owner of the service station, offers to testify, "I heard Sam Walsh tell Tim Downy that he had a bad tire."

(c) Adam Green, another mechanic at the service station, offers to testify, "I remember the morning when Sam Walsh came into the garage shaking his head and saying that he hoped Tim Downy would take his advice and not drive with a bad tire."

(d) Gloria Wilson, Downy's girlfriend, offers to testify, "Several days after the accident, Tim told me that he knew the tire was bad and that he never should have been driving on it."

(e) Frances Downy, Tim's mother, offers to testify, "Several days before the accident Tim mentioned that he wanted to have the left front tire on his car checked."

(f) Sam Walsh offers to testify, "When Tim Downy was at the service station on the morning of the accident, I heard him say 'I know the left front tire on my car is bad.'"

2. Which, if any, pieces of evidence in the preceding problem would be classified as hearsay if offered to prove that the tire on the defendant's car was bad?

3. Gary Burns has been charged with first-degree murder for killing Fred Byrd. Burns claims that he is innocent and that Byrd was his friend. His theory is that Elmer Ellis probably committed the crime. To show Ellis' dislike of Fred Byrd and possible motive for killing him, Burns offers the following evidence:

(a) W-1 offers to testify: "Several days before the killing, I heard Fred Byrd say to Elmer Ellis, 'You are the most vile person I've ever met.'"

(b) W-2 offers to testify: "One week before the killing Elmer Ellis confided to me that Fred Byrd had been blackmailing him for the last two years."

(c) W-3 offers to testify: "One week after Fred Byrd's death, Elmer Ellis said to me, 'That Fred Byrd was a real s.o.b. He deserved to die.'"

(d) W-4 offers to testify: "The day before his death, Fred Byrd told me that he had told Elmer Ellis that Ellis was the most vile person he had ever met."

(e) W-5 offers to testify: "The day before Fred Byrd was killed,

Elmer Ellis told me that Fred Byrd had said to him, 'You are the most vile person I have ever met.'"

Is any of this evidence objectionable as hearsay?

4. As Sharon Schunk, age seven, was walking home from school, she was induced by a soldier to go with him to a room where she was sexually assaulted. Following the incident, Sharon, her mother, and a police officer spent several days looking for the house to which Sharon had been taken. As a result of their investigation and Sharon's line-up identification of her assailant, Robert Bridges was charged with taking indecent liberties with a minor. Bridges, his wife, and their landlord plan to testify that they were all together at the time of the alleged crime. To help prove that Sharon had been at Bridges' apartment, the prosecution first established that Bridges resides in an apartment in a two-story brick house at 125 East Johnson street; that there are wooden steps leading up to the floor of the front porch, and that the steps are flanked by brick piers; that there are two separate entrances to the house; that the left door is an entrance to a stairway leading to Bridges' apartment; that the apartment contains a room with a bed, two dolls, an alarm clock, a radio, chest of drawers, a box, and a picture of a lady. The prosecution then offered the testimony of Sharon's mother and the police officer who conducted the investigation. Both are prepared to testify that prior to their coming upon Bridges' residence, Sharon gave the following description of the place where she was sexually assaulted: The house had gray wooden steps with bricks on the sides of the steps, and there were two doors going into the house. The room where the assault took place contained a bed, a chest of drawers, a dresser, a table with a picture of a lady on it, two dolls, and a chair by the bed with a radio and an alarm clock on it.

Should the testimony of the officer and Sharon's mother be excluded on the ground that it is hearsay?

C. *HEARSAY AND THE CONFRONTATION CLAUSE*

We are soon to consider various exceptions to and exemptions from the general prohibition against the use of hearsay evidence. Before turning to those matters though, we wish to explore briefly the extent to which the sixth amendment of the United States Constitution may provide an independent ban on the use of out-of-court statements.

The confrontation clause in the sixth amendment guarantees to criminal defendants the right "to be confronted with the witnesses against him." The meaning of this terse phrase is far from clear: There is virtually no legislative history shedding light on the framers' intent, and the words themselves are subject to a number of possible interpretations. Consider, for example, a situation in which the prosecutor wishes to introduce against the defendant some third person's hearsay statement that is not barred by the rules of evidence. Does the confrontation clause give a criminal defendant the right to confront all individuals that provide evidence against the defendant, only those individuals that happen to be available at the time of trial, or only those individuals that the prosecutor chooses to call as witnesses? If the person who made the hearsay statement also happens to be a witness, is merely having the witness in court sufficient to satisfy the confrontation clause, or must there be some meaningful opportunity to cross-examine the witness? If there is a requirement of meaningful cross-examination, is it satisfied when the prosecutor seeks to introduce a prior statement made by the witness and the witness claims to have forgotten either the events to which the statement relates or the making of the prior statement, or both? If there is a requirement for meaningful cross-examination, can it be satisfied by cross-examination or the opportunity for cross-examination at some time other than the trial—e.g., at a preliminary hearing?

In large measure because there were recognized exceptions to the hearsay rule when the Constitution was adopted, the Supreme Court has consistently taken the position that the confrontation clause does not bar the use of all hearsay against criminal defendants. The Court, however, has yet to articulate a satisfactory, comprehensive view of the relationship between the confrontation clause and the hearsay rule. What follows is a summary of and some brief comments on the Court's more important confrontation clause decisions.

1. The Early Cases

MATTOX v. UNITED STATES, 156 U.S. 237, 242-244 (1897): [Following the reversal of his first conviction, Mattox was retried for murder. At the retrial, the prosecutors introduced the transcript of testimony given by two now-deceased individuals who were witnesses as Mattox's first trial. (See FRE 804(b)(1) (former testimony exception).) The Supreme Court rejected Mattox's claim that the use of this hearsay evidence violated his sixth amendment confrontation right:]

The primary object of the constitutional provision in question was to prevent depositions or *ex parte* affidavits, such as were sometimes admitted in civil cases. . . . To say that a criminal, after having once been convicted by the testimony of a certain witness, should go scot free simply because death has closed the mouth of that witness, would be carrying his constitutional protection to an unwarrantable extent. The law in its wisdom declares that the rights of the public shall not be wholly sacrificed in order that an incidental benefit may be preserved to the accused.

We are bound to interpret the Constitution in the light of the law as it existed at the time it was adopted. . . . Many of its provisions in the nature

C. Hearsay and the Confrontation Clause

of a Bill of Rights are subject to exceptions, recognized long before the adoption of the Constitution. Such exceptions were obviously intended to be respected. . . . For instance, there could be nothing more directly contrary to the letter of the provision in question than the admission of dying declarations. [See FRE 804(b)(2) (dying declaration exception to hearsay rule).] They are rarely made in the presence of the accused; they are made without any opportunity for examination or cross-examination; nor is the witness brought face to face with the jury; yet from time immemorial they have been treated as competent testimony, and no one would have the hardihood at this day to question their admissibility. . . . [T]he sense of impending death is presumed to remove all temptation to falsehood. . . . If such declarations are admitted, because made by a person then dead, under circumstances which give his statements the same weight as if made under oath, there is equal if not greater reason for admitting testimony of his statements which were made under oath.

The substance of the constitutional protection is preserved to the prisoner in the advantage he has once had of seeing the witness face to face, and of subjecting him to the ordeal of cross-examination. This, the law says, he shall under no circumstances be deprived of.

KIRBY v. UNITED STATES, 174 U.S. 47 (1899): [The defendant was charged with receiving stolen property. To prove that the property in question was stolen, the government introduced evidence of the judgments of conviction of the individuals who stole the property. Referring again to dying declarations, the Supreme Court reaffirmed that the confrontation clause does not bar the use of all hearsay against criminal defendants. Nonetheless, the Court held use of the judgments rather than the testimony of live witnesses to prove that the property was stolen violated the defendant's sixth amendment confrontation clause right.]

2. The Emerging Right to Confrontation

There were no significant confrontation clause cases from the turn of the century until 1965. Then, within the span of a few years, it appeared that the confrontation clause had the potential for constitutionalizing much of the hearsay rule in criminal prosecutions.

POINTER v. TEXAS, 380 U.S. 400 (1965): [At the defendant's robbery trial the prosecution introduced the preliminary hearing testimony of a currently unavailable witness. Pointer had not been represented by counsel at the preliminary hearing, so one might have expected the Court to take the position that use of the preliminary hearing testimony violated Pointer's right to counsel. Instead, the Court used *Pointer* as the occasion for holding that the confrontation clause was incorporated into the fourteenth amendment and thus applicable to state as well as federal prosecutions. The Court then held that use of the preliminary hearing testimony violated the confrontation clause. In the course of its opinion, the Court reaffirmed the propriety of using dying declarations and former testimony against criminal defendants, and the Court suggested that the result in *Pointer* might have been different if the defendant had been represented by counsel who had the opportunity to cross-examine the preliminary hearing witness. The Court also observed that "a major reason underlying the constitutional confrontation rule is to give a defendant charged with crime an opportunity to cross-examine the witnesses against him." Id. at 406-407.]

DOUGLAS v. ALABAMA, 380 U.S. 415, 418, 420 (1965): [The defendant was charged with aggravated assault. A prosecution witness, Loyd, had made an earlier confession implicating both himself and the defendant. At trial, however, Loyd refused to answer any of the prosecutor's questions. Under the guise of refreshing the Loyd's memory, the prosecutor read the entire confession into the record. Technically, since the confession was not admitted into evidence, there was no denial of confrontation. Nonetheless, the Court relied on the confrontation clause to reverse the conviction. The Court stressed the probable impact of the confession on the jury and the absence of an opportunity for effective cross-examination of Loyd by the defendant. With respect to the latter point the Court observed:]

[A] primary interest secured by [the confrontation clause] is the right of cross-examination. . . .

[E]ffective confrontation of Loyd was possible only if Loyd affirmed the statement as his. However, Loyd did not do so, but . . . refuse[d] to answer.

BRUTON v. UNITED STATES, 391 U.S. 123 (1968): [Bruton and Evans were tried jointly for armed robbery. Evans did not testify, but the prosecution introduced into evidence an earlier confession by Evans that implicated both Evans and Bruton. The trial court instructed the jury that it could consider the confession as evidence against only Evans. The Supreme Court, relying in part on the probable inability of the jury to limit its consideration of the confession to Evans, held that introduction of the confession had violated Bruton's confrontation right.]

BARBER v. PAGE, 391 U.S. 719, 723-726 (1968): [Defendant and Woods were jointly charged with armed robbery by the state of Oklahoma. At the preliminary hearing Woods gave testimony that implicated the defendant. The defendant's counsel did not cross-examine Woods, although he presumably could have. Counsel for another co-defendant did cross-examine Woods. When the defendant came to trial, Woods was incarcerated in a federal prison in Texas. The prosecution introduced Woods' preliminary hearing testimony against the defendant pursuant to the state's former testimony exception. That exception, like the exception in most jurisdictions,

C. Hearsay and the Confrontation Clause

required that the hearsay declarant be unavailable. [See FRE 804(b)(1); Kirby v. United States, supra page 353.)]

... It must be acknowledged that various courts and commentators have heretofore assumed that the mere absence of a witness from the jurisdiction was sufficient ground for dispensing with confrontation on the theory that "it is impossible to compel his attendance, because the process of the trial Court is of no force without the jurisdiction, and the party desiring his testimony is therefore helpless." 5 Wigmore, Evidence §1401 (3d ed. 1940).

Whatever may have been the accuracy of that theory at one time, it is clear that at the present time increased cooperation between the States themselves and between the States and the Federal Government has largely deprived it of any continuing validity in the criminal law. For example, in the case of a prospective witness currently in federal custody, 28 U.S.C. §2241(c)(5) gives federal courts the power to issue writs of habeas corpus *ad testificandum* at the request of state prosecutorial authorities. . . . In addition, it is the policy of the United States Bureau of Prisons to permit federal prisoners to testify in state court criminal proceedings pursuant to writs of habeas corpus *ad testificandum* issued out of state courts. . . .

In this case the state authorities made no effort to avail themselves of either of the above alternative means of seeking to secure Woods' presence at petitioner's trial. . . . [A] witness is not "unavailable" for purposes of the foregoing exception to the confrontation requirement unless the prosecutorial authorities have made a good-faith effort to obtain his presence at trial. The State made no such effort here. . . .

[W]e would reach the same result on the facts of this case had petitioner's counsel actually cross-examined Woods at the preliminary hearing. . . . The right to confrontation is basically a trial right. It includes both the opportunity to cross-examine and the occasion for the jury to weigh the demeanor of the witness. A preliminary hearing is ordinarily a much less searching exploration into the merits of a case than a trial, simply because its function is the more limited one of determining whether probable cause exists to hold the accused for trial. While there may be some justification for holding that the opportunity for cross-examination of a witness at a preliminary hearing satisfies the demands of the confrontation clause where the witness is shown to be actually unavailable, this is not, as we have pointed out, such a case.

3. Retrenchment

The apparently emerging trend toward an expansive reading of the confrontation clause was short-lived. In Mancusi v. Stubbs,[52] for example, the Supreme Court limited Barber v. Page. *Stubbs* involved the defendant's second

---

52. 408 U.S. 204 (1972).

trial on a charge of murder. The prosecutor introduced into evidence testimony from the first trial of a key prosecution witness, Holms, who was then living in Sweden. Although the prosecutor had made no effort to secure Holms' attendance at trial, the Court held that use of the former testimony did not violate the confrontation clause. The Court distinguished *Barber* on two grounds: First, if Holms had refused to return voluntarily for the second trial, the prosecutor had no way force him to return. Second, because Holms was a key prosecution witness and because he had testified at the first trial rather than at a preliminary hearing, the opportunity and the incentive for cross-examination were much more substantial than they were in *Barber*; and in fact, defense counsel had cross-examined Holms at the first trial.

Consider also the following cases:

CALIFORNIA v. GREEN, 399 U.S. 149 (1970): [Defendant, Green, was charged with furnishing marijuana to a minor, Porter. Porter named Green as his supplier both in a statement made to a police officer following Porter's arrest for selling marijuana and in testimony at Green's preliminary hearing, where Porter was cross-examined extensively by Green's counsel. At trial Porter was a "markedly evasive and uncooperative" witness. He acknowledged making the prior statements and said that he was then telling the truth as he believed it to be. He also testified, however, that he had been high on LSD at the time he received the marijuana and that he could not now remember who furnished it to him. The trial court admitted for their truth both Porter's prior statement to the police officer and Porter's preliminary hearing testimony. These statements were admitted pursuant to Cal. Evid. Code §1235, which creates a hearsay exception for a witness' prior inconsistent statements. (Cf. FRE 801(d)(1)(A) (hearsay exemption for prior inconsistent statements under oath).[53]

[Green was convicted, and the Supreme Court rejected his confrontation clause claim. The Court first concluded that the purposes of confrontation—ensuring that statements are under oath, forcing the witness to submit to cross-examination, and permitting the jury to observe the witness' demeanor—are substantially satisfied when the out-of-court declarant is also available and testifying at the trial. The Court then held that, independently of the question whether Porter's presence satisfied the confrontation concerns, use of the preliminary hearing testimony did not violate the confrontation clause. The Court noted that counsel's opportunity to cross-examine Porter at the preliminary hearing was apparently no more restricted that it would have been at trial and that the evidence presumably would have been admissible if Porter had been unavailable. The Court suggested there was even less reason to exclude the statements when the declarant is present and testifying. Finally, the Court turned to the "narrow question . . . [w]hether Porter's apparent lapse of memory so affected Green's right to cross-examine

---

53. See pages 375-381 infra.

C. Hearsay and the Confrontation Clause

as to make a critical difference in the application of the Confrontation Clause in this case." Id. at 168. On that issue, the Court remanded the case.]

Green raises a host of questions and is subject to a number of different interpretations.[54] For example, how broadly should one read the portion of the opinion approving the use of the preliminary hearing testimony because of the prior opportunity for cross-examination? Is the mere opportunity for cross-examination sufficient to satisfy confrontation concerns? Is it or should it be important that defense counsel actually engage in cross-examination, as in fact Green's counsel did, at the preliminary hearing? Should it matter whether there is a strategic reason to forego cross-examination at the preliminary hearing, or is the lesson of *Green* that the proper strategy should almost always be to engage in extensive cross-examination of key prosecution witnesses? Even if there are good reasons that the Court would be willing to recognize for not engaging in extensive cross-examination at the preliminary hearing, should the combination of limited prior opportunity for cross-examination plus presence of the witness at trial be sufficient to satisfy confrontation concerns in (almost) all situations?

To the extent that Porter's presence at trial was sufficient to satisfy confrontation concerns, how important is it that Porter remembered at least making the prior statements? Consider, for example, whether confrontation concerns would have been satisfied if Porter claimed to have no present recollection of his prior statements as well as the underlying events.

If, as the Court suggested in the first part of its analysis, Porter's presence at trial was sufficient to satisfy confrontation concerns, why did the Court remand for a determination whether there had been an adequate opportunity to cross-examine Porter? What should the criteria be for making such a determination? (Nothing in the Court's opinion addresses this question.)

Consider the extent to which the ensuing cases shed light on the foregoing questions.

NELSON v. O'NEIL, 402 U.S. 622, 624-630 (1971): [The respondent, O'Neil, and Runnels were charged with kidnapping, robbery, and vehicle theft. At their joint trial the prosecutor introduced into evidence a confession made by Runnels that implicated both him and the respondent.] The trial judge . . . instructed the jury that it could not consider [the confession as evidence] against the respondent. When Runnels took the stand in his own defense, he was asked on direct examination whether he had made the statement, and he flatly denied having done so. He also vigorously asserted that the substance of the statement imputed to him was false. He was then intensively cross-examined by the prosecutor, but stuck to his story in every

---

54. See Graham, The Right of Confrontation and Rules of Evidence: Sir Walter Raleigh Rides Again, 9 Alaska L.J. (1971).

particular. The respondent's counsel did not cross-examine Runnels, although he was, of course, fully free to do so. . . .

The jury found both defendants guilty as charged. The Supreme Court rejected O'Neil's confrontation clause claim, which he based on Bruton v. United States, supra page 354.]

. . . In *Bruton* . . . we held that . . . a cautionary instruction to the jury is not an adequate protection for the defendant where the co-defendant does not take the witness stand. . . .

It was clear in *Bruton* that the "confrontation" guaranteed by the sixth and fourteenth amendments is a confrontation *at trial*—that is, that the absence of the defendant at the time the codefendant allegedly made the out-of-court statement is immaterial, so long as the declarant can be cross-examined on the witness stand at trial. This was confirmed in California v. Green, 399 U.S. 149 [(1970)], where we said that "[v]iewed historically . . . there is good reason to conclude that the Confrontation Clause is not violated by admitting a declarant's out-of-court statements, as long as the declarant is testifying as a witness and subject to full and effective cross-examination." Id. at 158. Moreover, "where the declarant is not absent, but is present to testify and to submit to cross-examination, our cases, if anything, support the conclusion that the admission of his out-of-court statements does not create a confrontation problem." Id. at 162. This is true, of course, even though the declarant's out-of-court statement is hearsay as to the defendant, so that its admission against him, in the absence of a cautionary instruction, would be reversible error under state law. The Constitution as construed in *Bruton*, in other words, is violated *only* where the out-of-court hearsay statement is that of a declarant who is unavailable at the trial for "full and effective" cross-examination.

The question presented by this case, then, is whether cross-examination can be full and effective where the declarant is present at trial, takes the witness stand, testifies fully as to his activities during the period described in his alleged out-of-court statement, but denies that he made the statement and claims that its substance is false.

[T]he Court of Appeals relied heavily on the dictum of this Court in Douglas v. Alabama, 380 U.S. 415, 420 [(1965)], that "effective confrontation" of a witness who has allegedly made an out-of-court statement implicating the defendant "was possible only if [the witness] affirmed the statement as his." . . . In *Douglas* and *Bruton* . . . there was in fact no question of the effect of an affirmance or denial of the incriminating statement, since the witness or codefendant was in each case totally unavailable. . . .

Had Runnels in this case "affirmed the statement as his," the respondent would certainly have been in far worse straits than those in which he found himself. . . . For then counsel for the respondent could only have attempted to show through cross-examination that Runnels had confessed to a crime he had not committed, or, slightly more plausibly, that those parts of the confession implicating the respondent were fabricated. . . . To be sure,

C. Hearsay and the Confrontation Clause 359

Runnels might have "affirmed the statement" but denied its truthfulness, claiming, for example, that it had been coerced, or made as part of a plea bargain. But cross-examination by the respondent's counsel would have been futile in that event as well. For once Runnels had testified that the statement was false, it could hardly have profited the respondent for his counsel through cross-examination to try to shake that testimony. . . .

Do you agree that O'Neil would have been "in far worse straits" if Runnels had admitted making the statement but claimed that it was false? In that situation, it would at least have been possible for the jury to assess the likelihood that the repudiation was honest in light of the explanation for the repudiation. By contrast, when Runnels denied making the statement, is it not likely that, in the jurors' minds, the question is whether to believe Runnels or the police officer who testified about Runnels' alleged confession? And if the case, as a practical matter, turns on a swearing context between a criminal defendant and a police officer, is it not clear whom the jury is likely to believe?

Even if O'Neil was in a less advantageous position because Runnels denied making the statement, should it follow that the admission of Runnels' confession violated O'Neil's confrontation right?

DUTTON v. EVANS, 400 U.S. 74, 77, 88-89 (1970): [Justice Stewart announced the Court's judgment in a plurality opinion joined by Chief Justice Burger and Justices White and Blackmun. Evans, along with Truett and Williams, was charged with murdering three police officers in Gwinnett County, Georgia. Truett was granted immunity and became the principal prosecution witness in Evans' trial. There were 19 other prosecution witnesses, one of whom was Shaw.] He testified that he and Williams had been fellow prisoners in the federal penitentiary in Atlanta, Georgia, at the time Williams was brought to Gwinnett County to be arraigned on the charges of murdering the police officers. Shaw said that when Williams was returned to the penitentiary from the arraignment, he had asked Williams: "How did you make out in court?" and that Williams had responded, "If it hadn't been for that dirty son-of-a-bitch Alex Evans, we wouldn't be in this now." Defense counsel's objection to the testimony on hearsay and confrontation grounds was overruled.

[Evans was convicted of murder. The basis for admitting Shaw's testimony was the state co-conspirator admission exception to the hearsay rule. (See FRE 801(d)(2)(E).) One of the standard requirements for this exception is that the statements be made during the course of the conspiracy, and in applying this requirement most jurisdictions take the position that the arrest of the conspirators terminates the conspiracy. In Georgia, however, the exception extends to the concealment phase of the conspiracy, and the

Georgia courts took the position that the concealment was continuing at the time of Williams' alleged statement.]

Evans was not deprived of any right of confrontation on the issue of whether Williams actually made the statement related by Shaw. Neither a hearsay nor a confrontation question would arise had Shaw's testimony been used to prove merely that the statement had been made. . . .

The confrontation issue arises because the jury was being invited to infer that Williams had implicitly identified Evans as the perpetrator of the murder when he blamed Evans for his predicament. But we conclude that there was no denial of the right of confrontation as to this question of identity. First, the statement contained no express assertion about past fact, and consequently it carried on its face a warning to the jury against giving the statement undue weight. Second, Williams' personal knowledge of the identity and role of the other participants in the triple murder is abundantly established by Truett's testimony and by Williams' prior conviction. It is inconceivable that cross-examination could have shown that Williams was not in a position to know whether or not Evans was involved in the murder. Third, the possibility that Williams' statement was founded on faulty recollection is remote in the extreme. Fourth, the circumstances under which Williams made the statement were such as to give reason to suppose that Williams did not misrepresent Evans' involvement in the crime. These circumstances go beyond a showing that Williams had no apparent reason to lie to Shaw. His statement was spontaneous, and it was against his penal interest to make it. These are indicia of reliability which have been widely viewed as determinative of whether a statement may be placed before the jury though there is no confrontation of the declarant. [See FRE 803(1), (2); FRE 804(b)(3).]

The decisions of this Court make it clear that the mission of the Confrontation Clause is to advance a practical concern for the accuracy of the truth-determining process in criminal trials by assuring that "the trier of fact [has] a satisfactory basis for evaluating the truth of the prior statement." California v. Green, 399 U.S. at 161. Evans exercised, and exercised effectively, his right to confrontation on the factual question whether Shaw had actually heard Williams make the statement Shaw related.[18] And the possibility that cross-examination of Williams could conceivably have shown the jury that the statement, though made, might have been unreliable was wholly unreal.

In portions of the plurality opinion not reproduced here, Justice Stewart stressed that the testimony about Williams' alleged statement was not critical evidence, and Chief Justice Burger and Justice Blackmun, who joined in

18. [The] cross-examination [of Shaw] was such as to cast serious doubt on Shaw's credibility and, more particularly, on whether the conversation which Shaw related ever took place.

C. Hearsay and the Confrontation Clause

the plurality opinion, maintained in a separate opinion that an alternative ground for disposing of the case was that any error was harmless.

What is the relationship between Barber v. Page (which had not yet been limited by *Stubbs*) and the *Evans* plurality view of the confrontation clause? More specifically, to what extent do the non-critical nature of the hearsay evidence and/or the indicia that the hearsay is reliable relieve the prosecutor of the obligation to make a good faith effort to produce live witnesses?

Justice Harlan concurred in the *Evans* judgment on the ground—espoused by Wigmore—that the primary objective of the confrontation clause is to guarantee to the defendant the right to confront and cross-examine those witnesses that the prosecutor chooses to call:

> The conversion of a clause intended to regulate trial procedure into a threat to much of the existing law of evidence and to future developments in that field is not an unnatural shift, for the paradigmatic evil the Confrontation Clause was aimed at—trial by affidavit—can be viewed almost equally well as a gross violation of the rule against hearsay and as the giving of evidence by the affiant out of the presence of the accused and not subject to cross-examination. But however natural the shift may be, once made it carries the seeds of great mischief for enlightened development in the law of evidence. . . .
>
> Nor am I now content with the position I took in concurrence in California v. Green, [399 U.S. 149 (1970)], that the Confrontation Clause was designed to establish a preferential rule, requiring the prosecutor to avoid the use of hearsay where it is reasonably possible for him to do so—in other words, to produce available witnesses. . . .
>
> A rule requiring production of available witnesses would significantly curtail development of the law of evidence to eliminate the necessity for production of declarants where production would be unduly inconvenient and of small utility to a defendant. Examples which come to mind are . . . the exceptions to the hearsay rule for [business records,] official statements, learned treatises, and trade reports. . . . If the hearsay exception involved in a given case is such as to commend itself to reasonable men, production of the declarant is likely to be difficult, unavailing, or pointless. In unusual cases . . . the Sixth Amendment guarantees federal and state defendants the right of compulsory process to obtain the presence of witnesses.
>
> [F]ederal and state trials . . . must be conducted in accordance with due process of law. It is by this standard that I would test federal and state rules of evidence. [400 U.S. at 94-97.]

In his *Green* concurrence, Justice Harlan specifically repudiated the Wigmore view, which he subsequently adopted in *Evans*:

> Wigmore's reading would have the practical consequence of rendering meaningless what was assuredly in some sense meant to be an enduring guarantee. It is inconceivable that if the Framers intended to constitutionalize a rule of

hearsay they would have licensed the judiciary to read it out of existence by creating new and unlimited exceptions. [399 U.S. at 179.]

Which of Justice Harlan's views is the more compelling?

OHIO v. ROBERTS, 448 U.S. 56, 58-59, 65-68, 70, 72-73 (1980): [Respondent] Roberts was charged with forgery of a check in the name of Bernard Isaacs, and with possession of stolen credit cards belonging to Isaacs and his wife Amy.

[At the preliminary hearing Roberts' counsel called] the Isaacs' daughter, Anita, . . . as the defense's only witness. . . . Defense counsel questioned Anita at some length and attempted to elicit from her an admission that she had given respondent the checks and the credit cards without informing him that she did not have permission to use them. Anita, however, denied this.

[F]ive subpoenas for four different trial dates were issued to Anita at her parents' Ohio residence. . . . She was not at the residence when these were executed. She did not telephone and she did not appear at trial.

[At trial Roberts testified that Anita had given him her parents' check book and credit cards with the understanding that he could use them. In rebuttal the prosecution offered the transcript of Anita's preliminary hearing testimony. To determine whether Anita was unavailable, the trial court conducted a voir dire hearing, at which Anita's mother, Amy, was the sole witness. Amy testified that Anita left for Arizona shortly after the preliminary hearing, that she had talked to Amy only twice since then, and that on the last occasion (seven months before trial) Anita said she would be traveling. Amy knew no way to reach her daughter and knew of nobody who knew where she was. The trial court admitted the transcript into evidence, and Roberts was convicted.]

The Confrontation Clause operates in two separate ways to restrict the range of admissible hearsay. First, in conformity with the Framers' preference for face-to-face accusation, the Sixth Amendment establishes a rule of necessity. In the usual case (including cases where prior cross-examination has occurred), the prosecution must either produce, or demonstrate the unavailability of, the declarant whose statement it wishes to use against the defendant. . . .

The second aspect operates once a witness is shown to be unavailable. Reflecting its underlying purpose to augment accuracy in the factfinding process by ensuring the defendant an effective means to test adverse evidence, the Clause countenances only hearsay marked with such trustworthiness that "there is no material departure from the reason of the general rule." Snyder v. Massachusetts, 291 U.S. [97, 107 (1934)]. . . .

The Court has applied this "indicia of reliability" requirement principally by concluding that certain hearsay exceptions rest upon such solid foundations that admission of virtually any evidence within them comports with the "substances of the constitutional protection." Mattox v. United

C. Hearsay and the Confrontation Clause 363

States, 156 U.S. [237, 244 (1895)]. . . . [When the evidence does not fall within a firmly rooted hearsay exception,] the evidence must be excluded, at least absent a showing of particularized guarantees of trustworthiness.

[The Court concluded that the unavailability requirement was satisfied.]

We turn . . . to [the question] whether Anita Isaacs' prior testimony at the preliminary hearing bore sufficient "indicia of reliability.". . .

[California v. Green, 399 U.S. 149 (1970), suggests] that the *opportunity* to cross-examine at a preliminary hearing—even absent actual cross-examination—satisfies the Confrontation Clause. Yet the record showed, and the Court recognized, that defense counsel in fact had cross-examined Porter at the earlier proceeding. . . .

We need not decide whether . . . the mere opportunity for cross-examination rendered the prior testimony admissible. . . . Nor need we decide whether *de minimis* questioning is sufficient, for defense counsel in this case tested Anita's testimony with the equivalent of significant cross-examination. . . .

We are also unpersuaded that *Green* is distinguishable on the ground that Anita Isaacs—unlike the declarant Porter in *Green*—was not personally available for questioning *at trial*. . . .

Finally, we reject respondent's attempt to fall back on general principles of confrontation, and his argument that this case falls among those in which the Court must undertake a particularized search for "indicia of reliability." . . . Anita, respondent says, had every reason to lie to avoid prosecution or parental reprobation. Her unknown whereabouts is explicable as an effort to avoid punishment, perjury, or self-incrimination. Given these facts, her prior testimony falls on the unreliable side, and should have been excluded.

In making this argument, respondent in effect asks us to disassociate preliminary hearing testimony previously subjected to cross-examination from previously cross-examined prior-trial testimony, which the Court has deemed generally immune from subsequent confrontation attack. Precedent requires us to decline this invitation. In *Green* the Court found guarantees of trustworthiness in the accouterments of the preliminary hearing itself; there was no mention of the inherent reliability or unreliability of Porter and his story. . . .

In sum, we perceive no reason to resolve the reliability issue differently here than the Court did in *Green*. "Since there was an adequate opportunity to cross-examine [the witness], and counsel . . . availed himself of that opportunity, the transcript . . . bore sufficient 'indicia of reliability' and afforded '"the trier of fact a satisfactory basis for evaluating the truth of the prior statement."'" [Mancusi v. Stubbs,] 408 U.S. [204, 216 (1972)].

Roberts is a notable decision because the Court set forth some broad guidelines for resolving confrontation clause problems. First, *Roberts* seems to establish the general proposition that the hearsay declarant must be either unavailable within the meaning of *Barber/Stubbs/Roberts* or present and testifying in court. Second, according to *Roberts*, if the hearsay declarant is unavailable, the hearsay must carry with it sufficient "indicia of reliability." There are apparently three ways of satisfying this second requirement. First, one can establish that the hearsay falls within a traditional hearsay exception. Second, one can demonstrate that the circumstances surrounding the making of the statement suggest that it is a sincere, accurate account of the events it relates. (See, e.g., the Court's discussion of the probable reliability of Williams' statement in Dutton v. Evans.) Third, one can show that the defendant subjected (or perhaps could have subjected) the hearsay declarant to cross-examination at the time the statement was made.

As we shall see, the traditional hearsay exceptions are based in large measure on the premise that the circumstances under which the hearsay statements were made tend to ensure their reliability. Thus, the first two methods of satisfying the "indicia" requirement are similar in that they suggest that the hearsay statement is accurate. The mere fact that a statement was subjected to earlier cross-examination does not, as the defendant in *Roberts* argued, necessarily guarantee that the statement is accurate. There has already been one opportunity to challenge the statement through cross-examination, however. If that opportunity was exercised with some degree of success, the defendant can introduce the cross-examination testimony to cast doubt on the prosecutor's hearsay evidence. On the other hand, if the cross-examination was unsuccessful in shaking the witness' story, it is arguably reasonable to assume that cross-examination at trial would be similarly unsuccessful. In any event, if the choice is between foregoing evidence altogether or admitting statements of a now unavailable witness whom the defendant once subjected to cross-examination, a decision to admit the evidence is arguably appropriate.

Despite the benefit of having a general framework for resolving confrontation clause issues, *Roberts* and the Court's earlier cases still leave a number of questions unsettled:

1. Particularly in light of Mancusi v. Stubbs, (page 355 supra), it is not clear how much of an effort or what kind of a showing the prosecutor must make to satisfy the unavailability requirement.
2. In *Roberts*, the Court expressed reservations about the broad dictum in *Green* that mere opportunity for cross-examination at a preliminary hearing was sufficient to satisfy the "indicia of reliability" requirement. It is not clear, however, when or whether *de minimis* cross-examination or the mere opportunity to cross-examine will suffice to satisfy the "indicia of reliability" requirement.
3. It is not clear how broadly one should read *Roberts'* "unavailable or present and testifying" requirement. As Justice Harlan pointed out in his *Green* concurrence, a number of traditional hearsay exceptions such as business records or trade reports do not, as a

C. Hearsay and the Confrontation Clause

matter of evidence law, require that the declarant be unavailable or present and testifying. The Court has not suggested that use of these exceptions against criminal defendants would violate the confrontation clause. Moreover, Dutton v. Evans suggests that either strong indicia of reliability or the non-critical nature of the hearsay or some combination of both may warrant dispensing with the unavailability requirement. For more on the unavailability requirement, see United States v. Inadi, page 366 infra.

4. Assuming that there is an unavailable or present and testifying requirement, it is not clear under what circumstances the presence of the hearsay declarant during the trial will be insufficient to satisfy the confrontation clause. Recall that in *Green* the Court remanded the case on the question "[w]hether Porter's apparent lapse of memory so affected Green's right to cross-examine as to make a critical difference in the application of the Confrontation Clause in this case." 399 U.S. at 168. How, in terms of the *Roberts* framework for analyzing confrontation cases should one approach the question upon which *Green* was remanded? Is memory lapse a kind of unavailability that requires an assessment of the second part of the *Roberts* test—indicia of reliability? Or does one apply a wholly different type of analysis to a present but forgetful witness? If so, what are the relevant criteria? See United States v. Owens, page 368 infra.

DELAWARE v. FENSTERER, 474 U.S. 15, 16-17, 20-24 (1985): Respondent was convicted of murdering his fiance, Stephanie Ann Swift. The State's case . . . proceeded on the theory that respondent had strangled Swift with a cat leash. To establish that the cat leash was the murder weapon, the State [introduced the testimony of an expert witness, Robillard, who testified that two hairs found on the cat leash were similar to Swift's hair and that the hairs had been forcibly removed.]

[Robillard] explained that, in his opinion, there are three methods of determining whether a hair has been forcibly removed [one of which is the presence of the follicular tag on the hair.] . . . However, Robillard went on to say that "I have reviewed my notes, and I have no specific knowledge as to the particular way that I determined the hair was forcibly removed other than the fact that one of those hairs was forcibly removed.". . . On cross-examination, Agent Robillard was again unable to recall which method he had employed. . . . He also explained that what he meant by "forcibly removed" was no more than that the hair could have been removed by as little force as is entailed in " 'brushing your hand through your head or brushing your hair.' " . . .

The defense offered its own expert in hair analysis. [The defense expert agreed that the hairs from the leash were similar to the victim's hair and that one of the hairs had a follicular tag. He further testified that in a telephone conversation Robillard had said that he based his forcible removal conclusion on the presence of the follicular tag. Finally, the defense expert stated that there is no adequate scientific basis for concluding that the presence of the follicular tag indicates forcible removal of the hair.]

We need not decide whether there are circumstances in which a witness' lapse of memory may so frustrate any opportunity for cross-examination that admission of the witness' direct testimony violates the Confrontation Clause. In this case, defense counsel's cross-examination of Agent Robillard demonstrated to the jury that Robillard could not even recall the theory on which his opinion was based. Moreover, through its own expert witness, the defense was able to suggest to the jury that Robillard had relied on a theory which the defense expert considered baseless. The Confrontation Clause certainly requires no more than this.

[California v. Green, 399 U.S. 149 (1970),] lends no support to respondent. . . .

[T]he question raised but not resolved in *Green* . . . arises only where a "prior statement," not itself subjected to cross-examination and the other safeguards of testimony at trial, is admitted as substantive evidence. Since there is no such out-of-court statement in this case, the adequacy of a later opportunity to cross examine, as a substitute for cross-examination at the time the declaration was made, is not in question here.

. . . The Confrontation Clause includes no guarantee that every witness called by the prosecution will refrain from giving testimony that is marred by forgetfulness, confusion, or evasion. To the contrary, the Confrontation Clause is generally satisfied when the defense is given a full and fair opportunity to probe and expose these infirmities through cross-examination, thereby calling to the attention of the factfinder the reasons for giving scant weight to the witness' testimony.

[In a concurring opinion Justice Stevens observed:] . . . I find the issue much closer to the question reserved in California v. Green. . . . The question reserved in *Green* concerned the admissibility of an earlier out-of-court statement by the witness Porter of which Porter disclaimed any present recollection at the time of trial. The question decided by the Court today concerns the admissibility of an earlier out-of-court conclusion reached by a witness who disclaims any present recollection of the *basis* for that conclusion.

UNITED STATES v. INADI, 475 U.S. 387, 394-399 (1986): [Inadi was convicted of conspiring to manufacture and distribute illegal drugs. The trial judge, over Inadi's objection, permitted the prosecutor to introduce into evidence the out-of-court statements of various non-testifying co-conspirators. The statements were introduced pursuant to the co-conspirator admission provision, FRE 801(d)(2)(E), without any showing that the co-conspirators were unavailable. The court of appeals, relying on Ohio v. Roberts, reversed Inadi's conviction on the ground that the admission of the co-conspirators'

C. Hearsay and the Confrontation Clause 367

statements without establishing the co-conspirators' unavailability violated the confrontation clause. The Supreme Court reversed.]

Roberts must be read consistently with the question it answered, the authority it cited, and its own facts. All of these indicate that *Roberts* simply reaffirmed a longstanding rule . . . that applies unavailability analysis to prior testimony. *Roberts* cannot fairly be read to stand for the radical proposition that no out-of-court statement can be introduced by the government without a showing that the declarant is unavailable. . . .

There are good reasons why the unavailability rule, developed in cases involving former testimony, is not applicable to co-conspirators' out-of-court statements. Unlike some other exceptions to the hearsay rule, or the exemption from the hearsay definition involved in this case, former testimony often is only a weaker substitute for live testimony. It seldom has independent evidentiary significance of its own, but is intended to replace live testimony. If the declarant is available and the same information can be presented to the trier of fact in the form of live testimony, with full cross-examination and the opportunity to view the demeanor of the declarant, there is little justification for relying on the weaker version. When two versions of the same evidence are available, longstanding principles of the law of hearsay, applicable as well to Confrontation Clause analysis, favor the better evidence. . . . But if the declarant is unavailable, no "better" version of the evidence exists, and the former testimony may be admitted as a substitute for live testimony on the same point.

Those same principles do not apply to co-conspirator statements. Because they are made while the conspiracy is in progress, such statements provide evidence of the conspiracy's context that cannot be replicated, even if the declarant testifies to the same matters in court. . . . Conspirators are likely to speak differently when talking to each other in furtherance of their illegal aims than when testifying on the witness stand. Even when the declarant takes the stand, his in-court testimony seldom will reproduce a significant portion of the evidentiary value of his statements during the course of the conspiracy.

In addition, the relative positions of the parties will have changed substantially between the time of the statements and the trial. The declarant and the defendant will have changed from partners in an illegal conspiracy to suspects or defendants in a criminal trial, each with information potentially damaging to the other. The declarant himself may be facing indictment or trial, in which case he has little incentive to aid the prosecution, and yet will be equally wary of coming to the aid of his former partners in crime. In that situation, it is extremely unlikely that in-court testimony will recapture the evidentiary significance of statements made when the conspiracy was operating in full force.

[C]o-conspirator statements derive much of their value from the fact that they are made in a context very different from trial, and therefore are usually irreplaceable as substantive evidence. . . . The admission of co-conspirators' declarations into evidence thus actually furthers the "Confrontation Clause's very mission" which is to "advance 'the accuracy of the truth-determining process in criminal trials.' " Tennessee v. Street, 471 U.S. 409, 415 (1985), quoting Dutton v. Evans, 400 U.S. 74, 89 (1970). . . .[3]

There appears to be little, if any, benefit to be accomplished by the Court of Appeals' unavailability rule. First, if the declarant either is unavailable, or is available and produced by the prosecution, the statements can be introduced into evidence. Thus, the unavailability rule cannot be defended as a constitutional "better evidence" rule, because it does not actually serve to exclude anything, unless the prosecution makes the mistake of not producing an otherwise available witness. . . .

Second, an unavailability rule is not likely to produce much testimony that adds anything to the "truth-determining process" over and above what would be produced without such a rule. Dutton [v. Evans, 400 U.S. 74, 89 (1970)]. Some of the available declarants already will have been subpoenaed by the prosecution or the defense, regardless of any Confrontation Clause requirements. Presumably only those declarants that neither side believes will be particularly helpful will not have been subpoenaed as witnesses. . . ."[11]

While the benefits seem slight, the burden imposed by the Court of Appeals' unavailability rule is significant. A constitutional rule requiring a determination of availability every time the prosecution seeks to introduce a co-conspirator's declaration automatically adds another avenue of appellate review in these complex cases. The co-conspirator rule apparently is the most frequently used exception to the hearsay rule. See 4 D. Louisell & C. Mueller, Federal Evidence §427, p.331 (1980). A rule that required each invocation of Rule 801(d)(2)(E) to be accompanied by a decision on the declarant's availability would impose a substantial burden on the entire criminal justice system.

Moreover, an unavailability rule places a significant practical burden on the prosecution. In every case involving co-conspirator statements, the prosecution would be required to identify with specificity each declarant, locate those declarants, and then endeavor to ensure their continuing availability for trial. . . .

---

3. The reliability of the out-of-court statements is not at issue in this case. The Court of Appeals determined that whether or not the statements are reliable, their admission violated the Sixth Amendment because the Government did not show that the declarant was unavailable to testify. . . . The sole issue before the Court is whether that decision was correct.

11. In addition to the reasons mentioned in the text why an unavailability rule would be of little value, many co-conspirator statements are not introduced to prove the truth of the matter asserted, and thus do not come within the traditional definition of hearsay, even without the special exemption of Federal Rule of Evidence 801(d)(2)(E). . . . We explained just last Term that admission of non-hearsay "raises no confrontation Clause concerns." Tennessee v. Street, 471 U.S. 409, 414 (1985). Cross-examination regarding such statements would contribute nothing to Confrontation Clause interests.

C. Hearsay and the Confrontation Clause

LEE v. ILLINOIS, 476 U.S. 530 (1986): [In a bench trial the judge relied in part on the confession of a non-testifying co-defendant to find the defendant guilty of murder. The Supreme Court held that use of the co-defendant's confession violated the defendant's sixth amendment confrontation clause right. Citing *Douglas*, page 354 supra and *Bruton*, page 354 supra, the Court observed that a co-defendant's confession is presumptively unreliable and held that there were not sufficient indicia of reliability in the present case to overcome the presumption.]

UNITED STATES v. OWENS, 108 S. Ct. 838, 840-843 (1988): On April 12, 1982, John Foster, a correctional counselor at the federal prison in Lompoc, California, was attacked and brutally beaten with a metal pipe. His skull was fractured, and he remained hospitalized for almost a month. As a result of his injuries, Foster's memory was severely impaired. When Thomas Mansfield, an FBI agent investigating the assault, first attempted to interview Foster, on April 19, he found Foster lethargic and unable to remember his attacker's name. On May 5, Mansfield again spoke to Foster, who was much improved and able to describe the attack. Foster named respondent as his attacker and identified respondent from an array of photographs.

Respondent was tried [and convicted of] assault with intent to commit murder. . . . At trial Foster recounted his activities just before the attack, and described feeling the blows to his head and seeing blood on the floor. He testified that he clearly remembered identifying respondent as his assailant during his May 5th interview with Mansfield. On cross-examination, he admitted that he could not remember seeing his assailant. He also admitted that, although there was evidence that he had received numerous visitors in the hospital, he was unable to remember any of them except Mansfield, and could not remember whether any of these visitors had suggested that respondent was the assailant. . . .

In California v. Green, 399 U.S. 149, 157-164 (1970), . . . we declined . . . to decide the admissibility of [a] witness's out-of-court statement to a police officer concerning events that at trial he was unable to recall. . . .

Here that question is squarely presented. . . . As [Delaware v. Fensterer, 474 U.S. 15 (1985),] demonstrates, [the] opportunity [for effective cross-examination] is not denied when a witness testifies as to his current belief but is unable to recollect the reason for that belief. It is sufficient that the defendant has the opportunity to bring out such matters as the witness's bias, his lack of care and attentiveness, his poor eyesight, and even (what is often a prime objective of cross-examination. . .) the very fact that he has a bad memory. If the ability to inquire into these matters suffices to establish the constitutionally requisite opportunity for cross-examination when a witness testifies as to his current belief, the basis for which he cannot recall, we see no reason why it should not suffice when the witness's past belief is introduced and he is unable to recollect the reason for that past belief. In both cases the foundation for the belief (current or past) cannot effectively be elicited, but other means of impugning the belief are available. Indeed, if there is any difference in persuasive impact between the statement "I believe this to be the man who assaulted me, but can't remember why" and the statement "I don't know whether this is the man who assaulted me, but I told the police I believed so earlier," the former would seem, if anything, more damaging and hence give rise to a greater need for memory-testing, if that is to be considered essential to an opportunity for effective cross-examination. We conclude with respect to this latter example, as we did in *Fensterer* with respect to the former, that it is not. The weapons available to impugn the witness's statement when memory loss is asserted will of course not always achieve success, but successful cross-examination is not the constitutional guarantee. They are, however, realistic weapons, as is demonstrated by defense counsel's summation in this very case, which emphasized Foster's memory loss and argued that his identification of respondent was the result of the suggestions of people who visited him in the hospital.

. . . The dangers associated with hearsay inspired the Court of Appeals in the present case to believe that the Constitution required the testimony to be examined for "indicia of reliability," Dutton v. Evans, 400 U.S. 74 (1970), or "particularized guarantees of trustworthiness," [Ohio v.] Roberts, [448 U.S. 56, 66 (1980)]. We do not think such an inquiry is called for when a hearsay declarant is present at trial and subject to unrestricted cross-examination. In that situation, as the Court recognized in *Green*, the traditional protections of the oath, cross-examination, and opportunity for the jury to observe the witness's demeanor satisfy the constitutional requirements. . . . We do not think that a constitutional line drawn by the Confrontation Clause falls between a forgetful witness's live testimony that he once believed this defendant to be the perpetrator of the crime, and the introduction of the witness's earlier statement to that effect.

As you will see when we turn to the exceptions to the hearsay rule, loss of memory is one of the things that satisfies the unavailability requirement for those hearsay exceptions that require unavailability. Why should Foster's memory loss not result in his being regarded as "unavailable" for the purposes of the confrontation clause analysis? Presumably if Foster had died, he would have been considered unavailable, and Foster's statement would have been admissible only if it satisfied the "indicia of reliability" test. Was defense counsel in any better position in *Owens* because "Foster survived the beating [but] his memory . . . did not"? 108 S. Ct. 845 (Brennan, J., dissenting).

In all of the pre-*Owens* cases in which the Court had rejected the defendant's confrontation clause challenge and the hearsay declarant had not been a witness, there had been either (1) an extensive prior examination of the hearsay declarant or (2) some reason to believe that the hearsay declaration was sincere and accurate (thereby reducing the need for cross-

C. Hearsay and the Confrontation Clause

examination). In the cases prior to *Owens* in which the Court had rejected the defendant's confrontation clause challenge and the hearsay declarant had been a witness, the Court had relied or could have relied on more than the mere availability of the declarant for cross-examination to reject the confrontation clause challenge. For example:

(a) In Nelson v. O'Neil, the witness was not forgetful, and there was a thorough questioning to which the witness was responsive about both the alleged prior statement and the underlying events.

(b) In California v. Green, Porter's statement to the police officer, like Williams' statement to a fellow inmate in Dutton v. Evans, was not likely to be inaccurate because of faulty memory or perceptions, unless perhaps Porter had been under the influence of LSD, as he claimed at trial. His assertion about LSD, however, was itself fully subject to exploration at trial. If the jury believed the LSD story, they presumably would be appropriately skeptical about Porter's earlier statements. There is, of course, the possibility that Porter's earlier statement was a lie, and, unlike the situation in *Evans*, there do not appear to be any circumstantial guarantees that Porter's statement was sincere. There was, however, an opportunity for the jury to get a sense of Porter's general sincerity, and cross-examination rarely exposes out-and-out lies in any event.

(c) In Delaware v. Fensterer, there was no suggestion that the expert witness was dishonest or had in any way tampered with or not actually examined the hairs found on the leash. Rather, the direct and cross-examination fully exposed the expert's forgetfulness and left it for the jurors to decide whether the forgetfulness was reasonable or a sign of ineptitude that should lead them to discount the expert's opinion.

By contrast, there is almost nothing except the physical presence of the witness to overcome the confrontation challenge in *Owens*. There admittedly is no reason to doubt the reality of Foster's memory loss, and there is no particular reason to question Foster's sincerity either at the time of trial or at the time of the earlier identification. There are, however, substantial perception and memory questions surrounding the earlier identification. Perhaps if Foster had not lost his memory, he would have identified Owens at trial and successfully withstood the defense counsel's cross-examination. We cannot even reasonably speculate that that would have been the case though. There are no "indicia of reliability" in the circumstances in which the prior identification was made to suggest the accuracy at that time of Foster's perception and memory; and except for the speculation that some unidentified person may have suggested to Foster that Owens was the assailant, there is nothing in the cross-examination itself to give the jury any kind of a sense of the accuracy of Foster's perception and memory when he made the identification.

The Supreme Court has never formally adopted the Wigmore-Harlan view that the confrontation clause guarantees a criminal defendant the right to confront and cross-examine only those witnesses that the prosecutor chooses to call. Are *Inadi* and *Owens* perhaps first steps in that direction?

D. EXEMPTIONS FROM THE DEFINITION OF HEARSAY

The Federal Rules classify two types of out-of-court declarations that may be offered for their truth as exemptions from the definition of hearsay, see FRE 801(d), rather than as exceptions to the hearsay rule, see FRE 803, 804. They are certain prior statements of a witness and "admissions" of a party opponent. Functionally, there is no difference between an FRE 801(d) exemption and an FRE 803 or FRE 804 exception.[55] We treat the exemptions separately here only as a matter of organizational convenience.

It is unclear why the drafters of the Federal Rules created both exemptions and exceptions. Perhaps they had in mind the following rationale: Most hearsay exceptions are based at least in part on the premise that the circumstances in which the declaration was made tend to minimize the likelihood of a serious problem with respect to one or more of the hearsay dangers. Thus, there is in theory less reason for concern about the absence of cross-examination. By contrast, there is little or nothing inherent in the circumstances that give rise to prior statements or admissions that would tend to ensure the trustworthiness of the declarations. In the case of prior statements, however, there is an opportunity for delayed cross-examination at the trial or hearing at which the prior statement is offered; and in the case of admissions of a party opponent, the party can take the stand and be subjected to direct and cross-examination.

One must be careful not to press this rationale too far. Only some prior statements of a witness fall within the Federal Rules hearsay exemption, and the restrictions on the use of prior statements for their truth appear to rest in part on general trustworthiness concerns—a rationale underlying the hearsay *exceptions*; and as we shall see, the opportunity for a party to take the witness stand and explain fully any prior statement is not a sufficient justification for the vicarious admission provisions.

As you examine the various hearsay exemptions and exceptions, keep in mind that an out-of-court statement may sometimes be potentially admissible pursuant to more than one exemption or exception. For example, the former grand jury testimony of a party-witness could be admissible against the party as an admission (FRE 801(d)(2)(A)) or as a prior inconsistent state-

---

55. But see page 386 n.75 infra.

D. Exemptions from the Definition of Hearsay

ment under oath (FRE 801(d)(1)(A)); a document may qualify for admission as past recollection recorded (FRE 803(5)) or as a business record (FRE 803(6)). When this is the case, it is sufficient to overcome a hearsay objection to show that the evidence falls within one exemption or exception. Similarly, except in one context that we will consider later,[56] the fact that evidence does *not* fit within a particular exemption or exception is not a good reason for sustaining a hearsay objection if there is some exemption or exception that is applicable to the evidence.[57]

1. Prior Statements of a Witness Generally

Although prior statements of a witness offered for their truth have traditionally been regarded as hearsay,[58] there are at least three reasons why one might want to admit a witness' prior statement to prove the truth of the statement. First, the witness is currently under oath and subject to cross-examination, and the jury will have an opportunity to view the witness' demeanor. Second, some prior statements may be more reliable than in-court testimony because the witness' memory will have been fresher at the time of the prior statement. Finally, some prior statements will be admissible for the non-hearsay purpose of impeaching or rehabilitating the credibility of a witness. For example, proof of a witness' prior inconsistent statement suggests that the person may be lying or forgetful or not careful with words. Whatever the reason for the inconsistency, there is reason to treat the person's testimony with some skepticism; and this skepticism arises from the mere fact of the inconsistency, not the truth of the prior statement. Similarly, if we know that a witness has been consistent in reporting a particular event, the mere fact of the consistency is at least a bit helpful to support the witness' credibility. (I.e., we are more likely to give credit to the statements of a person we know to be consistent than to someone about whose consistency we are ignorant.) If a prior statement is going to be admitted to impeach or rehabilitate a witness, it is arguably appropriate to admit the statement for its truth as well, rather than to trust that the jury will understand and apply a limiting instruction.[59]

---

56. See pages 462-467, 470-471 infra.
57. Both the House and the Senate Judiciary Committee Reports on the Federal Rules confirmed this general principle:

> [I]t is the Committee's understanding that a memorandum or report, although barred under [FRE 803(5), the past recollection recorded exception], would nonetheless be admissible if it came within another hearsay exception. This last stated principle is deemed applicable to all the hearsay rules. [House Report.]
>
> The committee . . . accepts the understanding of the House that a memorandum or report, although barred under [FRE 803(5)], would nonetheless be admissible if it came within another hearsay exception. We consider this principle to be applicable to all the hearsay rules. [Senate Report.]

58. See page 301-302 supra.
59. In Chapter Six we will consider the extent to which prior statements may be admissible for the non-hearsay purpose of showing inconsistency or consistency. Our focus here is on the use of prior statements for their truth.

2. Prior Inconsistent and Consistent Statements

At common law, prior inconsistent statements of a witness were admissible only for the non-hearsay purpose of impeaching the witness' credibility. The Federal Rules of Evidence promulgated by the Supreme Court and sent to Congress departed from the common law by providing that prior inconsistent statements should be exempted, without limitation, from the hearsay prohibition. This meant, in effect, that prior inconsistent statements could be used both for their traditional impeachment purpose and for the truth.

During the congressional debates on the Federal Rules, the Senate concurred with the Court. The House of Representatives, however, took the position that prior inconsistent statements should be admissible for their truth only if they were made under oath and were at the time subject to cross-examination. The final version of the Federal Rules represents a compromise between these two positions: Prior inconsistent statements are admissible for their truth only if they are made under oath, but they need not be subject to cross-examination. See FRE 801(d)(1)(A). This compromise satisfied one of the primary objectives of the advocates of a liberal non-hearsay treatment of prior inconsistent statements: the opportunity to use for its truth a witness' prior inconsistent grand jury testimony.[60]

Prior inconsistent statements not under oath may still be admissible for the non-hearsay purpose of impeaching the credibility of the witness. In such a situation, the party against whom the evidence was admitted would be entitled to a limiting instruction that the evidence could be considered only for its impeachment value and not for its truth.

Prior consistent statements were not admissible for their truth at common law, and the use of prior consistent statements for the non-hearsay purpose of supporting the credibility of a witness was usually limited to situations in which the prior consistent statement was offered to rebut an express or implied charge of recent fabrication or improper influence or motive. The Federal Rules in essence provide that in these situations in which the common law permitted prior consistent statements to be admissible for the non-hearsay purpose of supporting a witness' credibility, the statements may now also be admissible for their truth. See FRE 801(d)(1)(B). In other words, in these situations the party against whom the evidence is offered would not be entitled, under the Federal Rules, to a limiting instruction.

3. Preliminary Fact Finding With Respect to Prior Consistent and Inconsistent Statements

Since a prior consistent statement is relevant to rehabilitate a witness regardless of whether the statement is offered to rebut a charge of undue

---

60. Grand jury witnesses are placed under oath. Grand jury proceedings, however, are secret and ex parte. Thus, there is no opportunity for cross-examination.

D. Exemptions from the Definition of Hearsay

influence or improper motive, the question at common law whether the statement was offered for such a purpose should be and was generally regarded as an FRE 104(a)-type preliminary fact. The same should be true when the evidence is offered for the truth pursuant to FRE 801(d)(1)(B).

Sometimes there may be a question whether a prior statement is in fact consistent or, as was more often the case, inconsistent with a witness' trial testimony. For rehabilitation or impeachment purposes, this question in most jurisdictions was regarded as an FRE 104(b)-type preliminary fact. For example, if an allegedly inconsistent statement was ambiguous, or if the witness claimed to be able to explain away an apparent inconsistency, the extent to which there was in fact an inconsistency was treated as a matter of conditional relevance. The jury, not the judge, was the ultimate decision maker on this issue, unless, of course, the judge decided to exclude the evidence altogether because of the prejudice inherent in the risk that the jury might improperly consider the prior statement for its truth.

Consider what the preliminary fact standard for the question of consistency or inconsistency should be when a prior statement is offered for its truth pursuant to FRE 801(d)(1)(A) or (B). The relevance of the statement offered for its truth may not be dependent upon whether the statement is consistent or inconsistent with the witness' trial testimony. If this is the case, does it follow that the judge should make an FRE 104(a) determination of consistency or inconsistency as a condition of admitting the statement for its truth? Or should one regard the objective of FRE 801(d)(1)(A) and (B) as merely the removal of a hearsay objection to inconsistent statements that are under oath and consistent statements that meet the common law admissibility criteria for rehabilitation? If so, it would seem appropriate to apply FRE 104(b), the test used to determine consistency or inconsistency for rehabilitation and impeachment purposes.

4. Prior Statements of Identification

The Federal Rules also exempt from the definition of hearsay a witness' prior statement that is "one of identification of a person made after perceiving the person." FRE 801(d)(1)(C). Although the rule is not restricted to particular parties or actions, for several reasons it will be of primary benefit to prosecutors in criminal proceedings. First, identification is more often an issue in criminal than in civil actions. Second, and not surprisingly in light of the manner in which criminal cases are investigated and evidence is developed, it is usually the prosecutor and not the defendant who seeks to use prior identification evidence. Third, any rule that permits evidence to be used for a relatively broad purpose (e.g., for its truth, as well as for impeachment) is likely to be of most help to the party with the burden of proof; and in criminal cases, it is the prosecutor who bears a heavy burden of proof. Consider, for example, the existence of an unsworn statement of identification that is inconsistent with a witness' in-court testimony. If the witness testifies that the defendant did not commit the crime and the prior statement names the defendant as the assailant, the prosecutor's use of the prior statement for its truth may be essential to avoid a directed verdict of acquittal. On the other hand, if the witness' in-court testimony identified the defendant as the assailant but the prior statement named somebody else, the jury's assessment whether there is a reasonable doubt about the defendant's guilt may not depend much, if at all, upon whether the prior statement is admitted only for its impeachment value or for its truth.

The original version of the Federal Rules promulgated by the Supreme Court and sent to Congress contained FRE 801(d)(1)(C). The Federal Rules, which were enacted by Congress in 1974 and took effect in January, 1975, deleted this provision, primarily because of opposition to it by Senator Sam Ervin. He feared that criminal defendants would be convicted solely on the basis of unsworn, possibly unreliable out-of-court statements of identification.

Senator Ervin retired from the Senate when his term expired at the end of 1974. In the following year, Congress amended the Federal Rules by adding FRE 801(d)(1)(C). The Report of the Senate Judiciary Committee offered the following explanation for the amendment:

> In the course of processing the Rules of Evidence in the final weeks of the 93rd Congress, the provision excluding such statements of identification from the hearsay category was deleted. Although there was no suggestion in the committee report that prior identifications are not probative, concern was there expressed that a conviction could be based upon such unsworn, out-of-court testimony. Upon further reflection, that concern appears misdirected. First, this exception is addressed to the "admissibility" of evidence and not to the "sufficiency" of evidence to prove guilt. Secondly, except for the former testimony exception to the hearsay exclusion, all hearsay exceptions allow into evidence statements which may not have been made under oath. Moreover, under this rule, unlike a significant majority of the hearsay exceptions, the prior identification is admissible only when the person who made it testifies at trial and is subject to cross-examination. This assures that if any discrepancy occurs between the witness' in-court and out-of-court testimony, the opportunity is available to prove, with the witness under oath, the reasons for that discrepancy so that the trier of fact might determine which statement is to be believed.
>
> Upon reflection, then, it appears the rule is desirable. Since these identifications take place reasonably soon after an offense has been committed, the witness' observations are still fresh in his mind. The identification occurs before his recollection has been dimmed by the passage of time. Equally as important, it also takes place before the defendant or some other party has had the opportunity, through bribe or threat, to influence the witness to change his mind.

In the traditional laundry lists of hearsay exceptions, there is no specifically recognized common law hearsay exception for statements of prior identification; nonetheless, there is a good deal of precedent for the admis-

D. Exemptions from the Definition of Hearsay

sibility of prior statements of identification for their truth. The caselaw prior to the Federal Rules, at least at the appellate level, tended to focus not on the hearsay issue but on whether use of the prior identification violated a criminal defendant's constitutional right to counsel or due process of law.[61]

The inclusion of subdivision (C) in FRE 801(d)(1) raises a number of questions and concerns, most of which have not been adequately addressed in the literature or the caselaw. For example, consider the following:

(a) If it is desirable generally (which it may not be) to permit only *sworn* prior inconsistent statements to be used for their truth, why is there no oath requirement for prior inconsistent statements of identification? If one assumes that most statements of identification are likely to be made within minutes or at least a few days after the commission of a crime, are the likely absence of a memory problem and the at least occasional difficulty of arranging for the statement to be given under oath sufficient reasons to forego the oath requirement?

(b) If close temporal proximity between the observation and the statement of identification is at least part of the underlying rationale for FRE 801(d)(1)(C), see Report of the Senate Judiciary Committee quoted supra, would it be desirable to amend that section to provide that the statement of identification must be made "soon" or "shortly" after the witness perceived the person identified?[62]

(c) In addition to doing away with the oath requirement for inconsistent statements of identification, does FRE 801(d)(1)(C) add anything to subdivisions (A) and (B)? The answer is clearly "Yes, at least a little." Some in-court statements that are different from pre-trial statements arguably should not be regarded as manifesting an inconsistency. For example, present inability to identify the defendant due to loss of memory arguably should not be regarded as inconsistent with an earlier positive identification, at least if the loss of memory claim seems reasonable. In any event, it becomes unnecessary to grapple with the question whether there is an inconsistency when the in-court testimony is different from the prior identification declaration. Similarly, when the in-court testimony is consistent with the prior identification testimony, it is unnecessary to decide whether there has been an express or implied charge of recent fabrication or improper influence or motive. Indeed, the party offering the prior testimony can ask the witness about the prior identification on direct examination before there has even been an opportunity for the opposing party to suggest recent fabrication or improper influence.

---

61. See, e.g., Gilbert v. California, 388 U.S. 263 (1967) (criminal defendant has right to counsel at post-indictment confrontation between witness and defendant; denial of right to counsel requires exclusion of pretrial identification evidence); Manson v. Brathwaite, 432 U.S. 98 (1977) (due process requires exclusion of unnecessarily suggestive pretrial identification if identification is likely to be unreliable).

62. See Proposed Amendments to Uniform Rules of Evidence (1986) (suggesting such an amendment).

(d) Is it desirable to permit prior statements of identification that would not otherwise be admissible for impeachment purposes to be used for their truth? The person whose prior identification is admitted into evidence must be subject to cross-examination; the earlier statements may be more reliable because they were made closer in time to the event; and there is a risk that a witness may testify falsely at trial because of threats to family members. On the other hand, as we suggest in the next section, the present opportunity for cross-examination about the content of the prior identification may not be very helpful as a practical matter. Moreover, neither the witness nor even the police officers who arranged for the identification may have been aware of possible subtle suggestive factors that could have influenced the prior identification.

In assessing these competing concerns, there are at least two important variables to keep in mind. The first is the time lapse between the event and the statement of identification. Studies have demonstrated that individuals' memories fade quickly;[63] thus, the justification for the prior identification provision is strongest with respect to identifications made soon after the perception of the person identified. Second, it is important to develop some sense of the need for prior identification testimony. If one focuses on a case involving organized crime figures as the prototype for the use of prior identification evidence, the case for admissibility is relatively strong because of the concern with possible witness intimidation. On the other hand, if one focuses on the run-of-the-mill street crime, where witness intimidation is unlikely, there is relatively less need for prior identification testimony.

(e) What is and what should be the scope of FRE 801(d)(1)(C)? Obviously, the rule was intended to include statements of identification made at traditional line-ups and show-ups, and just as obviously the language of the rule excludes statements of identification of things other than persons. With respect to what is or may be included within FRE 801(d)(1)(C), there may be questions about how broadly the rule should be interpreted. For example, does it include statements about the identification of a *photograph* of a person?[64] descriptive statements to a police artist? the out-of-court declaration "John Smith raped me" to prove that the assailant was John Smith? And with respect to what is not included within FRE 801(d)(1)(C), why should identifications of persons but not, for example, automobiles be admissible? If descriptions of a person (e.g., those made to a police artist) are admissible, what about descriptions of the clothing worn by the person? In attempting to answer these and similar questions it is important to keep in mind two not necessarily consistent propositions. First, a rational system of

---

63. For an excellent summary of the psychological data bearing on the reliability of eyewitness identification testimony, see Note, Did Your Eyes Deceive You? Expert Psychological Testimony on the Unreliability of Eyewitness Identification, 29 Stan. L. Rev. 969, 975-988 (1977).

64. Courts have held that identification of persons in photographs falls within FRE 801(d)(1)(C). See, e.g., United States v. Lewis, 565 F.2d 1248 (2d Cir. 1977).

D. Exemptions from the Definition of Hearsay

rules of admissibility should strive for a reasonable degree of consistency with respect to what is and is not excluded; in gray areas, one should be able to identify reasons for exclusion or admission and argue by analogy for exclusion or admission of a particular piece of evidence. Second, particularly in light of the abandonment of the oath requirement for prior inconsistent identifications and the abandonment of the recent fabrication or improper influence requirement for prior consistent identifications, the words *identification of a person* should, it would seem, be regarded as a serious substantive limitation on the scope of FRE 801(d)(1)(C).

5. The Significance of the Opportunity to Cross-Examine

The FRE 801(d)(1) exemptions from the definition of hearsay all require that the out-of-court declarant "testifies at the trial or hearing and is subject to cross-examination concerning the statement." Cross-examination, however, may not always be a potentially effective device for evaluating the truth of the prior statement. At one extreme, cross-examination with respect to a witness' prior statement is likely to be most similar to cross-examination about in-court testimony when the witness fully affirms the prior statement and gives testimony that is consistent with the statement. In this type of situation, though, there is relatively little need for the prior statement.

At the other extreme, cross-examination is likely to be least effective when the witness denies or cannot recall making the statement (and perhaps the event to which the statement relates, as well). In this type of situation, although the jury will have the benefit of observing the witness' demeanor (for whatever that is worth), there will be little, if anything, that cross-examination of the witness who supposedly made the prior statement can do to shed light on the truth of the earlier statement. Rather, there is likely to be nothing more than a swearing contest between two witnesses— one who denies making or does not remember making the statement and the other who testifies that the statement was made. Moreover, at least in the context of prior statements offered by the prosecutor in a criminal case, the witness who claims to suffer from loss of memory may have an unsavory background, and the witness who reports the statement is likely to be a police officer. Thus, it is a good bet that the jury will believe that the prior statement was made. In theory, of course, cross-examination is fully available to test the credibility of the police officer with respect to whether the statement was made. Police perjury, however, is unfortunately not an uncommon phenomenon, and one may reasonably question whether cross-examination is likely often to expose the perjury.[65]

---

65. See, e.g., People v. Berrios, 28 N.Y.2d 361, 321 N.Y.S.2d 884, 270 N.E.2d 709 (1971) (discussion of "dropsy" evidence in narcotics possession cases; prosecutor supported defense argument that in light of frequency of dropsy testimony by police officers, burden of proving legal warrantless search should be on state). See generally P. Chevigny, Police Power (1969).

From the standpoint of an advocate, there are two vehicles for objecting to the admission of a witness' prior statement on the ground that there will not be an opportunity for effective cross-examination of the witness concerning the statement. First, in the context of a criminal prosecution where prior statements are offered against a criminal defendant, defense counsel can argue that the lack of a meaningful opportunity for cross-examination is a denial of the defendant's state or federal constitutional right "to be confronted with the witnesses against him."[66] Second, one can argue in terms of the language of FRE 801(d)(1) or similar state rule that there is not a *meaningful* opportunity for cross-examination of the witness "*concerning the statement.*" At least at the present time, however, both of these arguments seem doomed to failure as a matter of federal constitutional or evidentiary law in the case of a witness who claims loss of memory. In United States v. Owens,[67] the Supreme Court rejected both a confrontation clause and an FRE 801(d)(1) challenge to the prior identification evidence of a witness who had no present memory of the underlying events. A more detailed statement of the *Owens* facts along with the Court's confrontation clause analysis appears earlier.[68] With respect to the FRE 801(d)(1) issue the Court said:

> Ordinarily a witness is regarded as "subject to cross-examination" when he is placed on the stand, under oath, and responds willingly to questions. Just as with the constitutional prohibition, limitations on the scope of examination by the trial court or assertions of privilege by the witness may undermine the process to such a degree that meaningful cross-examination within the intent of the rule no longer exists. But that effect is not produced by the witness's assertion of memory loss—which . . . is often the very result sought to be produced by cross-examination. [108 S. Ct. at 844.]

The Court went on to emphasize that the Advisory Committee's Notes to FRE 801 express a preference for prior statements of identification because of the problem of fading memories. Since there is not a similar expression of preference for prior inconsistent and consistent statements governed by FRE 801(d)(1)(A) and (B), one might argue that *Owens* should not apply to non-identification prior statements. On the other hand, the absence of an opportunity for effective cross-examination perhaps should be regarded as even less critical in situations covered by FRE 801(d)(1)(A) and (B). In those situations, a witness' prior statement would probably be admissible in any event for the non-hearsay purpose of impeaching or supporting the witness' credibility. Thus, one arguably can justify admitting the prior statement for its truth on the independent ground that a limiting instruction is not likely to be very helpful.

---

66. The quoted language is in the sixth amendment to the United States Constitution. See generally pages 351-371 supra. Most state constitutions have identical or similar provisions.
67. 108 S. Ct. 838 (1988).
68. See pages 368-370 supra.

D. Exemptions from the Definition of Hearsay

An alternative would be to exclude the evidence for both purposes on the ground that the risk of jury misuse of the statement for its truth substantially outweighs the probative value of the statement for its legitimate non-hearsay purpose. See FRE 403. A judge, however, is unlikely to adopt this solution. At common law prior inconsistent and consistent statements that were usable for a legitimate non-hearsay impeachment or rehabilitation purpose were rarely excluded on prejudice or confusion grounds. Thus, as a practical matter, for most prior statements that have a legitimate non-hearsay use, the available choices are admission with limiting instructions or admission without limiting instructions.

Even if the limitations on effective cross-examination stemming from a witness' claimed memory loss will not operate to exclude the witness' prior statements, limitations on cross-examination imposed by the trial court or by the witness' refusal to respond may have that effect. *Owens* acknowledged this possibility in the quoted passage supra, and the Supreme Court has taken this position in the context of interpreting the sixth amendment confrontation clause.[69]

PROBLEMS

1. Larry Emerson is being tried for arson. The state's key witness, Alice Hastings, testified under a grant of immunity that she had cooperated with Larry in planning the arson. On cross-examination, defense counsel inquired about promises made to Ms. Hastings in return for her testimony and suggested that she was testifying against Mr. Emerson in order to shift responsibility for the crime from herself. On redirect examination the prosecutor asks Ms. Hastings about a statement consistent with her direct examination testimony that she made to the police during the early stages of the investigation of the crime. Can defense counsel successfully object to this question?

2. Jean Andrews has sued Barney Cox for injuries received in an automobile accident. Drew Foster, a passenger in Andrews' car, testified on direct examination that Cox caused the accident by turning without warning into the traffic lane occupied by the Andrews vehicle. On cross-examination, Foster specifically denied telling an insurance investigator for Foster's insurance company that Jean Andrews had been speeding at the time of the accident. Later in the trial the insurance investigator testified that Foster had told him that Ms. Andrews had been speeding. During the cross-examination of the insurance investigator, Andrews' attorney has the investigator authenticate the report of the interview that the agent prepared and Foster signed. The report contains the following: "We were in a hurry to get to an appointment, but I knew we would be late. The traffic was so bad that we just

---

69. See Davis v. Alaska, 415 U.S. 308 (1974), set forth in the Supplement accompanying this text; Douglas v. Alabama, 380 U.S. 415 (1965), described at page 354 supra.

couldn't move very quickly. And then Mr. Cox's car cut right in front of us." Andrews' attorney now offers the report into evidence. Should it be admitted?

3. Ed Larson is being prosecuted for armed robbery of a bank. Terry Davis, an alleged accomplice, pleaded guilty to the same charge and is currently serving a 20-year sentence. Davis was called as prosecution witness, and initially in response to the prosecutor's questions about the robbery, Davis refused to answer on the basis of the fifth amendment privilege against self-incrimination. Since Davis had already been convicted and sentenced for his role in the robbery, the judge ruled that Davis could not invoke the fifth amendment and ordered Davis to testify. Davis then admitted that he was involved in the robbery, but he claimed that he could not remember whether he had a partner or, if he did have one, who the partner might have been. He also claimed not to remember ever having made a statement to anyone about having a partner. To prove that Larson committed the robbery with Davis the prosecutor offers (a) a transcript of Davis' grand jury testimony naming Larson as his accomplice and (b) the testimony of a police officer to the effect that following Davis' arrest, he confessed to the robbery and named Larson as his accomplice. The defendant has objected to both pieces of evidence. What result?

4. In the same bank robbery prosecution described in Problem 3, the prosecutor established that Larson habitually wears bright red socks and white sneakers. The prosecutor then called as a witness, Alice James, who was a customer in the bank at the time of the robbery. She testified that there were two robbers and that she did not see either of their faces. When asked if she could recall any distinguishing characteristics of either robber, she responded negatively. She was then asked, over defense counsel's objection, if she remembers telling a police officer shortly after the robbery that one of the robbers was wearing red socks and white sneakers. The objection is overruled, and she responds, "Now that you mention it, yes, I do remember saying that, and if I said it, it must have been true. I just don't remember now though." Was the court's ruling proper?

6. Admissions of a Party Opponent Generally

The most commonly invoked exception to the hearsay rule, which has become an exemption from the definition of hearsay under the Federal Rules, is the admissions exception. (Since the term *exemption* does not appear in the Federal Rules, and since a person offering what is arguably an admission will probably have to offer a more precise explanation for admissibility than "not hearsay," we suspect that the traditional terminology—"admissions exception"—will continue in frequent use. In any event, we have chosen here to refer to admissions as "exceptions to" rather than "exemptions from" the hearsay rule.)

D. Exemptions from the Definition of Hearsay

Any out-of-court statement made by a party to an action and offered against that party is regarded as an admission and may be considered for its truth. In addition, as we will see shortly, statements of various third persons who have particular relationships with parties—e.g., co-conspirators and certain agents—fall within the scope of the admissions exception and can be used for their truth against parties to a law suit. For example, a statement made by an employee on a subject about which the employee was authorized to speak by the employer would be admissible as an admission against the employer.

If conduct is hearsay, it is a statement for the purposes of this or any other hearsay exception or exemption. Thus, in a jurisdiction that regarded nonassertive conduct as hearsay, the defendant's flight from the scene of a crime would be an admission. Similarly, in any jurisdiction, an individual's nod of assent in response to a question whether the individual threw the first punch would be admissible as an admission against that individual in a subsequent prosecution.

An admission obviously will in fact be adverse to the interest of the party against whom it is offered if the opposing party wishes to introduce it into evidence. For this reason, admissions are sometimes referred to as "admissions against interest." For two reasons, however, we strongly urge you to avoid—indeed, to become uncomfortable with—the phrase "admission against interest." First, as you will see, there is a completely distinct exception to the hearsay rule for "declarations against interest." Getting used to referring to admissions simply as admissions should help to avoid confusion between declarations against interest and admissions. Second, the admissions exception does not require that the party making the statement realize at the time that the statement was in any way against the party's interest. Assume, for example, that Marcia and Robert were arrested for their participation in a bank robbery in which one of the tellers was killed. Following a waiver of his *Miranda* rights, Robert, believing that he was making an exculpatory statement, said to the police interrogator, "It was Marcia who shot the teller." Now, in Robert's prosecution for murder on a felony-murder theory, the prosecutor wishes to introduce for its truth Robert's statement about Marcia. Even though Robert may have believed at the time that the statement was exculpatory, it was in fact inculpatory; and as long as the statement was not obtained in violation of Robert's constitutional rights,[70] it would be admissible against him for its truth—simply because he made the statement.

---

70. There are a number of potential constitutional objections, all of which are beyond the scope of the materials in this book, to the use against a criminal defendant of the defendant's statements. For example, the statement may be the product of an illegal arrest, see Brown v. Illinois, 422 U.S. 590 (1975); it may have been obtained in violation of the defendant's sixth amendment right to counsel, see Brewer v. Williams, 430 U.S. 387 (1977); it may have been obtained in violation of the defendant's fifth amendment rights under Miranda v. Arizona, 384 U.S. 436 (1966); it may be an involuntary confession, see Brown v. Mississippi, 297 U.S. 278 (1936); it may have been obtained as the result of electronic surveillance that violated the defendant's fourth amendment right to be free from unreasonable searches and seizures, see

7. A Party's Own Statements

The traditional rationale for permitting statements of a party to an action to be used against the party for their truth is straightforward and related directly to the rationale for the hearsay rule: In effect, a hearsay objection is an objection to the lack of an opportunity to expose weaknesses in the declarant's narration, sincerity, perception, and memory through cross-examination. With one possible exception, however, a party to an action cannot reasonably complain about the lack of an opportunity for self–cross-examination, for there is a viable alternative. The party can take the stand on direct examination and have a full opportunity to explain any difficulties with sincerity, narration, perception, or memory. In short, it seems absurd for a party to complain about not being able to cross-examine himself or herself.

The one situation in which the rationale for admitting a party's own statements against the party may not seem entirely satisfactory is in the context of an admission by a criminal defendant. While it is true that the defendant has the same right as any other litigant to testify, it is also true that the criminal defendant has the fifth amendment right to refuse to testify. Admitting a criminal defendant's statements may put some pressure on the defendant to abandon the fifth amendment right not to testify. The rationale for the admissions exception tacitly acknowledges that this burdening of the fifth amendment right is acceptable.

Professors Lempert and Saltzburg offer an alternative rationale for the admissions exception:

> The exception really seems rooted in ideas about the *responsibility* which individuals have for their actions. People are expected to tell the truth as a matter of course, not because the law requires veracity in everyday speech, but because accepted notions of morality require it. The law recognizes in the hearsay rule the fact that people do not always speak the truth; but this recognition does not mean that parties before the court will be assumed to have failed in their moral duty to tell the truth or be relieved of the responsibility for their actions if they have failed. [R. Lempert and S. Saltzburg, A Modern Approach to Evidence (1983 2d ed.) 384 (emphasis original).[71]]

Consider whether this is a viable *alternative* theory. Even if one concedes that there are general and generally accepted moral norms of personal accountability and honesty, is there really some shared sense of moral responsibility mandating that any litigant's statements can be used against the litigant to the litigant's legal deprivation? Why should somebody who perhaps quite unwillingly becomes a litigant be required to shoulder this particular

---

Katz v. United States, 389 U.S. 347 (1967). See generally R. Allen and R. Kuhns, Constitutional Criminal Procedure: An Examination of the Fourth, Fifth, and Sixth Amendments and Related Areas (1985).

71. See also Lev, The Law of Vicarious Admissions—An Estoppel, 26 U. Cinn. L. Rev. 17 (1957).

D. Exemptions from the Definition of Hearsay

responsibility? In any event, the moral responsibility rationale seems no better than the "opportunity to take the witness stand" rationale for admitting the statements made by the individual litigants. In the case of criminal defendants—the only situation in which the "opportunity to take the witness stand" rationale is arguably weak—the relevant constitutional law runs counter to the implications of the moral responsibility rationale. A criminal defendant's statements may be completely voluntary and at the same time excluded because of a violation of the defendant's right to counsel or right against self-incrimination.[72]

Perhaps a sufficient answer to the concern with burdening the fifth amendment right not to testify is to note that any number of factors may make a defendant feel pressured to testify, and only some of these factors raise constitutional problems. At one extreme, a direct threat of punishment for refusing to testify would be regarded as a violation of the fifth amendment right not to testify. A defendant, however, may feel pressure to testify simply because of the nature or strength of the prosecutor's case, and this type of pressure does not raise constitutional problems. In any event, it is well settled that the admissions exception applies to criminal defendants as well as to other parties to actions.

In two respects the admissions exception has tended to operate differently from other hearsay exceptions. The first relates to the relationship between the hearsay rule and the lay opinion rule. When hearsay evidence falling within an exception to the hearsay rule is objectionable as an impermissible lay opinion, courts have tended to be more liberal in admitting the objectionable opinion evidence if the evidence is an admission rather than hearsay falling under some other exception to the hearsay rule. Since the underlying justification for the lay opinion rule is to present to the fact finder information in the most specific form reasonably possible, and since the party against whom the opinion is offered can take the witness stand and explain why the opinion may be misleading in its generality, liberalizing the lay opinion rule in this context does not seem unreasonable. Indeed, what may be unreasonable is a more rigid application of the lay opinion rule to declarations falling within other hearsay exceptions. If the person offering the impermissible lay opinion is a witness on the stand, it will always be possible, after the opinion objection is sustained, to rephrase questions in order to elicit the desired information with more specificity. By contrast, there is no guarantee that the hearsay declarant will be available to testify. Thus, to sustain a lay opinion objection to hearsay evidence falling within an exception to the hearsay rule may have the effect of depriving the jury completely of relevant information.[73]

---

72. See note 70 supra. The moral responsibility rationale is considered with respect to vicarious admissions at note 81 infra.
73. The federal lay opinion rule need not operate as harshly as the common law rule. FRE 701 permits the use of lay opinions "which are (a) rationally based on the perception of the witness and (b) helpful to a clear understanding of his testimony *or the determination of a fact in issue.*" (Emphasis added.)

The second way in which admissions differ from other hearsay exceptions is in the application of the firsthand knowledge requirement. The requirement that a witness speak from firsthand knowledge, see FRE 602, applies generally to hearsay declarants as well as to in-court witnesses.[74] In the majority of jurisdictions, however, there is no requirement that an admission be based on the declarant's firsthand knowledge. Assume, for example, that a hearsay declarant's out-of-court statement satisfies the requirements of the excited utterance exception to the hearsay rule, see FRE 803(2), but that it can be shown that the declarant lacked firsthand knowledge of the event to which the excited utterance relates. A hearsay objection to this evidence would be overruled, but a lack of firsthand knowledge objection would be sustained. If the same statement were made under the same circumstances by a party to the action and were offered against that party, the evidence would be admissible in most jurisdictions.

The Advisory Committee's Note to FRE 801 expresses approval of the precedent for dispensing with the firsthand knowledge requirement in the case of admissions:

> The freedom which admissions have enjoyed from technical demands of searching for an assurance of trustworthiness in some against-interest circumstances, and from the restrictive influences of the opinion rule and the rule requiring firsthand knowledge, when taken with the apparently prevalent satisfaction with the results, call for generous treatment of this avenue to admissibility.[75]

McCormick offers the following justification for dispensing with the firsthand knowledge requirement for a party's own admissions:

> [Decisions refusing to apply the firsthand knowledge requirement to admissions] argue that when a man speaks against his own interest it is to be supposed that he has made an adequate investigation. While this self-disserving feature might attach to most admissions, we have seen that admissions are competent evidence though not against interest when made. As to these the argument does not apply, and it seems sufficient to justify the general dispensing with the knowledge qualification to say that admissions which become relevant in litigation usually concern some matter of substantial importance to the declarant upon which he would probably have informed himself so that they possess, even when not based on firsthand observation, greater reliability than the general run of hearsay. Moreover, the possibility is substantial that the

---

74. See FRE 803 Advisory Committee Note ("In a hearsay situation, the declarant is, of course, a witness, and neither this rule nor Rule 804 dispenses with the requirement of firsthand knowledge.")

75. The classification of admissions as not hearsay and the Advisory Committee's statement that the firsthand knowledge rule applies to hearsay declarants, see note 74 supra, may be another indication that the drafters of the Federal Rules did not intend for the firsthand knowledge requirement to apply to admissions. There is no suggestion in the Advisory Committee's Notes, however, that the decision to exempt some statements from the definition of hearsay had anything to do with the firsthand knowledge rule. —Eds.

D. Exemptions from the Definition of Hearsay

declarant may have come into possession of significant information not known to his opponent. [McCormick's Handbook on the Law of Evidence 778-779 (3d ed., Cleary, 1984).]

Do you find this justification convincing? Is there some other justification for dispensing with the firsthand knowledge requirement? Consider the alternative rationales for the admissions exemption dealt with in the discussion of vicarious admissions at pages 389-394 infra.

8. Adoptive Admissions

One type of admission recognized by common law courts and incorporated into the Federal Rules, see FRE 801(d)(2)(B), is the adoptive admission. A statement made by a third person, not a party to the action, may be admitted against a party who has manifested an adoption of the statement. There is no limitation on the type of language or conduct by a party that might be regarded as an adoption, but perhaps the most common type of adoptive admission is the admission by silence. Consider, for example, a situation in which Jim and Sally are having dinner with friends. Sally says, "You should see all the money that Jim and I got in the bank robbery," and Jim remains silent. At Jim's trial for bank robbery, one of the dinner companions will probably be permitted to testify about Sally's statement and Jim's silence.[76]

Except perhaps for the purpose of making clear that the drafters of the Federal Rules intended to include adoptive admissions within the admissions exception, there does not appear to be any need for a provision dealing specifically with adoptive admissions. Instead of regarding the party's conduct as an adoption of some third person's hearsay statement within the meaning of FRE 801(d)(2)(B), it is possible to consider the party's adoptive activity either as nonassertive activity falling outside the basic definition of hearsay in FRE 801(a)-(c) or as "the party's own statement" within the meaning of FRE 801(d)(2)(A). Under this theory, the third person's out-of-court statement—e.g., Sally's statement in the above illustration—would be admissible not for its truth but simply as part of the description of the circumstances that give relevance to the party's activity. To put the matter somewhat differently, instead of using the notion of adoption to credit the sincerity, narration, perception, and memory of some third person (e.g., Sally), we

---

76. If the accusation had been made by a police officer after Jim had been arrested and informed of his *Miranda* rights, the evidence would not be admissible. See Doyle v. Ohio, 426 U.S. 610 (1976) (post-arrest silence following *Miranda* warnings "insolubly ambiguous;" impeachment use of such silence violates due process). It is not unconstitutional, however, to impeach a criminal defendant by asking about the defendant's pre-arrest failure to come forward with exculpatory evidence, Jenkins v. Anderson, 447 U.S. 231 (1980), or by asking about post-arrest silence when the record does not indicate that *Miranda* warnings had been given, Fletcher v. Weir, 455 U.S. 603 (1982).

can rely directly on the sincerity, narration/ambiguity, perception, and memory of the party against whom the evidence is offered; the words spoken by the third person—without regard to their truth or the third person's belief—give content and meaning to the party's activity.

One possible difference between these two approaches to adoptive admissions is the appropriate preliminary fact standard to apply to the evidence. The fact of adoption, which is a condition of admissibility pursuant to FRE 801(d)(2)(B), is not likely to be critical to the relevance of the third person's declaration. Thus, the appropriate preliminary fact standard would be FRE 104(a): The judge should decide if there has been an adoption. On the other hand, if one views the supposedly adoptive activity (e.g., Jim's silence in our hypothetical) as the party's own admission pursuant to FRE 801(d)(2)(A), it may be appropriate to utilize the FRE 104(b) conditional relevance standard: The question whether a party's supposedly adoptive activity is in fact an indication of liability—like the question whether a supposedly inconsistent statement offered to impeach a witnesss is in fact inconsistent[77] —is one of relevance. If a reasonable person could find that the party's activity was relevant as an indication of liability, that finding arguably should ultimately be made by the jury, not the judge.

There is one difficulty with regarding a party's supposedly adoptive activity, or a witness' supposedly inconsistent statement, as raising only an issue of relevance. The accusation to which the supposedly adoptive activity is a response will have to be admitted into evidence in order to give meaning to the party's activity, and the accusation is relevant to prove the truth of the accusation even though, in theory, it may not be admitted for that purpose. Similarly, a supposedly inconsistent statement is relevant to prove the truth of what it asserts, even though it may not be admitted for that purpose. The policies underlying the general prohibition against hearsay arguably should require the judge to take a more active role in initially screening statements that the jury may consider for their truth even though the statements are not admitted for that purpose. Perhaps, however, the FRE 403 balancing process is adequate to meet this concern.

As we suggested in another context,[78] it may not make much difference which view of preliminary fact standards a court takes. In many instances, we believe, a judge is likely to have a strong enough instinctive feeling about whether the accusation and supposedly adoptive activity should be admissible that the preliminary fact standard is not likely to affect the admissibility decision. If a situation arises in which a judge believes that the FRE 104(b) relevance standard but not the more rigorous FRE 104(a) adoption standard has been satisfied, the judge is likely to be sympathetic to an argument for exclusion on FRE 403 grounds.

Regardless of whether one views a party's activity as an adoption of some

---

77. See pages 374-375 supra.
78. See pages 243-245 supra.

D. Exemptions from the Definition of Hearsay

third person's statement or as the party's own admission, a frequent problem, but one that seldom precludes admissibility, is the ambiguity of the party's conduct. In our illustration involving Sally and Bob, for example, Bob may not have heard Sally's statement; or he may have thought Sally's statement was too ridiculous to warrant a response; or because of his macho image, Bob might not have wanted to admit to friends that he had not robbed the bank. Bob, of course, can take the witness stand and offer such an explanation. Moreover, in some situations, particularly where the third person's statement relates to something about which the party has personal knowledge, the party may exercise the right to testify effectively. In other situations, however, because of lack of firsthand knowledge or for other reasons, the party may not be a very good witness. In such a case the jury will have to choose between the story told by the ineffective party-witness and the un-cross-examined hearsay of the third person. Consider, for example, Elliott's failure to respond to a bill sent by Jason for repairs made during the off-season to Elliott's summer cabin. If Elliott's failure to respond to the bill is considered an admission that the bill is not an accurate statement of the hours Jason worked or of the amount due, which it probably would be, Elliott could perhaps offer some explanation to the jury for his failure to respond to the bill. He is unlikely to be able to testify about the accuracy of the bill, however.[79]

In emphasizing the ambiguity and lack of firsthand knowledge problems that inhere in many adoptive admissions, we do not mean to suggest a general disapproval of admitting adoptive admissions. Rather, we would urge courts here, as well as with other questions of admissibility, to be sensitive to the obligation to balance probative value and prejudice pursuant to FRE 403: To the extent that the party's conduct is ambiguous, the probative value of the evidence *as an admission* is low; and whenever the evidence is admitted, there is potential prejudice because of the risk that the jury will consider the truth of the third person's statement without regard to the party's arguably adoptive or acquiescing conduct.

9. Admissions by Agents, Servants, and Employees

All jurisdictions include within the admissions exception some statements made by agents, servants, and employees of the party against whom the evidence is offered. For the sake of convenience we will refer to the party against whom the evidence is offered as the "principal" and the declarant as

---

79. If Jason is the plaintiff and will be testifying in his own behalf, it may make little difference, as a practical matter, whether the bill is admitted into evidence. Furthermore, it may be that Jason keeps careful records and that his copy of the bill would be admissible under the business records exception to the hearsay rule. See FRE 803(6). It may be, however, that Jason did not keep any records, that he is now dead, and that the action is being brought by his estate.

the "agent." Keep in mind, however, that the exception is not limited to formal principal-agency relationships.

Some jurisdictions admit only declarations that the agent was authorized to make, while other jurisdictions have extended admissibility to statements about matters within the scope of the agent's authority or control. The Federal Rules include within the agency admission rule both "a statement by a person authorized by the party to make a statement concerning the subject" and "a statement by the party's agent or servant concerning a matter within the scope of the agency or employment, made during the existence of the relationship." FRE 801(d)(2)(C) and (D).

The specific articulation of the rule in any particular jurisdiction may be misleading. Jurisdictions that purport to limit admissibility to authorized admissions sometimes take an extremely broad view of what is authorized; and jurisdictions that purport to have a broader rule of admissibility sometimes have given narrow interpretations to the scope of the agency admission rule. Indeed, there may be no other area of law, except perhaps the substantive law of agency, where it is as difficult to predict from the language of a rule or principle what that rule or principle is likely to mean in a particular case. The jargon of agency law (e.g., "actual authority," "implied authority," "apparent authority") is not very helpful in dealing with the issues to which the jargon relates. Assume, for example, in the context of the substantive law of agency, that an agent has caused some injury to a third person and then absconded to Acapulco. The third person sues the principal, and a court must decide whether the principal will be vicariously liable or whether the third person should bear the risk of loss from dealing with the agent. Terms such as "apparent or implied authority" or "frolic and detour" are simply conclusory labels; they do not suggest substantive criteria for resolving the question who should bear the risk of loss. Similarly, the jargon of agency law is not helpful in determining when, despite the general prohibition against hearsay evidence, it is appropriate to admit an agent's out-of-court statement against a principal. Nonetheless, it is a fair generalization to say that just as the scope of substantive vicarious liability has grown during the twentieth century, the breadth of the agency admissions exception to the hearsay rule has also grown; the narrowest decisions denying admissibility of agents' statements are likely to be the oldest.[80]

The appropriate scope of the agency admissions rule should depend upon evidentiary principles consistent with the hearsay rule, not the jargon of agency law. Since there is no guarantee that the agent will be available to testify, the rationale for admitting individual admissions is of no assistance in dealing with the agency admission rule. Some agents' admissions, how-

---

80. For example, a number of older, and even some fairly recent, decisions limit the "authorized admissions" exception to statements authorized to be made to third persons. Statements made by one agent to another agent or to the principal would not be admissible. See, e.g., Rudzinski v. Warner Theatres, Inc., 16 Wis. 2d 241, 114 N.W.2d 466 (1962).

D. Exemptions from the Definition of Hearsay

ever, can be justified in terms of the two general criteria that are used to justify other exceptions to the hearsay rule: necessity and reliability.[81]

The necessity stems from the facts that individuals and institutional entities use agents and employees to conduct their affairs, that the agents and employees constitute a primary source of information about their activities, and that as a matter of substantive law we have decided that individual and institutional parties are legally responsible for activities of their employees and agents. If individuals or institutions are to be liable for the acts of agents and employees and for the ramifications of policy decisions implemented by agents and employees, it is arguably appropriate as a matter of fairness between parties, and perhaps even essential for the proper functioning of our liability scheme, for some statements of agents and employees to be admissible against principals and employers.

The broadest possible agency admission rule consistent with the preceding necessity rationale would admit the statements of agents whenever the principal was (a) vicariously liable for the actions or words of the agent or (b) directly liable for activities in which the agent was in some way involved *as an agent*. For several reasons, however, such a rule would arguably be too broad. First, if the declarant were no longer an agent of the party at the time of the declaration, the severing of the relationship may have created animosity that would give the agent a desire to retaliate against the party.[82] Second, if the agent were only marginally involved in the activities to which the declaration relates, one might wonder whether the declarant had sufficient information to speak accurately about the matter. Indeed, one might wonder if there were some ulterior motive for making a statement about something only marginally related to one's agency.

On the other hand, some agents' statements occur in a context which gives them circumstantial guarantees of trustworthiness. First, if a statement is authorized, it is reasonable to infer that the principal has exercised some discretion in selecting a trustworthy and reliable spokesperson. Second, if a statement is authorized or is about a matter central to the activities of the agent, there is reason to believe that the agent has a solid basis for making the statement; and because it is central to the declarant's activities, one can infer that the statement is likely to be made carefully and accurately. Third, if the declarant is an agent at the time of the statement, it is reasonable to infer that the interests of the declarant and the principal are the same and, therefore, that the declarant would not lie to injure the principal. Finally, an agent's statement, like a party's own statement, will frequently be one

---

81. In discussing their "moral responsibility" rationale for the admissions exception, see page 384 supra, Professors Lempert and Saltzburg assert, "Notions of responsibility also explain why one will be held to the statements of agents, partners and coconspirators." R. Lempert and S. Saltzburg, A Modern Approach to Evidence 384 (2d ed. 1983). They do not state and we do not know what *moral* principles require this result.

82. If the agent is not available and if the declaration is one that a reasonable person at the time would have realized was against the *agent's* interest, the declaration may be admissible against the principal pursuant to the declaration against interest exception.

that is obviously against the declarant's interest at the time it is made. This "against interest" feature, when it exists, arguably is an additional circumstantial guarantee of trustworthiness.[83]

We suggest that the foregoing considerations are sufficient to justify the agency admission provisions at least as broad as those codified in FRE 801(d)(2)(C) and (D). At the same time, we want to point out that in articulating the necessity rationale we used the phrase "in some way involved *as an agent,*" and in articulating the trustworthiness rationale we used the phrases "marginally involved in the activities" and "a matter central to the activities of the agent or employee." These phrases are far from precise. They are no less precise, however, than the phrase "a matter within the scope of the agency or employment," which occurs in FRE 801(d)(2)(D).

Many courts dispense with the firsthand knowledge requirement for vicarious as well as individual admissions. Thus, it is possible for a statement made by an agent who may be reporting only rumor to be admissible against a principal—and the agent may be in Acapulco. This refusal to apply a firsthand knowledge requirement to vicarious admissions has been severely criticized.[84] We question whether this criticism is warranted, at least if one is willing to forego the firsthand knowledge requirement for individual admissions. If the declarant is unavailable and if it is unclear from other evidence whether the declarant had firsthand knowledge, the statement may be admissible even if the firsthand knowledge requirement were applicable. FRE 602, the firsthand knowledge rule, requires only that there be evidence "sufficient to support a finding that [the declarant] has personal knowledge." On the other hand, if it were clear that the agent lacked firsthand knowledge or if the agent were available to testify about the absence of firsthand knowledge, the principal should be able to establish that the agent did not have firsthand knowledge. And as we noted earlier,[85] a party whose own non-firsthand knowledge statement is admitted may be able to do nothing more than establish the absence of firsthand knowledge. Thus, it is by no means clear that the absence of a firsthand knowledge requirement creates any greater problems in the vicarious admission context than in the individual admission context.

10. Co-Conspirators' Admissions

A non-party declarant's statement is admissible for its truth under the co-conspirators' admissions exception if (1) the declarant and the party were both members of a conspiracy and the statement was made (2) during the course and (3) in furtherance of the conspiracy. The "furtherance" require-

---

83. But see pages 418-419 infra for our discussion of the "against interest" requirement for the declaration against interest exception to the hearsay rule.
84. See J. Weinstein and V. Berger, Evidence ¶801(d)(2)(C)[01]-(D)[01].
85. Reconsider the discussion at page 389 supra of the hypothetical involving Elliott.

D. Exemptions from the Definition of Hearsay

ment, however, is often not taken seriously. Declarations that are merely narrative statements of past events and that do nothing to advance the objectives of the conspiracy are frequently admitted.[86] The principal issue with respect to the "during" requirement is whether the exception includes statements made during the concealment phase of the conspiracy, after the conspiracy's objectives have been achieved. The majority position is that such statements are not within the scope of the exception.

There does not have to be a formal charge of conspiracy for the co-conspirators' admissions exception to apply. Indeed, the exception is not limited to criminal prosecutions. As a practical matter, however, the exception is most frequently invoked by prosecutors in criminal actions. Our discussion here reflects this common usage.

One largely artificial rationale for the co-conspirators' admissions exception is that each co-conspirator authorizes (or is deemed to have authorized) the statements of other co-conspirators. A more practical rationale is necessity: Conspiracies tend to be secret enterprises that are difficult to prove. Some of the best evidence—and perhaps essential evidence if a prosecutor is to prove a defendant's guilt beyond a reasonable doubt—will be statements made by co-conspirators. Thus, just as it is arguably appropriate to burden a principal who chooses to conduct affairs through an agent with the risk that the agent's statements will be used against the principal, so also it is arguably appropriate to burden a person who chooses to engage in a conspiracy with the risk that co-conspirators' statements will be used against that person.

There is also a somewhat weak reliability rationale for the exception: To the extent that the "in furtherance of the conspiracy" requirement is taken seriously, co-conspirators' declarations may tend to be trustworthy because of their importance to the enterprise. In addition, many co-conspirators' declarations will fairly obviously be against the interest of the declarant at the time the declaration is made, and this "against interest" feature is commonly regarded as a circumstantial guarantee of trustworthiness.[87] As we have noted, however, the furtherance requirement is often not taken seriously, and there is no requirement that the declaration appear to be against the declarant's interest at the time it is made. Furthermore, if the declaration is not obviously against the interest of the declarant and is obviously against the interest of the party against whom it is offered, there may be reason to doubt the declarant's trustworthiness. Perhaps the declarant is (falsely) trying to shift the blame to the party. Particularly if the "during" requirement extends to the concealment phase (where there is probably a

---

86. But see United States v. Urbanik, 801 F.2d 692 (4th Cir. 1986) (casual conversation following drug purchase about weightlifting during which seller mentioned defendant as excellent weightlifter and as the supplier of drugs not admissible against defendant because not in furtherance of conspiracy).

87. See pages 415-419 infra (discussion of the declarations against interest exception to the hearsay rule).

somewhat greater likelihood that each co-conspirator will be primarily concerned with self-protection), there is reason to question the reliability of statements implicating some person other than the declarant.

Another partial rationale for the exception is similar to one of the rationales for admitting for their truth prior statements of a witness: Just as some witnesses' prior statements will be admissible for non-hearsay impeachment purposes, some co-conspirators' statements will be independently admissible for some non-hearsay purposes. For example, in a prosecution of Smith for conspiracy with Jones (now deceased) to extort money from Abel and Baxter, the prosecutor might allege and try to prove that the conspiracy was carried out by acts of violence and threats of violence. Abel's testimony about Jones' statements that Smith had been violent toward Baxter would be relevant for two purposes. First, the words themselves, apart from their truth, were fear-inducing acts of intimidation; second, if we rely on the truth of Jones' statement, the acts of violence toward Baxter are also acts of intimidation. If the evidence would be admissible in any event for the first purpose, and if one doubts the jury's ability to comprehend and apply limiting instructions, perhaps the evidence should be admissible for its truth as well.

A question that has often been the focal point of litigation regarding the co-conspirator exception (and, perhaps surprisingly, seldom the focus of litigation with respect to other hearsay exceptions) is the role of the judge and jury in deciding whether the requirements of the exception have been satisfied. Prior to the adoption of the Federal Rules, the majority federal position was that the prosecutor had to introduce "some evidence" or "*prima facie* proof" that both the declarant and the party against whom the evidence was offered were involved in the conspiracy.[88] It is not clear precisely what these phrases meant, but apparently they were more akin to the conditional relevance standard of FRE 104(b) ("evidence sufficient to support a finding") than to the FRE 104(a) (judge decides by at least a preponderance of the evidence) standard. Once the "some" or "*prima facie*" evidence standard had been satisfied, the co-conspirators' declarations would be admissible. The jurors, however, would be instructed not to consider these statements for their truth unless they found that the declarant and the defendant were both members of the conspiracy. The instruction sometimes said that before they could consider the statements, the jurors had to find beyond a reasonable doubt that the declarant and the defendant were involved in the conspiracy.

Such a "beyond a reasonable doubt" standard is nonsensical if the only charge before the jury is conspiracy: If the jurors find a conspiracy beyond a reasonable doubt without considering the truth of the statements, there is no need for the statements in the first place. On the other hand, if there are substantive crimes charged, it is theoretically possible that the jury may find the conspiracy beyond a reasonable doubt without regard to the truth of the

---

88. The requirement existed with respect to the "during" and "furtherance" requirements, as well. There is not likely to be a factual dispute about these matters, however. There frequently are factual disputes about who members of the conspiracy are.

D. Exemptions from the Definition of Hearsay

co-conspirators' statements and that the truth of those statements would make the difference between a reasonable doubt and no reasonable doubt on the substantive counts. It seems unlikely, however, that the jurors would engage in such mental gymnastics.

There is no indication that the drafters of the Federal Rules had any intent to change the operation of the co-conspirators' admissions exception; and there is no indication that the drafters thought they were doing anything other than restating well-established common law principles in FRE 104(a) and (b). Indeed, the Advisory Committee's Note to FRE 104 characterizes FRE 104(a) as incorporating "accepted practice" and FRE 104(b) as providing "accepted treatment" that is "consistent with that given fact questions generally." Nonetheless, apparently as a result of the codification of standard preliminary fact rules in FRE 104 and the propensity to litigate preliminary fact issues in the context of the co-conspirators' admissions rule, the law has changed. In 1987, the Supreme Court in Bourjaily v. United States[89] adopted the position that had been taken by a majority of the federal circuits since the adoption of the Federal Rules: Whether the preliminary facts necessary for the co-conspirator exception have been satisfied is an FRE 104(a) question for the judge alone to decide by a preponderance of the evidence.

Bourjaily also addressed what is commonly referred to as the "bootstrap" issue: whether it is appropriate for the judge to consider the content of the hearsay declaration itself in deciding whether the preliminary facts that would warrant admissibility have been satisfied. In Glasser v. United States,[90] the Court took the position that co-conspirators' declarations "are admissible [for their truth] over the objection of [the defendant] . . . only if there is proof *aliunde* that he is connected with the conspiracy. . . . Otherwise, hearsay would lift itself by its own bootstraps to the level of competent evidence." 315 U.S. at 74-75.

Some lower courts interpreted *Glasser* only as prohibiting exclusive reliance on the content of the hearsay declaration to establish the preliminary facts. A majority of the federal circuits, however, both before and after the adoption of the Federal Rules of Evidence, interpreted *Glasser* as requiring that the preliminary facts for the co-conspirator exception be established by evidence completely independent of the hearsay declaration. *Bourjaily* adopted the minority position:

> Rule 104(a) provides: ". . . In making its [preliminary fact] determination [the court] is not bound by the rules of evidence except those with respect to privileges." Similarly, Rule 1101(d)(1) states that the Rules of Evidence (other than with respect to privileges) shall not apply to "[t]he determination of questions of fact preliminary to admissibility of evidence when the issue is to be determined by the court under rule 104." The question thus presented is

---

89. 107 S. Ct. 2775 (1987).
90. 315 U.S. 60 (1942).

whether any aspect of *Glasser's* bootstrapping rule remains viable after the enactment of the Federal Rules of Evidence. . . .

Petitioner claims that Congress evidenced no intent to disturb the bootstrapping rule, which was embedded in the previous approach, and we should not find that Congress altered the rule without affirmative evidence so indicating. It would be extraordinary to require legislative history to *confirm* the plain meaning of Rule 104. The Rule on its face allows the trial judge to consider any evidence whatsoever, bound only by the rules of privilege. We think that the Rule is sufficiently clear that to the extent that it is inconsistent with petitioner's interpretation of *Glasser* . . . , the Rule prevails.[2] . . .

We need not decide in this case whether the courts below could have relied solely upon [the alleged co-conspirator's] hearsay statements to determine that a conspiracy had been established by a preponderance of the evidence. To the extent that *Glasser* meant that courts could not look to the hearsay statements themselves for any purpose, it has clearly been superseded by Rule 104(a). It is sufficient for today to hold that a court, in making a preliminary factual determination under Rule 801(d)(2)(E), may examine the hearsay statements sought to be admitted. As we have held in other cases concerning admissibility determinations, "the judge should receive the evidence and give it such weight as his judgment and experience counsel." United States v.

---

2. The Advisory Committee Notes show that the Rule was not adopted in a fit of absent-mindedness. The Note to Rule 104 specifically addresses the process by which a federal court should make the factual determinations requisite to a finding of admissibility:

> If the question is factual in nature, the judge will of necessity receive evidence pro and con on the issue. The rule provides that the rules of evidence in general do not apply to this process. McCormick §53, p.123, n.8, points out that the authorities are "scattered and inconclusive," and observes:
> "Should the exclusionary law of evidence, 'the child of the system' in Thayer's phrase, be applied to this hearing before the judge? Sound sense backs the view that it should not, and that the judge should be empowered to hear *any relevant evidence, such as affidavits or other reliable hearsay.*" [28 U.S.C. App., p.681 (emphasis added [by the Court]).]

The Advisory Committee further noted, "An item, offered and objected to, *may itself be considered in ruling on admissibility,* though not yet admitted in evidence." Ibid. (emphasis added [by the Court]). We think this language makes plain the drafters' intent to abolish any kind of bootstrapping rule. Silence is at best ambiguous, and we decline the invitation to rely on speculation to import ambiguity into what is otherwise a clear rule.

[The entire paragraph containing the last italicized quotation from the Advisory Committee's Note comes immediately after the Advisory Committee's quotation from McCormick regarding the use of "any relevant evidence, such as affidavits or other reliable hearsay." That paragraph reads as follows:

> This view is reinforced by practical necessity in certain situations. An item, offered and objected to, may itself be considered in ruling on admissibility, though not yet admitted in evidence. Thus the content of an asserted declaration against interest must be considered in ruling whether it is against interest. Again, common practice calls for considering the testimony of a witness, particularly a child, in determining competency. Another example is the requirement of Rule 602 dealing with personal knowledge. In the case of hearsay, it is enough, if the declarant "so far as appears [has] had an opportunity to observe the fact declared." McCormick, §10, p.19.

Quite clearly, when placed in context, the Court's italicized language does not "make plain the drafter's intent to abolish any kind of bootstrapping rule." The language has nothing to do with the bootstrapping issue.—Eds.]

D. Exemptions from the Definition of Hearsay

Matlock, 415 U.S. 164, 175 (1974). [107 S. Ct. at 2780-2782 (emphasis in original).]

Justice Blackmun, in an opinion joined by Justices Brennan and Marshall, dissented from the Court's bootstrap holding on two grounds. First, he argued, as most lower courts had held, that FRE 104(a) should not be interpreted as overruling *Glasser*. Second, he maintained that the *Glasser* independent evidence requirement was an important, although admittedly limited, safeguard against the use potentially unreliable hearsay evidence. Id. at 2789-2790.

We can find no indication that either the Advisory Committee in proposing the Federal Rules of Evidence or Congress in enacting them had any idea that they were changing the law with respect to the co-conspirators' admissions exception. Indeed, as noted earlier, the Advisory Committee indicated that FRE 104 was nothing more than a statement of well-established evidentiary principles. Thus, in our view, the silence of the Advisory Committee on the bootstrap issue is significant. We believe there is substantial merit to the proposition that the language of FRE 104 should not be relied upon as the basis for overruling *Glasser*, or, for that matter, for changing the preliminary fact standard to apply to co-conspirators' declarations.

On the other hand, the conclusions that *Bourjaily* reached are quite sound. In most, if not all, instances in which declarations of alleged co-conspirators are offered for their truth against defendants, the statements will be relevant to establish the defendant's guilt without regard to whether the declarant is a co-conspirator. Thus, *Bourjaily's* adoption of the FRE 104(a) test for evaluating the preliminary facts for the co-conspirator exception seems desirable. Furthermore, *Bourjaily's* resolution of the bootstrap issue is reasonable. Since there may be reasons to distrust the reliability of alleged co-conspirators' declarations, it may well be that reliance on nothing but the out-of-court declaration to establish the preliminary facts would be inappropriate. Requiring that the preliminary fact evidence be completely independent of the hearsay declaration, however, is not likely, as even the dissent seemed to recognize, to be a significant safeguard against the introduction into evidence of unreliable hearsay. If judges can be trusted generally to assess hearsay in making preliminary fact determinations, we fail to see why they cannot be trusted to assess properly co-conspirators' declarations.

On its face *Bourjaily* purports to deal only with the co-conspirators' admissions exception to the hearsay rule. The same types of preliminary fact issues that *Bourjaily* addressed, however, can arise in cases involving declarations by alleged agents offered against principals. Indeed, as we noted at the outset of our discussion of the co-conspirator exception, the relationship between the declarant co-conspirator and the party is sometimes characterized as or analogized to an agent-principal relationship. Thus, it would be reasonable to expect *Bourjaily* to have an impact on the operation of FRE 801(d)(2)(C) and (D).

A significant practical problem frequently arises with the manner in which the co-conspirators' admission exception is invoked during a trial. For the sake of presenting an effective story to the jury and in order to minimize the need to call the same witness several times during a trial, the prosecutor may seek to present co-conspirators' admissions outside the normal order of proof, i.e., prior to establishing that the conditions of the exception have been satisfied. For example, if there is a charge of conspiracy, the prosecutor may want the jury to hear much of the same information that the judge must hear in order to make the FRE 104(a) preliminary fact decision about the existence of a conspiracy involving the defendant and the declarant.

FRE 104(b) specifically contemplates that evidence will sometimes be presented out of order: "[T]he court shall admit it upon, *or subject to*, the introduction of evidence sufficient to support a finding of the fulfillment of the condition." (Emphasis added.) There is no similar specific acknowledgment that evidence may be presented to the jury before the judge is satisfied that requisite FRE 104(a) preliminary facts have been established. It is well settled, however, that the court has discretion to alter the normal order of proof with respect to FRE 104(a) as well. Thus, if the prosecutor represents that the requisite foundation evidence will be forthcoming, the court may grant the prosecutor's request to admit conditionally alleged co-conspirators' hearsay statements. Once the co-conspirators' statements are conditionally admitted, however, it may be extremely difficult for the judge or anyone else to separate mentally the "good" evidence from the only conditionally admitted evidence for the purpose of determining whether there is sufficient independent evidence of a conspiracy to justify admission of the co-conspirators' statements. Furthermore, once a judge has conditionally admitted the co-conspirators' statements, the judge may be reluctant to find that the preliminary fact standard has not been satisfied. Such a finding would require the judge either to instruct the jury to disregard the co-conspirators' statements or to declare a mistrial. The former alternative is not a realistic solution in many cases; and because the prosecutor will have presented all—or at least a substantial part—of the state's case before it becomes clear that the preliminary facts cannot be satisfied, the mistrial alternative will frequently be quite expensive.

PROBLEMS

1. Day and Moore were tried jointly for preparing and filing a false partnership income tax return in 1980. The government's evidence tended to show that Day and Moore diverted money from the partnership to themselves by cashing partnership checks and not accounting for the proceeds in either the partnership or their own financial records and income tax returns. Moore testified in his defense and claimed that he did not receive any proceeds from cashing the checks and that he had always instructed Day to

D. Exemptions from the Definition of Hearsay   399

make a proper accounting of partnership funds. As part of its rebuttal, the government seeks to introduce against both Day and Moore a properly authenticated tape recording of a sworn statement that Moore made in an interview with an Internal Revenue Service agent. The recorded statements implicate both Day and Moore and are inconsistent with Moore's trial testimony. The interview took place in December, 1984. What objection, if any, can Day make to the use of this evidence against him?

2. Edith Lapham, whose income tax return was being audited, hired Sam Fisher, an attorney, to represent her in dealing with the IRS. During the course of the audit, Fisher told an IRS auditor that Lapham had unreported income but that Lapham did not know she was required to report the income. Lapham was subsequently indicted for income tax evasion, and at trial the prosecutor calls the IRS auditor to testify about Fisher's statement regarding unreported income. Defendant makes a hearsay objection. What result?

3. Daniel Mahlandt has sued the Wild Canid Survival & Research Center, Inc. and its director of Education, Kenneth Poos, for injuries sustained when Daniel was allegedly bitten by a wolf named Sophie. Sophie was enclosed in the yard at Mr. Poos' residence by a five-foot chain link fence and was chained to the fence with a six-foot-long chain. Daniel, who was $3\frac{1}{2}$ years old at the time of the alleged biting, somehow managed to get into the yard with Sophie. The plaintiff presented no eyewitnesses to the actual biting, but one witness testified that she heard a child's screams and observed Daniel on the ground with Sophie straddling him. Sophie's face was near Daniel's, and Sophie was wailing. (A defense witness will testify that Sophie, almost a year old, had been very gentle and was taken to various schools and institutions as part of a lecture program. Another defense witness, an expert on animal behavior, will testify that when a wolf licks a child's face, that is a sign of care, and that a wolf's wail is a sign of compassion.)

Mr. Poos arrived at his home shortly after the attack. After seeing that Daniel was taken to a hospital, Mr. Poos talked to neighbors about what happened and then went to the Center to report the incident to the Center's president. The president was not in, so Mr. Poos left the following note on his door:

> Please call me at home. Sophie bit a child that came in our back yard. All has been taken care of. I need to convey to you what happened. KP

Several weeks later there was a meeting of the Board of Directors of the Center. Mr. Poos was not present. The minutes of that meeting state that there was a "great deal of discussion about the legal aspects of the incident of Sophie biting the child."

Plaintiff has offered into evidence against both Mr. Poos and against the Center (a) the note written by Mr. Poos and (b) the foregoing passage from the minutes of the board meeting. Both defendants have objected on hearsay grounds to the admission of both pieces of evidence. With respect to each defendant, what result?

4. Zeke Silverman is charged with conspiracy to distribute cocaine. Willard, a prosecution witness, testified that he made three cocaine purchases from Zeke's sister, Pearl Phoenix. On each occasion Pearl left Willard, got in a taxi, and came back a short time later with the cocaine. Willard offers to testify that on each occasion Pearl said that she was going to get the cocaine from her brother and that he heard her direct the taxi driver to take her to a location that he, Willard, knows is near Zeke's residence. Willard also offers to testify that on various occasions Pearl stated that Zeke was her source for cocaine. Zeke objects to any testimony about what Pearl said on the ground that it is inadmissible hearsay. What result?

5. Janice Schultz is suing Walter White for injuries sustained when their automobiles ran into each other. Janice calls Officer Gerald Ames, who offers to testify that he arrived at the scene shortly after the accident and that he heard Walter say, "The entire front windshield was fogged over, and I couldn't see a thing." Walter objects to this evidence on hearsay grounds. Outside the presence of the jury, he testifies that he did not make the statement and that if anyone made the statement it must have been the plaintiff or Sam Smith, who had been a passenger in Walter's car. Officer Ames then testifies—still outside the presence of the jury—that he is positive that one of the men, not the plaintiff, made the statement but that since Walter and Sam were standing fairly near each other, there is a slight possibility that he is mistaken and that Sam made the statement. After hearing this testimony, the judge says she is at a complete loss to know which person made the statement. How should the judge rule on Walter's objection?

6. Same facts as in Problem 5 except that the statement the officer heard is "I had dozed off and was asleep at the moment of impact."

7. Defendant is charged with extortion and conspiracy to extort in a jurisdiction in which the judge must find by a preponderance of the evidence that the requirements for the co-conspirator admission exception have been satisfied. The prosecutor asks the judge to permit hearsay statements of alleged co-conspirators to be admitted prior to the requisite proof of the preliminary facts. The prosecutor represents that the preliminary facts will be established with the testimony of subsequent witnesses. The judge grants the prosecutor's request and at the time gives the following cautionary instruction to the jury: "I am provisionally admitting these hearsay statements pursuant to what is called the co-conspirator admission provision. If the prosecutor does not introduce sufficient independent evidence of the existence of a conspiracy, I may ask you later to disregard these hearsay statements." The prosecutor's subsequent evidence satisfies the judge that the co-conspirators' statements were properly admitted, and as a result the judge says nothing further to the jury about the evidence.

Was the judge's cautionary instruction wise? If defendant were convicted, would the instruction provide any basis for an appeal?

D. Exemptions from the Definition of Hearsay

8. A group of criminal defense attorneys has expressed concern about the frequent inability to evaluate through cross-examination the reliability of statements admitted pursuant to the co-conspirator admissions provision. As an alternative safeguard for criminal defendants they propose that standard jury instructions in cases in which statements are admitted pursuant to the co-conspirator admission provision should include an instruction that the jury must determine as a preliminary matter whether the defendant and the declarant were involved in a conspiracy. The jury would then be instructed to ignore the co-conspirators' admissions unless they first find by independent evidence that the defendant and the co-conspirator were involved in a conspiracy. Do you think this proposal is a good idea? Are there alternative, and perhaps better, ways to protect defendants against possibly unreliable hearsay statements of alleged co-conspirators?

9. Defendant Tom Adams is being tried for conspiracy to import drugs. He and his alleged co-conspirator, Henry Hopkins, were arrested together. The arresting officer offers to testify for the prosecution as follows: "At the time of the arrest, in Adams' presence Hopkins said, 'Oh, [expletive deleted]! We're caught.' Adams remained silent." Should Adams' hearsay objection be sustained? Does your answer depend on whether the prosecutor can convince the judge that there was a conspiracy involving Adams and Hopkins?

10. Alex Gamble is charged with extortion. An earlier trial on the same charge resulted in a mistrial when it was learned that Alex had attempted to bribe one of the jurors. At the retrial on the extortion charge the prosecutor calls the juror from the first trial, and the juror offers to testify about the bribe. Gamble objects on relevance and hearsay grounds. What result?

11. Jerry Martin has been charged with assault with intent to murder Walter Williams. Mary Albee, an eyewitness to the crime, testified before the grand jury that Martin hit Williams on the head with a baseball bat. At trial, Mary testified on direct examination that Williams attacked Martin, who acted in self-defense.

The prosecution then offers the following evidence:

(a) The testimony of Sharon Ashley that she was with Mary at Mary's residence two days after the attack when the door bell rang. Mary went to the door, and Sharon overheard a male voice say, "Jerry Martin sent me to talk to you. He knows he shouldn't have attacked Mr. Williams, and he is very sorry for his action. He will pay you $1,000 to testify that he acted in self-defense. If you agree to this, come to the Eat-Rite Cafe tomorrow at noon. I will give you $500 then, and you will get the rest after the trial."

(b) Mary's grand jury testimony about Jerry hitting Walter with a baseball bat.

Defense counsel objects to both pieces of evidence and offers the remainder of the grand jury transcript, which shows that Mary was never asked about the cause of the attack on Walter or any of the activities of Walter or Jerry prior to the attack.

Assuming that appropriate objections are made, for what purposes are the foregoing pieces of evidence arguably admissible?

E. THE UNAVAILABILITY EXCEPTIONS: FRE 804

As we noted earlier, the Federal Rules classify the hearsay exceptions into two catagories: Those that apply only if the hearsay declarant is unavailable (FRE 804), and those that apply regardless of whether the declarant is unavailable (FRE 803). Only four hearsay exceptions—former testimony, dying declarations, declarations against interest, and declarations of pedigree—are applicable only when the hearsay declarant is unavailable.[91] Why unavailability is a requirement for only these exceptions is by no means clear. The Advisory Committee's Note to FRE 803 suggests that unavailability is not required for the FRE 803 exceptions because they are reliable hearsay and, therefore, an acceptable substitute for live testimony even if the declarant is available. By contrast, according to the Advisory Committee, hearsay falling within an FRE 804 exception "is not equal in quality to testimony of the declarant on the stand. . . ." These hearsay statements are admissible only as a last resort, i.e., only if the declarant is unavailable to testify in person.

We question—and we urge you to question as you examine the various hearsay exceptions—whether the reliability explanation will withstand scrutiny as the reason for requiring or not requiring unavailability of the declarant. At the same time, we caution you against trying too hard to come up with an overarching theory to rationalize the existing law. It may be that historical accident is the best explanation for the current state of the unavailability requirement.

Part of the underlying rationale of some FRE 803 exceptions would be frustrated by the existence of an unavailability requirement. For example, the records exceptions—see, e.g., FRE 803(6), FRE 803(8)—are justified in part in terms of convenience: It would be extremely burdensome to require all the available individuals who may have contributed to a particular business record to appear in court and give live testimony. On the other hand, it

---

91. FRE 804 contains a fifth exception: the residual provision for a "statement not specifically covered by any of the foregoing exceptions but having equivalent circumstantial guarantees of trustworthiness. . . ." FRE 804(b)(5). An identical provision appears as the last of the FRE 803 exceptions. See FRE 803(24). Thus, it is clear that unavailability is not always required for the admission of a "statement not specifically covered. . . ." We consider the residual exception and why it appears in both FRE 803 and FRE 804 at pages 476-478 infra.

E. The Unavailability Exceptions: FRE 804

would not undermine the rationale for the spontaneous declaration exceptions to the hearsay rule, see FRE 803(1)(3), to require that the declarant be unavailable. The historical precedent for considering spontaneous declarations as res gestae and not hearsay may help explain why these exceptions can be invoked without regard to unavailability.[92]

As you study the various exceptions, consider whether you, as a rule drafter, would extend the unavailability requirement to some of the FRE 803 (or FRE 801(d)(2)(C)-(E)) exceptions or remove the requirement from some of the FRE 804 exceptions.

1. The Meaning of Unavailability

Prior to the adoption of the Federal Rules, what constituted unavailability would vary from jurisdiction to jurisdiction and even from hearsay exception to hearsay exception within a single jurisdiction. For some exceptions in some jurisdictions a claim of privilege or absence from the jurisdiction or, occasionally, even absence from the courtroom would suffice. For dying declarations, death was the only acceptable type of unavailability. The requirement of death, however, may not have been the result of an independent determination of what "unavailability" should mean, but rather a function of the fact that the dying declaration exception applied only in criminal homicide actions.

The Federal Rules and a growing number of states have improved on the common law substantially. FRE 804(a) contains a broad, reasonable definition of unavailability that applies uniformly to all of the exceptions requiring unavailability:

> "Unavailability as a witness" includes situations in which the declarant—
> (1) is exempted by ruling of the court on the ground of privilege from testifying concerning the subject matter of the declarant's statement; or
> (2) persists in refusing to testify concerning the subject matter of the declarant's statement despite an order of the court to do so; or
> (3) testifies to a lack of memory of the subject matter of the declarant's statement; or
> (4) is unable to be present or to testify at the hearing because of death or then existing physical or mental illness or infirmity; or
> (5) is absent from the hearing and the proponent of a statement has been unable to procure the declarant's attendance (or in the case of a hearsay exception under subdivision (b)(2), (3), or (4), the declarant's attendance or testimony) by process or other reasonable means.
> A declarant is not unavailable as a witness if exemption, refusal, claim

---

92. See page 423 infra.

of lack of memory, inability, or absence is due to the procurement or wrong-doing of the proponent of a statement for the purpose of preventing the witness from attending or testifying.

The parenthetical clause in FRE 804(a)(5) was added by Congress to the rule originally promulgated by the Supreme Court. The subdivisions referred to in that clause are, respectively, the exceptions for dying declarations, declarations against interest, and declarations of pedigree. The only FRE 804 exception not specifically listed, (b)(1), is for former testimony. The purpose of the parenthetical clause is to make it clear that the proponent of a dying declaration, a declaration against interest, or a declaration of pedigree must have attempted "to depose a witness (as well as to seek his attendance) as a precondition to the witness being deemed unavailable."[93] Do you think this congressional amendment improved the rule?

In the context of a criminal prosecution the question whether "reasonable means," FRE 804(a)(5), have been used to procure the attendance of an absent witness has constitutional overtones. In Barber v. Page,[94] the hearsay declarant was in federal prison in another state, but there was a federal policy to honor subpoenas for witnesses to testify. Thus, even though declarant was technically beyond subpoena power of state, it was likely that the prosecutor could have secured the declarant's attendance. The introduction of the declarant's former testimony in the absence of reasonable efforts by the prosecutor to procure the declarant's attendance, the Court held, violated the defendant's sixth amendment right to confront witnesses.[95]

PROBLEM

Consider which of the following may be sufficient to constitute unavailability for the purposes of the FRE 804 hearsay exceptions:

1. The hearsay declarant is on the witness stand but invokes the fifth amendment privilege against self-incrimination.
2. The party offering the hearsay evidence submits an affidavit stating that the declarant is in another state beyond the subpoena power of the court.
3. The party offering the hearsay evidence submits the declarant's affidavit stating that the declarant does not recall the events in question.

---

93. Report of the Committee on the Judiciary, H. Rep. No. 93-650.
94. 390 U.S. 719 (1968). The case is discussed more fully at pages 354-355 supra.
95. But cf. Mancusi v. Stubbs, 408 U.S. 204 (1972) (hearsay declarant was out of country and, unlike declarant in *Page*, had been extensively cross-examined at earlier proceeding; failure to try to contact declarant prior to use of former testimony not a violation of defendant's sixth amendment confrontation right), discussed at pages 355-356 supra.

E. The Unavailability Exceptions: FRE 804

4. The hearsay declarant is on the witness stand and claims to have no current memory of the events in question, and the judge believes this testimony.
5. The hearsay declarant is on the witness stand and claims to have no current memory of the events in question, and the judge does not believe this testimony.

2. Former Testimony

Consider the following situation:

> Paula has sued Drew for personal injuries caused in an automobile accident. Wilma testifies for Paula that Drew was drunk at the time and had been driving on the wrong side of the road. There is a judgment for Paula, but the judgment is reversed on appeal because of improper jury instructions. Wilma dies before the retrial, so Paula offers a transcript of Wilma's testimony from the first trial.

Even though Wilma's former testimony is hearsay, there are good reasons for admitting it into evidence at the second trial. Because exactly the same issues are involved in the retrial, the motives of Paula and Drew to develop fully the testimony were as great at the first trial as they are now. Moreover, the parties each had an opportunity to develop the testimony through direct and cross-examination; and if the cross-examination had cast any doubt on the truth of what Wilma said on direct examination, Drew could introduce relevant parts of the cross-examination at the retrial. Finally, since Wilma is dead, the available choice is not live testimony or hearsay, but rather hearsay or nothing.

This all-or-nothing choice, of course, always exists when the hearsay declarant is unavailable (although there may sometimes be other relevant evidence on the same point, so the need for the hearsay will in fact vary from case to case). Although perhaps the law should be otherwise, the all-or-nothing choice is not itself enough to justify the admission of hearsay evidence. There must also be circumstantial guarantees of trustworthiness or some other reasons to forego immediate cross-examination. With respect to former testimony, the prior opportunity to develop the testimony is the substitute for present cross-examination.

Given the existence of the prior opportunity to develop the testimony, why is it necessary to require that the declarant be unavailable in the first place?

Whatever you answer to the preceding question, it should not be surprising that the evidence in our hypothetical, where the declarant is unavailable, falls squarely within the former testimony exception to the hearsay rule: It is, in the language of FRE 804(b)(1), "testimony given as a witness at another hearing of the same or a different proceeding," and "the party against whom the evidence is now offered . . . had an opportunity and similar motive to develop the testimony by direct, cross, or redirect examination."

Some of the former testimony cases articulate a requirement that the evidence be offered on the *same issue*. Apart from ensuring that the motive to develop the testimony is the same, however, there is no reason to insist that the issue be precisely the same. Assume, for example, that the judgment in our hypothetical was reversed because the jury was instructed to apply a negligence rather than a gross negligence standard to the defendant's conduct. Wilma's former testimony should not be precluded at the second trial because the issue to which the testimony relates is now "gross negligence" instead of "negligence." The testimony is undoubtedly still relevant, and it is difficult to believe that the motive of the parties to develop the testimony is any different because of the different legal standard against which the defendant's culpability will be measured. Appropriately, FRE 804(b)(1) makes no reference to a same issue requirement.

Now, consider several further variations of our hypothetical:

> (a) Wilma surprised Paula by testifying on direct examination at the first trial that Paula had been speeding and that Paula drove across the center line and hit Drew's car. At the second trial, Drew offers this former testimony, and Paula objects on the ground that she did not have an opportunity to cross-examine Wilma.
>
> (b) Rhoda, a passenger in Paula's car, has sued Drew for personal injuries. By the time Rhoda's case goes to trial, Wilma has died, and Rhoda offers Wilma's testimony from the first Paula v. Drew trial about Drew being drunk and driving on the wrong side of the road.
>
> (c) Paula has sued Barney to recover damages for her injuries in the accident with Drew. Barney is the owner of the tavern where Drew had been drinking prior to the accident. Wilma has died, and Paula offers Wilma's testimony from the first Paula v. Drew trial about Drew being drunk and driving on the wrong side of the road.

Our first variation is easy to resolve. It does not matter that Paula did not have an opportunity to "cross-examine" Wilma. It is sufficient, in the language of FRE 804(b)(1) that Paula had the "opportunity and similar motive to develop the testimony by *direct*, cross, or *redirect* examination." (Emphasis added.) The Federal Rules specifically permit a party to impeach the credibility of any witness, including a witness called by the party, see FRE 607; and FRE 611, which sets forth general guidelines for the "mode and order" of presenting evidence, provides sufficient flexibility for Paula to develop fully and to explore weaknesses in Wilma's testimony. FRE 611(a) mandates that "the court shall exercise reasonable control over the mode . . . of interrogating witnesses . . . so as to . . . make the interrogation and pre-

E. The Unavailability Exceptions: FRE 804

sentation effective for the ascertainment of the truth"; and FRE 611(c) provides that "leading questions should not be used on direct examination of a witness *except as may be necessary to develop the witness' testimony.*" (Emphasis added.) Thus, unless the trial judge unduly restricted Paula's direct and redirect examination, she has nothing about which to complain.

At common law, a party was deemed to vouch for the credibility of witnesses called by the party and, as a result, was prohibited from impeaching those witnesses. If such a "voucher" rule were applicable to Paula, her ability to develop fully Wilma's testimony would have been restricted (unless Wilma had been declared a hostile witness by the court, in which case impeachment would have been appropriate). The former testimony, however, would still be admissible against Paula because she had vouched for Wilma's credibility in the first instance.[96]

The second variation of our hypothetical also presents no serious problem. Some of the older former testimony cases speak of an "identity of parties" requirement. Many modern cases and the Federal Rules, however, recognize there is no sound basis for such a requirement. There is no reason why the party offering the former testimony must have been a party to the proceeding in which the testimony was given. Rather, it is sufficient if the party *against whom the evidence is offered* had an opportunity to develop the testimony. In our hypothetical, since Drew had an opportunity to develop the testimony, it does not matter that the person now offering the testimony is Rhoda rather than Paula. The former testimony exception is applicable.[97]

The third variation of the hypothetical is somewhat troublesome. Here, Barney, the party against whom the evidence is offered did not have an opportunity to develop the testimony. Thus, to admit the evidence against him is, in effect, to impose upon him the selection of counsel that was made by Drew. If Drew had been represented by a mediocre attorney who did not do a good job of developing the testimony, Barney would be stuck with that result even though his attorney might have done a substantially better job of discrediting Wilma. On the other hand, Drew had the opportunity to develop the testimony and to discredit Wilma, and his motive for doing so was identical to Barney's. Given the fact that the alternative is to forego completely relevant evidence, the fact that Drew had the opportunity and a similar motive to develop the testimony is arguably sufficient to permit admission of the evidence against Barney. Moreover, as a practical matter,

---

96. The common law voucher rule and its abolition by FRE 607 are considered further in Chapter Six.
97. A similar "identity of parties" requirement once existed with respect to the doctrine of collateral estoppel: A party would be estopped from relitigating an issue only if that party and the party seeking estoppel had previously litigated the issue. In the collateral estoppel context, the identity of parties requirement has been substantially eroded, so that now the doctrine applies if the party against whom the estoppel is sought had litigated the issue. If there is no identity of parties requirement in the collateral estoppel context, where the consequence of the estoppel is inability to litigate an issue, it should follow *a fortiori* that identity of parties should not be a requirement for the former testimony exception, where the only consequence of applying the exception is admissibility of evidence.

Drew himself may not have been aware of the skills or able to control the actions of his attorney. Thus, while it may at first blush sound unfair to characterize use of the evidence against Barney as sticking Barney with Drew's choice of an attorney, it may be no more "unfair" to do this than to stick Drew with the choice of attorney that he initially made and that he may later regret.

The Federal Rules promulgated by the Supreme Court permitted the use of former testimony whenever the party against whom the evidence is offered or some third person with a similar motive had the opportunity to develop the testimony. The Judiciary Committee of the House of Representatives, however, took the view that

> it is generally unfair to impose upon the party against whom the hearsay evidence is being offered responsibility for the manner in which the witness was previously handled by another party. The sole exception to this, in the Committee's view, is when a party's predecessor in interest in a civil action or proceeding had an opportunity and similar motive to examine the witness.

As a result, FRE 804(b)(1) now defines the scope of the exception as follows:

> Testimony given as a witness at another hearing . . . , or in a deposition . . . , if the party against whom the testimony is now offered, or, in a [current] civil action . . . , a predecessor in interest [to the party against whom the evidence is now offered], had an opportunity and similar motive to develop the testimony by direct, cross, or redirect examination.

The rule as adopted—without the bracketed language—is grammatically correct, but its multiple clauses make it difficult to follow. We inserted the bracketed language to make it clear that "civil" action refers to the current action and that "predecessor in interest" refers to the predecessor of the civil litigant against whom the evidence is now offered.

If one thinks for a minute about the relationship between the prior action and the current action, this reading is the only one that makes sense substantively. There is no reason to have the admissibility of former testimony depend upon whether the former proceeding was civil or criminal. There may, however, be a reason for requiring that the party to a current criminal action and not some third person be the one that had the opportunity to develop the testimony earlier: Concern with a criminal defendant's right to confront and cross-examine witnesses may warrant such an evidentiary rule. Even if it would not be a violation of the sixth amendment confrontation clause to admit former testimony against a criminal defendant who did not have the opportunity to cross-examine the declarant—and the Advisory Committee was convinced that it would not be unconstitutional to do so[98]—it may be desirable as a matter of evidentiary policy or as part of a policy of

---

98. See FRE 804, Advisory Committee Note.

E. The Unavailability Exceptions: FRE 804

drafting rules to avoid possible constitutional issues to provide that criminal defendants must themselves have had the opportunity to develop the testimony in the earlier proceeding. In any event, under FRE 804(b)(1) former testimony is never admissible against a criminal defendant unless the defendant had an opportunity to develop the testimony; and former testimony is admissible against a civil litigant if either (a) the litigant or (b) a predecessor in interest to the litigant had an opportunity and a similar motive to develop the testimony.

If the opportunity of a predecessor in interest to develop the testimony is sufficient in civil actions, we cannot think of any good reason why it should not also be sufficient with respect to former testimony offered *against the government* in a criminal prosecution. Yet, if one reads FRE 804(b)(1) literally, the opportunity of a predecessor in interest to develop the testimony can satisfy the exception only in civil cases.

As you will see when we consider FRE 803(8), the official records exception, courts have interpreted a prohibition against the use of certain records in "criminal cases" to bar only prosecutors and not defendants from using the records. Consider whether a similar interpretation should be given to FRE 804(b)(1). (As a practical matter, the issue is unlikely to arise. When the same issues are the subject of both criminal and civil litigation, the criminal litigation is likely to precede the civil litigation.)

The question that remains in our final variation of the hypothetical is whether Drew, who had the opportunity to develop Wilma's testimony, is a predecessor in interest to Barney. Perhaps surprisingly, there is not a clear answer to this question. The term *predecessor in interest* is not defined in the Federal Rules or in the legislative history, and courts considering the issue have taken two quite different paths. Some interpret the term narrowly and include only relationships in which individuals stand in privity to each other in some traditional property or contract law sense.[99] According to this view, Wilma's former testimony would not be admissible against Barney. Other courts interpret predecessor in interest broadly by equating interest with motive.[100] According to this latter view, any party to an earlier proceeding who had a similar motive to develop fully the testimony is a predecessor in interest. Thus, the evidence would be admissible against Barney.

The Report of the Senate Judiciary Committee on the Federal Rules of Evidence lends some support to the broad reading of "predecessor in interest." In acceding to the House's narrowing of the Supreme Court's rule, the Senate Judiciary Committee stated:

> Although the committee recognizes considerable merit to the rule submitted by the Supreme Court, a position which has been advocated by many scholars

---

99. See, e.g., In re IBM Peripheral EDP Devices Antitrust Litigation, 444 F. Supp. 110 (N.D. Cal. 1978).
100. See, e.g., Lloyd v. American Export Lines, Inc., 580 F.2d 1179 (3d Cir.), *cert. denied*, 439 U.S. 969 (1978).

and judges, we have concluded that *the difference between the two versions is not great* and we accept the House amendment. [Emphasis added.]

Which interpretation of "predecessor in interest" do you think is preferable?

When former testimony is admissible, any witness with present knowledge of the content of the former testimony can relate what was said. The most common method of getting former testimony before the fact finder, however, is to introduce a properly authenticated transcript of the testimony. Use of a transcript for this purpose actually involves multiple hearsay. First, there is the out-of-court statement of the now unavailable witness; second, there is the activity of the court reporter in taking down what the witness says; and third, there is the activity of the court reporter in making a transcript of the testimony. There is at least the theoretical possibility that the court reporter may fabricate the testimony or make a perception error, either initially or during the transcription process. These risks, however, are probably slight; and as we shall see, the business or official records exception will apply to the court reporter's hearsay.

Regardless of what method is used to introduce former testimony, there is a possibility that the former testimony may itself be objectionable for some reason. For example, the former testimony may have been elicited in response to a leading question; it may have contained an impermissible lay opinion; it may have been privileged; or it may have been inadmissible hearsay. In these types of situations, the question arises whether objections can be made to exclude former testimony that meets all the requirements of the former testimony exception. The Federal Rules do not address this issue. McCormick, after noting that some courts say always and other courts say never, states:

> The more widely approved view, however, is that objections which go merely to the form of the testimony, as on the ground of leading questions, unresponsiveness, or opinion, must be made at the original hearing, when they can be corrected, but objections which go to the relevancy or the competency of the evidence may be asserted for the first time when the former testimony is offered at the present trial. [McCormick's Handbook on the Law of Evidence 770 (3d ed., Cleary, 1984).]

For the most part McCormick's summary represents sound policy. If the substance of an unavailable declarant's testimony would not be admissible in the event that the declarant were present in court, the mere fact that the information appears in the form of former testimony provides no reason for dispensing with the objection. On the other hand, if the objection is one that could have been overcome at the first proceeding by rephrasing questions to the witness, it is arguably inappropriate to sustain the objection at the present trial, where the unavailability of the witness precludes the rephrasing opportunity. Indeed, even if an objection to form had been made and er-

E. The Unavailability Exceptions: FRE 804

roneously overruled at the earlier proceeding, the party against whom the evidence is now offered arguably should not be entitled to have the objection sustained at the current proceedings. Rephrasing is just as impossible in this situation as in the situation in which the objection is made for the first time at the current proceeding.

PROBLEMS

1. Roland is the sole beneficiary of a will that his uncle, Thomas, executed in 1984. In 1985 Roland was the moving party in a proceeding to have Thomas committed to a mental institution. Roland called Anthony, Barbara, and Cleo, all of whom testified to various incidents of Thomas' irrational behavior during the past several years. Thomas died in 1986, and Preston, Thomas' adopted son, who would inherit Thomas' estate by intestate succession, is contesting the validity of the will on the ground that Thomas was incompetent when he executed the will. Preston offers into evidence the testimony from the commitment proceeding of Anthony, Barbara, and Cleo, all of whom are also now deceased. Is the evidence admissible?

2. Alex and Brenda Dawson are suing the Delta Insurance Company for the loss they sustained when a warehouse they jointly owned was destroyed in a fire. Delta has refused payment because a clause in the policy precludes recovery in the event that either owner is responsible for damage to the property. The insurance company claims that Alex arranged to have Eddy Hall burn the building. Eddy pleaded guilty to arson and testified against Alex at Alex's arson trial, which resulted in a hung jury. Delta calls Eddy to testify in the current action, and Eddy invokes the fifth amendment privilege against self-incrimination and refuses to testify. Delta then offers a properly authenticated transcript of Eddy's testimony at Alex's arson trial. Alex objects on the ground that he now has new information that would lead him to engage in a very different type of cross-examination than the cross-examination that actually occurred at the arson trial. Brenda objects on the ground that she did not have any opportunity to cross-examine Eddy. In addition, both Alex and Brenda object on the ground that Eddy is now unavailable. How should the court rule?

3. Assume that you represent the Delta Insurance Company in Problem 2 and that you anticipate being able to introduce the former testimony against at least one of the plaintiffs. Who, specifically, will you want to have with you in the courtroom and what steps, specifically, will you take to introduce this evidence?

4. Jake Matson is charged with possession of narcotics with the intent to sell. The prosecutor introduces narcotics found during a legal search of Jake's residence, and then calls Jake's girlfriend, Patty Armbrust, who had testified at Jake's preliminary hearing. When Patty refuses to testify at the trial, the prosecutor offers Patty's preliminary hearing testimony that she

overheard Jake's friend, Walter, talking on the telephone in Jake's kitchen. According to Patty at the preliminary hearing, Walter said, "Jake and I just made a big purchase. We can supply all of your needs without any difficulty." Jake objects to the admissibility of this evidence.

As part of his defense Jake wants to establish that the drugs discovered in his house belonged to Patty, who spends a good deal of time on the premises. Patty persists in her refusal to testify; however, Jake has the transcript of Patty's testimony in a criminal prosecution against Adam Gellers, who was charged with aggravated assault. Patty was one of several witnesses who testified for the prosecution that she observed Gellers enter the apartment house where the victim of the assault resided. During cross-examination Gellers' attorney asked Patty, "Isn't it true that you frequently use cocaine?" and Patty responded, "Yes." There was no further cross or redirect examination of Patty. Jake offers the cross-examination about the cocaine, and the prosecution objects.

Should either piece of Patty's former testimony be admissible?

5. Peter has sued Dolly for injuries received when Peter fell from an elevated walkway that crosses a stream on Dolly's property. Peter calls Alice as a witness. She testifies that she was with Peter at the time of the accident and the walkway was icy and extremely slippery. Alice was cross-examined vigorously about the condition of the bridge but she stuck to her story.

Later in the trial Dolly offers the transcript of Alice's deposition in which Alice said that there was lots of salt and sand on the walkway and that at the time Peter fell he was trying to do a handstand on edge of the walkway. Is this evidence admissible?

3. Dying Declarations

The dying declaration exception to the hearsay rule is one of the oldest exceptions and also one of the most problematic in terms of the soundness of its underlying rationale. At common law the exception could be invoked only in homicide prosecutions,[101] and it required (1) that the declarant be in imminent fear of death and (2) that the declaration be about the cause or circumstances of the impending death. The "imminent fear of death" requirement could be satisfied by the declarant's own statement or by circumstances such as the nature of the declarant's wound or evidence that the declarant was told that death was imminent. Some of the cases—particularly the older ones—required a strong showing that the declarant realized death was imminent.

Modern versions of the exception retain the "imminent fear" and "cause or circumstances" requirements, but many jurisdictions have broadened the

---

[101]. Prior to the early nineteenth century, the common law did not limit the exception to homicide actions. See McCormick's Handbook on the Law of Evidence 830 (3d ed., Cleary, 1984).

E. The Unavailability Exceptions: FRE 804

exception in two respects. First, although as a practical matter the person making a declaration in imminent fear of death is likely to die, the exception may require only unavailability, not death. Second, rule drafters invariably focus upon and frequently broaden the category of cases in which dying declarations may be admissible. The most likely criminal actions, besides homicides, to be included within the scope of the exception are rapes and other serious assaults; the most likely civil actions are those for wrongful death. FRE 804(b)(2) permits the use of dying declarations in any civil action and in criminal homicide prosecutions. The declarant need not be dead but only unavailable within the meaning of FRE 804(a).

The rationale for the exception is twofold. First, the unavailability of the declarant means that there may not be another means of obtaining the same or similar evidence. Moreover, many assaults occur in the privacy of a home or in situations in which there are not likely to be eyewitnesses to the assault. Thus, particularly with respect to information about the "cause or circumstances" of (what is likely to be) the death of the declarant, the necessity rationale may be particularly strong. Second, there is the notion that a person who realizes that death is imminent will be especially likely to be sincere. After all, it is in the declarant's interest to "meet The Maker" with clean hands, or least with hands that have not recently been soiled by falsehood.

Both rationales are subject to attack. It is not clear that the need for a dying declarant's statement about the cause or circumstances of death is any greater than the need for the statements of any unavailable witness. There may be an absence of available eyewitness to all sorts of events; and there may be alternative forms of evidence available—e.g., ballistics tests, confessions, skid marks, hair or fiber samples—to prove the cause of circumstances of death.

The notion that dying declarations are likely to be reliable is also suspect. The proposition that individuals who are in imminent fear of death are particularly likely to be sincere is sheer speculation. Even if it seems intuitively sound to hypothesize that deeply religious individuals who know they are dying will be sincere, there is no requirement that dying declarants be shown to be religious, and there is no reason to believe that dying declarants in general are disproportionately religious. Furthermore, even if one assumes that dying declarants are likely to be sincere, the circumstances surrounding a dying declaration may exacerbate other hearsay dangers. Studies have shown that individuals tend not to be very accurate observers of sudden unexpected events. Thus, if the declarant is the victim of a sudden attack, there is reason to question the accuracy of the victim's perceptions.[102] Additionally, even though most dying declarations may be made relatively soon

---

102. This same problem exists with respect to the excited utterance exception. See FRE 803(2), discussed at pages 426-429 infra. Indeed, some dying declarations may qualify as excited utterances. If so, they will be admissible regardless of the type of action in which they are offered (and without regard to whether there is adequate proof of imminent fear of death).

after the event described in the declaration, an individual who is suffering enough to believe that death is imminent may have a somewhat clouded memory—perhaps because of drugs that have been administered in order to revive the individual or at least reduce present suffering, or perhaps because of pain or trauma from the incident.

Something else that may be a matter of concern, although it does not relate to the hearsay dangers, is the unseemly manner in which dying declarations are sometimes obtained. In order for the declaration to be admissible, the proponent of the evidence (usually the prosecutor) must demonstrate to the satisfaction of the trial judge that the declarant was in imminent fear of death at time of the declaration. See FRE 104(a). The best way to do this, of course, is to have the declarant acknowledge that death is imminent. Sergeant Friday was a master at developing the requisite foundation in some of the old *Dragnet* television shows: The victim would be lying in a hospital bed with grieving relatives at his side when Sergeant Friday would enter the room, inform the victim that he was going to die, and get the victim to acknowledge the same. Sergeant Friday would then proceed to take the victim's statement.

The very content of the dying declaration exception is a reflection of ambivalence about the exception's underlying rationale:[103] If dying declarations are reliable, why is the scope of the exception limited to only certain types of actions and to only declarations about the cause and circumstances of one's death? Perhaps one can justify the latter limitation on the ground that the declarant is most likely to have firsthand knowledge about and be anxious to talk about the "cause or circumstances" of impending death. Indeed, one might argue that a declarant's statements about other matters at a time when death is apparently imminent casts doubt on either the declarant's sincerity or the declarant's belief in imminent fear of death or both.

The limitation of the exception to only certain actions is more troublesome. At least in all actions (both criminal and civil) based on the defendant's alleged assault on a now unavailable declarant, the need for the evidence to establish the charge would appear to be equal.[104] Thus, it would seem that only (a) a general concern with reliability or (b) a sense of particular need to be able to prove the requisite elements in some limited category of cases can justify the limitation of the dying declaration exception to only

---

103. Another indication of ambivalence is the fact that in some jurisdictions the party against whom a dying declaration is admitted is entitled to a jury instruction that dying declarations are to be considered with caution. (There is also some precedent for such an instruction with respect to hearsay generally, but this precedent is much more limited than the precedent for cautionary instructions about dying declarations.)

The strong showing of imminent fear of death that courts sometimes require is also probably an indication of ambivalence.

104. The need, of course, will not be the same in each individual case. Among the cases involving an assault by the defendant on the dying declarant, however, we can think of no basis for generalizing about the types of causes of action or offenses in which the need for the evidence to establish the elements is likely to be greater or lesser.

E. The Unavailability Exceptions: FRE 804

certain actions. Ironically, both of these factors appear to be at work: We admit the evidence in homicide (and perhaps other serious criminal) cases because we are especially anxious to convict the perpetrators of these crimes;[105] we exclude the evidence in other cases because we are concerned about its reliability—except perhaps we admit the evidence in civil cases, because we are less concerned with erroneous civil judgments than erroneous criminal convictions. The result, of course, is that we are willing to use evidence whose reliability we question in other contexts in order to obtain criminal convictions that carry the most severe sanctions!

FRE 804(b)(2), as promulgated by the Supreme Court and sent to Congress, contained no limitation on the type of actions in which dying declarations could be used. The current version of the rule came from the House Judiciary Committee, which justified its amendment as follows:

> The Committee did not consider dying declarations as among the most reliable forms of hearsay. Consequently, it amended the provision to limit their admissibility in criminal cases to homicide prosecutions, where exceptional need for the evidence is present.

Do you prefer the Supreme Court version because it avoids the anomaly described in the text and the House Committee Report? Or, given concerns about the reliability of dying declarations, is the current rule preferable because it imposes some limitations on the exception?

4. Declarations Against Interest

The declaration against interest exception applies to statements that a reasonable person in the declarant's position would regard as being against interest when made. Assume, for example, that Mark is suing Angela to obtain possession of an antique clock that had belonged to Angela's father, who is currently unavailable. Mark claims that Angela's father sold the clock to him, and Angela claims that her father gave the clock to her. Mark would be permitted to introduce the testimony of witnesses who claim to have heard Angela's father say that he no longer owned the clock. The fact that the statement is against the declarant's interest is thought to give the declaration a sufficient circumstantial guarantee of trustworthiness to warrant admissi-

---

105. Homicide defendants as well as prosecutors can invoke the dying declaration exception, and there is precedent for the introduction by homicide defendants of dying declarations in order to show that some third person committed the murder. As a practical matter, however, it will usually be prosecutors who want to take advantage of the dying declaration exception.

bility, at least if the alternative is foregoing the evidence altogether, which it is since the exception requires unavailability.[106]

In discussing the declaration against interest exception, some courts speak of the requirement that the declarant not have a motive to lie. Other courts and some commentators, however, have correctly pointed out that this should not be regarded as an independent requirement for the exception, but merely as a reminder of the need for the declaration to be against interest.

One difference between the "no motive to lie" formulation and the typical formulation of the against interest requirement is that the former is usually stated in terms of the motive of the individual declarant, whereas the against interest requirement is stated in terms of an "objective," reasonable person standard. This difference, however, has not been and should not be a matter for concern. We typically evaluate the probable motive or intent of an individual by asking what a reasonable person in that individual's position would be thinking; and we typically apply "objective," reasonable person standards in light of the circumstances and facts known to the particular individual whose conduct or statement is in issue. (There may, of course, be disagreement from time to time in various contexts about what particular attributes or circumstances to attribute to the reasonable person.)

The common law limited the declaration against interest exception to declarations against "proprietary" or "pecuniary" interest. Modern versions of the exception tend to take a broad view of what constitutes a pecuniary or proprietary interest and include within the scope of the exception declarations against penal interest. For example, FRE 804(b)(3) defines the exception as follows:

> A statement which was at the time of its making so far contrary to the declarant's pecuniary or proprietary interest, or so far tended to subject the declarant to civil or criminal liability, or to render invalid a claim by the declarant against another, that a reasonable person in the declarant's position would not have made the statement unless believing it to be true. A statement tending to expose the declarant to criminal liability and offered to exculpate the accused is not admissible unless corroborating circumstances clearly indicate the trustworthiness of the statement.

A few jurisdictions extend the exception to declarations against social interest, i.e., to declarations that are likely to subject the declarant to ridicule.[107]

It is important, as we suggested earlier, not to confuse admissions with declarations against interest. The latter exception requires that the declarant

---

106. See 5 J. Wigmore, Evidence in Trials at Common Law 329 (Chadbourn rev. 1974):

> The basis of the exception is the principle of experience that a statement asserting a fact distinctly against one's interest is unlikely to be deliberately false or heedlessly incorrect, and is thus sufficiently sanctioned, though oath and cross-examination are lacking.

107. See, e.g., Cal. Evid. Code §1230.

E. The Unavailability Exceptions: FRE 804

be unavailable, whereas the admissions exception applies to declarations of parties (or their agents or co-conspirators); the latter exception requires that a reasonable person in the declarant's position would realize that the declaration was against interest, whereas there is no similar requirement for admissions; the latter exception applies to only specified types of interest, whereas there is no such limitation with respect to admissions; and the latter exception, like other FRE 803 and 804 exceptions, requires that the declarant have firsthand knowledge, whereas courts generally do not apply this requirement to admissions.

There are two reasons for limiting the declaration against interest exception to statements that are against only specified kinds of interests or for imposing special corroboration requirements, as FRE 804(b)(3) does for declarations against penal interest offered by an accused. First, the rule formulators may have feared that declarations appearing to be against some types of interests are in fact frequently self-serving and, therefore, not trustworthy. For example, it has been suggested that convicted criminals may be willing to confess falsely to other crimes in order to curry favor with the police or to help a friend who has not yet been convicted. Second, there is a concern—again, one that has been expressed primarily with respect to declarations against penal interest—that witnesses may fabricate declarations against interest. For example, a friend of a criminal defendant may be willing to testify falsely that some currently unavailable individual confessed to committing the crime with which the defendant is charged.

Strictly speaking, this latter concern is not a hearsay problem. The witness who we suspect is lying is on the witness stand and subject to cross-examination. Nonetheless, it may be that friends of many criminal defendants are themselves rather unsavory characters, who as a class are more willing than other witnesses to perjure themselves. More importantly, even if witnesses for criminal defendants are not disproportionately willing to perjure themselves, it may be especially difficult to detect a falsehood about a declaration against interest. The supposed declarant is unavailable, and it is reasonable to expect that there may not be corroborative circumstantial evidence to support or cast doubt on the witness' assertion that such a statement was made. If a hearsay exception is likely to invite false testimony or create the opportunity for testimony that often cannot be corroborated, these may be sufficient reasons to forego or limit the exception.

A difficulty that sometimes arises in applying the declaration against interest exception stems from the fact that many declarations are against more than one type of interest. Consider, for example, an automobile accident involving vehicles driven by A, B, C, and D. D died in the accident, and several days after the accident C said that the accident was entirely her fault. C is currently unavailable. B is being prosecuted for vehicular homicide and is being sued for damages by A. C's statement is against both her pecuniary and her penal interest. Can B introduce C's statement in either the criminal or the civil action in a jurisdiction that extends the exception only to declarations against pecuniary and proprietary interest? In a jurisdiction that has adopted FRE 804(b)(3), is the corroboration requirement applicable to *C's* statement?

Except for the fact that the FRE 804(b)(3) corroboration requirement comes into play only when a *criminal defendant* offers a declaration against penal interest, the answers to these questions depend not on the type of action in which the evidence is offered but on the nature of the interest implicated by the statement. But what is that interest?

Perhaps surprisingly in light of the substantial overlap of potential criminal and civil liability, the questions raised by the preceding hypothetical have not received much attention. For the most part courts seems to apply some *a priori*, unarticulated notion that the activity or subject to which the declaration relates is typically in either the civil realm or the criminal realm. And, although the nature of the current action is not the stated criterion, the nature of the action probably has at least some subtle influence on the judge's determination whether the statement is against a penal or a civil interest.

The most serious problem with the declaration against interest exception, in our view, is its rationale. The premise underlying the exception, with which we agree, is that people seldom intentionally say things that are truly against their interest. We find absurd, however, the conclusion that when such statements are made, they are, therefore, likely to be trustworthy. Since people do not normally intentionally say things that are against their interest, it seems much more likely to us that a statement that appears to be against interest is in fact not against interest.

We believe that most statements that are characterized as declarations against interest are likely to fall into one of two categories:

1. They are insincere statements made for some ulterior motive. Consider, for example, the statement of a person trying to break a relationship with lover or spouse: "I'm really no good; I don't deserve somebody as good as you; I'm a terrible companion." We doubt that most declarants who utter these or similar words sincerely believe that all of these statements are objectively true self-characterizations.
2. They are sincere statements that the declarant has no idea may be in some sense against interest. This is likely to be true, for example, of the declaration of Angela's father in the hypothetical at the beginning of the discussion of declarations against interest.

The former type of statements presumably will be excluded if the court determines that there was an ulterior motive for the statement and that it was not, therefore, against interest. Sometimes, however, there may not be much available information bearing on this point. As a result, there is a risk

E. The Unavailability Exceptions: FRE 804

that the declaration against interest exception may result in the admissibility of untrustworthy statements.

To the extent that statements of the latter type are admitted pursuant to the declaration against interest exception, the exception may appear to be allowing the admission of statements that "a reasonable person in the declarant's position would not have made unless believing it to be true." FRE 804(b)(3). The fact that the statement may be characterized as being against interest, however, has nothing to do with the trustworthiness of the statement. Rather, the statement seems trustworthy because there is no apparent motive to lie; and in this respect the statement is no different from many other hearsay statements that do not fall within the declaration against interest (or any other hearsay) exception.

To put the entire matter somewhat differently, we strongly doubt the existence of a positive relationship between a meaningful "against interest" requirement and reliability. As a result, we believe that the exception inevitably operates to admit two quite different types of declarations: (a) statements that appear to be against interest and that have a high risk of being unreliable because the court has failed to see that the statements were not in fact against interest but rather were very much in the interest of the declarant to make; and (b) reliable statements, whose reliability has nothing to do with their "against interest" characterization.

Ideally, one would want to exclude the former type of statements and admit the latter type. Abolition of the declaration against interest exception would accomplish the first objective, but the second objective could be accomplished only by restructuring the hearsay rule to give the judge substantial discretion in admitting what appeared to be reliable hearsay.

Even if one is unwilling to restructure the hearsay rule, it may well be desirable to retain a declaration against interest exception in some form, despite the problems we have pointed out. If the exception in fact operates to admit more of the reliable type of statements than the suspect statements, the existence of the exception is a net plus in terms of its contribution to accurate fact finding. (Our hunch is that at least with respect to declarations that traditionally have been regarded as against pecuniary and proprietary interest, the operation of the exception is a net plus. We have serious doubts about whether the same is true with respect to declarations against penal interest.)

5. Declarations of Pedigree[108]

The common law hearsay exception for declarations of family history not only required that the declarant be unavailable but also required, as assur-

---

108. We deal here only with FRE 804(b)(4) and its common law counterpart, an exception that requires that the declarant be unavailable. You should keep in mind that there are other

ances of reliability, (a) that the declarant be related by blood or marriage to the person about whom the declaration is made and (b) that the declaration be made prior to the time of the controversy that is the subject of the litigation. The Federal Rules continue the unavailability requirement but abandon the other two common law requirements. FRE 804(b)(4) defines the exception as follows:

> (A) A statement concerning the declarant's own birth, adoption, marriage, divorce, legitimacy, relationship by blood, adoption, or marriage, ancestry, or other similar fact of personal or family history, even though declarant had no means of acquiring personal knowledge of the matter stated; or (B) a statement concerning the foregoing matters, and death also, of another person if the declarant was related to the other by blood, adoption, or marriage, *or was so intimately associated with the other's family* as to be likely to have accurate information concerning the matter declared. [Emphasis added.]

The Advisory Committee's Note to FRE 804(b)(4) explains the absence of a requirement that the declaration be made prior to the dispute to which the declaration relates on the ground that the timing of the statement has a "bearing more appropriately on weight than admissibility." McCormick suggests that in "extreme cases" a judge could rely on FRE 403 to exclude statements made after the dispute that is the subject of the litigation had arisen.[109] Do you agree that FRE 403 might be used for this purpose?

The common law pedigree exception, like FRE 804(b)(4)(A), did not require that the declarant have firsthand knowledge. Only a mother conscious during childbirth or a relative present at the time of birth will have direct firsthand knowledge of who a person's natural mother is; and usually only the mother and perhaps the father will know who a person's father is. At the same time, however, any declarant meeting the requirements of either the common law or the federal exception is inevitably going to have a good deal of circumstantial evidence of the family relationships from having observed how individuals relate to each other. Indeed, it may be that this type of circumstantial evidence would be sufficient to satisfy the firsthand knowledge requirement in any event.

Apparently because FRE 804(b)(4)(B) contains an expansion of the common law pedigree exception to close family members, the drafters of the Federal Rules did not extend the elimination of the firsthand knowledge requirement to that subsection. If the elimination of the firsthand knowledge requirement for declarations of pedigree is significant, however, the reasons for eliminating it would appear to be equally strong with respect to both (4)(A) and (4)(B) declarants.

---

hearsay exceptions, not requiring unavailability, that may be helpful in proving family history. See FRE 803(9)-(13) (all dealing with various records that may have family history information); FRE 803(19) (reputation concerning personal or family history); FRE 803(23) (judgments as to personal or family history).

109. See McCormick's Handbook on the Law of Evidence 902 (3d ed., Cleary, 1984).

E. The Unavailability Exceptions: FRE 804

PROBLEMS

1. Anne Applegate is charged with the murder of Harold White. The prosecutor's evidence shows that Anne lived next door to Harold and Janet White, and that there was a long history of bickering between Anne and the Whites. The primary subject of the disputes was a fence that ran between their lots. The fence was erected by the Whites, and Anne claimed that it was on her property. On two different occasions she had managed to rip down part of the fence before the Whites stopped her. On the night of July 24, somebody broke into the White residence and shot both Harold and Janet White. Harold died immediately. Although Janet later slipped into a coma, she is still alive.

The prosecutor offers the following testimony of Alice Turner, a nurse at Bayside Hospital where Janet White has been a patient since the shooting incident: "On July 27, one day before she went into a coma, Janet White said to me, 'Alice, I know I'm going to die, and I need your help. I want to be sure that Anne gets what is due her for all that she has done to Harold and me.'"

Anne Applegate's attorney objects to the admissibility of this evidence, and in a hearing outside the presence of the jury, calls to the witness stand Marcia Simpson, who has been Janet White's physician at Bayside Hospital. Dr. Simpson testifies as follows: "When I spoke with Janet on July 26, she seemed quite spunky. She spoke of wanting to get home soon so she could keep the next door neighbor from tearing down her fence. She did not then or at any other time indicate to me who shot her."

(a) Anne's attorney now objects to the admission of Alice Turner's testimony on the grounds that (i) Janet White was not in imminent fear of death, (ii) Janet's statement is not about the cause or circumstances of what she may believe to be her imminent death because the statement refers to the difference she and Anne have had about the fence and is not an identification of Anne as the assailant, and (iii) in any event, the statement is inadmissible as a dying declaration since Anne is not charged with the murder of Janet. How should the court rule on these objections?

(b) Assume that the court admits Alice Turner's testimony. Anne's attorney now offers the testimony of Dr. Simpson about her discussion with Janet White. The prosecutor objects that this evidence is inadmissible because it goes to the issues whether the requirements of the dying declaration exception have been satisfied and those are issues for the judge to decide. How should the court rule?

2. Velma, fully aware that she is about to die, says, "Dixon shot me." A faith healer then prays with Velma. She miraculously recovers and leaves the jurisdiction. Dixon is charged with aggravated assault on Velma. Can the prosecutor introduce Velma's statement?

3. Nancy Berger has been charged with the murder of Evan Williams. Her defense is an alibi. During the course of the trial, the court admitted,

over Nancy's objection, Evan's deathbed statement naming Nancy as his assailant. Nancy has requested that the following instruction regarding that statement be given to the jury:

> The court has admitted in evidence for your consideration an alleged dying declaration of the deceased. In so admitting the dying declaration the court has only passed upon its admissibility. In order that a statement of the deceased may properly be considered as a dying declaration it must have been made by the deceased with a consciousness of impending death, and if you find from the evidence that such statement by the deceased, if made, was without consciousness on the part of the deceased of impending death, you should not further consider it as a dying declaration.

Should the court give this instruction?

4. X, fully aware that she is about to die, says, "I killed Smith." D, who is on trial for the murder of Smith, offers to introduce this statement, and the prosecution objects. What result?

Would it matter if X's statement were, "Smith shot me and then I killed him" or "I stabbed Smith before he pulled his gun, but he shot me before he died"?

5. Hanna Mason has sued the Acme Rental Company for personal injuries that she sustained as a pedestrian when she was hit by an Acme truck driven by James Lowe, an Acme employee. Lowe was fired the day after the accident, and has recently moved to Acapulco. Before leaving the country, Lowe told his friend, Andy Becker, that he had been drinking at the time of the accident and had failed to stop at a stop sign. Lowe also made the same statement in a deposition taken during the discovery phase of the current law suit. Lowe has refused to respond to plaintiff's letter. At trial, Hanna calls Andy Becker to testify about Lowe's statement. Is the evidence admissible?

6. Sergio Bell is being prosecuted for possession of marijuana that was discovered in the pocket of a raincoat during a legal search of Sergio's apartment on May 23. As part of his defense Sergio offers the following testimony of Mary Wilson: "On the morning of May 23, it was raining hard. As my husband, Ed, was leaving for work, I remember his saying, 'Look at that rain! And I don't have my raincoat. I left it at Sergio's yesterday afternoon.'" Ed Wilson is now dead. Other witnesses confirm that it was raining on May 23. Is Mary Wilson's testimony admissible?

7. Cosimo Demasi sued the Whitney Trust & Savings Bank for $6500 dollars that the plaintiff claimed the bank held in a joint savings account that he maintained with his wife. The bank defended on the ground that all but $700 had been withdrawn by the plaintiff's daughter with the consent of Mr. or Mrs. Demasi. A judgment for the defendant was reversed on appeal, and before the new trial Mrs. Demasi sought to withdraw the $700 that the bank conceded remained in the account. In order to receive the

F. Hearsay Exceptions Not Requiring Unavailability: FRE 803

money, the bank required that Mrs. Demasi sign an affidavit indicating that she had consented to the prior withdrawals. Mrs. Demasi signed the affidavit, withdrew the $700, and died before the second trial began. At the retrial, the bank offers her affidavit. Should it be admitted?

8. Benson and Albrecht are being jointly tried for the crimes of sale and conspiracy to sell drugs. After establishing to the satisfaction of the judge that Benson and Albrecht had been co-conspirators, the prosecutor offers into evidence a police officer's testimony that Albrecht, following his arrest, had confessed to selling drugs. Benson objects to this evidence on hearsay grounds. Should the evidence be admitted?

9. In a suit to establish that Grace is the daughter of the testator, Ephram Enders, Katie Thompson offers to testify as follows: "During the last recess I was out in the corridor and I heard Lydia Lipton, a longtime friend of Ephram and his family, say, 'Grace is Ephram's daughter.'" Is the evidence admissible?

F. HEARSAY EXCEPTIONS NOT REQUIRING UNAVAILABILITY: FRE 803

1. Spontaneous Declarations Generally

From early in the nineteenth century, when the hearsay rule and its exceptions were not well developed, courts have admitted a number of relatively spontaneous out-of-court declarations pursuant to what has become known as the res gestae rule. Literally, *res gestae* means the "thing having been done." For example a Roman might have spoken of the events of the day as the "res gestae." Even in Latin, the term did not have a very precise usage.

Sometimes courts would characterize res gestae evidence as something different from hearsay, and sometimes courts would speak of the res gestae exception to the hearsay rule. Regardless of how the term was characterized, it was regularly applied to (1) declarations that posed no hearsay dangers, (2) declarations that posed only sincerity and narration dangers, and (3) declarations that posed all hearsay dangers. Inevitably, this indiscriminate use of the term detracted from rather than fostered sound analysis of the potential hearsay dangers associated with various spontaneous declarations.

As the law of hearsay developed, there eventually emerged four distinct hearsay exceptions—present sense impression, excited utterance, declaration of present mental state, and declaration of present physical state—whose combined scope encompasses all or at least most of the hearsay declarations that courts in the past have labeled *res gestae*. Because of these exceptions and because the term *res gestae* was attached to so many different kinds of out-of-court declarations, commentators have long urged that the term be abandoned completely. For the most part their pleas were ignored. In the past few years, however, the term *res gestae* seems to have lost some of its popularity among at least appellate judges. We suspect that this is because the Federal Rules, which have become a model for a number of states, do not use the term. In any event, we agree that the term *res gestae* should be abandoned, and we will not use it here. Nonetheless, it has been used pervasively enough in the past that you will undoubtedly encounter it in the library and perhaps even in some courtrooms. Be prepared as an advocate to use the term if you are before a judge that feels comfortable with it, but remember that the term will not be of assistance in a reasoned analysis of hearsay issues.

2. Present Sense Impressions

Of the hearsay exceptions that have grown out of the res gestae concept, the most recent one to receive formal recognition by courts is the present sense impression exception.[110] That exception, in terms of the language of FRE 803(1), covers "[a] statement describing or explaining an event or condition made while the declarant was perceiving the event or condition, or immediately thereafter." The primary rationale for the exception is that the contemporaneity of the declaration tends to ensure the declarant's sincerity. This rationale is based on the premise that the contemporaneity is an indication that the declaration is spontaneous rather than premeditated. If the declaration is indeed spontaneous, there has not been time to fabricate and thus it is sincere. Additionally, the contemporaneity of the declaration virtually eliminates any memory problem.

Consistently with the foregoing sincerity rationale, many courts have interpreted "immediately thereafter" to mean within a matter of seconds. Some courts, however, have relied on FRE 803(1) to admit apparently spontaneous statements made 10 to 15 minutes after the event they describe or explain.[111]

The FRE 803(1) requirement that the declaration be one "describing or explaining an event or condition" is also intended to be a limitation on the exception that is consistent with the exception's underlying rationale. The Advisory Committee explains this limitation by comparing the language of FRE 803(1) to the language of FRE 803(2), the excited utterance exception, which allows the use of spontaneous statements that are prompted by an exciting event:

> Permissible *subject matter* of the statement is limited under Exception (1) to description or explanation of the event or condition, the assumption

---

[110]. The leading case formally recognizing present sense impressions as an exception to the hearsay rule is Houston Oxygen Co. v. Davis, 139 Tex. 1, 161 S.W.2d 474 (1942).

[111]. See, e.g., United States v. Obayagbona, 627 F. Supp. 329 (E.D.N.Y. 1985).

F. Hearsay Exceptions Not Requiring Unavailability: FRE 803 425

being that spontaneity, in the absence of a startling event, may extend no farther. In Exception (2), however, the statement need only "relate" to the startling event or condition, thus affording a broader scope of subject matter coverage.

The Advisory Committee does not elaborate on the meaning of the terms *describing, explaining,* and *relating,* and it is not intuitively obvious how broadly or narrowly they should be defined.

Of course, not all contemporaneous declarations are spontaneous, and particularly if a contemporaneous declaration is obviously self-serving, one may doubt its spontaneity and, therefore, its sincerity. There are two ways in which courts have dealt with this problem. First, courts have tended to apply the time limitation much more rigorously in situations in which the spontaneity of the declaration is questionable.[112] Second, some courts require, as a condition of admitting a present sense impression declaration, that there be some independent corroboration of the substance of the declaration.[113]

We believe that proper attention to preliminary fact finding will remove any perceived need to read a corroboration requirement into FRE 803(1).[114] To satisfy the conditions of the exception, there must be a showing not only that the declaration is proximate in time to the supposed event or condition but also that there was in fact an event or condition that is described or explained by the declaration. This showing of an event or condition is a preliminary fact, and like most preliminary facts that are conditions for the admissibility of hearsay, it should be a fact for the judge to determine pursuant to FRE 104(a).[115] In order for a present sense impression declaration to be admissible, therefore, the court should be convinced by a preponderance of

---

112. Giving a narrow reading to the other words of limitation in the rule—"describing," "explaining," "event," "condition"—in some situations could accomplish the same result. Courts, however, have not focused on the meaning of these terms in applying FRE 803(1).

113. For conflicting views on the desirability of imposing a corroboration requirement on the present sense impression exception, compare McCormick's Handbook on the Law of Evidence 862-863 (3d ed., Cleary, 1984) (corroboration requirement undesirable) with Waltz, The Present Sense Impression Exception to the Rule Against Hearsay, 66 Iowa L. Rev. 869 (1981).

114. For an elaboration of this proposition and a demonstration of the advantages of a preliminary fact finding analysis over a corroboration requirement, see Comment, The Need for a New Approach to the Present Sense Impression Hearsay Exception After State v. Flesher, 67 Iowa L. Rev. 179, 194-204 (1981).

115. The evidence, of course, is relevant only if the declarant honestly and accurately describes what happened. Viewing the evidence from this perspective, one could say in terms of the language of FRE 104(b) that "the relevance of the evidence depends upon the fulfillment of a condition of fact" (i.e., the occurrence of the event or condition). Although analytically this statement is accurate, it is not a correct analysis in view of the hearsay rule. The rule's objective is to prevent the jury from considering the possible truthfulness of out-of-court statements, unless the statements have sufficient guarantees of trustworthiness to compensate for the absence of an opportunity to examine the hearsay declarant. It would undermine this objective to leave ultimately to the jury the question whether those guarantees (here, the occurrence of an event or condition) exist.

the evidence[116] that there was in fact an event occurring or a condition existing at the time of the declaration and that the event or condition is what is being described or explained.

Assuming that there is an event or condition, the judge can determine whether the words describe or explain that event or condition merely from looking at the words. A more difficult question is to what extent the judge should be able to rely on the words to establish the existence of the event or condition. This is the same "bootstrapping" issue that we discussed in the context of the co-conspirators' admissions exception to the hearsay rule,[117] and the analysis there is equally applicable here.

Frequently the witness offering to testify to the present sense impression declaration will be the declarant or someone who was with the declarant at the time of the event, and such a witness is likely to be able to verify the details of the event. Other times, however, detailed corroboration will not be available. Consider, for example, a situation in which the declarant of the apparent present sense impression was speaking to the witness on the telephone. In this type of situation, regardless of whether one speaks in terms of corroboration or preliminary fact finding, any requirement that there be some evidence, other than the declaration itself, of the event or condition necessarily raises the question how detailed the independent proof must be.

If there needs to be independent proof of all the critical details of the declaration, there is likely to be little need for the declaration and, therefore, little reason to have a present sense impression hearsay exception in the first place. It is theoretically possible for a situation to arise in which there is substantial independent but inadmissible evidence of the details of the event or condition but only the present sense impression declaration that is potentially admissible. In our judgment, such a situation is not very likely to arise, however. What is much more likely is that the independent information that the judge considers will also be admissible before the jury. Thus, if the judge requires independent evidence of all the details in the present sense impression declaration, the detailed independent evidence, we suspect, would frequently be enough to convince the jury of the existence of the event or condition described in the present sense impression declaration. On the other hand, if the independent evidence requirement is applied with extreme laxity, the purpose of the requirement may be frustrated.

As a solution to this potential dilemma, one commentator has advocated the following test:

> [C]ourts must be assured by a preponderance of the evidence . . . that (1) an event occurred which is (2) sufficiently consistent with the hearsay statement that it could be the event described by the statement. [Comment, The Need

---

116. As we have noted before, the preponderance standard is the standard that is applicable to most FRE 104(a) preliminary fact finding. If it is generally sufficient elsewhere, we can think of no good reason for applying a higher standard here.

117. See pages 395-397 supra.

F. Hearsay Exceptions Not Requiring Unavailability: FRE 803

for a New Approach to the Present Sense Impression Hearsay Exception After State v. Flesher, 67 Iowa L. Rev. 179, 197 (1981).]

Does this test give sufficient guidance to courts? How might one elaborate on it? Or would you reject it altogether?

3. Excited Utterances

An exception that often overlaps with the present sense impression exception is the exception for excited utterances. The Federal Rules version, contained in FRE 803(2), defines the exception as "[a] statement relating to a startling event or condition made while the declarant was under the stress of excitement caused by the event or condition." The rationale for the exception is virtually identical to the rationale for the present sense impression exception: The fact that a declaration is made under the stress of an exciting event or condition tends to ensure that the declaration is spontaneous and, therefore, sincere; and the likely closeness in time between the event or condition and the declaration minimizes the possibility of a memory problem. On the other hand, as commentators have long recognized, in the case of excited utterances, the very thing that provides the sincerity guarantee—the exciting event—may augment perception (and perhaps narration) problems.[118] Nonetheless, the exception is well established.

Some of the older decisions required that the declarant actually be involved in the exciting event and refused to admit excited utterances of mere bystanders. Other decisions admitted statements of bystanders if they appeared to be visibly shaken by the exciting event. Still other decisions refused to admit excited utterances made in response to a question. FRE 803(2) contains none of these specific limitations. Each of these factors, however, is relevant to the question whether the declarant was under the stress of the exciting event at the time of the declaration.

The fact that a statement is made under the stress of an exciting event or condition is at least as good and probably a better indication of the statement's spontaneity than the mere fact that the statement was made contemporaneously with an event or condition. As a result, as noted earlier, it is sufficient if the statement is "relating to" as opposed to "describing or explaining" the exciting event. The Advisory Committee's Note cites two cases that apparently, in the view of the Advisory Committee, would fall within the meaning of "relating to" but not "describing or explaining":

> See Sanitary Grocery Co. v. Snead, 67 App. D.C. 129, 90 F.2d 374 (1937), slip-and-fall case sustaining admissibility of clerk's statement, "That has been

---

118. See, e.g., Hutchins and Slesinger, Some Observations on the Law of Evidence: Spontaneous Exclamations, 28 Colum. L. Rev. 432 (1928); Note, Did Your Eyes Deceive You? Expert Psychological Testimony on the Unreliability of Eyewitness Identification, 29 Stan. L. Rev. 969, 975-988 (1977).

on the floor for a couple of hours," and Murphy Auto Parts Co. v. Ball, 101 U.S. App. D.C. 416, 249 F.2d 508 (1957), upholding admission, on issue of driver's agency, of his statement that he had to call on a customer and was in a hurry to get home.

Why do these statements "relate to" but not "describe or explain" an event or condition?

FRE 803(2) also places no specific time restraint on the scope of the exception. Time, however, is a relevant consideration in determining whether the exception is applicable. To the extent that the declaration is removed in time from the event, there is reason to doubt whether the statement was made under the stress of the event. Moreover, just as courts applying FRE 803(1) tend to be strict with the "immediately thereafter" requirement particularly when the declaration seems self-serving and sometimes liberal when the declaration seems trustworthy, courts applying FRE 803(2) tend to require a very close temporal relationship between exciting events and self-serving utterances and to permit long time lags when the declarations seem trustworthy.

The questions whether an exciting event occurred and whether the declaration was made under the influence of the exciting event involve the same type of preliminary fact issues that we raised in the discussion of the present sense impression exception. As a practical matter, however, preliminary fact issues will seldom arise with respect to excited utterances, since there will usually be ample independent evidence that an exciting event occurred. The nature of the event is likely to attract attention; and even if there are no eyewitnesses to the event other than the declarant, the declarant's nervousness or injuries or quivering voice would constitute at least some evidence of an exciting event. Nonetheless, there is precedent for the proposition that the declaration itself is sufficient to establish the exciting event.[119]

We can think of no justification for treating preliminary fact issues differently for excited utterances than for other hearsay exceptions. Moreover, we are puzzled by the Advisory Committee's apparent approval and discussion of this precedent. According to the Advisory Committee:

> [O]n occasion the only evidence may be the content of the statement itself, and rulings that it may be sufficient are described as "increasing," Slough, [Spontaneous Statements and State of Mind, 46 Iowa L. Rev. 224,] 246, and as the "prevailing practice," [McCormick's Handbook on the Law of Evidence (2d ed., Cleary, 1972)] §272, p.579. . . . Moreover, under Rule 104(a) the judge is not limited by the hearsay rule in passing upon preliminary questions of fact.
>
> [W]hen declarant is an unidentified bystander, the cases indicate hesitancy

---

119. There is at least one court that has taken this position with respect to present sense impression declarations. See State v. Flesher, 286 N.W.2d 215 (Iowa 1979), discussed in Comment, The Need for a New Approach to the Present Sense Impression Hearsay Exception After State v. Flesher, 67 Iowa L. Rev. 179 (1981).

F. Hearsay Exceptions Not Requiring Unavailability: FRE 803

in upholding the statement alone as sufficient, Garrett v. Howden, 73 N.M. 307, 387 P.2d 874 (1963); Beck v. Dye, 200 Wash. 1, 92 P.2d 1113 (1939), a result which would under appropriate circumstances be consistent with the rule.

The Advisory Committee's Note does not explain what knowing the identity of the declarant has to do with the question whether one can rely on the declaration alone to prove that there was an exciting event, nor does the Advisory Committee's Note elaborate on what the "appropriate circumstances" might be for requiring other evidence of the event. *Beck*, the second case cited by the Advisory Committee offers no reason for its conclusion. The other case, *Garrett*, relied on the ground that there was no basis for inferring that the unidentified declarant had firsthand knowledge. We suspect, however, that frequently the circumstances surrounding the making of the statement, even if the declarant is unidentified, will be *"sufficient to support a finding* that the [declarant] has personal knowledge of the matter." FRE 602 (emphasis added).

Even if it is reasonable to infer from the surrounding circumstances that an exciting event occurred and that the declarant had firsthand knowledge of it, is it nonetheless appropriate to exclude an unidentified declarant's statement on the ground that the lack of identity makes it impossible to discover and present any evidence that impeaches the credibility of the particular declarant? Are there other reasons for excluding always or under appropriate circumstances the hearsay statements of unidentified declarants?

PROBLEMS

1. Mort Meyers is being prosecuted for the rape of Victoria Villa. The prosecution calls Pamela Jones, who offers to testify: "Seven weeks after Vikki was raped, I was with her in a downtown department store. She suddenly became very agitated and excited, and pointing at a man at the next counter, she screamed, 'That's the guy that raped me!' The man that she pointed at was the defendant, Mort Meyers." Defendant has raised a hearsay objection to this evidence. Should the objection be sustained?

2. Alice Brown has sued Brenda White for personal injuries resulting from an automobile accident on a rural road. Brown's claim is that White, who was traveling from the north in a blue Chevrolet, was speeding and that the speeding was the cause of the accident. To show that White was speeding, Brown calls Ed Mackler to the stand. Mackler testifies that at approximately the time of the accident, he was on the shoulder of the road where the accident occurred and about two miles north of the site of the accident. He then offers to testify that he was not watching the road himself but that he suddenly heard somebody shout, "That blue car just went by my jacket going

over a hundred miles an hour!"[120] He then looked in the direction of the shout and saw a hitchhiker at the side of the road. What objections can the defendant make to the admissibility of the evidence? How should the court rule?

3. Defendant is charged with molesting his three-year-old daughter. The daughter's grandmother offers to testify that four days after the alleged incident, her granddaughter appeared upset, and that when questioned about her sadness the granddaughter spoke about the molestation. Should this evidence be admitted?

4. Jane McDonald is being prosecuted for the murder of her boyfriend, Tim Blake. The prosecution offers the following testimony of Tim's brother Walt: "On the morning that he was murdered I was talking on the telephone to my brother, Tim, who had stayed home from work with the flu. As we were talking, I heard the doorbell ring in the background and Tim said, 'Just a minute. There's someone at the door.' I then heard Tim's voice and another voice in the background. I couldn't make out who the other person or what they were saying. After about a minute, Tim returned to the phone and said, 'Jane just arrived, and I have some things I need to talk to her about. I'll call you later.' We said good-bye and hung up. That was the last time I talked to Tim." Should the defendant's hearsay objection to this evidence be sustained?

4. State-of-Mind Declarations

In our initial consideration of the hearsay concept, we noted that the relevance of some out-of-court declarations requires the fact finder to rely on the sincerity and narrative ability, but not the perception or memory, of the declarant.[121] In terms of the testimonial triangle, these are the declarations that require the fact finder to make the inference illustrated by only the left leg of the triangle. As we pointed out in our earlier discussion, the hearsay rule is never a bar to the admissibility of these types of declarations. If they are considered hearsay, they fall within the hearsay exception for declarations of a person's then existing (i.e., at the time of the declaration) state of mind.

The primary justification for the state-of-mind exception is that there are no perception or memory problems (except to the extent that they inhere in the narration problem). Another reason sometimes given for the exception is necessity: Mental states are such a pervasive part of our substantive law that it would be unwise to bar from admissibility one of the primary sources

---

120. The jacket, of course, was not going anyplace. If the hitchhiker was surprised by the closeness of his encounter with serious injury, however, perhaps his grammatical lapse can be excused.

121. See pages 308-311 supra. But see pages 346-349 supra, where we pointed out that perception and memory problems in fact inhere in the narration problem. For the purposes of our discussion here we will refer to declarations as *not* involving perception and memory problems if those problems inhere only in the narration problem.

F. Hearsay Exceptions Not Requiring Unavailability: FRE 803

for evidence about mental states. This rationale, however, is not especially compelling. The state-of-mind exception is not limited to situations in which a person's mental state is an ultimate issue in litigation, and frequently we infer mental states from the conduct of individuals. Indeed, if there is a conflict between what a person claims to believe and how a person acts, we are probably likely to rely on the person's actions more than the person's words in assessing the mental state. A third reason for the exception is the notion that declarations of present state of mind are likely to be spontaneous and, therefore, sincere. There is no independent requirement of spontaneity, however, and we believe there is no particular reason to believe that most declarations of present state of mind are spontaneous rather than reflective.

In addition to providing an exception from the hearsay prohibition for declarations of present state of mind, typical formulations of the state-of-mind exception extend it, in will contest cases, to statements about a testator's earlier state of mind. Even though these statements require reliance on the declarant's memory and perception, as well as sincerity and narrative ability, the likelihood that persons will speak carefully about their wills and the "necessity" that arises from the unavailability of the declarant are considered sufficient reasons for admitting these types of statements.[122]

The Federal Rules state-of-mind exception is FRE 803(3):

> A statement of the declarant's then existing state of mind, emotion, sensation, or physical condition (such as intent, plan, motive, design, mental feeling, pain, and bodily health), but not including a statement of memory or belief to prove the fact remembered or believed unless it relates to the execution, revocation, identification, or terms of a declarant's will.

In dealing with declarations of a person's then existing state of mind, it is important to keep in mind that the state of mind itself need not be an ultimate issue in the case in order for the declaration to be admissible. Rather, it is frequently the case that evidence of a person's then existing state of mind is just one step in the inferential process to the establishment of some fact. As long as the inferential process does not involve the inference from belief to truth illustrated by the right leg of the testimonial triangle, the hearsay rule will not be a bar to admissibility. Consider, for example, Mary's declaration on Monday, "I plan to leave on my vacation Tuesday" to prove that she in fact left for a vacation on Tuesday. We first must infer that Mary, at the time of the declaration, sincerely believed that she would leave on Tuesday. On the testimonial triangle, this inference would be illustrated by the left leg of the triangle. Then, on the basis of Mary's Monday belief, we can infer, without relying on her perception and memory, (1) that she

---

122. The California Evidence Code extends the will contest part of the state-of-mind exception to all situations in which the declarant is unavailable, subject to the qualification that the statement is not admissible if there are circumstances suggesting a lack of trustworthiness. See Cal. Evid. Code §§1251, 1252.

probably had the same belief on Tuesday and, therefore, (2) that she left for her vacation on Tuesday. The premises underlying these inferences are, respectively, that intentions of the type Mary had are not likely to change, at least in a relatively short period of time, and that people generally do the things that they intend to do.[123] On the testimonial triangle, these inferences are illustrated by a line from the top point of the triangle to "Issue" in the center. Because there is no reliance on Mary's perception or memory in making any of these inferences, the hearsay rule would not bar Mary's statement of intent to show what she did at some future time.

Consider also a situation in which a criminal defendant wishes to establish that some third person had a motive for killing the victim in order to suggest that the third person was the killer. The third person's statement, "I hate the victim," made a week before the killing is proof that one week before the killing the third person hated the victim. From hatred at that time we infer that there was probably still hatred a week later, when the killing occurred. Our inference is based on the assumption that strong emotional feelings about an individual are not likely to change over a relatively short period of time. Finally, we infer from hatred toward the victim at the time of the killing that the third person killed the victim. The first inference (i.e., from declaration to then existing state of mind) requires reliance on the declarant's sincerity and narration, but none of the inferences requires reliance on the declarant's perception and memory. Thus, the hearsay rule would not be a bar to admissibility.

Just as a declaration of a person's then existing state of mind can be used to prove some future event or state of mind without relying on the declarant's perception or memory, a declaration showing a person's then existing state of mind can sometimes be used to look backwards in time without relying on the declarant's perception or memory. Consider, for example, in our preceding murder case, the third person's declaration two days after the murder, "The victim was a really nasty fellow who deserved to die." The hearsay rule would bar this evidence to prove the truth of the fact that the victim was a nasty fellow or to prove the truth of the proposition that the declarant *remembers* having had a dislike for the victim. Both of these uses of the evidence necessarily require reliance on the declarant's memory. The declaration, however, is also relevant to suggest a present (i.e., at the time of the declaration) dislike for the victim. And if it is reasonable, as we suggested a few sentences ago, to infer that a present animosity is likely to continue into the future for some time, it is also reasonable to infer that a present animosity has existed for some time in the past. Thus, the evidence is relevant to show hatred at an earlier time—the time of the murder—without reliance on the declarant's perception and memory, and then to

---

123. The strength of the inferences will vary depending on the nature of the intended activity and the stated time frame. In some situations, the inferences may be so weak that it would be appropriate to sustain an FRE 401 or FRE 403 objection to the admissibility of the evidence.

F. Hearsay Exceptions Not Requiring Unavailability: FRE 803

infer, again without reliance on the declarant's perception and memory, action that is consistent with that hatred (i.e., killing the victim). Since none of the links in this chain of inferences requires reliance on the declarant's perception and memory, the hearsay rule would not bar using the evidence in this manner.

The biggest problem with the state-of-mind exception is that some courts have a great deal of difficulty understanding its contours. This difficulty stems in part from a failure to focus on the nature of the inferences involved in the use of the evidence and in part from some unfortunate dictum in one of the leading state-of-mind cases, Mutual Life Insurance Co. of New York v. Hillmon.[124]

Hillmon was an action by Sallie Hillmon to recover the proceeds of life insurance policies on the life of her husband John Hillmon, who, she alleged, died in Crooked Creek, Colorado, on March 17, 1879. The principal issue in the case was whether a body found in Crooked Creek was that of Hillmon, as the plaintiff contended. The defendants tried to establish that a man named Walters had traveled to Crooked Creek with Hillmon and that the body was Walters, not Hillmon. Their evidence included the contents of a letter Walters had written to his sister. The sister testified that she received the letter around March 4, 1879, that the letter was in Walters' handwriting, that she had searched for the letter but could not find it, and that she remembered the contents of the letter. She then orally related the contents:[125]

> Dear sister and all: I now in my usual style drop you a few lines to let you know that I expect to leave Wichita on or about March the 5th, with a certain Mr. Hillmon, a sheeptrader, for Colorado or parts unknown to me. I expect to see the country now. News are of no interest to you, as you are not acquainted here. I will close with compliments to all inquiring friends. Love to all.
>
> I am truly your brother,
> Fred. Adolph Walters

[145 U.S. at 288.]

The trial court sustained a hearsay objection to this and a similar letter from Walters, and the jury found in favor of the plaintiff. In reversing the judgment for the plaintiff, the Supreme Court explained:

> The letters in question were competent, not as narratives of facts communicated to the writer by others, nor yet as proof that he actually went away

---

124. 145 U.S. 285 (1892).
125. See FRE 901 (general authentication requirement); FRE 1002 (best evidence rule); FRE 1004 (exemptions from best evidence rule requirement).

from Wichita,[126] but as evidence that, shortly before the time when other evidence tended to show that he went away, he had the intention of going, *and of going with Hillmon*, which made it more probable both that he did go and that he went with Hillmon, than if there had been no proof of such intention. In view of the mass of conflicting testimony introduced upon the question whether it was the body of Walters that was found in Hillmon's camp, this evidence might properly influence the jury in determining that question. [Id. at 295-296 (emphasis added).]

Some courts, in apparent reliance on the italicized portions of the preceding quotation, have taken the position that *Hillmon* stands for the proposition that Walters' letters could be used to show that Hillmon went to Crooked Creek. As a result, they conclude that one person's declaration about what a third person plans to do should be admissible to prove what that third person in fact did.[127] For several reasons this interpretation of *Hillmon* is unwarranted.

First, the letters were offered by the insurance companies to prove that Walters had gone to Crooked Creek. Thus, to the extent that it is reasonable to interpret the preceding passage as saying something about what Hillmon did, the passage is dictum.

Second, to the extent that Walters' letter might be regarded as an assertion that Hillmon planned to go to Crooked Creek, the assertion is necessarily dependent upon Walters' perception and memory: Walters could know that Hillmon planned to go to Crooked Creek only if Walters had perceived and properly remembered something that Hillmon (or perhaps some third person) had said or done to indicate that Hillmon was going to Crooked Creek. Thus, all hearsay dangers are potentially present. Except in will contest cases, however, the state-of-mind exception applies only to declarations that do not have perception and memory problems. Indeed, the Court specifically stated in the first sentence of the quoted paragraph that the letters were not competent as "narratives of facts communicated to the writer by others."[128]

Third, if Walters' letter were admissible as an assertion, based on Wal-

---

126. Since the Court goes on in the same paragraph to say that the evidence can be used to show that Walters left Wichita, this "nor yet . . ." clause may initially seem confusing. A sensible reading of the clause, which we believe is supported from the context in which the quoted paragraph appears, is that "nor yet" refers to steps in the logical chain of inferences: One must first infer from Walters' expressed intent to leave that he actually intended to leave (i.e., that the words are a sincere expression of his intent). Until one makes that first inference, it is not (yet) possible to infer from the letter that Walters did leave Wichita.—Eds.

127. See United States v. Pheaster, 544 F.2d 353 (9th Cir. 1976); People v. Alcade, 24 Cal. 2d 177, 148 P.2d 627 (1944).

128. It is appropriate to regard Hillmon's state of mind as a "fact" within the meaning of the Court's statement. The Court was discussing the hearsay prohibition, and "facts" of which the hearsay rule bars proof are events, conditions, or phenomena that a declarant (here Walters) has perceived and remembered. As we noted in the text, Walters could have known Hillmon's state of mind only if Walters perceived and remembered something that Hillmon or some third person said or did to indicate that state of mind.

F. Hearsay Exceptions Not Requiring Unavailability: FRE 803

ters' perception and memory of what Hillmon planned to do, the hearsay rule would be completely undermined. The argument for applying the state-of-mind exception to permit this use of Walters' declaration would be that the declaration is offered to show the declarant's intent or state of mind for the purpose of inferring what caused that state of mind (e.g., what Hillmon said to Walters or the maps of Crooked Creek that Walters saw in Hillmon's home). That characterization of the declaration (i.e., that it is being used to show what caused the state of mind), however, can be made of any hearsay statement. Thus, the state-of-mind exception would completely swallow the hearsay prohibition.

Fourth, an alternative interpretation of the Court's language in *Hillmon* is consistent with the view that it is not appropriate to rely on Walters' perception and memory to prove that "he went with Hillmon." In his letter, Walters said that he was planning to go with Hillmon. The Court may have been suggesting that an appropriate inference to draw from this statement is that Walters planned to take the trip only if Hillmon would accompany him. To show what Walters planned to do, this inference does not require reliance on Walters' perception and memory. Rather it is merely an inference about an intent that is conditioned on the occurrence of an event (Hillmon's decision to accompany Walters) that may or may not occur. It is also, however, an inference that in the context of the *Hillmon* case permits the further inference—without reliance on Walters' perception or memory—that Hillmon went to Crooked Creek: Walters was not in Wichita. Thus, it is reasonable to infer that Walters acted on his intent to go to Crooked Creek. And if that intent was to leave only in the company of Hillmon, it is reasonable to infer that Hillmon decided to go to Crooked Creek.

This chain of inferences, of course, provides some support for the proposition that the body may have been Hillmon rather than Walters. The chain of inferences, however, also strengthens the probative value of the evidence for the purpose for which it was offerred, i.e., to prove that Walters went to Crooked Creek: If there is reason to believe that Hillmon was traveling with a companion—and, we can reasonably infer, it is more likely that Hillmon is traveling with a companion if Walters acts in conformity with his expressed intent—there is reason to believe that the body discovered in Crooked Creek may be that of the companion rather than Hillmon.[129]

We suspect that at this point some of you may have one of the following reactions to our discussion of how the state-of-mind exception should apply in a case like *Hillmon*:

> (a) The intricacies of the argument are so complex that even if I can understand how the state-of-mind exception should work, it is likely that in the midst of litigation lawyers and judges will have difficulty

---

129. Obviously, the litigants and the Supreme Court considered this latter inference to be the stronger one.

properly applying the exception. Therefore, the existence of the exception in its current form, even if logically defensible, is not a desirable rule of evidence.

(b) Regardless of the intricacies of the state-of-mind exception, it is silly to distinguish or to think that the jury can distinguish between using the letters to prove what Walters did and using the letters to prove what Hillmon did. If the evidence is legitimately admissible for one purpose, it should be legitimately admissible for both purposes.

We believe there are four reasonable responses to these concerns. First, one might take the position that the hearsay rule in its present form is generally sound and relatively easy to apply properly, accept the fact that proper application of the hearsay rule sometimes requires very complex analysis and sometimes makes distinctions that seem not to be significant, and concede that *Hillmon* is one of those not too frequent difficult cases. Second, one could abolish the hearsay exception for declarations of a person's then existing state of mind and include within the hearsay prohibition all declarations whose relevance required reliance on the declarant's sincerity and narrative ability.[130] Third, one could make the second reaction listed above a proposition of general applicability—at least with respect to out-of-court statements. Fourth, one could abolish the hearsay rule altogether.

As you proceed through the remainder of the hearsay materials, consider which of these four responses is preferable, and as you do so, keep in mind that concern with the inference from Walters' belief to Walters' action is *not* a hearsay problem. Rather, it is a problem of relevance that can be resolved by reference to FRE 401 and FRE 403. The belief-to-action inference is relevant to the hearsay issue only as a point of comparison: If we are willing to invest trial judges with discretion to decide whether to admit evidence whose relevance depends on the strength of the inference from belief to action in conformity with belief, why are we not also willing to commit to the trial judge's discretion the question whether to admit evidence whose relevance depends on the inference from belief to the event that caused the belief (i.e., the inference illustrated by the right leg of the testimonial triangle)?

PROBLEMS

1. Harold, one of three sons of the decedent, has brought an action to recover the entire estate of his father on the ground that he is the sole beneficiary under his father's will. Harold's father, it has been shown, ripped the will in half nine months before dying. Harold claims that his father's

---

130. If the hearsay rule exempted nonassertive activity generally, that exemption should apply to out-of-court declarations and conduct that present only potential sincerity and narration problems as well as out-of-court activity that presents all hearsay dangers.

F. Hearsay Exceptions Not Requiring Unavailability: FRE 803

action was an accident, and that his father never intended to revoke the will. To rebut this claim, Harold's brothers offer the following evidence:

> (a) W-1 to testify that the day before the will was destroyed the decedent said, "I don't want Harold to inherit anything."
>
> (b) W-2 to testify that the day after the will was destroyed the decedent said, "I don't want Harold to inherit anything."
>
> (c) W-3 to testify that six months after destroying the will the decedent said, "When I tore up the will, I didn't want Harold to inherit anything."

Harold has objected to all of the foregoing evidence on the ground that it is inadmissible hearsay. How should the judge rule?

2. Mary Adams has sued the Acme Delivery Company for injuries that she sustained as a pedestrian when she was hit by a car driven by Grover Greer. Mary claims that Greer was in the process of making a delivery for Acme to James Pepper. Acme has admitted that Greer was an employee and that he had been instructed to make a delivery to James Pepper, but Acme denies that Greer was acting within the scope of his employment at the time of the accident. The defense case rests in part on the fact that the route which Greer took was not the most direct route to Pepper's residence. Mary offers the following evidence:

> (a) W-1 to testify: "Immediately before he got in his car on the day of the accident, Grover Greer said to me, 'I think the route that I am about to take is a faster way to get to Pepper's house.'"
>
> (b) W-2 to testify: "Ten minutes after the accident, I heard Grover Greer say, 'This is usually a faster route to Pepper's house.' Mr. Greer seemed very calm at time."
>
> (c) W-3 to testify: "Fifteen minutes after the accident, I heard Grover Greer say, 'I thought this route would be a faster way to get to Pepper's house.' Mr. Greer seemed very calm at the time."
>
> (d) W-4 to testify: "Immediately after the accident, Greer jumped out of his car, ran over to Mary Adams, and said, 'I'm sorry; I'm sorry. It was my fault. I was on an errand for my boss, and I was in a hurry.'"

Acme has objected to all of the foregoing evidence on the ground that it is inadmissible hearsay. How should the judge rule?

3. Alvin North is being prosecuted for breaking and entering a vacant summer cottage on Leech Lake in mid-December. His defense is that he was in Minneapolis, over 100 miles away, at the time of the commission of the crime. To rebut this defense the prosecutor offers the following evidence:

> (a) A letter written in November by Janice Evans, a resident of Minneapolis. The letter states, "I plan to travel to Leech Lake with Alvin North in mid-December."

(b) The testimony of Harry Blackfoot, who resides near Leech Lake, that he saw Janice Evans in the Leech Lake area in mid-December and a letter written by Alvin North in early December. The letter states, "I plan to be traveling with Janice Evans later this month."

Is either piece of evidence admissible?

4. Charles Shepard is being prosecuted for the murder of his wife, Zenana, who died as a result of ingesting a poison, bichloride of mercury. The defendant's theory was that Zenana committed suicide, and he called several witnesses who testified about Zenana's depression and occasional talk of killing herself. In rebuttal the prosecution offers the following testimony of Zenana Shepard's nurse: "Shortly before she collapsed, Mrs. Shepard said the juice she just drank had tasted strange, and she said, 'Dr. Shepard has poisoned me.'" In response to the defendant's hearsay objection, the prosecution argues that there are three bases for admitting the evidence:

(a) as a dying declaration;
(b) as state-of-mind evidence to infer the behavior that caused her state of mind—i.e., that Dr. Shepard poisoned her; and
(c) as state-of-mind evidence to rebut evidence of Mrs. Shepard's depression and alleged suicidal tendencies.

How should the court respond to these prosecution arguments?

5. Elmer Olson is being prosecuted for the murder of Dorothy Peterson. Elmer claims that he had had several dates with Dorothy over the last two months; that on the night of her death, she accepted his invitation to come to his apartment for dinner; that after dinner she sexually assaulted him; and that he had to shoot her in self-defense. To rebut this claim, the prosecutor calls Lisa Johnson, who offers to testify as follows: "On the morning before she was killed, Dorothy said to me 'I'm afraid of Elmer Olson. He tried to rape me once, and I think he's going to kill me.'"

What objections to Lisa's testimony can the defendant make? How should the court rule?

6. Frank Jackson is charged with the murder of Kate Upton. Ms. Upton's brutally beaten body was found in a ditch on the morning of the first Sunday in April. When the police searched her apartment that afternoon, they found it to be orderly. There was no evidence of fighting or struggling.

(a) The prosecution offers the following testimony of Barbara Berry: "When I spoke with Kate on the Saturday before she was killed, she said, 'I'm going out with Frank Jackson tonight.'"

(b) Instead of the evidence in (a), the prosecution offers the following testimony of Carla Cole: "I spoke with Kate on the Saturday before she died. She indicated that she had to work all weekend to finish a report that was due Monday and that she planned to be in her

F. Hearsay Exceptions Not Requiring Unavailability: FRE 803

apartment the entire time except for a few hours that night. She said that Frank Jackson was coming to her apartment to take her out for a drink that evening."

Assuming that the prosecutor offers only the evidence in (a) or only the evidence in (b), is either piece of evidence admissible? Would your answer be any different if the prosecutor offered both pieces of evidence?

7. The police have been investigating illegal drug distribution by Gwen Gable and her connection with Helen Hogan, a suspected customer. At 1:00 A.M. on April 5 the police, as the result of a legal wiretap on Gwen Gable's telephone, intercepted a conversation between Gwen and Helen. The gist of the conversation was that Helen agreed to go immediately to Gwen's house which was on the other side of town. The police staked out Gwen's house. A short time later they observed Helen emerge from a car driven by Dirk Dwyer, her boyfriend and live-in companion. Helen entered Gwen's house, returned a few minutes later, and drove off with Dwyer.

Before the grand jury Dirk Dwyer testified that he had driven across town on April 5 to visit a friend of his, that Helen was just along for the ride, and that although she left the car for a short time, he had no idea why she had done so.

Dwyer is charged with perjury before the grand jury for giving a false reason for being in the vicinity of Gwen Gable's house. The prosecution offers the recording of Helen's statement to Gwen that she would come immediately to Gwen's house. Dwyer objects on the ground of hearsay. What result?

8. Mike Morris is charged with conspiracy to extort money from Rick Peters. The alleged co-conspirators are Able and Black. As part of his defense, Morris calls Williams, who offers to testify: "I overheard a conversation between Able and Black in which Able said, 'Morris would be shocked to learn of our plan to extort money from Peters. We have to be sure he doesn't find out about it.'" Is the evidence admissible?

9. Ed Rogers is being prosecuted for the murder of Emily Dawson. Ms. Dawson was tied up with ropes and strangled on the night of May 23. The prosecution's theory is that Rogers was present, along with his 18-month-old daughter, at the time of the killing and that he aided and abetted the actual killers. The prosecution offers the following testimony of Gloria Rogers, the defendant's wife:

> (a) On the morning of Tuesday, May 24 I noticed our 18-month-old daughter playing with the belt from my bathrobe. She appeared to be tying a knot with it.
>
> (b) Two weeks after Emily Dawson was killed, I was in the kitchen with my daughter. There was a mouse cartoon on television, and when one of the mice was tied up, she began to cry.

Rogers has objected to both pieces of evidence on the ground of hearsay. What result?

5. Declarations of Physical Condition

Declarations of physical condition that are the equivalent of declarations of mental state in that they do not require reliance on the declarant's perception or memory (e.g., I have a headache), fall within the scope of FRE 803(3): "A statement of the declarant's then existing . . . physical condition (such as . . . mental feeling, pain, and bodily health). . . ." A declaration of physical condition the relevance of which depends upon the declarant's perception or memory (e.g., my wrist is slashed and is bleeding badly) would appear not to fall within the scope of FRE 803(3), which equates physical condition with mental condition. Such a declaration, however, may fall within FRE 803(1) or FRE 803(2).

Declarations of physical condition falling within the scope of FRE 803(1)-FRE 803(3) may be made by anybody for any purpose. The rationales for admitting the declarations, as we have discussed previously, are probable spontaneity in the case of FRE 803(1) and (2) and absence of memory and perception problems in the case of FRE 803(3).

Declarations of physical condition made for the purposes of diagnosis or treatment—including declarations of *past* symptoms and conditions—are admissible under FRE 803(4), which excepts from the hearsay prohibition

> [s]tatements made for the purpose of medical diagnosis or treatment and describing medical history, or past or present symptoms, pain, or sensation, or the inception or general character of the cause or external source thereof insofar as reasonably pertinent to diagnosis or treatment.

With respect to statements offered for the purpose of treatment, the rationale for this exception is that a person seeking medical treatment is likely to speak honestly about symptoms and conditions. Thus, even though the declaration may not be spontaneous and even though there are perception and memory problems, the declaration is likely to be sincere. Declarations about the cause or source of an injury may or may not be pertinent to the diagnosis or treatment. When these statements are not pertinent, there is some reason to suspect their sincerity and thus they do not fall within the scope of the exception.

It would be more consistent with the sincerity rationale for the exception to ask whether the declarant *believed* that statements about the cause or external source were pertinent to the diagnosis or treatment, rather than whether the statements were in fact pertinent. We suspect, however, that situations in which it matters which question is asked will be rare.

The sincerity rationale, of course, does not apply when a statement of

F. Hearsay Exceptions Not Requiring Unavailability: FRE 803

physical condition is made for the purpose of diagnosis in preparation for litigation. The treatment motive for the declaration, which tends to ensure sincerity, is lacking. Moreover, the possibility of receiving a high damage award is an incentive to exaggerate present and past symptoms or suffering. For this reason, the common law physical condition exception did not apply to declarations made for the purpose of diagnosis in preparation for litigation. FRE 803(4), however, specifically abandons this common law limitation. Declarations of physical condition fall within the scope of the exception when made "for the purposes of medical diagnosis or treatment" (emphasis added) without any restriction on the purpose for which the diagnosis is made.

As a matter of first impression, this Federal Rules departure from the common law may seem unwise. The departure is understandable and reasonable, however, when one considers the physical condition exception in conjunction with the rules regulating expert opinion testimony. When a person's physical condition is at issue, there frequently will be an expert witness to testify about the nature of the condition. Moreover, the expert is likely to have reached conclusions about the person's physical condition at least in part on the basis of what the person related out of court about present and past symptoms. Given the fact, on the one hand, that the expert is likely, as a matter of course, to rely in part on the declarations of the person whose physical condition is in issue, and the fact, on the other hand, that we have reason to be suspicious of a declarant's self-serving statements to an expert consulted for the purpose of testifying at trial, what information should the rules of evidence permit to go to the jury?

The common law answer to this question was to ensure that self-serving hearsay statements of physical condition were not presented to the jury. To accomplish this objective, the common law required expert witnesses to base their opinions solely on admissible evidence. This requirement inevitably led to one of two consequences in situations in which the expert had relied on inadmissible hearsay. First, the expert might state falsely that the opinion is based solely on factors (e.g., the expert's personal observations) about which the expert could testify. Second, the person whose physical condition was in issue would testify (and be cross-examined) about the physical conditions, and the expert would then be asked to offer an opinion about a hypothetical question that incorporated the pain and symptoms to which the person previously testified. The hypothetical question served two important purposes. First, it ensured that the premises for the opinion had been the subject of earlier testimony. Second, it was a means of satisfying the common law requirement that the factual bases for an expert opinion be set forth before the opinion is given.[131]

---

131. If the expert had been sitting in the courtroom throughout the testimony that is pertinent to the diagnosis or opinion, and if there had been no conflicting evidence about the information the expert relied on, one could simply ask the expert to offer an opinion on the basis of the evidence previously introduced instead of using the hypothetical question. There

There are a number of reasons why one might be reluctant to force reliance on hypothetical questions to elicit expert testimony. The question can be time-consuming and boring for the jury; it can be improperly used by counsel as a device to summarize the evidence; and it inevitably presents the expert's information to the jury in a somewhat stilted form. Well aware of these problems, the drafters of the Federal Rules consciously tried to avoid the need for hypothetical questions to elicit expert information.[132] In addition, the drafters recognized that experts in various fields do not look to the rules of evidence for guidance in deciding how to reach their conclusions and that experts frequently rely on what the law would consider inadmissible evidence in reaching their conclusions. In order to take full advantage of the contribution that experts can make and to minimize the need for the hypothetical question, FRE 703 provides that the facts or data upon which an expert bases an opinion or inference, "if of a type reasonably relied upon by experts in the particular field," need not be admissible in evidence. Since experts typically state the bases for their opinions,[133] one effect of FRE 703 is that it provides the opportunity for otherwise inadmissible evidence to be presented to the jury.

A medical expert who has been consulted for diagnosis in preparation for litigation is almost certainly going to rely on the patient's declarations about past and present symptoms. As long as the declarations are of a type reasonably relied on by medical experts, the jury in all likelihood will hear the declarations when the expert explains the basis for the diagnosis. Having made this commitment to facilitate the testimony of experts, the drafters of the Federal Rules were left with two choices about declarations of physical condition: They could have taken the position, as they did, that since the evidence was likely to be admissible in any event, there was no reason to retain the common law restriction on the scope of the physical condition exception. Alternatively, they could have retained the common law restriction with the understanding that the judge, if requested, would instruct the jury that statements of physical condition were admissible only to explain the basis of the expert's opinion and not for their truth.

In fact, some common law courts, uncomfortable with the rigid restrictions on expert testimony, permitted experts to relate hearsay information and then instructed the jury that the hearsay could not be considered for its

---

will seldom be situations in which there is not conflicting evidence, and there will probably be even fewer situations in which a litigant would want to pay an expert to sit through the trial while the evidence is being developed. Additionally, the party calling the expert may want to use the hypothetical question in any event to focus the jury's attention on precisely what the bases for the opinion are.

132. See Fed. R. Evid. 702, 703, 705 Advisory Committee Notes.
133. See FRE 705, which provides:

The expert may testify in terms of opinion or inference and give his reasons therefor without prior disclosure of the underlying facts or data, unless the court requires otherwise. The expert may in any event be required to disclose the underlying facts or data on cross-examination.

F. Hearsay Exceptions Not Requiring Unavailability: FRE 803

truth, but only for showing the basis for the opinion.[134] Unlike most limiting instructions, which (although perhaps difficult for the jury to follow) are logically sound, this type of limiting instruction is nonsensical. Assuming that the expert's opinion is based on the truth of the declarations of physical condition, those declarations cannot be relevant in any meaningful way to the jury's evaluation of the expert's opinion unless the jury, like the expert, considers the statements for their truth.

To summarize, the common law—except in jurisdictions that adopted the limiting instruction alternative—gave priority to the notion that the jury should not hear inadmissible evidence, including declarations made for diagnosis in preparation for litigation; and the common law adjusted the rules governing expert testimony to foster this objective. By contrast, the Federal Rules give priority to the notion that it is desirable to take full advantage of the information that experts can supply; and the Federal Rules have adjusted the physical condition exception to accommodate this priority.

PROBLEMS

1. Martha Jones is suing the Friendly Daycare Center for injuries to herself and her infant child. Martha's claim is that the injuries are a result of the defendant's alleged failure to take reasonable precautions to avoid exposing her to rubella while she was pregnant. As part of her proof that she contracted rubella, Martha offers the following testimony of Martha's husband, Ben: "I was talking to Martha on the telephone, when she interrupted and said, 'Ben, I have red dots all over my arms.'" Is the evidence admissible?

2. Consider whether the following declarations would be admissible in a personal injury action if made (a) to the declarant's spouse, (b) to the declarant's physician for treatment, and (c) to a physician consulted for the purpose of giving expert testimony at trial:

"I have a severe headache."
"Yesterday, I had a severe headache."
"I was hit in the head with a baseball bat."
"John Jones hit me in the head with a baseball bat."

3. Ginger Gibbons has sued Mark Morley for injuries arising from a fall down defendant's steps. After filing the action, Ginger visited "Dr." William J. Quackster and paid him a fee to diagnose her injuries and testify for her at trial. Dr. Quackster, who has no formal education beyond the tenth grade, obtained his doctor's degree from a mail order company. He

---

134. Federal courts since the adoption of the Federal Rules have done the same thing with respect to non-medical experts who relied on hearsay not falling within any exception to the hearsay rule. See pages 746-749 infra.

bases his diagnoses and opinions on statements of his patients and on patterns formed by the plumes of smoke that emanate from a large, noxious cigar.

At her evaluative session with Dr. Quackster, Ginger said, in the presence of Dr. Quackster and his receptionist/assistant, Wanda Wilson, that for three weeks after the accident she suffered from severe headaches, and that she had never had severe headaches prior to the accident.

Dr. Quackster has fled the jurisdiction. At her trial Ginger calls Wanda Wilson, who offers to testify about the statements Ginger made in Dr. Quackster's office. Is the evidence admissible?

4. Larry Stevenson is charged with raping his 11-year-old stepdaughter, Mia Read. Dr. Logan, the family physician has testified that he examined Mia soon after the rape and that he saw her every other day for the next two weeks. During the first three meetings, according to Dr. Logan, Mia said almost nothing about what happened. He then offers the following testimony, to which the defendant objects on hearsay grounds: "At our fourth meeting, Mia seemed quite calm and collected for the first time. She was willing to talk about what happened to her and how she felt, and it was during this conversation that she said it was her stepfather that had raped her." How should the court rule on the hearsay objection?

6. Past Recollection Recorded

The past recollection recorded hearsay exception is unusual in that it requires both availability and unavailability. The person whose memory has been recorded must be on the witness stand, and the witness must be unavailable in the sense of having insufficient current memory to testify about the events recorded. The Federal Rules version of the exception appears in FRE 803(5):

> A memorandum or record[135] concerning a matter about which the witness once had knowledge but now has insufficient recollection to enable the witness to testify fully and accurately,[136] shown to have been made or adopted by the witness when the matter was fresh in the witness' memory and to reflect that knowledge correctly. If admitted, the memorandum or record may be read into evidence but may not itself be received as an exhibit unless offered by an adverse party.[137]

The absence of current memory creates the need for the hearsay, and the fact that the record was made when the matter was fresh in the witness' mind

---

135. Usually the record is a writing. The language of FRE 803(5), however, does not require that it be a writing. Other types of records—e.g., tape recordings—presumably qualify for the exception.—Eds.

136. Some of the older decisions speak of complete loss of memory.—Eds.

137. Even though FRE 803(5) provides that the record is not admissible as an exhibit, it is the contents of the record that is being proven. Thus, the proponent of a record of past recollection must comply with the best evidence rule. See FRE 1001-FRE 1008.—Eds.

F. Hearsay Exceptions Not Requiring Unavailability: FRE 803

minimizes any memory problem. Indeed, because of the "fresh in the witness' memory" requirement, there is probably less of a memory problem with past recollection recorded than with live testimony. The witness' current availability for general cross-examination, coupled with the fact that the witness has vouched for the accuracy of the statement, tends to reduce the risk that other hearsay dangers will go undetected.

If the witness cannot remember what happened, it will be theoretically impossible for the witness to swear that the record is a correct reflection of what the witness' knowledge had been. The best that the witness can really do is explain why it is likely to have been accurate. Frequently, however, in laying the foundation for the exception, the question is asked and answered without objection in terms of the language of the rule.

The reason for not receiving the record as an exhibit is a concern that jurors might put undue weight on the statements in the record merely because the record was before them as an exhibit. When deposition evidence is admitted into evidence, it is typically treated in the same manner: The contents of the deposition are read to the jury, but the deposition is not itself admitted as an exhibit—or at least the jury is not allowed to take it into the jury room during deliberations. There is no similar specific requirement that the record not be admitted as an exhibit in evidentiary rules dealing with other documents or records, see, e.g., FRE 803(6) (business records exception), and there is no specific prohibition against introducing as an exhibit documents that happen to contain admissible hearsay (e.g., a written dying declaration).

Is there some particular reason for treating records of past recollection differently from other records containing hearsay? Should the rules be amended to provide for similar treatment of other hearsay documents? Or should the last sentence of FRE 803(5) be repealed? Note that the party against whom the record of past recollection is introduced has the option of introducing the record as an exhibit. Why might the party against whom the evidence is offered want to do this?

An issue that sometimes arises and that FRE 803(5) does not specifically address is the effect of multiple person involvement in making the record. Assume, for example, that in the process of taking an inventory the witness (with no current memory) called out numbers to a third person, who recorded the numbers on the inventory record; or assume that an executive (with no current memory) dictated information to her secretary, who created the document in question.[138] If the witness reviewed the document prepared by the third person while the matter was still fresh in the witness' mind, the proponent of the evidence could rely on the "or adopted" language of FRE

---

138. Depending on the circumstances, both the inventory and the document prepared by the secretary may qualify as business records. See pages 451-459 infra. If they fall within the business records exception, they would be admissible under that exception to the hearsay rule regardless of whether they are admissible as past recollection recorded. See page 372 supra.

803(5). What should the result be if there were no adoption? The Advisory Committee's Note to FRE 803(5) states, "Multiple person involvement in the process of observing and recording . . . is entirely consistent with the exception."[139] The Advisory Committee, however, offers no suggestions or criteria for determining what, if any, limits should be placed on multiple person involvement in the making of the records.[140]

The potential problem with multiple person involvement in making the

---

139. The version of FRE 803(5) promulgated by the Supreme Court and sent to Congress did not contain the phrase *or adopted by the witness*. The phrase was added by the House Judiciary Committee, and the "by the witness" language could be read as a rejection of the Advisory Committee's approval of multiple person involvement in making the record.

Although the matter is not free from doubt, such a reading appears not to be warranted. The House Judiciary Committee's only explanation for the amendment is to make the "treatment consistent with the definition of 'statement' in the Jencks Act, 18 U.S.C. 3500 [regulating criminal defendants' rights to discovery of statements made by prosecution witnesses]." The Senate Judiciary Committee, in accepting the amendment, stated:

> The committee accepts the House amendment with the understanding and belief that it was not intended to narrow the scope of applicability of the rule. In fact, we understand it to clarify the rule's applicability to a memorandum adopted by the witness as well as one made by him. While the rule as submitted by the Court was silent on the question of who made the memorandum, we view the House amendment as a helpful clarification, noting, however, that the Advisory Committee's note to this rule suggests that the important thing is the accuracy of the memorandum rather than who made it.
>
> The committee does not view the House amendment as precluding admissibility in situations in which multiple participants were involved.

140. In discussing multiple person involvement in making the record, both the Advisory Committee and the Senate Judiciary Committee cited with approval Rathbun v. Brancatella, 93 N.J.L. 222, 107 A. 279 (1919). It is not clear, however, what the case has to do with hearsay, much less past recollection recorded. A witness to a pedestrian-automobile accident called out the license number of the automobile to a companion, who wrote down the number immediately and then related the number to a police officer 10 minutes later. The officer then "reported" the number at police headquarters. At trial, both the officer and the companion of the bystander who initially called out the number testified as to what the number was. In holding that it was proper to admit this evidence, the court said:

> When therefore Menandier testified that he called out a number to Miss Sullivan, and she testified that she at once committed it to paper, and remembered it from that fact, and from frequent iteration in judicial proceedings, and that she transmitted it to Officer Grant within a short time after she heard it called out, each of these witnesses was competent to verify the number, not for the purpose of furnishing substantive proof of the ownership of the defendant's car, but for the purpose of presenting the complete concatenation of circumstances arising out of an incidental fact, and evidencing that in the transmission the fact transmitted was identical from its inception to its ultimate delivery at police headquarters. [93 N.J.L. at 226; 107 A. at 281.]

Along with *Rathbun*, the Senate Judiciary Committee also cited Curtis v. Bradley, 65 Conn. 99, 31 A. 591 (1894), an equally unhelpful case, and McCormick's Handbook on the Law of Evidence §303 (2d ed., Cleary, 1972), which addresses the multiple person involvement issue as follows:

> A . . . type of cooperative report exists when a person (R) reports orally facts known to him to another person (W), who writes them down. A salesman or timekeeper, for example, may report sales or time to a bookkeeper. In this type of situation, courts have held the written statement admissible if R swears to the correctness of his oral report (although he may not remember the detailed facts) and W testifies that he faithfully transcribed R's oral report.

F. Hearsay Exceptions Not Requiring Unavailability: FRE 803

record, of course, is that the accuracy of the record depends on the narrative ability, sincerity, memory, and perception of each person involved in making the record. Thus, the proponent of a record made in whole or in part by some person other than the witness (who initially made the declarations and who now has no memory of the event) should try to alleviate these hearsay concerns. If the third person (who actually made the recording) is available, it would probably be desirable to call that person as a witness to testify about the recording process and to give the opposing party the opportunity to cross-examine the recorder. In some situations, however, putting the actual recorder on the witness stand will be of little practical value. When the recording is part of a regularized, routine activity, for example, the recorder may have no memory of the particular recording and may be able to say nothing more than that the recording was made in a routine, usually reliable fashion. Anyone familiar with the recorder's functions could offer the same testimony. Thus, presence of the recorder, while perhaps always desirable as a matter of strategy, should not be mandatory in every case of multiple person involvement in the recording.

We believe that, consistently with the rationale for the exception, multiple person involvement should be acceptable at least in those situations in which a third person recorder is performing a routine task and is only recording, as opposed to interpreting or editing, what the witness was saying and has now forgotten. The routine nature of the task tends to reduce the risks of insincerity or inadvertent error in recording,[141] and the absence of interpretation ensures that the witness' memory, not the recorder's consciously altered version of that memory, is what is recorded. On the other hand, if the third person recorder has played an interpretative role, there is a greater risk that what is recorded will be different from what was fresh in the mind of the witness who has now forgotten the event.

For hearsay exceptions generally, it is not essential that the hearsay be a verbatim recital of what the hearsay declarant said. Rather, it is sufficient for the witness to relate the gist of what the declarant said. Indeed, given the limitations of human memory, it would be impossible, as a practical matter, to insist on verbatim recall without substantially reducing the extent to which we admit hearsay evidence. Moreover, if the declaration were quite long and complicated, one might suspect the credibility of a witness who purported to remember the declaration word for word. Thus, for example, a witness who testifies to a party's admission or a declaration of physical condition does not have to recall the precise words that the declarant spoke. Similarly, if the witness who heard the admission or declaration of physical condition made a contemporaneous record summarizing the gist of the declaration and now could not remember its contents, the record of past recollection would be admissible to prove the admission. When more than one

---

141. Cf. pages 452-453 infra (discussion of the rationale for the business records exception).

person is involved in creating the record offered under the past recollection recorded exception and when the witness with no current memory is not the actual recorder, however, it may be essential that the recording be a verbatim statement of what the now forgetful witness said. Part of the rationale for the past recollection recorded exception is the assurance that the record is an accurate account of what the now forgetful witness knew when the matter was fresh in the witness' mind. Thus, interpretation of that memory by a third person recorder tends to undermine one of the rationales for, and thus is arguably inconsistent with, the past recollection recorded exception.

If the proposition at the end of the preceding paragraph is correct, it has two implications for the operation of the past recollection recorded exception. First, a third person's interpretative report of the declarant/witness' now failed recollection should not be admissible even if the interpretative reporter is prepared to testify from present memory that the interpretation was an accurate account of what the initial declarant/witness said. Second, the structure of FRE 803(5) makes it clear that present memory is preferred over past recorded memory. Thus, if the third person interpretative reporter were a witness with no current memory about the accuracy of the interpretation, one should not be able to rely on the past recollection recorded exception to get over the hearsay problem created by the interpretative recorder as well as the hearsay problem created by the loss of memory of the initial declarant/witness.

In dealing with the past recollection recorded exception, there are several important things to keep in mind. First, records of a person's past recollection often contain multiple hearsay (in addition to the multiple hearsay that may exist as a result of multiple person involvement in the recording). For example, the witness with no current memory may have made a memorandum about a conversation with a business associate, and it may be the truth of what that business associate said that is relevant. The past recollection recorded exception alone will not make the memorandum admissible in this situation. The record of past recollection does nothing more than act as a substitute for the memory of the witness on the stand. If a hearsay objection to the witness' testimony about what the business associate said would be sustained, so would a hearsay objection to the admission of the recorded recollection of what the business associate said. On the other hand, if the business associate's statement fell within some hearsay exception, the witness could testify to that statement; and if the witness had no current memory, the combination of the hearsay exception for the business associate and the past recollection recorded exception would suffice to overcome a hearsay objection to the record. Thus, as we suggested supra, a writing that qualifies for the past recollection recorded exception and that contains the gist of some third person's admission or declaration of physical condition would be admissible. Similarly, in our interpretative recording hypothetical if there were some hearsay exception other than past recollection recorded to cover the initial declarant's statement, and if the interpretive reporter had no current

F. Hearsay Exceptions Not Requiring Unavailability: FRE 803

memory of what was said, it would be appropriate to rely on the past recollection recorded exception as a substitute for the interpretive reporter's current memory and the other hearsay exception for the hearsay problem created by the initial declarant.

Second, you should be aware of the fact that the requirements for the past recollection recorded exception and the business records exception, to which we are about to turn, are quite different. We make special note of this because the two exceptions frequently overlap in the sense that it may be possible with respect to a particular document to lay a foundation for either past recollection recorded or business records. This overlap is sometimes confusing to both law students and lawyers. As long as you realize that the two exceptions are distinct and have separate requirements, you should have no difficulty in dealing with them.

Finally, be sure not to confuse, as some courts occasionally do, the past recollection recorded hearsay exception with the process of refreshing memory (sometimes referred to as "refreshing recollection" or "present recollection revived"). When a witness initially cannot recall something, it may be possible to refresh the witness' memory by presenting a witness with a document or something else that the examiner thinks or that the witness suggests may jog the witness' memory. There is limited precedent for the proposition that only documents satisfying the requirements of the recorded recollection hearsay exception can be used to refresh memory. These holdings may be the result of confusing the concepts of refreshing recollection and past recollection recorded. In any event, there is no sound reason for imposing the limitations of the past recollection recorded hearsay exception on what can be used to refresh memory. The view of most courts is more akin to that of Baker v. State:

> Although the use of a memorandum of some sort will continue quantitatively to dominate the field of refreshing recollection, we are better able to grasp the process conceptually if we appreciate that the use of a memorandum as a memory aid is not a legal phenomenon unto itself but only an instance of a far broader phenomenon. In a more conventional mode, the process might proceed, "Your Honor, I am about to show the witness a written report, ask him to read it and then inquire if he can now testify from his own memory thus refreshed." In a far less conventional mode, the process could as well proceed, "Your Honor, I am pleased to present to the court Miss Rosa Ponselle who will now sing 'Celeste Aida' for the witness, for that is what was playing on the night the burglar came through the window."[142] Whether by conventional or unconventional means, precisely the same end is sought. One is looking for the effective elixir to revitalize dimming memory and make it live again in the service of the search for truth. [35 Md. App. 593, 604-605, 371 A.2d 699, 705-706.]

---

142. Do you think Rosa Ponselle ever sang "Celeste Aida"—except perhaps in the shower?—Eds.

If some physical object, like a document, is used to refresh memory, it will be first marked as an exhibit for the purposes of identifying it in the transcript. Use of the object to refresh memory, however, is *not* using the document *as evidence*. Rather, the object is only a device to try to jog the witness' memory. If the witness' memory is refreshed, the witness will then proceed to testify on the basis of current (revived) recollection, and there will be no need for further reference to the object that revived the witness' memory.[143] Similarly, if the object does not revive the witness' memory, there will be no further occasion to refer to the object, unless the object happens to have some independent relevance to the law suit.

If the object is a document that could be shown to meet the requirements of a hearsay exception, it would then be admissible under that exception. For example, if the document did not refresh the witness' memory, if the document were one that the witness had made when the matter to which the document relates was fresh in the witness' mind, and if the witness testifies that the document contains an accurate reflection of what the witness knew, it would be admissible as a record of past recollection. Indeed, a standard part of laying the foundation for past recollection recorded is to show the witness the document and ask if the document refreshes the witness' memory.

With a friendly witness, the process of refreshing memory is likely to take place outside the courtroom while discussing and rehearsing the direct and anticipated cross-examination.

> IF DURING THIS OR ANY OTHER PREPARATION FOR COURTROOM OR DEPOSITION TESTIMONY THE WITNESS USES A WRITING TO REFRESH MEMORY, THE OPPOSING PARTY MAY BE ENTITLED TO INSPECT THE WRITING. SEE FRE 612.

We have indented and capitalized the preceding sentence because we believe that of all of the specific rules that you deal with in this course, FRE 612 is the most important one for you to remember after the course. It is not merely a rule of admissibility; it is also a rule of discovery. And one of the things it means is that any documents that a person looks at in preparing for a deposition may be discoverable by the opposing party—including perhaps documents that would otherwise be protected by the work-product doctrine or some privilege. Since many of you are likely to become involved in the process of taking depositions long before you have any immediate concern with the rules of admissibility, we urge you to find a special place in your memory for FRE 612.

---

143. If the object is a writing that refreshes the witness' memory, the opposing party is entitled to inspect the document and to introduce into evidence "those portions which relate to the testimony of the witness." FRE 612. If the writing has refreshed the witness' memory, however, it will probably contain information that corroborates what the witness has said. Thus, it is unlikely that the opposing party would want to introduce it into evidence.

F. Hearsay Exceptions Not Requiring Unavailability: FRE 803

PROBLEMS

1. Richard Dapple is being prosecuted for conspiracy to fix prices. Mary Wright was present at a meeting in which Dapple made incriminating statements, but Wright no longer has any recollection of what was said at the meeting. Are any of the following pieces of evidence admissible to prove what Dapple said at the meeting:

(a) A memorandum prepared under the following circumstances: Within three hours of the meeting, Wright dictated into a recording device her recollections of the gist of what Dapple had said. The next morning her secretary, as was her custom, typed all of the dictation from the night before. Wright read over the typed memorandum, initialed it, and placed it in a file drawer, where it remained until it was removed in preparation for this litigation.

(b) The same as (a), except that Mary Wright never read the typed memorandum.

(c) A memorandum prepared under the following circumstances: Within three hours of the meeting Mary Wright gave her secretary copious notes that she, Mary, had taken at the meeting. The secretary, as was her custom, typed a summary of the notes and, without showing the summary to Mary Wright, placed it in a file drawer, where it remained until it was removed in preparation for this litigation.

(d) The same as (c), except that the secretary is willing to testify from present memory as to the contents of the longhand notes.

2. While Andrew was crossing an intersection, he was hit by an automobile, which fled the scene of the accident. Sadie, Andrew's companion, rushed to his side, and asked, "Are you o.k.?" Andrew, who was still conscious, responded, "I don't know, but I got the license number of the car that hit me. It was 879-ACY. Write it down so we won't forget." Sadie took a pencil and paper from her purse, and wrote down the number. Andrew has brought an action for personal injuries against Roland Bowers, who is the registered owner of a green Plymouth with the license number 879-ACY. Be prepared to question both Andrew and Sadie on direct examination for the purpose of eliciting the license number of the car that hit Andrew. In your preparation, consider that either or both of them may have less than clear memories about the license number.

7. Business Records

Although the business records exception has vestiges in the common law, the development of the modern business records exception is the result of statutory enactment. The principal models for the business record exception in most jurisdictions have been the Commonwealth Fund Act (1927)[144] and the Uniform Business Records as Evidence Act (1933). Some jurisdictions retain statutes based on one of these models. A growing number of jurisdictions, however, has enacted by statute or promulgated by rule a version FRE 803(6), the Federal Rules business record exception. FRE 803(6), which is itself based on the Commonwealth Fund Act, defines the exception as follows:

> A memorandum, report, record, or data compilation, in any form, of acts, events, conditions, opinions, or diagnoses, made at or near the time by, or from information transmitted by, a person with knowledge, if kept in the course of a regularly conducted business activity, and if it was the regular practice of that business activity to make the memorandum, report, record, or data compilation, all as shown by the testimony of the custodian or other qualified witness, unless the source of the information or the method or circumstances of preparation indicate lack of trustworthiness. The term "business" as used in this paragraph includes business, institution, association, profession, occupation, and calling of every kind, whether or not conducted for profit.

Like many other exceptions, the business records exception is justified on the grounds of necessity and reliability. The necessity is twofold. First, there is frequently multiple person involvement in the production of a business record, and it would be time consuming and inconvenient to call to the witness stand each individual who had a part in generating the record. Moreover, some of the individuals responsible for making the record may no longer be associated with the business for which the record was made, and, therefore, they may be difficult to find. Second, even if the people who were responsible for making the record were on the witness stand, they might not have any present memory of matters contained in the record. When this is the case, which it is often likely to be with respect to routine matters recorded in the ordinary course of business, the record may be the only available source of the information.

The "necessity" for the business records exception is sometimes described as the need to bring the rules of evidence into conformity with modern business practices. Such an objective obviously includes, given present business practices, permitting reliance on computer-generated documents. See FRE 803 Advisory Committee Note:

> The form which the "record" may assume under the rule is described broadly. . . . The expression "data compilation" is used as broadly descriptive of any means of storing information other than the conventional words and figures in written or documentary form. It includes, but is by no means limited to, electronic computer storage.

---

144. See E. Morgan et al., The Law of Evidence: Some Proposals for Its Reform 51-63 (1927).

F. Hearsay Exceptions Not Requiring Unavailability: FRE 803

What particular problems can you foresee with the possible use of computer-generated business records?

The reliability rationale for the business records exception is based on several factors. The requirement that the record be made at or near the time of the matter recorded minimizes any memory problem; a person who makes a record in the ordinary course of business has an incentive to be honest and accurate in order to advance in the business; the fact that the record is kept in the ordinary course of business suggests that it may be checked for accuracy, which provides an added guarantee of trustworthiness and an incentive for the record maker to be accurate in the first place; the routine nature of many records that are made and kept in the ordinary course of business suggests that such records will be accurate because there is not likely to be an incentive to lie about routine matters; and finally, the regularity of the record-making process often gives the record maker some expertise in record making that tends to ensure accuracy.

Although the preceding factors contribute to the reliability of many business records, some documents that can reasonably be characterized as having been made and kept in the ordinary course of business are inherently suspect. Consider, for example, the medical records of a doctor who has been retained by the defendant in a personal injury action or the investigative report made for a corporation by its general counsel after suit had been filed against the corporation.

If one wants to exclude such records from the exception, there are two possibilities: First, one can include as part of the exception a general trustworthiness requirement as FRE 803(6) does. Alternatively, one can define the nature of the business very narrowly for the purpose of the business records exception. The Supreme Court took this latter approach in Palmer v. Hoffman,[145] a 1943 case interpreting the then-existing federal business record statute. The plaintiff, who was injured in a railroad grade crossing accident, claimed that the railroad was negligent in that the engineer failed to ring a bell, blow a whistle, or have a light burning in the front of the train. The defendant offered into evidence as a business record a written statement made by the engineer, who died prior to trial. The Supreme Court was willing to "assume that if the statement was made 'in the regular course' of business, it would satisfy the other provisions of the Act."[146] The Court, however, upheld the exclusion of the evidence:

> It is not a record made for the systematic conduct of the business as a business. An accident report may affect the business in the sense that it affords information on which the management may act. It is not, however, typical of entries made systematically or as a matter of routine to record events or occurrences, to reflect transactions with others, or to provide internal controls. . . . [T]he fact that a company makes a business out of recording its

---

145. 318 U.S. 109 (1943).
146. Id. at 111.

employees' versions of their accidents does not put those statements in the class of records made "in the regular course" of the business within the meaning of the Act. If it did, . . . [w]e would then have a real perversion of a rule designed to facilitate admission of records which experience has shown to be quite trustworthy. . . . Regularity of preparation would become the test rather than the character of the records and their earmarks of reliability . . . acquired from their source and origin and the nature of their compilation. . . .

In short, it is manifest that in this case those reports are not for the systematic conduct of the enterprise as a railroad business. Unlike payrolls, accounts receivable, accounts payable, bills of lading and the like, these reports are calculated for use essentially in the court, not in the business. Their primary utility is in litigating, not in railroading. [318 U.S. at 113-114.]

Do you agree with the Court's characterization of the utility of accident reports? Is the approach of Palmer v. Hoffman or the approach of FRE 803(6) preferable as a way to deal with potentially untrustworthy records generated in the course of regularly conducted activity?

One matter on which various formulations of a business records rule or statute differ is whether opinions and diagnoses contained within business records are admissible. For example, Calif. Evid. Code §1271 covers only records of "an act, condition, or event," whereas FRE 803(6) covers records of "acts, events, conditions, opinions, or diagnoses." The difficulty with freely admitting business records containing opinions and diagnoses is that there will not necessarily be an opportunity (1) to cross-examine the person who gave the opinion or diagnosis,[147] (2) to explore the underlying factual bases for the opinion or diagnosis, or (3) in the case of expert opinions, to explore the purported expert's degree of expertise.

The first of these three concerns—possible inability to cross-examine—inheres in the use of any kind of business record. It seems appropriate, therefore, to ask why cross-examination might be thought to be more important with respect to opinion givers than other declarants. The answer, we believe, is that cross-examination may be helpful in determining the bases for the opinion and the extent of a person's purported expertise. It does not appear to us, however, that cross-examination is any more critical to the exploration of these questions than it is in exploring other factual questions. Thus, as a practical matter, the important concerns are only the latter two—exploring the underlying bases for an opinion and determining the extent of the opinion giver's expertise.

---

147. See McCormick's Handbook on the Law of Evidence 884 (3d ed. E. Cleary 1984):

When an expert opinion is offered by a witness personally testifying, the expert is available for cross-examination on that opinion. If the opinion is offered by means of a hospital record, no cross-examination is possible. Consequently, there is a tendency somewhat to limit those opinions which can be introduced by this method. . . . If the opinion is in connection with a central dispute in the case, such as causation, a court may well be reluctant to permit a decision to be made upon the basis of an uncross-examined opinion, and require that the witness be produced.

F. Hearsay Exceptions Not Requiring Unavailability: FRE 803

We agree that it would be disturbing to admit what purports to be an expert opinion in the absence of an opportunity to explore the underlying bases for the opinion or the extent of the opinion giver's expertise. We do not believe, however, that it is necessary to exclude opinions and diagnoses from the business records exception in order to accomplish this objective. Frequently, information about these matters will be readily available without cross-examination of the opinion giver; and to the extent that such information is not available, the party against whom the evidence is offered can argue for exclusion on several possible grounds:

(a) The evidence is inadmissible pursuant to FRE 702 because the opinion giver has not been qualified as an expert.[148]
(b) The evidence is inadmissible pursuant to FRE 705 because it will be impossible to comply with the requirement that the bases for the expert opinion be disclosed.
(c) Because of uncertainty about the opinion giver's expertise and/or the bases for the opinion, the probative value of the evidence is substantially outweighed by the time that it will take to present the evidence and the risk that, in the absence of critical evaluation, the jury will give undue weight to the opinion. FRE 403.

Frequently, several individuals will be involved in the making of a business record, and there will be potential hearsay problems with respect to each of them. For example, a recording secretary may take notes on what happened at a board meeting and give those notes to a stenographer to transcribe; a doctor may orally recite observations about a patient that are recorded by a nurse. In the former case, the recording secretary may fabricate, misunderstand, or incorrectly remember what happened at the meeting, and the stenographer may fabricate or misunderstand what the recording secretary reported. In the latter case, the doctor may fabricate or misperceive the symptoms, and the nurse may fabricate or misunderstand what the doctor says. In both examples, the business records exception will operate to remove from the hearsay prohibition the out-of-court statements of both contributors to the record.

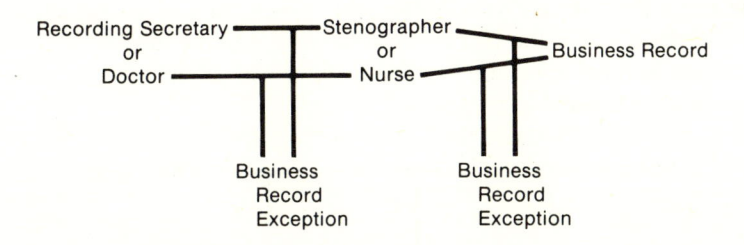

```
Recording Secretary ─┬─ Stenographer ─┐
        or           │       or       ├─ Business Record
      Doctor ────────┤     Nurse ─────┘
                     │                │
                     │                │
                  Business         Business
                   Record           Record
                 Exception        Exception
```

---

148. For a discussion of what standard the judge should apply in determining whether a witness has been qualified as an expert, see pages 740-741 supra.

The language of FRE 803(6) makes it clear that the business records exception can properly be used in multiple hearsay situations like those just described. The actual maker of the record does not have to have firsthand knowledge of the matters recorded. Rather, it is sufficient if the record was "made at or near the time *by, or from information transmitted by, a person with knowledge*. . . ." [Emphasis added.]

Unfortunately, the afore-quoted language in FRE 803(6), if applied literally, would in some situations bring about a result that the drafters of the Federal Rules did not intend. Consider, for example, a slight variation in the preceding doctor-nurse hypothetical:

> The doctor, instead of reporting observations of physical symptoms to the nurse, reports that the patient said, "John Jones hit me in the head with a baseball bat." In a prosecution of John Jones for assault, the district attorney, after properly authenticating the record and showing that it was kept in the ordinary course of the doctor's business and that it was the regular practice of the doctor to make such records, offers it into evidence to prove that John Jones committed the assault.

The business records exception may or may not still cover the hearsay steps from the doctor to the nurse and from the nurse to the record. It is probably reasonable to assume that the doctor is likely to relate accurately and that the nurse is likely to record accurately information that is obviously pertinent to the doctor's or the hospital's business—i.e., information relevant to the diagnosis or treatment of the patient's condition. When the information related and recorded is obviously not pertinent to the business activities (e.g., the patient's statement to a doctor about who is responsible for an injury), there is arguably reason for concern that the relating and recording of the information will not be carried out with the same care, even if such non-pertinent information is regularly recorded in records that are kept in the ordinary course of business. To the extent that this concern reasonably exists, it becomes a basis for arguing that the business records exception is not applicable because "the source of the information or the method or circumstances of preparation indicate lack of trustworthiness."

Even if the business records exception covers the hearsay steps from the doctor to the nurse to the report, we have an additional hearsay step—from the patient to the doctor; for it is the truth of the patient's declaration that the evidence is offered to prove:

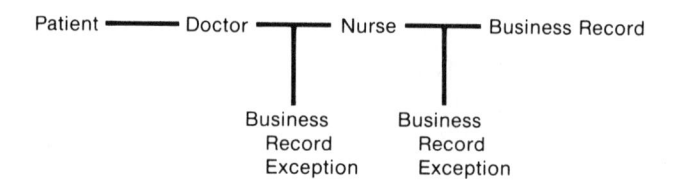

```
Patient ——— Doctor ——┬—— Nurse ——┬—— Business Record
                     │            │
                     │            │
                  Business     Business
                   Record       Record
                  Exception    Exception
```

F. Hearsay Exceptions Not Requiring Unavailability: FRE 803

If the patient's statement had been "I was hit in the head with a baseball bat," that statement might be admissible under FRE 803(4), the physical condition exception. If so, the combination of that exception for the initial declaration and the business records exception for the other two hearsay steps would make the record admissible. Naming the assailant, however, is not likely to be pertinent to diagnosis or treatment; therefore, FRE 803(4) would probably not be available. Moreover, the patient has no particular interest in the contents or accuracy of the doctor's records. Thus, the rationale for the business records exception is not applicable to the hearsay step from the patient to the doctor. Yet, because the record was made "from information transmitted by . . . a person with knowledge," FRE 803(6), if read literally, would appear to make the record admissible.

Perhaps one could rely on the general trustworthiness requirement in FRE 803(6) to exclude information in business records based on information from third persons who have nothing to do with the business. Giving the trial judge discretion to apply a general trustworthiness requirement on a case-by-case basis to hearsay *solely* because of the fortuity that it happens to be contained in a business record, however, seems inconsistent with the Federal Rules' general approach of requiring hearsay to fit within specifically articulated exceptions that, in theory, minimize the need for cross-examination. Moreover, according to the Advisory Committee's Note, the intent was to exclude, without regard to the trustworthiness clause, statements from persons with no business duty to the record keeper:

> Sources of information presented no substantial problem with ordinary business records. All participants, including the observer or participant furnishing the information to be recorded, were acting routinely, under a duty of accuracy, with employer reliance on the result, or in short "in the regular course of business." If, however, the supplier of the information does not act in the regular course, an essential link is broken; the assurance of accuracy does not extent to the information itself, and the fact that it may be recorded with scrupulous accuracy is of no avail. An illustration is the police report incorporating information obtained from a bystander: the officer qualifies as acting in the regular course but the informant does not. The leading case, Johnson v. Lutz, 253 N.Y. 124, 170 N.E. 517 (1930), held that a report thus prepared was inadmissible.

The version of FRE 803(6) submitted to Congress by the Supreme Court was somewhat more consistent with the expressed intent of the Advisory Committee than is the present version. The Supreme Court's version defined the exception as follows:

> A memorandum . . . made at or near the time by, or from information transmitted by, a person with knowledge, *all in the course of a regularly conducted activity*, as shown by the testimony of the custodian or other qualified witness. . . . [Emphasis added.]

The Advisory Committee apparently believed that the italicized clause—or perhaps just the word "all"—would accomplish the objective of excluding from the business records exception a statement like that of the patient in our hypothetical. See FRE 803, Advisory Committee Note:

> Model Code Rule 514 contains the requirement "that it was the regular course of that business for one with personal knowledge . . . to make such a memorandum or record or to transmit information thereof to be included in such a memorandum or record. . . ." *The rule follows the lead in requiring an informant with knowledge acting in the course of the regularly conducted activity.* [Emphasis added.]

Do you think the language in the Court's rule accomplishes the stated objective?

In its consideration of the Federal Rules, the House Judiciary Committee expressed the view that the Court's version of FRE 803(6) contained "insufficient guarantees of reliability." To remedy this perceived problem, the Committee amended the rule to provide that the activity must be a "business" activity and that it must be the "regular practice" of the business activity to make the record. The process of incorporating these limitations into the rule resulted in the current language. There is no indication in the legislative history that Congress disagreed with the Advisory Committee's position with regard to the source of the information. In light of this background, we believe that the rule, despite its language, should be interpreted consistently with the Advisory Committee's comments about the source of information in business records: Any declarant to whom the business records exception applies must have a business duty to make the declaration.

Consider how one might amend FRE 803(6) in order to make it conform to the Advisory Committee's expressed intent. Would it be sufficient, for example, to insert "and a business duty" immediately after "person with knowledge"?

In working with the business records exception it is critically important to understand what is and is not a business record. Consider, for example, the receipts that you receive when you have a car bumper replaced and the bills that you, as a consumer, receive in the mail from the telephone company and various credit card companies. These documents may be copies of the body shop's or the telephone company's or the credit card company's business record. You, however, have no firsthand knowledge about whether those institutions in fact have the records; you know only that the documents in your possession are your personal records reflecting your activities as a consumer of goods and services. Even if you can credibly characterize yourself as a Yuppie, we doubt that a court would find that you are in the business of being a consumer.

The way to ensure that you have what qualifies as a business record and that you will be able to admit it into evidence is to focus on the foundation

F. Hearsay Exceptions Not Requiring Unavailability: FRE 803

requirements for business records. You will need to establish that (1) the writing was made at near the time of the matter recorded, (2) the source of the information had knowledge of the subject matter, (3) the source had a business duty to report (or that the source's statement is not hearsay or falls within some independent hearsay exception), (4) the record is kept in the ordinary course of business activity, (5) it was the regular practice of the business activity to make the record, and (6) the trustworthiness requirement has been satisfied. In addition, you will have to be sure that you have satisfied the best evidence rule and authentication requirements. Usually the person who supplies the foundation for the business records exception will be able to provide the needed information for these requirements as well.

Unlike the past recollection recorded exception, which requires that the person whose statement is recorded be a witness, the business records exception does not require testimony from anyone with personal knowledge of the contents of the document. Rather, all that is needed is somebody to authenticate the document and to testify that it meets the requirements of the exception. An appropriate witness, for example, would be a custodian of records who may have no personal knowledge of the contents of the records but who can identify the records and testify about when and how they are made and kept in the ordinary course of business.

PROBLEMS

1. Reconsider Problem 1 at page 450. Would FRE 803(6) provide an alternative or a better basis for admitting any of the four pieces of evidence? If so, be prepared to discuss who you would call to the witness stand and what questions you would ask in order to lay the proper foundation.

2. Ed Larcher has brought an eviction action against Millie Tremble, a welfare recipient. Millie lives in a rooming house that she conveyed to Larcher several years ago. She claims that she had an oral agreement with Larcher that she could live in one of the rooms rent free for the rest of her life. Larcher claims that the agreement was for only six months. Millie offers into evidence records of the welfare department that were prepared by Millie's social worker in the ordinary course of her work and kept on file in the welfare department. The records indicate that Larcher had told Millie's social worker that Millie was entitled to stay rent free in the rooming house for the rest of her life. Larcher objects to the records as inadmissible hearsay. What result?

3. Angela Anderson has sued Harvey Hart for injuries she sustained when she fell from the second-story balcony of Harvey's apartment. Angela claims that Harvey, ignoring her protests, picked her up and tried to set her on the railing, that he lost control of her and dropped her over the side. Harvey, on the other hand, claims that Angela was drunk, that before he could stop her she tried to hang by her knees over the railing, and that she

lost her grip and fell. Following the incident, Harvey called an ambulance and accompanied Angela to the hospital, where she was treated for a broken leg and various bruises and scrapes. After establishing that plaintiff's Exhibit 3 for identification was the medical record of her hospital stay, that all entries were made in the ordinary course of business at or near the time of the events they record, and that it was the regular business of the hospital to make and keep such records, Angela offers the following portions of the record:

> (a) A notation by the intake nurse in the emergency room that Angela had said, "My leg hurts so much I think I'm going to die. Why did that idiot Harvey drop me off the balcony?"
>
> (b) A notation by the intake nurse in the emergency room that Harvey said, "I could have prevented this."

As part of his defense, Harvey offers the following portions of the same record:

> (c) A notation by the intake nurse that one of the ambulance attendants noted that Angela's breath smelled of alcohol and that she appeared to have been drinking heavily.
>
> (d) The results of a blood test which showed that Angela's blood-alcohol content was .17.

Should any of the preceding evidence be admissible?

4. Clarence Dempsey is being prosecuted for securities violations in conjunction with the illegal use of inside information. One of the beneficiaries of Dempsey's scheme, Sherman Pipps, has already pleaded guilty to securities violations and is cooperating with the government. Pipps has testified to various telephone conversations with Dempsey during which Dempsey advised Pipps to purchase certain stocks. According to Pipps, one conversation in January related to the purchase of Acme International and a second conversation in April related to the purchase of Ozone Airlines. Pipps' cannot, however, remember the exact date of the conversations, and establishing the date is critical to the government's case. To prove that Dempsey had been speaking on the telephone with Sherman Pipps on January 3 and on April 16, the government wants to introduce into evidence Pipps' desk calendar, which has notations in Pipps' handwriting on every page of various names and times. Dempsey's name appears on the January 3 page along with the notation "9:10 A.M." and on the April 16 page along with the notation "9:37 A.M." Is the government likely to be able to get the desk calendar admitted? What can the government do to maximize the chances of getting the desk calendar admitted?

5. Betty Harris has sued Joan Atkins for the conversion of a diamond ring. To prove the value of the ring Betty offers a written appraisal stating that a diamond ring matching the description of the ring allegedly converted

F. Hearsay Exceptions Not Requiring Unavailability: FRE 803

by Joan was worth $3500. The letterhead on the appraisal bears the name Haven's Jewelry. The appraisal bears what purports to be the signature of James Haven, who is described as "President, Haven's Jewelry." Betty testifies that she got the appraisal six months ago from James Haven, that she knows him as the president of Haven's Jewelry, and that she observed Mr. Haven examine the ring and prepare and sign the appraisal. Is the appraisal admissible?

6. Mary Thomas is suing Pam Martin for personal injuries resulting from an automobile accident. As part of her case, Mary called Frank Williams, a bystander who observed the accident. He testified that Mary was proceeding North on Main Street when Pam Martin, who had been traveling East on Pine, ran a red light and turned left onto Main immediately in front of Mary. As part of her defense Pam Martin offers a properly authenticated police report which contains the following statement: "Bystander Frank Williams stated that Mary Thomas ran red light." Should Mary Thomas' hearsay objection to this evidence be sustained?

8. Public Records and Reports

In addition to having a hearsay exception for private business records, every jurisdiction permits certain public records and reports to be admitted into evidence for their truth. The exception for public records has common law origins, but much of the law governing the admissibility of public records is statutory. It is not unusual, for example, to find in one jurisdiction a large number of statutes dealing with the admissibility of various public records. Often these statutes were enacted as part of the general statutory scheme dealing with a particular type of record. As such, they may provide not only for an exception to the hearsay rule but also for some means of self-authentication and for the admissibility of copies in lieu of the original. The rationale for a public records hearsay exception is virtually identical to the rationale for the business records exception: The inconvenience of calling public officials to testify[149] and the likelihood that public officials—particularly with respect to routine matters—may not recall the information in the records create the "necessity" for the exception; the public official's duty and the likelihood that public access to the records will reveal inaccuracies tend to ensure the records' reliability.

The Federal Rules public records exception is FRE 803(8). Before the rules became effective in 1975, Congress amended the version of FRE 803(8)

---

149. The hearsay exception alone does not solve the inconvenience problem, for there is still the matter of authentication. To ensure that somebody from the public office will not be required to testify as to the authenticity of the document and to avoid the inconvenience of temporary removal or perhaps even loss of public records, jurisdictions provide that copies of public records in a particular form—e.g., certified; bearing the seal of the office—are self-authenticating. See generally FRE 902.

that was promulgated by the Supreme Court. That amendment has been the subject of considerable litigation and inconsistent decisions. The text of FRE 803(8), the nature of the congressional amendment, and one view about what it all means is contained in the following case.

UNITED STATES v. OATES
560 F.2d 45 (2d Cir. 1977)

WATERMAN, Circuit Judge: This is an appeal from a judgment of the United States District Court for the Eastern District of New York convicting appellant . . . of possession of heroin with intent to distribute, and of conspiracy to commit that substantive offense. . . .

Appellant . . . claims that the trial court committed error by admitting into evidence at trial two documentary exhibits purporting to be the official report and accompanying worksheet of the United States Customs Service chemist who analyzed the white powdery substance seized from Isaac Daniels[, the defendant's alleged co-conspirator]. The documents, the crucial nature of which is beyond cavil, concluded that the powder examined was heroin. . . .

At trial the government had planned upon calling as one of its final witnesses a Mr. Milton Weinberg, a retired United States Customs Service chemist who allegedly had analyzed the white powder seized from Isaac Daniels. It seems that Mr. Weinberg had been present on the day the trial had been scheduled to commence but he was not able to testify then because of a delay occasioned by the unexpected length of the pretrial suppression hearing. The government claims that by the time Weinberg was rescheduled to testify he had become "unavailable." The Assistant United States Attorney explained the circumstances of this unavailability as follows: "I am told by his wife [that he is] very sick. Apparently he has some type of bronchial infection." After a short adjournment the prosecutor added the following comment: "Mr. Weinberg called my office this morning and I was made known about it about 10:30 this morning, prior to coming upstairs." Considering these two explanations to be consistent with each other, it appears that Weinberg called the United States Attorney's office to inform them of his unavailability and that subsequently the Assistant United States Attorney attempted to speak to Weinberg personally but was able, for some reason, to speak only to Weinberg's wife who advised that Weinberg had "some type of bronchial infection." There is no indication in the record as to why the Assistant United States Attorney was at that time unable to speak to Weinberg himself, although earlier that day Weinberg had been able to carry on a telephone conversation. Nor is there any other indication in the record that the prosecutor made any further attempts to confirm the fact that Weinberg was ill, and, if so, how ill he might be. No request was made of the district

F. Hearsay Exceptions Not Requiring Unavailability: FRE 803

court for a brief continuance for the purpose of determining the nature and expected duration of Weinberg's illness.

. . . When Weinberg became "unavailable," the government decided to call another Customs chemist, Shirley Harrington, who, although she did not know Weinberg personally, was able to testify concerning the regular practices and procedures used by the Customs Service chemists in analyzing unknown substances. Through Mrs. Harrington the government was successful in introducing Exhibits 13 and 12 which purported to be, respectively, the handwritten worksheet used by the chemist analyzing the substance seized from Daniels and the official typewritten report of the chemical analysis. The report summarizes salient features of the worksheet. Mrs. Harrington claimed to be able to ascertain from the face of the worksheet the various steps taken by Weinberg to determine whether the unknown substance was, as suspected, heroin. When the defense voiced vigorous objection to the attempt to introduce the documents through Mrs. Harrington, the government relied on [FRE 803(6) and FRE 803(8)] . . . to support its position that the documents were admissible. . . .

Mrs. Harrington was obviously an experienced chemist, having conducted thousands of tests while working for the Customs Service, including hundreds designed to identify heroin. She was also an experienced witness, having testified "probably a hundred or so" times in the course of her duties with the Customs Service. She had never worked with Weinberg personally and had never observed him perform any chemical tests. She had never received any notes or letters from him, but she identified Weinberg's writing on Exhibit 13 and his signature on Exhibit 12, presumably because she had, in accordance with Customs Service practices, reanalyzed, prior to destruction, substances Weinberg had previously analyzed shortly after the substances were seized.

The defense, in addition to having no opportunity to cross-examine Weinberg, the chemist who had performed the analysis, was also disturbed about two other circumstances surrounding the introduction of Exhibits 12 and 13. In particular the defense was surprised that Exhibit 12, the official typewritten report, contained Weinberg's signature, for no such signature had appeared on the copy of this exhibit given to the defense beforehand. Moreover, the defense was particularly, and understandably, distressed about the absence of Weinberg in view of the fact that the two exhibits differed in one important particular, a particular in which they certainly should have been identical. A notation pertaining to the chain of custody of the powder within the agency appeared on both exhibits, in typewritten form on the official report and in handwriting, presumably Weinberg's, on the worksheet. The notation read "Received from and returned to CSO Fromkin." On the typewritten official report, however, this statement had been crossed out, although it still was legible beneath the scribbling. Mrs. Harrington knew nothing about this deletion. There is nothing in the exhibits themselves or in the testimony of any witnesses that would explain why, when and by whom this deletion was made. . . .

It is eminently clear that the report and worksheet were "written assertions" . . . which were "offered . . . to prove the truth of the matters asserted. . . ." . . .

That the chemist's report and worksheet could not satisfy the requirements of the "public records and reports" exception seems evident merely from examining, on its face, the language of FRE 803(8). That rule insulates from the exclusionary effect of the hearsay rule certain:

> (8) *Public records and reports.*—Records, reports, statements, or data compilations, in any form, of public offices or agencies, setting forth (A) the activities of the office or agency, or (B) matters observed pursuant to duty imposed by law as to which matters there was a duty to report, excluding, however, in criminal cases matters observed by police officers and other law enforcement personnel, or (C) in civil cases and proceedings and against the Government in criminal cases, factual findings resulting from an investigation made pursuant to authority granted by law, unless the sources of information or other circumstances indicate lack of trustworthiness.

While there may be no sharp demarcation between the records covered by exception 8(B) and those referenced in exception 8(C), . . . and indeed there may in some cases be actual overlap, we conclude without hesitation that surely the language of item (C) is applicable to render the chemist's documents inadmissible as evidence in this case. . . .

. . . It seems indisputable to us that the chemist's official report and worksheet in the case at bar can be characterized as reports of "factual findings resulting from an investigation made pursuant to authority granted by law." The "factual finding" in each instance, the conclusion of the chemist that the substance analyzed was heroin, obviously is the product of an "investigation," see, e.g., Martin v. Reynolds Metal Corp. 297 F.2d 49, 57 (9th Cir. 1961) (" 'investigation', when liberally construed, includes the sampling and *testing* here contemplated") (emphasis supplied [by the court]),[150] supposedly involving on the part of the chemist employment of various techniques of scientific analysis. . . .

Though with less confidence, we believe that the chemist's documents might also fail to achieve status as public records under FRE 803(8)(B). . . . [T]he reports in this case conceivably could . . . be susceptible of the characterization that they are "reports . . . setting forth . . . (B) matters observed pursuant to a duty imposed by law as to which matters there was a duty to report." If this characterization is justified, the difficult question would be whether the chemists making the observations could be regarded as "other law enforcement personnel." We think this phraseology must be read broadly enough to make its prohibitions against the use of government-generated

---

150. The Federal Rules were approved by Congress in 1974 and became effective in 1975. Of what relevance to the meaning of "investigation" in FRE 803(8)(C) is the meaning of that same term in a single 1961 case?—Eds.

F. Hearsay Exceptions Not Requiring Unavailability: FRE 803

reports in criminal cases coterminous with the analogous prohibitions contained in FRE 803(8)(C). . . . We would thus construe "other law enforcement personnel" to include, at the least, any officer or employee of a governmental agency which has law enforcement responsibilities. Applying such a standard to the case at bar, we easily conclude that full-time chemists of the United States Customs Service are "law enforcement personnel." [The court then elaborated on the extensive role Customs Service chemists play in the development of evidence for criminal prosecutions.]

Our conclusion that the chemist's report and worksheet do not satisfy the standards of FRE 803(8) comports perfectly with what we discern to be clear legislative intent not only to exclude such documents from the scope of FRE 803(8) but from the scope of FRE 803(6) as well. . . . The Advisory Committee, in unequivocal language, offers the specter of collision with the confrontation clause as the explanation for the presence of FRE 803(8)(C) in its proposed (and, since FRE 803(8)(C) was unaltered during the legislative process, final) form:

> In one respect, however, the rule with respect to evaluative reports under [FRE 803(8)(C)] is very specific; they are admissible only in civil cases and against the government in criminal cases in view of the *almost certain collision with confrontation rights which would result from their use against an accused in a criminal case.* [Emphasis supplied by the court.]

. . . This preoccupation with preserving the confrontation rights of criminal defendants was shared by a Congress which established enhanced protection for those rights by substantially amending the proposed language of FRE 803(8)(B). [The] amendment offered by Representative David Dennis . . . [added to FRE 803(8)(B)] the language . . . "excluding, however, in criminal cases matters observed by police officers and other law enforcement personnel." . . . In the debate that followed the offer of this amendment, the accused's right to confront the witnesses against him was advanced as the impetus for the proposal. Speaking in support of the amendment, Representative Elizabeth Holtzman understood one of its purposes to be to "[reaffirm] the right of cross examination to the accused." . . . In a similar vein, Representative Dennis . . . emphasiz[ed] that the amendment pertained to "criminal cases, and in a criminal case the defendant should be confronted with the accuser to give him the chance to cross examine." . . .

. . . The *result* Congress intended was the absolute inadmissibility of records of this nature, and that this was, indeed, the result which Congress believed it had achieved by Rules 803(8)(B) and (C), could not have been articulated with any more clarity than it was by Representative William L. Hungate. As Chairman of the House Judiciary Subcommittee on Criminal Justice, Representative Hungate had been responsible for presiding over extensive hearings on the proposed Federal Rules of Evidence and must be regarded as one of the legislators most knowledgeable about the then pending legislation. Representative Hungate was also a floor manager for the legislation and a member of the Committee of Conference appointed to resolve the difference between the versions of the rules as approved by the House and Senate. . . . Representative Hungate presented to the House the official report of the Committee of Conference. At [that] time . . . , [h]e explained . . . : "As the rules of evidence now stand, police and law enforcement reports are not admissible against defendants in criminal cases. This is made quite clear by the provisions of rule 803(8)(B) and (C)." . . .

[The] very question of whether the so-called police reports disqualified under FRE 803(8) could nonetheless gain eventual admission by first satisfying the standards of some other hearsay exception was expressly raised by Representative Elizabeth Holtzman. [She] suggested that the police reports would now be able to qualify under another hearsay exception, specifically FRE 803(24) or 804(b)(5). . . . Representative David Dennis, an active participant in the floor debate, the sponsor of the amendment excluding police reports, a floor manager of the legislation and a member of the Committee of Conference, responded, politely but bluntly: ". . . I cannot see how anybody could suggest that introducing such a report is possible or a thing that could be done under these rules. . . ."

[T]he government argues . . . that the chemist's report and worksheet in the case at bar fall clearly within the literal terms of . . . FRE 803(6). . . .

[T]he government's argument . . . is not altogether unappealing if it is assessed strictly on the basis of the literal language of FRE 803(6). . . . For instance, it is true that, traditionally, a proponent's inability to satisfy the requirements of one hearsay exception does not deny him the opportunity to attempt to meet the standards of another. Secondly, it is clear from the explicit inclusion of the words "opinions" and "diagnoses" in FRE 803(6) that, in one sense, anyway, Congress intended to expand, or at least ratify, the view of prior court cases that had expanded the concept of what constitutes a "business record." . . . Thirdly, the testimony of Mrs. Harrington, a "qualified witness," established that it was a regular practice of the Customs laboratory to make written reports of their analyses and that these particular written reports were made in the regular course of the laboratory's activities. However, not nearly as clear is whether under the facts here the "method or circumstances of preparation" might not "indicate lack of trustworthiness." [The court repeated its description of the documents.] [W]hile we are troubled by these concededly unusual circumstances, . . . we prefer not to predicate our decision on a finding that the "circumstances of preparation indicate lack of trustworthiness." Instead, we assume for purpose of argument here, that . . . the chemist's report and worksheet might fall within the literal language of FRE 803(6).

. . . This would not be the first time that a court has encountered a situation pitting some literal language of a statute against a legislative intent that flies in the face of that literal language. Our function as an interpretive

F. Hearsay Exceptions Not Requiring Unavailability: FRE 803

body is, of course, to construe legislative enactments in such a way that the intent of the legislature is carried out. . . .

[P]olice and evaluative reports not satisfying the standards of FRE 803(8)(B) and (C) may not qualify for admission under FRE 803(6) or any of the other exceptions to the hearsay rule. . . .

[T]he introduction of the chemist's documents constituted reversible error and, accordingly, we reverse the judgment of conviction and remand for a new trial.

SOME THOUGHTS ABOUT OATES

Much of the court's analysis in *Oates*, we believe, was misguided. To suggest an alternative view of the public records exception, we begin as the *Oates* court did by focusing on the meaning of FRE 803(8)(C), which was left unaltered by Congress, and by then turning to the effect of the congressional amendment to FRE 803(8)(B). We conclude with a gratuitous response to the court's gratuitous comments about the absence of Mr. Weinberg and the apparent discrepancies in the documents.

Admittedly the Advisory Committee was concerned with possible confrontation clause problems if the government could take unrestrained advantage of FRE 803(8)(C) in criminal cases.[151] Moreover, the concern with avoiding possible confrontation problems was not unique to this particular hearsay exception. For example, the Advisory Committee explained a similar limitation on the judgments exception, FRE 803(22), as an effort to avoid "collision" with the confrontation clause. The Advisory Committee, however, correctly did not assume that all uses of hearsay evidence against a criminal defendant raised confrontation issues. Most exceptions do not contain limitations on the government's right to rely on them in criminal cases. Furthermore, the Advisory Committee, it seems to us, was not suggesting that *all* reports falling within FRE 803(8)(C) would, if offered against a criminal defendant, violate the confrontation clause. Rather, in discussing FRE 803(8)(C) the Advisory Committee noted that there had been conflicting decisions (in both civil and criminal cases) about the admissibility of what the Committee referred to throughout its discussion as " 'evaluative' reports." The Advisory Committee suggested that "the disagreement among the decisions has been due in part, no doubt, to the variety of situations encountered. . . ." Thus, it is reasonable to interpret the Advisory Committee as having a concern that in some but not necessarily all instances the use of FRE 803(8)(C) reports against criminal defendants might pose a confrontation problem.

The type of situation that is most likely to raise a confrontation issue is suggested both by the language of the rule and by the Advisory Committee's

---

151. See FRE 803, Advisory Committee Note, quoted by *Oates* at page 465 supra.

Note. The rule itself speaks of "factual findings resulting from an investigation." Since many investigations that result in factual findings are based on hearsay information, FRE 803(8)(C) in effect creates an exception that can cover multiple hearsay steps. For example, the factual findings might be based on the hearsay statements of persons interviewed by the fact finder. The only safeguards against the use of this hearsay from the interviewee are (1) the fact that the public agency decided to rely on the hearsay and (2) the court's application of the general trustworthiness requirement in FRE 803(8). Understandably, there might be a concern that this broad deference to the agency and the court to give credit to hearsay not falling within some other exception to the hearsay rule could at times run afoul of the confrontation clause. That this was the concern of the Advisory Committee is suggested by the Committee's continual reference to FRE 803(8)(C) as covering " 'evaluative' reports," a term that suggests reliance on or evaluation of information supplied by third persons. Particularly in light of the Advisory Committee's failure to limit the use against criminal defendants of "matters observed pursuant to a duty imposed by law," the Advisory Committee's reference to evaluative reports can reasonably be understood as expressing a concern with evaluations based on possibly unreliable information from third persons.

The Advisory Committee, of course, did not exclude the use against criminal defendants of evaluative reports or factual findings only if the reports or findings were based on otherwise inadmissible hearsay. The Committee excluded altogether the use of such evidence against criminal defendants. Presumably the Committee did so because of the view that a flat rule with respect to factual findings was preferable to a flexible rule whose applicability would have to be litigated in every case. If our view of the Advisory Committee's concern is correct, however, we have provided a reason for interpreting FRE 803(8)(C) in less than the broadest possible manner. More specifically, if a reasonable argument could be made that a report without multiple hearsay fell within the scope of both FRE 803(8)(B) (as proposed by the Court) and FRE 803(8)(C), it would be reasonable to place the report within (B) rather than (C) and to hold that the prohibition in (C) did not preclude reliance on (B) for making the report admissible.

One might counter that it would have been relatively easy for the Advisory Committee to draft the kind of limitation on the use of factual findings that we have suggested the Committee probably had in mind. Furthermore, one might maintain that the overlap between FRE 803(8)(B) and FRE 803(8)(C) is potentially so great that accepting our argument tends to negate what we assume was the Advisory Committee's reason for a generalized limitation on the scope of FRE 803(8)(C), namely the desire to avoid case-by-case litigation of the admissibility of what might reasonably be characterized as factual reports.

These are reasonable points to which we have no irrefutable response. We would merely point out that here, as elsewhere, the language of the rule and the comments of the Advisory Committee are less than clear about what

F. Hearsay Exceptions Not Requiring Unavailability: FRE 803

was intended. The objective in the face of this ambiguity is to try to develop a reasonable interpretation of the rule that is consistent with what appear to be the general objectives of the Federal Rules and that is not inconsistent with any clearly expressed legislative purpose. In these terms—or even in terms of the narrower (myopic?) focus of the *Oates* court on the particular legislative history of FRE 803(8)—we believe our account of FRE 803(8) compares favorably to that of the *Oates* court.

The question that remains is what impact the congressional amendment to FRE 803(8)(B) should have on the foregoing analysis. We disagree with *Oates'* conclusion that a general concern with the confrontation clause led Congress to impose a limitation on FRE 803(8)(B) that must be read broadly. First, the *Oates* court characterized Congress as sharing the Advisory Committee's "preoccupation with preserving the confrontation rights of criminal defendants." As we have already suggested, however, the *Oates* court seems to have an unwarranted view of the extent of the Advisory Committee's confrontation clause concern. Second, although some of the remarks during the legislative consideration of FRE 803(8)(B) suggest a broad concern with a criminal defendant's right to confront witnesses, the primary focus in the House discussion of Representative Dennis' amendment was quite narrow. The concern was whether it would be proper to use a *police report* in lieu of the testimony of a police officer, particularly in situations in which the police report contained the police officer's eyewitness account of criminal conduct:

> MR. DENNIS: . . . . What I am saying here is that in a criminal case, only, we should not be able to put in the police report to prove your case without calling the policeman. I think in a criminal case you ought to have to call the policeman on the beat and give the defendant the chance to cross examine him, rather than just reading the report into evidence, that is the purpose of this amendment. . . .
>
> MR. SMITH *of New York:* Mr. Chairman, I rise in opposition to the amendment. . . .
>
> I just think we are treading in an area the impact of which will be very unfortunate and the effect of which is to make police officers and law enforcement officers second-class citizens less trustworthy than social workers or garbage collectors. . . .
>
> MR. JOHNSON *of Colorado:* Mr. Chairman, as an ex-prosecutor I cannot imagine that the gentleman would be advocating that a policeman's report could come in to help convict a man, and not have the policeman himself subject to cross-examination. . . .
>
> . . . If the officer who made the investigation is not available for cross-examination, then you cannot have a fair trial.
>
> I cannot believe the gentleman would be saying that we should be able to convict people where the police officer's statement is not subject to cross-examination.
>
> MR. SMITH *of New York:* All I am saying . . . is that it seems to me that it should be allowed for the jury to consider such a report, together with

all of the other aspects of the case, if this report was made by a police officer pursuant to a duty imposed upon the police officer by law. . . .

MR. BRASCO: . . . As I understand it the gentleman from New York [Mr. Smith] is advocating . . . that if a police officer made a report that he saw Mr. X with a gun on such and such an occasion, and then thereafter that police officer is unavailable that that statement could be used in a criminal case against Mr. X without the defense attorney having the opportunity to cross-examine the officer with respect to his position with relation to Mr. X, the time of day, whether he was under a light, or whether there was no light, how much time did he have in which to see the gun, and all other observations relevant to the case.

MR. DENNIS: Mr. Chairman, I would say in answer to the question raised by the gentleman from New York [Mr. Brasco] that if the statements of the police officer in his report would, in the language of this bill, be "matters observed pursuant to a duty imposed by law, and as to which he was under a duty to make a report," and I rather think they might be, that then what the gentleman says is true, and would be true.

I am trying to remove that possibility. . . .

MR. HUNT: I had no intention of getting into this argument, but when the gentleman brings in the word "investigator," then I have to get in.

MR. BRASCO: I did not say it.

MR. HUNT: I know the gentleman from New York [Mr. Brasco] did not, but it was discussed. The only time I can recall in my 34 years of law enforcement that a report of an investigator was admissible in court was to test the credibility of an officer. . . . We would never even think about bringing in a report in lieu of the officer being there to have that officer cross-examined; but reports were admitted as evidentiary fact for the purpose of testing the officer's credibility and perhaps to refresh his memory.

MR. BRASCO: I do not think that the gentleman's amendment interferes with that at all. [120 Cong. Rec. 2387 (Feb. 6, 1974).]

In light of this concern, it seems reasonable to interpret "other law enforcement personnel" to include only individuals whose functions are similar to police officers.[152] Moreover, in light of the expressed concern with need to cross-examine police officers, it is arguable that very routine (and, therefore, probably reliable) observations, even if made by police officers and included within police reports, need not be excluded in criminal cases.[153]

---

152. See, e.g., United States v. Orozco, 590 F.2d 789 (9th Cir.), cert. denied, 442 U.S. 920 (1979) (Customs Service computer cards containing license numbers of cars crossing border admissible in narcotics prosecution).

153. See, e.g., United States v. Gilbert, 774 F.2d 962 (9th Cir. 1985) (card taken from files of state department of public safety which had fingerprint and notation by department criminologist indicating source of print admissible under FRE 803(8)(B); exclusionary provision in (B) not applicable because it was designed to exclude only "observations by officials at the scene of the crime or apprehension because observations made in an adversarial setting are less reliable than observations made by public officials in other settings"); United States v. Grady, 544 F.2d 598 (2d Cir. 1976) (Ulster Constabulary records of serial numbers of weapons received in Northern Ireland admissible in prosecution for unlawfully exporting firearms).

F. Hearsay Exceptions Not Requiring Unavailability: FRE 803

There is one matter about which we are in partial agreement with the *Oates* court. As we noted earlier, the rationales for the business records exception and the official records exception are almost identical. Thus, if a document is inadmissible under FRE 803(8) *because of* the limitations on the use of "matters observed" in (B) or "factual findings" in (C), it seems to us that it would be a subversion of the legislative intent to permit the document be used as an FRE 803(6) business record.[154] In addition, it should not be permissible to circumvent the specific limitations on the scope of FRE 803(8) by resorting to the residual exceptions, FRE 803(24) and FRE 804(b)(5). We do not believe, however, that the *Oates* dictum prohibiting resort to other exceptions is sound. The justification for the past recollection recorded exception, for example, is sufficiently different from the justification for the business and public records exceptions that a court should not deny the availability of the former exception to the government in criminal cases merely because the recorded recollection happens to be in a public record falling within FRE 803(8)(B) or (C).[155]

Regardless of whether we are right or the *Oates* court is right about the extent to which it is appropriate to look to other exceptions for "matters observed" or "factual findings" that are inadmissible pursuant to FRE 803(8), it is important to realize that some public records may contain information that is neither a "matter observed" nor a "factual finding." When that is the case, the report is not covered by FRE 803(8)(B) or (C) at all and, therefore, cannot fall within the specific limitations of FRE 803(8)(B) or (C). Thus, it would not be a subversion of those limitations to resort to FRE 803(6), or to any other hearsay exception.

Finally, we address the *Oates* court's comments about the absence of Mr. Weinberg and the apparent discrepancies in the documents. The court notes that these matters were totally unexplained, a circumstance that we find not surprising. If there were some reason to believe that there was an ulterior motive in not calling Mr. Weinberg or some reason for believing that the official report and worksheet were not accurate, we suspect that defense counsel would have tried to exploit these possibilities in concrete terms. The reality probably was that there was nothing to exploit. It does not seem unusual that Mr. Weinberg spoke to the prosecutor's office early in the day and that only his wife spoke with the prosecutor's office later. If Mr. Weinberg was sick and unable to attend the trial, it is reasonable to assume that he felt worse as the morning went on. Indeed, since he apparently had a bronchial condition, he may have lost his voice.

The discrepancies in the documents are also explainable. The copy that

---

154. At least one court, reasoning that the key to the limitations in FRE 803(8) was an inability to cross-examine the record maker, has applied FRE 803(6) to admit against a criminal defendant a public record that the court was willing to assume fell within the scope of the FRE 803(C) exclusion in a situation in which the record maker was a witness subject to cross-examination. United States v. King, 613 F.2d 670 (7th Cir. 1980).

155. See United States v. Sawyer, 607 F.2d 1190 (7th Cir. 1979) (document falling within exclusionary provision of FRE 803(8)(B) admissible under FRE 803(5)).

was given to the defense counsel was probably made before the original was given to Mr. Weinberg for his signature. Perhaps the chain of custody note was crossed out on the official report because it is not customary to include such notations on the official report. In any event, from the court's description of the deletion, it seems evident that there was no intent to conceal or alter pertinent information.

Our hypotheses about Mr. Weinberg's absence and the discrepancies in the documents may not be correct. They seem to us, however, to be more plausible than the innuendo of wrongdoing in the court's account of these matters. On the other hand, particularly in the context of evidence offered by a prosecutor against a criminal defendant, should the offerer always have the burden of at least making a good faith effort to account for such things as the absence of witnesses and discrepancies in documents?

9. The Absence of Entry Exceptions

FRE 803(7) and FRE 803(10) set forth hearsay exceptions for the absence of entries in business and public records offered for the purpose of proving the non-occurrence or non-existence of a matter that probably would have been included in the particular record if the matter had occurred or existed. As the Advisory Committee noted, it is unlikely that the failure to make the entry is the result of a conscious intent to assert the non-occurrence or non-existence of the event. Thus, the failure to make an entry may not constitute a hearsay "statement" in the first place. Nonetheless, there is some precedent for treating the absence of an entry as hearsay. The exceptions exist, according to the Advisory Committee, "[i]n order to set the question at rest in favor of admissibility. . . ."

PROBLEMS

1. Lois Loftis is suing Reggie Morris for injuries she received in an accident involving her bicycle and Morris' Volvo. A police report prepared and signed by Officer Frank Friendly several hours after the accident contains the following:

> Arrived at accident scene at 2:30 P.M. Officer Elaine Davis already at scene. She reports that bystander, Tom Willis, said Volvo did not stop at stop sign. I interviewed Volvo driver who claimed that stop sign was hard to see. 40-ft. skid marks into intersection to point of impact indicate Volvo did not stop at stop sign. Bicycle rider badly bruised and unconscious. May have broken neck. Called ambulance. Cited Volvo driver for reckless driving and failure to stop at stop sign.

F. Hearsay Exceptions Not Requiring Unavailability: FRE 803 473

How much of the preceding excerpt from the police report is Lois likely to be able to introduce against Morris?

2. Same facts as in Problem 1, except that Lois died as a result of her injuries and Morris is being prosecuted for vehicular homicide. How much of the excerpt from the police report is the prosecutor likely to be able to introduce against Morris?

3. Tammy Lincoln is being prosecuted for recklessly endangering the lives of others. Several witnesses testified for the prosecution that a car driven by a woman sped along the sidewalk in a crowded urban area and eventually crashed into a cement wall. None of these witnesses could specifically identify Tammy as the driver, and several witnesses testified that they thought there was a passenger in the car. Officer Elaine Davis testified that she arrived at the scene of the crash within seconds after its occurrence, that there were two unconscious people in the front seat, and that the person in the driver's seat was Tammy Lincoln. Tammy claims that she was the passenger, and that the car was being driven by her now deceased boyfriend, Fred Able. To help support her claim she offers into evidence the following portion of the police report on the accident prepared and signed by Officer Frank Friendly:

> Arrived at scene at 11:45 A.M. Officer Elaine Davis already at scene. Ambulance arrived and removed unconscious male body from driver's seat and unconscious female body from front passenger seat.

The prosecution objects to the admissibility of this evidence on the ground that its admission is barred by FRE 803(8)(B). How should the court rule?

4. Wilson is being prosecuted for illegally shipping arms to Libya. His defense is that he had an ongoing special relationship with the CIA, and that he shipped the arms with their tacit approval. To rebut this claim, the government offers an affidavit signed by the Executive Director of the CIA stating that he had ordered a diligent search of all CIA records and that the search revealed no evidence of any special relationship with Wilson. Wilson objects to the admissibility of the affidavit on the ground of hearsay. How should the court rule?

5. Paul Martin has brought a federal civil rights action against Wilford James, a police officer, for injuries Martin received when he was shot by James during a civil rights demonstration that had briefly become violent. James offers into evidence the report of the State Shooting Review Board, which concludes that James acted within the police guidelines for use of weapons. Martin objects that the report is inadmissible hearsay. What result?

10. Other Records Exceptions

In addition to the business and official records exceptions, FRE 803 contains a variety of exceptions for other types of records, e.g., marriage and baptismal records. These exceptions for the most part are based on the notion that the records are likely to be reliable. The scope and operation of these exceptions should be easily discernable from the language of the rule and the Advisory Committee's Notes.

11. Learned Treatises

The common law learned treatises exception to the hearsay rule was rarely of much value to parties because of severe foundation requirements that courts imposed on it. Some courts limited the exception to matters that were so well known they were virtually beyond dispute. In that case, to prove such matters, it probably would not have been necessary to rely on learned treatises. Non-hearsay evidence of obvious, well-known facts usually is readily available, or it may be possible to persuade a court to take judicial notice of such facts. See FRE 201.

Another foundation requirement imposed by some courts was that the treatise itself be one of virtual unquestioned authority. Few treatises could meet the standard. If a treatise were so basic and fundamental that it met the standard, it probably would have been relatively easy to establish the proposition contained in the treatise by other evidence.

The reasons for taking such a restrictive position as to the use of learned treatises was not limited solely to concerns about the hearsay dangers with respect to the treatise writer. There was also a concern that skillful advocates could manipulate the information in learned treatises to support propositions that the author never intended to support.[156] FRE 803(18) attempts to meet both the hearsay and the non-hearsay concerns in its much broader formulation of the learned treatises exception:

> To the extent called to the attention of an expert witness upon cross-examination or relied upon by the expert witness in direct examination, statements contained in published treatises, periodicals, or pamphlets on a subject of history, medicine, or other science or art, established as a reliable authority by the testimony or admission of the witness or by other expert testimony or

---

156. Despite these severe limitations on the use of learned treatises for their truth, courts have regularly permitted treatises to be used to impeach or rehabilitate expert witnesses. For example, if Dr. Ellen Jones testifies that she has relied on a particular treatise in making her diagnosis or, in some jurisdictions, if she merely acknowledges that a particular treatise is authoritative, she may be impeached by showing passages in the treatise that are inconsistent with her in-court testimony. Similarly, the common law permitted prior consistent statements in treatises relied upon—or in some jurisdictions merely recognized as authoritative—to be used to rehabilitate a witness after an express or implied charge of recent fabrication or improper influence. The rationale for this use of the treatises was that the witness, by relying on the treatise—or recognizing it as authoritative—had in effect vouched for or accepted as valid all of the statements in the treatise. Thus, statements in the treatise could be used in the same non-hearsay manner than prior inconsistent or consistent statements of any witness could be used.

F. Hearsay Exceptions Not Requiring Unavailability: FRE 803

by judicial notice. If admitted, the statements may be read into evidence but may not be received as exhibits.

According to the Advisory Committee:

> The writers have generally favored the admissibility of learned treatises, . . . but the great weight of authority has been that learned treatises are not admissible as substantive evidence. . . . The foundation of the minority view is that the hearsay objection must be regarded as unimpressive when directed against treatises since a high standard of accuracy is engendered by various factors: the treatise is written primarily and impartially for professionals, subject to scrutiny and exposure for inaccuracy, with the reputation of the writer at stake. . . . Sound as this position may be with respect to trustworthiness, there is, nevertheless, an additional difficulty in the likelihood that the treatise will be misunderstood and misapplied without expert assistance and supervision. . . . The rule avoids the danger of misunderstanding and misapplication by limiting the use of the treatises as substantive evidence to situations in which an expert is on the stand and available to explain and assist in the application of the treatise if declared.

12. Judgments

A judgment in a criminal or civil action is relevant evidence of the facts essential to support the judgment, and it is also hearsay evidence of those facts. Indeed, it is multiple hearsay. The judgment is the judge's official entry based on the jury's verdict or the judge's findings, or the criminal defendant's plea. The defendant's plea of guilty is itself a hearsay statement, and a judge's or a jury's factual conclusions from evidence presented in a trial are also hearsay statements based on what the witnesses at the trial said. Nonetheless, in at least some situations, it is reasonable to assume that a judgment is reliable proof of the facts essential to sustain the judgment. For example, in civil cases involving claims for substantial monetary damages or deeply felt principles or in criminal prosecutions where the potential penalty is substantial, it is reasonable to believe that the parties will put forth their best efforts in trying to vindicate their positions and, therefore, that the judgment will represent a reasonable conclusion or assessment about the relevant facts. On the other hand, if the stakes are small, a litigant may not have a serious interest in devoting the resources that would be necessary to vindicate the litigant's position. If this or some other reason suggests that the judgment may not be a reliable indication of the accuracy of the facts that in theory are essential to support the judgment, one should be reluctant to accept the judgment as evidence of those facts. Furthermore, even if it is reasonable to believe that the litigation leading to the judgment was seriously contested, one might be reluctant to admit a judgment based on a lower standard of proof than the standard applicable to the facts at issue in the action in which the judgment is offered. If the present fact finder learns that a previous fact finder reached certain conclusions, the present fact finder may be inclined to focus on the fact that certain conclusions were reached by that other, presumably reasonable, fact finder and be reluctant to find contrary facts even though the standard of proof in the prior action was lower than the standard of proof in the current action. The Federal Rules exception, contained in FRE 803 (22) attempts to accommodate these competing concerns by defining the judgments exception in the following manner:

> Evidence of a final judgment, entered after a trial or upon a plea of guilty (but not upon a plea of nolo contendere), adjudicating a person guilty of a crime punishable by death or imprisonment in excess of one year, to prove any fact essential to sustain the judgment, but not including, when offered by the Government in a criminal prosecution for purposes other than impeachment, judgments against persons other than the accused. The pendency of an appeal may be shown but does not affect admissibility.

The exclusion in current criminal cases of judgments against persons other than the defendant is based on a concern with the defendant's right to confront and cross-examine adverse witnesses; the exclusion of misdemeanor—and relatively small civil—judgments is based on the notion that there might not be a sufficient incentive to litigate those matters seriously; the exclusion of even serious criminal judgments entered after a plea of nolo contendere is based on the fact that a nolo plea, which can be entered only with the leave of the court, is specifically designed to resolve a criminal matter without the expense of a trial or the defendant's acknowledgment of guilt; and the exclusion of even major civil cases is based on the potential prejudice that may result from the current fact finder's possible inability to grasp fully the notion that the prior judgment may have been based on a relatively low standard of proof. Even if one wanted to include judgments from major civil cases, any attempt to define the difference between major and minor cases is likely to seem quite arbitrary.

In dealing with the judgments exception to the hearsay rule, keep in mind that the issue is whether it is appropriate to use the judgment only as *some evidence* of the facts that are essential to support the judgment. The exception does not raise questions of collateral estoppel or issue preclusion, which would, in effect, make moot any possible evidentiary use of a judgment.

13. The Residual Exceptions

The Federal Rules as promulgated by the Supreme Court provided an exception in both FRE 803 and FRE 804 for a "statement not specifically covered by any of the foregoing exceptions but having comparable circum-

F. Hearsay Exceptions Not Requiring Unavailability: FRE 803

stantial guarantees of trustworthiness." The Advisory Committee did not explain why this rule appeared in both FRE 803 and FRE 804. Apparently, the notion is that unavailability may be relevant but not critical to the application of the residual exception. It is not clear, however, what role unavailability should play. One might derive from FRE 803(24) and FRE 804(b)(5) the proposition that if the circumstantial guarantees of trustworthiness were more similar to the specific FRE 804 exceptions than the specific FRE 803 exceptions, unavailability should be required. Given what appears to us to be the absence of a principled basis of requiring or not requiring unavailability, however, we have no idea how to apply that proposition. Furthermore, we are not sure what role unavailability should play. On the one hand, unavailability of the hearsay declarant cuts in favor of admissibility since there may be no alternative source for the information contained in the hearsay statement. On the other hand, unavailability cuts against admissibility because unavailability means that it will be impossible to test by cross-examination the declarant's sincerity, narration, perception, and memory.

The House of Representatives initially approved the Federal Rules with the residual exceptions completely deleted. The Senate inserted more restrictive residual exceptions that became part of the Federal Rules adopted by Congress. The restrictive residual exceptions, FRE 803(24) and FRE 804(b)(5), create hearsay exceptions for:

> A statement not specifically covered by any of the foregoing exceptions but having equivalent circumstantial guarantees of trustworthiness, if the court determines that (A) the statement is offered as evidence of a material fact; (B) the statement is more probative on the point for which it is offered than any other evidence which the proponent can procure through reasonable efforts;[157] and (C) the general purposes of these rules and the interest of justice will best be served by admission of the statement into evidence. However, a statement may not be admitted under this exception unless the proponent of it makes known to the adverse party sufficiently in advance of the trial or hearing to provide the adverse party with a fair opportunity to prepare to meet it, the proponent's intention to offer the statement and the particulars of it, including the name and address of the declarant.[158]

According to the Senate Judiciary Committee:

---

157. Fairly obviously, the extent to which this requirement is applied rigorously will have a substantial impact on the utility of the residual exceptions.—Eds.

158. The advance notice provision was not part of the Senate proposal, but instead was an amendment added by the conference committee. Courts have held that, despite the language of the rule, notice "in advance of the trial or hearing" is not necessarily required, as long as there is a reasonable opportunity for the opposing party to be apprised of and have an opportunity to respond to the hearsay. See, e.g., United States v. Iaconetti, 406 F. Supp. 554 (E.D.N.Y.), aff'd, 540 F.2d 574 (2d Cir.), cert. denied, 429 U.S. 104 (1976); United States v. Bailey, 581 F.2d 341 (3d Cir. 1978).—Eds.

It is intended that the residual hearsay exceptions will be used very rarely, and only in exceptional circumstances. The committee does not intend to establish a broad license for trial judges to admit hearsay statements that do not fall within one of the other exceptions contained in rules 803 and 804(b). The residual exceptions are not meant to authorize major judicial revisions of the hearsay rule, including its present exceptions. Such major revisions are best accomplished by legislative action. It is intended that in any case in which evidence is sought to be admitted under these subsections, the trial judge will exercise no less care, reflection and caution than the courts did under the common law in establishing the now-recognized exceptions to the hearsay rule.

In order to establish a well-defined jurisprudence, the special facts and circumstances which, in the court's judgment, indicates [sic] that the statement has a sufficiently high degree of trustworthiness and necessity to justify its admission should be stated on the record.

Despite this admonition from the Senate Judiciary Committee, courts, perhaps not surprisingly, have taken quite divergent views about how broadly or narrowly to interpret the residual exceptions.

Regardless of the general mindset that one brings to the residual exceptions, there are several types of specific issues with which one must grapple. First, what is the significance of the availability or unavailability of the hearsay declarant? Second, what kinds of factors or information tend to establish that there are "equivalent circumstantial guarantees of trustworthiness"? Must there be circumstantial guarantees that are similar to the guarantees that justify specific hearsay exceptions, or is it sufficient to show by way of independent corroborating evidence that the particular hearsay statement is probably trustworthy? Finally, what is the significance of the fact that the offered hearsay almost, but not quite, fits within one of the specific hearsay exceptions? Does the closeness to an established exception enhance the likelihood of admissibility, or does the fact that declaration does not quite fit the contours of the exception mean that admitting the statement would be undermining the legislative intent with respect to that general category of hearsay? Not surprisingly, courts have taken different positions on these questions just as they have taken different positions on the more general question of the liberality with which they will treat the residual exceptions.

PROBLEMS

1. Al Tiger was charged with willfully placing a dynamite bomb in the St. Louis airport terminal. The bomb, which was discovered by police shortly before it exploded, was contained in a shoe box. Following his arrest and the posting of bail, Tiger fled the jurisdiction. He eluded recapture for nine years.

F. Hearsay Exceptions Not Requiring Unavailability: FRE 803

Shortly after the bombing when the investigation began to focus on Tiger, the police interviewed a number of his friends and acquaintances, including his landlady, Bertha Short. The landlady was called as a witness at Tiger's trial. She testified that she barely remembered having Tiger as a tenant, and she could recall no details about him or any dealings she had with him. Police Officer James Mills was then called as a witness. He testified that he had observed the bomb before it exploded and that it was contained in a Brown Shoe Co. box that was scotch taped at one end. He also testified that within one week of the bombing he interviewed Tiger's landlady and that he transcribed the interview on the same day. He then authenticated the prosecutor's "Exhibit J" as the original transcription of the interview. The transcription reads as follows:

> Mrs. Bertha Short advised Al Tiger has been a tenant, occupying an upstairs front room for about the past eight months. Mrs. Short informed that to her knowledge Al Tiger has not received the delivery of any kind of box at her rooming house within recent past. She stated Tiger asked her for a shoe box on Wednesday, December 22 [which was three days before the bombing] and that she put it in his room on that day. Mrs. Short stated the shoe box she furnished Tiger was a Brown Shoe Company shoe box, gray in color, bearing the brand name "Pedwin" on one end. She further advised that this box was broken at one end and had a piece of scotch tape on it to hold it together.

If you were the prosecutor and wanted to introduce the transcription into evidence, is there any additional information relating to the transcription that you would want to develop through the testimony of Officer Mills? Assume that you, as prosecutor, have completed the examination of Officer Mills and that you now offer the transcription into evidence. How should the court rule?

2. David Dixon has been charged with the sale of heroin. Two alleged purchasers, Brown and Green, were granted immunity and were prepared to testify against Dixon. Since Green had a long history of involvement with drugs and several drug-related convictions, the prosecution planned to make Brown the star witness. Brown, however, died of a heart attack several days prior to the trial. At Dixon's trial the prosecution authenticates and offers into evidence Brown's signed, written statement that contains the substance of what would have been his live testimony. Should the court admit the statement?

3. Ed Barns has sued Acme Used Cars for injuries that he sustained when he and a companion were examining an automobile at the Acme car lot. The car in which Barns was interested would not start, so Fred Anders, an Acme mechanic, offered his assistance. Barns was pouring gasoline from a small can into the carburetor while his companion attempted to start the engine. The engine backfired and ignited the can, and Barns suffered severe burn injuries. At trial, the parties disagreed over whether the plaintiff was

acting pursuant to Fred Anders' instructions, as the plaintiff claimed, or in disregard of Anders' warning, as the defendant claimed.

Anders died prior to the trial, and the defendant offers into evidence Exhibit B, a signed statement that supports the defendant's claim, along with the following testimony of Anders' supervisor, Georgia Breen:

> I learned of the accident within several hours of its occurrence, and I immediately instructed Fred Anders to go into a room, not to talk to anyone else, and to write down everything that happened. Anders obeyed my instruction and came back with a handwritten statement within 30 minutes. I recognized his handwriting and he signed the document in my presence. I recognize Exhibit B as that document.

Should Exhibit B be admitted into evidence? If your answer is yes, should the jury be permitted to inspect the exhibit, or should the statement only be read to the jury?

4. Alex Johnson has been charged with extortion and attempted murder. Elmer Peepers, a pawn shop owner and the victim of the alleged crimes, was to be the prosecution's star witness. Elmer, however, has adamantly refused to testify because of fear for the safety of his wife and children. He has been held in contempt and is currently incarcerated. The prosecutor offers into evidence Elmer's grand jury testimony that details the defendant's involvement in the charged crimes. Should the defendant's hearsay objection to this evidence be sustained?

G. REFLECTIONS ON THE HEARSAY RULE

NOTE, THE THEORETICAL FOUNDATION OF THE HEARSAY RULES
93 Harv. L. Rev. 1786, 1787-1791, 1793-1809, 1811-1812 (1980)

I. RATIONALIZING THE RULE AGAINST HEARSAY

A. A GENERAL MODEL FOR EXCLUSION

Motivated by the assumption that a primary goal of our legal system is to achieve accurate case results, this Section will develop a framework that premises the exclusion of a relevant piece of evidence upon an expectation that the jury will erroneously assess the credibility of that evidence. To determine the extent to which the jury's assessment is erroneous, that assessment must be measured against some standard. Although ideally one

G. Reflections on the Hearsay Rule

would choose a standard of "truth," such a standard is, of course, impossible in principle to ascertain in the context of a trial. Instead, the framework will use the best alternative: the credibility that would be assigned to the evidence by "experts"—judges, attorneys, and academicians. This criterion will be referred to as "absolute reliability." Any relevant evidence, including hearsay, has at least some absolute reliability because the existence of infirmities and uncertainties of a piece of evidence only justifies *discounting* the weight given to the evidence rather than *ignoring* the evidence through exclusion. . . .

If the jury's assessment is accurate by the standard of absolute reliability—that is, if the jury and the "expert" assessments coincide—the evidence should be admitted. When the jury cannot accurately assess the credibility of a piece of evidence, the error results in a gap between the jury's perception of the evidence and the absolute reliability of the evidence. Were the jury expected to *under*assess reliability, the controversy would not be over exclusion but over methods designed to increase the jury's reliance on the evidence. Exclusion is premised upon jury *over*assessment.

Any error that the jury commits in using the evidence to arrive at its verdict will depend upon the gap that remains at the conclusion of the trial—the residual gap—and not on the gap that existed after direct examination. Cross-examination and closing argument present opportunities to expose the weaknesses of testimony, improving the accuracy of the jury's assessment. . . .

The concept of residual gap measures the expected jury error—the cost of admitting evidence. Credibility, judged by the standard of absolute reliability, measures the expected value of the evidence—the expected benefit from admission. A cost-benefit decision rule aimed at maximizing the accuracy of the result in a given case would exclude evidence when the expected error exceeds the expected value. This formula is analogous to [FRE] 403. . . .

One way to examine the amount of error required to outweigh value, in order to justify exclusion, is to imagine a scale for recording assessments of the credibility of evidence. Zero would correspond to evidence given no credibility whatsoever; 100 to evidence believed with absolute certainty. Suppose the expert assessment (absolute reliability) of the evidence is above 50—for example, 51. Since the greatest value the jury could assign to the evidence is 100, the largest possible gap is 49. Thus the expected value (51) exceeds the gap (at most 49) and the evidence should be admitted under the decision rule. Alternatively, consider a case where the expert assessment of value was 30 and the jury assessment was 61. The resulting gap of 31 exceeds the value of 30, barely justifying exclusion. Exclusion requires that the gap exceed the value of the evidence, and, as this second example indicates, this condition is fulfilled only if the jury assessment exceeds twice the value of the evidence. The occurrence of this condition is unlikely since it requires the existence of factors that indicate to the experts in the legal profession the credibility of some evidence is very low but that are so far beyond the comprehension of laypersons that juries still would assess the credibility as being quite high.[14]

B. Exclusion on the Ground that Evidence is Hearsay

The process of determining the admissibility of a relevant piece of evidence by balancing its value against the residual gap between expected jury perception and absolute reliability is applicable to all types of evidence, and not just hearsay. Hearsay is distinguished from other evidence by the absence of the declarant. To justify the exclusion of evidence *because it is hearsay*, two conditions must be satisfied: (1) In the absence of the declarant (or when testimony is offered of the witness' own past statements), the gap must exceed value. (2) If the declarant is present (testifying to a current recollection of the events), the value must exceed the gap. If the first condition fails, there would be no reason to exclude. Without the second, exclusion would be justified even if the evidence were not hearsay. . . .

II. MISDIRECTION OF THE HEARSAY RULES: FAILURE ON THEIR OWN TERMS

A. The Mystery of the Available Declarant

. . . In the context of considering the accuracy of the result in a given case, arguments over the admission of the hearsay of available declarants make little sense because in any given case application of either of the two extreme approaches (always exclude or always admit) leads to the same result. If the declarant is available, (1) exclusion would be of little consequence to the party needing the evidence since the declarant can be called directly, and (2) admission would not damage the position of the party fearing jury overevaluation of the hearsay since the declarant can be called for cross-examination, which allows the same impeachment possibilities that would have existed were the opponent to have called the declarant for direct examination.[28] If exclusion is the general rule,[30] some special treatment of hearsay of available declarants may be justified on grounds unrelated to fears

---

14. . . . One qualification is necessary in the case of exceptionally unreliable hearsay evidence (for example, with a value of one on the 100 point scale) where it may be plausible that the jury assessment would exceed twice the value (in this example, an assessment of three). Such evidence may be excluded because of the waste of time, Fed. R. Evid. 403, and in any event the impact of such slight error would be de minimis. Moreover, for evidence of such low credibility, it is not clear that the jury will usually overassess the evidence instead of giving it too little weight or ignoring it completely.

28. . . . In civil cases, liberalized discovery makes the distinction even more academic.

30. Exclusion serves to minimize the potential for manipulation when the decision not to call the available declarant may provide some strategic benefit. Also, it avoids disruption that might result from allowing the opponent to cross-examine the declarant immediately after direct examination of the witness testifying to the hearsay statement, possible surprise to the opponent if no notice is required, and placing burdens on the opponent to procure the declarant.

G. Reflections on the Hearsay Rule

of jury overvaluation. For example, business records might be admitted to save the time and expense of calling the five employees who each had a hand in processing the data. . . . The remainder of this Part . . . implicitly considers only the unavailable declarant.

B. Traditional Justifications for the Hearsay Exceptions

Exceptions to the rule against hearsay are traditionally justified on the grounds that some hearsay is particularly reliable or necessary. . . .

1. *Reliability.*—The most common and accepted characterization of the hearsay problem is that such evidence is not sufficiently reliable and that exceptions are made for categories of hearsay that exhibit additional guarantees of trustworthiness. . . .

Current analyses are unpersuasive even in their attempts to identify which categories of hearsay are reliable. The reliability of hearsay is usually determined by examining the degree to which believing the evidence requires unsupported reliance upon the declarant's four testimonial capacities: narration, sincerity, memory, and perception. If circumstances indicate that no danger would result from reliance upon one or more of these capacities, an exception is sometimes said to be warranted. Yet it is not clear why the hearsay problem is "solved" when only one or two of the four defects have been removed. Analysis of an exception justified on the basis of circumstantial guarantees as to one capacity suggests that the three that remain unchecked present no significant ground for worry. After examination of several exceptions, each justified by guarantees as to a different capacity, one would conclude that *none* of the four capacities found wanting in circumstantial guarantees presents a significant problem. One might respond to this criticism by assuming that the degree to which the reliability gap exceeded the value of the evidence was small enough that the incremental decrease in the gap provided by the removal of one of the defects is sufficient to swing the balance in favor of admission. If that is the case, however, it seems curious that those implicitly making this assumption devote so much attention to determining which categories of hearsay should be admitted and which should be excluded. The assumption itself suggests that most questions regarding the admissibility of hearsay are nearly a toss-up.

The above criticism would not prove embarrassing to those wishing to inquire into the reliability of hearsay if one capacity could be isolated as the most important, with exceptions being made solely when there exist circumstantial guarantees for that capacity. In fact, most advocates of exceptions do emphasize circumstantial guarantees for one capacity—the sincerity of the out-of-court declarant. Acceptance of the principle that only appeals to sincerity can justify exceptions renders meaningless all current discussion of the other three capacities. More important, analysis within the framework of the first Part reveals how this justification backfires. Distinguishing hearsay from other evidence depends upon the testability of the hearsay declaration, assuming that it was offered as testimony in court. Few would doubt that cross-examination effectively remedies defects in the other three capacities: it exposes and resolves ambiguity, it tests or refreshes memory, and it brings into question possible defects in perception. By contrast, cross-examination may be less well suited to exposing insincerity.[49] Studies of jury reaction to eyewitness testimony indicate that the jury does not function as an effective lie detector.[50] Focus upon sincerity as the pivotal element could be justified if it is the most testable capacity; in fact, it may be the least. Alternatively, one might justify this focus on the ground that, although sincerity is less testable, sincerity problems occur far more frequently in the underlying population of potential hearsay evidence than do weaknesses in the other three capacities. This empirical assertion has not even been stated, much less proved, by those who appeal to circumstantial indications of sincerity when arguing for exceptions. . . .

2. *Necessity.*—. . .

The principle of necessity addresses the need for the specific evidence in a given case. This includes both consideration of other means of proving the issue on which the evidence is probative and determination of the importance of that issue to the case as a whole. But, aside from the desire not to waste time with redundant evidence, the importance of the issue to the case as a whole should have no bearing on admissibility. . . . Variations in the degree of importance have precisely the same effect on both the value of the evidence and the impact of the error. Consequently, the remainder of this subsection will address only the effect from considering other means of proving the issue.

Since necessity is a function of the other evidence available in a given case, it will be difficult to identify, *a priori*, any categories of hearsay—with the possible exception of dying declarations—that will be "necessary." Therefore, implementing the necessity principle involves according broad discretion to the trial judge. Even then, a circularity problem arises within a single trial because the necessity of any evidence depends upon what other evidence is admitted. This difficulty is compounded by problems raised by the order of presentation, the difficulty of changing previous rulings, the potential for parties to manipulate the judge by failing to investigate or present other sources of evidence, and the sheer complexity of making rulings that depend upon the variety of possible configurations of other evidence in a given case. . . .

The principle of necessity . . . directs attention away from the indi-

---

49. "While the exposure of deliberate falsehood is the most dramatic function of cross-examination, one needs only a brief experience in the courtroom to learn that its more frequently and effectively exercised functions are to bring to light faults in the perception, memory, and narration of the witnesses." Morgan, [The] Hearsay Rule, [12 Wash. L. Rev. 1], 4 [(1937)]. . . .

50. See, e.g., E. Loftus, Eyewitness Testimony (1979); Note, Did Your Eyes Deceive You? Expert Psychological Testimony on the Unreliability of Eyewitness Identification, 29 Stan. L. Rev. 969, 969-989 (1977).

G. Reflections on the Hearsay Rule

vidual pieces of evidence and towards its impact on the case as a whole. The correlation between necessity and the value of evidence to the case as a whole has always been recognized. What is generally ignored is the correlation between necessity and the impact of jury error upon its ultimate decision; the less other evidence is available, the less will be the opportunity to remedy or mitigate the impact of the jury error in evaluating the given piece of evidence.

A formal analysis of how the necessity of the evidence affects both its value and its danger reveals that, a priori, the implications of the necessity criterion for determining the admissibility of evidence are indeterminate. The expected jury error in processing the evidence to reach its ultimate decision and the value of the evidence both increase as necessity increases. This is illustrated in Figure 1. The amount and quality of other evidence is measured along the horizontal axis. The value of the evidence to the case as a whole—"Value"—and the expected error in the jury's decision resulting from admission—"Error"—are both measured along the vertical axis. For any category of hearsay, there are four possible cases. First, it is possible that error exceeds value for all degrees of necessity, justifying exclusion in all cases (illustrated in Figure 1). Second, value might exceed error for all degrees of necessity, justifying admission in all cases (Figure 2). In both cases the necessity of the evidence is irrelevant to the decision to admit or exclude.

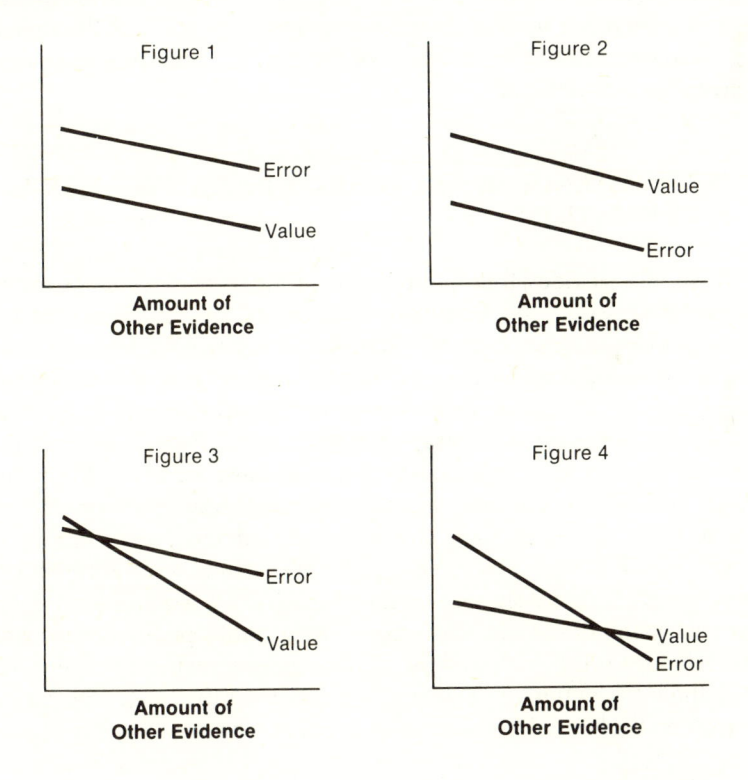

A third possibility is that value declines more rapidly than does error as the amount and quality of other evidence increases (i.e., as the necessity of the evidence in question decreases). In other words, where little other evidence is available, value outweighs error, and the evidence should be admitted; where much is available, error exceeds value, and the evidence should be excluded (Figure 3). The standard argument that necessity justifies the admission of hearsay assumes that this case is an accurate description of the world. The existence of a fourth case, however, indicates that the opposite result is equally plausible. This would occur if error is above value when little other evidence is available, justifying exclusion, but that error falls below value as more evidence is available, justifying admission (Figure 4). In both case three and case four, the admissibility decision when little other evidence is available will be the opposite of the ruling when much other evidence is available. Neither case is complete without specification of where that reversal occurs. For example, Figure 3 portrays a crossover where little other evidence on the issue is available, and in Figure 4 the crossover does not occur until far more evidence is available. In other words, one must determine how much other evidence must be available to change the decision. Asserting that the reversal occurs at *some* point is only a first step toward a workable principle either for discretionary implementation by judges or for application to the debate over the delineation of hearsay exceptions. No attempt has been made to support the implicit empirical judgment reflected by adherence to case three, to specify the location of the switching point, or to examine the significance of the gap between error and value for any given level of necessity.

III. INCONSISTENCY OF THE HEARSAY RULES WITH JUDGE-JURY RELATIONS

. . . [FRE 403 provides] that "[a]lthough relevant, evidence may be excluded if its probative value is substantially outweighed by the danger of unfair prejudice." Under this structure, exclusion is justified by fears of how the jury will be influenced by the evidence. However, it is not traditional to think of hearsay as merely a subdivision of this structure, and the Federal Rules do not conceive of hearsay in that manner. Prejudice refers to the jury's use of evidence for inferences other than those for which the evidence is legally relevant; by contrast, the rule against hearsay questions the jury's ability to evaluate the strength of a *legitimate* inference to be drawn from the evidence. For example, were a judge to exclude testimony because a witness was particularly smooth or convincing, there would be no doubt as to the usurpation of the jury's function. Thus, unlike prejudices recognized by the evidence rules, such as those stemming from racial or religious biases or from the introduction of photographs of a victim's final state, the exclusion of hearsay on the basis of misperception strikes at the root of the jury's function

G. Reflections on the Hearsay Rule

by usurping its power to process quite ordinary evidence, the type of information routinely encountered by jurors in their everyday lives.

Even if one were to accept the coherence of the two principles of reliability and necessity, hearsay provisions based on them would remain inconsistent with the common understanding of the role played by the rules of evidence in our system of adjudication. Outside the hearsay context, it is not generally required that evidence be necessary in order to be admissible. Furthermore, exclusion of evidence because it is unreliable is grossly inconsistent with our usual view of the jury's ability to process evidence and to make inferences. In considering absolute reliability, which is germane to the weight that should be given to evidence, the rulemakers and treatise writers approach the hearsay problems from the wrong perspective; they exclude evidence that they would discount or disbelieve if *they* were sitting as trier of fact rather than considering which evidence should be kept from a trier of fact. . . .

IV. THE HEARSAY RULES AS A MEANS OF ENHANCING THE SOCIAL ACCEPTANCE OF OUR SYSTEM OF ADJUDICATION

. . . Society needs to have confidence in the outcomes produced by its system of adjudication. . . . Social acceptance is a function of how the system is perceived, and not of how it actually performs. The hearsay rules, though incoherent when viewed from the perspective taken in the first three Parts, might seem more comprehensible when viewed from a cynical perspective, as aimed at enhancing social acceptance by directly addressing society's perception of the system rather than the system's performance.

First, the hearsay rules shield the system from possible embarrassment. Admitting hearsay generally creates the possibility that the declarant might later come forward to reveal that injustice resulted from the trier of fact's reliance on such evidence. Second, hearsay is distinctive in that its deficiencies can be observed readily by anyone outside the system. With other evidence, the jury functions as a "black box": its ability to observe demeanor, though limited in revealing truth, "justifies" deference to the jury's decision because the jury ostensibly has additional information that those absent could not possibly duplicate and those present could not fully communicate.[85]

These two considerations indicate how a rule against hearsay enhances

---

85. Nesson, Reasonable Doubt and Permissive Inferences: The Value of Complexity, 92 Harv. L. Rev. 1187, 1195-1198 (1979). "The trial system presents the jurors with an array of facts, assertions, contradictions, and ambiguities, and then obtains a verdict difficult to disagree with because the secrecy of the jurors' deliberations and the general nature of the verdict make it hard to know precisely on what it was based." Id. at 1195 (footnotes omitted). Professor Nesson's application of this analysis to demonstrate how prosecution cases relying exclusively upon circumstantial evidence fail to induce deference by outside observers, id. at 1198, is fully applicable to hearsay. (In fact, if "hearsay evidence" is substituted for "circumstantial evidence," his argument reads just as well.) . . .

social acceptance by excluding evidence. Yet extensive exclusion of hearsay may itself diminish acceptance since we like to believe that the trier considers all relevant information in reaching its decision. Therefore, maximizing social acceptance implies that hearsay exceptions are appropriate where the danger of *exposing* error is less, whereas the Part I framework justifies exceptions where the danger of jury misperception is less.

The danger of exposing error is minimized by creating exceptions to the rule against hearsay when later contradictory statements from the declarant are unlikely to arise or would not prove embarrassing. The clearest illustration is the exception for dying declarations, the classic example of an exception of dubious validity by traditionally accepted criteria. Admissions by a party opponent would be allowed in evidence since "[a] party can hardly object that he had no opportunity to cross-examine himself or that he is unworthy of credence save when speaking under sanction of an oath."[89] With respect to present sense impressions, excited utterances, and indications of the declarant's state of mind, the declarant's recollection of the events presented after a trial is no more and possibly less credible than the extrinsic (hearsay) evidence of the declarant's knowledge at the time of the incident. For business records and official public reports, the body responsible for the existence of the information is unlikely to surprise us later. Similarly, the admission of statements against interest by an unavailable declarant does not risk future embarrassment because declarants typically will not become available, and, even if one does, later contrary statements will not prove embarrassing.[97] As these examples illustrate, the current pattern of hearsay exceptions seems quite rational as a reflection of the desire to enhance social acceptance by shielding the system from possible embarrassment. . . .

If this rationalization of the hearsay structure were the true explanation for its existence, one still would not expect it to be explicitly advanced in support of the hearsay rules since stating this rationalization is self-defeating: rules cannot successfully protect the appearances of a system if the rules are openly presented as serving that end. It seems implausible that the hearsay rules were consciously designed and subsequently modified to shelter the system from embarrassment and to preserve the jury's ability to function as a "black box." It seems plausible, however, that those operating within our system of adjudication would be motivated by a desire, perhaps subconscious, to feel that the system to which they have devoted their energy is worthy of society's acceptance as a system of justice.

Since the underlying purposes may remain subconscious and, in any event, could not be openly expressed, other justifications would be offered in their place. These surrogate justifications would give rise to a set of rules that only approximately mirror the rules that would result if the actual objectives were openly admitted. After the process of adjusting and amending

---

89. E. Morgan, Basic Problems of Evidence 266 (1963). . . .
97. [O]ne recanting a confession carries little credibility.

the proffered justifications to fit the desired objectives more closely, one would expect the resultant patchwork of rules to appear confused and complex, much as the hearsay rules are today.

NOTES AND QUESTIONS

1. Consider the likely impact of abolishing the hearsay prohibition altogether. As the Note author suggests, there would probably be more reliance on hearsay evidence than there is today. This increased use of hearsay would probably be attributable not only to the fact that "good" hearsay evidence is now sometimes excluded but also that parties with the option to do so might choose to rely on hearsay even though other forms of proof were available to them. In cases in which the declarant was available, abolition of the hearsay rule would create a greater burden to call live witnesses on the party against whom the hearsay evidence is offered. In addition, since any liberalization of admissibility rules is likely to be of primary benefit to the party with the burden of proof,[159] abolition of the hearsay rule would tend to be of primary benefit to civil plaintiffs and prosecutors. The benefit to prosecutors, however, may be somewhat offset by the confrontation clause.[160] Would altering the status quo in these ways be desirable?

2. Typically, the hearsay rule is considered independently of the FRE Article 4 relevance rules. Moreover, the Advisory Committee's Note to FRE 403 states, "The rules which follow in this Article [but apparently not in Article 8, dealing with hearsay] are concrete applications evolved for particular situations." Thus, there is merit to the Note author's observation that "[i]t is not traditional to think of hearsay as merely a subdivision" of the structure that excludes evidence because of "fears of how the jury will be influenced by the evidence." To what extent has this propensity to separate the hearsay rule from the relevance rules contributed to improper analysis of hearsay issues?

3. Has the Note author taken too narrow a view of the relationship between hearsay and the objective of accurate fact finding? Is it possible that the risks of undetected witness error are greater with respect to testimony about what others have said or meant than with respect to testimony about other phenomena? Consider the times you have been involved in a discussion in which there was a disagreement over what happened or what someone said on a particular occasion. Our guess is that for many of you the disputes have arisen—or at least remained unresolved—more often with respect to what people said or meant. If so, perhaps the hearsay rule can be justified at least in part on the ground that the trial process, including the cross-examination of witnesses, will too often be unable to detect witnesses' mis-

---

159. See page 375 supra (discussion of prior identification rule).
160. See pages 351-371 supra.

perceptions and misunderstandings about what other people have intended to communicate. If one relies on this justification for a general hearsay prohibition, should some of the existing hearsay exceptions be eliminated? Should others be added?

4. Some proponents of the hearsay rule have rested their case in part on their distrust of trial judges to apply properly a more flexible rule.[161] If the question were whether to have a broad discretionary rule or a simple, easily applied exclusionary rule, we agree that distrust of trial judges' ability wisely to apply a discretionary rule might lead one to favor simple exclusionary rule. Given the intricacies of the hearsay rule, however, we wonder which way concerns about the capabilities of trial judges should cut. Furthermore, we wonder how much, given the pervasive scope of FRE 403, a relatively rigid hearsay rule will minimize abuses of judicial discretion.

5. Do you agree with the Note author's claim that a major function of the hearsay rule is to make verdicts socially acceptable? To the extent that this is the objective or the result of the hearsay rule, is it good or bad? Reconsider Professor Nesson's acceptability thesis and Professor Allen's response in Chapter 2 at pages 134-151 supra.

6. Consider the merits of the following possible amendments or alternatives to the hearsay rule:

a. Abolish the hearsay rule, and rely solely on an application of FRE 403 for determining the admissibility of hearsay.
b. Abolish the hearsay rule, and rely solely on a balancing rule that admits hearsay only if the probative value substantially outweighs the countervailing factors (i.e., a reverse 403 balancing test that favors exclusion instead of admissibility).
c. Modify the residual exceptions in FRE 803 and FRE 804 by deleting the language added by Congress.
d. Replace FRE 803 and FRE 804 with the following rules, which were initially proposed by the Federal Rules Advisory Committee in the first draft of the Proposed Federal Rules:

> 803. (a) A statement is not excluded by the hearsay rule if its nature and the special circumstances under which it was made offer assurances of accuracy not likely to be enhanced by calling the declarant as a witness, even though he is available.
>
> (b) By way of illustration only, and not by way of limitation, the following are examples of statements conforming with the requirements of the rule: [the rule then proceeded to list as illustrations what eventually became, with some modifications, the FRE 803 exceptions].
>
> 804. (a) A statement is not excluded by the hearsay rule if its nature and the special circumstances under which it was made offer strong

---

161. See, e.g., R. Lempert and S. Saltzburg, A Modern Approach to Evidence 523 (2d ed. 1982).

G. Reflections on the Hearsay Rule

assurance of accuracy and the declarant is unavailable as a witness.

(b) By way of illustration only, [the rule proceeded in the same fashion as Proposed FRE 803, with a version of the current FRE 804 exceptions listed as the illustrations].

e. Add to FRE 804 the following exception, which was deleted by Congress from FRE 804 as promulgated by the Supreme Court:

> A statement, not in response to the instigation of a person engaged in investigating, litigating, or settling a claim, which narrates, describes, or explains an event or condition recently perceived by the declarant, made in good faith, not in contemplation of pending or anticipated litigation in which he was interested, and while his recollection was clear.

f. Eliminate the hearsay prohibition for all declarations of unavailable declarants.

g. Prohibit the use of hearsay in all situations in which the declarant is available, unless there is a strong "necessity" rationale for an exception (as there may be, for example, with business and official records).

CHAPTER SIX

CROSS-EXAMINATION, IMPEACHMENT, AND REHABILITATION

Our concern in this chapter will be primarily with the theory and methods of impeaching and rehabilitating the credibility of witnesses. Before turning to that subject we wish to consider a significant departure from the common law by the Federal Rules—the elimination of the so-called voucher rule, which restricted the ability of a party to impeach witnesses on direct examination. We shall also review briefly the differences between direct and cross-examination. At this point you should examine carefully FRE 607 and review FRE 611.

A. THE VOUCHER RULE

Although its origins are obscure,[1] a rule developed in the common law and early statutory law of both England and the various states that has become known as the "voucher rule." According to this rule, a party who called a witness vouched for the credibility of that witness and thus could not impeach the witness' credibility.

The voucher rule prohibited only attempts to impeach credibility. It did not prevent a party from introducing contradictory testimony about some matter that was directly relevant to the resolution of the dispute between the parties. For example, if a prosecution witness were to deny that the defendant was the perpetrator of the crime charged, the prosecution could not introduce

---

1. See 3A J. Wigmore, Evidence in Trials at Common Law §896, pp.658-660 (Chadbourn rev. 1970).

the witness' prior statement naming the defendant as the perpetrator, nor could the prosecutor introduce evidence for the purpose of attacking the witness' character for trustworthiness. The prosecution, however, could introduce the testimony of a second witness who was prepared to identify the defendant as the perpetrator.

The voucher rule had exceptions that varied in scope from jurisdiction to jurisdiction and, to a lesser extent, from one type of impeachment technique to another.[2] The most common exceptions permitted impeachment of a witness who was the opposing party, an attesting witness (e.g., to a will) whom the law required to be called in order to establish the validity of a document, and a witness whose testimony was both surprising and damaging to the party calling the witness. With respect to this last category of witnesses, forgetfulness or equivocation was generally regarded as insufficiently damaging to qualify for the exception.

Judicial efforts to articulate a justification for the rule are for the most part quite obscure, but there appear to be several underlying rationales: a belief that impeachment of one's own witnesses is unnecessary because a party has the opportunity to choose friendly witnesses; a belief that a party is morally bound to present trustworthy evidence to the court, and that to permit impeachment of one's witnesses would be inconsistent with this moral obligation; a fear that permitting impeachment of one's own witnesses would permit a party to use the threat of impeachment as a means of coercing favorable but perhaps false testimony from a witness; a concern that a party who wished to introduce favorable evidence that was admissible only to impeach (e.g., a prior inconsistent statement) would call a witness solely for the purpose of impeaching the witness' credibility in order to get the impeaching information before the jury.

The last of these rationales has been at least somewhat weakened by the fact that the Federal Rules and their modern counterparts permit some prior statements to be used for their truth. The other rationales, to put it bluntly, do not bear much relationship to reality. Neither empirical evidence nor, in our judgment, common sense supports the proposition that litigants are so unscrupulous and potential witnesses so spineless that there is reason to fear that parties can coerce false testimony through threats of impeachment. Moreover, we fail to see why parties should be morally responsible for or be regarded as in fact vouching for the credibility of witnesses that they call. In some situations—e.g., selecting character witnesses and to a somewhat lesser extent in selecting expert witnesses—a party will have the opportunity to choose sympathetic witnesses; and it may well be that most witnesses are not overtly hostile to the party calling the witness. Nonetheless, the fact remains that to a great extent a party has no choice but to accept as witnesses the individuals who happen to know the most about the facts that are being

---

2. For example, the voucher rule was more likely to prohibit attempts to show a witness' bad character for trustworthiness than a witness bias. See generally 3A J. Wigmore, Evidence in Trials at Common Law §§900-918, pp.666-720 (Chadbourn rev. 1970).

A. The Voucher Rule

litigated, and there is no guarantee where these persons' sympathies will lie or how helpful they will be.

Our criticisms of the voucher rule are not new. Scholars have called for its abolition for years. Indeed, of all of the common law rules of evidence, none has received as much and as uniform derision as the voucher rule. Thus, it is not surprising that the drafters of the Federal Rules chose to abandon this relic of the common law. FRE 607 provides: "The credibility of a witness may be attacked by any party, including the party calling the witness."

The abandonment of the voucher rule, however, has created some potential problems that to date have not been adequately addressed. Consider, for example, the following situation:

> The defendant has been charged with various drug offenses. The prosecution plans to call Charlie Co-conspirator who had agreed to testify against the defendant. Two days before the trial Charlie recants his earlier story and tells the prosecutor that his testimony will exculpate the defendant. The prosecutor calls Charlie as a witness, and Charlie offers the exculpatory testimony that he said he would offer. Should the prosecutor now be able to introduce evidence of inconsistent, inculpatory statements that Charlie made after the termination of the conspiracy (1) to the grand jury and (2) to a friend, Bernice Brown?

Some courts have stated that, despite FRE 607, a party may not call a witness as a "mere subterfuge" to get the impeaching information before the jury.[3] Is that dictum wise? Should it apply to prohibit the prosecutor from impeaching Charlie in our hypothetical?

The statement allegedly made to Bernice was not made under oath, and, therefore, would not be admissible for its truth. It is doubtful, however, that the jurors could fully appreciate this distinction. Moreover, it may be that Bernice is lying about the making of the statement, a type of lie that may be difficult to expose on cross-examination. Thus, the effect of permitting the prosecutor to impeach Charlie would be to permit the prosecutor to get before the jury potentially unreliable and prejudicial information.

The inconsistent statement given to the grand jury would be admissible for its truth, since grand jury testimony is given under oath. See FRE 801(d)(1)(A). Moreover, the likelihood that somebody would fabricate the making of a statement is probably relatively small with what appear to be sworn statements. It is not clear, however, how much these facts should strengthen the prosecutor's argument for admissibility. It may be that the drafters' intent in removing certain inconsistent and consistent statements from the hearsay prohibition was not to make them freely admissible. Rather,

---

3. See, e.g., Whitehurst v. Wright, 592 F.2d 834 (5th Cir. 1979); United States v. Crouch, 731 F.2d 621 (9th Cir. 1984).

the intent may have been to make them admissible for the truth only when they would otherwise be admissible for impeachment or rehabilitation purposes.[4] Such an intent could be justified on the ground that an important reason for letting the statement in for the truth is to avoid giving a limiting instruction that the jury probably could not follow. To the extent that this is the rationale for the prior inconsistent and consistent statement provisions in FRE 801(d)(1)(A) and (B), the fact that a prior statement may be admissible for its truth provides no support for the proposition that a party can call a witness for the purpose of introducing impeaching testimony.

Perhaps introducing the impeaching evidence in our hypothetical would be appropriate if the prosecutor had a good faith belief that Charlie's earlier statements were in fact true and that, despite Charlie's promise to recant, the prosecutor believed that once on the witness stand and under oath Charlie would tell the truth. Indeed, even if the prosecutor subjectively believed that Charlie would recant his earlier version of the events, perhaps the prosecutor should be entitled to presume that Charlie would tell the truth on the witness stand. Otherwise, any reluctant witness could avoid being called simply by threatening to recant.

Should there be any limitations on the right of a party to impeach witnesses that the party calls? If there should be, is the foregoing rationale for permitting the prosecution to impeach Charlie in our hypothetical sufficient? Even if it is, should there be evidentiary or ethical constraints on the ability of a party in other contexts to impeach witnesses that the party calls? Would it be appropriate, for example, to rely on FRE 403 to limit the extent to which parties can impeach their own witnesses? If so, is FRE 403 a sufficient constraint, or should there be others?

PROBLEMS

1. In the preceding hypothetical involving Charlie, assume that Charlie's testimony was exculpatory for the defendant, that immediately after the exculpatory statement the prosecution offered into evidence a previously

---

4. The California Evidence Code explicitly adopts this approach to the use of prior statements for their truth. Cal. Evid. Code §1235 provides: "Evidence of a statement made by a witness is not made inadmissible by the hearsay rule if the statement is inconsistent with his testimony at the hearing and is offered in compliance with Section 770 [which governs the use of inconsistent statements for nonhearsay impeachment purposes]." In similar fashion, Cal. Evid. Code §1236 creates a hearsay exception for prior consistent statements that are "offered in compliance with Section 791," the section dealing with the non-hearsay use of prior consistent statements to rehabilitate witnesses.

The Advisory Committee's Note to FRE 801(d) cites with approval Cal. Evid. Code §1235 and notes that prior consistent statements covered by FRE 801(d)(1)(B) traditionally have been admissible for non-hearsay rehabilitation purposes. The Advisory Committee's Note, however, does not explicitly articulate the legislative intent that we hypothesize. Instead, the Note emphasizes that the traditional justifications for excluding hearsay—absence of oath, cross-examination, and opportunity to observe demeanor—are of limited applicability when the out-of-court declarant is also the witness.

A. The Voucher Rule

authenticated transcript of Charlie's grand jury testimony, and that the trial judge sustained the objection to the admissibility of the transcript. The prosecutor then proceeds as follows:

Q: Charlie, are you sure you are remembering accurately what happened?
A: Yes.
Q: Might you be mistaken?
A: I don't think so.
Q: Do you remember testifying about these events before the grand jury?
A: I believe I did, but I'm not sure.
Q: I have here an authenticated transcript of the grand jury proceedings. Charlie, I would like to read a passage from this transcript to see if it refreshes your memory about what happened. . . .

DEFENSE COUNSEL: Objection, your honor.

What possible grounds exist for an objection? Should the objection be sustained?

2. Drake has been charged with causing false information to be submitted to the Department of Housing and Urban Development. Drake was in the business of buying, rehabilitating, and selling old houses. Purchasers of the houses could receive favorable interest rates on FHA mortgages. The government's evidence tended to show that Drake would rent the houses and get the renters to fill out FHA mortgage applications, which were then processed through a local bank with the cooperation of Alice Allwine, an employee in the bank's escrow department. Allwine, who had previously been convicted of the same crime for her part in the scheme, was a government witness. She testified as to her and Drake's activities, which included her falsely completing down-payment deposit verifications of the "purchasers" and Drake's depositing down payments for the apparent purchasers after she delivered the verification forms to him. The prosecutor then asked Allwine why she falsely verified the down payments, and she responded that she thought verification was unnecessary. Contending that this response is untrue, the government seeks, over defendant's objection, to impeach Allwine with her false information conviction. What result?

3. Nick Dixon, a used car dealer, has been charged with fraudulently altering odometers on cars that he sold. An important prosecution witness, Walters, was another used car dealer who had sold some of the cars in question to Dixon and who testified that the odometer reading was higher on those cars when he sold them to Dixon than when Dixon resold the cars. While Walters was still testifying on direct examination, the prosecutor sought to elicit that Walters had been involved in a scheme of fraudulently altering automobile titles, that he had pled guilty to charges relating to that fraud, and that he was currently testifying pursuant to a plea bargain that

included the requirement that he testify truthfully. Dixon has objected to this evidence. What result?

4. Consider whether the party calling the witness should be able to impeach the witness' credibility in the following situations:

(a) A party has no interest in developing the substantive testimony of a witness, but rather wants only to elicit that the witness is an associate of the opposing party and then to impeach the witness by showing the witness' unsavory, untrustworthy character.

(b) The witness has consistently told the party who contemplates calling the witness a story that is helpful to the opposing party, but there is a third person who is willing to testify that the witness made an inconsistent statement, which is damaging to the opposing party.

(c) Instead of waiting to impeach the defendant's witnesses on cross-examination after they have had an opportunity to tell a coherent story on direct examination, the plaintiff decides to call the defense witnesses in order to get the impeaching evidence before the jury early in the trial.

B. DIRECT AND CROSS-EXAMINATION

We have provided examples of and talked about direct and cross-examination throughout these materials. If the terms were not familiar to you at the outset of the course, we trust that they are now. Lest there be any doubt, direct examination is the questioning of a witness by the party who called the witness; cross-examination is the questioning of a witness called by the opposing party. Similarly, re-direct examination is the questioning of a witness, following cross-examination, by the party who called the witness; and re-cross-examination is questioning by the opposing party following re-direct examination.

At common law there were two significant differences between direct and cross-examination. The cross-examiner, but not the direct examiner, was free to impeach witnesses and to ask leading questions. As we have seen, FRE 607 and its modern counterparts eliminate the first restriction on direct examination, but the second remains. See, e.g., FRE 611(c):

> Leading questions should not be used on the direct examination of a witness except as may be necessary to develop the witness' testimony. Ordinarily leading questions should be permitted on cross-examination. When a party calls a hostile witness, an adverse party, or a witness identified with an adverse party, interrogation may be by leading questions.

B. Direct and Cross-Examination

Leading questions are questions that suggest the answer, and as we observed in Chapter One all questions will be to some degree leading. If they were not, there would be no way to direct the witness' attention to the type of information the examiner is seeking. Some questions, though, are much more leading than others. The intent of FRE 611 is to prevent the direct examiner from asking questions in a manner that suggests particular answers to matters that are in dispute. The task of the direct examiner is to formulate questions in a neutral enough way to avoid this specific suggestiveness and at the same time to be sufficiently leading that the witness will respond about the subject matter that the direct examiner wants to explore. Obviously, there will sometimes be differences of opinion as to the boundary between "leading" and "non-leading."

The assumption underlying FRE 611(c) is that more often than not a witness is likely to be, if not friendly toward, at least cooperative with the party calling the witness, and that this same degree of cooperativeness may not extend to the cross-examiner. The presumed bias against the cross-examiner may make leading questions essential in order to get at the truth. If counsel were not permitted to ask a very specific "Isn't it true that . . . ?" question that calls for a "Yes" or "No" answer, it might be impossible adequately to explore the details and nuances of the witness' knowledge.

By contrast, because of the witness' presumed willingness to cooperate with the direct examiner, there is thought to be a risk that the suggestiveness in leading questions on direct examination may cause the witness to distort the truth in the direct examiner's favor. Of course, the most friendly and most cooperative witnesses will have spent hours with the attorney discussing the testimony and rehearsing the direct and cross-examinations. Thus, the form of the question at trial is likely to have little impact on the testimony. With this type of witness, though, the direct examiner has a positive incentive to avoid leading questions: The examiner does not want to give the jury the impression that the witness' testimony is the product of influence or suggestion. In short, in situations in which the rationale for prohibiting leading questions is strongest, there is an independent incentive for avoiding leading questions. Indeed, in these types of situations, it may be the cross-examiner who has an interest in ensuring that the direct examination is at least marginally suggestive. A very general, open-ended question on direct examination may invite a narrative response that contains objectionable information not anticipated by opposing counsel. On the other hand, to the extent that the direct examiner's witness has not cooperated with the examiner and rehearsed testimony prior to trial, there may be a need for the direct examiner to ask some leading questions to get at the details of the witness' knowledge.

Because not all witnesses are friendly to the direct examiner, there have always been exceptions to the general prohibition against leading questions on direct examination. Some of these exceptions are recognized in the last sentence of FRE 611(c), which also provides in the first sentence that leading questions may be used on direct examination when "necessary to develop the witness' testimony." Furthermore, by providing that leading questions should "ordinarily," but not necessarily as a matter of right, be permitted on cross-examination, FRE 611(c) gives the trial judge discretion to disallow needlessly suggestive questions to a cooperative witness on cross-examination.

One of the frequently stated exceptions to the general prohibition against leading questions on cross-examination is that leading questions are permissible on preliminary matters, such as a witness' name, address, and general background. This is not one of the exceptions in FRE 611(c), and unless the witness were extremely uncooperative, it seems unlikely that leading questions on these matters would be "necessary to develop the witness' testimony." Nonetheless, it may be unwise for opposing counsel to object. If the leading questions are limited to preliminary matters, it is hard to imagine how the opposing party could be prejudiced by them. Moreover, an objection may seem trivial to the jury and thus prejudice them against the objecting attorney. Finally, the use of leading questions may give the jury the impression that the direct examiner is putting words into the witness' mouth.

A matter upon which jurisdictions differ is the appropriate scope of cross-examination. The English or wide-open rule of cross-examination permits the opposing party to question witnesses about anything that is relevant to the resolution of the dispute between the parties. Most American jurisdictions have adopted some variation of the American or restrictive rule of cross-examination. This rule limits cross-examination to matters brought out on or suggested by the direct examination plus matters that are relevant to impeach the credibility of the witness. For example, FRE 611(b) provides:

> Cross-examination should be limited to the subject matter of the direct examination and matters affecting the credibility of the witness. The court may, in the exercise of discretion, permit inquiry into additional matters as if on direct examination.

The primary advantage of the American rule is that it allows the parties to develop their cases in an orderly fashion. For example, the plaintiff may wish to introduce a document into evidence early on in the trial and may need to call the defendant or somebody closely associated with the defendant in order to authenticate the document. Even if the witness has knowledge of other aspects of the case, the plaintiff does not need to go into those matters at this time or with this witness; and if the plaintiff limits the direct examination to the question of authentication, application of the restrictive cross-examination rule will prevent the defendant on cross-examination from exploring the witness' knowledge about other aspects of the case.

The advantages of the English rule are that it avoids the necessity of determining what the scope of direct examination was, and it avoids the necessity of recalling witnesses whose testimony may be sought about several issues in a case. With respect to such witnesses, the English rule is somewhat

B. Direct and Cross-Examination

more efficient for the court and considerably more convenient for the witnesses.

FRE 611(b) gives the trial judge discretion to ameliorate the rigidity of the restrictive cross-examination rule. When a cross-examiner is permitted to exceed the scope of direct examination, the examination, according to FRE 611(b) shall be "as if on direct examination." This means, in effect, that the witness has become the cross-examiner's witness and that, therefore, "leading questions should not be used . . . except as may be necessary to develop the witness' testimony." FRE 611(c).

A narrow construction of the limited scope of cross-examination rule coupled with a rigid application of the rule prohibiting leading questions on direct examination could in some instances hinder the search for truth. If there is a matter hinted at or implied or closely related to the subject matter of the direct examination testimony, it may be desirable to permit the cross-examiner to explore the matter immediately after the direct examination. If the cross-examiner is forced to wait and call the witness on direct examination, there is some risk that the witness will have had the time to consider carefully what to say about the matter in light of the earlier testimony. As a result the later testimony may be less spontaneous and, perhaps, less truthful than testimony elicited on cross-examination immediately after the direct examination. The problem would be compounded if the witness were sympathetic to the party who initially called the witness, because now leading questions would not be available to help develop the testimony.

FRE 611(b) and (c) are flexible enough to avoid the type of problem just described. The potential for the problem arising, however, could be eliminated completely by adopting the English scope of cross-examination rule. Are the risks of too rigid an application of the restricted scope of cross-examination rule worth the supposed benefit of allowing each party to present evidence in a relatively more orderly fashion?

Perhaps the most important question to consider in evaluating scope of cross-examination rules is the impact that the rules may have on the jury's truth-finding function. Two factors suggest that the English rule may contribute more than the restrictive rule to accurate fact finding. First, outside the trial context, our process of accumulating and evaluating information probably more closely reflects the wide-open rule of cross-examination. For example, when we learn about an event from what people say to us, we tend to hear and question each person we talk to about all aspects of the event. Because this is a customary way of obtaining and evaluating information, perhaps jurors could better evaluate the testimony of witnesses if it were presented to them in a similar manner. Second, there is empirical evidence suggesting that the first presenter of information has the opportunity to influence listeners in a manner that will make them not fully receptive to successive presenters.[5] To the extent that this phenomenon occurs with the

---

5. See, e.g., Lawson, Experimental Research on the Organization of Persuasive Arguments: An Application to Courtroom Communications, [1970] L. & Soc. Order 579.

presentation of evidence during a trial, it may be desirable to avoid enhancing the opportunity of the plaintiff to control the manner in which information is presented.

The preceding arguments in favor of the English rule are highly speculative. It may be true that we usually obtain information in a manner that is similar to the way in which it would be presented pursuant to the English rule. It does not follow, however, that this is the best way to reach accurate judgments. Furthermore, it may be that whatever benefits accrue to the initial presenter will be derived from an opening statement and, in any event, will not be much affected by the order of interrogating witnesses. We are not prepared to urge adoption of the English rule. Rather, we raise these concerns to suggest the type of inquiry that is appropriate and the type of information that we should seek in order to improve the quality of our evidentiary rules.

C. IMPEACHMENT AND REHABILITATION IN GENERAL

1. Impeachment: The Inferential Process

In our discussion of hearsay, we used the testimonial triangle primarily for the purpose of illustrating the logical inferences that one had to make in assessing the relevance of various out-of-court declarations. We also explained there that making the inferences illustrated by the triangle was essential in crediting the truth of what in-court witnesses say. Impeachment is the process of attempting to raise doubts about the strength of these inferences. It is, in other words, an attempt to show that a witness (or a hearsay declarant, if a declaration is admitted pursuant to a hearsay exception) may have lied (sincerity), misspoken (narration), misperceived the events about which the witness testified (perception), or forgotten some or all of what happened (memory).

The difference between evidence offered to impeach the credibility of a witness and evidence offered for other purposes, which we shall call "substantive" purposes, becomes important, as a practical matter, only when evidence offered for impeachment purposes is not admissible substantively. For example, in the case of a bank robbery, W-1 may testify for the prosecution that she was the teller who handed money over to the robber, but she may say that the defendant was not the robber. W-2 and W-3, customers in the bank, may then identify the defendant as the robber, and W-4 may establish that W-1 is the sister of the defendant. The testimony of W-2 and W-3 implicitly impeaches the credibility of W-1 (and vice versa), but each witness' testimony is independently admissible on the substantive question

C. Impeachment and Rehabilitation in General

of the robber's identity. The testimony of W-4 is not independently admissible; its only relevance is to impeach the credibility of W-1 by showing W-1's bias. In short, to admit evidence for the purpose of impeaching the credibility of a witness is to admit evidence that, but for its impeachment value, would not be admissible—either because it would be irrelevant, as in the preceding bias hypothetical, or because some exclusionary rule (e.g., the hearsay rule) would prohibit its substantive use. For example, according to the Federal Rules a prior inconsistent statement not made under oath is inadmissible for its truth, but it may be admissible for the impeachment purpose of showing the witness' inconsistency.

Ultimately, of course, evidence offered to impeach the credibility of a witness—like other evidence that is admitted—must be relevant to prove or disprove some fact that is in dispute between the parties. If it were not, the impeachment evidence would be inadmissible pursuant to FRE 402. The difference between evidence offered for "impeachment" purposes and evidence offered for "substantive" purposes is in the route to the ultimate destination, i.e., to proof or disproof of some disputed fact.

When a witness offers substantive testimony (e.g., "The defendant's car ran the red light"), we must, as we have noted, infer that the witness honestly believes this particular assertion and that the belief is based on accurate perception and memory. We do not, however, necessarily have nor do we require as a condition of admissibility any information about the witness' general sincerity, narrative ability, perception, and memory. The evidence is relevant because we assume, at least for the moment, that the witness' particular assertion is accurate. We make this assumption because more often than not people are truthful and accurate.

An essential step in the inferential process of impeachment evidence is that it must in some way discredit the witness. From this discrediting, the fact finder is then urged to infer that what the witness said is less likely to be accurate than if there had been no impeaching evidence. The discrediting may be fairly general (e.g., showing character for untrustworthiness), or it may be quite specific (e.g., showing a strong motive to lie about the particular statement). The discrediting, however, will never in theory be as direct as a specific repudiation or contradiction of a statement about some ultimate fact in the litigation. Such a specific repudiation or contradiction either would be admissible as substantive evidence, or, perhaps because of the hearsay rule, would not be admissible for that purpose. If the evidence were admissible to contradict or repudiate the statement, there would be no need to rely on some theory of impeachment for admissibility. If the evidence were not admissible for that purpose, the "impeachment" use would have to be different from its substantive use. Otherwise, the substantive prohibition would be undermined.

To illustrate the preceding point consider the following example. In our running the red light hypothetical, the defendant wishes to impeach the plaintiff's witness with the witness' earlier statement, not made under oath, that the light was green when the defendant entered the intersection. Because of the hearsay rule, we cannot use the prior statement as substantive evidence that the light was green. See FRE 801(d)(1)(A). In other words, unlike the direct examination testimony, it would not be admissible as direct evidence that the defendant did not run the red light. We can, however, use the prior statement, without regard to its truth, to infer that the witness' direct examination testimony is not accurate. Knowing that the witness has made inconsistent statements about the same subject, regardless of which statement is true, casts some doubt on the witness' credibility. On one of the two occasions the witness may have been lying; at the very least, the inconsistency shows that the witness is not particularly careful about what he or she says. All of us, of course, are occasionally inconsistent in our statements, but particularly when the inconsistency relates to something of consequence in the litigation, there is reason to be concerned. Thus, regardless of whether the underlying explanation for the inconsistency is dishonesty or lack of care, the inconsistency suggests that one must be more cautious about accepting at face value the witness' testimony about what happened at the intersection than one would need to be if there were no evidence of inconsistency about this matter. To the extent that one doubts the truth of the present testimony, some alternative possibility may have existed. In other words, there is a greater likelihood with the impeaching evidence than without it that the light was not red; and to the extent that it is likely that the light was not red, it must have been some other color, which in this case happens to be green— or perhaps amber.

Consider also the following example. Della Dean is charged with perjury and testifies in her own defense. To impeach Della's testimony, the prosecution offers evidence that Della was convicted of perjury two years ago. Because of the prohibition against using specific acts substantively to prove character to show action in conformity with character, it would be impermissible, if Della had not testified, to introduce evidence of past perjury to prove that Della committed perjury on the occasion charged in the current indictment. Since Della has testified as a witness, however, it may be permissible to introduce her prior conviction in order to impeach her credibility as a witness. See FRE 609(a). The inferential process is as follows: Because Della has committed perjury, she is a generally untrustworthy person; if she is a generally untrustworthy person, she may be lying as a witness. To the extent that she is lying, the facts may be other than she portrays them to be. Since she says she was not lying, that may be untrue and, therefore, she may have been lying.

In both of the preceding examples, the impeachment route to the ultimate relevance of the evidence is more circuitous than the substantive route, which is prohibited by the hearsay rule in the first example and by FRE 404(b) in the second. What basis is there in human experience to warrant permitting the jury to take the circuitous route but not the direct route to the ultimate relevance of the evidence? Even if there is a theoretically reasonable answer to the preceding question, do you believe that trial judges

C. Impeachment and Rehabilitation in General

are capable of instructing juries in the nuances of the inferential process or, if they are, that juries are capable of comprehending and acting upon those nuances?

If the distinction between the impeachment use and the substantive use of the prior inconsistent statement or the prior perjury is not one that judges and juries are likely to be able to appreciate and understand, there is a fundamental problem with our current approach to "impeachment" evidence. Moreover, it is a problem, that at least in practice, is not adequately addressed by the balancing process of FRE 403: In the overwhelming number of cases in which there is more than very marginal impeachment value to evidence that is inadmissible substantively, it will be admitted with limiting instructions. If we are serious about the "substantive" prohibitions, we should not be so ready to admit for impeachment purposes evidence that in theory is inadmissible for substantive purposes; or if we want to admit evidence for impeachment purposes that theoretically is not admissible substantively, we need to rethink the desirability of the substantive prohibitions.

Our own view is that it is nonsensical to expect juries to make the extremely subtle distinctions between the impeachment and substantive uses of evidence. Moreover, we seriously doubt that many judges are sensitive to the distinction. Rather, we believe, they are likely, without thinking clearly about what they are saying, glibly to instruct juries that a particular piece of evidence may be considered only for its impeachment value.

As a first step toward bringing some rationality to this process, we suggest that the current distinctions between impeachment and substantive uses of evidence should remain in place only for the purpose of deciding whether or at what point evidence will be admissible. In other words, for present purposes at least, we are willing to accept the notion that specific acts should not be admissible as part of a prosecutor's case-in-chief to prove character to show action in conformity with character and that unsworn prior statements should not initially be admissible for their truth. However, once this type of evidence gains added relevance because, in addition to its independent substantive value, it happens to impeach the credibility of a witness, it should be admissible, and it should be admissible for whatever purposes it may be relevant. In short, it may be appropriate to make relevance for impeachment purposes a condition of admissibility, but it is not appropriate to admit impeachment evidence only for the limited purpose of impeaching the credibility of a witness.

As you proceed through these impeachment materials, consider whether you agree with our suggestion and whether, after gaining familiarity with the traditional approach to impeachment, you would recommend other changes in the rules of evidence.

2. Bolstering Credibility

At common law the process of bolstering the credibility of a witness was referred to as rehabilitation. As the term *rehabilitation* implies, the common law prohibited a party from bolstering the credibility of a witness until after there had been an attempt to impeach the witness' credibility. Sometimes courts would justify this limitation on bolstering credibility by saying that the bolstering evidence was not relevant if the witness had not been impeached. This assertion, however, seems to be quite clearly incorrect. Regardless of whether a witness has been impeached, it is likely that jurors would be somewhat more willing to believe the story if they knew that the witness was a generally trustworthy person and that the witness was in no way biased toward the party for whom the witness was testifying. Nonetheless, refusing to permit a party to bolster the credibility of a witness prior to impeachment is probably sound in many instances. As we have noted before, a witness' statement that something happened is relevant to prove that the event occurred because our common experience tells us that more often than not people report events honestly and accurately. Without some particular reason to disbelieve a witness, jurors will probably apply the general assumption about truthtelling to the witness. Given this general assumption about truthtelling, the bolstering evidence is likely to have little independent probative value, and, therefore, it is not worth the court's time to hear the evidence.

The difficulty with the preceding justification for a general prohibition against bolstering prior to impeachment is that impeachment is not the only thing that may raise doubts about credibility. The physical appearance or nervousness of a witness may cause jurors to question the witness' credibility. If a witness' story seems somewhat improbable, the jurors may have doubts about the witness' credibility. If two witnesses tell contradictory stories, each implicitly impeaches the credibility of the other, but there may have been no formal attempt to impeach the credibility of either witness.

As we shall see, FRE 608(a) contains a prohibition against introducing reputation or opinion evidence of a witness' good character for trustworthiness unless the witness' character for trustworthiness has been attacked. The Federal Rules, however, contain no general prohibition against bolstering credibility prior to impeachment with other types of evidence. One inference to draw from the absence of such a rule is that the drafters intended that the use of bolstering evidence in other contexts be governed by FRE 401-403. Another possible inference is that the drafters' silence implies an acceptance of well-established common law prohibition against pre-impeachment bolstering in all contexts. Unfortunately, the Advisory Committee's Notes are not helpful in resolving this issue. The Advisory Committee's only reference to bolstering is the following passage in the Note accompanying FRE 608(a):

> Character evidence in support of credibility is admissible under the rule only after the witness' character has first been attacked, as has been the case at common law. . . . The enormous needless consumption of time which a contrary practice would entail justifies the limitation.

C. Impeachment and Rehabilitation in General

We have no objection to the specific prohibition against bolstering in FRE 608(a). It seems likely that the probative value of reputation or opinion evidence regarding good character for trustworthiness to prove truthfulness on the witness stand will be sufficiently low that it is not worth taking the time prior to impeachment to call the opinion or reputation witnesses, to question them about the bases for their reputation or opinion testimony, and then to subject them to cross-examination. With other types of bolstering evidence, we believe that the preferable approach is to evaluate the propriety of introducing the evidence in terms of FRE 401-403. Some pre-impeachment bolstering evidence—e.g., evidence of a prior consistent statement or information suggesting a lack of bias—can be elicited efficiently from the witness whose credibility may be in question, and as we have suggested the probative value of such evidence may sometimes be relatively high.

3. Extrinsic Evidence and Impeachment

Throughout this chapter we shall be referring to impeachment by examination (usually cross-examination) of the witness and impeachment by extrinsic evidence. Extrinsic evidence means any evidence other than that developed through direct or cross-examination of the witness; it may be, for example, a record of a prior conviction or another witness' testimony about the untrustworthiness or bias of the witness being impeached.

In some instances it would be patently unfair to prohibit the use of extrinsic evidence to impeach the credibility of a witness. For example, it may seem undesirable to limit the impeaching party to cross-examination about a witness' potential bias or inconsistent statement. If extrinsic evidence were inadmissible, the witness could deny the facts relevant to the impeachment, and the impeaching party would be at a loss to correct the witness' misimpression. On the other hand, excessive reliance on extrinsic impeachment evidence has the potential for substantially prolonging trials and deflecting emphasis from the critical substantive issues. Consider, for example, a prosecutor's effort to impeach a criminal defendant's character witness, W-1, by calling W-2 to testify to W-1's bias, followed by the criminal defendant calling W-3 to testify about W-2's bad character for trustworthiness, followed by the prosecutor calling W-4 to testify about W-3's inconsistent statements, etc. At some point—probably well before W-4 is called as a witness—this potentially endless chain of extrinsic impeachment evidence should be broken.

A common law response to this problem was the dictum that a party cannot introduce extrinsic evidence to impeach a witness with respect to a matter that is collateral to the litigation. For example, in the case of prior inconsistent statements, if the inconsistency related to some fact that was relevant to the dispute between the parties, it would be permissible to introduce extrinsic evidence of the statement unless the witness admitted the inconsistency.[6] On the other hand, if the inconsistency were about a matter that had no bearing on the case, i.e., if it were about a "collateral matter," the impeaching party was not permitted to introduce extrinsic evidence of the statement; instead, as it was frequently put, the impeaching party was bound by the witness' answer.

The general common law prohibition against use of extrinsic evidence to impeach on a collateral matter has never been consistently applied to all forms of impeachment—or, in the alternative, the notion of what constitutes "collateralness" is not intuitively obvious. For example, courts uniformly have permitted extrinsic evidence to prove bias or to prove a prior conviction offered to impeach the credibility of a witness. On the other hand, the rule has been fairly consistently invoked to prevent extrinsic evidence of prior inconsistent statements on subjects unrelated to the litigation, evidence that contradicted the witness' testimony on matters that are not relevant to the dispute between the parties, and evidence of prior acts that suggest untrustworthiness and that have not resulted in convictions.

The Federal Rules do not contain a general prohibition against the use of extrinsic impeaching evidence on a collateral matter. There is, however, a specific application of the general common law dictum in FRE 608(b), which deals with the use of prior bad acts of a witness. Moreover, in view of the frequently low probative value of extrinsic impeaching evidence on a collateral matter and the desire to avoid confusing the jury and wasting time with marginally relevant evidence, a proper application of FRE 403 should frequently lead to the same result that common law courts reached applying the "no extrinsic evidence to impeach on a collateral matter" dictum. As we discuss the specific impeachment devices in the following pages, we shall in each instance consider the propriety of using extrinsic evidence as well as direct or cross-examination to develop the impeaching information.

4. Impeachment and Self-Incrimination

Because of the centrality of cross-examination to our adversary system, the giving of testimony by a witness is regarded as a waiver or forfeiture of the witness' fifth amendment right against self-incrimination, at least with respect

---

6. The requirement that the statement not be about a collateral matter ensures that the truth of the prior statement will be relevant. As our earlier hypothetical involving inconsistent statements about the color of a traffic light illustrates, however, the hearsay rule would make the evidence inadmissible for its truth. Thus, requiring that the evidence be substantively relevant as a condition for admitting extrinsic evidence necessarily means there is a danger that the jury may misuse the evidence. At the same time, though, the requirement probably contributes to the probative value of the evidence for its legitimate purpose: All of us are at least occasionally inconsistent, so the mere showing of an isolated instance or two of inconsistency proves very little about a person's general credibility. When the inconsistencies relate to something about which we care, however, there is reason to be concerned about the person's accuracy with respect to that general subject matter.

C. Impeachment and Rehabilitation in General

to the subject matter of the witness' direct examination testimony. Thus, if a witness testifies on direct examination and refuses, on the basis of the fifth amendment to answer any questions on cross-examination, the court will strike the direct examination testimony.[7] It is not clear, though, to what extent testifying on direct examination precludes invoking the fifth amendment right against self-incrimination with respect to questions about matters beyond the scope of the direct examination.

Jurisdictions that have adopted the restrictive rule of cross-examination provide some measure of protection for a witness who is willing to testify but fearful of self-incrimination. Assuming that the court does not exercise its discretion to relax the restrictive cross-examination rule, the direct examiner, by avoiding the potentially incriminating subjects, can ensure that the cross-examiner will not be able to question the witness about those subjects, unless they happen to be relevant to impeach the credibility of the witness. For matters relevant to the witness' credibility—unless it becomes clear that the constitution requires the witness to be able to invoke the privilege against self-incrimination—some further exclusionary rule is needed if the witness is to be protected. FRE 608 provides such protection in its final paragraph:

> The giving of testimony, whether by an accused or by any other witness, does not operate as a waiver of the accused's or the witness' privilege against self-incrimination when examined with respect to matters which relate only to credibility.

Consider how this right should be invoked. If the purpose of the provision were merely to protect witnesses against potential self-incrimination, it perhaps would be sufficient for witnesses to claim their fifth amendment right on the witness stand in response to particular questions. The Advisory Committee's Note to FRE 608, however, suggests that this is only part of the rationale for the rule:

> . . . While it is clear that an ordinary witness cannot make a partial disclosure of incriminating matter and then invoke the privilege on cross-examination, no tenable contention can be made that merely by testifying he waives his right to foreclose inquiry on cross-examination into criminal activities for the purpose of attacking his credibility. So to hold would reduce the

---

7. Striking testimony is the most common remedy when cross-examination is not available. In some situations, however, it may be an insufficient remedy, and in others it may be an unnecessarily harsh remedy. For example, it may be unlikely that the jury could put out of its mind what it heard from a critical prosecution witness who refused to be cross-examined. If that seems likely, a mistrial would be appropriate. At the other extreme, in a civil action in which the direct examiner is in no way responsible for the inability to cross-examine (e.g., because the witness unexpectedly died after direct examination and before cross-examination), perhaps the judge can adequately compensate for the inability to cross-examine by giving the jury an instruction that explores the possible weaknesses in the now-deceased witness' testimony. For more on these types of problems, see 5 J. Wigmore, Evidence in Trials at Common Law §§1390-1394, pp.133-147 (Chadbourn rev. 1974); McCormick's Handbook on the Law of Evidence §19, pp.48-50 (3d ed., Cleary, 1984).

privilege to a nullity. While it is true that an accused, unlike an ordinary witness, has an option whether to testify, if the option can be exercised only at the price of opening up inquiry as to any and all criminal acts committed during his lifetime, the right to testify could scarcely be said to possess much vitality. . . . While no specific provision in terms confers constitutional status on the right of an accused to take the stand in his own defense, the existence of the right is so completely recognized that a denial of it or substantial infringement upon it would surely be of due process dimensions.

If a criminal defendant testifies on direct examination and then, in front of the jury, invokes the fifth amendment during cross-examination, there is a substantial risk that the jury may assume the answer would be incriminating and rely on that assumption in evaluating the defendant's guilt or innocence. Indeed, in many—probably most—instances it will be preferable for the defendant not to testify at all rather than to testify and openly claim the fifth amendment. Thus, to the extent that the last paragraph of Rule 608 is designed to remove an impediment that criminal defendants face in deciding whether to testify, it may not be sufficient merely to permit the defendant to claim the privilege on the witness stand. Instead, it may be appropriate for the defendant, outside the presence of the jury, to invoke the fifth amendment before testifying and seek a ruling that it is improper for the prosecution to ask potentially incriminating questions.

The defendant, of course, is free to seek an early ruling on a fifth amendment claim. It is not clear, however, that the defendant is entitled to such a ruling. Should FRE 608(b) be amended to provide criminal defendants or all party-witnesses or all witnesses such a right?

One puzzling feature of the Federal Rules provision dealing with self-incrimination and impeachment is its placement in FRE 608(b). FRE 608 deals with the means of impeaching a witness' general character for trustworthiness, and FRE 608(b) deals specifically with cross-examination designed to get at a witness' character for trustworthiness. Potential self-incrimination problems, however, can arise in impeachment contexts other than those involving questions related to character for trustworthiness. For example, evidence indicating bias may stem from the fact that a witness and a party were cohorts in some criminal enterprise; acknowledging having made a prior inconsistent statement may be incriminating if the statement is itself an admission of criminal activity. Does the witness have the right to invoke the last paragraph of FRE 608 with respect to questions about such matters? Neither the language of the provision nor anything about its rationale suggests a reason for limiting it to questions asked pursuant to FRE 608(b). Yet if it were intended as a provision of general applicability, one would think that it would be a distinct rule, or at least that there would be some reference to the same problem in other relevant rules.[8] Why do you suppose the provision is in FRE 608?

---

8. As we shall see, the Federal Rules do not address all of the possible impeachment methods. Probably the only other Federal Rule where reference to impeachment and self-incrimination would be appropriate is FRE 613.

D. IMPEACHMENT AND REHABILITATION WITH CHARACTER EVIDENCE

In Chapter Four we considered evidentiary restrictions on the substantive use of character evidence. We noted there that one of the FRE 404(a) exceptions to the general prohibition against using character evidence to show action in conformity with character was the use of character evidence for impeachment and rehabilitation purposes. See FRE 404(a)(3). It is to that subject that we now turn. We are concerned here with using evidence of a witness' character for trustworthiness to infer action by the witness in conformity with that character trait on a particular occasion, i.e., to infer that the witness is either lying or telling the truth on the witness stand.[9]

The rules governing the use of character evidence for impeachment and rehabilitation purposes are different from the rules governing the use of character evidence for substantive purposes. Impeachment and rehabilitation with character evidence can occur in civil as well as criminal trials, and defendants do not have the option to keep the door closed to inquiries about a witness' character for trustworthiness. The trustworthiness of any witness—including criminal defendants and other parties—is fair game for impeachment. In short, the rules governing impeachment and rehabilitation with character evidence, as well as the rules governing other forms of impeachment and rehabilitation evidence, apply to all witnesses; with some minor exceptions that we will discuss in due course, it makes no difference that the witness happens to be a party.

Because the rules governing the use of character evidence for impeachment purposes are different from the rules governing character evidence for substantive purposes and because both sets of rules are quite intricate, the general subject of character evidence may seem confusing. The best way to eliminate the confusion and to deal rationally with the rules is to focus initially on what should always be the first question: How is the evidence relevant? Once you answer this question, it should be relatively easy to apply the proper rules.

1. Reputation and Opinion Evidence

One method to impeach or to rehabilitate a witness is with reputation or opinion evidence offered to prove the witness' character for trustworthiness in order to suggest that the witness is lying or telling the truth on the witness stand. While it is theoretically possible for witnesses whose credibility is in

---

9. FRE 608 refers to a witness' "character for truthfulness or untruthfulness." Unless the context suggests a contrary meaning, our use of the term *trustworthiness* includes both truthfulness and untruthfulness.

question to offer an opinion about their own credibility or testify about their own reputation, we know of no case in which that has been done. This impeachment method is one that traditionally relies on the use of extrinsic evidence, i.e., the opinion or reputation testimony of one witness about another witness' character for trustworthiness.

The Federal Rule governing this form of impeachment is FRE 608(a):

> The credibility of a witness may be attacked or supported by evidence in the form of opinion or reputation, but subject to these limitations: (1) the evidence may refer only to the character for truthfulness or untruthfulness, and (2) evidence of truthful character is admissible only after the character of the witness for truthfulness has been attacked by opinion or reputation evidence or otherwise.

Just as the common law prohibited the use of opinion evidence to prove character to show action in conformity with character for substantive purposes, the common law also prohibited the use of opinion evidence to prove character for impeachment or rehabilitation purposes. The drafters of the Federal Rules rejected this common law limitation in both the substantive and the impeachment/rehabilitation contexts for the same reason: Character witnesses are likely to be testifying because of their opinions about a person's character, and we should not force them to couch that opinion in reputation rhetoric.[10]

Once a character witness has testified pursuant to FRE 608(a), the opposing party is permitted to impeach the character witness by asking questions about specific acts. This impeachment process is identical to the impeachment process described in Chapter Four, where we considered the substantive uses of character evidence.[11] It is specifically authorized by two Federal Rules. First, with no apparent intent to limit its applicability to Article Four, FRE 405(a) provides: "On cross-examination [of character witnesses who offer reputation or opinion testimony], inquiry is allowable into relevant specific instances of conduct." Second, and considerably more awkwardly, FRE 608(b) provides:

> Specific instances of the conduct of a witness . . . may . . . be inquired into on cross-examination of the witness . . . concerning the character for truthfulness or untruthfulness of another witness as to which character the witness being cross-examined has testified.

Why do you suppose the Federal Rules authorize the identical specific acts inquiry in two different places? Is this another example of different rules being drafted by different committees without sufficient attention being paid to the rules in their totality?

10. See pages 221-222 supra.
11. See pages 223-228 supra.

D. Impeachment and Rehabilitation with Character Evidence 513

A few jurisdictions have permitted witnesses to be impeached by evidence of general bad character or bad moral character. The limitation in FRE 608(a) to "character for truthfulness or untruthfulness" is intended as a repudiation of this position. According to the Advisory Committee's Note:

> In accordance with the bulk of judicial authority, the inquiry is strictly limited to character for veracity, rather than allowing evidence as to character generally. The result is to sharpen relevancy, to reduce surprise, waste of time, and confusion, and to make the lot of the witness somewhat less unattractive.

We have already noted that reputation or opinion testimony regarding a witness' good character for trustworthiness is not admissible until the witness' character has been impeached. It is not entirely clear, though, what kind of impeachment will permit rehabilitation with reputation or opinion evidence. As FRE 608(a) specifies, reputation or opinion evidence of bad character for trustworthiness will suffice, but what does "or otherwise" in the last sentence of the rule mean? Courts traditionally have regarded impeachment by showing prior convictions, see FRE 609, or bad acts that did not result in convictions, see FRE 608(b), as impeachment of a witness' character. Thus, rehabilitation with reputation or opinion evidence would be appropriate. On the other hand, proof of a witness' bias has not been regarded as impeachment of the witness character; thus, rehabilitation with reputation or opinion testimony has not been regarded as appropriate. When other impeachment devices—e.g., prior inconsistent statements or demonstration of contradiction—are used, courts are divided on the propriety of using reputation or opinion evidence to rehabilitate the witness.

The Advisory Committee's Note to FRE 608 expresses approval of the settled precedent but offers no guidance with respect to the areas of uncertainty:

> [E]vidence of misconduct, including conviction of a crime, and of corruption . . . fall within this category [of attacks on character for trustworthiness]. Evidence of bias or interest does not. . . . Whether evidence in the form of contradiction is an attack upon the character of the witness must depend upon the circumstances.

Why should proof of bias not be considered an attack on the character of the witness? With respect to impeachment by means other than proof of bad acts or prior convictions, what "circumstances" are relevant to determining whether the impeachment warrants rehabilitation with reputation or opinion evidence about the witness' good character for trustworthiness?

PROBLEMS

1. Darby is being prosecuted for the armed robbery of a liquor store proprietor. During the presentation of the prosecution's case the proprietor

made a positive identification of Darby as the robber. As part of the defense, Darby calls Williams to testify that the proprietor has a reputation in the community for not remembering faces and for misidentifying people. Is the evidence admissible?

2. Dan Dickson is charged with perjury and testifies in his own behalf. The prosecutor's cross-examination fails to shake Dickson's story or cast doubt on his credibility. Dickson then offers the testimony of Willa Wilson that Dickson has a good reputation in the community for truth and veracity. Is Ms. Wilson's testimony admissible?

3. Diana Daws has been charged with committing a bank robbery, which occurred at 9:15 A.M. on Friday, March 17. She is relying on an alibi defense. Daws calls Willie Watson, who testifies on direct examination that he is absolutely sure that he was with Diana Daws at his home between 8 A.M. and noon on Friday, March 17. Assume, alternatively, that on cross-examination of Willie the prosecutor:

(a) gets Willie to admit that two years ago he was convicted of child molesting.
(b) gets Willie to admit that last week he told his friend Sally that he had not been with Diana Daws on March 17.
(c) gets Willie to admit that he is engaged to be married to Diana Daws.
(d) gets Willie to concede that he is not absolutely sure whether the morning he was with Diana Daws was Friday, March 17 or Thursday, March 16, but that he thinks it was Friday.

To which of these items of impeachment may Diana Daws respond with witnesses who are willing to testify that, in their opinion, Willie is a generally truthful person?

2. Specific Acts Other Than Convictions

Although the Federal Rules and the common law prohibit the use of extrinsic evidence of a witness' specific acts to prove character for trustworthiness to show dishonesty or honesty on the witness stand, FRE 608(b)—as well as the majority of jurisdictions—permits inquiry into such acts during the examination of a witness. According to FRE 608(b):

> Specific instances of the conduct of a witness, for the purpose of attacking or supporting the witness' credibility, other than conviction of crime as provided in rule 609, may not be proved by extrinsic evidence. They may, however, in the discretion of the court, if probative of truthfulness or untruthfulness, be inquired into on cross-examination of the witness . . . concerning the witness' character for truthfulness or untruthfulness. . . .

D. Impeachment and Rehabilitation with Character Evidence

It is important initially to recognize a point we made in our earlier discussion of character evidence:[12] Although FRE 404(b) purports to prohibit absolutely the use of specific acts to prove character in order to show action in conformity with character, FRE 608(b)—as well as FRE 609, as we shall see—explicitly authorizes the use of specific acts for this purpose. Although the means of eliciting the specific acts evidence is limited to cross-examination in FRE 608(b), the rule explicitly acknowledges that the reason for inquiring into these acts is to prove something about the "witness' character for truthfulness or untruthfulness"; and the only reason a witness' character for truthfulness or untruthfulness is relevant is to show action in conformity with that character trait—i.e., telling the truth or lying on the witness stand.

As we noted earlier, the inconsistency between FRE 404(b) and the impeachment provisions in FRE 608(b) and 609 has not troubled courts. Without discussing or perhaps even being aware of the contradiction, courts readily rely on FRE 608(b) to permit specific acts inquiries. This approach to the contradiction is consistent with the canon of construction holding that the specific should take precedence over the general. Moreover, particularly in light of the references to FRE 608 and 609 in FRE 404(a)(3), this result clearly appears to be consistent with the intent of the drafters. Nonetheless, the inconsistency is troublesome because of what it suggests about the general lack of care in the drafting process.

One reason why the inconsistency between FRE 404(b) and the character impeachment rules may not have troubled courts is that in terms of underlying evidentiary policy there is not a conflict, or at least not a serious conflict, between a prohibition on the use of specific acts evidence to prove character to show action in conformity with character for substantive purposes and the permissible uses of specific acts evidence in FRE 608(b) and 609. In our earlier discussion of FRE 404(b), we observed that that rule could be justified on the ground that it is not worth taking the time to become involved in litigation over specific acts when the only purpose of resolving the dispute was to prove character in order to make a very speculative inference to action in conformity with character. In the impeachment context, one might speculate that the inference from character for trustworthiness to action on the witness stand is stronger than other inferences from character to action in conformity with character. Even if it is not stronger, the danger that significant amounts of time will be spent litigating collateral matters is almost nonexistent in the impeachment context. In the case of prior convictions governed by FRE 609, the existence of a conviction is not likely to be subject to dispute, and in the case of an FRE 608(b) specific act, the examiner is bound by the answer of a witness.

Not permitting the examiner to challenge the witness' answer with extrinsic evidence may sometimes appear unfair. Assume, for example, that on cross-examination the witness is asked about and denies having lied on

---

12. See page 223 note 7 supra.

a job application form. Assume further, that the cross-examiner is prepared to authenticate the job application form and to call 10 witnesses who will testify that the facts stated in the application are false. What could be better impeaching evidence than this extrinsic proof that the witness had lied not only on the job application form but also on the witness stand?

Perhaps the answer is that there could not be a more relevant or more effective impeachment. The relevance of the impeachment, however, depends upon the certainty with which the impeaching party can establish the lie. If the impeacher is permitted to introduce the extrinsic evidence, the party whose witness was impeached should be able to rebut that evidence. It may be, for example, that the job application form is a forgery, that the statements on the job application are reasonably subject to more than one interpretation, or that the witnesses who would testify that the first witness lied on the application are themselves dishonest. If the impeaching party is allowed to introduce the extrinsic evidence, the party whose witness was impeached should have an opportunity to counter that evidence. And if that opportunity exists, a substantial amount of time and energy could be devoted to litigating the truth or falsity of facts whose sole or primary value is to impeach the credibility of a witness. Moreover, there would be the potential for this type of litigation with every witness. Thus, while it may be true that catching the witness in a lie on the stand would be extremely effective impeachment, FRE 608(b), out of concern with the time and distraction that could result from litigating collateral matters, prohibits the impeaching party from introducing extrinsic evidence to prove the lie.

Just as some common law jurisdictions permitted impeachment with reputation evidence about general moral character, some jurisdictions permitted inquiry about specific acts that were relevant to prove something about a person's general moral character for impeachment purposes. The result, of course, was that almost any bad act was relevant; and if the act was regarded as relevant, asking about it was almost invariably permitted.

Consistently with FRE 608(a), FRE 608(b), as well as the majority of common law courts, takes the position that the specific act must relate to character for trustworthiness. According to the Advisory Committee's Note:

> . . . Effective cross-examination demands that some allowance be made for going into matters of this kind, but the possibilities of abuse are substantial. Consequently, safeguards are erected in the form of specific requirements that the instances inquired into be probative of truthfulness or its opposite.

The term *safeguards* in the preceding passage is plural because FRE 608(b), as originally drafted and as promulgated by the Supreme Court, also contained the requirement that the acts be "not remote in time." That language was deleted and the "in the discretion of the court" language was inserted by Congress. According to the House Judiciary Committee:

D. Impeachment and Rehabilitation with Character Evidence

The Committee amended the Rule to emphasize the discretionary power of the court in permitting such testimony and deleted the reference to remoteness in time as being unnecessary and confusing (remoteness from time of trial or remoteness from the incident involved?)[13]

Despite the deletion of the time limitation, the time factor is obviously relevant in assessing probative value. Moreover, in considering the time factor, it should be appropriate to reason by analogy to FRE 609, which, as you will see shortly, imposes specific time restrictions on prior convictions that can be used to impeach a witness.

Consider what meaning should be given to the "in the discretion of the court" language that is currently part of FRE 608(b). Even without that language, it is clear that potentially admissible specific acts questions—like almost all other evidence—could be excluded on FRE 403 grounds. Thus, there is no need for providing specifically for judicial discretion with respect to FRE 608(b). Perhaps the clause is intended to do nothing more than remind the court and the litigants that FRE 403 may be a basis for exclusion. But is that kind of reminder really necessary? And if it is, why are there not similar reminders in other rules?

If the "discretion" language has any independent content for the trial judge, it must be either that the judge can exclude specific acts questions that would not be excluded by FRE 403 or that the judge can permit specific acts questions that would be excluded by FRE 403. This latter alternative is nonsensical: If the probative value is substantially outweighed by the countervailing factors, the evidence should be excluded. Thus, if the language means anything, it must be that the trial judge has more discretionary power to *exclude* specific acts questions pursuant to FRE 608(b) than to exclude other evidence pursuant to FRE 403.

Another possibility is that the "discretion" language in FRE 608 is directed primarily to appellate courts as a suggestion that they should be especially deferential to trial judges' decisions regarding the use of specific acts questions to impeach. Unfortunately, it is impossible to tell from the brief comment of the House Judiciary Committee which of these—or perhaps other—reasons it had for its addition to FRE 608(b).

Although most jurisdictions have a long history of permitting inquiry about specific acts that have not resulted in convictions to prove character for impeachment purposes, the majority federal position prior to the adoption of the Federal Rules was that such inquiry is inappropriate. Neither the Advisory Committee's Note to FRE 608 nor the congressional legislative history offers any indication that the drafters realized they were changing the federal law.

---

13. Since the theory of relevance is that the witness' character for (un)truthfulness indicates that the witness may be lying or truthful on the stand, quite obviously the concern is with the witness' current character. Thus, the remoteness reference must be a reference to remoteness in time from the trial.—Eds.

The primary justification for the minority common law and pre-FRE majority federal position is that the specific acts inquiries—even if the witness denies doing the act—may be extremely prejudicial, particularly when the witness is a party. If the question suggests, as it is likely to, that the cross-examiner knows the bad act occurred,[14] the jury may not believe a witness' denial. The denial and any surrounding circumstances that make the denial plausible could be explored, at least briefly, on re-direct examination, but the general prohibition against extrinsic evidence would prevent introducing other evidence to support the denial. If the jury believes that a party/witness committed a bad act, the jury may be prone to decide against the party/witness because the individual appears to be a general unsavory character. Moreover, if the act inquired about on cross-examination is similar to something that a party/witness allegedly did that gave rise to the current litigation, there is the risk that the jury will make not only the inference from bad character to lying on the stand but also the inference, prohibited by FRE 404(b), from bad character to conduct that is the subject of the litigation.

Are the foregoing reasons sufficient to preclude inquiry into specific acts to prove character for impeachment purposes, or is the Advisory Committee correct in asserting that "[e]ffective cross-examination demands that some allowance be made for going into matters of this kind, . . ."?

PROBLEMS

1. Dwight Dixon is charged with murder. The prosecutor anticipates that Dixon will testify in his own behalf and that he will call Walt Waters to testify that Dixon has a good reputation for peacefulness. Assuming that the prosecutor has a factual basis for the questions, can the prosecutor

   (a) ask Dixon if he was arrested for bribery five years ago?
   (b) ask Waters if he has heard that Dixon was arrested for bribery five years ago?

2. Doris Delorme has been charged with possession of heroin with intent to sell. The heroin was discovered in a small private airplane in which Doris and Wally Winter, an alleged co-conspirator, were riding. Wally initially testified that Doris was part of their conspiracy and that Doris knew the heroin was on the airplane. The prosecutor then offered to elicit from Wally that he had pled guilty pursuant to a plea agreement that included a commitment to testify truthfully against Doris and, if requested, to take lie detector tests. What objection can Doris make to this evidence? What objection could Doris make if the prosecutor offered the evidence only after

---

14. The cross-examiner has an ethical obligation to have a good faith belief that the witness committed the act, or the question is improper. See ABA, Model Rules of Professional Conduct, Rules 3.3 and 3.4.

D. Impeachment and Rehabilitation with Character Evidence 519

Doris had established that she had just obtained a divorce from Wally's brother and that Wally was convicted of perjury three years ago?

3. The defendant is being tried for sexually molesting his twelve-year-old adopted daughter. The daughter is the prosecution's sole witness. Consider whether any of the following evidence should be admissible:

> (a) After the prosecution has presented its case, the defendant calls several witnesses who offer to testify that the daughter is manipulative and often lies.
>
> (b) After the defendant has testified and denied molesting his adopted daughter, the prosecutor wishes to inquire on cross-examination about whether the defendant misrepresented his college class standing in campaign speeches made 10 years earlier during an unsuccessful attempt to win a state legislative seat. (The prosecutor has affidavits of several campaign workers verifying that the incident occurred.)
>
> (c) During cross-examination of the defendant, the prosecutor also wishes to inquire about whether the defendant's first marriage ended in divorce because he allegedly molested his first wife's daughter. (The prosecutor knows that there was a complaint filed against the defendant with respect to that incident, that the charges were dropped, and that the defendant and his first wife were divorced shortly thereafter.)
>
> (d) If the prosecutor is permitted to make the inquiry in (c), can defense counsel on re-direct examination inquire about the disposition of any criminal charges growing out of the incident?
>
> (e) As part of its rebuttal, the prosecution offers the testimony of a social worker who has counselled the daughter that on the basis of the counselling sessions the social worker is of the opinion that the daughter's account of the alleged molestation is trustworthy.

3. Prior Convictions

To the extent that a prior conviction is relevant to impeach the credibility of a witness, it is relevant in the same way that a prior bad act governed by FRE 608(b) is relevant: The witness' activity that led to the conviction shows a general character trait or disposition inconsistent with truthtelling from which one can infer that the witness may not be telling the truth on the witness stand. Nonetheless, in many jurisdictions convictions based on conduct that could not be inquired into in the absence of a conviction may be admissible. For example, FRE 609(a) permits a trial judge to balance probative value and prejudice in deciding whether to admit evidence of convictions punishable by imprisonment in excess of one year, regardless of whether the underlying conduct could reasonably be described as having a bearing on the witness' character for trustworthiness.[15] Moreover, *all* jurisdictions, including those that prohibit inquiry into specific acts that have not resulted in convictions, permit the use of some types of prior convictions to impeach the credibility of a witness.

The common law origins of the prior conviction impeachment device probably account in part for its breadth and its uniform acceptance:

> At common law the conviction of a person of treason or any felony, or of a misdemeanor involving dishonesty (*crimin falsi*), or the obstruction of justice, rendered the convicted person altogether incompetent as a witness. These were said to be "infamous" crimes. By statutes or rules which are virtually universal in the common law world, this primitive absolutism has been abandoned and the disqualification for conviction of crime has been abrogated, and by specific provision or by decision has been reduced to a mere ground of impeachment of credibility. [McCormick's Handbook on the Law of Evidence §43, p.93 (3d ed., Cleary, 1984).]

The uniform acceptance and broad scope of rules permitting impeachment by prior convictions undoubtedly also rests in part on the belief that prior convictions, even if they are based on activity that does not relate very directly to trustworthiness, may be especially relevant to the question of the witness' general trustworthiness. Neither courts nor commentators, however, attempt to explain the apparent contradiction in the notion that convictions for acts only remotely related to trustworthiness (e.g., aggravated assaults) may be especially probative of trustworthiness. Consider to what extent the following explanation accounts for the apparent contradiction:

A person of generally bad moral character is more likely to lie than a person of generally good moral character. Indeed, compelling proof of bad moral character may be particularly probative of trustworthiness. All of us, however, from time to time engage in "bad" acts that tend to suggest bad moral character; and since few, if any, of us are likely to consider ourselves to be of bad moral character, it must follow that a single bad act—or even a series of bad acts—is not necessarily very probative of general moral character. Thus, in the absence of a conviction, most jurisdictions prohibit inquiry into these acts unless they are likely to have more than very marginal value to the question whether the witness is lying—i.e., unless they relate fairly directly to that issue by suggesting a character trait of untruthfulness as opposed to general bad moral character. On the other hand, because the criminal law tends to proscribe only the most reprehensible activity, con-

---

15. One might maintain that all bad conduct is, at least in a minimal FRE 401 sense, relevant to trustworthiness. Perhaps that is so, but the Advisory Committee's Note to FRE 608 indicates that the drafters considered there to be a distinction between trustworthiness and general moral character, the former notion being narrower than the latter, and FRE 608 limits impeachment with reputation, opinion, or non-conviction specific acts to evidence that shows a witness' character for trustworthiness. There is no similar absolute prohibition in FRE 609(a).

D. Impeachment and Rehabilitation with Character Evidence

victions—especially when they are for serious crimes—are likely to be particularly probative of bad moral character and, therefore, untruthfulness.

From a cynical perspective one might further justify use of prior convictions to impeach on the ground that criminal defendants are disproportionately likely both to have records of prior convictions and to lie in the hope of obtaining acquittals. Thus, the threat of impeachment with prior convictions may deter criminal defendants from testifying and, as a result, reduce the amount of false testimony that might otherwise be presented in a criminal trial.

This last rationale, of course, is inconsistent with the rationale underlying the final paragraph of FRE 608, which permits a witness to invoke the right against self-incrimination with respect to questions "which relate only to credibility."[16] In addition, by emphasizing deterrence from testifying rather than probative value, the rationale implicitly relies on prejudice as a reason for admitting rather than excluding the evidence.

Regardless of how probative of trustworthiness prior convictions are and regardless of whether they are generally more probative than bad acts that have not resulted in convictions, most prior convictions are likely to be quite prejudicial—probably more prejudicial than most non-conviction bad act evidence. This is so because the substantive law tends to criminalize the most reprehensible behavior, because police and prosecutors tend to focus their limited resources on the most serious offenders, and because the fact of conviction represents the community's judgment of moral condemnation. As a result, there is a relatively high risk that juries may be predisposed against witnesses who are shown to have prior convictions. Whenever the witness is a party or somebody closely associated with the party, jurors' attitudes about the witness may improperly affect their decision.

FRE 609 deals with the concerns of probative value and prejudice in the following manner:

> (a) For the purpose of attacking the credibility of a witness, evidence that the witness has been convicted of a crime shall be admitted if elicited from the witness or established by public record during cross-examination but only if the crime (1) was punishable by death or imprisonment in excess of one year under the law under which the witness was convicted,[17] and the court determines that the probative value of admitting this evidence outweighs its prejudicial effect to the defendant, or (2) involved dishonesty or false statement, regardless of the punishment.
>
> (b) Evidence of a conviction under this rule is not admissible if a period of more than 10 years has elapsed since the date of the conviction or of the release of the witness from the confinement imposed for the conviction, whichever is the later date, unless the court determines, in the interests of

---

16. See pages 508-510 supra.
17. The federal definition of a felony is "an offense punishable by death or imprisonment for a term exceeding one year." 18 U.S.C. §1(a).—Eds.

justice, that the probative value of the conviction supported by specific facts and circumstances substantially outweighs its prejudicial effect. However, evidence of a conviction more than 10 years old as calculated herein, is not admissible unless the proponent gives to the adverse party sufficient advance written notice of intent to use such evidence to provide the adverse party with a fair opportunity to contest the use of such evidence.

The remaining subdivisions of FRE 609 limit the admissibility of convictions that have been the subject of pardon, annulment, or finding of rehabilitation, severely restrict the admissibility of juvenile adjudications, and provide that the pendency of an appeal does not make the conviction inadmissible. See FRE 609(c)-(e).

To the extent that one equates "dishonesty" with "illegality," all crimes are crimes of dishonesty. Clearly, however, the term *dishonesty* in FRE 609(a)(2) should not be interpreted that broadly, for FRE 609(a)(1) would then be meaningless. The admissibility of FRE 609(a)(1) crimes is limited by both a potential term of imprisonment requirement and a balancing test. Crimes of dishonesty and false statement are admissible without these restrictions.

The Advisory Committee's Note to FRE 609 equates "dishonesty or false statement" with the common law classification *crimen falsi*. According to Professor Greenleaf's treatise on evidence,

> the extent and meaning of the term "crimen falsi," in our law, is nowhere laid down with precision. . . . [It does not include] deceits in the quality of provisions, deceits by false weights and measures, [and] conspiracy to defraud by spreading false news, [but it does include] forgery, perjury, subornation of perjury, suppression of testimony by bribery, or conspiracy to procure the absence of a witness, or other conspiracy, to accuse one of a crime, and barratry. And from these decisions it may be deduced, that the "crimen falsi" of the Common Law not only involves the charge of falsehood, but also is one which may injuriously affect the administration of justice, by the introduction of falsehood and fraud. At least it may be said, in the language of Sir William Scott, "so far the law has gone, affirmatively; and it is not for me to say where it should stop, negatively." [S. Greenleaf, Evidence §373 (1842) *quoted in* 2 J. Wigmore, Evidence in Trials at Common Law §520, pp. 729-730 (Chadbourn rev. 1970) (footnotes omitted).]

The Senate Judiciary Committee Report and the Conference Report on the Federal Rules appear to go a little further before stopping. The two reports contain the following identical elaboration on the meaning of dishonesty or false statement:

> [It means] crimes such as perjury or subornation of perjury, false statement, criminal fraud, embezzlement or false pretenses, or any other offense, in the nature of *crimen falsi* the commission of which involves some element of

D. Impeachment and Rehabilitation with Character Evidence

untruthfulness, deceit or falsification bearing on the accused's propensity to testify truthfully.

Despite the ambiguity in this description, it is fair to say that most federal courts have interpreted the phrase *dishonesty and false statement* relatively narrowly and that the caselaw tends to limit the phrase quite closely to the crimes named as examples in the preceding excerpts.

In assessing probative value and prejudice pursuant to FRE 609(a)(1) and FRE 609(b), it is important to keep two things in mind. First, as we noted in the discussion of FRE 608(b), when the witness is a party, the similarity between the crime charged and the facts underlying the impeachment evidence enhances the *prejudice*, not the probative value of the prior conviction: The proper impeachment inference is from conviction to bad character to lying on the witness stand; the inference from conviction to bad character to action that is the basis for the current charge is improper. See FRE 404(b). Second, like the balancing test in FRE 412, the rape shield provision, the balancing tests in FRE 609(a) and (b) are "reverse FRE 403" tests. Rather than authorizing exclusion if the prejudice and other factors substantially outweigh the probative value, they require exclusion if the probative value does not "outweigh" (FRE 609(a)(1)) or "substantially outweigh" (FRE 609(b)) the prejudice. In other words, whereas the FRE 403 balancing test favors admissibility and, in effect, puts the burden on the party seeking exclusion to justify that result, the FRE 609 tests favor exclusion and, in effect, put the burden on the party seeking admission to establish that probative value outweighs prejudice.

FRE 609(a) does not preclude the use of extrinsic evidence to prove the conviction. Thus, if the witness denies having been convicted, it is appropriate for the impeaching party to introduce into evidence the record of conviction. As we suggested earlier, the reason for permitting extrinsic evidence of convictions but not of bad acts that have not resulted in convictions is that the existence or nonexistence of a conviction can be established quickly and with a high degree of certainty. By contrast, there may be disputes about the occurrence or nature of bad acts that have not resulted in convictions. Attempts to resolve these disputes with extrinsic evidence could result in time-consuming litigation about collateral matters.

Just as there is an interest in avoiding lengthy inquiry into the underlying facts with extrinsic evidence, there is also an interest in not spending a great deal of time exploring with the witness the facts underlying the conviction. Thus a court frequently will permit the impeaching party to do no more than mention the name of the crime, when and where it occurred, and what sentence was imposed. Some courts also prohibit the impeached witness from offering any explanation for the conviction. A number of courts, however, will permit the witness, particularly if the witness is also a party, to testify briefly about any mitigating or extenuating circumstances.

Regardless of whether the prior conviction is elicited from the witness or proved extrinsically with the record of conviction, the evidence is hearsay: A conviction, even if the witness was factually innocent, may make the witness hostile to the judicial system and therefore more willing to lie than somebody who has not been convicted. Clearly, though, the theory underlying both the use of convictions for impeachment generally and the distinction in FRE 609 between crimes of dishonesty and false statement and other crimes is that the acts underlying the conviction suggest something important about the witness' credibility. When the conviction is used for this purpose, it is a manifestation of the jury's or the judge's assertion in an earlier proceeding that the facts essential to the conviction are true.

The Federal Rules, as well as a number of other jurisdictions, have a judgments exception to the hearsay rule. Typically, however, the judgments exception is narrower than the rule authorizing impeachment with prior convictions. For example, FRE 803(22) extends the judgments exception only to convictions for crimes punishable by imprisonment for more than one year, whereas FRE 609(a)(2) authorizes the use of dishonesty and false statement convictions regardless of the potential penalty. If courts have even noticed this conflict between FRE 609(a) and FRE 803(22), they have not been bothered by it. Quite properly, in our view, courts considering the admissibility of prior convictions for impeachment have relied on the FRE 609, the rule dealing specifically with that issue, and have ignored the limitations in the more general FRE 803(22).

When Congress was considering the Federal Rules, both houses devoted considerable attention to FRE 609. Some members of Congress were especially concerned with the potential prejudice, particularly to criminal defendants who take the witness stand, that can result from impeachment with prior convictions. Others were adamant that at least the most probative convictions—those involving dishonesty and false statement—should be admissible. As a result of these concerns, the version of FRE 609 that became part of the Federal Rules is quite different from the version approved by the Advisory Committee. FRE 609 is a political compromise of competing concerns about the use of prior convictions, and to some extent the language of the rule is more a manifestation of that compromise than a coherent, comprehensive rule governing prior convictions. As you consider the following case and problems, pay especially close attention to the language of FRE 609(a), and consider to what extent it is appropriate to take the language at face value.

CAMPBELL v. GREER
831 F.2d 700 (7th Cir. 1987)

POSNER, Circuit Judge. Rudolph Campbell, an inmate at the Illinois state prison at Menard, appeals from a judgment for the Illinois prison officials and guards whom Campbell sued under section 1 of the Civil Rights Act of

D. Impeachment and Rehabilitation with Character Evidence

1871, now 42 U.S.C. §1983. The suit charged them with having deprived Campbell of his right to be free from cruel and unusual punishment, a right granted federal prisoners by the Eighth Amendment and extended to state prisoners by interpretation of the Fourteenth Amendment. By consent of the parties, the trial was conducted before a federal magistrate. Campbell and his witnesses (inmates all) testified that he had learned he was the target for a "hit" by other inmates and had requested the defendants to be sure to leave his cell on "deadlock," but that they had neglected to do so and, as a result, when the cells were opened from a centrally located locking-and-unlocking station the "hit men" entered his cell and stabbed him repeatedly. To "deadlock" a cell so that it remains locked when the master switch is thrown open requires the guard to turn a second lock in the door, and this wasn't done. The defendants did not deny the stabbing but said that Campbell had never asked any of them to deadlock his cell. The jury brought in a verdict for the defendants. Campbell wants a new trial. He says that . . . the defendants' counsel should not have been allowed to bring out, in cross-examining him, the fact that he was in Menard as a result of having been convicted of rape. . . .

. . . Campbell's first submission is that subsection (1) of [FRE 609(a)] required the magistrate, before admitting the evidence of Campbell's conviction for rape, to balance its prejudicial effect against its probative value. We disagree. The rule requires such balancing only when there is prejudicial effect "to the defendant," and Campbell is the plaintiff. If the defendant is not prejudiced, and the evidence otherwise satisfies the requirements of the rule, it is admissible, period; at least that is what the rule seems to say. Campbell argues that it would be absurd to read the rule literally, for that would allow a defendant in a civil case, but not a plaintiff, to complain about the use of his criminal record to impeach. That would indeed be absurd. It would load the dice in favor of defendants in civil cases, even though it is often a matter of happenstance in a civil suit which party is plaintiff and which defendant. As is true of many rules and statutes, Rule 609(a) can't mean what it says. It needs judicial patchwork. We merely disagree with Campbell's suggested patch, which would require a balancing of probative value and prejudicial effect with regard to every witness in every federal trial, civil and criminal, whose testimony the opposing party wanted to impeach with a conviction.

An interpretation of the rule that is more in keeping with its background and legislative history is that the only witness who may demand a balancing of the prejudicial value of his criminal record against its probative effect is the defendant in a criminal trial. As pointed out in the Note of the Advisory Committee on Proposed Rule 609, the dominant approach at common law was "to allow use of felonies generally, without regard to the nature of the particular offense," to be used to impeach a witness's credibility, even when the witness was a criminal defendant, who might be inhibited from taking the witness stand by fear of the adverse impact on his chances of acquittal if the jury learned he was a convicted felon. Despite this danger, Rule 609(a) as drafted by the Advisory Committee and approved by the Supreme Court followed the dominant approach of the common law and thus allowed, without any balancing test for any witness, impeachment by means of felony convictions. . . . [The House Judiciary Committee confined] impeachment by conviction to convictions of crimes involving dishonesty or false statements. . . .

The Senate Judiciary Committee adopted a modified version of the House bill. The Senate bill confined the use of convictions to impeach the credibility of a criminal defendant to prior crimes (whether felonies or misdemeanors) involving dishonesty or false statements, but as to [all] other witnesses . . . [adopted a] balancing test for convictions, except that, as in the case of criminal defendants, convictions involving dishonesty or false statement could be used to impeach a witness without bothering with a balancing test. . . . If the Senate bill had been enacted, Campbell would be correct that the magistrate was required to balance the probative value (as impeachment) of his conviction for rape (not a crime of dishonesty or false statement as these terms are understood in the present context) against the prejudicial effect of the conviction on his civil case. But the Senate bill was not enacted, as is obvious from a glance at the text of Rule 609(a). . . .

The change is explained in the Conference Report:

> [T]he Conference determined that the prejudicial effect to be weighed against the probative value of the conviction is specifically the prejudicial effect *to the defendant*. The danger of prejudice to a witness other than the defendant (such as injury to the witness' reputation in his community) was considered and rejected by the Conference as an element to be weighed in determining admissibility. It was the judgment of the Conference that the danger of prejudice to a nondefendant witness is outweighed by the need for the trier of fact to have as much relevant evidence on the issue of credibility as possible. Such evidence should only be excluded where it presents a danger of improperly influencing the outcome of the trial by persuading the trier of fact to convict the defendant on the basis of his prior criminal record. [H.R. Rep. 1597, 93d Cong., 2d Sess. 9-10 (1974) (emphasis in original).]

This could not be clearer. The only prejudicial effect that the judge is to consider in ruling on the admissibility of a prior conviction is the prejudicial effect on the defendant in a criminal trial. . . .

Some cases, illustrated by Petty v. Ideco, 761 F.2d 1146, 1152 (5th Cir. 1985), disagree with this conclusion and hold that the balancing test is applicable to any witness, but we do not find these cases persuasive in light of the language and legislative history of Rule 609(a). . . .

Campbell has a back-up submission, however. It is that a conviction offered for purposes of impeachment can be excluded under Rule 403. . . . Campbell's argument is not entirely of the back-door variety. Rule 403 is less restrictive than Rule 609(a) is. . . . In addition, while it is plain from

D. Impeachment and Rehabilitation with Character Evidence

the legislative history that Congress (or at least those members who took an interest in this legislation) was aware and intended to make provision for the situation where a conviction is used to impeach the testimony of a witness in a criminal trial whether or not he is the defendant, it is less clear that Congress intended Rule 609(a) to establish the standard of admissibility for the use of convictions against any witness in a civil trial. Neither the Advisory Committee's note nor the committee reports mention civil trials; and though the hearings and floor debates do—see 120 Cong. Rec. 2376-2377, 2379 (1974) . . .—there is always a question whether expressions of view in these settings represent majority sentiment. The use of convictions to impeach a witness in a civil trial appears to be rare, and this may mean that few Congressmen would have been aware of the implications of Rule 609(a) for civil trials such as the one in this case. (Of course, it may be rare only because the threat of impeachment deters parties from calling witnesses who have been convicted of felonies.)

However, the rule is not limited in terms to criminal trials, and some Congressmen as we have just noted thought it would apply to civil trials as well. Moreover, the impression conveyed by the detail of the rule and by the legislative history is that Congress and the Advisory Committee thought they were dealing exhaustively in Rule 609 with the subject of using criminal convictions to impeach witnesses' testimony. If so, Rule 403 is not applicable. That rule is a catch-all. It was not meant to overlap, supplant, or contradict the policy premises of more specific rules, such as Rule 609. The Advisory Committee's Note to Rule 403 says it "is designed as a guide for the handling of situations for which no specific rules have been formulated." Rule 609(a) is a specific rule governing the admissibility of convictions to impeach a witness's testimony.

We do not pretend that these arguments are conclusive; we point out that one Congressman thought that what is now Rule 403 would permit the exclusion of a previous conviction in exceptional cases. . . . See 120 Cong. Rec. 2381 (1974). For us the clinching argument against the applicability of Rule 403 is the unacceptable implication of the argument, which is that a district judge or magistrate could exclude even convictions for crimes of dishonesty or false statement if convinced that the probative value of such evidence in the circumstances of the case was substantially outweighed by its prejudicial effect. For remember that the balancing test of Rule 403 is not limited to any particular class of evidence. If it overrides the express statement in Rule 609(a)(1) that evidence of prior convictions shall be admissible unless prejudice *to the defendant* outweighs the probative value of the evidence, then it overrides the express statement in Rule 609(a)(2) that evidence of prior convictions involving dishonesty or false statement is admissible regardless of prejudice to the defendant or anyone else. Yet Congress plainly decided that such evidence should be admissible regardless of its prejudicial effect, even against a criminal defendant. . . .

The point can be generalized: the concerns that drove Congress in Rule

609(a) to modify the common law rule of automatic admissibility of prior convictions for impeachment purposes were focused on the use of such convictions against criminal defendants. Congress was not concerned with the prejudicial effects of their use against any witness in civil proceedings and did not in Rule 403 seek to undo the common law rule that would permit such use against any witness in a civil or criminal proceeding. It is true that when the Federal Rules of Evidence were adopted the courts were moving away from the common law rule and allowing a criminal defendant to seek exclusion of his prior convictions, whatever the crimes for which he had been convicted, on the basis of undue prejudice. See, e.g., Luck v. United States, 348 F.2d 763 (D.C. Cir. 1965). . . . But Congress cut back on that trend, by providing for the automatic admission of convictions for crimes involving dishonesty or false statements. There is no indication that by the catch-all provision in Rule 403 Congress meant to approve the trend in a field where the argument for exclusion was so much weaker: civil trials.

We conclude that . . . a civil plaintiff cannot complain about the use of his prior felony convictions to impeach his testimony, no matter how harmful that use is to his chances in the trial. . . . There is contrary authority, . . . all stemming from Shows v. M/V Red Eagle, 695 F.2d 114, 118 (5th Cir. 1983), which treats Rule 403 as "a rule of exclusion that cuts across the rules of evidence," including Rule 609(a). However, *Shows* failed to note the comment of the Advisory Committee that Rule 403 is inapplicable where another rule has dealt exhaustively with the admissibility of a particular class of evidence. Moreover, the only basis that *Shows* offered for its conclusion that Rule 403 applied to impeachment by convictions was a citation to Rozier v. Ford Motor Co., 573 F.2d 1332, 1347 (5th Cir. 1978), which holds only, and unexceptionably, that evidence not barred by the hearsay rule may still be barred by Rule 403. Evidence may be inadmissible for more than one reason; but where, as in Rule 609(a), Congress has taken pains to specify the conditions for both the admission and the exclusion of a specific class of evidence (convictions), district courts may not use Rule 403 to set that specification at naught. . . .

Affirmed.

WILL, Senior District Judge, concurring. . . . [Since] the trial judge's errors, if any, on the admissibility of evidence . . . were not material, the jury's verdict should be affirmed. I write separately . . . because I believe some of Judge Posner's opinion is erroneous dictum.

. . . If Rule 609(a) is read, through judicial patchwork, to apply only to criminal cases, I find it illogical, as well as unnecessary, to conclude that Rule 403 is never applicable to prior conviction evidence in civil cases. That conclusion is inconsistent with what some members of Congress clearly intended as Judge Posner's opinion points out, as well as a number of prior decisions. . . .

Moreover, since Rule 403 specifically provides for the balancing of other potentially less prejudicial evidence, it seems logical that, in civil cases, it

D. Impeachment and Rehabilitation with Character Evidence

should require balancing with respect to prior convictions whether of parties or witnesses. This is no great burden on the trial judge and obviates the certainty that, in cases where the prejudice clearly outweighs the probative value, the evidence will nevertheless be admitted since the trial judge, under Judge Posner's analysis, has *no* discretion in civil cases to exclude it.

In support of this conclusion, Judge Posner finds it an "unacceptable implication" that Rule 403 would permit a district judge or magistrate to exclude in a civil case convictions for crimes of dishonesty or false statement. . . . This, he points out, would give the trial judge in civil cases broader discretion than Rule 609(a)(2) does in a criminal case. As a result, he concludes that Rule 403 is *never* applicable in a civil case.

This, I believe, is throwing the baby out with the bath. Rule 609(a)(1) provides for balancing probative value only against "prejudicial effect to the *defendant*". . . . I find it an "unacceptable implication" that so narrow a specific rule should be generalized to foreclose application of the broad provisions of Rule 403 in all cases. Rather the only acceptable implication to me is that Rule 609 forecloses application of Rule 403 only to those specific circumstances to which Rule 609 is applicable. . . .

PROBLEMS

1. Alex Dean is being prosecuted for the murder of Viola Adams. Alex has testified that he was with another woman at the time of the alleged murder. On cross-examination the prosecutor asked Alex if he had falsely stated that he had no criminal record on a job application filed with the Acme Parts Co. three years ago. Alex responded that he had applied for a job with Acme and that he had not lied on the job application form. The prosecutor now offers into evidence Alex's job application form in which he responded "No" to the question whether he had ever been convicted of a crime and a public record of Alex's conviction for armed robbery seven years ago. Alex has objected to the admissibility of both documents. What result?

2. Jane Dillon has been charged with conspiracy to sell narcotics, and she plans to testify in her own defense. Three years ago Jane entered a nolo contendere plea to a charge of perjury. Citing FRE 410 and FRE 803(22) she has filed a motion in limine for a court order that the prosecutor refrain from introducing extrinsic evidence of or asking her about the perjury conviction. How should the court rule?

3. Dirk Dooley is charged with perjury and testifies in his own behalf. On cross-examination the prosecutor wants to introduce evidence that on two previous occasions—once five years ago and once twelve years ago—Dirk was convicted of perjury. Is the evidence admissible?

4. Doren Decker is charged with the sale of narcotics. He calls a government informant as a witness, and after the informant gives testimony

unfavorable to Doren, Doren offers to introduce evidence that the informant was convicted of theft eight years ago. Is the evidence admissible?

5. Dawn Drabble is charged with robbery. In cross-examining a prosecution witness, Dawn wishes to show that the witness was convicted of felonious assault eight years ago. Later, Dawn testifies in her own defense, and the prosecution offers to show that she was convicted of felonious assault eight years ago. Are the convictions admissible?

6. Pamela Parsons has brought a federal civil rights action against Duane Davis, a correctional officer, for alleged sexual assaults while Ms. Parsons was an inmate. On cross-examination of Ms. Parsons, defense counsel wishes to inquire about a six-year-old felony conviction for sale of heroin. In a motion in limine Ms. Parsons has objected to any reference by the defense to this conviction. What result?

7. Ed Dobisch is being prosecuted for writing checks on an account with insufficient funds. Four years ago Ed was convicted of grand theft for embezzling funds from his employer. The embezzlement involved falsifying company records and making numerous false representations over a two-year period. Ed plans to testify in his defense and he has filed a motion in limine asking that the court order the prosecutor to refrain from making any reference to the grand theft conviction or, in the alternative, to order the prosecutor to refer to the crime only as a "felony" and to make no reference to grand theft, embezzlement, or the details of the crime. The prosecutor has filed a motion in limine seeking a ruling that the conviction is admissible and that it is appropriate to bring out the details of the false representations that form the basis for the conviction. How should the court rule?

8. Sam Leonard has been convicted of conspiracy to sell narcotics. Prior to Sam's trial he filed a motion in limine stating that he wanted to testify and seeking a ruling that a three-year-old heroin possession conviction and a five-year-old armed robbery conviction could not be used to impeach him. The court declined to rule on the motion prior to trial, and the defendant renewed his motion at the close of the prosecutor's case. Although the defendant argued that an advance ruling was essential in order for the defendant to decide whether to exercise his right to testify, the court once again refused to rule on the motion. Sam did not testify in his defense, and is now appealing on the ground that it was reversible error for the trial judge not to grant the motion in limine prior to the time that defendant had to elect whether to testify. What result?

E. IMPEACHMENT AND REHABILITATION WITH A WITNESS' PRIOR STATEMENTS

Prior statements of a witness traditionally have been regarded as inadmissible hearsay to prove the truth of the statements. Prior inconsistent and consistent

E. Impeachment and Rehabilitation with a Witness' Prior Statements

statements, however, are relevant and have been admissible for the non-hearsay purposes of impeaching and rehabilitating a witness' credibility: Proof of an inconsistency, regardless of which statement is true, suggests that the witness may have lied in making one of the statements or that the witness for some other reason—e.g., faulty memory or general lack of interest in the subject matter—has on one occasion not reported accurately what happened.

Since all of us occasionally make inconsistent statements, proof of an apparently trivial inconsistency does little, if anything, to impeach a witness' credibility. If the inconsistency relates to the subject matter of the law suit, however, it provides a reason to be wary generally of the witness' testimony even when the most likely explanation for the inconsistency is memory lapse or general lack of care in speaking about the matter either at trial or in the prior inconsistent statement. Regardless of which statement may be inaccurate, it is reasonable to infer that the witness' testimony relating generally to the same subject matter may be careless and inaccurate.

If it is reasonable to infer from proof of an inconsistency that one statement is a deliberate falsehood, the proof of an apparent willingness to lie on one occasion—regardless of whether it is on the witness stand during the current law suit or in the prior statement—suggests that the witness may be willing to lie on other occasions. Therefore, some or all of the witness' testimony may be false. The probative value of the inconsistency will be greatest if the apparently deliberate falsehood relates to the subject matter or parties involved in the litigation or to something intrinsically important.

Proof of consistency, without regard to the truth of either consistent statement, suggests that the witness is careful and thoughtful in speaking about the matter to which the statement relates. Thus, except to the extent that there is reason to believe the witness is deliberately telling consistent lies, knowing about the consistency gives us more reason to credit and rely on the witness' testimony than we would have without evidence of the consistency.

Occasionally a prior statement may fall within one of the traditional exceptions to the hearsay rule. For example, a prior inconsistent statement offered against a party to an action would be admissible for its truth as an admission. Moreover, as we pointed out in Chapter Five, the Federal Rules and other modern codifications of evidence rules permit the use of some prior statements for their truth. See FRE 801(d)(1). If a prior statement is admissible for its truth, there is no need to consider whether it may *also* be admissible for the non-hearsay purpose of impeaching or rehabilitating a witness. Relying on the truth of the prior statement will inevitably do more to discredit or to rehabilitate trial testimony than relying merely on the fact of inconsistency or consistency. Our focus here is on the non-hearsay impeachment and rehabilitation use of prior inconsistent and consistent statements that are not independently admissible for their truth.

1. Prior Inconsistent Statements

Since prior inconsistent statements were not generally admissible for their truth at common law, their admissibility usually depended on whether they could be used for the non-hearsay purpose of impeaching a witness' credibility. Under the Federal Rules, the question whether a prior inconsistent statement is admissible for impeachment purposes is important in at least one and possibly two contexts. First, the FRE 801(d)(1)(A) hearsay exemption applies only to inconsistent statements under oath. Thus, a prior inconsistent statement not under oath is potentially admissible only for its non-hearsay impeachment value, unless the statement is one of identification, FRE 801(d)(1)(C), or falls within some other hearsay exemption or exception. Second, as we suggested in the discussion of the voucher rule,[18] the FRE 801(d)(1)(A) hearsay exemption for prior inconsistent statements under oath arguably should apply only to those statements that are independently admissible for non-hearsay impeachment purposes. If this is the case, it will be necessary to decide whether the evidence could be admitted for the non-hearsay impeachment purpose in order to determine whether it is admissible for its truth.

At common law there were two limitations on the right to ask a witness about prior inconsistent statements. One was the voucher rule. The other, derived from the Queen's Case,[19] required that, at least with respect to written statements, the witness had to be shown the statement prior to any questioning about the statement. The rationale for this requirement is a concern that the witness may honestly have forgotten what is or what may appear to be an inconsistent statement. If such a witness were not shown the statement prior to questioning, a clever cross-examiner might be able to get the witness to deny having made the statement, thereby giving the false impression that the witness is a liar. On the other hand, showing the statement to the witness prior to questioning gives the dishonest witness the opportunity to concoct a false story that minimizes the impact of the inconsistency, and for this reason many commentators have criticized the rule. Although a number of courts and some legislatures at one time or another formally adopted the rule of the Queen's Case, it is seldom invoked in practice. FRE 613(a) specifically rejects it:

> In examining a witness concerning a prior statement made by the witness, whether written or not, the statement need not be shown or its contents disclosed to the witness at that time, but on request the same shall be shown or disclosed to opposing counsel.[20]

---

18. See pages 495-496 supra.
19. 2 Broad. & Bing. 284, 129 Eng. Rep. 976 (1820).
20. The Advisory Committee's Note to FRE 613(a) states, "The provision for disclosure to counsel is designed to protect against unwarranted insinuations that a statement has been made when the fact is to the contrary."—Eds.

E. Impeachment and Rehabilitation with a Witness' Prior Statements

There is no absolute prohibition against the use of extrinsic evidence to prove a prior inconsistent statement. The common law, however, conditioned the use of extrinsic evidence on compliance with a fairly rigid foundation requirement: Although typically the impeaching party could ask the witness questions about the statement without first revealing the statement to the witness, the impeaching party could not introduce extrinsic evidence of the statement without first indicating the precise time and place of the statement and the person to whom it was made and then asking the witness whether the witness made the statement. This foundation requirement serves at least three purposes. First, it ensures that the witness will not have to bear the inconvenience of being recalled later in the trial to explain the apparent inconsistency. Second, since witnesses occasionally will not be available to be recalled, the requirement ensures that the witness will have an opportunity to explain or account for the apparent inconsistency. Finally, since there will be no need for extrinsic evidence if the witness admits the inconsistency, the foundation requirement contributes to the efficient resolution of disputes. Indeed, most courts prohibit the use of extrinsic evidence if the witness admits having made the inconsistent statement. However, if the witness' version of the statement is different from what the extrinsic evidence will show or if the witness testifies to "maybe" or "probably" having made the statement, the impeaching party should be able to introduce the extrinsic evidence.

FRE 613(b) substantially alters the common law foundation requirement:

> Extrinsic evidence of a prior inconsistent statement by a witness is not admissible unless the witness is afforded an opportunity to explain or deny the same and the opposite party is afforded an opportunity to interrogate the witness thereon, or the interests of justice otherwise require. This provision does not apply to admissions of a party-opponent as defined in rule 801(d)(2).[21]

According to the Advisory Committee:

> . . . The traditional insistence that the attention of the witness be directed to the statement on cross-examination is relaxed in favor of simply providing the witness an opportunity to explain and the opposite party an opportunity to examine on the statement, with no specification of any particular time or sequence. Under this procedure, several collusive witnesses can be examined before disclosure of a joint prior inconsistent statement. . . .
>
> In order to allow for such eventualities as the witness becoming unavailable by the time the statement is discovered, a measure of discretion is conferred upon the judge. . . .

---

21. This last sentence is consistent with the common law. If the statement is independently admissible as an admission, its admissibility does not depend upon whether the declarant testifies, much less whether the declarant, if a witness, is questioned about the statement.—Eds.

Would it be preferable to retain the common law foundation requirement and perhaps create specific exceptions for the types of situations contemplated by the Advisory Committee? Are there reasons other than those advanced by the Advisory Committee that justify the Federal Rules' departure from the common law foundation requirement?

Even if it is appropriate to forego the rigors of the common law foundation requirement, should a party who knew about a prior inconsistent statement at the time of cross-examination and who made no effort to ask the witness about it be permitted to introduce extrinsic evidence of the statement later in the trial? Perhaps surprisingly in light of the wording of FRE 613(b), some courts have upheld exclusion of the evidence even though there is no showing that it would have been impossible or inconvenient to recall the witness.[22] Should there be limits on a judge's discretion to exclude extrinsic evidence in this type of situation?

As we noted in our initial discussion of the use of extrinsic evidence to impeach, the common law applied the "no extrinsic evidence to impeach on a collateral matter" dictum to impeachment with prior inconsistent statements. Thus, even if the impeaching party had laid a proper foundation, extrinsic evidence would be inadmissible and the impeaching party would be forced to accept a witness' denial if the inconsistency were about a "collateral" matter, i.e., some matter that had no bearing on the litigation.

Applying the no extrinsic evidence dictum may make sense in the context of an inconsistency that appears to be explainable in terms of lack of care or attention to detail: Lack of care or attention to one detail may suggest lack of care or attention to the general subject matter to which the detail relates, but it probably suggests very little about the witness' credibility or accuracy with respect to other matters. Thus, it may be desirable to avoid time-consuming and potentially distracting inquiries with extrinsic evidence into these types of collateral inconsistencies. When the most likely explanation for the inconsistency is that one statement is a lie, however, the justification for excluding extrinsic evidence of a statement about a collateral matter is considerably weaker. Since the impeachment theory relies on the fact of inconsistency rather than the truth of the prior inconsistent statement to discredit the witness, the gravity of the apparent lie, not whether the subject matter is non-collateral, would appear to be the most significant factor affecting probative value. Moreover, to the extent that there is a concern that the jury may improperly consider an inconsistent statement for its truth, it would seem preferable to permit proof of an inconsistency about a collateral matter rather than a non-collateral matter.

As we noted earlier the Federal Rules do not contain a general prohibition against the use of extrinsic evidence to impeach on a collateral matter. The only Federal Rule barring extrinsic evidence is FRE 608(b), which applies to "specific instances of conduct." A prior inconsistent statement

---

22. See, e.g., United States v. Geer, 806 F.2d 556 (5th Cir. 1986).

E. Impeachment and Rehabilitation with a Witness' Prior Statements

cannot be "conduct" within the meaning of FRE 608(b), because FRE 613(b) specifically contemplates the use of extrinsic evidence of prior inconsistent statements. Thus, under the Federal Rules the propriety of using extrinsic evidence of prior inconsistent statements should be governed not by FRE 608(b) or by an inquiry about "collateralness" but by the balancing process of FRE 403.

Apparently in an attempt to stress the point that FRE 608(b) and FRE 613 deal with different methods of impeachment, the Advisory Committee's Note to FRE 613 states, "Under the principles of *expression unius* the rule does not apply to impeachment by evidence of prior inconsistent conduct." [Emphasis in original.] This statement may mean nothing more than that a party cannot admit extrinsic evidence for the purpose of establishing a witness' prior dishonest act on the theory that proof of the act is "inconsistent" with the witness' denial of having committed the act. If so, we agree with the Advisory Committee, for to accept such an argument in favor of admissibility would subvert the FRE 608(b) prohibition against extrinsic evidence to prove bad acts probative of a witness' trustworthiness. It should be permissible, however, to introduce extrinsic evidence of prior inconsistent conduct pursuant to FRE 613(b) if the conduct is offered to prove an express or implied communication that is inconsistent with the witness' testimony.

Consider, for example, the following situation: A cross-examiner, for the purpose of impeaching a witness' credibility, asks if the witness robbed a jewelry store, and the witness denies having robbed the jewelry store. Assuming the inquiry is a proper FRE 608(b) inquiry in the first place, FRE 608(b) should prohibit introduction of eyewitness identification testimony or other extrinsic evidence offered for the purpose of proving that the witness committed the robbery to show that the witness is an untrustworthy character and, therefore, perhaps being dishonest on the witness stand. FRE 608(b), however, should not prohibit and, subject only to FRE 403, FRE 613 should permit extrinsic evidence (1) that the witness previously wrote a note admitting the robbery, (2) that the witness nodded affirmatively when accused of committing the robbery, and (3) that the witness was seen fleeing from the scene of the robbery. In each of these latter instances the evidence is legitimately usable not to prove the truth of the matter asserted or implied by the writing or conduct but rather to prove an inconsistency between what the witness asserted on the witness stand and what the witness asserted or appeared to imply earlier.

FRE 806 affirms the propriety of impeaching a witness with evidence of inconsistent conduct of the type illustrated in the preceding paragraph. We noted in Chapter Five that hearsay declarants, like other witnesses, are subject to impeachment and rehabilitation. FRE 806 recognizes this possibility. Since the hearsay declarant may be unavailable, FRE 806 sensibly provides that the FRE 613 requirement of an opportunity for the witness to explain the inconsistency does not apply to the impeachment of hearsay declarants. The rule also sensibly provides that the inconsistency need not occur prior to the time of the hearsay declaration. In so providing, the rule refers to impeachment by inconsistent statements *or conduct*:

> . . . Evidence of a statement or conduct by the declarant at any time, inconsistent with the declarant's hearsay statement, is not subject to any requirement that the declarant may have been afforded an opportunity to deny or explain. . . .

Why do you suppose there is reference to inconsistent conduct here and a reference to prohibiting evidence of inconsistent conduct in the Advisory Committee's Note to FRE 613?

PROBLEMS

1. Diane Draper has been charged with illegal possession of heroin. Seeking to establish that Ms. Draper had made a false exculpatory statement, the prosecution called Emily Klein and asked her whether Ms. Draper said that the police had planted the heroin in her apartment. Emily Klein responded that she did not remember whether Ms. Draper made such a statement. The prosecution now calls an assistant prosecutor to testify that in a pre-trial interview Emily Klein did make such a statement. Is the evidence admissible?

2. Danny Dickson has been charged with murdering a fellow prison inmate. Three inmates testified for the prosecution that Danny committed the murder, and none of them was cross-examined. Later in the trial Danny offered the testimony of two other inmates to the effect that the prosecution witnesses had told them that Danny had not committed the murder. The prosecution objects to this evidence. What result?

3. David Dooley is being prosecuted for conspiracy to distribute narcotics. Carl Cooper, a co-conspirator who had pleaded guilty to the same offense was the chief prosecution witness. During cross-examination Cooper asserted that he did not know until after his guilty plea that he would be required to testify against Dooley. Later in the trial Dooley called Cooper's former girl friend Willa Watson, who offers to testify that prior to pleading guilty Cooper told her that part of the plea agreement was his willingness to testify for the government. Should the government's objection to this evidence be sustained?

4. Dawson is being prosecuted for vehicular homicide. Williams, a police officer, testifies for the prosecution: "Immediately before the accident I observed Dawson's car traveling at a high rate of speed in violation of the posted speed limit." Later in the trial Dawson offers William's accident report, which says nothing about the speed of Dawson's car. Should the evidence be admitted?

E. **Impeachment and Rehabilitation with a Witness' Prior Statements**   537

2. Prior Consistent Statements

We noted at the beginning of this chapter that it is impermissible to bolster a witness' credibility until the witness' credibility has been impeached. Since proof of a prior consistent statement tends to bolster credibility, the critical question with respect to the use of prior consistent statements is what type of impeachment will warrant responding with proof of such a statement. The common law rule was that a prior consistent statement is admissible only to rebut an express or implied charge of recent fabrication or improper influence. Thus, for example, if defense counsel established that a plaintiff's witness might be biased because the defendant had recently fired the witness, a consistent statement made by the witness prior to the time of the events that led to the firing would be admissible. There was no prohibition against the use of extrinsic evidence, so the consistency could be established either through the examination of the witness or with other evidence.

If the consistent statement in our firing hypothetical were made subsequent to the firing, the statement would not be admissible. The same motive to fabricate existed then that exists at the time of trial, and the motive to fabricate appears to be a likely explanation for the consistency. If the evidence has any probative value to rehabilitate, i.e., to suggest care and accuracy in speaking about the matter that is the subject of the testimony, the probative value is likely to be so low that the countervailing FRE 403 factors will justify exclusion. Discussions of the common law use of prior consistent statements typically articulate a generally applicable requirement that the consistent statement be made prior to the time of the alleged bias, improper influence, or other circumstances providing the motive to fabricate.

At common law witnesses who were impeached with evidence of bad character for trustworthiness were generally not subject to rehabilitation with prior consistent statements. The rationale for this limitation is that proving consistency does not tend to rebut the character trait. The difficulty with the rationale is that a witness' character for trustworthiness is not itself an issue in the case. Rather, the character evidence is introduced for the purpose of inferring action in conformity with character, i.e., being untrustworthy on the witness stand. Even if the character trait is firmly established, individuals do not always act in conformity with character. A prior consistent statement may suggest that the witness' testimony is not behavior in conformity with the supposed dishonest character trait. On the other hand, the consistency may show nothing more than that the witness with a dishonest character trait is consistently dishonest.

Which of these inferences is the more reasonable one probably depends primarily on whether the witness had some particular motive to fabricate and whether the statement was made prior to the time that the motive to fabricate arose. If there were some particular reason—in addition to evidence of bad character for trustworthiness—for believing that the trial testimony was recently fabricated, then, as in the preceding firing example, evidence of the prior consistent statement should be admissible or inadmissible depending on whether the statement was made prior or subsequent to the time that the particular motive to fabricate arose. If there were no evidence of recent fabrication or improper influence, there would be no particular reason to believe that the witness was consistently lying in the two statements. Thus, a reasonable inference to draw from the consistency would be that the witness' testimony was not action in conformity with the witness' supposedly dishonest character trait. Whether this inference is sufficiently strong in an individual case to warrant admissibility should turn on an FRE 403-type balancing of probative value and countervailing concerns, not on a flat rule that rehabilitation with prior consistent statements is impermissible when the impeachment is limited to showing bad character for trustworthiness.

Most common law courts also precluded rehabilitation with proof of a prior consistent statement after impeachment with an inconsistent statement. Some courts maintained that evidence of the consistency was irrelevant because it could not undo the inconsistency; other courts stressed a desire to avoid turning the litigation into a battle over prior statements. Whatever the reason for the traditional common law approach, we believe that a flat prohibition against the use of consistent statements to rehabilitate a witness following evidence of an inconsistency is undesirable. The use of prior consistent statements to rehabilitate following evidence of inconsistency, like the use of prior consistent statements following evidence of bad character for trustworthiness, should be evaluated in terms of an FRE 403 balancing test. We take this position for two reasons.

First, a possible explanation for the inconsistency may be—indeed, we believe it is often likely to be—that the trial court testimony is recently fabricated. To the extent that this inference depends on crediting the truth of the prior inconsistent statement, it is a theoretically impermissible inference if the inconsistent statement was admitted only for the non-hearsay purpose of proving inconsistency. It is, nonetheless, an inference that the jury may draw. Moreover, it is arguably reasonable to infer, if not recent fabrication, at least improper influence or motive from the mere fact of inconsistency: The inconsistency suggests that something, perhaps some improper pressure, led to the inconsistency; and even though the trial testimony, not the inconsistent statement, may be true, the pressure or motive may have led the witness to testify falsely in other respects. In short, even though courts in dealing with prior consistent statements traditionally have distinguished between rebutting a mere inconsistency (impermissible) and rebutting a charge of recent fabrication or improper influence or motive (permissible), the distinction is largely nonexistent.

The second problem with a general prohibition against the use of prior consistent statements to rehabilitate following evidence of an inconsistency is that the consistent statements may frequently be quite relevant apart from their probative value to rebut a charge of recent fabrication or improper influence or motive. If the most likely explanation for the inconsistency is

E. Impeachment and Rehabilitation with a Witness' Prior Statements

not lying but lack of care or attention to the subject matter, proof of numerous other statements consistent with the trial statement suggests that the prior inconsistent statement was an incorrect slip of the tongue. More importantly, there may frequently be a dispute over whether or in what context the inconsistent statement was made. Proof of a prior statement consistent with the trial testimony suggests that the alleged prior inconsistent statement may not have been made or that in context it may not have been as inconsistent as the impeaching party claims it is.

The only provision in the Federal Rules dealing with the use of prior consistent statements is FRE 801(d)(1)(B), which exempts from the definition of hearsay a witness' statement that is "consistent with the declarant's testimony and is offered to rebut an express or implied charge against the declarant of recent fabrication or improper influence or motive." As the Advisory Committee acknowledges, these are the purposes for which prior consistent statements "traditionally have been admissible" for non-hearsay rehabilitation purposes. Thus, as we noted in Chapter Five, FRE 801(d)(1)(B) makes admissible for their truth prior consistent statements that at common law were admissible only to rehabilitate a witness.

What is not clear is whether FRE 801(d)(1)(B) implicitly limits the extent to which prior consistent statements may be used in federal courts for non-hearsay rehabilitation purposes. According to one view, FRE 801(d)(1)(B) is nothing more than a hearsay exemption.[23] Since there is no rule restricting the use of prior consistent statements for non-hearsay purposes, the admissibility of prior consistent statements to rehabilitate should be governed by FRE 401-403. Thus, for example, there will be times when it is appropriate to introduce a prior consistent statement following evidence of a "mere" inconsistency or evidence of bad character for trustworthiness, and the party against whom the evidence is admitted will be entitled to an instruction that the jury cannot consider the prior consistent statement for its truth.

An alternative view is that the drafters' implicit objective was to prohibit the use of prior consistent statements for non-hearsay as well as hearsay purposes unless the statements were offered to rebut an express or implied charge of recent fabrication or improper influence or motive.[24] In other words, the intent of the drafters was to create a hearsay exemption for all of the situations in which they assumed prior consistent statements would be admissible for non-hearsay purposes.

Although our personal preference is for an interpretation of the Federal Rules that liberalizes the potential admissibility of prior consistent statements, we doubt that the drafters of the Federal Rules contemplated this possibility. There is nothing in the legislative history to suggest that the Advisory Committee or Congress thought prior statements not meeting the criteria of FRE 801(d)(1)(B) would be admissible for non-hearsay purposes. More impor-

---

23. See, e.g., United States v. Pierre, 781 F.2d 329 (2d Cir. 1986).
24. See, e.g., United States v. Quinto, 582 F.2d 224 (2d Cir. 1978).

tantly, we can think of no reason why a sensible drafter would provide that only some prior consistent statements could be admitted for their truth, much less why the permissible uses of an admissible consistent statement should turn on whether the statement was offered to rebut a charge of recent fabrication or improper influence or motive.[25]

If our assumption about the drafters' intent is correct, what impact should that assumption have on the interpretation of FRE 801(d)(2)(B)? Should the impact depend upon a determination whether the drafters affirmatively contemplated restricting the use of prior consistent statements for non-hearsay purposes or whether the drafters merely assumed without examination that the common law uses were the only appropriate ones? If so, how can you discern what the drafters had in mind? And if you cannot determine what they thought, what implication does this fact have for interpreting FRE 801(d)(2)(B)?

PROBLEMS

1. Dan Dawley is charged with a robbery that occurred on August 23. The trial is taking place in the second week of November. Alice Alibi testifies for Dawley that she was with him at a movie when the robbery occurred.

The prosecution, after laying an appropriate foundation for a prior inconsistent statement and eliciting Alice's denial of the statement, calls Wilma Woods who offers to testify as follows: "Last week Alice told me that when she was with Dan Dawley several months ago they had gotten some easy money." The court, over Dawley's objection, admits the evidence.

Now Dawley wants to introduce the testimony of Rene Rogers, a police officer, that during her investigation of the robbery and prior to the time of Alice's alleged statement to Wilma Woods Alice told her that she had been at a movie with Dawley when the robbery occurred.

Was the trial court's ruling on the admissibility of Wilma Woods' testimony correct? Should Rene Rogers' testimony be admitted over the prosecution's objection?

2. Pam Peters has brought an action for personal injuries against the Ace Department Store for injuries that she claims to have sustained when

---

25. One might raise a similar question regarding the wisdom of FRE 801(d)(1)(A), which permits prior inconsistent statements to be used for their truth only if they were made under oath: Why should only inconsistent statements under oath be admissible for their truth, particularly if statements not under oath may be admissible for non-hearsay impeachment purposes? The answer is clear, if not enlightened. Prior inconsistent statements have traditionally been admissible to impeach without regard to whether they were made under oath, and the version of FRE 801(d)(1)(A) promulgated by the Supreme Court, which did not contain the oath restriction, in effect made all of these statements admissible for their truth. The FRE 801(d)(1)(A) oath requirement was added during congressional consideration of the Federal Rules as a compromise between those who favored the Supreme Court version of the rule and those who wanted to prohibit the use of prior inconsistent statements for their truth unless the statements had been both under oath and subject to cross-examination.

E. Impeachment and Rehabilitation with a Witness' Prior Statements 541

she fell on some ice in the parking lot on January 23. Ms. Peters first consulted an attorney in March, and the suit was filed in April. The trial is taking place the following December. On direct examination Ms. Peters testified about the accident, the severe bruises that she suffered, and the continuing back and head aches that she has had almost continuously from the day of the injury. During cross-examination defense counsel elicited the fact that Ms. Peters did not mention the fall or her alleged injuries when she visited her doctor for a routine check-up on March 1. Later in the trial the defendant offered the testimony of two women who have monthly bridge games with Ms. Peters to the effect that Ms. Peters said nothing about the fall or any injuries at their bridge games on January 30 and on February 28. Plaintiff objects to the admissibility of this evidence.

In rebuttal, the plaintiff offers the testimony of Ed Peters, Ms. Peters' husband, that she told him about the accident on January 23 and that she has frequently mentioned head and back aches—at least two or three times a week ever since January 23. The plaintiff also offers the testimony of one of her bridge partners that she discussed the accident and her injuries at the May bridge party. The defendant has objected to the testimony of both witnesses.

Should either plaintiff's or the defendant's objection be sustained? Does your answer depend upon whether the jurisdiction follows the common law or the Federal Rules?

3. Reconsider Problem 1 at page 381 supra. For what purposes is the evidence relevant? admissible?

3. Impeachment of Experts With Statements in Treatises

Prior to the adoption of the Federal Rules some jurisdictions recognized a hearsay exception for learned treatises. The exception, however, did not receive broad acceptance, and where it existed courts tended to interpret it narrowly. Nonetheless, statements in learned treatises were frequently admissible for the non-hearsay purpose of impeaching the credibility of an expert witness. Analytically, the process of using treatises in this manner is analogous to the use of prior statements for non-hearsay purposes: Initially, the witness had to acknowledge either reliance on the treatise or, in some jurisdictions, that the treatise was authoritative. This acknowledgment, in effect, constituted an adoption of the statements in the treatise. If statements in the treatise happened to be inconsistent with the witness' testimony, they were then admissible for the non-hearsay purpose of impeaching the witness' credibility.

Just as a witness impeached with an ordinary inconsistent statement has an opportunity to account for the inconsistency, the expert could attempt to account for the apparent inconsistency in the treatise. Such an explanation might involve reading additional statements from the treatise for the purpose of putting the supposedly inconsistent statement in proper context or explaining why it was not appropriate to rely on that part of the treatise. As in the use of ordinary prior statements, however, it would not be appropriate to read consistent passages in the treatise to bolster the expert's testimony: Traditionally, the mere showing of an inconsistency, as opposed to making an express or implied charge of recent fabrication or improper influence or motive, is not the type of impeachment that permits response with evidence of a prior consistent statement.

FRE 803(18) contains a relatively broad hearsay exception for learned treatises. The Advisory Committee acknowledged that in part the rationale for this hearsay exception is that it "avoids the unreality of admitting evidence for the purpose of impeachment only, with an instruction to the jury not to consider it otherwise." The hearsay exception, however, does not require that any particular expert rely on or acknowledge the treatise as authoritative, nor does it require that the statements in the treatise be inconsistent with any expert's testimony. Thus, as other portions of the Advisory Committee's Note make clear, the purpose of the exception is to permit affirmative use of statements in learned treatises apart from whatever impeachment value they may have.

If a statement in a treatise is admissible for its truth, there is no need to consider its possible admissibility for impeachment purposes. If the statement is not admissible for its truth, then one must turn to the prior statement analogy to find a possible non-hearsay basis for admission.

F. OTHER IMPEACHMENT TECHNIQUES

In addition to permitting evidence of bad character for trustworthiness and of inconsistent statements, the common law permitted the impeachment of witnesses with evidence relevant to four other subjects: unorthodox religious beliefs, bias, mental or sensory incapacity, and contradiction. FRE 610 specifically prohibits relying on the content of a witness' religious beliefs to assess credibility:

> Evidence of the beliefs or opinions of a witness on matters of religion is not admissible for the purpose of showing that by reason of their nature, the witness' credibility is impaired or enhanced.

The Federal Rules do not address the other impeachment techniques at all. Thus, admissibility of evidence for the purpose of showing something about

F. Other Impeachment Techniques

a witness' bias or mental or sensory capacity or for the purpose of contradicting a witness should be governed by FRE 401-403.[26]

1. Bias

Modern courts and commentators frequently attach the label "bias" to what Wigmore identified as three methods of showing a witness' "emotional incapacity." According to Wigmore:

> Three different *kinds of emotion* constituting untrustworthy partiality may be broadly distinguished—bias, interest, and corruption:
>
> *Bias*, in common acceptance, covers all varieties of hostility or prejudice against the opponent *personally* or of favor to the proponent personally. [E.g., intimate family relationship with one of the parties.]
>
> *Interest* signifies the specific inclination which is apt to be produced by the relation between the witness and the *cause at issue* in the litigation. [E.g., the expectation of favorable treatment from the prosecutor or sentencing judge in return for the testimony.]
>
> *Corruption* is here to be understood as the *conscious false intent* which is inferrible from giving or taking a bribe or from expressions of a general unscupulousness [sic] for the case at hand. [E.g., an attempt to bribe another witness[27] or the receipt of money for testimony.]
>
> The kinds of evidence available are two:
>
> (a) the *circumstances of the witness' situation*, making it "a priori" probable that he has some partiality of emotion for one party's cause;
> (b) the *conduct of the witness* himself, indicating the presence of such partiality, the inference here being from the expression of the feeling to the feeling itself. [3A J. Wigmore, Evidence in Trials at Common Law §947, p.782 (Chadbourn rev. 1976) (emphasis original).]

---

26. Earlier in noting the absence of any rule dealing with the non-hearsay use of prior consistent statements, we suggested that it may be reasonable to infer that the drafters intended for courts to make admissibility determinations in accordance with the common law rules governing the use of consistent statements rather than in accordance with FRE 401-401. To the extent that suggestion is sound, it rests on the fact that we could not understand why only some prior consistent statements—those meeting the common law criteria for admissibility—should be admissible for their truth. There is no similar reason to believe that evidence of bias, mental or sensory capacity, or contradiction should be governed by common law principles rather than FRE 401-403.

27. If a party attempts to bribe a witness, evidence of the attempted bribe is admissible, regardless of whether the party is a witness, to infer that the party is guilty or liable. Since the conduct is probably not intended as an assertion of guilt or liability, it would probably not be regarded as hearsay. If it were classified as hearsay within the meaning of FRE 801(a)-(c), it would still be admissible against the party as an admission. FRE 801(d)(2)(A).

In the case of a witness who is not a party, the relevance of words or conduct suggesting corruption or some other form of bias is to suggest a mind-set that may lead the witness to be untruthful on the witness stand. If the evidence is characterized as hearsay, the state-of-mind exception will be available to overcome the hearsay objection.—Eds.

We shall follow the common practice of referring to all of these matters as "bias."

All common law courts permitted proof of a witness' bias both by way of examination of the witness and with extrinsic evidence. Some, but not all, courts required the impeaching party to lay a foundation similar to the prior inconsistent foundation as a condition of admitting extrinsic evidence of bias: The witness had to be asked specifically about the bias before extrinsic evidence of bias could be introduced.

Had the Federal Rules retained the common law foundation requirement in the prior inconsistent statement context, there would be a plausible argument that the same requirement should apply with respect to evidence of bias. As we noted earlier, however, FRE 613(b) imposes only the minimal requirement that the witness have an opportunity to explain or deny the statement. Neither FRE 613(b) nor the Advisory Committee's Note suggests that a similar requirement should apply to impeachment with bias. Prior to the adoption of the Federal Rules, however, a number of federal courts had held that the common law foundation requirement for extrinsic evidence of inconsistent statements was applicable to impeachment with evidence of bias; and following the adoption of the Federal Rules, some courts have held that the relaxed FRE 613 requirement is applicable to impeachment with evidence of bias. Since the requirement is only that the witness have an opportunity to explain or deny the statement (or bias), and since FRE 613(b) acknowledges that "the interests of justice" may warrant foregoing even this requirement, application of FRE 613 to both bias and inconsistent statements should not be a significant roadblock to effective impeachment.

A troublesome issue that sometimes arises—particularly with the type of evidence that Wigmore refers to as "corruption"—is whether the evidence should fit within the "bias" category or the "character" category. For example, is proof that the witness attempted to bribe another witness evidence of corruption/bias, or is it evidence of character? The issue is important because extrinsic evidence of the witness' conduct is admissible to prove bias but not to prove character.

The issue is difficult to resolve in part because the term *character* is not defined and probably not definable in any very helpful sense. The *approach* to resolving the issue, however, is relatively straightforward and consistent with the manner in which courts distinguish between inadmissible "character" evidence and potentially admissible specific acts evidence in applying FRE 404(b): To the extent that it is reasonable to infer from the corrupt act that the witness has some particular concern about or interest in the outcome of the present litigation, the evidence has relatively high probative value on the question whether the witness' testimony is truthful. Thus, it seems appropriate to attach the bias label to the evidence in order to permit exploration of the matter with extrinsic evidence. On the other hand, if the most reasonable inference to draw from the corrupt act is that the individual has a general lack of integrity or disregard for the proper operation of the judicial

F. Other Impeachment Techniques

system, the probative value of the evidence to suggest untruthfulness on one specific occasion on the witness stand is relatively low. This evidence should receive the "character" label in order to prevent the possibility of time-consuming and distracting exploration of the matter with extrinsic evidence. In short, as Wigmore observed, "The only distinction that is here legitimate is between conduct indicating a corrupt moral character in general and conduct indicating a specific corrupt intention for the case at hand." Id. at §963, pp. 808-810.

Would it be desirable to abandon the distinction between "character" and "bias" and always to treat the question whether extrinsic acts evidence can be introduced in terms of FRE 403? Reconsider pages 248-265 supra, which raises the same question with respect to the character evidence prohibition in FRE 404(b).

PROBLEMS

1. Jack Lucas is being prosecuted for mail fraud and theft. Edward Eads, a victim of the alleged mail fraud scheme, is an important prosecution witness. Zeke Zamora is a character witness for the defendant.

   (a) On cross-examination of Eads, Lucas seeks to inquire about the details of several civil actions that Eads has filed against Lucas. The desired inquiry includes reference to the amount of damages sought in each suit, the total amount of which is over $500,000. These civil actions are based on the same facts that have given rise to the present criminal prosecution.

   (b) On cross-examination of Zamora, the prosecution seeks to inquire about the fact that in an earlier civil action involving Mrs. Zamora, Eads had given testimony that was adverse to Mrs. Zamora's interest.

To what extent should the court permit these inquiries?

2. Stella Starlet is a rising movie star, rock singer, and television personality. She has sued Frances Fisher, her former manager and agent, for fraud and breach of contract. Stella's services were in great demand, and according to the complaint Ms. Fisher would negotiate contracts only with individuals willing to pay a substantial sum, above the negotiated contract amount, in cash directly to Frances. One of Stella's key witnesses is Ken Olsen, a former employee of Frances Fisher. Olsen testified in detail about Ms. Fisher's demanding and receiving sums to book Stella that were never accounted for. The following cross-examination of Olsen took place without objection:

Q: Do you know Stella Starlet personally?

546   Chapter Six. Cross-Examination, Impeachment, and Rehabilitation

A: Yes.
Q: You're quite fond of her, aren't you?
A: Well, I like her and respect her.
Q: You feel indebted to her, don't you?
A: Indebted? No.
Q: Isn't it true that in the two months prior to this trial she has taken you to dinner at expensive restaurants on at least seven occasions?
A: No, she has never done that.
Q: And isn't it true that last month she bought you diamond cuff links and a new set of expensive golf clubs?
A: No.
Q: Two weeks ago when you were having lunch with your friend Tom Thompson at the River Edge Cafe, didn't you tell Thompson that Stella had taken you to dinner seven times in the last two months and that she had bought you diamond cuff links and new golf clubs?
A: No.

As part of its defense, the defendant calls Tom Thompson to testify that two weeks ago at the River Edge Cafe, Ken Olsen was bragging that he had had dinner with Stella Starlet on seven occasions in the last two months and that she recently bought him diamond cuff links and new golf clubs. Should this evidence be admitted over plaintiff's objection?

3. Clarence Green, an inmate, has filed a federal civil rights action against Bull Brackton, a prison guard who shot and severely wounded Green. Green claims that the shooting was an unprovoked attack, and Brackton claims that he shot Green in self-defense. Elmer Novak, another prison guard, testifies for the defense that he observed the entire incident, that Green attacked Brackton, and that Brackton shot Green to avoid the infliction of serious bodily injury by Green. Green is a black man; Brackton and Novak are white. Consider whether the following evidence should be admitted over the opposing party's objection:

On cross-examination of Novak, plaintiff's counsel asks:

(a) whether Novak is a member of the John Birch Society;
(b) whether Novak had referred to Green as a "no good nigger";
(c) whether Novak physically assaulted a black youth following a minor automobile accident involving the youth and Novak;
(d) whether Elmer Novak had told the warden that Brackton had been taunting Green with racial slurs prior to the attack.

(Assume that the plaintiff has a reasonable factual basis for asking each of the preceding questions. Assume further that if the objections are overruled the witness will respond affirmatively to the first question and negatively to the last three questions.)

On re-direct examination, defense counsel seeks to establish:

F. Other Impeachment Techniques

(e) that Novak is an active member of the Christian Church of Holiness, whose membership is 40 percent black.

As part of its rebuttal, the plaintiff calls a black youth to testify:

(f) that last month he accidentally backed his car into Brackton's car in a parking lot, that Brackton became enraged, used racial epithets, and beat him.

In rebuttal the plaintiff also offers the following testimony of Al Jensen, Green's cellmate:

(g) that he has known Elmer Novak and people that know Elmer Novak both in prison and in the community for the last 15 years and that Elmer Novak has a reputation both within the prison and in the outside community for racial prejudice and bigotry;
(h) that he had heard Novak call Green a "no good nigger" on a number of occasions;
(i) that he had heard Novak tell the warden that immediately before the attack Brackton had been taunting Green with racial slurs.
(j) that he personally had witnessed two occasions on which Novak and Brackton together made unprovoked attacks on black inmates.

In rebuttal, the defendant offers the following evidence:

(k) the evidence in (e), supra, in the event that it was excluded previously;
(l) testimony of the warden that he was away from the prison at the time of the attack, that he arrived at the prison six hours later and immediately sought to interview all witnesses, and that at that time Elmer Novak said to him, "Warden, the tall black prisoner, Clarence Green, made an unprovoked attack on Bull Brackton, who had to shoot Green in self-defense."
(m) the testimony of Glen Smith, another inmate, that he did not see the attack, but that Clarence Green threatened to slit his throat if he, Smith, did not volunteer to testify that the defendant made an unprovoked attack on the plaintiff.

2. Mental or Sensory Incapacity

Any sensory or mental deficiency that inhibits a witness' ability to perceive events accurately at the time they occur or to remember and to narrate accurately what happened at the time of trial is relevant to cast doubt on the witness' credibility. Thus, for example, it is relevant to prove that a witness suffers from faulty memory, some form of mental illness that contributes to a witness' inability to distinguish fact from fantasy, intoxication at the time of the event to which the testimony relates or while on the witness stand, or color blindness if accuracy with respect to color is important. Subject, of course, to a court's discretion to control the mode of cross-examination (see, e.g., FRE 611(a)) and to balance probative value against prejudice, confusion, and consumption of time (see, e.g., FRE 403), it is permissible to inquire about these matters during the examination of the witness whose sensory or mental condition is at issue. In addition, evidence of sensory or mental deficiency traditionally has not been regarded as evidence of a character trait; it is evidence of a sensory or mental incapacity, not a moral incapacity. Thus, the restrictions on the use of character evidence are inapplicable, and courts frequently hold that it is permissible to introduce extrinsic evidence on these matters. For example, courts have permitted extrinsic evidence of strange, seemingly irrational acts of a witness, expert testimony from a psychiatrist about a witness' mental capacity, and courtroom experiments to demonstrate a witness' poor memory.

Despite the general recognition of the proposition that evidence of sensory or mental incapacity is not character evidence, a number of decisions preclude the use of extrinsic evidence to prove sensory or mental incapacity. Commentators tend to look for general principles to explain these decisions. For example, McCormick states that a mental or sensory " 'abnormality' " may be shown by extrinsic evidence but that the decisions "are divided" on the question whether it is permissible to introduce extrinsic evidence to prove "defects of mind within the range of normality, such as a slower than average mind or poorer than usual memory."[28] These types of generalizations may be roughly accurate descriptive statements. The decisions, however, are quite diverse, and the generalizations are often quite imprecise. Moreover, as McCormick and other commentators recognize, it is not desirable to have general rules of exclusion in this area. Rather, it is appropriate to decide on a case-by-case basis how extensive a cross-examination to permit and how much, if any, extrinsic evidence to introduce on a witness' sensory or mental incapacity. The Federal Rules take this approach. In the absence of any exclusionary rule, admissibility decisions must be made in terms of FRE 401-403, FRE 611(a), and if expert testimony is offered, FRE 702-706.

In considering an individual's mental incapacity it is important not to confuse mental incapacity as a subject matter for impeachment with mental incapacity as a complete bar to testimony. Early in the development of the common law, courts barred individuals regarded as mentally deranged or defective from testifying. Over time, however, courts and legislatures relaxed or abandoned this and other prohibitions against testifying (e.g., lack of religious beliefs, conviction of certain crimes). Today there is no general

---

28. McCormick's Handbook on the Law of Evidence §45, pp. 104-105 (3d ed., Cleary, 1984).

F. Other Impeachment Techniques

prohibition against receiving the testimony of individuals with mental defects or mental illness. If an individual's mental deficiency prevents the individual from understanding the oath or the obligation to testify truthfully, however, that would be a legitimate reason for refusing to let the individual testify. See, e.g., FRE 603 ("Before testifying, every witness shall be required to declare that the witness will testify truthfully, by oath or affirmation administered in a form calculated to awaken the witness' conscience and impress the witness' mind with the duty to do so.")

PROBLEM

Al Drummond has been charged with possession and sale of cocaine. The key government witness is Jimmy Jones, an informant and, according to the government, a former co-conspirator in drug trafficking with Drummond. Jones had already pleaded guilty and been sentenced for his involvement in the drug incident for which Drummond is on trial. On cross-examination of Jones, defense counsel (with a factual basis for each question) asks:

(a) "Isn't it true that you are a heroin addict?"
(b) "Isn't it true that you are under the influence of heroin right now on the witness stand?"
(c) "Isn't it true that last week you sold two ounces of heroin to James Edwards?"

Are any of these questions objectionable? If objections are not made or are overruled, can the defendant later introduce extrinsic evidence to prove that Jones is an addict? was under the influence of heroin on the witness stand? sold heroin last week to James Edwards?

The defense calls as a witness Dr. Helen James, who is qualified as an expert on mental disorders. She offers to testify that she recently diagnosed Jimmy Jones as suffering from Allen-Kuhns syndrome, a severe mental disorder. Should plaintiff's objection to this evidence be sustained?

3. Contradiction

The last of the traditional methods of impeaching a witness' credibility is by means of contradiction—introducing evidence that contradicts something the witness has said. For example, if the witness said that she was wearing a yellow dress when she saw the automobile accident, it would contradict her testimony to establish that she was wearing a blue dress on that occasion; and if the witness can be shown to be incorrect about one thing, it is arguably appropriate to infer that the witness may be wrong about other things, including perhaps the substantively important aspects of the witness' testimony.

As Wigmore observed:

> The peculiar feature of [the] probative fact of error on a particular point [i.e., contradiction] is its *deficiency with respect to definiteness* and its *wide range with respect to possible significance*. Looking back over the various [impeachment devices] already considered, it will be seen that the evidence in those classes of cases was aimed clearly and specifically at a particular defect; it showed either that or nothing. Former perjury would indicate probably a deficient sense of moral duty to speak truth; relationship to the party, a probable inclination to distort the facts, consciously or unconsciously. . . .
>
> [Evidence of contradiction] is not offered as definitely showing any specific defect of any of these kinds, and yet it may justify an inference of the existence of any one or more of them. We know simply that an erroneous statement has been made on one point, and we infer that the witness is capable of making an erroneous statement on other points. We are not asked, and we do not attempt to specify, the particular defect which was the source of the proved error and which might therefore be the source of another error. The source might be a mental defect as to powers of observation or recollection; it might be a lack of veracity character; it might be bias or corruption. . . . The inference is only that since, for this proved error, there was *some unspecified defect* which became a source of error, the same defect may equally exist as the source of some other error, otherwise not apparent. [3A J. Wigmore, Evidence in Trials at Common Law §1000, pp. 957-958 (Chadbourn rev. 1970) (emphasis original).]

All of us, of course, from time to time make erroneous statements that can be contradicted. Thus, proof of a contradiction about something unrelated to the issues being litigated—e.g., that the witness in the preceding example was wearing a blue dress instead of a yellow dress—is often of only marginal probative value to impeach the witness' credibility.[29] For this reason, common law courts applied the "no extrinsic evidence to impeach on a collateral matter" dictum to impeachment with evidence of contradiction. Thus, for example, it may be permissible to permit some cross-examination about the color of the witness' dress at the time of the accident, but if the witness did not admit being wrong about the color of her dress, it would be impermissible to introduce extrinsic evidence on the matter.

What constitutes "collateralness" for the purpose of determining whether extrinsic evidence is admissible is not intuitively obvious. McCormick suggests that "the inquiry is best answered by determining what facts are not within the term," and then proceeds to list three such types of facts: facts relevant to the substantive issues in the case; facts relevant, apart from the

---

29. But consider the possibility of proving numerous erroneous statements about matters unrelated to the litigation. See 3A J. Wigmore, Evidence in Trials at Common Law §1000, p. 958 (Chadbourn rev. 1970).

F. Other Impeachment Techniques

contradiction, to impeach the credibility of a witness, if extrinsic evidence is generally admissible for the non-contradiction impeachment purpose; and facts recited by the witness that, if untrue, logically undermine the witness' story.[30]

The first of these categories of evidence should present no problem. Evidence that is directly relevant to the issues in litigation can be introduced for its substantive value apart from any impeachment value that it may have. Indeed, even the voucher rule does not prevent a party from calling a witness who will contradict another witness. In effect, the impeachment value of the evidence as a contradiction is secondary. As we stated earlier, if evidence is independently admissible, there is no need to consider whether it is also admissible for impeachment purposes. Thus, the value of stressing that this type of evidence is not precluded by the collateralness doctrine is only to make clear that the collateralness doctrine should not operate to preclude the use of otherwise independently admissible evidence.

The second category—contradiction on matters relevant, apart from contradiction to impeach, if extrinsic evidence would be admissible for the independent impeachment purpose—is only slightly more troublesome. Just as the collateralness doctrine should not prohibit the use of independently admissible substantive evidence, it should not prohibit use of extrinsic evidence that both contradicts the witness and also impeaches credibility in some other way, as long as it is clear that extrinsic evidence would be admissible for that independent impeachment purpose (e.g., to prove bias or a prior conviction). On the other hand, if a specific impeachment rule prohibits extrinsic evidence as FRE 608(b) does, it seems appropriate not to undermine that prohibition on the theory that proving a bad act the witness has denied contradicts the witness.

There is only one minor problem with the way the term *collateral* is traditionally applied to this second category of evidence. It is difficult to understand why, if "collateralness" has any independent substantive content, some impeachment devices are collateral and others are not. The answer, of course, is that, at least in this context, the concept "collateralness" does not have any independent coherent content. The term could be given a coherent meaning in one of two ways. First, one could maintain that contradiction that also impeaches a witness by showing what Wigmore called "a particular defect" is never collateral. When extrinsic evidence would not be admissible to prove the particular defect, however, the probative value of extrinsic evidence to establish a mere contradiction is substantially outweighed by the likelihood that the jury will improperly use the extrinsic evidence as proof of the particular defect. Alternatively, one could say that a contradiction that also impeaches a witness by showing a particular defect is always impeachment on a collateral matter, but recognize that the col-

---

30. McCormick's Handbook on the Law of Evidence §47, pp. 110-112 (3d ed., Cleary, 1984).

lateralness doctrine in the contradiction context does not take precedence over the rules permitting extrinsic evidence to prove a particular defect.

Whatever explanation seems more suitable, the result is clear: The ban on using extrinsic evidence to contradict on a collateral matter does not prohibit introducing extrinsic evidence to disprove the witness' denial when the evidence is relevant to impeach by one of the means for which extrinsic evidence is admissible; and if a rule prohibits extrinsic evidence for a particular impeachment evidence as FRE 608(b) does, one cannot get around that prohibition by arguing that the evidence is offered not for the prohibited purpose but to prove contradiction.

McCormick's third category of non-collateral contradiction evidence—contradictions that are not independently relevant to the issues in the law suit or to impeach the witness by showing a "particular defect" but that nonetheless logically undermine the witness' story—is probably the most significant. Here, since the extrinsic evidence by definition is not independently admissible, the only basis for admitting it is to establish that the contradiction is not on a collateral matter. To illustrate this third category, consider a personal injury action in which Sadie testifies for the plaintiff and explains that she happened to see the accident as she was walking home from the grocery store where she had gone to purchase milk for her children. Proof that Sadie bought cigarettes and beer instead of milk would contradict her story, but such proof would not logically undermine her testimony. What she bought is collateral. Thus, counsel on cross-examination could question Sadie about what she bought, but the counsel would have to accept her answers; extrinsic evidence would be inadmissible. On the other hand, evidence that Sadie had not been in the area of the grocery store at all suggests that she may not have seen the critical events to which she testified. Just as there would be no general prohibition against extrinsic evidence that Sadie was almost blind, there should be no prohibition against the use of extrinsic evidence suggesting that Sadie might not physically have been in a position to observe what she claimed to have seen. In short, proof that Sadie had not been in the vicinity of the grocery store at all on the day of the accident tends logically to undermine her story about the accident. Thus, it should not be regarded as collateral, and extrinsic evidence of her absence from the store should be admissible.

There is a commonly stated test for collateralness that, if properly understood and applied, is consistent with all we have said so far:

> Could the fact have been proven with extrinsic evidence for any purpose except to show a (mere) contradiction?

If the answer is "Yes," if, in other words, there is some permissible use for extrinsic evidence above and beyond its value as showing a mere contradiction, it is not collateral. On the other hand, if the only legitimate probative value of the evidence is to prove a contradiction, the extrinsic evidence is

F. Other Impeachment Techniques

collateral. Thus, for example, in our preceding illustrations it would not be collateral to prove by extrinsic evidence (a) a prior conviction that the witness denied committing, (b) facts constituting bias that the witness denied, (c) substantively relevant events that the witness denied, or (d) Sadie's absence from the grocery store. It would be collateral to prove (a) that the witness was wearing a blue dress instead of a yellow dress, (b) that the witness falsely denied committing a dishonest act, or (c) that Sadie bought cigarettes and beer. Moreover, if the jurisdiction had a general prohibition against the use of extrinsic evidence of a prior inconsistent statement about a collateral matter, and if the witness denied making such a statement, it would be inappropriate to introduce extrinsic evidence of that statement on the theory that it contradicted the witness: Because of the extrinsic evidence prohibition for collateral inconsistent statements, "the fact could not have been proven with extrinsic evidence for any purpose except to show a (mere) contradiction."

The only Federal Rules governing the use of extrinsic evidence to contradict are FRE 401-403. Nonetheless, the common law doctrine upon which we have been elaborating remains important in a jurisdiction that has adopted the Federal Rules for two reasons. First, mastering the common law doctrine of collateralness requires focusing on the inferential process involved in the use of evidence that contradicts a witness. This very focus on the inferential process is critical to a reasoned, persuasive argument about admissibility in FRE 403 terms. Second, since the common law collateralness doctrine is itself based on FRE 403-type concerns, we suspect that the question whether extrinsic evidence will be admissible to impeach by way of contradiction will usually be resolved in the same manner under both the common law and the Federal Rules.

Consider whether the court in the following case properly applied the common law collateralness test and whether the result would be the same under the Federal Rules.

STATE v. OSWALT
62 Wash. 2d 118, 381 P.2d 617 (1963)

HAMILTON, Judge. Defendant appeals, upon a short record, from a conviction of robbery and first degree burglary. During trial, a defense of alibi was introduced. Error is assigned to the admission of certain rebuttal testimony, defendant contending such evidence constituted impeachment on a collateral matter.

The short record before us (testimony of two witnesses) indicates that on July 14, 1961, two armed men entered the King County residence of Frank L. Goodell. One man stood guard over a number of people at the home. The other man took Mr. Goodell to a Tradewell store and forced him to open the safe and turn over the money therein. Defendant was identified as one of the two men.

In presenting his defense of alibi, defendant called a Mr. August Ardiss of Portland, Oregon. On direct examination Mr. Ardiss testified in substance that: his wife and he operated a restaurant in Portland; he was acquainted with the defendant, as a fairly regular patron of the restaurant; defendant was in the restaurant at such times on July 14, 1961, as to render it impossible, as a practical matter, for defendant to be in Seattle at the time of the offense charged; and he remembered this occasion because defendant had accompanied a restaurant employee to work, assisted in a part of her work, and escorted her home.

On cross-examination by the state, the following exchange took place:

Q: To the best of your knowledge would you say Oswalt had been in every day for the last couple of months or did he miss occasional periods of three or four days, or what was it?
A: No, I think he was in there every day. I really think he was in there every day.
Q: For the last couple months?
A: Yes.

In rebuttal, a police detective was permitted to testify, over defense objections, as follows:

Q: Did you see and talk to the defendant Mr. Oswalt on June 12, 1961?
A: I did.
Q: And in what city did you talk to him?
A: In the City of Seattle.
Q: And did you during that conversation ask him how long he had been in this city of Seattle at that time? . . .
A: I did.
Q: And how long did he state he had been in the City of Seattle?
A: He stated he had arrived in Seattle a couple days before I talked to him.
Q: Did he state where he had come from?
A: Portland, Oregon.

During colloquy between the trial court and counsel relative to the admissibility of the detective's testimony, the trial court commented: "There is no claim by Oswalt he wasn't in Seattle, Gilman [a co-defendant] claims that, but Oswalt doesn't."

It is to the rebuttal testimony of the police detective that defendant assigns error. The state, in response, contends such testimony to be admissible not only because it challenges the credibility of witness Ardiss, but also establishes defendant's presence in Seattle preparatory to the offense. It is a well-recognized and firmly established rule in this jurisdiction, and else-

F. Other Impeachment Techniques

where, that a witness cannot be impeached upon matters collateral to the principal issues being tried. . . .

The purpose of the rule is basically twofold: (1) avoidance of undue confusion of issues, and (2) prevention of unfair advantage over a witness unprepared to answer concerning matters unrelated or remote to the issues at hand. . . .

We, in common with other jurisdictions, have stated the test of collateralness to be: Could the fact, as to which error is predicated, have been shown in evidence for any purpose independently of the contradiction? . . .

We are handicapped by the limited record before us in evaluating the relationship of the contradictory evidence in question to the general issues presented in the trial.

So far as appears by this record, the sole issue raised by defendant's defense of alibi, through the direct testimony of witness Ardiss, was whether or not the defendant was or could have been in Seattle at the time of the offense on July 14, 1961. The defendant did not contend or seek to prove by this witness that he had not been in Seattle prior to such date. Thus, for purposes of impeaching this witness, whether the defendant was in Seattle on a given occasion one month prior to July 14th, was irrelevant and collateral. While a cross-examiner is, within the sound discretion of the trial court, permitted to inquire into collateral matters testing the credibility of a witness, he does so at the risk of being concluded by the answers given. State v. Anderson, 46 Wash. 2d 864, 285 P.2d 879.

The state, however, contends that the quoted testimony of Ardiss, as elicited by its cross-examination, carries with it an inference that defendant could not have been in Seattle sufficiently in advance of July 14, 1961, to have participated in necessary planning of and preparation for the offense. Upon the inference so erected, the state asserts the questioned testimony becomes material and admissible independently of its contradictory nature. The state further supports this argument by testimony elicited from the police detective to the effect that defendant admitted, in the interview of June 12, 1961, that he had purchased some adhesive tape.

Admittedly, relevant and probative evidence of preparations by an accused for the commission of a crime is admissible. State v. Stevenson, 169 Wash. 20, 13 P.2d 47. Based upon the limited record before us, however, the state's argument requires us to speculate that the defendant could not readily commute between Portland and Seattle, and that his presence in Seattle and acquisition of adhesive tape, upon an isolated occasion approximately a month before the offense in question, constituted significant evidence of planning and preparation for the offense in question, the particular mechanics of which are unrevealed by the record. This we decline to do, absent effort upon the part of the state to obtain a more complete record.

Upon the record before us, we must conclude it was error to admit the questioned testimony.

Having so concluded, we must next determine whether the error was prejudicial. State v. Moore, 35 Wash. 2d 106, 211 P.2d 172.

In State v. Britton, 27 Wash. 2d 336, 341, 178 P.2d 341, we said:

> A harmless error is an error which is trivial, or formal, or merely academic, and was not prejudicial to the substantial rights of the party assigning it, and in no way affected the final outcome of the case. . . . A prejudicial error is an error which affected the final result of the case and was prejudicial to a substantial right of the party assigning it.

In the instant case, the state's charge apparently rested upon an identification of the defendant by witnesses at the scene of the crime. The defense apparently rested upon alibi. The state seemingly considered the testimony of witness Ardiss sufficiently credible to require this attack. The defendant was convicted. It is difficult, therefore, to classify admission of the testimony in question trivial, formal, academic, or harmless, and to conclude that such did not affect the outcome of the case. The alternative is that it was prejudicial. We so hold.

The judgment is reversed and the cause remanded for new trial.

Ott, C.J., and Donworth, Hunter, and Finley, JJ., concur.

QUESTIONS AND PROBLEM

1. Was the evidence in *Oswalt* both irrelevant and collateral? Do you suppose that the alibi witness in *Oswalt* actually remembered the day of the crime, or is it possible that the witness merely assumed Oswalt had been in Portland on the day in question because of the witness' general recollection that Oswalt had been there every day for a month?

2. How was the evidence prejudicial? Assuming the unlikely possibility that the evidence was both collateral and outcome determinative, why should the erroneous admission of this collateral evidence warrant reversal?

3. D is charged with a liquor store robbery that occurred at eleven o'clock on a Sunday morning. To establish an alibi, W-1 testifies for D as follows: "On Sunday morning at 11:00 A.M., as I was walking out of church, I observed D across the street." (Other testimony establishes that the church and the liquor store are at opposite ends of the city.)

W-2 offers to testify for the prosecution that on Sunday morning at about 11:00 A.M. he saw W-1 walking out of an all-night bar. D objects to this evidence on the ground that it violates both FRE 608(b)'s prohibition against extrinsic evidence of specific instances of conduct and the general prohibition against the use of extrinsic evidence to impeach on a collateral matter. How should the court rule?

CHAPTER SEVEN

PROCESS OF PROOF IN CIVIL CASES: Burdens, Presumptions, Judicial Summary and Comment

We have studied in great detail the proof process at the level of individual elements. We have considered the way the law structures the relationship between the evidence produced by the parties and the substantive elements of any particular litigation. We have looked closely at the respective responsibilities of the trial judge and jury, and the way in which that relationship is governed by the specific relevancy rules. We turn now to a consideration of the manner in which trials are structured. This inquiry builds on what has come before in a number of different ways. As we saw in Chapter Three, the trial judge must make a preliminary determination of the possible relevancy of each proffer of proof. Those rulings will affect the ability of a party to prove a specific element of a case, and the ability to prove a specific element will in turn influence the likelihood of a party prevailing in litigation.

Even if all the evidence each party wishes to produce is admitted into evidence, the role of the trial judge is not at an end. Just as the trial judge must make a preliminary determination concerning the logical force of any offered evidence, so too does the judge make a preliminary determination of the overall strength of each party's case. The trial judge is empowered to issue preclusive rulings—rulings that terminate the litigation—at various stages in the proceedings based in large measure on the judge's assessment as to how reasonable people would analyze the evidence offered at trial. It is in part the rules governing this process that are the subject matter of this chapter. Whereas previously we analyzed the judge-jury relationship from the perspective of individual elements, here we view that relationship from the perspective of the case as a whole.

We shall also see that in addition to simply determining the sufficiency of the evidence to go to the jury, the trial judge has various means to influence the jury's deliberations on the evidence. We have already seen one indirect instance of such a power. By ruling on the admissibility of specific proffers, the judge can dramatically influence the jury's perspective. For example, if a judge finds that a proposed witness lacks personal knowledge and thus cannot be placed on the stand, the jury will not have before it that witness' testimony. Suppose that witness would have contradicted an important witness of the adversary. By excluding the witness, the judge affects the proof process by constraining the jury's perspective. Similarly, a judge will decide whether to admit evidence that casts doubt on the credibility of the testimony of a witness. A jury that has heard that a witness has reason to be biased against a party is likely to view the evidence that witness provides quite differently from a jury that did not have access to the impeaching testimony. Thus the judge, by deciding questions of the admissibility of evidence, has significant power to influence the deliberative process.

There are other ways in which the judge influences the jury's perspective. In some jurisdictions the judge has the power to sum up the evidence for the benefit of the jury. Subtle shifts of emphasis by the judge in summing up, even if unintended, may communicate to the jury the judge's view of aspects of the case. That, of course, may influence the jury's view, since the judge is likely to be an authority figure of some importance. In some jurisdictions the judge has the power to influence directly the jury's deliberations by expressing an opinion about the evidence by commenting on it. When this occurs, the jury is informed of the judge's appraisal of the evidence and its implications, and again this surely has an impact in many cases. These processes, too, will be studied here.

We consider here the process of proof in civil cases only. Civil cases must be treated separately from criminal cases because the constitutional requirement of proof beyond reasonable doubt affects the discretion legislatures have in allocating burdens of proof in criminal cases. In Chapter Eight, we turn our attention to process of proof in criminal cases.

A. BURDENS OF PROOF IN CIVIL CASES: THE BURDEN OF PRODUCING EVIDENCE AND RELATED ISSUES

Rules structuring the process of proof are derived from, and implement, a theory of dispute resolution. The dominant theory of dispute resolution in this country, and the one to which the rules of evidence are particularly important, is the adversarial process. The adversarial process, in turn, is derived from underlying conceptions of the appropriate role of the organized institutions of government in the resolution of disputes between private individuals. In the Anglo-American tradition, that role has generally been

A. The Burden of Production

perceived as primarily facilitative. The government has the obligation to provide a fair and disinterested forum for the impartial resolution of private disputes; and for the most part that is all the government has an obligation, or a right, to do.

This conception of the role of the government in the resolution of disputes is not universally shared, of course. In many Western European countries disputes are not "private" matters to the extent that they are in the United States, and the government plays a much more active role in virtually all phases of litigation. The government often is actively involved in investigation, and the trial process is controlled much more by the court than by the litigants. To the extent the resolution of disputes is viewed as a matter of collective concern, such procedures make very good sense. For a discussion of this and related matters, see Damaska, The Faces of Justice and State Authority (1986), and Damaska, Evidentiary Barriers to Conviction and Two Models of Criminal Procedure, 121 U. Pa. L. Rev. 506 (1973). In this country, by contrast, since private disputes are not understood to be matters of social concern for the most part, the government plays a much less active role. The parties are responsible for investigating the case, preparing the case for trial, and in large measure controlling the presentation of evidence at trial. Similarly, appellate courts often purport to decide cases based only on the arguments presented to them by the parties, thus generating the possibility that cases with virtually identical facts will be decided differently due to the legal arguments advanced.[1] The point is, of course, that the obligation of the court extends to deciding the case correctly based on what the parties have put forth rather than to decide it "correctly" for all purposes.

The differences between "adversarial" and "inquisitorial" systems of dispute resolution also are a function of different beliefs concerning how effective each is in producing "the truth." In this country, there is a generally held view that adversarial investigation and presentation of evidence is more likely to yield a verdict consistent with the truth than is a process more dominated by a tribunal. Needless to say, those who favor continental systems are inclined to the view that control by a disinterested tribunal will lead to less abuse and manipulation of the evidence, thus increasing the chances that verdicts consistent with the truth will emerge. For a discussion, see Langbein, The German Advantage in Civil Procedure, 52 U. Chi. L. Rev. 823 (1985); Allen, Koeck, Reichenberg, and Rosen, The German Advantage in Civil Procedure: A Plea for More Details and Fewer Generalities in Comparative Scholarship, 82 Nw. U.L. Rev. 705 (1988).

In the United States, the adversarial process remains the dominant theory of litigation, and the conception of disputes as being, for the most part, private matters of private individuals does not seem under serious re-

---

1. In United States v. Ross, 456 U.S. 798 (1982), the Court overruled a case decided just two years earlier on an argument that had not been made in the earlier case.

consideration on a broad scale.[2] If private individuals are going to resolve those disputes in the courts, however, the process by which that is done must be structured. The first step is the initiation of the litigation, which is done by filing pleadings that state a cause of action and announce an intent to litigate a matter with another party. The pleading puts both the court and the adversary on notice of the fact that litigation is to be pursued; it also presents the basic parameters of the cause of action. The adversary is then typically required to file a responsive pleading, and in some jurisdictions must raise specific issues if the party wishes those issues to be litigated in addition to the issues raised by the plaintiff. For example, affirmative defenses often must be pleaded by the defendant. See generally Cleary, Presuming and Pleading: An Essay on Juristic Immaturity, 12 Stan. L. Rev. 5 (1959). This, of course, is the subject matter of civil procedure, and will not be pursued further here.

After a case is fully pleaded and discovery has been completed, the case is ready for presentation at trial. Here we observe once more a division of authority between judge and jury, and the parties for that matter. The judge is presumed to know the law relevant to the litigation, although the judge will often be informed of it by the parties (and the parties will often challenge the judge's understanding of it on appeal). The point of the trial is to determine the facts based upon the evidence produced by the parties, and it is the jury's responsibility to do that.

When the parties are ready to proceed at trial, there is the need to structure how they are to proceed: who goes first, what happens after one party produces a witness, etc. This is done in the first instance through rules governing the allocation of burdens of production. Each issue to be litigated, whether it is an element or an affirmative defense, has a burden of production associated with it that requires one party or the other to produce evidence relevant to the particular issue (hence the name "burden of production"). If the party with a burden of production fails to produce sufficient evidence on a particular issue, that party will not be allowed to take the issue to the jury and will lose on that issue. Thus, the burden of production informs the parties how issues will be decided if no evidence is produced; and if the parties wish an outcome different from what would result if no evidence is produced, they must produce evidence on the relevant issues.

How, though, is one to know when a party with a burden of production has produced sufficient evidence to avoid a preclusive ruling that would decide an issue for purposes of the litigation? A burden of production should be satisfied when the underlying purpose of the requirement is met. In civil cases, the primary purpose of a burden of production is to ensure that there are issues in the case that need to be resolved by the jury. Issues need to be resolved by juries when there could be reasonable disagreement about which

---

2. An increasing proportion of the business of the federal courts may involve matters of public law rather than private dispute resolution. For an interesting discussion, see Chayes, The Role of the Judge in Public Law Litigation, 89 Harv. L. Rev. 1281 (1976).

A. The Burden of Production

party should prevail. If there could be no reasonable disagreement, there is no reason to go to the expense and trouble of a trial, and the judge should, and will, render a verdict for the appropriate party (or otherwise dispose of the case, by dismissal for example). Thus, another implication of a burden of production is that the failure to satisfy its requirements will result in the adversary "winning" on that particular issue.

To decide if there could be reasonable disagreement about which party should prevail, the judge must test the evidence produced by a party by reference to a procedural rule of decision, typically referred to as a "burden of persuasion." A burden of persuasion informs the decision maker how to decide a case in light of the evidence. For example, one possible rule of decision is that a plaintiff should prevail only if the evidence establishes the plaintiff's case to a certainty. This rule would require a verdict for the defendant if there is any doubt about the truth of the facts that must be established by the plaintiff.

A decision rule of certainty has an intuitive appeal to it—people (defendants) should not be required to pay unless they have done something wrong. Notwithstanding this intuitive appeal, it is not the rule generally found in civil litigation because it would put plaintiffs at a serious disadvantage. It is difficult if not impossible to prove any fact to certainty. Requiring plaintiffs to do so, it is believed, would result in a disproportionate number of wrongful verdicts for defendants at the expense of deserving plaintiffs. The opposite rule—requiring defendants to show to a certainty that they should not be held liable—would have the opposite effect, of course. Rather than adopt either of these two extremes, the virtually uniform practice in civil litigation is to adopt a burden of persuasion of a preponderance of the evidence. Plaintiffs must prove each of their necessary factual claims to a preponderance of the evidence, and defendants must establish affirmative defenses by the same standard. Accordingly, juries are instructed in civil cases to analyze the evidence, and render a verdict for the party in whose favor the evidence "preponderates." This is usually defined as meaning "more than a 50 percent chance of being true." Thus, the task for juries is to determine whether the evidence favors the plaintiff's story with respect to the factual elements of a cause of action and to determine whether the evidence favors the defendant's story with respect to affirmative defenses.

We will elaborate on the implications of rules governing burdens of persuasion below. Now the task is to see how burdens of persuasion relate to burdens of production. Reflect on our description of burdens of productions. A burden of production should be deemed satisfied if enough evidence has been produced to indicate that there is a need for judicial resolution of the relevant factual question, and that occurs when reasonable people could disagree about the matter. The disagreement would be over whether or not the rule of decision—the burden of persuasion—has been satisfied. If no reasonable person could disagree that a plaintiff or defendant has satisfied the relevant burden of persuasion, then there is no reason to try the fact in question or to prolong any judicial proceedings that have already occurred. Thus, as Professor McNaughton developed in an important article, the burden of production is a function of the burden of persuasion. McNaughton, Burden of Production of Evidence: A Function of a Burden of Persuasion, 68 Harv. L. Rev. 1382 (1955). The test to determine if a burden of production has been met is whether, in light of the evidence, there could be reasonable disagreement over which party should win. If there could be such disagreement, a jury question has been generated. If not, the judge may as well dispose of the case as expeditiously as possible.

The relationship between burdens of production and burdens of persuasion deserves a closer look. Presumably jurors evaluate evidence in conventional probabilistic terms, as do the rest of us, by making rough estimates of the probability of facts being true. Whether juries think in these terms or not, they are instructed to apply a probabilistic concept in deciding cases whenever the standard preponderance of the evidence instruction is given. For purposes of simplicity, we will assume for now that jurors do think in roughly probabilistic terms and that a preponderance of the evidence means more than a 50 percent chance of the relevant fact being true.

Under these assumptions, the evidentiary process can be diagramed in such a way as to highlight the relationship between burdens of production and burdens of persuasion. Assume that the party with a burden of production produces some evidence. That evidence will indicate that there is a certain chance that the relevant facts are true. However, the evidence is likely to be not perfectly clear as to what probability it generates. Looking at that evidence, reasonable people could disagree about the probability to which the evidence establishes some necessary fact. Does that mean that every time evidence is produced a jury issue is generated because there always will be reasonable disagreement about its implications? No, because a jury issue will be generated only when there is disagreement about which party should win, and that requires referring to the burden of persuasion. Consider now the three possibilities charted below:

(1) ─────────

(2)   ─────────

(3)   ─────────

0%   50%   100%

A. The Burden of Production

After a party produces evidence on an issue, this chart reflects the three relevant possibilities in terms of the implications of the evidence. First, the evidence produced may not be very convincing. A reasonable person looking at it may conclude that it has some persuasive force, but not very much. That possibility is represented by (1) above. It indicates that, given the evidence, the probability of the relevant fact being true (the fact the evidence is being relied upon to establish) ranges from about 10 to 35 percent (we could have drawn that line segment anywhere between 0 and 49.9 percent, just so long as it did not exceed 50 percent). In this case, the burden of production has not been satisfied. Since no reasonable person could conclude that the party producing the evidence should win, there is no reason to send this issue to the jury. In case (2), a jury issue has been generated. The evidence indicates a range of reasonable persuasiveness from about 40 to 60 percent (here we could have drawn the line segment in any fashion so long as it ranged over 50 percent). Since reasonable people could disagree about the implications of the evidence in this case, the issue will be sent to the jury. Case (3) is similar to case (1) in that again no reasonable disagreement could exist as to the implications of the evidence. The evidence indicates somewhere between a 65 and 90 percent chance of the relevant fact being true (here the line could be drawn anywhere to the right of 50 percent).

Case (3) is different from case (1) in one respect. We have been assuming that the party with the burden of production has produced evidence. In case (1), the burden has not been met, and thus there is no reason to proceed further. In case (2), the burden of production has been met, and the case will proceed. In case (3), the burden has not only been met, but exceeded. No reasonable person could disagree about who should win. This conclusion, though, is based solely on the evidence produced by one party. Case (3) differs from case (1) in that rather than the judge disposing of the issue, case (3) requires that the adversary be given a chance to produce contrary evidence in order to demonstrate that there is a reasonable dispute about the relevant fact. In case (1), there is no reason to have the adversary proceed because the party's evidence itself indicates that the relevant fact cannot be established. Having the adversary produce still more information substantiating that conclusion would be a waste of time and money. In case (3), however, the adversary has not yet been heard and may be in possession of information that would affect the analysis of how likely the relevant fact is, given all the evidence (including the adversary's). Accordingly, in case (3), the judge will not dispose of the relevant issue; rather, the adversary will be given a chance to respond.

After the adversary responds, the judge once more may be asked to test the sufficiency of the evidence by one or both of the parties. To determine how the judge ought to proceed in light of such requests, we must consider how the evidentiary process proceeds. Assume that the party with the burden of production produces sufficient evidence so that something akin to case

(2) is generated. At that point, the adversary will have the right to respond. The adversary's evidence will likely decrease the probability of the relevant fact being true, thus shifting the probability range on the chart to the left. In most jurisdictions, after the adversary has responded the party with the initial burden of production is entitled to produce "rebutting" evidence, evidence that responds to the evidence produced by the adversary, and typically the adversary may respond to that new offer of evidence. This process continues until neither party has anything new to offer, at which point the evidence taken as a whole will approximate one of the three cases from the chart. If the evidence fits into case (1), the judge should decide the issue in favor of the adversary; if the evidence fits into case (2), the issue should go to the jury; if the evidence fits into case (3), the judge should decide the issue in favor of the party who initially bore the burden of production.

The manner in which the judge is asked to decide the case in favor of one party or another depends upon the time at which the judge is asked to do so, and here we see the interaction between the law of evidence and civil procedure. One possibility is that before any evidence is produced a party can move for summary judgment. The motion will be granted if the judge can determine from the pleadings and any supporting documentation that there are no issues in need of judicial resolution in the case. Such a decision, however, is equivalent to saying that either case (1) or case (3) is present—either the party with the burden of production will not be able to meet it or the adversary will not be able to show that the party's evidence does not justify taking the case away from a jury. If case (2) is present, the motion for summary judgment (by either party) will be denied, and the litigation will proceed. The important point to note, though, is that the judge's decision will rest upon the ability of a party to meet its burden of production and the adversary's ability to respond to a party's proof with sufficient evidence to justify taking the issue to a jury. Although summary judgments are not conventionally discussed as being intimately related to burdens of production and burdens of persuasion, the concepts are obviously closely related. The Supreme Court has recently noticed this relationship in Anderson v. Liberty Lobby, Inc., 106 S. Ct. 2505 (1986) and Celotex Corporation v. Catrett, 106 S. Ct. 2549 (1986).

Another possibility is that, if a case goes to the evidence-taking phase, the judge may be asked to test the strength of the evidence by a motion for directed verdict at the end of the party's case. The analysis here is quite similar to the analysis of summary judgment motions; in fact there is only one significant difference. After the party with the burden of production rests its case-in-chief, if case (1) is present the court should direct a verdict for the adversary; if case (2) is present, the trial obviously should proceed. It will also proceed if case (3) is present because the adversary has not yet been heard from. So long as the party resisting a preclusive motion has evidence to offer that might affect the judge's analysis of the case, preclusive motions should not be granted. Again, the analysis of directed verdicts is not typically

A. The Burden of Production

approached from the perspective of burdens of production and persuasion, but the consanguinity of the ideas is obvious. The preclusive motions are the means by which the implications of the evidence are tested; and the implications of the evidence are a function of the burdens of proof, in particular the burden of persuasion. Thus, not only are burdens of production a function of burdens of persuasion, but preclusive motions are as well.

Who bears the burden of production with respect to any particular issue is a function more of tradition than of either rules or reason. Consider the following excerpt:

JAMES, BURDENS OF PROOF
47 Va. L. Rev. 51, 58-61 (1961)

There is no satisfactory test for allocating the burden of proof . . . on any given issue. The allocation is made on the basis of one or more of several variable factors. Before considering these, however, we should note three formal tests which have some currency but are not very helpful.

(1) It is often said that the party who must establish the affirmative proposition has the burden of proof on the issue. But language can be manipulated so as to state most propositions either negatively or affirmatively. Breach of promise may be called non-fulfillment. Negligence is often described as the lack of or failure to exercise due care. An action in which plaintiff seeks a declaration of non-liability is just as truly one seeking a declaration that good defenses exist to the claim asserted by the defendant.

(2) It is sometimes said that the burden of proof is upon the party to whose case the fact in question is essential, and so it is, but this test simply poses another question: to which party's case is the fact essential? And the second question is no easier to answer than the first; indeed it is but a restatement of the same question.

(3) It is often said that the party who has the burden of pleading a fact must prove it. This is in large part true and where there is clear authority on the pleading rule this is a fairly good, though not infallible, indication that the rule of burden of proof will parallel it. Three things should, however, be noted. The burden of proof does not follow the burden of pleading in all cases. Many jurisdictions for example require a plaintiff to plead non-payment of an obligation sued upon but do not require him to prove it. . . . The second difficulty with the suggested test is that there is often no clear authority upon the pleading rule. The burden of pleading is itself allocated on the basis of pragmatic considerations of fairness, convenience, and policy, rather than on any general principle of pleading. Since the burden of proof is allocated on very much the same basis, a similar inquiry must be made to determine the pleading rule (where there is no clear authority) as would suffice to answer the burden of proof rule in the first instance. This fact, incidentally, suggests why burden of pleading and burden of proof are usually

parallel; they are both manifestations of the same or similar considerations. A third difficulty with the proposed rule is that under modern systems, pleadings are cut off with the answer[53] so that issues often have to be tried that do not appear in the pleadings at all.

Another rule for allocating the burden of proof would put it on the party having the readier access to knowledge about the fact in question. This, it will be noted, is not merely a formal rule. It refers rather to one of the considerations which should and do in fact influence the allocation of the burden of proof. But it is not the only consideration and it is by no means always controlling. It is an everyday occurrence in litigation that a party has the burden to prove what his opponent's conduct was. Examples are negligence, contributory negligence, and breach of contract, in many common situations. In these instances the consideration arising from greater access to evidence is overcome by a feeling that a charge of wrongdoing should in fairness be proven by the party making it.

Another factor to be considered is the extent to which a party's contention departs from what would be expected in the light of ordinary human experience. It is a matter of convenience to assume that things occurred as they usually do and to make the party who asserts the uncommon occurrence prove that it did happen as he claims. Thus where services are performed for another in an ordinary business or professional context, it is unlikely that they were understood to be gratuitous. It is not surprising, therefore, to find that the burden of proving such an understanding is on the one who claims it. By way of contrast, where services are performed for other members of the immediate family, living together, the likelihood of an agreement to pay for them is not so great and must be proved by him who claims the right to be paid.

Substantive considerations may also be influential. For real or supposed reasons of policy the law sometimes disfavors claims and defenses which it nevertheless allows. Where that is the case procedural devices like burden of proof are often used as handicaps, to use Judge Clark's felicitous phrase, against the disfavored contention. [58] Thus whoever charges his adversary with fraud, be he plaintiff or defendant, must prove it. And although falsity is often included in the definitions of defamatory statements, yet the defendant in libel or slander must plead and prove the truth of the objectionable words if he would use that as a defense. In many of the older states, plaintiff, in a negligence action, had to prove his own due care, but as the defense of contributory negligence became increasingly unpopular with courts and legislatures, the tendency has been increasingly to make defendants plead and prove it.

53. See, e.g., Fed. R. Civ. P. 7(a); N.Y. Civ. Prac. Act §§260, 272, 274.
58. Clark, Code Pleading 609-610 (2d ed. 1947).

A. The Burden of Production

NOTES AND QUESTIONS

1. Typically the plaintiff or moving party on a motion bears both the burden of pleading and the burden of production. In general, then, whoever is asking the courts to modify the status quo, which is either the plaintiff or a party who has made a motion for some sort of relief, must introduce sufficient evidence of the relevant factual claims to justify a finding of fact consistent with those claims. Thus, who bears the burden of production will normally be a function of the position of the parties. If X sues Y over a contract, X will bear the burden of production on most factual issues. If, by contrast, Y sues X in a declaratory judgment action, Y will bear the burden of production on most of the identical factual issues. The burden of production, in short, is primarily a rule of convenience. It is in the exceptions to the normal rule of burden of production where issues of policy become relevant.

2. What should justify an exception to the normal rule that plaintiffs and moving parties bear the burden of production? As Professor James demonstrates, most of the articulated tests are simply circular, and thus completely unenlightening. Any fact can be described in positive or negative terms; either party can be made to plead a particular fact or its negation; and the proof of a fact or its negation can be placed in the case of either party. Do Professor James' suggestions advance much beyond these somewhat circular tests? What is the significance of one party or another having readier access to knowledge? In particular, what is its significance in the context of mature discovery procedures? In addition, should this test be applied on a case-by-case basis or to general categories of factual issues? Similarly, what is the significance of the fact that some claims may not be what would be expected in the light of ordinary human experience? Does all litigation involve matters that are not normally "what would be expected in the light of ordinary human experience"? Finally, how does the allocation of a burden of production "disfavor claims"?[3]

3. Are any of the issues concerning allocation of burdens of production a function of the nature of the relevant discovery rules or of one's belief as to how well discovery functions? Should burdens of production ever be used to sanction the failure of the discovery process? Is there ever a time when that should be done if the sanctions provided in the discovery rules are inadequate for one reason or another?

4. The dominant model of litigation in this country is the private law model developed in the text. In an interesting article, Professor Chayes questions the adequacy of that model. Consider the following excerpt:

---

3. Professor James was referring to both burdens of production and persuasion, and the manipulation of burdens of persuasion may make it more difficult for a party to establish a claim or defense.

CHAYES, THE ROLE OF THE JUDGE IN PUBLIC LAW LITIGATION
89 Harv. L. Rev. 1281, 1282-1283, 1284, 1297-1298, 1302 (1976)

The characteristic features of the public law model are very different from those of the traditional model. The party structure is sprawling and amorphous, subject to change over the course of the litigation. The traditional adversary relationship is suffused and intermixed with negotiating and mediating processes at every point. The judge is the dominant figure in organizing and guiding the case, and he draws for support not only on the parties and their counsel, but on a wide range of outsiders—masters, experts, and oversight personnel. Most important, the trial judge has increasingly become the creator and manager of complex forms of ongoing relief, which have widespread effects on persons not before the court and require the judge's continuing involvement in administration and implementation. School desegregation, employment discrimination, and prisoners' or inmates' rights cases come readily to mind as avatars of this new form of litigation. But it would be mistaken to suppose that it is confined to these areas. Antitrust, securities fraud and other aspects of the conduct of corporate business, bankruptcy and reorganizations, union governance, consumer fraud, housing discrimination, electoral reapportionment, environmental management—cases in all these fields display in varying degrees the features of public law litigation. . . .

In our received tradition, the lawsuit is a vehicle for settling disputes between private parties about private rights. The defining features of this conception of civil adjudication are:

(1) The lawsuit is bipolar. Litigation is organized as a contest between two individuals or at least two unitary interests, diametrically opposed, to be decided on a winner-takes-all basis.

(2) Litigation is retrospective. The controversy is about an identified set of completed events: whether they occurred, and if so, with what consequences for the legal relations of the parties.

(3) Right and remedy are interdependent. The scope of the relief is derived more or less logically from the substantive violation under the general theory that the plaintiff will get compensation measured by the harm caused by the defendant's breach of duty—in contract by giving plaintiff the money he would have had absent the breach; in tort by paying the value of the damage caused.

(4) The lawsuit is a self-contained episode. The impact of the judgment is confined to the parties. If plaintiff prevails there is a simple compensatory transfer, usually of money, but occasionally the return of a thing or the performance of a definite act. If defendant prevails, a loss lies where it has fallen. In either case, entry of judgment ends the court's involvement.

A. The Burden of Production

(5) The process is party-initiated and party-controlled. The case is organized and the issues defined by exchange between the parties. Responsibility for fact development is theirs. The trial judge is a neutral arbiter of their interactions who decides questions of law only if they are put in issue by an appropriate move of a party. . . .

The public law litigation model portrayed in this paper [that is becoming increasingly prevalent in federal courts] reverses many of the crucial characteristics and assumptions of the traditional concept of adjudication:

(1) The scope of the lawsuit is not exogenously given but is shaped primarily by the court and parties.
(2) The party structure is not rigidly bilateral but sprawling and amorphous.
(3) The fact inquiry is not historical and adjudicative but predictive and legislative.
(4) Relief is not conceived as compensation for past wrong in a form logically derived from the substantive liability and confined in its impact to the immediate parties; instead, it is forward looking, fashioned ad hoc on flexible and broadly remedial lines, often having important consequences for many persons including absentees.
(5) The remedy is not imposed but negotiated.
(6) The decree does not terminate judicial involvement in the affair: its administration requires the continuing participation of the court.
(7) The judge is not passive, his function limited to analysis and statement of governing legal rules; he is active, with responsibility not only for credible fact evaluation but for organizing and shaping the litigation to ensure a just and viable outcome.
(8) The subject matter of the lawsuit is not a dispute between private individuals about private rights, but a grievance about the operation of public policy. . . .

[As a consequence of this changing model of litigation] [t]he courts . . . continue to rely primarily on the litigants to produce and develop factual materials, but a number of factors make it impossible to leave the organization of the trial exclusively in their hands. With the diffusion of the party structure, fact issues are no longer sharply drawn in a confrontation between two adversaries, one asserting the affirmative and the other the negative. The litigation is often extraordinarily complex and extended in time, with a continuous and intricate interplay between factual and legal elements. It is hardly feasible and, absent a jury, unnecessary to set aside a contiguous block of time for a "trial stage" at which all significant factual issues will be presented. The scope of the fact investigation and the sheer volume of factual material that can be exhumed by the discovery process pose enormous problems of organization and assimilation. All these factors thrust the trial judge into an active role in shaping, organizing and facilitating the litigation. We may not yet have reached the investigative judge of the continental systems, but we have left the passive arbiter of the traditional model a long way behind.

B. THE BURDEN OF PERSUASION

As mentioned above, a legal system that does not purport to rest verdicts only on facts that are established to certainty must provide rules that instruct fact finders how to decide cases in the face of uncertainty. These rules are normally referred to as burdens of persuasion. The typical burden of persuasion in civil cases is the preponderance of the evidence rule: Plaintiffs and moving parties must establish those facts necessary to their claims by a preponderance of the evidence. "Preponderance of the evidence," in turn is defined as "more probable than not" or as "50 percent +"—which means a probability that slightly favors the party with the burden of persuasion. For a discussion, see McCormick, Handbook of the Law of Evidence §339 (3d ed. 1984).

The preponderance rule incorporates an underlying assumption concerning the participants in litigation: that plaintiffs as a class and defendants as a class generally ought to be treated in equivalent ways. The reason for this is that before a case is resolved, one cannot know who should win; it is as likely that the defendant should win as the plaintiff. Assume that the plaintiff is suing the defendant for $200 allegedly owed under a contract. Before the evidence relevant to this dispute is produced, how should the case be conceptualized? Should it be thought of as a case where the plaintiff is trying to get $200 of the defendant's money, as a case where the defendant is wrongfully refusing to pay, or as a case where two individuals are contesting whose $200 it is? The latter view is intuitively more compelling. Without knowing the facts, it seems just as likely that the defendant is refusing to pay what is owed as that the plaintiff is attempting to obtain that to which he does not have a right.

The preponderance of the evidence standard generalizes this basic point into a statement that plaintiffs as a class and defendants as a class generally ought to be treated equivalently (with defendants, and the status quo, favored if there is a "tie" in which the evidence does not preponderate in either direction). As Professor Kaye has demonstrated algebraically, if certain conditions are met the preponderance of the evidence standard should result in about the same number of errors being made for plaintiffs as for defendants. Kaye, The Limits of the Preponderance of the Evidence Standard: Justifiably Naked Statistical Evidence and Multiple Causation, 1982 A.B.F.J. 487.

B. The Burden of Persuasion

Professor Kaye's demonstration can be understood without the mathematics he employs. Assume that in the set of all cases going to trial there are approximately as many deserving plaintiffs as deserving defendants. Assume further that the jury will make a rough probability assessment of the strength of each case presented by the parties. Presumably those probability assessments will range from 0.0 to 1.0. Now compare the set of cases where plaintiffs deserve to win to the set of cases where defendants deserve to win. It is not unreasonable to suppose that in most of the cases where plaintiffs deserve to win the facts will support that conclusion, thus creating a probability assessment of more than 0.5, which will result in a verdict for the plaintiff. Only in those cases in which the probability assessment is 0.5 or less will wrongful verdicts for defendants be entered. This is also true with respect to the set of cases where defendants deserve to win. Presumably the evidence in most of those cases will demonstrate that the defendant deserves to win, thus creating a probability assessment of 0.5 or less. Only in those cases in which the probability assessment is more than 0.5 will there be wrongful verdicts for plaintiffs. If one assumes that the probability assessments for these two sets are in a normal distribution over the range of 0.0 to 1.0, then the number of errors made for plaintiffs will approximate the number of errors made for defendants, and the preponderance of the evidence standard will have done its job.

The following graph demonstrates this argument geometrically.[4] The horizontal axis is the probability that juries assign to cases, and the vertical axis is the number of cases assigned a particular probability. Graph I is the set of cases in which defendants deserve to win (which means if we knew all the facts to certainty, the defendant would win); graph II is the set of cases in which plaintiffs deserve to win.

Errors are represented in graph I by all those cases to the right of the 0.5 level, which is the area heavily shaded in the graph. In graph II, errors are represented by the area to the left of the 0.5 level, which again is the heavily shaded area. The number of errors is represented by the area under the graph—the larger the area the more errors and the smaller the area the

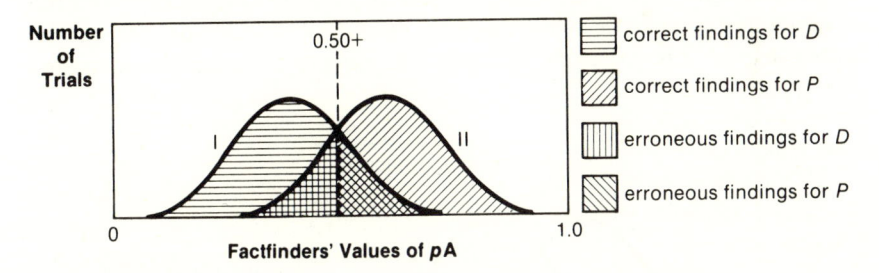

---

4. We are heavily indebted for what follows, including the graphs, to Bell, Decision Theory and Due Process: A Critique of the Supreme Court's Lawmaking for Burdens of Proof, 78 J. Crim. L. & Crim. 557 (1987).

fewer errors. So long as the heavily shaded areas under the two graphs are of approximately equal size, then the preponderance standard will have done its appointed task of equalizing errors among plaintiffs and defendants. Note, however, that this will be so only when the relevant areas under the two graphs are roughly equal in size, which is an empirical question. If the contours of the two graphs differ markedly from what we have presented, or if the number of cases in which plaintiffs deserve to win is substantially larger or smaller than the number of cases in which defendants deserve to win, then the size of those areas under the graphs would change, with the result being that errors may not be allocated equally over plaintiffs and defendants. The manner in which we have drawn these graphs reflects assumptions that are pertinent to civil cases but that are dubious in criminal cases, a matter we will return to below.

These graphs also demonstrate why alternative burdens of persuasion are occasionally relied upon in civil cases. Many jurisdictions require allegations in civil cases of fraud or of activity that would be criminal to be proven by clear and convincing evidence. Because of the seriousness of such allegations, errors should favor the person against whom such allegations are made (which also explains the higher burden of persuasion in criminal cases). Making the same assumptions as we did above, the effect of raising the burden of persuasion from a preponderance to "clear and convincing evidence" can be seen in the second graph. The shaded area again represents errors, and the effect of raising the burden of proof is obvious. Errors favoring defendants are increased and errors favoring plaintiffs are decreased, which is precisely the effect that the higher burden of persuasion is designed to accomplish. Again, though, bear in mind that what these graphs would look like in reality is an empirical question. Should reliable data ever be obtained on that issue, it might be justifiable to modify the burden of persuasion in light of that information. For example, we might decide after reviewing the data that too many errors favoring defendants are made where there is an allegation of fraud. The rate of such errors can be affected by lowering the burden of persuasion.

Although our primary concern here is with civil cases, note that the requirement of proof beyond reasonable doubt in criminal cases can also be explicated by this approach. Indeed, the graph of "clear and convincing

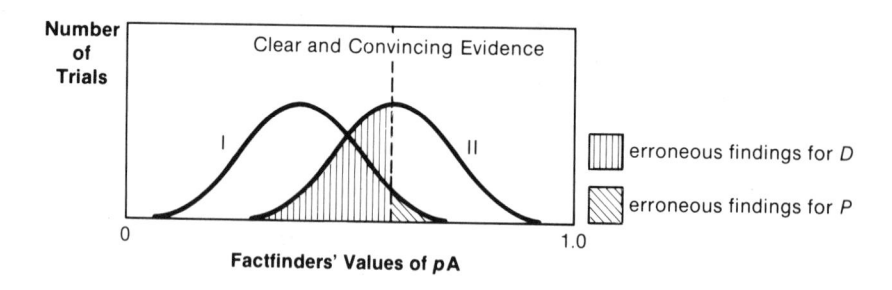

B. The Burden of Persuasion

evidence" with but slight modification can become one of proof beyond reasonable doubt. What do you think graph I of such a schema would look like? That would be the set of all innocent people who go to trial in criminal cases. If that set is quite small, and it may well be given all the diversion mechanisms in criminal cases, there may be few cases of wrongful convictions to offset whatever wrongful acquittals occur. If that is so, does it amount to an argument for lowering the burden of persuasion in criminal cases? Perhaps not, for one would need to determine the secondary consequences of lowering the standard of proof. Presumably one factor that prosecutors take into account in deciding how far to pursue a case is the standard of proof. If it is lowered, prosecutors might bring more problematic cases to trial, which would then change the size and configuration of graph I, thus resulting in more errors of innocent individuals being convicted.

Compare the implications of these graphic demonstrations with the discussion in Chapter Two of the significance of the decision maker's utilities. You will see that in certain respects these graphs give a geometric representation to that discussion. In the normal civil case, the disutility of a wrongful plaintiff's verdict is viewed as equivalent to the disutility of a wrongful defendant's verdict. There will be times, though, when that will not be true, such as in cases where there are allegations of fraud. In Chapter Two we relied on this idea to elaborate on the concept of prejudice to show how the effect of prejudicial evidence can be understood to modify implicitly the burden of persuasion. Here we are elaborating on how other considerations may affect explicitly the burden of persuasion. Apart from those differences, however, the analysis is virtually identical—one is an algebraic and the other a geometric demonstration—altlhough earlier we were dealing with inappropriate reasons for implicitly modifying the burden of persuasion while here we are dealing with acceptable reasons for doing so directly.

The burden of persuasion of each necessary element of a cause of action must be allocated to one party or the other, just as is true of burdens of production. Typically the same question-begging indicia are asserted as the basis for the allocation of burdens of persuasion as are employed in determining where the burden of production lies. Thus, the most that sensibly can be said of the allocation of the burden of persuasion is that the normal rule is that plaintiffs and moving parties bear the burden to prove by a preponderance all the facts necessary to justify a verdict or judgment in their behalf.

There are exceptions to the normal rule. On occasion, defendants are required to bear the burden of persuasion on specified factual questions that are typically referred to as "affirmative defenses." It is not unusual, for example, to find a defendant in a negligence action having the burden to prove the plaintiff's contributory negligence. There are also jurisdictions that require one party to plead an issue and the other party to bear both the burden of production and the burden of persuasion with respect to that issue. Similarly, there are situations where one party bears the burden of production with respect to a fact, but the opposing party must disprove the fact (or prove its negation, however you want to view it) by the relevant burden of persuasion. Such cases fit no general rule, but you should be aware that they do occasionally arise. In any event, states are free to allocate burdens of proof in civil cases virtually any way they like. Lavine v. Milne, 424 U.S. 577 (1976) ("Outside the criminal area, where special concerns attend, the locus of the burden of persuasion is normally not an issue of federal constitutional concern"). States on occasion exercise that power in interesting ways. Consider the following case.

SCHECHTER v. KLANFER
321 N.Y.S.2d 99, 269 N.E.2d 812, 28 N.Y.2d 228 (1971)

BREITEL, Judge. In this negligence action for personal injuries, the issue is whether the jury should have been instructed to hold plaintiff, who had by amnesia lost his memory of the events causing his injury, to a lesser degree of proof than a plaintiff who could have testified to the events.

Upon the trial, a verdict in favor of defendants was returned. The trial court initially instructed the jury to hold plaintiff to a lesser degree of proof if it found his amnesia to be genuine. Upon defendants' objection, however, the charge was withdrawn, plaintiff taking exception.

There should be a reversal and a new trial in order that the jury may consider whether plaintiff should be held to a lesser degree of proof.

Robert Schechter and his companion, Alice Stone, were involved in a motorboat collision on the night of August 25, 1964. Both were then 14 years old. They had left a party at a lakeshore home and, with Robert operating his father's boat, had begun motoring across the lake. Alice sat in the front seat, to the left of Robert. Alice testified that the night was clear and moonlit, that the boat's lights were on, and that Robert was taking a straight course at about four miles an hour. They had not gone far, Alice continued, when she looked to her right and saw a motorboat some 50 feet distant heading towards them, its bow out of water. About one second later, she estimated, the other boat, operated by defendant Robert Klanfer, struck the Schechter boat near the driver's seat. Alice estimated that the Klanfer boat was traveling at 30 miles an hour. The nighttime speed limit on the lake was 10 miles an hour. The defendants disputed Alice's testimony as to the speed of their boat and the lighting of the Schechter boat. Robert testified but not as to the accident, claiming that, as a result of the collision, he had no memory of the events. He had sustained a fractured skull, fractured arm, fractured jaw, and other physical injuries. He had been comatose for several days. Plaintiff's medical expert testified that Robert had suffered severe emotional shock and psychiatric change, including amnesia, due to brain damage.

The rule providing when a plaintiff may prevail on a lesser degree of

B. The Burden of Persuasion

proof was best crystalized in Noseworthy v. City of New York, 80 N.E.2d 744. The court there held that "in a death case a plaintiff is not held to as high a degree of proof of the cause of action as where an injured plaintiff can himself describe the occurrence." Moreover, despite some contrary notions, the rule has been applied in wrongful death cases where the plaintiff has called an eyewitness. . . .

The Committee on Pattern Jury Instruction of the Association of Supreme Court Justices recommends, in a pattern instruction, that the amnesiac plaintiff be held to a lesser degree of proof if the jury is satisfied from medical and other evidence that plaintiff is suffering from loss of memory and that the injuries plaintiff incurred were a substantial factor in causing plaintiff's loss of memory (PJI 1:62).* In a thoughtful and well-documented comment to the instruction, the committee explains: "The limitation that the accident must have been a substantial factor in causing the loss of memory is predicated on the rationale of the *Noseworthy* case, which is not merely plaintiff's inability to present proof, but the unfairness of allowing the defendant, who has knowledge of the facts, to benefit by standing mute when plaintiff's inability results from defendant's acts." (1 N.Y. PJI 36, emphasis in original.)

Of course, an amnesiac plaintiff can no more "describe the occurrence" that produced his injury than can a plaintiff's decedent, a toddler or an imbecile. Other States, faced with an analogous choice of extending to amnesiac plaintiffs a "presumption of due care" normally accorded plaintiffs' decedents, have reasoned that the amnesiac's inability to testify entitles him to the preferential rule.

The rule even as applied to amnesiacs does not, however, shift the burden of proof or eliminate the need for plaintiffs to introduce evidence of a *prima facie* case. The jury must rest its findings on some evidence to establish negligence and also the absence of contributory negligence. In this case, however, plaintiff did introduce evidence to make out a *prima facie* case, so that there was an opportunity to apply the lesser burden of persuasion. If the jury had been told to apply a lesser burden of persuasion, it could have and, therefore, might have found plaintiff free from contributory negligence. The circumstances testified to by Alice Stone that Robert drove the boat in a straight line, at a speed of four miles an hour, and with the boat lights on, were relevant on the issue of contributory negligence. It also could have found defendants negligent upon Alice's testimony of the speed and course of the Klanfer boat.

The danger is, of course, that amnesia is easily feigned. The dangers may be ameliorated. Plaintiff has the burden of proof on the issue of amnesia as on other issues. A jury should be instructed that before the lesser burden

---

*"If, however, you are satisfied from the medical and other evidence presented that plaintiff is suffering from a loss of memory that makes it impossible for him to recall events at or about the time of the accident and that the injuries plaintiff incurred in the accident were a substantial factor in causing his loss of memory, the plaintiff is not held to as high a degree of proof as would be a plaintiff who can himself describe the occurrence."

of persuasion is applied, because of the danger of shamming, they must be satisfied that the evidence of amnesia is clear and convincing, supported by the objective nature and extent of any other physical injuries sustained, and that the amnesia was clearly a result of the accident.

The above is undoubtedly a more severe test than that suggested by the Pattern Jury Instructions. Yet it would seem a small price to pay for a liberal rule treating amnesiac plaintiffs on a par with the representatives of decedents in death actions. The reasons for so treating amnesiacs are similar to those advanced for representatives of persons silenced in fatal accidents, but the risk and ease of shamming are measurably greater.

Accordingly, the order of the Appellate Division should be reversed and a new trial ordered, with costs to abide the event.

Order reversed, etc.

NOTES AND QUESTIONS

1. Do the justifications for allocating burdens of production given by Professor James make any more sense applied to burdens of persuasion? Assuming a mature discovery system is in place, of what significance is it that one party may have readier access to evidence than another? Does it make sense to handicap certain claims by allocating to their proponents the burden of persuasion either because such claims are typically unlikely to be true or because such claims are disfavored? If burdens of persuasion operate as they are intended to operate, precisely what cases would come out differently under a rule that allocated the burden of persuasion to one party instead of the other? Isn't the answer only those cases in which the jury is in equipoise and is unable to say whether the burden of persuasion is met or not? How large a class of cases do you think that is likely to be? Raising or lowering a burden of persuasion, by contrast, is more likely to affect the results in cases, again assuming burdens of persuasion operate roughly as intended.

2. Burdens of persuasion, at least the standard burden of a preponderance of the evidence, may not operate as they are intended to. In an interesting study, Rita James Simon and Linda Mahan obtained data that indicate that jurors may understand "preponderance of the evidence" to mean a probability somewhere between 0.7 and 0.8, while judges consistently indicate that it means slightly more than 0.5. Simon and Mahon, Quantifying Burdens of Proof, 5 Law & Soc. Rev. 319 (1971). In this study, jurors were asked to translate the phrase *preponderance of the evidence* into a probability assessment rather than being informed that the phrase means "50% +." When so informed, there is data that indicate that individuals can follow such instructions. Kagehiro and Stanton, Legal v. Quantified Definitions of Standards of Proof, 9 L. & H. Beh. 159 (1985). In this study, individuals were given a data set and varying instructions on the burden of persuasion; some

B. The Burden of Persuasion

were instructed in legal terminology such as "a preponderance of the evidence" and "clear and convincing evidence" and others in probabilities ranging from 0.51 to 0.91. The results showed that the legal definitions of burdens of persuasion did not much affect the outcome in cases, whereas the instructions in probabilistic terms did. If you were convinced that this study accurately reflected how most individuals react to such instructions, what implications does it have for the structuring of trials?

3. There are statements in many cases, in particular the older ones, that the "burden of proof never shifts; it always rests with the party to whom it was originally allocated." For the most part this shibboleth is true, but it is more misleading than helpful. Reconsider the charts, supra. When a party has demonstrated such a strong case that no reasonable person could disagree that the party deserves on the evidence so far produced to win, a directed verdict will be entered unless the adversary produces more evidence that lowers the probabilities to a point where reasonable people could disagree. In such a case, the adversary bears a functional burden of production; the adversary can produce evidence or lose. In this sense, the "burden of production" can shift numerous times during the course of a trial. Typically, though, a judge would not say that an adversary who fails to produce more evidence in this circumstance has not met a burden of production. Rather, the judge would merely enter a directed verdict without referring to the idea of a burden of production. Note that regardless of what a judge would say in this situation, conceptually the adversary has failed to meet a "burden of production."

Unlike burdens of production, burdens of persuasion do not tend to get shifted around even functionally during a trial. In this sense, wherever the law initially allocates a burden of persuasion is generally where it remains from beginning to end of the litigation. We will examine the one significant exception to this below when presumptions are considered.

4. We earlier mentioned Professor Kaye's demonstration that a preponderance of the evidence rule minimizes errors. But that depends on what an error is. If an error is conceived of as an erroneous determination that plaintiff should win or that defendant should lose, Kaye is correct. If, however, an error is conceived of as dollars wrongly being paid, he is not. From this latter perspective, two erroneous judgments against defendants for $100 each is less of an error than one erroneous judgment for $300 because fewer dollars will "wrongly" change hands. If the objective is to minimize the total number of dollars that wrongly change hands, an expected value rule should be adopted that requires parties to pay an amount equal to the likelihood that they are liable times the amount of damages. If, for example, there is a 60 percent likelihood that defendant is liable and damages are $10,000, the defendant should pay $6000. For a discussion, see Orloff and Stedinger, A Framework for Evaluating the Preponderance of the Evidence Standard, 131 U. Pa. L. Rev. 1159 (1983).

5. Not all states define the burden of persuasion in civil cases in quasi-

mathematical terms. Some states, such as Kentucky, instruct jurors that they are to return a verdict for the plaintiff only if the the jury "believes from the evidence" that the plaintiff's allegations are true. In such states, it is not altogether clear what the measure of "belief" is.

C. JUDICIAL SUMMARY OF AND COMMENT ON THE EVIDENCE

At common law, trial judges had the power to sum up the evidence at the close of the trial and to comment upon its implications. These are two quite different matters. The power to sum up the evidence allowed the judge to review for the jury all the evidence that had been presented by the parties on both sides of all the relevant issues. The value of summary is that it provides for the jury an impartial review of the evidence. The power to comment on the evidence went considerably further. It permitted the court to express its own views on the implications of the evidence, thus injecting the judge's personal opinion into the litigation.

The common law was rejected in many states. Indeed, some states still have constitutional or statutory provisions prohibiting summary or comment, or both.[5] The concern that led to curtailing the common law authority to summarize and comment on the evidence was that such powers allowed an elite—the trial judges—too much opportunity to influence the fact-finding process. This could occur in two ways. The trial judges have their own individual biases and prejudices that could influence how a trial judge summarized or commented upon the evidence. In addition, any small and coherent group, such as trial judges were and probably still are, tends to have unconsciously held beliefs and attitudes that may affect how evidence is perceived as well as what inferences are drawn from that evidence. Allowing summary and comment would permit those unconsciously held beliefs and attitudes to creep into the fact-finding process, skewing it in favor of the interests of this particular elite.[6]

There is another objection to judicial comment in particular, although it is also applicable to a lesser degree to summary. Some argue that comment is unnecessary because the attorneys for the parties are in a position to provide whatever argument about the evidence that they believe would prove useful or necessary. If the parties do not wish to develop certain implications of the evidence, that decision ought not to be second guessed by the trial judge.

---

5. The classic discussions are Wright, Instructions to the Jury: Summary Without Comment, [1954] Wash. U.L.Q. 177; and Wright, The Invasion of the Jury: Temperature of the War, 27 Temp. L.Q. 137 (1953).

6. See J. Hurst, The Growth of American Law: The Lawmakers, 97-98, 104, 145, 351-352 (1940).

C. Judicial Summary of and Comment on the Evidence

Moreover, the parties cannot easily respond to what the trial judge says in summary or comment, thus potentially putting them at a disadvantage. This latter point is deserving of some elaboration.

The attractiveness of comment and summary is that it may inject into the trial process a disinterested element that is valuable to the jury in its appraisal of the evidence. To the extent one believes that there is such a thing as a "disinterested observer," and to the extent one distinguishes the "evidence" presented at trial from "inferences" one draws from the evidence, one may be convinced that summary and comment are laudable features of trials. Both of these points have another side to them, however.

Trial judges certainly are disinterested in certain respects, but they, like the rest of us, have their own way of looking at things that undoubtedly affects both what they observe and retain as well as what inferences they draw from evidence. Reconsider the discussion of relevancy in Chapter Two. When evidence is presented to a fact finder, that evidence presumably is evaluated in the context of the fact finder's belief system—his or her way of looking at the world. Suppose, for example, that a person returns home one night and before entering the house wonders if his wife is at home. He notices that the evening paper is not on the doorstep and there is no mail in the mailbox. Moreover he knows from prior experience that when his spouse returns home she invariably gets the mail and picks up the paper. He also knows that the mail was delivered that day—he received some at the office—and that he has a reliable paper delivery service. By comparing what he observes—no mail or newspaper—he can infer that his spouse has already arrived at home.

Of course, the inference drawn may be in error. It is possible, for example, that the paper blew away and that there was no mail to be delivered to that house that day. These matters, too, might be considered in light of observations made at the time, which would also be compared to previous experience. Is it a windy day? What happens to the paper on such a day? How often do days occur in which no mail is delivered, etc.? The process of inference, in short, requires that evidence be compared to previous experience. That is what jurors do when evidence is considered, and indeed it explains in large measure why we cherish the jury system. In deciding the facts of a case, we want a representative mix of the population to bring their differing views to bear upon the question of what inferences may be drawn from evidence.

This also explains in large measure the resistance to judicial comment on the evidence, and to some extent summary as well. Judges commenting on the implications of evidence are, in a very real sense, commenting upon their previous experience. Moreover, the judge does so in such a way that it is very difficult for the parties to respond since typically comment comes at the time of instructing the jury. One can also reasonably wonder whether the judge is so powerful an authority figure in many instances that nothing the parties could do in response to judicial comment would be of any consequence in the eyes of the jury.

Judicial comment, then, presents a fundamental dilemma. It is in fact a source of further evidence, but of a very different kind than is normally produced at trial. The "evidence" comes from the bench rather than from the adversaries, and it is presented in such a way that the jury may not perceive it for what it is. On the other hand, judges presumably have substantial experience with the kinds of matters involved in the trials before them. They have observed many situations that are undoubtedly similar in nature, and quite likely they are more sophisticated in their appraisal of evidence than are most jurors. To deprive the jurors of the views of the judge may deprive the fact-finding process of an extremely valuable source of "evidence."

As mentioned above, the response to this dilemma in many states has been to forbid judges from commenting on and summing up the evidence. As we discuss in the next section, the response of the judiciary to this limitation upon judicial power has been to create ways to circumvent it. In the federal courts, by contrast, the common law power to summarize and comment has never been called into question. The fundamental dilemma of comment and summary has been dealt with by rulings that attempt to walk the fine line between the judge being helpful as compared to "intruding" too far into the jury process. Summary and comment are appropriate "to assist [the jury] in arriving at a just conclusion." Vicksburg & M.R.R. v. Putnam, 118 U.S. 545, 553 (1886). The difficulty is that the criteria for determining when a jury has been properly assisted are not clear. For example, in Quercia v. United States, 289 U.S. 466 (1933), a criminal case, the trial judge instructed the jury in the following manner:

> And now I am going to tell you what I think of the defendant's testimony. You may have noticed, Mr. Foreman and gentlemen, that he wiped his hands during his testimony. It is rather a curious thing, but that is almost always an indication of lying. Why it should be so we don't know, but that is the fact. I think that every single word that man said, except when he agreed with the Government's testimony, was a lie.
>
> Now, that opinion is an opinion of evidence and is not binding on you, and if you don't agree with it, it is your duty to find him not guilty.

In reversing the ensuing conviction, the Supreme Court stated:

> This privilege of the judge to comment on the facts has its inherent limitations. His discretion is not arbitrary and uncontrolled, but judicial, to be exercised in conformity with the standards governing the judicial office. In commenting upon testimony he may not assume the role of a witness. He may analyze and dissect the evidence, but he may not either distort it or add to it. His privilege of comment in order to give appropriate assistance to the jury is too important to be left without safeguards against abuses.

C. Judicial Summary of and Comment on the Evidence

Nor do we think that the error was cured by the statement of the trial judge that his opinion of the evidence was not binding on the jury and that if they did not agree with it they should find the defendant not guilty. His definite and concrete assertion of fact, which he had made with all the persuasiveness of judicial utterance, as to the basis of his opinion, was not withdrawn.

NOTES AND QUESTIONS

1. *Quercia* was a criminal case, but at least ostensibly the standards are the same for comment in civil and criminal cases. See, e.g., Capital Traction Co. v. Hof, 174 U.S. 1 (1899).

2. Is the standard implicit in *Quercia* inherently inconsistent? How can one "analyze and dissect the evidence" without "adding to it"? For a discussion, see Allen, More on Constitutional Process-of-Proof Problems, 94 Harv. L. Rev. 1795 (1981); and Nesson, Rationality, Presumptions, and Judicial Comment: A Response to Professor Allen, 94 Harv. L. Rev. 1574, 1589-1590 (1981). In addition, if comment is going to be allowed, why should it not be allowed when the judge possesses clear and apparently convincing views? Either the material commented upon is obvious or it is not. If it is obvious, the reiteration of the obvious by the trial judge should not be grounds for reversal. On the other hand, if what is commented upon is not obvious, and the trial judge is correct, the comment moves the jury toward a rational result. Only if the trial judge is in error in the comment should there be grounds for reversal, but the Supreme Court in *Quercia* did not address the factual accuracy of the comment.

Why do you suppose the Court did not address the factual basis of the comment? Do you agree with the thrust of the preceding paragraph? By reference to what standards should comment be judged?

3. The courts of appeals do not hesitate to reverse judgments on the grounds that trial judges have exceeded legitimate bounds of appropriate comment. For example, in Nunley v. Pettway Oil Co., 346 F.2d 95 (6th Cir. 1965), the jury was unable to decide if the plaintiff had been an invitee or a licensee. In order to encourage the jury to break the impasse, the judge gave the jury the following instruction during a break from deliberations:

> Now, the jury of course is the sole and exclusive judge of the facts in this lawsuit. It is appropriate that the court in an effort to be possibly of some help to the jury may comment upon the evidence. I refrain from doing that and have refrained until this time from doing it in this case. However, in an effort to be of some possible assistance to you I think that I should under these circumstances make some comment upon the evidence upon this issue of invitee-licensee. I want you to understand, however, that in making these comments that you are not in any degree, in any respect, obligated to receive or accept or agree with what I may say. It is your duty to accept what I say

with regard to the law in the case, but it is not your duty to accept any comment that I may make or any evaluation that I make or conclusion that I might reach on the evidence. That is solely your responsibility and solely your duty. But, with that understanding, it is the opinion of the court in this case that, from all the evidence upon the issue of invitee or licensee, that the evidence will establish that at the time and place of the accident the plaintiff was a licensee and not an invitee. Now, I say that just for the purpose, as I say, of possibly being of some help to you, but I want you to understand that making that comment you are not obligated whatsoever to accept that comment as your comment or as your opinion in the case, because it is your job and your responsibility to resolve that issue. I only make that with the thought and the hope that it may be of some possible assistance to you. At any rate, I want to ask you once again to retire and consider your verdict and see if you cannot come to some agreement, some verdict that will reflect the views of all of the jurors. Have respect for the views of your fellow jurors. If you find there are jurors that have different views from you, don't hesitate to change your mind if you should be persuaded by reason and logic to accept a different view. Attempt if you can in good conscience to arrive at a unanimous verdict. After you have considered the views of all others you shouldn't give up a firm conviction that you have just for the purpose of arriving at a unanimous verdict, but see if you cannot resolve this issue. Make one more effort, please.

In reversing a judgment for the defendant, the court of appeals, while recognizing the common law power to comment on the evidence, said that "the trial judge's opinion on the licensee-invitee issue was an opinion on an ultimate fact question peculiarly for jury consideration and amounted to an instructed verdict as to defendant. . . ." Do you agree?

4. The drafters of the Federal Rules proposed the following rule:

SUMMING-UP AND COMMENT BY JUDGE

After the close of the evidence and arguments of counsel, the judge may fairly and impartially sum up the evidence and comment to the jury upon the weight of the evidence and the credibility of the witnesses, if he also instructs the jury that they are to determine for themselves the weight of the evidence and the credit to be given to the witnesses and that they are not bound by the judge's summation or comment.

According to the commentary to the proposed rules, this rule was meant to codify the common law in the federal courts. The rule was rejected by Congress on the ground that such a rule is more properly one of procedure than evidence. The intention, though, was not to affect or change the existing power of the trial judge.

5. Perhaps in response to the formal and informal restraints on the power to summarize and comment, there has developed a practice of providing "standardized inferences." These are instructions to the jury that inform it that proof of one fact gives rise to an inference of another fact.

Such instructions come in a variety of forms, and for that reason to some extent defy generalization. For examples, see Longenecker v. General Motors, 594 F.2d 1283 (9th Cir. 1979)(inference of a defect from a product failure is permissible); Ina Aviation Corp. v. United States, 468 F. Supp. 695, (E.D.N.Y.), *aff'd*, 610 F.2d 806 (1st Cir. 1979)(inference that evidence in a party's control but not produced at trial would have been unfavorable to that party). For a discussion see McCormick's Handbook on the Law of Evidence 966-967 (3d ed. 1984).

The sources of a standardized inference can be statutory or common law. When the source is the common law, the standardized inference is, in essence, a summary of collected judicial wisdom with respect to a certain matter. For a more complete consideration of this issue, see Barnes v. United States, infra page 653. Such a standardized inference may be preferable to a normal comment on the evidence because the personal views of the trial judge are relegated to a lesser role. The trial judge will not be commenting on the evidence from his or her own perspective; rather, the judge will be providing a summation of the collected wisdom of the judiciary. To some extent the same is true of standardized inferences that are authorized by statute, except that the source of the inference is legislative rather than judicial wisdom. In any event, a judge's personal views are not involved in the giving of a statutory inference just as they are not when the source is the common law. But, is there a difference between the two sources nonetheless that has its roots in the nature of the judicial function? Consider this issue as you study the remaining materials in this chapter.

D. *PRESUMPTIONS IN CIVIL ACTIONS*

1. The Concept, Such As It Is, Of Presumptions

We have seen that the process of proof at trial is structured through various evidentiary practices. Burdens of production and persuasion must be allocated among the parties; the judge must decide if burdens of production are satisfied and whether reasonable people could disagree about which party to a law suit should win, given the evidence and the appropriate burden of persuasion; summaries of and comments upon the evidence may be given that can influence the deliberative process of juries; and standardized inference instructions are employed that are distinguishable from comments on the evidence only in that they emanate from some other source than the trial judge's personal views and typically are not as fact or case specific as a comment on the evidence.

These evidentiary practices can be employed in various ways that can have a substantial impact on the progression of a trial. Moreover, they can be employed by trial judges to implement various purposes or goals of the judiciary. We have already seen numerous examples of this. The allocation of burdens of production and persuasion are often justified on the grounds of implementing various policies. Comments on the evidence result from a trial judge's concern that the jury reach an accurate result. In fact, these various evidentiary practices can be employed in quite complicated ways, much more complicated than we have so far observed. For example, an allocation of a burden of persuasion can be made to depend upon proof of some other fact. One case where this occurs with some frequency concerns notice. If notice is an element in a cause of action, the plaintiff normally will be required to prove that notice was given to the defendant. If the plaintiff proves that he mailed notice to the defendant under circumstances where in the regular course of things the defendant would have received the mailed notice, then often the defendant is required to prove that he received no notice (from the allegedly mailed notice or from any other source). Similarly, it is not unusual to find a requirement that if a burden of production on one issue is met, the opponent then must bear the burden of persuasion on that or some other issue.

The reason for such manipulations of the process of proof is the sense of the judiciary that they will advance the goal of rational and accurate outcomes at trial. The format for these creative uses of the process of proof techniques is often referred to as a "presumption." What goes by the name "presumption" is invariably a standard evidentiary device or technique being employed in a slightly unusual fashion. For example, burdens of persuasion are normally set before trial begins and do not shift during a trial. However, if experience indicates that if some fact is true (such as the mailing of a letter), some other fact is very likely to be true (such as receipt of the letter resulting in notice), then rational decision making perhaps can be advanced by making the person who denies receipt, and thus notice, prove the matter.

In complex cases, the claim that creative use of burdens of proof through the medium of presumptions may advance the legitimate goals of trials has some merit, although as a general proposition the primary effect of the use of presumptions is confusion. We will consider the confusion presumptions generate, but first consider the possible value of the creative use of burdens of proof in structuring litigation as contained in the following case.

TEXAS DEPT. OF COMMUNITY AFFAIRS v. BURDINE
450 U.S. 248, 101 S. Ct. 1089, 67 L. Ed. 2d 207 (1981)

Justice POWELL delivered the opinion of the Court. This case requires us to address again the nature of the evidentiary burden placed upon the defendant in an employment discrimination suit brought under Title VII of the Civil Rights Act of 1964, 42 U.S.C. §§2000e et seq. The narrow question presented is whether, after the plaintiff has proved a *prima facie* case of

D. Presumptions in Civil Actions

discriminatory treatment, the burden shifts to the defendant to persuade the court by a preponderance of the evidence that legitimate, nondiscriminatory reasons for the challenged employment action existed.

I

Petitioner, the Texas Department of Community Affairs (TDCA), hired respondent, a female, in January 1972, for the position of accounting clerk in the Public Service Careers Division (PSC). PSC provided training and employment opportunities in the public sector for unskilled workers. When hired, respondent possessed several years' experience in employment training. She was promoted to Field Services Coordinator in July 1972. Her supervisor was reassigned in November of that year, and respondent was assigned additional duties. Although she applied for the supervisor's position of Project Director, the position remained vacant for six months.

PSC was funded completely by the United States Department of Labor. The Department was seriously concerned about inefficiencies at PSC. In February 1973, the Department notified the Executive Director of TDCA, B. R. Fuller, that it would terminate PSC the following month. TDCA officials, assisted by respondent, persuaded the Department to continue funding the program, conditioned upon PSC's reforming its operations. Among the agreed conditions were the appointment of a permanent Project Director and a complete reorganization of the PSC staff.

After consulting with personnel within TDCA, Fuller hired a male from another division of the agency as Project Director. In reducing the PSC staff, he fired respondent along with two other employees, and retained another male, Walz, as the only professional employee in the division. It is undisputed that respondent had maintained her application for the position of Project Director and had requested to remain with TDCA. Respondent soon was rehired by TDCA and assigned to another division of the agency. She received the exact salary paid to the Project Director at PSC, and the subsequent promotions she has received have kept her salary and responsibility commensurate with what she would have received had she been appointed Project Director.

Respondent filed this suit in the United States District Court for the Western District of Texas. She alleged that the failure to promote and the subsequent decision to terminate her had been predicated on gender discrimination in violation of Title VII. After a bench trial, the District Court held that neither decision was based on gender discrimination. The court relied on the testimony of Fuller that the employment decisions necessitated by the commands of the Department of Labor were based on consultation among trusted advisers and a nondiscriminatory evaluation of the relative qualifications of the individuals involved. He testified that the three individuals terminated did not work well together, and that TDCA thought that eliminating this problem would improve PSC's efficiency. The court accepted this explanation as rational and, in effect, found no evidence that the decisions not to promote and to terminate respondent were prompted by gender discrimination.

The Court of Appeals for the Fifth Circuit reversed in part. The court held that the District Court's "implicit evidentiary finding" that the male hired as Project Director was better qualified for that position than respondent was not clearly erroneous. Accordingly, the court affirmed the District Court's finding that respondent was not discriminated against when she was not promoted. The Court of Appeals, however, reversed the District Court's finding that Fuller's testimony sufficiently had rebutted respondent's *prima facie* case of gender discrimination in the decision to terminate her employment at PSC. The court reaffirmed its previously announced views that the defendant in a Title VII case bears the burden of proving by a preponderance of the evidence the existence of legitimate nondiscriminatory reasons for the employment action. . . . The court found that Fuller's testimony did not carry [this] evidentiary burden. It, therefore, reversed the judgment of the District Court and remanded the case for computation of backpay. Because the decision of the Court of Appeals as to the burden of proof borne by the defendant conflicts with interpretations of our precedents adopted by other Courts of Appeals, we granted certiorari. We now vacate the Fifth Circuit's decision and remand for application of the correct standard.

II

In McDonnell Douglas Corp. v. Green, 411 U.S. 792 (1973), we set forth the basic allocation of burdens and order of presentation of proof in a Title VII case alleging discriminatory treatment. First, the plaintiff has the burden of proving by the preponderance of the evidence a *prima facie* case of discrimination. Second, if the plaintiff succeeds in proving the *prima facie* case, the burden shifts to the defendant "to articulate some legitimate, nondiscriminatory reason for the employee's rejection." Id., at 802. Third, should the defendant carry this burden, the plaintiff must then have an opportunity to prove by a preponderance of the evidence that the legitimate reasons offered by the defendant were not its true reasons, but were a pretext for discrimination. Id., at 804.

The nature of the burden that shifts to the defendant should be understood in light of the plaintiff's ultimate and intermediate burdens. The ultimate burden of persuading the trier of fact that the defendant intentionally discriminated against the plaintiff remains at all times with the plaintiff. The *McDonnell Douglas* division of intermediate evidentiary burdens serves to bring the litigants and the court expeditiously and fairly to this ultimate question.

The burden of establishing a *prima facie* case of disparate treatment is

D. Presumptions in Civil Actions

not onerous. The plaintiff must prove by a preponderance of the evidence that she applied for an available position for which she was qualified, but was rejected under circumstances which give rise to an inference of unlawful discrimination.[6] The *prima facie* case serves an important function in the litigation: it eliminates the most common nondiscriminatory reasons for the plaintiff's rejection. . . . As the Court explained in Furnco Construction Corp. v. Waters, 438 U.S. 567, 577 (1978), the *prima facie* case "raises an inference of discrimination only because we presume these acts, if otherwise unexplained, are more likely than not based on the consideration of impermissible factors." Establishment of the *prima facie* case in effect creates a presumption that the employer unlawfully discriminated against the employee. If the trier of fact believes the plaintiff's evidence, and if the employer is silent in the face of the presumption, the court must enter judgment for the plaintiff because no issue of fact remains in the case.[7]

The burden that shifts to the defendant, therefore, is to rebut the presumption of discrimination by producing evidence that the plaintiff was rejected, or someone else was preferred, for a legitimate, nondiscriminatory reason. The defendant need not persuade the court that it was actually motivated by the proffered reasons. It is sufficient if the defendant's evidence raises a genuine issue of fact as to whether it discriminated against the plaintiff.[8] To accomplish this, the defendant must clearly set forth, through the introduction of admissible evidence, the reasons for the plaintiff's rejection. The explanation provided must be legally sufficient to justify a judgment for the defendant. If the defendant carries this burden of production, the

---

6. In *McDonnell Douglas*, supra, we described an appropriate model for a *prima facie* case of racial discrimination. The plaintiff must show: "(i) that he belongs to a racial minority; (ii) that he applied and was qualified for a job for which the employer was seeking applicants; (iii) that, despite his qualifications, he was rejected; and (iv) that, after his rejection, the position remained open and the employer continued to seek applicants from persons of complainant's qualifications." 411 U.S., at 802. We added, however, that this standard is not inflexible, as "(t)he facts necessarily will vary in Title VII cases, and the specification above of the prima facie proof required from respondent is not necessarily applicable in every respect in differing factual situations." Id., at 802, n.13. In the instant case, it is not seriously contested that respondent has proved a *prima facie* case. She showed that she was a qualified woman who sought an available position, but the position was left open for several months before she finally was rejected in favor of a male, Walz, who had been under her supervision.

7. The phrase *"prima facie* case" not only may denote the establishment of a legally mandatory, rebuttable presumption, but also may be used by courts to describe the plaintiff's burden of producing enough evidence to permit the trier of fact to infer the fact at issue. 9 J. Wigmore, Evidence §2494 (3d ed. 1940). *McDonnell Douglas* should have made it apparent that in the Title VII context we use *"prima facie* case" in the former sense.

8. This evidentiary relationship between the presumption created by a *prima facie* case and the consequential burden of production placed on the defendant is a traditional feature of the common law. "The word 'presumption' properly used refers only to a device for allocating the production burden." F. James and G. Hazard, Civil Procedure §7.9, p.255 (2d ed. 1977) (footnote omitted). See Fed. Rule Evid. 301. Usually, assessing the burden of production helps the judge determine whether the litigants have created an issue of fact to be decided by the jury. In a Title VII case, the allocation of burdens and the creation of a presumption by the establishment of a *prima facie* case is intended progressively to sharpen the inquiry into the elusive factual question of intentional discrimination.

presumption raised by the *prima facie* case is rebutted,[10] and the factual inquiry proceeds to a new level of specificity. Placing this burden of production on the defendant thus serves simultaneously to meet the plaintiff's *prima facie* case by presenting a legitimate reason for the action and to frame the factual issue with sufficient clarity so that the plaintiff will have a full and fair opportunity to demonstrate pretext. The sufficiency of the defendant's evidence should be evaluated by the extent to which it fulfills these functions.

The plaintiff retains the burden of persuasion. She now must have the opportunity to demonstrate that the proffered reason was not the true reason for the employment decision. This burden now merges with the ultimate burden of persuading the court that she has been the victim of intentional discrimination. She may succeed in this either directly by persuading the court that a discriminatory reason more likely motivated the employer or indirectly by showing that the employer's proffered explanation is unworthy of credence.

III

In reversing the judgment of the District Court that the discharge of respondent from PSC was unrelated to her sex, the Court of Appeals adhered to [the] rule it had developed to elaborate the defendant's burden of proof [that] the defendant must prove by a preponderance of the evidence that legitimate, nondiscriminatory reasons for the discharge existed.

A

The Court of Appeals has misconstrued the nature of the burden that *McDonnell Douglas* and its progeny place on the defendant. We stated in *Sweeney* that "the employer's burden is satisfied if he simply 'explains what he has done' or 'produc(es) evidence of legitimate nondiscriminatory reasons.'" 439 U.S., at 25, n.2, quoting id., at 28, 29 (Stevens, J., dissenting). It is plain that the Court of Appeals required much more: it placed on the defendant the burden of persuading the court that it had convincing, objective reasons for preferring the chosen applicant above the plaintiff.

The Court of Appeals distinguished *Sweeney* on the ground that the case held only that the defendant did not have the burden of proving the absence of discriminatory intent. But this distinction slights the rationale of

---

10. See generally J. Thayer, Preliminary Treatise on Evidence 346 (1898). In saying that the presumption drops from the case, we do not imply that the trier of fact no longer may consider evidence previously introduced by the plaintiff to establish a *prima facie* case. A satisfactory explanation by the defendant destroys the legally mandatory inference of discrimination arising from the plaintiff's initial evidence. Nonetheless, this evidence and inferences properly drawn therefrom may be considered by the trier of fact on the issue of whether the defendant's explanation is pretextual. Indeed, there may be some cases where the plaintiff's initial evidence, combined with effective cross-examination of the defendant, will suffice to discredit the defendant's explanation.

D. Presumptions in Civil Actions 589

Sweeney and of our other cases. We have stated consistently that the employee's *prima facie* case of discrimination will be rebutted if the employer articulates lawful reasons for the action; that is, to satisfy this intermediate burden, the employer need only produce admissible evidence which would allow the trier of fact rationally to conclude that the employment decision had not been motivated by discriminatory animus. The Court of Appeals would require the defendant to introduce evidence which, in the absence of any evidence of pretext, would persuade the trier of fact that the employment action was lawful. This exceeds what properly can be demanded to satisfy a burden of production.

The court placed the burden of persuasion on the defendant apparently because it feared that "(i)f an employer need only articulate—not prove—a legitimate, nondiscriminatory reason for his action, he may compose fictitious, but legitimate, reasons for his actions." Turner v. Texas Instruments, Inc., [555 F.2d 1251] at 1255 (5th cir. 1977). We do not believe, however, that limiting the defendant's evidentiary obligation to a burden of production will unduly hinder the plaintiff. First, as noted above, the defendant's explanation of its legitimate reasons must be clear and reasonably specific. This obligation arises both from the necessity of rebutting the inference of discrimination arising from the *prima facie* case and from the requirement that the plaintiff be afforded "a full and fair opportunity" to demonstrate pretext. Second, although the defendant does not bear a formal burden of persuasion, the defendant nevertheless retains an incentive to persuade the trier of fact that the employment decision was lawful. Thus, the defendant normally will attempt to prove the factual basis for its explanation. Third, the liberal discovery rules applicable to any civil suit in federal court are supplemented in a Title VII suit by the plaintiff's access to the Equal Employment Opportunity Commission's investigatory files concerning her complaint. Given these factors, we are unpersuaded that the plaintiff will find it particularly difficult to prove that a proffered explanation lacking a factual basis is a pretext. We remain confident that the *McDonnell Douglas* framework permits the plaintiff meriting relief to demonstrate intentional discrimination. . . .

IV

In summary, the Court of Appeals erred by requiring the defendant to prove by a preponderance of the evidence the existence of nondiscriminatory reasons for terminating the respondent. . . . When the plaintiff has proved a *prima facie* case of discrimination, the defendant bears only the burden of explaining clearly the nondiscriminatory reasons for its actions. The judgment of the Court of Appeals is vacated, and the case is remanded for further proceedings consistent with this opinion.

It is so ordered.

What is occurring in *Burdine* is simple enough to explain. The plaintiff has to produce enough evidence so that a reasonable person could conclude that she has been discriminated against. The employer must then provide evidence of a non-discriminatory reason for the employer's action. This requirement focuses inquiry on a particular set of issues. If the employer satisfies this requirement, the plaintiff must prove by a preponderance of the evidence that discrimination rather than the employer's proffered reason is the true cause of the employer's action. In this way, burdens of proof, in particular burdens of production, have been employed to structure and order the proof process. Note, however, the many different phrases used by the Court to accomplish this result. The Court refers to a *"prima facie* case," to the "consequential burden of production," to a "legally mandated inference," to a "legally mandatory rebuttable presumption," among others. Most of these phrases probably mean the same thing. There are only three different requirements that can be placed upon litigants in the context of a case like *Burdine*: A party can be required to plead an issue, bear a burden of production, and bear a burden of persuasion. All the various formulations in the opinion refer to one or the other of these requirements, or some combination of the requirements. Unfortunately, the primary effect of using the complicated legal terminology of the Court is to increase confusion and perhaps to obfuscate the laudatory objectives that the Court achieves through its structuring of the proof process.

If the primary effect of using the complicated terminology is confusion, why does the Court use it? There is no ready answer for that, although a few plausible hypotheses may be advanced. First, the terminology the Court employs has the stamp of history upon it. In addition, the use of such legal technicalities may permit a court to intrude considerably into the evidentiary process while purporting not to do so (and perhaps believing that it is not doing so, as well). Reconsider *Burdine* from that perspective. Normally the manner in which the proof process unfolds is a matter for the litigants to decide, and the inferences that are to be drawn from the evidence is for the jury to decide. In *Burdine*, however, the Supreme Court has provided a very detailed structure for the process of proof in trials of alleged discrimination in the workplace. Would the Court be subject to complaints that it had exceeded its appropriate bounds if it simply said directly what it said indirectly? In that regard, how do the following articulations differ from each other:

(a) Upon evidence of discrimination a presumption of discrimination arises that can be rebutted by evidence of a non-discriminatory purpose, and if such evidence is forthcoming, the plaintiff's "ultimate burden" must then be satisfied.

(b) The plaintiff must establish a certain probability of having been discriminated against, at which point the defendant must establish a certain probability of having acted for an acceptable reason, at

D. Presumptions in Civil Actions

which point the plaintiff must then establish by a preponderance of the evidence that the actual cause of her complaint was discrimination by the employer.

These two articulations are identical in function, differing only in the terminology employed to reach identical outcomes. Does the first sound less intrusive and more "judicial" than the second, thus appearing to be more respectful of the traditional roles of the parties and the jury? Does the second sound more like a statute than the first? If so, does that provide an explanation for the Court's approach?

In addition to allocating burdens of production in various ways (as in *Burdine*), courts also use presumption language to change the substantive law, to create affirmative defenses, to shift burdens of proof around during trial, and to provide for comments on the evidence while appearing to respect the constraints upon comment imposed by various jurisdictions. Each of these uses will now be examined in greater detail in order to demonstrate that there is nothing unique to presumptions that permits these results to be achieved; rather, standard evidentiary techniques are being employed under the rubric of "presumptions."[7]

a. *Constructing Substantive Rules*

Presumption terminology has been employed to allow changes in the law to be effected. Although one still sees it today, this particular use was especially important in earlier times when courts purported only to discover, not to make, law. As times changed, cases decided at a previous time would on occasion appear to be a bit outdated. The courts could not just change their earlier arrived-at positions, however, for to do so would be to undermine the legitimacy of the common law. A dilemma was faced. The courts perceived that changes in the law were in order, but the basis of their legitimacy forbad them from acting directly. Not surprisingly, the judges acted indirectly through the creation of various fictions, including various presumptions, that had the effect of changing the law. A good example of this is the role of the violation of a safety statute in establishing negligence. At an early time in the common law development of negligence, the violation of a safety statute was admissible as evidence of negligence. Courts began instructing juries that the violation of a safety statute gave rise to a presumption of negligence that was "evidence" of negligence (a modified comment on the evidence), and soon thereafter cases appeared in which violation of a safety statute was held to give rise to a "conclusive presumption" of negligence. What that meant was that "negligence" no longer had to be shown; it would suffice to

---

7. Much of what follows is based upon Allen, Presumptions in Civil Actions Reconsidered, 66 Iowa L. Rev. 843 (1981), which should be consulted for elaborations and complete citations.

show the violation of a safety statute. For a fascinating account of the use of legal fictions, including presumptions, to change the law, see the three-part article Fuller, Legal Fictions, 25 Ill. L. Rev. 363, 513, 877 (1930-1931).

Presumptions have also been put to other substantive uses, in particular to determine the outcome of cases that depend upon an issue for which there is no satisfactory evidence. An example is the determination of survivorship in cases in which the parties died in the same accident and there is no evidence as to who died first. Distribution of the property to the heirs may depend upon who survived, and thus without evidence of survivorship an impasse may develop that could interfere with the distribution. Moreover, relying on the normal rules of burden of persuasion may yield unjust results. In order to avoid a possible impasse and unfairness, various presumptions have been created to supply an answer to the question of survivorship.

Creating such presumptions does, to be sure, resolve the problem of survivorship, but the resolution is not accomplished because of something unique in the nature of a presumption. Rather, the problem is resolved because a substantive rule has been constructed. For example, one solution to the problem of determining the order of death would be to "create the presumption" that each party survived the other and to distribute the property accordingly. This is equivalent, however, to constructing the rule that, in the absence of evidence of survivorship, the property of the parties shall be distributed without reference to the death of the other party. There is nothing peculiar to the nature of presumptions that would facilitate accomplishing that objective. Rather, the label "presumption" would simply have been applied to the construction of a rule that was created for reasons entirely independent of any concept implicit in the nature of presumptions, and a functionally identical rule could be constructed without using the word *presumption*.

The failure to confront directly the relevant evidentiary issues has generated some confusion, however, as can be seen by considering the presumption of death after seven years absence and the concomitant presumption as to time of death. When a person has been absent and unheard of for seven years, a presumption of death is said to arise.[8] Again, a rule of decision has been constructed under the guise of a presumption: After seven years of unbroken absence and silence, the legal system will proceed as if the person were dead. The policy behind the rule is that it is unfair to require that the affairs of other persons affected by those of the missing person be held in abeyance indeterminately, especially when there is a good chance that the missing person is in fact dead. It may be of importance, however, to determine precisely when the missing person died. For example, the rights of heirs might be affected by the date. Accordingly, a second presumption is usually created that the person died on the last day of the seventh year.[9]

---

8. Morgan, Presumptions, 12 Wash. L. Rev. 255, 258 (1937).
9. Morgan, Instructing the Jury Upon Presumptions and Burden of Proof, 47 Harv. L. Rev. 59, 78 (1933).

D. Presumptions in Civil Actions

Unfortunately, the use of these two presumptions in tandem raises problems when one is rebutted at trial. By one view, all an opponent of a presumption need do to rebut it is produce sufficient evidence to the contrary of the presumed fact to justify a jury verdict.[10] Assume that an action in a jurisdiction with such a rule is brought to contest the distribution of the property of a person who has been missing for seven years. Assume further that if the person died on the last day of the seventh year the property would be distributed in one manner, but if he died on some other day, the property would be distributed differently. Finally, assume that the opponent of the presumption of time of death manages to produce sufficient evidence to justify a jury verdict that the decedent did not die on the last day of the seventh year, but that the jury does not believe the evidence.

The result in such a case would be another impasse. The presumption of time of death, having been "rebutted," is out of the case, but there is no convincing evidence establishing the date of death. Thus, the probable outcome will be that the plaintiff will lose, because the plaintiff will not be able to satisfy the burden of persuasion. However, it hardly makes sense to let the outcome of disputes in cases such as these hinge on the fortuity of who filed suit if such a result can be avoided. Moreover, fortuity will control only if one assumes that there is a rebuttable presumption at work in the case.

If, by contrast, the substantive rule is viewed without the distortion caused by referring to it as a presumption, the resolution of the difficulty becomes clear. The rule has been constructed to avoid an impasse. Accordingly, the resolution is to construct a slightly different rule that accommodates the possibility of another impasse. For example, one resolution would be to provide that the property will be distributed as though the decedent died on the last day of the seventh year, unless the actual date of death is established. Under this rule, the property will be distributed according to the substantive rules of the jurisdiction rather than according to the fortuity of who filed suit, which should better serve the policies of the jurisdiction.

Unnecessary problems of a slightly different nature can also arise from the failure to perceive that the presumption of death from seven years absence is simply a substantive rule constructed to resolve certain problems of proof. What happens, for example, if the spouse of the absent person remarries after five years? Has bigamy occurred? Since seven years have not passed, the missing person is presumed to be alive, thus casting doubt on the validity of the second marriage. However, there is also a presumption of the validity of marriages that is applicable to the remarriage. Thus, these two presumptions are seen to be in conflict, and the resolution of the conflict by the courts normally follows after a lengthy discussion of "conflicting presumptions."[11] Typically, the answer given is that the presumption of the validity of the marriage "outweighs" that of the absent person being alive.

10. See Diederich v. Walters, 65 Ill. 2d 95, 102 357 N.E. 1128, 1131 (1976).
11. See Louisell, Construing Rule 301: Instructing the Jury on Presumptions in Civil Actions and Proceedings, 63 Va. L. Rev. 281, 293-295 (1977).

The rhetoric of conflicting presumptions would not be necessary if the courts would simply do directly what is now done indirectly through the use of presumptions. There are certain interests served by requiring seven years to pass before declaring a person legally dead. There are other equally important interests served by the institution of marriage. The issue posed by cases such as the one hypothesized is how those interests intersect. It may very well be that the societal concern for the family unit justifies remarriage after five years' absence; it may also be that it does not. However that issue is resolved, the resolution is *not* facilitated by viewing the issue as a case of conflicting presumptions. The real issue is whether a rule should be created that allows remarriage after a spouse has been absent for five years. Focusing on the label "conflicting presumptions" merely diverts attention from that issue.

b. *Allocating Burdens of Persuasion*

When the burden of persuasion of an issue is placed directly on a defendant, it is normally referred to as an "affirmative defense." For example, rule 8(c) of the Federal Rules of Civil Procedure lists a number of affirmative defenses that must be pled and proven by defendants. Occasionally, though, burdens of persuasion are said to be allocated by presumptions that shift the burden of persuasion to the opponent of the presumption. In paternity suits in which the husband denies legitimacy, for example, there is said to be a presumption of legitimacy of a child born during wedlock that requires the defendant to persuade the fact finder of the child's illegitimacy.

To say, however, that there is a "presumption of legitimacy that allocates or shifts the burden of persuasion" to the defendant and that there is an "affirmative defense of illegitimacy" that requires the defendant to prove the fact is to make functionally identical statements. Indeed, the only reason for referring to a presumption as shifting or allocating the burden is to emphasize that an exception has been created to the normal rule that plaintiffs bear the burden of persuasion in civil cases. Accordingly, a "presumption that allocates the burden of persuasion" is simply an alternative label applied to an affirmative defense. As with presumptions that create substantive rules, there is nothing in the concept of a presumption that facilitates the allocation of a burden of persuasion. Rather, presumptions that shift the burden of persuasion are simply affirmative defenses that are created for the same reasons of policy that generally inform the decision to allocate burdens of persuasion. Indeed, whether an affirmative defense goes by its usual label or that of a presumption seems entirely fortuitous.

There is one variant of burden shifting presumptions that requires closer examination, however. The label "presumption" is occasionally applied to a set of evidentiary relationships that may profitably be referred to as "con-

D. Presumptions in Civil Actions

ditional imperatives."[12] Under a conditional imperative, the burden of persuasion shifts if, but only if, the party first establishes some other fact.

The distinction between a conditional imperative and an affirmative defense can be easily demonstrated by a simple example. Assume that an heir sues to compel distribution of the estate of a person who has been missing and unheard of for over seven years. A jurisdiction could, if it chose to do so, place the burden of proving the testator alive on the conservator of the estate in all cases. Were that done here, the result would be to create an affirmative defense. Thus, when an heir sues a conservator, the conservator could prevail by proving the testator to be alive. Alternatively, a jurisdiction could require claimants to prove the death of the testator, but also provide that if the testator is proven to be missing and unheard of for more than seven years, the conservator must then prove the testator is alive. Thus, the burden of proving the relevant fact normally would rest upon the plaintiff; but if seven years' absence were established, the burden of proving the testator alive would shift to the defendant. In the latter case, a conditional imperative would be created—upon proof of a basic fact, the conservator must prove a second fact or lose.

Often this conditional imperative is said to be created by a presumption. This class of presumptions differs from a normal affirmative defense in one crucial aspect: the jury is often instructed in the alternative. In such cases, the judge instructs the jury that the burden of persuasion lies on the plaintiff unless the jury is persuaded that the testator has been missing and unheard of for seven years. If the jury is so persuaded, then the burden of persuasion to show the testator is alive shifts to the conservator.

However, the use of the word *presumption* when referring to a conditional imperative demonstrates once again how the application of that label can have deleterious results. Because presumptions of this type are generally viewed as devices to regulate jury decision making, the jury is often responsible for determining the truth or falsity of the basic fact—here, absence for seven years. Yet, when this process is viewed without the distorting effect that results from thinking of it as involving a presumption, it becomes quite clear that the jury should *not* determine the existence of the basic fact for purposes of allocating the burden of persuasion of the conditional fact. That determination involves a preliminary fact, and thus it should be made by the judge.

Consider why a jurisdiction would condition the burden of persuasion of a fact on the existence of some other fact. The reason is that the decision to allocate burdens of persuasion is influenced by the truth or falsity of the fact in question. Assume, for example, that a jurisdiction allocates burdens of persuasion consistently with its *a priori* appraisal of probability. It may then conclude that since testators are normally alive, anyone alleging one is not should prove it. However, once the testator has been proven to have

---

12. See J. Maguire, Evidence: Common Sense and Common Law 175 (1947).

been missing or unheard of for seven years, the *a priori* probability may change, making it more likely that the testator is dead. Accordingly an application of the general rule of decision to this subset of cases produces the result that the conservator should now bear the burden of persuading the fact finder that the testator is alive.

Seven years' absence, then, is a fact upon which a rule of evidence depends. In that regard, it is quite similar to determining whether two people are married for purposes of the rules on privilege, whether an offer of proof is within the parol evidence rule, or, for that matter, whether a burden of production has been satisfied. Accordingly, for the same reasons of expediency, consistency, and expertise that allocate the finding of these facts to the judge, so too should the judge make a preliminary determination whether or not the testator has been unheard of and missing for seven years and then allocate the burden of persuasion accordingly.

In the case of allocating burdens of persuasion, the primary value secured by having the judge determine the preliminary facts is convenience. That value is not offset by any serious loss to the jury's role. The only effect of determining the preliminary fact is to determine who bears the burden of persuasion. But, in the normal civil case, the purpose of burdens of persuasion is to provide a rule for deciding cases in which the evidence is very nearly balanced. Thus, even if a judge's determination of a preliminary fact differed from how the jury would have decided it, the result is not likely to be very significant since only cases in which the evidence is essentially in equipoise should be affected. That possibility does not seem to outweigh the confusion that may result from the greatly increased complexity of jury instructions that results if juries are instructed on these preliminary facts.

The frequent failure to appreciate the proper role of the trial judge seems primarily to be a function of the ambiguity generated by erroneously viewing the resolution of these evidentiary problems as a function of the nature of presumptions and the concomitant error that juries should decide the basic facts. This failure of perception has led to a number of other significant misunderstandings. One of these, once again involving conflicting presumptions, also bears closer scrutiny. Consider the following example from McCormick:

> W, asserting that she is the widow of H, claims her share of his property, and proves that on a certain day she and H were married. The adversary then proves that three or four years before her marriage to H, the alleged widow married another man. W's proof gives her the benefit of the presumption of the validity of a marriage. The adversary's proof gives rise to a general presumption of the continuance of a status or condition once proved to exist, and a specific presumption of the continuance of a marriage relationship.[13]

---

13. McCormick's Law of Evidence §344, at 976-977 (3d ed., Cleary, 1984).

D. Presumptions in Civil Actions

If the continuation of the first marriage disposes of the validity of the second, and vice versa, then the presumptions described by Dean McCormick cannot logically exist simultaneously. Only one party can bear a burden of persuasion on an issue at a given point in time for otherwise there would be a situation in which both parties would lose. Thus, the presumptions are said to conflict, and the issue is how to resolve the conflict. The answer Dean McCormick supplied is that the "weightier" presumption should survive—the validity of the second marriage in his hypothetical—or, alternatively, that there should be created a new presumption that in successive marriages the earlier ones were terminated, thus requiring the opponent of that proposition to prove the contrary. Dean McCormick's solutions would work, but they would do so for reasons having nothing to do with some concept inherent in presumptions. In fact, they demonstrate further the bankruptcy of the term.

First, the two suggested solutions are in reality one. If the presumption of the validity of the second marriage "survives," that would require the opponent to prove that the first marriage was never terminated, which is precisely what the second proposed solution does. More importantly, however, the talk of "new" or "surviving" presumptions merely obfuscates the fact that what Dean McCormick did was to suggest a solution to a fairly standard problem as to sufficiency of the evidence. The presumption of the continuation of a marriage reflects a belief that the creation of a relationship implies that it continues. The presumption of the validity of a marriage, by contrast, reflects the importance we attach to that institution. Because of that importance, it is certainly comprehensible to require someone attacking the validity of a marriage to prove its invalidity by a high standard of persuasion, and proof of another marriage three or four years earlier, without more, can certainly be viewed as being inadequate to achieve the level of proof necessary to prove the later marriage invalid.

Suppose, however, that the first marriage had occurred three or four weeks (or hours) before the second marriage. Would the "weightier" presumption of the validity of the second marriage still survive? If Dean McCormick's solution were taken at face value, the answer would be in the affirmative. However, the response *should* be in the negative because the more recent the first marriage, the less likely is the second to be valid. At some point, that likelihood will be sufficiently low to justify concluding that the second marriage is invalid. The "conflict in presumptions," in short, collapses into a sufficiency of the evidence problem, as does practically every other purported conflict in presumptions that shift burdens of persuasion.

The problem of conflicting presumptions in this context further illustrates that nothing but ambiguity comes from relying on presumptions to do that which can be done directly. There are yet other examples of unnecessary confusion and ambiguity that corroborate that conclusion, but the point has been adequately made. The power of the courts and legislatures to allocate burdens of persuasion and of courts to make determinations of sufficiency of the evidence is quite well established. Relying on presumptions does not add to that power in any way. Since it generates a risk of confusion, there is no reason to continue to use the misleading term in this fashion.

c. *Allocating Burdens of Production*

Although plaintiffs normally bear the burden of production of most issues relevant to a litigated case, just as they also normally bear the burden of persuasion, occasionally a presumption is said to exist that shifts a burden of production to a defendant. However, underlying the label of presumption is a quite common decision concerning the proper evidentiary relationship of the parties that is made for reasons entirely independent of any concept attributable to presumptions.

If a jurisdiction wishes to place a burden of production on a party, it may do so directly. Doing so by use of the word *presumption* in no way affects the scope of the power. Furthermore, an examination of the two justifications normally given for the creation of a presumption that shifts a burden of production—to encourage the production of evidence and to expedite trials[14]—not only will demonstrate that there is no independent concept at play, but also that reliance on presumptions in this context produces unnecessary confusion and controversy.

Placing a burden of production on a party may in fact encourage the production of evidence, but no greater encouragement comes from referring to the process of allocation as a presumption. Placing a burden of production on a party does provide a sanction for failing to produce evidence—dismissal or a directed verdict—but the sanction is a function of the meaning of a burden of production rather than an independent attribute of presumptions. Moreover, it is difficult to imagine a case today in which the sanction of possible dismissal would generate more evidence than discovery schemes. Thus, reliance on a presumption to shift a burden of production in order to generate evidence is not only doing indirectly what can be done directly, but it also no longer serves the stated purpose.

The second justification for using presumptions that shift burdens of production—to expedite trials—fares no better than the first. There are some issues that are so inherently unlikely to be relevant at trial that we normally can proceed without reference to them. One way to describe that process is to say that we will "presume" the issue is not to be contested unless the defendant "rebuts" the presumption by producing evidence on the issue.

---

14. Presumptions are also used to satisfy a party's burden of production, thus ensuring against a directed verdict. Legislatures may or may not have the power to direct that certain types of cases go to the jury. Unites States v. Gainey, 380 U.S. 63, 67-71 (1965). But whether they do or not is not affected by the existence of presumptions. Rather, the word *presumption* is simply used on occasion to describe the decision to direct trial courts to send certain kinds of cases to the jury.

D. Presumptions in Civil Actions

This is simply another way of saying that a burden of production has been allocated to a party, and the use of the word *presumption* is nothing more than a handy label in this context. Unfortunately, however, again there has been confusion caused by the use of the label that can and should be avoided. The most important example of the confusion is the controversy that has developed concerning how presumptions of this kind can be rebutted.

"Rebutting the presumption" in this context merely means satisfying the burden of production. Nevertheless, because of the failure to see presumptions as involving nothing but the application of a label to a decision reached for other reasons, a number of courts have concluded that presumptions shifting the burden of production can be rebutted and that the jury should make that determination. As a result, a scheme for determining whether these presumptions have been rebutted has developed that can only be described as bizarre. For example, some courts have held that a presumption is rebutted if the opponent of the presumption produces sufficient evidence believed by the jury that would justify a finding to the contrary even though the jury is not convinced by it. Others have held that an opponent must produce sufficient evidence to justify a jury verdict that is not positively disbelieved by the jury.[15] And there are still other views that need not be recited here.[16]

Were these courts not operating under the mistaken assumption that something called a presumption was at play, they surely would have realized that none of this is necessary. Whether a burden of production is satisfied, regardless of the reasons for the allocation of that burden, is a question for the trial judge to decide employing whatever standard the jurisdiction wishes the judge to employ. Were this simple fact to be realized, this aspect of the controversy surrounding presumptions that shift burdens of production would simply disappear, as indeed it should.

d. Commenting on the Relationship Between Facts

Suppose you are a trial judge of some experience, and that over time you have observed that jurors tend consistently to misevaluate a certain type of evidence. One way to correct that systemic flaw is to comment on that evidence for the benefit of the jurors and to inform them of what your experience has been. Suppose further, however, that the legislature enacts a blanket prohibition on judicial comment on the evidence. That is not going to change the fact that jurors misevaluate this evidence from your perspective, and so you now face a dilemma. Do you passively accept the legislature's admonition and thus allow a series of erroneous results to occur?

Not surprisingly, the judiciary in this country when faced with basically

---

15. G. Lilly, An Introduction to the Law of Evidence 56 (1978).
16. Ibid.

this problem did not passively accept the inevitability of erroneous outcomes but instead searched for alternatives. The alternative that was found was, again, "presumptions."[17] Rather than comment on the evidence, judges began instructing jurors that proof of certain facts gave rise to a "presumption" that permitted an inference of some other fact, that the "presumption is evidence" of some other fact,[18] or that it "has weight as" evidence that the jury was to consider in its deliberations.[19] All this mumbo-jumbo amounts to, however, is comment on the evidence in disguised form. As the Supreme Court has commented, it is "often . . . tempting to cast in terms of a 'presumption' a conclusion which a court thinks probable from given facts."[20] Similar instructions are given when the proven fact's logical relationship to the second fact is tenuous at best. An instruction in the latter case is justified, it is said, because legislatures and courts are entitled to give "additional weight" to proven facts by presumptions if they are so inclined. Again, however, the metaphysics of presumptions merely obscures what is in fact occurring. Providing proven facts with an effect greater than that justified by their logical significance is a method of manipulating the burden of persuasion of the second fact.

Consider first an instruction that once fact A is proven there is a presumption of fact B, and that the jury is to weigh fact A, or the presumption itself, as evidence of fact B. Assume further that the judiciary or the legislature has concluded that fact B normally is inferable from fact A. The point of such an instruction, obviously, is to encourage the jury to find fact B once fact A is established. The encouragement comes from the judge's indicating to the jury in a conclusory fashion the judge's or the legislature's perception of the relationship between the facts. The judge would so instruct, presumably, when it was feared that the jury might not appreciate the relationship between the facts, thus increasing the likelihood that the jury would reach what the judge believed to be an erroneous result. Consequently, the instruction would be designed to put the jury in the position of an informed decisionmaker, thus increasing the likelihood of the jury arriving at a result the judge or legislature deems correct.

The effect of such an instruction is to modify the manner in which the jury's inferential process occurs by enhancing the role of fact A. That effect is indistinguishable from the effect of a judicial comment on the strength of the evidence. The reason for giving this type of presumptive instruction is identical to that of judicial comment, as is the anticipated outcome. Thus, presumptions of this sort are nothing but a form of judicial comment on the evidence.

    17. Reaugh, Presumptions and the Burden of Proof, 36 Ill. L. Rev. 703, 719 n.103 (1942).
    18. Ibid. (and see authorities cited therein).
    19. Brosman, The Statutory Presumption (pt. II), 5 Tul. L. Rev. 178, 204-205 (1931); Louisell, Construing Rule 302: Instructing the Jury on Presumptions in Civil Actions and Proceedings, 63 Va. L. Rev. 281, 302-303 (1977).
    20. Morrissette v. United States, 342 U.S. 246, 274 (1952).

D. Presumptions in Civil Actions

There is, however, one difference between this type of presumptive instruction and traditional judicial comment on the evidence that further demonstrates the deleterious effect of our ill-advised reliance on presumptions. While explicit judicial comment attempts to inform the jury of the factors that may be relevant to its decision, and why they may be relevant, presumptive instructions do little more than inform the jury that upon proof of fact A a presumption arises of fact B. Little or no effort is made to inform the jury *what* the instruction means or *why* a particular result might be appropriate.[21] Consequently, a presumptive instruction may tend to promote an irrational decision-making process, even though it may also enhance the probability of a more accurate result to the extent the underlying inference is valid.

An irrational inferential process is promoted by a presumptive instruction that recommends to the jury that it engage in the impossible mental feat of "weighing the presumption as evidence." As Professor Morgan has asked, "How can one weigh a presumption against, or with, or as, evidence? Just what will be the mental process?"[22] The answer, is, of course, that the jury cannot "weigh the presumption" as evidence, for it is not evidence. It is merely a label that has been applied to a perceived relationship between facts. Thus, the aim of the instruction is to encourage the jury to "weigh the facts underlying the presumption and the inferences that may follow from those facts." The jury, however, is rarely informed in realistic terms of what it should do; it is only informed that it should weigh the presumption as evidence, which is an impossible task. Obviously, then, the irrationality of the resultant decision-making process may tend to be enhanced by an instruction of this sort since the jury has no basis for rationally evaluating the instruction.

What is particularly troublesome about a jury instruction to weigh a presumption as evidence, even if the underlying inference is valid, is that it may diminish the role of the jury. The jury may reach a decision not on the basis of its independent consideration of the facts and the inferences from the facts that it concludes are reasonable, but rather by deference to the legislative or judicial judgment expressed in the instruction that a presumption has arisen that is proof of some other fact. While one may applaud the potential for improved accuracy in results, the question remains whether accuracy should be obtained at the expense of diminishing the role of juries in the trial process in this manner.

Consider now those instructions that provide for a presumption to be weighed as evidence where the presumption is used to give "additional weight" to fact A beyond its logical significance. Normally in these cases fact A has little logical relevance to B, but the instruction is still given that proof of

---

21. See McCormick, Charges on Presumptions and Burdens of Proof, 5 N.C.L. Rev. 291, 299-301 (1972).
22. Morgan, Instructing the Jury upon Presumptions and Burden of Proof, 47 Harv. L. Rev. 59, 73 (1933).

fact A gives rise to a presumption that is to be weighed as evidence of fact B. One way of viewing such an instruction is that it is an inaccurate comment on the evidence. The effect of an inaccurate comment, however, is to implicitly shift the burden of persuasion, a point which can best be clarified by an example.

Consider a negligence trial in which there is an issue of contributory negligence that must be disproved by the plaintiff by a preponderance of the evidence. Assume that on the basis of the evidence adduced, a well-informed, rational jury would conclude that it is just as likely as not that the plaintiff was contributorily negligent. The verdict would be for the defendant, since the plaintiff would have failed to meet the burden of persuasion. Assume, however, that the trial judge instructs the jury that proof of plaintiff's injuries gives rise to a presumption of due care on the part of the plaintiff that is evidence to be weighed by the jury in its deliberations. Assume further that as a result of that instruction, the same jury would now conclude that there is only a 40 percent chance that the plaintiff was contributorily negligent. The verdict now would be for the plaintiff. In order to escape the verdict, the defendant would have to adduce stronger evidence of the plaintiff's negligence.

Assume that the defendant, in anticipation of the instruction, adduced stronger evidence, that the trial judge instructed on the presumption, and that the evidence was now so strong that the jury nonetheless would conclude that it is just as likely as not that the plaintiff was contributorily negligent, thus finding for the defendant. If the well-informed jury had evaluated the much stronger evidence *without* the instruction having been given, it surely would have concluded that there was a much higher chance of contributory negligence than 50 percent. As a result of the instruction, then, the defendant had to do more than merely establish that contributory negligence was as likely as not, as judged by what a rational, well-informed fact finder would conclude. The defendant was required to make a showing sufficient to reach some higher, unarticulated standard.

The functional effect of such an instruction is to create an affirmative defense. Although the jury formally will be applying the normal rule that the burden of proving lack of contributory negligence is on the plaintiff, the reality is that the instruction has lowered the plaintiff's burden of proving lack of contributory negligence, and concomitantly has raised the defendant's burden of establishing the issue. And whenever a defendant has to meet a higher standard of proof than the normal rule allows, an affirmative defense has been created.

Thus, the effect of instructing on a presumption that is to be weighed as evidence is either to make a comment on the evidence or to manipulate a burden of persuasion. In neither case does reliance on the concept of a presumption facilitate the process, but it does obfuscate the issues at hand. By relying on presumptions to make judicial comment on the evidence, the question of the proper role of comment on the evidence is avoided. At the

D. Presumptions in Civil Actions

same time such instructions inject an irrational component into the jury decision-making process. Instructions of this sort that shift burdens of persuasion must inject an even greater irrational element into the decision-making process, since there is no way of knowing just how high a burden of persuasion these instructions will be translated into by juries. Moreover, various juries will undoubtedly view the instruction, and the burden it implicitly imposes, in differing ways. Thus, the instruction probably has the additional undesirable effect of contributing to ad hoc decision making by juries.

The message of this section has been that presumptions do not exist independently of common evidentiary techniques such as burdens of proof and comment on the evidence. The courts, and to a lesser extent legislatures, have employed the label "presumption" to refer to complex interactions of these various techniques. Do you think that the result has been for the better, or should we instead reduce the intrusions into the jury process that presumptions normally entail? In any event, borrowing but modifying an idea first developed in R. Lempert and S. Saltzburg, A Modern Approach to Evidence 805 (2d ed. 1982), the various ways in which the label "presumption" has been used, and the consequence of the various uses, have been charted below. Work your way through each step in the chart to ensure that you completely grasp the manner in which the label "presumption" has been employed:

The beneficiary of the presumption introduces evidence of the basic fact and the presumption:	The party opposing the presumption introduces:	The consequences of the presumption are:
1. Is conclusive.	No evidence bearing on the presumption.	A substantive rule has been created making the "presumed" fact irrelevant. Therefore, the jury will be instructed either that liability is determined by the basic fact or that if it finds the basic fact it must find the presumed fact. A directed verdict will be in order if reasonable people could not disagree about the existence of the basic fact.
	Evidence tending to contradict the basic fact.	Same as above.

	Evidence tending to contradict the presumed fact.	Same as above, except that the jury should be admonished to disregard any evidence relevant only to the presumed fact.
2. Shifts the burden of persuasion.	No evidence bearing on the presumption.	If the jury finds the basic fact, it must find the presumed fact (since opponent will not have met its burden of persuasion). If the jury does not find the basic fact, the burden of persuasion remains with the beneficiary with respect to the presumed fact. A partial directed verdict on the basic fact would be entered if reasonable people would not disagree about its existence. If a verdict is directed on the basic fact, a verdict will also be directed on the presumed fact.
	Evidence tending to contradict the basic fact.	Same as above.
	Evidence tending to contradict the presumed fact.	Same as above, except that a verdict would not be directed on the presumed fact if there is sufficient evidence to generate a jury question.
3. Shifts the burden of production.	No evidence bearing on the presumption.	If the jury finds the basic fact, it must find the presumed fact (since opponent will not have met its burden of persuasion).
	Evidence tending to contradict the basic fact.	Same as above.
	Evidence tending to contradict the presumed fact.	There will be no jury instruction relating the basic fact to the presumed fact.

D. Presumptions in Civil Actions

4. Is a permissible inference.	No evidence bearing on the presumption.	The jury will be instructed in one of a variety of ways that if it finds the basic fact it may infer the presumed fact. This is a disguised comment on the evidence. In some jurisdictions evidence of the basic fact will guarantee the beneficiary that it will not have a verdict directed against it on the presumed fact. This amounts to a legislative determination that proof of the basic fact generates a jury question on the presumed fact.
	Evidence tending to contradict the basic fact.	Same as above.
	Evidence tending to contradict the presumed fact.	Same as above. If the evidence contradicting the presumed fact is quite strong, a directed verdict might be granted, but it is unlikely.

PROBLEMS

1. Patty Price is the beneficiary of a life insurance policy issued on the life of her husband, Robert, by the Delta Insurance Company. Patty claims that Robert is dead, and when Delta refuses to pay on the policy, she brings suit against Delta in state court. Delta's sole defense is that Robert is not dead. The jurisdiction where the law suit is being tried has a statutory provision that one not heard from for seven years is presumed to be dead. This presumption has the effect of imposing upon the party against whom it operates the burden of persuasion as to the nonexistence of the presumed fact.

Patty introduces the testimony of several individuals who claim that they saw Robert killed by a fleeing felon five years ago. The defendant introduces evidence suggesting that the person killed was not Robert. The judge should

   (a) instruct the jury that Patty has the burden of persuading the jury that the body in question was Robert;

(b) instruct the jury that Delta has the burden of persuading the jury that the body in question was not Robert;

(c) instruct the jury that Delta merely has an obligation to present some evidence suggesting that the body in question may not be Robert; or

(d) instruct the jury that both the burden of producing evidence and the burden of persuading the jury rest with the plaintiff.

2. Instead of the evidence in Problem 1, Patty and a number of Robert's friends testify that Robert mysteriously disappeared nine years ago, and that none of them has seen or heard from Robert since that time. Patty introduces no further evidence. At this point the judge should

(a) grant the plaintiff's motion for a directed verdict;
(b) grant the defendant's motion for a directed verdict;
(c) take judicial notice of the fact that Robert is dead; or
(d) do none of the above.

3. Assume that Patty introduces only the evidence referred to in Problem 2 and that neither party moved for a directed verdict at the conclusion of the plaintiff's case. If Delta calls as its sole witness a person who claims to be Robert Price and then rests, the judge should

(a) direct a verdict for the plaintiff if he believes the defense witness is lying;

(b) instruct the jury that, if it believes plaintiff's evidence, it must find for the plaintiff unless it has been persuaded by a preponderance of the evidence that the defense witness is Robert Price;

(c) instruct the jury that the law presumes that one not heard from in seven years is dead, and that this presumption may be considered as evidence; or

(d) give the jury the instructions outlined in both (b) and (c).

4. Instead of the evidence in Problem 3, Delta offers as its sole evidence the following: a letter purportedly written by Robert and the testimony of Robert's brother that he is familiar with Robert's handwriting and that the letter was indeed written by Robert. Both the letter and the postmark on the envelope bear a date that is five years old. The plaintiff objects to the admissibility of the letter and offers the testimony of expert witnesses to the effect that they have compared the letter in question with verified samples of Robert's handwriting, and in their opinion Robert did not write the letter in question.

(a) The trial judge should exclude the letter regardless of what Patty's experts say because Delta has not properly authenticated it.

D. Presumptions in Civil Actions

(b) The trial judge should exclude the letter if he believes the experts and thinks Robert's brother is lying.

(c) If the trial judge believes that the letter was written by Robert, he should admit the letter and tell the jury that he has found the letter to be authentic but that the jury is not bound by that finding.

(d) The trial judge should admit the letter regardless of whether he thinks it is authentic and say nothing to the jury about his belief as to its authenticity so long as the judge concludes that a reasonable person could find the letter authentic.

5. Casanova, a life beneficiary, and Linus and Lucy, two remaindermen of a testamentary trust, seek to accelerate and thereby terminate the trust. They argue that the class of remaindermen who are the issue of Casanova has been effectively closed by reason of a vasectomy performed upon Casanova, which rendered him sterile. The Trustee defends on the ground that there is in this jurisdiction an irrebuttable presumption that a man or woman irrespective of his or her age or physical capacity is conclusively presumed to be capable of producing children. Moreover, the Trustee argues, despite Casanova's vasectomy future advances in medical science may be able to reverse the effect of a vasectomy and to restore fertility. Accordingly, the Trustee moves for a directed verdict. Should it be granted?

6. Husband is being sued by Wife for support for a child born to wife during the marriage to Husband. The marriage has since ended in divorce, and Husband defends on the ground that he and his wife had not had sexual relations for two years prior to the birth of the child and that his wife's infidelity, leading to her pregnancy, was one of the reasons for the breakup of the marriage. Wife asks the trial judge to instruct the jury on the irrebuttable presumption that a child born during wedlock is legitimate. Should such an instruction be given, assuming that the law is as Wife asserts? Would it make any difference if Husband could prove beyond any doubt, based on blood test for example, that he is not the father of the child?

7. Ima Bowski has sued Fast Eddy's Meat Supply for damages under a contract that called for Fast Eddy's to supply a specified amount of tenderloin to Bowski at the contract price. Fast Eddy's asserts that no notice of Bowski's acceptance of the contract was ever received, and thus no contract was entered into. Bowski has produced evidence that he mailed his acceptance to Fast Eddy's, and he has asked the trial judge to instruct the jury on the presumption that a mailed letter is received, thus establishing that Fast Eddy's received Bowski's acceptance. The trial judge concurred with Bowski that such a presumption exists in the jurisdiction, and accordingly the following instruction was given:

> You are instructed that the law creates a presumption that a mailed letter is received. This presumption stands until rebutted by credible evidence of non-receipt by the opponent of the presumption, who in

this case is the defendant. Under this presumption, if you find that the plaintiff mailed his acceptance to the defendant, receipt of that acceptance is to be presumed and the burden shifts to the defendant to rebut the presumption. The defendant may rebut this presumption by producing credible evidence of nonreceipt. Thus, if you find that the acceptance was mailed, you must find that it was received unless you further find that the defendant has produced credible evidence of non-receipt. If you find that credible evidence of non-receipt has been produced, the burden to prove acceptance remains with the plaintiff. If you do not find that the acceptance was mailed, then again the burden of proving acceptance remains with the plaintiff.

What is the point of this instruction? Can it be accomplished without such a complicated instruction?

8. Jane Remington sued to recover $100,000 under a certificate of accidental death insurance. The insured, her husband Joe Remington, died of a gunshot wound. The issue at trial was whether Joe died as a result of accidental bodily injury or as a result of suicide. The trial judge instructed the jury as follows:

> I instruct you that the law never presumes that one accused of committing a suicide is guilty therof. The presumption is against suicide. It is presumed that a person accused of doing a wrongful act is innocent of such accusation. Such a presumption is the equivalent of evidence and the plaintiff is entitled to its benefit throughout the trial of this case and throughout your deliberations on the facts until such time, if ever, as sufficient evidence may satisfy your minds to the contrary. It is therefore presumed that the gunshot wounds received by the deceased Joe Remington were the result of an accident and were not intentionally self-inflicted. If you find that the gunshot wounds caused the death of Joe Remington then, unless the presumption against suicide has been overcome by sufficient evidence to satisfy you, it is presumed that Joe Remington's death was the result of an accidental bodily injury and was not the result of suicide. Generally, if you find that Remington's injury and death were accidental, plaintiff is entitled to recover. If you find that Remington intentionally shot himself, resulting in his death, the defendant should recover.

Defense counsel objects to the presumption of accidental death on the ground that it has the effect of shifting the burden of proof to the defendants. What result?

9. Tim Johnson was injured when his car was struck by a truck driven by Leonard Walters. Walters died as a result of the crash. Johnson is suing Walters' estate on a negligence theory. At trial, the judge instructs the jury as follows:

D. Presumptions in Civil Actions

I instruct you that there is a legal presumption that the deceased, Leonard Walters, was obeying the law at the time and place of the accident in question and that he was exercising ordinary care for his own concerns at the time and place of said accident. This presumption is in itself a species of evidence, and it shall prevail and control your deliberations until and unless it is overcome by satisfactory evidence. This presumption is disputable, but unless it is adequately and sufficiently controverted, you, the jury, are bound to find in accordance with the presumption that the deceased, Leonard Walters, was obeying the law and was exercising ordinary care for his own concerns and was not negligent at the time and place of the accident. It is evidence in the case and is sufficient in and of itself to support a verdict on your part that the said deceased was careful at the time and place of the accident in question.

Counsel for plaintiff objects. Result?

2. Federal Rule 301

Congress attempted to deal with the problem of presumptions in FRE 301.[23] As promulgated by Congress, FRE 301 provides that the effect of a presumption is to place a burden of production upon the party against whom the presumption operates:

> In all civil actions and proceedings not otherwise provided for by Act of Congress or by these rules, a presumption imposes on the party against whom it is directed the burden of going forward with evidence to rebut or meet the presumption, but does not shift to such party the burden of proof in the sense of the risk of nonpersuasion, which remains throughout the trial upon the party on whom it was originally cast.

Although the matter is not entirely clear, FRE 301 seems to be a fairly standard example of a rule that allocates or shifts burdens of production through the use of presumptions (such rules are sometimes called "bursting bubble" rules because the presumption is satisfied by the opponent's production of evidence—the presumption "bubble" bursts, in other words, upon the production of contrary evidence). Indeed, whatever ambiguity there is about the matter is primarily attributable to loose language in the commentary to the rule rather than to the wording of the rule itself. The problem stems from the statements in the Conference Report to the effect that, if the

---

23. Much of the analysis of FRE 301 is based upon Allen, Presumptions, Inferences and Burden of Proof in Federal Civil Actions—An Anatomy of Unnecessary Ambiguity and a Proposal for Reform, 76 Nw. U.L. Rev. 892-895, 904-912 (1982), which may be consulted for full citations.

opponent of a presumption offers no evidence opposing the presumed fact, the court should instruct the jury that it *may* presume the existence of the presumed fact. If, however, FRE 301 is a "bursting bubble" rule, the instruction should be that the jury *must* presume the existence of the presumed fact.

Even if the intended effect of FRE 301 is clear, the rule nevertheless is seriously inadequate. FRE 301 purports to deal with presumptions without reference to a judge's authority to allocate burdens of production and persuasion, to instruct the jury on inferences, or to comment on the evidence. Yet as we have seen, the word *presumption* is merely a label applied to various manipulations of these other judicial prerogatives. To define the scope of presumptions without dealing with these related areas is thus to engage in an effort preordained to be futile at best and at worst, confusing. Not surprisingly, the dominant judicial response to FRE 301 has been either to ignore it or to misapply it.

The Supreme Court has apparently (and ironically) noted the impotency of FRE 301. In NLRB v. Transportation Management Corp., 462 U.S. 393, (1983), the Court reviewed a change in NLRB rules that required employers to bear the burden of persuasion on the issue whether discharge of an employee was for a permissible reason. The employer argued that this shift in the burden of persuasion was in contravention of FRE 301. The Court concluded to the contrary, but in such a way that demonstrates that the rule has virtually no significance. "The Rule merely defines the term 'presumption.' It in no way restricts the authority of a court or an agency to change the customary burdens of persuasion in a manner that otherwise would be permissible."

Examples abound of the rule's inadequacies resulting from its failure to address the relevant evidentiary areas. First, FRE 301 does not purport to limit the federal courts' power to allocate burdens of persuasion; it merely says presumptions do not have that effect. May a court allocate a burden of persuasion consistently with the allocation of a burden of production effected by FRE 301? Understandably, the answer is unclear. Some courts have suggested that FRE 301 prohibits such an allocation by implication, while others view FRE 301 either as not applicable or as impliedly authorizing such allocations.[24] Perhaps in response to this ambiguity, other courts seem simply to ignore FRE 301's existence. Moreover, the effect of FRE 301 on pre-FRE 301 decisions is not clear,[25] and the relationship between FRE 301

---

24. In NLRB v. Tahoe Nugget, Inc., 584 F.2d 293 (9th Cir. 1978), *cert. denied*, 442 U.S. 921 (1979), the court said, "Respondents contend a presumption cannot [shift a burden of persuasion] . . . under rule 301. . . . Only a superficial reading of the rule supports this contention. The courts have approved the presumption's [burden of persuasion shifting effect] . . . both before and after the adoption of the Federal Rules of Evidence." Id. at 297. Unfortunately, the court neglected to provide its more sophisticated reading of FRE 301, so its assertion is difficult to appraise. See also Bunge Corp. v. M/V Furness Bridge, 558 F.2d 790, 794-795 (5th Cir. 1977), *cert. denied*, 435 U.S. 924 (1978).

25. Compare Plough, Inc. v. The Mason & Dixon Lines, 630 F.2d 468, 471-472 (6th

D. Presumptions in Civil Actions

and the remaining evidentiary powers of the courts is simply unaddressed.

There are further difficulties with FRE 301. There is, as mentioned above, a dispute in the cases concerning whether FRE 301 is a "bursting bubble" rule.[26] Similarly, there is doubt about whether an opponent's failure to adduce evidence contrary to the presumed fact justifies a directed verdict, although the Supreme Court seems to have resolved that issue correctly in the affirmative.[27] Further, it is not clear whether FRE 301 prohibits a directed verdict against the proponent of a presumption when the opponent has responded with convincing evidence.

The inadequacies of FRE 301 press even deeper. It has been suggested, but not resolved, that FRE 301 may restrict the federal courts' power to create new presumptions, and thus indirectly limit their authority over these evidentiary matters. Moreover, whether FRE 301 was meant to apply to common law presumptions or to statutory presumptions, or to both, is not clear. Indeed, this absence highlights the futility of FRE 301. If it was meant to apply to common law "presumptions," nothing seems to prohibit the courts from simply replacing a presumption that allocated a burden of persuasion with an affirmative defense.[28] In fact, the only "change" would be in the label used. If, on the other hand, FRE 301 was meant to apply to statutory presumptions, it is not clear what is included thereby—whether, for example, the category includes presumptions that do not directly shift the burden of persuasion but that have been interpreted as doing so, and whether it extends to all the variations of language that Congress in its wisdom has chosen to employ in formulating evidentiary burdens created by statute.[29]

Cir. 1980) (rule found to have no effect since presumption used before and after rule's adoption) and NLRB v. Tahoe Nugget, Inc., 584 F.2d 293, 297 (9th Cir. 1978) *cert. denied*, 442 U.S. 921 (1979) (same) with Legille v. Dann, 544 F.2d 1, 5-7 n.37 (D.C. 1976) (court suggests that rule's application would change decision rendered).

26. Compare Bunge Corp. v. M/V Furness Bridge, 558 F.2d 790, 795 n.3 (5th Cir. 1977), *cert. denied*, 435 U.S. 924 (1978) (Court rejected interpretation of FRE 301 as "bursting bubble") with Legille v. Dann, 544 F.2d 1, 6-7 (D.C. Cir. 1976) (court embraced notion of FRE 301 as a "bursting bubble" rule).

27. Texas Dept. of Community Affairs v. Burdine, 450 U.S. 248, 254 (1981). See also United States v. Ahrens, 530 F.2d 781, 787 n.9 (8th Cir. 1976).

28. As an example of presumption language used to create an affirmative defense, as well as an example of the uselessness of FRE 301, see James v. River Parishes Co., 686 F.2d 1129, 1133 (5th Cir. 1982). In *James*, a barge broke away from its moorings and rammed into plaintiff's ship, causing considerable destruction. At trial, the judge relied upon the following presumption:

> [W]here a collision occurs between a moving vessel and a moored vessel, a presumption of fault is raised against the offending vessel; that is, an inference arises as a matter of law that the vessel was adrift through negligence. This presumption must be rebutted by a preponderance of the evidence . . . . The custodian of the drifting vessel bears the burden of disproving fault by a preponderance of the evidence. . . . This inference or presumption of negligence is a rule of law based on the logical deduction that a vessel found floating loose was improperly moored. See 9 J. Wigmore, Evidence §2487 (Chadbourne rev. 1981). It is not governed by Rule 301 of the Federal Rules of Evidence. The weight and effect of such a presumption is determined, as a matter of substantive law, in the light of the considerations that prompted its adoption.

29. For a collection of federal statutes employing various formulations, see 1 J. Weinstein

If FRE 301 does not apply to a wide variety of statutes, and is limited in its applicability to those that clearly allocate burdens of production, it is, of course, superfluous. If, by contrast, it were intended to have a wider application, Congress has effected significant change in federal law in the form of a simple rule of evidence.

FRE 301 is, in essence, a case study of the problems presented by the view that there should be a single rule for presumptions. To isolate a single meaning for the word *presumption* is possible only if all of the related evidentiary areas are also accommodated. If they are not, the courts will almost certainly proceed without serious regard for the rule, applying it where to do so facilitates reaching a desired result, but simply avoiding it when it is expeditious to do so.[30]

To satisfactorily accommodate the relevant factors, a rule on presumptions must provide express authorization for the evidentiary decisions the courts need to make, clarify the relationships among the various decisions, and indicate in a general way the appropriate basis for those decisions. Consider the following suggested replacement for FRE 301, which is followed by commentary explaining its more important aspects.

RULE 301-1: BURDEN OF PRODUCTION AND PERSUASION IN CIVIL ACTIONS AND PROCEEDINGS

(A) DEFINITIONS

1. A burden of production is a requirement that a party produce sufficient evidence on an issue to avoid a directed verdict on that issue.

2. A burden of persuasion is a requirement that a party convince the finder of fact to a previously specified level of certainty of the truth of an issue.

(B) GENERAL PROVISIONS

1. In the absence of controlling statutory authority, plaintiffs or moving parties generally shall bear the burden of production and persuasion on all contested issues. The courts of the United States may provide exceptions to this rule based on general principles derived in light of reason and experience, but any such exception and its justification must be specifically articulated and is subject to review in the appellate courts.

2. A statute that creates a presumption, specifies a prima facie or sufficient case, or employs any similar language shall be interpreted as

---

and M. Berger, Weinstein's Evidence 303-42 to 303-50 (1986). See also Poncy v. Johnson & Johnson, 460 F. Supp. 795, 803 (D.N.J. 1978), where the court found FRE 301 to control a federal statute that contained a provision for a *prima facie* case.

30. For an example of the lack of effect of FRE 301, see Sharp v. Coopers & Lybrand, 649 F.2d 175, 188 (3rd Cir. 1981).

D. Presumptions in Civil Actions

allocating a burden of production, unless the statute expressly (i) allocates a burden of persuasion, in which case the burden shall be allocated to the specified party, or (ii) indicates an appropriate matter for comment, in which case the court may comment as provided in Rule 301-2.

3. A question of fact upon which allocation of a burden of production or persuasion is conditioned shall be decided by the court for the purpose of allocating the burden of production or persuasion.

RULE 301-2: COMMENT ON THE EVIDENCE IN CIVIL ACTIONS AND PROCEEDINGS

After the close of the evidence and arguments of counsel, the court may accurately sum up the evidence and comment upon the weight of the evidence and the credibility of the witnesses, provided that the court does not intrude upon the prerogative of the jury to determine the weight of the evidence and the credibility of witnesses. The court may examine the logical implications of the evidence for the benefit of the jury, and may provide the jury with the court's opinion as to the significance of the evidence, but the court shall not instruct the jury on an inference without explaining the basis of that inference, nor shall the court employ any presumption as a form of comment. Notice of intended comment shall be provided to counsel, and an opportunity to respond with evidence or argument shall be permitted.

Section 301-1(a)(1) defines "burden of production" and determines its effect as requiring enough evidence to avoid a directed verdict. If that standard is not met, the issue is dropped from the case, a result which accomplishes the purpose of burdens of production.

Section 301-1(a)(2) defines "burden of persuasion" in the standard fashion as a requirement of convincing the fact finder to some level of certainty. Section 301-1(a)(2) contains two features worthy of comment, though. It does not provide for the level of certainty which is required; it only requires that the level be specified previously. This allows the courts to impose a standard of proof higher than a preponderance of the evidence; but the requirement of previous specification would prevent ad hoc manipulation of the standard of persuasion, thus ensuring greater consistency among cases. This requirement could be met, however, by a pre-trial ruling; it would not require a prospective ruling in the final adjudication of a previous case.

Section 301-1(b)(1) is the heart of the rule. It provides for the normal allocation of burdens, but also permits exceptions to be made "in light of reason and experience." Factors justifying exceptions are too numerous to specify; hence no list of them is provided. However, ad hoc manipulations of burdens should not be permitted. Consequently, any exception to the general rule must be justified in light of general common law principles developed by the courts. The purpose of the last phrase, specifically authorizing appellate review, is to emphasize that this common law process is the proper mode of decision. That point may not need to be stated; however, given the confusion so long rampant in this area, caution seems advisable. The first phrase, referring to controlling legislation, merely reiterates the congressional power to allocate burdens.

Section 301-1(b)(2) removes much of the ambiguity over statutory presumptions that affect the burden of production by making it clear that there is no difference between a direct allocation of the burden and one that employs the word *presumption* or similar language. This clarification would effect some change in the case law.[31] If a statute does shift a burden of persuasion, this section provides that such a result is identical to a direct allocation of the burden of persuasion. Thus, the spurious issue of what it takes to "rebut" a presumption is eliminated. If a statute is designed to authorize comment, the rule refers the court to Rule 301-2, which leaves it to the court to decide whether or not to comment in light of all the evidence presented at trial.

Section 301-1(b)(3) simply makes it clear that juries are not to be given confusing instructions in the alternative concerning burdens of proof—"If you find A, defendant has the burden of B; if you do not find A, plaintiff has the burden." The court will determine whatever facts need to be determined in order to allocate burdens, but that determination will not be communicated to the jury. A parallel amendment to FRE 104 might also be advisable.

Rule 301-2 is somewhat similar to Proposed Rule 105 of the Federal Rules—which Congress did not enact—but it also contains significant differences. Rule 105 contained language directing the court to sum up and comment "fairly and impartially" and to instruct the jury that it is to determine the weight and credibility of the evidence. The suggested rule, by contrast, simply requires the court's summary and comment to be accurate and not to intrude upon the prerogatives of the jury. These two conditions are the primary concerns associated with summary and comment by the court, and should be addressed directly. The problems with Proposed Rule 105's language are twofold: it may be difficult to give a "fair and impartial" summary or comment in a one-sided case, and an instruction to the jury on its powers may be inadequate to offset what otherwise would be overreaching behavior by the judge. The suggested rule accommodates these concerns by requiring that comment be accurate, not "fair and impartial," and by not allowing a simple instruction on the jury's powers to insulate the instructions from scrutiny on the basis of their possible over-intrusiveness.

Rule 301-2 would also promote clarity by its requirement that inference instructions be explained to the jury, thus converting those indirect and

---

31. See, e.g., NLRB v. Tahoe Nugget, Inc., 584 F.2d 293, 297 (9th Cir. 1978), *cert. denied*, 442 U.S. 921 (1979) (court held that a presumption allocating the burden of persuasion in labor relations case survived FRE 301).

D. Presumptions in Civil Actions

potentially troublesome comments into direct and hopefully helpful ones. The provision that presumptions are not to be used as a form of comment will prohibit "presumption as evidence" instructions, and should further reduce the confusion surrounding presumptions.

Finally, the court is required to give notice of comment, but not of summary. The reason for this differing requirement is that comment involves imparting information to the jury. Thus, the parties before the court should have an opportunity to respond to that information in order to ensure that the decision-making process is not, from their perspective, skewed.[32] The notice requirement could pose some minor inconveniences at trial; but those inconveniences are outweighed by the value of allowing the parties to adduce evidence and provide argument on those matters to which comment is directed.[33]

3. The Legislative Role in Structuring the Process of Proof

Bear in mind that the legislature is an actor in this drama, too. What role should it play in structuring the proof process? Reconsider the nature of the specific relevancy rules studied in Chapter Four, keeping in mind that they are, for the most part, statutory creatures (or at least codifications of the common law). Bear in mind, also, the close affinity of statutory and common law rules, and think about whether the source of the rule makes any difference. One option, of course, is to have no rules governing the process of proof. Let the adversaries present what they want to present, and let the jury believe what it wants to believe. On the opposite end of the spectrum are rules tightly governing the proof process. Consider the following case.

USERY v. TURNER ELKHORN MINING CO. et al.
428 U.S. 1, 96 S. Ct. 2882, 49 L. Ed. 2d 752 (1976)

Mr. Justice MARSHALL delivered the opinion of the Court. Twenty-two coal mine operators (Operators) brought this suit to test the constitutionality of certain aspects of Title IV of the Federal Coal Mine Health and Safety Act of 1969. The Operators, potentially liable under the amended Act to

---

32. This is analogous to the opportunity to be heard before judicial notice is taken. See FRE 201(e).

33. The federal courts also employ the phrase *res ipsa loquitur* to refer to comment on the evidence. See Sweeney v. Erving, 228 U.S. 233, 238-239 (1913) (res ipsa loquitur means that the facts give rise to an inference of negligence). Other courts use the phrase to refer to burden-shifting arrangements. See Prosser, Law of Torts §40 at 230 (4th ed. 1971). This is simply another example of a loose use of language that should be eliminated.

Providing notice and an opportunity to respond need not run afoul of Fed. R. Civ. P. 51, which requires that instruction of juries occur "after the arguments are completed." Counsel could adduce evidence or make argument before instructions if they are on notice.

compensate certain miners, former miners, and their survivors for death or total disability due to pneumoconiosis arising out of employment in coal mines, sought declaratory and injunctive relief against the Secretary of Labor and the Secretary of Health, Education, and Welfare, who are responsible for the administration of the Act and the promulgation of regulations under the Act.

On cross-motions for summary judgment, a three-judge District Court for the Eastern District of Kentucky . . . found the amended Act constitutional on its face, except in regard to two provisions concerning the determination of a miner's total disability due to pneumoconiosis. The court enjoined the Secretary of Labor from further application of those two provisions. After granting a stay of the three-judge court's order, we noted probable jurisdiction of the cross-appeals. We conclude that the amended Act, as interpreted, is constitutionally sound against the Operators' challenges.

I

Coal workers' pneumoconiosis black lung disease affects a high percentage of American coal miners with severe, and frequently crippling, chronic respiratory impairment. The disease is caused by long-term inhalation of coal dust. Coal workers' pneumoconiosis (hereafter pneumoconiosis) is generally diagnosed on the basis of X-ray opacities indicating nodular lesions on the lungs of a patient with a long history of coal dust exposure. As the Surgeon General has stated, however, post-mortem examination data have indicated a greater prevalence of the disease than X-ray diagnosis reveals.

According to the Surgeon General, pneumoconiosis is customarily classified as "simple" or "complicated." Simple pneumoconiosis, ordinarily identified by X-ray opacities of a limited extent, is generally regarded by physicians as seldom productive of significant respiratory impairment. Complicated pneumoconiosis, generally far more serious, involves progressive massive fibrosis as a complex reaction to dust and other factors (which may include tuberculosis or other infection), and usually produces significant pulmonary impairment and marked respiratory disability. This disability limits the victim's physical capabilities, may induce death by cardiac failure, and may contribute to other causes of death.

Removing the miner from the source of coal dust has so far proved the only effective means of preventing the contraction of pneumoconiosis, and once contracted the disease is irreversible in both its simple and complicated stages. No therapy has been developed. Finally, because the disease is progressive, at least in its complicated stage, its symptoms may become apparent only after a miner has left the coal mines.

In order to curb the incidence of pneumoconiosis, Congress provided in Title II of the Federal Coal Mine Health and Safety Act of 1969 for limits

D. Presumptions in Civil Actions

on the amount of dust to be permitted in the ambient air of coal mines. Additionally, in view of the then-established prevalence of irreversible pneumoconiosis among miners, and the insufficiency of state compensation programs, Congress passed Title IV of the 1969 Act to provide benefits to afflicted miners and their survivors. These benefit provisions were subsequently broadened by the Black Lung Benefits Act of 1972.

As amended, the Act divides the financial responsibility for payment of benefits into three parts. Under Part B of Title IV, claims filed between December 30, 1969, the date of enactment, and June 30, 1973, are adjudicated by the Secretary of Health, Education, and Welfare and paid by the United States.

Under Part C of Title IV, claims filed after December 31, 1973, are to be processed under an applicable state workmen's compensation law approved by the Secretary of Labor under the standards set forth in §421. In the absence of such an approved state program, and to date no state program has been approved, claims are to be filed with and adjudicated by the Secretary of Labor, and paid by the mine operators. Under §422 an operator who is entitled to a hearing in connection with these claims is liable for Part C benefits with respect to death or total disability due to pneumoconiosis arising out of employment in a mine for which the operator is responsible. The operator's liability for Part C benefits covers the period from January 1, 1974, to December 30, 1981. Payments of benefits under Part C are to the same categories of persons—a miner or certain survivors—and in the same amounts, as under Part B.

Claims filed during the transition period between the Federal Government benefit provision under Part B, and state plan or operator benefit provision under Part C that is, July 1 to December 31, 1973 are adjudicated under §415 of Part B, by the Secretary of Labor. The United States is responsible for payment of these claims until December 31, 1973. Responsible operators, having been notified of a claim and entitled to participate in a hearing thereon, are thereafter liable for benefits as if the claim had been filed pursuant to Part C and §422 had been applicable to the operator.

The Act provides that a miner shall be considered "totally disabled," and consequently entitled to compensation, "when pneumoconiosis prevents him from engaging in gainful employment requiring the skills and abilities comparable to those of any employment in a mine or mines in which he previously engaged with some regularity and over a substantial period of time." §402(f). The Act also prescribes several "presumptions" for use in determining compensable disability. Under §411(c)(3), a miner shown by X-ray or other clinical evidence to be afflicted with complicated pneumoconiosis is "irrebuttably presumed" to be totally disabled due to pneumoconiosis; if he has died, it is irrebuttably presumed that he was totally disabled by pneumoconiosis at the time of his death, and that his death was due to pneumoconiosis. In any event, the presumption operates conclusively to establish entitlement to benefits.

The other presumptions are each explicitly rebuttable by an operator seeking to avoid liability. There are three such presumptions. First, if a miner with 10 or more years' employment in the mines contracts pneumoconiosis, it is rebuttably presumed that the disease arose out of such employment. §411(c)(1). Second, if a miner with 10 or more years' employment in the mines died from a "respirable disease", it is rebuttably presumed that his death was due to pneumoconiosis. §411(c)(2). Finally, if a miner, or the survivor of a miner, with 15 or more years' employment in underground coal mines is able, despite the absence of clinical evidence of complicated pneumoconiosis, to demonstrate a totally disabling respiratory or pulmonary impairment, the Act rebuttably presumes that the total disability is due to pneumoconiosis, that the miner was totally disabled by pneumoconiosis when he died, and that the miner's death was due to pneumoconiosis. §411(c)(4). Section 411(c)(4) specifically provides: "The Secretary may rebut (this latter) presumption only by establishing that (A) such miner does not, or did not, have pneumoconiosis, or that (B) his respiratory or pulmonary impairment did not arise out of, or in connection with, employment in a coal mine." Moreover, under §413(b), none of these three rebuttable presumptions may be defeated solely on the basis of a chest X-ray.

II

In initiating this suit against the defendant Secretaries (hereafter Federal Parties), the Operators contended that the amended Act is unconstitutional insofar as it requires the payment of benefits with respect to miners who left employment in the industry before the effective date of the Act; that the Act's definitions, presumptions, and limitations on rebuttal evidence unconstitutionally impair the Operators' ability to defend against benefit claims; and that certain regulations promulgated by the Secretary of Labor regarding the apportionment of liability for benefits among Operators, and the provision of medical benefits, are inconsistent with the Act and constitutionally defective.

The three-judge District Court held that all issues as to the validity of the challenged regulations were within the jurisdiction of a single district judge, and the court entered an order so remanding them. The District Court upheld each challenged statutory provision as constitutional, with two exceptions. First, the District Court held that §411(c)(3)'s irrebuttable presumption is unconstitutional as an unreasonable and arbitrary legislative finding of total disability "in terms other than those provided by the Act as standards for total disability." 385 F. Supp., at 430. Second, reading the limitation on evidence in rebuttal to §411(c)(4)'s presumption of total disability due to pneumoconiosis to apply to an operator's defense in a §415 transition-period case, the District Court found that limitation unconstitutional in two respects. It held the limitation arbitrary and unreasonable in

D. Presumptions in Civil Actions

not permitting a rebuttal showing that the case of pneumoconiosis afflicting the miner was not disabling. And taking the provision to mean that an operator may defend against liability only on the ground that the pneumoconiosis did not arise out of employment in any coal mine, rather than on the ground that it did not arise out of employment in a coal mine for which the operator was responsible, the District Court found the provision an unreasonable and arbitrary limitation on rebuttal evidence relevant and proper under §422(c). The District Court accordingly entered an order declaring unconstitutional, and enjoining the Secretary of Labor from seeking to apply, §411(c)(3)'s irrebuttable presumption and §411(c)(4)'s limitation on rebuttable evidence.

The Operators' appeal, No. 74-1316, reasserts the constitutional challenges rejected by the District Court. The appeal of the Federal Parties, No. 74-1302, seeks reversal of the declaration and injunction respecting the constitutionality of §§411(c)(3) and (4). Neither side here questions the District Court's decision not to address the issues raised with respect to the Secretary of Labor's regulations. As we have already noted, we uphold the statute against all the constitutional contentions properly presented here. Because we read the limitation on rebuttal evidence in §411(c)(4) as inapplicable to the Operators, however, we vacate that portion of the District Court's order which invalidates that limitation. . . .

IV

The Operators contend that the amended Act violates the Fifth Amendment Due Process Clause by requiring them to compensate former employees who terminated their work in the industry before the Act was passed, and the survivors of such employees. The Operators accept the liability imposed upon them to compensate employees working in coal mines now and in the future who are disabled by pneumoconiosis; and they recognize Congress' power to create a program for compensation of disabled inactive coal miners. But the Operators complain that to impose liability upon them for former employees' disabilities is impermissibly to charge them with an unexpected liability for past, completed acts that were legally proper and, at least in part, unknown to be dangerous at the time.

[The Court discussed congressional power to "adjust . . . the burdens and benefits of economic life," finding that these statutes were within the power of Congress.]

In sum, the Due Process Clause poses no bar to requiring an operator to provide compensation for a former employee's death or disability due to pneumoconiosis arising out of employment in its mines, even if the former employee terminated his employment in the industry before the Act was passed.

V

We turn next to a consideration of the Operators' challenge to the "presumptions" and evidentiary rules governing adjudications of compensable disability under the Act.

A

The Act prescribes two alternative methods for showing "total disability," which is a prerequisite to compensation. First, a miner is "totally disabled" under the definition contained in §402(f), if pneumoconiosis, simple or complicated,

> prevents him from engaging in gainful employment requiring the skills and abilities comparable to those of any employment in a mine or mines in which he previously engaged with some regularity and over a substantial period of time.

Second, if a miner can show by clinical evidence (ordinarily X-ray evidence) that he is afflicted with complicated pneumoconiosis, the incurable and final stage of the disease, then the miner is deemed to be totally disabled under §411(c)(3). Thus, Congress has mandated that the final stage of the disease is always compensable if its existence can be shown by positive clinical evidence, and that any stage of the disease is compensable when physically disabling under the terms of §402(f). The Operators maintain that both of these standards are constitutionally untenable.

(1)

The Operators contend that the definition of "total disability" set up in §402(f) is unconstitutionally arbitrary and irrational, because it provides for the compensation of former miners who might well be employable in other lines of work, and who therefore are not truly disabled by their mining-generated afflictions. We think it patent that this attack on §402(f) must fail. A miner disabled under §402(f) standards has suffered in at least two ways: His health is impaired, and he has been rendered unable to perform the kind of work to which he has adapted himself. Whether these interferences merit compensation is a public policy matter left primarily to the determination of the legislature. We cannot say that they are so insignificant as not to be a rational basis for compensation. Indeed, we long ago upheld against similar attack a workmen's compensation scheme providing benefits for injuries not depriving the employee of his ability to work.

(2)

The District Court, relying on such cases as Stanley v. Illinois, 405 U.S. 645 (1972), and Vlandis v. Kline, 412 U.S. 441 (1973), invalidated

D. Presumptions in Civil Actions 621

§411(c)(3)'s "irrebuttable presumption" of total disability due to pneumoconiosis based on clinical evidence of complicated pneumoconiosis. The presumption, the court explained,

> forecloses all fact finding as to the effect of that disease upon a particular coal miner.... To the extent that such presumption purports to making a finding of total disability in terms other than those provided by [§402(f)] as standards for total disability, it is unreasonable and arbitrary. As written, section [411(c)(3)] is violative of due process in precluding the opportunity to present evidence as to the effect of a chronic dust disease upon an individual in determining whether or not he is disabled." 385 F. Supp., at 429-430.

We think the District Court erred in equating this case with those in the mold of *Stanley* and *Vlandis*.

As an operational matter, the effect of §411(c)(3)'s "irrebuttable presumption" of total disability is simply to establish entitlement in the case of a miner who is clinically diagnosable as extremely ill with pneumoconiosis arising out of coal mine employment. Indeed, the legislative history discloses that it was precisely this advanced and progressive stage of the disease that Congress sought most certainly to compensate. Were the Act phrased simply and directly to provide that operators were bound to provide benefits for all miners clinically demonstrating their affliction with complicated pneumoconiosis arising out of employment in the mines, we think it clear that there could be no due process objection to it. For, as we have already observed, destruction of earning capacity is not the sole legitimate basis for compulsory compensation of employees by their employers. New York Central R. Co. v. Bianc, supra. We cannot say that it would be irrational for Congress to conclude that impairment of health alone warrants compensation. Since Congress can clearly draft a statute to accomplish precisely what it has accomplished through §411(c)(3)'s presumption of disability, the argument is essentially that Congress has accomplished its result in an impermissible manner by defining eligibility in terms of "total disability" and erecting an "irrebuttable presumption" of total disability upon a factual showing that does not necessarily satisfy the statutory definition of total disability. But in a statute such as this, regulating purely economic matters, we do not think that Congress' choice of statutory language can invalidate the enactment when its operation and effect are clearly permissible.

(3)

In addition to creating an irrebuttable presumption of total disability, §411(c)(3) provides that clinical evidence of a miner's complicated pneumoconiosis gives rise to an irrebuttable presumption that he was totally disabled by pneumoconiosis at the time of his death, and that his death was due to pneumoconiosis. The effect of these presumptions, in particular the presumption of death due to pneumoconiosis, is to grant benefits to the survivors of any miner who during his lifetime had complicated pneumoconiosis arising out of employment in the mines, regardless of whether the miner's death was caused by pneumoconiosis. The Operators raise no separate challenge to these presumptions, and we would have no occasion to comment separately on them were it not for the Operators' general complaint against the application of the Act to employees who terminated their employment before the Act was passed. To the extent that the presumption of death due to pneumoconiosis is viewed as requiring compensation for damages resulting from death unrelated to the operator's conduct, its application to employees who terminated their employment before the Act was passed would present difficulties not encountered in our prior discussion of retroactivity. The justification we found for the retrospective application of the Act is that it serves to spread costs in a rational manner by allocating to the operator an actual cost of his business, the avoidance of which might be thought to have enlarged the operator's profits. The damage resulting from a miner's death that is due to causes other than the operator's conduct can hardly be termed a "cost" of the operator's business.

We think it clear, however, that the benefits authorized by §411(c)(3)'s presumption of death due to pneumoconiosis were intended not simply as compensation for damages due to the miner's death, but as deferred compensation for injury suffered during the miner's lifetime as a result of his illness itself. Thus, the Senate Report accompanying the 1972 amendments makes clear Congress' purpose to award benefits not only to widows whose husbands "(gave) their lives," but also to widows whose husbands "gave their health . . . in the service of the nation's critical coal needs."

In the case of a miner who died with, but not from, pneumoconiosis before the Act was passed, the benefits serve as deferred compensation for the suffering endured by his dependents by virtue of his illness. And in the case of a miner who died with, but not from, pneumoconiosis after the Act was passed, the benefits serve an additional purpose: The miner's knowledge that his dependent survivors would receive benefits serves to compensate him for the suffering he endures. In short, §411(c)(3)'s presumption of death due to pneumoconiosis authorizes compensation for injury attributable to the operator's business, and viewed as such it poses no retroactivity problems distinct from those considered in our prior discussion.

It might be suggested that the payment of benefits to defendant survivors is irrational as a scheme of compensation for injury suffered as a result of a miner's disability. But we cannot say that the scheme is wholly unreasonable in providing benefits for those who were most likely to have shared the miner's suffering. Nor can we say that the scheme is arbitrary simply because it spreads the payment of benefits over a period of time.

We might face a more difficult problem in applying §411(c)(3)'s presumption of death due to pneumoconiosis on a retrospective basis if the presumption authorized benefits to the survivors of a miner who did not die from pneumoconiosis, and who during his life was completely unaware of

D. Presumptions in Civil Actions 623

and unaffected by his illness; or, in the case of a miner who died before the Act was passed, if the presumption authorized benefits to the survivors of a miner who did not die from pneumoconiosis, who nevertheless was aware of and affected by his illness, but whose dependents were completely unaware of and unaffected by his illness. But the Operators in their facial attack on the Act have not suggested that a miner whose condition was serious enough to activate the §411(c)(3) presumptions might not have been affected in any way by his condition, or that the family of such a miner might not have noticed it. Under the circumstances, we decline to engage in speculation as to whether such cases may arise.

B

Turning our attention to the statutory regulations of §402(f) disability, we focus initially on the Operators' challenge to the presumptions contained in §§411(c)(1) and (2). Section 411(c)(1) provides that a coal miner with 10 years' employment in the mines who suffers from pneumoconiosis will be presumed to have contracted the disease from his employment. Section 411(c)(2) provides that if a coal miner with 10 years' employment in the mines dies from a respiratory disease, his death will be presumed to have been due to pneumoconiosis. Each presumption is explicitly rebuttable, and the effect of each is simply to shift the burden of going forward with evidence from the claimant to the operator. See Fed. Rule Evid. 301.

We have consistently tested presumptions arising in civil statutes such as this, involving matters of economic regulation, against the standard articulated in Mobile, J.& K. C. R. Co. v. Turnipseed, 219 U.S. 35, 43 (1910):

> That a legislative presumption of one fact from evidence of another may not constitute a denial of due process of law or a denial of the equal protection of the law it is only essential that there shall be some rational connection between the fact proved and the ultimate fact presumed, and that the inference of one fact from proof of another shall not be so unreasonable as to be a purely arbitrary mandate.

Moreover, as we have recognized:

> The process of making the determination of rationality is, by its nature, highly empirical, and in matters not within specialized judicial competence or completely commonplace, significant weight should be accorded the capacity of Congress to amass the stuff of actual experience and cull conclusions from it. United States v. Gainey, 380 U.S. 63, 67 (1965).

Judged by these standards, the presumptions contained in §§411(c)(1) and (2) are constitutionally valid. The Operators focus their attack on the rationality of the presumptions' bases in duration of employment. But it is agreed here that pneumoconiosis is caused by breathing coal dust, and that the likelihood of a miner's developing the disease rests upon both the concentration of dust to which he was exposed and the duration of his exposure. Against this scientific background, it was not beyond Congress' authority to refer to exposure factors in establishing a presumption that throws the burden of going forward on the operators. And in view of the medical evidence before Congress indicating the noticeable incidence of pneumoconiosis in cases of miners with 10 years' employment in the mines, we cannot say that it was "purely arbitrary" for Congress to select the 10-year figure as a point of reference for these presumptions. No greater mathematical precision is required.

The Operators insist, however, that the 10-year presumptions are arbitrary, because they fail to account for varying degrees of exposure, some of which would pose lesser dangers than others. We reject this contention. In providing for a shifting of the burden in going forward to the operators, Congress was no more constrained to require a preliminary showing of the degree of dust concentration to which a miner was exposed, a historical fact difficult for the miner to prove, than it was to require a preliminary showing with respect to all other factors that might bear on the danger of infection. It is worth repeating that mine employment for 10 years does not serve by itself to activate any presumption of pneumoconiosis; it simply serves along with proof of pneumoconiosis under §411(c)(1) to presumptively establish the cause of pneumoconiosis, and along with proof of death from a respiratory disease under §411(c)(2) to presumptively establish that death was due to pneumoconiosis. In its "rough accommodations," Metropolis Theatre Co. v. Chicago, 228 U.S. 61, 69 (1913), Congress was surely entitled to select duration of employment, to the exclusion of the degree of dust exposure and other relevant factors, as signaling the point at which the operator must come forward with evidence of the cause of pneumoconiosis or death, as the case may be. We certainly cannot say that the presumptions, by excluding other relevant factors, operate in a "purely arbitrary" manner. Mobile, J. & K. C. R. Co. v. Turnipseed, supra, at 43.

The Operators press the same due process attack upon the durational basis of the rebuttable presumption in §411(c)(4), which provides, inter alia, that a miner employed for 15 years in underground mines, who is able to marshal evidence demonstrating a totally disabling respiratory or pulmonary impairment, shall be rebuttably presumed to be totally disabled by pneumoconiosis. Particularly in light of the Surgeon General's testimony at the Senate hearings on the 1969 Act to the effect that the 15-year point marks the beginning of linear increase in the prevalence of the disease with years spent underground, we think it clear that the durational basis of this presumption is equally unassailable.

C

The Operators also challenge §413(b) of the Act, which provides that "no claim for benefits . . . shall be denied solely on the basis of the results of a

D. Presumptions in Civil Actions 625

chest roentgenogram (X-ray)." Congress, of course, has plenary authority over the promulgation of evidentiary rules for the federal courts. See, e.g., Hawkins v. United States, 358 U.S. 74, 78 (1958); Tot v. United States, 319 U.S., at 467. The Operators contend, however, that §413(b) denies them due process because X-ray evidence is frequently the sole evidence they can marshal to rebut a claim of pneumoconiosis.[32] We conclude that, given Congress' reasoned reservations regarding the reliability of negative X-ray evidence, it was entitled to preclude exclusive reliance on such evidence.

Congress was presented with significant evidence demonstrating that X-ray testing that fails to disclose pneumoconiosis cannot be depended upon as a trustworthy indicator of the absence of the disease. In particular, the findings of the Surgeon General and others indicated that although X-ray evidence was generally the most important diagnostic tool in identifying the presence or absence of pneumoconiosis, when considered alone it was not a wholly reliable indicator of the absence of the disease; that autopsy frequently disclosed pneumoconiosis where X-ray evidence had disclosed none; and that pneumoconiosis may be masked from X-ray detection by other disease.

Taking these indications of the unreliability of negative X-ray diagnosis at face value, Congress was faced with the problem of determining which side should bear the burden of the unreliability. On the one hand, preclusion of any reliance on negative X-ray evidence would risk the success of some nonmeritorious claims; on the other hand, reliance on uncorroborated negative X-ray evidence would risk the denial of benefits in a significant number of meritorious cases. Congress addressed the problem by adopting a rule which, while preserving some of the utility, avoided the worst dangers of X-ray evidence. Section 413(b) does not make negative X-ray evidence inadmissible, or ineligible to be considered as ultimately persuasive evidence when taken together with other factors, for example, a low level of coal dust concentration in the operator's mine, a relatively short duration of exposure to coal dust, or the likelihood that the miner is disabled by some other cause. The prohibition is only against sole reliance upon negative X-ray evidence in rejecting a claim.

The Operators attack the limitation on the use of negative X-ray evidence by suggesting that Congress' conclusion as to the unreliability of negative X-ray evidence is constitutionally unsupportable. Relying on other evidence submitted to Congress in 1972,[36] the Operators contend that the consensus

---

32. The Operators frame their argument by saying that the effect of §413(b) is to render the rebuttable presumptions of §411(c) effectively irrebuttable. But this dressing adds nothing. Once it is determined that the limitation on X-ray evidence is permissible generally, it is irrelevant that the burden of going forward with some rebuttal evidence is thrown upon the operator by a permissible presumption rather than by the claimant's affirmative factual showing.

36. This evidence was brought to the hearings by the Social Security Administration, whose rules the §413(b) limitation was designed to overrule, and was credited by the minority of the House Committee on Education and Labor. H. Rep. No. 92-460, supra, at 22, 29-30.

of medical judgment on the question is that good quality X-ray evidence does reliably indicate the presence or absence of pneumoconiosis. In essence, the Operators seek a judicial reconsideration of the judgment of Congress on this issue. But the reliability of negative X-ray evidence was debated forcefully on both sides before the Congress, and the Operators here suggest nothing new to add to the debate; they are simply dissatisfied with Congress' conclusion. As we have recognized in the past, however, when it comes to evidentiary rules in matters "not within specialized judicial competence or completely commonplace," it is primarily for Congress "to amass the stuff of actual experience and cull conclusions from it." United States v. Gainey, 380 U.S., at 67. It is sufficient that the evidence before Congress showed doubts about the reliability of negative X-ray evidence. That Congress ultimately determined "to resolve doubts in favor of the disabled miner"[38] does not render the enactment arbitrary under the standard of rationality appropriate to this legislation. . . .

D

Finally, the Operators challenge the limitation on rebuttal evidence contained in §411(c)(4). That section, as we have indicated, provides that a miner employed for 15 years in underground mines who is able to demonstrate a totally disabling respiratory or pulmonary impairment shall be rebuttably presumed to be totally disabled by pneumoconiosis, and his death shall be rebuttably presumed to be due to pneumoconiosis. The final sentence of §411(c)(4) provides that

> (t)he Secretary may rebut (the presumption provided herein) only by establishing that (A) such miner does not, or did not, have pneumoconiosis, or that (B) his respiratory or pulmonary impairment did not arise out of, or in connection with, employment in a coal mine.

The effect of this limitation on rebuttal evidence is, inter alia, to grant benefits to any miner with 15 years' employment in the mines, if he is totally disabled by some respiratory or pulmonary impairment arising in connection with his employment, and has a case of pneumoconiosis. The Operators contend that this limitation erects an impermissible irrebuttable presumption, because it establishes liability even though it might be medically demonstrable in an individual case that the miner's pneumoconiosis was mild and did not cause the disability—that the disability was wholly a product of other disease, such as tuberculosis or emphysema. Disability due to these diseases, as the Operators note, is not otherwise compensable under the Act.

[The Court disposed of this contention by construing the relevant section to be inapplicable to the Operators.]

38. S. Rep. No.92-743, supra, at 11, U.S. Code Cong. & Admin. News 1972, p.2315.

D. Presumptions in Civil Actions

VI

In sum, the challenged provisions, as construed, are constitutionally sound against the Operators' facial attack. The judgment of the District Court as appealed from in No. 74-1316 is affirmed. The judgment of the District Court as appealed from in No. 74-1302 is reversed, except insofar as it declares unconstitutional, and enjoins the operation of, the limitation on rebuttal evidence contained in §411(c)(4) of the Act. In this latter respect, the judgment in No. 74-1302 is vacated, and the case remanded with directions to dismiss.

It is so ordered.

The Chief Justice concurs in the judgment.

Mr. Justice Stevens took no part in the consideration or decision of these cases.

Mr. Justice Powell's opinion, concurring in part and concurring in the judgment in part, is omitted.

Mr. Justice Stewart's opinion, with whom Mr. Justice Rehnquist joins, concurring in part and dissenting in part, is omitted.

NOTES AND QUESTIONS

1. *Usery* is an example of a legislature providing complicated evidentiary rules through the use of "presumptions." As the Court rightly points out, each of the uses of the word *presumption* amounts to one or another of the standard evidentiary practices involved in process of proof. In Part V(A)(2), for example, the Court recognizes that the "irrebuttable presumption" language merely creates a right to compensation if the appropriate conditions are met. The Court had difficulty with irrebuttable presumptions in earlier cases, the ones cited in *Usery*, primarily because it failed to recognize that "irrebuttable presumptions" do not involve the drawing of inferences but instead comprise a somewhat awkward method of articulating legal categories. Thus, the appropriate question, as the Court concluded here, is whether the categories constructed by the relevant statute are acceptable. That question is not informed at all by the method employed by Congress to reach a result. The fact that Congress chose awkward or indirect language to reach an acceptable result does not give rise to a constitutional issue.

2. Note the impotence, as well as the positive confusion, generated by FRE 301. The Court has recognized that legislatures can allocate burdens of proof as they like. See Lavine v. Milne, 424 U.S. 577 (1976). Thus, the use of a presumption to allocate a burden of production (or a burden of persuasion for that matter) should give rise to no difficulty. Yet, the Court felt constrained to talk about the "rationality" of certain of the presumptions involved in *Usery*. See Part V(B) of the Court's opinion. Why? If the implications of *Lavine* are correct, presumably Congress could allocate burdens

of persuasion or production in these cases as it chooses to do so. Why, then, discuss "rationality" when Congress chooses to allocate burdens of proof but uses the label "presumption"?

3. Indeed, why did the Court *not* discuss FRE 301 in its "irrebuttable presumption" discussion? Why are presumptions sometimes, but not other times, "governed" by FRE 301?

4. Compare *Usery* to the following passage from Lavine v. Milne, 424 U.S. 577 (1976), a case that we have mentioned previously. In *Lavine*, the Court considered the constitutionality of a statute that "deemed" a person applying for welfare within 75 days after voluntarily terminating his employment or reducing his earning capacity to have done so "for the purpose of qualifying for such assistance or a larger amount thereof, in the absence of evidence to the contrary supplied by such person. N.Y. Soc. Serv. Law §131(11) (McKinney Supp. 1975)":

> Although the District Court found this [provision] to be an unconstitutional "rebuttable presumption," the sole purpose of the provision is to indicate that, as with other eligibility requirements, the applicant rather than the State must establish that he did not leave employment for the purpose of qualifying for benefits. The provision carries with it no procedural consequence; it shifts to the applicant neither the burden of going forward nor the burden of proof, for he appears to carry the burden from the outset.
>
> The offending sentence could be interpreted as a rather circumlocutory direction to welfare authorities to employ a standardized inference that if the Home Relief applicant supplies no information on the issue, he will be presumed to have quit his job to obtain welfare benefits. However, such an instruction would be superfluous for the obvious reason that the failure of an applicant to prove an essential element of eligibility will always result in a nonsuit. The only "rebuttable presumption"—if, indeed, it can be so called—at work here is the normal assumption that an applicant is not entitled to benefits unless and until he proves his eligibility.
>
> Despite the rebuttable presumption aura that the second sentence of §131(11) radiates, it merely makes absolutely clear the fact that the applicant bears the burden of proof on this issue, as he does on all others. And since appellees do not object to the substantive requirement that Home Relief applicants must be free of the impermissible benefit-seeking motive, their underlying complaint may be that the burden of proof on this issue has been unfairly placed on welfare applicants rather than on the State [a complaint that the Court rejected]. [424 U.S. at 583-585 (footnote omitted)].

Note that the Court said that there was no "procedural consequence," as though it is one thing to structure burdens of proof before any evidence is heard, and another to provide for burdens of proof to shift after evidence is heard. Can you make any sense out of that distinction?

5. Compare *Usery* to United States v. Klein, 80 U.S. (13 Wall.) 128 (1872). *Klein* dealt with congressional statutes passed during the reconstruction era that purported to modify the effect of Presidential pardons of former

E. Reflections on Presumptions 629

southern loyalists. Congress passed a statute that in essence provided that the oath that a person to be pardoned had to take to receive the pardon was proof of disloyalty in any proceeding where the pardoned person was attempting to obtain his or her property that had fallen into the possession of the forces of the United States. The Presidential pardon, by contrast, provided for the return of such property to those who had received pardons, with certain specified exceptions. As the Court said: "The substance of this enactment is that an acceptance of a pardon . . . shall be conclusive evidence of the acts pardoned, but shall be null and void as evidence of the rights conferred by it, both in the Court of Claims and in this court on appeal." The Court held the statute to be unconstitutional as an attempt of Congress to provide "a rule of decision, in causes pending, prescribed by Congress." In addition, the Court said, "the court is forbidden to give the effect to evidence which, in its own judgment, such evidence should have, and is directed to give to it an effect precisely contrary. We must think that Congress has inadvertently passed the limit which separates the legislative from the judicial power." How is *Klein* different from *Usery?* Is a rule of evidence different from a rule of decision in causes pending? How? If there is a difference, what are or ought to be the standards that permit Congress to provide for rules of evidence, and when do factual matters come within judicial competence? If the standard actually is "matters 'not within specialized judicial competence or completely commonplace,' " how do the specific relevancy rules fare?

6. Burden of proof issues also arise in the administrative context. See, e.g., Steadman v. SEC, 450 U.S. 91 (1981); Woodby v. Immigration & Naturalization Serv., 385 U.S. 276 (1966).

E. *REFLECTIONS ON PRESUMPTIONS*

The message of this chapter is that in all of its various manifestations, a presumption is simply a label applied to a choice concerning the evidentiary relationships of the parties that is reached for policy reasons having nothing to do with any independent meaning of the word *presumption*. As Justice Holmes once commented: "A presumption upon a matter of fact, when it is not merely a disguise for some other principle, means that common experience shows the fact to be so generally true that courts may notice the truth."[34] Moreover, the use of the label has had significant negative effects without providing, at least not anymore,[35] compensatory benefits. Accord-

---

34. Greer v. United States, 245 U.S. 559, 561 (1918).
35. Presumptions, like other legal fictions, originally served a very important purpose. See generally, Fuller, Legal Fictions (pts. I-III), 25 Ill. L. Rev. 363, 513, 877 (1930-1931). Before the courts' common law power was understood to include the power to change the

ingly, the only sensible solution to the "problem of presumptions" is to stop using the term and to face directly whatever evidentiary issues may be posed for resolution by our system of adjudication.

One conceivable consequence that would follow from foregoing the use of presumptions is that the courts, freed from whatever constraints may be imposed by the law of presumptions, would begin to provide even more diverse solutions to the various evidentiary questions they face. In one sense, this proposal is similar to early suggestions that the effect of each presumption should be determined according to the reasons that gave rise to it.[36] That suggestion was quickly termed "an almost impossible task, a curse worse than the disease, and a solution more rational, but less to be preferred than that offered by a simple rule."[37] Similarly, Dean McCormick concluded that "[t]o attempt to handle [presumptions] differently, according to a classification based upon their varying origins in trial convenience, in experimental probability, in superiority of access of one party to proof of the fact, or in external considerations of policy, seems impractical."[38]

These criticisms, however well reasoned, are misdirected. It may very well be impractical to replace whatever uniformity the law of presumptions supplies with a multitude of rules governing the placement of burdens of proof and judicial comments on the evidence. Nonetheless, the reason it would be impractical has nothing to do with presumptions; rather, it would be impractical because the result may be an overly complex set of rules governing judicial comment and burden of proof practices.

Curiously enough, one does not find complaints in the cases or the literature that the comment and burden of proof rules generally are overly

---

law, a court presented with a legitimate need to modify the law faced a dilemma. New developments called for change, but the power to change the common law resided elsewhere. The common law courts explicated the common law; the legislature changed it. With relatively quiescent legislatures, however, the proper role of the courts, as assigned by the theory of the common law, was inadequate. Change needed to be accomplished, and the legislatures were slow to respond. Accordingly, the courts searched for methods to facilitate the process of change, and one method that was created was the use of the legal fiction of the presumption. By "discovering" presumptions, the courts could change the common law quite significantly while still maintaining the facade that the courts were limited to explication and forbidden from legislating. In a similar fashion, the courts also discovered that presumptions could be used to control the decision-making process of juries. And again, the control could be accomplished without appearing to intrude upon the legitimate domain of another institution. See 9 W. Holdsworth, A History of English Common Law 139-142 (1926); J. Thayer, A Preliminary Treatise on Evidence at the Common Law 316-331 (1898); Bohlen, The Effect of Rebuttable Presumptions of Law upon the Burden of Proof, 68 U. Pa. L. Rev. 307, 310-312 (1920); Cleary, Presuming and Pleading: An Essay on Juristic Immaturity, 12 Stan. L. Rev. 24 (1959). Legislatures also created presumptions quite early, probably for somewhat similar reasons. See J. Thayer, supra, at 327-330.

36. Morgan, Some Observations Concerning Presumptions, 44 Harv. L. Rev. 906, 931-932 (1931).

37. Levin, Pennsylvania and the Uniform Rules of Evidence: Presumptions and Dead Man Statutes, 103 U. Pa. L. Rev. 1, 12 (1954). See also Gausewitz, Presumptions, 40 Minn. L. Rev. 391, 411 (1956).

38. McCormick, What Shall the Trial Judge Tell the Jury About Presumptions?, 13 Wash. L. Rev. 185, 188 (1938).

E. Reflections on Presumptions

complex.[39] Such complaints are limited to the law of presumptions, even by those who recognize the relationship between presumptions and burden of proof analysis.[40] The reason for this apparent inconsistency is readily understandable, however. To determine where the burdens of proof lie with respect to any litigated issue, or whether comment is permitted, one needs simply to check the statutes and precedents. Where, by contrast, a statute or opinion refers to a presumption, there is no way to be certain of the meaning of the term unless, as is rarely the case, the legislature or court took pains to provide an adequate definition. One way to avoid this ambiguity is to have a uniform rule for presumptions in a jurisdiction, and it is the desire to avoid ambiguity that generates the demands for a single rule concerning presumptions. The better solution would be to forego the use of presumptions entirely and do directly through the use of explicit evidentiary rules and an examination of the underlying policies what is now being done indirectly through the use of presumptions.[41]

There is a final issue that deserves attention. Our central thesis is that there is no such thing as a presumption, yet the foremost names in the field of evidence have argued long and hard over the "nature" of something that we have attempted to show does not exist. The most famous aspect of the controversy has been that involving Thayer and Wigmore on one side and Morgan on the other. Thayer and Wigmore popularized the "bursting bubble" view of presumptions that presumptions shift only burdens of production, and thus upon evidence contrary to the presumption being produced the presumption "bursts like a bubble" and is no longer of consequence to the case.[42] Morgan concluded that presumptions should shift burdens of persuasion.[43] A closer examination of this debate merely confirms the conclusion that presumptions have no independent meaning.

Wigmore and Thayer limited "presumptions" to shifting burdens of

---

39. See, e.g., McBaine, Burden of Proof: Presumptions, 2 UCLA L. Rev. 13, 15 (1954). See also 9 J. Wigmore, Evidence §2485, at 278 (3rd ed. 1940):

> There is, then, no one principle, or set of harmonious principles, which afford a sure and universal test for the solution of a given class of cases. The logic of the situation does not demand such a test; it would be useless to attempt to discover or to invent one; and the state of the law does not justify us in saying that it has accepted any. There are merely specific rules for specific classes of cases, resting for their ultimate basis upon broad reasons of experience and fairness. [*Ibid.* (footnotes omitted).]

40. See, e.g., Cleary, Presuming and Pleading: An Essay on Juristic Immaturity, 12 Stan. L. Rev. 5, 21-23, 27 (1959). Compare Morgan, Presumptions, 12 Wash. L. Rev. 255, 279-281 (1973).

41. Sections 600 to 688 of the California Evidence Code are a tentative step in that direction. Cal. Evid. Code §§600-688 (West 1966 & Supps. 1976 & 1979). To some extent, the lack of complex burden of proof practices may be attributed to the fact that a lot of intricate tinkering with burdens of proof has been done through the use of presumptions. Nonetheless, elimination of the confusion generated by the use of presumptions to accomplish indirectly that which can be accomplished directly would be valuable, even if that would also result in somewhat more complex burden of proof practices.

42. J. Thayer, A Preliminary Treatise on Evidence at the Common Law 336-337 (1898); 9 J. Wigmore, Evidence §2490, at 287-288 (3rd ed. 1940).

43. Morgan, Presumptions, 12 Wash. L. Rev. 255, 281 (1937).

production for the simple reason that every other use of the term involved the exercise of a power already possessed by the courts and legislatures and for which a label was already provided. Both believed that burdens of persuasion could be allocated for reasons of policy,[44] and both embraced the judicial power to comment on the evidence.[45] Thus, the only purpose to be served by presumptions was to provide a convenient method of referring to "legal rulings affecting the duty of producing evidence."[46]

Morgan also appears to have recognized quite early that what the courts were doing under the rubric "presumptions" could be done directly. In fact, his earliest treatment of presumptions suggested that "presumptions should be classified according to the reasons which justify their creation and existence."[47] He also recognized that his "proposal calls only for the same sort of reasoning as has actually been applied in allocating the burden of persuasion generally, even though its results have there been expressed in mechanical formulae."[48]

Morgan's proposal did not have a significant effect on the courts, however. The ambiguity and confusion surrounding presumptions continued unabated, and Morgan quite obviously became convinced that the confusion would continue until a simple rule was propounded that gave the word *presumption* a consistent meaning. Moreover, that meaning could not be the one suggested by Wigmore and Thayer, for that would give to most presumptions an inadequate role.[49] Accordingly, Morgan concluded that the general rule should be that presumptions shift burdens of persuasion. Yet even as he embraced that rule, he recognized what an admission of defeat it entailed. In the words of Professor Morgan:

> In wrongful death cases the courts have used the term presumption to express the effect to be given in a lawsuit to the fact that decedent met his death by accident upon the issue of decedent's due care or negligence. It seems naive to the point of foolishness to suppose that the courts first decided there was a presumption of due care and then by consulting dictionaries, text-writers, words and phrases judicially interpreted, and other lexicographic sources, determined the meaning of presumption. If that were the process, then the courts must have consisted of mere mechanical jurists. Giving them credit for proceeding with ordinary judicial competence, they must have tried to decide just what effect the decedent's death was to be given in the process of determining the quality of his conduct. . . . In so far as precedents are persuasive, the definition which other courts used in similar situations will make clear their opinions, and enable the instant court to determine what effect has elsewhere

---

44. J. Thayer, supra, at 376.
45. Id. at 188 n.2; J. Wigmore, supra §2551a, at 330, 509-534.
46. J. Wigmore, supra, §2490, at 287-288; see J. Thayer, supra, at 336-337.
47. Morgan, Some Observations Concerning Presumptions, 44 Harv. L. Rev. 906, 931-932 (1931).
48. Id. at 932.
49. Morgan, Instructing the Jury Upon Presumptions and Burden of Proof, 47 Harv. L. Rev. 59, 77-81 (1933).

E. Reflections on Presumptions

been given to the same facts. The question fundamentally is not one of terminology but one the decision of which is to be made upon considerations of fairness, convenience, and sound social policy. These considerations must be weighed in the light of what every judge and lawyer knows: that our adversary system of administering justice provides a very crude machine from the operation of which we can expect only approximately accurate results at best, and in the operation of which it is useless to attempt to apply meticulously nice rules, requiring the capacity for keen intellectual distinctions. Such admirable processes and capacities may be used to the utmost in framing rules of substantive law and rules of procedure. But the rules of procedure when framed must be simple and easily understandable as to be capable of ready apprehension and easy application by ordinary minds.[50]

In short, the well-publicized debate between Thayer, Wigmore, and Morgan does not rest on a difference over the nature of presumptions; instead, it rests on a disagreement over the legal system's ability to exercise its responsibilities rationally. Once again quoting Professor Morgan:

> Since the rules as to presumptions must be applied by the trial judge in the heat and hurry of the trial, will it be practicable to classify presumptions and assign to each an effect dependent upon the considerations which caused the courts to create it? If such classification were made by statute with an enumeration of all presumptions, this might work. If most presumptions were to be given a specified effect and only a few other effects, it might be practicable. With the present confusion in the authorities, however, any attempt at a statutory codification would be fanciful. What of an attempt to simplify by statute? The role which presumptions are theoretically deemed to play in actual litigation is almost negligible when compared with the confusion, uncertainty, and opportunities for error and alleged error which they create. In some classes of litigation by resort to them as a device for either taking a question from the jury or putting a question into the province of the jury, the result of a lawsuit is determined. If a court has become convinced that good policy requires that a particular issue should be tried by the judge or by the jury, and the device of presumption is taken away, judicial ingenuity will soon invent a new one. And outside this use of presumption, the confusion could be cleared away, it is suggested, without harm to courts, clients, or lawyers by a statute enacting a rule similar to the common law rule of Pennsylvania—that the sole effect of a presumption is to put upon the opponent the so-called burden of proof, in the double sense of producing evidence and of persuading the jury that the presumed fact did not exist. This would make it unnecessary ever to mention the presumption to the jury, and could be very easy of application by the trial judge. To be sure, it would be arbitrary, but it would abolish the prevailing confusion and complexities.[51]

---

50. Morgan, Presumptions, 12 Wash. L. Rev. 255, 279-280 (1937).
51. Id. at 280-281.

CHAPTER EIGHT

PROCESS OF PROOF IN CRIMINAL CASES:
Burdens, Presumptions, Judicial Summary and Comment

Burdens of proof in criminal cases are similar but not identical to burdens of proof in civil cases. As in civil cases, the law determines what facts need to be proven in order to establish that a crime has occurred. The criminal law also possesses virtually the same rule for the allocation of burdens of proof as in civil cases. The "plaintiff," which is the State, must plead and prove the necessary elements of the crime. Moreover, in many jurisdictions there are affirmative defenses that defendants must plead and with respect to which defendants bear the burden of production or persuasion. The primary differences between the civil and criminal arenas are that the normal burden of persuasion in criminal cases is proof beyond reasonable doubt and that as a result of In re Winship, 397 U.S. 358 (1970), the state always carries that burden with respect to the necessary elements of the offense.

In *Winship*, the Court considered the constitutionality of a New York statute that required findings of juvenile delinquency to be made by a preponderance of the evidence. The Court first ruled that a finding of juvenile delinquency in New York was equivalent to a finding of criminality, notwithstanding the purported beneficent general purpose of delinquency proceedings (or, for that matter, the label that New York had attached to the proceedings). Accordingly, the dictates of due process were fully applicable to these proceedings, and the Court found that due process required the state to prove its case in a criminal proceeding beyond reasonable doubt. In so holding, the Court asserted that the requirement of proof beyond reasonable doubt extends to "every fact necessary to constitute the crime with which [the accused] is charged." 397 U.S. at 364. Unfortunately, the Court did not elaborate on the meaning of this ambiguous phrase, and a moment's thought exposes how problematic it is. Reconsider the discussion of burdens of proof in Chapter Seven, where we saw that the only difference between an element of a plaintiff's case and an affirmative defense is who bears the burden of persuasion. The "element" of negligence can be converted into the "affirmative defense" of lack of negligence by legislative (or judicial) fiat. The same is obviously true in criminal cases. The "element" of intentionality can be converted into an "affirmative defense" of lack of intentionality. *Winship* failed to offer any means of distinguishing *constitutionally* necessary elements with respect to which the state cannot place the burden of persuasion on the defendant from factual matters that the state may allocate to the defendant's case if it wishes to do so.

Predictably, this crucial ambiguity in a major and innovative case soon led to considerable confusion, and the Supreme Court had little choice but to attempt to clarify the area of constitutional burden of proof practices. It did so first in the context of affirmative defenses and then in the context of presumptions. We will take up these two developments in turn by first discussing the proper scope of *Winship* in the context of affirmative defenses. This will be followed by materials dealing with the implications of the requirement of proof beyond reasonable doubt for presumptions in criminal cases.

A. THE SCOPE OF THE REQUIREMENT OF PROOF BEYOND REASONABLE DOUBT[1]

Winship was soon followed by two cases construing its mandate: Mullaney v. Wilbur, 421 U.S. 624 (1975), and Patterson v. New York, 432 U.S. 197 (1977). In *Mullaney*, the Court struck down Maine's homicide provisions that placed the burden of persuasion of provocation on the defendant. Under Maine law, the prosecution was required to establish intentionality and unlawfulness of the defendant's act of killing the victim in order to obtain a conviction for murder. Once the state established these elements, state law provided that "malice aforethought" was to be "conclusively implied" unless the defendant proved "by a fair preponderance of the evidence that he acted in the heat of passion on sudden provocation." Notwithstanding the "conclusively implied" language, Maine law did not provide for any inferences to be drawn; rather, that language simply meant that provocation was an affirmative defense that had to be established by the defendant in order to reduce a possible first-degree murder conviction to manslaughter.

In *Patterson*, the Court upheld New York's defense of extreme emotional disturbance that is distinguishable from the Maine statute only in that it is

---

1. Much of what follows is indebted to Allen, The Restoration of *In re Winship*: A Comment on Burdens of Persuasion in Criminal Cases after *Patterson v. New York*, 76 Mich. L. Rev. 30 (1977), and Allen, *Mullaney v. Wilbur*, The Supreme Court, and the Substantive Criminal Law—An Examination of the Limits of Legitimate Intervention, 55 Tex. L. Rev. 269, 279-281 (1977), which should be consulted for elaborations and more complete citations.

A. The Scope of the Requirement of Proof Beyond Reasonable Doubt

the modern version of the common law defense that was in force in Maine. Under New York law, the prosecution was required to establish an intentional killing in order to obtain a conviction for murder. Once this was established, the defendant, in order to reduce a murder conviction to manslaughter, was required to prove by a preponderance of the evidence that he "acted under the influence of extreme emotional disturbance for which there was a reasonable explanation or excuse."

The only significant difference between the New York and Maine statutes is that New York employed more modern terminology in its homicide provisions than did Maine. In particular, Maine employed the awkward "conclusively implied" language to create an affirmative defense, whereas New York created an affirmative defense through the use of more conventional language. Thus, unless there is something magical about the use of conventional language, these two cases are flatly inconsistent with one another, an inconsistency that we analyze in this section. We do so notwithstanding that recently the Supreme Court rendered a decision in Martin v. Ohio, which is reproduced immediately following our discussion, that seems to eviscerate the significance of both *Mullaney* and *Patterson*. You might wonder, why bother with studying the theory underlying affirmative defenses, which is the subject matter of this section? The reason for doing so is that the theory underlying affirmative defenses is also relevant to the analysis of presumptions. Thus, to understand constitutionally motivated presumption analysis, one must first work through these ideas. Given that *Mullaney* and *Patterson* no longer seem to be of any consequence, however, there is inadequate justification to reproduce them here. Nevertheless, you may wish to consult them (they are reproduced in the supplement), if for no other purpose than to assure yourself that the following discussion treats the cases fairly.

Winship was the first Supreme Court decision to hold explicitly that the reasonable doubt standard possesses constitutional dimensions. Since no state had ever allowed criminal conviction on less than proof beyond reasonable doubt, with a qualified exception for affirmative defenses, the Court had never been called upon to impose the reasonable doubt standard as a constitutional mandate.

The Court reached its conclusion in *Winship* concerning the due process attributes of the reasonable doubt standard by noting that the universal acceptance of that standard strongly implied its fundamental nature or, to put the matter more precisely, strongly implied the necessity of employing the reasonable doubt standard to protect a fundamental value. The value protected is the policy of preferring errors benefitting the accused over those favoring the prosecution. The Court then supplemented its analysis by articulating the interests that this value preference protects—principally the accused's liberty and good name—in order to demonstrate that they were of sufficient magnitude to justify including the procedure safeguarding them among the elements of due process. Accordingly, the states were forbidden from withdrawing a procedure that served values and interests of constitutional dimension from a hearing in which those interests were at stake in a fashion indistinguishable from a criminal trial.

The important point to note about the *Winship* Court's treatment of burdens of proof in criminal cases is that the Court's due process analysis relied heavily on the common practice in the states and only supported the implications of that practice by reference to the interests protected. The Court attempted no thorough examination of those interests and did not purport to consider fully the states' burden-of-persuasion practices. Indeed, affirmative defenses were never even mentioned by the Court. In *Mullaney*, by contrast, the Court reversed its order of reasoning, concentrating almost exclusively on the interests protected by the reasonable doubt standard rather than on whether Maine's statute was consistent with common practices in the states. This reversal of the analysis in *Mullaney* was the cause of *Patterson*'s subsequent disavowal of *Mullaney*, for it had implications far beyond what *Winship* could support.

In *Mullaney*, the Court noted that the interests protected by the reasonable doubt standard are implicated when a state chooses to distinguish murder from manslaughter, since a conviction for murder entails a more serious punishment. That is true, but what the Court failed to note was that these interests are implicated every time a state draws a distinction between offenses by the use of an affirmative defense, since invariably that distinction will carry with it a difference in the applicable sentence. Thus, *Mullaney* carried to its logical extreme would forbid the use of all affirmative defenses. Yet consider once again the genesis of this analysis in *Winship*. There the Court relied heavily on existing law in order to demonstrate the constitutional interest in the reasonable doubt standard. The existing law, however, included affirmative defenses. Thus, on the basis of *Winship*, states should indeed be forbidden generally from employing the preponderance standard in criminal cases but, in light of the Court's analysis, they should also be allowed to employ affirmative defenses in that setting.

One can now see more clearly the shift of analysis in *Mullaney* that permitted it to accomplish a result that *Winship* could not sustain. *Mullaney* invoked *Winship* not to invalidate a burden-of-proof practice demonstrably inconsistent with the "traditions and conscience of our people," but instead used that case in a fashion that would provide the means to invalidate a practice long accepted throughout the country. Thus *Mullaney*, which purported to "apply" *Winship*, drastically altered that case from one that looks to traditional practice and prevailing usage by the states to aid in due process analysis to one that frees the federal courts to impose their own view about the appropriate use of the reasonable doubt standard on the states notwithstanding widely shared views to the contrary. Moreover, this was the case even though the states had not eviscerated the prosecution's burden of proof so that "innocents" were being exposed to erroneous convictions. It is this overextension of *Winship* by *Mullaney* that the Court condemned in *Patterson*:

A. The Scope of the Requirement of Proof Beyond Reasonable Doubt 639

> Long before *Winship*, the universal rule in this country was that the prosecution must prove guilt beyond reasonable doubt. At the same time, the long-accepted rule was that it was constitutionally permissible to provide that various affirmative defenses were to be proved by the defendant. This did not lead to such abuses or to such widespread redefinition of crime and reduction of the prosecution's burden that a new constitutional rule was required. This was not the problem to which *Winship* was addressed. [432 U.S. at 211.]

Merely noting the effect of *Patterson* is inadequate, however, for quite possibly the erroneous decision is *Patterson* rather than *Mullaney*. This possibility is made evident by reconsidering what it means to protect "innocent" defendants by the reasonable doubt standard. We suggested above that affirmative defenses do not enhance the likelihood of erroneous convictions since the prosecution must meet its burden for the designated elements of the crime before an affirmative defense ever becomes relevant. Yet what does it mean to protect against "erroneous convictions"? If it means simply that the prosecution must establish enough to justify a conviction, our suggestion is correct. If, on the other hand, it means that the prosecution must establish each fact that bears on an accused's culpability or sentence, the suggestion is in error. Whenever a defendant fails to establish an affirmative defense, the possibility is presented that, had the prosecution been required to disprove the defense beyond reasonable doubt, the trier of fact would have either convicted the defendant of a lesser offense or acquitted altogether. This would result in exposing the defendant to a lesser punishment or no punishment at all. Affirmative defenses, in short, undeniably affect the interests articulated in *Winship*. Thus, to determine which case—*Patterson* or *Mullaney*—was decided correctly, the analysis must proceed to an examination of the interests protected by the reasonable doubt standard. That examination will demonstrate that the interests articulated in *Winship* and employed in *Mullaney* cannot reasonably justify the implications of *Mullaney*, although those interests, as implicitly accommodated in *Patterson*, do indicate the extent of the federal interest in the reasonable doubt standard.

Winship articulated three interests that the reasonable doubt standard tends to protect: the community's confidence in the criminal law, the defendant's interests in avoiding unwarranted stigmatization and being free from unjustified loss of liberty. This list has apparently been considerably shortened by *Patterson*. Neither the majority nor the dissent in *Patterson* made any reference to the community confidence notion, presumably because the Court now recognizes that insofar as this interest does more than reiterate the defendant's interest in avoiding undeserved punishment, it is a concern of the states, not the federal government. The matter of stigmatization, also omitted from the majority's analysis, parallels the deprivation of liberty and hence does not require separate treatment. In short, the interests informing due process analysis of the reasonable doubt standard under the Constitution can be reduced to the defendant's liberty interest (we are excluding the unlikely case where the only purpose of a criminal trial is to stigmatize. See, e.g., Paul v. Davis, 424 U.S. 693 (1976) (reputation alone is not "liberty" or "property" within the due process clause)).

The *Mullaney* Court insisted that the determination of which of two related offenses the defendant has committed affects his constitutional liberty interest no less than the judgment of guilt or innocence. Undeniably, the presence or absence of the mitigating factor may have a substantial impact on the severity of the punishment a convicted defendant receives. Yet one cannot jump from this fact to the conclusion that requiring the prosecutor to prove the distinguishing factor beyond a reasonable doubt serves the due process interest. Assuming that the punishment for the higher offense is constitutionally acceptable, given what the prosecution must prove beyond a reasonable doubt, the allocation of the persuasion burden of the mitigating factor has no bearing on whether the defendant suffers unconstitutional punishment.

An example may help to clarify this argument. Consider a state with an intentional homicide statute that punishes every intentional homicide with 30 years of imprisonment; if the state proves that the defendant intentionally killed the victim, then a flat sentence of 30 years is imposed regardless of the presence of any mitigating factor. Assume that such a statute is constitutional. Now, consider how the constitutionality of that statute is affected if we simply add to it a provision that no more than 20 years of imprisonment may be imposed if the defendant proves by a preponderance of the evidence that he acted under the influence of extreme emotional disturbance. If the constitutional interest in the reasonable doubt standard centers on liberty deprivation, the addition of a chance to mitigate a constitutional punishment cannot invalidate the statute. To put it another way, if a state may constitutionally imprison all intentional murderers for 30 years by proving beyond reasonable doubt only intent and causation, then whatever liberty interest the defendant constitutionally possesses in the context of homicide prosecutions surely is fully accommodated by such a statute. The addition of a mitigating circumstance in the form of an affirmative defense—a factor that reduces punishment—cannot violate the already fully accommodated interest.

Patterson appears on close inspection to have adopted this line of reasoning:

> The Due Process Clause, as we see it, does not put New York to the choice of abandoning [affirmative] defenses or undertaking to disprove their existence in order to convict of a crime which otherwise is within its constitutional powers to sanction by substantial punishment. [432 U.S. at 207-208.]

The key to this passage is the word *otherwise*. What the Court is saying is that if a state may "otherwise" impose a particular sentence on the basis of what the state has proven beyond a reasonable doubt, then permitting a

A. The Scope of the Requirement of Proof Beyond Reasonable Doubt

defendant to reduce the sentence he receives below the permissible level through proof of an affirmative defense is constitutional.

If the Court now subscribes to this theory—sometimes referred to as the theory that "the greater includes the lesser"—the analysis of the constitutionality of an affirmative defense must proceed to another level. One must ask whether the greater punishment—the punishment authorized in the event the defendant fails to establish the affirmative defense—is constitutional. And to answer that question, one must turn to the eighth amendment.

Through most of the nineteenth century, the eighth amendment was thought to forbid only rather hideous punishments. But within the last century the cruel and unusual punishment clause has been interpreted to require a rough proportionality between the culpability of an offense and the punishment that is imposed. This requirement of proportionality provides the method of testing the accuracy of the assumption of constitutionality in the hypothetical, and it also provides the means of delineating the extent of the federal interest in the reasonable doubt standard. If the courts conclude that a given punishment is not disproportional to what the state has proved beyond reasonable doubt, notwithstanding the presence or absence of any mitigating factors, then a defendant's liberty interest would obviously be satisfied by a statute that required proof of only those elements and that imposed that particular punishment. Accordingly, the mere addition to that statute of an affirmative defense, which after all could constitutionally be ignored, should be equally satisfactory. The import of the proportionality principle is, then, that the state should be required to prove enough to justify the imposition of the maximum sentence permissible under the statute. Once that is accomplished, the accused has been fully protected against an unwarranted deprivation of liberty, and the state should be permitted to elaborate on the basic statute as it sees fit.

The thesis that due process requires proof beyond a reasonable doubt only with respect to those elements of the offense that are "essential" by virtue of the eighth amendment concretely expresses the role of the reasonable doubt standard. Due process and the eighth amendment protect criminal defendants from unwarranted deprivations of liberty by requiring the state to establish sufficient factual elements to justify the allotted punishment and by requiring the state, in establishing those elements, to minimize the risk of error adverse to the defendant. Once the overriding constitutional command is satisfied, however, the need for the protective procedure is likewise satisfied, and the traditional state power should reassert itself, permitting the states to allocate burdens of proof as they desire.

One of the more attractive features of the proportionality theory is that it ties the federal constitutional mandate to a relatively unambiguous constitutional command that has the further advantage of leaving the states substantially free to fashion their own policies. Moreover, it does so in such a way as to reconcile *Winship* and *Patterson* while concomitantly demonstrating the errors of *Mullaney*. *Winship* merely articulated what a state must do if a factor is a necessary element of the offense as defined by law. *Patterson*, by contrast, provides the method to determine whether a state's definition of a crime is constitutionally permissible. *Mullaney* erred in failing to inquire whether there are limits to the federal concern in the accused's liberty and reputational interests and whether the markedly different setting of *Mullaney*, as compared to *Winship*, was of any constitutional significance. *Patterson* rectified these errors, if it is viewed as embracing the proportionality concept, by making clear that although the interests articulated in *Winship* are of great importance, standing alone they are inadequate to prohibit a state's allocation of the burden of proof that otherwise is constitutional. *Patterson* makes clear, in other words, to what extent the factors present in *Winship* but absent in *Mullaney* are relevant to due process adjudication in this area and to what extent the accused's liberty and reputational interests are independently significant.

There are two other principal theories of the constitutional standards applicable to affirmative defenses that compete with the proportionality theory—the "elements" theory and the "political compromise" theory. Under the elements theory, the state must prove beyond reasonable doubt whatever factual issues it labels an element of the offense. A component of this theory is the "physical location" rule, a rule of statutory construction providing that a particular factual issue is an element of an offense only if it is incorporated into the text of the basic statute describing the offense.

At various points throughout the *Patterson* opinion the Court alluded to the elements test, most explicitly in the statement that the Court "will not disturb the balance struck in previous cases holding that the Due Process Clause requires the prosecution to prove beyond reasonable doubt all of the elements included in the definition of the offense of which the defendant is charged." 432 U.S. at 210. Both examples given by the Court of unconstitutional burden shifts also tend to support this view. The Court noted that the legislature cannot delcare an individual guilty or presumptively guilty, nor can it declare that the finding of an indictment or proof of the identity of the accused shall create a presumption of the existence of all the facts essential to guilt. These are situations in which no elements are included within the definition of "crime," which may suggest that any affirmative defense will be sustained so long as the legislature does not drain all substantive content from a crime's definition.

Nevertheless, we doubt that the Court meant to embrace the elements test as its criterion of constitutionality. It is difficult to see what constitutional interest is served by the elements theory. The physical location rule is obviously an arbitrary means of determining the "definition" of an offense. The legislature may wish to "define" an offense in one way but determine the elements of the prosecution's case in another, and either could be considered the "definition" of the crime. There is no reason why the validity of a state statute placing the burden of proving provocation on the defendant should depend on whether the state "defines" murder as intent, causation,

A. The Scope of the Requirement of Proof Beyond Reasonable Doubt

and no provocation in one statute and in another places the burden of proving provocation on the defendant, or simply as intent and causation with another statute authorizing provocation as an affirmative defense. Surely *Patterson*'s references to the elements theory were intended simply to indicate that the elements as defined in the statute under review permitted the state to provide for the affirmative defense of extreme emotional disturbance.

The second standard that has been proposed for judging the validity of an affirmative defense, while somewhat more sophisticated than the elements theory, is no more persuasive. This is the "political compromise" test, which permits affirmative defenses that result from the compromise of competing forces in the legislature. This test responds to the fear that states may be unwilling to provide certain affirmative defenses if they cannot place on the defendant the burden of proof for the factual issue created. Commentators have often pointed out that a decision like *Mullaney*, if followed, would likely inhibit experimentation with new affirmative defenses. To avoid that harsh irony, the political compromise test looks to whether the legislature would have refused to adopt the defense but for the provision imposing the burden of proof on the defendant.

Of this theory's many problems, the most disturbing is its paradoxical quality. It is paradoxical in the sense that if the only justification for allowing affirmative defenses is that otherwise the legislature will be forced to choose between two diametrically opposed but constitutional alternatives, then the argument implicitly assumes the unconstitutionality of affirmative defenses. The real point, in other words, is that affirmative defenses are unconstitutional but that such a conclusion may result in an unfortunate legislative choice, and thus the better tack is to permit an unconstitutional choice as an expedient.

Our discussion to this point has been based on the conclusion that *Patterson* overruled *Mullaney*, as we think it did. A majority of the Court purported to see it otherwise, however, and the Court's effort to distinguish *Mullaney* raises a number of questions about the motives of the Court. The answers to those questions make it clear that the purported distinction yields no insights into the federal interest in the reasonable doubt standard. However, the attempt to distinguish *Mullaney* is not without interest for reasons quite removed from the burden-of-proof analysis of *Patterson*.

The *Patterson* Court argued that the New York statute differed from the Maine statute in that the latter created a statutory presumption whereas New York's involved a true affirmative defense. Thus, the Court read Maine's homicide statute as making the absence of provocation an element of murder, and the Court reaffirmed the holding of *Mullaney* that due process does not allow a state to shift "the burden of persuasion with respect to a fact which the State deems so important that it must be either proved or presumed." In contrast, under the New York statute, "nothing was presumed or implied against Patterson." Consequently, in the Court's view New York had proved beyond a reasonable doubt every element of its definition of murder.

Unfortunately the purported distinctions between presumptions and affirmative defenses fail to sustain the contrasting outcomes of *Mullaney* and *Patterson*. The Maine statute, as construed by the Maine courts, did not set up a statutory presumption in the sense of providing for an inference from one fact to another. Nonetheless, the Court somewhat inexplicably depicted Maine law as directing the trial judge to instruct the jury that fact C, a necessary element of the offense, could be inferred from proof of facts A and B. That is not the case. Maine had not provided a rule of evidence concerning inferential relationships; instead, it had placed the burden of proving provocation on the defendant, precisely as New York had done with extreme emotional disturbance. Indeed, if a few words are changed, the description of Maine's statute fits New York's perfectly. The absence of extreme emotional disturbance is just as much a "part of the definition of" murder in New York as provocation was in Maine. Moreover, New York "presumes" lack of extreme emotional disturbance to the same extent as did Maine. All it meant in Maine to presume lack of provocation until the "presumption" was "rebutted" by the defendant was that the defendant had the burden of proving that he had been provoked. That is precisely the situation in New York. Still, by characterizing *Mullaney* as a statutory presumption case, the Court could assert that it had no impact on garden-variety affirmative defenses where no inferential process is involved. This analysis allowed the Court to reach the opposite conclusion in *Patterson* than it reached in *Mullaney* without having to overrule the earlier case.

One wonders why the Court struggled to construct such a spurious argument. The most plausible explanation of the Court's behavior is that it recognized it had erred in *Mullaney* and wished to rectify that mistake. Unfortunately, *Mullaney* was only two years old, and, to complicate matters, the decision was unanimous. These factors, plus a natural reluctance to confess error, no doubt sent the Court down the path it took.

In any event, if *Mullaney* is overruled what is left of *Winship*?

MARTIN v. OHIO
—U.S.—, 107 S. Ct. 1098,—L. Ed. 2d —(1987)

Justice WHITE delivered the opinion of the Court. The Ohio Code provides that "(e)very person accused of an offense is presumed innocent until proven guilty beyond a reasonable doubt, and the burden of proof for all elements of the offense is upon the prosecution. The burden of going forward with the evidence of an affirmative defense, and the burden of proof by a preponderance of the evidence, for an affirmative defense, is upon the accused." Ohio Rev. Code Ann. §2901.05(A) (1982). An affirmative defense is one involving "an excuse or justification peculiarly within the knowledge of the accused, on which he can fairly be required to adduce supporting evidence." Ohio Rev. Code Ann. §2901.05(C)(2) (1982). The Ohio courts

A. The Scope of the Requirement of Proof Beyond Reasonable Doubt 645

have "long determined that self-defense is an affirmative defense," and that the defendant has the burden of proving it as required by §2901.05(A).

As defined by the trial court in its instructions in this case, the elements of self-defense that the defendant must prove are (1) that the defendant was not at fault in creating the situation giving rise to the argument; (2) the defendant had an honest belief that she was in imminent danger of death or great bodily harm and that her only means of escape from such danger was in the use of such force; and (3) the defendant must not have violated any duty to retreat or avoid danger. The question before us is whether the Due Process Clause of the Fourteenth Amendment forbids placing the burden of proving self-defense on the defendant when she is charged by the State of Ohio with committing the crime of aggravated murder, which, as relevant to this case, is defined by the Revised Code of Ohio as "purposely, and with prior calculation and design, caus(ing) the death of another." Ohio Rev. Code Ann. §2903.01 (1982).

The facts of the case, taken from the opinions of the courts below, may be succinctly stated. On July 21, 1983, petitioner Earline Martin and her husband, Walter Martin, argued over grocery money. Petitioner claimed that her husband struck her in the head during the argument. Petitioner's version of what then transpired was that she went upstairs, put on a robe, and later came back down with her husband's gun which she intended to dispose of. Her husband saw something in her hand and questioned her about it. He came at her, she lost her head and fired the gun at him. Five or six shots were fired, three of them striking and killing Mr. Martin. She was charged with and tried for aggravated murder. She pleaded self-defense and testified in her own defense. The judge charged the jury with respect to the elements of the crime and of self-defense and rejected petitioner's Due Process Clause challenge to the charge placing on her the burden of proving self-defense. The jury found her guilty.

Both the Ohio Court of Appeals and the Supreme Court of Ohio affirmed the conviction. . . . We granted certiorari, and affirm the decision of the Supreme Court of Ohio.

In re Winship declared that the Due Process Clause "protects the accused against conviction except upon proof beyond a reasonable doubt of every fact necessary to constitute the crime with which he is charged." A few years later, we held that *Winship*'s mandate was fully satisfied where the State of New York had proved beyond reasonable doubt, each of the elements of murder, but placed on the defendant the burden of proving the affirmative defense of extreme emotional disturbance, which, if proved, would have reduced the crime from murder to manslaughter. Patterson v. New York[, 432 U.S. 197 (1977)]. . . . Referring to Leland v. Oregon, 343 U.S. 790 and Rivera v. Delaware, 429 U.S. 877, we added that New York "did no more than *Leland* and *Rivera* permitted it to do without violating the Due Process Clause" and declined to reconsider those cases. 432 U.S., at 206, 207. It was also observed that "the fact that a majority of the States have now assumed the burden of disproving affirmative defenses—for whatever reasons—(does not) mean that those States that strike a different balance are in violation of the Constitution." Id., at 211.

As in *Patterson*, the jury was here instructed that to convict it must find, in light of all the evidence, that each of the elements of the crime of aggravated murder must be proved by the State beyond reasonable doubt and that the burden of proof with respect to these elements did not shift. To find guilt, the jury had to be convinced that none of the evidence, whether offered by the State or by Martin in connection with her plea of self-defense, raised a reasonable doubt that Martin had killed her husband, that she had the specific purpose and intent to cause his death, or that she had done so with prior calculation and design. It was also told, however, that it could acquit if it found by a preponderance of the evidence that Martin had not precipitated the confrontation, that she had an honest belief that she was in imminent danger of death or great bodily harm, and that she had satisfied any duty to retreat or avoid danger. The jury convicted Martin.

We agree with the State and its Supreme Court that this conviction did not violate the Due Process Clause. The State did not exceed its authority in defining the crime of murder as purposely causing the death of another with prior calculation or design. It did not seek to shift to Martin the burden of proving any of those elements, and the jury's verdict reflects that none of her self-defense evidence raised a reasonable doubt about the state's proof that she purposefully killed with prior calculation and design. She nevertheless had the opportunity under state law and the instructions given to justify the killing and show herself to be blameless by proving that she acted in self-defense. The jury thought she had failed to do so, and Ohio is as entitled to punish Martin as one guilty of murder as New York was to punish Patterson.

It would be quite different if the jury had been instructed that self-defense evidence could not be considered in determining whether there was a reasonable doubt about the state's case, i.e., that self-defense evidence must be put aside for all purposes unless it satisfied the preponderance standard. Such instruction would relieve the state of its burden and plainly run afoul of *Winship*'s mandate. The instructions in this case could be clearer in this respect, but when read as a whole, we think they are adequate to convey to the jury that all of the evidence, including the evidence going to self-defense, must be considered in deciding whether there was a reasonable doubt about the sufficiency of the state's proof of the elements of the crime.

We are thus not moved by assertions that the elements of aggravated murder and self-defense overlap in the sense that evidence to prove the latter will often tend to negate the former. It may be that most encounters in which self-defense is claimed arise suddenly and involve no prior plan or specific purpose to take life. In those cases, evidence offered to support the defense may negate a purposeful killing by prior calculation and design, but Ohio does not shift to the defendant the burden of disproving any element

A. The Scope of the Requirement of Proof Beyond Reasonable Doubt 647

of the state's case. When the prosecution has made out a *prima facie* case and survives a motion to acquit, the jury may nevertheless not convict if the evidence offered by the defendant raises any reasonable doubt about the existence of any fact necessary for the finding of guilt. Evidence creating a reasonable doubt could easily fall far short of proving self-defense by a preponderance of the evidence. Of course, if such doubt is not raised in the jury's mind and each juror is convinced that the defendant purposely and with prior calculation and design took life, the killing will still be excused if the elements of the defense are satisfactorily established. We note here, but need not rely on it, the observation of the Supreme Court of Ohio that "Appellant did not dispute the existence of (the elements of aggravated murder), but rather sought to justify her actions on grounds she acted in self-defense."

Petitioner submits that there can be no conviction under Ohio law unless the defendant's conduct is unlawful and that because self-defense renders lawful what would otherwise be a crime, unlawfulness is an element of the offense that the state must prove by disproving self-defense. This argument founders on state law, for it has been rejected by the Ohio Supreme Court and by the Court of Appeals for the Sixth Circuit. It is true that unlawfulness is essential for conviction, but the Ohio courts hold that the unlawfulness in cases like this is the conduct satisfying the elements of aggravated murder—an interpretation of state law that we are not in a position to dispute. The same is true of the claim that it is necessary to prove a "criminal" intent to convict for serious crimes, which cannot occur if self-defense is shown: the necessary mental state for aggravated murder under Ohio law is the specific purpose to take life pursuant to prior calculation and design.

As we noted in *Patterson*, the common law rule was that affirmative defenses, including self-defense, were matters for the defendant to prove. "This was the rule when the Fifth Amendment was adopted, and it was the American rule when the Fourteenth Amendment was ratified." 432 U.S., at 202. Indeed, well into this century, a number of States followed the common law rule and required a defendant to shoulder the burden of proving that he acted in self-defense. We are aware that all but two of the States, Ohio and South Carolina, have abandoned the common law rule and require the prosecution to prove the absence of self-defense when it is properly raised by the defendant. But the question remains whether those States are in violation of the Constitution; and, as we observed in *Patterson*, that question is not answered by cataloging the practices of other States. We are no more convinced that the Ohio practice of requiring self-defense to be proved by the defendant is unconstitutional than we are that the Constitution requires the prosecution to prove the sanity of a defendant who pleads not guilty by reason of insanity. We have had the opportunity to depart from Leland v. Oregon but have refused to do so. Rivera v. Delaware, 429 U.S. 877 (1976). These cases were important to the *Patterson* decision and they, along with *Patterson*, are authority for our decision today.

The judgment of the Ohio Supreme Court is accordingly affirmed.

Justice POWELL, with whom Justice Brennan and Justice Marshall join, and with whom Justice Blackmun joins with respect to Parts I and III, dissenting.

Today the Court holds that a defendant can be convicted of aggravated murder even though the jury may have a reasonable doubt whether the accused acted in self-defense, and thus, whether he is guilty of a crime. Because I think this decision is inconsistent with both precedent and fundamental fairness, I dissent.

I

. . . The Court today relies on the *Patterson* reasoning in affirming the Ohio decision. If one accepts *Patterson* as the proper method of analysis for this case, I believe that the Court's opinion ignores its central meaning.

In *Patterson*, the Court upheld a state statute that shifted the burden of proof for an affirmative defense to the accused. New York law required the prosecutor to prove all of the statutorily defined elements of murder beyond a reasonable doubt, but permitted a defendant to reduce the charge to manslaughter by showing that he acted while suffering an "extreme emotional disturbance." The Court found that this burden-shifting did not violate due process, largely because the affirmative defense did "not serve to negative any facts of the crime which the State is to prove in order to convict of murder." 432 U.S., at 207. The clear implication of this ruling is that when an affirmative defense does negate an element of the crime, the state may not shift the burden. In such a case, In re Winship requires the state to prove the nonexistence of the defense beyond a reasonable doubt.

The reason for treating a defense that negates an element of the crime differently from other affirmative defenses is plain. If the jury is told that the prosecution has the burden of proving all the elements of a crime, but then also is instructed that the defendant has the burden of disproving one of those same elements, there is a danger that the jurors will resolve the inconsistency in a way that lessens the presumption of innocence. For example, the jury might reasonably believe that by raising the defense, the accused has assumed the ultimate burden of proving that particular element. Or, it might reconcile the instructions simply by balancing the evidence that supports the prosecutor's case against the evidence supporting the affirmative defense, and conclude that the state has satisfied its burden if the prosecution's version is more persuasive. In either case, the jury is given the unmistakable but erroneous impression that the defendant shares the risk of nonpersuasion as to a fact necessary for conviction.[1]

---

1. Indeed, this type of instruction has an inherently illogical aspect. It makes no sense to say that the prosecution has the burden of proving an element beyond a reasonable doubt

A. The Scope of the Requirement of Proof Beyond Reasonable Doubt 649

Given these principles, the Court's reliance on *Patterson* is puzzling. Under Ohio law, the element of "prior calculation and design" is satisfied only when the accused has engaged in a "definite process of reasoning in advance of the killing," i.e., when he has given the plan at least some "studied consideration." In contrast, when a defendant such as Martin raises a claim of self-defense, the jury also is instructed that the accused must prove that she "had an honest belief that she was in imminent danger of death or great bodily harm." In many cases, a defendant who finds himself in immediate danger and reacts with deadly force will not have formed a prior intent to kill. The Court recognizes this when it states: "It may be that most encounters in which self-defense is claimed arise suddenly and involve no prior plan or specific purpose to take life. In those cases, evidence offered to support the defense may negate a purposeful killing by prior calculation and design. . . ."

Under *Patterson*, this conclusion should suggest that Ohio is precluded from shifting the burden as to self-defense. The Court nevertheless concludes that Martin was properly required to prove self-defense, simply because "Ohio does not shift to the defendant the burden of disproving any element of the state's case."

The Court gives no explanation for this apparent rejection of *Patterson*. The only justification advanced for the Court's decision is that the jury could have used the evidence of self-defense to find that the state failed to carry its burden of proof. Because the jurors were free to consider both Martin's and the state's evidence, the argument goes, the verdict of guilt necessarily means that they were convinced that the defendant acted with prior calculation and design, and were unpersuaded that she acted in self-defense. The Court thus seems to conclude that as long as the jury is told that the state has the burden of proving all elements of the crime, the overlap between the offense and defense is immaterial.

This reasoning is flawed in two respects. First, it simply ignores the problem that arises from inconsistent jury instructions in a criminal case. The Court's holding implicitly assumes that the jury in fact understands that the ultimate burden remains with the prosecutor at all times, despite a conflicting instruction that places the burden on the accused to disprove the same element. But as pointed out above, the *Patterson* distinction between defenses that negate an element of the crime and those that do not is based

---

and that the defense has the burden of proving the contrary by a preponderance of the evidence. If the jury finds that the prosecutor has not met his burden, it of course will have no occasion to consider the affirmative defense. And if the jury finds that each element of the crime has been proved beyond a reasonable doubt, it necessarily has decided that the defendant has not disproved an element of the crime. In either situation the instructions on the affirmative defense are surplusage. Because a reasonable jury will attempt to ascribe some significance to the court's instructions, the likelihood that it will impermissibly shift the burden is increased. Of course, whether the jury will in fact improperly shift the burden away from the state is uncertain. But it is "settled law . . . that when there exists a reasonable possibility that the jury relied on an unconstitutional understanding of the law in reaching a guilty verdict, that verdict must be set aside." Francis v. Franklin, 471 U.S. 307, 323 n.8.

on the legitimate concern that the jury will mistakenly lower the state's burden. In short, the Court's rationale fails to explain why the overlap in this case does not create the risk that *Patterson* suggested was unacceptable.

Second, the Court significantly, and without explanation, extends the deference granted to state legislatures in this area. Today's decision could be read to say that virtually all state attempts to shift the burden of proof for affirmative defenses will be upheld, regardless of the relationship between the elements of the defense and the elements of the crime. As I understand it, *Patterson* allowed burden-shifting because evidence of an extreme emotional disturbance did not negate the mens rea of the underlying offense. After today's decision, however, even if proof of the defense does negate an element of the offense, burden-shifting still may be permitted because the jury can consider the defendant's evidence when reaching its verdict.

I agree, of course, that States must have substantial leeway in defining their criminal laws and administering their criminal justice systems. But none of our precedents suggests that courts must give complete deference to a State's judgment about whether a shift in the burden of proof is consistent with the presumption of innocence. In the past we have emphasized that in some circumstances it may be necessary to look beyond the text of the State's burden-shifting laws to satisfy ourselves that the requirements of *Winship* have been satisfied. In Mullaney v. Wilbur, we explicitly noted the danger of granting the State unchecked discretion to shift the burden as to any element of proof in a criminal case.[4] The Court today fails to discuss or even cite *Mullaney*, despite our unanimous agreement in that case that this danger would justify judicial intervention in some cases. Even *Patterson*, from which I dissented, recognized that "there are obviously constitutional limits beyond which the States may not go (in labeling elements of a crime as an affirmative defense)."[5] 432 U.S., at 210. Today, however, the Court simply asserts that Ohio law properly allocates the burdens, without giving any indication of where those limits lie.

Because our precedent establishes that the burden of proof may not be shifted when the elements of the defense and the elements of the offense conflict, and because it seems clear that they do so in this case, I would reverse the decision of the Ohio Supreme Court.

II

Although I believe that this case is wrongly decided even under the principles set forth in *Patterson*, my differences with the Court's approach are more

---

4. We noted, for example: "(I)f Winship were limited to those facts that constitute a crime as defined by state law, a State could undermine many of the interests that decision sought to protect without effecting any substantive change in its law. It would only be necessary to redefine the elements that constitute different crimes, characterizing them as factors that bear solely on the extent of punishment." 421 U.S., at 698.

5. See also McMillan v. Pennsylvania, 477 U.S. 79 (1986) ("(I)n certain limited circumstances *Winship*'s reasonable-doubt requirement applies to facts not formally identified as elements of the offense charged").

A. The Scope of the Requirement of Proof Beyond Reasonable Doubt

fundamental. I continue to believe that the better method for deciding when a state may shift the burden of proof is outlined in the Court's opinion in *Mullaney* and in my dissenting opinion in *Patterson*. In *Mullaney*, we emphasized that the state's obligation to prove certain facts beyond a reasonable doubt was not necessarily restricted to legislative distinctions between offenses and affirmative defenses. The boundaries of the state's authority in this respect were elaborated in the *Patterson* dissent, where I proposed a two-part inquiry:

> The Due Process Clause requires that the prosecutor bear the burden of persuasion beyond a reasonable doubt only if the factor at issue makes a substantial difference in punishment and stigma. The requirement of course applies a fortiori if the factor makes the difference between guilt and innocence. . . . It also must be shown that in the Anglo-American legal tradition the factor in question historically has held that level of importance. If either branch of the test is not met, then the legislature retains its traditional authority over matters of proof. . . .

There are at least two benefits to this approach. First, it ensures that the critical facts necessary to sustain a conviction will be proved by the state. Because the Court would be willing to look beyond the text of a state statute, legislatures would have no incentive to redefine essential elements of an offense to make them part of an affirmative defense, thereby shifting the burden of proof in a manner inconsistent with *Winship* and *Mullaney*. Second, it would leave the states free in all other respects to recognize new factors that may mitigate the degree of criminality or punishment, without requiring that they also bear the burden of disproving these defenses.

Under this analysis, it plainly is impermissible to require the accused to prove self-defense. If petitioner could have carried her burden, the result would have been decisively different as to both guilt and punishment. There also is no dispute that self-defense historically is one of the primary justifications for otherwise unlawful conduct. Thus, while I acknowledge that the two-part test may be difficult to apply at times, it is hard to imagine a more clear-cut application than the one presented here.

III

In its willingness to defer to the State's legislative definitions of crimes and defenses, the Court apparently has failed to recognize the practical effect of its decision. Martin alleged that she was innocent because she acted in self-defense, a complete justification under Ohio law. Because she had the burden of proof on this issue, the jury could have believed that it was just as likely as not that Martin's conduct was justified, and yet still have voted to convict. In other words, even though the jury may have had a substantial doubt whether Martin committed a crime, she was found guilty under Ohio law.

I do not agree that the Court's authority to review state legislative choices is so limited that it justifies increasing the risk of convicting a person who may not be blameworthy. The complexity of the inquiry as to when a state may shift the burden of proof should not lead the Court to fashion simple rules of deference that could lead to such unjust results.

NOTES AND QUESTIONS

1. Does the proportionality theory provide a workable solution to the problem of the scope of the constitutional interest in the reasonable doubt standard? Is there a better approach? Does *Martin* suggest an approach? Justice White asserts that *Patterson* and *Leland* are "authority" for the decision in *Martin*. Is this an example of authority without reason?

2. For the Supreme Court's most recent decisions on proportionality, see Rummell v. Estelle, 445 U.S. 263 (1980), upholding the constitutionality of a recidivist statute under which the defendant received a mandatory life sentence for three crimes of fraud that netted a total sum of less than $230; Hutto v. Davis, 454 U.S. 370 (1982), upholding a 40-year prison term for possession and distribution of approximately nine ounces of marijuana; Solem v. Helm, 463 U.S. 277 (1983), striking down a life sentence for uttering a "no-account" check for less than $100.

B. PRESUMPTION ANALYSIS IN CRIMINAL CASES

As you can tell from the preceding material, "presumptions" play an important role in burden of proof analysis in criminal cases, as they do in civil cases. In criminal cases, the word typically refers to a permissible inference, and the traditional approach has been to ask if there is a rational basis for that inference. This does not mean that presumptions have caused no difficulty in criminal cases, however, as the next three cases demonstrate. *Barnes* is an excellent example of the traditional approach. *Ulster County Court* and *Sandstrom* demonstrate the difficulties that have developed with that traditional analysis; in addition, these latter two cases are more directly responding to the requirement of proof beyond reasonable doubt than was *Barnes*. As you read *Ulster County Court* and *Sandstrom*, see if you can make sense of them without answering the question posed by cases such as *Martin*: What is the scope of the constitutional interest in the requirement of proof beyond reasonable doubt?

B. Presumption Analysis in Criminal Cases

BARNES v. UNITED STATES
412 U.S. 837, 93 S. Ct. 2357, 37 L. Ed. 2d 380 (1973)

Justice POWELL delivered the opinion of the Court. Petitioner Barnes was convicted in United States District Court on two counts of possessing United States Treasury checks stolen from the mails, knowing them to be stolen, two counts of forging the checks, and two counts of uttering the checks, knowing the endorsements to be forged. The trial court instructed the jury that ordinarily it would be justified in inferring from unexplained possession of recently stolen mail that the defendant possessed the mail with knowledge that it was stolen. We granted certiorari to consider whether this instruction comports with due process.

The evidence at petitioner's trial established that on June 2, 1971, he opened a checking account using the pseudonym "Clarence Smith." On July 1, and July 3, 1971, the United States Disbursing Office at San Francisco mailed four Government checks in the amounts of $269.02, $154.70, $184, and $268.80 to Nettie Lewis, Albert Young, Arthur Salazar, and Mary Hernandez, respectively. On July 8, 1971, petitioner deposited these four checks into the "Smith" account. Each check bore the apparent endorsement of the payee and a second endorsement by "Clarence Smith."

At petitioner's trial the four payees testified that they had never received, endorsed, or authorized endorsement of the checks. A Government handwriting expert testified that petitioner had made the "Clarence Smith" endorsement on all four checks and that he had signed the payees' names on the Lewis and Hernandez checks. Although petitioner did not take the stand, a postal inspector testified to certain statements made by petitioner at a post-arrest interview. Petitioner explained to the inspector that he received the checks in question from people who sold furniture for him door to door and that the checks had been signed in the payees' names when he received them. Petitioner further stated that he could not name or identify any of the salespeople. Nor could he substantiate the existence of any furniture orders because the salespeople allegedly wrote their orders on scratch paper that had not been retained. Petitioner admitted that he executed the Clarence Smith endorsements and deposited the checks but denied making the payees' endorsements.

The District Court instructed the jury that "(p)ossession of recently stolen property, if not satisfactorily explained, is ordinarily a circumstance from which you may reasonably draw the inference and find, in the light of the surrounding circumstances shown by the evidence in the case, that the person in possession knew the property had been stolen."[3]

---

[3]. The full instruction on the inference arising from possession of stolen property stated:

Possession of recently stolen property, if not satisfactorily explained, is ordinarily a circumstance from which you may reasonably draw the inference and find, in the light of the surrounding circumstances shown by the evidence in the case, that the person

The jury brought in guilty verdicts on all six counts, and the District Court sentenced petitioner to concurrent three-year prison terms. The Court of Appeals for the Ninth Circuit affirmed, finding no lack of "rational connection" between unexplained possession of recently stolen property and knowledge that the property was stolen. Because petitioner received identical concurrent sentences on all six counts, the court declined to consider his challenges to conviction on the forgery and uttering counts. We affirm.

I

We begin our consideration of the challenged jury instruction with a review of four recent decisions which have considered the validity under the Due Process Clause of criminal law presumptions and inferences. Turner v. United States, 396 U.S. 398 (1970); Leary v. United States, 395 U.S. 6 (1969); United States v. Romano, 382 U.S. 136 (1965); United States v. Gainey, 380 U.S. 63 (1965).

In United States v. Gainey, the Court sustained the constitutionality of an instruction tracking a statute which authorized the jury to infer from defendant's unexplained presence at an illegal still that he was carrying on "the business of a distiller or rectifier without having given bond as required by law." Relying on the holding of Tot v. United States, 319 U.S. 463, 467 (1943), that there must be "a rational connection between the fact proved and the ultimate fact presumed," the Court upheld the inference on the basis of the comprehensive nature of the "carrying on" offense and the common knowledge that illegal stills are secluded, secret operations. The following Term the Court determined, however, that presence at an illegal still could not support the inference that the defendant was in possession, custody, or control of the still, a narrower offense. "Presence is relevant and

---

in possession knew the property had been stolen. However, you are never required to make this inference. It is the exclusive province of the jury to determine whether the facts and circumstances shown by the evidence in this case warrant any inference which the law permits the jury to draw from the possession of recently stolen property. The term "recently" is a relative term, and has no fixed meaning. Whether property may be considered as recently stolen depends upon the nature of the property, and all the facts and circumstances shown by the evidence in the case. The longer the period of time since the theft the more doubtful becomes the inference which may reasonably be drawn from unexplained possession. If you should find beyond a reasonable doubt from the evidence in the case that the mail described in the indictment was stolen, and that while recently stolen the contents of said mail here, the four United States Treasury checks, were in the possession of the defendant you would ordinarily be justified in drawing from those facts the inference that the contents were possessed by the accused with knowledge that it was stolen property, unless such possession is explained by facts and circumstances in this case which are in some way consistent with the defendant's innocence. In considering whether possession of recently stolen property has been satisfactorily explained, you are reminded that in the exercise of constitutional rights the accused need not take the witness stand and testify. Possession may be satisfactorily explained through other circumstances, other evidence, independent of any testimony of the accused.

B. Presumption Analysis in Criminal Cases

admissible evidence in a trial on a possession charge; but absent some showing of the defendant's function at the still, its connection with possession is too tenuous to permit a reasonable inference of guilt—'the inference of the one from proof of the other is arbitrary. . . .' Tot v. United States, 319 U.S. 463, 467." United States v. Romano, supra, at 141.

Three and one-half years after *Romano*, the Court in Leary v. United States considered a challenge to a statutory inference that possession of marijuana, unless satisfactorily explained, was sufficient to prove that the defendant knew that the marijuana had been illegally imported into the United States. The Court concluded that in view of the significant possibility that any given marijuana was domestically grown and the improbability that a marijuana user would know whether his marijuana was of domestic or imported origin, the inference did not meet the standards set by *Tot, Gainey,* and *Romano*. Referring to these three cases, the *Leary* Court stated that an inference is "irrational or arbitrary, and hence unconstitutional, unless it can at least be said with substantial assurance that the presumed fact is more likely than not to flow from the proved fact on which it is made to depend." 395 U.S. at 36. In a footnote the Court stated that since the challenged inference failed to satisfy the more-likely-than-not standard, it did not have to "reach the question whether a criminal presumption which passes muster when so judged must also satisfy the criminal 'reasonable doubt' standard if proof of the crime charged or an essential element thereof depends upon its use." Id., at n.64.

Finally, in Turner v. United States, decided the year following *Leary*, the Court considered the constitutionality of instructing the jury that it may infer from possession of heroin and cocaine that the defendant knew these drugs had been illegally imported. The Court noted that *Leary* reserved the question of whether the more-likely-than-not or the reasonable doubt standard controlled in criminal cases, but it likewise found no need to resolve that question. It held that the inference with regard to heroin was valid judged by either standard. With regard to cocaine, the inference failed to satisfy even the more-likely-than-not standard.

The teaching of the foregoing cases is not altogether clear. To the extent that the "rational connection," "more likely than not," and "reasonable doubt" standards bear ambiguous relationships to one another, the ambiguity is traceable in large part to variations in language and focus rather than to differences of substance. What has been established by the cases, however, is at least this: that if a statutory inference submitted to the jury as sufficient to support conviction satisfies the reasonable-doubt standard (that is, the evidence necessary to invoke the inference is sufficient for a rational juror to find the inferred fact beyond a reasonable doubt) as well as the more-likely-than-not standard, then it clearly accords with due process.

In the present case we deal with a traditional common-law inference deeply rooted in our law. For centuries courts have instructed juries that an inference of guilty knowledge may be drawn from the fact of unexplained possession of stolen goods. James Thayer, writing in his Preliminary Treatise on Evidence (1898), cited this inference as the descendant of a presumption "running through a dozen centuries." Id., at 327. Early American cases consistently upheld instructions permitting conviction upon such an inference, and the courts of appeals on numerous occasions have approved instructions essentially identical to the instruction given in this case. This longstanding and consistent judicial approval of the instruction, reflecting accumulated common experience, provides strong indication that the instruction comports with due process.

This impressive historical basis, however, is not in itself sufficient to establish the instruction's constitutionality. Common-law inferences, like their statutory counterparts, must satisfy due process standards in light of present-day experience.[8]

In the present case the challenged instruction only permitted the inference of guilt from unexplained possession of recently stolen property.[9] The evidence established that petitioner possessed recently stolen Treasury checks payable to persons he did not know, and it provided no plausible explanation for such possession consistent with innocence. On the basis of this evidence alone common sense and experience tell us that petitioner must have known or been aware of the high probability that the checks were stolen. Such evidence was clearly sufficient to enable the jury to find beyond a reasonable doubt that petitioner knew the checks were stolen. Since the inference thus satisfies the reasonable doubt standard, the most stringent standard the Court has applied in judging permissive criminal law inferences, we conclude that it satisfies the requirements of due process.[11]

II

Petitioner also argues that the permissive inference in question infringes his privilege against self-incrimination. The Court has twice rejected this ar-

---

8. The reasoning of the statutory-inference cases is applicable to analysis of common-law inferences. Cf. United States v. Gainey, 38 U.S. 63, 70, 85, (1965). . . . Common-law inferences, however, present fewer constitutional problems. Such inferences are invoked only in the discretion of the trial judge. While statutes creating criminal law inferences may be interpreted also to preserve the trial court's traditional discretion in determining whether there is sufficient evidence to go to the jury and in charging the jury, such discretion is inherent in the use of common law inferences.

9. Of course, the mere fact that there is some evidence tending to explain a defendant's possession consistent with innocence does not bar instructing the jury on the inference. The jury must weigh the explanation to determine whether it is "satisfactory." The jury is not bound to accept or believe any particular explanation any more than it is bound to accept the correctness of the inference. But the burden of proving beyond a reasonable doubt that the defendant did have knowledge that the property was stolen, an essential element of the crime, remains on the Government.

11. It is true that the practical effect of instructing the jury on the inference arising from unexplained possession of recently stolen property is to shift the burden of going forward with

B. Presumption Analysis in Criminal Cases

gument,[12] Turner v. United States, supra, 396 U.S., at 417-418; Yee Hem v. United States, 268 U.S. 178, 185 (1925), and we find no reason to reexamine the issue at length. The trial court specifically instructed the jury that petitioner had a constitutional right not to take the witness stand and that possession could be satisfactorily explained by evidence independent of petitioner's testimony. Introduction of any evidence, direct or circumstantial, tending to implicate the defendant in the alleged crime increases the pressure on him to testify. The mere massing of evidence against a defendant cannot be regarded as a violation of his privilege against self-incrimination. . . .

Affirmed.

Justice Douglas's dissenting opinion is omitted.

Justice BRENNAN, with whom Justice Marshall joins, dissenting.

Petitioner was charged in two counts of a six-count indictment with possession of United States Treasury checks stolen from the mails, knowing them to be stolen. The essential elements of such an offense are (1) that the defendant was in possession of the checks, (2) that the checks were stolen from the mails, and (3) that the defendant knew that the checks were stolen. The Government proved that petitioner had been in possession of the checks and that the checks had been stolen from the mails; and, in addition, the Government introduced some evidence intended to show that petitioner knew or should have known that the checks were stolen. But rather than leaving the jury to determine the element of "knowledge" on the basis of that evidence, the trial court instructed it that it was free to infer the essential element of "knowledge" from petitioner's unexplained possession of the checks. In my view, that instruction violated the Due Process Clause of the Fifth Amendment because it permitted the jury to convict even though the actual evidence bearing on "knowledge" may have been insufficient to establish guilt beyond a reasonable doubt. I therefore dissent.

We held in In re Winship that the Due Process Clause requires "proof beyond a reasonable doubt of every fact necessary to constitute the crime. . . ." Thus, in Turner v. United States we approved the inference of "knowledge" from the fact of possessing smuggled heroin because " '(c)ommon sense' . . . tells us that those who traffic in heroin will inev-

---

evidence to the defendant. If the Government proves possession and nothing more, this evidence remains unexplained unless the defendant introduces evidence, since ordinarily the Government's evidence will not provide an explanation of his possession consistent with innocence. In Tot v. United States, 319 U.S. 463, (1943), the Court stated that the burden of going forward may not be freely shifted to the defendant. *Tot* held, however, that where there is a "rational connection" between the facts proved and the fact presumed or inferred, it is permissible to shift the burden of going forward to the defendant. Where an inference satisfies the reasonable-doubt standard, as in the present case, there will certainly be a rational connection between the fact presumed or inferred (in this case, knowledge) and the facts the Government must prove in order to shift the burden of going forward (possession of recently stolen property). We do not decide today whether a judge-formulated inference of less antiquity or authority may properly be emphasized by a jury instruction.

12. Nor can the instruction "be fairly understood as a comment on the petitioner's failure to testify." United States v. Gainey, 380 U.S., at 70-71.

itably become aware that the product they deal in is smuggled. . . ." The basis of that "common sense" judgment was, of course, the indisputable fact that all or virtually all heroin in this country is necessarily smuggled. Here, however, it cannot be said that all or virtually all endorsed United States Treasury checks have been stolen. Indeed, it is neither unlawful nor unusual for people to use such checks as direct payment for goods and services. Thus, unlike Turner, "common sense" simply will not permit the inference that the possessor of stolen Treasury checks "inevitably" knew that the checks were stolen.

In short, the practical effect of the challenged instruction was to permit the jury to convict petitioner even if it found insufficient or disbelieved all of the Government's evidence bearing directly on the issue of "knowledge." By authorizing the jury to rely exclusively on the inference in determining the element of "knowledge," the instruction relieved the Government of the burden of proving that element beyond a reasonable doubt. The instruction thereby violated the principle of *Winship* that every essential element of the crime must be proved beyond a reasonable doubt.

COUNTY COURT OF ULSTER COUNTY v. ALLEN et al.
442 U.S. 140, 99 S. Ct. 2213, 60 L. Ed. 2d 777 (1979)

Justice STEVENS delivered the opinion of the Court. A New York statute provides that, with certain exceptions, the presence of a firearm in an automobile is presumptive evidence of its illegal possession by all persons then occupying the vehicle. The United States Court of Appeals for the Second Circuit held that respondents may challenge the constitutionality of this statute in a federal habeas corpus proceeding and that the statute is "unconstitutional on its face." We granted certiorari to review these holdings and also to consider whether the statute is constitutional in its application to respondents.

Four persons, three adult males (respondents) and a 16-year-old girl (Jane Doe, who is not a respondent here), were jointly tried on charges that they possessed two loaded handguns, a loaded machinegun, and over a pound of heroin found in a Chevrolet in which they were riding when it was stopped for speeding on the New York Thruway shortly after noon on March 28, 1973. The two large-caliber handguns, which together with their ammunition weighed approximately six pounds, were seen through the window of the car by the investigating police officer. They were positioned crosswise in an open handbag on either the front floor or the front seat of the car on the passenger side where Jane Doe was sitting. Jane Doe admitted that the handbag was hers. The machinegun and the heroin were discovered in the trunk after the police pried it open. The car had been borrowed from the driver's brother earlier that day; the key to the trunk could not be found in the car or on the person of any of its occupants, although there was testimony

B. Presumption Analysis in Criminal Cases

that two of the occupants had placed something in the trunk before embarking in the borrowed car.[3] The jury convicted all four of possession of the handguns and acquitted them of possession of the contents of the trunk.

Counsel for all four defendants objected to the introduction into evidence of the two handguns, the machinegun, and the drugs, arguing that the State had not adequately demonstrated a connection between their clients and the contraband. The trial court overruled the objection, relying on the presumption of possession created by the New York statute. . . .

At the close of the trial, the judge instructed the jurors that they were entitled to infer possession from the defendants' presence in the car. . . .

Defendants filed a post-trial motion in which they challenged the constitutionality of the New York statute as applied in this case. The challenge was made in support of their argument that the evidence, apart from the presumption, was insufficient to sustain the convictions. The motion was denied, and the convictions were affirmed by the Appellate Division without opinion.

The New York Court of Appeals also affirmed. . . .

Respondents filed a petition for a writ of habeas corpus in the United States District Court for the Southern District of New York contending that they were denied due process of law by the application of the statutory presumption of possession. The District Court issued the writ. . . .

The Court of Appeals for the Second Circuit affirmed. . . . The majority of the court, without deciding whether the presumption was constitutional as applied in this case, concluded that the statute is unconstitutional on its face because the "presumption obviously sweeps within its compass (1) many occupants who may not know they are riding with a gun (which may be out of their sight), and (2) many who may be aware of the presence of the gun but not permitted access to it."[4]

The petition for a writ of certiorari presented [two] questions: (1) whether it was proper for the Court of Appeals to decide the facial constitutionality issue; and (2) whether the application of the presumption in this case is unconstitutional. We answer the first question in the negative. We accordingly reverse. . . .

---

3. Early that morning, the four defendants had arrived at the Rochester, N.Y., home of the driver's sister in a Cadillac. Using her telephone, the driver called their brother, advised him that "his car ran hot" on the way there from Detroit and asked to borrow the Chevrolet so that the four could continue on to New York City. The brother brought the Chevrolet to the sister's home. He testified that he had recently cleaned out the trunk and had seen no weapons or drugs. The sister also testified, stating that she saw two of the defendants transfer some unidentified item or items from the trunk of one vehicle to the trunk of the other while both cars were parked in her driveway.

4. The majority continued: "Nothing about a gun, which may be only a few inches in length (e.g., a Baretta or Derringer) and concealed under a seat, in a glove compartment or beyond the reach of all but one of the car's occupants, assures that its presence is known to occupants who may be hitchhikers or other casual passengers, much less that they have any dominion or control over it." 568 F.2d, at 1007.

II

. . . A party has standing to challenge the constitutionality of a statute only insofar as it has an adverse impact on his own rights. As a general rule, if there is no constitutional defect in the application of the statute to a litigant, he does not have standing to argue that it would be unconstitutional if applied to third parties in hypothetical situations. Broadrick v. Oklahoma, 413 U.S. 601, 610 (and cases cited). . . .

In this case, the Court of Appeals undertook the task of deciding the constitutionality of the New York statute "on its face." Its conclusion that the statutory presumption was arbitrary rested entirely on its view of the fairness of applying the presumption in hypothetical situations—situations, indeed, in which it is improbable that a jury would return a conviction,[14] one that a prosecution would ever be instituted. We must accordingly inquire whether these respondents had standing to advance the arguments that the Court of Appeals considered decisive. An analysis of our prior cases indicates that the answer to this inquiry depends on the type of presumption that is involved in the case.

Inferences and presumptions are a staple of our adversary system of factfinding. It is often necessary for the trier of fact to determine the existence of an element of the crime—that is, an "ultimate" or "elemental" fact—from the existence of one or more "evidentiary" or "basic" facts. The value of these evidentiary devices, and their validity under the Due Process Clause, vary from case to case, however, depending on the strength of the connection between the particular basic and elemental facts involved and on the degree to which the device curtails the factfinder's freedom to assess the evidence independently. Nonetheless, in criminal cases, the ultimate test of any device's constitutional validity in a given case remains constant: the device must not undermine the factfinder's responsibility at trial, based on evidence adduced by the State, to find the ultimate facts beyond a reasonable doubt.

The most common evidentiary device is the entirely permissive inference or presumption, which allows—but does not require—the trier of fact to infer the elemental fact from proof by the prosecutor of the basic one and

---

14. Indeed, in this very case the permissive presumptions in §265.15(3) and its companion drug statute, N.Y. Penal Law §220.25(1) (McKinney Supp. 1978), were insufficient to persuade the jury to convict the defendants of possession of the loaded machinegun and heroin in the trunk of the car notwithstanding the supporting testimony that at least two of them had been seen transferring something into the trunk that morning.

The hypothetical, even implausible, nature of the situations relied upon by the Court of Appeals is illustrated by the fact that there are no reported cases in which the presumption led to convictions in circumstances even remotely similar to the posited situations. In those occasional cases in which a jury has reached a guilty verdict on the basis of evidence insufficient to justify an inference of possession from presence, the New York appellate courts have not hesitated to reverse.

In light of the improbable character of the situations hypothesized by the Court of Appeals, its facial analysis would still be unconvincing even were that type of analysis appropriate. This Court has never required that a presumption be accurate in every imaginable case.

B. Presumption Analysis in Criminal Cases

which places no burden of any kind on the defendant. In that situation the basic fact may constitute *prima facie* evidence of the elemental fact. When reviewing this type of device, the Court has required the party challenging it to demonstrate its invalidity as applied to him. Because this permissive presumption leaves the trier of fact free to credit or reject the inference and does not shift the burden of proof, it affects the application of the "beyond a reasonable doubt" standard only if, under the facts of the case, there is no rational way the trier could make the connection permitted by the inference. For only in that situation is there any risk that an explanation of the permissible inference to a jury, or its use by a jury, has caused the presumptively rational factfinder to make an erroneous factual determination.

A mandatory presumption is a far more troublesome evidentiary device. For it may affect not only the strength of the "no reasonable doubt" burden but also the placement of that burden; it tells the trier that he or they must find the elemental fact upon proof of the basic fact, at least unless the defendant has come forward with some evidence to rebut the presumed connection between the two facts.[16] In this situation, the Court has generally

---

16. This class of more or less mandatory presumptions can be subdivided into two parts: presumptions that merely shift the burden of production to the defendant, following the satisfaction of which the ultimate burden of persuasion returns to the prosecution; and presumptions that entirely shift the burden of proof to the defendant. The mandatory presumptions examined by our cases have almost uniformly fit into the former subclass, in that they never totally removed the ultimate burden of proof beyond a reasonable doubt from the prosecution.

To the extent that a presumption imposes an extremely low burden of production—e.g., being satisfied by "any" evidence—it may well be that its impact is no greater than that of a permissive inference, and it may be proper to analyze it as such. See generally Mullaney v. Wilbur, 421 U.S. 684, 703 n.31.

In deciding what type of inference or presumption is involved in a case, the jury instructions will generally be controlling, although their interpretation may require recourse to the statute involved and the cases decided under it. . . .

The importance of focusing attention on the precise presentation of the presumption to the jury and the scope of that presumption is illustrated by a comparison of United States v. Gainey, 380 U.S. 63, with United States v. Romano. Both cases involved statutory presumptions based on proof that the defendant was present at the site of an illegal still. In *Gainey* the Court sustained a conviction "for carrying on" the business of the distillery in violation of 26 U.S.C. §5601(a)(4), whereas in *Romano*, the Court set aside a conviction for being in "possession, or custody, or . . . control" of such a distillery in violation of §5601(a)(1). The difference in outcome was attributable to two important differences between the cases. Because the statute involved in *Gainey* was a sweeping prohibition of almost any activity associated with the still, whereas the *Romano* statute involved only one narrow aspect of the total undertaking, there was a much higher probability that mere presence could support an inference of guilt in the former case than in the latter.

Of perhaps greater importance, however, was the difference between the trial judge's instructions to the jury in the two cases. In *Gainey*, the judge had explained that the presumption was permissive; it did not require the jury to convict the defendant even if it was convinced that he was present at the site. On the contrary, the instructions made it clear that presence was only "a circumstance to be considered along with all the other circumstances in the case." As we emphasized, the "jury was thus specifically told that the statutory inference was not conclusive." 380 U.S., at 69-70. In *Romano*, the trial judge told the jury that the defendant's presence at the still "shall be deemed sufficient evidence to authorize conviction." 382 U.S., at 138. Although there was other evidence of guilt, that instruction authorized conviction even if the jury disbelieved all of the testimony except the proof of presence at the site. This Court's holding that the statutory presumption could not support the *Romano*

examined the presumption on its face to determine the extent to which the basic and elemental facts coincide. To the extent that the trier of fact is forced to abide by the presumption, and may not reject it based on an independent evaluation of the particular facts presented [at trial], the analysis of the presumption's constitutional validity is logically divorced from those facts and based on the presumption's accuracy in the run of cases.[17] It is for this reason that the Court has held it irrelevant in analyzing a mandatory presumption, but not in analyzing a purely permissive one, that there is ample evidence in the record other than the presumption to support a conviction.

Without determining whether the presumption in this case was mandatory, the Court of Appeals analyzed it on its face as if it were. In fact, it was not. . . .

The trial judge's instructions make it clear that the presumption was merely a part of the prosecution's case,[19] that it gave rise to a permissive

---

conviction was thus dependent, in part, on the specific instructions given by the trial judge. Under those instructions it was necessary to decide whether, regardless of the specific circumstances of the particular case, the statutory presumption adequately supported the guilty verdict.

17. In addition to the discussion of *Romano* in n.16, supra, this point is illustrated by Leary v. United States. In that case, Dr. Timothy Leary, a professor at Harvard University, was stopped by customs inspectors in Laredo, Tex., as he was returning from the Mexican side of the international border. Marihuana seeds and a silver snuffbox filled with semirefined marihuana and three partially smoked marihuana cigarettes were discovered in his car. He was convicted of having knowingly transported marihuana which he knew had been illegally imported into this country in violation of 21 U.S.C. §176a (1964 ed.). That statute included a mandatory presumption: "possession shall be deemed sufficient evidence to authorize conviction (for importation) unless the defendant explains his possession to the satisfaction of the jury." Leary admitted possession of the marihuana and claimed that he had carried it from New York to Mexico and then back.

Mr. Justice Harlan for the Court noted that under one theory of the case, the jury could have found direct proof of all of the necessary elements of the offense without recourse to the presumption. But he deemed that insufficient reason to affirm the conviction because under another theory the jury might have found knowledge of importation on the basis of either direct evidence or the presumption, and there was accordingly no certainty that the jury had not relied on the presumption. 395 U.S., at 31-32. The Court therefore found it necessary to test the presumption against the Due Process Clause. Its analysis was facial. Despite the fact that the defendant was well educated and had recently traveled to a country that is a major exporter of marihuana to this country, the Court found the presumption of knowledge of importation from possession irrational. It did so, not because Dr. Leary was unlikely to know the source of the marihuana, but instead because "a majority of possessors" were unlikely to have such knowledge. Id., at 53. Because the jury had been instructed to rely on the presumption even if it did not believe the Government's direct evidence of knowledge of importation (unless, of course, the defendant met his burden of "satisfying" the jury to the contrary), the Court reversed the conviction.

19. "It is your duty to consider all the testimony in this case, to weigh it carefully and to test the credit to be given to a witness by his apparent intention to speak the truth and by the accuracy of his memory to reconcile, if possible, conflicting statements as to material facts and in such ways to try and get at the truth and to reach a verdict upon the evidence.

"To establish the unlawful possession of the weapons, again the People relied upon the presumption and, in addition thereto, the testimony of Anderson and Lemmons who testified in their case in chief.

"Accordingly, you would be warranted in returning a verdict of guilt against the defendants or defendant if you find the defendants or defendant was in possession of a machine gun and

B. Presumption Analysis in Criminal Cases

inference available only in certain circumstances, rather than a mandatory conclusion of possession, and that it could be ignored by the jury even if there was no affirmative proof offered by defendants in rebuttal.[20] The judge explained that possession could be actual or constructive, but that constructive possession could not exist without the intent and ability to exercise control or dominion over the weapons. He also carefully instructed the jury that there is a mandatory presumption of innocence in favor of the defendants that controls unless it, as the exclusive trier of fact, is satisfied beyond a reasonable doubt that the defendants possessed the handguns in the manner described by the judge. In short, the instructions plainly directed the jury to consider all the circumstances tending to support or contradict the inference that all four occupants of the car had possession of the two loaded handguns and to decide the matter for itself without regard to how much evidence the defendants introduced.[23]

Our cases considering the validity of permissive statutory presumptions such as the one involved here have rested on an evaluation of the presumption as applied to the record before the Court. None suggests that a court should pass on the constitutionality of this kind of statute "on its face." It was error for the Court of Appeals to make such a determination in this case.

III

As applied to the facts of this case, the presumption of possession is entirely rational. Notwithstanding the Court of Appeals' analysis, respondents were not "hitchhikers or other casual passengers," and the guns were neither "a few inches in length" nor "out of [respondents'] sight." See note 4, supra,

---

the other weapons and that the fact of possession was proven to you by the People beyond a reasonable doubt, and an element of such proof is the reasonable presumption of illegal possession of a machine gun or the presumption of illegal possession of firearms, as I have just before explained to you."

20. "Our Penal Law also provides that the presence in an automobile of any machine gun or of any handgun or firearm which is loaded is presumptive evidence of their unlawful possession.

"In other words, these presumptions or this latter presumption upon proof of the presence of the machine gun and the hand weapons, you may infer and draw a conclusion that such prohibited weapon was possessed by each of the defendants who occupied the automobile at the time when such instruments were found. The presumption or presumptions is effective only so long as there is no substantial evidence contradicting the conclusion flowing from the presumption, and the presumption is said to disappear when such contradictory evidence is adduced.

"The presumption or presumptions which I discussed with the jury relative to the drugs or weapons in this case need not be rebutted by affirmative proof or affirmative evidence but may be rebutted by any evidence or lack of evidence in the case."

23. The verdict announced by the jury clearly indicates that it understood its duty to evaluate the presumption independently and to reject it if it was not supported in the record. Despite receiving almost identical instructions on the applicability of the presumption of possession to the contraband found in the front seat and in the trunk, the jury convicted all four defendants of possession of the former but acquitted all of them of possession of the latter. See note 14, supra.

and accompanying text. The argument against possession by any of the respondents was predicated solely on the fact that the guns were in Jane Doe's pocketbook. But several circumstances—which, not surprisingly, her counsel repeatedly emphasized in his questions and his argument—made it highly improbable that she was the sole custodian of those weapons.

Even if it was reasonable to conclude that she had placed the guns in her purse before the car was stopped by police, the facts strongly suggest that Jane Doe was not the only person able to exercise dominion over them. The two guns were too large to be concealed in her handbag.[24] The bag was consequently open, and part of one of the guns was in plain view, within easy access of the driver of the car and even, perhaps, of the other two respondents who were riding in the rear seat.

Moreover, it is highly improbable that the loaded guns belonged to Jane Doe or that she was solely responsible for their being in her purse. As a 16-year-old girl in the company of three adult men she was the least likely of the four to be carrying one, let alone two, heavy handguns. It is far more probable that she relied on the pocketknife found in her brassiere for any necessary self-protection. Under these circumstances, it was not unreasonable for her counsel to argue and for the jury to infer that when the car was halted for speeding, the other passengers in the car anticipated the risk of a search and attempted to conceal their weapons in a pocketbook in the front seat. The inference is surely more likely than the notion that these weapons were the sole property of the 16-year-old girl.

Under these circumstances, the jury would have been entirely reasonable in rejecting the suggestion—which, incidentally, defense counsel did not even advance in their closing arguments to the jury—that the handguns were in the sole possession of Jane Doe. Assuming that the jury did reject it, the case is tantamount to one in which the guns were lying on the floor or the seat of the car in the plain view of the three other occupants of the automobile. In such a case, it is surely rational to infer that each of the respondents was fully aware of the presence of the guns and had both the ability and the intent to exercise dominion and control over the weapons. The application of the statutory presumption in this case therefore comports with the standard laid down in Tot v. United States, and restated in Leary v. United States. For there is a "rational connection" between the basic facts that the prosecution proved and the ultimate fact presumed, and the latter is "more likely than not to flow from" the former. Respondents argue, however, that the validity of the New York presumption must be judged by a "reasonable doubt" test rather than the "more likely than not" standard employed in *Leary*. Under the more stringent test, it is argued that a statutory presumption must be rejected unless the evidence necessary to invoke the inference is sufficient for a rational jury to find the inferred fact beyond a reasonable doubt. Respondent's argument again overlooks the distinction

24. Jane Doe's counsel referred to the .45-caliber automatic pistol as a "cannon."

B. Presumption Analysis in Criminal Cases

between a permissive presumption on which the prosecution is entitled to rely as one not necessarily sufficient part of its proof and a mandatory presumption which the jury must accept even if it is the sole evidence of an element of the offense.[29]

In the latter situation, since the prosecution bears the burden of establishing guilt, it may not rest its case entirely on a presumption unless the fact proved is sufficient to support the inference of guilt beyond a reasonable doubt. But in the former situation, the prosecution may rely on all of the evidence in the record to meet the reasonable-doubt standard. There is no more reason to require a permissive statutory presumption to meet a reasonable-doubt standard before it may be permitted to play any part in a trial than there is to require that degree of probative force for other relevant evidence before it may be admitted. As long as it is clear that the presumption is not the sole and sufficient basis for a finding of guilt, it need only satisfy the test described in *Leary*.

The judgment is reversed. So ordered.

Chief Justice Burger's concurring opinion is omitted.

Justice POWELL, with whom Justice Brennan, Justice Stewart and Justice Marshall join, dissenting.

I agree with the Court that there is no procedural bar to our considering the underlying constitutional question presented by this case. I am not in agreement, however, with the Court's conclusion that the presumption as charged to the jury in this case meets the constitutional requirements of due process as set forth in our prior decisions. On the contrary, an individual's mere presence in an automobile where there is a handgun does not even make it "more likely than not" that the individual possesses the weapon.

I

In the criminal law, presumptions are used to encourage the jury to find certain facts, with respect to which no direct evidence is presented, solely because other facts have been proved. The purpose of such presumptions is plain: Like certain other jury instructions, they provide guidance for jurors' thinking in considering the evidence laid before them. Once in the juryroom, jurors necessarily draw inferences from the evidence—both direct and circumstantial. Through the use of presumptions, certain inferences are commended to the attention of jurors by legislatures or courts.

---

29. The dissenting argument rests on the assumption that "the jury [may have] rejected all of the prosecution's evidence concerning the location and origin of the guns." Even if that assumption were plausible, the jury was plainly told that it was free to disregard the presumption. But the dissent's assumption is not plausible; for if the jury rejected the testimony describing where the guns were found, it would necessarily also have rejected the only evidence in the record proving that the guns were found in the car. The conclusion that the jury attached significance to the particular location of the handguns follows inexorably from the acquittal on the charge of possession of the machine gun and heroin in the trunk.

Legitimate guidance of a jury's deliberations is an indispensable part of our criminal justice system. Nonetheless, the use of presumptions in criminal cases poses at least two distinct perils for defendants' constitutional rights. The Court accurately identifies the first of these as being the danger of interference with "the factfinder's responsibility at trial, based on evidence adduced by the State, to find the ultimate facts beyond a reasonable doubt." If the jury is instructed that it must infer some ultimate fact (that is, some element of the offense) from proof of other facts unless the defendant disproves the ultimate fact by a preponderance of the evidence, then the presumption shifts the burden of proof to the defendant concerning the element thus inferred.

But I do not agree with the Court's conclusion that the only constitutional difficulty with presumptions lies in the danger of lessening the burden of proof the prosecution must bear. As the Court notes, the presumptions thus far reviewed by the Court have not shifted the burden of persuasion; instead, they either have required only that the defendant produce some evidence to rebut the inference suggested by the prosecution's evidence, or merely have been suggestions to the jury that it would be sensible to draw certain conclusions on the basis of the evidence presented. Evolving from our decisions, therefore, is a second standard for judging the constitutionality of criminal presumptions which is based—not on the constitutional requirement that the State be put to its proof—but rather on the due process rule that when the jury is encouraged to make factual inferences, those inferences must reflect some valid general observation about the natural connection between events as they occur in our society.

This due process rule was first articulated by the Court in Tot v. United States, in which the Court reviewed the constitutionality of §2(f) of the Federal Firearms Act. That statute provided in part that "possession of a firearm or ammunition by any . . . person [who has been convicted of a crime of violence] shall be presumptive evidence that such firearm or ammunition was shipped or transported [in interstate or foreign commerce]." As the Court interpreted the presumption, it placed upon a defendant only the obligation of presenting some exculpatory evidence concerning the origins of a firearm or ammunition, once the Government proved that the defendant had possessed the weapon and had been convicted of a crime of violence. Noting that juries must be permitted to infer from one fact the existence of another essential to guilt, "if reason and experience support the inference," 319 U.S., at 467, the Court concluded that under some circumstances juries may be guided in making these inferences by legislative or common-law presumptions, even though they may be based "upon a view of relation broader than that a jury might take in a specific case," id., at 468. To provide due process, however, there must be at least a "rational connection between the fact proved and the ultimate fact presumed"—a connection grounded in "common experience." Id., at 467-468. In *Tot*, the Court found that connection to be lacking. . . .

B. Presumption Analysis in Criminal Cases

In sum, our decisions uniformly have recognized that due process requires more than merely that the prosecution be put to its proof.[6] In addition, the Constitution restricts the court in its charge to the jury by requiring that, when particular factual inferences are recommended to the jury, those factual inferences be accurate reflections of what history, common sense, and experience tell us about the relations between events in our society. Generally, this due process rule has been articulated as requiring that the truth of the inferred fact be more likely than not whenever the premise for the inference is true. Thus, to be constitutional a presumption must be at least more likely than not true.

II

. . . Undeniably, the presumption charged in this case encouraged the jury to draw a particular factual inference regardless of any other evidence presented: to infer that respondents possessed the weapons found in the automobile "upon proof of the presence of the machine gun and the hand weapon" and proof that respondents "occupied the automobile at the time such instruments were found." I believe that the presumption thus charged was unconstitutional because it did not fairly reflect what common sense and experience tell us about passengers in automobiles and the possession of handguns. People present in automobiles where there are weapons simply are not "more likely than not" the possessors of those weapons. . . .

As I understand it, the Court today does not contend that in general those who are present in automobiles are more likely than not to possess any gun contained within their vehicles. It argues, however, that the nature of the presumption here involved requires that we look, not only to the immediate facts upon which the jury was encouraged to base its inference, but to the other facts "proved" by the prosecution as well. The Court suggests that this is the proper approach when reviewing what it calls "permissive" presumptions because the jury was urged "to consider all the circumstances tending to support or contradict the inference."

It seems to me that the Court mischaracterizes the function of the presumption charged in this case. As it acknowledges was the case in *Romano*, the "instruction authorized conviction even if the jury disbelieved all of the testimony except the proof of presence" in the automobile.[7] The Court

---

6. The Court apparently disagrees, contending that "the factfinder's responsibility . . . to find the ultimate facts beyond a reasonable doubt" is the only constitutional restraint upon the use of criminal presumptions at trial.

7. In commending the presumption to the jury, the court gave no instruction that would have required a finding of possession to be based on anything more than mere presence in the automobile. Thus, the jury was not instructed that it should infer that respondents possessed the handguns only if it found that the guns were too large to be concealed in Jane Doe's handbag; that the guns accordingly were in the plain view of respondents; that the weapons were within "easy access of the driver of the car and even, perhaps, of the other two respondents

nevertheless relies on all of the evidence introduced by the prosecution and argues that the "permissive" presumption could not have prejudiced defendants. The possibility that the jury disbelieved all of this evidence, and relied on the presumption, is simply ignored.

I agree that the circumstances relied upon by the Court in determining the plausibility of the presumption charged in this case would have made it reasonable for the jury to "infer that each of the respondents was fully aware of the presence of the guns and had both the ability and the intent to exercise dominion and control over the weapons." But the jury was told that it could conclude that respondents possessed the weapons found therein from proof of the mere fact of respondents' presence in the automobile. For all we know, the jury rejected all of the prosecution's evidence concerning the location and origin of the guns, and based its conclusion that respondents possessed the weapons solely upon its belief that respondents had been present in the automobile.[8] For purposes of reviewing the constitutionality of the presumption at issue here, we must assume that this was the case.

The Court's novel approach in this case appears to contradict prior decisions of this Court reviewing such presumptions. Under the Court's analysis, whenever it is determined that an inference is "permissive," the only question is whether, in light of all of the evidence adduced at trial, the inference recommended to the jury is a reasonable one. The Court has never suggested that the inquiry into the rational basis of a permissible inference may be circumvented in this manner. Quite the contrary, the Court has required that the "evidence *necessary to invoke the inference* [be] sufficient for a rational juror to find the inferred fact. . . ." Barnes v. United States, 412 U.S., at 843 (emphasis supplied). Under the presumption charged in this case, the only evidence necessary to invoke the inference was the presence of the weapons in the automobile with respondents—an inference that is plainly irrational.

In sum, it seems to me that the Court today ignores the teaching of our prior decisions. By speculating about what the jury may have done with the factual inference thrust upon it, the Court in effect assumes away the inference altogether, constructing a rule that permits the use of any infer-

---

who were riding in the rear seat"; that it was unlikely that Jane Doe was solely responsible for the placement of the weapons in her purse; or that the case was "tantamount to one in which the guns were lying on the floor or the seat of the car in the plain view of the three other occupants of the automobile."

8. The Court is therefore mistaken in its conclusion that, because "respondents were not 'hitchhikers or other casual passengers,' and the guns were neither 'a few inches in length' nor 'out of (respondents') sight,' " reference to these possibilities is inappropriate in considering the constitutionality of the presumption as charged in this case. To be sure, respondents' challenge is to the presumption as charged to the jury in this case. But in assessing its application here, we are not free, as the Court apparently believes, to disregard the possibility that the jury may have disbelieved all other evidence supporting an inference of possession. The jury may have concluded that respondents—like hitchhikers—had only an incidental relationship to the auto in which they were traveling, or that, contrary to some of the testimony at trial, the weapons were indeed out of respondents' sight.

B. Presumption Analysis in Criminal Cases

ence—no matter how irrational in itself—provided that otherwise there is sufficient evidence in the record to support a finding of guilt. Applying this novel analysis to the present case, the Court upholds the use of a presumption that it makes no effort to defend in isolation. In substance, the Court—applying an unarticulated harmless-error standard—simply finds that the respondents were guilty as charged. They may well have been but rather than acknowledging this rationale, the Court seems to have made new law with respect to presumptions that could seriously jeopardize a defendant's right to a fair trial. Accordingly, I dissent.

SANDSTROM v. MONTANA
442 U.S. 510, 99 S. Ct. 2450, 61 L. Ed. 2d 39 (1979)

Justice BRENNAN delivered the opinion of the Court. The question presented is whether, in a case in which intent is an element of the crime charged, the jury instruction, "the law presumes that a person intends the ordinary consequences of his voluntary acts," violates the Fourteenth Amendment's requirement that the State prove every element of a criminal offense beyond a reasonable doubt.

I

On November 22, 1976, 18-year-old David Sandstrom confessed to the slaying of Annie Jessen. Based upon the confession and corroborating evidence, petitioner was charged on December 2 with "deliberate homicide," in that he "purposely or knowingly caused the death of Annie Jessen." At trial, Sandstrom's attorney informed the jury that, although his client admitted killing Jessen, he did not do so "purposely or knowingly," and was therefore not guilty of "deliberate homicide" but of a lesser crime. The basic support for this contention was the testimony of two court-appointed mental health experts, each of whom described for the jury petitioner's mental state at the time of the incident. Sandstrom's attorney argued that this testimony demonstrated that petitioner, due to a personality disorder aggravated by alcohol consumption, did not kill Annie Jessen "purposely or knowingly."

The prosecution requested the trial judge to instruct the jury that "(t)he law presumes that a person intends the ordinary consequences of his voluntary acts." Petitioner's counsel objected, arguing that "the instruction has the effect of shifting the burden of proof on the issue of" purpose or knowledge to the defense, and that "that is impermissible under the Federal Constitution, due process of law." He offered to provide a number of federal decisions in support of the objection, including this Court's holding in Mullaney v. Wilbur, but was told by the judge: "You can give those to the Supreme Court. The objection is overruled." The instruction was delivered, the jury found petitioner guilty of deliberate homicide and petitioner was sentenced to 100 years in prison.

Sandstrom appealed to the Supreme Court of Montana, again contending that the instruction shifted to the defendant the burden of disproving an element of the crime charged, in violation of Mullaney v. Wilbur, In re Winship, and Patterson v. New York. The Montana court conceded that these cases did prohibit shifting the burden of proof to the defendant by means of a presumption, but held that the cases "do not prohibit allocation of some burden of proof to a defendant under certain circumstances." 580 P.2d 106, 109 (1978). Since in the court's view, "(d)efendant's sole burden under instruction No. 5 was to produce some evidence that he did not intend the ordinary consequences of his voluntary acts, not to disprove that he acted 'purposely' or 'knowingly,' . . . the instruction does not violate due process standards as defined by the United States or Montana Constitution. . . ."

Both federal and state courts have held, under a variety of rationales, that the giving of an instruction similar to that challenged here is fatal to the validity of a criminal conviction. We granted certiorari to decide the important question of the instruction's constitutionality. We reverse.

II

The threshold inquiry in ascertaining the constitutional analysis applicable to this kind of jury instruction is to determine the nature of the presumption it describes. See Ulster County Court v. Allen. That determination requires careful attention to the words actually spoken to the jury, for whether a defendant has been accorded his constitutional rights depends upon the way in which a reasonable juror could have interpreted the instruction.

[G]iven the lack of qualifying instructions as to the legal effect of the presumption, we cannot discount the possibility that the jury may have interpreted the instruction in either of two . . . ways [that would violate the defendant's rights].

First, a reasonable jury could well have interpreted the presumption as "conclusive," that is, not technically as a presumption at all, but rather as an irrebuttable direction by the court to find intent once convinced of the facts triggering the presumption. Alternatively, the jury may have interpreted the instruction as a direction to find intent upon proof of the defendant's voluntary actions (and their "ordinary" consequences), unless the defendant proved the contrary by some quantum of proof which may well have been considerably greater than "some" evidence—thus effectively shifting the burden of persuasion on the element of intent. . . .

We do not reject the possibility that some jurors may have interpreted the challenged instruction as permissive, or, if mandatory, as requiring only that the defendant come forward with "some" evidence in rebuttal. However, the fact that a reasonable juror could have given the presumption conclusive

B. Presumption Analysis in Criminal Cases

or persuasion-shifting effect means that we cannot discount the possibility that Sandstrom's jurors actually did proceed upon one or the other of these latter interpretations. And that means that unless these kinds of presumptions are constitutional, the instruction cannot be adjudged valid. . . . It is the line of cases urged by petitioner, and exemplified by In re Winship, that provides the appropriate mode of constitutional analysis for these kinds of presumptions.

III

In *Winship*, this Court stated:

> Lest there remain any doubt about the constitutional stature of the reasonable-doubt standard, we explicitly hold that the Due Process Clause protects the accused against conviction except upon proof beyond a reasonable doubt of every fact necessary to constitute the crime with which he is charged.

The petitioner here was charged with and convicted of deliberate homicide, committed purposely or knowingly. It is clear that under Montana law, whether the crime was committed purposely or knowingly is a fact necessary to constitute the crime of deliberate homicide. Indeed, it was the lone element of the offense at issue in Sandstrom's trial, as he confessed to causing the death of the victim, told the jury that knowledge and purpose were the only questions he was controverting, and introduced evidence solely on those points. Moreover, it is conceded that proof of defendant's "intent" would be sufficient to establish this element. Thus, the question before this Court is whether the challenged jury instruction had the effect of relieving the State of the burden of proof enunciated in *Winship* on the critical question of petitioner's state of mind. We conclude that under either of the two possible interpretations of the instruction set out above, precisely that effect would result, and that the instruction therefore represents constitutional error.

We consider first the validity of a conclusive presumption. This Court has considered such a presumption on at least two prior occasions. In Morissette v. United States, 342 U.S. 246 (1952), the defendant was charged with willful and knowing theft of Government property. Although his attorney argued that for his client to be found guilty, "the taking must have been with felonious intent," the trial judge ruled that "(t)hat is presumed by his own act." Id., at 249. After first concluding that intent was in fact an element of the crime charged, and after declaring that "(w)here intent of the accused is an ingredient of the crime charged, its existence is . . . a jury issue," *Morissette* held:

> It follows that the trial court may not withdraw or prejudge the issue by instruction that the law raises a presumption of intent from an act. It often is tempting to cast in terms of a "presumption" a conclusion which a court thinks

probable from given facts. . . . (But) (w)e think presumptive intent has no place in this case. A *conclusive presumption which testimony could not overthrow would effectively eliminate intent as an ingredient of the offense.* A presumption which would permit but not require the jury to assume intent from an isolated fact would prejudge a conclusion which the jury should reach of its own volition. A presumption which would permit the jury to make an assumption which all the evidence considered together does not logically establish would give to a proven fact an artificial and fictional effect. In either case, *this presumption would conflict with the overriding presumption of innocence with which the law endows the accused and which extends to every element of the crime.* Id., at 274-275. (Emphasis added; footnote omitted.)

Just last Term, in United States v. United States Gypsum Co., 438 U.S. 422 (1978), we reaffirmed the holding of *Morissette*. In that case defendants, who were charged with criminal violations of the Sherman Act, challenged the following jury instruction:

The law presumes that a person intends the necessary and natural consequences of his acts. Therefore, if the effect of the exchanges of pricing information was to raise, fix, maintain and stabilize prices, then the parties to them are presumed, as a matter of law, to have intended that result. 438 U.S., at 430.

After again determining that the offense included the element of intent, we held:

(A) defendant's state of mind or *intent is an element of a criminal antitrust offense which . . . cannot be taken from the trier of fact through reliance on a legal presumption* of wrongful intent from proof of an effect on prices. Cf. Morissette v. United States. . . .

Although an effect on prices may well support an inference that the defendant had knowledge of the probability of such a consequence at the time he acted, the jury must remain free to consider additional evidence before accepting or rejecting the inference. . . . (U)ltimately the decision on the issue of intent must be left to the trier of fact alone. The instruction given invaded this factfinding function. Id., at 435, 446 (emphasis added).

As in *Morissette* and *United States Gypsum Co.*, a conclusive presumption in this case would "conflict with the overriding presumption of innocence with which the law endows the accused and which extends to every element of the crime," and would "invade (the) factfinding function" which in a criminal case the law assigns solely to the jury. The instruction announced to David Sandstrom's jury may well have had exactly these consequences. Upon finding proof of one element of the crime (causing death), and of facts insufficient to establish the second (the voluntariness and "ordinary consequences" of defendant's action), Sandstrom's jurors could reasonably have concluded that they were directed to find against defendant on the element of intent. The State was thus not forced to prove "beyond

B. Presumption Analysis in Criminal Cases

a reasonable doubt . . . every fact necessary to constitute the crime . . . charged," 397 U.S., at 364, and defendant was deprived of his constitutional rights as explicated in *Winship*.

A presumption which, although not conclusive, had the effect of shifting the burden of persuasion to the defendant, would have suffered from similar infirmities. If Sandstrom's jury interpreted the presumption in that manner, it could have concluded that upon proof by the State of the slaying, and of additional facts not themselves establishing the element of intent, the burden was shifted to the defendant to prove that he lacked the requisite mental state. Such a presumption was found constitutionally deficient in Mullaney v. Wilbur. In *Mullaney*, the charge was murder, which under Maine law required proof not only of intent but of malice. The trial court charged the jury that "malice aforethought is an essential and indispensable element of the crime of murder." However, it also instructed that if the prosecution established that the homicide was both intentional and unlawful, malice aforethought was to be implied unless the defendant proved by a fair preponderance of the evidence that he acted in the heat of passion on sudden provocation. As we recounted just two Terms ago in Patterson v. New York, "(t)his Court . . . unanimously agreed with the Court of Appeals that Wilbur's due process rights had been invaded by the presumption casting upon him the burden of proving by a preponderance of the evidence that he had acted in the heat of passion upon sudden provocation." 432 U.S., at 214. And *Patterson* reaffirmed that "a State must prove every ingredient of an offense beyond a reasonable doubt, and . . . may not shift the burden of proof to the defendant" by means of such a presumption. Id., at 215.

Because David Sandstrom's jury may have interpreted the judge's instruction as constituting either a burden-shifting presumption like that in *Mullaney*, or a conclusive presumption like those in *Morissette* and *United States Gypsum Co.*, and because either interpretation would have deprived defendant of his right to the due process of law, we hold the instruction given in this case unconstitutional. . . .

Accordingly, the judgment of the Supreme Court of Montana is reversed, and the case is remanded for further proceedings not inconsistent with this opinion.

It is so ordered.

Justice Rehnquist's concurring opinion is omitted.

Can *Barnes*, *Ulster*, and *Sandstrom* be reconciled, or are they hopelessly inconsistent? Many commentators think that the cases are hopelessly at odds with one another, see, e.g., Lushing, Faces Without Features: The Surface Validity of Criminal Inferences, 72 J. Crim. L. & Criminology 82 (1981), and there are a multitude of problems.[2]

---

2. For further elaboration on many of the themes that follow, see Allen and DeGrazia, The Constitutional Requirement of Proof Beyond Reasonable Doubt in Criminal Cases: A Comment Upon Incipient Chaos in the Lower Courts, 20 Am. Crim. L. Rev. 1, 8, 10-15 (1982).

Among the most pressing problems is the fact that the opinion in *Barnes* essentially finessed the difficulty posed by the interaction of the rational relationship test and proof beyond reasonable doubt, but in a way that highlights the problem. Instructions on inferences and presumptions are either awkward methods of allocating burdens of proof or they are comments on the evidence designed to inform the jury of the inferential relationships between facts. In either case, the rational relationship test is an ill-conceived standard by which to judge such an instruction. If an instruction allocates a burden of persuasion, whatever standard emerges in the line of cases from *Winship* to *Martin* to judge such allocation ought to be employed. If, on the other hand, an instruction is a comment on the evidence, whatever standard is appropriate to judge comment on the evidence ought to be utilized. The unadorned rational relationship test is unacceptable in either case.

If an instruction allocates a burden of persuasion to a defendant, there is no rational relationship to test in the sense meant by the standard. If an instruction is a comment on the evidence, it may be a comment on an ultimate fact or it may be a comment on an evidentiary fact. It may accurately point out that one fact may be inferred from another beyond reasonable doubt or it may, just as accurately, point out that one fact may be inferred from another without meeting the reasonable doubt standard. Alternatively, a comment could be inaccurate, but in such a way as to be helpful to either the prosecution or the defense. The rational relationship test, as employed in *Barnes*, is inadequate to deal with these and other nuances.

To take just one example, a court could accurately comment to a jury that a certain piece of evidence tends to prove an element of a crime and thus support an inference of guilt, but that standing alone it is insufficient. It is unclear whether this is acceptable under *Barnes*, which suggests that instructions on necessary elements must meet the beyond reasonable doubt standard (although this suggestion was apparently disavowed in *Ulster County Court*). In the hypothetical, that standard is not met. Nonetheless, it is difficult to see what difference this makes. Since the instruction is accurate, the jury's decision-making process should not be undermined; indeed, it should be enhanced. If this is true, then the jury's employment of the appropriate burdens of persuasion should also be enhanced, thus resulting in greater, rather than lesser, protection of constitutional interests. The difficulty with the *Barnes* approach is its crudeness. By looking to only one factor, it is unresponsive to the complexities of the process of proof at trial and tends to be counterproductive if rigorously applied.

In *Ulster*, the Court implicitly responded to the inadequacies of *Barnes*, but the response itself was inadequate. In upholding the instruction that the jury may infer the defendants' possession of guns from their presence in the car the Court reasoned that the inference made sense in this situation because the guns were found sticking out of the handbag of a 16-year-old girl riding in the car with three adult defendants. *Ulster* differs from *Barnes* in that the Court purportedly analyzed the instructions on the basis of the evidence in

B. Presumption Analysis in Criminal Cases 675

the trial record. *Barnes*, by contrast, clearly had referents outside the record. The Court in *Ulster* maintained that the proper test was not to assess the hypothetical relationship between the facts, which was how the Court applied the rational relationship test in *Barnes*, but rather to determine the likelihood that the instruction was factually accurate in light of the particular facts of the case.

This distinction cannot be maintained. The inference in *Ulster* that the guns were possessed by the defendants is not supported solely by the facts of the case. Rather, common sense dictates that under such circumstances it is highly probable that the guns belonged to the adult men in the car. To rely on common sense for that conclusion is to rely on evidence outside the record. Our shared experience and common knowledge of normal human behavior—which obviously comprise extra-judicial "evidence"—suggest that a young girl is less likely than the three older men in her company to possess the guns. In sum, the Court in *Ulster* implicitly judged the instruction's validity by relying on considerations beyond the trial record. That, of course, is precisely what the Court did in *Barnes* as well, although in that case the reference to evidence outside the record was explicit.

One result of the *Ulster* Court's heavy emphasis on the evidence adduced at trial appears to be to transform the analysis of the instructions into a harmless error analysis. As Justice Powell noted in his dissent, "the Court . . . simply finds that the respondents were guilty as charged." The Court in *Barnes*, by contrast, was careful to avoid that approach, and for a very good reason. The Court's look-at-all-the-evidence approach ignores the possibility of the jury's disbelieving all the other evidence and convicting only on the basis of the inference. The jury could have believed that the prosecution had proved the defendants' presence in the car, disbelieved the rest of the evidence, and yet still convicted because of the inference. A harmless error standard that looks heavily to the facts in the record can permit an instruction to be upheld, and a conviction affirmed, primarily on the basis of facts that a jury did not believe beyond reasonable doubt. The effect is to undercut both the right to a jury trial and the reasonable doubt standard.

To be sure, the chances of the jury's disbelieving all the other evidence may be small, as was the case in *Ulster* itself, but another problem is more troublesome. Consider once again the actual instruction given:

> Our Penal Law also provides that the presence in an automobile of any machine gun or of any handgun or firearm which is loaded is presumptive evidence of their unlawful possession. In other words, [under] these presumptions or this latter presumption upon proof of the presence of the machine gun and the hand weapons, you may infer and draw a conclusion that such prohibited weapon was possessed by each of the defendants who occupied the automobile at the time when such instruments were found.

This instruction did not tell the jury that it may infer possession because of the other facts in the case. Thus, when the Supreme Court upheld the instruction on the basis of those facts, it permitted the other facts to have a double effect. After the evidence had its normal effect on the jury, that effect may have been enhanced beyond what the evidence justified by an instruction that, unknown to the jury, was based on the same evidence. The result could very well have been a conviction based on the incremental effect of the instruction even though the jury, rationally evaluating the other evidence, might have acquitted without the instruction. The deleterious effect on the right to trial by jury and the reasonable doubt standard is obvious.

The Court's opinion in Sandstrom v. Montana, which was handed down only two weeks after *Ulster*, fares no better under this analysis. The Court was certainly correct to approach the case from the point of view of the jury. Moreover, the Court's interpretation of the effect of the instruction is plausible. The Court's analysis of the two possible constructions of the jury instruction, however, is not entirely satisfactory.

Consider first the Court's treatment of the "conclusive presumption" interpretation. On its face, the Court's analysis seems reasonable, amounting to little more than a reaffirmation of the impermissibility of directing verdicts on elements of crimes. There are, however, more accurate ways of characterizing such an instruction. If the instruction is given in every case of murder, a traditional element of the definition of the crime has been removed. If the instruction accurately describes state law, intent is not included as an element of murder; rather, the state must show only a voluntary act and its ordinary consequences. Alternatively, the instruction may be read to define the crime to require either proof of intent or proof that the defendant's act was voluntary and that the ordinary consequences of that act would be death. In either case, the instruction merely provides an untraditional definition of homicide that forgoes the usual requirement of intent. This involves no burden shifting at all; the issue has simply been removed as an absolute requirement. Consequently, neither alternative should have been objectionable to the Court on the grounds that the reasonable doubt requirement was violated. Montana may very well have defined homicide in an unusual fashion, but under the Court's theory all it did was define the crime. Without a constitutional limitation on a state's definition of crime, Montana's statute should have been perfectly acceptable.

The Court's treatment of the second burden-shifting interpretation of the jury instruction is also troublesome. In viewing the instruction as shifting the burden of persuasion, the Court again engaged in the confusing and unsatisfying analysis that marred its opinions dealing with the constitutionality of affirmative defenses. In fact, *Sandstrom* demonstrates the deficiencies in the reasoning of the earlier decisions that held unconstitutional the creation of an affirmative defense through the use of presumptive language. The Court in *Sandstrom* appears to approve of traditionally constructed affirmative defenses, but to regard as constitutionally impermissible the unorthodox method of creating affirmative defenses through presumptions. This distinc-

B. Presumption Analysis in Criminal Cases

tion is difficult to support because placing a burden of persuasion on a defendant by a presumption is the functional equivalent of creating an affirmative defense in the conventional manner. Thus, the second theory of the Court in *Sandstrom* would make the constitutionality of functionally similar devices depend solely on how the device is created. To be constitutional, the state need only use the correct words in its statute. If the state makes the mistake of effectively creating an affirmative defense through the use of mandatory presumption language rather than in the manner approved in *Patterson*, then the statute is unacceptable even though there is no functional difference between the two methods. Unless the Court intended to elevate such formalistic distinctions to the level of constitutional doctrine, the *Sandstrom* Court's analysis of the second interpretation also must be rejected. It should be pointed out, however, that the failure of the Court to explicitly overrule *Mullaney* in either *Patterson* or *Martin* gives some plausibility to this otherwise unimpressive argument.

The decisions in *Ulster* and *Sandstrom* are not only internally troublesome, but also difficult to reconcile. They appear to construct two very different ways of looking at similar problems. For example, the Court in *Ulster* seemed to create a dichotomy between permissive and mandatory presumptions based primarily upon whether or not the jury "is forced to abide by the presumption," an example of a mandatory presumption being an affirmative defense created by presumptive language. In such a case, the Court implied, the presumption's constitutionality is "based on the presumption's accuracy in the run of cases." How an affirmative defense can be analyzed based upon the accuracy of the language creating it—or why it should be—is left undiscussed, and indeed, is a bit of a mystery.

In *Sandstrom*, by contrast, the Court dealt with what two weeks earlier it apparently would have classified as a mandatory presumption. Nonetheless, it did not utilize the method of analysis suggested in *Ulster* as the appropriate constitutional approach. Why the Court did not do so is, again, completely unexplained. The *Ulster* Court also took care to distinguish "as applied" analysis from "on its face" analysis, yet the *Sandstrom* Court two weeks later never mentioned this distinction. Most puzzling of all, the Court in *Sandstrom* focused heavily on the possible effect of the instruction on the jury. The *Ulster* Court, by contrast, noted the effect of the instruction and proceeded to analyze the case as if the instruction had not been given through the use of a harmless error standard.

How the Court determined that it was dealing with a permissive presumption in *Ulster* but with something else in *Sandstrom* also is unexplained. In both cases, the jury was informed that the state had to prove its case beyond reasonable doubt. In both cases, the jury was instructed on the presumption of innocence. Most importantly, *Sandstrom* suggests that the Court followed the path it did because of the use of derivations of the word "presume" in the instruction. By Professor Lushing's count, derivations of the word *presume* were used 12 times in the instruction reviewed in *Ulster*, foreclosing this potential reconciliation as well.[3]

The Court was consistent in *Ulster* and *Sandstrom* with respect to one point. In both cases, the Court began its analysis by attempting to determine the effect of the challenged instruction on the jury. Although the Court's effort to do so in *Ulster* is incomplete, the Court's starting point is appropriate. The issue posed by instructions on inferences, presumptions, and affirmative defenses is precisely the compatibility of the instructions with the requirement of proof beyond reasonable doubt. That, in turn, can be determined only by analyzing the effect of the instructions on the jury. If, for example, the judge said "green" but the jury understood "red" (and we know that that is so), it is the height of formalistic triviality to analyze the instruction as though the jury heard "green." The issue is not the judge's utterances; rather, it is the jury's understanding, although the two are usually intimately related.

The problem with the Supreme Court's efforts in this general area is that it is attempting to deal with the unruly nature of the proof process with a set of rules tailored to individual cases. That is an effort doomed to failure. Every case presents a different factual context, and rules governing the inferential process must respond to more generalized concerns than those emanating from particular cases. Can such rules be formulated? We have so far seen that all of the evidentiary devices studied in this Chapter and in Chapter Seven have the effect of manipulating burdens of persuasion. Remember that this is also true of comments on the evidence (and instructions on inferences and presumptions that are the functional equivalent of judicial comment). To emphasize the point, and to assist you in translating it into the criminal context, compare two cases in which the only distinguishing feature is that one does not contain judicial comment and the other does. To make the exercise more concrete, assume the cases involve the charge of knowing possession of stolen goods. In each case, the only evidence of knowledge is the fact of possession of recently stolen goods. Assume further that judicial experience has yielded the insight that the possession of recently stolen goods is very highly correlated with knowledge of the nature of the goods. And finally, assume that the judicial insight is not widely possessed by the general populace who make up juries.

In the first case, without judicial comment, the jury might conceivably convict, but certainly the chance of acquittal is higher than in the second case, in which the judge explains the implications of possessing recently stolen goods. The judge's comment increases the chance of conviction by enhancing the effect of the state's evidence. In order for the defendant to have the same chance of acquittal in the second case as in the first, the defendant would have to adduce more persuasive rebuttal evidence than that advanced in the first case. Although the formal relationship between the

---

3. Lushing, Faces Without Features: The Surface Validity of Criminal Inferences, 72 J. Crim. L. & Criminology 82 (1981).

state and the defendant has remained the same—the jury has applied the reasonable doubt standard in each case—the comment has modified the relative burdens of persuasion by altering the factual matrix within which the jury reached its decision.[4] The effect of judicial comment, then, is to shift the positions of the parties by modifying the relative burden of persuasion that a defendant bears on an issue. Note further that since the relative burden of persuasion simply describes the functional relationship between the parties, a shift in the explicit burden works a shift in the relative burden as well. The reverse is not true, however. Comments on the evidence can affect the relative burden of persuasion even though the explicit burden of persuasion remains the same.

The significance of the fact that comments on the evidence also affect burdens of persuasion is that the constitutional analysis of the various evidentiary devices that we have been studying can concentrate on that variable. Consider the effort to construct a unified constitutional analysis in the following excerpt.

ALLEN, STRUCTURING JURY DECISIONMAKING IN CRIMINAL CASES: A UNIFIED CONSTITUTIONAL APPROACH TO EVIDENTIARY DEVICES
94 Harv. L. Rev. 321-354 (1980)

We have seen that the superficially distinct evidentiary devices employed in criminal trials—affirmative defenses, placement of burdens of production and the concomitant possibility of a directed verdict on an issue, judicial comment on the evidence, and instructions on presumptions and inferences—are actually very similar. Their primary unifying trait is that they all modify the evidentiary relationship of the parties at trial by manipulating burdens of persuasion. Affirmative defenses and burdens of production manipulate the relative burden of persuasion explicitly, the other devices do so implicitly.

Moreover, these devices cannot be distinguished on the basis of the

---

4. Cool v. United States, 409 U.S. 100 (1972) (per curiam), provides an excellent example of the concept of a shift in the relative burden of persuasion. The Court reversed a conviction when the trial court had instructed the jury that it was to consider exculpatory accomplice testimony only if it believed beyond reasonable doubt that the testimony was credible. The Court accurately perceived the problem:

> By creating an artificial barrier to the consideration of relevant defense testimony putatively credible by a preponderance of the evidence, the trial judge reduced the level of proof necessary for the Government to carry its burden. Indeed, where, as here, the defendant's case rests almost entirely on accomplice testimony, the effect of the judge's instructions is to require the defendant to establish his innocence beyond a reasonable doubt.

Id. at 104. For a similar example, see Hughes v. Mathews, 576 F.2d 1250, 1255 (7th Cir.), *cert. denied*, 439 U.S. 801 (1978).

magnitude of their effect on the burden of persuasion, for that effect unmistakably varies within each category. Comments on the evidence, or presumptive instructions, may be very influential with a jury, and thus have a great impact on the relative burden of persuasion, or may have little influence and little or no effect on the relative burden. Similarly, one affirmative defense may be much easier to establish than another, even though the formal burden of persuasion is the same in both cases. Moreover, instructions that comment on the evidence, either explicitly or implicitly, involve essentially the same problems of ensuring the accuracy of the comment. Both explicit judicial comment and presumptive instructions may enhance the likelihood of a correct outcome; but both may also do just the opposite, thereby unconstitutionally abridging the defendant's right to have the state prove its case against him beyond a reasonable doubt.

Finally, the detrimental impact on the defendant does not adequately distinguish any of these evidentiary devices. Compare, for example, shifts in burdens of "persuasion" and "production." As a rule, it may be more damaging to a defendant to have to prove something by a preponderance of the evidence instead of to some lower degree. If, however, the defendant has access to little or no convincing evidence on an issue, he will not be able to meet either standard. Similarly, the prevailing view that shifts in burdens of persuasion are more damaging than instructions on inferences seems erroneous. A shift in the explicit burden of persuasion conceivably may have no impact upon the outcome. If, for example, after all the evidence is in, the jury would conclude that there is a 65 percent chance that the defendant committed a homicide in the heat of passion, then the result will be the same—mitigation to manslaughter—regardless of whether the state has to prove the absence of provocation beyond reasonable doubt or the defendant has to establish it by a preponderance of the evidence. By contrast, judicial comment on that evidence conceivably could cause the same jury to find that provocation has been disproven beyond reasonable doubt.

The actual effect in a particular case of any of the evidentiary devices discussed above is an empirical question that probably is not subject to very satisfactory empirical investigation, but the devices all share the function of allocating burdens of persuasion to the state and to the defendant. Consequently, they all raise essentially the same two issues, despite the diversity of their manifestations in the current case law. The first issue is the compatibility of the devices with In re Winship's imposition of the reasonable doubt standard as a constitutional mandate. The second is the effect of the devices on our conception of the right to a jury trial.

Because of the functional similarity of these devices, a unified analysis of their constitutionality can be developed. As noted earlier, affirmative defenses and burdens of production placed on defendants depart from the reasonable doubt standard by allowing guilt to be determined in part on the basis of the defendant's failure to prove exculpatory facts. In the same way, jury instructions outlining presumptions or inferences create a functionally

B. Presumption Analysis in Criminal Cases

similar exception to *Winship*'s standard of proof by encouraging the jury to conclude that one incriminating fact has been established on the basis of proof of another less incriminating one. In addition, judicial comment unfavorable to the defendant lowers the state's burden by making a conviction more likely. It should also be clear at this point that affirmative defenses and burdens of production allocate burdens of persuasion directly, while the other devices do so indirectly through comment on the evidence. The framework for testing the constitutionality of these burden-shifting devices must ensure both that the state's duty to prove guilt beyond a reasonable doubt is not diluted, and that the defendant's right to a jury trial is not eroded by judicial or legislative usurpation of the jury's factfinding role.

Such a framework can be constructed by asking three fundamental questions. The first two questions respond specifically to *Winship*'s requirement of proof beyond a reasonable doubt, and the last relates to both *Winship* and the right to a jury trial. First, we must determine whether the evidentiary device has a favorable or unfavorable effect on the defendant's case, since there is no danger of the state's burden being lowered and therefore no question of constitutionality if the effect is favorable. Second, if the effect is unfavorable, we must establish whether the device affects a fact that the state is constitutionally required to demonstrate as an element of criminality. This step is a necessary part of the analysis because imposing a constitutional standard of proof makes sense only if it is linked to a theory that indicates what facts constitutionally must be proved under the standard; otherwise, the standard could be circumvented by a state choosing to redefine the factual elements constituting a crime. The third step of this analysis, which applies if the fact affected is one that the state cannot constitutionally remove from its definition of the crime in question, is to ask whether the device amounts to an accurate judicial comment on the evidence. Manipulations of the burden of persuasion are permitted only if the device moves the jury toward a more rational, accurate result. This last inquiry guards against undermining the jury's factfinding role, and ensures that the jury does not reach its conclusion on the basis of inaccurate commentary that would lower the state's burden of proof.

A. A FAVORABLE EFFECT

The first standard applicable to the evidentiary devices is obvious and requires no extended discussion. If a state employs an evidentiary device that is favorable to a defendant, it should not be struck down on constitutional grounds. "Favorable" in this context means only that the explicit burden of persuasion on the issue involved remains with the government at least to the level of beyond reasonable doubt,[76] and that the comment, whether accurate

---

76. The analysis of affirmative defenses will always require proceeding to the second step of the test because these defenses function to the detriment of the defendant.

or not, tends to dispose the jury more in favor of the defendant on that issue than the jury would have been without the comment. Under such circumstances, a defendant has no basis for complaint. The constitutionally required burden of persuasion has been maintained, and the jury's evaluation of the factual issue will be at least as fair as he has a right to expect.

B. THE CONSTITUTIONAL NECESSITY OF PROVING THE FACT IN ISSUE

In the second step of the analysis, the nature of a particular fact in issue is examined to determine whether it is one that the state is required by the Constitution to prove beyond a reasonable doubt. Because forcing a defendant to bear the burden of persuasion in proving facts that establish a defense is functionally the same as requiring the state to prove the absence of those facts, constitutional analysis must not depend upon whether a state legislature chose to label a factual issue a defense [rather than] an "element of the offense." Without some substantive restriction on a legislature's discretion to define crime, *Winship* may be eviscerated. Therefore, step two inquires whether the state has increased the defendant's relative burden of persuasion with respect to an issue that is critical to culpability.

The need for a conceptual and doctrinal bridge between *Winship*'s reasonable doubt standard and a substantive theory of criminal law that would limit a state's power to define a crime has been discussed at length elsewhere, and thus will only be outlined here. Two principal constitutional sources for such a limitation have been suggested: the eighth amendment's proportionality standard and substantive due process concepts. No matter which label is used, however, the fundamental constitutional concern with protecting the defendant's liberty interest articulated in *Winship* can be fully satisfied only if the procedural safeguard of the reasonable doubt standard is linked to a substantive standard guaranteeing that the state's definition of criminal conduct is fair and does not carry the potential for disproportionate punishment. Thus, it is not surprising that on close analysis the underlying rationale of those who have suggested that burden of persuasion analysis be tested by a "flexible due process framework" does not differ significantly from an analysis based on proportionality.

Commentators who advocate the substantive due process test argue that "in evaluating the constitutionality of an affirmative defense, the ultimate question should be whether the issue is so critical to culpability that it would offend 'the deepest notions of what is fair and right and just' to obtain a conviction where a reasonable doubt remains as to that issue."[86] To say that a fact "so critical to culpability" has not been proven beyond reasonable

---

86. Comment, The Constitutionality of Affirmative Defenses After Patterson v. New York, 78 Colum. L. Rev. 655, 670 (1978) (quoting Solesbee v. Balkcom, 339 U.S. 9, 16 (1950) (Frankfurter, J., dissenting)).

doubt, however, is simply another way of saying that the conditions for imposing punishment have not been satisfied. To subject a person to substantial punishment when such a critical fact has not been proven beyond reasonable doubt would distort the relationship between what the defendant has been proven to have done and what the state does to him. Unmistakably, this "due process" test is yet another manifestation of the concern that a proper relationship between crime and punishment be maintained, and thus is simply a variation on the theme of maintaining proportionate punishment. . . .

In sum, if a state limits its manipulation of burdens of persuasion to issues that need not be proved under the eighth amendment's proportionality standard or principles of substantive fairness imposed by due process, then whatever the state does should be acceptable. If, by contrast, the state manipulates a burden on an issue that constitutionally it must establish, then it must do so in a way that either favors the defendant or amounts to accurate judicial comment.

C. ACCURATE JUDICIAL COMMENT

Judicial comment on the evidence may be either accurate or inaccurate. Comment that is accurate enhances the jury's conception of reality, and permits the jury to deliberate in a more accurate and realistic factual matrix. Inaccurate comment also changes the factual matrix within which the jury operates, but it skews the decision-making process away from reality.

The effect of accurate and inaccurate comment can best be demonstrated with the aid of an example. Consider a murder trial where the defendant has injected the "defense" of alibi. Assume that on the basis of the evidence adduced without judicial comment, a well-informed, rational jury would conclude that there is a 15 percent chance that the facts of the alibi story are true. The verdict would be not guilty, since a 15 percent chance of error surely is a "reasonable doubt." First, take the case in which the trial judge comments on the evidence tending to prove or disprove the alibi and assume that the comment is factually inaccurate. Assume further that as a result of the inaccurate comment, the same jury would conclude that there is only a very small chance that the alibi is true.[101] The verdict, then, all other things remaining the same, would be guilty. In order to escape the guilty verdict, and the effect of the trial judge's comments, the defendant would unfairly be forced to produce stronger, more persuasive evidence of the alibi.[102] In effect, his burden of persuasion has been increased beyond that of merely raising a reasonable doubt.

101. The jury would be acting rationally, but on the basis of factually erroneous information.
102. Cf. Allen v. Ulster County Court, 568 F.2d 998, 1009 (2d Cir. 1977) ("The evil of the presumptions that the Supreme Court has struck down has not been that they could not be dispelled, but rather that they forced defendants to meet inferences that could not rationally be drawn from the facts proved."), *rev'd on other grounds*, 442 U.S. 140 (1979).

Now consider the case where the judge's comments on the evidence are accurate. Assume again that the comments caused the jury to discredit the alibi sufficiently to render a guilty verdict. Once again, the defendant's burden of persuasion has been increased—he would have to present stronger evidence to gain an acquittal—but this time the defendant has no constitutional grounds to complain. By altering the jury's factual matrix to one more in accordance with reality, the judicial comment has enabled the jury to perceive that guilt was indeed proven beyond reasonable doubt.

The example illustrates that inaccurate judicial comment detrimental to the defendant, on an issue that constitutionally must be included in a state's definition of a crime, violates the mandate of In re Winship by effectively lowering the state's burden of proving guilt beyond a reasonable doubt. In fact, inaccurate comment on an issue is tantamount to creating an affirmative defense since the defendant is forced to show the existence of more than a reasonable doubt on the issue. Accurate comment, on the other hand, can prevent an erroneous verdict when the jury is unable to appreciate the implications of certain facts proven at trial. Certainly a state should be permitted to fill in gaps in the jury's knowledge. Since accurate judicial comment serves this important function without undercutting the reasonable doubt standard, it should be constitutionally permissible—as should its functional equivalents—so long as the comment does not violate the right to a jury trial. Accordingly, the impact of judicial comment on that right must be examined.

The effect of judicial comment on the right to a jury trial raises three questions that may generate constitutional problems: first, does the right to a jury trial limit the manner in which the jury may acquire information; second, how constrained may a jury be made to feel concerning the content of the comment; and third, what is the significance of ambiguity or incoherence in the comment?

1. THE MANNER OF PRESENTING INFORMATION TO THE JURY

The first difficulty results from the very nature of judicial comment. Judicial comment is, in essence, a method of presenting evidence to the jury. Legislative investigation or judicial experience may result in the conclusion that certain facts usually present themselves in a certain relationship, a relationship that may not be known by the jury. One method of communicating the substance of that relationship is by judicial comment, which is precisely the dynamic the Supreme Court was referring to when it commented that "a valid presumption may . . . be created upon a view of relation broader than that a jury might take in a specific case."[107]

There are alternatives to comment, however. The facts that the comment is based upon could be presented to the jury. Prosecutorial argument

---

107. Tot v. United States, 319 U.S. 463, 468 (1943) (footnote omitted).

B. Presumption Analysis in Criminal Cases

on the basis of those data and the other evidence in the case may often be sufficient. Nonetheless, there does not seem to be any constitutional basis for preferring these procedures to judicial comment. Since the Constitution does not dictate a specific method of introducing evidence, accurate judicial comment does not contravene any constitutional command.[110]

Two interrelated lines of cases emphasize the general lack of constitutional constraints on the method of adducing evidence. The long line of Supreme Court cases permitting instructions on inferences and presumptions, and the equally long line permitting judicial comment, have established the proposition that evidence may be presented to the jury in the form of comment. The Supreme Court has yet to recognize publicly that a comment is a method of adducing evidence and that an instruction on an inference is a comment, but nonetheless, the implication of those two lines of cases, considered together, would be difficult to deny.

In addition to this precedent favoring comment, it must be remembered that jurors do not deliberate simply on the basis of the evidence adduced at trial in the traditional manner. To require that the jury limit its consideration to the matters presented as evidence would mean that all the life experiences that form the juror's individual perceptions of reality would have to be matters of proof. "Common sense" and "judgment" would not be entities that jurors brought with them to their task; rather, they would have to be established at trial. Because that is impossible, jurors are allowed, indeed instructed, to rely on their common sense, general knowledge, and judgment. By instructing a jury to rely on general knowledge or common sense, however, a judge invites consideration of "evidence" not adduced in a traditional fashion. Thus, the cases permitting comment, combined with the need to rely on "evidence" such as common sense not introduced in the traditional manner, suggest quite clearly that accurate judicial comment, which is merely an alternative method of presenting facts to a jury, is not categorically unconstitutional.

---

110. Another difficulty is the potential conflict between comment and the sixth amendment right of confrontation. The judge, in commenting, reports on data compiled extrajudicially in order to fill in possible gaps in the jury's knowledge or understanding. Arguably the defendant is thereby denied the chance to confront his accusers. Presenting evidence through a comment, however, is not significantly different from presenting evidence through the use of admissible hearsay. Cf. California v. Green, 399 U.S. 149 (1970) (permitting use of out-of-court statements against the accused). See generally Westen, Confrontation and Compulsory Process: A Unified Theory of Evidence for Criminal Cases, 91 Harv. L. Rev. 567 (1978). The task faced by an advocate responding to hearsay is virtually identical to that of an advocate responding to judicial comment, presuming, of course, that the trial judge will not let himself be examined by the attorneys. Cf. Fed. R. Evid. 605 (judge may not be a witness). In both cases independent evidence of the fact in issue may be proffered, and in both cases the credibility of an absent declarant may be attacked. Accordingly, so long as the defendant is entitled to respond to whatever comment is made, as he can respond to any other evidence adduced, cf. United States v. Vargas, 583 F.2d 380 (7th Cir. 1978) (striking down conviction because prosecutor's argument to jury should have been presented as evidence to allow rebuttal by defendant), no problem of constitutional magnitude should arise.

2. Jury Independence from Judicial Comment

Though judicial comment is a permissible method of presenting evidence, it still raises problems with respect to the right to an independent evaluation of the evidence by a jury, which is implicit in the constitutional right to a jury trial. To be permissible, judicial comment must not convey to the jury a sense that it is bound by the content of the comment. The comment must be in permissive language and make very clear that the jury is simply being presented with another matter for its consideration. Obviously, the jury may be influenced by the comment, but if the comment is accurate, it ought to be influential. It ought to be influential, however, only to its degree of accuracy as determined by the jury, which raises the third problem with judicial comment.

3. Ambiguity in Judicial Comment

The judge is quite likely to be viewed with some respect by the jurors, and there will surely be a strong inclination to accept what he says as true. Accordingly, he must be careful to make sure that his comment is clear and coherent. Thus, instructions that say only that a jury "may but need not" infer or presume one fact from another should be struck down on the ground that they lead to irrational jury decision making in contravention of the right to a trial by jury. The judge should be required to elaborate on what the word *may* means—what is the basis for concluding that one fact implies another, how close does the relationship seem to be, what are the levels of confidence that the data possess? These questions, of course, prompted the development of the "rational relationship" test in the first place. This test was created in order to ensure that a reasonable connection exists between an "inferred fact" and one proved at trial so that an instruction on the inference would not skew the jury's deliberations away from reality. However, the rational relationship test is, at best, only a crude guarantor of jury rationality because the instructions on inferences and presumptions are usually so ambiguous that it is difficult to assess their impact on the jury's inferential process. The goal of the test would be accomplished better by requiring thorough, cautious comment in place of current instructions. . . .[123]

One final point deserves emphasis. To say that the primary constraints on judicial comment are that it be accurate and coherent and that it not impose too much on the jury is not to say that judicial comments should proliferate. Strong policy reasons may motivate a state to restrict comment. More important, the sine qua non of comment—accuracy—will often be difficult to establish. Since the issue is one that affects the truth-determining

---

123. For a good example of how a sterile instruction on an inference can be transformed into a helpful comment, see Hickory v. United States, 160 U.S. 408, 419 (1896). Another reason for replacing inferences and presumptions with judicial comment is that this would avoid reliance on the rational relationship test.

B. Presumption Analysis in Criminal Cases

process, the state should be required to establish the appropriateness of judicial comment in any particular case. If the state establishes that, in a particular case, these considerations are outweighed by the potential benefit of accurate, coherent, and nonintrusive comment, then the Constitution does not appear to forbid the judge to express an opinion on the weight and implications of the evidence.

NOTES AND QUESTIONS

1. Is a directed verdict against a defendant on any issue ever permissible? There is language in the cases that you have just read that suggests that the answer is no. If that is so, though, how can a burden of production ever be placed upon a criminal defendant? See, e.g., n.11 in *Barnes,* supra. How would you characterize the refusal of a judge to instruct the jury on a particular defense on the grounds that insufficient evidence of that defense has been produced? That happens frequently, and the Supreme Court has given the process its imprimatur.

In United States v. Bailey, 444 U.S. 394 (1980), the Supreme Court upheld the defendants' convictions for escaping from a federal institution, rejecting their claims that the trial court erred in failing to instruct the jury on the common law defenses of duress and necessity. The question was whether the defendants' testimony of threats of death as the reason they failed to turn themselves in immediately after escaping required an instruction on duress or necessity. One could certainly conclude that good faith fears of death constitute an acceptable excuse for escaping from a penal institution and remaining at large. If that is so, the jury should have been instructed to acquit if there was a reasonable doubt about whether the defendants actually held such beliefs, unless such defenses are unavailable. The Court concluded that even if Congress intended to allow such defenses, a point left undecided, the defendants failed to make a sufficient showing of duress or necessity to justify a jury instruction. The defendants, in other words, failed to meet a burden of production, and the district court directed a verdict on their defense by refusing to instruct on it.

What the Court did not do, unless it did so implicitly, was to inquire into the constitutional necessity of establishing the fact in issue—in this case, whether or not the defendants had acted under duress or necessity. Without that inquiry, the Court's analysis is incomplete. If the fact in issue was one that must be established in order to justify the potential sanction, then permitting the district court to remove that issue from the case resulted in a conviction when one essential fact had not been proven beyond reasonable doubt to the jury's satisfaction, which is inconsistent with In re Winship. If it does not need to be established, then *Bailey* provides an acceptable, if not ideal, analysis of burdens of production on nonessential elements. The analysis is not ideal because of the majority's position that personal testimony of the defendants did not justify a jury instruction. 444 U.S. at 415. The Court is playing the role of fact finder with such a test and concluding that the defendants' testimony is incredible. As a matter of policy, such questions should be left to the jury even on non-essential issues.

Analyzing burdens of production in this fashion not only tidies up the analytical scheme, but also has significant pragmatic appeal. The present rules governing the placement of burdens of production are not altogether clear. Were a court today to strike down a statute placing a burden of production on a defendant, it probably would do so on the basis of the comparative convenience and rational relationship tests, but analyzing burdens of production functionally provides a much clearer articulation of the appropriate question: whether the Constitution requires that the fact in issue be established by the state.

One pragmatic objection to analyzing burdens of production functionally is that the result would be too burdensome—the state would have to disprove a series of issues that quite clearly have nothing to do with the case at hand. The force of the objection, however, is considerably blunted by two factors. First, normally not that many factors are crucial to liability, and the ones that are will not create extraordinary problems of proof for the government. In *Bailey*, for example, if the lack of a genuine fear of death did have to be established by the Government, it would have to show only that these defendants were treated no differently than other inmates, and that protective custody was available to them if requested. Second, the absence of the "unusual" exculpatory factor will frequently be inferable from the circumstances that the government has proven.[5] Accordingly, the defendant will be forced to introduce some evidence of the unusual exculpatory factor before it arises in the case in any real sense, although the defendant should be entitled to an instruction on it (if requested) regardless of whether he has presented evidence.

2. The Oregon Supreme Court has recognized that most presumptions in criminal cases are awkward comments on the evidence and that they tend to disadvantage defendants. Accordingly, the court forbad such instructions from being given. State v. Rainey, 298 Or. 459, 693 P.2d 635 (1985).

3. An example of the controversial nature of comment on the evidence in criminal cases is presented by People v. Cook, 658 P.2d 86 (Cal. 1983). In *Cook*, the California Supreme Court held that judicial comment on the ultimate question of guilt or innocence is grounds for reversal of a conviction even though the state constitution explicitly permits comment. For a discussion, see Note, 5 Whittier L. Rev. 693 (1983).

4. The area of constitutional burden of proof requirements has spawned a rich and wide-ranging literature. In addition to the articles previously cited,

---

5. Cf. Rossi v. United States, 289 U.S. 89, 91 (1933) ("The general principle, and we think the correct one . . . is that it is not incumbent on the prosecution to adduce positive evidence to support a negative averment the truth of which is fairly indicated by established circumstances. . . .").

B. Presumption Analysis in Criminal Cases

see Nesson, Reasonable Doubt and Permissive Inferences: The Value of Complexity, 92 Harv. L. Rev. 1187 (1979). Also, compare Nesson, Rationality, Presumptions, and Judicial Comment: A Response to Professor Allen, 94 Harv. L. Rev. 1574 (1980) with Allen, More on Constitutional Process-of-Proof Problems in Criminal Cases, 94 Harv. L. Rev. 1795 (1981), and Saltzburg, Burdens of Persuasion in Criminal Cases: Harmonizing the Views of the Justices, 20 Am. Crim. L. Rev. 393 (1983) with Allen, Rationality and Accuracy in the Criminal Process: A Discordant Note on the Harmonizing of the Justices' Views on Burdens of Persuasion in Criminal Cases, 74 J. Crim. L. & Criminology 1147 (1983). See also Dripps, The Constitutional Status of the Reasonable Doubt Rule, 75 Calif. L. Rev. 1665 (1987).

5. The Supreme Court has engaged in burden-of-proof analysis in a multitude of contexts. In addition to the various cases cited and discussed previously, see Addington v. Texas, 441 U.S. 418 (1979) (civil commitment proceeding under state law must employ "clear and convincing" standard of proof); Santosky v. Kramer, 102 S. Ct. 1388 (1982) (parental rights termination proceeding must employ "clear and convincing" standard of proof); Vance v. Terrazas, 444 U.S. 252 (1980) (Congress may determine the standard of persuasion to be employed in expatriation proceedings); Rivera v. Minnich, 107 S. Ct. 3001 (1987) (state's adoption of a preponderance of the evidence standard to establish paternity does not violate due process, distinguishing *Santosky*). In McMillan v. Pennsylvania, 106 S. Ct. 2411 (1986), the Court upheld a Pennsylvania statute that increased the minimum sentence for a felony if the defendant "visibly possessed a firearm" during the commission of the felony. Under the statute, the state had to prove "visible possession" by a preponderance of the evidence.

CHAPTER NINE

JUDICIAL NOTICE

Reconsider the discussion of relevancy in Chapter Two where the point was developed that to determine "relevancy" requires that evidence be analyzed by reference to something external to that evidence, which typically is the experience and understanding of the fact finder. The significance of this point, in large measure, is that the criteria by which evidence is judged—the experience and understanding of the fact finder—could themselves be a matter of proof. For example, a purported eyewitness' perceptual abilities are obviously relevant to an evaluation of the witness' testimony, but we normally let fact finders appraise such matters "in light of their experience and common sense" without the benefit of formal proof. Nevertheless, there is nothing that prohibits proof on such matters, and suppose that evidence is introduced about the witness' eyesight. Whoever testifies about the matter, ophthalmologists perhaps, could now have their perceptual abilities examined as well, and off we go into an infinite regress. Indeed, any evidence whatsoever generates a similar descent into a potentially endless regression. Even the meaning of the language employed at a trial has this attribute. Words are not self-defining. Why, then, is not every word uttered at trial a matter of proof as to its definition? Of course, the definitions in a dictionary quickly become circular (if you don't believe that, pick even a common word, find its definition, and then look up the words used to define it; you will soon find yourself in a circle), which requires once more that something external to the dictionary be employed to give "meaning" to language.

Consider one last example. Assume that one of the parties wishes to impeach the credibility of a witness by introducing evidence that the witness had been drinking on the day the witness purportedly observed the event in question. The point of the impeachment would be to trigger in the minds of the fact finders the generally held belief that the perceptual abilities of an

691

individual who had ingested alcohol are likely to be impaired, a matter with which most of us would agree based upon our experiences in life. Suppose, however, that the adversary wished to produce evidence that contradicted this generally shared belief. Perhaps the adversary had evidence that tended to show that alcohol affects perception in certain ways, but not ways relevant to this litigated event. Or suppose that the adversary wished to make such an argument in closing to that effect. Would either be allowed? Of course. The evidence would clearly be relevant to a fact in issue, and the argument would certainly be within the bounds of examining the implications of the evidence. The point, though, is that the "evidence" produced at trial—proof of alcohol ingestion—could itself be the subject of further proof or of argument by counsel. Moreover, the process of making evidence that is produced the subject of yet further evidence could go on endlessly.

The legal system responds to this epistemological problem in two ways. Its primary response is to instruct the jury to evaluate whatever evidence is presented in light of the jurors' "common sense," "everyday experience," and "shared human knowledge." See, e.g., Rostad v. Portland Railway, Light & Power Co., 101 Or. 569, 201 P. 184 (1921). That instruction means, however, that a substantial amount of "evidence" is before the jury before either party calls a witness or produces an exhibit. It also means that every trial presents a unique question concerning how far the parties will be allowed to go in pushing the evidentiary process back into the experience and understanding of the jurors. At some point, the trial court will conclude that the evidence is descending too far into the jurors' "experience," which will result in rulings that certain proffers are "matters for argument." This means that the trial judge has concluded, whether consciously or not, that the party offering the evidence has pushed the evidentiary chain back far enough that the time, effort, and expense of producing the evidence now being offered is not justifiable (which is related to the subject matter of FRE 403). Obviously, where the line is to be drawn is very difficult to say, which probably explains why the matter is virtually never discussed by cases or commentators.

There is a second, and more formal, manner in which the evidentiary process is cut off. This is through judicial notice. Here, rather than relegating matters to the wisdom of the jury, the judge will affirmatively instruct the jury that certain matters are to be taken as true because they have been "judicially noticed" by the judge. The Federal Rules provide for judicial notice in FRE 201, which should be reviewed carefully at this point.

It will probably come as no surprise to you that the scope of judicial notice is a matter of dispute. One view is that judicial notice should be exercised only when a matter is indisputable.[1] The opposing view is that judicial notice should occur whenever it is "convenient" and "fair" to notice a fact.[2] "Convenience" usually refers to the impossibility or expense of "prov-

---

1. Morgan, Judicial Notice, 57 Harv. L. Rev. 269 (1944).
2. Davis, Judicial Notice, 55 Colum. L. Rev. 945 (198-55).

ing" every fact relevant to a litigated event at trial, and "fair" refers to the need to allow a party who might be adversely affected by judicial notice to be heard on the matter. The Federal Rules adopted the second view, and you should now carefully consider the Advisory Committee Note to FRE 201.

In our view, judicial notice is another example of a subject matter traditionally viewed as a distinct subset of evidence law suitable for specialized treatment by rule whereas in reality judicial notice is not distinct from the various process-of-proof rules governing proof of facts at trial.[3] Indeed, it primarily supplements those rules by permitting the judge to expedite the trial process and to dispose of trivial questions of fact. There are two other related ideas that often go by the label "judicial notice"—the power to preserve obviously correct verdicts and the power to make factual determinations necessary for the rational operation of the judicial system. In a manner similar to the misuse of the word *presumption*, the label *judicial notice* is applied to these three areas indiscriminately, which has the predictable effect of obfuscating the nature of judicial notice. By recognizing that "judicial notice" is primarily a collection of methods of ordering aspects of the process-of-proof and the judge-jury relationship, ambiguity surrounding judicial notice can be reduced, and in addition it can be accommodated to those process-of-proof rules that typically are found under the label "presumption."

The most important function of judicial notice is to accommodate the formal model of proof at trial, which requires evidence of all factual issues, with the fact that such a model is, if not incoherent, certainly too inefficient to be taken seriously. Thus, we loosen the restrictions of our model of proof that calls for evidence on every issue by not requiring evidence on undisputed issues and by removing some of those undisputed issues from the jury. There is no mystery here, although there is a problem. If some things need to be proven at trial, what are these things?

One can draw the line between what must and what must not be proven at trial in any number of places, and precisely where it is drawn does not matter very much so long as the reason for drawing the line is agreed upon. The primary reason for drawing the line is to save time by removing from trials factual issues over which there is no serious dispute. Thus, rules on judicial notice tend to have standards, such as that in FRE 201(b), that allow notice of facts "(1) generally known within the territorial jurisdiction of the trial court or (2) capable of accurate and ready determination by resort to sources whose accuracy cannot reasonably be questioned."

In terms of the trial dynamic, when would we say some fact is "generally known" or "capable of accurate and ready determination"? Assuming that we do not wish to limit indirectly the role of the jury, we would equate these

---

3. For elaborations on some of these themes, see Allen, The Explanatory Value of Analyzing Codifications by Reference to Organizing Principles Other Than Those Employed in the Codification, 79 Nw. U. L. Rev. 1080, 1091-1094 (1984-1985).

phrases with whether reasonable jurors, employing the relevant burden of persuasion, could possibly disagree on the outcome. If the answer is no, then there is no reason for protracted proceedings on the issue. If the answer is yes, then we should leave the matter to the jury. This is the directed verdict standard. On the other hand, if we wish to reduce the jury's fact-finding role, we can either expand the scope of judicial notice or encourage judges to grant preclusive motions like directed verdict motions, which yield virtually indistinguishable results. Thus, the first function of judicial notice merely provides for extending ideas of burden of proof and directed verdicts prior to the time of the formal presentation of proof, or to excuse its absence for analogous reasons. This form of judicial notice is not separate and distinct from other evidentiary rules; rather, it is merely a supplement to normal process-of-proof rules that order one aspect of the judge-jury relationship.

The second general type of event that goes under the label "judicial notice" serves to protect verdicts when there has been a lapse of proof. Such verdicts should be protected only when the lapse would not have affected the outcome. Thus, when a court is convinced that reasonable jurors would have produced the same verdict had no lapse of proof occurred, there is no need to engage in the expense of a new trial. To make clear the court's power to engage in this inquiry, rules provide, as FRE 201(f) does, that "judicial notice may be taken at any stage of the proceeding" and further provide, as in FRE 201(e), for the court to hear "information" concerning the propriety of taking notice. The word *information* is obviously just a euphemism for "evidence," and thus such rules provide for judges to hear evidence in order to determine if there is an issue in dispute. Again, though, that sounds like directed verdict or summary judgment language, and indeed it is.

So far, then, when viewed from the perspective of the judge-jury relationship, judicial notice appears to be nothing more than a minor variant of process-of-proof rules governing proof of fact at trial. This perspective also explains what on its face is perhaps the most curious rule in the Federal Rules—FRE 201(g)'s provision that "[i]n a criminal case, the court shall instruct the jury that it may, but is not required to, accept as conclusive any fact judicially noticed." It is contradictory to tell the jury that it "may" accept a fact that has been judicially noticed. Judicial notice is supposed to dispose of issues. The incongruity is explained by the recognition that judges are allowed less authority over the facts in criminal cases than in civil cases, which is reflected in the misleading shibboleth that there are no directed verdicts in criminal cases.[4] To notice a fact is to direct a verdict on it, since the issue is removed from the jury, and that conflicts with the conventional view of the role of jurors in criminal cases. FRE 201(g) responds to the apparent conflict of the normal understanding of notice and the normal

---

4. It is misleading because it is false. See the discussion of United States v. Bailey, supra page 687 (refusing to instruct a jury on a defense for which the defendant bears but has not met the burden of production is in effect a directed verdict against the defendant on that defense).

approach in criminal cases by purporting to allow non-binding notice. The response may appear to be quite incoherent, but that may be preferable to consciously limiting the jury's fact-finding role in criminal cases.

In fact, the resolution of FRE 201(g) is not as curious as it seems at first blush. It permits a court to refuse to direct a verdict for the defendant where there has been a lapse in the prosecution's case concerning a fact that the judge thinks is indisputable. More importantly, by allowing the jury to be instructed on "noticed" facts, FRE 201(g) authorizes a form of comment on the evidence that can benefit either party. If the judge believes a fact is almost certainly true, the judge may tell the jury that it "may" accept it as true if it chooses to do so. This allows the judge to comment on the obvious, the generally known, or the indisputable even though evidence on the particular point has not been adduced. There is nothing particularly mysterious about such a rule when fully understood, even though it may be politically controversial. The only truly curious aspect of FRE 201(g) is its placement and its consequent peculiar wording. Instead of being placed in a rule on judicial notice, it should be in a rule that directly authorizes the court to comment on the evidence.

The third meaning of "judicial notice" deals with the judicial power to find facts that are more intimately related to the orderly maintenance of the judicial system than to the resolution of a particular dispute—such as "facts" relevant to the interpretation of statutes (legislative intent or policy, etc.). As we have seen, juries decide facts that are more intimately related to the parties while judges decide facts that are more intimately related to the legal system. This division of authority is often referred to by the misleadingly precise assertion that juries decide adjudicatory facts and judges decide legislative facts (and note that FRE 201 is limited to adjudicative facts). These are, however, spheres of influence and not clearly distinct categories. For example, what a law means is a question of general application, but it also is raised by the case at bar with all its factual idiosyncrasies. Conversely, the inferences that can be drawn from certain behavior to, say, state of mind is of importance to the particular case, but that same inferential relationship is also relevant to all similar cases. Nonetheless, our political choice has been to carve out a fact-finding role for lay persons, and we construct it by reference to the end of the factual spectrum more closely associated with the particular parties. We assign virtually everything else to the judge, often labeling this authority the power to judicially notice legislative facts. On other occasions the identical purpose is accomplished by labeling certain facts as "preliminary facts" or "questions of law," although this seems to occur more when the concern is with jury fact finding than it is with the orderly maintenance of the judicial system.[5]

Each of the meanings of "judicial notice" refers to one aspect or another

---

5. See, e.g., UCC §2-302 (1978) (Unconscionable Contract or Clause), which makes unconscionability a matter of law solely for the judge to decide, even where evidence on the question is introduced.

of the process of proof, and regulates in one way or another the judge-jury relationship. Viewed from this perspective, the analytical similarity of notice, presumptions, and process-of-proof rules is obvious. Furthermore, the various meanings of judicial notice, presumptions, and all the process-of-proof rules can easily be integrated into a unified rule. In addition, the ambiguities of FRE 104(a) and (b) can also be clarified.[6] Consider the following outline of such a rule:

> 1. *Definitions.* The rule would begin with a few basic definitions, most notably definitions of burden of production and burden of persuasion.
> 2. *Role of Jury and Judge.* The rule would allocate to the jury the power to determine "historical facts" pursuant to the appropriate burden of persuasion and subject to the authority of the judge to decide those facts allocated to the court. The rule would not attempt to define "historical facts," resting instead on the existing general understanding and the fact that specific allocations of authority will be made to the judge. These allocations would come next and would be divided into two categories. The first category would contain facts that the judge would accept as true if sufficient evidence to support a finding of them were introduced. Included in this category would be such matters as are now contained in FRE 104(b), 901, 1008, and perhaps those in FRE 602, 702, and 703, depending upon the resolution of the relevant policy issues. Next, the court's responsibility would be detailed to decide facts that would bind the jury in the appropriate circumstances. The present subject matter of FRE 104(a) would be included here, as well as a reference to the court's power to determine facts concerning the requirements of the law. In addition, the standard of persuasion the court is to employ would be specified. The only difficulties are resolving the political question of the scope of the jury's role and accepting that the distinction between historical facts and legislative facts cannot be made sharply and clearly.
> 3. *Assignment of Burden of Proof.* The rule would assign the parties the burdens of production and persuasion, as well as determine the appropriate scope of the various standards of persuasion.
> 4. *Comment on and Summary of the Evidence.* The only issue raised by the judicial power to sum up and comment on the evidence is the political issue of the scope of such a power.[7] The section would make rules such as Rule 201(g) unnecessary.
> 5. *Judicial Power To Dispose of Factual Issues Without the Formal*

---

6. Indeed, such a rule could and perhaps should encompass preemptive motions as well, such as motions for summary judgment, directed verdict, judgment notwithstanding the verdict, etc.

7. See, e.g., Saltzburg, The Unnecessarily Expanding Role of the American Trial Judge, 64 Va. L. Rev. 1 (1978); Pope, The Proper Function of Jurors, 14 Baylor L. Rev. 365 (1962).

Presentation of Evidence. This section would provide for the power of the judiciary to find facts that normally would be viewed as historical facts and for the procedure to be employed in such cases.

NOTES AND QUESTIONS

1. Do you find the analysis above compelling or the suggested approach attractive? If it is all that simple, why does judicial notice exist as an independent doctrine? One reason may be historical. Judicial notice arose at a time when pre-emptive motions such as directed verdicts and summary judgments were either not allowed or very sparingly employed. Once procedures are in place, they often tend to be immune to subsequent changes. For an interesting discussion, see Schwartz, A Suggestion for the Demise of Judicial Notice of "Judicial Facts," 45 Tex. L. Rev. 1212 (1967). At least one court of appeals has held that judicial notice of adjudicative facts should be limited "to self-evident truths that no reasonable person could question, truisms that approach platitudes or banalities." Hardy v. Johns-Mansville Sales Corp., 681 F.2d 334, 347 (5th Cir. 1982). Why, then, have such a thing as judicial notice?

2. As is evident in FRE 201(g), judicial notice in criminal cases poses somewhat different problems than judicial notice in civil cases. The primary difference results from the fact that juries are given greater deference in criminal cases than in civil, thus there is a greater reluctance to remove factual matters from the jury. This is understandable, but it poses some difficulties. Suppose there has been a lapse of proof on an issue, but on one which could certainly be established. One example might be failure of proof in a grand larceny trial that the car stolen was worth more than the statutory amount that converts larceny into grand larceny. What should a judge do in such a case? The most attractive solution would be to open up the evidentiary process for evidence on that point. On occasion that course might be unavailable, however. The defendant might move for a directed acquittal after the jury has begun to deliberate. In addition, some states have rules forbidding the re-opening of a case after a side has rested. In such cases, the trial judge must either grant the motion for acquittal, and free a guilty person, or take judicial notice of the relevant fact. If the latter course is followed, the case will often be reversed on appeal precisely because judicial notice of a necessary element in a criminal case intrudes too far into the jury process. Still, taking judicial notice and being reversed may be more attractive than freeing a guilty person. The real point, though, is that this whole game does not seem worth the effort. Why should such energy be expended on appeals and re-trials merely to establish an incontestable proposition? See, e.g., State v. Lawrence, 120 Utah 323, 234 P.2d 600 (1951), where the trial court in a fact situation similar to that hypothesized above had the option to reopen the evidentiary process but chose instead to take judicial notice of the value

of a car. Maine has rejected FRE 201(g) and provides for the mandatory instruction in criminal cases. See MRE 201(g).

3. Questions of foreign law have proved troublesome. A court may notice, or is "presumed" to know, the law of its own jurisdiction, but at common law a party was required to plead and prove the content of foreign law. This has been eliminated in the federal courts by Fed. R. Civ. P. 44.1 and Fed. R. Crim. P. 26.1, which commits the question of foreign law to the judge, whose "determination shall be treated as a ruling on a question of law." Many states still possess the common law rule, however.

4. The fact that jurors must rely on their common sense and common knowledge in thinking about and deliberating upon the evidence is occasionally referred to, especially in the older texts, as "jury notice." See, e.g., 9 Wigmore, Evidence in Trials at Common Law §2570 (1940). As is predictable of anything in the legal system that has a name, litigation developed over "jury notice." To generalize, the nature of this litigation has to do with the extent to which the jury may rely upon its own creativity in accomplishing its tasks. In a wrongful death case involving an electrocution, for example, it was error for a juror to read about electricity on his own and share his newly acquired knowledge with his fellow jurors. Thomas v. Kansas Power & Light Co., 185 Kan. 6, 340 P.2d 379 (1959).

Can the appropriate bounds of judicial notice be specified with any clarity? Consider the following case:

IN RE THE MARRIAGE OF LINDA LOU TRESNAK AND EMIL JAMES TRESNAK
297 N.W.2d 109 (Iowa 1980)

McCormick, Justice. This appeal involves a parental dispute over custody of two sons, Rick, age eleven, and Ryan, age nine. The parents are Emil James Tresnak (Jim) and Linda Lou Tresnak (Linda) who were married in 1965. In the August 1979 decree dissolving the marriage, the trial court awarded custody of the children to Jim. Linda appeals. We reverse and remand.

Jim was 24 at the time of the marriage and had three years of college. Linda was 19, had one year of college and had worked for one year. They resided in Dodge, Nebraska, where Jim worked with his father in the insurance business. In 1969 he sold his interest in the insurance agency and the parties sold their home. Jim returned to college and obtained his degree. In 1970 the family moved to Omaha where Jim taught in a private girls' college. In 1971 they moved to Chariton where Jim taught high school business courses, a position which he still held at the time of trial.

Chapter Nine. Judicial Notice 699

Linda worked in a nursing home in 1967 but otherwise was not employed outside the home during the marriage.

Jim obtained a master's degree in 1978 after three years' of summer school study at Northeast Missouri State University in Kirksville.

In the fall of 1975 Linda entered junior college at Centerville. She attended summer sessions at the university in Kirksville in 1976 through 1978, while Jim was there. In addition, she attended the university full-time from January 1978 until the spring of 1979. At that time she graduated with a B.A. degree in psychology. She planned to enter law school at the University of Iowa in the fall of that year.

The children stayed in Chariton with Jim from January through May 1978 while Linda was in school at Kirksville. The whole family was in Kirksville that summer while both parents were in school. In the fall, the children remained with Linda and enrolled in school in Kirksville for the 1978-79 school year while Jim returned to Chariton. The children have been in the continuous custody of Linda since then.

In awarding custody of the children to Jim, the trial court said:

> The Petitioner at this time in life now desires to continue her education by attending law school at the University of Iowa. Although this is commendable insofar as her ambition for a career is concerned, in the opinion of the Court, it is not necessarily for the best interest and welfare of her minor children, who are now ten and eight years of age. Anyone who has attained a legal education can well appreciate the time that studies consume. Although the Petitioner, during her undergraduate work, was able to care for the children while attending the Northeast Missouri University at Kirksville by studying after the children were placed in bed, the study of law is somewhat different in that it usually requires library study, where reference material is required. Also, other than time in class during the day, there will be study periods during the day in the library necessary, as well as in the evening, and which would necessarily require the children being in the hands of a babysitter for many hours a day when not attending school. The weekends are usually occupied by study periods, and although the Petitioner has a high academic ability, she will find that by reason thereof there will be additional activities bestowed upon her, such as becoming a member of a law review, which is time-consuming. Although the Petitioner may believe that she would not have to engage in such, she by not doing so would be interfering with her own achievements for her own benefit and welfare in future years.
>
> The Respondent father has a stable position in the Chariton school system, president of the teachers' association, and, so far as known now, can remain in the Chariton schools for many years in the future. The Respondent's salary, though not exceptionally high, is adequate to maintain the children properly, and give them all the necessities of life. The Respondent father will be able to engage in various activities with the boys, such as athletic events, fishing, hunting, mechanical training, and other activities that boys are interested in. It would also be a benefit to the children if they were allowed to remain in the Chariton school system where they have attended school and have many

friends and acquaintances. Placing custody with the Petitioner would require the children to be placed in the Iowa City school system for only a temporary time of three years, and again undoubtedly removed and placed in another system where the Petitioner would locate to practice her profession.

Linda, supported by the amicus briefs, challenges the trial court's statements concerning the demands of law school and the appropriateness of awarding custody of male children to their fathers. She asks that the custody decision be reversed.

I. THE TRIAL COURT'S ANALYSIS

In challenging the trial court's reasoning, Linda contends no evidentiary support existed for the court's assumptions about law school and the children's activities. She also contends the assumed facts are not a proper subject of judicial notice.

A. THE DEMANDS OF LAW SCHOOL

The only evidence about the demands of law school appeared in Linda's testimony. She acknowledged on cross-examination that law school would require many hours of study. However, she also said she did not expect to leave the children with babysitters often, she would take them to the library with her if necessary, and she did not believe her studies would interfere with her care of the children. Thus, while the record supports the trial court's inference that law school studies would occupy much of Linda's time, it does not lend much support to the court's statements about the necessity of library work away from the children, the likelihood of her involvement in extracurricular activities, or the effect of such factors on her care of the children.

Nor are these matters subject to judicial notice. "To be capable of being judicially noticed a matter must be of common knowledge or capable of certain verification." Motor Club of Iowa v. Department of Transportation, 251 N.W.2d 510, 517 (Iowa 1977). Courts are permitted to dispense with formal proof of matters which everyone knows. In this case, in overruling Linda's motion for new trial, the trial court defended its findings by asserting a "personal acquaintanceship with the studies of law school." However, judicial notice "is limited to what a judge may properly know in his judicial capacity, and he is not authorized to make his (personal) knowledge of a fact not generally or professionally known the basis of his action." Bervid v. Iowa State Tax Commission, 78 N.W.2d 812, 816 (1956). It is common knowledge in the legal profession that law school studies are demanding and time-consuming, but the requirements of a specific law school curriculum are not generally or professionally known.

Chapter Nine. Judicial Notice

The trial court's statements about the necessity of extensive library study and likelihood of Linda's work on the law review at the University of Iowa law school are not matters of common knowledge or capable of certain verification within the meaning of the judicial notice principle. Because the statements have only tenuous support in the evidence, they are entitled to little weight in evaluating the merits of the custody dispute. In saying this, however, we do not suggest the court could not consider the demands of law school which were shown in the evidence.

B. THE CHILDREN'S PREFERRED ACTIVITIES

Linda testified that the boys enjoy fishing, reading, baking cookies, bicycling, swimming, soccer, and basketball. They do not play baseball or football. She fishes, reads, bakes cookies, bicycles and swims with them. Jim testified he swam and played soccer with the children, although he said his age and smoking limited his participation in soccer to about 15 minutes. Linda said he refused to take the boys fishing.

This record does not support the court's statement that Jim "will be able to engage in various activities with the boys, such as athletic events, fishing, hunting, mechanical training and other activities that boys are interested in." No evidence was received that these boys were interested in hunting or mechanical training, that the enumerated pursuits are more appropriate to males, that "other activities" exist in which males have a necessary interest, or that these children will necessarily have the same interests as other males. Nor does the record contain any evidence that Jim was capable of participating in any activities with the children that Linda could not participate in with them equally well.

Apart from the lack of evidentiary support, the statement has at least two other flaws. It contains matters which are not subject to judicial notice, and it represents a stereotypical view of sexual roles which has no place in child custody adjudication.

We have emphasized that child custody cases are to be decided "upon what the evidence actually reveals in each case, not upon what someone predicts it will show in many cases." Each case must be decided on its own facts. As we said in *Bowen*, neither parent has an edge on the other based merely on sex: "The real issue is not the sex of the parent but which parent will do better in raising the children." 219 N.W.2d at 688. It logically follows that neither parent has an edge on the other based on the sex of the children either. We reject the idea that any *a priori* notion of parental fitness should be based on the sex of parent or child.

The trial court was not justified in basing the award in this case in part on assumptions related to the sex of the parents and children which are not supported by the record.

II. THE MERITS OF THE CUSTODY AWARD

Our review of the record is de novo. Although we give weight to the court's findings, we are not bound by them.

Because either parent would be a good custodian of the children, the decision on the merits is difficult. Linda and Jim are stable and responsible persons who love their children and are capable of giving them adequate care.

Prior to returning to school, Linda fulfilled a traditional role as housewife and mother while Jim was the breadwinner. Until Linda moved to Kirksville in January 1978, she continued to have primary responsibility for the day-to-day parenting of the children. This was true even when she was attending junior college full-time. Although Jim had primary responsibility for the children from January through May 1978, Linda came home each weekend to clean house, help with the laundry, cook meals, and prepare foods to be served during the following week. During that period Rick required assistance at home with his spelling. After first agreeing to help, Jim later asserted he was too busy to do so. Linda provided the assistance during her weekends at home. She has had primary care of the children since the fall of 1978.

Linda is a fastidious housekeeper and obviously a highly-motivated and organized person. She has been active in school affairs. She plays with the children and has counseled with them concerning their development as adolescents.

Jim likes his work and keeps busy with it. He is not as concerned about household cleanliness as Linda. Nor did he display her concern about the children's meals and clothing during the period he had their primary care. He has not been active in their school affairs, and he was not aware of several of their allergies. Although this is explained in part by the necessity of devoting his time and energy to making a living, the record shows that even when he had primary responsibility for the care of the children, he was not as attentive as Linda to the details of their lives. Moreover, she maintained her attentiveness even during the times when her studies were demanding as much time as Jim's work.

A psychologist who interviewed the children testified in Linda's behalf. He said the children were exceptionally well-adjusted and would not suffer from moving with their mother to Iowa City. He reasoned that the stability of their relationship with their mother was more important than continuity in their place of residence. The children are normal, although Rick has had problems with spelling and underachievement at school. Linda has worked with him on these problems. The children are close, well-mannered and disciplined.

The trial court believed Linda's pursuit of a legal education would be detrimental to the children's interests. We do not think the record bears out this concern. She very capably cared for the children during her undergraduate studies. During that time Jim did not complain of her ability to do so. Moreover, the children did not suffer when, by agreement of the parties, they lived with Linda and attended the Kirksville schools in the 1978-79 school year. No question existed about their moving again. The only issue was whether they would return to Chariton or accompany Linda to Iowa City.

Furthermore, no basis exists for characterizing Linda's law school years as unstable. She has demonstrated she can control the time she spends on her studies as well as Jim can control the time he spends on his work. Although she may move again when she finishes law school, this prospect differs little from Jim's readiness to move to a junior college teaching position if an opportunity arises.

It is common knowledge that in many homes today both parents have demanding out-of-home activities, whether in employment, school or community affairs. Neither should necessarily be penalized in child custody cases for engaging in such activities. In this case, Linda seeks a legal education for self-fulfillment and as a means of achieving financial independence. These goals are not inimical to the children's best interests. Because the record shows she is capable of continuing to provide the children with the same high quality of care she has given them in the past, her attendance at law school should not disqualify her from having their custody. We perceive no reason for believing she will not give the children excellent care during her law school years and thereafter.

. . .We believe the long-range best interests of the children will be better served if Linda has their custody. Therefore we reverse the trial court and remand to permit the court to enter appropriate orders relating to child support and visitation.

Reversed and remanded.

NOTES AND QUESTIONS

1. Is the court's reliance in *Tresnak* on "common knowledge" somewhat ironic, given its discussion of the trial court's decision? Can you tell, based on the opinion, when judicial notice is acceptable in Iowa? Does it matter what stage the litigation is at? Should it matter? Note that the Federal Rules permit notice at any stage in the proceedings, which includes the appellate process.

2. What is the real lesson of cases like *Tresnak*? Is it that trial judges should not explain the basis of their reasoning if they wish to avoid being reversed? Is that a disturbing commentary on the legal system?

3. As you might expect, the examples of judicial notice, and problems resulting from taking notice, are incredibly varied, precisely because judicial notice is yet another mirror for the inferential process that occurs at trial. For an excellent collection of cases that presents a good sampling of the

range of problems, see P. Rothstein, Evidence: Cases, Materials and Problems 1293-1310 (1986).

PROBLEMS

1. The defendant was convicted of speeding on the basis of radar readings taken by the police. The police testified to the operation of the radar gun, but did not testify to the reliability of the device nor how it operated. The trial judge took judicial notice of how radar operates, thus obviating the need to bring in experts to establish the scientific basis of the radar gun. Permissible or not?

2. In an employment discrimination suit, can a court judicially notice either that "men as a group have had considerably more working experience in the industrial work place than women" or that "the extent of one's experience on a particular job does not necessarily mean that [a] person is more competent than a person with less experience"?

3. Federal law forbids the importation of "Schedule II controlled substances." Schedule II includes "derivatives of coca leaves." If a defendant is alleged to have committed this offense because of the possession of cocaine hydrochloride, must the government present expert testimony that cocaine hydrochloride is derived from coca leaves or may the court instruct the jury that "if you find the substance was cocaine hydrochloride, you are instructed that cocaine hydrochloride is a schedule II controlled substance under the laws of the United States"?

4. An action was brought under the Federal Tort Claims Act by 24 plaintiffs to recover for cancer of various kinds, including leukemia, allegedly caused by the Atomic Energy Commission's testing of atomic devices prior to 1963. At trial, for purposes of scientific analysis concerning radioactivity generally and the nature of decay of radioactive isotopes specifically, the court took judicial notice of the "Table of the Isotopes" and of the table of "Gamma Energies and Intensities of Radionuclides," contained in the Handbook of Chemistry and Physics. Proper?

5. Plaintiffs in a class action seek nullification of a New York statute that prohibits the sale of contraceptives to persons under the age of 16 years. The state argues that the statute is justifiable because it is designed to limit the sexual activity of minors. At trial, the judge is asked by the plaintiffs to take notice of the fact that "some young persons do engage in sexual intercourse and that the consequences of such activity is often venereal disease, unwanted pregnancy, or both, and that the ready accessibility of contraceptives ameliorates these problems." The plaintiffs cite a magazine article entitled "The Health And Social Consequences of Teenage Childbearing" that discusses the existence and prevalence of teenage intercourse, venereal disease, and pregnancy, and that discusses how contraceptives can minimize the risks involved. Should the judge take judicial notice?

Chapter Nine. Judicial Notice 705

6. The famous Hollywood actor Rocky Bedford is being sued by his ex-girlfriend, Mary Medusa, for an increase in financial support of their illegitimate child. The jurisdiction permits an order for the support and education of an illegitimate child to be made by the court in the exercise of its sound discretion, considering the needs of the child and the financial ability of the father. No evidence is offered by Medusa concerning Bedford's standard and condition of living, his position in society, the value of his property, nor of his indebtedness—all of which are elements that must be considered in determining Bedford's liability to Medusa. At trial, the judge takes judicial notice of a series of articles from newspapers and magazines that confirms the widely held view that Bedford is the wealthiest man in Hollywood, with a vast amount of real and personal property, including extensive holdings in the motion picture industry, sufficient to pay Medusa the amount of any order or judgment in the action. Proper?

7. The Atlantic States Bankcard Association (ASBA) brought an action against the Internal Revenue Service, seeking a refund of a portion of federal income taxes attributable to a disallowance of ASBA's $64,000 business deduction. The ASBA was incorporated by 22 member banks to avoid duplication of services and provide economy of scale in processing bankcard data. The issue at trial is whether the deduction taken by the member banks for the services was to "carry on any trade or business," and thus allowable, or whether the member banks are establishing a new business venture, where a deduction is not allowable. The court is asked to take judicial notice of the "vital role which bank credit cards play in modern American society and that bank cards represent nothing more than a new method of providing services which most banks have always rendered." Should notice be taken?

8. Alison Kleen is suing the Belsch Corporation to recover damages claimed to be a result of alleged pollution from Belsch's Coke Works, one mile from Kleen's home. Kleen alleges that Belsch willfully emitted into the ambient air large quantities of gaseous and solid pollutants that are both "harmful and noxious." Kleen has supplied the court with a list of chemical compounds that she alleges were used, or produced as by-products, and then emitted into the air. Kleen has requested the court to take judicial notice of the "dangerous properties" of these substances. Result?

9. In 1981, the Empress Corporation brought an action seeking an order to limit its liability on certain letters of credit issued to it by The First National Bank of Cicero ("Cicero") as part of a contract between Empress and the Iranian government. The contract provided that all disputes between the parties relative to the contract be settled by competent Iranian Courts. The letter of credit agreement between Empress and Cicero exempts Cicero for liability for actions taken by it in good faith in connection with the letters of credit. Empress moved for a preliminary injunction, where it must show irreparable injury if the injunction is not granted. The jurisdiction recognizes that, in letter of credit cases, the question of whether the plaintiff is likely to suffer irreparable injury absent an injunction boils down to whether it has

an adequate remedy at law—here, a lawsuit against the Iranian government. At trial the court takes notice of the fact that the present domestic situation in Iran has rendered access to Iranian courts "futile." Error?

10. Greg Neeld, a one-eyed hockey player, brought an action against the National Hockey League on a claim that a National Hockey League by-law that precludes a player with only one eye from playing in the NHL violates the Sherman Act. The issue is whether adoption of the by-law was motivated by anti-competitiveness. At trial, the court takes judicial notice that the motivation for the by-law is that ice hockey is a very rough contact sport and that there is bound to be danger to players who happen to be on a one-eyed player's blind side. Error?

11. Claude Ballew was apprehended while "distributing obscene materials," a misdemeanor triable by a five-person jury under the state law of Georgia. At his trial, Ballew moved for a 12-person jury, arguing that a jury of only five was constitutionally inadequate to assess the "contemporary standards of the community." The motion was overruled and Ballew was convicted. On appeal, the court took notice that "empirical data suggests that progressively smaller juries are less likely to foster effective group deliberation. At some point this determination leads to inaccurate fact finding and incorrect application of the common sense of the community to the facts." Proper?

12. Dr. Brown, a research employee of Phoenix Phone Labs, Inc., seeks a patent on his new invention, the "Flux-Capacitor," a telephonic sound device. In order to obtain a patent, Brown must demonstrate to the Patent Office that there has been an "invention," which is determined by the "character" of the inventor's contribution (there being no invention without inventive genius). Neither step-by-step improvements on existing technology nor the final steps in a developing technology qualify as "inventions." The Patent Office found that despite the improvements which Dr. Brown added to earlier sound devices to create his "Flux-Capacitor," and the fact that those improvements required a high degree of skill in the art of phone physics, he could not demonstrate "invention" since the "Flux-Capacitor" represented simply a combination of ideas disclosed by former patents issued to Phoenix Phone Labs, Inc. Dr. Brown sues the Commissioner of Patents. In order to evaluate the contribution of Dr. Brown the court must reconstruct the conditions under which he worked, with emphasis on the contribution of other employees of Phoenix Phone Labs, Inc. The court has been asked to take judicial notice that today routine experimentation can produce results beyond the imagination of people twenty years ago and that contributions to industrial art are more often than not the step-by-step progress of an entire group rather than achievement of an individual. The judge has also been asked to take judicial notice that "all the great research labs operate on this principle."

Counsel for Dr. Brown objects. Result?

13. Felicia Sunquist has brought an action against Faustman Builders, Inc., alleging negligence in the construction of a mass produced, pre-fab-

ricated home she had purchased after seeing a "model home" on Faustman's lot. Sundquist's six-month-old son was seriously scalded when a hot water tap malfunctioned in the home's shower, releasing water at an extremely high temperature. At trial, Sunquist argues that Faustman "knew or should have known of the highly dangerous condition created by the use of scalding hot water at a temperature that was dangerously high for ordinary domestic use," and that Faustman provided no notice or warning of such condition. Faustman is defending on the basis that a builder is not liable to the purchaser for damages resulting from latent defects in the absence of express warranties in the deed or fraud or concealment. The caselaw in this jurisdiction holds that mass-produced products (e.g., automobiles) are impliedly warranted against defect, but that real estate is warranted only by the express terms of a deed of sale. The trial judge, however, takes notice of the fact that

> the law should be based on current concepts of what is right and just and the judiciary should be alert to the never-ending need for keeping its common law principles abreast of the times. Ancient distinctions which make no sense in today's society and tend to discredit the law should be readily rejected. The court considers that there are no meaningful distinctions between Faustman's mass production and sale of homes and the mass production and sale of automobiles and that the pertinent overriding policy considerations are the same.

Defense counsel objects. Result?

14. Hal Shamlon published and distributed a newsletter on stock activity entitled "Hal's Wallstreet Review," which recommended the purchase of particular stocks. The Securities and Exchange Commission brought a securities fraud action against Shamlon seeking to show that shortly before the newsletter was mailed, Hal and his cronies purchased shares of the particular stocks consistent with Hal's forthcoming recommendations, and in one instance, where the newsletter suggested that the stock was too high, Hal sold short. The SEC points to the fact that there were small market rises in each of the stocks following publication and that Hal sold the stocks previously purchased within a week thereafter. At Shamlon's trial, he argues that newsletters have no effect on market activity. Nevertheless, the trial judge takes notice that "Wallstreet newsletters affect the market." Proper?

15. Cherry Salinas and Fae Miracle were stopped by U.S. Customs Agent Wilkie at the United States-Mexico border checkpoint in San Ysidro, California. Wilkie directed a search of the automobile and discovered 300 pounds of marijuana hidden in the trunk. The two were indicted. At trial, the prosecution asks the judge to take notice of Wilkie's expertise at identifying drug runners, as developed and analyzed by the court (but a different judge) in a prior criminal proceeding. Result?

16. The ship SS *Norton* broke from its moorings and was grounded, releasing 200,000 barrels of crude oil into the ocean near Guam. The owner,

Kramden, sued the captain and the charterers for negligence, arguing that the ship's being moored in Guam during the month of November—the peak of the typhoon season—posed a great danger both to the cargo of oil and to the environment. At trial the judge is asked to take notice that Guam is seriously vulnerable to typhoons and that the month of November is the peak of the typhoon season. Objection?

17. Defendant was on trial for murder, and defended on the basis of self-defense. He asserted that the deceased had assaulted him, and in the ensuing fray Defendant managed to grab the deceased's gun. During the struggle, according to Defendant, the deceased hit Defendant, knocking him backwards, and as he fell the gun went off killing deceased. According to Defendant, he was no more than "two or three feet" from the deceased when the gun went off. There were no powder burns on deceased, however. During jury deliberations, the jurors procured a gun similar to that involved in the case and test fired it to determine at what distance powder burns would be left at the site of a wound. According to the jury's experiment, the gun had to be at least five feet away from the target not to leave powder burns. Following this discovery, the jury convicted Defendant. What result on appeal?

CHAPTER TEN

REFLECTIONS ON THE PROCESS OF PROOF

There are numerous profound problems lurking just beneath the calm veneer of the rules structuring the process of proof at trial. Most of these problems are at least indirectly observable in the preceding materials of this text, in particular in those detailing the continuing struggle to mark the boundary between the judge and jury on questions of fact. We limit the question in such a fashion because the justification for allocating responsibility to the trial judge over matters (of fact and law) more relevant to the structure of the system of litigation than to the particular dispute before the court is reasonably persuasive. That justification, of course, is simple expediency. Judges are trained in the law and presumably have a much more sophisticated grasp of the implications and limitations of a legal system than do jurors. In addition, judges should generally be accurate interpreters of the law's demands for the benefit of the jury.

Nonetheless, there is something that can be said for increasing the jury's involvement even with respect to matters concerning the structure of the legal system and the interpretation of legal requirements. Judges are an elite group in virtually every way that matters. They tend to be upper middle-class, white males, and are located toward the upper range of income and status in this society. Moreover, in most jurisdictions they are insulated to one degree or another from popular political pressure. As a consequence, one might predict (and indeed surely observe) that judges as a group are a conservative and stabilizing force in society. To some people, perhaps most, that may seem to be a positive factor, but to others it may not. To the extent one wishes the interpreter of the laws to be more in tune with or under the influence of the views of the populace, one may wish to increase the power of juries over questions of law.

The same political concerns that inform the allocation of responsibility for law-related matters also inform the choice of allocating responsibility over historical facts. Here, though, the institutional competence of judges and juries is not so clear (which, frankly, it may not be with respect to questions of law, either). In addition, this particular issue is complicated by the implications of the epistemological assumptions that underlie the system of litigation.

The legal system for the most part operates under the influence of, and attempts to implement, a "correspondence theory" of knowledge. This is the notion that there is a reality that exists beyond each individual that can be known or discovered by the operation of the various senses of perception. Indeed, this is such a strong assumption, and so much taken for granted, that this discussion may seem odd to you. Of course the law attempts in litigation to establish "what happened." The light was red or it was green. The defendant intended to kill or did not. The facts may be incomplete or ambiguous, but there is no question that *in fact* the light was one color or another and the defendant either did or did not intend to kill.

Perhaps; but are you sure? Do you "see" the color of the light (or anything else) or are you merely aware of the input of your senses? And how do you "know" how those implications coincide with "reality" even if you assume "reality" exists? How do you know that what you perceive is not a function of unconscious or undetectable dynamics of mind and body?

There is yet another level that ought to be considered. The legal system requires that a reconstruction of reality be developed and that labels be applied to it. "Such and such evidence demonstrates that the light was red, which means that the defendant was negligent," and so on. This approach requires that the evidence be considered and the concrete implications of it be abstracted, so that we can conclude with the appropriate degree of certainty that a particular event had the precise and determinate attributes required for legal judgment to be entered. What does it mean, though, for something to have "precise and determinate" attributes, legal or otherwise? Take a simple example—the book that you are reading at this moment. Now we all know what a book is, and this is one. But is it "really" a book? Have you ever used this book, or any other equally definite book to hold down papers? Does that make that book a paperweight? Have you ever propped open a door with a book? Does that make that book a doorstop? Have you ever put your feet up on a book? That, presumably, converts the book into an ottoman. Is it really so clear that a "book" has a definite and knowable existence?

Perhaps you are objecting to this line of inquiry for the reason that a book remains a book even if it is used for some other purpose, and you know what a book is because it can be read. What if a note were pinned to a "real" ottoman? Would that make that ottoman a book? There is a hillside in California that has "HOLLYWOOD" on it. Is that hillside a book? Can you, in short, "abstract" what it means to be a book in the sense of articulating its essence independent of all relevant (and maybe just all) surrounding

Chapter Ten. Reflections on the Process of Proof

circumstances? If not, does that mean that books do not have an essence, and instead just have a relationship with other objects and events in the universe, and only in such a context does it make sense to talk of "books" or anything else? If that is so, what do you think of the implicit requirement of the legal system that the "definite" traits of a litigated event be determined? Can one say that a person acted negligently or only that a person acted in such and such a way with such and such a result?

One way of thinking about this line of inquiry is to ask whether the idea of categories makes sense. That, of course, is one of the central problems of philosophy and logic, which for our purposes is best represented in the work of the Skeptics. The thrust of skepticism is not that there is not a "knowable universe" that exists outside the mind. Rather, it is that the nature of that universe is open to doubt and at best appears to be relative. Things have attributes only in relationship with everything else.

Put these two strands of thought together, the one that raises doubts about the universe beyond the mind and the other that doubts that it makes much sense to talk about the "attributes" of things. These points may seem far removed from the legal system, but reflect for a moment on many of the core issues of litigation. Much of what gets litigated has referents in mental states. Even if you doubt the significance of the points made here for descriptions of physical reality, what about their significance for descriptions of mental states? What does it mean, and how is it concluded, that someone intended something?

Assume that Billy-Joe is on trial for the murder of his stepfather, Brutus Seizher. From the time Brutus married Billy-Joe's mother and moved into their home, he abused Billy-Joe physically and forced him to do humiliating acts. Eventually Billy-Joe left the home, telling Brutus that if Brutus ever crossed him again, Billy-Joe would kill him. Billy-Joe had a younger brother, whom Brutus had also physically abused, and a younger sister toward whom Brutus had made advances.

After Billy-Joe left home, he got a job. He was soon fired, and he learned that he was fired because Brutus had lied to his employer about him. Furious, Billy-Joe went looking for Brutus. "That does it," thought Billy-Joe, "I am going to kill that s.o.b." As he approached his former home, he heard his younger brother screaming, and his sister sobbing. He burst in the door and saw what looked to be Brutus beating his brother, and his sister in what appeared to be a state of partial undress. Overcome with rage, Billy-Joe picked up a fire poker and advanced towards Brutus, yelling at him to let go of his brother. Brutus, who was obviously drunk, told Billy-Joe to "shove it," and that if he did not put down the poker, "I will whip your a--, too." Enraged, Billy-Joe hit him with the poker. The blow was not hard enough to kill a normal person, but it caused a weak blood vessel to break in Brutus's brain, which caused his death.

What crime has Billy-Joe committed? More precisely, what was his state of mind? Did he intend to kill? Does it matter whether Brutus was, in fact, assaulting either the brother or the sister? Does it matter whether Brutus had lied to the employer or whether he had previously beaten Billy-Joe? Can you say what happened independently of the entire context? Are the skeptics right about this one?

Moreover, will the "facts" of what happened be a function of who is observing? Will the brother and sister have a view of Billy-Joe's liability that may differ from a judge's view, or a law professor's view, his mother's view, or the view of the members of his community? Even if facts do exist apart from their being perceived, what about values? More importantly, what about the underlying experience that we all bring to bear to evidence that permits inferences to be drawn? Even if there is a knowable reality, what occurs at trial is a reconstruction that is premised in large measure upon the experiences of those who draw the inferences based upon the evidence.

Now, reconsider the relationship between judge and jury. If doubts about either the existence of a knowable reality or the ability to reconstruct it accurately are at all persuasive, what should the role of the judge be? Why should the judge decide if evidence is relevant or if a burden of production has been met? If all that can be obtained is a relativistic reconstruction, what warrant is there to let the judge intrude into that process? Now relax the assumption about the unknowability of the universe, and assume that we can reconstruct reality. Under this assumption, the inferences that are drawn will be in part a function of our prior experience. Again, what warrant is there for judges to intrude into that process? In fact, is there a positive disutility to allowing them to do so? If judges are an elite in any important sense, will they not tend to have similar experiences and thus draw more uniform inferences from evidence? Only if judges as a group are more insightful than the rest of us, or more accurately perceive the nature of their own existence, is that uniformity likely to lead to increased accuracy. What it is clearly going to lead to is decision making skewed toward the biases, prejudices, and interests of the group making the decisions. That, of course, is in large measure why we have juries. Here the question is why judges are given such power to influence the jury process.

One answer may be that judges as a group do have a better grasp upon reality or are more insightful. In that case, why preserve juries? In any event, can you rationalize the various boundaries between judge and jury that you have been studying in light of the points made here? What do considerations of efficiency add in that effort?

There is a related problem that underlies the system of litigation. As we have seen, the rules structuring the process of litigation employ in various ways the conventional conception of probability that assigns a number between 0.0 and 1.0 to the occurrence of any event, and that assumes that the probability of an event plus the probability of its negation must equal 1. The probability of getting a head if an evenly balanced coin is flipped is 0.5 and the probability of getting a head or not getting a head (that is, getting a tail) is $0.5 + 0.5 = 1.0$. This basic concept is obviously crucial to many of the

Chapter Ten. Reflections on the Process of Proof

rules of evidence, and indeed juries are instructed in this concept when told to apply the preponderance of evidence standard, defined as more than a 0.5 probability (more than a 50 percent chance of the element being true).

If jurors are to employ conventional ideas of probability, they must understand them. There is some reason to believe that people generally do not think in conventional probabilistic terms; nor do they easily apply such concepts to problems. In fact, we will now do a small field study to test how well people—you—do in applying concepts of conventional probability.

Assume that the United States is preparing for the outbreak of an unusual disease, which is expected to kill 600 people. Two alternative programs to combat the disease have been proposed. Assume that the exact scientific estimate of the consequences of the program are as follows: If program A is adopted, 200 people will be saved. If Program B is adopted there is a one-third probability that all 600 people will be saved, and a two-thirds probability that no people will be saved. Which of the two programs would you favor? When this question was asked to a large number of respondents, 72 percent favored Program A while Program B was favored by 28 percent. Tversky and Kahneman, The Framing of Decisions and the Psychology of Choice, 11 Science 453 (1981). Are the two programs different, though? In Program A, 400 people will die. In Program B, the expected value is the same. If Program B is selected, over time on the average 400 people will die (two-thirds of 600). There is a difference in the programs in that in any particular case there is the risk in Program B that all 600 will die. Indeed, eventually that will happen if Program B is selected repetitively. Thus, perhaps it is sensible for people who are risk adverse to choose the certainty of 200 people living in any particular case to the possibility of all 600 dying in any particular case. It bears noting, however, that there is also a chance that everybody will be saved, which makes it more difficult to believe that the great disparity in responses (72 percent to 28 percent) can be explained on the basis of the respondents clearly understanding these implications.

Compare these results to your answer to the next question. Assume the exact facts as above. Assume further that if Program C is adopted 400 people will die, where if Program D is adopted, there is one-third probability that nobody will die and a two-thirds probability that 600 will die. Which of these two programs would you favor? In the study done by Kahneman and Tversky, under these conditions 22 percent favored Program C, while 78 percent favored Program D, which is the exact opposite of what people choose in comparing Program A and B, above. Did you make the same choice in this case, or a different one? Whatever choice you made, in fact these two problems are identical. The only difference between Programs A and B on the one hand and C and D on the other is in their emphasis on people dying instead of living. In Program A 200 people out of 600 will live, whereas in Program C 400 out of 600 will die. Those, obviously, are identical, as are Programs B and D. Why, then, does the mere change in articulation engender such radically different responses? Some draw the conclusion from these and similar experiments that the disparity is a function of the fact that people generally do not think "logically" or "rationally," by which it is meant that people do not think in conventional probabilistic terms. For an interesting presentation of this particular point of view, see Kahneman, Slovic, and Tversky (eds.), Judgment Under Uncertainty: Heuristics and Biases (1982).

Another example of curious modes of thinking given by Professor Tversky is discussed by Professor Jonathan Cohen, The Probable and the Provable 261 n.6 (1977):

> Fighter-pilots in the Pacific during World War II encountered situations requiring incendiary shells about one-third of the time and armour-piercing shells about two-thirds of the time. When left to their own devices, pilots armed themselves with incendiary and armour-piercing shells in the proportion of 1 to 2. Tversky argues that, since there was no general procedure for predicting on every mission which type of shells would be required, the optimal policy was to use armour-piercing shells on every mission, and that thus the pilots reasoned fallaciously even when their own lives were at stake.

As Professor Cohen points out, this may establish that the pilots did not reason as Tversky would, but does it establish "irrationality" (defined in some other way than inconsistency with "predicted" outcome)? As Cohen says: "[D]id [the pilots] reason fallaciously? A pilot might well think that Tversky's policy was, in the long run, a recipe for certain suicide while the other policy offered at least some chance of personal survival—of having the right shells on each occasion. . . ."

Cohen's point is that a "rational" answer depends upon what question is being asked. In the context of the fighter pilots, the "rational" answer from the point of view of conventional probability will result in a large number of planes being shot down. Thus, from the individual's point of view, is it "irrational" to rely on intuition as to when to arm the plane in one fashion instead of another? Perhaps not.

Suppose that people do not think naturally in "probabilistic" ways or at least in not very sophisticated probabilistic ways. Should jurors be instructed in the methodology of statistical reasoning? Perhaps experts in Bayesian theory could be brought in. This thought has stimulated an interesting debate. Professor Tribe has argued that in criminal cases a greater emphasis on probabilistic reasoning is unwise in that it may tend to dehumanize the process, although he does not argue that jurors do not think in at least roughly probabilistic ways. Tribe, Trial by Mathematics: Precision and Ritual in the Legal Process, 84 Harv. L. Rev. 1329 (1971). For at least mild disagreement with Tribe, see Saks and Kidd, Human Information Processing and Adjudication: Trial by Heuristics, 15 Law and Soc. Rev. 123 (1980). Professors Saks and Kid, while not specifically endorsing the use of experts on probability as a standard practice, present considerable evidence that casts doubts upon certain assumptions that Tribe seemed to have made.

Chapter Ten. Reflections on the Process of Proof

There is another side to the "probability debates." Not only is there some question whether people can or do think in conventional probability terms, and whether they should, but also conventional probability has curious implications for the structure of litigation.[1] These result from the rules for conjunction that specify that the probability of two independent events occurring is the product of their separate probabilities. If the probability of getting a head on the flip of a coin is 0.5, the probability of getting two in a row—or of getting two heads from two identical coins—is 0.5×0.5, or .25. This is a serious problem for an account of civil trials in conventional probability terms since jurors are typically instructed that the plaintiff must prove each element by a preponderance of the evidence, which is usually defined as "more probable than not" or as "50 percent +."[2]

The problem posed by conventional probability approaches at trial stems from the fact that a plaintiff deserves to win a civil trial only if all of the elements of the cause of action are true. We would say that an error had been made if a plaintiff recovered for an intentional tort where the defendant caused the injury but did not intend it, or intended it but did not cause it. This understanding, however, is not consistent with the conjunction rule.

Suppose a jury found the probability of intentionality to be 0.6 and that of causation to be 0.6 as well. Assuming that these elements are independent, the probability of their conjunction is .36. Thus, the probability of at least one of them not being true—which should result in a defendant's verdict—is $1 - .36 = .64$. The significance of this phenomenon is that there is a divergence between how we instruct juries and how we wish trials to come out. If these numbers were to be at all accurate assessments of the class of cases into which this individual case fell—that is to say that over the long run in about two-thirds of such cases at least one of the necessary elements of recovery is not true—then the system will be biased against defendants, and more errors favoring plaintiffs than defendants will be made.

Another implication of the conjunction principle is that it injects a certain inequality of treatment into the trial of disputes that is a function of the number of elements of a cause of action. Compare two causes of action. Assume that the first has two elements and that the second has three. To see the inequality of treatment, assume that in both causes of action each element is established to a probability of .75, which more than satisfies the requirement of a preponderance of the evidence. But note the consequences of the conjunction principle. In the first case, the probability of both elements being true, again assuming independence, is $.75 \times .75$, or .56. In that case, a verdict for the plaintiff is obviously justifiable notwithstanding the effect of conjunction. Now, consider the result in the second case where the probability that all three elements are true is $.75 \times .75 \times .75$, or .42. Here

---

1. Much of what follows is indebted to Allen, A Reconceptualization of Civil Trials, 66 B.U.L. Rev. 401 (1986), and the symposium of which it was a part.
2. McCormick's Law of Evidence §339 (3d ed., Cleary, 1984).

we have an example where errors will favor plaintiffs over defendants if the jury is given the normal instruction to return a verdict for the plaintiff if it finds each element to be true by a preponderance of the evidence. In addition, we have another problem that emerges from comparing the results in the two cases. Defendants as a class are considerably worse off in the second case than in the first even if the jury finds each individual element in both cases by a preponderance of the evidence.

To generalize, a verdict may be returned for a plaintiff if there are two issues whenever there is a slightly lower probability than $1 - (0.5 \times 0.5)$, or .75, that a defendant ought not to be liable. When there are three issues, a verdict for a plaintiff may be returned whenever there is a slightly lower probability than $1 - (0.5 \times 0.5 \times 0.5)$, or .875, that a defendant ought not to be liable. Moreover, inequality cannot be eliminated by requiring the product of the individual elements to exceed 0.5. The effect of doing that merely shifts the differential treatment from defendants to plaintiffs. Since each additional element will generally lower the probability of the conjunction, the more elements there are the higher is the probability to which, on average, each will have to be established in order to reach a specified level, regardless whether it is 0.5 or something else. Thus, according to conventional probability theory as it would apply in this modified situation, plaintiffs' tasks will become more difficult as each new independent element is added. As a result, plaintiffs will be treated differentially based upon the fortuity of the number of elements in a cause of action, whereas under our present rules defendants are treated differentially based on the number of elements. If conventional probability theory is applicable to the trial of disputes, one or the other disparity must exist, given our present conceptualization of trials.

There is yet another curiosity emanating from the interaction of the conjunction principle of conventional probability and the conventional view of trials. Compare two cases, each containing three elements. Assume that in the first case each element is established to a probability of 0.6, thus resulting in a verdict for the plaintiff. Assume that in the second case two elements are established to a probability of 0.9 and the third element is established to a probability of 0.4. Since a probability of 0.4 would not meet the preponderance of the evidence standard, the second case would result in a verdict for the defendant. However, if the three elements are independent, there is a $1 - (0.6 \times 0.6 \times 0.6)$, or .78, probability that at least one of the elements is not true in the first case, and a $1 - (0.9 \times 0.9 \times 0.4)$, or .68, probability that at least one element is not true in the second case. In other words, the probability is higher in the first case than in the second that the defendant is *not* factually liable, yet under the conventional view of trials a verdict will be returned for a plaintiff in the first case and the defendant in the second.

There is one last problem implicit in the conventional conceptualization of trials. Consider from a somewhat different perspective the nature of erroneous judgments that will result if jurors are instructed to find for plaintiffs

Chapter Ten. Reflections on the Process of Proof

only if each necessary element is established to a specified probability. Assume that a cause of action has two elements, X and Y. There are four subsets that can be created of all such cases: (1) X and Y are both factually true; (2) X and Y are both factually false; (3) X is true and Y is false; (4) X is false and Y is true. In subset (1), there are three types of errors that can be made; an error can be made on either element separately or on both of them. In each case, however, the result will favor defendants. Plaintiffs are entitled to a verdict in subset (1), and any error will result in a verdict for the defendant.

Now consider subset (2). Here two out of the three possible types of errors will not result in an erroneous judgment. Only if the fact finder makes an error with respect to both issues will an erroneous judgment for plaintiffs result. Thus, defendants again seem to be relatively advantaged by this phenomenon, although the precise effect is a function of the actual distribution of errors that occurs.

Combining the analysis of these two subsets, one in which plaintiffs deserve a verdict and one in which defendants deserve a verdict, demonstrates that erroneous verdicts for defendants will be reached as a result of three types of errors whereas erroneous verdicts for plaintiffs will be reached as a result of only one type of error. If the objective at trials is in part to equalize errors among defendants and plaintiffs, this phenomenon should be troublesome.

A consideration of subsets (3) and (4) is not as startling, but it is of some interest. In both cases, defendants deserve verdicts. Thus, the only erroneous verdict that can result is for plaintiffs. Of the six kinds of errors that can be made, only two of them will result in erroneous verdicts for plaintiffs, namely those in which an error is made with respect to the factually false issue in each subset. All other errors will result in verdicts for defendants.

To some extent these consequences may be explained away by asserting that sometimes defendants are favored and sometimes plaintiffs are. That, however, is a weak explanation of what appears to be a crazy-quilt process. Although it is true that of the 12 kinds of errors that can be made—three result in erroneous verdicts for plaintiffs, three result in erroneous verdicts for defendants, while six leave the ultimate verdict unchanged—they are nonetheless distributed by an apparently nonsensical rule: When both elements are true or both false, defendants are favored; when one is true and one false, plaintiffs are favored.

There have been efforts to salvage the utility of conventional probability analysis from these difficulties. In a very interesting article, Professor David Kaye hypothesized a case where the litigated issue is causation.[3] He then demonstrated that applying to that issue a burden of persuasion rule of a preponderance of the evidence conceptualized as a probability measure of

---

3. Kaye, The Limits of the Preponderance of the Evidence Standard: Justifiably Naked Statistical Evidence and Multiple Causation, 1982 A.B.F.R.J. 487.

greater than 0.5 will minimize the sum of defendants who are wrongfully required to compensate plaintiffs and plaintiffs who are wrongfully denied recovery. In addition, it will result in minimizing the total amount of money wrongfully paid by factually liable defendants and not obtained by factually deserving plaintiffs. Professors Orloff and Stedinger extended Kaye's analysis to show that a different burden of persuasion rule is optimal if the policy is to reduce the incidence of large errors.[4] If that is the policy, an expected value rule should be employed that provides for a plaintiff to recover an amount equal to the magnitude of the damages multiplied by the probability that the defendant is liable. While both of these efforts are impressive and insightful, each makes a simplifying assumption that is highly unrealistic, which is that in each case there is only a single litigated issue. Without that simplifying assumption, the prescriptions of these works begin to diverge radically from the present system of trials.

This is most evident in Kaye's work. By assuming that there is only a single issue, Kaye has assumed away the problem of conjunction, which is the primary source of the difficulties. He assumes that all relevant issues other than the one under consideration are proven to a probability of 1. If that assumption is relaxed, then his argument requires that the probability of the conjunction of all elements of the relevant cause of action be greater than 0.5. In other words, while he purports to be discussing the system of civil trials, his discussion entails a radical change in the system from one where jurors are instructed to apply the relevant burden of persuasion to each element to a system where they would be instructed to apply the burden of persuasion to the conjunction of all elements.

In fact, Professor Kaye's discussion entails an even more radical approach. When he expands the analysis to include the possibility that there is more than one person who could be liable, the result he reaches is that liability should attach to that person, including the plaintiff, for whom the probability of liability is greatest, and without regard to whether the probability of the most probable culprit exceeds 0.5 or anything else for that matter. Thus, upon generalization, Kaye is defending the normal preponderance rule only in a very narrowly constricted context. His analysis, rather than showing the consanguinity of conventional probability theory and the normal rules of civil trials, argues instead for a radical modification of civil trials. The work of Orloff and Stedinger has an analogous attribute. The example that they employ assumes that the probability of causation is the only litigated issue. When that assumption is relaxed, liability becomes a function of the conjunction of all legally relevant elements, as it does in Kaye's work. Moreover, Orloff and Stedinger do not consider the possibility of multiple defendants. Had they done so, presumably their analysis would have lead them to the conclusion that, if reduction of large errors is the goal, a plaintiff

---

4. Orloff and Stedinger, A Framework for Evaluating the Preponderance of the Evidence Standard, 131 Pa. L. Rev. 1159 (1983).

Chapter Ten. Reflections on the Process of Proof

should be allowed to recover the "expected value" from all possible defendants.

While some of the works elaborating the implications of probability theory do not appear upon examination to be defending or explicating the present system of civil trials, other efforts that more directly attempt to demonstrate that there is no "fundamental dissonance between mathematical probability theory and forensic proof"[5] somewhat paradoxically tend to demonstrate precisely that there is such a dissonance. The best example of this is the dispute between Professors Kaye and Cohen over the now famous "Paradox of the Gatecrasher." To understand how odd the debate over the gatecrasher hypothetical seems, one must bear in mind that all the disputants have the reduction of errors at trial as an important value. Indeed, it appears to be the primary value of Professor Kaye.[6] In light of that, consider his response to that part of Professor Cohen's challenge to conventional probability implicit in his gatecrasher hypothetical. Professor Kaye, essentially quoting from Cohen, presents the hypothetical thusly:

> Consider a case in which it is common ground that 499 people paid for admission to a rodeo, and that 1000 are counted on the seats, of whom A is one. Suppose no tickets were issued and there can be no testimony as to whether A paid for admission or climbed over the fence. So there is a .501 probability, on the admitted facts, that he did not pay. The conventionally accepted theory of probability would apparently imply that in such circumstances the rodeo organizers are entitled to judgment against A for the admission money, since the balance of the probability would lie in their favor. But it seems manifestly unjust that A should lose when there is an agreed probability of as high as .499 that he in fact paid for admission.
>
> Indeed, if the organizers were really entitled to judgment against A, they would be entitled to judgment against each person in the same position as A. So they might conceivably be entitled to recover 1000 admission prices, when it was admitted that 499 had actually been paid. The absurd injustice of this suffices to show that there is something wrong somewhere. But where?[7]

Professor Kaye defends against this example of the troubling implications of conventional probability theory for the trial of civil disputes in two ways.

---

5. Kaye, Paradoxes, Gedanken Experiments and The Burden of Proof: A Response to Dr. Cohen's Reply, 1981 Ariz. St. L.J. 635, 645.

6. Kaye, The Laws of Probability and the Law of the Land, 47 Chi. L. Rev. 35-36, 38 (1979). Cohen's views are less clear. He may simply be trying to describe in a more accurate fashion what he thinks is going on in the trial of disputes. His book, The Probable and the Provable, contains no suggestion that errors will be reduced by embracing his analysis. Nor does it offer any suggestions for changing any currently employed procedure at or before trial. Cohen has asserted that "the thesis for which I have . . . contended is essentially a normative one, concerned with answering the question 'What is the legally correct way to judge proofs?,' not a factual one, concerned with answering the question 'What is the way proofs are actually judged?'" Cohen, The Role of Evidential Weight in Criminal Proof, 66 B.U.L. Rev. 635 (1986). The "ought," however, must refer to analysts of the trial process, not to judges or juries, for once again no suggestions for change are offered.

7. Kaye, The Paradox of the Gatecrasher and Other Stories, 1979 Ariz. St. L.J. 101.

First, he asserts that although the "objective probability" of plaintiff's story being accurate is .501, "it may be appropriate to treat the subjective probability as less than one-half, and therefore insufficient to support a verdict for plaintiff, simply to create an incentive for plaintiffs to do more than establish the background statistics."[8] There are two problems with this explanation, however. First, it is obviously an example of explaining away the troublesome aspects of the hypothetical by implicitly rejecting them. The only sensible way to understand the hypothetical is that it asks what should be done when this is all the evidence there is. The answer Professor Kaye gives is to get more evidence. That may be a good idea, but it does not respond to this problem. In the context of this problem the answer translates into the plaintiff losing—even though Professor Kaye, in the same article, recognizes that the proper conclusion from the point of view of conventional probability is that the plaintiff should win.[9]

A second problem emerges if Professor Kaye's modification of the hypothetical is accepted. If the plaintiff can produce more evidence, then so can the defendant. If this statistical data is all that is presented, it is because that is all both parties wish to present. If one assumes that the classes of plaintiffs and defendants should be treated as equivalently as possible, then one class ought not to bear the costs of the defaults of both classes. If the parties are willing to let the dispute be resolved on this basis, as a general rule they should be allowed to make that choice. Professor Kaye's argument conflates appropriate rules of decision with appropriate discovery sanctions. The only time a court should follow Professor Kaye's advice is if it believes either party is refusing to disclose relevant information in the discovery process.

At any rate, Professor Kaye's first response sounds very much like an ad hoc rationalization rather than a convincing argument that there is not as much of a conflict as Professor Cohen asserts between the present system of civil litigation and conventional conceptualizations of probability. His second response is in the same vein. Relying on Bayes's Theorem, he argues:

> The very fact that the paradoxical plaintiffs, at the conclusion of their case, have failed to supply any particularized evidence about defendant is itself an important datum. Suppose a juror accepts the statistic about the number of paying customers at face value. For him, the subjective probability, $P(X)$, that defendant did not pay is .501. But, if he stops to reflect on the fact that this is all there is to the case, he should revise this probability in light of this new item of "evidence." Under the preponderance of the evidence standard, he should find for defendant if the revised subjective probability, $P(X/E)$, is one-half or less. This will be the case only if the fraction f [in a Bayesian calculation] is more than $P(X)/[1-P(X)]$, or 1.004. Hence, if it is even slightly more likely that the rodeo organizers would have been able to come forward with more

8. Id. at 106.
9. Id. at 103.

evidence about how the defendant A came onto the premises without paying if he had actually done so, the f could be taken to exceed this figure. Consequently, at the conclusion of plaintiff's case, this rational juror, following the dictates of the probability theory as it is conventionally understood, will think the probability that A is liable is one-half or less and find for A.[10]

Professor Kaye again has responded to the problem by changing it. The problem is what should happen if the hypothesized evidence is all there is at the end of the entire case rather than the plaintiff's case-in-chief. At the end of the entire case, both the plaintiff and the defendant would have had the chance to produce more evidence, and both would have failed to do so. The result, one would think, would be that the inference Kaye discusses would arise on both sides and cancel each other out. Indeed, this conclusion can be avoided only by a series of ad hoc moves, for example asserting that plaintiff's default gives rise to a stronger inference than defendant's or vice versa.

Another curious aspect of Professor Kaye's argument is that it defeats the objective of minimizing error. If one understands Professor Cohen's hypothetical to include the fact that the statistical data is all that can be offered in each case, Professor Kaye would apparently deny recovery in each case. That would result in 499 correct decisions and 501 incorrect ones. If recovery were allowed in each case, by contrast, fewer mistakes would be made (499 instead of 501) and less money would be wrongfully paid (whatever the cost of the ticket is times the number of mistakes). This would result in a windfall to the plaintiff, but denying recovery results in a larger windfall, overall, to defendants.

The most curious aspect of arguments similar to Kaye's response to the gatecrasher hypothetical is that they are ill defined and appear to be somewhat internally inconsistent. Implicit in much of the literature on the implications of conventional probability theory for the trial of civil disputes is a dichotomy of evidence into that which is quantified and that which is not. This distinction often is articulated in terms of "statistical evidence" or some derivative thereof on the one hand, and evidence that "personalizes" the case on the other. The former is usually categorical and definite ("501 out of a 1000 did not buy tickets") and the latter is specific to an individual and complex ("I saw X take money out of his wallet and exchange it for what appeared to be tickets to the rodeo"). These categories do not exist as mutually exclusive sets, however, although they may reflect points on a spectrum with respect to certain variables.

What distinguishes quantified from unquantified evidence is merely the "clarity of the ambiguity" of the evidence. As curious as that assertion might seem upon first reading, it is nonetheless accurate. For example, testimony that 501 out of 1000 people in attendance at the rodeo did not pay for

10. Id. at 107-108.

admission is not to make a cold and unassailable statement of a universal truth. It is instead to assert an inference drawn from a set of observations, or to assert the observations (or a summary thereof) themselves, any of which may contain error. Moreover, to make such assertions is to "personalize" data with respect to any person for whom another set of assertions places that person in the audience. Such a person has been culled out from all the rest of humanity and placed in a group of individuals with respect to whom there is some reason to believe that they have committed an actionable wrong. Such evidence may not be very personal, but the point remains that it is "personal" to some degree. What is omitted in the writings about statistical evidence and probability theory is any effort to specify why any particular degree of "personalness" should be treated differently from some other, where and why the line is to be drawn.

Look at the matter from the flip side of the coin. Suppose in the gatecrasher hypothetical the operator of the rodeo testified that a particular defendant did not buy a ticket. He knows this, he asserts, because the defendant looks unusual to the operator, and as the operator sold all the tickets himself, he would have remembered such an unusual character. This evidence would appear to meet the standards of admission to the set of unquantified data. Now consider how a fact finder will analyze that data. If the fact finder will analyze it by reference to his own experience, the data will be compared, consciously or unconsciously, to the fact finder's own experience and the inferences drawn from those experiences. Regardless whether that is done in a deductive, inductive or analogical manner, eventually a generalization will be formed (again even if unconsciously) and the "evidence" compared to it. A fact finder, in short, will convert "personalized" data into categorical data to analyze them. Thus, again the distinction between quantified and unquantified evidence is exposed as one of degree in its most crucial variable.

This perspective also demonstrates the curious inconsistency that meanders through arguments about quantified evidence. The resistance to statistical evidence paradoxically amounts to favoring evidence with ambiguous limits over evidence with limits that are clearer, and even creates a bias against increased sophistication in the evidentiary process. As knowledge increases about some matter so that more and more confident statements can be made about it, greater skepticism is engendered about its admissibility as evidence and whether verdicts may rest upon it. The implications of probability theory are directly to the contrary, of course. Probability theory teaches that as ambiguity increases, reliance on the data should decrease.[11]

Do the problems we have been examining here indicate that conventional probability should play no role in structuring trials? We think to the contrary. The problem is not with probability but with the conventional

---

11. See D. Barnes, Statistics as Proof: Fundamentals of Quantitative Evidence 143-230 (1983).

Chapter Ten. Reflections on the Process of Proof 723

conception of trials. The unsettling implications of conventional analyses of civil trials are a function primarily of the fact that the conventional conception of civil trials requires comparing the probability of the plaintiff's elements to that of their negation. If one determines the probability of the plaintiff's elements being true by reference to a conventionally conceived burden of persuasion rule, and then allows a verdict for the plaintiff when each element is established, rather than when the conjunction of them is established, the paradoxes do occur. Many of the unsettling implications of our understanding of probability can be eliminated or ameliorated by conceptualizing trials in a slightly different way. Rather than conceiving of trials as comparing a plaintiff's case to its negations, trials could be conceived of as comparing the probability of the fully specified case of the plaintiff to the probability of the equally well specified case of the defendant. Just as plaintiffs presently are required to specify with particularity at some point the nature of their claims and factual assertions (through such devices as pleading, discovery, pre-trial conferences, and the like) defendants could also be required to respond with equally specific and affirmative allegations rather than with simple denials. The trier of fact could then compare its view of the likelihood of the plaintiff's case to that of the defendant.

Such a conceptualization has numerous advantages over the present conceptualization of trials. First, it moves toward greater equality of treatment of plaintiffs and defendants. Second, the problem of conjunction is obviated in large measure because the probability of two series of allegations would be compared rather than a series of allegations with their negations. Third, this view requires a greater concentration on specific factual allegations on the part of the defendant, which may lead to a sharper focus on disputed factual matters. That in turn may lead to a commensurate reduction in the amount of extraneous material dealt with at trials, thus not only saving time and money but simplifying the fact finding process as well.

Perhaps most importantly of all, this conceptualization may lead to fewer errors being made at trial. This can be demonstrated by freeing Professor Kaye's treatment of multiple possible sources of liability for an actionable wrong from its present artificial limitation of assuming only a single litigated issue. If one replaces in his efforts the probabilities of single elements with probabilities of the conjunction of all elements, one obtains a more general theory that liability should attach to the most likely sequence of events that explains the litigated occurrence. The proposed conceptualization of trials would implicate this more general theory by requiring the parties to assert what they believe are the most likely sequence of events leading to the event in question and then instructing the jury to choose between them. To be sure, this would allow a plaintiff to recover from a defendant when the jury concludes that the probability of the plaintiff's case is low, but that of the defendant lower. This would be inconsistent with minimizing errors only when there is yet another possible sequence of events leading to the event in question, such as some other person who is more probably liable than the defendant. In that case, however, the defendant would be allowed to implead that third party.

This proposal also can accommodate the Orloff and Stedinger view of allocation rules after it, too, is freed of the artificial constraint of assuming a single litigated issue. Orloff and Stedinger's work may be generalized in precisely the same manner as Kaye's. The question that would then remain is simply the political one of which allocation scheme is preferred.

A number of implications of this proposal deserve elaboration. The first is that it involves a dramatically different role for single elements than the current system of trials possesses. If a plaintiff and a defendant assert quite different factual allegations, with only a few common points, a fact finder could determine that the probability of a common element favors the defendant but that, taking each case as whole, the probabilities favor the plaintiff. Nonetheless, the work of Kaye and of Orloff and Stedinger shows upon generalization that to return a verdict for the defendant in this circumstance would lead to increased errors. Thus, the real lesson here is the counterproductive consequences of the present focus at trials on the individual elements of the plaintiff's case. If, however, there is a dispute over only one fact that has mutually exclusive possibilities (for example, was the light red or green when the car entered the intersection), then the probability of the respective cases will be determined by the appraisal of that single fact. In that case, the proposal would operate as the system does presently.

This conception of trials also eliminates the formal problems resulting from instructing the jury to find each, rather than all, elements to a specified level of probability. The jury will be comparing two fully specified versions of reality, rather than comparing discrete issues to their negations. As a result, the problems of conjunction do not create paradoxes where verdicts will be returned for plaintiffs even though there is an enormously high probability that at least one of the plaintiffs' necessary elements is not true. Rather, the conjunction effect will be contained within *both* parties' evidentiary proffers. Similarly, the bizarre effect of distributing errors differentially over the parties based upon whether all or some of the elements are in fact true will not occur. Errors will occur, of course, but they will affect both parties in the same manner.

NOTES AND QUESTIONS

1. The conceptualization of trials developed in the text is stimulated by criticisms of the conventional view of trials that are based in large measure upon the assumption that elements of a cause of action are statistically independent. This means that the occurrence or non-occurrence of one element does not affect the probability that some other element occurred. This is a highly unrealistic assumption. It would mean, for example, that the likelihood of negligence is not associated with the likelihood of harm.

Chapter Ten. Reflections on the Process of Proof

A more realistic appraisal would be that elements of a cause of action are dependent, that is, related to one another. Even if this is so, though, the analysis in the text is essentially accurate. The likelihood of two dependent events occurring will always be less than the likelihood of either one occurring. Thus, the conjunction effect discussed in the text does occur with dependent events, but its effect is less extreme. Dependence was not discussed in the text in an effort to simplify an already complex discussion.

2. For the proposal advanced in the text to make sense, one must be able to distinguish an affirmative story from a denial. Is that distinction a coherent one?

3. Should a plaintiff or a defendant be allowed to advance multiple stories, as they presently are under the Federal Rules of Civil Procedure? If so, what should the decision rule be? Suppose that each party advances two competing versions of reality. Assume further that the jury would assess the likelihood of plaintiff's Version I to be 0.05 and Version II to be 0.3, while it would assess the likelihood of the defendant's Version I to be 0.2 and Version II to be 0.2. Assume further that these four versions of reality are completely independent of each other. Who should win? The single most probable story is one of the plaintiff's. Still, the probability is greater that one of the defendant's versions is correct, even though we do not know which one, than that one of the plaintiff's versions is correct. Thus, if the objective is to reduce errors, a verdict should be returned for the defendant rather than for the plaintiff.

Does this make the discussion in the text a rather convoluted justification for the status quo? It may, since the plaintiff's burden will be to establish some version of the facts consistent with what the law requires for a verdict. Accordingly, the plaintiff will attempt to prove factual propositions that if believed will result in an inference of the necessary elements of his cause of action. The defendant, on the other hand, will attempt to prove factual assertions that will result in the inference that at least one of the necessary elements in the plaintiff's cause of action is not true. Thus, the final form of the inferential process under the theory developed in the text may appear to be identical to that which occurs now. If the probability of the plaintiff's factual assertions concerning any single element is less than 0.5, the defendant can admit all other elements and defend solely with respect to this particular element. If the plaintiff can only establish an element to some probability less than 0.5, then the defendant has established that this element did *not* occur to more than 0.5, and the single most likely sequence, or sequences, of events favors the defendant.

There is one crucial difference, however. A jury in evaluating evidence should conclude that the probability of the defendant's versions of reality is the probability of the plaintiff's versions subtracted from one *only* if it feels that it has before it all relevant versions of reality. Although it is an empirical matter, we suggest that it is often not the case.

To see this point, assume there is a cause of action that in the jury's view entails 10 factual explanations. Assume further that the plaintiff asserts four of them to be true and supports those assertions with credible evidence. In addition, assume that the defendant asserts three of the 10 possibilities as true, and supports those assertions with credible evidence. Lastly, assume that the versions asserted by each party justify a verdict for that party. In this hypothetical, under the conventional view of trials, presumably the defendant should win. Of the 10 possibilities that the jury thinks may explain the relevant state of affairs, the plaintiff has provided evidence that only four of those may be true. If there are 10 possible explanations of an event, four of which favor the plaintiff and thus six of which do not, certainly the plaintiff has not proven his case to a preponderance of the evidence. Indeed, this is true regardless of whether the defendant produces any evidence with respect to its three factual assertions.

The difficulty with this explanation, which highlights the single most troublesome aspect of the present conceptualization of trials, is that it results in resolving all ambiguity against the plaintiff. The "thus" in the penultimate sentence of the preceding paragraph is inaccurate, in other words. Presumably the jury does not know how to evaluate the three possibilities for which no evidence has been produced. In that case, a verdict for the defendant results in all possible inferences for which neither party has produced evidence being drawn against the plaintiff. A better view is that the ambiguity in a case should be distributed over the parties. That is what the conceptualization of civil trials we have advanced would do, and why on the facts of this hypothetical a verdict should be returned for the plaintiff.

4. Can you make any sense of the textual discussion as applied to criminal cases? Is this inability to generalize a weakness in the argument, or does it indicate that the purposes of civil and criminal trials may differ dramatically?

5. Does our approach to litigation make economic sense? Parties do not bear the entire cost of litigation. There is a public subsidy in the form of the capital costs of constructing court houses, judge's salaries, judicial employee's salaries, etc. In civil cases, this public subsidy rather perversely seems inversely related to need. As the cases get bigger, with greater monied interests involved, presumably the proceedings tend to get more protracted, absorbing more judicial resources. As that occurs, the public subsidy increases. Does this strike you as odd? What rationalization is there for increasing the size of the subsidy as the ability of the parties to pay increases as well?

A similar economic approach deserves to be taken with respect to rules of evidence and procedure. There are both public and private interests advanced by litigation. The public interests are rule formation and enforcement; the private interest is in dividing up the spoils. To the extent litigation and rules of evidence serve the public interest, an argument for subsidization can be made; but to the extent litigation serves private interests, such arguments become attenuated.

Chapter Ten. Reflections on the Process of Proof

Rules of evidence and procedure can also induce waste of resources. Burden of proof rules are a good example. A is suing B. Before evidence is produced, the fact finder may assess the odds as even that A deserves to win (and thus that B deserves to win). A then produces evidence that tilts the fact finder in the direction of the plaintiff. But B responds and tilts the fact finder back in the opposite direction. Suppose at this point the fact finder's assessment is where it began, at equipoise. Because of the demands of the rules of evidence and procedure, the parties have invested substantial resources to no purpose. Still, so what? Is this just a necessary by-product of a dispute resolution system that must be tolerated, or is there more to be said about the matter? For more on this kind of analysis of the legal process, see G. Tullock, Trials on Trial: The Pure Theory of Legal Procedure (1980).

CHAPTER ELEVEN

LAY OPINIONS, SCIENTIFIC EVIDENCE, AND EXPERT WITNESSES

The subject matter of this chapter is not new to you. The transcript and problems in Chapter One offered examples of lay opinion testimony, scientific evidence, and expert testimony, and we have returned to these topics throughout the course. For example, in Chapter Two we considered the propriety of utilizing statistical evidence; in Chapter Three we raised the question what standard the judge should apply in deciding whether a witness was qualified to testify as an expert; in Chapter Five we examined the process of eliciting expert testimony in the context of discussing the physical condition exception to the hearsay rule; in Chapter Six we discussed the process of impeaching expert witnesses with passages from scientific treatises; and in Chapter Seven, in the context of examining the process of litigating civil rights claims, we saw examples of the use of statistical evidence.

At their most fundamental level, the issues raised by the topics considered here are ones of relevance, preliminary fact finding, and FRE 403 balancing—issues with which by now you should be familiar. We have included a separate chapter on scientific and opinion evidence in part to provide an opportunity to review some fundamental aspects of those issues and in part because both judicial decisions and rules of evidence articulate specific criteria for the admission of scientific and opinion evidence. FRE 701 addresses the subject of lay opinion testimony, and FRE 702-706 deal with expert testimony.

A. LAY OPINIONS

The rhetoric of the common law was that witnesses could testify only about facts and could not offer opinions. The purported distinction between "fact" and "opinion," however, is nonexistent. A witness' testimony that something did or will occur is only evidence. Regardless of how certain the witness purports to be, we have no way of knowing that the witness is correct. Rather, all that we have is the witness' expression of a belief about the existence or nonexistence of some fact. And what is an "opinion" if it is not an expression of a belief about some "fact"?

One possible way to distinguish between opinion and fact is in terms of the degree of certainty with which a belief is expressed: An opinion would be an expression made with some significant degree of uncertainty, whereas a fact would be an expression made with a high degree of certainty. Perhaps a witness' extreme uncertainty about some event should be regarded as making the witness' testimony irrelevant or at least not sufficiently probative to warrant admissibility in light of countervailing FRE 403 considerations. There is no need, however, for a separate exclusionary rule that distinguishes between fact and opinion in terms of the degree of a witness' certainty. The line between the two would remain inevitably murky. Moreover, the existence of such a rule might be an incentive for witnesses to be less than fully candid about their doubts. Fortunately, degree of certainty has not been a critical factor in giving content to the lay opinion prohibition.

A second possible distinction between fact and opinion is in terms of the bases for a witness' knowledge: A belief based on firsthand knowledge would be a fact, and a belief based on hearsay would be an opinion. In this country, however, the opinion rule did not develop as a manifestation of this distinction. Indeed, there is no need for such an opinion rule, for courts generally have recognized the firsthand knowledge requirement and the hearsay prohibition as independent evidentiary rules.

A third way to get at the supposed difference between fact and opinion— and this is what many common law courts appeared to do—is by applying some common sense "I know it when I see it" notion in defining an opinion. Thus, most courts would probably agree that the statement "The platform was dangerous" is an opinion whereas the assertions "John shot me" or "The object is a chair" would be statements of fact. The difficulty with this approach is that it does not provide much guidance for classifying statements generally. For example, what about a statement that the defendant was "drunk" or was "speeding" or was driving "recklessly" or was driving "too fast given the weather conditions"? Moreover, even the supposedly clear examples may be unclear in some contexts. Is the statement "John shot me" one of fact or opinion if we know that John and Jim are identical twins and if there is conflicting evidence about which twin shot the witness? With respect to the statement about the chair, assume that the object is being imported into the country and that the import duty depends upon the classification of the item as a piece of furniture or as an art object. Is the identification of the object as a chair a statement of fact or opinion?

The legitimate concern underlying the prohibition against lay opinions is that we do not want witnesses to substitute their conclusions for data that

A. Lay Opinions

would be helpful to the jury. Thus, in the dangerous platform case, we would prefer to have the witness describe to the jury the condition of the platform in some detail. Without the detailed information about the condition of the platform, the jury's only choice would be whether to rely on the conclusion of the witness. By contrast, with the detailed information the jurors would be in a better position to determine for themselves whether the platform was dangerous, and this is what we want them to do.

Similarly, in the identical twin case, we would prefer to have the victim describe the particular characteristics of the assailant or the prior encounters with John that led the victim to conclude that the assailant was John rather than Jim. And in the case in which the question was whether the object was a chair or a piece of art, we would prefer a detailed description of the object to the witness' summary conclusion. In short, sustaining a lay opinion objection forces the witness to articulate the underlying details that gave rise to the "opinion."

In some cases, insisting upon details rather than conclusions may be counterproductive. Consider, for example, testimony about the identity of an assailant who is an acquaintance of the victim and not an identical twin. Should we insist that the witness describe the particular physical features of the assailant—e.g., blue eyes, red hair, dimples, bushy eyebrows—or is it sufficient for the witness to name the assailant as John, along with testimony indicating the nature of the witness' acquaintance with John and the opportunity that the witness had to observe John during the attack? Or consider testimony about whether an object is a chair when the purpose of the testimony is to describe pieces of furniture in a room. Should the witness be required to describe the physical features of the object—e.g., a square horizontal cushion with a wood base supported by four carved 20-inch long vertical pieces of wood at each corner and with a solid piece along one side of the horizontal cushion that rises approximately two feet above the horizontal cushion—or should it be sufficient for the witness to describe the object as a chair with a high, solid back?

Fairly clearly the detailed descriptions should not be required in the two preceding examples. The reasons for not requiring the detail relate to how people tend to perceive individuals, chairs, and other phenomena. Consider the thought process that you go through when you see a friend or enter a furnished room. At least at a conscious, purposeful level you are not likely to think, "There is an individual with red hair, dimples, bushy eyebrows, etc.; therefore, that person is John" or "That object has a horizontal cushion supported by four vertical poles, etc.; therefore, it must be a chair." Rather, you are likely to think, "There is John" or "That is a chair."

To the extent that individuals tend to perceive people, objects, or other phenomena in the aggregate, describing the phenomena in the aggregate is likely to contribute to helpful and efficient communication in at least three ways. First, since the witness probably has not consciously perceived or thought about the discrete attributes of the phenomenon (e.g., "John" or "chair"), requiring the witness, after the fact, to try to break down the phenomenon into its component parts would lend an aura of artificiality to the testimony. Second, regardless of the witness' actual thought process at the time of perceiving the phenomenon, it may be difficult for the witness at the time of the trial to reconstruct and articulate the underlying details (e.g., the physical characteristics of John or the chair). To the extent that this is the case, requiring the witness to describe the component parts may, in effect, tongue tie the witness with the result that the jury will receive little or nothing of value. Finally, to the extent that jurors tend to perceive a phenomenon in the aggregate rather than in its component parts, the jurors may be disconcerted and confused about testimony that describes the component parts of the phenomenon. Jurors are likely to expect that witnesses will describe a phenomenon in terms that are familiar to them. If the phenomenon is inexplicably broken down into detailed component parts, the jurors may for that reason alone tend to suspect and discredit the evidence.

To summarize, the legitimate concern underlying the common law prohibition against lay opinions is that a witness' opinion—or summary or conclusion—may sometimes deprive the jurors of important data with which to perform their fact-finding role. Whether that is likely to be the case, however, does not depend upon some *a priori* distinction between fact and opinion. Rather, it depends upon an assessment in the context of each particular case of what information will be optimally helpful to jurors in their fact-finding role. If a summary or conclusion that forgoes underlying details will be adequate for the jury's purposes, the testimony in that form should be admissible. On the other hand, if jurors need underlying details, the witness should be required to provide those details rather than the witness' own summary or conclusion.

There is no logical need for a special evidentiary provision dealing with these concerns. A court could rely on FRE 402 and FRE 403 to exclude opinions or conclusions that are not helpful to the fact finder. The absence of a lay opinion provision in a general codification of evidentiary rules, however, might suggest that the common law prohibition against opinions should not be disturbed. In language that is sufficiently flexible to accommodate the objectives that we have been discussing, FRE 701 makes it clear that there is no absolute exclusion of lay opinions:

> If a witness is not testifying as an expert, the witness' testimony in the form of opinions or inferences is limited to those opinions or inferences which are (a) rationally based on the perceptions of the witness and (b) helpful to a clear understanding of the witness' testimony or the determination of a fact in issue.

As the Advisory Committee's Note points out, the limitation in (a) is merely a restatement of the firsthand knowledge requirement. Moreover, the Advisory Committee's Note expresses an expectation that the helpfulness limitation in (b) will seldom be a ground for exclusion:

A. Lay Opinions

The rule assumes that the natural characteristics of the adversary system will generally lead to an acceptable result, since the detailed account carries more conviction than the broad assertion, and a lawyer can be expected to display his witness to the best advantage. If he fails to do so, cross-examination and argument will point up the weakness. . . . If, despite these considerations, attempts are made to introduce meaningless assertions which amount to little more than choosing up sides, exclusion for lack of helpfulness is called for by the rule.

In contrast to the general tenor of this language in the Advisory Committee's Note, some courts stress that FRE 701 vests substantial discretion in the judge to exclude lay opinion testimony.[1] For the most part, though, courts operating under the Federal Rules have been fairly liberal in overruling objections based on FRE 701.

Regardless of what position a court takes with respect to FRE 701 objections to the testimony of a witness on the stand, a court should be particularly reluctant to exclude otherwise admissible hearsay evidence on the ground that the hearsay constitutes an impermissible lay opinion. The live witness can always respond to a successful lay opinion objection by testifying about the "factual" details upon which the "opinion" is based. The hearsay declarant, however, will not necessarily be available to offer the detailed information. Thus, in the hearsay situation, the effect of sustaining the objection may be to deprive the fact finder completely of any input from the hearsay declarant.

PROBLEMS

1. Review Problems 2 and 11 at the end of Chapter One.

2. Ed Hall is being prosecuted for aggravated assault. After spending several hours drinking, Ed, his wife Emma, and Emma's brother, George, returned to the Hall residence. Ed and George got into a heated argument about local politics. Ed took a loaded revolver from a desk drawer, pointed it at Emma and George and in a slurred voice threatened to shoot them. George moved toward Ed and asked him to drop the gun. Ed took several steps back and tripped over an ottoman, at which point the gun discharged, severely wounding George. As part of his defense Ed plans to call Emma and George and ask them whether, in their opinions, the shooting was accidental. Should the prosecutor's lay opinion objection to this testimony be sustained?

3. Vera Wells is being prosecuted for the murder of her infant son, Todd, by drowning. A neighbor and prosecution witness offers to testify as follows: "On the morning that the baby drowned I observed Vera walking toward the creek that runs behind our properties. I was about 100 feet away

---

1. See, e.g., United States v. Skeet, 665 F.2d 983, 985-986 (9th Cir. 1982).

from her. She had a bundle in her hands. While I can't be certain, it is my best impression that she was carrying Todd." Should this evidence be admissible over defendant's lay opinion objection?

B. SCIENTIFIC OR SPECIALIZED EVIDENCE

By "scientific" or "specialized" evidence we mean evidence that is generated by persons who have some specialized or unusual training, experience, or ability that permits them to piece together or to interpret data in a manner that would not be readily apparent to the average layperson fact finder. This type of information is typically presented to the fact finder through the testimony of expert witnesses. We will examine the rules governing the qualification and questioning of experts in the next section. Our focus here is limited to the permissible subject matter of scientific or specialized evidence.

Frequently scientific or specialized evidence will be highly probative in a law suit, and with a proper foundation (e.g., qualifying the witness as an expert and demonstrating how the information relates to the issues being litigated) such evidence may be admitted. For example, a person experienced in the practices of a particular business or industry can testify about those practices. Similarly, courts regularly admit ballistics and finger print evidence, expert testimony about valuation in a condemnation proceeding, and expert medical testimony about a criminal defendant's competence to stand trial or insanity at the time of the alleged crime. On the other hand, courts have traditionally been reluctant to admit, in the absence of prior stipulation by the parties, the results of lie detector tests, and most courts have excluded expert testimony about the vagaries of eyewitness identification. A court would almost certainly exclude an astrologer's or palm reader's "expert" testimony about an individual's violent tendencies or life expectancy.

Courts may base decisions about the admissibility of scientific or specialized evidence either on the general nature of the alleged science or specialty or on the foundation for the evidence that the proponent establishes in the individual case. For example, a court would be likely to exclude the palm reader's testimony on the ground that the information is not relevant regardless of the qualifications of the palm reader. Indeed, the court may preclude the proponent from even attempting to lay a foundation for such evidence. On the other hand, although a court would be willing to admit expert testimony about valuation in a condemnation proceeding, the court may exclude a particular witness' testimony because the proponent has failed to establish that that witness is an expert in the area. Similarly, the admissibility of expert testimony about the vagaries of eyewitness identification may turn on the nature of the foundation that the proponent is able to

B. Scientific or Specialized Evidence

establish. If the expert witness could establish that significant numbers of misidentifications occur in situations that are in relevant respects similar to the situation in which the identification was made in the current case, a court would be more likely to admit this evidence than more generalized evidence about misidentification.

As the foregoing illustrations suggest, the question whether scientific or specialized evidence should be admitted turns on an evaluation of the relevance of the evidence and the countervailing FRE 403 factors. Some purportedly specialized evidence may appear to have no probative value. Evidence with slight probative value arguably should be excluded because of FRE 403 concerns: The evidence may be misleading if scientific jargon gives the evidence a sense of legitimacy that it does not deserve; the complexity of the evidence may tend to confuse rather than help jurors; and perhaps most importantly, the speculative nature or low probative value of some specialized evidence may not warrant spending the time, first, to demonstrate the possible relevance of the evidence and, second, to explore all of the possible weaknesses in the evidence.

Perhaps FRE 401-403 are adequate tools for dealing with the potential problems raised by scientific and specialized evidence. Indeed, it is arguable that courts should be especially reluctant to exclude specialized evidence pursuant to FRE 402 or FRE 403, for there are at least three factors inherent in the litigation process that are likely to inhibit parties from procuring unreliable specialized evidence.

First, the attorney will need to develop some familiarity with any specialization about which the attorney desires to interrogate a witness, and the specialist is likely to demand a fee for preparing for the litigation and testifying. These expenditures of time and money are likely to make the cost of procuring specialized evidence higher than the cost of procuring other evidence.

Second, the seemingly bizarre nature of some specialized evidence may lead jurors to reject it out of hand. Even if there appears to be an initial aura of legitimacy to the specialized evidence, opposing counsel will have the opportunity through cross-examination and rebuttal to demonstrate the irrelevance or low probative value of the evidence. In either situation, jurors' skepticism about the specialized evidence may lead them not merely to reject the specialized evidence; it may lead them to draw an inference similar to the inference that one can draw from the exposure of an attempt to bribe a witness or the knowing presentation of perjured testimony: If the party must resort to this type of unreliable evidence, the party's case must be a weak one.

Third, although we regard cross-examination as an important vehicle for testing the reliability of all witnesses, cross-examination is at best a very imperfect vehicle for assessing reliability of witnesses generally. Some witnesses may lie with impunity, and even a vigorous cross-examination may not shake the testimony of a confident witness who in fact misperceived or improperly remembered what happened. By contrast, except perhaps in the case of a specialist who claims to have special insights as a result of some admittedly not fully understood psychic power, the probative value of specialized evidence is likely to depend in large measure on the rationality and methodology of allegedly scientific processes. These are matters that can be fully exposed and considered during the examination of witnesses. The witnesses, of course, may be lying or may have misperceived or forgotten something that will not come to light during the examination. We can think of no reason, however, why this problem is likely to be any greater with purported specialists than with other witnesses.

Admittedly, these factors will not ensure the reliability of all specialized evidence. Particularly in the context of a criminal prosecution, where discovery may not be readily available, opposing counsel may not be sufficiently knowledgeable about the specialty or adequately prepared to cross-examine specialists and offer opposing experts. Moreover, a litigant with a weak case may rationally decide that the best chance of prevailing is through the confusion that may be generated by the presentation of unreliable or extremely complex specialized evidence; and it is arguably inappropriate to place on opposing counsel the burden of having to respond to specialized evidence unless the offering party first demonstrates that it has a relatively high degree of probative value. Finally, jurors may tend to give an aura of legitimacy to even bizarre specialized evidence merely because the evidence is presented to them: Why would the judge let us hear this evidence if it were not relevant? On the other hand, a judge's proclivity to exclude unusual types of specialized evidence can prevent litigants from taking advantage of innovative, highly probative information and, as a result, detract from the search for truth.

In Frye v. United States,[2] decided in 1923, the federal circuit court for the District of Columbia adopted a special rule for the admissibility of scientific evidence. The defendant, Frye, sought to introduce into evidence the results of an early type of lie detection device—a systolic blood pressure test. In upholding the trial court's exclusion of the evidence the Court of Appeals stated:

> Just when a scientific principle or discovery crosses the line between the experimental and demonstrable stages is difficult to define. Somewhere in this twilight zone the evidential force of the principle must be recognized, and while courts will go a long way in admitting expert testimony deduced from well-recognized scientific principle or discovery, *the thing from which the deduction is made must be sufficiently established to have gained general acceptance in the particular field in which it belongs.* [293 F.2d at 1014 (emphasis added).]

As McCormick has pointed out, the *Frye* opinion is unclear about whether "the thing" that must have gained "general acceptance" is the relationship between truthtelling and blood pressure or the ability of an expert to measure

2. 293 F.2d 1013 (D.C. Cir. 1923).

B. Scientific or Specialized Evidence

and interpret the changes in blood pressure, or both.[3] Nonetheless, despite this ambiguity and despite the court's failure to explain further or to cite precedent for its holding, a number of courts adopted the "general acceptance" test, commonly referred to as the *"Frye test."*

Polygraphy,[7] graphology,[7.5] hypnotic and drug induced testimony,[8] voice stress analysis,[9] voice spectrograms,[10] ion microprobe mass spectroscopy,[11] infrared sensing of aircraft,[12] retesting of breath samples for alcohol content,[12.5] psychological profiles of battered women,[13] post traumatic stress disorder as indicating rape,[13.5] astronomical calculations,[14] and blood group typings[15] all have fallen prey to its influence. [McCormick's Handbook on the Law of Evidence §203 (3d ed., Cleary, 1984 & 1987 Pocket Part).]

Particularly in recent years the *Frye* test has been the subject of extensive criticism, primarily because a rigorous application of the test prevents use of scientific evidence based on emerging disciplines or cross-disciplinary studies. The Federal Rules make no reference to the "general acceptance" standard. Rather, FRE 702, which authorizes the admission of scientific or specialized evidence provides:

> If scientific, technical, or other specialized knowledge will assist the trier of fact to understand the evidence or to determine a fact in issue, a witness

---

3. McCormick's Handbook on the Law of Evidence §203, p.605 (3d ed., Cleary, 1984).
7. [See, e.g., State v. Mitchell, 402 A.2d 479, 482 (Me. 1979).]
7.5. State v. Anderson, 379 N.W.2d 70, 79 (Minn. 1985), *cert. denied*, 106 S. Ct. 2248.
8. [E.g., People v. Shirley, 31 Cal. 3d 18, 181 Cal. Rptr. 243, 250-252, 641 P.2d 775, 782-784 (1982) (reviewing cases involving hypnosis), *cert. denied*, 103 S. Ct. 133; Cain v. State, 549 S.W.2d 707, 712 (Tex. Cr. App. 1977) (citing cases to show that "[t]he weight of authority in this country regards results of truth serum tests as inadmissible inasmuch as they have not yet attained scientific acceptance as reliable and accurate means of ascertaining truth or deception"), *cert. denied*, 434 U.S. 845.]
9. [See McCormick's Handbook on the Law of Evidence §206, p. 628 (3d ed., Cleary, 1984).]
10. [United States v. Addison, 498 F.2d 741 (D.C. Cir. 1947), questioned in United States v. McDaniels, 538 F.2d 408, 413 (D.C. Cir. 1976).]
11. United States v. Brown, 557 F.2d 541, 556-557 (6th Cir. 1977) (as applied to hair samples).
12. United States v. Kilgus, 571 F.2d 508, 510 (9th Cir. 1978) (customs officer tried to use military forward looking infrared tracking system to distinguish the aircraft he had previously followed from others of the same type).
12.5. Commonwealth v. Neal, 392 Mass. 1, 464 N.E.2d 1356, 1364-1365 (1984).
13. [Ibn-Tamas v. United States, 407 A.2d 626, 634 D.C. App. 1979) (erroneously excluded, but properly excluded after hearing on remand).]
13.5. People v. Bledsoe, 36 Cal. 3d 236, 251, 203 Cal. Rptr. 450, 460, 681 P.2d 291 301 (1984); State v. Taylor, 663 S.W.2d 235, 240 (Mo. 1984).
14. United States v. Tranowski, 659 F.2d 750, 755-757 (7th Cir. 1981) (analysis of shadow length to determine time at which photograph taken).
15. See Huntington v. Crowley, 64 Cal. 2d 647, 51 Cal. Rptr. 254, 414 P.2d 382 (1966) (Kell-Cellano test not generally accepted as giving accurate results); State v. Damm, 62 S.D. 123, 252 N.W. 7 (1933) (medical sciences not shown to be sufficiently agreed on "the transmissibility of blood characteristics"), *on reh'g*, 64 S.D. 309, 266 N.W. 667 (1936) (science found unanimously agreed.)

qualified as an expert by knowledge, skill, experience, training, or education, may testify thereto in the form of an opinion or otherwise.

On its face, the "assist the trier of fact" criterion appears, with one possible exception, to be nothing more than an incorporation of the basic relevance concepts embodied in FRE 401-403. The possible exception is that there may be a subtle shift in the burden of proof on the question of admissibility. The "substantially outweighed" language in FRE 403 in effect places the burden on the party seeking exclusion of the evidence, whereas the "assist the trier of fact" language in FRE 702 arguably is a condition of admissibility that the proponent of the evidence must satisfy. It is not clear, however, what standard the judge is to apply in making the "assist the trier" determination.[4] If the judge must make an FRE 104(a) determination that, in light of FRE 403 factors, the evidence will assist the jury, there has been a shift in the burden of proof to the proponent of the evidence. On the other hand, if the judge's role is to make an FRE 104(b)-like determination that the evidence *could be*, but not necessarily will be, helpful to the jury, there is no shift in the burden of proof.

In any event, it is not surprising in view of the language of FRE 702 that some commentators take the position that the Federal Rules have rejected the *Frye* test.[5] It is arguable, however, that the Federal Rules' failure explicitly to repudiate a well-established rule indicates that the drafters intended for courts to continue to apply the "general acceptance" requirement.[6] Courts are divided on the issue,[7] although the trend in both federal courts and state courts is in the direction of abandoning or at least not rigorously applying the *Frye* test.

If the *Frye* test is abandoned, should there be some substitute test for the admissibility of scientific and specialized evidence that is more rigorous than the standards embodied in FRE 401-403? Instead of focusing on standards of admissibility, would it be desirable for there to be some mandatory process—perhaps implemented through discovery and pre-trial conferences—that would ensure that both the lawyers and the judge were sufficiently versed in the specialty to address questions of admissibility in a reasonable and helpful way? Should there be a panel of experts either to make decisions about the admissibility of specialized evidence or perhaps

---

4. See Imwinkelried, Judge Versus Jury: Who Should Decide Questions of Preliminary Facts Conditioning the Admissibility of Scientific Evidence, 25 Wm. & Mary L. Rev. 577 (1984).

5. E.g., 3 J. Weinstein and M. Berger, Weinstein's Evidence ¶702[03], at 702-16 (1982).

6. See S. Saltzburg and K. Redden, Federal Rules of Evidence Manual 633 (4th ed. 1986); Giannelli, The Admissibility of Novel Scientific Evidence: Frye v. United States, a Half-Century Later, 80 Colum. L. Rev. 1197, 1229 (1980).

7. E.g., compare United States v. Brown, 557 F.2d 541 (6th Cir. 1977) (applying *Frye*) with United States v. Williams, 583 F.2d 1194 (2d Cir. 1978), *cert. denied*, 439 U.S. 1117 (1979).

B. Scientific or Specialized Evidence

even to make the ultimate factual determination of questions that turn on the evaluation of scientific evidence?

Whatever the precise standards for the admission of specialized testimony, the evidentiary principles involved in dealing with the evidence are quite simple and straightforward: They are, as we have suggested, the principles embodied in FRE 401-403 and 104. What is not simple and what is by far the most important aspect of dealing with specialized evidence is that the attorney must have a solid working grasp of the specialized or scientific principles to which the testimony relates, for it is the attorney who will be responsible for developing and refuting the information through the direct and cross-examination of witnesses. In short, the attorney must be an expert.

A TRUE PARABLE

Plaintiff, Rudolfo Sanchez, brought a products liability action for injuries sustained when he was attempting to clean a glue-spreading machine manufactured by the defendant. The jury returned a verdict for the defendant. Sanchez appealed on the ground, inter alia, that it was error to prevent him from impeaching the defendant's expert witness with a speech that the witness had given to a group of engineers. The court upheld the plaintiff's claim and reversed the judgment. A portion of the speech is quoted in a concurring opinion:

> The way I counteracted the thing, I used another technique. I used the technique [of] science as a foreign language. I made a statement to the attorney that absolutely nobody could understand. Now, what it amounts to, it's going to terminate the cross-examination, and it's going to terminate it in a hurry.
>
> *I want the jury to understand what I say when I feel there are certain conditions. Under direct examination, the jury understands everything that I say. Under cross-examination, there are some things I will allow the jury to understand and there are some things which I will not allow the jury to understand.*
>
> If you don't want the jury to understand something, then what you do is you answer the question precisely, you see. If somebody is working with a form of inertia, why I use a form of inertia. I say, "Do you mean the second bolt above the first bolt," you know. Just get into something which is a very precise way of saying something.
>
> The interval of minus infinity to plus infinity of X times X, X_2, and you know the—no one is going to be able to do much with that kind of thing.
>
> And he says, "Can you simplify it?" You say, "See, there's too much simplification already. This is the only way that I can state it to you so there will be no misunderstanding." [Sanchez v. Black Bros. Co., 98 Ill. App. 264, 423 N.E.2d 1309, 1320 (1981) (emphasis added by the court).]

C. EXPERT WITNESSES

1. Qualifications

Once there has been a determination that specialized information will assist the trier of fact, there must be a determination whether the person presenting the information is qualified to do so. The qualifications need not include formal education in the subject matter. Rather, as FRE 702 provides, one can be a qualified expert as a result of one's "knowledge, skill, experience, [or] training," as well as education.

The most interesting evidentiary issue governing the qualification of expert witnesses is the preliminary fact issue we raised in Chapter Three: Should the judge decide pursuant to FRE 104(a) whether, in the judge's view, the witness is an expert? Or should the judge—subject, of course, to FRE 403—permit the witness to testify if there is "evidence sufficient to support a finding," FRE 104(b), that the witness' "knowledge, skill, experience, training, or education" give the witness "scientific, technical, or other specialized knowledge [that] will assist the trier of fact"?

Prior to the adoption of the Federal Rules, courts considered the question whether a witness was qualified to give expert testimony to be one for the judge to decide. Without close analysis, courts and commentators assume that the role of the judge remains the same under the Federal Rules. It is arguable, however, that the question of a witness' expertise should be evaluated in terms an FRE 104(b)-type "evidence sufficient to support a finding" standard. The witness' expertise has a direct bearing on the relevance of the testimony; and the question whether an expert witness is adequately qualified is closely analogous to the question whether a lay witness has firsthand knowledge.[8] The Federal Rules explicitly mandate in FRE 602 that judges apply an FRE 104(b)-type sufficiency standard to the firsthand knowledge question.

On the other hand, there is nothing in the Federal Rules to indicate that the drafters intended to depart from the common law on this issue. Moreover, FRE 104(a) specifically refers to the "qualifications of a person to be a witness" in the list of preliminary facts that are for the judge to decide. Except for the FRE 602 firsthand-knowledge requirement and the infrequently invoked prohibitions against testimony from presiding judges (FRE 605) and sitting jurors (FRE 606), FRE 702's requirement that the witness

---

8. See McCormick's Handbook on the Law of Evidence §13, p.33 (3d ed., Cleary, 1984):

> An observer is qualified to testify because he has firsthand knowledge of the situation or transaction at issue. The expert has something different to contribute. This is the power to draw inferences from the facts which a jury would not be competent to draw.

See also R. Lempert and S. Saltzburg, A Modern Approach to the Law of Evidence 864 (2d ed. 1982) ("[T]he purported expert who lacks expertise is a bit like the proffered witness who lacks firsthand knowledge.").

C. Expert Witnesses

be "qualified as an expert" is the only explicit witness qualification provision in the Federal Rules. Thus, even though FRE 104(a) operates "subject to the provisions" in FRE 104(b), it seems reasonable to infer that the drafters of the rules assumed that the expert qualification requirement would be one for the court to resolve pursuant to FRE 104(a).[9]

2. Disclosure of the Bases for an Opinion

At common law, once a witness was qualified to testify as an expert it was necessary to elicit the bases for the opinion prior to asking the witness about the opinion. In our discussion of the physical condition hearsay exception[10] we noted that this requirement, coupled with the requirement that opinions be based on admissible evidence, tended to force reliance on the use of hypothetical questions. We considered there why and how the Federal Rules minimize the need for asking hypothetical questions to experts. You should take a few minutes now to review that discussion.

The Federal Rule governing the disclosure of the bases for an expert's opinion is FRE 705, which provides:

> The expert may testify in terms of opinion or inference and give reasons therefor without prior disclosure of the underlying facts or data, unless the court requires otherwise. The expert may in any event be required to disclose the underlying facts or data on cross-examination.

In addition to obviating the need for hypothetical questions, FRE 705 sensibly gives the direct examiner the flexibility to elicit the opinion or conclusion prior to developing all the details that support it. If the direct examiner had to present to the jury the detailed facts upon which the opinion was based prior to presenting the opinion, there is the risk that in at least some instances the jurors would pay insufficient attention to the details

---

9. There is one related preliminary fact issue that is worth considering in assessing how a court should deal with the preliminary fact of a witness' expertise. FRE 603 provides:

> Before testifying, every witness shall be required to declare that the witness will testify truthfully, by oath or affirmation administered in a form calculated to awaken the witness' conscience and impress the witness' mind with the duty to do so.

Consider whether or to what extent this provision gives the judge authority to find a prospective witness unqualified on the ground that the witness cannot understand or appreciate the obligation to testify truthfully. The ability to understand and appreciate the oath or affirmation would appear to be a "qualification of a person to be a witness." FRE 104(a). But is it a qualification that the court decides pursuant to FRE 104(a) or FRE 104(b)? See 3 J. Weinstein and V. Berger, Weinstein's Evidence ¶603[01], p.603-6 (1982) (suggesting that judge should apply FRE 104(b) standard in determining whether witness is "inherently untruthful"). Do you agree that that is the proper test to apply? If it is the proper test for this qualification to be a witness, why is it not also the proper test for determining whether a witness is sufficiently qualified as an expert?

10. Pages 439-443 supra.

because they would not know how the details were relevant. On the other hand, if there is reason to suspect that the information upon which the expert bases the opinion is so unreliable that it may be appropriate to exclude the opinion altogether, it would be desirable to test that suspicion before rather than after the jury hears the opinion. By explicitly giving the judge authority to require that the bases for an opinion be elicited prior to the opinion, FRE 705 provides a reasonable basis for solving this type of problem. Unfortunately, however, neither the rule nor the Advisory Committee's Note suggests any criteria for the judge to apply in deciding whether to require that the bases for the opinion precede the opinion.

An unsubstantiated opinion is not likely to impress the jury as much as one that has a demonstrably solid basis. Thus, as a matter of strategy, the direct examiner is likely to explore the bases for an expert's opinion sometime during the direct examination. There may be times, however, when the attorney's voluntary exploration of the bases for the testimony on direct examination is less than complete. Rather than ensuring in every case that direct examination will reveal the bases for an opinion, FRE 705 contents itself with the possibility of developing the bases on cross-examination. According to the Advisory Committee's Note:

> If the objection is made that leaving it to the cross-examiner to bring out the supporting data is essentially unfair, the answer is that he is under no compulsion to bring out any facts or data except those unfavorable to the opinion. *The answer assumes that the cross-examiner has the advance knowledge which is essential for effective cross-examination.* This advance knowledge has been afforded, though imperfectly, by the traditional foundation requirement. *Rule 26(b)(4) of the Rules of Civil Procedure, as revised, provides for substantial discovery in this area, obviating in large measure the obstacles which have been raised in some instances to discovery of findings, underlying data, and even the identity of the experts.* (Emphasis added.)

The Advisory Committee's answer may be sufficient for civil cases. In criminal cases, where discovery traditionally has been more limited, however, the cross-examiner may be at a serious disadvantage if the underlying facts and data are not revealed on direct examination. In such a case it would be appropriate for the trial judge to require that the bases for the opinion be elicited on direct examination.

3. Opinions Based on Otherwise Inadmissible Evidence

As we pointed out in the discussion of the physical condition hearsay exception, many common law courts required witnesses to base their opinions only on admissible evidence. By contrast, FRE 703 expressly authorizes the use of opinions based on inadmissible evidence:

C. Expert Witnesses

The facts or data in the particular case upon which an expert bases an opinion or inference may be those perceived by or made known to the expert at or before the hearing. If of a type reasonably relied upon by experts in the particular field in forming opinions or inferences upon the subject, the facts or data need not be admissible in evidence.

When an expert bases an opinion in whole or in part on inadmissible evidence, there is an inevitable tension between whatever rule makes the evidence inadmissible and FRE 705, which contemplates disclosure of the bases for an opinion. Most often this is a tension between FRE 705 and the hearsay rule,[11] but data upon which an opinion is based may be inadmissible for other reasons as well. For example, the expert may have relied on the oral recitation of the contents of an X-ray, whereas the best evidence rule would require reliance on the X-ray itself; or the expert may have relied on writings that have been insufficiently authenticated. In these types of situations, should FRE 703 operate as a rule of admissibility that can take precedence over various specific exclusionary rules, or does FRE 703 merely permit an expert to express an opinion based on inadmissible evidence? If the latter, how does one accommodate this interpretation of FRE 703 with the usual practice of permitting experts to state the bases for their opinions?

Neither the Federal Rules nor the Advisory Committee's Notes address these questions, and courts have taken inconsistent approaches to the problem. We believe that courts should treat FRE 703's inadmissible evidence provision as a broad rule of admissibility.

One possible alternative solution to the problem is to limit the data upon which expert opinions may be based. For example, some courts have interpreted the "reasonably relied upon" language in FRE 703 very narrowly.[12] According to this narrow view of FRE 703, the court has the right, indeed the obligation, to make an independent evaluation of the trustworthiness of the information upon which the expert relies. A few courts have suggested that it is reasonable to rely on hearsay information only if the hearsay is sufficiently reliable to meet some exception to the hearsay rule.

In our view, judicial reliance upon the "reasonably relied" language to second-guess the expert—and particularly to scrutinize carefully hearsay information—is unwarranted. Such an interpretation of the "reasonably relied" language is tantamount to saying that an expert cannot base an opinion on inadmissible evidence—or at least on inadmissible hearsay; and the one thing that is clear about FRE 703 is that the drafters did not intend experts

---

11. In the context of a criminal case, the prosecutor's use of an opinion based on hearsay may also raise a sixth amendment confrontation clause issue. In Chapter Five we explored briefly the relationship between the hearsay rule and the confrontation clause. See pages 351-371 supra. That discussion is fully applicable to hearsay evidence that the jury may hear as the result of an expert's reliance on hearsay.

12. See 3 J. Weinstein and V. Berger, ¶703[03], pp. 703-18 to 703-33 (1988) (collecting and discussing cases).

to be so limited in what they can rely upon. According to the Advisory Committee's Note to FRE 703:

> Facts or data upon which expert opinions are based may, under the rule, be derived from three possible sources. The first is firsthand observation of the witness, with opinions based thereon traditionally allowed. A treating physician affords an example. . . . The second source, presentation at the trial, also reflects existing practice. The technique may be the familiar hypothetical question or having the expert attend the trial and hear the testimony establishing the facts. . . . The third source contemplated by the rule consists of presentation of data to the expert outside of court and other than by his own perception. *In this respect the rule is designed to broaden the basis for expert opinions beyond that current in many jurisdictions and to bring the judicial practice into line with the practice of experts themselves when not in court. Thus a physician in his own practice bases his diagnosis on information from numerous sources and of considerable variety, including statements by patients and relatives, reports and opinions from nurses, technicians and other doctors, hospital records, and X-rays. Most of them are admissible in evidence, but only with the expenditure of substantial time in producing and examining various authenticating witnesses. The physician makes life-and-death decisions in reliance upon them. His validation, expertly performed and subject to cross-examination, ought to suffice for judicial purposes.* . . .
>
> If it be feared that enlargement of permissible data may tend to break down the rules of exclusion unduly, notice should be taken that the rule requires that the facts and data "be of a type reasonably relied upon by experts in the particular field." The language would not warrant admitting in evidence the opinion of an "accidentologist" as to the point of impact in an automobile collision based on statements of bystanders, since this requirement is not satisfied. [Emphasis added.]

Both the phrase "*reasonably* relied" and the Advisory Committee's discussion of the accidentologist example indicate that the court should play some evaluative role in determining whether an expert may offer an opinion based on inadmissible evidence. At the same time, however, it seems clear from the italicized portion of the Advisory Committee's Note that the court's evaluative role should be more limited than the very restrictive interpretations of FRE 703 described above. We agree with those decisions holding that the court's role in interpreting and applying FRE 703's "reasonably relied upon" clause should be largely limited to determining whether experts in the field customarily rely or would rely on the information in question, without regard to whether the rules of evidence make the information admissible.

By urging this broad, permissive interpretation of the "reasonably relied upon" clause, we do not mean to suggest that judges are or should be entirely at the mercy of an expert. The proponent of the expert opinion must establish at a minimum that the facts and data relied upon by the expert are of the type customarily relied upon by other experts in the field. In addition, as

C. Expert Witnesses

we have just noted, the Advisory Committee apparently contemplated at least some minimal evaluative role for the court in assessing the reasonableness of the reliance. Finally, one should keep in mind that FRE 703 does not provide the only basis for excluding unreliable opinion testimony. FRE 702 requires that the subject matter be one that requires specialized knowledge to be understood, that the purported expert have that knowledge, and that the expert's opinion be of assistance to the fact finder. In addition, FRE 403 permits the exclusion of evidence whose probative value is substantially outweighed by various countervailing concerns of unreliability and inefficiency. Indeed, it may be that these other rules provide sounder bases than the "reasonably relied upon" language in FRE 703 for excluding the opinion in the Advisory Committee's accidentologist example. It would arguably be appropriate to exclude the accidentologist's opinion because the opinion is so inherently speculative that it is not very helpful (FRE 702), because the purported expert does not bring sufficient specialized knowledge to the subject to make the opinion helpful (FRE 702), or because the probative value of the opinion is so low that it does not warrant presenting to the jury hearsay evidence that the jury may misevaluate (FRE 403). Courts, however, should not rely upon FRE 702 and FRE 403 to exclude an opinion merely because the opinion is based on inadmissible evidence. Such a use of FRE 702 and FRE 403 would undermine the objective of FRE 703 just as much as an extremely restrictive interpretation of FRE 703's "reasonably relied upon" language.

Thus far our focus has been on the propriety of excluding opinions based on inadmissible evidence as a means of accommodating the tension between various exclusionary rules and the practice of disclosing the bases for an opinion. A second possible way of accommodating the tension is by limiting the disclosure. Consider, for example, the situation hypothesized in the Advisory Committee's Note to FRE 703 in which a doctor bases a diagnosis not only on some statements that may fall within the physical condition hearsay exception, but also on some inadmissible hearsay statements of nurses, other doctors, and relatives of the patient. If the court were concerned about the jury hearing the inadmissible hearsay, the court could instruct the expert to state only that the opinion is based in part on the statements of nurses, doctors, and relatives without revealing the content of those statements. The evidentiary basis for such a ruling would be FRE 403: The probative value of the specific hearsay statements in evaluating the expert's opinion is substantially outweighed (a) by the risk that the jury may overestimate the probative value of the uncross-examined hearsay and, (b) by the risk, if the hearsay is relevant to some issue other than evaluating the expert's opinion, that the jury will use the inadmissible hearsay for this other purpose. Such a ruling would prohibit the proponent of the opinion testimony from using the expert witness as a device to get before the jury otherwise inadmissible evidence.

Any ruling that limits the extent to which an expert may testify about the factual bases for an opinion should probably be limited to the direct examination. If the cross-examiner wishes to risk exposing the inadmissible hearsay in challenging the expert's opinion, there would appear to be no good reason to prevent the cross-examiner from doing so.[13]

We have noted previously that FRE 403, which requires that the probative value be *"substantially outweighed"* by the countervailing factors, is a rule that favors admissibility. Consistently with this general approach to FRE 403, we believe that the rule should be used only sparingly to limit experts from detailing the bases for their opinions. Although FRE 705 does not require, in the absence of a judicial order, that the facts and data underlying an opinion be presented to the jury, disclosure of the specific facts and data has been the norm both at common law and under the Federal Rules. Moreover, restricting evidence about the underlying facts and data necessarily deprives the jury of information that can be extremely useful in evaluating an expert's opinion. Admittedly, if the judge does restrict the expert's explanation, the jury will still be able to learn about the general *type* of facts and upon which the expert relied, and this information can be of some help in evaluating the strength of the expert's testimony. This general information, however, is a far cry from the specific facts and data.

The third and most common way to attempt to restrict the use of inadmissible evidence upon which an opinion is based is through a limiting instruction.[14] The typical limiting instruction, however, is nonsensical: The jury is told that it may not consider the inadmissible evidence for its truth but only as something to consider in assessing the expert's opinion. The problem with this instruction, of course, is that the only way in which the inadmissible hearsay is relevant to an evaluation of the expert's opinion is if the hearsay is considered for its truth.

It would not be nonsensical to tell jurors that they may not consider the content of hearsay statements but that they may consider the fact that hearsay statements were relied upon. If this is what a judge intends to convey to the jury, however, there is no need to admit the content of the statements in the first place. Instead, the judge should initially follow the previously suggested alternative of restricting the extent to which the expert is allowed to state the bases for the opinion.

There are two other types of limiting instructions about the underlying facts and data of an opinion that would not be logically nonsensical. First, it would be coherent to tell jurors that they may consider an otherwise

---

13. In some situations the cross-examiner may feel that as a matter of reasonable trial strategy, the only available option is to expose the inadmissible hearsay in the hope of undermining the expert. When this is the case, limiting the direct examiner has no practical utility. The court should either forgo limiting the disclosure on direct examination or exclude the opinion altogether on the ground that the probative value of the opinion is substantially outweighed by the possible misevaluation or misuse of the hearsay statements upon which the opinion is based.

14. See, e.g., Paddack v. Dave Christiansen, Inc., 745 F.2d 1254, 1262 (9th Cir. 1984); United States v. Madrid, 673 F.2d 1114, 1122 (10th Cir.), *cert. denied*, 459 U.S. 843 (1982).

C. Expert Witnesses

inadmissible hearsay statement for its truth in evaluating the opinion but that they may not consider the truth of the statement for any other purpose. Thus, for example, if the expert based an opinion in part on an eyewitness account of a third person and if the jury rejected the expert's opinion because of doubts about the expert's qualifications, the jury could not consider for its truth the hearsay recitation of the eyewitness account.

If one is content generally with the use of limiting instructions to regulate a jury's use of evidence, there is no compelling reason to avoid the type of instruction described in the preceding paragraph. We believe, however, that there are serious problems that inhere in all limiting instructions: The complexity and subtlety of most limiting instructions inevitably raise the question whether jurors are likely to understand and appreciate the instructions; even if jurors understand a limiting instruction, the instruction has the undesirable effect of increasing the complexity of the jurors' already complex task; and finally, it is at best questionable whether even conscientious, understanding jurors are capable of performing the mental gymnastics that a limiting instruction requires. We are aware of no precedent for the type of limiting instruction under consideration now, and since we have grave doubts about the efficacy of limiting instructions generally, we are loath to recommend new uses for them.

The remaining type of logically sound limiting instruction about the facts and data underlying an expert's opinion would be one that in effect instructs jurors that even though the expert relied on inadmissible evidence, they may not do so. For example:

> Ladies and gentlemen of the jury, you have heard Dr. Agnes Smith base an opinion about the plaintiff's condition in part on what various relatives and other doctors told her. You may not consider those out of court statements of the relatives and doctors for their truth. However, to the extent that witnesses other than Dr. Smith have testified in this courtroom about the information that the relatives and doctors relayed to Dr. Smith, you may, to the extent that you believe that information, take it into account in evaluating Dr. Smith's opinion. To the extent that Dr. Smith based her opinion on information that was relayed to her by the relatives and nurses and that has not been the subject of testimony by witnesses in this trial, you must disregard Dr. Smith's opinion.

In other words, the expert can give an opinion even though the expert has relied on inadmissible evidence, and the expert can testify about the specific facts and data relied upon. The jury, however, may not rely on the otherwise inadmissible evidence reported by the expert, and the jury can credit the expert's opinion only to the extent that there is admissible evidence tending to prove the facts and data upon which the expert relied.

The arguably attractive features of this type of limiting instruction are that (1) it permits the proponent of expert testimony to avoid the hypothetical question and (2), at the same time, it tells the *jury* to rely only on admissible evidence. Moreover, although the typical limiting instruction that courts give—"you may consider statements that the expert relied on not for their truth but only for the purpose of evaluating the expert opinion"—is at best ambiguous, it may be that this is the notion that courts are trying to convey. The only alternative, suggested earlier, is that the instruction is completely nonsensical.

There are three difficulties with telling jurors that they may rely only on admissible evidence in evaluating an expert opinion. First, such an instruction suffers from all of the previously mentioned problems that inhere in limiting instructions. In this regard, consider how an instruction might read when the doctor relied in part on admissible hearsay and in part on inadmissible hearsay. It would be necessary both to make the basic point made in the preceding hypothetical instruction and also to distinguish which of the hearsay statements the jury could rely upon.

Second, if one is serious about ensuring that juries rely only on admissible evidence in evaluating expert opinions, there will frequently be a better way to accomplish the objective. The judge can require a preliminary showing or at least an oral representation on the part of the proponent of expert testimony that the proponent is prepared to introduce evidence supporting the facts upon which the expert relied. If there were reason to believe that the proponent of the expert testimony may not be able to meet this requirement, the judge could invoke FRE 705 and require disclosure—in the form of admissible evidence—of the facts and data underlying an opinion before the opinion is given.

Third, instructing the jury to rely only on admissible evidence in evaluating an expert opinion appears to be inconsistent with the Advisory Committee's understanding of FRE 703, and there is nothing in the legislative history of FRE 703 to suggest a rejection of the Advisory Committee's understanding. In discussing the type of information upon which a doctor typically relies, the Advisory Committee pointed out that most of the data relied upon could be admitted into evidence "*but only with the expenditure of substantial time in producing and examining various authenticating witnesses.*" (Emphasis added.) This language suggests that the Advisory Committee considered it unnecessary for the proponent of expert testimony to present admissible evidence of all the underlying facts and data. Moreover, in the next sentence, the Advisory Committee commented that the doctor's "validation, *expertly performed and subject to cross-examination, ought to suffice for judicial purposes.*" (Emphasis added.) Here the Advisory Committee seems to be saying that these factors provide a basis for crediting fully otherwise inadmissible evidence. Finally, in introducing its consideration the accidentologist's testimony, the Advisory Committee stated, "*If it be feared that enlargement of permissible data may tend to break down the rules of exclusion unduly, notice should be taken that the rule requires that the facts or data 'be of a type reasonably relied upon by experts in the particular field.'*" (Emphasis added.) If the jury could not consider an expert's opinion unless there were independently admissible evidence to support it, there would be no reason to be concerned with the possibility of a "break down of the rules of exclusion." Moreover, if the Advisory Committee envisioned that the jury could credit an expert's opinion only to the extent that there was admissible evidence supporting the underlying facts and data, one could reasonably expect the Advisory Committee to have made that very point in explaining why there was no need to fear a "break down."

To summarize, there are three possible ways to prevent or limit jury consideration of inadmissible evidence upon which an expert bases an opinion. First, one could exclude the opinion and thereby obviate any reason for exploring the otherwise inadmissible underlying facts and data. Second, one could order the expert to avoid mentioning, at least on direct examination, some or all of the specific facts and details upon which the expert relied. Finally, one could permit the expert both to state the opinion and to relate the underlying facts and data and try to restrict the use of the otherwise admissible evidence with a limiting instruction. We have argued that the limiting instruction alternative, regardless of the form of the instruction, is always inappropriate. FRE 403, 702, and 703 provide grounds for effectuating both of the first two alternatives, and in some cases it will undoubtedly be appropriate to invoke these alternatives. The mere fact that the rules of evidence happen to make the facts and data upon which the expert relied inadmissible, however, should not be a reason for prohibiting an expert from expressing an opinion or explaining the underlying facts and data; and in applying the "reasonably relied upon" requirement in FRE 703 judges should give substantial deference to experts' testimony about what it is reasonable to rely upon. In short, FRE 703's reliance on an inadmissible evidence provision is an exception to potentially every evidentiary exclusionary rule, and it certainly should be regarded as an exception to the hearsay rule.

PROBLEMS

1. Ann Tyson has sued the Horner Equipment Company for injuries that she received in an accident involving her car and a Horner truck. As a result of the accident Ann was unable to work or do household chores for more than a year. The defendant concedes liability, and the only issues at trial relate to damages. After establishing that she is married, the mother of a teenage son, 45 years old, and working full-time, Ann offers the following testimony of an expert economist: The economist's opinion, based on a study entitled "The Dollar Value of Household Work" by Gauger and Walker, that a married woman between 40 and 54 who is employed outside the home and has a 16-year-old child provides about $8000 worth of services to the family during a year. The offer of proof includes no information about the details of the study or the authors' backgrounds, but the economist does

testify that the study was a highly recognized work among economists. Should the evidence be admitted over defendant's objection?

2. William Smith is being prosecuted for molesting his teenage daughter. The daughter first complained of the molestation to school authorities and said that it had been going on since she was five years old. The daughter has indicated that at the trial she will recant her earlier statements and deny that her father had molested her. According to her present story, she made the false charge because she was angry with her father for disciplining her and refusing to let her see her boyfriend. There is no physical evidence of abuse. The prosecution's case will rest in large part on the prior statements of the daughter, some of which had been tape recorded and some of which were related to her mother, various therapists, and friends. (The statements are admissible pursuant to an evidentiary rule permitting the use of prior inconsistent statements for their truth without regard to whether the statements were made under oath.) In addition, the prosecution wishes to introduce testimony from various psychologists and psychiatrists who are conceded to be experts in dealing with child molestation. Consider to what extent the following expert testimony should be admissible:

(a) testimony that the daughter appeared angry and that anger is a typical reaction of child molestation victims;

(b) testimony that it is common for child molestation victims to recant their stories at some point; that this occurs because the victims have the sense that they are responsible for holding the family together, and if the family falls apart, it is their fault; that the easiest way out of this situation is to recant;

(c) testimony that the witness had been asked to do an evaluation to determine whether the daughter had been sexually molested and that the witness' findings based on objective personality tests were consistent with the results one would get with an individual who had been molested;

(d) testimony that on the basis of various tests and interviews with the daughter, the witness is of the opinion that the daughter's statements about the molestation were truthful.

3. Wally Daniels is charged with murder and arson. The prosecution's theory is that Wally killed his wife and then, at about 7 P.M., set fire to the house in order to make the death look like an accident. Wally claims that he was not near the house at the relevant times and that the fire was the result of bad electrical wiring. The prosecutor's expert, a fire marshall, offers to testify that in his opinion the fire was the result of arson. The fire marshall is prepared to testify about the bases for his opinion which include, inter alia, the following:

C. Expert Witnesses

(a) interviews with next door neighbors, John and Wilma Smith, who say they saw Wally running from the house about 7 P.M. shortly before they noticed the fire;

(b) a written police report prepared by Officer June Adkins, stating that she was patrolling the area shortly before the fire was discovered and that she observed an adult male running from the defendant's house at about 7 P.M.; and

(c) the fact that Wally had twice previously been convicted of arson.

Wally has objected to all of this evidence. To support the objection, he offers to prove that John Smith is an alcoholic who almost daily is in an alcohol-induced stupor from 3 P.M. until midnight. What result?

4. Frank Edwards and two companions have been charged with conspiracy to pass and with passing counterfeit bills. During the week of July 23 a number of counterfeit $50 bills—all with the same serial number—were passed to various employees of the Fun Time Amusement Park. The park owners circulated the number to employees and asked them to look for additional bills. Edwards and two companions were arrested after a park employee identified Edwards as the individual that had given him a counterfeit bill. When the three men were arrested, one of Edwards' companions was carrying a bag that contained 95 of the counterfeit bills. Both companions' fingerprints were found on some of the bills. Edwards' fingerprints were not discovered on the bills, and he was not in possession of any of the counterfeit bills.

At Edwards' trial the government offers the testimony of a federal agent, Angela Draper, about the modus operandi of individuals who pass counterfeit bills. According to the offer, the agent has 18 years of experience investigating persons who pass counterfeit bills and has testified frequently about the techniques employed by such persons. She will testify that it is common for individuals conspiring to pass counterfeit bills to divide functions so that one person carries a bag containing large sums of counterfeit currency while another actually passes the money; that the conspirators frequently switch functions; and that it is common for the holder of counterfeit bills to possess genuine currency as well. Should this testimony be admitted over defendant's objection?

5. Pam Peters is suing David Dean for personal injuries she received when Dean's automobile ran into her motorcycle. Dean claims that the accident was the result of an unexpected, uncontrollable acceleration of his vehicle. Both parties plan to introduce expert witnesses whose qualifications are not in dispute. Dean's expert is prepared to testify that the cause of the accident was uncontrollable acceleration. This conclusion is based in part on tests that the defendant performed on an automobile of the same year and model as defendant's and in part on consumer complaint reports (many from owners of the same year and model automobile) made to the National Highway Traffic Safety Agency. Pam has filed a motion in limine seeking

a ruling barring any reference to the fact of complaints or the content of the complaints during the examination of Dean's expert or the cross-examination of her expert. She has further moved that any opinion based on these reports be excluded. To what extent should the court grant her motion?

D. OPINIONS ON AN ULTIMATE ISSUE

In the nineteenth and early twentieth century a number of courts adopted the rule that witnesses—lay as well as expert—could not offer opinions on an ultimate issue in a case. The typical rationale for this rule was that such an opinion would invade the province of the jury. As Wigmore[15] and others[16] have pointed out, however, it is not clear how or why an opinion on an ultimate issue "invades the province of the jury." Indeed, it is not entirely clear what constitutes an opinion on an ultimate issue. Consider a case in which the defendant is charged with possessing drugs with the intent to sell them. Presumably it would be an opinion on an ultimate issue for a narcotics officer to testify that in her opinion the amount of drugs possessed by the defendant indicated to her that the defendant intended to sell the drugs. But would it be an opinion on an ultimate issue for the officer (1) to testify that in her opinion the amount possessed was far in excess of what one would possess for personal use or (2) to offer her opinion about how much of the particular drug a typical user or addict is likely to consume in a given period of time? If not, the prohibition against opinions on an ultimate issue would appear to be more one of form than of substance.

The foregoing example illustrates both the benefit and one of the potential problems with opinions about matters that are, or are closely related to, ultimate issues in a law suit. Jurors unfamiliar with the use of drugs may not know what quantities of a particular drug individuals are likely to possess for personal use. Thus, the narcotics officer's testimony can be helpful— indeed, perhaps critical—to the jury's evaluation of the defendant's intent. On the other hand, the narcotics officer's testimony would be most helpful if the jury was assured of learning the bases for the officer's opinion, e.g., how much of the particular drug a person can be expected to use in a given period of time and the habits of drug users with respect to stockpiling. Yet, the prosecutor may fail to bring out all of the underlying data on direct examination, in which case defense counsel may be reluctant to explore the matter on cross-examination for fear of bolstering the officer's testimony.

If the subject matter of the opinion testimony is not critical to the

---

15. 7 J. Wigmore, Evidence in Trials at Common Law §1920, p.18 (Chadbourn rev. 1978).

16. E.g., McCormick's Handbook on the Law of Evidence §12, p.30 (3d ed., Cleary, 1984).

D. Opinions on an Ultimate Issue

resolution of the law suit, the failure to develop the underlying facts may not be a problem of major concern.[17] It is particularly important, however, that jurors have as much detailed factual information as possible on the ultimate issues in a lawsuit, for the resolution of those issues is their primary responsibility.

There are at least two other potential problems with opinions about ultimate issues. First, even if jurors have all of the underlying facts and data and are fully capable of resolving the ultimate issues, the mere fact that they hear witnesses express opinions on those issues may mislead them into believing that they should give some special deference to the opinions. Why else would the evidence be presented to them? Second, if an opinion on an ultimate issue embraces a legal concept or conclusion, there may be uncertainty about whether the expert is using that concept in the same manner in which the law uses it.

Adequate means exist for dealing with these potential problems without altogether prohibiting opinions on an ultimate issue. The judge has the discretion to exclude opinions that are not helpful (see, e.g., FRE 701, 702) or whose probative value is substantially outweighed by the possibility of confusing or misleading the jury (see, e.g., FRE 403). If there is a concern that the underlying facts and data may not be forthcoming, the judge can require that they be set forth prior to the opinion (see, e.g., FRE 705); and if there is concern that the expert's use of a particular term may differ from the legal definition of a term, the judge can deal with this possibility in the instructions to the jury.

During the last several decades a number of courts have rejected an absolute prohibition against opinions on ultimate issues. The 1972 edition of McCormick's hornbook reports that a majority of courts had rejected the rule with respect to opinions on ultimate factual issues.[18] The same section of text, however, in both that edition and the more recent 1984 edition,[19] observes that courts generally prohibit opinions on questions of law.

If by "questions of law" one means questions that are for the judge rather than the jury to decide, it is obviously appropriate that jurors not hear evidence on the issue in any form. The evidence from their perspective would be irrelevant. On the other hand, if the issue is one for the jury to decide, there would appear to be no sound reason to prohibit an opinion merely because one can characterize the issue as embodying "law" or a "legal concept." Indeed, to have a rule that prohibits opinions on jury issues that are characterized as questions of law—or, as some courts have said, "mixed

---

17. Indeed, as we noted in our discussion of character evidence, see pages 221-222 supra, the Advisory Committee's Note to FRE 405 indicates that the court should prohibit proponents of opinion evidence about a person's character from exploring the factual details that support the opinion.
18. McCormick's Handbook on the Law of Evidence §12, p.27 (2d ed., Cleary, 1972).
19. Id. at §12, p.28; id. at §12, p.31 (3d ed., Cleary, 1984).

questions of law and fact"[20]—and, at the same time, to permit opinions about ultimate issues of "fact" may lead to an abstract, meaningless debate about whether the issue is one of "fact" or "law."[21]

There may, of course, be times when an opinion embracing a legal concept would be confusing (e.g., if the witness were using the term differently from the manner in which the law used it) or not very helpful (e.g., if it were a substitute for the underlying facts and data). Courts, however, can deal adequately with these problems on a case-by-case basis, just as they can deal adequately on a case-by-case basis with opinions on ultimate issues of "fact." Regardless of how one characterizes the issue to which the opinion is directed, the critical question should be whether the opinion will be helpful to the jury.

FRE 704, as promulgated by the Supreme Court and initially adopted by Congress, followed the lead of those courts that had rejected the prohibition against opinions on an ultimate issue. FRE 704 provided that there was no such general prohibition for opinions on an "ultimate issue to be decided by the trier of fact." According to the Advisory Committee:

> The older cases often contained strictures against allowing witnesses to express opinions upon ultimate issues. . . . The rule was unduly restrictive, difficult of application, and generally served only to deprive the trier of fact of useful information. . . . Efforts to meet the felt needs of particular situations led to odd verbal circumlocutions which were said not to violate the rule. Thus a witness could express his estimate of the criminal responsibility of an accused in terms of sanity or insanity, but not in terms of ability to tell right from wrong or other more modern standard. [sic] And in cases of medical causation, witnesses were sometimes required to couch their opinions in cautious phrases of "might or could," rather than "did," though the result was to deprive many opinions of the positiveness to which they were entitled, accompanied by the hazard of a ruling of insufficiency to support a verdict. In other instances the rule was simply disregarded, and, as concessions to need, opinions were allowed upon such matters as intoxication, speed, handwriting, and value, although more precise coincidence with an ultimate issue would scarcely be possible.

In 1984, in the aftermath of John Hinckley's acquittal on insanity grounds of the attempt to assassinate President Reagan, there was substantial

---

20. See, e.g., Grismore v. Consolidated Products Co., 232 Iowa 328, 5 N.W.2d 646, 663 (1942) (opinions on ultimate questions of fact permissible, but opinions on questions of law or questions of mixed fact and law not permissible). Ironically, *Grismore* is the case that McCormick cites as beginning the trend toward abolishing the prohibition against opinions on ultimate issues. McCormick's Handbook on the Law of Evidence §12, p.30 n.7 (3d ed., Cleary, 1984).

21. See, e.g., State v. Ogg, 243 N.W.2d 620 (Iowa 1976) (in prosecution for possession of LSD with intent to distribute, prosecution witness testified that in his opinion the amount of drugs possessed by defendant far exceeded the amount one would possess for personal use; majority and dissent disagree on whether witness' testimony is impermissible opinion of law with majority labeling opinion as one of law).

D. Opinions on an Ultimate Issue

public debate about and criticism of the insanity defense. Congress enacted legislation that for the first time provided a federal statutory definition for insanity and that made insanity an affirmative defense that must be proved by the defendant. As part of that legislation, Congress amended FRE 704, which now reads as follows (with the amendment in italics):

> (a) Except as provided in subdivision (b), testimony in the form of an opinion or inference otherwise admissible is not objectionable because it embraces an ultimate issue to be decided by the trier of fact.
>
> *(b) No expert witness testifying with respect to the mental state or condition of a defendant in a criminal case may state an opinion or inference as to whether the defendant did or did not have the mental state or condition constituting an element of the crime charged or of a defense thereto. Such ultimate issues are matters for the trier of fact alone.*

According to the Report of the House Judiciary Committee (quoting an earlier Senate Judiciary Committee Report):

> The purpose of this amendment is to eliminate the confusing spectacle of competing expert witnesses testifying to directly contradictory conclusions as to the ultimate legal issue to be found by the trier of fact. Under this proposal, expert psychiatric testimony would be limited to presenting and explaining their diagnoses, such as whether the defendant had a severe mental disease or defect and what the characteristics of such a disease or defect, if any, may have been. . . .
>
> Moreover, the rationale for precluding ultimate opinion psychiatric testimony extends beyond the insanity defense to any ultimate mental state of the defendant that is relevant to the legal conclusion sought to be proven. The Committee has fashioned its Rule 704 provision to reach all such "ultimate" issues, e.g., premeditation in a homicide case, or lack of predisposition in entrapment.

In support of this view, the Committee quoted from the American Psychiatric Association's Statement on the Insanity Defense (1982):

> [I]t is clear that psychiatrists are experts in medicine, not the law. As such, it is clear that the psychiatrist's first obligation and expertise in the courtroom is to "do psychiatry," i.e., to present medical information and opinion about the defendant's mental state and motivation and to explain in detail the reason for his medical-psychiatric conclusions. When, however, "ultimate issue" questions are formulated by the law and put to the expert witness who must then say "yea" or "nay," then the expert witness is required to make a leap in logic. He no longer addresses himself to medical concepts but instead must infer or intuit what is in fact unspeakable, namely, the probable relationship between medical concepts and legal or moral constructs such as free will. These impermissible leaps in logic made by expert witnesses confuse the jury. [Footnotes omitted.] Juries thus find themselves listening to conclusory psychiatric testimony that defendants are either "sane" or "insane"

or that they do or do not meet the relevant legal test for insanity. This state of affairs does considerable injustice to psychiatry and, we believe, possibly to criminal defendants. In fact, in many criminal insanity trials both prosecution and defense psychiatrists do agree about the nature and even the extent of mental disorder exhibited by the defendant at the time of the act.

Psychiatrists, of course, must be permitted to testify fully about the defendant's diagnosis, mental state and motivation (in clinical and commonsense terms) at the time of the alleged act so as to permit the jury or judge to reach the ultimate conclusion about which they and only they are expert. Determining whether a criminal defendant was legally insane is a matter for legal fact finders, not for experts.

Do you think that jurors may sometimes have difficulty relating a psychiatrist's diagnosis to the legal standard for insanity without some expert assistance? If so, does the problem lie with the amendment to FRE 704 or with the legal definition of insanity or both?

Even if a witness cannot offer an opinion about a defendant's "sanity," "premeditation," "predisposition," or other mental state, is it likely that jurors will be unaware of what the witness feels about such an issue? If not, of what practical benefit is the amendment to FRE 704? Keeping in mind that FRE 403, 701, 702, and 705 are available to regulate opinion testimony about ultimate issues, do you believe that the amendment to FRE 704 improved the Federal Rules of Evidence?

PROBLEMS

1. Reconsider the narcotics possession hypothetical set forth at page 752, supra. To what extent and in what manner does the amendment to FRE 704 restrict the ability of the narcotics officer from offering helpful evidence about the defendant's intent?

2. Velma Bland is charged with bank robbery and claims duress. A prosecution psychiatrist, after being qualified as an expert, offers to testify that Velma acted voluntarily and was not under duress at the time of the robbery. The defendant objects on the ground that this is an impermissible opinion on an ultimate issue. What result?

3. Dr. Steven Jones has been charged with distributing controlled substances "in bad faith and not in the usual course of a professional practice and not in accordance with standard medical practice." The prosecution calls Dr. Shirley Evans, who offers to testify that on the basis of her review of what Dr. Jones did it is her opinion that his prescribing of drugs was not done in the usual course of professional practice or for a legitimate medical purpose. Should the defendant's objection to this testimony be sustained?

4. Edgar Graves has sued the Bi-State Railway Co. for injuries he sustained in a nighttime accident involving his automobile and one of the defendant's trains. The plaintiff's theory is that the crossing was not adequately

D. Opinions on an Ultimate Issue

marked and lighted. Because it is conceded that the defendant had complied with all applicable regulations relating to the crossing, the plaintiff must establish that the crossing was "extra hazardous." The plaintiff plans to introduce photographs of the crossing, evidence of other accidents that have occurred there, and the testimony of a civil engineer whose area of expertise is railroad crossings. The civil engineer has examined the crossing in question as well as numerous other crossings. Should the plaintiff be permitted to ask the civil engineer whether in his opinion the crossing is "extra hazardous"? What (else) can the plaintiff ask the civil engineer that would be helpful for the plaintiff's case?

5. Tim Brown has been charged with making false statements to a federally insured savings and loan institution (18 U.S.C. §1014) and with making false statements about a matter within the jurisdiction of a federal agency (18 U.S.C. §1001). Both statutes have been interpreted as requiring that the statements be material. The allegedly false statements in this prosecution were contained in income tax returns and financial statements that Brown submitted to a savings and loan company in conjunction with an application for a real estate loan. As part of his defense Brown offers the testimony of an independent consultant and certified financial examiner who is knowledgeable about savings and loan real estate practices. The witness offers to testify that in making the type of loan involved in this case a savings and loan company would look only to the value of the property securing the loan and not consider the income, net worth, or employment of the borrower. Should this evidence be admitted over the prosecutor's objection?

CHAPTER TWELVE
PRIVILEGES

All of the rules and principles that we have considered thus far have as their primary objective the facilitation of accurate fact finding in the context of the adversary system. Rules of privilege are different. They exclude evidence that may be extremely helpful in order to foster some objective unrelated to accurate fact finding.[1] For example, in all jurisdictions an individual may invoke the attorney-client privilege to exclude evidence of the individual's confidential communications to an attorney, even though the communications may contain an admission of past criminal conduct. Similarly, in many jurisdictions a spouse may invoke the marital communications privilege to prevent evidence of confidential communications between spouses,

---

1. There are constitutional exclusionary rules that inhibit accurate fact finding, for example, the fourth amendment exclusionary rule for evidence obtained as the result of an illegal search or seizure; the sixth amendment right to exclude statements obtained in violation of one's right to counsel; and the fifth amendment right not to be a witness against oneself, commonly referred to as the "privilege" against self-incrimination. These rules typically are considered in criminal procedure courses, and they will not be addressed here. Our focus will be on non-constitutional evidentiary privileges with common law or statutory origins.

There also are some constitutional limitations on privileges in criminal prosecutions. A criminal defendant has a due process right to confront and cross-examine witnesses and sixth amendment/due process rights to compulsory process and to confront and cross-examine adverse witnesses. Privileges that significantly impede these rights may be unconstitutional, at least as applied in particular cases. See Nixon v. United States, 418 U.S. 683 (1974) (claim of absolute executive privilege for presidential communications will not prevail over demonstrated need for particular evidence); Davis v. Alaska, 415 U.S. 308 (1974) (defendant's right to confront and cross-examine key prosecution witness includes right to bring out witness' juvenile record despite state statute making those records confidential); Washington v. Texas, 388 U.S. 14 (1967) (state statute prohibiting individuals charged with participating in same crime from testifying for each other violates right to compulsory process). Cf. Chambers v. Mississippi, 410 U.S. 284 (1973) (application of state's voucher rule and hearsay rule to prevent defendant from presenting critical exculpatory evidence violated due process). These matters too will not be considered further in this chapter.

even though the communications may be highly relevant to the resolution of some factual dispute.

The existence and the scope of privileges vary from jurisdiction to jurisdiction. The most prevalent privileges protect confidential communications. Common privileges of this type, in addition to the attorney-client privilege and the privilege for confidential communications between spouses, are the physician-patient privilege, the psychotherapist-patient privilege, and the privilege for confidential communications to ministers, priests, rabbis, and similar functionaries (traditionally referred to as the "priest-penitent" privilege).

Other privileges, which usually are not as broadly recognized, protect against the disclosure of specific types of information. For example, there are privileges for trade secrets and the identity of news reporters' sources. Commonly recognized privileges of this type protect diplomatic secrets and other sensitive government information, such as the identity of informants.

Finally, in a number of jurisdictions there is a privilege to prevent a witness spouse from testifying against a party spouse. This testimonial privilege, which typically applies only in criminal prosecutions, is distinct from and should not be confused with the marital confidential communications privilege. The testimonial privilege excludes testimony about any subject matter by one spouse against the other; the confidential communications privilege, as its name indicates, applies only to confidential communications between spouses and excludes evidence from any source of such communications.

The traditional justification for the rules of privilege is utilitarian and is based on an underlying, untested empirical assumption: The benefit derived from recognizing the privilege—e.g., open communications between an attorney and client or between spouses—outweighs the cost of forgoing relevant evidence. More recently, proponents of some privileges have offered justifications that do not depend upon an empirical assumption about how the existence of the privilege affects individual behavior. For example, the existence of a marital communication privilege may have little if any impact on the extent to which spouses engage in confidential communications; nonetheless, the privilege is arguably desirable because it provides some recognition of and protection for the privacy of intimate aspects of the marital relationship.[2]

A. *THE UNIQUE OPERATION OF PRIVILEGE RULES*

Regardless of the particular justification, rules of privilege operate differently from other rules of evidence in at least two and sometimes three respects.

---

2. In Chapter Four we noted that similar utilitarian and non-utilitarian justifications provide partial support for some of the relevance rules. See pages 274-275 supra.

A. The Unique Operation of Privilege Rules

First, since the objective of the privilege would be frustrated by forced disclosure of privileged information at any time, the rules of privilege apply to all stages of judicial proceedings. Other rules of evidence, however, are designed primarily to enhance the accuracy of fact finding, particularly in jury trials, and they therefore do not apply to various preliminary or relatively informal aspects of the adjudicatory process. For example, FRE 1101 provides that the rules of evidence, other than those relating to privileges, do not apply to FRE 104(a) preliminary fact determinations, grand jury proceedings, and other specified relatively informal proceedings.

Second, the person who can invoke a rule of privilege to exclude evidence will not necessarily be one of the litigants. Because the rules of evidence other than the rules of privilege are designed to enhance the fact-finding process, they exist for the benefit of and may be invoked only by the parties to the dispute. By contrast, rules of privilege exist for the benefit of the persons whose communications or actions are covered by a privilege. Only these intended beneficiaries of a privilege (or persons acting on their behalf), who need not be parties to the action, can claim or forgo a privilege. For example, a non-party eye-witness to the event that is the subject of litigation may have made a confidential communication about the event to the non-party's attorney. The out-of-court communication of some historical fact, of course, is hearsay, but the communication may fall within a hearsay exception. Assume, for example, that the declaration is an excited utterance, or that declarant is presently unavailable and the communication is a declaration against interest. The non-party declarant may invoke the privilege; and in the absence of the declarant, the declarant's attorney or the court may invoke the privilege *on behalf of* the declarant. If the declarant has expressed a desire not to claim the privilege, nobody can invoke the privilege.

The third way in which rules of privilege sometimes differ—and perhaps should always differ—from other evidentiary rules relates to the impact on appeal of an erroneous trial court decision regarding the admissibility of allegedly privileged information. If the trial judge erroneously excludes the evidence, the party who would have benefitted from the evidence will be able to raise the improper exclusion on appeal: As is true whenever a judge erroneously excludes relevant evidence, the exclusion deprives the fact finder of information that would have enhanced the likelihood of a factually accurate result. Consider, however, what the result should be when the trial judge erroneously overrules a claim of privilege. Appellate courts frequently entertain such appeals, particularly in situations in which the appellant is also the primary beneficiary of the privilege. Unfortunately, however, the courts' opinions do not analyze carefully what interests are being vindicated by permitting the appeals.[3]

---

3. Notable exceptions to this judicial propensity for lack of analysis occur in the context of judicial interpretations of the fourth amendment right against illegal searches and seizures and the fifth amendment right against self-incrimination. With respect to these constitutional issues the initial constitutional violation—e.g., an illegal search or seizure; obtaining a confes-

Assuming that there is no basis other than a claim of privilege for excluding a piece of evidence, a trial judge's erroneous admission of privileged information results in the jurors having before them more relevant, helpful information than they would otherwise have had. The only impact of such an error is to enhance the likelihood of a factually accurate result. Thus, even if the person entitled to invoke the privilege happens to be one of the litigants, the "injury" from the erroneous admission of the evidence does not adversely affect the person's legitimate interests *as a litigant*. Moreover, the injury caused by the wrongful denial of the privilege is complete at the time the privileged information is presented to the fact finder. Reversal on appeal cannot unring the bell. Unless there is reason to believe that the possibility of reversal on appeal is a desirable way to make litigants and trial judges more sensitive to and more prone to accept claims of privilege, the error should not be grounds for reversal. And if the erroneous denial of a privilege claim is recognized as a possible ground for reversal on appeal, it should make no difference whether the person entitled to claim the privilege happens to be one of the litigants.

B. THE HISTORICAL SOURCES AND CURRENT STATUS OF PRIVILEGE RULES

The earliest privileges that courts recognized were the attorney-client privilege and the marital testimonial privilege. The attorney-client privilege, which has Roman law roots, finds its first expressions in the common law in the sixteenth century. The privilege of a witness spouse not to testify against a party spouse also dates back to the sixteenth century. Although the marital testimonial privilege is frequently associated with the general common law rule of competency that prevented interested parties from testifying as witnesses, the origins of this privilege are obscure.

The privilege for confidential communications between spouses received wide recognition in the latter part of the nineteenth century, and it is frequently said to have common law origins. The privilege, however, received substantial support and recognition through legislative action both in this country and in England.

During the last half of the nineteenth century, courts became increasingly reluctant to expand existing privileges or to create new ones. Since that

---

sion in violation of the mandate of Miranda v. Arizona—is the equivalent of the wrongful admission of privileged information, and the admission of the unconstitutionally obtained evidence is the equivalent of entertaining an appeal on the ground that privileged information was wrongfully admitted. The Supreme Court has made it clear that only those individuals who were directly injured by the fourth or fifth amendment violation may benefit from the rule excluding the unconstitutionally obtained evidence. Moreover, in the fourth amendment context, both the caselaw and the scholarly literature discuss at length the relationship between the initial violation (illegal search or seizure) and the remedy (exclusion).

B. The Historical Sources and Current Status of Privilege Rules

time the fashioning of privileges has been primarily—but not exclusively—a legislative function. For example, both the physician-patient and the priest-penitent privileges are creatures of the legislature, not the common law. The legislative adoption of both of these privileges, however, has been pervasive; and the Supreme Court has suggested recently in dictum that it would give them common law recognition.[4]

The Federal Rules of Evidence as promulgated by the Supreme Court set forth nine distinct privileges. These privileges covered required reports, attorney-client confidential communications, psychotherapist-patient confidential communications, prevention of spousal testimony, clergy-communicant confidential communications, political vote, trade secrets, state secrets and other official information, and the identity of an informer.[5] Noticeably absent were the physician-patient and the marital confidential communication privileges. Proposed Rule 501 made it clear that, in the absence of a constitutional mandate, courts were not at liberty to alter the list:

> Except as otherwise required by the Constitution of the United States or provided by Act of Congress, and except as provided in these rules or in other rules adopted by the Supreme Court, no person has a privilege to:
> (1) Refuse to be a witness; or
> (2) Refuse to disclose any matter; or
> (3) Refuse to produce any object or writing; or
> (4) Prevent another from being a witness or disclosing any matter or producing any object or writing.

When the Proposed Rules were submitted to Congress, the rules of privilege created substantial controversy. There were disagreements about the scope of some of the proposed privileges, about whether the proposed list of privileges was sufficiently inclusive, and about the extent to which state or federal rules of privilege should be applicable in diversity actions. The culmination of this controversy was a congressional decision not to enact the Proposed Rules relating to privilege. In their place Congress enacted only one rule relating to privileges, FRE 501:

> Except as otherwise required by the Constitution of the United States or provided by Act of Congress or in rules prescribed by the Supreme Court pursuant to statutory authority, the privilege of a witness, person, government, State, or political subdivision thereof shall be governed by the principles of the common law as they may be interpreted by the courts of the United States in the light of reason and experience. However, in civil actions and proceedings, with respect to an element of a claim or defense as to which state law supplies the rule of decision, the privilege of a witness, person, government, State, or political subdivision thereof shall be determined in accordance with State law.

---

4. Trammel v. United States, 445 U.S. 40, 51 (1980).
5. See Proposed FRE 502-510.

At the same time, Congress abolished the Supreme Court's rule-making power with respect to rules of privilege.[6]

The objective of the second sentence in FRE 501 is to let state policy with respect to privileges govern in those situations in which a federal court is applying state substantive law. For the most part, this means that state rules of privilege apply in diversity cases. Difficulties, however, sometimes arise in determining whether or what state privilege law to apply. Consider a situation in which there is both a federal claim and a state claim over which a federal court has concurrent or pendant jurisdiction. If the same evidence is relevant to both claims and is protected by a state privilege but not a federal privilege, should the evidence be admissible?[7] Consider also a situation in which the issue is which state privilege rule to apply in litigation involving contacts with several states. Should the court use the pre-FRE approach of federal courts,[8] which was to apply the choice-of-law rule of the forum state to determine what state privilege rules to apply? Or should the court view FRE 501 as a federal choice-of-law rule that permits the court to decide which state's privilege rules will apply?[9]

In the situations in which federal law governs the applicability of privileges, FRE 501's reference to "principles of the common law . . . interpreted . . . in light of reason and experience" gives courts discretion both to modify common law privileges and to create new ones:

> In rejecting the proposed Rules and enacting Rule 501, Congress manifested an affirmative intention not to freeze the law of privilege. Its purpose rather was to "provide the courts with the flexibility to develop rules of privilege on a case-by-case basis" and to leave the door open to change. [Trammel v. United States, 445 U.S. 40, 47 (1980) (quoting Statement by Representative Hungate, 120 Cong. Rec. 40891 (1974).]

Pursuant to this mandate the Supreme Court, as we shall see shortly, has substantially narrowed the scope of one common law privilege,[10] and other courts have created new privileges.[11]

---

6. See 28 U.S.C. §2076 (1976) (any amendment to Federal Rules of Evidence "creating, abolishing or modifying a privilege shall have no force or effect unless it shall be approved by act of Congress").

7. See William T. Thompson Co. v. General Nutrition Corp., Inc., 671 F.2d 100 (3d Cir. 1982) (refusing to apply state accountant-client privilege in situation involving federal and pendant state claims).

8. See, e.g., Hare v. Family Publications Service, Inc., 342 F. Supp. 678 (D. Md. 1972), 334 F. Supp. 953 (D. Md. 1971).

9. Most courts continue to follow the pre-FRE approach, see, e.g., Samuelson v. Susen, 576 F.2d 546 (3d Cir. 1978); but some commentators have advocated the alternative approach, see, e.g., Berger, Privileges, Presumptions, and Competency of Witnesses in the Federal Court: A Federal Choice of Law Rule, 42 Brooklyn L. Rev. 417 (1976).

10. See Trammel v. United States, page 799 infra.

11. See, e.g., In re Grand Jury Subpoena Dated January 4, 1984, 750 F.2d 223 (3d Cir. 1984) (acknowledging propriety of limited scholar's privilege); In re Zuniga, 714 F.2d 632 (6th Cir.), *cert. denied*, 464 U.S. 983 (1983) (acknowledging but not applying psychotherapist-patient privilege); People v. Doe, 61 A.D.2d 426, 403 N.Y.S.2d 375 (1978) (recognizing limited parent-child privilege).

B. The Historical Sources and Current Status of Privilege Rules

One resource for determining whether to recognize or how to apply a federal privilege is the Proposed Rules of privilege that were not adopted.[12] As Judge Weinstein has observed:

> [Congress eliminated the proposed rules of privilege] primarily because they were considered substantive in nature and not a fit subject for rule making.[13]
>
> The specific rules on privilege promulgated by the Supreme Court are reflective of "reason and experience." They are the culmination of three drafts prepared by an Advisory Committee consisting of judges, practicing lawyers and academicians. In its many years of work, the Committee considered hundreds of suggestions received in response to the circulation of the drafts throughout the legal community. Finally, they were adopted by the Supreme Court. . . .
>
> As its commentary indicates, the Advisory Committee in drafting the privilege rules was for the most part restating the law applied in the federal courts. These rules or standards, therefore, are a convenient comprehensive guide to the federal law of privileges as it now stands, subject of course to a considerable flexibility of construction. [United States v. Mackey, 405 F. Supp. 854, 857 (E.D.N.Y. 1975).]

Both the sources for and the content of state privilege rules vary considerably. Although well over half of the states have adopted rules of evidence based on the Federal Rules, the fact that Congress eliminated the specific privilege provisions in the Federal Rules has contributed to less uniformity among the states in this area of evidence law. Approximately one-third of the states that have promulgated rules of evidence since the adoption of the Federal Rules have followed the lead of the Federal Rules and omitted specific privilege provisions. In these states the pre-existing statutory and common law rules of privilege govern. Most of the remaining states have tended to use as models the Proposed Federal Rules relating to privilege or the privilege provisions in the Revised Uniform Rules of Evidence (1974). The Revised Uniform Rules are themselves based on the Proposed Federal Rules, but the Revised Uniform Rules differ from the Proposed Federal Rules in some important respects.[14] States using either model have not been reluctant to deviate from it.[15]

---

12. The Proposed Rules and the Advisory Committee's Notes are included in the rules Supplement that accompanies this text.

13. There was also substantial disagreement about the content of the proposed rules. See generally Krattenmaker, Interpersonal Testimonial Privileges Under the Federal Rules of Evidence: A Suggested Approach, 64 Geo. L.J. 613, 635-645 (1976).—Eds.

14. See generally 2 J. Weinstein and V. Berger, Evidence ¶502[01]-510[08], pp. 502-1 to 510-70 (1988).

15. See generally 1 G. Joseph and S. Saltzburg, Evidence in America: The Federal Rules in the States ch. 23-34 (1987).

C. CONFIDENTIAL COMMUNICATION PRIVILEGES GENERALLY

Here we provide an overview of the confidential communication privileges, which are all similar in their structure and operation. At the same time, we raise questions about the scope and coverage of some of the confidential communication privileges.

1. Persons and Relationships Covered by a Privilege

Initially, there is the matter of definition: Precisely what types of individuals or relationships does the privilege cover? For example, what are the qualifications for an "attorney," or "psychotherapist," and what does it take to be a "client" or a "patient"?

With respect to confidential communication privileges for professional relationships, there typically is no problem defining the client,[16] who is the individual seeking the services offered by the professional. Defining the professional, however, can present difficulties. For example, a decision to limit the category "psychotherapist" to physicians or psychiatrists would have the effect of discriminating against female professionals and relatively poor clients. Including licensed social workers and psychologists within the definition of "psychotherapist" would go far toward eliminating any sexual bias in the privilege, but to what extent would it eliminate the wealth discrimination? How available are social services to poor people? To what extent do the needy or other individuals tend to rely on non-licensed counselors or perhaps men and women of the clergy for psychotherapy? To what extent is it appropriate to include or exclude these types of relationships from the privilege?

In order to protect the reasonable expectations of an individual who consults a professional, it is common to define the professional not only as an individual meeting the specified qualifications but also as a person reasonably believed by the client or patient to have the qualifications. The Proposed Federal Rules and the Revised Uniform Rules include such provisions in the attorney-client privilege and the privilege for communications to clergy. The psychotherapist-patient privilege in Proposed FRE 504 includes within the definition of psychotherapist "a person authorized to practice medicine" and "a person licensed or certified as a psychologist." The "reasonably believed by the patient" clause, however, applies only to individuals reasonably believed to be licensed physicians and not to individuals reasonably believed to be licensed psychologists. According to the Advisory Committee's Note to Proposed FRE 504:

---

16. But see Upjohn Co. v. United States, page 781 infra.

C. Confidential Communication Privileges Generally

The requirement that the psychologist be in fact licensed, and not merely be believed to be so, is believed to be justified by the number of persons, other than psychiatrists, purporting to render psychotherapeutic aid and the variety of their theories.

Do you agree?

The privilege for confidential communications between husband and wife typically does not include a "reasonably believed to be a spouse" provision. Should the privilege be broadened in this manner? Should the privilege extend to individuals—both heterosexual and homosexual—who live and function in long-term intimate relationships that are similar to the traditional husband-wife relationship?

The attorney-client privilege applies not only to communications between the attorney and the client but also to communications between the client and a representative of the attorney, i.e., a person such as an expert witness who is "employed to assist the lawyer in the rendition of professional services." Proposed FRE 503(a)(3). Consider whether it would be appropriate to include such a provision in other confidential communication privileges.

2. Communications—And More?

For the privileges covering professional relationships, communications falling within the privilege typically must be made in the course or for the purpose of obtaining services that the professional offers. For example, Proposed FRE 504 limits the psychotherapist-patient privilege to confidential communications "made [by the patient] for the purpose of diagnosis or treatment of his mental or emotional condition, including drug addiction." California's psychotherapist-patient privilege is unusual in that it extends the privilege to communications made "for the purpose of scientific research on mental or emotional problems." Cal. Evid. Code §1011. Do you think the California provision is wise?

The confidential communication privileges do not protect the substance of information conveyed in confidential communications but only the communications themselves. Thus, although clients, patients, and spouses can refuse to answer questions about what they said during a privileged confidential communication, they cannot claim the privilege to refuse to answer questions about an event that was the subject of a confidential communication. Similarly, if clients, patients, or spouses make a confidential communication in writing, they may insist that the writing that is the communication remain confidential. They may not, however, shield an otherwise discoverable writing from disclosure merely by referring to it or enclosing it in a confidential communication.

On occasion individuals have argued—primarily in the context of the attorney-client privilege—that the privilege should extend beyond communications to information about the relationship, such as the identity of the client or the dates on which the client consulted an attorney. The prevailing view is that the attorney-client privilege does not extend beyond confidential communications. Some courts, however, have acknowledged that there may be limited situations in which the privilege can be invoked to prevent disclosure of facts relating to the attorney-client relationship. For example, in In re Kaplan,[17] an attorney, at the client's request, informed the authorities about a client's report of public corruption but refused to identify the client; and in Baird v. Koerner,[18] an attorney made payment to the IRS of back taxes for a client but refused to reveal the name of the client. In both cases the courts upheld the refusal to disclose the identity of the client.

Should the attorney-client privilege give the client the right to remain anonymous in the preceding or in other situations? According to McCormick:

> One who reviews the cases in this area will be struck by the prevailing flavor of chicanery and sharp practice pervading most of the attempts to suppress proof of professional employment, and general application of a rule of disclosure seems the approach most consonant with the preservation of the repute of the lawyer's high calling. At the same time, much should depend upon the client's objective in seeking preservation of anonymity, and cases will arise in which protection of the client's identity is both proper and in the public interest. [McCormick's Handbook on the Law of Evidence §90, pp.216-217 (3d ed., Cleary, 1984).]

McCormick cites *Kaplan* as an example of a case where protecting the client's identity is proper, and it is clear from the context of the quotation that McCormick disapproves of protecting the client's identity in *Baird*. Do you agree with McCormick's general assessment or the specific conclusions about *Kaplan* and *Baird*?

A similar issue about whether the privilege is limited to communications sometimes arises with respect to the spousal confidential communication privilege. The prevailing federal view is that the privilege applies only to words and deeds that are intended as communications. There is substantial state court authority, however, for applying this privilege to preclude testimony about apparently non-communicative acts in which one spouse engages in the presence of the other. For example, in People v. Daghita,[19] the court held that it was a violation of the confidential communication privilege to admit a wife's testimony that her husband hid proceeds of a theft under the bed. Can one justify *Daghita's* application of the marital communication

---

17. 8 N.Y.2d 214, 203 N.Y.S.2d 836, 168 N.E.2d 660 (1969).
18. 279 F.2d 623 (9th Cir. 1960).
19. 299 N.Y. 194, 86 N.E.2d 172 (1949).

C. Confidential Communication Privileges Generally

privilege to seemingly non-communicative acts on the ground that the husband's activity inevitably involved some communicative aspect that led the wife to understand that he was dealing with the proceeds of a theft?

If not, *Daghita* and similar cases are not really about the marital confidential communications privilege. Rather, these cases in effect are limited, seemingly ad hoc applications of the privilege of a witness spouse not to testify against a party spouse.

3. Confidentiality

As their names indicate, the confidential communications privileges apply only to communications that are *confidential*. Whether a communication is confidential depends on the intent of the communicator. In the absence of an explicit assertion, one must infer the intent from the circumstances in which the communication is made.

The presence of third persons who are not necessary to accomplish the object for which the communication is made is an almost certain indication that the requisite intent of confidentiality is lacking. If a child is old enough to comprehend what is being said, spousal statements made in the presence of the child—e.g., at the dinner table or on a drive in the family automobile—will probably not be privileged. Similarly, the presence of a client's friend or confidant at an attorney-client meeting will make the attorney-client privilege inoperative if the friend or confidant has no legal interest in the matters being discussed.

There are two types of situations in which the presence of more than two individuals is perfectly consistent with an intent to maintain confidentiality. First, there may be times when individuals are jointly seeking the assistance of a professional. For example, several individuals may consult an attorney for a legal problem that they have in common, or several individuals may be participating with a psychotherapist in group therapy sessions. Second, there may be present third persons who are necessary for the proper functioning of the privileged relationship. Thus, in a meeting with an attorney, it may be necessary for an interpreter to be present, or the attorney may introduce a secretary to take notes about or to transcribe the interview.

Occasionally conversations that the participants later claim were intended to be confidential will have been overheard by some third person. There is substantial authority in the older cases for the proposition that the third person who overheard a conversation can relate the contents of the conversation, even if that person was an eavesdropper about whom the participants in the conversation could not reasonably have known. The modern trend is to reject this precedent and allow the claim of privilege to prevent testimony by the eavesdropper as long as the setting of the conversation suggests that the speakers intended the conversation to be confidential. If the conversation took place in a setting where it was likely to be overheard, this fact would tend to negate the claim that the participants intended the conversation to be confidential in the first place.

4. Holder of the Privilege

A critically important concept in dealing with the rules of privilege is that of "holder" of a privilege. The holder is the person to whom the privilege belongs. The holder may claim the privilege, and the holder is the only person who may waive it.

Modern privilege rules frequently distinguish between holders of the privilege and individuals who may claim the privilege. For example, Proposed FRE 504 (psychotherapist-patient privilege) provides:

> **(b) General rule of privilege.**—A patient has a privilege to refuse to disclose and to prevent any other person from disclosing confidential communications made for the purposes of diagnosis or treatment of his mental or emotional condition. . . .
>
> **(c) Who may claim the privilege.**—The privilege may be claimed by the patient, by his guardian or conservator, or by the personal representative of a deceased patient. The person who was the psychotherapist may claim the privilege but only on behalf of the patient. . . .

No person, however, can claim the privilege once the holder has waived it; and as is true with Proposed FRE 504, the individuals other than the holder who can claim an unwaived privilege on their own behalf are representatives of the holder and, therefore, in effect acting on behalf of the holder or the holder's estate. To summarize, only the holder may waive a privilege, and only the holder—or some person acting on behalf of the holder or the holder's estate—is entitled to claim the privilege.

Early in its common law development, courts regarded the attorney-client privilege as belonging to the lawyer, on the theory that it would be unprofessional for the lawyer to have to reveal confidential communications from the client. In other words, the lawyer was the holder of the privilege. Today, jurisdictions uniformly recognize that the attorney-client privilege exists for the benefit of the client, who is now understood to be the holder of the privilege. If the client affirmatively waives the privilege, or if neither the client nor some person acting on behalf of the client invokes the privilege, the attorney cannot refuse to reveal the confidential communications.

The other privileges for confidential communications between a professional and a client or patient usually make the client or patient the holder of the privilege. For example, despite whatever ethical or moral obligation to silence a doctor may assert, the doctor is not a holder of the physician-

C. Confidential Communication Privileges Generally

patient privilege. If the holder has not specifically waived the privilege, the doctor may be able to claim the privilege on behalf of the holder. Unless the holder (or somebody acting for the holder) claims the privilege, however, a court can compel—with threat of a contempt sanction—the doctor's testimony about a confidential communication.

With respect to the priest-penitent privilege, some jurisdictions give the privilege to the individual making the communication and others give the privilege to the priest, clergy member, or similar functionary. Who should be the holder of this privilege?

Jurisdictions also differ on the question of the holder of the marital confidential communications privilege. Some jurisdictions make both spouses holders of the privilege; some make each spouse the holder for his or her own statements; and others, assuming that one spouse is likely to be a witness and the other a party, make either the witness spouse or the party spouse the holder of the privilege.[20] Who should be the holder(s) of this privilege?

5. Waiver

There are three ways in which the holder of a privilege may waive the privilege. First, the holder may indicate through words or conduct a desire to forgo the privilege. Second, if the holder forgoes an opportunity to claim the privilege, the failure to assert the privilege will be regarded as a waiver. Finally, the voluntary disclosure of the confidential communication will constitute a waiver, except that voluntary disclosure of a confidential communication in the context of another privileged confidential communication will not be a waiver. See, e.g., Proposed FRE 511:

> A person upon whom these rules confer a privilege against disclosure of the confidential matter or communication waives the privilege if he or his predecessor while holder of the privilege voluntarily discloses or consents to disclosure of any significant part of the matter or communication. This rule does not apply if the disclosure is itself a privileged communication.

With respect to waiver by disclosure, it is important to note that the voluntary disclosure must be a disclosure of *the confidential communication itself.* Just as a court without violating the privilege can compel an individual to testify about a subject that happened to have been related in a confidential communication, a voluntary statement—either as a witness or in a casual conversation—about the same subject matter that happened to have been related in confidential communication is not a waiver of the privilege. Voluntary statements about the subject matter to third persons, however, may

---

20. This focus on witness and party may be a result of confusing the marital communications privilege with the marital testimonial privilege. See page 799 infra.

be a circumstantial indication that there was no intent for the communication in question to be confidential in the first place.

In some situations privileged information may be disclosed without any waiver from the holder of the privilege. A court may erroneously reject a holder's claim of privilege and compel, under the threat of a contempt penalty, the holder to testify about the confidential communication; or the communication may be related by some third person during a proceeding in which the holder is not present and able to claim the privilege. Similarly, if both spouses are holders of the marital communications privilege or if several individuals consult a lawyer jointly or participate in group therapy, one holder but not the other(s) may have waived the privilege. Can a nonwaiving holder subsequently claim the privilege?

In each of the foregoing situations the confidence has been breached through no fault of and perhaps against the will of the holder—or at least one of the holders—of the privilege. The fact that the information is no longer confidential suggests that permitting the holder to invoke the privilege may do little to promote the objective of the privilege. On the other hand, an added disclosure may compound the injury; and when the reason for the disclosure is an erroneous denial of the privilege by the trial judge, it is arguable, as we suggested earlier, that permitting invocation of the privilege may be an appropriate means of making judges more sensitive to privileges.

The caselaw dealing with these types of problems is relatively sparse,[21] and the decisions are not consistent.[22] Codifications tend to deal with some, but not necessarily all, of these problems. For example, Proposed FRE 512 provides:

> Evidence of a statement or other disclosure of privileged information is not admissible against the holder of the privilege if the disclosure was (a) compelled erroneously or (b) made without opportunity to claim the privilege.

The Proposed Federal Rules do not deal with the problem of disclosure by one of two or more co-holders of the privilege. In discussing the attorney-client privilege, Wigmore suggests that the following principles should govern waiver determinations in situations involving co-holders:

> Where the consultation was had by *several clients jointly*, the waiver should be joint for joint statements, and neither could waive for the disclosure of the other's statements; yet neither should be able to obstruct the other in the disclosure of the latter's own statements. [8 J. Wigmore, Evidence in Trials

---

21. See, e.g., 8 J. Wigmore, Evidence in Trials at Common Law §2328, p.639 n.3 (McNaughton rev. 1961) (noting that there are few rulings on the effect of waiver by one of several joint clients of a single attorney).

22. See, e.g., McCormick's Handbook on the Law of Evidence §82, p.196 n.6 (3d ed., Cleary, 1984) (citing conflicting cases involving waiver of marital communication privilege by one spouse).

C. Confidential Communication Privileges Generally

at Common Law §2328, p. 639 (McNaughton rev. 1961) (emphasis in original).]

6. The Effect of the Unavailability of the Holder

If the holder of a privilege is not present to claim the privilege, the holder's conservator or guardian may claim the privilege, and in the case of privileges covering conversations between a patient or client and a professional, the professional may claim the privilege on behalf of the patient or client. See, e.g., Proposed FRE 504 at page 770 supra. In addition, there is precedent permitting the trial judge to invoke a privilege on behalf of an absent holder.[23] Judge Weinstein and Professor Berger have suggested that this is an inherent judicial power that is not abrogated by the failure of a rule specifically to mention the authority of the judge to act on the holder's behalf.[24]

The confidential communication privileges survive the death of the holders. The personal representative of the deceased holder, however, may choose not to invoke the privilege; and there is a commonly recognized exception to the attorney-client privilege for communications "relevant to an issue between parties who claim through the same deceased client." Proposed FRE 503(d)(2). See also Proposed FRE 504(d)(3) (exception to the proposed psychotherapist-patient privilege, discussed in the next section).

7. Exceptions

There are specified exceptions to most privileges. In addition to the exception noted in the preceding paragraph, the attorney-client privilege is typically inapplicable to communications made for the purpose of furthering a crime or fraud, to communications relevant to an alleged breach of duty by the lawyer to the client or the client to the lawyer, to communications relevant to an issue involving a document attested to by the lawyer, and to communications relevant to an issue in an action between clients who were joint holders of the privilege. See Proposed FRE 503(d).

The three most common exceptions to the psychotherapist-patient privilege are those set forth in Proposed FRE 504(d):

> (1) Proceedings for hospitalization. There is no privilege under this rule for communications relevant to an issue in proceedings to hospitalize the patient for mental illness, if the psychotherapist in the course of diagnosis or treatment has determined that the patient is in need of hospitalization.
>
> (2) Examination by order of judge. If the judge orders an examination of the mental or emotional condition of the patient, communications made in

---
23. See, e.g., Coles v. Harsch, 129 Or. 11, 276 P.2d 248, 255 (1929).
24. 2 J. Weinstein and V. Berger, Evidence ¶503(c)[1], p.503-67 (1988).

the course thereof are not privileged under this rule with respect to the particular purpose for which the examination is ordered unless the judge orders otherwise.

(3) Condition an element of claim or defense. There is no privilege under this rule as to communications relevant to an issue of the mental or emotional condition of the patient in any proceeding in which he relies upon the condition as an element of his claim or defense, or, after the patient's death, in any proceeding in which any party relies upon the condition as an element of his claim or defense.

As Judge Weinstein and Professor Berger have observed, the last part of the third exception largely nullifies the opportunity for the deceased patient's personal representative to claim the privilege.[25] Some jurisdictions narrow somewhat the third exception by limiting the last part of the exception to situations in which the party is claiming through or as a beneficiary of the deceased patient.[26]

The physician-patient privilege typically contains exceptions similar to those in Proposed FRE 504 plus others that vary widely from jurisdiction to jurisdiction. Frequently there is an exception for all criminal prosecutions. The Advisory Committee's Note to Proposed FRE 504 observed:

> While many states have by statute created the [physician-patient] privilege, the exceptions which have been found necessary in order to obtain information required by the public interest or to avoid fraud are so numerous as to leave little if any basis for the privilege.

As a result the Proposed Federal Rules did not include a physician-patient privilege.

The spousal communication privilege—like the spousal testimonial privilege—typically does not apply to civil and criminal proceedings involving injury to the person or property of the other spouse or to a child of either spouse. There usually are no stated exceptions to the privilege for confidential communications to members of the clergy.

8. Drawing an Adverse Inference From Invoking a Privilege

In Griffin v. California,[27] the Supreme Court held that it is a violation of a criminal defendant's fifth amendment right against self-incrimination for there to be comment on the defendant's election not to testify. According to the Court, permitting such comment would "cut[] down on the privilege by making its assertion costly."[28] Proposed FRE 513 applies the *Griffin* principle to privileges generally:

25. Id. at ¶504[07], p.504-31.
26. See, e.g., Cal. Evid. Code §1016.
27. 380 U.S. 609 (1965).
28. Id. at 614.

C. Confidential Communication Privileges Generally

(a) Comment or inference not permitted. The claim of a privilege, whether in the present proceeding or upon a prior occasion, is not a proper subject of comment by judge or counsel. No inference may be drawn therefrom.

(b) Claiming privilege without knowledge of jury. In jury cases, proceedings shall be conducted, to the extent practicable, so as to facilitate the making of claims of privilege without knowledge of the jury.

(c) Jury instruction. Upon request, any party against whom the jury might draw an adverse inference from a claim of privilege is entitled to an instruction that no inference may be drawn therefrom.

There would appear to be no general *constitutional* barrier to comments about the invocation of a confidential communication privilege, and the caselaw is divided[29] as to the propriety of comment about invoking privileges outside the *Griffin* context.[30] Decisions permitting comment frequently draw an analogy to the long-established practice of permitting comments on and adverse inferences from the destruction of evidence or the failure to produce available witnesses or documents. Decisions not permitting the practice echo *Griffin's* concern that comment or adverse inferences undermine the privilege.

If the person claiming a privilege is not a party and not closely associated with either of the parties, it would seem inappropriate to commend any adverse inference to the fact finder. With no reason to believe that the witness has an interest or bias in the matter being litigated, there is no basis for drawing an inference that the witness' testimony would be unfavorable to either party.

On the other hand, it seems unlikely that a party would invoke a confidential communication privilege to shield information that would be helpful in winning the lawsuit. A criminal defendant, however, may invoke the fifth amendment right not to testify for fear of making a bad impression on the jury or being prejudiced by impeachment with prior convictions. Is this difference sufficient to justify drawing an adverse inference from a party's claim of a confidential communication privilege? How strong is the possibility that the party claiming the confidential communication privilege is doing so not because the information is harmful, but because the information is neutral and the party desires to keep it private?

Can hypotheses about the reasonableness of inferences that one might draw from invoking a privilege provide a basis for distinguishing between a criminal defendant's fifth amendment right not to testify and some or all confidential communication privileges? Or if one is to make such a distinction, must it be in terms of the importance of the interests protected by the privilege in the first instance?

---

29. See 2 J. Weinstein and V. Berger, Evidence ¶513[02], pp. 524-529 (Supp. 1988).

30. *Griffin* itself applies only to comments about a criminal defendant's invocation of the privilege in a criminal prosecution. See Baxter v. Palmigiano, 425 U.S. 308 (1976); Brink's, Inc. v. City of New York, 717 F.2d 700 (2d Cir. 1983).

9. Unprivileged Confidential Communications

Consider the individuals to whom you entrust your most private thoughts. For many of you, we suspect, the people who come to mind are a sibling, another law student, a close family friend, a parent or child, or perhaps even an administrator or teacher. Except for a few jurisdictions that recognize a limited parent-child privilege, there is no privilege to protect these confidential relationships. Should we have additional privileges? Or does the fact that there is no privilege for so much of what we treat as confidential, coupled with the fact that there are exceptions for most privileges, suggest that we really do not need confidential communication privileges?

PROBLEMS

If a privilege that is or could be asserted in any of the Problems in this Chapter is included within the Proposed Federal Rules on privilege, assume that the content of the privilege is identical to that of the proposed rule.

1. Sam Evans is being prosecuted for sexually assaulting his twelve-year-old stepdaughter. Shortly after the incident that is the subject of the prosecution Sam and his wife began seeing their minister for marriage counseling. Only Sam, his wife, and the minister were present at the sessions, and they all regarded them as confidential. During one of the early sessions Sam admitted that he had sexually assaulted the stepdaughter, and Sam's wife informed the minister that Sam had confessed to her the night before. The prosecution plans to call Sam's wife, who is willing to testify about both of Sam's admissions. The prosecution also plans to call the minister and ask him about what both Sam and his wife said at the counseling session. The minister, however, has expressed an unwillingness to testify about these matters, and the minister is disturbed that Sam's wife is willing to testify.

Does the minister have any personal right not to testify or to prevent Sam's wife from testifying? What objections can Sam make to the testimony of his wife and the minister?

2. At Alex Draper's murder prosecution the state offers to introduce the following evidence. Shortly after the victim's death, an individual called the state mental hospital and asked to speak with a doctor. When the receptionist who had answered the phone asked about the nature of the caller's business, the caller responded, "Murder. I just killed a man." The psychiatrist on duty then spoke with the caller long enough for the receptionist to call the police and for the police to trace the telephone call to a telephone booth, where they found and arrested Draper. Draper has objected to evidence of what he said to the receptionist or the psychiatrist on the ground that his statements fall within the psychotherapist-patient privilege. What result?

3. Alice Gordon has filed a civil rights action against the school board

D. The Attorney-Client Privilege

for allegedly dismissing her because of her political views. Alice has sought to depose Sister Anne Cassidy, who was Alice's spiritual adviser when Alice was a postulate studying to become a nun. Sister Cassidy has refused to answer any questions about what Alice said to her during spiritual counseling. Is Sister Cassidy's refusal proper?

4. Jim Jones joined a mail order church for a fee of $100, which entitled him to the offices of "bishop" and "apostle." Shortly after joining the church Jones claimed to have had a revelation from God, who told him that all of his income was exempt from taxation. The government is prosecuting Jones for income tax evasion and plans to call Edward McNulty, the minister of a legitimate, established church. If McNulty is ordered to testify, he will state that he had several conversations with Jones about the supposed tax advantages of the ministry, and that he advised Jones that his income was not exempt from taxation. Should either Jones' or McNulty's objection to this testimony be sustained?

D. THE ATTORNEY-CLIENT PRIVILEGE

Except for one deliberate omission that we will consider shortly, Proposed FRE 503 is a representative statement of the modern attorney-client privilege:

> (a) Definitions. As used in this rule:
> (1) A "client" is a person, public officer, or corporation, association, or other organization or entity, either public or private, who is rendered professional legal services by a lawyer, or who consults a lawyer with a view to obtaining professional legal services from him.
> (2) A "lawyer" is a person authorized, or reasonably believed by the client to be authorized, to practice law in any state or nation.
> (3) A "representative of the lawyer" is one employed to assist the lawyer in the rendition of professional legal services.
> (4) A communication is "confidential" if not intended to be disclosed to third persons other than those to whom disclosure is in furtherance of the rendition of professional legal services to the client or those reasonably necessary for the transmission of the communication.
> (b) General rule of privilege. A client has a privilege to refuse to disclose and to prevent any other person from disclosing confidential communications made for the purpose of facilitating the rendition of professional legal services to the client,
> (1) between himself or his representative and his lawyer or his lawyer's representative, or
> (2) between his lawyer and the lawyer's representative, or
> (3) by him or his lawyer to a lawyer representing another in a matter of common interest, or

(4) between representatives of the client or between the client and a representative of the client, or

(5) between lawyers representing the client.

(c) Who may claim the privilege. The privilege may be claimed by the client, his guardian or conservator, the personal representative of a deceased client, or the successor, trustee, or similar representative of a corporation, association, or other organization, whether or not in existence. The person who was the lawyer at the time of the communication may claim the privilege but only on behalf of the client. His authority to do so is presumed in the absence of evidence to the contrary.

(d) Exceptions. There is no privilege under this rule:

(1) Furtherance of crime or fraud. If the services of the lawyer were sought or obtained to enable or aid anyone to commit or plan to commit what the client knew or reasonably should have known to be a crime or fraud; or

(2) Claimants through same deceased client. As to a communication relevant to an issue between parties who claim through the same deceased client, regardless of whether the claims are by testate or intestate succession or by *inter vivos* transaction; or

(3) Breach of duty by lawyer or client. As to a communication relevant to an issue of breach of duty by the lawyer to his client or by the client to his lawyer; or

(4) Document attested by lawyer. As to a communication relevant to an issue concerning an attested document to which the lawyer is an attesting witness; or

(5) Joint clients. As to a communication relevant to a matter of common interest between two or more clients if the communication was made by any of them to a lawyer retained or consulted in common, when offered in an action between any of the clients.

PROBLEMS

1. Brent Carson and Gloria Green were charged with importing cocaine, and retained separate counsel. At a meeting involving Brent, Gloria, and Gloria's attorney, Gloria supposedly said that Brent did not know anything about the plan to import cocaine. Gloria subsequently fled the jurisdiction, and Brent is now on trial. He calls Gloria's attorney to testify about her statement that he was not involved in the cocaine scheme. The prosecutor has objected to this testimony and asserted the attorney-client privilege on behalf of Gloria. How should the court rule?

2. Ed Brown has been charged with sexual assault. At a pre-trial hearing to determine Brown's competence to stand trial, the attorney called himself as a witness for the purpose of explaining how difficult it was to communicate with Brown. The attorney's testimony included the details of three quite different stories that Brown had told at various times about the incident in question. The court found Brown competent to stand trial. At trial, where

D. The Attorney-Client Privilege

Brown was represented by a different attorney, the prosecutor called the former attorney to testify about Brown's earlier inconsistent statements regarding the crime. Brown has objected on the ground that his statements are protected by the attorney-client privilege. What result?

3. The defendants, former officers of the Acme Drug Co., are charged with fraud for their role in falsifying records of drug tests that were sent to the Federal Drug Administration. During the course of the investigation of the record falsification scheme, the defendants made incriminating admissions in sessions with an attorney hired by Acme. Acme has waived the attorney-client privilege, and the prosecutor plans to call the attorney to testify about the defendants' admissions. Should the court sustain the defendants' attorney-client privilege objection to the evidence?

4. Following Claus von Bulow's acquittal on charges of assaulting and attempting to kill his wife, defense counsel Alan Dershowitz published a book entitled *Reversal of Fortune—Inside the von Bulow Case*. The children of von Bulow's wife have brought a civil action against von Bulow based on the same facts involved in criminal prosecution, and they are seeking to discover the content of conversations between von Bulow and his attorney that relate to communications that are referred to in the book. To what extent should the publication of Professor Dershowitz's book, assuming that it was done with von Bulow's consent, constitute a waiver of the attorney-client privilege for conversations not specifically revealed in the book?

As is true of Proposed FRE 503, the attorney-client privilege traditionally has applied not only to individual clients but also to corporate and other organizational clients. An organization, however, can make confidential communications only through individual members. Thus, the question necessarily arises: Who can speak for the organization for the purposes of the attorney-client privilege? Or to phrase the issue in terms of the language of FRE 503: Who is a "representative of the client"?

At the time Proposed FRE 503 was promulgated lower federal courts had given different answers to this question. According to one view, any officer, employee, or member of an organization was a representative of the organization.[31] Although this definition has the advantage of ease in application, it is perhaps too broad. Consider a situation in which an employee and a visitor to a plant happen to witness an industrial accident. Under this broad definition of representative of the client, a communication about the accident from the employee to the company's lawyer would be privileged. Yet, it is difficult to see why the employee's communication should be treated differently from that of the visitor or other eyewitnesses to accidents. For the purposes of litigation that might arise out of the accident, the employee is

---

31. See, e.g., United States v. United Shoe Mach. Corp., 89 F. Supp. 357 (D. Mass. 1950).

no different from any other witness; the fact of the employment status is a fortuity.

A second approach to defining representative of the client was the "control group" test. According to this test an employee's communication is privileged only if the employee

> is in a position to control or even to take a substantial part in a decision about any action which the corporation may take upon the advice of the attorney, or if he is an authorized member of a body or group which has that authority. . . . [City of Philadelphia v. Westinghouse Elec. Corp., 210 F. Supp. 483, 485 (E.D. Pa. 1962).]

Although widely adopted, the control group test was subject to criticism on two grounds. First, it was unclear precisely to whom the privilege would apply, and this lack of certainty would inhibit candid communication. Second, because the control-group test tended to limit the attorney-client privilege to communications by upper-level management, the test did not go far enough in protecting communications of employees who might have information that would be critical in order for the attorney to give sound legal advice to the organization.

A third approach to defining representative of the client was the subject matter test[32]: An employee's communication is privileged if the employee "makes the communication at the direction of his superiors" and the subject matter of the communication "is the performance by the employee of the duties of his employment."[33] This test avoids both the problem of bringing within the scope of the privilege communications by mere witness employees and the problem of limiting the privilege to communications from members of the control-group. But is the subject matter test itself too broad? Would the first prong of the test be satisfied if every employee were routinely directed to channel all business reports through corporate counsel?[34] Would the first prong be satisfied if *any* superior for *any* reason directed the employee to communicate with the attorney?[35]

The drafters of the Federal Rules chose not to define "representative of the client." Without elaboration, the Advisory Committee concluded that "the matter is better left to resolution by decision on a case-by-case basis."[36] The Supreme Court addressed the issue in the following case:

---

32. See Harper & Row Publishers, Inc. v. Decker, 423 F.2d 487 (7th Cir. 1970), *aff'd mem.*, 400 U.S. 955 (1971).
33. Id. at 491-492.
34. See Note, Evidence—Privileged Communications—The Attorney-Client Privilege in the Corporate Setting: A Suggested Approach, 62 Mich. L. Rev. 360 (1970).
35. See 2 J. Weinstein and V. Berger, Evidence ¶503(b)[04], pp. 503-47 to 503-51 (1988).
36. In earlier drafts the Advisory Committee had included a version of the control-group test in the definition section of Proposed FRE 503. Prior to the final draft, however, the Supreme Court affirmed by an equally divided vote the decision that had announced the

D. The Attorney-Client Privilege

UPJOHN CO. v. UNITED STATES
449 U.S. 383, 101 S. Ct. 677, 66 L. Ed. 2d 584 (1981)

Justice REHNQUIST delivered the opinion of the Court. We granted certiorari in this case to address important questions concerning the scope of the attorney-client privilege in the corporate context and the applicability of the work-product doctrine in proceedings to enforce tax summonses. . . . We . . . conclude that the attorney-client privilege protects the communications involved in this case from compelled disclosure and that the work-product doctrine does apply in tax summons enforcement proceedings.

I

Petitioner Upjohn Co. manufactures and sells pharmaceuticals here and abroad. In January 1976 independent accountants conducting an audit of one of Upjohn's foreign subsidiaries discovered that the subsidiary made payments to or for the benefit of foreign government officials in order to secure government business. The accountants so informed petitioner Mr. Gerard Thomas, Upjohn's Vice President, Secretary, and General Counsel. Thomas is a member of the Michigan and New York Bars, and has been Upjohn's General Counsel for 20 years. He consulted with outside counsel and R. T. Parfet, Jr., Upjohn's Chairman of the Board. It was decided that the company would conduct an internal investigation of what were termed "questionable payments." As part of this investigation the attorneys prepared a letter containing a questionnaire which was sent to "All Foreign General and Area Managers" over the Chairman's signature. The letter began by noting recent disclosures that several American companies made "possibly illegal" payments to foreign government officials and emphasized that the management needed full information concerning any such payments made by Upjohn. The letter indicated that the Chairman had asked Thomas, identified as "the company's General Counsel," "to conduct an investigation for the purpose of determining the nature and magnitude of any payments made by the Upjohn Company or any of its subsidiaries to any employee or official of a foreign government." The questionnaire sought detailed information concerning such payments. Managers were instructed to treat the investigation as "highly confidential" and not to discuss it with anyone other than Upjohn employees who might be helpful in providing the requested information. Responses were to be sent directly to Thomas. Thomas and

---

subject matter test. See note 32 supra.

> The Advisory Committee recognized that lack of consensus in the Supreme Court precluded the possibility of drafting a rule satisfactory to a majority of the justices. Consequently, the committee eliminated the definition of "representative of the client" in subdivision (a) of the rule. [2 J. Weinstein and V. Berger, Evidence ¶503(b)[04], p. 503-47 (1988).]

outside counsel also interviewed the recipients of the questionnaire and some 33 other Upjohn officers or employees as part of the investigation.

On March 26, 1976, the company voluntarily submitted a preliminary report to the Securities and Exchange Commission on Form 8-K disclosing certain questionable payments. A copy of the report was simultaneously submitted to the Internal Revenue Service, which immediately began an investigation to determine the tax consequences of the payments. Special agents conducting the investigation were given lists by Upjohn of all those interviewed and all who had responded to the questionnaire. On November 23, 1976, the Service issued a summons pursuant to 26 U.S.C. §7602 demanding production of:

> All files relative to the investigation conducted under the supervision of Gerard Thomas to identify payments to employees of foreign governments and any political contributions made by the Upjohn Company or any of its affiliates since January 1, 1971 and to determine whether any funds of the Upjohn Company had been improperly accounted for on the corporate books during the same period.
>
> The records should include but not be limited to written questionnaires sent to managers of the Upjohn Company's foreign affiliates, and memorandums or notes of the interviews conducted in the United States and abroad with officers and employees of the Upjohn Company and its subsidiaries. . . .

The company declined to produce the documents specified in the second paragraph on the grounds that they were protected from disclosure by the attorney-client privilege and constituted the work product of attorneys prepared in anticipation of litigation. . . . [T]he United States filed a petition seeking enforcement of the summons . . . in the United States District Court for the Western District of Michigan. That court adopted the recommmendation of a Magistrate who concluded that the summons should be enforced. Petitioners appealed to the Court of Appeals for the Sixth Circuit which rejected the Magistrate's finding of a waiver of the attorney-client privilege, . . . but agreed that the privilege did not apply "[t]o the extent that the communications were made by officers and agents not responsible for directing Upjohn's actions in response to legal advice . . . for the simple reason that the communications were not the client's." . . . The court reasoned that accepting petitioners' claim for a broader application of the privilege would encourage upper-echelon management to ignore unpleasant facts and create too broad a "zone of silence." Noting that Upjohn's counsel had interviewed officials such as the Chairman and President, the Court of Appeals remanded to the District Court so that a determination of who was within the "control group" could be made. In a concluding footnote the court stated that the work-product doctrine "is not applicable to administrative summonses issued under 26 U.S.C. §7602." . . .

D. The Attorney-Client Privilege

II

. . . The attorney-client privilege is the oldest of the privileges for confidential communications known to the common law. . . . Its purpose is to encourage full and frank communication between attorneys and their clients and thereby promote broader public interests in the observance of law and administration of justice. The privilege recognizes that sound legal advice or advocacy serves public ends and that such advice or advocacy depends upon the lawyer's being fully informed by the client. [I]n Fisher v. United States, 425 U.S. 391, 403 (1976), we recognized the purpose of the privilege to be "to encourage clients to make full disclosure to their attorneys." This rationale for the privilege has long been recognized by the Court. . . . Admittedly complications in the application of the privilege arise when the client is a corporation, which in theory is an artificial creature of the law, and not an individual; but this Court has assumed that the privilege applies when the client is a corporation, . . . and the Government does not contest the general proposition.

The Court of Appeals, however, considered the application of the privilege in the corporate context to present a "different problem," since the client was an inanimate entity and "only the senior management, guiding and integrating the several operations, . . . can be said to possess an identity analogous to the corporation as a whole." . . . The first case to articulate the so-called "control group test" adopted by the court below, Philadelphia v. Westinghouse Electric Corp., 210 F. Supp. 483, 485 (ED Pa.), *petition for mandamus and prohibition denied* sub nom. General Electric Co. v. Kirkpatrick, 312 F.2d 742 (CA3 1962), *cert. denied*, 372 U.S. 943 (1963), reflected a similar conceptual approach:

> Keeping in mind that the question is, Is it the corporation which is seeking the lawyer's advice when the asserted privileged communication is made?, the most satisfactory solution, I think, is that if the employee making the communication, of whatever rank he may be, is in a position to control or even to take a substantial part in a decision about any action which the corporation may take upon the advice of the attorney, . . . then, in effect, *he is (or personifies) the corporation* when he makes his disclosure to the lawyer and the privilege would apply. (Emphasis supplied [by the Court].)

Such a view, we think, overlooks the fact that the privilege exists to protect not only the giving of professional advice to those who can act on it but also the giving of information to the lawyer to enable them to give sound and informed advice. The first step in the resolution of any legal problem is ascertaining the factual background and sifting through the facts with an eye to the legally relevant. See ABA Code of Professional Responsibility, Ethical Consideration 4-1:

> A lawyer should be fully informed of all the facts of the matter he is handling in order for his client to obtain the full advantage of our legal system. It is for

the lawyer in the exercise of his independent professional judgment to separate the relevant and important from the irrelevant and unimportant. The observance of the ethical obligation of a lawyer to hold inviolate the confidences and secrets of his client not only facilitates the full development of facts essential to proper representation of the client but also encourages laymen to seek early legal assistance.

. . . In the case of the individual client the provider of information and the person who acts on the lawyer's advice are one and the same. In the corporate context, however, it will frequently be employees beyond the control group as defined by the court below—"officers and agents . . . responsible for directing [the company's] actions in response to legal advice" —who will possess the information needed by the corporation's lawyers. Middle-level—and indeed lower-level—employees can, by actions within the scope of their employment, embroil the corporation in serious legal difficulties, and it is only natural that these employees would have the relevant information needed by corporate counsel if he is adequately to advise the client with respect to such actual or potential difficulties. . . .

The control group test adopted by the court below thus frustrates the very purpose of the privilege by discouraging the communication of relevant information by employees of the client to attorneys seeking to render legal advice to the client corporation. The attorney's advice will also frequently be more significant to noncontrol group members than to those who officially sanction the advice, and the control group test makes it more difficult to convey full and frank legal advice to the employees who will put into effect the client corporation's policy. See, e.g., Duplan Corp. v. Deering Milliken, Inc., 397 F. Supp. 1146, 1164 (S.C. 1974) ("After the lawyer forms his or her opinion, it is of no immediate benefit to the Chairman of the Board or the President. It must be given to the corporate personnel who will apply it").

The narrow scope given the attorney-client privilege by the court below not only makes it difficult for corporate attorneys to formulate sound advice when their client is faced with a specific legal problem but also threatens to limit the valuable efforts of corporate counsel to ensure their client's compliance with the law. In light of the vast and complicated array of regulatory legislation confronting the modern corporation, corporations, unlike most individuals, "constantly go to lawyers to find out how to obey the law," Burnham, The Attorney-Client Privilege in the Corporate Arena, 24 Bus. Law. 901, 913 (1969), particularly since compliance with the law in this area is hardly an instinctive matter, see, e.g., United States v. United States Gypsum Co., 438 U.S. 422, 440-441 (1978) ("the behavior proscribed by the [Sherman] Act is often difficult to distinguish from the gray zone of socially acceptable and economically justifiable business conduct").[2]

---

2. The Government argues that the risk of civil or criminal liability suffices to ensure

D. The Attorney-Client Privilege

The communications at issue were made by Upjohn employees[3] to counsel for Upjohn acting as such, at the direction of corporate superiors in order to secure legal advice from counsel. As the Magistrate found, "Mr. Thomas consulted with the Chairman of the Board and outside counsel and thereafter conducted a factual investigation to determine the nature and extent of the questionable payments *and to be in a position to give legal advice to the company with respect to the payments.*" (Emphasis supplied [by the Court].). . . . Information, not available from upper-echelon management, was needed to supply a basis for legal advice concerning compliance with securities and tax laws, foreign laws, currency regulations, duties to shareholders, and potential litigation in each of these areas. The communications concerned matters within the scope of the employees' corporate duties, and the employees themselves were sufficiently aware that they were being questioned in order that the corporation could obtain legal advice. The questionnaire identified Thomas as "the company's General Counsel" and referred in its opening sentence to the possible illegality of payments such as the ones on which information was sought. . . . A statement of policy accompanying the questionnaire clearly indicated the legal implications of the investigation. The policy statement was issued "in order that there be no uncertainty in the future as to the policy with respect to the practices which are the subject of this investigation." It began "Upjohn will comply with all laws and regulations," and stated that commissions or payments "will not be used as a subterfuge for bribes or illegal payments" and that all payments must be "proper and legal." Any future agreements with foreign distributors or agents were to be approved "by a company attorney" and any questions concerning the policy were to be referred "to the company's general Counsel." . . . This statement was issued to Upjohn employees worldwide, so that even those interviewees not receiving a questionnaire were aware of the legal implications of the interviews. Pursuant to explicit instructions from the Chairman of the Board, the communications were considered "highly confidential" when made, . . . and have been kept confidential by the company. Consistent with the underlying purposes of the attorney-client privilege, these communications must be protected against compelled disclosure.

---

that corporations will seek legal advice in the absence of the protection of the privilege. This response ignores the fact that the depth and quality of any investigations to ensure compliance with the law would suffer, even were they undertaken. The response also proves too much, since it applies to all communications covered by the privilege: an individual trying to comply with the law or faced with a legal problem also has strong incentive to disclose information to his lawyer, yet the common law has recognized the value of the privilege in further facilitating communications.

3. Seven of the eighty-six employees interviewed by counsel had terminated their employment with Upjohn at the time of the interview. . . . Petitioners argue that the privilege should nonetheless apply to communications by these former employees concerning activities during their period of employment. Neither the District Court nor the Court of Appeals had occasion to address this issue, and we decline to decide it without the benefit of treatment below.

The Court of Appeals declined to extend the attorney-client privilege beyond the limits of the control group test for fear that doing so would entail severe burdens on discovery and create a broad "zone of silence" over corporate affairs. Application of the attorney-client privilege to communications such as those involved here, however, puts the adversary in no worse position than if the communications had never taken place. The privilege only protects disclosure of communications; it does not protect disclosure of the underlying facts by those who communicated with the attorney. . . . Here the Government was free to question the employees who communicated with Thomas and outside counsel. Upjohn has provided the IRS with a list of such employees, and the IRS has already interviewed some 25 of them. While it would probably be more convenient for the Government to secure the results of petitioner's internal investigation by simply subpoenaing the questionnaires and notes taken by petitioner's attorneys, such considerations of convenience do not overcome the policies served by the attorney-client privilege. . . .

Needless to say, we decide only the case before us, and do not undertake to draft a set of rules which should govern challenge to investigatory subpoenas. Any such approach would violate the spirit of Federal Rule of Evidence 501. See S. Rep. No. 93-1277, p.13 (1974) ("the recognition of a privilege based on a confidential relationship . . . should be determined on a case-by-case basis"). . . . While such a "case-by-case" basis may to some slight extent undermine desirable certainty in the boundaries of the attorney-client privilege, it obeys the spirit of the Rules. At the same time we conclude that the narrow "control group test" sanctioned by the Court of Appeals in this case cannot, consistent with "the principles of the common law as . . . interpreted . . . in the light of reason and experience," Fed. Rule Evid. 501, govern the development of the law in this area.

III

Our decision that the communications by Upjohn employees to counsel are covered by the attorney-client privilege disposes of the case so far as the responses to the questionnaires and any notes reflecting responses to interview questions are concerned. The summons reaches further, however, and Thomas has testified that his notes and memoranda of interviews go beyond recording responses to his questions. . . . To the extent that the material subject to the summons is not protected by the attorney-client privilege as disclosing communications between an employee and counsel, we must reach the ruling by the Court of Appeals that the work-product doctrine does not apply to summonses issued under 26 U.S.C. §7602.[6]

6. The following discussion will also be relevant to counsel's notes and memoranda of interviews with the seven former employees should it be determined that the attorney-client privilege does not apply to them. See n.3, supra.

D. The Attorney-Client Privilege

The Government concedes, wisely, that the Court of Appeals erred and that the work-product doctrine does apply to IRS summonses. . . . This doctrine was announced by the Court over 30 years ago in Hickman v. Taylor, 329 U.S. 495 (1947). In that case the Court rejected "an attempt, without purported necessity or justification, to secure written statements, private memoranda and personal recollections prepared or formed by an adverse party's counsel in the course of his legal duties." Id., at 510. The Court noted that "it is essential that a lawyer work with a certain degree of privacy" and reasoned that if discovery of the material sought were permitted

> much of what is now put down in writing would remain unwritten. An attorney's thoughts, heretofore inviolate, would not be his own. Inefficiency, unfairness and sharp practices would inevitably develop in the giving of legal advice and in the preparation of cases for trial. The effect on the legal profession would be demoralizing. And the interests of the clients and the cause of justice would be poorly served. [Id., at 511.]

The "strong public policy" underlying the work-product doctrine was reaffirmed recently in United States v. Nobles, 422 U.S. 225, 236-240 (1975), and has been substantially incorporated in Federal Rule of Civil Procedure 26(b)(3).[7]

. . . While conceding the applicability of the work-product doctrine, the Government asserts that it has made a sufficient showing of necessity to overcome its protections. The Magistrate apparently so found. . . . The Government relies on the following language in *Hickman:*

> We do not mean to say that all written materials obtained or prepared by an adversary's counsel with an eye toward litigation are necessarily free from discovery in all cases. Where relevant and nonprivileged facts remain hidden in an attorney's file and where production of those facts is essential to the preparation of one's case, discovery may properly be had. . . . And production might be justified where the witnesses are no longer available or can be reached only with difficulty. [329 U.S., at 511.]

The Government stresses that interviewees are scattered across the globe and that Upjohn has forbidden its employees to answer questions it considers

---

7. This provides, in pertinent part:

[A] party may obtain discovery of documents and tangible things otherwise discoverable under subdivision (b)(1) of this rule and prepared in anticipation of litigation or for trial by or for another party or by or for that other party's representative (including his attorney, consultant, surety, indemnitor, insurer, or agent) only upon a showing that the party seeking discovery has substantial need of the materials in the preparation of his case and that he is unable without undue hardship to obtain the substantial equivalent of the materials by other means. In ordering discovery of such materials when the required showing has been made, the court shall protect against disclosure of the mental impressions, conclusions, opinions, or legal theories of an attorney or other representative of a party concerning the litigation.

irrelevant. The above-quoted language from *Hickman*, however, did not apply to "oral statements made by witnesses . . . whether presently in the form of [the attorney's] mental impressions or memoranda." Id., at 512. As to such material the Court did "not believe that any showing of necessity can be made under the circumstances of this case so as to justify production . . . . If there should be a rare situation justifying production of these matters, petitioner's case is not of that type." Id., at 512-513. . . . Forcing an attorney to disclose notes and memoranda of witnesses' oral statements is particularly disfavored because it tends to reveal the attorney's mental processes, 329 U.S., at 513 ("what he saw fit to write down regarding witnesses' remarks"); id., at 516-517 ("the statement would be his [the attorney's] language, permeated with his inferences") (Jackson, J., concurring).[8]

Rule 26 accords special protection to work product revealing the attorney's mental processes. The Rule permits disclosure of documents and tangible things constituting attorney work product upon a showing of substantial need and inability to obtain the equivalent without undue hardship. This was the standard applied by the Magistrate. . . . Rule 26 goes on, however, to state that "[i]n ordering discovery of such materials when the required showing has been made, the court shall protect against disclosure of the mental impressions, conclusions, opinions or legal theories of an attorney or other representative of a party concerning the litigation." Although this language does not specifically refer to memoranda based on oral statements of witnesses the *Hickman* court stressed the danger that compelled disclosure of such memoranda would reveal the attorney's mental processes. It is clear that this is the sort of material the draftsmen of the Rule had in mind as deserving special protection. See Notes of Advisory Committee on 1970 Amendment to Rules, 28, U.S.C. App., p. 442 ("The subdivision . . . goes on to protect against disclosure the mental impressions, conclusions, opinions, or legal theories . . . of an attorney or other representative of a party. The *Hickman* opinion drew special attention to the need for protecting an attorney against discovery of memoranda prepared from recollection of oral interviews. The courts have steadfastly safeguarded against disclosure of lawyers' mental impressions and legal theories . . . .").

Based on the foregoing, some courts have concluded that *no* showing of necessity can overcome protection of work product which is based on oral statements from witnesses. . . . Those courts declining to adopt an absolute rule have nonetheless recognized that such material is entitled to special protection. . . .

We do not decide the issue at this time. It is clear that the Magistrate applied the wrong standard when he concluded that the Government had

---

8. Thomas described his notes of the interviews as containing "what I considered to be the important questions, the substance of the responses to them, my beliefs, as to the importance of these, my beliefs as to how they related to the inquiry, my thoughts as to how they related to other questions. In some instances they might even suggest other questions that I would have to ask or things that I needed to find elsewhere." . . .

D. The Attorney-Client Privilege

made a sufficient showing of necessity to overcome the protections of the work-product doctrine. The Magistrate applied the "substantial need" and "without undue hardship" standard articulated in the first part of Rule 26(b)(3). The notes and memoranda sought by the Government here, however, are work product based on oral statements. If they reveal communications, they are, in this case, protected by the attorney-client privilege. To the extent they do not reveal communications, they reveal the attorneys' mental processes in evaluating the communications. As Rule 26 and *Hickman* make clear, such work product cannot be disclosed simply on a showing of substantial need and inability to obtain the equivalent without undue hardship.

While we are not prepared at this juncture to say that such material is always protected by the work-product rule, we think a far stronger showing of necessity and unavailability by other means than was made by the Government or applied by the Magistrate in this case would be necessary to compel disclosure. . . . [W]e . . . reverse the judgment of the Court of Appeals for the Sixth Circuit and remand the case to it for such further proceedings in connection with the work-product claim as are consistent with this opinion. . . .

Chief Justice BURGER, concurring in part and concurring in the judgment.

I join in Parts I and III of the opinion of the Court and in the judgment. As to Part II, I agree fully with the Court's rejection of the so-called "control group" test, its reasons for doing so, and its ultimate holding that the communications at issue are privileged. As the Court states, however, "if the purpose of the attorney-client privilege is to be served, the attorney and client must be able to predict with some degree of certainty whether particular discussions will be protected." . . . For this very reason, I believe that we should articulate a standard that will govern similar cases and afford guidance to corporations, counsel advising them, and federal courts.

The Court properly relies on a variety of factors in concluding that the communications now before us are privileged. . . . Because of the great importance of the issue, in my view the Court should make clear now that, as a general rule, a communication is privileged at least when, as here, an employee or former employee speaks at the direction of the management with an attorney regarding conduct or proposed conduct within the scope of employment. The attorney must be one authorized by the management to inquire into the subject and must be seeking information to assist counsel in performing any of the following functions: (a) evaluating whether the employee's conduct has bound or would bind the corporation; (b) assessing the legal consequences, if any, of that conduct; or (c) formulating appropriate legal responses to actions that have been or may be taken by others with regard to that conduct. . . . Other communications between employees and corporate counsel may indeed be privileged . . . but the need for certainty does not compel us now to prescribe all the details of the privilege in this case.

Nevertheless, to say we should not reach all facets of the privilege does not mean that we should neglect our duty to provide guidance in a case that squarely presents the question in a traditional adversary context. Indeed, because Federal Rule of Evidence 501 provides that the law of privileges "shall be governed by the principles of the common law as they may be interpreted by the courts of the United States in the light of reason and experience," this Court has a special duty to clarify aspects of the law of privileges properly before us. Simply asserting that this failure "may to some slight extent undermine desirable certainty," . . . neither minimizes the consequences of continuing uncertainty and confusion nor harmonizes the inherent dissonance of acknowledging that uncertainty while declining to clarify it within the frame of issues presented.

NOTES AND QUESTIONS

1. Both the majority and the concurring opinions stress and rely heavily upon the traditional justification for the attorney-client privilege—the need to encourage clients to be fully candid with their attorneys. Consider whether this justification is sound. Leaving aside the possibility of a criminal prosecution,[37] we believe it is unlikely that a rational client would choose to withhold information from an attorney because of the absence of an attorney-client privilege.[38] Unless the attorney is under an ethical or legal obligation to reveal confidences (in which case the privilege would not apply in the first place), the client should not have to fear voluntary disclosure from an honest attorney. Realizing that clients generally desire confidentiality, the attorney's professional self-interest provides an incentive to maintain confidences. Moreover, most of the information that the client provides the attorney will be independently discoverable. Since the substance of what is

---

37. A client's fifth amendment right against compulsory self-incrimination would not protect the client against the lawyer's disclosure of confidential communications because communications to an attorney are not "compelled." Thus, in the absence of an attorney-client privilege a client may be reluctant to be candid with an attorney because of a fear that the attorney would be powerless to prevent disclosure of information for which the client could invoke the fifth amendment. See Fisher v. United States, 425 U.S. 391 (1976) (attorney-client privilege protects against disclosure documents turned over to lawyer for legal advice if fifth amendment would have protected documents from disclosure when in hands of client). Moreover, if there were a criminal prosecution, the failure to protect the confidentiality of the defendant-client's communications to the lawyer may be a violation of the defendant-client's sixth amendment right to the assistance of counsel. The omission of these concerns from the analysis in the text is admittedly a large one. The traditional justification for the attorney-client privilege, however, extends well beyond these concerns and does not focus on them. Our analysis is a response to the traditional justification. We have no quarrel with an attorney-client privilege that is based on and limited to the advancement of a client's fifth and sixth amendment rights.

38. For an elaboration on the material in this and the following five Notes, see Allen, Grady, Polsby, and Yashko, Confidentiality of Legal Affairs (forthcoming).

D. The Attorney-Client Privilege

communicated to the attorney can be made known to an opposing party either in pre-trial discovery or when the client is a witness, the absence of an attorney-client privilege usually should not deter the rational client from communicating fully and openly with the attorney. Indeed, it would be against the client's best interest to have the attorney learn of some fact for the first time when the client is on the witness stand during the trial.

We can think of only three types of situations in which the existence of the privilege might increase the client's candor with the attorney. First, the client may believe that opposing counsel will not have the foresight to inquire about the subject matter of a confidential communication but that opposing counsel would routinely ask about confidential communications. To the extent that this is a possibility, the existence of the privilege will augment the client's candor. Second, the client might not understand the points made in the foregoing paragraph and, thus, might believe erroneously that candor in the absence of the privilege would be detrimental. Finally, a dishonest client might believe candor with counsel in a confidential situation will increase the client's ability to lie effectively to the opponent.

The foregoing possibilities should not be regarded as sufficient to justify the privilege. It seems unlikely that a client would have the foresight to anticipate the possible failure of opposing counsel to engage in thorough discovery and investigation. Moreover, a good attorney should advise a client against trying to rely on such a possibility, just as a good attorney should explain to the client why the absence of a privilege will not adversely affect the client's interest in confidentiality. This leaves only the dishonest client who desires confidentiality in order to become a more effective purveyor of falsehoods. We can think of no reason why there should be a rule to promote this type of behavior.

2. The speculations in the preceding Note may be incorrect; perhaps in the absence of an attorney-client privilege honest clients would withhold information from their attorneys. If so, presumably they would want to withhold only information that they thought might be ultimately harmful to them. Consider the consequences of a client's decision to withhold information that the client believes to be harmful because of the absence of an attorney-client privilege.

A client's communication often will be partly harmful, partly helpful, and partly neutral. The client, however, may not properly assess the ultimate value of the information.

> (a) *Neutral information.* If the information is neutral, it makes no difference whether it becomes known. Thus, it is irrelevant that the information happens to be suppressed by the client initially rather than by the confidentiality requirement of the privilege.
>
> (b) *Harmful information.* If the information happens to be harmful to the client, it makes no difference in terms of ultimate disclosure *to an opposing party* whether there is a privilege: Either the client will

withhold the information, or if the privilege induces the client to reveal the information, the privilege will ensure that the communication remains confidential. In either case, withholding the information will contribute to an inaccurate result in litigation if the opposing party fails to develop the information independently through investigation and discovery.

There may, however, be situations in which the client's failure to communicate harmful information because of the absence of a privilege is harmful to the client. In such situations, if the attorney had the information, the attorney often could give better legal advice to the client. Consider, however, the situations in which revealing harmful confidential information will be most important to the client. The value in the attorney's knowing the harmful information is likely to be that the attorney can advise the client to forgo illegal activity, advise the client how best to proceed with marginally legal activity, or devise a litigation strategy that will avoid or minimize the damaging information.

Clients who would forgo clearly illegal activity or who would engage openly in marginally legal activity are likely to have little interest in whether there is a rule of confidentiality. In the former situation, the only risk is the very marginal one that the attorney may act against self-interest and embarrass the client by revealing the communication; and in the latter situation, the openness of the client's activity is likely to negate any need for confidentiality of the earlier communications. Indeed, if the legality of the activity is called into question, the client may very well want to reveal the communications with counsel. On the other hand, clients who wish to engage in clearly illegal activity or to maintain an aura of secrecy around their marginally legal activities have something to gain by the confidentiality of their communications, as do the litigants who can benefit from an attorney's expertise in trying to avoid or minimize damaging information. But why should we have a rule that protects and facilitates these interests?[39]

(c) *Helpful information.* If the information that the client refuses to reveal is in fact helpful to the client, the absence of the attorney-client privilege can make a great difference. With the privilege, the client could reveal the information to the attorney, who then could explain to the client how it is in the client's interest to use the information in litigation or in other contexts. Why, though, should we have a rule to facilitate the interests of a misguided withholder of information, particularly when the motive for withholding is suppression of the truth for personal gain?

---

39. Typically the attorney-client privilege does not extend to situations in which legal advice is sought to enable a person to commit a crime or fraud. See, e.g., Proposed FRE 503(d)(1).

D. The Attorney-Client Privilege

3. We have suggested that the individuals who would be the most likely to withhold information in the absence of an attorney-client privilege may not deserve the benefits of the privilege. Perhaps, however, we should retain the attorney-client privilege not because we want to encourage those individuals to be candid with their lawyers for their benefit, but rather because we want them to be candid for our benefit. A client's failure to disclose information to a lawyer may contribute both to faulty legal advice about how the client should conduct the client's affairs and to inaccurate results in litigation. There is, we submit, a societal interest both in having individuals conduct their affairs with sound legal advice and in trying to ensure factually accurate results in litigation.

Sound legal advice that is provided earlier rather than later in the course of a client's conduct should enable the client to anticipate and minimize legal problems. This, in turn, should reduce legal costs for the client, for those who deal with the client, and for the public, whose tax dollars help support our judicial system. These benefits, of course, are less likely to exist when the client, after making the communication, utilizes the lawyer's advice in carrying out some marginally legal activity. Frequently, however, the client will not know before discussing the matter with a lawyer whether the information that the client imparts is harmful or the extent to which contemplated future action may be illegal or marginally legal. It is unlikely that one could create a rule of confidentiality that successfully incorporates these nuances. Rather, the most one is likely to be able to do is to exclude the extreme situations from the privilege. See, e.g., Proposed FRE 503(d)(1) (attorney-client privilege inapplicable when client consults attorney for advice on how to commit crime or fraud).

Accurate results in litigation can benefit not only the parties to a law suit but society in general by reinforcing the law's general deterrence value— its "educational" and "moralizing" value.[40] The importance of any single case for this purpose is not likely to be great, but accurate results over the long run may be important. Consider a case in which a pedestrian sues a driver for injuries that occurred when the pedestrian stepped in front of the driver's car. If we regularly had good information about the extent to which pedestrians took precautions before stepping in front of cars, we might want a rule of law that limited pedestrians' recovery in situations in which they were inattentive; and if so, we would want to reinforce that rule at every opportunity in order to encourage pedestrians to use caution. Without good information in most cases about the precautions that pedestrians take, however, we might develop a rule of strict liability and thereby defeat whatever deterrent effect the law could have on the carefulness of pedestrians. If the absence of an attorney-client privilege would induce pedestrians to withhold from their lawyers details about the precautions they took, the absence of

---

40. Andenaes, General Prevention, 43 J. Crim. L.C. & P.S. 176, 179-180 (1952).

the privilege could contribute to this undermining of the deterrence value of the law.

The preceding scenario is highly speculative. Moreover, it is based on the probably unrealistic premise that the absence of the attorney-client privilege would have an impact initially on what clients tell their lawyers. Nonetheless, it does suggest that in assessing the propriety and/or scope of the attorney-client privilege there is more at stake than the incentives and ultimate fate of the individual client.

4. Perhaps one can make a better case for the attorney-client privilege by focusing on its probable impact on the lawyer rather than on the client. The lawyer's task is a creative one that consists of gathering and synthesizing facts and developing legal theories or contexts within which to explain the facts. The discussions between the lawyer and client are not merely a static collection of data; rather, they are an important creative component of the process. The lawyer's probing, tone of voice, gestures, decision to pursue one avenue of inquiry instead of another—all have an impact on what the client says. In short, the information that comes from attorney-client communications is very much the result of the creative efforts of the lawyer. If the lawyer could not derive any special benefit from this effort, if opposing counsel could regularly compel the disclosure of the results of this creative process, the lawyer's effort is likely to be less thorough than it would otherwise be. Moreover, the process of producing the information for the opposing party would often be extremely time consuming and, therefore, expensive. Unless there were a recorded transcript (which the lawyer may try to avoid because it would give so much to the opponent), the opposing party would probably not be content with the lawyer's written summary of what was said but would want to depose both the lawyer and the client. The lawyer and client would then have the extremely difficult task of trying to recreate the nuances of what was said, being careful to qualify statements and to explain contexts and subtle meanings.

5. Even if abolishing the attorney-client privilege would tend to have the effect just described, it does not follow that the privilege should be retained. Presumably some—perhaps most—lawyers will continue to engage in reasonably comprehensive creative efforts on behalf of their clients, and if we were concerned about the cost of discovering confidential communications, we could place that cost on the person seeking discovery. Even without the attorney-client privilege, all lawyers are playing by the same rules, and each client is free (within his or her financial constraints) to select a lawyer. What is the *public* interest in a rule designed to protect the confidentiality of the creative energies of the lawyer?

The public interest, we submit, is the dual concern discussed in Note 3 supra: the benefits of sound legal advice by attorneys and accurate fact finding in adjudication. Moreover, it seems likely to us that a lawyer's decision whether to engage in a thorough, creative job of lawyering is more likely to have an impact on these matters than a client's initial decision

D. The Attorney-Client Privilege

(which may be changed by a persuasive, creative lawyer) to withhold information. Indeed, in the context of considering the impact of a lawyer's creative effort, it seems reasonable to expand the second potential benefit beyond mere accurate fact finding to the advancement of socially desirable legal theories and concepts through litigation.

6. To summarize the points in the preceding Notes, the traditional justification for the attorney-client privilege rests on the empirical assumption that abolition of the privilege would deter individuals from being candid with their attorneys. We believe this assumption is highly dubious, and we have suggested an alternative empirical assumption—that abolition of the attorney-client privilege would adversely affect the extent to which attorneys would engage in the thorough, creative practice of their profession. If one rejects both empirical assumptions, it is difficult, if not impossible, to make a viable case for the attorney-client privilege.[41] Accepting either or both empirical assumptions, however, is not enough alone to justify the privilege. In addition, there should be some public benefit derived from recognizing a rule that on its face suppresses information, thereby apparently detracting from accurate fact finding. The benefit, we suggest, lies in the public interest in sound legal advice and accurate, socially desirable results of litigation, both of which may ensue from recognizing the privilege. These benefits, however, are admittedly speculative and difficult to value.

7. The work-product doctrine discussed in *Upjohn* often overlaps or supplements the attorney-client privilege. The Supreme Court initially announced the doctrine, now codified in Fed. R. Civ. P. 26(b)(3) (which is set forth in *Upjohn* at Court's footnote 7 supra), in Hickman v. Taylor:[42]

> Proper preparation of a client's case demands that [the lawyer] assemble information, sift what he considers to be the relevant from the irrelevant facts, prepare his legal theories and plan his strategy without undue and needless interference. . . .
>
> . . . This work is reflected, of course, in interviews, statements, memoranda, correspondence, briefs, mental impressions, personal beliefs, and the countless other tangible and intangible ways—aptly though roughly termed by the Circuit Court of Appeals in this case as the "work product of the lawyer." Were such materials open to opposing counsel on mere demand, much of what is now put down in writing would remain unwritten. An attorney's thought, heretofore inviolate, would not be his own. Inefficiency, unfairness and sharp practices would inevitably develop in the giving of legal advice and in preparation of cases for trial. The effect on the legal profession would be

---

41. We have avoided here any attempt to justify the privilege on some non-empirical privacy-like ground. See, e.g., Louisell, Confidentiality, Conformity and Confusion: Privileges in Federal Court Today, 31 Tul. L. Rev. 101 (1956); see also Fried, Correspondence, 86 Yale L.J. 573 (1977). These attempted justifications merely assert the purported value of the privilege without any careful attempt to assess what is at stake.

42. 329 U.S. 495 (1947).

demoralizing. And the interests of the clients and the cause of justice would be poorly served. [329 U.S. at 511.]

Although the Court's rhetoric may be a bit extreme, this language suggests a rationale for the work-product doctrine that is similar to that suggested for the attorney-client privilege in Notes 4 and 5 supra.

8. Note that the work-product doctrine, at least with respect to "documents and tangible things" as opposed to "mental impressions, conclusions, opinions, or legal theories of an attorney," is not absolute. Rather, there is a substantial need test. By contrast, the attorney-client privilege is usually considered absolute. If the privilege is applicable, a showing of need will not overcome the privilege. How absolute should the protection be for a client's confidential communications or a lawyer's thought processes and other creative efforts? If a witness uses a document protected by the attorney-client privilege or the work-product doctrine to refresh the witness' memory prior to testifying, should the judge be able to order production of the document pursuant to FRE 612?

9. A third source—in addition to the attorney-client privilege and the work-product doctrine—for the protection of confidentiality in attorney-client relations is the ethical obligation of a lawyer to keep confidential matters about a client's affairs. The American Bar Association's Model Rules of Professional Conduct set forth this obligation in Rule 1.6:

> (a) A lawyer shall not reveal information relating to representation of a client unless the client consents after consultation, except for disclosures that are implicitly authorized in order to carry out the representation, and except as stated in paragraph (b).
>
> (b) A lawyer may reveal such information to the extent the lawyer reasonably believes necessary:
>
> (1) to prevent the client from committing a criminal act that the lawyer believes is likely to result in imminent death or substantial bodily harm; or
>
> (2) to establish a claim or defense on behalf of the lawyer in a controversy between the lawyer and the client, to establish a defense to a criminal charge or civil claim against the lawyer based upon conduct in which the client was involved, or to respond to allegations in any proceeding concerning the lawyer's representation of the client.

The Comment accompanying Model Rule 1.6 provides the following explanation for the ethical obligation of confidentiality:

> The lawyer is part of a judicial system charged with upholding the law. One of the lawyer's functions is to advise clients so that they avoid any violation of the law in the proper exercise of their rights.
>
> The observance of the ethical obligation of a lawyer to hold inviolate confidential information of the client not only facilitates the full development

D. The Attorney-Client Privilege

of facts essential to proper representation of the client but also encourages people to seek early legal assistance.

Almost without exception, clients come to lawyers in order to determine what their rights are and what is, in the maze of laws and regulations, deemed to be legal and correct. The common law recognizes that the client's confidences must be protected from disclosure. Based upon experience, lawyers know that almost all clients follow the advice given, and the law is upheld.

A fundamental principle in the client-lawyer relationship is that the lawyer maintain confidentiality of information relating to the representation. The client is thereby encouraged to communicate fully and frankly with the lawyer even as to embarrassing or legally damaging subject matter.

The principle of confidentiality is given effect in two related bodies of law, the attorney-client privilege (which includes the work product doctrine) in the law of evidence and the rule of confidentiality established in professional ethics. The attorney-client privilege applies in judicial and other proceedings in which a lawyer may be called as a witness or otherwise required to produce evidence concerning a client. The rule of client-lawyer confidentiality applies in situations other than those where evidence is sought from the lawyer through compulsion of law. The confidentiality rule applies not merely to matters communicated in confidence by the client but also to all information relating to the representation, whatever its source. A lawyer may not disclose such information except as authorized or required by the Rules of Professional Conduct or other law. . . .

The American Bar Association's Model Code of Professional Responsibility, the predecessor to the Model Rules of Professional Conduct, included a similar confidentiality provision. ABA Model Code of Professional Responsibility Disciplinary Rule 4-101. The exception for contemplated criminal conduct by a client, however, extended to *all* crimes, and there was also an exception permitting a lawyer to reveal confidences "when required by law or court order." With respect to the omission of this latter exception in the Model Rules, the Comment accompanying Rule 1.6 states: "Whether another provision of law supersedes Rule 1.6 is a matter of interpretation beyond the scope of these Rules, but a presumption should exist against such a supersession."

How compelling a case for confidentiality does the Comment to Rule 1.6 make? Do the rule and commentary deal adequately with the relationship between the ethical obligation of confidentiality and the attorney-client privilege? Is the Rule 1.6 permission for a lawyer to disclose a client's contemplated criminal conduct too narrow? Why should there be a "presumption" that provisions of law mandating disclosure do not supersede Rule 1.6's obligation of confidentiality?

There is one situation in which the Model Rules of Professional Conduct specifically provide that the rule of confidentiality is superceded. See Model Rule 3.3:

(a) A lawyer shall not knowingly:
  (1) make a false statement of material fact or law to a tribunal;
  (2) fail to disclose a material fact to a tribunal when disclosure is necessary to avoid assisting a criminal or fraudulent act by the client;
  (3) fail to disclose to the tribunal legal authority in the controlling jurisdiction known to the lawyer to be directly adverse to the position of the client and not disclosed by opposing counsel; or
  (4) offer evidence that the lawyer knows to be false. If a lawyer has offered material evidence and comes to know of its falsity, the lawyer shall take reasonable remedial measures.

(b) The duties stated in paragraph (a) continue to the conclusion of the proceeding, and apply even if compliance requires disclosure of information otherwise protected by rule 1.6.

(c) A lawyer may refuse to offer evidence that the lawyer reasonably believes is false.

PROBLEMS

1. Al Driver, who is suspected of bank robbery tells his attorney, George Shippers, where to locate the mask and gun used in the robbery. Shippers retrieves the mask and gun and places them in the office safe. Has Shippers acted unethically? What disclosures about the gun and mask is he now permitted or required to make?

What if it had been Shippers' secretary who, without Shippers' permission, had retrieved the mask and gun? In either case, should it matter (a) whether the police or some third person would have been likely to find the mask and gun or (b) whether the initial information about the mask and gun came from some person other than the client?

After Shippers first learned about the mask and gun, what would have been the appropriate course of action for him to take?

2. Sarah Johnson, an attorney, represents Oscar Rivers, who has been charged with murder. Rivers and his girlfriend, Elsie Lewis, are both prepared to testify that they were together at Elsie's apartment at the time of the killing. Oscar has consistently told Sarah this alibi story; Elsie, however, has confided in Sarah that she was not with Oscar at the time of the killing and that Oscar admitted to her that he was the murderer. The only eyewitness to the killing, Elvira Dugan, is an elderly lady with failing eyesight.

What should Sarah do if both Oscar and Elsie are adamant about testifying that they were together at Elsie's apartment when the murder was committed? Does your answer depend upon whether Sarah believes Oscar or Elsie?

Sarah is convinced that she can neutralize Elvira Dugan's eyewitness testimony during cross-examination. Is there any problem with her doing so if she is convinced that Oscar is guilty and that Elvira's identification is in fact accurate?

E. THE MARITAL PRIVILEGES

There are two distinct marital privileges—one to protect confidential communications between spouses and the other (usually applicable only in criminal prosecutions) to prevent a witness spouse from testifying against the party spouse. A particular jurisdiction may have either or both privileges. Federal courts recognized both privileges prior to the adoption of the Federal Rules of Evidence. The proposed Federal Rules on privilege included only the marital testimonial privilege. The Supreme Court, however, subsequently indicated in dictum that it would continue to apply the marital confidential communications privilege.[43]

As we suggested earlier, there are two justifications that have been offered for confidential communications: to encourage open and frank discussions between spouses and (2) regardless of the privilege's encouraging effect, to protect the privacy of intimate spousal communications. Consistently with both of these rationales, the privilege applies to communications that take place during the marriage relationship, and the privilege does not end with the termination of the marriage. The privilege, however, may not apply to communications made while the parties were married but separated.[44] A holder of the privilege—who may be, depending on the jurisdiction, the spouses jointly, the communicating spouse, the witness spouse, or the party spouse—is entitled to claim the privilege even though the holder is no longer married to the individual with whom the communication occurred.

The modern justification for the spousal testimonial privilege is that it exists to promote harmony in an on-going marriage relationship; without the privilege, it is feared that one spouse testifying against the other may bring disharmony to the marriage. Consistently with this rationale, the privilege is not limited to testimony about confidential communications, and for the privilege to apply the witness and the party must be married at the time the privilege is invoked.[45]

Just as jurisdictions differ on the issue who is the holder of the marital communications privilege, jurisdictions differ on the question who is the holder of the marital testimonial privilege. The Supreme Court most recently addressed the issue in the following case:

TRAMMEL v. UNITED STATES
445 U.S. 40, 100 S. Ct. 906, 63 L. Ed. 2d 186 (1980)

Mr. Chief Justice BURGER delivered the opinion of the Court. . . .

---

43. Trammel v. United States, 445 U.S. 40, 51 (1980).
44. See United States v. Fulk, 816 F.2d 1202 (7th Cir. 1987).
45. The privilege may not apply if the marriage relationship is no longer viable at the time the testimony is sought. See In re Witness Before the Grand Jury, 20 Fed. R. Evid. Ser. 987 (2d Cir. 1986).

I

On March 10, 1976, petitioner Otis Trammel was indicted with two others, Edwin Lee Roberts and Joseph Freeman, for importing heroin into the United States from Thailand and the Philippine Islands and for conspiracy to import heroin in violation of 21 U.S.C. §§952(a), 962(a), and 963. The indictment also named six unindicted co-conspirators, including petitioner's wife Elizabeth Ann Trammel.

According to the indictment, petitioner and his wife flew from the Philippines to California in August 1975, carrying with them a quantity of heroin. Freeman and Roberts assisted them in its distribution. Elizabeth Trammel then traveled to Thailand where she purchased another supply of the drug. On November 3, 1975, with four ounces of heroin on her person, she boarded a plane for the United States. During a routine customs search in Hawaii, she was searched, the heroin was discovered, and she was arrested. After discussions with Drug Enforcement Administration agents, she agreed to cooperate with the Government.

Prior to trial on this indictment, petitioner moved to sever his case from that of Roberts and Freeman. He advised the court that the Government intended to call his wife as an adverse witness and asserted his claim to a privilege to prevent her from testifying against him. At a hearing on the motion, Mrs. Trammel was called as a Government witness under a grant of use immunity. She testified that she and petitioner were married in May 1975 and that they remained married.[1] She explained that her cooperation with the Government was based on assurances that she would be given lenient treatment.[2] She then described, in considerable detail, her role and that of her husband in the heroin distribution conspiracy.

After hearing this testimony, the District Court ruled that Mrs. Trammel could testify in support of the Government's case to any act she observed during the marriage and to any communication "made in the presence of a third person;" however, confidential communications between petitioner and his wife were held to be privileged and inadmissible. The motion to sever was denied.

At trial, Elizabeth Trammel testified within the limits of the court's pretrial ruling; her testimony, as the Government concedes, constituted virtually its entire case against petitioner. He was found guilty on both the substantive and conspiracy charges and sentenced to an indeterminate term of years pursuant to the Federal Youth Corrections Act, 18 U.S.C. §5010 (b). . . . [The Court of Appeals affirmed the conviction.]

---

1. In response to the question whether divorce was contemplated, Mrs. Trammel testified that her husband had said that "I would go my way and he would go his."

2. The Government represents to the Court that Elizabeth Trammel has not been prosecuted for her role in the conspiracy.

E. The Marital Privileges 801

II

The privilege claimed by petitioner has ancient roots. Writing in 1628, Lord Coke observed that "it hath been resolved by the Justices that a wife cannot be produced either against or for her husband." 1 E. Coke, A Commentarie upon Littleton 6b (1628). See, generally, 8 J. Wigmore, Evidence §2227 (McNaughton rev. 1961). This spousal disqualification sprang from two canons of medieval jurisprudence: first, the rule that an accused was not permitted to testify in his own behalf because of his interest in the proceeding; second, the concept that husband and wife were one, and that since the woman had no recognized separate legal existence, the husband was that one. From those two now long-abandoned doctrines, it followed that what was inadmissible from the lips of the defendant-husband was also inadmissible from his wife.

Despite its medieval origins, this rule of spousal disqualification remained intact in most common-law jurisdictions well into the 19th century. . . . Indeed, it was not until 1933, in Funk v. United States, 290 U.S. 371, that this Court abolished the testimonial disqualification in the federal courts, so as to permit the spouse of a defendant to testify in the defendant's behalf. *Funk*, however, left undisturbed the rule that either spouse could prevent the other from giving adverse testimony. Id., at 373. The rule thus evolved into one of privilege rather than one of absolute disqualification. . . .

The modern justification for this privilege against adverse spousal testimony is its perceived role in fostering the harmony and sanctity of the marriage relationship. Notwithstanding this benign purpose, the rule was sharply criticized. Professor Wigmore termed it "the merest anachronism in legal theory and an indefensible obstruction to truth in practice." 8 Wigmore §2228, at 221. The Committee on Improvements in the Law of Evidence of the American Bar Association called for its abolition. 63 American Bar Association Reports 594-595 (1938). In its place, Wigmore and others suggested a privilege protecting only private marital communications, modeled on the privilege between priest and penitent, attorney and client, and physician and patient. See 8 Wigmore §§2332 et seq.[5]

These criticisms influenced the American Law Institute, which, in its 1942 Model Code of Evidence, advocated a privilege for marital confidences, but expressly rejected a rule vesting in the defendant the right to exclude all adverse testimony of his spouse. See American Law Institute, Model Code

5. This Court recognized just such a confidential marital communications privilege in Wolfe v. United States, 291 U.S. 7 (1934), and in Blau v. United States, 340 U.S. 332 (1951). In neither case, however, did the Court adopt the Wigmore view that the communications privilege be substituted *in place of* the privilege against adverse spousal testimony. The privilege as to confidential marital communications is not at issue in the instant case; accordingly, our holding today does not disturb *Wolfe* and *Blau*.

of Evidence, Rule 215 (1942). In 1953 the Uniform Rules of Evidence, drafted by the National Conference of Commissioners on Uniform State Laws, followed a similar course; it limited the privilege to confidential communications and "abolishe[d] the rule, still existing in some states, and largely a sentimental relic, of not requiring one spouse to testify against the other in a criminal action." See Rule 23(2) and comments. Several state legislatures enacted similarly patterned provisions into law.

In Hawkins v. United States, 358 U.S. 74 (1958), this Court considered the continued vitality of the privilege against adverse spousal testimony in the federal courts. There the District Court had permitted petitioner's wife, over his objection, to testify against him. With one questioning concurring opinion, the Court held the wife's testimony inadmissible; it took note of the critical comments that the common-law rule had engendered, . . . but chose not to abandon it. Also rejected was the Government's suggestion that the Court modify the privilege by vesting it in the witness-spouse, with freedom to testify or not independent of the defendant's control. The Court viewed this proposed modification as antithetical to the widespread belief, evidenced in the rules then in effect in a majority of the States and in England, "that the law should not force or encourage testimony which might alienate husband and wife, or further inflame existing domestic differences." Id., at 79.

Hawkins, then, left the federal privilege for adverse spousal testimony where it found it, continuing "a rule which bars the testimony of one spouse against the other unless both consent." Id., at 78. . . . However, in so doing, the Court made clear that its decision was not meant to "foreclose whatever changes in the rule may eventually be dictated by 'reason and experience.' " [Id.], at 79.

III

. . . The Federal Rules of Evidence acknowledge the authority of the federal courts to continue the evolutionary development of testimonial privileges in federal criminal trials "governed by the principles of the common law as they may be interpreted . . . in the light of reason and experience." Fed. Rule Evid. 501. . . . The general mandate of Rule 501 was substituted by the Congress for a set of privilege rules drafted by the Judicial Conference Advisory Committee on Rules of Evidence and approved by the Judicial Conference of the United States and by this Court. . . . In rejecting the proposed Rules and Enacting Rule 501, Congress manifested an affirmative intention not to freeze the law of privilege. Its purpose rather was to "provide the courts with the flexibility to develop rules of privilege on a case-by-case basis," 120 Cong. Rec. 40891 (1974) (statement of Rep. Hungate), and to leave the door open to change. . . .[8]

8. Petitioner's reliance on 28 U.S.C. §2076 for the proposition that this Court is without

E. The Marital Privileges

Although Rule 501 confirms the authority of the federal courts to reconsider the continued validity of the *Hawkins* rule, the long history of the privilege suggests that it ought not to be casually cast aside. That the privilege is one affecting marriage, home, and family relationships—already subject to much erosion in our day—also counsels caution. At the same time, we cannot escape the reality that the law on occasion adheres to doctrinal concepts long after experience suggests the need for change. . . .

Since 1958, when *Hawkins* was decided, support for the privilege against adverse spousal testimony has been eroded further. Thirty-one jurisdictions, including Alaska and Hawaii, then allowed an accused a privilege to prevent adverse spousal testimony. . . . The number has now declined to 24. In 1974, the National Conference on Uniform State Laws revised its Uniform Rules of Evidence, but again rejected the *Hawkins* rule in favor of a limited privilege for confidential communications. See Uniform Rules of Evidence, Rule 504. That proposed rule has been enacted in Arkansas, North Dakota, and Oklahoma—each of which in 1958 permitted an accused to exclude adverse spousal testimony.[10] The trend in state law toward divesting the accused of the privilege to bar adverse spousal testimony has special relevance because the laws of marriage and domestic relations are concerns traditionally reserved to the states. . . .

Testimonial exclusionary rules and privileges contravene the fundamental principle that " 'the public . . . has a right to every man's evidence.' " United States v. Bryan, 339 U.S. 323, 331 (1950). As such, they must be strictly construed and accepted "only to the very limited extent that permitting a refusal to testify or excluding relevant evidence has a public good transcending the normally predominant principle of utilizing all rational means for ascertaining truth." Elkins v. United States, 364 U.S. 206, 234 (1960) (Frankfurter, J., dissenting). . . . Here we must decide whether the

---

power to reconsider *Hawkins* is ill-founded. That provision limits this Court's *statutory* rule-making authority by providing that rules "creating, abolishing, or modifying a privilege shall have no force or effect unless . . . approved by act of Congress." It was enacted principally to insure that state rules of privilege would apply in diversity jurisdiction cases unless Congress authorized otherwise. In Rule 501 Congress makes clear that §2076 was not intended to prevent the federal courts from developing testimonial privilege law in federal criminal cases on a case-by-case basis "in light of reason and experience"; indeed Congress encouraged such development.

10. In 1965, California took the privilege from the defendant-spouse and vested it in the witness-spouse, accepting a study commission recommendation that the "latter [was] more likely than the former to determine whether or not to claim the privilege on the basis of the probable effect on the marital relationship." See Cal. Evid. Code Ann. §§970-973 (West 1966 and Supp. 1979) and 1 California Law Revision Commission, Recommendation and Study relating to The Marital "For and Against" Testimonial Privilege, at F-5 (1956). See also 6 California Law Revision Commission, Tentative Privileges Recommendation—Rule 27.5, pp. 243-244 (1964).

Support for the common-law rule has also diminished in England. In 1972, a study group there proposed giving the privilege to the witness-spouse, on the ground that "if [the wife] is willing to give evidence . . . the law would be showing excessive concern for the preservation of marital harmony if it were to say that she must not do so." Criminal Law Revision Committee, Eleventh Report, Evidence (General) 93.

privilege against adverse spousal testimony promotes sufficiently important interests to outweigh the need for probative evidence in the administration of criminal justice.

It is essential to remember that the *Hawkins* privilege is not needed to protect information privately disclosed between husband and wife in the confidence of the marital relationship. . . . Those confidences are privileged under the independent rule protecting confidential marital communications. . . . The *Hawkins* privilege is invoked, not to exclude private marital communications, but rather to exclude evidence of criminal acts and of communications made in the presence of third persons.

No other testimonial privilege sweeps so broadly. The privileges between priest and penitent, attorney and client, and physician and patient limit protection to private communications. These privileges are rooted in the imperative need for confidence and trust. The priest-penitent privilege recognizes the human need to disclose to a spiritual counselor, in total and absolute confidence, what are believed to be flawed acts or thoughts and to receive priestly consolation and guidance in return. The lawyer-client privilege rests on the need for the advocate and counselor to know all that relates to the client's reasons for seeking representation if the professional mission is to be carried out. Similarly, the physician must know all that a patient can articulate in order to identify and to treat disease; barriers to full disclosure would impair diagnosis and treatment.

The *Hawkins* rule stands in marked contrast to these three privileges. Its protection is not limited to confidential communications; rather it permits an accused to exclude all adverse spousal testimony. As Jeremy Bentham observed more than a century and a half ago, such a privilege goes far beyond making "every man's house his castle," and permits a person to convert his house into "a den of thieves." 5 Rationale of Judicial Evidence 340 (1827). It "secures, to every man, one safe and unquestionable and ever ready accomplice for every imaginable crime." Id., at 338.

The ancient foundations for so sweeping a privilege have long since disappeared. Nowhere in the common-law world—indeed in any modern society—is a woman regarded as chattel or demeaned by denial of a separate legal identity and the dignity associated with recognition as a whole human being. Chip by chip, over the years those archaic notions have been cast aside so that "[n]o longer is the female destined solely for the home and the rearing of the family, and only the male for the marketplace and the world of ideas." Stanton v. Stanton, 421 U.S. 7, 14-15 (1975).

The contemporary justification for affording an accused such a privilege is also unpersuasive. When one spouse is willing to testify against the other in a criminal proceeding—whatever the motivation—their relationship is almost certainly in disrepair; there is probably little in the way of marital harmony for the privilege to preserve. In these circumstances, a rule of evidence that permits an accused to prevent adverse spousal testimony seems

E. The Marital Privileges

far more likely to frustrate justice than to foster family peace.[12] Indeed, there is reason to believe that vesting the privilege in the accused could actually undermine the marital relationship. For example, in a case such as this, the Government is unlikely to offer a wife immunity and lenient treatment if it knows that her husband can prevent her from giving adverse testimony. If the Government is dissuaded from making such an offer, the privilege can have the untoward effect of permitting one spouse to escape justice at the expense of the other. It hardly seems conducive to the preservation of the marital relation to place a wife in jeopardy solely by virtue of her husband's control over her testimony.

IV

Our consideration of the foundations for the privilege and its history satisfy us that "reason and experience" no longer justify so sweeping a rule as that found acceptable by the Court in *Hawkins*. Accordingly, we conclude that the existing rule should be modified so that the witness-spouse alone has a privilege to refuse to testify adversely; the witness may be neither compelled to testify nor foreclosed from testifying. This modification—vesting the privilege in the witness-spouse—furthers the important public interest in marital harmony without unduly burdening legitimate law enforcement needs.

Here, petitioner's spouse chose to testify against him. That she did so after a grant of immunity and assurances of lenient treatment does not render her testimony involuntary. . . . Accordingly, the District Court and the Court of Appeals were correct in rejecting petitioner's claim of privilege, and the judgment of the Court of Appeals is affirmed.

[The concurring opinion of Justice Stewart is omitted.]

Consider carefully footnote 12 and the accompanying text in the Court's opinion. As the Court acknowledged early in its opinion, Mrs. Trammel was heavily involved in drug trafficking and thus faced the possibility of serious criminal penalties. Thus, the government's offer of immunity to her was a substantial incentive for her to testify against her husband. Perhaps the Trammel's marriage was likely to end regardless of the immunity, and perhaps she would have been willing to testify against her husband in any event. If it were clear that she would have testified without a grant of immunity, however, it seems unlikely that the prosecutor would have offered her immunity. In any event, if we are serious about trying to preserve marital

---

12. It is argued that abolishing the privilege will permit the Government to come between husband and wife, pitting one against the other. That, too, misses the mark. Neither *Hawkins*, nor any other privilege, prevents the Government from enlisting one spouse to give information concerning the other or to aid in the other's apprehension. It is only the spouse's testimony in the courtroom that is prohibited.

harmony—as recognizing the testimonial privilege suggests we are—why should we formulate the privilege in a way that encourages prosecutors to pressure one spouse into testifying against the other? If the accused spouse could claim the privilege, the government, as the Court recognized, would have no incentive to try to drive a wedge between the husband and wife with an offer of leniency or immunity in cases where the spouses were cohorts in crime or by trying to pit an innocent spouse against the charged spouse.

PROBLEMS

1. A state trial judge, Edgar Robbins, and two of his friends are being prosecuted for selling liquor seized in a dry county to a bar in a wet county. The prosecutor claims that Judge Robbins owns the bar in the wet county, and to help establish this fact the prosecutor plans to call the judge's wife, Emily Robbins. If Ms. Robbins testifies, she will say that she found a bill of sale for some professional bar supplies in the dresser drawer and that when she confronted her husband with the bill of sale he tore it up. Can either the judge or his wife prevent the jury from hearing this evidence? Does your answer depend upon whether the Robbins are still married?

2. Sam Temple has been charged with armed robbery. His wife, from whom he is now separated, is prepared to testify pursuant to a grant of immunity that she observed Sam come home one evening with a bag of money, that Sam said he had stolen the money from a courier, and that she helped Sam count, hide, and launder the money. Should this testimony be admissible over Sam's objection?

3. Ellen Graves has been subpoenaed to provide a handwriting exemplar and fingerprints to the grand jury, which is investigating the filing of false joint income tax returns by Ms. Graves and her husband. Ms. Graves moves to quash the subpoena on the ground that compliance would violate her privilege not to testify against her husband. What result?

F. DRAFTING RULES OF PRIVILEGE

The rules of privilege provide a manageable but challenging task for the rule drafter. The scope of each privilege is relatively narrow and discrete, but close attention to detail is critical if the rule is to operate as the drafter intends it to. As an exercise in legislative or rule drafting we suggest that each of you try your hand at modifying one of the traditional privileges or creating a new one. If you choose a traditional privilege, you should choose one that you want to modify in some significant manner. The Proposed Federal Rules can act as a model, and you may want to borrow entire sections or subsections

F. Drafting Rules of Privilege

from some of those or other rules of privilege. A substantial part of your effort (but not necessarily of the words you use), however, should be your original creation. You should accompany your draft with an explanatory Note that is similar to the Advisory Committee's Notes.

By way of suggestion and not limitation, we encourage you to try your hand at one of the following:

(a) The attorney-client privilege, with an emphasis on the definition of "representative of the client" and on a provision that would qualify the privilege by making privileged communications sometimes discoverable.

(b) A confidential communications privilege for some types of counsellors or social workers other than physicians and psychologists. Here a primary focus will have to be on how to define the types of individuals to whom privileged communications may be made and the subject matter of the communications that will be privileged.

(c) A priest-penitent privilege broader in scope from Proposed FRE 507. Here the difficult issues will be how to define "clergy member," and how to define the types of communications that will be covered by the privilege in view of the fact that members of the clergy often provide a variety of counselling functions. Also, as the privilege is expanded, should there be exceptions?

(d) A parent-child privilege. Here there are a number of problems with which to deal. Who qualifies as a parent? Should the privilege exist only during the child's minority; and if so, is the critical time the time of the communication or the time the information is sought? Who should the holders of the privilege be? If there is more than one holder, how should one resolve disputes between the holders over whether to waive the privilege? What exceptions to the privilege should there be?

TABLE OF CASES

Addington v. Texas, 150, 689
Addison, United States v., 737
Ahrens, United States v., 611
Alcade, People v., 434
Alexander Dawson, Inc. v. NLRB, 179
Anderson v. Liberty Lobby, Inc., 564
Anderson, State v., 379 N.W.2d 70, 737
Anderson, State v., 285 P.2d 879, 555

Bailey, United States v., 444 U.S. 394, 687, 688, 694
Bailey, United States v., 581 F.2d 341, 477
Baird v. Koerner, 768
Baker v. State, 449
Ball, State v., 120
Barber v. Page, 354, 360, 363, 404
Barnes v. United States, 583, 653, 668, 673-675
Barrett, United States v., 239
Baxter v. Palmigiano, 775
Beck v. Dye, 428
Beechum, United States v., 242, 243, 244
Benton, United States v., 238
Bermudez, United States v., 235
Berrios, People v., 379
Bervid v. Iowa State Tax Commn., 700
Blau v. United States, 801
Bledsoe, People v., 737
Bloom, United States v., 262
Borum v. United States, 142
Bourjaily v. United States, 168, 336, 395, 397
Brewer v. Williams, 383
Brink's, Inc. v. City of New York, 775

Britton, State v., 556
Broadrick v. Oklahoma, 660
Brooks, United States v., 235
Brown v. Illinois, 383
Brown v. Mississippi, 383
Brown, State v., 239
Brown, United States v., 737, 738
Bruton v. United States, 354, 357
Bryan, United States v., 803
Bunge Corp. v. M/V Furness Bridge, 610, 611
Burch v. Reading Co., 138
Burke, United States v., 217
Burton, United States v., 118

Cain v. State, 737
California v. Green, 356, 360-364, 366, 369-370, 685
Campbell v. Greer, 524
Capital Traction Co. v. Hof, 581
Cardenas, People v., 238
Carriger, United States v., 176
Carrillo, United States v., 260
Carroll, United States v., 235
Carson, United States v., 206
Celotex Corp. v. Catrett, 564
Cepulonis, United States v., 235
Cervantes, People v., 263
Chambers v. Mississippi, 269, 759
City of Philadelphia v. Westinghouse Elec. Corp., 780, 783
Coles v. Harsch, 773
Commonwealth v. Kline, 237
Commonwealth v. Neal, 737
Commonwealth v. Shively, 237

Cook, People v., 688, 689
Cool v. United States, 679
County Court of Ulster County v. Allen et al., 652, 658, 670, 673-678, 684
Crouch, United States v., 495
Cyphers, United States v., 238
Curtis v. Bradley, 446

Daghita, People v., 768
Dallas County v. Commercial Union Assur. Co., 302
Damm, State v., 737
Darden v. Wainwright, 83
Davis v. Alaska, 269, 381, 759
DeJohn, United States v., 239
Delaware v. Fensterer, 365, 369
DeLoach, United States v., 237
Diederich v. Walters, 593
Doe, People v., 765
Donnelly v. DeChristoforo, 83
Dothard, United States v., 235
Douglas v. Alabama, 354, 358, 381
Doyle v. Ohio, 387
Duplan Corp. v. Deering Milliken, Inc., 784
Dutton v. Evans, 359, 367, 370

Elkins v. United States, 803
Engel v. United Traction Co., 120

Faretta v. California, 242
Featherman, State v., 239
Findley v. State, 237
Fisher v. United States, 783, 790
Flesher, State v., 428
Fletcher v. Weir, 387
Foskey, United States v., 239
Francis v. Franklin, 649
Frye v. United States, 736
Fulk, United States v., 799
Funk v. United States, 801
Furnco Constr. Corp. v. Waters, 587

Gainey, United States v., 598, 623, 626, 654-658, 661
Gambino, People v., 238
Gano, United States v., 236
Garrett v. Howden, 428
Geaney, United States v., 206
Geer, United States v., 534
General Electric Co. v. Kirkpatrick, 783
Gibbs v. State, 238
Gila Valley Ry. Co. v. Hall, 162
Gilbert, United States v., 470
Gilbert v. California, 376
Glasser v. United States, 395, 396, 397

Government of the Virgin Islands v. Toto, 115
Grady, United States v., 470
Grand Jury Subpoena Dated January 4, 1984, In Re, 764, 765
Great American Ins. Co. v. Horab, 113
Great Atl. & Pac. Tea Co. v. Custin, 285
Green, State v., 238
Greer v. United States, 629
Griffin v. California, 774, 775
Grismore v. Consolidated Prod. Co., 754
Guerrero, United States v., 239

Haddad v. Lockheed, 116
Haldeman, United States v., 176, 238
Halloran v. Virginia Chemicals, Inc., 230
Hardy v. Johns-Mansville Sales Corp., 697
Hare v. Family Publications Serv., 764
Harper & Row Publishers, Inc. v. Decker, 780
Harris, United States v., 237
Hassell, United States v., 176
Hawkins v. United States, 625, 802, 803, 804, 805
Hearst, United States v., 237
Hickman v. Taylor, 787, 788, 795
Hickory v. United States, 686
Holland v. United States, 176
Holman, United States v., 237
Houston Oxygen Co. v. Davis, 424
Huddleston v. United States, 169, 242, 243, 244
Hughes v. Mathews, 679
Huntington v. Crowley, 737
Hutto v. Davis, 652

Iaconetti, United States v., 477
IBM Peripheral EDP Devices Antitrust Litig., In Re, 409
Ibn-Tamas v. United States, 737
Ina Aviation Corp. v. United States, 583
Inadi, United States v., 366
In Re Grand Jury Subpoena Dated January 4, 1984, 764, 765
In Re IBM Peripheral EDP Devices Antitrust Litigation, 409
In re Japanese Elec. Prod. Antitrust Litig., 168
In Re Kaplan, 768
In re Michael, 151
In Re the Marriage of Linda Lou Tresnak and Emil James Tresnak, 698
In Re Winship, 150, 635-653, 657, 670-674, 681, 682
In Re Witness Before the Grand Jury, 799
In Re Zuniga, 765

Table of Cases

James v. River Parishes Co., Inc., 611
James, United States v., 168
James R. Snyder Co. v. Associated Gen. Contractors of America, 168
Japanese Elec. Prod. Antitrust Litig., In re, 168
Jenkins v. Anderson, 387
Johnson v. Lutz, 457
Johnson, United States v., 237

Kaplan, In Re, 768
Katz v. United States, 383
Kilgus, United States v., 737
King, State v., 239
King, United States v., 471
Kirby v. United States, 353, 354
Klein, United States v., 628
Kline, Commonwealth v., 237
Klotter, State v., 235
Knapp v. State, 107, 119

Lakeside v. Oregon, 12
Lamar v. State, 237
LaPage, State v., 123
Lavine v. Milne, 574, 627, 628
Lawrence, State v., 697
Leary v. United States, 654, 655, 664, 665
Lee v. Illinois, 368
Leftwich, United States v., 235
Legille v. Dann, 611
Lego v. Twomey, 336
Leland v. Oregon, 645, 647, 652
Lewis, United States v., 693 F.2d 189, 235, 378
Lewis, United States v., 565 F.2d 1248, 378
Lloyd v. American Export Lines, Inc., 409
Lockhart v. McCree, 146
Long, State v., 235
Longenecker v. General Motors, 583
Luck v. United States, 528

Madrid, United States v., 746
Mancusi v. Stubbs, 355, 360, 363, 364, 404
Manrique, State v., 235
Manson v. Braithwaite, 174, 376
Marriage of Linda Lou Tresnak and Emil James Tresnak, In Re the, 698
Martin v. Ohio, 644, 652, 677
Martin v. Reynolds Metal Corp., 464
Masters, United States v., 235
Matlock, United States v., 396
Mattox v. United States, 352, 362
McDaniels, United States v., 737

McDonnell Douglas Corp. v. Green, 586-589
McFarlin, State v., 237
McGahee v. Massey, 236
McMillan v. Pennsylvania, 650, 689
McMillan, United States v., 176
McQueeney v. Wilmington Trust Co., 109, 119
Metropolis Theatre Co. v. Chicago, 624
Michael, In re, 151
Michaelson v. United States, 220, 225, 227
Miller v. Fenton, 169
Miranda v. Arizona, 383, 387, 762
Mitchell, State v., 737
Mitchell, United States v., 239
Mobile, J. & K. C.R. Co. v. Turnipseed, 623, 624
Monica, United States v., 206
Moore, State v., 556
Morissette v. United States, 600, 671, 672
Motor Club of Iowa v. Department of Transp., 700
Mullaney v. Wilbur, 636-653, 661, 670, 677
Murphy Auto Parts Co. v. Ball, 427
Mutual Life Ins. Co. of New York v. Hillmon, 432-436
Myers, United States v., 236

Neal, Commonwealth v., 737
Nelson v. O'Neil, 357, 370
Newark Stereotyper's Union v. Newark Morning Ledger, 113
New York Central R.R. Co. v. Bianc, 621
Nix v. Whiteside, 151
Nixon v. United States, 759
NLRB v. Tahoe Nugget, Inc., 610, 611, 614
NLRB v. Transportation Mgmt. Corp., 610
Nobles, United States v., 787
Noseworthy v. City of New York, 575
Nunley v. Pettway Oil Co., 581

Oates, United States v., 462, 467-472
Obayagbona, United States v., 424
Odum, People v., 239
Ogg, State v., 754
Ohio v. Roberts, 361, 363, 364, 365, 366
Orozco, United States v., 470
Oswalt, State v., 553
Owens, United States v., 368, 380

Paddack v. Dave Christiansen, Inc., 746
Palmer v. Hoffman, 453
Parnell, United States v., 235
Patterson v. New York, 636-653, 670, 677

Table of Cases

Paul v. Davis, 640
Peete, People v., 236
People v. Alcade, 434
People v. Bledsoe, 737
People v. Berrios, 379
People v. Cardenas, 238
People v. Cervantes, 263
People v. Cook, 688, 689
People v. Doe, 765
People v. Daghita, 768
People v. Gambino, 238
People v. Odum, 239
People v. Peete, 236
People v. Shirley, 737
People v. Spaulding, 238
People v. Williams, 237
Petty v. Ideco, 526
Pheaster, United States v., 434
Pierre, United States v., 539
Pisari, United States v., 236
Plough, Inc. v. The Mason & Dixon Line, 610
Pointer v. Texas, 353
Poncy v. Johnson & Johnson, 612
Price, State v., 235

Queen's Case, 532
Quercia v. United States, 580, 581
Quinto, United States v., 539

Rainey, State v., 688
Rathbun v. Brancatella, 446
Rex v. Smith, 236
Rivera v. Delaware, 645, 647
Rivera v. Minnich, 689
Robitaille v. Netoco Community Theatres of North Attleboro, 272
Robtoy, State v., 239
Rogers v. Missouri Pac. R.R., 150
Romano, United States v., 654, 655, 661, 662
Ross, United States v., 321 F.2d 61, 237
Ross, United States v., 456 U.S. 798, 559
Rossi v. United States, 688
Rostad v. Portland Ry., Light & Power Co., 692
Rozier v. Ford Motor Co., 528
Rubio-Gonzalez, United States v., 238
Rudzinski v. Warner Theatres, Inc., 390
Rummell v. Estelle, 652

Samuelson v. Susen, 764
Sanchez v. Black Bros. Co., 739
Sandstrom v. Montana, 652, 669, 673, 676-678
Sanitary Grocery Co. v. Snead, 427
Santosky v. Kramer, 689

Santobello v. New York, 288
Sauter, State v., 236
Sawyer, United States v., 471
Schecter v. Klanfer, 574
Schlak, State v., 237
Schut, State v., 237
Scully, United States v., 173
Seiler v. Lucasfilm, Ltd., 191
Sharp v. Coopers & Lybrand, 612
Shaw, State v., 238
Shirley, People v., 737
Shively, Commonwealth v., 237
Shows v. M/V Red Eagle, 528
Simborski, State v., 239, 256
Singer v. United States, 242
Skeet, United States v., 733
Sliker, United States v., 200
Solem v. Helm, 652
Solesbee v. Balkcom, 683
Snyder v. Massachusetts, 362
Spaulding, People v., 238
Stanley v. Illinois, 620, 621
Stanton v. Stanton, 804
State v. Anderson, 379 N.W.2d 70, 737
State v. Anderson, 285 P.2d 879, 555
State v. Ball, 120
State v. Britton, 556
State v. Brown, 239
State v. Damm, 737
State v. Featherman, 239
State v. Flesher, 428
State v. Green, 238
State v. King, 239
State v. Klotter, 235
State v. LaPage, 123
State v. Lawrence, 697
State v. Long, 235
State v. Manrique, 235
State v. McFarlin, 237
State v. Mitchell, 737
State v. Moore, 556
State v. Ogg, 754
State v. Oswalt, 553
State v. Price, 235
State v. Rainey, 688
State v. Robtoy, 239
State v. Sauter, 236
State v. Schlak, 237
State v. Schut, 237
State v. Shaw, 238
State v. Simborski, 239, 256
State v. Stevenson, 555
State v. Taylor, 737
State v. Toshishige Yoshino, 235
State v. Trujillo, 238
State v. Villavicencio, 235, 260
State v. Williams, 149
Steadman v. SEC, 629
Steele, United States v., 112
Stevenson v. Stuart, 108

Table of Cases

Stevenson, State v., 555
Sweeny v. Erving, 588, 615

Tanner v. United States, 12
Taylor, State v., 737
Tennessee v. Street, 367, 368
Texas v. McCullough, 146
Texas Dept. of Community Affairs v. Burdine, 584, 611
Thomas v. Kansas Power & Light Co., 698
Toshishige Yoshino, State v., 235
Tot v. United States, 625, 654-655, 664, 666, 685
Trammel v. United States, 763, 764, 799
Tranowski, United States v., 737
Trujillo, State v., 238
Turner v. Texas Instruments, Inc., 589
Turner v. United States, 654, 655

Ulland, United States v., 235
Union Paint & Varnish Co. v. Dean, 122
United Shoe Mach. Corp., United States v., 779
United States v. Addison, 737
United States v. Ahrens, 611
United States v. Bailey, 444 U.S. 394, 687, 688, 694
United States v. Bailey, 581 F.2d 341, 477
United States v. Barrett, 239
United States v. Beechum, 242, 243, 244
United States v. Benton, 238
United States v. Bermudez, 235
United States v. Bloom, 262
United States v. Brooks, 235
United States v. Brown, 737, 738
United States v. Bryan, 803
United States v. Burke, 217
United States v. Burton, 118
United States v. Carriger, 176
United States v. Carrillo, 260
United States v. Carroll, 235
United States v. Carson, 206
United States v. Cepulonis, 235
United States v. Crouch, 495
United States v. Cyphers, 238
United States v. DeJohn, 239
United States v. DeLoach, 237
United States v. Dothard, 235
United States v. Foskey, 239
United States v. Fulk, 799
United States v. Gainey, 598, 623, 654-658, 661
United States v. Gano, 236
United States v. Geaney, 206
United States v. Geer, 534
United States v. Gilbert, 470
United States v. Grady, 470

United States v. Guerrero, 239
United States v. Haldeman, 176, 238
United States v. Harris, 237
United States v. Hassell, 176
United States v. Hearst, 237
United States v. Holman, 237
United States v. Iaconetti, 477
United States v. Inadi, 366
United States v. James, 168
United States v. Johnson, 237
United States v. Kilgus, 737
United States v. King, 471
United States v. Klein, 628
United States v. Leftwich, 235
United States v. Lewis, 693 F.2d 189, 235
United States v. Lewis, 565 F.2d 1248, 378
United States v. Madrid, 746
United States v. Masters, 235
United States v. Matlock, 396
United States v. McDaniels, 737
United States v. McMillan, 176
United States v. Mitchell, 239
United States v. Monica, 206
United States v. Myers, 236
United States v. Nobles, 787
United States v. Oates, 462, 467-472
United States v. Obayagbona, 424
United States v. Orozco, 470
United States v. Owens, 368, 380
United States v. Parnell, 235
United States v. Pheaster, 434
United States v. Pierre, 539
United States v. Pisari, 236
United States v. Quinto, 539
United States v. Romano, 654, 655, 661, 662
United States v. Ross, 456 U.S. 798, 559
United States v. Ross, 321 F.2d 61, 237
United States v. Rubio-Gonzalez, 238
United States v. Sawyer, 471
United States v. Scully, 173
United States v. Skeet, 733
United States v. Sliker, 200
United States v. Steele, 112
United States v. Tranowski, 737
United States v. Ulland, 235
United States v. United Shoe Mach. Corp., 779
United States v. United States Gypsum Co., 672, 784
United States v. Urbanik, 392
United States v. Vargas, 685
United States v. Wasler, 238
United States v. Williams, 738
United States v. Witschner, 237
United States v. Wixom, 238, 258
United States v. Woods, 236
United States v. Young, 83

United States Gypsum Co., United States v., 672, 784
Upjohn v. United States, 766, 781
Urbanik, United States v., 392
Usery v. Turner Elkhorn Mining Co. et al., 615

Vance v. Terrazas, 689
Vargas, United States v., 685
Vicksburg & M.R.R. v. Putnum, 580
Villavicencio, State v., 235, 260
Vlandis v. Kline, 620, 621

Waldman v. Shipyard Marina, 122
Washington v. Texas, 759
Wasler, United States v., 238
Whitehurst v. Wright, 495
Whiteman v. State, 236
William T. Thompson Co. v. General Nutrition Corp., 764

Williams v. State, 236
Williams, People v., 237
Williams, State v., 149
Williams, United States v., 738
Winship, In Re, 150, 635-653, 657, 670-674, 681, 682
Witness Before the Grand Jury, In Re, 799
Witschner, United States v., 237
Wixom, United States v., 238, 258
Wolfe v. United States, 801
Woodby v. Immigration & Naturalization Serv., 629
Woods v. State, 236
Woods, United States v., 236
Wright v. Doe d. Tatham, 320-329, 332, 340, 341

Yee Hem v. United States, 657
Young, United States v., 83

Zuniga, In Re, 765

TABLE OF AUTHORITIES

Allen, A Reconceptualization of Civil Trials, 66 B.U.L. Rev. 401 (1986), 715
———, More on Constitutional Process-of-Proof Problems, 94 Harv. L. Rev. 1795 (1981), 581, 689
———, *Mullaney v. Wilbur*, The Supreme Court, and the Substantive Criminal Law—An Examination of the Limits of Legitimate Intervention, 55 Tex. L. Rev. 269 (1977), 636
———, Presumptions, Inferences and Burden of Proof in Federal Civil Action—An Anatomy of Unnecessary Ambiguity and a Proposal for Reform, 76 Nw. U.L. Rev. 892 (1982), 609
———, Presumptions in Civil Actions Reconsidered, 66 Iowa L. Rev. 843 (1981), 591
———, Rationality and Accuracy in the Criminal Process: A Discordant Note on the Harmonizing of the Justices' Views on Burdens of Persuasion in Criminal Cases, 74 J. Crim. L. & Criminology 1147 (1983), 689
———, Rationality, Mythology and the "Acceptability of Verdicts" Thesis, 66 B.U.L. Rev. 541 (1986), 143
———, Structuring Jury Decisionmaking in Criminal Cases: A Unified Constitutional Approach to Evidentiary Devices, 94 Harv. L. Rev. 321 (1980), 679
———, The Explanatory Value of Analyzing Codifications by Reference to Organizing Principles Other Than Those Employed in the Codification, 79 Nw. U.L. Rev., 1080 (1984-85), 167, 693
———, The Restoration of *In Re Winship*: A Comment on Burdens of Persuasion in Criminal Cases after *Patterson v. New York*, 76 Mich. L. Rev. 30 (1977), 636
Allen & DeGrazia, The Constitutional Requirement of Proof Beyond Reasonable Doubt in Criminal Cases: A Comment Upon Incipient Chaos in the Lower Courts, 20 Am. Crim. L. Rev. 1 (1982), 674

Allen, Grady, Polsby, & Yashiko, A Positive Theory of the Attorney-Client Privilege and Work-Product Doctrine (forthcoming), 790

Allen, Koeck, Reichenberg, & Rosen, The German Advantage in Civil Procedure: A Plea for More Details and Fewer Generalities in Comparative Scholarship, 82 Nw. U.L. Rev. 705 (1988), 559

Allen, R., & Kuhns, R., Constitutional Criminal Procedure: An Examination of the Fourth, Fifth, and Sixth Amendments and Related Areas (1985), 383

American Bar Association Model Rules of Professional Conduct, 518

Andenaes, General Prevention, 43 J. Crim. L.C. & P.S. 176 (1952), 793

Ball, The Moment of Truth: Probability Theory and Standards of Proof, 14 Vand. L. Rev. 807 (1961), 127

Ball, The Myth of Conditional Relevancy, 14 Ga. L. Rev. 435 (1980), 166

Barnes D., Statistics as Proof: Fundamentals of Quantitative Evidence (1983), 722

Bell, Decision Theory and Due Process: A Critique of the Supreme Court's Lawmaking for Burdens of Proof, 78 J.Crim. L. & Crim. 557 (1987), 571

Bentham, J., 5 Rationale of Judicial Evidence 340 (1827), 804

Berger, Man's Trial, Women's Tribulation, 77 Colum. L. Rev. 1 (1977), 265

Berger, Presumptions, and Competency of Witnesses in the Federal Court: A Federal Choice of Law Rule, 42 Brooklyn L. Rev. 417 (1976), 764

Bohlen, The Effect of Rebuttable Presumptions of Law upon Burden of Proof, 68 U. Pa. L. Rev. 307 (1920), 630

Brosman, The Statutory Presumption (pt. II), 5 Tul. L. Rev. 178 (1931), 600

Brownmiller, S., Against Our Will: Men, Women and Rape (1975), 265, 267

Burnham, The Attorney-Client Privilege in the Corporate Arena, 24 Bus. Law. 901 (1969), 784

California Law Revision Commission, Tentative Privileges Recommendation (1964), 803

Carter, The Admissibility of Evidence of Similar Facts, 70 Law Q. Rev. 214 (1954), 255

Casper, Benedict, & Perry, Juror Decision-Making, Attitudes and the Hindsight Bias, 13 Law & Hum. Behav. (1989), 124

———, The Tort Remedy in Search and Seizure Cases: A Case Study in Juror Decision-Making, Law & Soc. Inquiry 279 (1988), 124

Cather, W., The Professor's House (1925) (Vintage Books Edition, 1973), 151

Chafee, Book Review, Wigmore on Evidence, 37 Harv. L. Rev. 513 (1924), 158

Chayes, The Role of the Judge in Public Law Litigation, 89 Harv. L. Rev. 1281 (1976), 560, 568-570

Table of Authorities

Chevigny, P., Police Power (1969), 379
Christie, A. Curtain (1975), 318
Clark, C., Handbook of the Law of Code Pleading (2d ed. 1947), 566
Cleary, Presuming and Pleading: An Essay on Juristic Immaturity, 12 Stan. L. Rev. 5 (1959), 560, 630, 631
Cohen, L., The Probable and the Provable (1977), 126, 714
Cohen, Freedom of Proof, in Facts in Law (1983), 103
———, The Role of Evidential Weight in Criminal Proof, 66 B.U.L. Rev. 635 (1986), 719
Coke, A Commentarie upon Littleton (1628), 801
Comment, The Need for a New Approach to the Present Sense Impression Hearsay Exception After *State v. Flesher*, 67 Iowa L. Rev. 179 (1981), 425, 426, 428
———, Rape Laws: Sexism in Society and Law, 61 Calif. L. Rev. 919 (1973), 267

Damaska, M., The Faces of Justice and State Authority (1986), 559
———, Evidentiary Barriers to Conviction and Two Models of Criminal Procedure, 121 U. Pa. L. Rev. 506 (1973), 559
———, The Death of Legal Torture, 87 Yale L.J. 860 (1978), 103
Davis, Judicial Notice, 55 Colum. L. Rev. 945 (1985), 692
Devitt, E., & Blackmar, C., Federal Jury Practice and Instructions (3d ed. 1977) 138
Dickens, C., Hard Times, 152
Dripps, The Constitutional Status of the Reasonable Doubt Rule, 75 Calif. L. Rev. 1665 (1987), 689

Estrich, Rape, 95 Yale L.J. 1087 (1986), 265

Falknor, The "Hear-say" Rule as a "See-Do" Rule: Evidence of Conduct, 33 Rocky Mt. L. Rev. 741 (1964), 318
———, Silence as Hearsay, 89 U. Pa. L. Rev. 192 (1940), 318
Field, R., Kaplan, B., & Clermont, K., Materials for a Basic Course in Civil Procedure (5th ed. 1984), 141
Finman, Implied Assertions as Hearsay: Some Criticisms of the Uniform Rules of Evidence, 14 Stan. L. Rev. 682 (1962), 318, 324, 332, 333, 339, 341
Fried, Correspondence, 86 Yale L.J. 573 (1977), 795
Friedman, Route Analysis of Credibility and Hearsay, 96 Yale L.J. 667 (1987), 107
Fuller, Legal Fictions, 25 Ill. L. Rev. 363 (1930-31), 592, 629

Gausewitz, Presumptions, 40 Minn. L. Rev. 391 (1956), 630
Giannelli, The Admissibility of Novel Scientific Evidence: *Frye v. United States*, a Half-Century Later, 80 Colum. L. Rev. 1197 (1980), 738
Goldstein, The State and the Accused: Balance of Advantage in Criminal Procedure, 69 Yale L.J. 1149 (1960), 142
Graham, The Right of Confrontation and Rules of Evidence: Sir Walter Raleigh Rides Again, 9 Alaska L.J. (1971), 356

Hacking, I., The Emergence of Probability (1975), 148
Hart & McNaughton, Evidence and Inference in the Law, 87 Daedalus 40 (Fall 1958), 126
Hart & Sacks, The Legal Process: Basic Problems in the Making and Application of Law (1958), 163
Hay, Property, Authority and the Criminal Law, in Albion's Fatal Tree 17 (1975), 134, 144
Henver & Penrod, Increasing Jurors' Participation in Trials: A Field Experiment with Jury Notetaking and Question Asking, 12 Law & Hum. Behav. 231 (1988), 70
Holdsworth, W., A History of English Common Law (1926), 630
House Committee on Education and Labor, H.R. Rep. No. 92-460, 625
Hurst, J., The Growth of American Law: The Lawmakers (1940), 578
Hutchins & Slesinger, Some Observations on the Law of Evidence: Spontaneous Exclamations, 28 Colum. L. Rev. 432 (1928), 427

Imwinkelried, E., Evidentiary Foundations (1980), 26, 171
———, Judge Versus Jury: Who Should Decide Questions of Preliminary Facts Conditioning the Admissibility of Scientific Evidence, 25 Wm. & Mary L. Rev. 577 (1984), 738

James, Burdens of Proof, 47 Va. L. Rev. 51 (1961), 565-567
———, Relevancy, Probability and the Law, 29 Cal. L. Rev. 689 (1941), 122
James, F., & Hazard, G., Civil Procedure (2d ed. 1977), 587
Joseph, G., & Saltzburg, S., Evidence in America: The Federal Rules in the States (1987), 765

Kagehiro & Stanton, Legal v. Quantified Definitions of Standards of Proof, 9 Law & Hum. Behav. 159 (1985), 576
Kahneman, D., Slovic, P., & Tversky, A. (eds.), Judgment Under Uncertainty: Heuristics and Biases (1982), 713
Kalven, H. & Zeisel, H., The American Jury (1966), 268

Table of Authorities

Kaplan, Decision Theory and the Factfinding Process, 20 Stan. L. Rev. 1065 (1968), 127, 129
———, Of Marbus and Zorgs—An Essay in Honor of David Louisell, 66 Calif. L. Rev. 987 (1978), 169
Kaye, The Laws of Probability and the Law of the Land, 47 Chi. L. Rev. 35 (1979), 719
———, The Limits of the Preponderance of the Evidence Standard: Justifiably Naked Statistical Evidence and Multiple Causation, 1982 A.B.F.J. 487, 570, 717
———, Paradoxes, Gedanken Experiments and the Burden of Proof: A Response to Dr. Cohen's Reply, 1981 Ariz. St. L.J. 635, 719
———, The Paradox of the Gatecrasher and Other Stories, 1979 Ariz. St. L.J. 101, 719
Kornstein, A Bayesian Model of Harmless Error, 5 J. Legal Stud. 121 (1976), 115
Krattenmaker, Interpersonal Privileges Under the Federal Rules of Evidence: A Suggested Approach, 64 Geo. L.J. 613 (1976), 765
Kuhns, The Propensity to Misunderstand the Character of Specific Acts Evidence, 66 Iowa L. Rev. 777 (1981), 250

Ladd, Techniques and Theory of Character Testimony, 24 Iowa L. Rev. 498 (1939), 219
Langbein, The German Advantage in Civil Procedure, 52 U. Chi. L. Rev. 823 (1985), 559
———, J., Torture and the Law of Proof: Europe and England in the Ancien Régime (1977), 103
Lawson, Experimental Research on the Organization of Persuasive Arguments: An Application to Courtroom Communications, 1970 Law & Soc. Order 579, 501
Lempert, Modeling Relevance, 75 Mich. L. Rev. 1021 (1977), 127
Lempert, R. & Saltzburg, S., A Modern Approach to Evidence (2d ed. 1982), 245, 258, 264, 296, 384, 390, 490, 603, 740
Letwin, "Unchaste Character," Ideology, and the California Rape Evidence Laws, 54 S. Cal. L. Rev. 35 (1980), 265
Lev, The Law of Vicarious Admissions—An Estoppel, 26 U. Cinn. L. Rev. 17 (1957), 384
Levin, Pennsylvania and the Uniform Rules of Evidence: Presumptions and Dead Man Statutes, 103 U. Pa. L. Rev. 1 (1954), 630
Lilly G., An Introduction to the Law of Evidence (1978), 599
Linebaugh, Social History and Legal History: A Reply to Professor Langbein, 60 N.Y.U.L. Rev. 212 (1985), 144
Loftus, E., Eyewitness Testimony (1979), 484
Louisell, Confidentiality, Conformity and Confusion: Privileges in Federal Court Today, 31 Tul. L. Rev. 101 (1956), 795

———, Construing Rule 301: Instructing the Jury on Presumptions in Civil Actions and Proceedings, 63 Va. L. Rev. 281 (1977), 593, 600
Louisell, D., & Mueller, C., Federal Evidence (1977), 230, 235
———, Federal Evidence (1980), 368
Lushing, Faces Without Features: The Surface Validity of Criminal Inferences, 72 J. Crim. L. & Criminology 82 (1981), 673, 678

Maguire, J., Evidence: Common Sense and Common Law (1947), 595
———, The Hearsay System: Around and Through the Thicket, 14 Vand. L. Rev. 741 (1961), 318, 320, 339
Maguire & Epstein, Preliminary Questions of Fact in Determining the Admissibility of Evidence, 40 Harv. L. Rev. 392 (1927), 163
Marjorbanks, For the Defence: The Life of Edward Marshall Hall (1937), 236
McBaine, Burden of Proof: Presumptions, 2 UCLA L. Rev. 13 (1954), 631
McCormick, Charges on Presumptions and Burdens of Proofs, 5 N.C.L. Rev. 291 (1972), 601
McCormick, Handbook on the Law of Evidence (2d ed., Cleary, 1972), 193, 344, 345, 396, 428, 446, 753
———, Handbook on the Law of Evidence (3d ed., Cleary, 1984), 223, 231, 234-240, 249, 272, 280, 290, 309, 344, 386, 410, 412, 420, 425, 454, 509, 520, 548, 551, 583, 596, 715, 737, 740, 752, 754, 768, 772
———, The Borderland of Hearsay, 39 Yale L.J. 489 (1930), 332, 339
———, What Shall the Trial Judge Tell the Jury About Presumptions?, 13 Wash. L. Rev. 185 (1938), 630
McCormick, C., Sutton, J., & Wellborn, O., Cases and Materials on Evidence (6th ed. 1987), 272
McNaughton, Burden of Production of Evidence: A Function of a Burden of Persuasion, 68 Harv. L. Rev. 1382 (1955), 562
Mileski, Courtroom Encounters: An Observation Study of Lower Criminal Court, 5 Law & Soc. Rev. 473 (1971), 144
Miller, A., Death of a Salesman, 345
Monaghan, Constitutional Fact Review, 85 Colum. L. Rev. 229 (1985), 169
Morgan, E., Basic Problems of Evidence (1963), 488
———, Hearsay and Non Hearsay, 48 Harv. L. Rev. 1138 (1935), 318
———, Hearsay Dangers and the Application of the Hearsay Concept, 62 Harv. L. Rev. 177 (1948), 302, 320, 332, 339
———, Instructing the Jury Upon Presumptions and Burden of Proof, 47 Harv. L. Rev. 59 (1933), 592, 601, 632
———, Judicial Notice, 57 Harv. L. Rev. 269 (1944), 692
———, Presumptions, 12 Wash. L. Rev. 255 (1937), 592, 631, 632, 633
———, Some Observations Concerning Presumptions, 44 Harv. L. Rev. 906 (1931), 630
———, The Hearsay Rule, 12 Wash. L. Rev. 1 (1937), 484
———, The Law of Evidence: Some Proposals for Its Reform (1927), 451

Table of Authorities

Nance, The Best Evidence Principle, 73 Iowa L. Rev. 227 (1988), 67

Nesson, Rationality, Presumptions, and Judicial Comment: A Response to Professor Allen, 94 Harv. L. Rev. 1574 (1981), 581, 689

———, Reasonable Doubt and Permissive Inferences: The Value of Complexity, 92 Harv. L. Rev. 1187 (1979), 487, 689

———, The Evidence or the Event? On Judicial Proof and the Acceptability of Verdicts, 98 Harv. L. Rev. 1357 (1985), 134, 144, 146, 151

Note, Did Your Eyes Deceive You? Expert Psychological Testimony on the Unreliability of Eyewitness Identification, 29 Stan. L. Rev. 969 (1977), 378, 427, 484

———, Evidence—Privileged Communications—The Attorney-Client Privilege in the Corporate Setting: A Suggested Approach, 62 Mich. L. Rev. 360 (1970), 780

———, The Constitutionality of Affirmative Defenses After *Patterson v. New York*, 78 Colum. L. Rev. 655 (1978), 683

———, The Theoretical Foundation of the Hearsay Rules, 93 Harv. L. Rev. 1786 (1980), 480

Ogden, C., & Richards, I., The Meaning of Meaning (1927), 296

Orloff & Stedinger, A Framework for Evaluating the Preponderance of the Evidence Standard, 131 U. Pa. L. Rev. 1159 (1983), 577, 718

Park, *McCormick on Evidence* and the Concept of Hearsay: A Critical Analysis Followed by Suggestions to Law Teachers, 65 Minn. L. Rev. 423 (1981), 311

Pope, The Proper Function of Jurors, 14 Baylor L. Rev. 365 (1962), 696

President's Commission on Law Enforcement and the Administration of Justice, Task Force Report: The Courts (1967), 144

Prosser, Law of Torts (4th ed. 1971), 615

Reaugh, Presumptions and the Burden of Proof, 36 Ill. L. Rev. 703 (1942), 600

Rothstein, P., Evidence: Cases, Materials and Problems (1986), 704

Saks & Kid, Human Information Processing and Adjudication: Trial by Heuristics, 15 Law and Soc. Rev. 123 (1980), 714

Saltzburg, A Special Aspect of Relevance: Countering Negative Inferences Associated with the Absence of Evidence, 66 Calif. L. Rev. 1011 (1978), 260

———, Burdens of Persuasion in Criminal Cases: Harmonizing the Views of the Justices, 20 Am. Crim. L. Rev. 393 (1983), 689

———, The Unnecessarily Expanding Role of the American Trial Judge, 64 Va. L. Rev. 1 (1978), 696
Saltzburg, S., & Redden, K., Federal Rules of Evidence Manual (2d ed. 1977), 258
———, Federal Rules of Evidence Manual (4th ed. 1986), 172, 190, 738
Savage, L., The Foundations of Statistics (1954), 135
Schwartz, A Suggestion for the Demise of Judicial Notice of "Judicial Facts," 45 Tex. L. Rev. 1212 (1967), 697
Seligman, An Exception to the Hearsay Rule, 26 Harv. L. Rev. 146 (1912), 318
Simon & Mahon, Quantifying Burdens of Proof, 5 Law & Soc. Rev. 319 (1971), 576
Slough, Spontaneous Statements and State of Mind, 46 Iowa L. Rev. 224, 428
Stone, Exclusion of Similar Fact Evidence: America, 51 Harv. L. Rev. 988 (1938), 234

Thayer, J., Preliminary Treatise on Evidence at the Common Law (1898), 104, 208, 588, 630, 631, 632
Tribe, Trial By Mathematics: Precision and Ritual in the Legal Process, 84 Harv. L. Rev. 1329 (1971), 135, 151, 714
———, Triangulating Hearsay, 87 Harv. L. Rev. 957 (1974), 296
Tullock, G., Trials on Trial: The Pure Theory of Legal Procedure (1980), 727

Waltz, J., & Kaplan, J., Making the Record (1982), 19
Waltz, The Present Sense Impression Exception to the Rule Against Hearsay, 66 Iowa L. Rev., 869 (1981), 425
Weinstein, J., & Berger, M., Weinstein's Evidence, 174, 209, 210, 392, 611, 741, 743, 765, 773, 775, 780, 781
Westen, Confrontation and Compulsory Process: A Unified Theory of Evidence for Criminal Cases, 91 Harv. L. Rev. 567 (1978), 685
Wigmore, J., Evidence in Trials at Common Law, 102, 113, 116, 120, 151, 193, 230, 232, 291, 293, 300, 415, 493, 494, 509, 543, 550, 587, 611, 631, 632, 698, 752, 772
Williams, T., Cat on a Hot Tin Roof, 346
Wright, Instructions to the Jury: Summary Without Comment (1954) Wash. U.L.Q. 177, 578
Wright, The Invasion of the Jury: Temperature of the War, 27 Temp. L.Q. 137 (1953), 578

INDEX

Absence of entry, hearsay exception for, 472
Admissions of a party
  Adoptive, 387-389
  agents' declarations, 389-392
  co-conspirators' declarations, 392-398
  declarations against interest, compared, 383, 416
  nolo contendere pleas, 286-289
  offers of compromise, 282-285
  party's own statement, 383-387
  personal knowledge, 385-387
  rationale, 382-383
  silence, 387-389
  subsequent remedial measures, 276-281
  vicarious, 389-398
Adverse spousal testimony, privilege against, 759, 762, 768-769, 774, 799-806
Appeal, preserving issues for, 19
Arrest
  cross-examination of character witnesses, 225
  hearsay, 331-332
Attorney-client privilege
  client
    defined, 766
    identity of, 768
  confidentiality, indications of, 769-770
  "control group" test, 780, 784-785
  corporation as client, 779-790, 807
  crime or fraud exception, 778, 792, 793
  disclosure, effect of, 769-770, 771-772
  elements of, 777-778
  erroneous rulings, effect of, 761-762
  history, 762, 783-785
  holder, 770
  rationale, 760, 783-785, 790-795
  representative of attorney, 767, 769
  representative of client, 779-790, 807
  third persons present at discussions, 769
  waiver, 771-773
  work-product doctrine, 786-789, 795-796
Authentication and identification
  business records, 458-459
  chain of custody, 171-176
  foundation for introduction of evidence, 172
  similarity of underlying form, 179-182

Bad acts
  character evidence, 219-221
  impeachment, 514-518
  non-character uses, 234-265
Bayes' theorem, 126-132
Best evidence rule, 187-195
Bias or prejudice
  character evidence distinguished, 544-545
  extrinsic evidence, 544
  impeachment of witnesses with evidence of, 543-547
Burden of proof
  affirmative defenses
    civil cases, 573-574
    criminal cases, 635-652
  allocating, 565-567, 656-667
  beyond a reasonable doubt, 635-652
  burden of persuasion, 570-578, 635-652, 679-687
  burden of production, 558-570, 635, 679-687

823

directed verdict, 562-565, 687
instructing juries on, 578-581, 599-603, 679-687
preponderance of the evidence, 570-574
Business custom, 232-233
Business records
  absence of entry, 472
  computer-generated records, 452
  factual findings, 465-471
  foundation, 458-459
  law enforcement reports, 465-471
  multiple hearsay, 455-458
  opinions, 454
  trustworthiness, 453-454

Character evidence
  cross-examination of character witnesses, 223-227
  foundation for proposed testimony, 219
  habit evidence distinguished, 230-232
  hearsay exception, 218
  impeachment and rehabilitation of witnesses, 217, 223-227, 511-530
  jury instructions following admission of prior bad acts, 264
  methods of proving character, 218-222
  nature of testimony permissible, 219-220
  offered to prove
    action in conformity with character, 215-217, 511-530
    character trait that is element of claim or defense, 215
  opinion and reputation evidence compared, 221-222
  opinion evidence, admissibility, 219-220, 512
  prior arrests or convictions, inquiry on cross-examination, 225, 512-513
  prior sexual conduct of sexual assault victim, 265-272
  reputation evidence, admissibility, 219-220, 512
  specific instances of conduct
    character as essential element, to prove, 219-220
    impeachment, admissibility for, 514-519
    prohibition against substantive use, 218-221
Clergy-penitent privilege, 760, 763, 766, 771, 774, 807
Co-conspirators. See Admissions of a party; Confrontation clause
Comments of judge, 578, 653, 683
Compromise, offers of, 282-284
Conclusive presumptions, 591-594
Confidential information. See Privileges
Confrontation clause

  co-conspirators' declarations, 354, 357-360, 366-368
  cross-examination, opportunity for, 356-359, 361-366, 368-371
  hearsay rule, relationship to, 351-371
  prior inconsistent statements, 356-357
  prior testimony, 352-357, 361-365
  reliability of hearsay evidence, 359-360, 362-363
Contemporaneous declarations, 423-440
Contradiction, 493-494, 549-556
Convictions
  hearsay exception for, 475-476
  impeachment with, 519-530
Corporations. See Attorney-client privilege
Cross-examination. See also Impeachment of witnesses
  bias, to prove, 544
  character witnesses, impeachment of, 223-227
  contradiction, to prove, 550
  expert witnesses, impeachment of, 541-542
  prior convictions, to prove, 521, 523-524
  prior inconsistent statements, to prove, 532-534
  psychiatric condition, to prove, 548
  purpose, 299-300, 498-500
  questions, form of, 39, 498-499
  restrictive rule of, 42, 500-502
  scope of, 42, 500-502
  self-incrimination, 508-510
  specific instances of conduct, to prove, 514-518
  wide-open rule, 42, 500-502
Curative admissibility, 289-291

Declarations against interest, 415-419
Declarations of physical condition, 439-444
Declarations of state of mind, 308-311, 344-349, 430-439
Demonstrative evidence, 170-172
Direct examination, 498-500
Drunkenness
  habit or character, 230-232
  opinion evidence by lay person, 730
Dying declarations, 412-415

Error, requirements for review on appeal, 19
Examination of witnesses. See Cross-examination; Direct examination; Impeachment of witnesses
Exceptions to hearsay rule. See specific entries under Hearsay, e.g., dying declarations
Excited utterances, 426-430
Exemptions from hearsay definition

Index

Admissions, 382-398
Prior statements of a witness, 373-382
Expert testimony
  attorney's role, 739
  basis of expert opinion, 441-443, 742-745
  "beyond lay kin" test, 734
  confusion of jury, 752-754
  cross-examination, 541-542
  customary reliance on material by expert, 743-745
  disclosure of basis for opinion, 741-742, 745-749
  Federal Rules of Evidence, expansion of scope of, 737-739, 742-743, 754
  hearsay, based on, 442-443, 743-749
  helpfulness or "of assistance to jury" requirement, 737-739
  hypothetical questions, 441-442
  impeachment with treatises, 541-542
  inadmissible evidence, based on, 442, 743-749
  proper subject for, 734-739, 754-756
  qualifications of expert, 740-741
  reasonable reliance on material, 743-745
  sanity, opinion as to, 745-756
  scientific evidence, 734-739
  subjects for, 734-739
  treatises, use of, 474-475, 541-542
  ultimate fact in issue, admissibility of opinion on, 752-757
  usurpation of jury's function, 752-754

Family history, hearsay exceptions for, 419-420
"Fighting fire with fire," 289-291
Firsthand knowledge
  admissions, 385-387, 392
  hearsay declarants, 302-303
  witnesses generally, 15, 26, 169-170, 740
Former statements of witnesses
  identification, statements of, 375-379
  prior consistent statements
    admissibility for their truth, 373-375, 379-381
    admissibility to rehabilitate, 537-541
  prior inconsistent statements
    admissibility for their truth, 373-375, 379-381
    admissibility to impeach, 532-536
Former testimony
  confrontation issues, 352-357, 361-365
  hearsay exception for, 401-412
Foundation. *See* Authentication and identification; Business records
Fraud
  attorney-client privilege, exception to, 778, 792, 793

prior convictions for crimes of, impeachment with, 521-523

Government records, hearsay exceptions for, 461-480
Guilty pleas, 286-288

Habit and custom or routine practice, 230-234
Hearsay
  absence of entry exceptions, 472
  admissions, 382-398
  assertive intent of declarant as determinative, 313-324, 331-341
  bloodhounds, 325
  business records, 351-361
  co-conspirator exemption, 392-398
  conduct, 313-324
  confrontation clause, 351-371
  contemporaneous declarations, 423-440
  declarations against interest, 415-419
  declarations of physical condition, 439-443
  declarations of state of mind, 308-311, 344-349, 430-439
  dying declarations, 412-415
  exceptions. *See specific subentries, e.g.,* declarations against interest
  excited utterances, 426-430
  expert testimony based on, 419-420, 742-749
  family history exceptions, 419-420
  former statements of witnesses, 382-398
  former testimony, 402-412
  future of hearsay, 480-491
  government records, 461-480
  hearsay within hearsay, 303-304
  identification, statements of, 375-379
  implied statements, 315-324, 332-341
  judgments, 475-476
  learned treatises, 474-475
  mechanical devices, 330-331
  non-jury trials, 299
  operative facts, 304-308
  past recollection recorded, 444-450
  pedigree, 419-420
  preliminary hearing testimony, 353-357, 361-363
  present memory refreshed, distinguished from past recollection recorded, 449-450
  present sense impression, 424-426
  prior consistent statements, admissibility for truth, 373-375
  prior identifications, 375-379
  prior inconsistent statements, admissibility for truth, 373-375
  public records, 461-472

Index

purpose of statement as determinative whether, 304-311
rationale, 295, 489
reputation exception, 218
residual exceptions, 476-478
scientific publications, 474-475
silence, 387-389
spontaneous declarations, 423-440
state-of-mind declarations, 308-311, 344-349, 430-439
"statement," defined to exclude nonassertive conduct, 314-324
statements implied from words or conduct, 314-324, 332-341
testimonial triangle, 296-299, 305-306, 308-309, 346
treatises, 474-475
unavailability of declarant
  constitutional implications, 354-356, 361-364, 366-368
  requirement for hearsay exceptions, 402-423
verbal acts, 304-308
Hypothetical questions, 441-442, 741

Identification, statements of, 375-379
Impeachment of witnesses
  bad acts, 514-519
  bias, 543-547
  character for untruthfulness, 217, 511-530
  collateral matters, 507-508, 534-535, 550-556
  contradiction, 549-556
  conviction of crime, 519-530
  cross-examination of character witnesses, 223-227
  experts, 541-542, 549
  extrinsic evidence rule, 507-508, 534-535, 550-556
  good faith basis for questions, 225
  inconsistent statements, 530-536
  inferential process, 502-505
  mental incapacity, condition, or defect, 547-549
  opinion about untruthfulness, 511-514
  own witness, 493-498
  prior convictions, 519-530
  prior inconsistent statements, 530-536
  psychiatric condition, 547-549
  reputation for untruthfulness, 511-514
  sensory defect, 547-549
  treatises used for, 541-542
  voucher rule, 493-498
Inferences. *See also* Presumptions
  circumstantial evidence, 120-121
  criminal cases, 653-658
  hearsay, 295-311
  impeachment, 502-505

inference upon inference rule, 121-122
statutory, 615-627
Instructions to jury. *See* Jury instructions
Insurance, evidence of, 285-286
Intoxication
  character or habit, 230-232
  opinion by lay person, 730

Judges, power to
  comment on evidence, 578-583
  pass on preliminary questions, 167
Judge and jury
  admissions, 387-388, 394-397
  burden of proof, 167
  co-conspirators' statements, 394-397
  conditional relevance, 165-167
  dying declarations, 420-422
  prior statements, 374-375
  spontaneous declarations, 425-426, 428-429
Judgments
  hearsay exception, 475-476
  impeachment with prior convictions, 519-530
Judicial notice, 691-697
Jury instructions
  burden of proof and presumptions in civil cases, 583-604
  facts upon which expert opinion is based, 442, 746-749
  inadmissible and stricken evidence, 11-12
  judicial notice, 691-697
  limited admissibility generally, 11-12, 212, 263-264, 306, 442, 539, 746-749
  out-of-court declarations, 306, 539
  prior bad acts, 263-264
  prior statements of witnesses, 539
  weight of evidence, comments by judge, 578-583

Lay person opinion testimony, 729-734
Leading questions, 22, 498-499
Learned treatises
  hearsay exception, 474-475
  impeachment and rehabilitation with, 541-542
Limited admissibility. *See* Jury instructions

Mandatory presumptions, 658-673
Marital privileges
  adverse spousal testimony, 759, 762, 768-769, 774, 799-806
  confidential communications, 759-760, 762, 767, 768-769, 771, 774, 799-800

Index

Materiality, 104-105
Medical care and treatment
  hearsay exception, 440-443
  payment of expenses, 284-285
  privileged information, 760, 763, 770-771, 774
Medical treatises. *See* Treatises

Not guilty pleas, 286-288

Objections
  form of, 19, 39
  instructions to jury, 11
Offers of compromise, 282-284
Offers of proof, 19
Opinions
  basis for, 441-443, 742-749
  character evidence, 218-223, 511-514
  expert testimony, 440-443, 740-757
  firsthand knowledge, 303, 741-743
  hearsay containing, 385
  lay person's testimony, 729-734
  ultimate issue, 752-757
Original documents rule, 187-195
Other crimes
  character evidence, 219-221
  impeachment, 514-530
  non-character uses, 234-265

Parent-child confidential communications, 776, 807
Past recollection recorded, 444-450
Pedigree, declarations of, 419-420
Personal knowledge
  admissions, 385-387, 392
  hearsay declarants, 302-303
  witnesses generally, 15, 26, 169-170, 740
Physical condition, declarations of, 439-444
Prejudice. *See* Bias or prejudice; Relevance
Preliminary questions. *See* Judge and jury
Present memory refreshed, 449-450
Present sense impression, 424-426
Presumptions
  burden of producing evidence, affecting, 598-599, 679-687
  burdens of proof related to, 594-599, 679-687
  "bursting bubble theory," 609
  civil cases, 853
  constitutional issues, 635-689
  criminal cases, 652
  employment discrimination, 584
  extreme emotional disturbance, 635-644
  heat of passion on sudden provocation, 635-644
  homicide, 635-652
  intent, establishment of, 669-679

  mandatory, 658-673
  measures of validity for statutory, 615-627
  Morgan approach, 629-633
  possession of gun, 658-669
  rational connection test, 673-675
  shifting burdens of proof, 594-599, 635, 679-687
  statutory inferences, 582-583, 615-627
  Thayerian doctrine, 629-633
  Winship standard for prosecution burden of proof, 635-644
Priest-penitent privilege, 760, 763, 766, 771, 774, 807
Prior consistent statements
  hearsay exemption for, 373-375
  rehabilitation with, 537-541
Prior identifications, 375-379
Prior inconsistent statements
  hearsay exemption for, 373-375
  impeachment with, 530-537
Prior sexual conduct, 265-272
Privileges
  adverse inference from invoking, 774-775
  adverse spousal testimony, 759, 762, 768-769, 774, 799-806
  attorney-client, 759, 762, 766-770, 773, 777-795, 807
  clergy-penitent, 760, 763, 766, 771, 774, 807
  compromise, 282-284
  confidential communications generally, 766-777
  conflict of laws, 764
  effect of erroneous ruling on, 761-762
  exceptions, 773-774
  federal rule, 763-765
  government privileges, 763
  holder, 761, 770-771
  illegally obtained evidence, right to exclude, 759, 761-762
  marital, 759-760, 762, 767, 768-769, 774, 799-806
  offers of compromise, 282-284
  parent-child, 776, 807
  physician-patient, 760, 774
  priest-penitent, 760, 763, 766, 771, 774, 807
  professional-client relationship, 766-767, 769, 807
  psychotherapist-patient, 760, 766, 767, 770, 773-774
  settlement, 282-284
  spousal confidential communications, 759-760, 762, 767, 768-769, 771, 774, 799-800
  subsequent remedial measures, 276-281
  unique operation of rules of, 760-762
  waiver, 771-773
  work-product doctrine, 786-789, 795-796

Products liability, admissibility of remedial measure evidence, 276-281
Professional conduct of attorneys, 796-798
Psychotherapist-patient privilege, 760, 766, 767, 770, 773-774
Public records, 461-472

Rape shield laws, 265-272
Real evidence, 170-176
Reasonable doubt. *See* Burden of proof
Recordings
   authentication, 200-211
   best evidence rule, 187-197
Records
   authentication, 167-176
   business, 451-459
   past recollection recorded, 444-449
   public, 461-472
Refreshing memory, 449-450
Rehabilitating witnesses
   character evidence, 513
   impeachment as prerequisite, 505-507
   prior consistent statements, 537-541
Relevance
   Bayes' theorem, 126-132
   conditional, 165-167
   exclusion of relevant evidence generally, 104-107
   inferences, 123
   materiality, 104-105
   prejudice, 104-107
   probative force, 100-107
Remedial measures, 276-281
Reports, hearsay exceptions for, 451-474
Reputation. *See also* Character evidence
   hearsay exception, 218
   to prove character, 218-220, 511-514
Res gestae, 423
Residual hearsay exceptions, 476-480
Risk of non-persuasion. *See* Burden of proof
Routine practice of an organization, 232-233

Scientific evidence, 734-739
Scientific publications
   hearsay exception, 474-475
   impeachment and rehabilitation with, 541-542

Sensory defects, 547-549
Settlements and offers to settle, 282-284
Sexual conduct evidence, 265-272
Similar happenings, 272-274
Spontaneous declarations, 423-430
Spousal privileges
   confidential communications, 759-760, 762, 767, 768-769, 771, 774, 799-800
   testimonial, 759, 762, 768-769, 774, 799-806
State-of-mind declarations, 308-311, 344-349, 430-439
Subsequent remedial measures, 276-281
Summing up and comment by judge, 578-583

Tape recordings, 200-211
Treatises
   hearsay exception, 474-475
   impeachment and rehabilitation with, 541-542

Voucher rule, 493-498

Witnesses. *See also* Impeachment of witnesses
   character, 219-227, 511-514
   cross-examination, 498-502
   direct examination, 498-500
   experts, 740-752
   firsthand knowledge, 15, 26, 169-170, 740
   leading questions, 39, 498-500
   narrative by witness, 22
   prior statements by, 373-379, 530-541
   redirect and recross-examination, 498
   refreshing recollection, 449-450
   rehabilitating, 505-507, 513, 537-541
   voucher rule, 493-498
Work-product doctrine, 786-789, 795-796
Writings
   authentication, 172-176
   best evidence rule, 187-195
   past recollection recorded, 444-450
   records exceptions to hearsay rule, 451-472